BUSINESS POLICY: The Art of Strategic Management

BUSINESS POLICY

The Art of Strategic Management

William R. Boulton *University of Georgia*

MACMILLAN PUBLISHING COMPANY
New York
Collier Macmillan Publishers
London

Macmillan Publishing Company
866 Third Avenue, New York, New York 10022
Collier Macmillan Canada, Inc.

Library of Congress Cataloging in Publication Data

Boulton, William R.
Business policy.

Includes index.
1. Corporate planning. I. Title.
HD30.28.B68 1984 658.4'012 83-13630

PRINTING: 3 4 5 6 7 8 YEAR: 4 5 6 7 8 9 0 1 2

ISBN 0-02-312840-2

PREFACE

As we watch the field of Business Policy continue to evolve, we must constantly work to update our research and teaching paradigms to encompass current knowledge and understanding. In *Business Policy: The Art of Strategic Management,* I have attempted to incorporate those theories that will most likely have their greatest impact on managers, students and educators in the 1980s. The text's development has been heavily influenced by three streams of research. First, it has attempted to maintain the tradition of the field as established by the Harvard Business School faculty and set forth by C. Roland Christensen, Kenneth R. Andrews and Joseph L. Bower in *Business Policy: Text and Cases.* However, the research of McKinsey and Company, which has been popularized by T. Peters and R. Waterman in *In Search of Excellence* and by R. Pascale and A. Athos in *The Art of Japanese Management,* influenced both the content and organization of the text portion of this book. Finally, Michael Porter's *Competitive Strategy* was considered when writing the chapters on business strategy. While acknowledging the importance of these works, my motivation in writing this book was based on the perceived need to present an updated text and cases for the strategic management and business policy course of the 1980s.

In the tradition of the field, *Business Policy: The Art of Strategic Management* focuses on the application of theories and the development of management skills through the use of case studies. The cases developed and assembled for this book include topics of concern to today's managers and are consistent with the McKinsey "7-S" paradigm. While the heaviest emphasis has been given to the understanding of strategy; structure, systems, superordinate goals, style, staff, and skills are specifically dealt with in both the text and case materials.

The case materials incorporate issues that are of growing concern to today's managers. For example, cases on Hewlett-Packard, Tracor, Texas Instruments MODPLAN, and CALMA give special emphasis to the issues of technology and its rapid change. Cases on Republic Steel, DuPont, Lotus, and Chrysler show the impact of government in the development of competitive strategies. Cases on the Japanese steel industry, Toyo Kogyo, and the motorcycle industry provide insights into the competitive strategies required for global competition. While these cases raise strategic issues for today's managers, the focus is still on the need for managers to make decisions about strategy and then work to make those decisions successful.

Concern for the implementation of strategic decisions is encompassed in many of the cases. The "B" cases provided in both the book and instructor's manual provide significant coverage of the management and administrative issues. The cases on Bankers Trust and Georgia Federal were developed to encompass the McKinsey 7-S paradigm and, therefore, provide a comprehensive examination of these organizations. Cases on Lincoln Electric, Lou Holtz, BCI, Independent Publishing Company, Texas Air Corporation, and Majestic Hardware show the importance of top management's style and the systems they impose on the organization. However, let us not lose sight of the fact that these cases are included here to help develop skills needed by managers in both their analytic and administrative roles.

The rapid development and evolution of the Business Policy course requires us to update the materials used in the classroom. I hope that this book will make a significant contribution toward that effort.

W.R.B.

ACKNOWLEDGEMENTS

Special thanks must be given to all those individuals who have contributed to the development of this book. At the University of Georgia, I would like to thank Arnold Balk for the continuous support he has provided in obtaining important library material. Dean Flewellen and Richard Huseman provided the resources and time required to carry out such a project. Finally, Curtis Tate provided the encouragement and incentive to tackle the project.

The selection of case materials is always vital to a good Business Policy course. In this text, I owe thanks to all those who have contributed to such case development: Ed Roach and Jack Eure, Jr. for Mr. Gatti's; Jeanne Lynch for Majestic Hardware Co., Inc.; the Bank Marketing Association for Bankers Trust of South Carolina; Roger Atherton for Hewlett-Packard (A) and (B); Dennis Crites for Hewlett-Packard (A); Jim Chrisman for Note on the Analytical Instruments Industry, Tracor Incorporated (A) and (B); The World Motorcycle Industry, and The British Motorcycle Industry (A); Jesse Dougherty and Michael Porter for EG&G, Inc. (A) and (B); Phyllis Holland for Coca-Cola Wine Spectrum (A); Donald Scotton and Eleanor Schwartz for Republic Steel (A) and (B); Mike Alford for The Japanese Steel Industry and Toyo Kogyo Co., Ltd.; Jeffery Ellis for Group Lotus Car Companies Ltd.; Robert Hay for Lou Holtz's Razorback Football Image; Charles Summer for BCI Ltd.; Owen Weber and Warren DeBord for Nichols Equipment Inc.; Dan Thomas for Independent Publishing Company and The Chrysler Corporation; Arthur Sharplin for The Lincoln Electric Company; Tim Singleton and Robert McGlashan for Texas Air Corporation (A); Elizabeth Gatewood for Texas Air Corporation (B); Christine Blouke for The Chrysler Corporation and CALMA Company (A); James Verbrugge for Georgia Federal Savings & Loan Association; Charles Kight for Texas Instruments MODPLAN; and Jay Bourgeois for CALMA Company.

As with any writing project, special thanks must also be given to those who transformed words into manuscript form. Nancy Parks, Billie Najour, Karen Turner, and Jackie Ogletree were essential for their help in completing this project.

The reviewers were Kurt Christensen, Northwestern University; Jon P. Goodman, University of Houston; Robert Hay, University of Arkansas; Phyllis Holland, Georgia State University; Tom Lenz, Indiana University; Agnes Missirian, Bentley College; Leslie W. Rue, Georgia State University; John A. Seeger, Bentley College; and Lew Taylor, University of Nebraska—Lincoln.

Finally, I give special thanks to my wife Mary and my sons Gregory and Michael for the sacrifices they have made so that this text could become a reality.

W.R.B.

CONTENTS

Part I: Introduction to Strategic Management

Part II: Formulating Business Strategies

Part IV: Cases in Organizational Missions and Objectives

Part V: Cases in Business and Corporate-Level Strategies

Part VI: Cases in the Global Competitive Business Environment

Part VII: Cases in Managing the Organization

Part VIII: Cases in Managing the Organization's Future

LIST OF EXHIBITS

PART I

Introduction to Strategic Management

1 An Introduction to Strategic Management Education

Business policy is the study of how organizations determine and achieve their purposes. The study is concerned with the ability of organizations to achieve their objectives in a specific environment and with the top-level managers of organizations who must both lead and motivate people to achieve those objectives. It is the actions of setting organizational policies that we refer to as *strategic management.*

Since few managers ever begin their own companies from scratch, this text discusses concepts that deal with the analysis of existing organizations, their objectives and their strategies. To this extent, students will work to develop skills that are required to (1) identify the realities of ongoing organizational activities, (2) diagnose the health of those activities, and (3) determine what changes need to be made. It is through logical and systematic analysis that problems and opportunities of today's organizations can be identified and acted upon by top management.

Understanding the logic of analysis does not in itself cause one to become a good manager. In fact, some writers argue that good managers are born, not developed. Others believe, however, that education can equip managers with a variety of business skills to help them deal with the complex issues, events, and tasks which face today's business decision makers. More specific to this text is its focus on the broad role of general managers and the perspectives, understandings, and skills necessary for success in that role.

This text focuses on the job of top-level general managers who must integrate and coordinate the activities of many staff and line functions. The general manager's job includes

1. setting strategic direction through evaluation of external influences, weighting future trends and issues, and determining alternative business responses.
2. designing organizational structures and administrative systems that affect strategy implementation.
3. providing managerial leadership to develop climate, structure jobs, set rewards and motivations, and use power to achieve organizational goals.
4. managing operations and resource allocations through a variety of analytic techniques.
5. dealing with environmental issues, changing societal values, evolving

business ethics, growth of governmental involvement, and the impact of world business.

In concern for the organization's long- and short-term viability, the top or chief executive must ensure that proper balance is given to those decisions that affect the future of the organization as well as those decisions which affect the organization's ability to perform at present. To keep such a balance, chief executives often designate staff executives to manage the long-range planning process for the organization. Financial staff may also be used to evaluate major investment decisions that affect more medium-range results. The accounting staff tend to track ongoing operations. In all three of these time frames, the personnel manager must ensure that adequate attention and procedures are in place to staff long- and short-term operating needs. We now consider the strategic areas of management.

UNDERSTANDING STRATEGIC MANAGEMENT FUNCTIONS

Strategic management goes beyond the management of one functional area. Without an understanding of the problems of various functions and the complexity of interfunctional cooperation, it is difficult to maximize the overall performance of the organization. The larger the organization the more critical this coordination becomes and the more difficult it becomes to manage its complexities. Planning, allocating, and controlling both financial and human resources then become the essence of strategic management.

The Chief Executive's Job

Responsibility for the objectives, strategies, and performance of the overall organization rests in the hands of the chief executive of the firm. Most critical of his or her job is creating an organizational character that will deal with change, goal setting, interpersonal communication, and organizational demands. It is, therefore, the chief executive who has primary responsibility for strategic management and business policy.

Strategy. The chief executive may be compared to the conductor of an orchestra. As managing director, he or she has considerable influence over the choice of music and the way it is played. At the strategic level, the question becomes one of determining what music will generate enough demand to cover the costs of performance. Once the audience is attracted, the style or quality of the music must be adequate to keep the audience members coming back with their friends. Functional efficiency is of little help if there is no demand for the output.

Organization. The chief executive's organization includes both line and staff functions. The line functions generally refer to the create-make-market functions. The staff functions generally include key support functions for managing the total organization. Planning, finance and accounting, and personnel functions are the most familiar of these staff roles. They aid the chief executive in doing his or her job.

Operations. The relationship between the chief executive and the board of directors is often dependent upon company performance and image. Depending on the size and complexity of the company, the chief executive's role will change—moving further away from line operations as complexity and size increase. Growth then brings growing demands for staff functions that will provide information, help plan operations, and track results.

The Planning Function

The planning function generally gains popularity in organizations after expected performance is not met or losses in sales or profits become significant. A decline in results raises questions about the organization's ability to achieve its objectives and calls for new attempts to generate stability in sales or profits. At the same time, it brings into focus the need for reevaluation of the firm's direction and goals.

Strategy. The planning department crystallizes the objectives of the firm (e.g., expected profitability, profit growth, and sales growth) and of each business. Defining what businesses the firm is in, or should be in, will also determine who the competition is, what substitutes exist, what potential competitors may enter, and who the key suppliers and buyers are. The ultimate impact of the planning function is to establish a process for setting priorities and allocating resources that will affect the long-term success and direction of the organization. Consistency in planning over a long period will eventually tie long-range objectives to current operations and gain credibility for the planning function.

Organization. As in key functional areas, good interdepartmental information and communication are required for successful planning. It is not the role of the planner to produce the plans, but to provide the concepts and systems needed to support long-range programs that are consistent with company objectives. The planner's key function is to manage the planning system for top management and to ensure that this function is being carried out. The planner's credibility will depend on the importance given to this role by the chief executive.

Operations. Quantifying long-range plans and tracking their implementation requires tremendous effort and information-processing capabilities. If plans are not reviewed and results not tied to rewards, this effort will not be taken seriously. Ensuring that resources are allocated in time for additional facilities to be brought on line to meet forecasts is critical. As a result, identification and tracking of strategic accomplishments of milestones is essential in keeping long-range programs on track.

The Finance Function

Managing corporate cash flow has become increasingly important in past years. As the value of money continues to rise, financial structure and cash prove to be critical aspects of profitability and growth.

Strategy. The primary function of the financial area is to manage the structure of the balance sheet. Managing the cash assets proved to be quite profitable in the early 1980s. On the liabilities side, the structure of both debt and equity have a significant impact on profitability and the risk of doing business. Financial strategy becomes critical as to when and how new equity and debt instruments are issued or how capital structure affects the firm's competitive ability. Managing the release of funds to managers also serves as the most significant control mechanism available to top management.

Organization. Tracking the implementation of long-range plans and short-term budgets is essential to basic cash management. Financial personnel specify the financial requirements for investment planning and management ratios, and work closely with line areas in determining proper investment alternatives. Financial personnel are also important in external relations with the financial community.

Operations. Finding and managing the funds flow of the firm is a critical job that requires close cooperation with top management in planning finance strategy as well as maintaining good progress reports on current financial performance. Managing balance sheet accounts and investment criteria are key to maintaining stability in bottom-line performance.

The Accounting Function

The essence of business communication comes in the form of numbers that are primarily financial in nature. In order to assess the financial health and performance of the organization, there is a need for financial statements that will reflect the status of the organization.

Strategy. The accountant's primary function is to determine the appropriate policies for keeping accounts and meeting the legal and tax requirements of the firm. In support of financial strategies, accounting policies may be adjusted so as to manage profitability and surpluses.

Organization. The accounting department is a critical information center for the firm. This is a professional department responsible for information collection and dissemination. As a result, primary information-processing systems are generally established to link this department with all others.

Operations. The accurate collection and storage of data, and the presentation of information is the primary accounting function. To meet the legal liabilities and to ensure integrity of the data, the accountant and the auditing function of this department need to work closely with top management. This auditing function frequently meets directly with members of the board of directors to ensure that practices are appropriate and legal.

The Personnel Function

Possibly the most critical of all management functions is the recruiting of quality personnel with needed skills or qualities, and their continued development. Since the primary resource of organizations is its human resources, this function needs special attention and support from top management.

Strategy. Managing the firm's programs for recruiting, training, paying, appraising, and promoting individuals must be tied to long-term needs of the organization. Recognition of required skills to support major business objectives should guide this function. Indoctrination and training programs for personnel development should support current organizational strategies and policies or communicate the need and direction of change in such policies.

Organization. Personnel becomes a key interface between all departments in the organization for human resource requirements. It also provides the entry point for new employees, the record-keeping function for employees, and the reporting for government reports.

Operations. Besides intervening in hiring, training, and firing of employees, personnel is now responsible for job measurement, salary or pay determination, and employee benefit programs. Where unions are involved, this department often handles union communication and relations. One key problem area in the 1980s has been responding to equal employment and discrimination complaints and regulations.

In summary, there are strategic, organizational, and operational considerations in both line and staff functions of the organization. Problems may occur in any one or in a variety of these functions. The ability to recognize the nature of the problems and issues and to pose viable solutions is seldom an easy task. That is the reason we provide the repetition of case study discussions to develop the required skills needed for this analysis.

Case method discussions of actual business problems will aid participants in understanding the impact that attitudes of leadership have on organizational performance. Individual involvement in group activities allows their own leadership styles, abilities, and limitations to affect relationships, communication, motivation, group enterprise, and effective task accomplishment. In strategic management, these attitudes and styles of leadership must be applied to organizations in which diverse groups and personalities and power struggles and conflicts are not uncommon. The requirements of leadership, therefore, go beyond knowledge and skills, and require attitudes and integrity commonly seen in our greatest leaders. Leadership appears most successful when it is tempered with a large portion of humility and concern for others.

THE VALUE OF CASE STUDIES

Integration of the broad range of knowledge described in later chapters occurs through discussions of case studies included at the end of the text. In applying your knowledge to the cases, you will be asked to put yourself in the position of the responsible manager when analyzing the situation and deciding how to deal with the problems and issues at hand. This analysis requires the identification of relevant information, the application of analytic techniques, the determination of appropriate alternatives, and the use of judgment in your choice of actions.

Consider the nature of the organization being analyzed. The smaller the firm, the greater the likelihood that top managers will overlook important issues or problems simply because they lack interest or specialized skills or adequate time. In larger organizations, managers may be too far removed from operations to understand the problems occurring in different departments or the impact those problems are having on other operations. In all cases, managers must handle people, managing their operations through people. When managers fail to provide adequate leadership and motivation, problems are likely to follow.

In considering the nature of managerial work, one can distinguish between operational, organizational, and strategic concerns. "Strategic" analysis deals with long-term decisions that can be postponed without affecting day-to-day business results. The focus of strategic decisions is to take advantage of external opportunities through changes in organizational activities or direction. "Organizational" analysis deals with how one allocates people and skills and how one plans, controls, and motivates those people to achieve both operational and strategic objectives. "Operational" analysis relates to maintaining current day-to-day operations at a successful level.

Strategic concerns in the single business organization are most likely to occur as markets become mature or when past levels of growth and profits can no longer be maintained. Such problems often lead to a search for new products or markets that will allow continued use of current resources or continued growth and profits. Operational problems, oftentimes, are only symptoms of strategic or organizational problems. Because of these complications, experience with business analysis is required to develop the manager's problem-solving skills and knowledge.

The environment in which case discussions are carried out is critical to the study of strategic management and business policy. Learning from others is a key activity for managers. Problem-solving activities require communication between people through speaking, listening, reading, and writing. Building on others' thoughts, altering how they think, and inspiring action all require communication. Whether dealing with new strategies, operating crises, or succession, the general manager must be effective as a communicator. The classroom provides a low-risk environment for developing these skills.

Since case studies have no single solution, participants have an opportunity to express themselves as well as to hear a diversity of other approaches and ideas. Case preparation can therefore be expanded from that of the individual reader, to small group discussions, and, finally, to classroom discussion. Through increasing levels of preparation and discussion, participants will gain greater appreciation for the skills required in situational analysis and the variety of approaches to solving a specific problem. As a result, participants need to quickly develop their own skills of analysis and problem solving.

THE PROCESS OF CASE ANALYSIS

The process of preparing for a case discussion requires that an individual become familiar with the case material, analyzing the situation to determine what issues need attention and deciding what actions are most likely to resolve the issues. Figure 1-1 outlines these steps. Though we suggest a systematic, sequential movement through these steps, good preparation does not necessarily mean that other approaches cannot be used. It is important, however, that plans of action consider the points of view of the key executive(s) in the case.

Readers must first become familiar with the case and then develop techniques that are quick and effective. After an initial scanning of the material to gain an overall understanding of the available material, two key functions are required: (1) to make a detailed reading of the material for note taking, and (2) to examine exhibits in detail and do elementary numerical analysis. The sequence or intensity with which these functions are carried out is up to the individual. Depending on the available time, it may be advantageous to read the material and to think about it before attacking a more in-depth analysis.

Taking notes and making an analysis of the case situation requires some

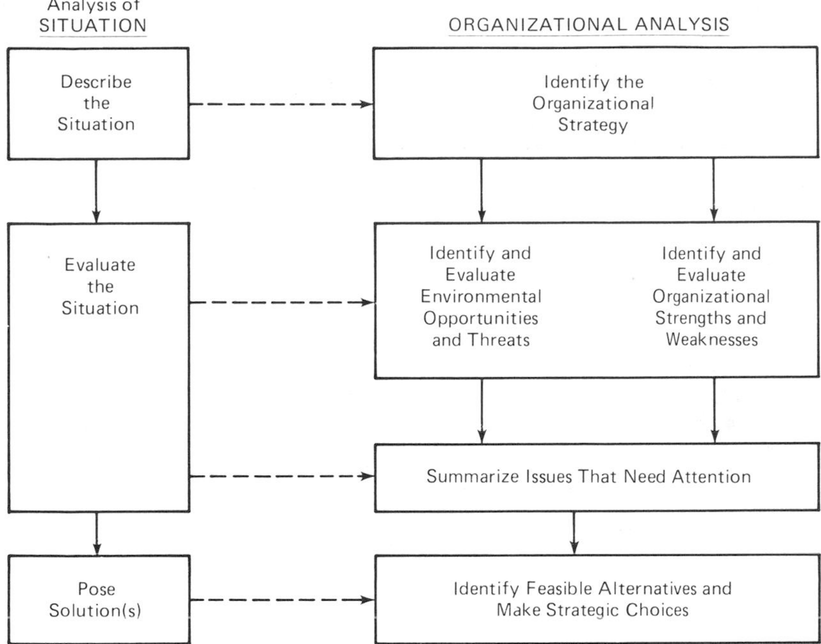

FIGURE 1-1: Case Analysis Process

system on the part of the reader. Since most cases present more information than is necessary for understanding and dealing with the problem, it is essential that readers determine the information required to understand and deal with the issues. Figure 1-2 provides one approach to organizing case data.

Descriptions of an organization's overall objectives, business involvement and strategy, and organizational characteristics allow for a complete understanding of the case situation. An overall evaluation of both internal and external characteristics refers to the process of determining what strategic, organizational and operational problems exist and which issues need to be addressed. Problems may suggest a lack of coherent strategy, weak management, inappropriate organizational structure, ineffective planning, and the like. Issues relate to those areas where management attention can make a strategic difference such as recognizing new market or product opportunities, responding to competitive or environmental changes, or changing the nature of a firm's competitive skills (i.e., changing technology, products, or cost structures).

The identification of specific problems or strategic issues may come directly from the case or be buried in case facts. The process of identification requires a careful understanding of the facts and a discovery of the key relationships between different sets of facts. Sensitivity to the facts of the case then allows the reader to use various analytic techniques to understand and find an approach for handling the case problems or issues.

Numerous techniques and concepts can be used for case analysis. The following chapters provide much of the conceptual materials that can be used in the course. However, the intuitive or systematic analysis by readers may draw

Overall Objectives Description	Objectives	Time Frame
Where do we want to go? What accomplishments are key? When do we want to get there?		

Business Description
What is our product-performance position? What is our price performance position? What is our functional expertise? What is our distinctive competence? What has power in the industry?

Organizational Description
What structure do we have? What planning, control, and incentive systems do we have? What skills do we have? What staff (people) do we have? What style (of management) do we have?

Overall Evaluation
What opportunities exist for us? What are our major strengths? What problems do we face? What are our major weaknesses?

Key Alternatives To Be Addressed
How do you use strengths to: (1) take advantage of opportunities? (2) overcome problems? How do you overcome weaknesses to: (1) take advantage of opportunities? (2) overcome problems? How do you set priorities?

Choice of Alternatives
Which alternatives will meet goals? Which alternatives will improve position? Which alternatives will improve operations? What changes are critical? What resources are critical? What time schedules are critical?

FIGURE 1-2: Case Analysis Framework

heavily on their own experience or insights. There are no right answers in the field of strategic management and concepts described here are only examples of current management thought. New approaches will continue to be developed in the future as we gain understanding of the field.

The final step in case analysis is to formulate a decision that will most likely solve the problem or deal effectively with the issues at hand. This phase will be based on the reader's final judgment after the various analytic tools are applied. Judgment incorporates all the various quantitative and qualitative, structured and unstructured, and sophisticated and primitive approaches to analysis used in coming to a decision. The quality of one's judgments can be determined only over time, by watching the final outcomes of decisions made over a long period of time.

The content of one's decisions must, of course, include the plans for implementation and action. The context and approach to plans vary by case, but depend heavily on the priorities assigned and the time available for action. In some cases, detailed action plans with time schedules and staff assignments will be called for. Other cases may call for additional analysis or information before action can be taken. The final approach is up to the reader to decide and defend in the classroom.

SUMMARY

These suggestions are only one set of approaches to case analysis. The key to learning rests in the hands of the reader. Case preparation can be carried out only by the reader. It is useful to prepare a summary of the problems and issues identified through one's analysis with recommended actions as preparation for classroom discussion.

The case study, then, provides a means by which managers can learn to size up a situation in a timely and accurate manner, to evaluate operations and policies as they relate to both environmental and organizational conditions. Sizing up case situations provides experience in analysis, identification of external opportunities and threats, recognition of organizational strengths and weaknesses, determination of critical problems and issues, and recommendation of the best available alternatives. The development of solutions and action plans further requires consideration of administrative factors, integrating solutions across functional areas. Success in developing these skills requires involvement, repetition and a commitment on the part of the students to the use of cases in this skill-development process.

FOCUS QUESTIONS

1. What are the major management concerns of the chief executives?
2. How do case studies aid in the understanding of strategic management requirements and skills?
3. What is the student's responsibility in this case method course? What should the student get out of it?
4. What process would you use to analyze a case?

2 An Introduction to Strategic Management

Have you ever stopped to consider what makes an organization successful? Why are some organizations able to survive for generations whereas others come and go? What lets "outstanding" organizations demonstrate above-average performance and growth? Some might argue that it is the basic business strategy of the firm. Some might argue that it is luck. Some might argue that it is the firm's officers and employees and their unique skills. Some might argue that it is the effective structuring of the organization and its planning and control systems. Still others might argue that it is the unique style of management and its values which generate support from all those who are associated with the organization. In fact, all of these characteristics become important to the making of successful organizations. It is the consistency with which these characteristics "fit" together and their effectiveness in meeting the needs of the organization and its environment that ultimately determines the organization's success.

Whereas business policy and strategic management are concerned with the achievement of organizational purpose, it is the decisions and actions of top management that set the tone, direction, and environment which will commit and motivate members of the organization to achieve the goals prescribed by top management. Without the support and commitment of the organization's members to its purpose, it is unlikely that an organization can be successful for any significant period of time. For example, the separation of employees and managers through rigid unionization reduces the flexibility of the organization to adapt in a timely manner to competitive changes. Both the steel and automobile industries in the United States can testify to these phenomena. More importantly, employees must feel some commitment and belief in what an organization is attempting to accomplish before they will dedicate their efforts to that purpose.

Today, *strategic management* is the term used to describe the process of managing the total organization and developing its distinctive competencies. Because of its concern for the total organization, strategic management deals primarily with the roles and functions of top-level general management. This top management point of view focuses our attention on those management functions that determine overall direction, develop the character of the organization, and coordinate and integrate organizational resources and actions.

Strategic management is the study of the functions and responsibilities of those who lead and manage purposeful organizations. It is devoted to the problems of the total organization as seen by top managers. It is concerned with the process and problems of determining the purpose of the organization, and the ends it hopes to achieve, and then committing critical resources to the accomplishment of those ends. It is concerned with understanding those characteristics that make organizations successful, and managing the development and transition of each organization's unique set of characteristics and competencies so as to achieve its desired purpose and goals.

TERRITORY OF STRATEGIC MANAGEMENT

Organizational success relates to the ability of an organization to achieve its purpose in the most efficient manner. In academic circles, this is described as the accomplishment of desired "ends" through various "means" that allow for long-term survival. Strategic management is carried out by those in the organization who make decisions about both the "ends" to which the organization aspires and the "means" by which they attempt to get there. To understand the nature of decisions that affect both ends and means, let us consider the areas in which strategic management is required.

Successful top managers must seek a balance or fit between the ends to which an organization's leadership aspires and the ways and means available to the organization to get there. A study carried out by the consulting firm of McKinsey and Company of thirty-seven well-run American companies found seven policy areas that affected long-term organizational success. These policy areas included three "hard" management areas of *strategy, structure,* and *systems,* plus four less understood areas of *staff, skills, style,* and *shared values or goals.* To these seven policy areas, succession is added to emphasize the need to manage transition in organizational policies. These eight "Ss" are described as follows: [1]

Strategy

Strategy is the means by which an organization attempts to achieve its purpose. There is often confusion here because strategy as the means for achieving a specified ends can be established at any level of an organization. In organizations that have a narrow range of products or services, such as soft drinks or fast foods, functional strategies may have the most important impact on achieving the organization's goals. For example, Coca-Cola's marketing strategy maintains its product image and market position. Although Coca-Cola is able to outspend its competitors in advertising, it still has the lowest advertising cost per unit of sales.

Marketing strategies often determine how one positions a product or service in the eyes of the intended consumer. The level of price, features, and performance relative to competitive products will generate a specific image in the mind of the consumer. Inconsistencies in marketing programs can jeopardize investments in image building and product positioning. This basic positioning

[1] Richard T. Pascale and Anthony G. Athos, *The Art of Japanese Management* (New York: Warner Books, Inc., 1982), p. 125.

strategy should then determine what selling methods to use, e.g., selling performance or unique features, using trade or consumer discounts, advertising and promotional programs, and approaches to training. Marketing strategy incorporates concepts of market segmentation, product life cycle, and marketing mix to develop a competitive position, enter new markets, and modify product lines. The product and the approach to fulfilling the consumer's needs will also dictate the degree of required direct consumer contact and servicing support. Lower priced products should generate higher sales levels. Recent studies suggest that low-price, high-quality strategies are most profitable as a result of growth in market share and economies of scale.

Production strategies are becoming increasingly important today. With growing competition and inflation, managers are recognizing the need to improve both the efficiency and quality of production output. With the advent of computers to improve information-processing capabilities, service-based organizations are also applying these strategies to information management. Depending on the volume of throughput, a variety of manufacturing techniques are available that require varying amounts of labor and capital. The production strategy must decide which of these alternatives is most advantageous. Some strategies may require too much capital; some may risk machinery obsolescence; some may be too specialized to find competent staff; some may require more expensive raw materials than competitors. For any given firm, trade-offs will have to be made between flexibility, capital and labor availability, production volume and economics, and break-even risks. Decisions, of course, need to be consistent with the ends to be achieved.

Research and development strategies tend to focus on longer range payoffs and goals. Research and development problems and issues often force trade-offs between improving current products and operating processes and developing new products and ideas. Making commitments to research and development requires greater risk taking because payoffs are uncertain and in the distant future. To ensure some investment in the future, management may need to commit a certain amount of money or percentage of sales to this function. Patents resulting from this activity may have a significant impact on the organization's future performance.

At the *business level,* the level to which functional managers report, decisions must be made as to what functional strategies will best accomplish the goals for that business. However, once there are a variety of businesses in an organization, *corporate level* managers must further decide which business strategies will help them best achieve the overall purpose and goals of the organization. This is discussed further in Chapter 3.

Developing or modifying strategy requires an understanding of the environment in which the organization operates as well as the strengths and competencies that might provide opportunity for success. Threats to future success come from changes in the social, political, legal, technological, economic, or competitive aspects of the environment. When such changes are great, or when the organization's weaknesses are significant, the organization often fails. Strategy, therefore, should seek to build on an organization's strengths or advantages, while seeking to overcome or minimize its weaknesses. Strategy also needs to be flexible enough to adapt the organization to its changing environment.

Structure

Structure refers to the basic framework that management uses to designate responsibilities for specific business functions, communication and information, and decision-making processes. The structure determines to a large degree how well people communicate, through which lines they communicate, and what needs they have for communication. The existence of line and staff functions, with corresponding levels of responsibility and authority, determines the degree of centralization or decentralization given to the decision-making process. As is the case with strategy, structure also needs flexibility to adapt to its environment and facilitate the accomplishment of strategy.

As organizations move from a narrow purpose, e.g. a single function or business, to a more complex multipurpose or multibusiness institution, the ability of top management to directly manage day-to-day operations is greatly diminished. In fact, growth in organizational size and complexity forces top management to rely on others in staying informed about the organization's operations and performance. As the organization grows beyond the abilities of a single manager to make all decisions, the addition of managers and delegation of day-to-day decisions to those managers will be required.

For example, Figure 2-1 shows the evolution of structure as size and complexity force top management to rely on others. In the smallest entrepreneurial organizations, very little decision-making authority is given to others since one person can "do it all." Size alone can force the top manager to rationalize the structure into key operating *functions* such as marketing, manufacturing, and research and development (R&D). As the complexity increases with additional businesses or programs, further rationalization may require some form of *divisional* organization such as product lines or business units.

As the number of divisional managers increases, top management may find it difficult to effectively maintain the communication required to ensure appropriate coordination in determining the most effective allocation of resources, selecting strategies and achieving objectives. The greater the autonomy given to divisional or functional managers, the greater is the need for systems to provide top management with information about their organization's operations and performance.

Systems

As organizations grow in size and complexity, systems become an important management tool. Systems not only facilitate communication but impact heavily on decision-making behavior. Systems have both planning and control components. Planning systems focus attention on developing strategic plans to achieve functional, business, or organizational objectives. Through the planning process, goals and objectives with varying time frames are established for both the organization and its subunits. The control system is generally the responsibility of the accounting function. The purpose of the control system is to determine in a timely fashion the variances between planned and actual performance so that corrective actions can be taken.

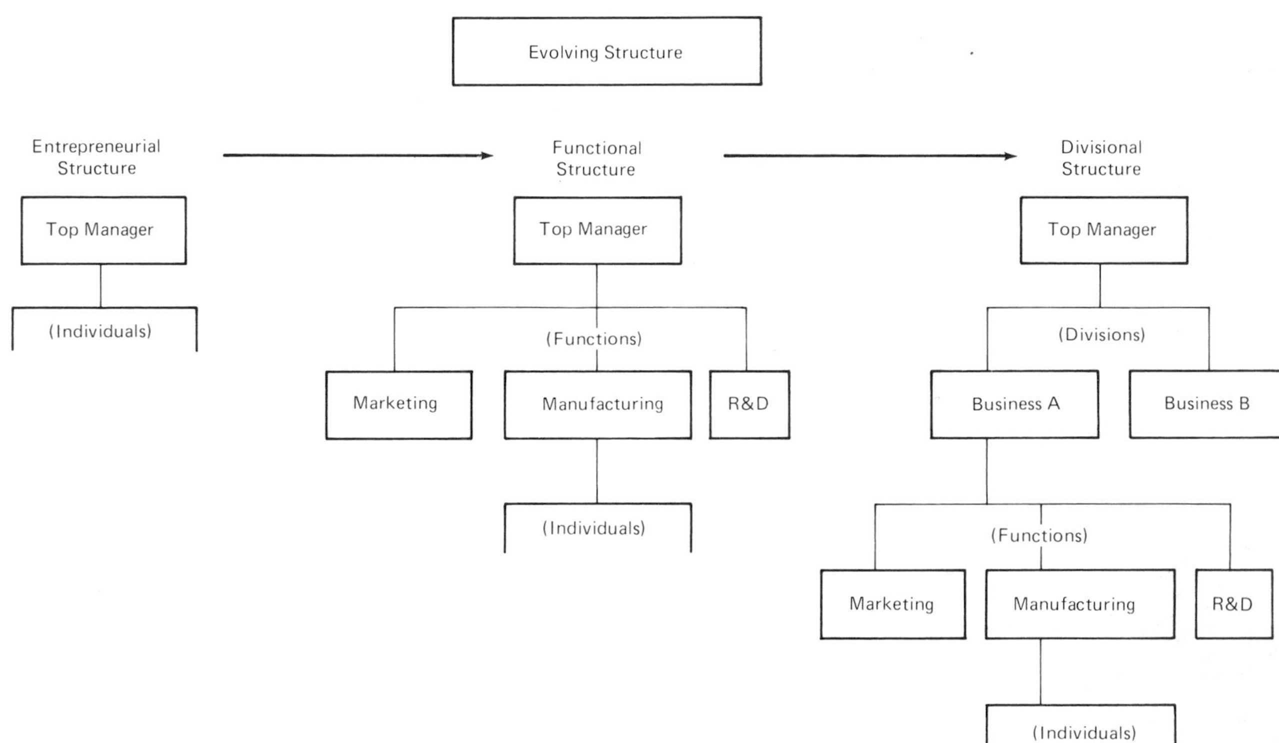

FIGURE 2-1: Evolving Organizational Structures

Staff

Staff refers to the demographic description of an organization's human resources. Since the most basic organizational resource is its people, the importance of "staff" must be recognized. Staff needs for development and communication are significantly impacted by the strategy, structure, and systems of the organization. The staff, in turn, affects the success of those strategies, structures, and systems. This requires that care be taken in the selection, long-term employment, socialization, training, and promotion of individuals who have goals and values congruent with those of the organization. Criticism and rewards can be effectively used in linking individual performance with organizational goals. In the same vein, the organization must commit itself to each employee to develop those skills that are required for individual and organizational success. Development through job rotation and internal merit-based promotions can increase motivation and internal competition.

Skills

Skills are the capabilities of an organization's staff and of the overall organization. Critical executive skills are often described in terms of the personality, culture, training, or experiences of the organization. The culture of the organization can be influenced through indoctrination, socialization, promotions, and training programs. When "outsiders" are brought into an organization, proper selection and integration become essential if the basic skills of the organization are to be maintained.

At management levels, dealing with people requires effective communication skills; evaluating performance requires effective analytic skills; and accomplishing individual tasks requires appropriate job skills. Through training and management development programs, the organization can update or improve these skills. However, fundamental to the maintenance of critical organizational skills is understanding what those skills are so that they may be protected and developed, and ultimately facilitate the organization's success in achieving its superordinate goals.

Superordinate Goals or Shared Values

Superordinate goals are the objectives, goals, and values that an organization's leaders instill in its members. These shared values encompass the purpose and mission of the organization and become the glue or common objectives or visions that often reinforce the areas of organizational competence or strength. For example, at McDonalds it was the stress on quality food; at IBM it was the stress on customer service. However, in most American companies, the shared values tend to include a demand for information, measurable short-term goals, and an impersonal work environment. In contrast, most Japanese companies stress two-way communication, long-term strategic goals, and a work environment that values individual loyalties, commitments, harmony, and consultation. In most Japanese companies, this policy area tends to be the guiding policy area, not just one of the eight Ss.

Style

"Style" describes how top managers behave in leading and motivating their organizations to achieve their desired ends. The manager's style will affect the policies they set and the priorities they use in allocating resources. In the most successful businesses, managers encourage communication between employees and demonstrate the importance of organizational values through their behavior.[2] Tough-minded, pragmatic, hands-on management also characterizes successful organizations. The use of meetings to generate information and foster face-to-face confrontation was also found to be a common practice in successful U.S. firms. The key to successful style, according to IBM's Watson, was to "generate extraordinary qualities in ordinary men." He wrote: "I believe the real difference between success and failure in a corporation can very often be traced to the question of how well the organization brings out the great energies and talents of its people."[3]

Treating people with respect and trust can foster individual commitment and cooperation and encourage employee contributions and organizational success. For example, increased autonomy and responsibility of employees reduced the need for supervision and overhead in McKinsey's excellent companies.

Succession

An eighth "S" that was not described by the McKinsey study is that of *succession.* Special attention needs to be given to maintaining or managing change in the first seven Ss. Through employee development and extensive socialization, top management can implant its values and management systems. However, because of the interrelationship between the seven Ss, a change in top management can significantly impact *style* and, thereby, affect the other Ss. Succession at any level of management seldom occurs without requiring a revision in the "fit" between the seven Ss.

Summary

Managing organizational change in any of the Ss requires careful analysis of these policy areas and their interrelatedness. By understanding and accepting the interrelated policies of organizations, top management can better understand the underlying forces behind its success formula and can take special care to perpetuate them. It is not an easy job and may ultimately be the key to long-term performance and success. But it is the job of the chief executive to ensure that this strategic management of the organization takes place. Figure 2-2 outlines some of the tools, concepts, and techniques that can be applied in each of these major policy areas. These concepts and methods used by strategic managers are discussed in later chapters.

[2]Thomas J. Peters and Robert H. Waterman, Jr., *In Search of Excellence* (New York: Harper & Row, Publishers, 1982), pp. 321–322.

[3]Thomas J. Watson, Jr., *A Business and Its Beliefs, the Ideas That Helped Build IBM* (New York: McGraw-Hill Book Company, 1963), p. 4.

Policy Concerns	Strategic Management Tools, Concepts and Techniques
Shared Goals & Values Chapter 3	Concept of Purpose and Mission Hierarchy of Goals and Objectives Stakeholder Analysis Assumptions Analysis Critical Success Factors
Strategy Chapters 4-7	Environmental Scanning Product-Market Analysis Competitive Analysis Life Cycle Analysis Strengths-Weaknesses-Opportunities-Threats Analysis Scenario Analysis
Structure Chapter 8	Organizational Structure Strategy-Structure Linkages Centralized-Decentralized Responsibilities
Systems Chapter 9	Planning and Control Systems Milestones and Measurements Resource Allocation Techniques Information Processing Methods
Staff Chapter 10	Skill Analysis Organizational Life Cycle Analysis
Skills Chapter 10	Critical Success Factors Capabilities—Use of Analytic, Administrative and Operating Techniques Levels of Resource Support
Style Chapter 11	Value/Assumption Analysis Cost/Benefit Analysis Decision-Making/Power Analysis
Succession Chapter 12	Managing Change

FIGURE 2-2: Strategic Management Concepts and Methods

THE ORGANIZATION'S STRATEGY: UNDERSTANDING THE TERRITORY

The purpose of a course in business policy or strategic management is to pull students above their functional or specialist orientation to understand the top manager's point of view. The top management perspective causes students to consider the total organization and its problems rather than the narrow focus of any one of its parts, whether that be a policy area or specific line or staff job. For the most part, business curricula concentrate on the functional areas of marketing, production, finance, and accounting. There are also courses that deal with social, political, legal, and economic aspects of the business environment.

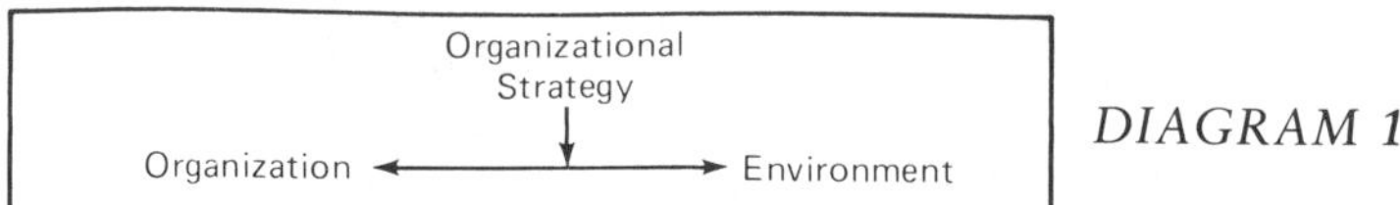

DIAGRAM 1

Other courses also cover management principles, organizational design, and behavior. Although these courses are important for understanding the functions of the organization and the nature of its environment, they often must neglect the problems of managing the total organization, integrating all of its diverse parts, or making trade-offs between those parts. It is this area of neglect that is the intended focus of business policy and strategic management.

The concept of corporate or *organizational strategy* provides managers with a concept by which they can organize their thinking about the basic relationship between the organization and its environment as shown in Diagram 1 above. The common use of the term *strategy* to define the "means" used to achieve the "ends" leads to some confusion here. At the organizational level, strategy must encompass the total organization in its attempt to achieve its overall purpose. In this sense, the organization and all of its policy areas, i.e., the eight Ss described earlier, make up the means by which the organization attempts to achieve its overall purpose or ends. Therefore, at the top management level, *organizational strategy* will encompass the superordinate goals, functional and business strategies, structures, systems, staff, skills, style, and succession policies used to accomplish the organization's purpose. Strategic management is the process of determining the character and content of those policy decisions in attempting to achieve the long-range objectives and purpose of the organization.

Without attempting to confuse the reader, we also use the term *business strategy* to refer to "means" used to accomplish a specific business objective. For example, Texas Instruments' strategic planning system is called OST, which is an acronym for objectives, strategies, and tactics. This is a system whereby explicit business objectives are supported by strategies as to how those objectives will be achieved and tactical resource allocation plans approved to implement those strategies. In practice, each of Texas Instruments' long-term (5-to-10 year) business objectives is supported by an average of five intermediate-term (3-to-5 year) business strategies. Each business strategy is then supported by an average of five short-term (6-to-18 months) tactical resource allocation or action plans.

To clarify the difference between "business strategy" and "organizational strategy" at Texas Instruments, the reader can think of the OST system as the strategic planning "system" characteristic. It is the OST system with its built-in reviews that Texas Instruments' management uses to recognize problems and make revisions in the face of the company's rapidly changing environment. The OST system allows top management to make trade-offs between resource allocations to different business objectives, thereby allowing Texas Instruments to achieve its overall organizational objectives. In this way TI's OST system becomes the planning and control system for its organizational strategy.

DIAGRAM 2: Organizational Considerations

UNDERSTANDING ORGANIZATIONAL STRATEGY

In an attempt to determine the strategic "fit" between the organization and its environment, top management must match its overall goals with the opportunities, obligations, and resources of the organization.[4] Organizational strategy requires that top management recognizes those opportunities that support the accomplishment of its purposes and can be effectively pursued with the organization's competencies and limited resources. At the same time, long-term viability also requires that society value the contributions of the organization and that the organization recognize noneconomic responsibilities which the organization has to those in society who are affected by its existence. Consider the nature of this "fit" as shown in Diagram 2.

Organizational Resources and Competencies

Finding an appropriate organizational strategy or "fit" between the organization and its environment requires that management recognize those opportunities that can be effectively pursued with the given resources and competencies of the organization. For example, Diagram 3 highlights those areas in which major organizational strengths can be found.

The most fundamental strength of organizations comes from its human resources. It is the human resources that provide the organization with its basic competence, bringing with them the basic skills and technical know-how required to manage the organization and develop and produce the products and services which are offered by the organization. It is the degree of economic or physical resources supporting this "staff" that ultimately determines the degree of strength the organization has relative to its competing institutions. Understanding the strengths and weaknesses of the organization's total resource base

[4]These concepts are discussed by C. R. Christensen et al., *Business Policy: Text and Cases* (Homewood, Ill.: Richard D. Irwin, Inc., 1978), p. 131.

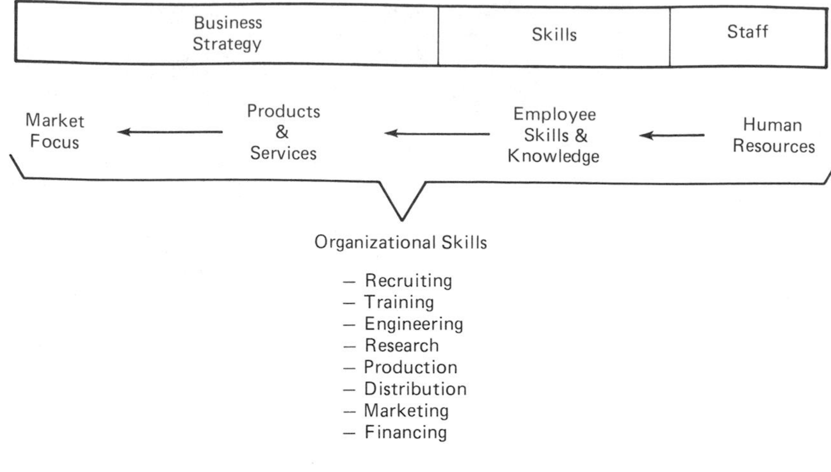

DIAGRAM 3

is critical in determining the business objectives and strategies used in approaching the marketplace.

Environmental Opportunities and Threats

Decisions about organizational strategy require careful analysis of the organization's environment, determining the nature and trend of those external characteristics and weighing the basic economic and noneconomic opportunities and threats. Those opportunities and threats only have meaning when they relate to the basic organizational operations, its values, its objectives, and its resources. For example, noneconomic concerns of society, such as the desire for clean air, can eventually have significant economic consequences for organizations that cause air pollution.

The problem with understanding societal issues is one of timing—knowing when such issues will impact on the political and legal structure of the organization's environment. Economic concerns tend to focus more directly on competitive issues—the nature of the product or service, the ability to meet the price and quality needs of the market, and the availability and consistency of the product or service. Technological changes, such as we see in electronics, can significantly impact on the price and quality of the offering as in the computer industry, or in service delivery, as in the telecommunications industry. Depending on an organization's values, commitments, and resources, such environmental trends can significantly alter an organization's financial position and future success.

The Role of Top Management

Those with the power to make or influence the critical "fit" of organizational strategy have primary responsibility for strategic management. The "superordinate goals" of the organization are heavily impacted by the experiences, values, and environmental perceptions of key directors and executives. Their definition of the mission, goals, and objectives of the organization will reflect their understanding and commitment to those superordinate goals. Inconsistencies or changes in such definitions can confuse employees and seriously impact on organizational morale and decision making.

The organization's philosophy and culture will also be impacted by management's "style" and its approach to operating policies and procedures. Management "style" has a strong influence on the kind of "systems" used to plan and control the allocation of organizational resources. It is this "systems" infrastructure that allows management (1) to allocate resources between long- and short-term programs in its effort to accomplish organizational objectives; (2) to keep informed about the health of the organization and its accomplishment of established objectives, strategies, and resource allocation plans; and (3) to provide the controls or measures of performance which allow individual payoffs or penalties for achieving specific levels of performance. The guidelines for developing systems come from the nature of the organizational strategy. These systems must be consistent with or "fit" with the business strategies being pursued and the structure used to support and manage the accomplishment of specific business and organizational objectives.

Diagram 4 shows the interrelatedness of the strategic management functions. The critical policies affecting the eight Ss are top management's responsibility and impact the overall character and success of the organization.

The effectiveness of *organizational strategy* depends on top management's strategic management skills. Strategic management requires both analytic and administrative skills. Making organizational strategy work requires both externally focused strategies (involving resources, products, and markets) and internally focused administration (involving structure and systems).

Strategy accomplishment requires goal directing and motivation systems by which individual rewards can be tied to organizational goals. Designing the structure and systems that support the organization's unique strategy requires administrative skills to structure individual relationships, to determine the degree of specialization and coordination, controls and measurements, and the incentives and motivations needed for success.

The Risks of Inflexibility

As is natural with individuals, much of our behavior becomes habitual in nature. Getting dressed and driving to work are routine behaviors to us. The only time we recognize that routine, however, is when we need to change it. How many people have left their money home because it was moved from its normal location? Or how many have found themselves at work when they were supposed to go some different place that day? Once we relegate our behavior to a routine it becomes difficult for us to change.

Habitual behavior patterns are also developed and perpetuated by organizations. The use of common practices, policies, or procedures causes behaviors to become routine and habitual. It is the nature of these habitual practices that impact most heavily on the basic character and culture of the organization. The stronger such habits or "traditions" become, the more difficult it becomes to change the behaviors of employees. As a result, ingrained habits and traditions

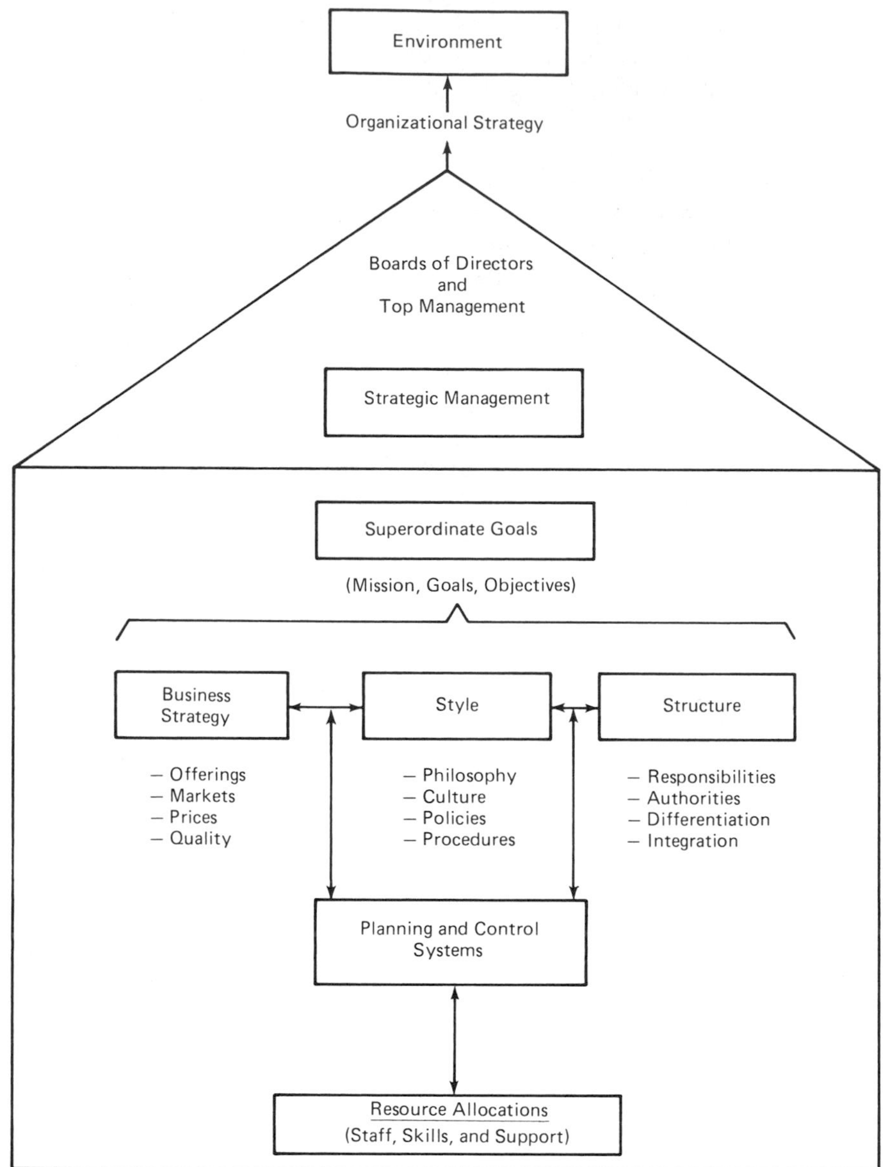

DIAGRAM 4

will impose constraints on the type of administrative tools and decisions that are available to strategic managers.

In contrast with the routinization of an organization is its ever changing or dynamic environment. Changes in the environment impact directly on the organization's requirements for success. For example, regulatory actions covering pollution, worker safety, equal employment, consumer safety, and trade activities have had significant impacts on business over the past ten years. Pollution standards for automobiles have required that industry to invest billions of dollars in pollution research and engineering. Deregulation of air transportation, financial institutions, and communications has obsoleted traditional strategies used in those industries. Rising energy costs and interest rates have affected the basic economic structure of energy users, such as steel, and debt-intensive industries, such as construction.

Rapidly changing environments will require organizations to change more quickly in the future. Complications derived from changing external and internal factors affect the performance and administration of the organization. Depending on the character of change, management attention will focus on opportunities for growth, pressures of maturity and decline, or demands of turnaround situations. Unfortunately, there is no easy way to develop the variety of skills and understanding needed by today's top managers. At best, we can help managers develop those analytic skills that will help them identify, understand, sort, and decide those areas that need their attention.

FORMULATING AND IMPLEMENTING ORGANIZATIONAL STRATEGY

Finding the appropriate strategy for an organization begins with the analytic process of determining what policies should best provide a successful "fit" between the organization and its environment. It should be obvious that this formulation process does not ensure success. Once strategic managers have decided what needs to be done, they must then implement appropriate policies in a manner that will hopefully achieve the desired results. This is not always easy since organizations tend to become inflexible over time. Therefore, decisions to change organizational strategy must also consider the constraints imposed by tradition, managerial preferences and skills, administrative systems, and procedures that make change difficult. Changing Ss can require the development of a whole new "fit" between the seven policy areas, which makes it difficult for organizations to make dramatic changes in their strategy. It is far more likely that only incremental changes will be acceptable in response to perceived dangers.

The interdependence of strategy formulation and implementation is most visible in large, multibusiness organizations where the "structure" and "systems" make it difficult to change "strategies." In such cases, changes in "structure," "systems," and "staff" may be required as the first step toward new strategic directions. This difficulty only reaffirms that strategic management is a complex field of study. Our attempts to simplify this complexity aid only in understanding its complexity, not in making the strategic manager's job any easier.

FOCUS QUESTIONS

1. What is strategic management?
2. What is an organization?
3. How does an organization relate to its environment?
4. What is organizational strategy?
5. What problems are inherent in managing organizational strategy?

6. What is the role of top management in formulating and implementing organizational strategy?

ADDITIONAL READINGS

ANDREWS, KENNETH R. *The Concept of Corporate Strategy.* Homewood, Ill.: Dow Jones Irwin, Inc., 1980.

BARNARD, CHESTER I. *The Functions of the Executive.* Cambridge, Mass.: Harvard University Press, 1938.

DRUCKER, PETER F. *The Practice of Management.* New York: Harper & Row Publishers, Inc., 1954.

PASCALE, RICHARD T. and Anthony G. Athos. *The Art of Japanese Management.* New York: Warner Books Inc., 1981.

SLOAN, ALFRED P. *My Years with General Motors.* New York: Doubleday & Co., Inc., 1964.

3 Introduction to Organizational Strategy and Its Key Components

At its most conceptual level, organizational strategy can be described in terms of the policy decisions that top managers have made over time. The "pattern of these decisions" and their impact on the eight Ss can be thought of as the organization's overall strategy. An organization's strategy may include a single business, relying heavily on functional operations; a business group; or a total complex of business groups. The description of the organizational strategy will differ depending on the size and complexity of the organization's business structure.

Unfortunately, members of organizations are not always aware of the elements that make up its strategy or cause its success. The organization's policies and procedures (i.e., the eight Ss) often have evolved as a result of conscious and unconscious decisions made in the past. As these policies and procedures affect the behavior and direction of the organization, management may lose control or understanding of the driving forces behind the organization's decisions and strategy. In the same sense, accomplishment of explicit organizational strategy can only be assured through strong organizational commitments and consistent decision making over a period of time.

The impetus for strategy identification, and its ultimate evaluation, comes most often during times of trouble. When the future success of the organization is in question, the difficult, painful, and time-consuming process of strategy identification and evaluation often begins. Answers to critical questions are not always agreed upon by managers and often meet with varied levels of disagreement. For example, the manufacturing vice-president of American Motors might argue that the primary reason for the company's poor profits comes from its lack of integrated production and the resulting high costs. The vice-president of finance, however, may argue that the low break-even level resulting from little integration has allowed American Motors to stay in business. These inconsistent beliefs result from the functional or operating perspectives of the management team. The closer these beliefs match the realities of their organization's environment, the greater is their likelihood of success. The greater the inconsistencies between management beliefs and environmental realities, the more likely it is that management conflicts will arise and strategies will fail. As a result, strategy description must challenge management beliefs to ensure that they match the realities of the organization's environment.

IDENTIFYING ORGANIZATIONAL STRATEGY

To begin the process of identifying organizational strategy, the following basic questions are useful in examining the critical factors and policy areas affecting the organization's past successes and failures.

1. Given our competitors' patterns of doing business, what has caused us to be successful in the past?
2. What are the nature and characteristics of our activities and policies that we have consistently followed?
3. What market position has these activities caused us to acquire?
4. What are the critical factors and policies that could make a difference in the success of our strategies?
5. To what extent are critical factors and policies likely to undergo change? What may be the direction of such change?

The process of identifying organizational strategy begins with a description of the actual scope of organizational activities, which encompass the "Ss" described in Chapter 2. A description of the products, markets, customers, and organizational policies will indicate the character of the current organizational strategy. Depending on the number and size of operating units within the organization, the concepts and tools used to assess the shared goals, strategy, structure, systems, staff, skills, style, and performance of the organization will differ. As organizations move away from simple operations to complex multibusiness combinations, the concepts and tools needed to understand organizational strategy will increase in number and complexity.

The Organizational Aims or Missions (Shared Goals)

The aims or missions are used to describe the purpose of the organization or products/markets/customers being served by a business. They establish the basic territory or playing field in which the organization will operate or compete. Specific objectives can be established as a basis for judging organizational success against the accomplishment of these aims or missions. The description of organizational strategy should then begin with the basic questions:

1. What are the aims or missions being followed by the organization in terms of priorities and with respect to stakeholders, current profits, future profits, growth, cash generation, resource development and utilization, and risk taking?
2. What is the general strategy for attaining the organizational aims and missions in terms of management's overall organizational, business, or functional concepts?

Exhibit 3-1 shows how the description of organization aims and missions changes with increasing organizational business complexity.

The organization's aims or missions often go beyond simply describing the business or businesses of the organization. For example, Mark Shepherd, the chairman of the board of Texas Instruments explained in 1976 the nature of his organization's mission.

EXHIBIT 3-1: Patterns of Aims, Missions, Goals and Objectives

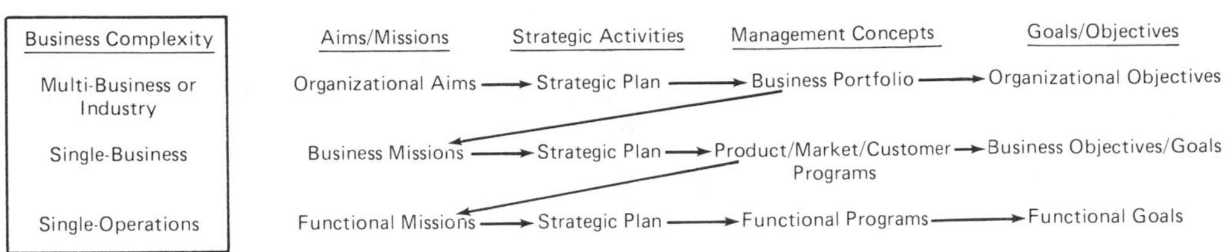

Source: Adapted from T. A. Smith, *Dynamic Business Strategy* (New York: McGraw-Hill Book Co., 1977), p. 138.

> Texas Instruments exists to create, make and market useful products and services to satisfy the needs of our customers throughout the world. Because economic wealth is essential to the development of society, we measure ourselves by the extent to which we contribute to that economic wealth—as expressed by our sales growth and our asset return. Our effectiveness in serving our customers and contributing to the economic wealth of society will be determined by our innovative skills.
>
> But Texas Instruments is permitted to operate by the society it serves, and that privilege does not include the inherent right to make a profit. There is an opportunity to earn a profit and that is our incentive as well as our reward for doing our job well. But unless any company meets genuine needs and solves vital problems, it will not earn the profit reward. That will be society's verdict that the organization is no longer useful. Without adequate profits it will cease to exist.
>
> This underlying philosophy implies much more about social responsibility. In the non-Communist world the corporation is responsible for managing a majority of the physical assets of society. And it must do so in a way which produces the *maximum return to society*—in new and better products, in creation of jobs, in a concern for the environment and community well-being. In short, it must provide a higher living standard, in both quantity and quality, for its employees and its customers. That is an enormous responsibility. The job of management is to create the unique corporate "culture" that will maximize the *return* to society in the fields where the corporation is active, and will minimize the *costs to society*—costs of all kinds—in achieving those returns.

Such a statement of organizational purpose goes beyond the specification of business activities into the realms of philosophy. It encompasses the inherent beliefs that management holds concerning the role of an organization in its environment.

It should also be stressed that such statements of mission or purpose only begin the process of strategic management. Without translating these philosophical concepts into specific objectives and goals, there is little that can be done to accomplish the mission or purpose of the organization. Mark Shepherd emphasized this point:

> The basic elements in managing the corporation are to define its goals. To make certain they are measurable, and to establish a system for tracking the progress achieved and assuring necessary feedback. Corporate leaders must be teachers. For unless the goals can be convincingly communicated, and unless the necessary corporate "culture" can be created to meet them, they will never be achieved. They must be achieved if the corporation is to do a proper job in society.

> In doing this job, we must not forget our basic corporate purpose—the delivery of goods and services at the lowest possible cost. The corporation will ultimately be judged by society on the basis of its ability to meet the world's material needs. We must do so with the highest standards of ethics, with a deep sense of obligation to the societies in which we operate, and with a willingness to stand before the public and defend our commitment as well as our capacity to carry them through.[1]

Deployment of Organizational Resources

The resources available to carry out the strategic activities identified in Exhibit 3-1 will significantly impact the ability of the organization to achieve its goals and objectives. Understanding the allocation of scarce organizational resources, such as funds, management talent, and technological know-how, therefore becomes critical in describing organizational strategy. For example, current strategy for a company such as Texas Instruments may include heavy investment in semiconductor research and development to maintain or achieve new technological leadership. Also, the assignment of qualified managers with skills to manage the implementation of that functional strategy may be a critical part of the organizational strategy.

The discretionary resources available to support strategic organizational activities need to be specifically identified. Describing the nature of these resource allocation patterns is an important part of strategy identification. Questions that may help in identifying resource deployment patterns include:

1. What is the strategy for employing critical resources (funds, managers and know-how) to get the most out of them?
2. How are resources being deployed to reinforce strategic strengths and/or overcome strategic weaknesses?
3. How are resource values being preserved (i.e., against inflation, turnover, and obsolescence)?
4. Are there any extremely vital resources? If so, what is the strategy for their use? Does it influence the total organizational strategy?

This description of resource deployment should show which businesses, functions, or programs have received the greatest management emphasis and where the greatest pool of resources and strengths currently lies.

For example, Texas Instruments began tracking its resource deployment through its strategic planning system in the early 1960s. In 1965, the then chairman of Texas Instruments, Patrick Haggerty, explained:

> Today, each division at T.I. has its own formally identified strategies and tactical action programs to implement them. There are additional intra-company strategies and tactical action programs (TAPS). In essence, these are identified as intra-company because more than one division is involved. Supervision and responsibility may be assigned to the lead division or, if of sufficient importance or involving several divisional and corporate activities, supervision and responsibility may be at the corporate level. We now have a total of 65 different strategies and 422 tactical

[1]Mark Shepherd, "Setting Goals and Objectives," *Top Management Report On: The Management of International Corporate Citizenship* (Washington D.C.: International Management and Development Institute, 1976), p. 19.

> action programs being carried out in pursuit of these strategies. Of even greater significance, perhaps, are the 21 strategies we identified as of potentially major impact on the corporation if successful. We define a major impact strategy as one which will generate at least $20 million a year of net sales billed over a period of at most five years. By contrast, three years ago there were only four major impact strategies.[2]

Although not all firms will utilize the same criteria or methods for identifying their resource deployment, it is crucial that some method be developed for understanding what resources are being committed to accomplish corporate, business, and functional level goals.

Organizational Competence and Competitive Position

Given the identification of business activities and resource deployment, an attempt should be made to deduce the actual bases upon which the company has been competing. Most successful strategies, for example, can be classified into one of the following three categories:

1. "Overall cost leadership" that results from investments in cost reduction for production, distribution, and product designs, and support with effective cost controls and targets.
2. "Product differentiation" that results from heavy investments in marketing and engineering to develop strong customer and dealer support and product features and leaders.
3. "Focus" that results from various combinations of the first two factors as they are applied to specific product/market/customer targets.[3]

Competitive advantages or distinctive competencies derived from these various approaches will have impacted past and present performance. To recognize the reasons for current competitive positions, consider the following strategic elements:

1. *Degree of specialization:* the degree to which product lines, geographic areas, and customer segments are limited.
2. *Degree of brand identification:* the degree to which brand recognition influences consumer demand for the product.
3. *Degree of marketing effort:* the degree to which resources are committed to "push" products through the distribution channels via sales force and special deals and "pull" products through the distribution channels via advertising and brand identification efforts.
4. *Selection of distribution channels:* the approach used to reach customers and provide market coverage range from ownership of retail outlets, use of mass merchandising chains, use of selected channels or specialized wholesale dealer networks, and direct selling to customers.
5. *Level of product quality:* adherence to high standards for raw material inputs, operating tolerances, and performance levels.

[2] P. E. Haggerty, *Management Philosophies and Practices of Texas Instruments* (Dallas: Texas Instruments, 1965), pp. 85–86.

[3] See Michael E. Porter, *Competitive Strategy* (New York: Free Press, 1980), pp. 40–41.

6. *Degree of technological leadership:* maintaining leadership in technological improvements and innovations rather than imitating or following competitive leadership.
7. *Degree of cost reductions:* the degree to which cost-minimization efforts are applied to engineering, marketing, manufacturing, and administrative operations to reduce overall product cost structures.
8. *Level of service:* the degree to which all ancillary customer needs are being met with regards to the product's purchase, including delivery, installation, training, repairs, financing, and the like.
9. *Competitive pricing levels:* the relative price position of the product compared to competitive levels of price, quality, features, and service.
10. *Level of vertical integration:* the degree to which "value added" levels are maximized through inclusion of all aspects of the production and marketing functions from raw material supplies to final customers or their purchasing outlets.
11. *Level of outside financial support:* the degree to which operations and assets are financed through borrowings and supplier credit.
12. *Level of external cooperation and support:* the degree to which external working relationships with government or private organizations support the efforts of the business.[4]

Once the strategic elements of an organizational strategy have been identified, a comprehensive description can be summarized by asking the following questions:

1. What strategy is being used to participate in each business or industrial field? What areas are being concentrated on? Are there restrictions on the areas being served? What is the "market" strategy?
2. What strategic position is being sought in the field? What strategy is being used to obtain or maintain it? What strategy is being used to adjust to future maturity phases?

As the semiconductor market began to develop in the early 1960s, Texas Instruments' management recognized the need of its customers. As chairman Haggerty explained in 1964:

> For electronics to be truly pervasive, it must be readily and commonly used by the mechanical engineer, the chemical engineer, the civil engineer, the retail merchant, and by the average citizen in broader ways than just for bringing entertainment to the home. Electronics cannot be truly pervasive unless such persons whose needs call for the powerful tools of electronics are capable of using them. It hardly seems feasible that highly skilled practitioners in other professions must also become skilled in the internal complexities of ours. The problem is considerably simplified, however, if the electronics skills which they require are limited to the comprehension or specification of the input and output parameters of electronics functions they need. And, it is exactly here that integrated electronics may prove to remove a large percentage of these communication limitations.[5]

By 1969, Texas Instruments had developed a whole line of standard "off-the-shelf" products. Mark Shepherd explained at the annual shareholders meeting:

[4] Michael E. Porter, *Competitive Strategy* (New York: Free Press, 1980), Chapter VII.
[5] Ibid., P. E. Haggerty.

> The standard market is exemplified by the expanding applications of low-cost, plastic-encapsulated integrated circuits. . . . We have developed a very strong product line to serve this market on a worldwide basis. Because of their low cost, they are being designed into many industrial products whose manufacturers heretofore could not afford to apply electronics to the solution of their equipment problems.

For custom designed electronic solutions, Texas Instruments worked to improve design time, as Shepherd continued:

> Design automation or computer aided design is a key element in this problem solving process. By using computers to do many of the repetitive design functions, we are able to reduce significantly the time to get a prototype design into the customer's hands and to release technical skills for more creative work.
>
> As an example, we reduced from eight weeks to three weeks the time it takes to generate a set of photomasks used in production of an integrated equipment component. This system is producing perfect masks the first time through the cycle. This rapid response helps our customer achieve his goals, and in so doing, enhances our efforts in building our share of his purchases.

Understanding the needs of the market and institutionalizing activities to meet those needs is fundamental to developing a strategic position in that market.

The Organizational Decision-Making Process

Since organizational strategy is a result of organizational decision-making behavior, the description of strategy must also include a description of those performance criteria and management priorities and assumptions that have governed the strategic choices and activities carried out by the organization. Since the "real world" factors are never clear, management's assumptions and beliefs are critical parts of strategy. Assumptions about the external and internal environments must therefore be specified if they are to be effectively monitored. For example, assumptions need to be recognized with regards to such areas as

1. stability of costs.
2. stability of resource availability.
3. stability of technology.
4. stability of resource values.
5. stability of market factors (e.g., market share, prices, distribution).
6. stability of organizational relationships and environmental dependencies.
7. stability of regulations and regulatory pressures.
8. stability of success factors.

Questions about the impact that such assumptions have on strategic activities include:

1. What strategy is used to keep the organizational aims and missions compatible with general environmental changes?
2. How will major environmental assumptions be monitored and strategic adjustments be made to deal with environmental changes?

For example, to facilitate the decision-making process at Texas Instruments, the company introduced a method for prioritizing projects that were competing for scarce financial resources. Mark Shepherd explained in 1969:

> Each year when we prepare our annual plans, we target billings and manufacturing cost goals which determines how much is left to cover our total expense package and profits. These expenses are in two categories: (1) operating expenses related to the maintenance of the current business, and (2) discretionary expenses related to future business. These "discretionary expenses," unlike the operational expenses, can be avoided, or delayed. Thus our problem is to decide how much to invest in discretionary expenses to support our strategic programs versus today's profits.
>
> To assist in making these choices, each unit or package or activity on which an independent decision logically could be made—we call it a "decision package"—was analyzed, scored on a set of criteria and ranked. This system allowed each program manager to score his own program, which then was reviewed and ranked at successively higher levels. . . . The decision packages were sorted and evaluated by strategy, technology, and business type. The goals were to minimize duplication, make sure we were not overemphasizing slow-growing aspects of the business to the detriment of faster-growing ones, relate common technologies, and select the best mix between low-risk, low-payoff and high-risk, high-payoff activities.

After ranking decision packages, programs were funded upon the level of discretionary funds. Unfunded packages left a "creative backlog" for future funding.

CHARACTERISTICS OF SUCCESSFUL ORGANIZATIONAL STRATEGIES

To understand the nature of "good" organizational strategies, McKinsey & Company studied thirty-seven companies that were considered to be well run. These firms relied on simple organizational structures, simple strategies, simple goals, and simple communications. Their approaches to organizational strategy were characterized by eight attributes:

1. a bias toward action.
2. a simple structure and lean staff.
3. continued contact with customers.
4. productivity improvements via people.
5. operational autonomy to encourage entrepreneurship.
6. stressing one key business value.
7. emphasizing doing what they know best.
8. simultaneous loose-tight controls.[6]

These eight characteristics of successful organizations deal with implementing ideas and getting the job done. This is not the same thing as using the latest strategic management techniques. The use of strategic management concepts does not guarantee success, since these concepts do not guarantee that the success variables are properly isolated or that proper action is taken. In fact, success seems to imply good organizational policies and their effective implementation.

Fast Action and Good Execution

The successful firms studied by McKinsey & Company were especially concerned about getting new product ideas off the ground. Long, complex business

[6]Thomas J. Peters and Robert H. Waterman, Jr., *In Search of Excellence* (New York: Harper & Row Publishers, 1982), pp. 13–15.

plans were being avoided. Instead, experiments were constantly being encouraged through the use of task forces made up of the best people to get the job done. The use of a task force was encouraged by management. It was made up of volunteers and was short lived. It involved little paperwork and received rapid feedback about its results. Extensive planning was left for the introduction phase of new products into the marketplace.

The success in action and execution appeared to come from having a limited number of well-defined goals and assigning organization-wide responsibility for specific goal or problem areas. Texas Instruments' management decided that more than two objectives for any manager was no objective at all. IBM also involves its busiest people in problem-solving projects: "We only put people on them who are so busy that their major objective is to get the problem solved and to get back to their main jobs."[7] At Texas Instruments results are reviewed and the time spent is justified to senior management, the focus is on results.

Simple Structures and Lean Staffs

Successful firms have concentrated on keeping organizations small and simple. To encourage the spirit of entrepreneurship, units are kept small, experiments are encouraged, task forces are common, and autonomy is supported. Product divisions are kept small. Staff positions are few and involve noncareer positions to discourage bureaucracies. Simplified interfaces between structural units come from project centers, such as task forces, which are used to break old habits and find innovative solutions to problems. Finally, controls are limited to only a few variables, leaving managerial autonomy in deciding how to achieve results.

Continued Contact with Customers

Successful organizations are customer-driven with customer contacts providing the insights that direct the company, its products, its technologies, and its strategies. Most ideas come from customers, not from market research. As a result, top management stays close to customers, talks to them, and sends out customer surveys. This allows successful organizations to become better listeners, to hear user ideas, and to stay in touch with their customers. It also encourages them to provide good customer service since complaints reach the top. In fact, at IBM, customer complaints must be processed within twenty-four hours. This guarantees that the customer becomes an integral part of the business.

Productivity Improvements Through People

Successful organizations have developed a culture in which people are highly valued and trusted to do the job. Group autonomy and entrepreneurship are fostered through the use of small groups, plants, and divisions. Care in maintaining quality and managing details is encouraged. Rewards, other than mone-

[7]Thomas J. Peters, "Putting Excellence into Management" *Business Week,* July 21, 1980.

tary ones, are given to successful workers. Experimentation, relentlessness, and persistence are values that cause productivity to occur inside the organization.

Operational Autonomy to Encourage Entrepreneurship

Maintaining organizational vitality proves to be a major concern of successful organizations. Overcontrol and complex decision-making procedures restrict entrepreneurs from pushing new ideas. Successful organizations have attempted to overcome these problems by instituting a management philosophy to encourage entrepreneurship. Key components of that philosophy include

1. encouraging volunteer champions of new ideas for product developments, process research, and development and productivity work.
2. forming self-sufficient, fully staffed groups incorporating all functional skills and encouraging competition between groups.
3. making divisional managers responsible for new ideas and product development for purposes of division self-renewal through reinvestment of their own profits.
4. training general managers through job rotation in tough, short, targeted assignments with a hard end-product focus.
5. spinning off winners (new products) into separate divisions so that entrepreneurs can pursue new activities.
6. increasing idea flows through constant changes in the organization and regular peer reviews.

The components of an entrepreneurial philosophy are simple in nature, but successful organizations have found that it takes real commitment and persistence from top management to make it work. It requires realism in goal setting, an action orientation, and tight control over a few important variables.

Stress One Key Business Value

Successful companies have developed shared goals that set the standard for what is valued in their corporate culture. Whether it is customer service, cost reduction, productivity, or quality, these organizations make certain that every employee is properly indoctrinated and believes in this goal. The common socialization process often insists that employees begin by "getting their hands dirty" to learn the basic skills required by the organization. Employees require realistic and innovative thinking to excel, and use constant peer comparisons and role models to set standards for employee performance and behavior. Those who do not fit the mold or do not believe in the values leave early. The focus on basic business values also provides the basis for rewards. Individuals who do "something special" to get the job done and foster the organization's goals win.

Emphasize What They Know Best

Successful organizations have understood their strengths—whether marketing, customer service, product innovations, or low-cost production—and built on those strengths. They have resisted the temptation or learned from experience and not moved into business that they did not understand or lacked the corporate skills to make successful. In many cases, bad experiences have caused them to recognize their strengths and stay close to home.

Simultaneous Loose-Tight Management

Successful organizations have spent much energy creating entrepreneurial organizations that have a great degree of autonomy. To encourage a loose atmosphere, some organizations have developed campuslike cultures with flexible structures and strong social networks. To encourage volunteer champions of new ideas and experimentation, other organizations have attempted to maximize individual, team, and division autonomy, and to give positive feedback to such behavior.

Successful organizations, however, have also maintained tight control over certain elements of the organization.They insist on tightly shared goals that relate most directly to the predominate discipline in the organization. To ensure that those disciplines are maintained, these organizations watch closely only a few key numbers, relying heavily on action-focused reviews, quick feedback, concise paperwork, and peer pressure. Many of these reviews are customer-focused.

In conclusion, McKinsey & Company found that these successful companies fought to avoid bureaucratic behavior in their organizations. Exhibit 3-2 shows the results of the research and contrasts what might be considered less successful practices. Organizations that overanalyze, overcontrol, overstructure, or let managers become too removed from the business are likely to run into trouble. Exhibit 3-3 points out that these successful characteristics relate to the eight policy areas described in Chapter 2. As top managers begin to assess their own organizational strategies, discrepancies between their own policies and practices and the ones described here can help focus on areas that need evaluation.

EXHIBIT 3-2: Findings from Excellent Companies Study

Practice	*Avoid*
1. Action and execution	"Analyze it,": "Complicate it," "Debate it"
2. Simple organization forms with lean staffs	Matrixing and layering
3. Staying close to customer/distributor	Frills, Statue of Liberty plays
4. Obtaining productivity through people	Cost control by overcontrol
5. Allowing autonomy/entrepreneurship	"Be creative, damn it"
6. Hands-on management that is value driven	Being driven by remote control
7. Sticking to their knitting	Apples + oranges = synergy
8. Simultaneous loose-tight management	Unbridled decisions or unbending controls

Source: Adapted from "Findings from the Excellent Companies" (New York: McKinsey & Company, Inc., 1980), p. 117.

EXHIBIT 3-3: Successful Policy Characteristics

Successful Organizational Characteristics/Policies	Shared goals	Style	Staff	Skills	Strategy	Structure	Systems	Succession
Action oriented		X						
Simple structure						X		
Lean staff		X	X					
Customer contact					X			
Productivity through people		X	X					
Autonomy		X	X	X				
Stress one value	X							X
Emphasize distinctive competence	X			X				X
Loose-tight controls							X	

SUMMARIZING ORGANIZATIONAL STRATEGY

The identification of organizational philosophy and objectives is fundamental in understanding what management wants the organization to become. This should state the organization's mission and aims; its economic purpose; its product, market, and technical goals; its responsibilities to employees, shareholders, community, and society; and its financial goals in specific and measurable terms, such as sales, earnings, return on assets, and product mix.

Specific business objectives for multibusiness organizations should support the corporate goals. The scope of each business should be defined, identifying the markets to be served within the scope of the business charter, major market and technical trends, and the industry structure. From this information, performance measures and goals can be identified for sales, earnings, return on investment, market penetration, and technical innovations.

Each business objective can then be described in terms of the functionally based programs aimed to accomplish the specific performance goals. Each strategic program can be described in terms of those actions that are expected to achieve significant results, identifying potential competitive responses to those actions, major policy commitments required by management, and contingent programs depending on results. All of this must be described in terms of those milestones that must be accomplished over time, and against which performance can be measured. Finally, the description needs to recognize the financial impact of a successful program and the probability of positive and negative factors influencing the achievement of those results.

FOCUS QUESTIONS

1. What would be an example of an organizational mission statement for (a) a single business firm, and (b) a multibusiness firm?
2. Find industry examples in which success is based on (a) cost leadership, (b) product differentiation, and (c) focus strategies.
3. Identify a product or firm that uses each of the twelve strategic elements described in the section entitled, "Organizational Competence and Competitive Position."
4. What assumptions would you make about each of the eight stability factors listed in the section entitled, "The Organizational Decision-Making Process."

ADDITIONAL READINGS

DRUCKER, PETER F. *Management: Tasks, Responsibilities, Practices.* New York: Harper & Row Publishers, Inc., 1974.

ROTHSCHILD, WILLIAM E. *Putting It All Together: A Guide to Strategic Thinking.* New York: AMACOM, 1976.

UYTERHOEVEN, HUGO E. R. et al.: *Strategy and Organization.* Homewood, Ill.: Richard D. Irwin, 1973.

VANCIL, RICHARD F. "Strategy Formulation in Complex Organizations." *Sloan Management Review,* 17, no. 2 (Winter 1976).

PART II

Formulating Business Strategies

4 Business Level Objectives and Strategies

As described in Chapter 3, strategic management is concerned with finding the appropriate fit between the organization and its environment. Of the eight "S's" described earlier, however, it is "strategy" that provides the primary link between most organizations and their environments in attempting to achieve their missions, goals, and objectives. This chapter describes the nature of "strategy" as it relates to the business and functional levels of the organization.

In organizations with a single business focus, the organization's mission statement and objectives are likely to include a product or market focus. To limit confusion here, the term *product* refers to the offerings of the organization whether it be a product or service. In fact, service organizations are increasingly using the strategic management concepts used commonly in manufacturing organizations. This trend is likely to continue as we move into computer-based information systems as discussed in the Texas Instruments MODPLAN case.

At the business level, strategy relies most heavily on coordination of the create-make-market functions. As shown in Exhibit 4-1, the *create* function includes both product and market research and development tasks. The *make* function includes the tasks of purchasing, manufacturing or assembly, and inventory management. The *market* function includes distribution, sales, advertising, and promotional responsibilities.

It is the capabilities of these functional areas that impact the product focus of the organization. Ultimately, it is the functional skills that determine how closely the product meets the needs of the marketplace. Either operating or coordination problems in these functions can impact on a strategy's success in achieving its objectives. Proper coordination requires an appropriate information system to ensure that plans and results of operations can be adapted to market realities.

In understanding the importance of having a product-market focus for functional activities, consider the comments of Texas Instrument's Pat Haggerty in 1964:

> Our growth and diversification led us in 1954 to decentralize our organization along product lines. In so doing we moved toward organization around entities of engineering, manufacturing and marketing functions and began to evolve the basic premise that today we say is fundamental to our entire philosophy of management.
>
> The essence of our capabilities to control and advance our business is based on the premise that we must be product-customer centered. Product-customer centering means that we must *not* be functionally-centered—that is, sales-centered,

EXHIBIT 4-1: Single Business Strategies

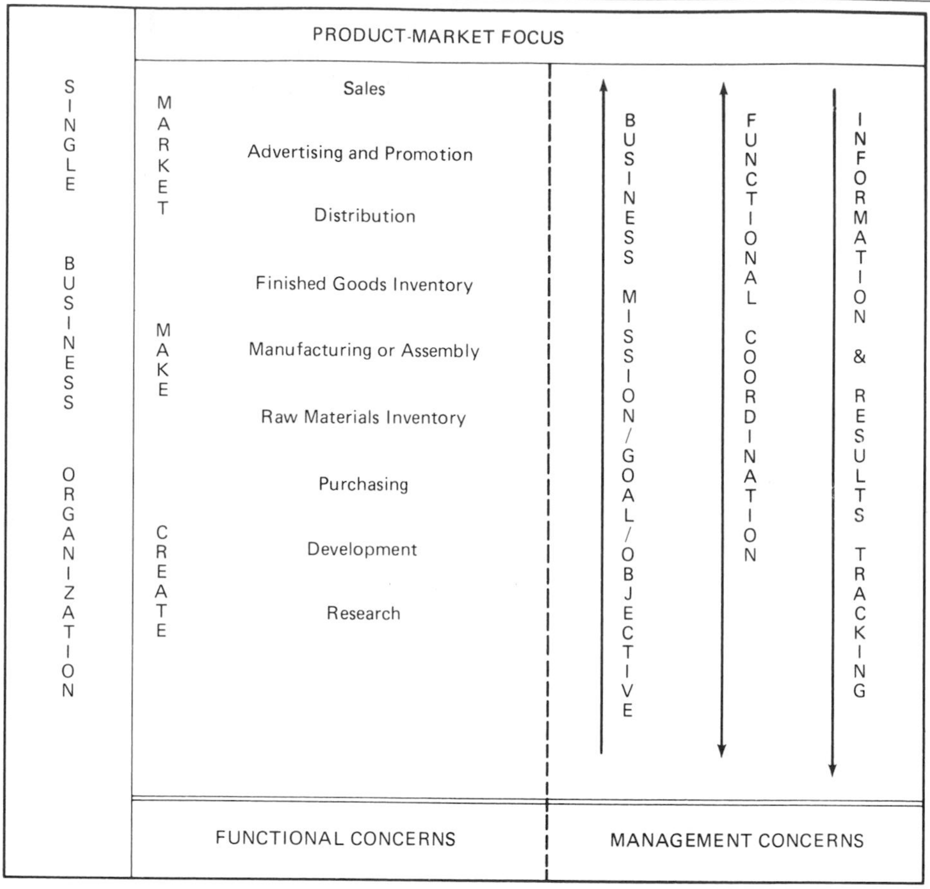

SINGLE BUSINESS ORGANIZATION

PRODUCT-MARKET FOCUS

MARKET
- Sales
- Advertising and Promotion
- Distribution
- Finished Goods Inventory

MAKE
- Manufacturing or Assembly
- Raw Materials Inventory
- Purchasing

CREATE
- Development
- Research

BUSINESS MISSION/GOAL/OBJECTIVE

FUNCTIONAL COORDINATION

INFORMATION & RESULTS TRACKING

FUNCTIONAL CONCERNS | MANAGEMENT CONCERNS

manufacturing-centered, engineering-centered, or even personnel-centered. It means that we *must* so orient ourselves as to ensure that our major organization emphasis is on the recognition of the needs of our customers and the creation and manufacture of products and services to satisfy those needs.

The three line functions through which we attempt to accomplish our product-customer centering are "creating" the product, "making" the product, and "marketing" the product—all are of major and equal importance.[1]

Functional capabilities are critical in the development of a product-market focus. As shown in Exhibit 4-2, business strategy must include (1) an understanding of market needs, (2) an appropriate product concept, and (3) adequate functional skills to efficiently and effectively make and/or deliver products to the designated market.

Time horizons are a second dimension that also needs some clarification in our discussion of objectives and strategies. For example, it will take longer to achieve business objectives than functional objectives since the functional objec-

[1]Patrick Haggerty, "Three Lectures at the Salzburg Seminar on Multinational Enterprises" (Dallas: Texas Instruments, 1977), pp. 11–12.

EXHIBIT 4-2: Business Level Objectives and Strategies

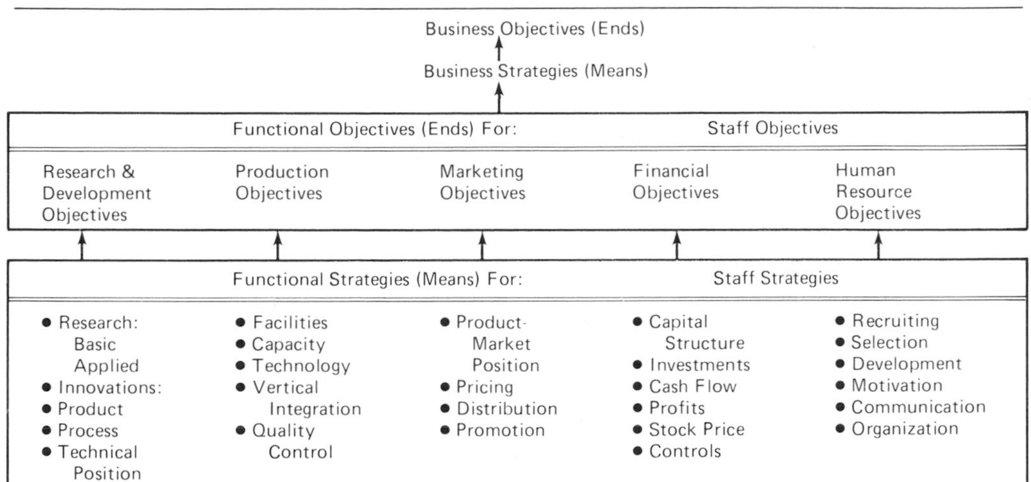

tives enable us to achieve business objectives. Funding decisions for capacity are required far in advance of achieving actual sales. Without the production facilities in place at the time sales demand is projected, there is no way that projected sales can be achieved. In this sense, then, lower level functional objectives and strategies are likely to have a shorter time horizon than business or organizational level objectives.

THE ROLE OF FUNCTIONAL OBJECTIVES AND STRATEGIES

The distinctive competencies of the organization at the functional level have the greatest impact on business level strategies. As a result, it is important to gain some understanding about the impact that functional strategies can have on the organization. In this section, some characteristics of the create-make-market functions are discussed.

Research and Development Characteristics

Understanding the role of research and development in business strategies requires that four key areas be understood in relation to the management and investment strategies for the business (e.g., depending on whether management intends to grow, defend, or harvest the business). These descriptive areas include:

1. *Technical competence.* The skills and talents of the technical organization will determine what expertise can be used to support the business strategy. This is especially critical in developing new products, innovations, or cost reductions to support growth or defense strategies.

2. *Ability to respond.* The response time required to meet competitive actions will influence the business strategy, depending on whether rapid, slow, or no response is demanded. The area of response is also important since it can be

in terms of applications, support systems, or product improvements. Each area requires a different set of skills.

3. *Technical position.* The business strategy often relies on maintaining an image as industry leader (IBM), technological leader (Hewlett-Packard), or follower (Radio Shack). The more technologically sophisticated one becomes, the greater is the chance of developing patents or skills that protect one's business niche. Management's commitment and continued investment is critical to maintaining such a position.

4. *Facilities and equipment.* The development of appropriate engineering and research support facilities is critical to institutionalizing a basic research and development strategy. Since resources are generally in short supply, the position and prestige of the department will impact its long-term development.

Manufacturing Characteristics

The organization that produces its own products must also ensure that the manufacturing function is integrated into the management and investment strategies. Critical areas include:

1. *Nature of production facilities.* The size, condition, degree of specialization, and location of production facilities will impact the firm's ability to carry out a growth, defense, or harvest strategy. Large specialized facilities may support defense and hold strategies through low-cost production capabilities. Growth strategies require flexibility in adding capacity and supporting small production operations. Harvest or exit strategies are easier to manage with leased facilities that might be later abandoned.

2. *Capacity utilization.* Capacity will affect both profitability (break-even levels) and the ability to meet demand. Growth strategies require that capacity be available ahead of demand, but, for large facilities, this can also be a risky investment which requires adequate capital for investment.

3. *Productivity.* Industry automation and cost structures are increasingly important as new competitors with new technologies enter the marketplace. Determining relative cost positions and planning process innovations and automation are especially important in defense and harvest strategies.

4. *Supplier characteristics.* Supplier dependencies will add to the risk of operating in industries in which materials are in short supply. Material stockpiles or backward integration may be required as part of the investment and management strategies for the business.

5. *Buyer characteristics.* Buyer dependencies and location will impact the production and distribution requirements for carrying out the business strategy. Inventory availability and speed of delivery become increasingly important in more mature industries and are critical to defense and hold strategies.

Marketing Characteristics

Although marketing comes last in this presentation, it is extremely important. In fact, most techniques used for strategy analysis spend a great deal of time on marketing decisions. Product planning, sales, distribution, service, promotion, and pricing are all critical elements of a business strategy.

1. *Product positioning.* Being in the position of product leader or follower

depends heavily on the joint response of marketing and engineering. Development of a complete product line, components, or subsystems requires market assessments, engineering development, and production availability. Tight coordination through management and investment decisions is fundamental.

2. *Product distribution.* Relatively new and complex products require more exclusive, customer-oriented distribution channels. However, as markets mature and products become more standardized, a wide range of jobbers, retailers, and even mail-order channels can be used.

3. *Sales approach.* Depending on the distribution system, the sales force will need to focus on building technical, problem-solving, personal selling, or promotional skills. Growth strategies will rely on a more knowledgeable, application-oriented sales force than is necessary with broad channel defense strategies.

4. *Available services.* Services are most critical in early stages of product development, including pre=to=postsales service, instruction, maintenance, repair, and product-upgrading activities. With more mature products and defense strategies, such services may be unbundled and offered for a price. Along with service strategies comes the availability of inventory, parts, or service to keep customer inconvenience or downtime to a minimum. This approach is especially important for defense strategies.

5. *Promotional orientation.* Customer awareness and information are necessary to sell products. Growth strategies based on new product innovations require more aggressive promotion and support than more standardized, well-known products. Strategies to switch customers to your products require heavy promotional budgets to publicize your products and brands.

6. *Pricing approach.* Pricing decisions are fundamental to market position, development, and profitability. Pricing to costs, being the price leader, or discounting price will all affect the business strategy. Growth strategies with innovative products can support higher prices than mature products. Defense strategies may rely on cost-based pricing. Uniqueness and quality images of products may also allow premium prices. It is important that the pricing approach be consistent with the needs of the business strategy.

In designing the overall business strategy, it is necessary that these functional strategies fit the total business strategy and be internally consistent with the management and investment strategies for the business. Engineering innovations, manufacturing, capacity, and marketing activities must all be coordinated to accomplish the same business objective. Without engineering support you will be a slow follower: without efficient production you will be a high-cost producer. Without market planning and promotion you will end up in a weak position. A good description of your functional strategies will help make this evaluation.

SETTING BUSINESS LEVEL OBJECTIVES AND STRATEGIES

The functional capabilities of an organization have a direct impact on what alternatives or options are available. The overall strengths and weaknesses of functional units will affect the organization's ability to compete in the marketplace and maintain profitable operations. Business strategies must, therefore, relate directly to the abilities of the functional units to carry out their roles. Whereas the functional units support and constrain business strategies, the attractiveness of the business environment also plays an important part in determining business-level objectives and strategies.

The primary business objectives can be grouped into four basic types of objectives:

1. objectives that follow the product life cycle.
2. objectives to focus on a market niche.
3. objectives to rebuild the business.
4. objectives to withdraw from the business.

Product life-cycle objectives include business strategies for starting, growing with the industry, gaining market position, defending market position, and, ultimately, harvesting the business as shown in the appendix to this chapter. A variety of functional strategies might be used to carry out the business strategy ranging from product-market expansion to restructuring through integration.

Many of the same functional strategies can also be used to achieve "market niche" objectives through business strategies of finding, expanding, and holding market niches.

"Rebuilding" objectives may include such strategies as catching up with competition, renewing product, turning around performance, and prolonging the business's existence. When rebuilding does not work, the objective may be to "withdraw" from the market. Withdrawal can include withdrawal strategies for rationalizing the business, more severe elimination or divestment of operations, or final abandonment of the business through divestiture.

Depending on the attractiveness of the business environment and the business unit's competitive strengths, the business objective will be to grow to maintain position or to withdraw from the market. Exhibit 4-3 identifies a number of more explicit objectives and strategies that can be established for a business depending on the assessment made as to its position. For example, an invest/grow strategy still leaves options such as (1) investing in advertising and sales force to increase market share and future profitability, (2) increasing research and development, or (3) reducing price to hold market share. If the product falls in the harvest/divest area, strategies could include (1) selling or liquidating the business, (2) cost cutting through plant and product-line consolidation, or (3) relinquishing market share to hold price and margin.

Products that fall into the selectivity/earnings area raise other questions about selective pricing and market segmentation strategies. Depending on the business strengths and attractiveness of the industry, alternative strategies for such product units include:[2]

1. *Finding a vacant product niche.* Finding a low-volume, price-insensitive market that large competitors have ignored is an effective survival strategy. For example, American Motor's (AMC) "Jeep" has kept AMC alive for many years after it became unable to compete effectively with the large automakers. Dr. Pepper and Mountain Dew had similar success against Coca-Cola and Pepsi in the soft drink market.

[2]R. G. Hammermesh, M. J. Anderson, Jr., and J. E. Harris, "Strategies for Low Market Share Businesses," *Harvard Business Review,* **56**, no. 3 (May–June 1978): 95–102.

EXHIBIT 4-3: Business Objectives and Strategies

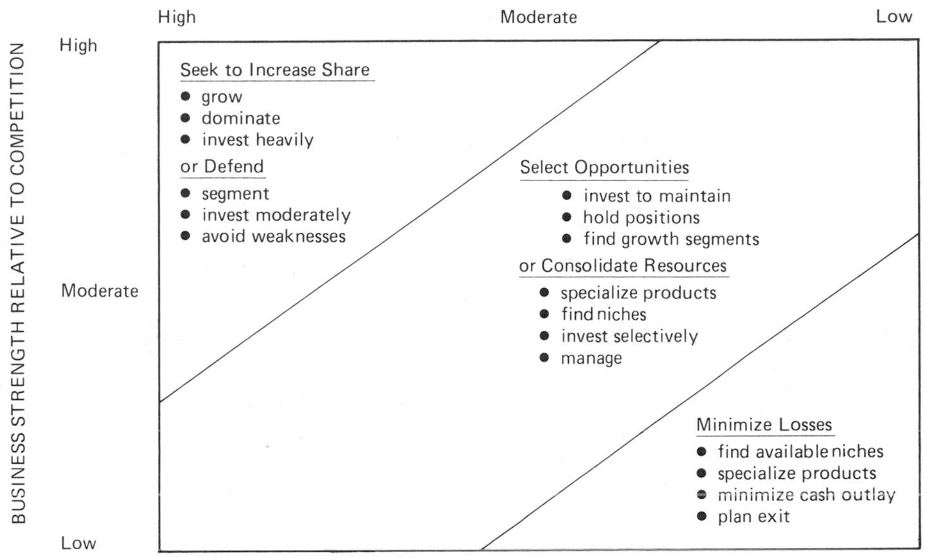

2. *Specializing in a specific market segment.* As large competitors seek to dominate all market segments, they lose their ability to provide specialized service and expertise to all segments of the market. In the computer market, for example, Burroughs has been able to dominate the banking segment of the industry.

3. *Providing a higher quality product.* There is always a segment in the market that insists on high-quality products. Small firms can effectively compete against the giants, like BMW in the quality auto segment of that industry. The Germans and Japanese have traditionally been successful at entering new markets by offering the highest quality at competitive prices.

4. *Finding new channels of distribution.* Being first to sell your product in a new or existing channel offers great opportunity. For example, drug products are now being offered in food stores and discount chains. Food products and snacks are increasingly being offered in drug chains. Auto tires and minor maintenance are being carried now by discount chains and department stores. Appliances are now being sold by tire stores. Today's television is becoming a new channel for direct sales through the use of "800" telephone numbers, providing opportunities for relatively unknown products to be sold across the nation.

5. *Offering something special.* A number of products have few distinctions in the mind of the customer. By offering something extra, like an extended warranty or extra feature, it is possible to stimulate new sales. General Motor's three-year extended warranties were a way to compete with the Japanese quality image. Sony's "fast forward" feature on its videotape player was a way to compare with Zenith's player. Tylenol's 800-milligram pain reliever was compared against 650-milligram products as a better pain killer.

The *Wall Street Journal* described one firm in 1982 that had found its niche:[3]

Rockford Headed Products, Inc., was losing its screw, bolt, and fastener sales to cheap imports in the late 1970s. In 1978, fifty-six-year-old Frank Taylor bought the small, privately owned firm that sold 85 per cent of its standard screws and bolts to distributors who resold them to end users. Since distributors bought on price, Rockford had to underprice competitors and importers to win orders.

To get out of this high-volume, low-cost, low-margin business, Taylor moved into special fasteners. He focused on a self-threading screw that speeds assembly and holds better than ordinary fasteners in certain materials. It had been developed by the previous owner but only accounted for a small portion of sales. These fasteners were sold directly to end users who demanded quality and on-time delivery above price. These special items sold for $55 to $100 a thousand compared to $5 for standard fasteners.

Moving into direct sales, however, required a total change in operations. Sloppy production had caused 20 per cent of raw materials to end up as scrap. At a cost of 40 cents a pound it brought only two cents a pound as scrap. The scrap rate is now 8 per cent with a goal of 6 per cent.

Quality was key to the new business. According to Taylor, "Quality is an attitude, and it is a long education process to change attitudes." Much of his new business was taken from competitors whose products had interrupted customers' assembly operations. Being able to move quicker in designing and producing special parts, Rockford will take on the "big boys."

He replaced his 100-year-old plant and outdated equipment in January 1981 with a newly designed and built 44,000-square foot plant. A $1.25 million industrial bond sold to a local bank provided $725,000 to build the factory and $525,000 for new equipment. Today, 47 production workers tend 65 machines in the new plant. He also signed 25 manufacturing representatives to develop new business for a 5 per cent sales commission. He expected a 10 per cent sales increase in 1982, to $4.4 million.

For business units that lack the resources or have already lost the dominant position within a product or industry area, opportunities still exist for developing effective product strategies. For example, effective low-share competitive strategies incorporate such elements as (1) high-quality products, (2) low competitive prices, (3) limited research and development, (4) low vertical integration, and (5) modest discretionary spending for marketing or administration areas.[4] The intention of such a strategy is to offer maximum "value" to hold market position and customer loyalty.

THE EVOLUTION OF BUSINESS LEVEL OBJECTIVES AND STRATEGIES

The nature of the problems faced by business-level managers may have very similar characteristics even though their products and market settings may be totally different. If we think of products like instant cameras, electronic watches,

[3]Stanford L. Jacobs, "How an Entrepreneur Revived Faltering Firm Despite Slump," *Wall Street Journal,* June 7, 1982, p. 23.

[4]Presentation made by C. Woo and A. Cooper, "Strategies of Effective Low Market Share Business," at the 1980 Annual Academy of Management meeting.

EXHIBIT 4-4: Stages of Life Cycle

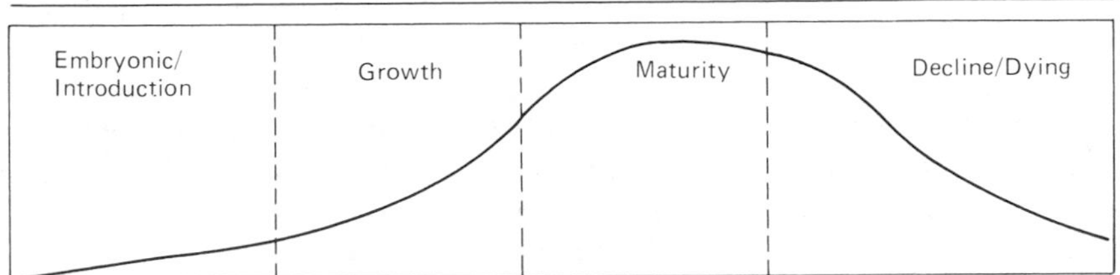

calculators, or home computers, we could identify a number of similar problems that they have faced since their introduction. For example, the early quality problems of these products caused delays in consumer acceptance as did their high costs. Once those problems were overcome, the distribution of the products to reach their various markets became important. Increasing variety and standardization of product designs by established and new competitors lead to tougher competition and lower prices. Today, Kodak and Polaroid are battling for position in the instant camera market. Texas Instruments held a leading position in the calculator market and the home computer market was dominated by IBM and Apple, but Texas Instruments and other competitors are coming on strong. To discuss the similarity between these products, let us consider the concept of product life cycle.

The hypothesis for using product life cycle is that a product or industry passes through evolutionary phases or stages—embryonic, growth, maturity, and decline as shown in Exhibit 4-4. The flat introductory stage reflects the difficulty of early product development and buyer resistance to new products. When the product proves itself, rapid growth occurs as news spreads and buyers rush into the market. Once heavy penetration of the potential markets or buyers has been reached, growth will slow down or level off to the growth or user rate of the market itself. After alternative or substitute products begin to appear, the growth rate will begin to decline.

The nature of the competitive forces within the marketplace will change dramatically as a product's life cycle evolves. One simplified description is the following:

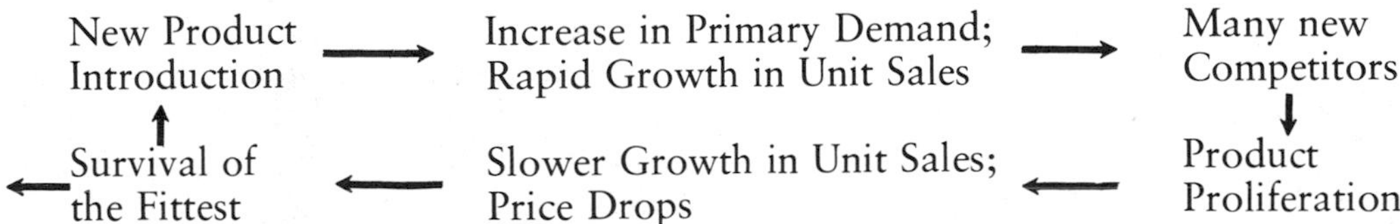

This indicates that product growth brings on competing firms and products which can eventually lead to heavy price competition and survival of the financially strongest or lowest cost producers.

Embryonic Product Strategies. In developing a product strategy for the embryonic stage in the life cycle, the primary focus should be on identifying relatively new industries where growth is high and competitors have relatively low market share positions. The primary business strategy should then be to develop new products that provide entry into the market. The basic business strategy would include:

1. Investing in and encouraging product research and development of new product innovations. Setting the industry standard for product design, quality of performance, or cost levels can lead to a market leadership position.
2. Identifying new market opportunities or product applications through consideration of technological, economic, social, political, and legal changes in the environment or marketplace. For example, the addition of occupational safety and health regulations (OSHA) created a whole new industry of workers' safety equipment. The move toward informal attire created enormous growth in blue jeans sales. Increasing energy costs have spurred small car sales and the retrofitting of buildings with energy-saving equipment. Satellites and computer technology have changed the whole structure of information processing and could significantly reduce the use of paper documents in large organizations. Being the first to identify and gain a position in such opportunity areas may allow high-price skimming strategies to support relatively high marketing costs needed to significantly affect market position.
3. Developing designs and production techniques to utilize all available experience in minimizing product costs. High labor content and low-volume production runs increase product costs. Rapid cost reductions can lead to price reductions and additional market growth opportunities.
4. Allocating specified resource levels for new product developments. The reliance on R&D and engineering functions and the high risk levels of coming up with major product breakthroughs suggest that a specified amount of resources be allocated at such risk levels.

The following example of the costs and risks inherent in new-product development was described in 1982 in the *Wall Street Journal.*[5]

RSP Laboratories, Inc., developed a nonsurgical technique using a hysteroscope and the company's proprietary devices to inject a silicone-rubber solution into a woman's Fallopian tubes. The procedure closes off the Fallopian tubes so that eggs cannot pass to the uterus. The procedure takes less than an hour and, unlike some methods, is reversible. At present, the method is expected to work on 75 to 90 per cent of the women on whom it is employed; some women's tubes are too small or not accessible to the current device.

The firm's president, John Schorsch, was optimistic that he would get approval from the Food and Drug Administration for the use of the device, but approval is never certain. All that is certain is that the company had invested $3 million since 1976 in its effort to build a business on this new medical approach. Schorsch, who had been used to running a profitable enterprise, expressed his frustration: "I haven't produced a profit since 1976. It takes a big mental adjustment." After experiencing difficulty in obtaining outside investors, he and Paul Guggenheim, his partner in a precious-metals recovery firm, funded the startup.

RSP's founders spent $650,000 in the first two years of the company's existence and in 1978, they sold 30 per cent to two investors for $350,000—the year the first human implants began. In 1980, a pharmaceutical firm bought 25

[5]Stanford L. Jacobs, "New Method of Birth Control Is Pioneered by Small Concern," *Wall Street Journal,* June 21, 1982, p. 19.

per cent of the firm for $1.4 million and the rights to the product should the company fail. In 1982, a group of venture capital companies invested $1,060,000 for 10 per cent ownership and an option for 7 per cent more at $600,000. This incremental funding has allowed the founders to keep a greater percentage of ownership than would have been the case if they had attempted to raise capital all at once.

Should the FDA approve the procedure, and should the RSP procedure be accepted worldwide, Schorsch estimated a market worth $100 million per year. In the United States alone, over six hundred thousand women are surgically sterilized each year. The problem is in training gynecologists to use the procedure; the current cost of training the thirteen who know how to use the device has been $15,000 each.

Growth Product Strategies. Once new products begin to achieve market acceptance, primary demand can rapidly push product sales into the growth phase of the product life cycle. During this growth phase, the primary focus should be on building market share so that long-term market position will generate substantial economies of scale and profitability. The basic business strategy could include:

1. Investing as many resources as required or available to build a strong position in current markets and to enter new markets. By maximizing sales relative to competition, economies of scale can lead to a competitive advantage in cost structure. Exhibit 4-5 describes the relationship between market share and product costs as related to the concept of the experience curve.
2. Using creative marketing techniques to introduce product improvements, performance, and reliability differences for maximum product and market diversification and product leadership. Heavy product advertising and expansion of distribution channels will maximize market coverage.
3. Utilizing economies of scale and experience curve effects to drive costs down so that price reductions can be used to exploit price/value elasticity and growth in primary demand. Relative price reductions, or even price maintenance in times of high inflation, can give a firm an entrenched position in the market or increase the amount of resources available to the firm for market expansion.
4. Accepting investment risks within the structure and limits of the firm's resources. If resources do not allow the organization to obtain a leadership position, then resources might be allocated to a specific market or segment where price is less important and profits can be maintained.

One example of the kinds of problems a firm can face once growth comes was described in 1982 in *Forbes.*[6]

Altos Computer Systems' president, David Jackson, received a contract from the $2.8 billion giant Control Data Corporation. The contract, which was worth $30 to $50 million over five years, called on Altos to provide a small, powerful "supermicro" business system computer using advanced 16-bit technology. This

[6]Barbara Ettone, "Faces Behind the Figures," *Forbes,* July 5, 1982, p. 160.

EXHIBIT 4-5: Experience Curve

For a firm to attain price leadership in its markets, it must seek a market share position which will allow it to reduce its cost levels. The decline in average price for integrated circuits as the total number of units increased shows the impact of the experience curve—the impact of increased productivity from learning to do a job faster, increased task specialization, growth in volume, increased investment in new capacity and equipment, and general increased economies of scale. The combined effect of learning, specialization, investment, and scale allows an approximation of the experience curve effect.

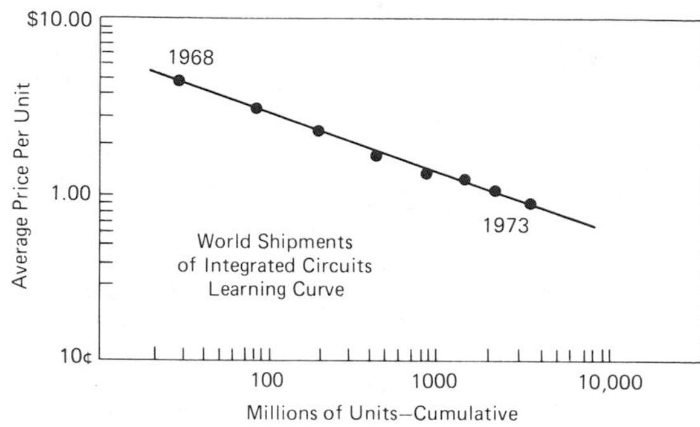

Declining industry prices obviously require that individual company costs also decline if a firm is to survive in the industry. As indicated in the following figures, the current industry price is illustrated by the horizontal dashed line. Companies A, B, and C have different cost positions depending on their accumulated volume. The volume of market share to Company A shows an excellent profit margin while Company B shows only marginal profits and Company C operates at a loss.

The key factor in developing the more competitive cost position comes from a firm's relative ability to ourgrow its competitors. For example, the figure below illustrates the difference in pricing abilities between a firm growing at 5 percent per year and a firm growing at 30 percent per year. In order to achieve such growth differentials, however, a firm must stress the importance of its world market share and corresponding productivity improvements.

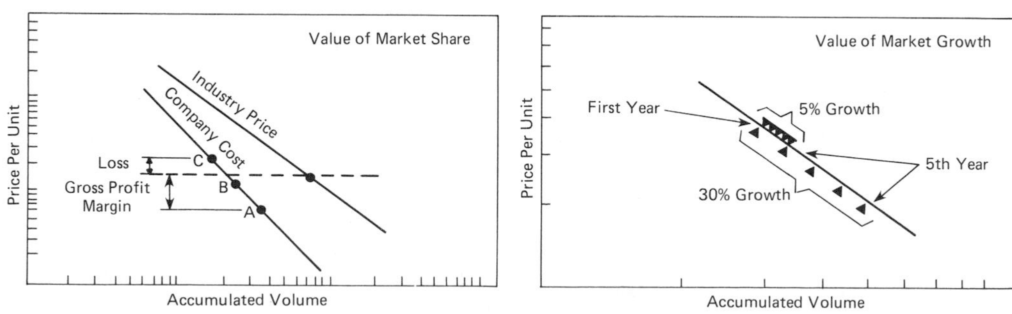

Source: Texas Instruments First Quarter Report to Shareholders, 1973.

contract established Altos as a credible original equipment supplier and was expected to bring the company other new contracts.

At $52 million in sales and 250 employees, Altos had done well in its five years of existence. Its largest OEM contract of $22 million was signed in 1981 by Moore Business Forms. David Jackson still owned 70 per cent of the firm, but expected the company's growth to create some problems. Altos will require 150 more people and will need working capital for marketing, inventory, and engineering. Because Altos buys most of its microprocessors, disc drives, and other components from others, Jackson will not require heavy capital investments to fill orders. "We're not running out of cash, but in terms of what we plan to do, you bet we have to get some money." That probably means that the company will go public.

Mature Product Strategies. During the mature phase of the product life cycle, the primary focus should be to maximize short-term earnings and to begin generating cash flows that can be used to support the development or marketing of new growth products. Earnings and cash flow become the reward of successful growth and market development strategies (see Exhibit 4-6). The basic business strategy would include

1. Selectively investing in new areas of growth opportunity or high return segments where additional market position can be gained and economies of scale achieved. Invest as necessary to maintain current product position and leadership in mature markets without expending excess resources on marketing activities.
2. Cutting creative marketing expenses while maintaining market coverage and product differentiation through the product's performance, specialization, and product applications.
3. Cutting production costs through long production runs with standardized techniques, designing to reduce costs, reducing overhead, and stabilizing prices to maximize profitability and cash generation.
4. Limiting risks to those acceptable to the business unit itself and planning for cyclicality to impact future performance.

For example, maintaining profitability in a mature market, such as consumer foods, can require drastic actions as described in the following example by *Business Week:* [7]

Swift & Co.'s president, Joseph P. Sullivan, began his job in April 1980 of improving the company's poor performance. For five years, Swift had returned a low 4 per cent return on assets. Swift's better-known products included Butterball turkeys, Peter Pan peanut butter, and Sizzlean bacon strips. Sullivan's challenge was to obtain a 15 per cent return on assets or for Swift to be divested by its parent company Esmark Inc.

By 1981, Swift posted an operating profit of $38.4 million on $1.5 billion in sales after a 1980 loss of $9.8 billion on $1.3 billion in sales. Return on assets reached 10 per cent. The first half of 1982 showed an additional 35 per cent gain in profits with just a 2 per cent increase in sales, and a projected 14.4 per cent return on assets for 1982.

In gaining control over profitability, Sullivan had to take some major actions. He got rid of his fresh-meat operations by selling its stock to the public, which removed him from the cyclical commodity markets. He decentralized the organization into four divisions—poultry and processed meat, dry grocery, cheese, and international—each with profit center responsibility. Critical tasks of pur-

[7] "Swift: Cutting Costs and Adding Products to Beat a Profit Deadline," *Business Week*, June 21, 1982, p. 65.

chasing, sales, and distribution were pushed back to the divisions. Each division now has its own sales force, dramatically reducing the number of products a salesperson carries.

The reorganization leaves only four managers between the plant foreman and the president and saves nearly $10 million a year in salary costs by eliminating 340 corporate staff jobs. Working capital requirements were reduced 23 per cent through more efficient inventory and receivables control. Cheese inventories were reduced $15 million through better purchasing practices. Turkey inventories were reduced $36 million to respond to the slow market acceptance. Now with current operations under control, Sullivan is looking for new opportunities for growth.

EXHIBIT 4-6: The Product Matrix

The Product Matrix provides a concept for analyzing the cash flow position resulting from a firm's products. Through the association of growth rate to cash use and market share to cash generation, a diagram can be developed which indicates:

1. STARS: High growth, cash using businesses which are self sufficient in cash flow because they are leaders that generate large amounts of cash.
2. CASH COWS: Businesses which generate more cash than they can use because they have high market share but are growing slowly.
3. DOGS: Businesses that use far more cash than they can generate because they have slow growth and low market share.
4. QUESTION MARKS: Businesses that require far more cash input than they can ever generate because of their high growth with low market share.

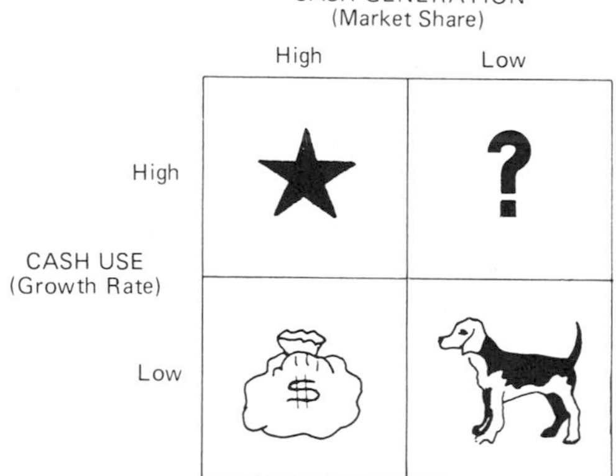

Market share serves as an indicator of competitive cost differentials taken from the experience curve. It is estimated that a market share of 2 to 1 will produce a differential in pre tax cost of value added of about 20 percent for the largest competitor. Achieving such a differential requires adequate investment, good management and a limitation in shared experience between firms.

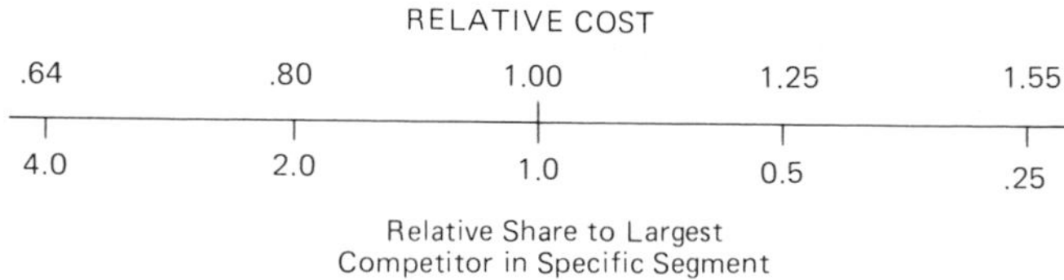

In analyzing a firm's market share, care must be taken to appropriately determine product-market segmentations since the largest firm in a single industry may not be a leader in any single segment. It is also important to compare each segment's growth rate against the industry growth rate since lower than industry growth rates means declining market share and ultimately makes the product a dog or question mark.

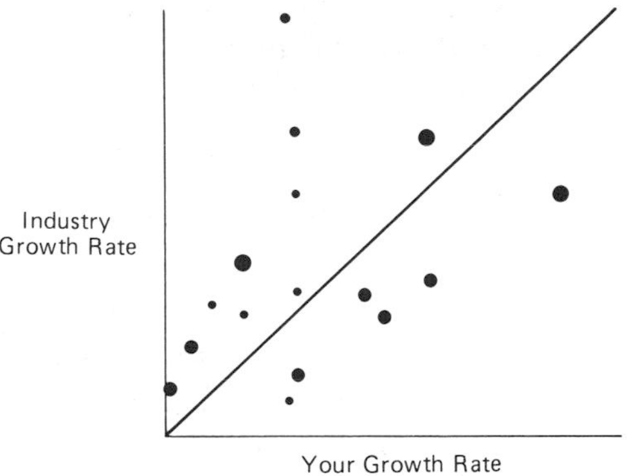

Declining Product Strategies. Once the market begins to shrink in size, it is likely that sales for all firms will be reduced. During the aging phase of the life cycle, the primary focus should be on maximizing the cash flow generated from the business and getting rid of losers. The basic business strategy would include:

1. Minimizing investments in dying segments and disposing of them when the opportunity arises, foregoing market share for maximization of profits and cash flow.
2. Cutting marketing expenses, holding prices, and eliminating less profitable products from the line.
3. As sales decline, rapidly consolidating facilities to minimize all fixed costs.
4. Avoiding any risks of further investment and liquidating unnecessary investments.

The decline in railcar sales is an example described in 1982 by *Forbes:*[8]

Pullman Standard, Inc., an industry giant in the railcar business, was in trouble in this highly cyclical business with declining product sales. In 1977 the company made $2 million; in 1978 and 1979, it made $16 and $51 million, respectively; but in 1981, it lost $1.4 million.

Boxcars, Pullman's mainstay, were in significant overcapacity with an estimated 70,000 of the nation's 384,000 units idle. Intermodal trailers that can be carried by trucks or trains have replaced them. Only now is Pullman focusing on intermodal cars to carry trailers, covered hopper cars for grain, fertilizer, and so on, and coal cars. But overspecialization on one product is a lesson well learned.

To handle the decline in sales, all manufacturing facilities had to be shut down. Some 5000 employees were discharged and given severance pay. Production capacity was cut from 25,000 cars to 10,000 to 12,000 cars annually, about

[8] John R. Doufman, "Bye-bye Boxcars," *Forbes*, June 7, 1982, pp. 135–36.

the size of ACF Industries, the next largest manufacturer. In addition, Pullman's new 61-year-old president, Jack Kruizenger, planned to keep only one production facility at which labor unions would have less control—"When we reopen we'll either have a different union or no union at all."

Kruizenger also planned to be more responsive to customers. Smaller competitors such as ACF, Berwick, Ortner, Thrall, and United American had been eager to profitably custom build cars for its customers. "In the 21 days it would take Pullman to change tooling, a smaller company could have the order built," he said. Pullman was able to get production economies, but it lost customers' goodwill. To fund Pullman's attempt to come back, Mellon Bank provided it with a $50 million loan for working capital.

Recognizing Strengths and Weaknesses

As summarized in Exhibit 4-7, business strategies and their functional requirements can be heavily affected by product life cycle. Research and development and production engineering are the primary requirements of business strategy at the embryonic stages. Without the development of viable products, there is little chance of the company's becoming a significant player at a later stage.

Once viable products have been developed, primary emphasis shifts to production and marketing activities. The ability to maintain market coverage of high-value products requires aggressive marketing and efficient and high-quality production operations. The success of production and marketing strategies will determine whether or not the business will enjoy the maturing phase of the industry.

In maturity, the market leader with the lowest cost production will reap the benefits of its hard work. The more it is able to reduce overall expenses and costs because of economies of scale or experience curve strategies, the more profitable it will become compared to its competition. At this point, little new investment is required other than what is required to maintain a leadership position.

Once the market begins to decline, it is necessary to avoid risks and to reduce invested resources. This is the opposite of the growth phase when new resources were needed to meet growth needs. In decline, contraction is needed to meet reduced demand. Care, however, must be taken here to distinguish between cyclical fluctuations and actual declines. Technological innovations are most likely to cause decline to occur, but it may take many years to occur. Being the last one out of a market can be very profitable.

Forecasting Performance Assumptions

No matter what strategic alternatives are being evaluated as potential business options, the projected financial statistics will depend on the actual state of the environment and competitive activities in the marketplace. The assumptions developed about the state of the environment and industry need to be identified and tracked, along with the performance appraisal. A few external events, such as legislation or supply shortages, or internal events, such as capacity constraints, can have significant effects on projected performance.

Some of the critical factors that need attention during the forecasting stage of strategy evaluation include

EXHIBIT 4-7: Developing Business Strategies

ANALYSIS
INDUSTRY MATURITY & BUSINESS CHARACTERISTICS ↓ COMPETITIVE POSITION & INVESTMENT/ PROFIT ATTRACTIVENESS

PORTFOLIO CATEGORY	EMBRYONIC	GROWTH	MATURE	AGING/DYING
INDUSTRY-MARKET CHARACTERISTICS	HIGH GROWTH-LOW SHARES	HIGH GROWTH-HIGH SHARES	LOW GROWTH-HIGH SHARES	LOW/NEGATIVE GROWTH LOW/DECLINING SHARES
PRIMARY OBJECTIVE	DEVELOP VIABLE ENTRY PRODUCTS	BUILD MARKET SHARE	MAXIMIZE EARNINGS WITH MODERATE CASH FLOW	MAXIMIZE CASH FLOW
BASIC STRATEGY				
(1) Investment	New product research and development	Market share development maximization	Limit to specific growth/market share targets	Minimize investments, sell or liquidate assets
(2) Product-market	Identify growth opportunities	Provide product leadership via diversify, market coverage, creativity, and price reductions	Maintain market coverage, product differentiation, and prices with less marketing	Cut expenses, hold price and eliminate losers
(3) Production	Develop low cost designs and production methods	Maximize use of scale (experience) to cut costs	Maximize profits with reduced product and fixed costs	Consolidate and close facilities
(4) Risk Taking	Designate specific amounts	Take acceptable risks	Limit risks	Avoid risks

1. key environment assumptions.
2. assumptions about buyers and their wants and needs.
3. assumptions about resources and assets.
4. assumptions about technologies.
5. assumptions about competitor behavior.
6. assumptions about barriers to competition.
7. assumptions about products and services.
8. assumptions about organization.

A change in any of these assumptions from positive to negative, or vice versa, can significantly impact the performance of a business unit. These factors are discussed in depth in the following chapter.

SUMMARY

The life cycle concept can have a significant impact on one's assessment of industry attractiveness. Let us now reconsider the business objectives and strategies described in Exhibit 4-3 as they relate to life cycle and competitive position.

EXHIBIT 4-8: Strategies Contingent Upon Competitive Position

Stage of Maturity: Embryonic, Growth, Mature, Aging

Competitive Position: Dominant, Strong, Favorable, Tenable, Weak

DEVELOPMENT STRATEGIES
Defend Position
Grow With Industry
Gain Position
Harvest
Start Up

SELECTIVE STRATEGIES
Hold Niche
Exploit Niche
Find Niche

PROVE VIABILITY
Catch Up
Renew
Hang In
Turn Around

WITHDRAWAL
Withdraw
Divest
Abandon

Source: Adapted from *A Management System for the 1980s* (Cambridge: Arthur D. Little, Inc., 1979), p. 17.

Exhibit 4-8 shows the business objectives and strategies that are most appropriate according to the strengths of an organization's competitors. The appendix to this chapter lists in more detail the specific functional strategies that may be used to accomplish these business objectives and strategies. It should be apparent that development strategies require increasingly strong competitive positions as the market matures. As discussed in this chapter, the origin of that competitive strength is in the evolution of functional strategies which support the product's evolution.

For organizations that have not been able to keep up with competition or have lacked appropriate functional strategies and support, the pressure to find a special niche or withdraw increases as the market matures. Once again, relative market position becomes critical to survival since overall economics and costs of larger competitors allow for price reductions that cannot be met by small producers.

Even though life cycle is a critical factor, overall market attractiveness can be further affected by government regulations, investment requirement, technological change, or union and community attitudes. The use of life cycle, however, gives us a good feel for the functional requirements of business strategies and the competitive requirements for creating make and market activities.

FOCUS QUESTIONS

1. Give an example of a business strategy. How do you relate the functional strategies to the business strategy?
2. Give examples of firms that have developed their business strategy through (a) research and development, (b) manufacturing, and (c) marketing. How would you characterize their distinctive competencies?
3. How will competitive position impact on a business strategy?
4. How might a business strategy change as you move through the product life cycle?

ADDITIONAL READINGS

ABELL, DEREK F. *Defining the Business: The Starting Point of Strategic Planning.* Englewood Cliffs, N.J.: Prentice-Hall, Inc., 1980.

BLOOM, PAUL N., and PHILIP KOTLER, "Strategies for High Market Share Companies." *Harvard Business Review,* **53,** no. 6 (November-December 1975): 63–72.

BUZZELL, ROBERT D. "Competitive Behavior and Product Life Cycle." *New Ideas for Successful Marketing.* Chicago: American Marketing Association, 1966, pp. 46–68.

HAMMERMESH, RICHARD G. et al., "Strategies for Low Market Share Companies." *Harvard Business Review,* **56,** no. 3 (May-June 1978): 95–102.

KOTTER, PHILIP. "Harvesting Strategies for Wear Products." *Business Horizons,* **21,** 5 (August 1978).

APPENDIX
Strategy Alternatives
a) Following Life Cycle Objectives

Business Strategy	*Functional Strategies*
Start up Business	Build excess capacity for new business.
	Invest to develop primary demand.
	Penetrate market via price, service, advertising, and product-line breadth.
Grow with Industry	Integrate backwards into purchased operations and functions that add value.
	Expand into overseas markets.
	Invest in overseas facilities.
	Integrate forward to control distribution and marketing to consumer.
	License abroad; expand markets and income.
	Improve operating efficiencies with new techniques.
	Add, modify, or replace products being sold.
	Add market segments or geographic areas.
	Maintain present product/market strategy.
Gain Market Position	Enter new market segments.
	Enter overseas markets.
	Develop overseas facilities.
	Add excess capacity.
	Integrate forward to consumers.
	Penetrate market via price, service, advertising, and expanded product line.
	Improve operating efficiencies via plant, equipment, and processes.
	Develop, manufacture, and market new products in new markets.
Defend Market Position	Integrate backwards to increase value added and reduce supply risks.
	Develop overseas facilities.

	Improve operating efficiencies.
	Maintain present product/market strategy.
Harvest	Rationalize distribution network and regions.
	Restrict investments and expenses.
	Rationalize to only profitable products.
	Rationalize to most profitable or concentrated market segments.
	Rationalize for product or process standardization or subcontract.
	Maintain current product/market strategy.
	Cut costs via management edicts.

b) Following Market Niche Objectives

Business Strategy	*Functional Strategies*
Find Market Niche	Integrate backwards to incorporate key functions, operations, or products.
	Integrate forward to increase control over distribution and customer service.
	Develop primary demand for new product via technological advances.
	Penetrate market via price, service, advertising, or expanded product line.
	Rationalize market focus to regions, profitable segments of volume segments.
	Rationalize products to most profitable.
	Maintain current product/market strategy.
Expand Market Niche	Expand overseas.
	Develop overseas facilities.
	Build excess capacity.
	Penetrate market via price, service, advertising, or product breadth.
	Improve operating efficiencies.
	Add, develop, or replace products in current markets.
	Maintain current product/market strategy.

Hold Market Niche	Develop overseas facilities.
	Rationalize distribution networks and regions.
	Improve operating efficiencies.
	Rationalize for production standardization or subcontract.
	Maintain current product/market strategy.

c) "Last Chance" Rebuilding Objectives

Business Strategy	*Functional Strategies*
Catch Up with Competition	Rationalize distribution networks and regions.
	Build excess capacity for future growth.
	Penetrate market via price, service, advertising, or expanded product line.
	Rationalize market focus for profit, volume, or geographic segments.
	Add, develop, or replace products in current markets.
	Rationalize for standardized production or subcontract.
	Rationalize to profitable products.
Renew Products	Rationalize distribution networks and regions.
	Rationalize market focus for profits, volume, or geographic segments.
	Develop, produce, and market new products to new markets.
	Add, develop, or replace current products in current markets.
	Rationalize for standardization of production or subcontract.
	Rationalize to profitable products.
	Maintain current product/market strategy.
Turn Around Performance	Rationalize distribution networks and regions.
	Penetrate market via price, service, advertising, or expanded product line.
	Rationalize market focus for profits, volume, or geographic segments.

	Improve generating efficiencies.
	Rationalize for standardized production or subcontract.
	Rationalize to profit products.
	Cut costs via management edict.
Prolong Existence	Integrate backwards to ensure supply sources and increase value added.
	Rationalize distribution networks and regions.
	Export products overseas.
	License products/technology abroad.
	Rationalize business to profitable areas only.
	Rationalize markets for profits, volume, and geographic regions.
	Improve operating efficiencies.
	Rationalize for standardization production or subcontract.
	Rationalize products for profits.
	Survive with reduced functions, products, and funds.
	Enter new markets and regions.
	Cut costs via management edict.

d) "Withdrawal" Objectives

Business Strategy	*Functional Strategy*
Withdraw from Market	Rationalization of distribution networks and regions.
	Rationalization of market focus to profits, volume or geographic area.
	Rationalize for standardized products or subcontract.
	Rationalization of products for profits.
	Cut costs by management edict.
Divest Operations	Rationalization of distribution networks and regions.
	Rationalize business for profits.

	Rationalize for standardized production of subcontract.
	Rationalization of products for profits.
	Eliminate products, functions, and finanical support.
Abandon Operations	Divest the business unit.

5 Multiple Business Objectives and Strategies

Thus far we have concentrated on business level strategies. As we add new business units, however, attention needs to be given to the relationships that exist between businesses. To analyze these relationships it is useful once again to use the three components of strategy: functional capabilities, product focus, and market focus. This chapter discusses concepts for determining multiple business direction.

PRODUCT-MARKET ANALYSIS

As a firm begins to consider the vast range of alternatives for product-market expansion, it can be useful for it to assess the potential for growth and profitability. This is most critical when trade-offs are being made between internal product-market expansion and external expansion through mergers and acquisitions. The concept of product-market life cycle can be helpful in this analysis.

PRODUCT-MARKET MATURITY

The level or opportunity and risk related to entering a new business can vary greatly based on industry maturity. Industries, like product-market segments, usually begin in an embryonic stage, pass through growth to maturity, and eventually begin to age or decline. Exhibit 5-1 shows examples of industries in various stages of product maturity.

Industry evolution can vary greatly in terms of the time it takes an industry to move through the cycle. It is not uncommon for new inventions or innovations to require twenty to forty years before they enter the growth phase as we have seen with solar energy products and computers. Emphasis on health and safety have generated significant growth in such products as sporting goods and smoke alarms, although the latter are rapidly maturing with market saturation. Golf equipment has already matured, whereas steel is rapidly moving toward decline as substitute materials become available. Men's hats and rail cars continue to age. As shown in Exhibit 5-1 for roller skates, sales can also rapidly reverse themselves through the introduction of new technologies or applications such as skateboards.

EXHIBIT 5-1: Examples of U.S. Industry Maturity

EMBRYONIC	GROWTH	MATURE	AGING
Home Computers • →			Rail Cars •
	Home Smoke Alarms • →	Steel • →	
• Solar Energy Devices			Men's Hats •
	• Sporting Goods	Golf • Equipment	
Paddle Tennis •			Baseball • Equipment
	• ←	Roller Skates	——•

Source: Arthur D. Little, Inc., "A Management System for the 1980s," p. 16.

Embryonic industries will experience rapid sales growth, frequent changes in technology, and fragmented, shifting market positions. Cash requirements are relatively high compared to sales as a result of expenses for technology, facilities, and market development. Profitability will generally not exist until market position can be achieved.

The growth stage comes from a rapid expansion in sales as a result of market development. As customer relationships, technology, and competitive position become established, new entry can become difficult. These industries require added resources to fund continued growth and market position.

With industry maturity comes increased stability in competitors' technology, customers, and market positions. Growth will compare to GNP while earnings and cash generation can be high.

Aging industries have declining demand, fewer competitors, and reduced product line variety. Little investment is required to ride the wave as remaining competitors work out of the market.

Understanding the maturity position of an industry will add focus to the strategies to be utilized by the strategic business unit, and to expectations of future performance. The problem comes in selecting strategies that are most appropriate to the competitive position of the business area and the maturity of the industry.

Determining Competitive Position

One of the most difficult tasks for the strategist in assessing the potential performance of new product-market introductions is to determine competitive positions. Competitive analysis requires that business strengths and weaknesses be related to competition. This requires that the manager understand the competition well enough to also identify their opportunities and problems.

Determining the competition's basic strategies may not be as difficult as assessing its financial performance. For larger organizations, financial reporting of costs, sales, expenses for marketing, research and administration, and net income will be lumped together with other business units. In the same sense, information on the competition's assets and return on investment (ROI) may be difficult to obtain. Careful observation and data collection, however, can allow estimates to be made.

In the same way that the strategic characteristics of a business must be identified, the manager needs to assess the key success factors of the competition. Factors to be encompassed in such an analysis include (1) technological strength, (2) breadth of product line, (3) total cost position, (4) management skills, (5) industry image and franchise, (6) regulatory compliance, and (7) financial and growth performance. These factors change in their priority or importance over the life of the product.

The classification of strategic business units in competitive positions can be made in several ways. Such firms as General Electric, McKinsey and Company, and Shell use three competitive levels: low, medium, and high. Arthur D. Little uses five classifications (Exhibit 5-2) of competitive position: (1) dominant positions such as DeBeers'; (2) strong positions such as General Motors'; (3) favorable positions such as Wendy's; (4) tenable positions such as Jones & Laughlin's; and (5) weak positions such as A&P's. Some of the criteria used for this classification include

1. strength, loyalty, and exclusivity of supplier and distributor networks.
2. level of forward and backward integration and overall cost position.
3. market coverage and relative strength of competition.
4. technological and R&D superiority.
5. position of leadership in price and quality.
6. utilization of operating capacity.
7. breadth of product-line compared to competition and customer needs.
8. relative management control and responsiveness to external changes.

The significance of each item will depend on the specific industry being analyzed. The importance of each item and the relative position of the strategic business

EXHIBIT 5-2: Competitive Positions of Strategic Business Units

Competitive Position	
Dominant	DE BEERS in diamonds
Strong	GENERAL MOTORS in automobiles
Favorable	WENDY'S in fast-food operations
Tenable	JONES & LAUGHLIN in steel
Weak	A&P in retail grocery

Source: Arthur D. Little, Inc., "A Management System for the 1980s," p. 13.

unit need to be summarized to assess the overall competitive strengths or weakness of the business.

THE CONCEPT OF BUSINESS FIT

The long-term objectives of most organizations require transitions from one business to more than one business as a way to continue growth and/or profitability. In deciding what business(es) to add to the existing organization, three basic alternatives need to be considered. First, expansion can be made along product line dimensions. Second, expansion can be made along market dimensions. Third, the requirement of functional capabilities must also be determined.

Adding new products or markets to an organization may be treated as either part of the existing business or as a new business segment. Adding a complementary product to the current product line may not be seen as a new business, even though it expands the potential for sales (e.g., adding electronic toys to a mechanical toy line). Within a given business unit, there can be a wide variety of products and markets represented. Adding totally new business units, such as small computers, to existing products, such as toys, may require a whole new set of production and marketing skills.

Exhibit 5-3 suggests that at either the corporate or business level, product decisions can be classified as either pursuing the organization's current mission or adding a new mission to the organization. When existing products are used, the goal will be either to increase the penetration of current markets or to develop new markets. When new products are added, emphasis will be on developing products for existing markets or diversifying into totally new markets.

Deciding whether an organization is staying in a business field or moving into a new business can often be a confusing distinction. Consider the Taft Broadcasting example described by *Forbes* in 1982:[1]

Taft Broadcasting's chief executive officer, Charles Mechem, has moved far beyond the five TV stations and seven radio stations owned when he took office in 1967. Taft, at $358 million in revenues, is now involved in cable TV, the production and distribution of TV shows, amusement parks, the Philadelphia Phillies baseball team, and Kinder-Care Learning Centers.

Taft owns seven TV stations from Birmingham to Buffalo and eleven radio stations that account for 54 per cent of corporate profits and 35 per cent of revenues. Mechem purchased two of the TV stations and four of the radio stations at a cost of $81 million. He has also entered into a partnership to acquire and invest $175 million to develop regional cable TV systems from Massachusetts to Michigan. This groups' operating margins are currently 36 per cent, down from 44 per cent three years ago, but they generated over $40 million in cash flow in 1981.

Taft also owns three television-production houses, one movie-production operation, and a distributor of television programming. Taft already owned Hanna-Barbera, the TV animation creator of "The Flintstones," "Yogi Bear," and "Scooby-Doo," which had $40 million in sales. Mechem acquired QM Productions for $13.5 million to get into adult programming such as its past hits,

[1] Thomas Jaffe, "We Want Some Respect," *Forbes,* June 21, 1982, pp. 92–97.

EXHIBIT 5-3: Strategic Growth Alternatives

Mission \ Product	Present	New
Present	Market Penetration	Product Development
New	Market Development	Diversification

Source: H. I. Ansoff, *Corporate Strategy* (New York: McGraw-Hill, 1965), p. 109. Reprinted by permission.

"The Fugitive" and "Barnaby Jones." To get into TV program syndication, he acquired Worldvision Enterprises for $13 million, which has foreign rights to "Little House on the Prairie," "Love Boat," and "Dallas." Entertainment sales for 1981 reached $102 million, up 20 per cent. Motion picture projects had yet to make a profit.

Amusement park investments include Ohio's Kings Island for $35 million in 1972; and 70 per cent of the $100 million Wonderland park outside Toronto, which had 2 million in attendance, $40 million in sales, and $5 million in profits its first year. Taft also owns Virginia's Kings Dominion and North Carolina's Carowinds parks of which Kroger Foods had owned 50 per cent prior to 1981. Although these investments had yet to make a profit, Mechem expected to turn them around in 1982.

Mechem also purchased 20 per cent of fast-growing Kinder-Care Learning Centers for $5 million and 47.5 percent of the Philadelphia Phillies for $15 million. Even with a 32 per cent growth in earnings, to $38.8 million, Wall Street seemed confused over these moves. Taft's stock price traded at eight times earnings, $30 per share, compared to fifteen times earnings for competitive broadcasting firms. Average return on equity, at a five-year 15.4 per cent average, was admittedly below competition.

Mechem argued that his diversification strategy made sense. His amusement parks generated nearly $40 million in cash, enough to fund annual capital investments in the business. Miniparks, called Hanna-Barbera Lands, were being developed at $15 million each. In regard to the Phillies, Mechem expects his radio station in Philadelphia to increase its operating profits $3.5 million a year just from its broadcasting of away games. "You see, we are practical! We do have our feet on the ground," he says.

When we evaluate the diverse activities of Taft Broadcasting, it might be useful to consider the following diagram:

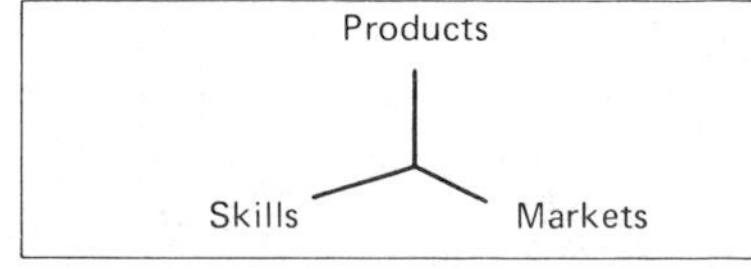

If we consider the "market" for children's entertainment, Mechem has Hanna-Barbera to produce children's programs and programs to use in his miniparks. The amusement park management skills allow him to use the Hanna-Barbera creations to further his penetration of the market. One might consider this relationship as shown in Exhibit 5-4.

Taft's broadcasting business might be seen in Exhibit 5-5 as an integration of programming, production, and distribution of programs used in radio and television operations. Taft's eleven radio, seven television, and cable operations give significant programming experience and skills. Hanna-Barbera, QM Production, the Phillies, and Kinder-Care Learning Centers all provide opportunities for developing programs that could gain acceptance in the entertainment markets. Worldvision Enterprises then provides for broader control and distribution of such program development.

THE CONCEPT OF DIVERSIFICATION

Such complex strategies as shown in the Taft Broadcasting example are seldom understood because of the inability of management to conceptualize them as we have just done. As a result, Wall Street and other investors may appear to undervalue such strategies. The actual value of a business strategy today appears to be higher when it is simple and easy to understand.

The more "related" the activities, the easier it is to understand them. Ex-

EXHIBIT 5-4: Taft Broadcasting Company Businesses

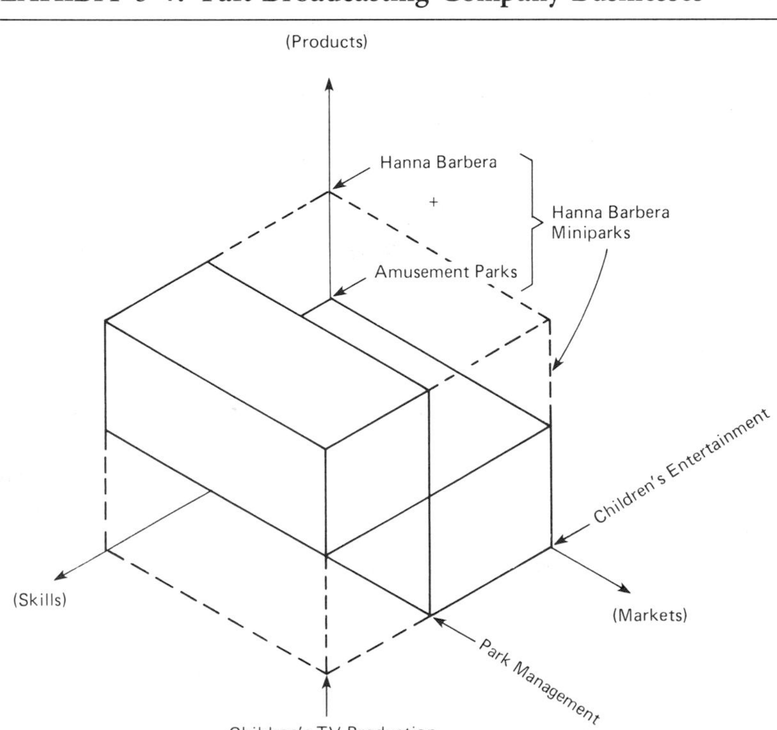

EXHIBIT 5-5: Taft Broadcasting Company Businesses

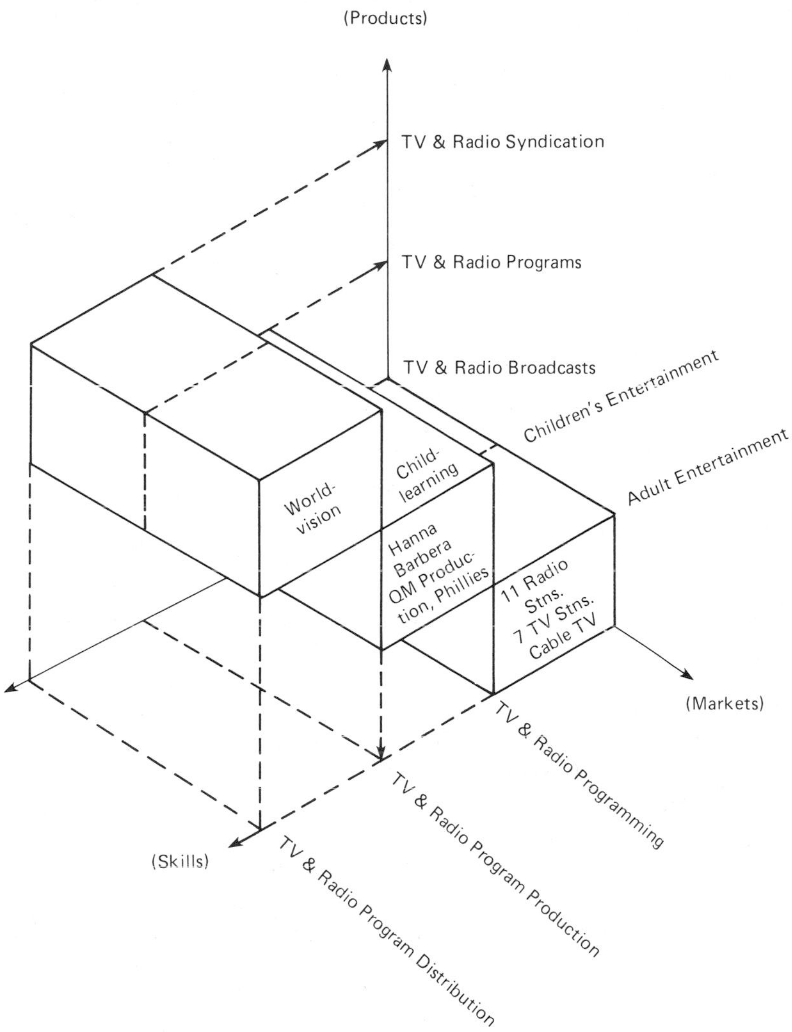

hibit 5-6, for example, suggests approaches or alternatives that affect the complexity of business strategies. Products are most often differentiated by the functional skills or know-how required to develop them or their markets. When we produce more products for our own needs, increasing the value we add to the end product, we refer to it as functional diversification or vertical integration. When we provide more products to our current markets, we call it product diversification. As we move into new products and new markets, we call it related or unrelated diversification.

Diversification is referred to as "related" or "unrelated" depending on whether or not our *current* functional capabilities can be applied to the new business direction. For example, related diversification would allow us to easily transfer our resources or functional skills to the new product or to use excess capacity that exists in our research, production, or marketing operations. Unre-

EXHIBIT 5-6: Product/Market Diversification Strategies

		New Product Directions	
		Related Know-how or Functional Capabilities ⟷	Unrelated Know-how or Functional Capabilities
New Marketing Missions or Customer Focus	Organization Is Its Own Customer	Functional Diversification (add more functions)	
	Use Same Type of Customers	Product Diversification	
	Similar Types of Customers	Market and Functionally Related Product Diversification	Market-Related Product Diversification
	New Types of Customers	Functionally Related Product-Market Diversification	Unrelated Product-Market

Source: Adapted from H. I. Ansoff, *Corporate Strategy* (New York: McGraw-Hill Book Company, 1965), p. 132.

lated diversification suggests that we lack resources or skills and must therefore rely on good management to quickly recognize the critical success factors and develop or acquire needed resources and skills.

Diversification strategies are generally related to the performance objectives of the organization. Growth objectives increase the pressure to add new businesses, especially when current businesses begin to mature or decline. Once organizations find themselves with excess marginal talent, excess cash, underutilized research and development skills, idle production or marketing facilities, or low-profit operations, they will search for new ways to utilize available resources.

Expanding into New Markets

Although there are a number of diversification alternatives and strategies, one of the most commonly used approaches is to simply find new markets for current products. This approach is especially attractive in international markets where countries may be in less developed stages of the product life cycle and where competition may be less intense.

The difficulty in selecting international markets comes in determining where opportunities are the greatest. One rather simple approach is shown in Exhibit 5-7 in which the Boston Consulting Group approach has been used for Japanese products. This analysis shows that products such as textiles, cutlery, and clothing have been losing their competitive position to imports. In fact, as unskilled, labor-intensive U.S. industries migrate to less developed Asian countries, Japanese domestic markets have opened up and are being penetrated.

EXHIBIT 5-7: Growth of Japanese Exports and Imports for Selected Manufactured Product Categories Relative to Growth of Total Japanese Exports and Imports 1968–1977

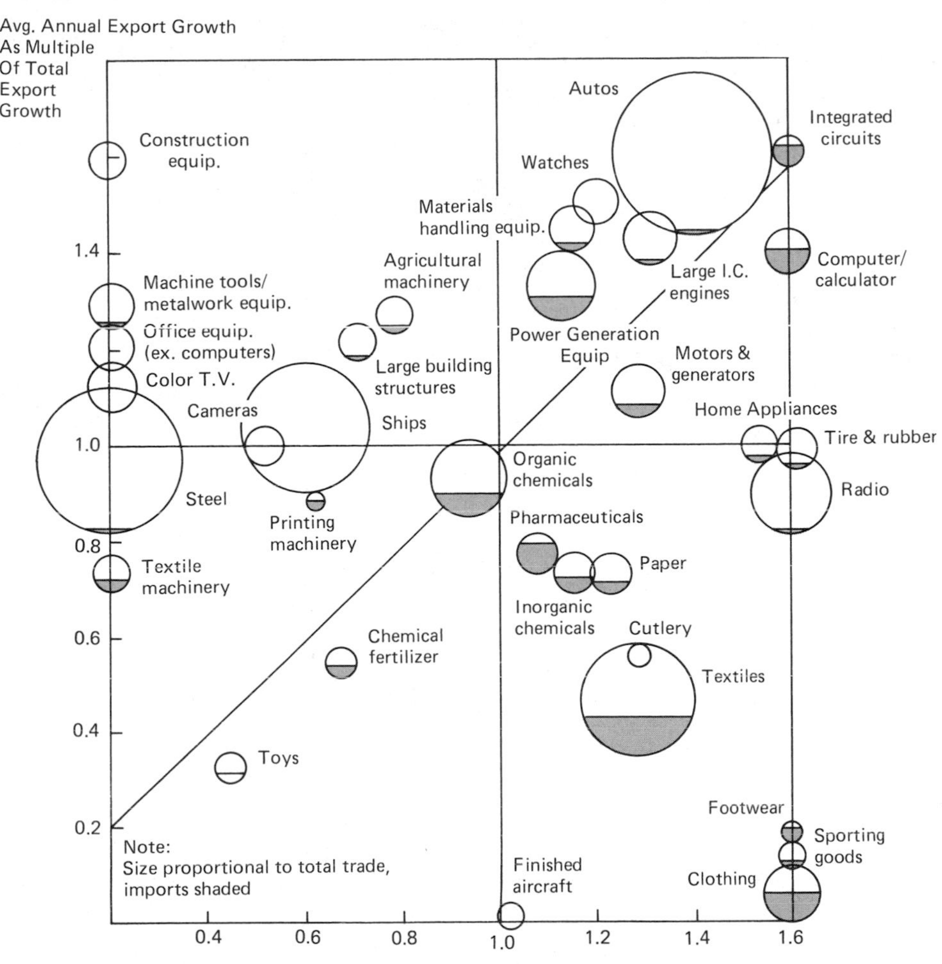

Source: Summary Reports Trade of Japan (Ministry of Finance) and BCG.

DIVERSIFICATION INTO INTERNATIONAL MARKETS

We can deal with the management of international strategies in the same way that we deal with product-market strategies. The difference in focus, however, is that our objective is to determine priorities for country-product investment strategies. Consider the matrix in Exhibit 5-8 used by Ford Tractor International.[2] To compute the country attractiveness scale, Ford used the following formula:

[2]Gilbert D. Harrell and Richard O. Kiefer, "Multinational Strategic Market Portfolios," *MSU Business Topics* (Winter 1981): 5–15.

EXHIBIT 5-8: Key Country Matrix

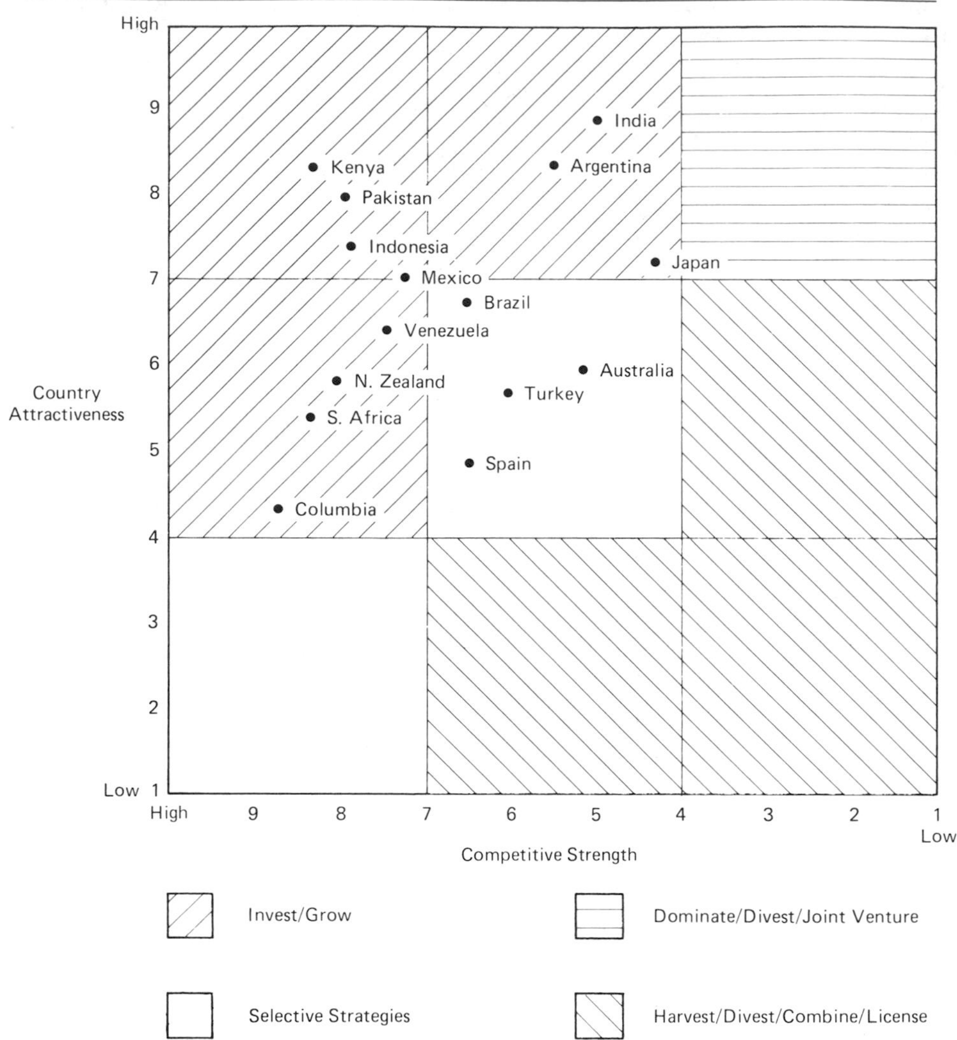

Source: G. D. Harrell and R. O. Kiefer, "Multinational Strategic Market Portfolios," *MSU Business Topics,* Winter 1981, pp. 5–15. Reprinted by permission.

Country Attractiveness Scale = Market Size + 2 × Market Growth + (.5 × Price Control/Regulation + .25 × Nontariff Barriers + .25 × Local Content Compensatory Export Requirements) + (.35 × Inflation + .35 × Trade Balance + .3 × Political Factors).

Market size was a three-year average of industry sales. Levels of unit sales were ranked 1 to 10 based on required levels to achieve economies of scale and to cover technical assistance and training. Market growth was rated on a ten-year average projection. Government regulation rated the degree of price controls, nontariff restrictions, and other requirements of doing business. Economic and political ratings included the inflation rate and trade balance. The combined rating then provided a single number that is then transposed to a ten-point rating.

To determine competitive strength, Ford used the following formula:

Competitive Strength = 2 × (.5 × Absolute Market Share + .5 × Industry Position) + Product Fit + (.5 × Profit Per Unit + .5 × Profit Percentage of Net Dealer Cost) + Market Support.

Relative market share may be critical because of experience curve volume and cost potentials. Product fit is a measure of how well the product fits the market's need. Profit contribution relates to local operating efficiencies as well as pricing flexibility as a result of government and competition. Market support measures the quantity and quality of local personnel, service and parts availability, advertising and promotional availability, and general company image. The resulting number from the computation was again converted to a ten-point scale.

The use of risk measuring and monitoring techniques is increasing in importance as today's environment becomes more turbulent. Strategy managers in larger and more complex, multinational organizations are finding it difficult to manage the environmental uncertainties with which they are currently faced. As a result, such techniques as those described here will become increasingly common as a tool of the strategy manager.

Multiple Business Managing

A variety of concepts can be used to aid the strategy manager in conceptualizing and determining multiple business objectives and strategies. Exhibit 5-9, for example, shows the life cycle matrix. Businesses are located according to market growth and competitive position. In addition, sales and market share information is also incorporated into the circle. Exhibit 5-10 shows how the total business portfolio can be related back to corporate level objectives for growth, profits, or some balance between the two.

Diversification strategies influence the overall balance or focus given to the business map. Organizations with mature and profitable businesses may find themselves with excessive cash reserves and heavily tied into economic downturns or cycles. On the other hand, heavy growth emphasis requires tremendous cash infusion, a fact that makes mergers between large mature firms and small growth firms quite common in practice. Declining businesses lead to underutilized resources and capacity that allows for low-cost product-market diversification. The important fact in minimizing overall business risk, however, is to find those businesses that can best utilize the functional capabilities of the diversifying organization.

EXHIBIT 5-9: Business Portfolio Using Product Life Cycle

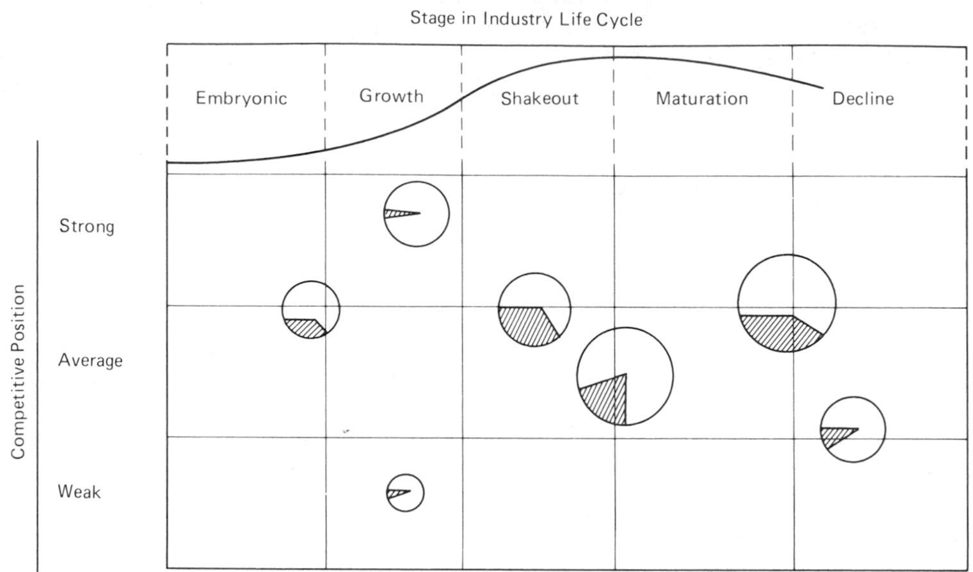

1. Circle shows size of sales.
2. Pie section shows market share.

Source: Adapted from C. W. Hofer, "Conceptual Constructs for Formulating Corporate and Business Strategies" (Boston: Intercollegiate Case Clearing House, #9-378-754, 1977), p. 3.

CONSISTENT SUPERORDINATE GOALS

In considering the types of products, markets, and capabilities that the organization desires to develop, it is important to recognize the interdependence of these strategy components. In evaluating diversification alternatives, preferences for product-market positions must tie into the organization's functional capabilities. Exhibit 5-11 provides the alternative positioning strategies that the organization can decide for its businesses. For example, Procter & Gamble has insisted that its products be high performance, for which higher prices are generally charged. This positioning goal for the corporation requires heavy emphasis on research and development activities for both products and processes.

At the other extreme, most commodities are sold at the lowest prices since no value or differentiation can be added to the standard product. Cost-based strategies, therefore, require tight control over all costs in order to stay profitable. Critical functional capabilities relate to purchasing, manufacturing, or tight management controls.

Companies with performance goals are not likely to be able to compete well with organizations that have cost-related goals. Procter & Gamble is finding it most difficult to compete with Kroger's "Cost Cutter" brands. Kroger invests little in additional advertising and purchases at marginal costs from suppliers who have excess capacity. It is unlikely that anyone can beat this cost-based strategy. The problem for Procter & Gamble is to reduce its own costs to

EXHIBIT 5-10: Comparative Portfolio Life Cycle Emphasis

	Stage of Product/Market Life Cycle				
Evaluation of Portfolio	Embryonic	Growth	Saturation	Maturation	Decline
Growth emphasis					
Profit emphasis					
Balanced emphasis					

1. Circle shows size of sales. 2. Pie section shows market share.

Source: Adapted from C. W. Hofer, "Conceptual Constraints for Formulating Corporate and Business Strategies" (Boston: Intercollegiate Case Clearing House, #9-378-754), 1977.

a level where the customer's received discrepancy between "Cost Cutter" brands and "P&G" brands will maintain P&G's market share. If Procter & Gamble cannot make this adjustment, its future performance strategy may be in jeopardy.

EXHIBIT 5-11: Price-Performance Matrix

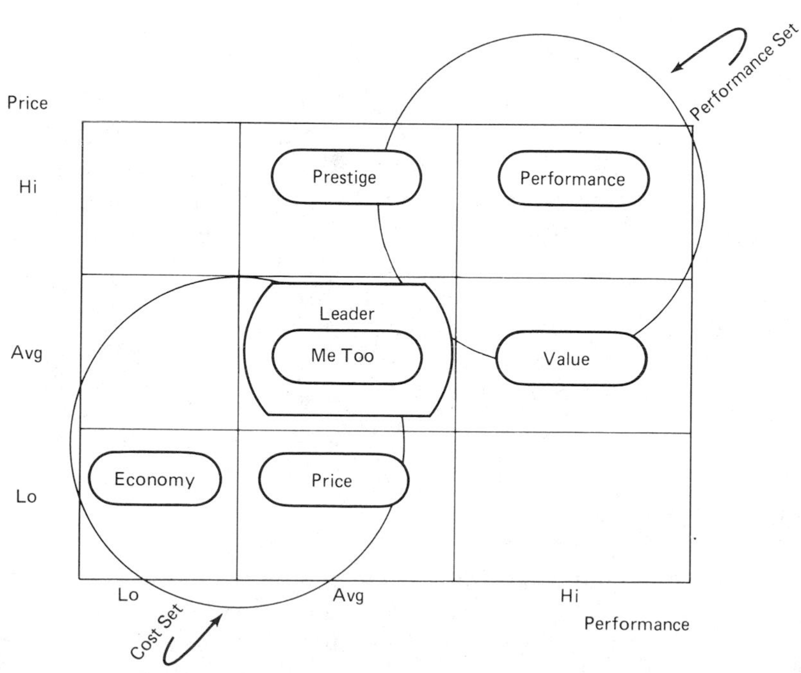

EXHIBIT 5-12: Position Matrix

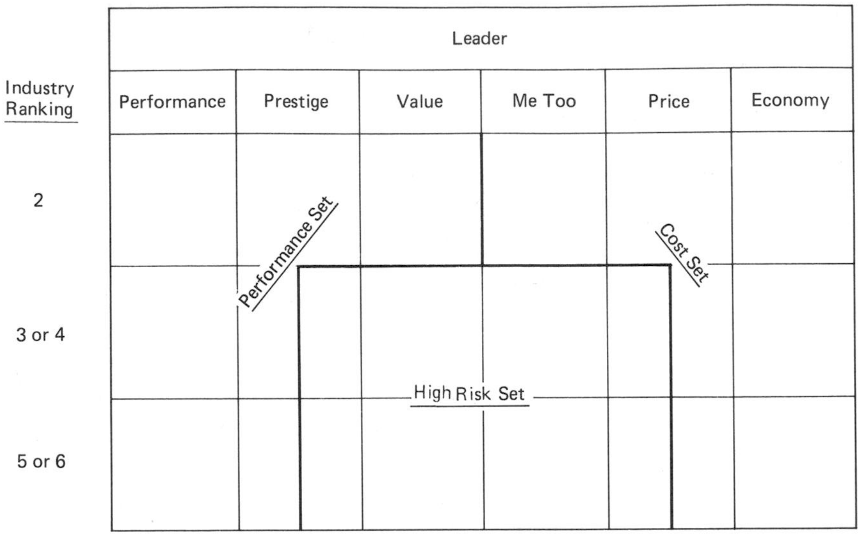

Industry Ranking	Leader					
	Performance	Prestige	Value	Me Too	Price	Economy
2						
3 or 4						
5 or 6						

Performance Set

Cost Set

High Risk Set

In linking product-market positions to functional capabilities, market share goals are also important. As shown in Exhibit 5-12, the position strategies require fairly strong industry positions to meet the requirements of either cost or performance. In competition with the "leader," "value," "me too," and "price" strategies will have lower volumes and, therefore, fewer economies of scale. As they move further behind the leader, the more difficult it will become for them to maintain adequate financial performance for survival.

SUMMARY

The skills required to manage single business strategies are not greatly different from the skills required to manage multiple-business strategies. In both cases, special attention has to be given to understanding the attractiveness of the market and the competitive positions of the key players. The move toward multiple-business strategies, however, does require special attention to the goals of the organization and consistency between product-market positioning strategies and functional capabilities. Without consistency in these business decisions and constant attention to competitors' relative positions, it is only a matter of time before trouble begins. Financial performance is only symptomatic of these more strategic problems.

FOCUS QUESTIONS

1. How do single business strategies differ from multibusiness strategies?
2. What kinds of problems are likely in diversification decisions?
3. Why aren't there more developed countries in the invest-grow category for Ford Tractors?

4. What is critical in using matrices for multibusiness strategies?
5. Give an example of a firm and industry dominated by each positioning strategy (e.g., pricing and performance combinations).

ADDITIONAL READINGS

ANSOFF, H. I. *Corporate Strategy.* New York: McGraw-Hill Book Company, 1965.

BRIGHT, WILLIAM M. "Alternative Strategies for Diversification." *Research Management,* **12,** no. 4 (July 1969): 24–253.

CANNON, J. THOMAS. *Business Strategy and Policy.* New York: Harcourt Brace and World, 1968.

FERGUSON, CHARLES. *Measuring Corporate Strategy.* Homewood, Ill.: Dow-Jones-Irwin, 1974.

HALL, WILLIAM K. "SBU's: Hot, New Topic in the Management Diversification." *Business Horizons,* **2,** No. 1 (Feb. 1978): 17–25.

HOFER, CHARLES W. "Conceptual Constructs for Formulating Corporate and Business Strategies." Boston: Intercollegiate Case Clearing House #9-378-754, 1977.

HOFER, CHARLES W., and DAN SCHENDEL. *Strategy Formulation: Analytical Concepts.* St. Paul, Minn.: West Publishing Co., 1978.

KOTTER, PHILIP. *Marketing Management: Analysis, Planning and Control.* Englewood Cliffs, N.J.: Prentice Hall Inc., 1980.

MELICHER, RONALD W., and DAVID F. RUSH. "Evidence on the Acquisition-related Performance of Conglomerate Firms." *Journal of Finance,* **29,** no. 1 (March 1974).

STEINER, GEORGE A. "Why and How to Diversify." *California Management Review,* **6,** no. 4 (Summer 1964).

VANCIL, RICHARD F., and PETER LORANGE, "Strategic Planning in Diversified Companies." *Harvard Business Review,* **53,** no. 1 (Jan.-Feb. 1975): 81–90.

6 Industry Attractiveness: The Impact of Industry Structure

As described in Chapter 4, business objectives and strategies vary greatly depending on the attractiveness of the industry and the competitive position of the organization. This chapter introduces several techniques that will aid the strategist in understanding the attractiveness of industries and in determining what opportunities and threats exist.

THE CONCEPT OF AN INDUSTRY[1]

A well-known example of an industry is the home appliance industry. Seven full-line manufacturers, including giants such as General Electric, General Motors, Ford, and Westinghouse, represent about 75 per cent of total industry output. Sears, however, sells nearly 30 per cent of this output through its vast retail network without being in the manufacturing area. Other firms, such as D&M, produce only a narrow product line and produce private-branded products for distributors. Some of the producers also have high technological capabilities (General Electric, Westinghouse, and Philco-Ford) and supply many of the component parts (electric motors and controls) for the industry. The consumer market, on the other hand, includes about 70 per cent homeowners and 30 per cent home and apartment builders and contractors. Only General Electric and Sears have national afterservice capabilities for all their products. With the complex interrelationships of this industry, it is difficult to exclude any part of the process from component supplier to retailer.

A second important dimension is the competitive structure of the industry. New competitors can enter an industry, such as the Japanese have done in computers and Saudi Arabians are doing in petrochemical refining. There is also the potential for substitute products to take over market share. For example, plastics are replacing metal in automobiles to reduce weight and energy consumption. Oil consumption is also likely to be replaced by solar, nuclear, and coal-based energy.

Finally, other stakeholders such as stockholders, labor unions, regulators, and interest groups can influence the nature of the competitive environment. The

[1] See Michael E. Porter's *Competitive Strategy* (New York: Free Press, 1980) for further discussion on this subject.

Bureau of Tobacco and Firearms, for example, regulates the nature of tobacco and liquor advertising, and challenged Coca-Cola's right to use comparative advertising in promoting its wine. Union wage demands are now affecting the competitiveness of the U.S. automobile industry. Picketing of nuclear facilities by environmentalist groups and the pressure of these groups for regulations have all but brought the U.S. nuclear energy industry to a complete standstill. The demands of stockholders for competitive returns on their investments in the high interest rate market of the early 1980s made capital extremely difficult to attract for needed expansion and rebuilding of such industries as steel and railroads. Any one, or all, of these factors, as shown in Exhibit 6-1, may be important in analyzing the opportunities and threats facing competitors within any single industry. Before discussing this framework in more detail, the following industry sketches will help the reader understand how different aspects of this framework affect different industries.

Automobiles. In 1979 the United States was a net importer of $10.5 billion worth of automobiles. During the first quarter of 1980, net imports of automobiles had increased to $20 billion. While the U.S. automakers delayed production of competitive models, Japanese and German manufacturers built plants in the United States. By the time the U.S. manufacturers are equipped to recapture their market share, foreign manufacturers will have established dealer organizations in this country with new facilities operating smoothly.

Given the new competitive structure of the automobile industry, other firms besides Chrysler may need financial support to reestablish their competitive position. If Chrysler, why not Ford or International Harvester, or suppliers of parts

EXHIBIT 6-1: The Competitive Industry Environment

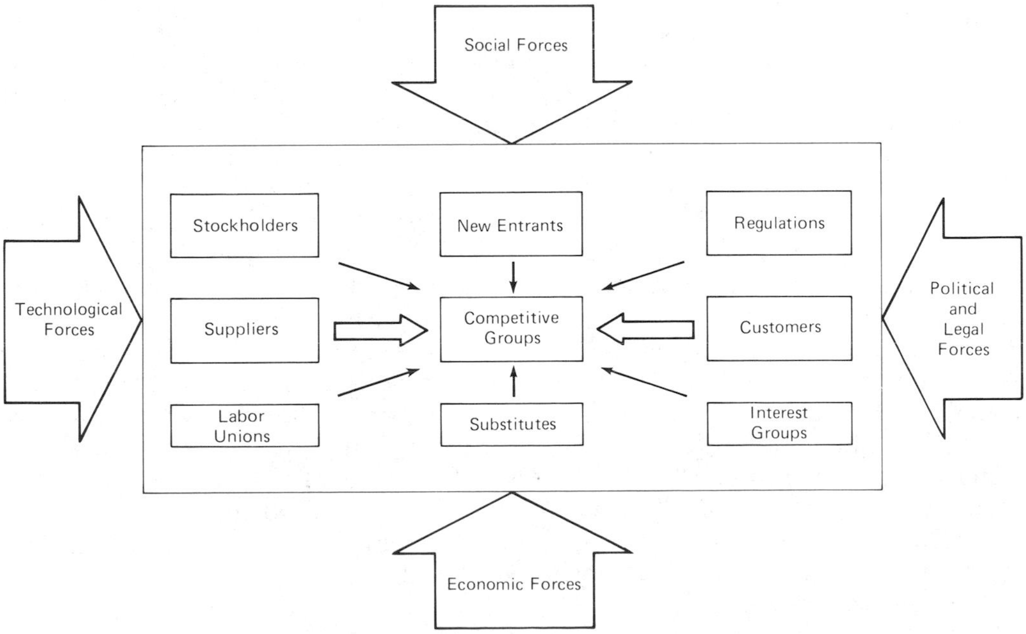

Social Forces

Technological Forces

Stockholders

New Entrants

Regulations

Suppliers

Competitive Groups

Customers

Labor Unions

Substitutes

Interest Groups

Political and Legal Forces

Economic Forces

Source: Adapted from Michael Porter, *Competitive Strategy* (New York: Free Press, 1980).

that are no longer needed? Such financial restructuring is likely to involve banks, dealers, employees, and stockholders alike. To the extent that the federal government is asked to participate in such bailouts, it will be difficult to complain about future governmental interference in corporate decision making.

The Tire Industry. Closely tied to the U.S. automobile manufacturers is the tire industry, which, rather than concentrating on making better tires, committed to supply the U.S. automakers abroad with plants in Europe, Africa, Asia, and Latin America. This heavy capital investment in less advanced technology left little surplus capital for research and development.

As the U.S. tire industry invested in global expansion, Michelin poured hundreds of millions of dollars into developing radial tires and building new radial tire plants in Europe. The family-owned French business also owned 53 per cent in France's Citröen and, therefore, had access to the European automobile industry. Michelin's invention of the steel-belted tire in 1960 soon dominated Europe and took markets from conventional U.S. tiremakers. By 1966, Michelin produced Sears tires in the United States, but it was not until 1969 that General Motors altered its model's suspension systems to accommodate radial tires. Ford then followed with its Lincoln Continental.

Today, Michelin is the fourth largest seller of tires in the United States. Since 1970, over 91,000 American workers in the tire industry have lost their jobs. The United States has become the world's leading tire importer, spending over $1 billion per year on foreign tires. Tire manufacturers in the United States are in trouble and are struggling to find new partners and new businesses to enter.

Aerospace. Firms such as Boeing, McDonnell-Douglas, General Dynamics, Northrop, and Lockheed have for years been in the forefront of advances in aircraft manufacture and in aerospace technology. Exports of American-made aircraft were over $11 billion in 1980, but this was not without problems. The industry's preeminence in commercial aircraft was directly attributable to defense spending for research and development (R&D) military aircraft. Military research has now moved to missiles and away from commercial applications. In addition, competition from abroad now comes from state-owned companies.

Airbus Industries, a European consortium consisting of French, German, Dutch, and British investors, was formed in 1976. By 1980, Airbus had obtained 257 firm orders and sold 147 options, passing all aircraft companies except Boeing in total orders. The Airbus airframe is built by the French government's Aerospatiale, with the government making up early losses. The French alone shipped $25 billion worth of aeronautical products in 1979.

The Airbus has involved technological leaders that makes the transfer of technology more likely in the future. The German partner is a combination of the old Messerschmitt company (MBB) and a German-Dutch partnership (VFW-Fokker). United Technologies owns 26 per cent interest in VFW and Boeing owns 8.9 per cent interest in MBB. The assembly of the Airbus begins in Bremen, West Germany, with final assembly in Toulouse, France.

The U.S. concern was for the future of Boeing. How can the U.S. aircraft industry, which is not directly subsidized, face the state competition represented by the Airbus consortium?

Computer Hardware. In 1971, IBM accounted for nearly 80 per cent of the U.S. computer mainframe market and was the dominant force in computers worldwide. The Japanese had only begun to design computers using integrated circuit (IC) technology. Since Japan's computer industry was faced with keen competition, the Japanese government by the end of 1971 reformed the computer industry into three groups: Fujitsu-Hitachi, NEC-Toshiba, and Iki-Mitsubishi. In addition, the Japanese government funded computer development projects expected to contribute to Japanese international competitive power in the 1980s. The Japanese government's approach was to motivate private firms to solve the problem. Its 1973 plan stated:

> We will select seven high-technology companies and invite them to bid on computer manufacture. Each will submit plans and budgets. Out of the seven we will select three and suggest that their budgets be funded by the government, since our study of IBM has clearly indicated the extent to which the industry is capital-intense. We will not question the budgets submitted but will advise the companies that by 1978 one of them will be eliminated and by 1980 probably a second one. By then, we will have succeeded, and competition will no longer be necessary.

In 1980, both Fujitsu and Hitachi succeeded in manufacturing computer hardware and exporting to the United States. Meantime, the U.S. Department of Justice continued to attempt to break up IBM under the antitrust laws. While the United States continues to protect individual entrepreneurs against the power of large competitors, the Japanese develop products deemed necessary to the nation, subordinating the individual or business to the national need. The future structure of the computer industry remains in doubt.

Semiconductors. Companies such as IBM, Texas Instruments, National Semiconductor, Motorola, and Intel have kept the United States in the forefront of technological advances in microprocessors and very large-scale integrated circuits (VLSI). As semiconductor chips become smaller, their capacity for information storage and processing also increases. As with computers, however, the Japanese government saw the need for VLSI technology and made it top priority in 1973. Funds were made available by the Japanese government to purchase the technology on a one-payment basis regardless of cost. In addition, three high-technology firms were invited to join a government-funded research foundation in which they were allowed to keep their patents on any new developments. In 1980, seven VLSI (64-K RAM) circuit plants were under construction in Japan, including plants for IBM and Texas Instruments.

In addition to the entry of Japanese competition, there is a shortage of qualified U.S. personnel to develop and use the new technology. There is a need for highly specialized engineers to develop computer software for applications which can improve productivity in every industry. The number of graduates in science and engineering per 10,000 labor force in the United States fell from 64.1 in 1965 to 57.4 in 1977. There is also a shortage of new facilities to train engineers and faculty to train them as inflation tightens budgets and high industry salaries attract faculty.

Robotics. The availability of cheaper, more advanced semiconductors and computerized systems has led to the development of robots that can perform many manufacturing duties. Japan, with its shortage of labor, more than doubled its investment in capital equipment per worker between 1970 and 1978 and has become the leader in reducing the availability of dull, repetitive jobs through the use of computer-controlled manufacturing processes, numerical-controlled machine tools, and industrial robots. By 1980, Nissan's new Datsun plant had 96 per cent of the welding done by robots. Matsushita's new TV plant used computer-controlled insertion of electronic components to reduce defects to 0.5 per cent of finished products. At Toyota, the third shift is managed by robots. Use of machine-controlled tools rather than workers for welding and nut tightening has given the Japanese high standardization and quality products.

Whereas the United States auto industry invested early in mass-production techniques, it has been slow to use this new robotics technology. It is almost as though General Motors wanted to keep employment high. American firms, such as Condec's Unimation division, have sold their technology to the Japanese because of the reluctance of U.S. firms to use the technology. Governmental pressure in the United States to hire unskilled workers requires that the simplest tasks be made available to them. However, the better-paid and better-educated unionized workers are demanding less mechanical jobs and higher wages which require job upgrading to justify the added costs. Whereas the Japanese auto production per factory worker was 45 in 1980, it is planned to be 81 per worker by 1985. The American auto plants have now reached about 20 cars per worker. In the United States it is projected that 50,000 robots will be in use by 1990 compared to 7,000 in use in 1980. The Japanese are expected to dominate the market with its governmental-supported 190 industrial robot makers.

Chemicals and Petrochemicals. In 1979, exports of U.S. chemicals and raw materials were nearly $19 billion and rising. In the past, the low price of oil and gas and their ready availability brought about these industries' rapid development and strong trade position. The rise in the cost of gas and oil has increased petrochemical prices, and deregulation promises to further aggravate the problem. More important, however, is the rapid investment by oil-producing countries into refineries to process crude oil into petrochemicals. Saudi Arabia's project to produce 1.6 million metric tons a year (4 per cent of the world market) of basic petrochemicals will be completed by 1985. By 1990, Saudi Arabia, Mexico, Canada, and Brazil may all enter the field. These plants will be new and have the latest technological innovations, creating tough competition for U.S. producers.

Pharmaceuticals. Like the chemical industry, the U.S. pharmaceutical industry has been one of the most technologically advanced in the world. Government grants and research investments provided a strong base for international expansion. Recent U.S. government policies of the Food and Drug Administration, however, have restricted distribution of drugs in the United States that have been used abroad. This has increased the cost of drug research in the United States and reduced the competitiveness of American pharmaceutical firms. The ability to establish drug standards for industrialized nations will determine the industry's viability and U.S. leadership in pharmaceuticals over the coming decades.

Nuclear Energy. Because of Presidents Roosevelt and Truman's efforts to create uses of the atom for both war and peace, the United States developed technological leadership in the nuclear age. Today, this leadership has been passed on to both France and the Soviet Union. Under President Carter in 1977, the federal government decided not to permit commercial reprocessing of spent nuclear fuel in the United States or to go ahead with the development of breeder reactors. This approach was thought to reduce the risks of nuclear proliferation and the availability of plutonium to Third World countries.

The French, with no oil, little coal reserves, and limited uranium, moved quickly toward nuclear energy and breeder reactor technology. France now has a commercial breeder reactor that could be eventually imported into the United States. Along with its technological leadership and prestige, the United States has given up much of its future role in determining the direction of nuclear technology.

UNDERSTANDING INDUSTRY STRUCTURE

It is easy to conceptualize an industry in terms of (1) those needs that are being met by the industry's products, (2) those companies competing and supplying the market needs, and (3) those companies supplying critical factors (raw materials, components, technology, and the like) to the competing companies in the industry. This is represented as follows:

Suppliers→Competitors→Buyers

The actual separation between suppliers, competitors, and buyers depends on the nature of the industry. As described previously for the appliance industry, major competitors may range from components producers to retailers. To begin to understand the nature of industry competitors, let us consider the create-make-market functions. For example, an industry may focus on only one or any combination of these functions. In fact, many of the service industries are found in the create and market functions. For example, advertising agencies serve an important role in marketing. Universities, research labs, and market research organizations serve key roles in the creative functions. Other consulting firms focus more on the linkages between functions. However, it must be recognized that the focus of strategy must be in terms of market needs through specific product designs and developments.

CLASSIFYING BUYER CHARACTERISTICS

One of the first steps in defining an industry is to ask, "Who are the buyers?" Depending on the industry, the buyer may be the ultimate user or consumer, the retailer, the wholesaler, or the manufacturer. Semiconductor manufacturers will generally sell to distributors or other manufacturers. Computer manufacturers may sell to wholesalers or dealers, such as with Apple, or sell to retailers, such as IBM has done with Sears. Radio Shack is a retailer who has integrated backwards and sells directly to the consumer.

It is important to identify the buyers in order to determine what factors will influence their purchasing decisions. For example, as you move toward more durable products, the price may have less effect on the purchasing decision than actual setup costs and maintenance costs. In the same sense, the features neces-

EXHIBIT 6-2: Factors Affecting Buyer Decisions

FACTORS INFLUENCING CONSUMER BUYING DECISIONS DECISIONS	
Prices	Purchase convenience
Product information	Credit availability
Product reputation	Product warranty
Product service	Product selection
Product availability	Product's life cycle
FACTORS INFLUENCING RETAILER/WHOLESALER BUYING DECISIONS	
Relative profitability	Product line
Promotional support	Product turnover
Merchandising support	Supply dependability
Consumer recognition	Distributor support
Competitive products	Product availability
FACTORS INFLUENCING MANUFACTURER BUYING DECISIONS	
Relative profitability	Source availability
Promotional support	Product performance
Technical assistance	Product availability
Relative product importance	Product line
Consumer demands	Product information

sary to sell a product may also include financing arrangements, as with automobiles, marketing support for advertising and promotions, product availability, or technical support.

Exhibit 6-2 lists some of the factors that impact on buyer decisions. However, the importance of the buyers to the industry can influence their bargaining power. Some key factors in determining their relationship include

1. the relative number of buyers and the importance of their volume.
2. the relative profitability of the buyers and their threat to integrate backwards.
3. the amount of information the buyers have about the products and their costs.
4. the uniqueness of the product in meeting the buyers' needs.
5. the availability of substitute products to meet the buyers' needs.
6. the effect that the buyers can have on the cost and quality of the product.

The more important the buyer is to the seller, the greater power the buyer is likely to have in negotiating price or features. General Motors has been able to buy tires at very low prices because of its volume and threat of integrating backwards. Retail chains get substantial price breaks because of their importance to manufacturers.

CLASSIFYING COMPETITIVE GROUPS

The comparative analysis of firms within an industry is necessary if one is to understand some of the basic opportunities and threats that exist in the short run. In the following section we discuss opportunities and threats that relate to buyers, suppliers, and potential competitors.

To simplify our analysis of competitive groups, let us consider three that make up a competitor's position within an industry. The first two components are the product and market strategies. The basis of business strategy is (1) to identify a market or buyer need that is not being properly filled, and (2) to design and develop a product or product line which best meets that need. The third component incorporates the functional capabilities being used to effectively and efficiently implement the product-market strategy. These three components can be thought of as shown in Exhibit 6-3.

Product-Market Focus. The basis for understanding competitive business strategies is first to understand the nature of product positioning. Consider the following competitive business strategies:

1. maintaining product-market "leadership."
2. following the leader with "me too" products.
3. selling higher priced "prestige image" products.
4. selling higher priced-higher performance "premium priced" products.
5. selling competitive priced-higher performance "value" products.
6. using lower "price" to sell competitive products.
7. setting lower priced-lower performance "economy" products.

The Price-Performance Matrix shown in Chapter 5 (Exhibit 5-11) provides meaning to these competitive strategies.

The "leader" is by definition the center position of the price-performance matrix. Competitive strategies only make sense when compared against those products with which the consumer most quickly identifies or uses for comparison. The "me too" strategy is often a copycat strategy aimed at getting into growing markets. Coca-Cola's introduction of Mr. PIBB to compete with Dr. Pepper, or its introduction of Sprite to compete with 7-Up are examples of such strategies. "Me too" strategies are also common second-source or supplier strategies where it is important that the buying institution never be without available sources of supply. This is most common with military contracts and large manufacturers.

EXHIBIT 6-3: Competitive Strategy Components

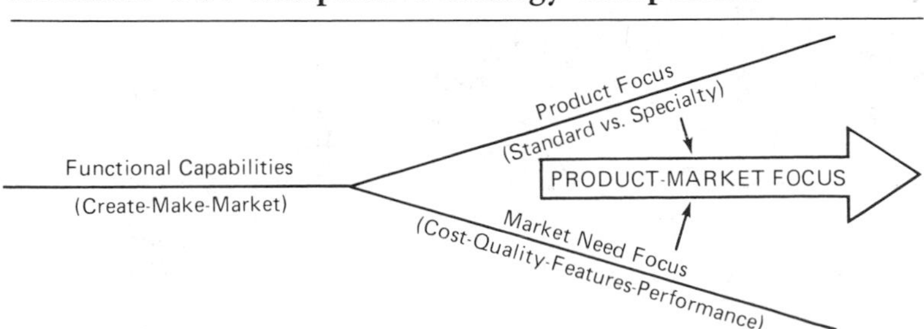

Alternative strategies to compete with the industry leader(s) are price-based strategies. For example, most discount houses use "price" strategies in which competitive brand-name products can be purchased at lower prices. Most bidding such as for military or construction contracts is based on generating competitors who will use this "price" strategy. The "economy" strategy provides low prices for lower performance or fewer features. We are seeing this happen in the food and drug industries where "generic" products are being introduced. Kroger food stores, for example, offers its Cost-Cutter brand at significantly lower prices and, in most cases, with lower quality than the brand names. The success of "economy" strategies depends on the minimum level for quality that the consumer will accept. If the consumer can find brand names at comparable prices, the "economy" strategy can fail as W. T. Grant discount stores discovered.

There are also competitive strategies that are based on product features and performance levels. For example, "value" strategies provide more features or higher quality at a competitive price. We have watched the Japanese auto manufacturers use this strategy to build a significant position in the auto industry. In electronics, Sony used a "premium" strategy in which it charged a higher price for high-quality and unique features. General Motors has effectively used a "prestige" strategy to position the Buick, Oldsmobile, and Cadillac lines. Through heavy advertising for image building, perfume companies are also notorious for their high-priced "prestige" strategies.

The importance of competitive strategy can be seen in Exhibit 6-4. According to the Strategic Planning Institute's PIMS data base, low-price, high-quality strategies gain an average 1.1 per cent in market share per year. In contrast, high-price, low-quality strategies lose an average 0.7 per cent market share per year. This suggests that a relative market share shift of 1.8 per cent per year can occur between the two extreme positions.

Quality, however, is only one dimension of performance. Product design and features must also be included in considering the consumer's perception of needs. For example, Exhibit 6-5 shows the relative comparison between 1982

EXHIBIT 6-4: Price-Quality Impact on Market Share

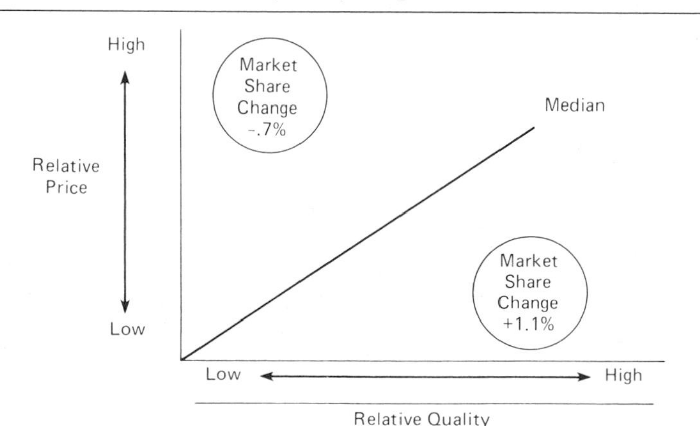

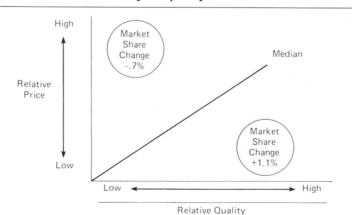

Source: Strategic Planning Institute.

EXHIBIT 6-5: Price-Maintenance Comparisons in U.S. Automobile Industry

1982 Purchase Prices	Much Worse (-35%)	Average	Much Better (+35%)
Higher Priced Cars	Corvette Seville	BMW Audi Continental Deville	Mercedes 280ZX Volvo
$15,000	Firebird Camaro Skylark	Regal, LTD Grand Prix, Olds 98 Cougar Saab, Olds 88 Marquis Granada Zephyr T-Bird	Cressida 626 Prelude
$9,000 Lower Priced Cars	Horizon Concord	LaBaron, Rabbit Newport Renault Aspen, Chevette Volare, Pinto	Corona Colt Champ Corolla Datsun 210 Subaru/GLC
	High Maintenance		Low Maintenance

Frequency of Maintenance*

Source: *Consumer Reports* 1982.

price categories of automobiles and their 1981 maintenance requirements. It can be seen that there were no American-made models in the low-maintenance category, and there were no foreign-made cars in the high-maintenance category. In spite of the poor maintenance record for Firebird and Camaro, these were General Motors' top-selling models. The styling and features offered customers can be of greater importance than quality. However, for more standard designs in the lower-price categories, the Japanese have continued to build market share.

Functional Capabilities. The competitive strategy used by a firm depends on the functional expertise of the organization. Competing on costs, performance, or features requires appropriate support from the make, create, and market functions. For example, "economy," "price," "me too," and "value" strategies require special capabilities in the *make* function to minimize purchasing or manufacturing costs. K-Mart's ability to purchase at low prices and keep operating costs down is essential for its "price" strategy. This has slowly eaten away at Sears's "leadership" position. In contrast, the "prestige," "premium," and "value" strategies require special expertise in the create and market functions. Research and development activities are of special importance in developing special features and in improving product performance. For Sony or Hewlett-Packard to continue to charge higher prices, it must be able to continue developing new products and features.

Identifying Competitive Strategies

Whereas some organizations may be lucky just by being in the right place at the right time, for purposes of analysis, let us consider functionally based strategies that can affect a competitor's product-market focus.

The Create Strategies. Corporations invest in R&D because they believe that such investments will lead to their maintaining or developing a stronger competitive position. Patents for product or process innovations can ensure market leadership for many years, as Polaroid demonstrated with its instant cameras. This has also been true for pharmaceutical and chemical firms. As technological development begins to mature, however, the costs of entering the industry can become very great. In semiconductor circuits, the cost of entering very large-scale integration is many hundreds of millions of dollars today, compared to less than $1 million in the early 1970s. On the other hand, this technology has stimulated the development of a vast number of new products.

The majority of create strategies can be classified into (1) new product strategies, (2) product improvement strategies, and (3) process development strategies. Leadership and premium position strategies rely most heavily on new product innovations and improvements. Value positions rely most heavily on product improvements and process development strategies.

The Make Strategies. Competitors who rely on low-cost positions are likely to have strong process development strategies, integration strategies to reduce costs and maximize value added by the organization, and strong purchasing strategies. Process engineering for equipment development and innovations is basic to increasing overall productivity and reducing material, labor, and processing costs. To achieve economies of scale, industries such as petrochemicals or steel require several years and hundreds of millions of dollars in capital investments. Finally, sources of supply can be critical to stable production and cost positions. Rapid increases in oil prices had a significant impact on heavy energy-using industries and their strategic positions.

Supply strategies may be a critical part of the cost strategy. Such strategies include (1) the reduction of a materials content in a product such as removing steel from automobiles, (2) signing long-term contracts with suppliers, (3) integrating backwards into critical components and materials, and (4) ensuring multiple sources of supply or "me too" strategies.

The Market Strategies. "Product-market" strategies can be limited to a specific market segment or to multiple markets. Depending on the breadth of the markets being addressed, market strategies can differ widely. The more critical market strategies can be classified into (1) limited product-market focus and (2) broad product-market focus. Do not confuse the breadth of market coverage with competitive position since competitive positions can be determined in every key product-market segment.

"Distribution-push" strategies recognize the importance of wholesalers and retailers in the selling process. These strategies are most important in industries in which products are relatively complex or specialty in nature. In such industries, direct sales forces or exclusive distributorships and high dealer margins will encourage training and sales support efforts. Push strategies are most critical where firms (1) have weak finances, unknown brand names, or unique products;

(2) have financial strength and brand name, but weak sales support; or (3) have standard products that require high sales volume to keep costs and prices down. Franchising has been heavily used in fast foods as a way to increase exposure, minimize investment requirements, and still have control over product quality and brand name.

"Demand-pull" strategies attempt to bypass the distribution system by directly influencing buyer behavior. Pull strategies rely on heavy promotion and advertising of product features or brand image. By preselling customers, this strategy can allow less margins and promotions to be used at the wholesale and retail levels. Such strategies increase the firm's ability to introduce new products, extend product life, and maintain the customer's image or the products' position.

Pull strategies can use price, features, performance, or image as the focus in their advertising. Kodak's continued position in instant cameras has used price that has resulted in a price war with Polaroid. Procter & Gamble stresses product features and performance. Coca-Cola stresses a "way of life" or image for its products. All of these firms use aggressive pull strategies.

Strong "customer focus" strategies may concentrate on providing special services in support of a customer sale. Special financing arrangements, technical training, or designs to meet customer needs are also part of market strategies. IBM was known for its user training and technical support. Sears has the largest service operation in the United States to support its appliance business. Such strategies ensure a minimum of downtime to the customer, thereby increasing perceived performance by the customer.

"Segment focus" strategies are becoming increasingly used as industries expand into global competition. Only the largest multinationals will be able to actively compete in all markets. An increasing number of U.S. firms have been withdrawing from the Japanese market as a result of their inability to compete. Firms have continued to withdraw from India as a result of their inability to make or withdraw profits.

Factors Affecting Levels of Competition

Within an industry, one can group competitors according to their combination of functional-product-market strategies. However, when one begins to assess the nature of the competition, the following factors become important:

1. the relative size and number of competitors.
2. the relative importance of the industry to competitors' survival.
3. the relative diversity of competitors.
4. the rate of industry growth.
5. the level of fixed costs, capital intensity, and value added of competitors.
6. the level of product differentiation and customer franchise.
7. the ability of the firm to exit from the industry.

The more committed a competitor is to one market, the greater is the likelihood that competition will increase when growth slows or times get tough. If they have no alternatives, competitors will fight for survival to the end.

CLASSIFYING SUPPLIER CHARACTERISTICS

Suppliers to an industry can have a critical impact on the industry's health and success. The less control that industry competitors have over important supplies, the greater is their risk of losing profits in times of short supply. As long as substitutes are not readily available, industry profitability can be transferred to suppliers who have a dominant position in times of shortage. OPEC countries have demonstrated this principle. In times of excess supply, however, profits can also shift back to the industry as OPEC has also found.

The importance of suppliers to an industry is similar to the importance of the buyers. Key factors determining the relationship include

1. the relative number of suppliers.
2. the relative importance of the industry volume to the supplier.
3. the threat of forward integration by the supplier.
4. the uniqueness of the product in meeting the industry's needs.
5. the availability of substitute supplies to meet industry needs.
6. the relative impact that supplier cost and quality have on the industry's product.

As with buyers, the more significant the role of the supplier in the industry, the greater is the power of the supplier in extracting profits from the industry.

CHARACTERISTICS OF POTENTIAL COMPETITION

To complete the framework for analyzing industry attractiveness, it is necessary to consider the nature of potential competition. Two kinds of potential competitors need to be discussed here: the threat of new entrants and the threat of substitute products. To include these, we can expand the basic framework as follows:

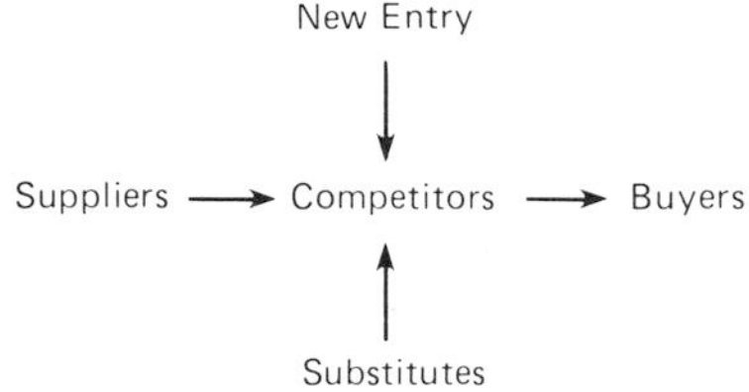

In considering the threat of new entrants into the industry, we need to understand the nature of barriers that exist which might keep them out. Some of the more important factors include

1. the investment and capital requirements necessary to get into the industry.
2. the economies of scale required to compete in the industry.
3. the cost advantages that competitors have in addition to economies of scale (e.g. access to low-cost raw materials).
4. the availability of channels of distribution.
5. the importance of the industry to competitors and their threat of retaliation.

6. the level of product differentiation and consumer franchise held by competitors.
7. the cost to the industry buyers to switch competitors.
8. the impact of government policy and regulation on the industry.

The more capital intensive the industry, the greater are the economies of scale required; and the more differentiated the products; the less likely it is for new competitors to enter an industry. DuPont's position in the titanium dioxide market describes such a situation (see the DuPont de Nemours case). The greater the barriers to entry, the less likely it is that new competition will develop. However, when investments are great and capacity becomes excess, the fight for the existing market by existing competitors can become severe.

The second major threat of competition comes from substitute products. New technology, such as word processors, may better meet the needs of customers than traditional products such as typewriters. The critical factors here include

1. avoiding marketing myopia to ensure that products are meeting buyer needs.
2. anticipating changes in product substitutability.

In the automobile industry, for example, Ford removed over one thousand three hundred pounds of steel from its cars between 1979 and 1982. This steel was replaced mostly by plastics and reducing the size of vehicles. The result was a reduction in both cost and car fuel consumption as a result of the reduced weight.

The Move to Global Competition

With the uneven distribution of resources, capital, food, and technology around the world, and all in short supply, more efficient global institutions will be required for effective production and distribution of essential goods and services. World trade will therefore continue to grow through the development of multinational and global corporations. Industries that are a part of the trading infrastructure (e.g., shipping, credit, and distribution) will be of great importance to future corporations. Access to world markets, especially developing nations that continue to offer growth opportunities, will require special attention to develop mechanisms to facilitate balanced trade.

As world competition continues to increase, United States-based multinationals will be faced with fundamental problems such as described in the industry section earlier in this chapter. As recognized in these industry discussions, the role of the U.S. government will be critical in balancing the competitive position of foreign government-supported industries. Exhibit 6-6 identifies some of the specific problem areas that will need to be addressed when assessing multinational industries. These are by no means the only problems to be addressed, but they will become increasingly important as trade expands.

Industry Performance

As we complete the basic framework of industry analysis, it is necessary to identify some of the key elements of industry performance. This analysis can

EXHIBIT 6-6: Problems Facing U.S. Industry in World Competition

1. U.S. products are not competitive because of quality levels.
2. Government assistance is not competitive with that of foreign governments.
3. Business behavior is not competitive with foreign firms as a result of U.S. legislated tax rules, environmental standards, and morality (antibribery).
4. Salaries of U.S. workers are two to four times the salaries of foreigners, and are also taxed by the United States when earned abroad.
5. High freight costs from the United States make American exports less competitive abroad.
6. The United States no longer holds technological superiority.
7. Foreign competition works closely with their governments in obtaining major contracts, obtaining government insurance and financial supports.

differ depending on whether the primary focus of the industry is aimed at the supplier, competitor, or buyer level of the product or service delivery process.

At the supplier level of the industry, the primary performance characteristics relate to technological advances, product quality, and development of future market position. For example, in energy resources, the future success of suppliers will be heavily based in technologies for coal gasification, deep-well drilling, solar technology, and nuclear energy. As lower quality crude oil is used, heavy investments will be required in refining facilities to maintain supplies of high-quality products. Control of current energy resources will provide power to the supplier until such alternatives are developed.

At the competitor level of the industry, capacity utilization will be increasingly important as overall fixed costs of operation continue to rise. This will require continued innovations to maintain productivity and market position. In capital-intensive industries, such as steel, large-scale operations will be essential to maintain competitive cost structure in commodity products. The problem with such large-scale investments, such as U.S. Steel's latest 7 million ton, $4 billion plant, is that market fluctuations can quickly put capacity utilization levels below the break-even operating level.

At the buyer level of industry analysis, the maintenance of demand and the consumer franchise is critical to performance. Measures such as product availability (stock-out rates) and product performance (returns and service requirements) will have a dramatic effect on the consumer franchise. Inflation is more difficult to control and can either negatively affect demand through price increases or profitability by raising costs. Depending on the nature of the elasticity of demand, price increases can possibly be passed on to the consumer.

DETERMINING INDUSTRY ATTRACTIVENESS

The attractiveness of an industry or market is not easy to determine. It is influenced by the structure of the industry and factors that may influence that structure. The industry structure includes a description of industry size, growth rates (past, present, and future), and key influences that affect growth and competitors' strengths and market position (both current and projected).

Industry attractiveness also depends on the degree of industry integration, ease of entry, and status of production facilities. Industry capacity, raw material

EXHIBIT 6-7: Factors Determining Market and Industry Attractiveness

Market	1. size (present and potential) 2. growth (stage in life cycle) 3. diversity of user segments 4. foreign opportunities 5. cyclicality
Competition	1. concentration ratio 2. capacity utilization 3. structural changes (entry or exits) 4. position changes (change in strategic groups) 5. vertical integration (levels, threats, opportunities) 6. sensitivity of price/service/and so on to market size and shares 7. degree of captive business
Profitabiltiy	1. level and trends of leaders 2. contribution rates (value added) 3. leverage factors and trends (economies of scale and pricing) 4. barriers to entry
Technology	1. maturity/volatility 2. complexity 3. patent protection 4. product/process opportunities or threats
Other	1. social/environmental 2. government/political 3. unions 4. human factors

Source: George S. Day, "A Strategic Perspective on Product Planning," *Journal of Contemporary Business* (Spring 1975): 27. Reprinted by permission.

availability, economic plant sizes, and new plant start-up times all impact on industry assessments. Government regulation, foreign competition, and distribution requirements also affect industry attractiveness. Finally, financial performance in terms of cost structure, asset turnover, price trends, and sale conditions ultimately has a significant influence on whether or not the industry is attractive to a specific organization.

Size and diversity of the overall market, competitive structure and power of industry participants, industry profitability, regulatory and legal developments, social and human concerns, role of technology, and environmental dynamics all impact the attractiveness of the industry. More favorable industries may receive greater attention and resources than industries that have significant problems. Exhibit 6-7 summarizes the factors used to determine industry and market attractiveness.

CRITERIA FOR SUCCESSFUL STRATEGIES

Although we have attempted to outline the kind of information needed for industry evaluations, we have not indicated what strategies are best for specific environmental, competitive, and organizational situations. Whereas generic success elements have yet to be developed in the field of strategic management, a number of important evaluative areas provide some direction. Some of these strategic points that can aid competitive performance are now described.

Have a Strong Competitive Position

Having a strong position in your industry is always helpful in developing and maintaining successful strategies. Some of the criteria for a strong position include

1. having no competition that is able to dominate the market.
2. having a significant market share.
3. having one of the three leading shares in the market.
4. having market share that is increasing.
5. gaining market share on the market leader.
6. having remaining market share divided between several competitors with significant market shares.
7. having markets that are truly competitive.
8. having a position protected by significant factors such as antitrust.

Build on Competitive Strengths

Building on the structural characteristics of the industry and its relationships can create significant competitive strengths for an organization. Some of the key elements for success include

1. concentrating on businesses in which your company's strengths are the key elements of industry competition.
2. finding businesses that are not as attractive to most of your competition.
3. finding businesses in which most of your competitors are not emotionally committed to the industry.
4. finding businesses in which your technology is strong relative to your competition.
5. finding markets in which you are protected by patents or customer contracts.
6. concentrating on businesses in which you have special relationships with sources of supply, major distributors, customers, and/or organizational support groups.
7. finding businesses in which you are at least as integrated, forward and backward, as your competition.

Strong relationships and protected markets allow for more successful strategic control of business operations. Such competitive advantages can lead to more successful implementation of functional strategies.

Build Marketing Strengths

Whereas structural relationships are important in the conduct of successful business strategies, they will not guarantee success. Some basic marketing characteristics are also necessary to support business success. Some of the key issues include

1. finding markets that attach value to your corporate name or brand.
2. finding markets in which your product line is broad relative to your competition.
3. finding markets in which you are the price leader, or in which there is no price leader.
4. finding markets in which prices range widely around the average.
5. finding markets in which you need not depend on only a few customers.
6. finding markets in which your volume justifies using the optimal distribution system for the industry.

In essence, the more differentiated the product and diverse the customer base, the stronger is the market position.

Build Production Strengths

Maintaining a strong marketing position requires that production operations provide a strong cost position for the business. Key production characteristics that are necessary for successful business strategies include

1. finding businesses where no competitor is planning to add significant new capacity.
2. building production facilities that are larger than currently viable larger units.
3. running operations near their optimal capacity levels.
4. keeping variable manufacturing costs below your competitors.
5. keeping total costs below the competition.
6. finding profitable alternative uses for your excess production capacities.

Use Financial and Managerial Strengths

Profitability and net cash generation are fundamental to successful business operations. However, without adequate management decision making, such success may, in reality, be starving operations from future success. Key organizational characteristics for ensuring future success include

1. building a managerial system that supports risk taking.
2. having the capital availability, balanced business portfolio, and competitive position that allows a company to take risks.
3. having a management team and organization that responds quickly to competitive and environmental changes.

PROJECTIONS FOR THE FUTURE

Thus far, we have only attempted to describe the current situation, not to project an industry's health into the future. Forecasting the future is not nearly as easy as describing the past or present. Forecasts can only be accomplished by making a lot of assumptions about what might happen in the future; not only in local markets, but in regional, national, and international markets.

Primary industry assumptions will include projections of industry growth, stability, availability of supplies, competitive actions, technological developments, demand fluctuations, cost and price trends, demographics, and corporate commitments. External influences such as legislation, the labor climate, social actions, and demographics also require assumptions to be developed. Alternative assumptions, or scenarios, can have dramatically different affects on the future of an industry.

Through industry analysis, the primary opportunities and threats of industry participants should be recognized. The changing character of each industry segment provides a new set of opportunities and risks for both strong and weak participants alike. As we begin to recognize some basic industry characteristics, however, we should also be able to identify the potential impact those characteristics will have on a firm. The following characteristics are shown with some common problems:

Characteristic	*Problem*
Small plant size	High relative cost
Small firm size	Limited capital availability
Old plant and equipment	High replacement cost
Urban locations	Limits to expansion
Rural locations	Lack municipal facilities
Heavy pollution	High cost of compliance
Heavy energy use	High cost of operations

As we relate aspects of industry analysis to some of the industries identified in the beginning of this chapter, we can recognize critical features of each industry:

Industry	*Critical Issues*
Automobiles	Low productivity and quality
Tires	Obsolete technology and facilities
Aerospace	Government-owned competition
Computer hardware	Government-funded research
Semiconductors	Government-funded research
Robotics	Slow acceptance
Chemicals	High capital and pollution-abatement cost
Pharmaceuticals	High research costs
Nuclear energy	Loss of technology

Critical issues in other industries include:

Primary Industry	*Critical Characteristics*
Steel	Mature growth
Utilities	High capital costs
Packaging	Ready substitutes
Paper	Low market concentration
Textiles	Unequal abatement costs
Copper smelting	High important competition

In understanding the continued changes in the business environment, we can also project some industries that are likely to have high growth potential in the future. Some of these include:

Energy suppliers:	coal
	hydrocarbon energy sources
	energy services
	energy conservation
Food suppliers:	agribusiness
Health and Safety:	protection and safety
	chemicals (drugs)
	medical instruments
	dental supplies and service
Productivity:	electronics
	communications
	transportation equipment and service
	production equipment and services
Capital:	financial services
	banks
	inflation hedges

Once major industry characteristics and trends are identified, it is then time to begin identifying the specific position, and the opportunities and problems which the individual firm must recognize in developing its future.

FOCUS QUESTIONS

1. Identify industries whose primary competitive groupings concentrate on each state of the product delivery cycle:
   a. raw materials.
   b. technology.
   c. manufacturing.
   d. distribution.
   e. retailing.
   f. service.
2. Take one industry with which you are familiar and identify (a) the industry characteristics and (b) the characteristics of the strategic groups.

ADDITIONAL READINGS

ADAMS, WALTER. *The Structure of American Industry.* New York: Macmillan Publishing Company, 1971.

ABELL, DEREK F., and JOHN S. HAMMOND. *Strategic Market Planning.* Englewood Cliffs, N.J.: Prentice Hall, Inc., 1979.

CAVES, RICHARD. *American Industry: Structure, Conduct, Performance.* Englewood Cliffs, N.J.: Prentice Hall, 1972.

LEVITT, THEODORE. "Marketing Myopia." *Harvard Business Review* (July–Aug., 1960): 45.

PORTER, MICHAEL E. *Interbrand Choice, Strategy and Bilateral Market Power.* Cambridge, Mass.: Harvard University Press, 1976.

———. "How Competitive Forces Share Strategy." *Harvard Business Review,* **57,** no. 2 (March–April 1979): 137–145.

———. *Competitive Strategy Techniques for Analyzing Industry and Competitors.* New York: Free Press, 1980.

WALL, JERRY. "What the Competition Is Doing: You Need to Know." *Harvard Business Review,* **52,** no. 6 (Nov.–Dec., 1974).

7 Industry Attractiveness: Impact of the General Business Environment

Beyond an understanding of industry structure is the need to understand the longer-range impact that external environmental changes are likely to have on the industry and its competitive strategies.

Exhibit 7-1 shows the variety of social, political, economic, and technological forces that can impact on a firm's business environment. Some of the social factors that affect us relate to the expectations, norms, and attitudes of the communities in which we operate. Political and legal factors that develop out of social concerns include ecological legislation, health and safety regulations, and the resulting concerns over too many regulatory and administrative controls. Economic issues include a growing concern over national economic policies, inflation rates, demographic changes, employment levels, and savings rates. Technological forces also play an increasing role in competition as a result of materials shortages, need for productivity improvements, plant modernization, and increased investment in research and development. The growing impact of these issues on business makes it difficult to consider them independently, or even to set priorities as to their relative importance.

The relationship between the organization and the environment in which it operates is highly interactive in nature. An example is the successful factory, back in the 1950s, which contributed to the high employment level and economy of its community. At that time, the black smoke belching from its stacks was looked upon with admiration as an indication of the factory's success. The employees of the factory and, as a result, the local economy as well, had higher income levels and the employees were able to enjoy their leisure time. The only problem was that, when they went outdoors or opened their windows, they would get black soot all over themselves.

Since people don't appreciate social irritants, such as black soot, the employees began to complain. The local factory owner was so busy running the operations and training new employees he could find little time from his eighty-hour work schedule to consider any new problems. This meant that the community would have to take action, if anything was to be done about the soot. Fortunately, an enterprising young man who wished to enter politics took up the cause and promised that, "If you vote for me, I'll do something about the soot!" Because of the social irritant, the members of the community were happy to find someone who would represent their cause, and he was elected to represent them.

EXHIBIT 7-1: Forces Influencing the Competitive Business Environment

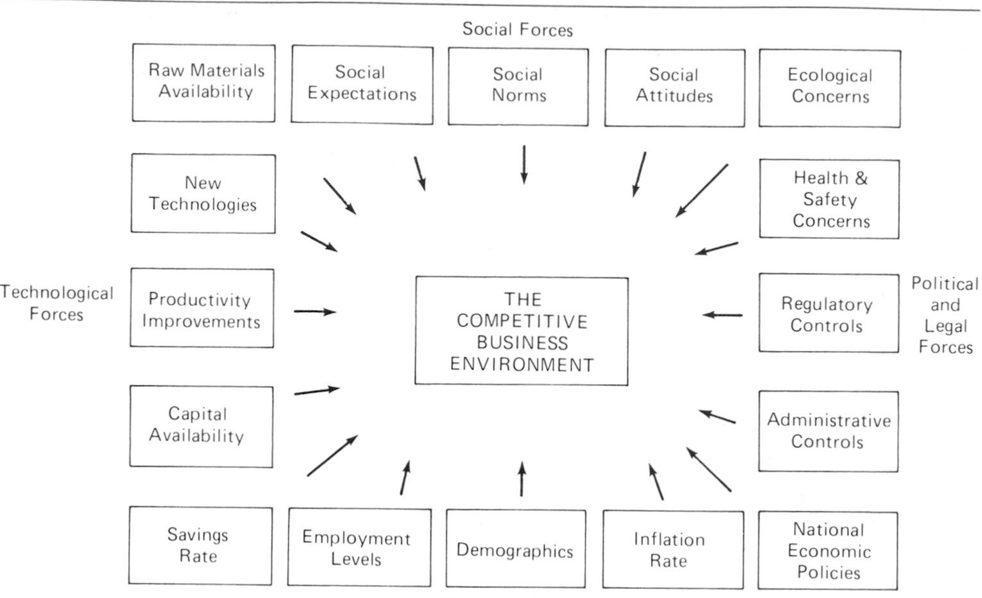

By the 1960s, the new politician had been able to collect thousands of letters, signatures, and petitions to take action against factory-caused pollution. The legislation that he had sponsored required that all smokestacks install equipment to eliminate soot from the vapors. By now, however, business at the factory had leveled off and had become more competitive and less profitable. The factory owner would be required by the new legislation to install expensive equipment that would cost as much as his original plant, and add nothing to its performance. Besides that, he needed new machines to replace his worn-out equipment. The factory owner decided to buy production equipment first, to keep the plant operating. Government officials were not satisfied with this performance and shut the plant down. Since the owner could not pay the company's creditors, bankruptcy followed and, now, employment in the community has fallen off by 15 per cent and the community's economy is badly suffering. The creditors sold off the factory's assets and the building is no longer in use.

Although this example is very simple, one can note that the relationship between the business organization and environment cannot be easily separated. Social concerns become political issues, political issues become law, and laws effectively impact on the ability of people to make decisions at either the individual or organizational level. Such laws have economic consequences that have social costs. In this example, the community's environment may be cleaner now, but fewer people there have jobs. Technology may have been an answer to this situation, but it was not available and nothing was done as part of the legislation to ensure its availability.

Understanding the nature of the changing environment is of growing importance to today's business strategists. These changes can best be thought of in terms of social, political, legal, technological, and economic factors. In assessing industry attractiveness, we need to consider how these environmental factors will affect our industry and strategy in the future. Let us consider some of these factors.

SOME SOCIAL FORCES

As we move through the 1980s, fundamental changes in demographics and the labor force, and shortages in the supply of critical skills will impact the structure of society and its institutions. In the United States, for example, some of the factors affecting the general organizational environment include the following:

Demographic and Labor Force Changes. The aging of the postwar baby boom generation will have an impact throughout the 1980s. This group will become the prime work force (age twenty-five to forty-five) and the prime consuming public. The relative importance of teenagers and young adults as consumers and workers will decline, thereby increasing the general stability of the work force and its potential productivity. This group will also be better educated than in the past.

The major problems caused by these demographic changes will relate to the shortage of skilled entry-level employees, and the reduced opportunities for promotion. This will not necessarily reduce the unemployment levels among blacks and minorities, but it may improve the chances for teenagers to get jobs.

Changes in the Nonworker/Worker Ratio. The ratio of nonworkers to workers in our society will affect productivity, living standards, Social Security burdens, and the degree of economic conflicts that exist. This ratio is likely to increase with increases in length of schooling, early retirements, shorter work weeks, and fewer workdays per year for full-time workers. By the year 2010, the baby boom generation will reach retirement age and pose a tremendous economic burden on society. As a result, Social Security and pension programs will be of special importance in the next several decades.

Changes in Work Structure. By 1979, over 50 per cent of the work force was classified as white collar, with less than one third being blue collar. Over 25 per cent were professionals and managers. In the decades ahead, growth will continue in information-related, technical, service-type jobs, as computer technology impacts every phase of our activities.

Applications of new technology will cause the office of the future to rapidly evolve. With this change will come job redesigning, and growing attempts at humanizing the workplace and quality of work life. Innovative techniques like job sharing and homework arrangements will provide increased flexibility to the growing number of women, minorities, and elderly people in the work force.

Increased Employee Participation. The growth in service institutions, technology-based worker environments, and worker education levels will cause increased pressure for employees to become involved in decision-making activities. The increased problem-solving focus of service activities will further require multiskilled worker participation. Such forces will require changed operating procedures, shared information sources, and shared authority.

Changing Educational Requirements. Pressures for the traditional educational system to adapt to the changing needs of students are likely to continue in the years ahead. Declining student-age populations, growing numbers of disadvantaged minorities, needs for income-earning skills, and explosions in information availability will cause significant changes in educational objectives and curricula. In addition, educational costs need to be controlled with the application of new technology and management techniques.

SOME POLITICAL FORCES

Whereas it may be apparent in the United States that social concerns eventually affect the political structure, this relationship is less clear in other countries. For example, European governments often own state monopolies in various industries that are not very responsive to consumer needs. In the Soviet Union the state owns all productive assets and leaves little freedom to the individual. Understanding the nature of this interaction, therefore, will be a significant challenge to future organizations operating across national boundaries. Only through an understanding of these relationships can operating risks be assessed.

Move Toward the Welfare State. In democratic countries, business excesses have generated disenchantment and growing demands for more "humanist" goals to equalize income distributions and end poverty and suffering. Such pressures have caused the trend toward "welfare states" in which the state (a) diverts resources into various welfare projects, (b) establishes compulsory insurance schemes, e.g., national health care, and (c) affects worker motivations to contribute. In the United States, for example, rent subsidy, negative income tax, welfare payments, and food stamp programs have been established to raise the living standards of the poor. The federal spending deficit for the United States from 1982 to 1985 is expected to add over $500 billion to the national debt, requiring over 60 per cent of the projected savings pool for government use.

Continued pressure for "welfare states" will likely grow and impact nations, organizations, and individuals in the following ways.

1. Total taxes and government spending will increase drastically.
2. Worker penalties for welfare recipients will create dysfunctional worker motivation.
3. New government administrations will be unable to reverse the trend toward more welfare benefits.
4. Resource allocation decisions will increasingly be made on philosophical or political grounds rather than on economic criteria.
5. Increased worker taxation on incremental income will encourage worker absenteeism.
6. Government dependence will decrease worker motivation through lack of "care" or "worry."

In essence, although the welfare state has popular support, the economic consequences are less certain. In the United States, however, business sales have stagnated in the 1980s, real long-term interest rates have remained high, industrial plants and equipment continue to deteriorate, and export markets shrink.

SOME TECHNOLOGICAL FORCES

Technological change results when new ideas are applied to existing problems for the purpose of economic or social development. As with all economic and social changes, the acceptance of technological innovations takes a significant period of time.

The Need for Innovation. Innovation needs to be distinguished from scientific discovery, which involves previously unknown knowledge, and from invention, which is the creation of a novel product, process, or service. Though inventions may provide the initial concept leading to the innovation, the time period between first conception and the successful introduction of a commercially viable innovation into the marketplace takes many years.

Exhibit 7-2 shows the duration in years of ten innovations that have reached the market. You will note that in the exhibit the average time period was 19.2 years. Research carried out on these innovations found that the reason for their development came from the recognition of technological opportunity.

The heart pacemaker alone utilized five technologies, all of which were initially developed prior to 1900. Semiconductor electronics developments were commercialized in the 1950s. Pacemaker battery requirements were not refined until 1959. Surgical techniques for open heart surgery were first successful in 1953. Cardiac stimulation techniques were not developed until the 1950s. Biomaterials and electrodes were not available until 1950. The first human implant of a cardiac pacemaker occurred in 1960.

Another of the more recent innovations was the videotape recorder in 1956 by CBS. Six technologies were incorporated into the VTR with all but one dating back to the late 1800s. These technologies included magnetic theory, magnetic recording, electronics, frequency modulation, control theory, and magnetic and recording materials developments. By 1950, all these developments were brought together and became VTR projects at Ampex and RCA. In 1956, CBS

EXHIBIT 7-2: Duration of the Innovative Process for Ten Innovations

Innovation	*Year of First Conceptualization*	*Year of First Realization*	*Duration (years)*
Heart Pacemaker	1928	1960	32
Hybrid Corn	1908	1933	25
Hybrid Small Grains	1937	1956	19
Green Revolution Wheat	1950	1966	16
Electrophotography	1937	1959	22
Input-Output Economic Analysis	1936	1964	28
Organophosphorous Insecticides	1934	1947	13
Oral Contraceptives	1951	1960	9
Magnetic Ferrites	1933	1955	22
Videotape Recorder	1950	1956	6
Average Time Span			19.2

Source: Battelle Memorial Institute, *Interactions of Science and Technology in the Innovative Process.* National Science Foundation Contract 667, 1973, pp. 4–10.

EXHIBIT 7-3: Developments Using Semiconductor Technology

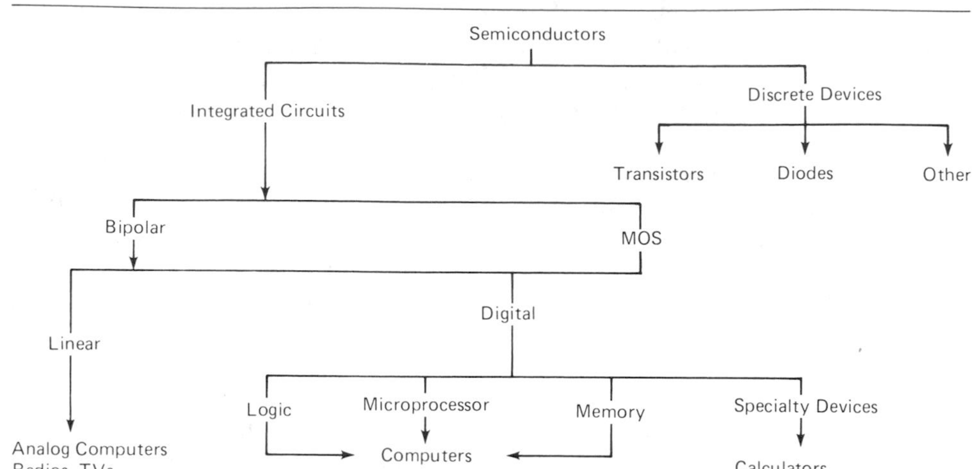

was the first to use the Ampex monochrome videotape recorder. Current commercialization of the VTR continues into the consumer market in the 1980s.

The Need for Continued Development. Today, we are seeing the impact of semiconductor technology in a wide range of products. Exhibit 7-3, for example, shows the evolution of technology that now affects most of us on a daily basis. Radios, television sets, computers, watches, calculators, and games all rely on semiconductor advancements. With the advancements in computers, we are now beginning to see the integration of information-processing technologies through the use of telecommunications, satellites, and laser technologies. These will be keys in future developments of information-processing innovations.

The slowness with which technological innovations develop makes these investments high risk. The potential payoff for winning innovations, however, can be significant and continues to encourage investments in research and development. Exhibit 7-4 shows that over $32 billion was invested in R&D by U.S. firms in 1981, over 30 per cent of which was accounted for by automobile, electronics, and computer research. Research in drugs, chemicals, and fuels accounted for another 22 per cent of the total. Without such long-term investments, the competitive position of these U.S. industries would be called into question.

As we look at the success of the Japanese in commercializing innovations, we can begin to identify some of the key characteristics that have brought success to the Japanese. Besides their basic strategy of improving on innovations, we also find some key environmental supports in Japan:

1. There is a national policy for setting up research and development facilities for new technologies.
2. There are tax and interest incentives for investors in designated technologies.
3. Capital is made available for designated technological investments at preferred interest rates.
4. Investment in new technology is readily accepted by employees.

EXHIBIT 7-4: R&D Scoreboard—1981

Industry (number of firms)	*Million Dollars*	*Per Cent of Sales*	*Per Cent of Profits*	*Dollars per Employee*
Aerospace (15)	2363.2	4.8	141.6	3717
Appliances (8)	159.7	2.0	82.9	1136
Automotive (7)	4545.1	3.7	−231.3	3426
Automotive parts (15)	350.9	2.0	59.9	1406
Building materials (20)	175.3	1.2	42.1	1053
Chemicals (45)	2635.2	2.5	47.1	2879
Conglomerates (14)	1280.7	2.0	41.4	1343
Containers (5)	119.4	0.8	22.4	689
Drugs (28)	2450.6	5.3	57.1	4044
Electrical (34)	1487.1	2.9	48.8	1862
Electronics (62)	841.3	3.1	74.3	1829
Food and Beverage (37)	578.1	0.7	16.3	761
Fuel (19)	2261.1	0.5	8.9	2287
Information processing:				
Computers (26)	3845.5	6.4	72.4	4231
Office equipment (13)	729.2	5.0	94.6	3324
Peripherals (44)	344.1	5.9	94.2	3284
Instruments (64)	647.5	4.6	87.5	2571
Leisure time (23)	896.1	4.4	55.5	3288
Machinery:				
Farm and Construction (18)	726.9	2.9	61.1	2679
Machine tools (55)	494.5	1.9	35.7	1370
Metals and Mining (16)	245.1	1.1	21.8	1239
Oil services (20)	623.6	1.8	16.5	1360
Paper (16)	255.9	0.9	16.4	930
Personal care (22)	590.1	2.0	33.1	2168
Semiconductors (9)	713.5	7.1	174.0	3109
Steel (7)	179.7	0.6	10.7	577
Telecommunications (14)	878.7	1.2	10.9	770
Textiles (15)	47.8	0.4	19.0	237
Tires and Rubber (10)	451.2	2.0	70.9	1435
Tobacco (2)	22.4	0.5	5.2	403
All-Industry Composite	32106.5	2.0	39.3	2161

Source: "R&D Scoreboard—1981," *Business Week,* July 5, 1982.

5. Growth in new technologies has become part of the culture and economic system.

Few, if any, real inventions have come out of Japan in the past, but Japanese developments in technology are being felt around the world.

Future developments have a wide range of technologies to draw from. Predicting new developments and innovations will be increasingly important. Consider the problem of depleting oil resources and their increasing costs. We are beginning to see a new emphasis on energy-related technologies that have yet to become commercial. Consider the following classes of technology:

1. nuclear fission.
2. nuclear fusion.
3. synthetic hydrocarbon fuels.
4. solar energy.
5. wind energy.
6. geothermal energy.
7. hydrostatic, tidal, and ocean current energy.
8. temperature gradient energy.
9. advanced energy storage and distribution.

Trying to decide on which of these technologies to invest research and development funds is a real gamble.

SOME ECONOMIC FORCES

Over the past century, the United States has led most nations in its ability to produce efficiently, to grow, to innovate, and to assure adequate services for a large and diverse population. In the past decade, however, the U.S. rate of productivity increase has fallen below that of most industrialized nations. According to the Bureau of Labor Statistics, productivity growth in the United States declined from an average of 3.2 per cent between 1947 and 1966, to 2.1 per cent between 1967 and 1973, to 1.6 per cent between 1973 and 1979. By 1979, productivity growth had reached an all-time low of .7 per cent. Moreover, the United States lags behind its principal industrial competitors in capital investments, savings, and research and development expenses as a percentage of gross national product. The continued decline in U.S. productivity can only be expected to hurt profitability and, thereby, further restrict capital investment and research and development expenditures.

The U.S. investment and savings problems relate to the rise in the U.S. inflation rate in the late 1970s to double-digit inflation. Over the past decade, individual savings dropped from nearly 6 per cent of disposable income to 3.5 per cent in 1979. This decline in savings reduces available capital for investments and added pressure for rising interest rates. Japan and Germany, however, continued with savings ratios of 20 per cent and 14 per cent, respectively, in 1980. R&D expenditures in the United States have also been influenced, dropping from 2.1 per cent of GNP in 1964 to 1.6 per cent in 1979, as more conservative, low-risk approaches are taken for U.S. investments.

The economic strength and vitality of the U.S. economy will depend in the future on its willingness to save and invest, to remove regulations that unduly stifle competition, to stimulate technological progress, and to increase productivity. The attainment of key domestic social and economic goals—such as revitalization of cities, cleaner environment, quality education, and security in old age—as well as assuring adequate strength in national security and foreign policy—will require improved productivity, improved competition, and control of inflation. The basic problem, however, is finding new ways to break the vicious circle of inflation and declining productivity.

Controlling Inflation. A major long-term political issue in combatting inflation is whether high employment and noninflationary economic growth can be achieved simultaneously. The continuation of economic restraint and unemployment to suppress inflation can only lead to the further development of a "welfare state." The inflationary impact of demand expansion policies, however, will require greater wage and price flexibility, productivity, and advanced capital investment to ensure supply availability. Such growth policies would, therefore, require changes in environmental and other regulatory provisions that hamper construction and production. Where commodity shortages are likely, international commodity agreements and investment in stockpile will be required in advance of inflationary shortages.

Modernizing Industry. To be internationally competitive, industry must seek economies of scale to sustain comparative advantages in efficiency and productivity. This requires continued capital investments and the application of technological innovations from research and development to reduce unit costs and to lead to the introduction of new and more efficient products and processes.

Inadequate incentives for capital investment and innovation, unrealistic depreciation guidelines, excessively burdensome regulatory structures, and institutionalized inflation lead to progressive liquidation of the capital base of a nation's economic system. Problems of the high cost of new capital, the long lead times required for capacity expansion or modernization or new product introductions, the use of unrealistic accounting practices, and tax policies for depreciation and long-term research expenditures will continue to plague industry in justifying required capacity or productivity investments that have inadequate real returns on investment. Industries such as steel, railroads, airlines, and utilities have lost their competitiveness both domestically and internationally. These problems are likely to increase administrative pressure for nationalization, rather than revitalization through special accounting and tax incentives.

Living with Energy Shortages. The U.S. and world economies will be living with the gradual depletion of oil, gas, and ultimately, coal reserves. The long lead times required to develop and apply new energy technologies require special action and incentives for the development of renewable energy resources such as solar and fusion energy. Until such alternatives are able to meet future needs, special attention will be required to deal with the interim supply-and-demand problems. National energy policies for the conservation and development of alternative supply are likely. Trade-offs between the use of coal, nuclear power, and synthetic fuels will involve difficult social and ecological issues.

Better Labor-Management Relationships. The growing complexity and interrelatedness of today's economic problems are likely to increase pressure for joint labor-management problem solving. For example, local joint committees and no-strike agreements are now used in the steel industry and may move into other problem industries. A common concern is developing for increasing productivity that may lead to productivity bargaining.

Growing International Interdependence. The rapid increase in movement of goods, people, money, ideas, and problems across national boundaries is complicating the ability of nations to manage their own economic affairs. Economic export policies of Japan, for example, have significantly influenced U.S. steel, auto, radio, and television industries. The transfer of Eurodollars into high-interest-paying countries can significantly affect exchange rates and corresponding corporate currency adjustments (often forcing significant accounting losses or gains to be reported). The growth in world trade also causes inflation to be spread rapidly from one economy to another.

Less developed countries that control scarce resources, such as oil, have increased the abundance of capital at their disposal. Important exporting nations such as Brazil, Korea, and Taiwan are becoming industrialized and important members of the developing world whereas others are near bankruptcy. Countries with balance of payments surpluses are becoming significant world bankers. Countries with balance of payments difficulties will be forced into severe retrenchment and basic problems of survival.

ASSESSING COUNTRY RISKS

With the growth in multinational business operations, both business and organizational strategies need to assess country risks. Country risk may be defined as the exposure to a loss in cross-border activity, caused by events in a particular country, where events are under the control of the government and not under the control of the private organization or individual. Bankruptcy, for example, could be considered a country risk if the bankruptcy is the result of the government's mismanagement of the economy. It would be a commercial risk if the bankruptcy were to result from mismanagement of the firm. Unforseeable natural calamities, such as earthquakes, cannot be considered country risks. However, where typhoons and monsoons are common, government preparations can minimize their harmful effects and thereby affect country risk.

The most common factors used in assessing country risk are political, social, and economic in nature. Examples of these include:

1. Political risks: war, occupation by foreign powers, riots, disorders caused by territorial claims, ideological differences, conflict of economic interests, regionalism, political polarization, and so on.
2. Social risks: civil wars, riots, disorders caused by such phenomena as tribal strife, unequal income distribution, union militancy, religious divisions, antagonism between social classes, and so on.
3. Economic risks: continuous slow GNP growth, strikes, rapid rise in production costs, fall in export earnings, sudden increase in food or energy imports, and so on.

Besides classifying country risks by political, social, and economic factors, risks can also be broken down by geographic areas and degree of risk inherent in cross-border activities.

Country risks can be quantified by asking the following questions:

1. What is the likelihood that an adverse event will occur?
2. When is this event most likely to occur?
3. What is the likelihood that risk materializes if the event occurs?
4. What is the likelihood of total loss?
5. Under what conditions is total loss likely to occur?

These risk factors can be quantified through the use of such formats as shown in Exhibit 7-5.

Whereas the format looks simple enough, accurate assessments require a good knowledge about the country: (1) its political, economic, and social structure; (2) its legislative, institutional, and regulatory framework; (3) the individual and collective character of its people and government leaders; and (4) past and current economic, political, and social trends. The more extensive the knowledge about these facts, the better the final assessment will be.

Let us consider some of the factors that are likely to affect country risk:

Social and Political Risk Factors

Political risk assessment is an art in itself. The risk of war is increased when disputes over territory and ideology have created deep-seated antagonism and

EXHIBIT 7-5: Quantification of Country Risk

Country: Date:
Borrower: Private bank/nonbank (no government guarantee)
Time Horizon: . . . . years

	Events/situations that may lead to the materialization of a risk:	What is the likelihood of										
		event occurring?		any risk materializing	default		renegotiation		rescheduling, etc.		transfer impossibility	
				if the event does occur?								
		Rating: 0 to 10										
			Yr.			Yr.		Yr.		Yr.		Yr.
		1	2	3	4	5	6	7	8	9	10	11
POLITICAL	War											
POLITICAL	Occupation by foreign power											
POLITICAL	Civil war, revolution											
POLITICAL	Riots, disorders											
POLITICAL	Take-over by extremist government											
POLICY	State take-over of enterprise											
POLICY	Indigenization, creeping indigenization											
	Natural calamities											
ECONOMIC	Depression or severe recession											
ECONOMIC	Mismanagement of the economy											
ECONOMIC	Credit squeeze											
ECONOMIC	Long run slowdown in G.N.P. growth											
ECONOMIC	Strikes											
ECONOMIC	Rapid rise in production costs											

EXHIBIT 7-5: (Continued)

	Events/situations that may lead to the materialization of a risk:	What is the likelihood of										
		event occurring?		any risk materializing	default		renegotiation		rescheduling, etc.		transfer impossibility	
				if the event does occur?								
		Rating: 0 to 10										
			Yr.			Yr.		Yr.		Yr.		Yr.
		1	2	3	4	5	6	7	8	9	10	11
B.O.P. & DEBT	Fall in export earnings											
	Sudden increase in food or energy imports											
	Overextension in external borrowing											
	Devaluation/depreciation of currency											
	Deterioration of the balance of payments*											
	Any other (specify):											

*for reasons not mentioned above.

Signature:

Name:

Source: P. J. Nagy, *Country Risk: How to Assess, Quantify, and Monitor It* (London: Euromoney Publications, 1979).

high tensions, and government is irresponsible or lacking in moderation. Risk of foreign occupation in such situations is increased when powerful, less moderate neighbors claim the right to intervene in the case of unacceptable takeovers or governmental acts.

The risk of internal riots or disorders is increased when deep-seated antagonism exists as a result of ethnic, tribal, religious, or ideological differences. When government is weak or unsuccessful in reducing tensions and the opposing factors are well organized, well armed, and/or have strong leaders, the risks become greater. The extent to which a given group might take control depends on the strength of government and the power of the extremist group.

The extent to which a government is likely to renegotiate its obligations to a foreign investor depends often on its wealth, its capacity for debt, its political leanings, and the political leverage available from outside the country. State takeovers of all foreign investments are most likely where governments and their support have socialist philosophies and believe that they can manage the operations. Economic nationalization, a slower process, is likely when the quality of the nationalist government is poor and inefficient.

Economic Risk Factors

Natural calamities are likely to cause economic losses in locations where monsoons, floods, typhoons, and earthquakes are severe and large-scale facilities exist. On the other hand, economic downturns are likely to hurt performance in overheated economies where labor markets are tight, prices and interest rates are accelerating, trade balances are deteriorating, raw material shortages exist, or capacity is unavailable. Indicators such as declining new orders, rising inventory levels, declining construction starts, and declining business confidence suggest increased risk of recession and slowdown.

The ability of governments to manage cyclical swings depends on their understanding of rational economic management and the availability of economic information. Lack of statistical reports, forecasting, and long-range objectives to improve the country indicate a lack of management and a higher risk of economic losses. Economic squeezes can also hurt performance when balance of payments, inflation, or overheating requires credit controls. Economic slowdowns, however, need not affect long-term risk assessments unless political or social factors cause a loss in confidence in the country's future.

Indicators of general confidence in a country's future include (1) growth of investments, (2) nature of investments in infrastructure, (3) availability of labor, and the (4) productivity of labor. Where unions are strong and militant the risk of long and frequent strikes increases. Wage costs are likely to rise rapidly in countries where rapid growth occurs, current wages are extremely low, or labor discontent is great. A fall in export earnings can seriously affect currency rates, inflation, and investments in infrastructure. Therefore, the nature and variety of exports and export markets can affect risk. The need for food and energy imports has the same effect on government spending. However, ultimate negative balance of payments and heavy debt financing levels can severely raise the long-term risks of a country. Heavy inflation and devaluation with weak government can lead to long-term economic disasters.

Monitoring Risk Assumptions

Since a country's risk status can rapidly change, it is necessary to keep track of the critical assumptions used in its assessment. Exhibit 7-6, for example, shows how basic assumptions for Mexico might have been evaluated in 1977 and 1978. Most of these assumptions have deteriorated in recent years. As long as the assumption proves valid, a zero is placed in the square. Should the assumption prove to be too positive, then a negative number is placed in the square. If the assumption is greatly surpassed, a positive number is used. As long as the range in assumption ratings stays within a specified range, say fifty points, then the current risk profile remains in use. If the spread goes over that range, then a revised analysis is probably indicated.

PREDICTING ENVIRONMENTAL CHANGES

As we move toward greater interdependencies and growing concern for the individual, we may find it more difficult to control our economic destiny. Poor economic performance will also lead to capital shortages and to further restrictions on investments in technology. Interaction between the social, political, technical, and economic environments of today's organizations will place greater pressure on strategists to monitor and forecast the organization's future business

EXHIBIT 7-6: Monitoring Sheet of Crucial Assumptions

Country: Mexico
Latest rating (date) . . . .

Date of latest study: April 1977
Previous rating (date) . . . .

Assumption / Date of evaluation	Nov. 1977	April 1978	June 1978				
1. Present system of government maintained	0	0	–10				
2. Quality of economic management to improve	0	0	0				
3. Conservative economic policies pursued	0	0	0				
4. Pragmatic approach to foreign direct investment	0	–5	–5				
5. Moderate growth of main foreign markets	+30	0	0				
6. Crude oil output to reach 1.8m b/d by 1982	+10	+20	+20				
7. Domestic oil demand increases 8% p.a. or less	0	0	0				
8. Moderation of inflation	+40	–20	–20				
9. Peso to regain stability	+5	0	–5				
10.							
11.							
12.							
Spread between highest + and – deviations	40	40	40				

Figures denote percentage deviations from postulated trends.

Remarks:

Economist

Source: P. J. Nagy. *Country Risk: How to Assess, Quantify, and Monitor It* (London: Euromoney Publications, 1979).

environment. It is important to understand that most federal legislation—that action which may affect us most directly—requires six to ten years to move from a social concern to legislative action. Ten years is likely to elapse before confrontation causes enough momentum and pressure to force government to take action. International issues require even greater time spans before action is taken unless a national crisis occurs.

Graham Molitor, in his 1977 article, suggests that public-policy issues can be anticipated and forecasted through proper tracking of issues. By understanding the development process for public policy, organizations should be able to

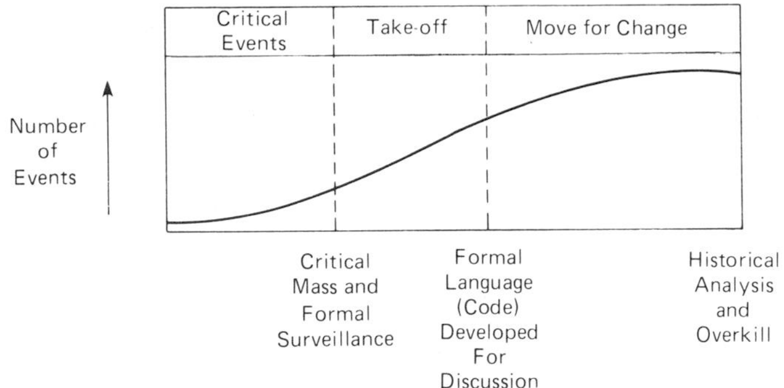

DIAGRAM 1: Leading Events Build to Take-off[1]

foresee public policy changes and accommodate them with minimal disruption. The Molitor model includes:

1. Tracking events over time that begin to attract leading authorities or advocates. Frequency of such events as thalidomide poisoning eventually reach a "critical" level at which time the "takeoff point" for political action is reached and becomes "virtually irreversible." Diagram 1 shows this sequence of events.

2. Leading authorities and advocates eventually recognize an event's significance and begin interpreting the implications of the event. Victims, though less capable of articulating the problem, are able to generate emotional support for the cause. Politicians are relatively late to join compared with other groups and institutions as shown in Diagram 2.

3. Written documentation and publication of the events and issues serve to fully explore the issues involved and, eventually, reach the mass media for public exposure and consumption. "Early warnings" about emerging problems can be obtained, therefore, from a careful review of the literature. Once scientific, technical, or professional publications confirm the details, public exposure and take-off are not far behind, as shown in Diagram 3.

4. Institutional support for action generally forces public-policy officials to consider the issue seriously. Such support generally begins at the local level, and moves to broader state and national coverages. Diagram 4 shows that once these organizations, people, and resources support the action, the "point of no return" has been reached and the implementation of change is not far behind.

[1] Moliton, Graham T., "How to Anticipate Public Policy Changes." S.A.M. *Advanced Management Journal* (Summer, 1977), pp. 4–13.

DIAGRAM 2: Leading Authorities and Advocates for Change

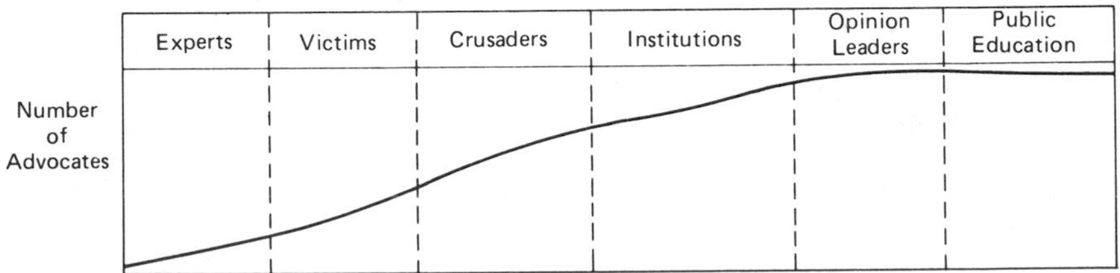

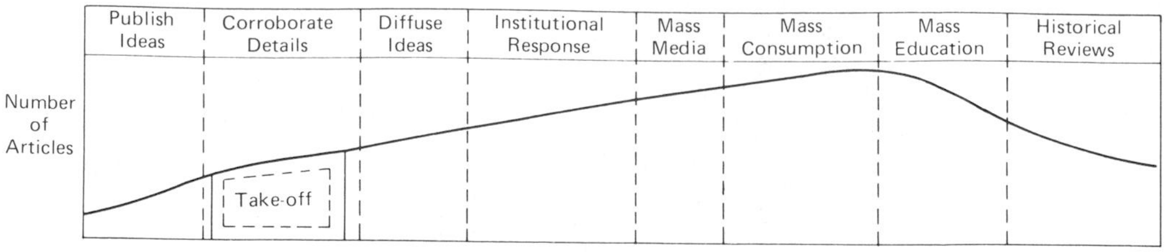

Publish Ideas | Corroborate Details | Diffuse Ideas | Institutional Response | Mass Media | Mass Consumption | Mass Education | Historical Reviews

Number of Articles

Take-off

DIAGRAM 3: Leading Literature Support for Change

5. Along with growth in institutional support over larger geographic areas comes increased concern by local, state, national, and international governments. Local legislation will be diffused to other domestic or international governments. Countries such as Sweden have become "early adopters" of social legislation. The United States has been rather slow to implement some two thousand consumer issues—some of which were implemented twenty years ago in Sweden, as suggested in Diagram 5.

Diagram 6 summarizes the effect that public issues can have on political actions. By overlaying the five dimensions of political action, the point at which a "critical mass" of support comes together can be identified as the "takeoff" point for action. From that point on, momentum can be expected to increase and create intense pressures for action. From this point onward, little chance remains to alter the direction of action. By tracking the social pressure for political action, organizations have ample lead time to either (a) attempt to impact the direction of change, (b) plan for alternatives, or (c) reallocate resources to deal with expected change.

The importance of tracking social issues should be apparent. Without recognizing the currents of change, managers are quite likely to be caught off guard—surprised at the implementation of new policies and unable to adapt effectively. This approach, therefore, simply outlines a methodology for environmental scanning in a complex, rapidly changing environment.

TRACKING ENVIRONMENTAL ISSUES

The growing interdependence and speed of economic changes will require greater adjustments and more efficient means of adjusting to change. Some of the changes that will impact economic decisions include (1) changing trade and investment

DIAGRAM 4: Organizational Support for Change

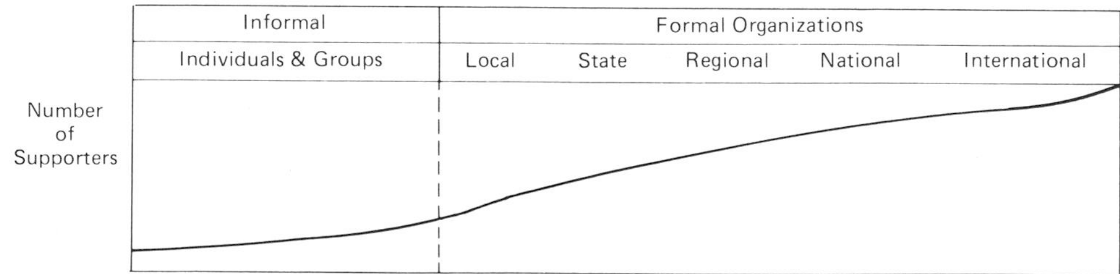

	Early Innovators	Early Adopters	Early Majority	Late Majority	Laggards
Number of Laws					
Domestic	Florida/ New York	Mass./ Ill./ Calif.			Deep South Rural Areas
International	Sweden/ Denmark	Germany	U.S./ Canada	Bulk of Countries	Less Dev. Countries

DIAGRAM 5: Political Leaders in Implementing Change

patterns, (2) changing economic importance of various regions and nations, (3) changing impacts of productivity and technology on employment and locations, and (4) changing government intervention into pricing and production decisions. Such changes will impose hardships on affected individuals, firms, industries, communities, and nations that cannot effectively adjust to the new conditions.

Adjustments and solutions to common world problems, such as inflation, recession, and energy and food shortages, will require improved coordination of national economic policies. International organizations such as the International Monetary Fund, the International Bank for Reconstruction and Development, the Organization for Economic Cooperation and Development, the General Agreement on Tariffs and Trade, and the United Nations will have to take more active roles in such cooperation.

Economic summit meetings, voluntary private-sector cooperation, regional cooperation and integration, and the like will also be required. For example, Mexico's role as a supplier of energy to the United States and U.S.-Canada energy cooperation will increase pressure for fewer trade and investment restrictions between the three countries. Regional economic integration would, how-

DIAGRAM 6: Forecasting Political Actions

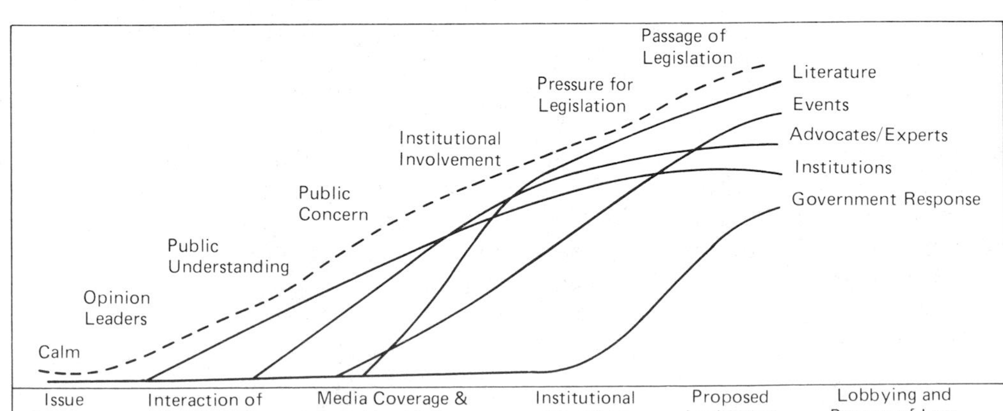

EXHIBIT 7-7: Identifying High Priority Environmental Issues

Impact on Business ←

Probability of Impact	(High)	(Medium)	(Low)
(High)	Critical	High Priority	Low Priority
(Medium)	High Priority	High Priority	Low Priority
(Low)	To Be Watched	Low Priority	Low Priority

ever, have implications for Mexican immigration and potential conflict about unemployment policies. Cooperation between common resource suppliers, such as OPEC members have had, may also increase as shortages develop for other commodities.

Given the variety of changes taking place in the general business environment, it will be difficult for management to set priorities and decide what strategies are required to cope with complex environmental problems. It will be necessary, therefore, for managers to develop a methodology for tracking environmental issues and determining priorities for action. One method for managers to prioritize those issues they will track in more specific detail is shown in Exhibit 7-7. For a given organization, environmental issues can be placed in one of the nine cells of the matrix. Those issues that will have a high impact on the business and have a probability of political action are "critical" to management and need formal attention and specific strategies developed to cope with imminent change. Those issues in the moderate impact cells need high-priority attention in order to possibly influence political outcomes. Low-priority issues still need watching in case they develop in combination with other issues which may change their importance.

For those issues that are identified as critical or high-priority, a more detailed tracking methodology is required. For example, Exhibit 7-8 shows a chart for summarizing the development of a specific environmental issue. This chart provides a way of tracking environmental changes and helping management assess the time horizons available for their action. As described in a previous section, "Predicting Environmental Changes," those forces important to the change process can be adequately tracked and recognized. Specific individuals, opinion leaders, media, communities, institutions, agencies, politicians, or nations in support of change can be identified according to the pressure they are generating for change and be identified within the appropriate cell. In this way, management will be able to know the degree and nature of support and be better equipped to predict its impact. Understanding the direction of change can better equip managers to respond in a realistic manner.

EXHIBIT 7-8: Analysis of Pressure for Political/Economic Change

Focus of Change (Issue) ______________________ Priority __________

Probable Nature of Change ______________________ When __________

Potential Impact on Business ______________________ Response Time __________

Forces for Change / Pressure for Change	Summary	Individuals	Opinion Leaders	Media	Public	Institutions	Agencies	Politicians	Nations
High									
Medium									
Low									

ENVIRONMENTAL ISSUES: A SUMMARY

As described earlier, a variety of problems will confront managers in the decades ahead. The solutions to these problems are in no way final, but a number of alternatives are being proposed. Several of these alternatives described later, are shown in Exhibit 7-9.

Industry Renewal

One area in which increasing support is developing for change can be summarized as the reindustrialization of America. The major elements of such a plan stress levels of consumption, investment, and research activities. For example, Amitai Etzioni, a former adviser in the Executive Office of President Carter, calls for a systematic program placing priority on four fronts: the development of

EXHIBIT 7-9: Environmental Change Movements

Movement	Organizational Impact
Reindustrialization	
– Retooling industry – Research and development	– Increased debt – Job retraining – Labor-management cooperation – Decreased dividends
Quality of Work Life	
– Individual needs – Work environment	– Equity in compensation – Health and safety – Social integration of work – Employee development
Labor-Management Relations	
– Participatory decision-making – Joint problem solving	– Board representation – Joint responsibility – Labor-management-government cooperation – Joint communication, education, and training

alternative sources of energy; an increase of plowback investment in capital goods; improvement of the national infrastructure of transportation systems; and a program of defense spending to build back military capacity for national security (*New York Times,* June 29, 1980). A second program presented by Felix Rohatyn, chairman of New York City's Municipal Assistance Corporation, emphasized industrial policy, arguing that the United States should select the key industries in which it holds distinctive competence, support them, and write off the others. That along with the development of alternative energy sources, a tax program favoring investment and productivity, and a balanced budget, Rohatyn argues, might save America from impending "national bankruptcy" (*Business Week,* March 10, 1980).

Each of these programs, in emphasizing the economic nature of the national problem, is calling for mass mobilization of the American people. Each program calls for prolonged belt tightening, drastic cuts in public and private spending, an informed public that trusts its leadership, a committed government, and a supportive industrial sector. Organizations, if they are to cooperate in the process of reindustrialization, will need to invest vast sums of capital in retooling. Debt/equity ratio will increase, thereby decreasing the market appeal of company stock. At the same time, to deal with the more sophisticated production technologies, universities and public educational systems will prove increasingly inadequate in supplying industry with skilled workers. Training programs will have to be designed for developing the job specific skills that organizations will require. To inhibit the inflation rate, organizations will have to play their part in keeping wage increments down, which implies the cooperation of labor unions in the process.

Quality of Working Life

A second major movement is under way to improve the quality of individual work life. This social movement is concerned with the degree to which organizational members are able to satisfy their personal needs through their experience in the organization. Conferences of managers, union leaders, government officials, and behavioral scientists are being held worldwide to understand and solve human problems in the workplace. The national Quality of Work Center, the Center for Quality of Working Life at UCLA, the Ohio Quality of Work Center, and the Work in America Institute are organizations committed to this movement. Some of the major issues being studied by such organizations include: (1) adequate and fair compensation; (2) safe and healthy work environments; (3) development of human capacities; (4) security; and (5) integration of the family, work, and leisure activities.

Labor-Management Relations

A third major movement relates to overcoming problems of collective bargaining. This movement is to redistribute power between the institutions of labor and management. Increased participation by labor in operating, management, and business decisions is likely. To this extent, mechanisms like suggestion boxes, work councils, quality circles, and board representation will be used to facilitate joint participation.

To determine U.S. energy and industrial policies for the future, the Economic Revitalization Board has attempted to bring labor, industry, and government representatives together. To allow such joint cooperation to work, conflicts between labor, management, and government need resolution and trust must be developed. Shared information, education, and training need to become common practices. A pretense of cooperation will not allow the kind of action necessary to resolve the complex problems of the future.

SUMMARY

As we consider the future of any organization, we need to understand the dynamics of the general environment in which that organization operates. As we move through the 1980s, it will be increasingly difficult to track the growing number of changes that can impact our likelihood of success or failure. In the area of business, all of the forces described in this chapter can be important to the future of the organization.

Political and legal factors already developing out of social concerns include growing ecological concerns, healthy and safety concerns, as well as concern over regulatory and administrative controls. Economic issues include growing concern over national economic policies, inflation rates, demographic changes, employment levels, and savings rates. Finally, technological forces are playing an increasing role in competition because of material shortages, need for new technological investments, productivity improvements, and investments to modernize old plants and facilities. We need not consider any one of these as most important, since they are all of growing concern to the competitive business environment.

FOCUS QUESTIONS

1. Identify how industry will be most affected by:
   a. Government regulation of interstate transportation, federal communications, and foods and drugs.
   b. Government and OPEC energy decisions.
   c. Government and consumer spending and inflation.
   d. Government and union impacts on productivity.
   e. Government impact on employment benefits and salary decisions.
   f. Government impact on marketing decisions.
   g. New electronic, computer, and communication technology.
2. Using Molitor's political forecasting chart, track the development of an issue that is currently receiving heavy media coverage. What industry will be most affected by this issue?
3. For each movement identified in Exhibit 7-9, identify an industry that is, or will be, heavily affected.

ADDITIONAL READINGS

Ackoff, Russell L. *Creating the Corporate Future.* New York: John Wiley & Sons, 1981.

Battelle Memorial Institute. *Interactions of Science and Technology in the Innovative Process.* National Science Foundation Contract 667, 1973.

Basil, Douglas C., and Curtis W. Cook. *The Management of Change.* London: McGraw-Hill Book Company, 1974.

Boelinger, Henry M. "Technology in the Manager's Future." *Harvard Business Review* (Nov.-Dec. 1970): 5.

The Business Roundtable. *Cost of Government Regulation.* Chicago: Arthur Andersen & Co., 1979.

Crawford, C. Merle. *The Future Environment for Marketing.* Ann Arbor, Mich.: University of Michigan Press, 1969.

Farmer, Richard N. "Management of Complex Organizations." *Academy of Management Proceedings* (1969): 4–13.

Gerstenfeld, Arthur. *Technological Innovation: Government/Industry Cooperation.* New York: John Wiley & Sons, 1979.

Molitor, Graham T. "How to Anticipate Public Policy Changes." *S.A.M. Advanced Management Journal* (Summer 1977): 4–13.

Murphy, A. D. "The New 'Mass' Audience Emerging." *Variety* (August 1973): 19.

Robock, S. H. "Political Risks: Identification and Assessment." *Columbus Journal of World Business* (July-August 1971): 6–20.

Rostow, Walter W. " 'The Stages of Growth' as a Key to Policy." *Fortune,* **60,** no. 6 (1959): 135–136, 201–209.

Sawyer, George C. "Social Issues and Social Change: Impact on Strategic Decisions." *MSU Business Topics* (Summer 1973): 17.

Thomas, Philip S. "Environmental Analysis for Corporate Planning." *Business Horizons* (October 1974): 36.

Toffler, Alvin. *Future Shock.* New York: Random House, 1970.

Wills, Gordon. et al.: *Technological Forecasting and Corporate Strategy.* New York: American Elsevier Publishing Co., Inc., 1969.

Wilson, Robert W. et al. *Innovation, Competition, and Government Policy in the Semiconductor Industry.* Lexington, Mass.: Lexington Books, 1980.

PART III

Managing the Organization

8 Aligning Organizational Strategy and Structure

As we consider the nature of organizational structure, we should keep in mind two fundamental concepts. The first is that the basic purpose of the organization is to create, make, and market products or services which will meet the needs of our customers. The second is that these overall activities must be managed or coordinated to achieve the purpose of the organization. In small, single business organizations, these two concepts can be incorporated into relatively simple structures with all responsibilities being carried out by the owner-manager or chief executive officer. It is only when the number of products and markets being served by the organization increases that more complex forms of structure must be used.

The key to successful business strategies is the flexibility and control provided to the manager over those resources and skills that are considered critical. The small organization that encompasses all those requisite resources has the ability to make rapid decisions and to adapt quickly to changes in competition, customer needs, or the environment. The more disbursed these resources become across the organization, the more difficult it becomes to obtain needed decisions or to adapt to external changes. As organizations grow in size and in business complexity, it becomes increasingly difficult to maintain their flexibility.

The Evolving Organization

As described in earlier chapters, the business strategy is composed of product-market offerings that are created, made, and/or marketed by the organization. Depending on the strategy, specific functional skills will be required; different businesses will rely more heavily on some functions than others. For example, Exhibit 8-1 lists nine specific functional areas and suggests businesses that rely most heavily on that function. Any organization in one of these businesses would, therefore, probably have someone with direct responsibility for this critical function. Depending on the level of integration required by the strategy of these organizations, responsibilities for other functions would also be assigned.

As shown in Exhibit 8-2, organizations with single businesses can generally be managed by one person. The use of the functional organization is efficient in carrying out the required tasks but may cause communication between functions to break down and constrain creativity and flexibility. As the business grows,

EXHIBIT 8-1: Dominant Business Functions

Function Area	*Business*
Raw material sourcing	Oil
Production facilities	Steel
Product design	Stereo equipment
Production technology	Semiconductors
Product range and variety	Components
Applications engineering	Microprocessors
Sales force	Automobile sales
Distribution network	Beer
Servicing	Elevators

the functional structure requires more and more staff functions to facilitate coordination between functions and to attempt to encourage communication between functions. At some point in time, it becomes better to re-form the organization into smaller units, called divisions.

THE MATSUSHITA EXAMPLE

The growth and development of organizations has been a problem for successful organizations for many years. Alfred D. Chandler's *Strategy and Structure* and Alfred Sloan's *My Years with General Motors* describe early attempts in American history to develop and manage complex organizational structures at DuPont, Sears, Exxon, and General Motors. However, this problem was not only an American problem. At about the same time, Konosuke Matsushita was encountering the same problems in Japan.

In 1918, at the age of twenty-three, Matsushita founded a company to produce electric light sockets. By 1922, he had fifty employees and began to produce long-life batteries for bicycles. After the great earthquake in Japan in 1923, the demand for electrical appliances grew rapidly. By 1928, Matsushita had built a second plant and had three hundred employees. In 1931, he began

EXHIBIT 8-2: Structural Alternatives

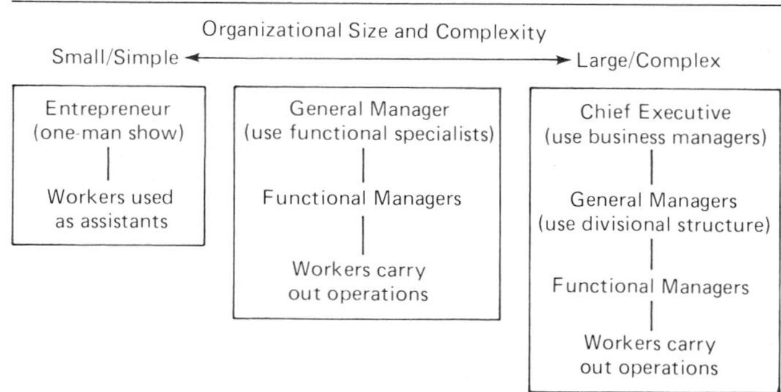

producing radios, and in 1935, he established the Matsushita Trading Company and later established plants in Korea and Taiwan. Until 1945, Matsushita's employees numbered forty thousand.

As Matsushita diversified his product line, it became impossible for him to control all of the functions or to make all of the different decisions necessary to carry on the daily activities of the company. After the company began to produce electric heaters in 1927 and radios in 1933, Matsushita began delegating responsibility to his two plant managers. After the company was reorganized into a public company in 1935, Matsushita established nine departments that were equal to independent companies. He established his headquarters in Osaka and operated it as a holding company.

The holding company system was considered to give efficiency to the organization rather than giving power to the head office. The department heads were given total responsibility for the success and operations of their businesses. During the years of World War II, total control was brought back to the headquarters. However, after the war, American occupation forces disorganized Matsushita's holding company and restricted him from doing business. During this time, the departments became independent subsidiaries.

In 1950, Matsushita was allowed to resume his business. Survival in the postwar era of inflation required greater control over the independent subsidiaries. However, the subsidiary managers were not willing to cooperate and new management concepts had to be developed.

As a result of this decentralized system, Matsushita centralized controls at the head office over four areas:

1. Headquarters had final decisions over product pricing decisions.
2. All hiring, training, and transfers of management or white-collar personnel was carried out by the head office.
3. All financial loans had to be obtained from the head office bank and required audits from head office accounting staff.
4. All company-related advertising that was not product-related had to be carried out by the head office.

The subsidiaries continued to act as independent companies in all other areas.

By the mid-1960s, Matsushita had fifty departments. In order to increase operating efficiency and to facilitate communications, the departments were grouped into divisions. The division heads were made directors of the company and had control over the departments or business units reporting to them. The departments were then transferred from one division to another as the company grew and changed. This added flexibility to the company as it continued to evolve and grow.

The departmental structure gave product-market responsibility and authority to the department manager. Each department manager could establish objectives and strategies without worrying about the other departments. This structure gave good experience to managers and also made it easy to detect and remove poor managers. However, this structure also increased management costs and overhead since the required management, research and development, manufacturing, and marketing functions are duplicated in each department. The merits of the system were considered to outweigh this cost.

Those areas of headquarters control had special significance to Matsushita's corporate strategy. Matsushita recognized the importance of gaining market share in order to increase production volume and reduce costs. Therefore, the headquarters had the final decision over product prices since competitive pricing was essential in making this strategy work. Matsushita further recognized the value of brand recognition and consumer brand loyalty. As a result, Matsushita established the *National* brand name in Japan and developed his own channel of independent *National* retail stores. The development and maintenance of the *National* image was therefore the responsibility of the head office.

Matsushita had tended to finance his own capital investments and therefore used the head office bank to fund its department's needs. Each department was provided necessary working capital and investment capital based on its budgeted sales and operating forecasts. Balance-sheet items such as accounts receivable and accounts payable were budgeted for thirty-day receipt and payment. Once the cash requirements were budgeted, it was up to the department manager to operate within the constraints of the budget. Managers were expected to know their sales and profit figures at all times. If his department's performance fell below budget, the manager had to go to the head office bank for additional cash, which required an immediate audit of operations. The bank then ensured that problems were found before they got too serious.

Matsushita's decentralized operations required that it develop and train good management personnel. Since the organization could operate only if it had able people placed in the right job, the personnel department played a key role. It was the personnel department's job to ensure that employees understood the philosophy of the organization and the value of their work in the organization. To stress this point, employees were encouraged to suggest improvements or new ideas for doing their jobs. This was one way in which the "management by everyone" philosophy was indoctrinated. Numerous self-development and training programs were made available. Finally, the development of managers was controlled by the personnel department as it transfered them from function to function across the various departments. The move into the general management position as department head was often made from the head office accounting function.

THE DANGERS OF POLITICS

Traditionally, the addition of new management levels such as departments, divisions or groups has been a solution to managing complex organizations. As layers of management and staff are added between the chief executive and the business or product-market level of the organization, the chief executive must rely more and more on other managers' judgments and motivations. These middle-level managers become increasingly important in interpreting the corporate level objectives and strategies into business-level objectives and strategies. They also become the primary source of support for business-level managers in their efforts to obtain necessary resources for their business needs.

Middle-level management plays a crucial role in coordinating business unit strategies and ensuring that they fit into the broad corporate objectives. The nature of these activities will be affected by the degree of control maintained at the corporate level. The motivation and level of risk that these managers take in carrying out their jobs depend on their own personal objectives and expected rewards. If failure of a business unit's strategy is likely to jeopardize a manager's future position or power, it is unlikely that he or she will support that strategy. As a result, what may be good for the organization may be perceived as being too risky for the middle manager. For this reason, special care must be made to limit the number of levels added to the organization and to allow strategic decisions to be reviewed at the corporate level.

THE USE OF COMMITTEES

When the size and complexity of the organization makes it difficult for corporate-level managers to keep track of business-level operations, it may be necessary to establish specialized committees to manage organizational strategy. For example, at Texas Instruments, three corporate-level committees were established in 1972 to oversee the development of business strategies, manage the investment in assets, and track ongoing operations. As Mark Shepherd explained to shareholders of Texas Instruments in 1972:

> Our management process concentrates on three kinds of questions: strategic plans, current operating decisions, and management of assets. At the corporate level, these are dealt with by three interlocking committees (Exhibit 8-3). The four group managers and I are members of all three, along with other members appropriate for each particular committee. These committees involve our senior line managers in running the corporation, as well as their own business units. It takes a lot of their time, but it does generate better decisions along with better understanding and commitment to corporate goals and decisions.

Factors affecting top management's need for such coordinating mechanisms are shown in Exhibit 8-4. As an organization increases the number of its functional operations, it will be more likely that some committee structure will become necessary to coordinate its activities. It is also likely that some committee structure will be needed as communication requirements increase for complex

EXHIBIT 8-3: Texas Instruments' Committee Structure (1972)

O.S.T. COMMITTEE | MANAGEMENT COMMITTEE | ASSET COMMITTEE

President
Group Vice Presidents
VP Corporate Development

VP Corporate Research
Key R&D Managers
Key Marketing Managers

SR. VP Finance & Legal
VP Controller
SR. VP Resources & Services
VP Personnel & Management Services

Treasurer

EXHIBIT 8-4: Factors Affecting Organizational Integration

Confounding Factors	Ease of Coordination: Easy	Hard
1. Degree of functional specialization	Little	Great
2. Number of units that require coordination	Few	Many
3. Direction of communication	Uni-directional	Reciprocal & multi-directional
4. Required frequency of communication	Seldom	Daily
5. Strategic importance of communication	Low	High
6. Complexity and uncertainty of information	Simple and certain	Complex and uncertain

Source: Adapted from Jay W. Lorsch, "Organizational Design: A Situational Perspective," *Organizational Dynamics*, Autumn 1977, pp. 2–14.

information. The shortage of critical resources, such as money, will also lead to greater coordination of planning and control activities at the corporate level.

As organizations continue to grow in size and complexity, some form of specialized committee (often referred to as meetings) becomes established to meet management's coordination and communication needs. These committees will be given the primary responsibility for collecting and disseminating specific information and making related policies and decisions. Such committees may be developed in six areas.

Legal Requirements. Given the nature and complexity of legal matters, large corporations generally find it necessary to have a legal staff that is capable of handling the diversity of regulations and increasing litigation which comes with increased size. Heavy reliance is placed on legal counsel to ensure that the corporation is fulfilling its legal obligations.

Financial Requirements. The problems of processing investment proposals and tracking actual results generally involves both the chief financial officer and controller. These managers become key in developing appropriate reports and procedures that communicate the health of the corporation. Review of investment proposals may also be carried out by committees that review the ongoing requirements for new equipment and facilities. Because of the different types of expertise required, separate committees may be set up for equipment and facilities reviews. Once these investment decisions are undertaken, the controller becomes key in accurately tracking performance during implementation.

Objectives and Policies. Responsibility for setting and revising overall objectives and policies in large organizations rests with the top executive organization, generally labeled the operating committee. Major questions of policy and goal setting will be resolved by the operating committee. In one large, multinational corporation, this committee's role was described as follows:

> The operating committee's objectives are to discuss and help shape the operating policies and practices. . . ; to determine annual and long-range planning goals; to

consider [short-term] plan changes; wage and salary actions; and to consider integration of [growth and productivity] efforts into operating decisions.

Strategic and Business Matters. Whereas the reviews of strategic programs (required to achieve specific business objectives) frequently may be carried out during strategic planning review meetings, in large organizations it is necessary that divisional strategies be continuously reviewed to ensure that they are consistent with overall corporate objectives and strategies. A corporate-level, strategic guidance committee, such as Texas Instruments' OST Committee, (generally labeled the corporate development committee) can include key staff, business, and area executives who broadly represent the corporation's organization. One such committee's charter read:

> The corporate development committee has as its objectives to consider the intermediate and long-term direction. . . , in terms of billings growth and product/service directions and emphasis; to set goals and allocate . . . resources (particularly in new areas of business); review and approve resource allocation within (business) objectives; to initiate new ventures; and appraise overall technical effort within the company.

Personnel and Organizational Matters. With the need for increased coordination and focus on long-range objectives and strategies, large organizations must provide equivalent attention to the development of managerial talent capable of successfully carrying out such programs. This requires increased emphasis on corporate-wide programs to develop and motivate employees and managers to carry out required programs, as well as improving overall organizational performance and productivity. A committee, such as a human resources and productivity committee, whose function is to review the development and motivation of the overall organization can ensure that all areas of the organization are consistent in applying salary administration, MBO programs, management development programs, and productivity improvement programs, such as work simplification programs. The charter of one such committee stated:

> [This] committee has as its objectives to achieve the financial and productivity goals of the company; to improve . . . ability to solve customer's problems through increased productivity of our people and our assets; to encourage participation of [employees] to the greatest extent practical in the planning and control of their work; and to maintain an environment of compatible employee and company goals.

External and Environmental Matters. The increasing turbulence of today's economic, social, and political environments is placing additional pressures on the corporation to improve its responsiveness to its environment, i.e., the community in which it operates: consumers, employees, shareholders, and so on. A committee, such as a community and corporate relations committee, can be used to review corporate activities and to ensure the appropriateness of corporate actions and response to community needs and to the various environmental changes.

Corporate-level structures must allow planning and control functions to be carried out effectively. As organizations evolve in size and complexity, top management, through its participation on various committees, can keep in touch with a broad representation of organizational executives who have direct operating responsibilities. This provides a wider representation in the development

EXHIBIT 8-5: Executive Information and Its Committee Organizational Structure

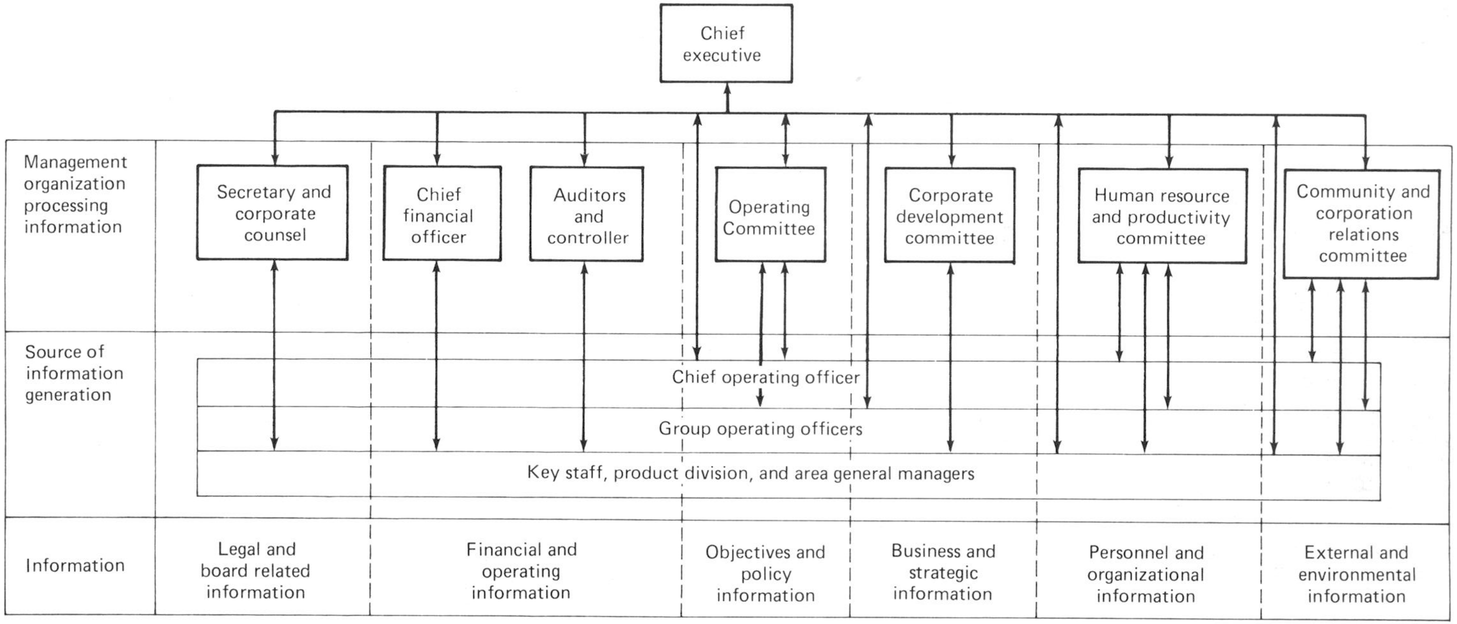

Chief executive

Management organization processing information	Secretary and corporate counsel	Chief financial officer	Auditors and controller	Operating Committee	Corporate development committee	Human resource and productivity committee	Community and corporation relations committee
Source of information generation	Chief operating officer						
	Group operating officers						
	Key staff, product division, and area general managers						
Information	Legal and board related information	Financial and operating information		Objectives and policy information	Business and strategic information	Personnel and organizational information	External and environmental information

Source: William R. Boulton, "The Changing Requirements for Managing Corporate Information Systems," *MSU Business Topics*, Summer 1978, p. 9. Reprinted by permission.

of overall corporate plans and policies and, hopefully, a greater likelihood of acceptance by the organization. The use of committees also allows a role for staff members of providing expertise and guidance to the committees while increasing middle managers' involvement in establishing and implementing corporate plans and policies. An example of an ideal corporate level structure is described in Exhibit 8-5.

It should also be apparent that processing executive information through this committee structure can cause the executive organization to continuously review the accomplishment of the critical management functions. As a result of this availability of management information, the corporation's board of directors is also able to monitor the accomplishments of the top management organization in carrying out its functions of ensuring that the long-term growth and viability of the institution will be maintained.

THE BOARD OF DIRECTORS' ROLE

It is difficult to discuss the structure of large organizations today without including a discussion of the role of the board of directors. The continued enforcement of the Federal Securities Laws is causing boards of directors to be more active in monitoring the activities of the top management organization. The board's primary role is to ensure that the "strategic management" of the organization is adequate to meet its long- and short-term needs. To the extent that the organization has appropriately established its objectives and strategies and developed a structure to facilitate their accomplishment, then strategic management exists.

Since organizational success is of major concern to today's organizations, the board of directors has become structured in a manner that allows them to more effectively monitor the organization's management efforts. Monitoring planning and control is fundamental to the achievement of organizational objectives and strategies. This monitoring function is being carried out through the development of board committees that parallel the management structure of the executive organization, including the monitoring of the following.

1. *Legal matters:* A board organization committee would review the legal liabilities and responsibilities of the corporation and ensure the adequacy of the board's organization, information, and director composition.
2. *Financial statements and reports:* An audit committee would be responsible for reviewing the accuracy of financial and operating information, and for ensuring that controls and auditing procedures are appropriate.
3. *Objectives and policies:* An executive committee would review corporate objectives and policies as well as critical decisions that relate to them.
4. *Strategies and businesses:* A strategy review committee would review the nature and adequacy of business strategies to accomplish corporate objectives and policies.
5. *Personnel and organizational information:* A compensation and human resources committee would review the adequacy of organizational development, productivity, and motivation systems within the organization.

EXHIBIT 8-6: Board Structure: Monitoring the Executive Information Flows

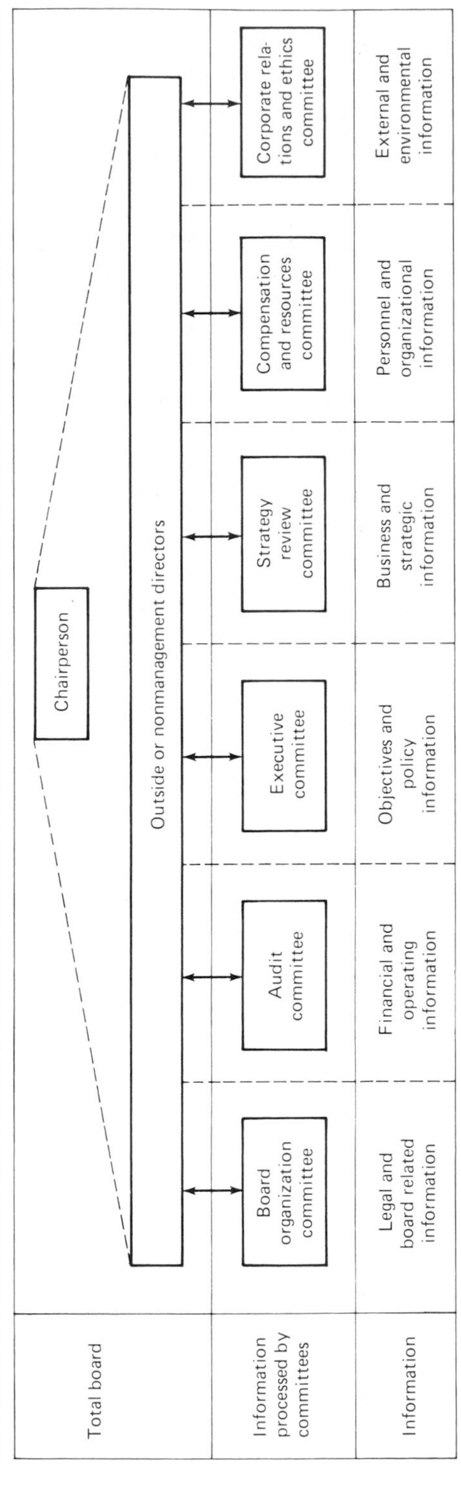

Source: Op. cit., p. 10.

6. *External and environmental matters:* A corporate relations and ethics committee would review the character and impact of corporate actions on its committees and environment.

Exhibit 8-6 shows the basic structure of a board organization designed to monitor corporate management's performance.

These board committees improve board-management communications by allowing the board to review in greater detail and to develop a better understanding of the organization's operations. It should be emphasized that these committees *do not* replace the board in its responsibilities for making decisions and showing due diligence in its actions, but simply allow it to effectively monitor organizational operations and management.

SUMMARIZING STRUCTURAL CONCEPTS

As organizations grow in size and complexity, top management must be more explicit in defining organizational purpose, objectives, and policies, and in ensuring that organizational strategies and structure are consistent with the needs of achieving those objectives. Monitoring organizational performance, therefore, is of primary concern and requires increased information-processing capabilities.

Refining or processing additional information requires a variety of specialized staff and/or committee operations that can review greater amounts and detail than can single individuals. This same information that is generated and processed by the corporate organization can then be monitored and utilized by the firm's board of directors through its own committee structure. This system of managing the flow of information not only allows the executive organization to manage the overall growth and development of the organization but also allows its board of directors to monitor the information and utilize it in reviewing overall executive performance and in providing long-range direction to the firm.

A major problem in this structure comes in coordinating the flow of management information through the various committees or staff positions. Agendas become the critical mechanism for both executives and directors to ensure that discussion priorities are established for meetings—be they reviews by the management organization, board organization, or joint committee reviews.

By incorporating the "committee" structure at the management and director levels, the flow of information across all levels of organization can be integrated. In coordinating the flow of information, the chairman of the board and the chief executive have the crucial roles of identifying critical, high-priority items for review. More importantly, specialization of committee functions at both the executive and board levels allows for efficient communications to be maintained between these levels (Exhibit 8-7). Executive and director expertise can also be effectively utilized on these specialized committees, and areas can be identified where needed expertise is lacking. Staying informed will require much more explicit information systems and more effective use of such committees that were described for tracking corporate performance and development in the future.

EXHIBIT 8-7: Processing Executive and Director Information Flows: A Tentative Model

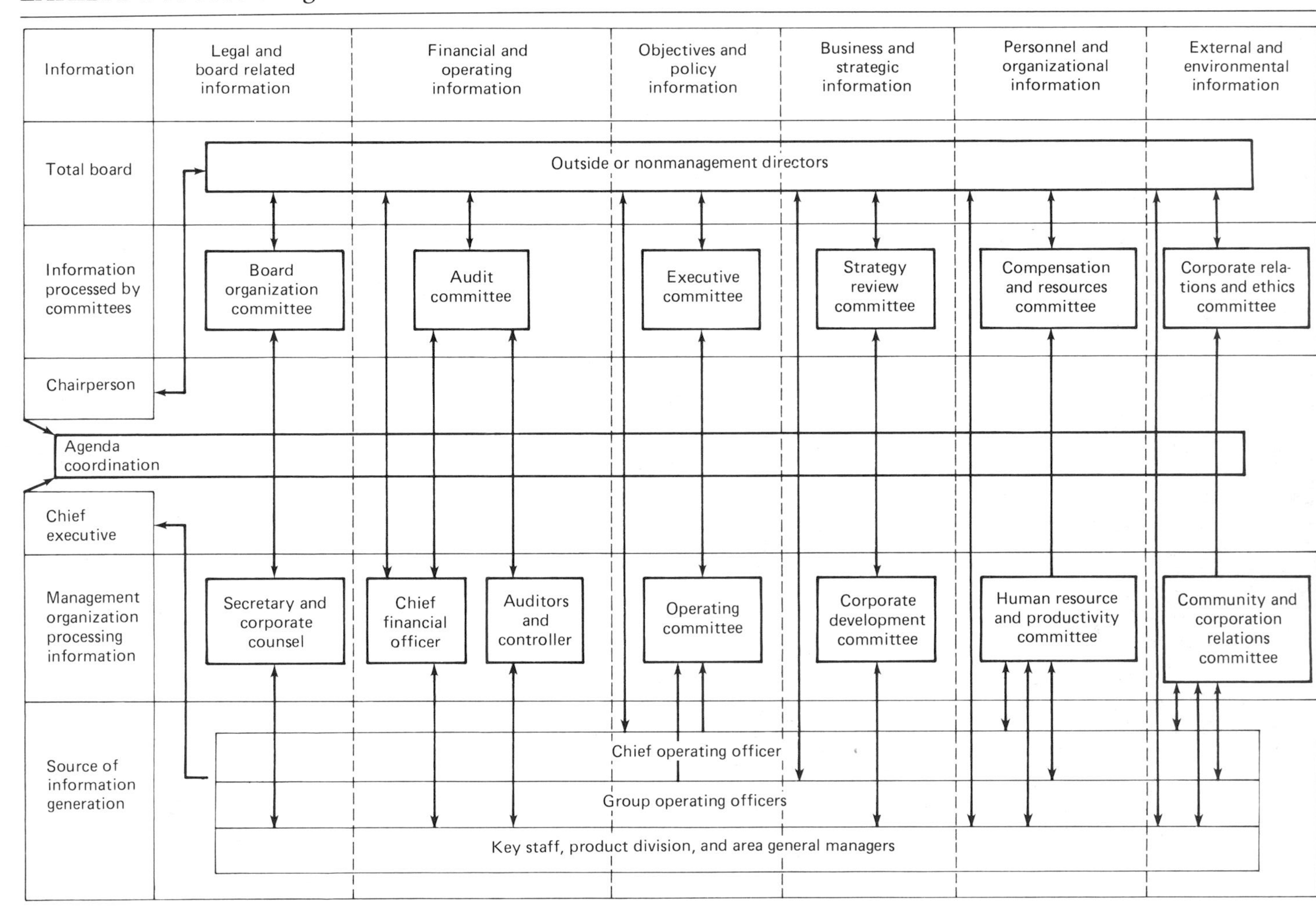

Source: Op. cit., p. 11.

FOCUS QUESTIONS

1. How does Matsushita separate the management of its businesses from the management of its organization?
2. If you were going to predict the evolution of an organization's structure, how would you expect it to evolve? Why?
3. With increased size and growth, what problems would you expect an organization to develop? How would you overcome those problems?
4. If you were asked to become the director of a large company, what would you want to know before you accepted?

ADDITIONAL READINGS

CHANDLER, A. D. *Strategy and Structure.* Cambridge, Mass.: M.I.T. Press, 1962.

GALBRAITH, JAY R. "Matrix Organization Designs." *Business Horizons* (Feb. 1971).

LAWRENCE, PAUL, and J. LORSCH. *Organization and Environment.* Boston: Harvard Business School Division of Research, 1967.

LIKERT, R. *The Human Organization.* New York: McGraw-Hill Book Company, 1967.

LORSCH, JAY W. "Organizational Design: A Situational Perspective." *Organizational Dynamics* (Autumn 1977): 2–14.

——— and P. R. LAWRENCE, eds. *Studies in Organizational Design.* Homewood, Ill.: Richard D. Irwin, 1970.

PETERS, THOMAS J. "Beyond the Matrix Organization." *Business Horizons* (October 1979).

9 Developing Planning and Control Systems

Strategic management requires continuous reviews of the organization's objectives, strategies, operations, and performance. As shown in Exhibit 9-1, both strategic and operational planning are important systems in strategic management. It is the strategic planning system that attempts to find a realistic balance between objectives and the strategic options available to the organization. Operational planning is the process by which these objectives become translated into specific actions to achieve those objectives.

Strategic planning includes the review of market conditions, customer needs, competitive strengths and weaknesses, and sociopolitical and economic conditions that lead to the identification of specific threats or opportunities facing the organization. This review should lead to the recognition of those strategic issues that need attention, such as shifts in technology, evolutions in market life cycles, changes in consumer needs, new competition, or new requirements for resources or skills. The development of strategic options should relate directly to overcoming or taking advantage of these strategic problems and opportunities. Upon completion of this process, decisions must be converted into the operational plans for implementation.

Although we have a fair understanding of the strategic planning process, tying this process to the organization's operating systems is a significant challenge and requires special attention. One of the prime difficulties is in translating strategic plans into the operating plans of the organization. It is only through the careful incorporation of strategic goals into operating decisions that this can be achieved. For example, Exhibit 9-2 identifies some of the key resource and budgeting elements that reflect the business goals. By ensuring that the resource and budget planning process reflects the business objectives in well-specified operating goals, strategic plans can be effectively integrated into current operations.

Strategic management requires the explicit integration of long-and short-range objectives. In Exhibit 9-3, we have identified some of the key planning elements by level of organization. It begins with setting objectives at both the corporate and business levels. Once objectives are decided, specific business and functional objectives must also be finalized and approved. The actual level of commitment and resources provided to support a strategic program should be determined through the resource and budget-planning process. Limited resources will require that priorities be set as to which programs are undertaken first. Final

EXHIBIT 9-1: Strategic Planning Process

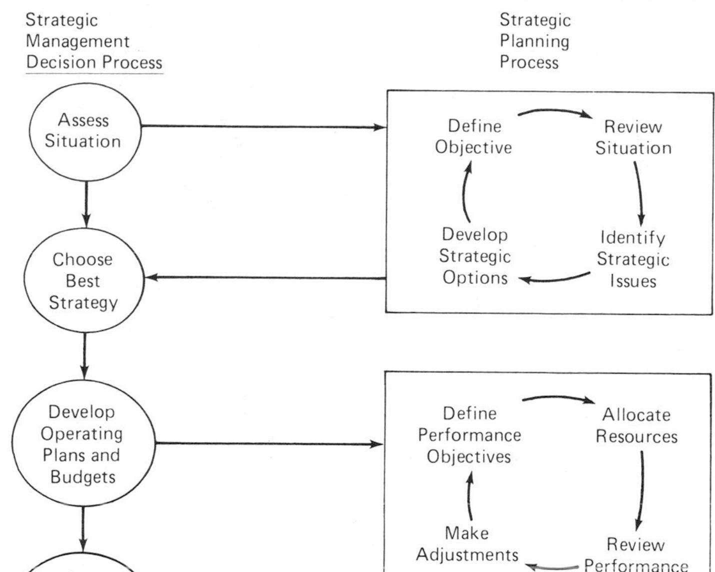

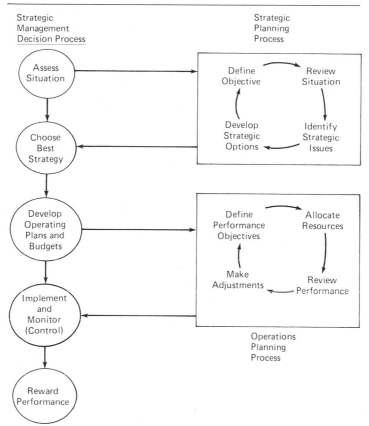

implementation and operational activities are then monitored and controlled through the establishment and review of specific operating goals. Rewarding good performance, or making changes in operations when performance is poor, is required if individual or group goals are to be linked to organizational objectives. To develop a unity of purpose across the organization, the strategic planning process and the operational planning system must be tied to corporate objectives. Strategic plans and operational plans must be consistent in integrating objectives and goals at functional, business, and corporate levels.

Whereas the corporate structure provides the skeleton of the organization, it is the planning and control system that provides its muscle. Priorities, communication, and resources are affected by these systems. At Matsushita, for example, department managers provide three plans every six months. The first is a five-year plan, which incorporates technological and environmental changes. The second is a two-year plan, which translates strategies into new products and new plant capacity. These plans are reviewed by the division of group managers.

The third and most important plan for department managers is the six-month operating plan, which includes monthly projections for production, sales, profits, inventories, accounts receivables, personnel requirements, quality control

EXHIBIT 9-2: Linking Strategic Objectives to Performance Goals

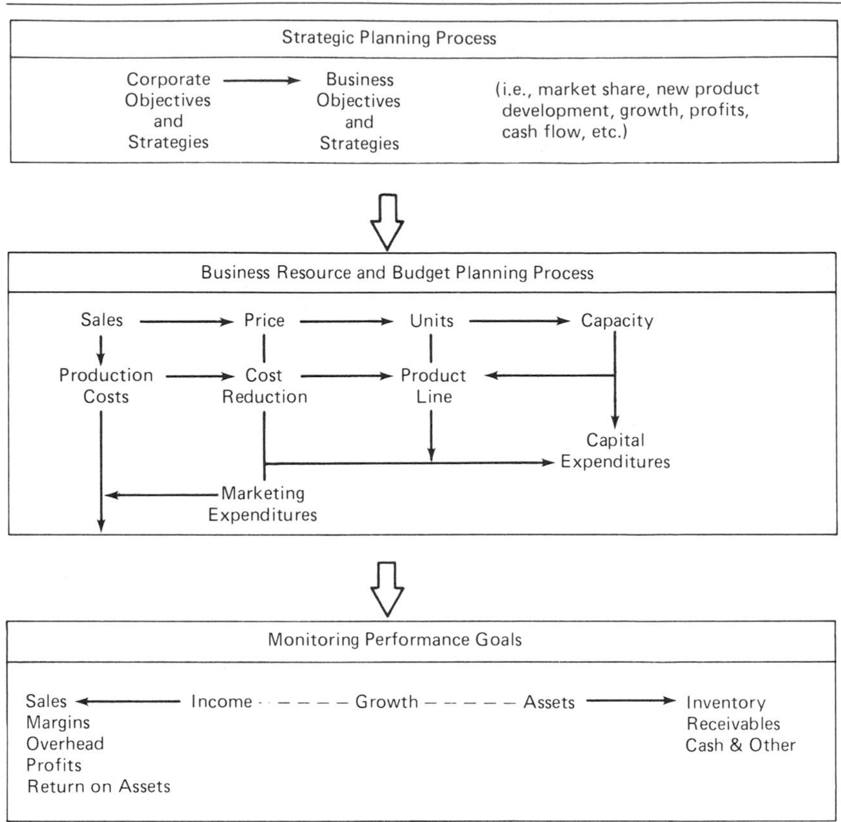

targets, and capital investments.[1] Once this plan is established, detailed accounting systems identify any variances monthly. Performance is then judged and rewards distributed based on results to plans. Each department is also allowed to keep 40 per cent of its before-tax profits for reinvestment and business development. These funds, however, stay in the head office bank until appropriate plans are approved.

Monthly and quarterly reviews provide the essence of Matsushita's controls. The chief financial officer reviews variance reports monthly. Department managers then go to the head office to review the results in detail before presenting them to corporate management. Primary attention is paid to operating variances and how well Matsushita's managers perform against competition. Department performance is ranked into groups A, B, C, and D. The D group (i.e., the poorest performers) makes its presentations last. As a result, there is strong peer motivation not to stay in the lower performance group.

[1]See Richard T. Pascale and Anthony G. Athos, *The Art of Japanese Management* (New York: Warner Books, 1981), p. 51.

EXHIBIT 9-3: Operationalizing Strategic Management

(⟶) Sequence of Communication And Planning

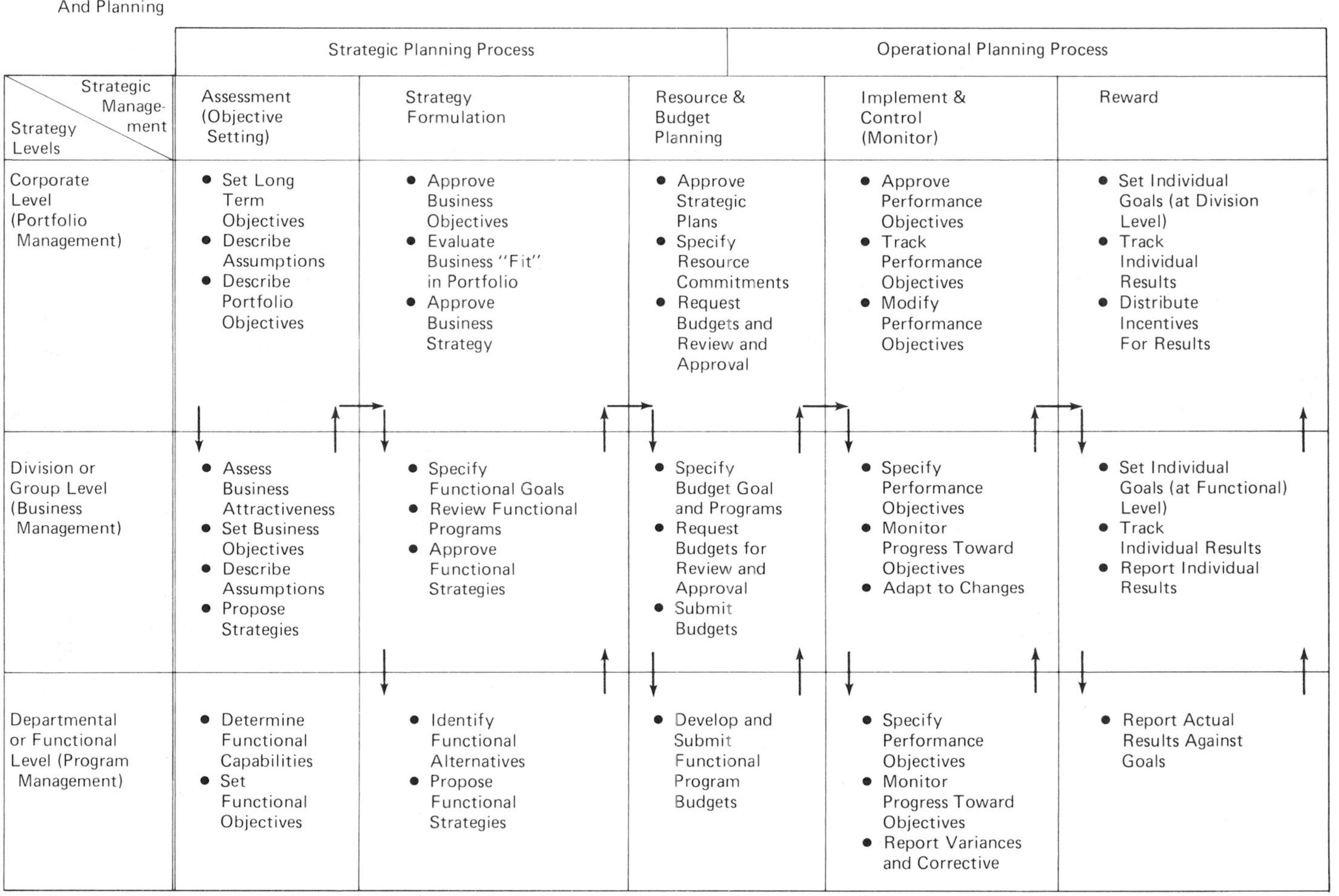

	Strategic Planning Process		Operational Planning Process		
Strategic Management / Strategy Levels	Assessment (Objective Setting)	Strategy Formulation	Resource & Budget Planning	Implement & Control (Monitor)	Reward
Corporate Level (Portfolio Management)	• Set Long Term Objectives • Describe Assumptions • Describe Portfolio Objectives	• Approve Business Objectives • Evaluate Business "Fit" in Portfolio • Approve Business Strategy	• Approve Strategic Plans • Specify Resource Commitments • Request Budgets and Review and Approval	• Approve Performance Objectives • Track Performance Objectives • Modify Performance Objectives	• Set Individual Goals (at Division Level) • Track Individual Results • Distribute Incentives For Results
Division or Group Level (Business Management)	• Assess Business Attractiveness • Set Business Objectives • Describe Assumptions • Propose Strategies	• Specify Functional Goals • Review Functional Programs • Approve Functional Strategies	• Specify Budget Goal and Programs • Request Budgets for Review and Approval • Submit Budgets	• Specify Performance Objectives • Monitor Progress Toward Objectives • Adapt to Changes	• Set Individual Goals (at Functional) Level) • Track Individual Results • Report Individual Results
Departmental or Functional Level (Program Management)	• Determine Functional Capabilities • Set Functional Objectives	• Identify Functional Alternatives • Propose Functional Strategies	• Develop and Submit Functional Program Budgets	• Specify Performance Objectives • Monitor Progress Toward Objectives • Report Variances and Corrective	• Report Actual Results Against Goals

Source: Adapted from Peter Lorange, *Corporate Planning: An Executive Viewpoint* (Englewood Cliffs, N.J.: Prentice-Hall, Inc., 1980), pp. 55–60.

INTEGRATING PLANNING AND CONTROL SYSTEMS

Whereas previous chapters focused on the content of strategies, there was no attempt made to show the complexity of integrating overall strategic management processes. Such integration requires that attention be paid to (1) the process of planning and control, (2) the planning horizon of each phase of planning and control systems, and (3) the strategic level of the organization being considered. These three components of planning and control systems are incorporated into the schedule shown in Exhibit 9-4.

Exhibit 9-4 indicates that the strategic assessment and objective setting function has the longest planning horizon (five to ten years into the future) and is generally concentrated at the upper levels of the organization. The strategy formulation process has an intermediate planning focus (two to five years) and is generally reviewed annually at the corporate, business, and functional levels (often using semiannual reviews at the business level). The third phase of resource and operational planning has a shorter planning focus (six months to two years), but it may be updated quarterly at the business level, and reviewed semiannually at the corporate level. This resource-planning function is especially important since it is this process that provides greatest control through its quarterly funding authorizations.

The ongoing operating phase provides control through frequent, often monthly, reviews at both the business and corporate levels. It is this review

EXHIBIT 9-4: Integrating the Strategic Management Systems

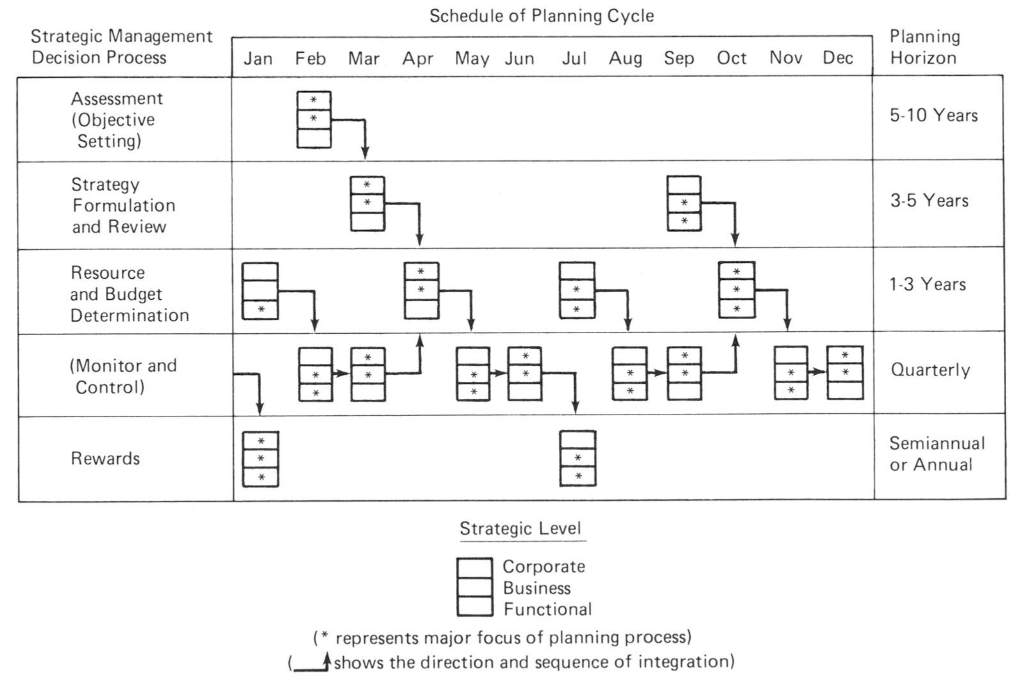

Strategic Management Decision Process	Schedule of Planning Cycle												Planning Horizon
	Jan	Feb	Mar	Apr	May	Jun	Jul	Aug	Sep	Oct	Nov	Dec	
Assessment (Objective Setting)													5-10 Years
Strategy Formulation and Review													3-5 Years
Resource and Budget Determination													1-3 Years
(Monitor and Control)													Quarterly
Rewards													Semiannual or Annual

Strategic Level

Corporate
Business
Functional

(* represents major focus of planning process)

(shows the direction and sequence of integration)

function of the process that keeps track of actual goal accomplishment and provides the early warning system of impending problems. This phase of the management process puts the greatest pressure on the business level of management because of ongoing reviews with functional and corporate level managers. As a result, the business level manager also carries the greatest burden in the integration process.

The final reward phase is geared to the time horizons of the strategic levels of the organization. Rewards can be made more short term for lower levels, but are generally more long range (e.g., stock options) for high levels. In fact, whereas rewards may be given annually, incentives such as stock options can be structured to payoff if organizational goals are achieved in future time periods. It is critical that management decisions be tied to future results as well as to current performance. If this is not done, trade-offs will frequently give preference to short-term results.

Exhibit 9-4 also shows the direction and sequence of information and communication through the integration process. For example, the process leads off with the annual assessment and objective-setting meetings that set the stage for more detailed planning. The strategy formulation and review meetings require more focused attention on business units and lead to actual budget determinations and major resource commitments during sequential meetings. The quarterly reviews are a bottom-up communication device that provides inputs into the budget and resource-determination process.

STRATEGIC MANAGEMENT RESPONSIBILITIES

The responsibilities for strategic management can be delegated to various members of the management team. Smaller organizations would not have the staff available to establish elaborate organizational structures and systems to monitor the management functions. However, as size and complexity increase, additional executives and staff will be required to carry out these responsibilities.

As shown in Exhibit 9-5, the strategic and operational planning systems are frequently assigned to corporate planning and chief financial officers, respectively. Designing and maintaining systems that meet the organization's planning needs requires that operations and control functions be designated to specific individuals or committees. Since there is no single system that meets the needs of all organizations, these functions require special attention and architecture to fit the unique characteristics of the organization.

Corporate level and business level executives have primary responsibility for the actual decisions made within the planning and operating systems frameworks. Tracking and integrating all of the information entering these systems also requires more sophisticated corporate information and management reporting systems. In fact, computer-based corporate information systems are rapidly becoming essential for today's planning and control systems. Such information systems require that strategic and operating plans be appropriately quantified so that reporting, tracking, and controlling results can be easily carried out on the computer.

EXHIBIT 9-5: Strategic Management Responsibilities

Responsibility of / Strategic Management Decision Process	Senior Executives & Directors (Responsibilities for Corporate Results)	Operating Executives (Responsibilities For Operating Results)	Corporate Planning Officer (Strategic Planning System)	Chief Financial Officer (Operating Planning System)	Integrative Mechanism
Assessment & Objective Setting	Define	Provide Inputs	Provide Inputs	Provide Inputs	Board Meetings and Committee Discussions
Strategic Plans	Review & Approve	Define	Design & Maintain System	Provide Inputs	Executive Meetings and Committee Discussions
Resource and Budget Determination	Set Goals & Standards	Review & Approve	Design & Maintain System	Design & Maintain System	Budgeting Meetings and Committee Discussions
Implementation (Monitor and Control)	Review	Set Goals & Standards		Design & Maintain System	Review Meetings and Committee Discussions
Reward	Set Goals & Standards; Review and Approve	Review & Approve			Board and Executive Reviews and Committee Discussions

The Texas Instruments Example

Becoming a growth company was a deliberate decision at Texas Instruments. As early as 1949, Texas Instruments' management began setting goals for the company. Retired chairman Patrick Haggerty explained in 1976:

> In 1949, when we had reached a sales billed level of about $5 million, we set the objective of becoming a good, big company, which we defined then as one with $200 million per year in billings and not less than $10 million in earnings. We went well past the earnings goal in 1959 and surpassed the billings goal with $233 million in 1960.
>
> By then, we had a new goal of $1 billion a year in billings and net earnings on that volume of at least $55 million, with a target set for 1973. Sales billed in 1973 were nearly $1.3 billion with earnings of more than $83 million.
>
> We were more than halfway to our $1 billion goal in 1966 and announced our new goal of $3 billion with the late 1970's as its target period. In March 1974, when about halfway to the $3 billion level, we set another goal of $10 billion in sales billed for the late 1980's.[8]

To achieve its $10 billion goal, several guidelines were set forth in 1976 by chairman Mark Shepherd at the annual shareholders meeting:

> We will model T.I.'s businesses to self-fund growth. If successful in realizing model performance, we will reach the goal without significantly diluting equity or increasing the debt-to-equity ratio beyond our traditional conservative index. We are now well below that index and have reserve financial capacity for periods of above-average growth in the future;

[2]Patrick Haggerty, "Three Lectures at the Salzburg Seminar on Multinational Enterprise" (Dallas: Texas Instruments, 1977), p. 9.

> We intend to rely primarily on internal growth rather than on major acquisitions;
>
> We will concentrate our resources for major market share positions;
>
> We will emphasize expansion of served markets into contiguous new segments, taking advantage of shared experience;
>
> We will rely primarily on opportunities related to electronics, particularly those in which our semiconductor skills can be decisive.

The importance of electronics to Texas Instruments' goal was further emphasized by Shepherd:

> Electronics—and particularly semiconductor technology—has been the driving force for T.I.'s growth. In 1975, the combined volume of the five business objectives devoted to electronics was 70 percent of T.I.'s total. Adding the electronic segments from the other four business objectives—industrial controls, connectors, computer processing of seismic data, and distribution of electronics products—84 percent of T.I.'s total business is electronics based.
>
> By the late 1980s the electronics-based portion is expected to increase to about 93 percent of T.I.'s total. The objectives totally devoted to electronics will grow faster. And the electronics-based portion of the other objectives will increase as electronics replaces electromechanical functions.

Texas Instruments' corporate strategy was to emphasize those products and services for which the company could maximize its value added. This emphasis was to utilize Texas Instruments' materials, components, equipment, and services capabilities to maximize its value added in developing products and services. Managing these efforts was considered critical if the company's corporate goals were to be achieved.

Texas Instruments' OST system for managing objectives, strategies, and tactics had become a fundamental element of its organizational strategy. It is a system for stating in writing the business strategies to be followed for further growth and development of the company and the tactics or functional strategies intended to implement those business strategies. The OST system is a system for management. It establishes a hierarchy of quantitative goals, measures performance against those goals, and separates discretionary from operational resources. Mr. Haggerty described the characteristics of the OST system in 1976:

> The fundamentals of the OST system are simply "institutionalized common sense." OST begins with a hierarchy of quantitative goals. It requires that a single statement of quantitative goals be made at the top of the organization and that these goals be translated into objectives for the individual business's strategies that support each of these objectives, and tactics that support each of the strategies. It is essential to this system that performance be measured against agreed-upon quantitative goals.
>
> Perhaps the most important feature of OST is that it clearly separates strategic from operational activities. This healthy dichotomy structures our thinking, organizations, resource allocation techniques, and reporting of results.
>
> Finally, it is essential that OST funds belong to the entire organization, and not to the divisions or departments that generate them. This gives us the flexibility to pursue new markets and new technologies within the larger scope of the entire organization's interests.
>
> First of all, we have a "corporate objective," a document that sets forth the overall goals of the corporation. Supporting the corporate objective, we presently

have 11 "business objectives." A business objective is a document that establishes a strategic organization of people under a business objective manager.

An actual example of a business objective manager will illustrate how OST managers wear two hats. For many years we had a vice president who had "operating" responsibility for semiconductor operations in the U. S., but not for any overseas locations. However, he was also the manager of our broader "electronic functions business objective," and in this role he had "strategic" responsibility throughout the company, including the related international operations.

The business objective document defines the scope of the business, including a business charter, appraisal of the market potential within this charter, projections of the technical and market trends, and the projected industry structure.

The heart of each business objective is its performance measures. These spell out, in quantitative terms, the parameters against which the organization will be measured. The most important of these measures are sales, profits, return on assets, and market penetration in terms of percentage of served available market. These are specified for five and ten years ahead. Typically, the closest two years are planned by quarter, and remaining years are planned by annual results.

Each business objective also examines the market and product goals in considerable detail as to projected market share penetration. Technical goals are examined, so that we can identify constraints clearly. Once these constraints have been identified, it becomes much more obvious that technical innovations will be required. Finally, the objective manager includes a critique. It covers evaluations of competition, threats and contingency plans, and possibilities of market shifts. The objective is long range, covering the next ten years.

Although each business objective is reviewed in detail at least once a year, major revisions are required infrequently in response to (1) success or failure in our pursuit of the specific strategies and tactics, (2) external economic environmental changes which are major in scope, or (3) unexpected successes or failures by competitors.

Each of the 11 business objectives is supported by a number of strategies. At present there is a total of 50 strategies, or an average of nearly five for each business objective.

Each strategy is the responsibility of a strategy manager. Under our "consumer objective," for example, we have a "calculator strategy manager" responsible for all strategic calculator activity through TI worldwide. He also happens to be the operating manager of the U. S. calculator division.

The strategy document explores the opportunity environment in terms of projected market growth. We try to identify the innovations in technology, manufacturing, and marketing that will be necessary to have a major impact on the business opportunity. We try to understand what competitive reaction might be, and we plan for contingencies. An important part of the strategy is to determine whether major new commitments must be made by the corporation to ensure success of the strategy. For example, do we need to acquire new skills, approach new markets, or create some other major change in the way we do business?

The strategy document also includes major long-range checkpoints, and the expected contribution to the business objective in financial terms. We try to weigh the probability of success of the strategy as a basis for applying judgement to the projection of the strategy's financial contribution. Strategies have lifetimes of several years or more, but they are reviewed and revised much more often than are objectives.

Each strategy is supported by a number of tactical action programs—or TAPs—each under a program manager. A TAP document includes a statement of the contribution the program will make to the strategy of which it is a part. It also sets forth the quantitative goals for the program.

This TAP is a resource allocation document that both specifies and commits resources in terms of manpower and capital. Moreover, it pinpoints responsibilities for accomplishment of each part of the program by listing the individual responsible, his organization, and the completion dates to which he is committed.

These action programs cover the full spectrum of business activities. Many are research and development programs—calling for invention to order and the development of specific new products or services. Some cover cost-reducing programs; others cover feasibility testing; still others cover innovative marketing techniques.

While most TAPs have relatively short lifetimes, typically from six to eighteen months, other programs covered by TAPs are much longer, such as some research and development projects. These normally would be covered by a sequence of TAPs keyed to appropriate stages in the R&D program.

The TAP is truly an action plan, because it triggers our "program management system." This begins with a "program evaluation and research techniques" (PERT) network, or a "schedule bar chart," for the project. This schedule, in turn, is translated into a "personnel task assignment schedule" and an "OST input form" that outlines facilities and support requirements, as well as procurement, manufacturing, and marketing plans.[3]

Because of its success in managing innovation Texas Instruments' OST system has been cited as one of the best systems in the country. However, by 1980, the slow OST process began to cause delayed product introductions and some missed market opportunities. By 1981, management decided to close its digital watch business, stop its $50 million magnetic bubble memory program, and stop its multichip microprocessor development. These changes brought a 10 per cent reduction in the workforce, over ten thousand layoffs. In response to these poor results and environmental changes, Texas Instruments reorganized and changed its OST system to allow more discretionary decisions to be made at lower levels in the organization.

The Texas Instruments' experience demonstrates the dynamics of organizational life. The continuing change in the external environment requires business decisions to be made close to the market. The ability to decentralize and still maintain an appropriate amount of control over strategic factors becomes the essence of the strategic manager's job. There is no formula for achieving this since our world is seldom stable in all its dimensions. Continued growth in organizational size and complexity can also limit an organization's flexibility and slow down its responsiveness to the market through bureaucratic decision-making processes. This is the challenge in setting and managing organizational strategy.

STRATEGIC MANAGEMENT OF INFORMATION

As strategic and operating plans become increasingly formalized, it becomes easier to apply today's computer and information-processing technologies to the task of managing these processes. The development of these new computer-based

[3] Op. cit.

systems is now allowing top managers to have more direct access to both strategic and operating data bases. However, before we can effectively apply these information-processing technologies to strategic management, we first need to systematize the internal processing of information. As described in Chapter 8, we can realign our corporate structure and staff according to the needs of strategic management.

For ease of discussion, we have reproduced Exhibit 8-5 as Exhibit 9-6. As shown here, it would not be unreasonable to expect computer-based information to be developed in each of the management areas: legal, environmental, objectives and policies, strategies, human resources, and financial and control areas. Although each of these six areas requires its own information and data storage, the strategic and operational planning process may require inputs from each of these areas.

To provide integration and coordination of the planning process, it becomes necessary that serious thought be given to the nature and priority of each information area. For example, consider the relationship of the information areas shown in Exhibit 9-7. Whereas we constantly emphasize the importance of objective setting, the structure of information requires that environmental conditions and assumptions, as well as legal requirements and constraints, be evaluated as an integral part of the objective-setting process. This requires that social, political, and legal data bases be developed in the future. Without these developments, setting realistic objectives and policies will continue to be difficult, if not impossible, for large and complex organizations.

The three information data bases that are most likely to be developed early, however, are in the strategy, human resource, and financial areas.

Strategy Models. Although strategy-related data bases are relatively new, they are becoming quite sophisticated. Firms, such as General Electric, have been working for many years to develop their own in-house strategy models. The Boston Consulting Group's and Strategic Planning Institute's PIMS data bases are commonly used in building strategy models. As strategic planners become increasingly more sophisticated in building strategy models, we are likely to see an integration of key elements from a number of these strategy models.

To give the reader a feeling for the kinds of variables that are likely to be considered in strategic information systems, consider those elements in Exhibit 9-8. PIMS' data base is used to assess business unit performance such as productivity, capital intensity, capacity utilization, working capital, price levels, product quality, marketing levels, and research levels. Whereas the current PIMS data base allows managers to assess their current performance levels and project the impact that changes in these variables are likely to have on performance, it does not allow managers to assess the impact of different competitive strategies in a specific industry. The importance of industry level analysis is likely to shift this analysis to industry levels in the future.

The Boston Consulting Group's analysis is used most effectively for projections of cash flow requirements and to test the consistency of specific strategies against their cash flow projections. The use of the experience curve analysis as seen in the motorcycle industry series can aid in determining where competitive advantages can be found. Finally, the search for improved productivity will put increased emphasis on experience curve strategies that improve both the effectiveness of people and assets.

EXHIBIT 9-6: Executive Information and Its Committee Organizational Structure

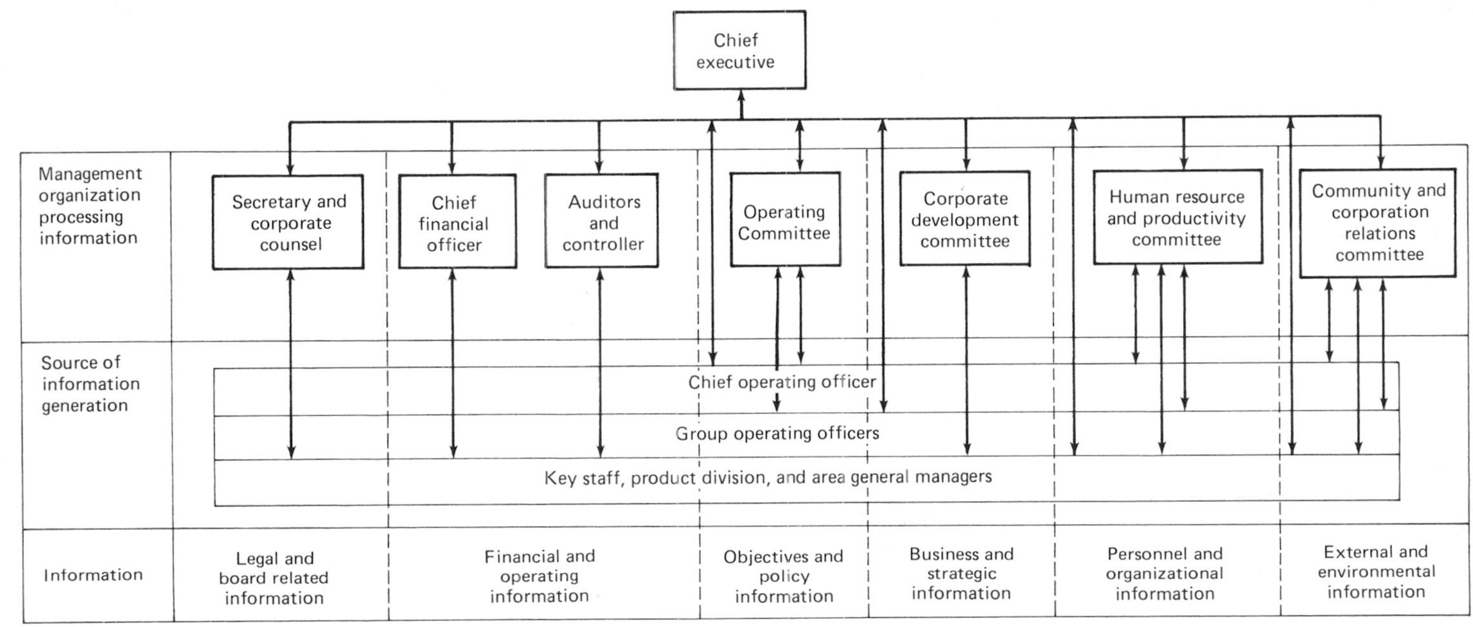

Source: William R. Boulton, "The Changing Requirements for Managing Corporate Information Systems," *MSU Business Topics,* Summer 1978, p. 9. Reprinted by permission.

EXHIBIT 9-7: Interrelated Strategic Management Information Systems

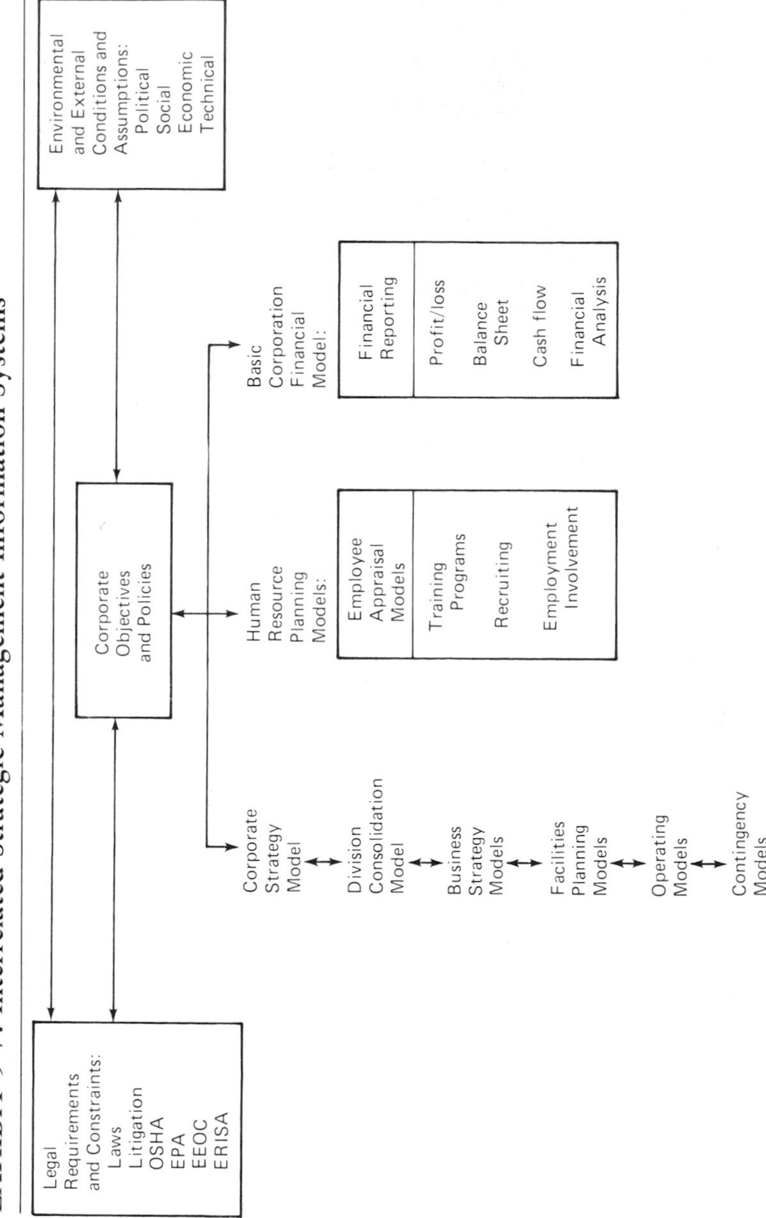

EXHIBIT 9-8: Strategic Information System

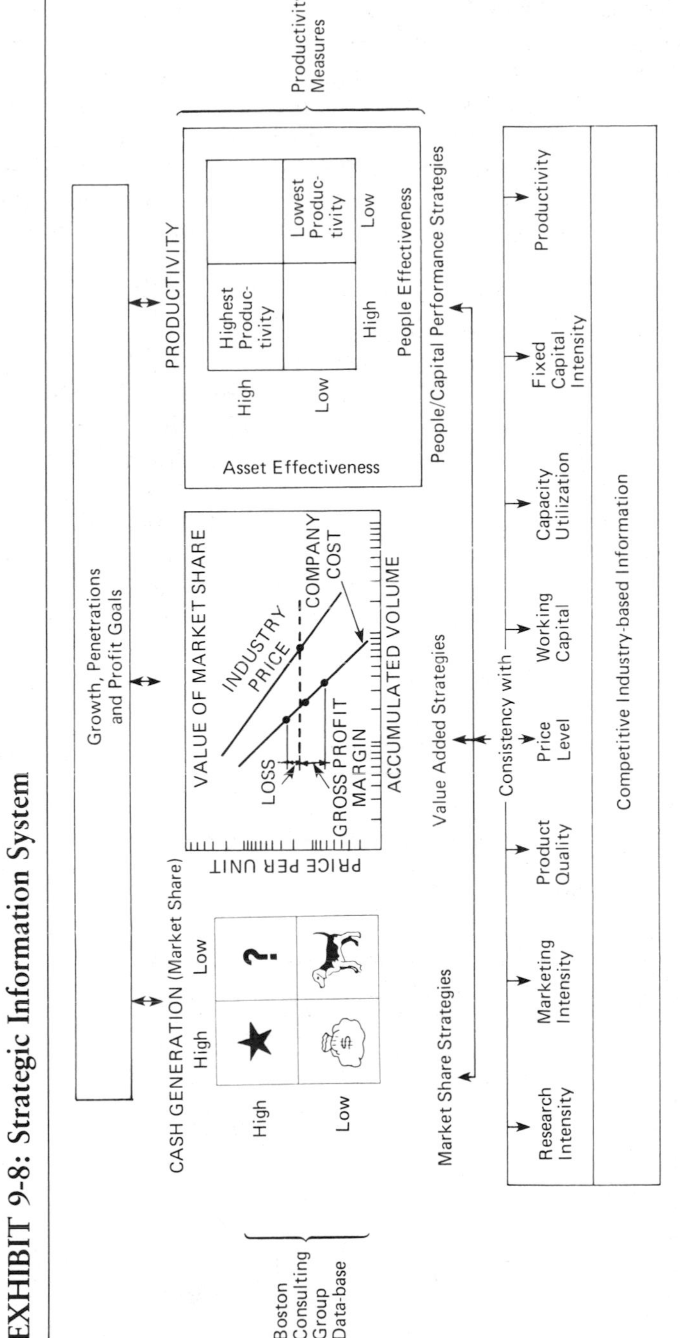

Human Resource Models. As we begin to better understand the strategic needs of an organization, the real challenge will come in making sure that we have the skills necessary to meet those needs. Human resource data bases will be needed to track the availability and development of skills needed to implement strategic and operating plans. In the human resource area, the Hay and Associates' type compensation data bases are among the few that are available. However, because of the increasing need to know and track the skills available within the organization, corporations are beginning to build their own human resource data bases.

As shown in Exhibit 9-9, an organization might identify its needs for managerial skills. Once it identifies key skills, the organization can begin to assess employee skill levels, develop specialized training programs to raise specific skill levels, and more effectively select individuals for specific job requirements. As we begin to better understand the traits or skills required to manage strategies effectively, we will find that pressures will increase for the development of such an information system.

Financial Information Models. Probably the most developed of current information systems, financial data bases were developed as one of the early applications of the computer. As a result of legal reporting requirements and budgeting practices, it has been cost effective for nearly two decades to use the computer for this purpose. Today, financial information systems are a basic management control tool used to track both strategic and operational performance.

Corporate financial information models have been in existence since the

EXHIBIT 9-9: Human Resource Information System

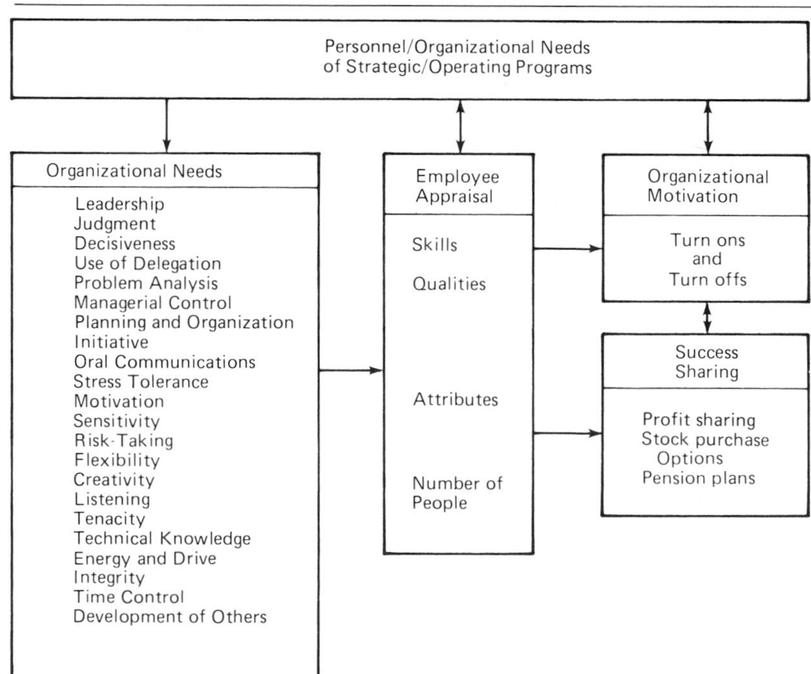

EXHIBIT 9-10: Financial Information Model

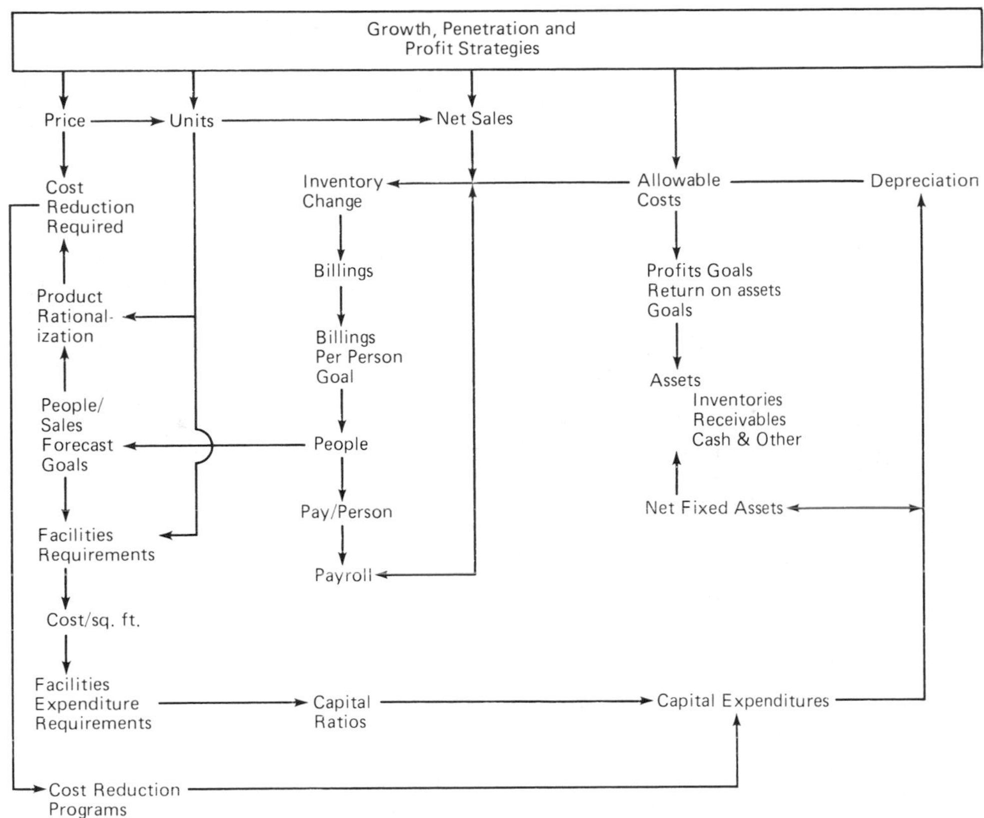

late 1960s. The model shown in Exhibit 9-10, for example, monitors profit and return on asset objectives by tracking unit sales, prices, production costs, payroll levels, and investment expenditures. Productivity or cost level objectives are also measured in terms of billings per person and asset turnover performance.

Commercially available modeling languages such as SIMPLAN and Execucom's Interactive Financial Planning System (IFPS) make it easy for managers to build their own systems for planning cash management, forecasting, budgeting, and financial consolidations. The use of such languages will continue to grow as we attempt to improve our productivity and effectiveness at information management.

As we continue to increase our use of financially based information systems, thought will also have to be given to the need for standardized reporting formats. For example, if data bases are kept at each business or product level, management will need the capability of consolidating all business or products into a single report. This may require that specific lines in the data base be reserved for specific information. A second need is to have a single data base for both strategic and operating financial data. Without a common data base, it will be difficult to check short-term and long-term plans for overall consistency. To overcome this problem, Texas Instruments' MODPLAN uses a common data base with standard reporting formats as shown in Exhibit 9-11. Through the

EXHIBIT 9-11: Standard Financial Reporting Formats

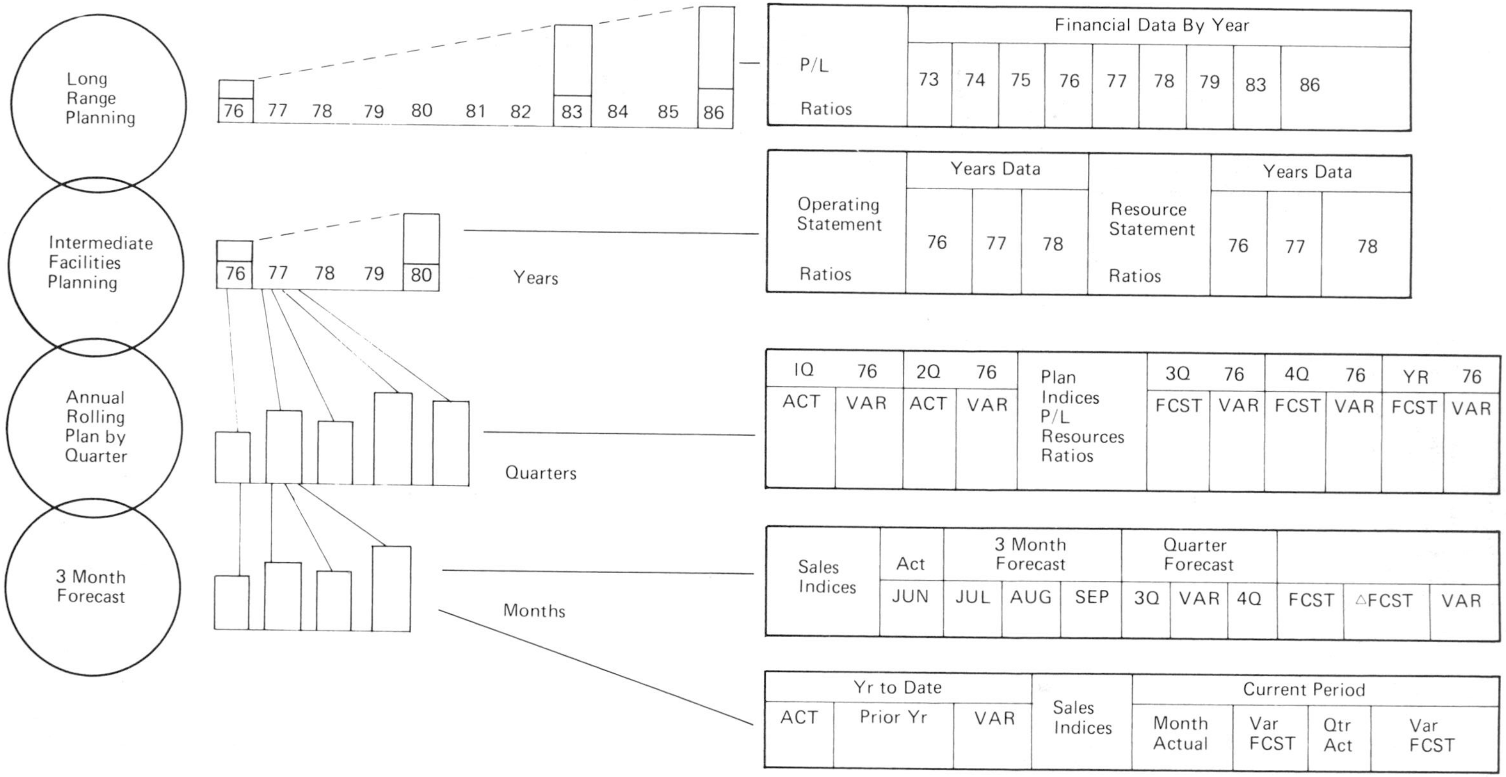

Long Range Planning

76 77 78 79 80 81 82 83 84 85 86

P/L Ratios	Financial Data By Year								
	73	74	75	76	77	78	79	83	86

Intermediate Facilities Planning

76 77 78 79 80

Years

Operating Statement Ratios	Years Data			Resource Statement Ratios	Years Data		
	76	77	78		76	77	78

Annual Rolling Plan by Quarter

Quarters

IQ 76		2Q 76		Plan Indices P/L Resources Ratios	3Q 76		4Q 76		YR 76	
ACT	VAR	ACT	VAR		FCST	VAR	FCST	VAR	FCST	VAR

3 Month Forecast

Months

Sales Indices	Act	3 Month Forecast			Quarter Forecast					
	JUN	JUL	AUG	SEP	3Q	VAR	4Q	FCST	△FCST	VAR

Yr to Date			Sales Indices	Current Period			
ACT	Prior Yr	VAR		Month Actual	Var FCST	Qtr Act	Var FCST

use of a common data base with standardized time periods, any change in strategic or operating plan can be quickly assessed as to its impact on the corporation.

As the job of corporate executive becomes increasingly complex and difficult to manage, computer-based corporate information systems will become an increasingly used management tool. The development of effective systems, however, will require that executives understand the need for corporate information systems and take a systematic and integrated approach to the development and application of specialized data bases which will make key staff functions more effective. Whereas such systems are still in the early stage of development, the direction in which corporate executives should already be moving is apparent. Successful implementation of strategic management systems will require executive time and commitment to information management.

AVOIDING BUREAUCRATIC PLANNING AND OPERATING SYSTEMS

As we begin to develop standard information systems, we will tend to become increasingly rigid and bureaucratic in managing the organization. This may work well in times of stability when planning and operating responsibilities are easier to manage. The difficulty comes in times of change when past practices no longer seem to work. The more rigid the systems, the less likely it will be that the organization can adapt in a timely manner.

In systems that are highly centralized, strategic managers will need performance measures which are easily obtainable so that they can readily balance systems for planning, operating, controlling, and motivating the organization. Unfortunately, in large and complex organizations where the environment is changing rapidly, it is not likely that meaningful performance measures will be found easily.

More specific performance measures, such as objectives, program schedules, and budgets, require careful design and considerable investment in time and thought to work effectively. As a result, there is a tendency in centralized organizations to develop controls over which decisions can be delegated. Such controls force centralization of decisions by not allowing managers to use their own judgments in determining how to achieve broader performance goals. This tendency leads to more bureaucratic management techniques than suggested by the concept of strategic management described in this text.

Exhibit 9-12 compares some of the basic differences between the concepts of strategic management and bureaucratic management. As shown, whereas strategic management concentrates on strategic business objectives, bureaucratic management is overwhelmed by details and the desire for control. Whereas strategic management concentrates on the review of strategic goals, bureaucratic management concentrates on control over decisions. Strategic management involves its line managers in strategy reviews, whereas bureaucratic management uses redundant staff reviews to track results. Finally, strategic management limits information requirements to data that contribute to strategic decision making and goal accomplishment, whereas bureaucratic systems require extensive data processing to keep decision makers throughout the organization involved. The lack of strategic focus in bureaucratic organizations causes more politics to evolve,

EXHIBIT 9-12: Alternative Planning and Control Systems

Strategic Management: *Strategic Control → Operating Flexibility*	*Bureaucratic Management:* *Strategic Freedom → Operating Control*
Summary PLANNING → GLOBAL CONTROL → REVIEWS	MOMENTUM → CASE CONTROL → POWER AND COMFORT
1. Focus attention on strategic issues. 2. Controls at business level. 3. Approvals at business level. 4. Use objectives, schedules, and budgets. 5. Review and track strategic issues and goals. 6. Act strategically and put responsibility for solution close to problem. 7. Align objectives with control elements and performance goals.	1. No attempt to recognize reasons for success and profit. 2. Approvals required by line and staff officials. 3. Report and monitor details. 4. Heavy controls from above for decisions. 5. Apply standard solutions to all problems. 6. Desire increased control.
Focus PLANNING STRATEGICALLY	ACCUMULATION OF DETAIL
1. Plans focus on key assumptions and strategic issues. 2. Outside inputs are used in strategic reviews. 3. Planning staff used to system for use by line management. 4. Use best/worst range of projections. 5. Keep track of objectives.	1. Planning process is data accumulation without questions. 2. Assumptions do not necessarily fit the realities. 3. Planning carried out by staff and not line management. 4. Overwhelming detail smothers objectives.
Controls USE OF GLOBAL CONTROLS	USE OF DECISION CONTROLS
1. Use business center structures with strategic goals. 2. Allow business centers to develop own systems. 3. Use reviews and audits to minimize communication. 4. Develop well-organized information systems.	1. Decision making. 2. Approvals required for all decisions. 3. Communication dilutes responsibility. 4. Approvals duplicated for some decisions. 5. Controls tend to be limited to areas of easy control.
Tracking USE OF REVIEWS	USE OF POWER
1. Concentrate on what to review. 2. Focus on achieving objectives. 3. Limit levels of hierarchy and focus on strategic decisions. 4. Line managers carry out reviews.	1. Concentrate on how to control. 2. Use redundant controls. 3. Add levels of hierarchy to process details. 4. Centralized decision making will lead to large headquarter's staff that carries out reviews.

Information USE OF CONCEPTS	USE OF DETAILS
1. Limit data to strategic needs.	5. Data needed by all participants in the decision-making process.
2. Transmit information on a need-to-know basis.	2. Details are passed up through the hierarchy.
3. Evaluate facts for contribution before submitting.	3. Data accumulation restricts ideas from passing through hierarchies.
4. Shallow hierarchy allows more direct communication.	4. Information provides power and rewards.

Source: Adapted from David Mitchell, *Control Without Bureaucracy* (London: McGraw-Hill Books Company, 1979).

where individuals focus on their own needs for survival rather than organizational goals.

Overcoming the dysfunctional consequences of bureaucratic management systems requires that management focus on overall organizational goals and develop managers who are able to determine contemporary methods of accomplishing those objectives. At the same time, individual performance measures and rewards need to be related to organizational goals. For organizations that have not yet used strategic management concepts, the move away from bureaucratic management requires a major emphasis on human resource evaluation, training and development. Restructuring, however, does not come easily.

SUMMARY

Information is essential to strategic managers. The planning and control system provides that needed information in a timely and useful manner. These systems facilitate information utilization and help to link corporate-level objectives to both business- and functional-level activities. Although we may use computers to aid the tracking of information, these machines do not communicate in any meaningful way. Only people can communicate, and therefore, our planning and control systems must fit the organization and people using them, not vice versa.

The development of effective planning and control systems requires several critical steps:

1. Business objectives and strategies must be articulated so that they can be tracked.
2. Critical success factors or milestones must be monitored.
3. Effective information-processing solutions need to be developed to meet planning and control requirements.
4. The priority and position of planning and control systems need to be well documented as an essential part of the computer information system.

Today, most organizations are only beginning to consider their real needs for information and resource management systems. This requires a close look at their organizational structure, business strategies, and management processes. Planning and control systems should, therefore, match the company's structure and strategy and meet its managers' need for information.

FOCUS QUESTIONS

1. How would you explain the differences between strategic and operational planning systems?
2. What is the role of systems in strategic management?
3. What systems would you establish in a growing organization? What systems would you establish first? What systems would you establish last? Why?

ADDITIONAL READINGS

BARNARD, CHESTER I. *The Functions of the Executive.* Cambridge, Mass.: Harvard University Press, 1938.

BLAU, PETER M. *The Dynamics of Bureaucracy.* Chicago: University of Chicago Press, 1963.

CROZIER, MICHAEL. *The Bureaucratic Phenomenon.* Chicago: University of Chicago Press, 1964.

DOWNS, ANTHONY. *Inside Bureaucracy.* Boston: Little, Brown and Co., 1967.

HOBBS, JOHN M., and D. F. HEANY, "Coupling Strategy to Operating Plans." *Harvard Business Review* (May–June, 1977); 121–126.

LIONS, GARRETT E. *Measuring Strategic Performance: A Management System for the 1980s.* Cambridge, Mass.: Arthur D. Little, Inc., 1979.

LORANGE, PETER. *Corporate Planning: An Executive Viewpoint.* Englewood Cliffs, N.J.: Prentice-Hall, Inc., 1980.

MITCHELL, DAVID. *Control Without Bureaucracy.* New York: McGraw-Hill Book Company, 1979.

10 Strategic Management of Human Resources

Whereas success may depend heavily upon the organization's ability to develop strategies, structures, and systems that fit the needs of its environment, it ultimately takes people with appropriate skills and knowledge to make the organization succeed. Planning for and managing human resources requires that management define the skills, know-how, and management qualities required throughout the organization. Selection, placement, and training of organizational members are essential functions for ensuring that appropriate skills, knowledge, and qualities are available. Human resource planning, therefore, must be treated as an integral part of the strategic management process.

Exhibit 10-1 shows how closely the human resource requirements are tied to organizational strategies and operating results. We can begin to understand this relationship by thinking of the objective and strategy setting phases as attempts to manage the organization's effectiveness, i.e., its ability to accomplish what it sets out to do. Whether or not an organization can achieve its objectives or accomplish its strategies depends on the basic skills and abilities of its human resource base. Over the longer term, it is management's ability to recruit, select, train, motivate, and replace its people that will determine how strong management's basic skills and capabilities remain.

Managing organizational efficiency relates more directly to short-term operating performance. For example, to achieve profitable operations, an operating unit must generate sufficient revenues to cover its total expenditures. The level of profitability is measured in terms of invested capital, such that:

$$\text{Profitability} = \frac{\text{Revenues} - \text{Expenditures}}{\text{Investment}}$$

"Revenues" become a function of the external demand for the organization's goods and services plus the ability of its marketing personnel to effectively reach its potential customers. "Expenditures" relate most directly to input costs and output per labor hour. "Investment" most directly affects overall productivity in terms of technology, skills, and output per employee. To maximize "efficiency" then, managers would generate the greatest level of revenues at the lowest expense for the least investment.

It should be apparent, however, that trade-offs will always have to be made

EXHIBIT 10-1: Human Resource Planning

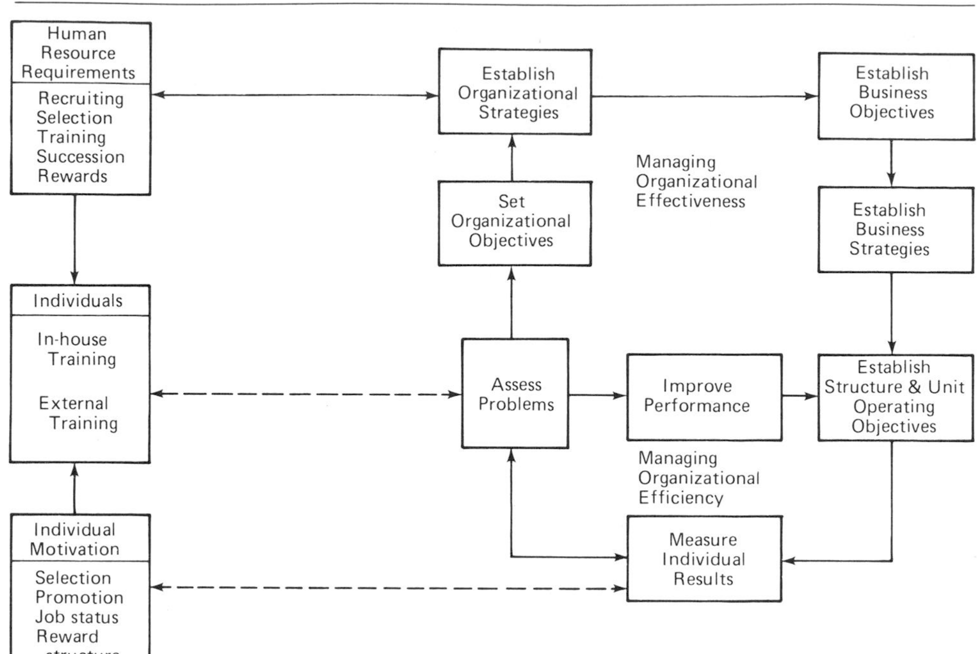

between managing organizational effectiveness and efficiency. The shift in objectives and strategies will lead to relatively low revenues for new ventures, with relatively high expenditures as a result of start-up and lack of experience, and high investment costs relative to profits. Given the nature of such changes, training and motivation of individuals to achieve ever changing objectives and strategies require more attention than has been given in the past. The drive for efficiency puts continuous pressure on cutting expenditures such as training costs and rewards.

THE IMPORTANCE OF HUMAN RESOURCES[1]

An organization's human resources affect its ability to be effective in achieving its objectives and strategies, as well as its ability to be efficient or profitable in achieving those ends. As shown in Exhibit 10-2, human resource productivity will become increasingly important as output per employee and employee cost percentages are used as standard measures to evaluate corporate performance. The importance of job security on labor relations and work force attitudes will also become increasingly important to management.

Overall work force motivation and stability will further impact on the organization's overall capabilities. Longer employee tenures will lead to increased

[1]See James W. Walker, *Human Resource Planning* (New York: McGraw-Hill Book Company, 1980) for further discussion.

EXHIBIT 10-2: Impact of Human Resources

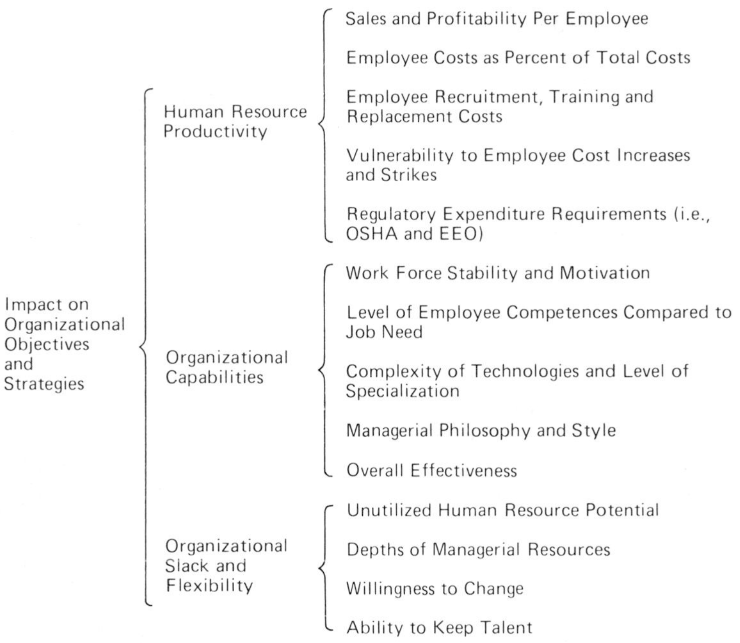

Source: Adapted from James W. Walker, *Human Resource Planning* (New York: McGraw-Hill Book Co., 1980), p. 82.

levels of competence and more effective organizations. More complex technologies and high levels of specialization can only benefit from a more stable work force. All of this, however, will depend heavily on the philosophy and style of management toward its work force.

Finally, the ability of an organization to change or adapt to its environment requires excess capabilities (slack) and flexibility in its work force. This requires excess human resource capabilities and talent to move the organization beyond its current operations. It also requires management depth to develop and coordinate the new activities and capabilities. Being able to recruit and keep employees who are overqualified for their current jobs is essential if such slack is to be part of the organization.

Critical Human Resource Issues

Attempts to manage the human capabilities of an organization require that human resource planning becomes an integrated part of the strategic planning process. This requires that management include human resource information as part of its planning and forecasting activities. Management must also be concerned with senior level management succession planning; assessing management candidates; and arranging for promotions, transfers, and executive education programs. Ensuring that training needs are recognized and that programs are developed or found to meet these needs is critical to human resource management. Finally, maintaining recruiting contacts and a staff capable of recruiting top candidates will allow the organization to, in essence, "overstaff" with competent people.

Some primary policy issues that need to be addressed in human resource planning include:

1. Intentions to promote from within or recruit from outside.
2. Intentions to be competitive on wage levels.
3. Degrees to which security will be offered as compared to high rewards and promotions for performance.
4. Degrees to which management controls and coordination requirements will be centralized or decentralized.

These policies will have a significant impact on the overall climate of the organization and the attitudes of its work force.

Formal hiring and development systems, like performance measurement and reward systems, can be quite elaborate, very simple, or nonexistent. Whereas these activities may be carried out informally in small organizations, large organizations generally have quite extensive educational and development programs. For example, IBM's education budget is larger than the budget of Harvard University.

Companies today are becoming increasingly aware of competitive wage level policies. Such organizations as Hay and Associates have been instrumental in developing standardized job-rating procedures and corresponding wage and salary information. As a result, managers are able to establish wage and salary level policies that relate to the external market. For example, a number of very aggressive firms may have salary levels that are in the upper quartile of the U.S. market, or 10 per cent above their local market rates. Staying abreast with competitive wage rates requires that a firm participate in one of the salary and wage survey programs. Results of annual surveys then allow managers to make appropriate wage and salary level adjustments.

In setting wage and salary level policies, a number of variables can be taken into consideration. Some of the key variables include:

1. *The Job.* Job specifications provide a basic mechanism for evaluating the job content and skill requirements of employees.

2. *Employee Specifications.* The need for education, experience, skills, and ability identifies the individual requirements and defines the size of the pool from which applicants can be recruited or selected.

3. *Supply and Demand.* Short-range market forces can drive up the price of those talents or skills that are in short supply. This is currently being seen in the engineering fields. Making compensation packages competitive can be a key factor in keeping such talent in an organization.

4. *Level of Specialization.* The more specialized the knowledge or skills required on the job, the smaller the pool of available talent is likely to be. This can affect both the supply and demand of talent by having such people in limited supply while also limiting the availability of outside alternatives for such specialists. Recognizing and keeping talents that are critical to the organization's capabilities can affect its compensation policies.

5. *Security.* Organizations with "hire and fire" reputations may need to pay a premium to compensate employees for the risk of losing their jobs. Under Harold Geneen, for example, ITT payed an average of 15 per cent over the

market price for managers. If the managers did not perform, however, they did not last. Lifetime security, on the other hand, may result in salaries below the market price.

6. *Benefits.* Benefits are becoming an increasing percentage of total employee compensation. Some firms allow their employees to decide what benefits they desire through what is called "cafeteria plans." Lincoln Electric Company, on the other hand, takes only required deductions from its employees incomes, thereby allowing the employees to maximize their total take-home pay. In Britain, where tax levels are extremely high, salaries are extremely low, whereas pensions are nearly 70 per cent of income and benefits such as company cars are common for executives.

7. *Incentive Payments.* Incentive payments, such as bonuses, stock options, and profit-sharing programs, are used to reward performance at the individual, group, and/or organizational levels. In organizations where such rewards are tied directly to individual or group efforts (i.e., Lincoln Electric Company), employees are likely to put in longer hours and to exert greater effort. Profit-sharing programs, on the other hand, direct individual or group efforts toward overall organizational performance. The difficulty with focusing on profit is its emphasis on short-term performance. Giving stock options to employees based on the organization's future performance, however, is used to cause individuals to also consider future performance. The key difficulty in designing incentive payments is to tie individual or group needs and goals to those of the organization. Finding the appropriate measures for performance at various levels in the organization, which direct individual or group behavior toward desired goals, is far from being a science. In the Independent Publishing Company case, the use of multiple goals forces the individual to consider organizational goals to achieve personal rewards.

Developing Incentive Systems

The overall purpose of incentive systems is to develop attitudes of involvement, participation, and responsibility for achieving the desired individual, group, and/or organizational goals. Properly conceived incentive income systems can have a strong influence on job performance. Since incentives are proposed to motivate employees to work toward specific goals, the following elements need consideration:

1. The identification of the goal.
2. The efforts required to achieve the goal.
3. The time required to achieve the goal.

The goals relate most often to revenues, expenditures, and profitability or productivity variables. The greatest difficulty, however, is in designing incentive systems that reward the appropriate behaviors on a timely basis to reinforce goal-directed behavior.

Since every incentive system has its own strengths and weaknesses, it is necessary that some flexibility be used to construct an incentive system which meets the needs of the organizational situation. This may require that incentives be developed for individual specific work group and/or organizational goals.

No matter which level of goals is being considered, specific characteristics that need to be considered include:

1. The situation in which the behavior is desired.
2. The variables that would reinforce the desired behavior.
3. The incentives that should be a consequence of the desired behavior.
4. The behavior that is expected.
5. The appropriate timing in which incentives should be distributed for the desired behavior.

By closely linking the situation-behavior-incentive factors, the desired performance has a greater likelihood of being achieved.

The schedule used to link the three performance factors (situation, behavior, incentive) can vary greatly between organizations. Ongoing incentives would reward individuals every time they performed as desired, which is the fastest method to establish new behavior. This is very difficult to employ in organizations because of administrative problems as well as the fact that desired behavior at higher levels cannot always be identified. The easiest method to administer is the use of fixed internal incentives, which may be provided weekly, biweekly, or monthly. This form provides the least incentive because reinforcement does not follow a specific behavior.

Individuals can also be paid based on their levels of performance within specified periods of time. The impact of these systems is dependent upon the time interval and level of incentive being used. Fixed-interval incentives are generally preferred, with shorter time intervals between performance and rewards to provide greater incentives. Frequent fixed-interval payments with a high percentage of performance-based income (e.g., commission payments) provide the greatest incentives and are generally used for sales personnel.

Compensation and wage level policies affect the ability of an organization to recruit and keep people whose skills, experience, and attitudes meet the needs of an organization's objectives and strategies. However, once employees enter the organization, training and development programs are needed to further develop the perspectives, knowledge, and skills needed to become an effective member of the organization.

THE IMPORTANCE OF ORGANIZATIONAL CULTURE

Rewards that employees receive for their contributions to an organization can be both monetary and nonmonetary in nature. Inducements for an individual to participate in an organization can be intrinsic in the job itself, with a job that is meaningful, challenging, and interesting. Inducements can also be social, with a close feeling of family support or comradeship. When the use or value of nonmonetary inducements declines, monetary inducements become increasingly called upon by employers to compensate for the lack of nonmonetary-based motivation.

Nonmonetary Rewards

A number of factors other than money affect the motivation of employees to perform for the organization. Some of these factors relate directly to individual needs such as needs for achievement, recognition, responsibility, advancement, growth, and the like. Other factors relate to group or organizational needs such as peer relations, supervision, status, job security, and company policies and administration. Japanese companies appear to rely much more on nonmonetary rewards than do typical American firms.

The Organization's Reputation. For the most part, employees want to be a part of a winning organization, and they want to work for a respectable organization that is involved in respectable affairs. Firms involved in questionable affairs or that hire and fire easily may have difficulty keeping good people. The greater the prestige and success of the organization, take IBM as an example, the more readily employees will identify themselves with the company rather than with their jobs.

The Organization's Climate. The success of an organization does not necessarily relate to how well the organization is being managed or how conducive the organizational environment is to long-term employee motivation. The relative level and perceived fairness of intrinsic and extrinsic rewards will determine the climate and culture of the organization. As management actions are repeated time and again, employees will come to expect similar actions in the future. The more predictable such behaviors become, the stronger the corporate culture is likely to become. Such a culture will have a positive affect on the organization's working climate if employees believe it to be appropriate or within their perceived range of acceptable practice.

Status. Rank, title, and the key to the executive washroom are often more important to an employee than income. Personal pride in one's job and external recognition can have a significant impact on one's satisfaction. However, when status is not provided by the organization, such as with garbage collectors, money may be demanded to allow the individuals to obtain status outside of the organization.

Job Satisfaction. Most people are in search of jobs that use their talents, challenge them, and expand their capabilities. Job satisfaction is likely when the individual's needs, goals, and values can be achieved through the job.

In research carried out by the consulting firm of McKinsey and Company, four characteristics were found to be especially important to Japan's past success. According to McKinsey's James S. Balloun:

1. They treat *people* as members of the organization, not as employees.
2. They use *shared values,* not detailed procedures and controls to guide operations.
3. They take a "*big think*" approach to business strategy.
4. They are *good listeners.*[2]

In Japan, the *organization* is its people, not the shareholders. The employees are considered lifetime members of the organization and have job security as long as the company performs well. Salary increases are tied to seniority with salaries being kept low until the employees enter management ranks usually when they are over the age of thirty-five. No Japanese employee of a large organization is fired to improve earnings, and employees are only asked to leave when the organization's survival is at stake. The personnel department is the primary

[2] James S. Balloun's speach entitled "Japan and the Excellent Organization," Atlanta, 1980.

agent for hiring employees and controlling their development through transfers across the organization. It is not unusual for employees of Japanese companies to work in sales, accounting, and production. This education and organizational understanding eventually makes these employees more effective participants and managers.

Japanese organizations have a shared sense of values. It is the chief executive's job to provide a kind of spiritual leadership and set the tone for the organization. Daily meetings begin with songs or talks that emphasize the organizational spirit and values. Over time, this brings about a common set of values and goals for the organization.

Japanese organizations tackle big problems by assigning groups to work full time to find a solution to the problem. Such groups are fully staffed and are charged with long-termed solutions to the problem. Rather than striving for short-term earnings, these groups look at market share, long-term position, and eventual profits. In every decision, innovative approaches are the focus of the search. As a result, the solutions developed by these groups eventually eliminate the problems.

Japanese are good listeners since they involve a lot of middle managers in the decision process. This involvement causes deep thinking to occur across organizational boundaries and develops group commitments to finding solutions. The intensive focus toward innovation and the listening skills with customers make product innovations especially successful.

Whereas McKinsey found that successful U.S. companies also had many of the same traits as Japanese firms, the practices of these successful firms were not consistent with traditional management theory. For example, much of today's theory is still based on the belief that man is a "rational" being. That belief is in conflict with the characteristics of these successful firms.

Conflicts with Management Theory

When we look at approaches to people, shared values, thinking big, and listening, we find that the rational-man approaches lead to different conclusions. For example, treating people as organizational members rather than as employees negates management's need to hire and fire. Management theory has suggested that to gain efficiency, one should limit the scope of the job, specify the job description, and then find someone to fill the job. Authority should be commensurate with responsibility, but one should do the job without questioning policies or responsibilities. We know now that such practices are much more likely to alienate individuals and reduce performance than treating them as organizational members. In fact, Japan loses only about 10 per cent as many hours as a result of strikes as does the United States. This level is significant even in view of the fact that, over time, only about 5 per cent of U.S. union negotiations result in strikes.

The use of shared values to direct behavior also conflicts with the theory that what gets measured gets done, and that results must be compared monthly against plans. It goes against the belief that good financial controls allow any company to be well managed. It also goes against the belief that decision processes should be made explicit, specifying responsibilities for analysis, reviews, recommendations, and approvals. In all, the concept of global controls is not consistent with current management theory that espouses detailed controls.

Finally, careful listening to members of the organization before making decisions is in conflict with current practice of appointing superstars to specialized staff positions. Current theory requires detailed information systems to elimate the need for listening, and to support the superstar's "dog and pony show" decision making. This growing importance and control over information is causing shifts in organizational power, but does little to facilitate listening.

ORGANIZATIONAL CONSISTENCIES

Developing an organization that supports the achievement of organizational objectives and strategies is a critical function of strategic management. The organization's elements must be consistent with the strategic needs of the organization. There must be consistency between the various goals, strategies, structures, people, management styles, individual skills, and supporting systems. It should also be apparent from the descriptions of business strategies described in earlier chapters that management, marketing, research, engineering, and manufacturing must work together as a team to accomplish any given strategy. Plants must be located to optimize not only manufacturing, shipping, and duty costs but also marketing, development, and management costs.

In addition to the business strategies, each department's strategies must be coordinated to achieve overall organizational objectives. Specific coordination strategies include such areas as

1. development of a viable strategic planning system.
2. development of human resource development programs to support strategic and operational requirements of the organization.
3. development of reward and control systems to meet the varied needs of different strategic and operating units.
4. development of communication systems to meet the varied needs of different organizational units and the corporation.
5. development of appraisal or measuring systems to assess individual and organizational performance.
6. development of reporting systems and formats to meet the various needs of different organizational units and the corporation.

The importance of these coordinating management systems can be better understood as we discuss the implications of managing a portfolio of multiple businesses and strategies.

Relating Organization to Product Life Cycle

If one agrees that life cycle has a profound effect on business strategy, then life cycle must also have a corresponding effect on how one should plan, organize, motivate, control, and measure the accomplishment of those different strategies.

To begin with, let us consider the different managerial requirements for each of the four life-cycle stages. During the embryonic or introduction stage, it is necessary to have an entrepreneurial commitment to see the opportunity available and to take the risks inherent in developing and getting a new product off the ground. As the business enters its growth stage, it becomes essential to have more sophisticated market managers who relate to the conditions of the market and its production requirements. More mature businesses require tough-minded administrators who can make critical decisions about capital and human investment decisions to maximize the opportunities in the business. Finally, aging businesses require a manager who can consolidate, sell, or close down business as opportunities arise to milk all of its available cash. To further understand the managerial implications of these different business strategies, let us look at the differing needs for planning, organizing, motivating, controlling, and measuring business units in the life cycle's phases as shown in Exhibit 10-3.

Organizing for Introduction. The entrepreneur managing an embryonic business will require the following managerial environment and systems:

1. Planning must be long range to comprehend the product life cycle and its product/customer implications.
2. Organization must be relatively informal but task oriented to find new market opportunities and to develop new products.
3. Rewards should be for individual performance, allowing individual involvement and freedom in carrying out tasks.
4. Controls should be qualitative with market guidelines and informal or tailored communication systems.
5. Performance measures should be relatively few in number, with a minimum of detail and frequent measurement.

The purpose of this system is to encourage individual creativity and promote an entrepreneurial environment in which to generate and develop new ideas and products. That requires a minimum of procedures and controls and a reward for individual efforts.

Organizing for Growth. The sophisticated market manager of a growth business requires a managerial environment and systems that are different from that of the entrepreneur.

1. Planning will be long range but focused on investment plans for specific products and their strategic programs.
2. The organization will need to be more established to focus on product and market development. Special attention will be needed to develop new people to manage the growing organization and to expand and get new production facilities in operation.
3. The organization will need strong leadership with rewards provided for both individual and group performance for achieving objectives.
4. Controls should include both qualitative and quantitative guidelines for all individuals with communications tailored to meet the specific objectives of the business unit.
5. Multiple objectives require multiple, detailed performance measures to be used and often measured.

The basic characteristics of this system will lead to disciplined growth and the development of market share. It requires strong leadership and control because

EXHIBIT 10-3: Managing Multiple Product Strategies

ANALYSIS

INDUSTRY MATURITY & BUSINESS CHARACTERISTICS → COMPETITIVE POSITION & INVESTMENT ATTRACTIVENESS

IMPLEMENTATION

MANAGERIAL RESOURCES & SYSTEMS

PORTFOLIO CATEGORY	EMBRYONIC	GROWTH	MATURE	AGING/DYING
INDUSTRY MARKET CHARACTERISTICS	HIGH GROWTH LOW SHARES	HIGH GROWTH HIGH SHARES	LOW GROWTH HIGH SHARES	LOW/NEGATIVE GROWTH LOW/DECLINING SHARES
PRIMARY BUSINESS OBJECTIVE	DEVELOP VIABLE ENTRY PRODUCTS	BUILD MARKET SHARE	MAXIMIZE EARNINGS WITH MODERATE CASH	MAXIMIZE CASH FLOW
MANAGERIAL REQUIREMENT	ENTREPRENEUR	SOPHISTICATED MARKET MANAGER	TOUGH-MINDED ADMINISTRATOR	OPPORTUNISTIC MILKER
MANAGERIAL NEEDS:				
(1) Planning	Long range life-cycle for planning and customers	Long range investments for products and programs	Formal intermediate planning for products, markets and functions	Formal short range planning by plant
(2) Organization emphasis	Informal or task force; market research & new product development	Established task force, product & market divisions; operations research & organization development	Business division & renewal task force; value analysis, better reporting & expense control	Stripped down division; better purchasing & scheduling
(3) Motivation & rewards	Reward individual performance with high variables compensation; participative management	Reward individual & group performance with balanced fixed & variable compensation; strong leadership	Reward group performance with low variable & high fixed compensation; guidance with strong loyalty	Fixed compensation, with strong loyalty and direction
(4) Controls & communication	Limited qualitative and marketing guidelines with informal or tailored communications	Some qualitative & quantitative guidelines for all functions but tailored communications	Many written, production oriented guidelines with uniform & formal communications	Many numerical guidelines with balance sheet orientation and little formal communication
(5) Measures	Few, less detailed but frequently measured	Multiple, detailed and often measured	Multiple, very detailed and periodically measured	Few, fixed with less detail and less often measured

of continuing growth in all functions and the addition of new personnel and facilities. Without specific objectives, measures, and rewards, the organization can easily get out of control.

Organizing for Maturity. As the organization enters maturity, the "tough-minded" administrator needs an even more rigid managerial environment and more formal systems.

1. Planning becomes formal for all products, markets, and functions and focuses attention on more intermediate time periods.
2. The organization can be more formal with business unit definitions and task force designation to develop new business opportunities.
3. Organizational performance becomes increasingly important and requires highly loyal employees who will do their jobs with minimum guidance and accept rewards for group performance.
4. The need for increased efficiency and profits requires tighter controls with more written, quantitative, production-oriented objectives communicated in a formal and uniform way.
5. Multiple objectives require multiple measures that are very detailed to track every element of operations and which are periodically reviewed.

The mature business must be tightly controlled to take advantage of its cash-generating and profit potential. However, because every detail must be well managed, the mature business requires the highest degree of decentralized management with a group whose organizational orientation is achieved through individual loyalty and group rewards.

Organizing for Decline. The manager of an aging or dying business needs to be very objective and opportunistic to get the most cash out of a shrinking business. This requires the following, more restrictive managerial environment and systems:

1. Planning will be short run with the major focus being placed on plant consolidation and cash generation.
2. The organization will need to be stripped down of all excess overhead and staff, with the major emphasis being given to purchasing and scheduling for shrinking operations.
3. Rewards will need to be fixed with strong reliance on employee loyalty and direction.
4. Controls should be numerical with a balance sheet.
5. A limited number of fixed measures is needed to occasionally measure balance sheet performance.

As organizations become larger and add businesses, the variety of organizational systems used should increase. This requires more managers and better training and development programs to ensure that managers understand the needs of their organizations. In an attempt to limit the diversity of organizational needs, many firms have attempted to stay in businesses that can be encompassed in one area of the life cycle. Growth companies carry the features of the growth organization, but have difficulty in managing mature businesses. Firms that have managed mature businesses over a long period of time often have difficulty getting new businesses off the ground. The penchant for having "one way of managing" can build rigidities into the organization that keep "portfolio management" from becoming a reality.

THE IMPORTANCE OF ORGANIZATIONAL SUCCESSION

Human resource motivation and management are linked directly to the philosophy and style of management. Explicit rewards can be used to motivate individuals and groups. However, to increase the probability that the rewards offered attract, retain, and motivate employees toward achievement of organizational goals in a cost-effective manner, the philosophy of management needs to be shared throughout the organization. This philosophy can best be reflected in the climate and reward and control systems of the organization. Succession, therefore, becomes a primary concern in human resource management, since changes in leadership can affect the basic philosophy and motivational elements of the organization.

A succession plan, as shown in Exhibit 10-4, can quickly point out the areas in which recruiting and development are needed. By identifying job structures, both current and projected, and the individuals being groomed for those positions, the gap between current supply and projected demands can be readily identified. In addition, the training and development requirements for the organization can be recognized so that appropriate programs (either inhouse or external) can be developed to meet those needs. By moving individuals across business and functional areas during on-the-job training, better organizational perspectives and understanding can be developed. This is especially important as individuals move upwards in the organization since they will affect larger portions of the organization. Systematic succession, therefore, becomes increasingly important as we near the top of the organization.

THE TEXAS INSTRUMENTS EXAMPLE

Texas Instruments' early attempt to measure and motivate key personnel was explained to the company's shareholders by Pat Haggerty in 1964:

> Our whole management system at Texas Instruments is organized around the premise that we must be goal oriented. It is perfectly consistent, therefore, that one important way we identify and evaluate key TI managers is via our annual Key Personnel Analysis (KPA), a highly systematized and formalized analysis of all salaried personnel up to and including company officers. With it we try to establish an index of contribution to company objectives for each such individual for the coming year. Department heads examine and select the top 20 percent of all their personnel. The performance of these persons is reviewed with the division head who, in turn, singles out the top 5 percent. This process enables us to correct inequities in compensation and responsibility and (at our present size) to find the top 325 TI people.

As part of the KPA review, top management then ranked its top people according to contribution. Once this was done, stock options were then given to key personnel. Haggerty continued:

EXHIBIT 10-4: Human Resource Requirements

Company X
Division Y
Department Z
Date:

HIGHLY CONFIDENTIAL

SUCCESSION PLAN

Job Title	Present Job Holder	Estimated Date of Leaving & Reason, e.g., Retirement	Immediate Successor	Age	Company Service	Present Job	Service in Present Job	Performance Rating	Readiness	Training & Experience Required

> We have always endeavored to relate personnel interest and advancement to company interest and progress. . . . One of the most effective ways we have done this with key personnel is with our Stock Option plan, in which there are now 263,730 shares under option to 148 key personnel.
>
> All stock option plans are incentive-oriented, of course, but in 1963 we amended TI's plan further to emphasize the incentive feature. We related exercise privileges to planned growth in TI earnings.
>
> That options became exercisable two years after the date of the grant, and cannot be exercised at a greater rate than 20 percent per year for five years, is conventional and in our plan. But . . . we added a requirement which clearly associates gains for the individual with corporate goals and gains for the stockholders. We tied the annual right to exercise options to a 15 percent increase in TI earnings every year for nine years. Installments are exercisable in January, based on the immediately prior year's earnings.

In addition to stock options, annual bonuses were given to key personnel.

At Texas Instruments, top management was especially concerned with the development of organizational practices and a climate that would foster long-term employee motivation. In 1964, as Pat Haggerty explained to shareholders:

> We have sought to avoid the inhibiting influences of slavish adherence to conventional administrative practices and have always attempted to achieve our goals by the most expedient means possible, provided, of course, that no TIer should be required or permitted to compromise moral or ethical standards in the achievement of his task. Consider, for example, the nature of the interpersonal relationships among TIers.
>
> As one moves up in the traditional organization, opportunities increase to surround oneself with physical evidence of his greater status. We at TI are not categorically opposed to status symbols. However, we are selective in the choice or permission of those which can have impact on our TI administrative climate. We say that status symbols are not harmful provided: (1) they do not inhibit communication, (2) they do not reinforce or increase social distances, and (3) they are available through a democratic process. Apart from the impact which status symbols can have on interpersonal relations, we, as a profit-conscious organization, have an obligation to our customers and shareholders to avoid expenditures which will not contribute to the value of our products and services and the profits we earn.
>
> To name a few practices which characterize our relationship and our climate: common dining room facilities—only using our meeting rooms sometimes for luncheons with customers or for business conferences—equal parking privileges, tenure-related identification badges, assignment of office space in accordance with actual need, functional office furnishings, informality in attire, and the use of the informal first name in our day-to-day relationships. Alone, none of these would have a significant impact, but, collectively, they become significant. Administered as is intended, they tend to reinforce the TI spirit. In many companies, where these areas provide a basis for rather elaborate status symbols, the more sharply divided are management and labor. At TI, we cannot support a system of symbols which, because it is based on special privilege, connotes favoritism and provides the basis to divide TIers into "them" and "us" groups. How can we in good conscience advance a philosophy which unifies TIers and support status practices which divide us?
>
> Status symbols sometimes do serve to bolster feelings of security in individuals. At TI we like to think that our managers gain their feelings of security from

> achievement of significant responsibility and recognition of that contribution with other than physical trappings.
>
> Not unrelated to our philosophy is the way in which we communicate in TI. One of the inevitable consequences of company growth is the tendency to formalize communications. Many large organizations fall into a pattern of avoiding verbal orders and ultimately try to commit everything to paper. We hope to avoid that trap and encourage face to face communication and use of the telephone, for it provides open-access from any direction and harnesses and reinforces the spontaneous relationships which exist in every company. Although such informal communication shortens management action time and reduces clerical costs, it carries a parallel responsibility to keep adequately posted all intervening levels, line and functional, in the formal organization. We do not say to abandon the memorandum. Surely, it has its place. We do say, and encourage managers, to use deliberate judgement in deciding what must be committed to paper as an act of good management and what is best achieved less formally. We have introduced formal media to communicate important information to TIers at all levels of responsibility, but their success and that of any communication system depends as much on an atmosphere in which they are received—security, fairness and friendliness—as on how they are stated.
>
> Another TI climate factor I would mention is job stability. I refer primarily to our long-established policy to lay off TIers only as a last resort. This goes back to the very beginnings of this company and has been applied consistently throughout the years. We feel it influences in an important way the productivity, the creativity and dignity of TIers who comprise the organization. With competent people and utilization of overtime instead of overstaffing, in most times of decreasing business we have been able to shift employees and reduce hours. Such job stability surely must have a substantial impact on TIers' feelings of job security.

Many of the characteristics incorporated into Texas Instruments' early development have been found to be equally important today.

At Texas Instruments, succession policies had been well specified by 1973. As Pat Haggerty explained to shareholders:

> Assurance of present and future managerial competencies is especially important for Texas Instruments. The management practices and procedures we follow in running our business every day to help us attain our ambitious long-range objectives—such management policies and practices as our detailed rolling annual and ten-year planning programs, the intensive controls systems exemplified by our objectives-strategies-tactics system—are effective; however, they demand not just competent management but rigorous discipline, thorough comprehension, many years of experience in utilizing them, and an intense commitment to their pursuit from each and every key manager. This is especially so for those who occupy our top positions as senior and group vice presidents, executive vice presidents, president, and chairman.
>
> This responsibility for ensuring competent management succession is one I have always judged to be among the most important responsibilities—perhaps the most important—I assumed as president, or now as chairman of Texas Instruments. And I know that judgement was and is held equally important by my immediate predecessor, Erik Johson, and my very capable successor as president and chief executive officer, Mark Shepherd.
>
> Over the past year, our directors have examined intensively how we might improve still further the practices and policies we followed to assure completely competent and sufficiently experienced top management succession for Texas Instruments. This examination is particularly appropriate now, first, because of the

long-range corporate growth objectives set for TI—objectives not only for growth in size and profitability but in products and services, in organization and in overall competence—not just here in the United States but in much of the rest of the world as well; and, second because the extraordinary depth of good managers of which TI is now possessed allows us to consider how best to assure competent top management succession rather than simply respond expediently as our needs for top executives develop.

As a culmination of these deliberations, at its regular meeting last month, TI's board of directors decided to adopt and implement the following policies and practices:

1. Retirement for TI's chairman, president, and executive vice presidents will be compulsory shortly after they attain age 62. This policy will affect me first, since I will be 62 in March, 1976.
2. TI's chairman, president, or executive vice president, with board approval and after serving a specified number of years in these posts, may choose early retirement after their 55th birthday. Executive vice-presidents ordinarily will retire shortly after they reach their 55th birthday, but they may be expected to serve to a later age when TI's needs may so require or in order to attain the minimum length in that post.
3. TI's chairman, president, and executive vice-presidents will be elected by TI's board with these retirement ages and the following minimum lengths of time in mind:

	Years in position or cumulative years	
	minimum	*optimum*
Chairman	4	—
President and chief executive	4	8–10
As president and chairman	8	
Executive vice president	3	
As president, chairman and executive vice president	11	

An executive vice-president will be expected to serve at least three years as such. A president and chief executive officer will be expected to serve at least four years and then normally will be elected to be TI's board chairman and serve for not less than four additional years. Further, whenever possible, TI's president will be elected so as to be able to serve an optimum term of 8 to 10 years followed by a minimum of four years as chairman.

4. These key officers, on early retirement, will be paid a supplementary retirement allowance sufficient to bring their total retirement allowance up to an amount which is a percentage of the retirement allowance to which they would normally have been entitled at age 65. This retirement allowance will be reduced by 1½ percent per year for each year retirement is early; that is, a chairman retiring at age 62 will be entitled to 95½ percent of the amount he would have received, had he continued working to age 65, at the same average pay he received in the last five full calendar years he served. An executive vice president retiring at 55 would receive 85 percent of that amount.

Obviously, these policies will mean that, ordinarily TI's executive vice presidents will not be older than 52 and usually will be younger when elected; a president will not be more than 50 at election.

To give you some feeling for the significant effect of these policies, let me point out that if our present president, chairman, and three executive vice presidents served to our present retirement age of 65, there would be just three vacancies allowing promotion to these posts over the next 15 years; that is, until 1988. With these new policies there are likely to be no less than seven such major promotions over the same 15 years.

By using such words as "usually" and "ordinarily" in their policy statement, TI's board and top management were also given flexibility in implementing the policy. In case of ordinary circumstances, it was felt that the policy would be implemented. However, to protect against unforeseen situations, flexibility was felt to be important.

SUMMARY

Managing the human resource elements of the organization depends quite heavily on the overall needs of the organization for specific skills and knowledge. However, achieving a high level of motivation requires management attention of both the intrinsic and extrinsic characteristics of the organization. Providing a good climate while aligning individual goals and rewards to organizational goals will maximize overall motivation. Once the proper alignment and climate are achieved, succession will be critical to their maintainance.

FOCUS QUESTIONS

1. What are the key concerns for the strategic management of human resources? How do these concerns change with the evolution of organizational size and complexity?
2. What are the key differences between Japanese and American philosophies in regards to human resources? How do these differences affect performance?
3. How would you change an organization's human resource management as a business matures? How would you manage the human resources of highly diversified companies?

ADDITIONAL READINGS

DRUCKER, PETER F. "What we can learn from Japanese management." *Harvard Business Review* (March–April, 1971).

HENEMAN, HERBERT G. et al. *Personnel/Human Resource Management.* Homewood, Ill.: Richard D. Irwin, Inc., 1980.

JOHNSON, RICHARD T., and W. G. OUCHI, "Made in America (under Japanese management)." *Harvard Business Review* (September–October, 1974).

OUCHI, WILLIAM G., and A. M. JAEGER. "Type Z Organizations: Stability in the Midst of Mobility." *Academy of Management Review* (April 1978): 305–313.

PETERS, THOMAS J. "Putting Excellence into Management." *Business Week,* July 21, 1980.

ROBBINS, STEPHEN P. "Reconciling Management Theory with Management Practices." *Business Horizons* (February 1977).

WALKER, JAMES W. *Human Resource Planning.* New York: McGraw-Hill Book Company, 1980.

YOSHINO, M. Y. *Japan's Managerial System: Tradition and Innovation.* Boston: The M.I.T. Press, 1968.

11 The Role of Top Management (Style)

Anyone with organizational experience understands the impact that the top manager or chief executive officer has on the organization. The behavior and expectations of top management determine the character and environment of the organization. Top management will decide who gets hired or promoted into key positions, what functions or skills get their support or commitment in resources, and will approve the basic product-market strategies to be followed by the organization. The structure and systems of top management will influence the distribution of responsibilities and authorities across the organization. And the basic values and style of top management will determine the way in which other members of the organization behave and make decisions. And ultimately, top management's decision about its successors will determine whether these "rules of the game" continue or not into the future.

To understand the broad impact of management on the organization, consider the following example described in 1981 by *Forbes:*

Top management's influence is greatest in determining organizational strategies. Consider the changes made by Hasbro Industries, Inc.'s president, Stephen Hassenfeld, after he took office in 1979. The toy manufacturer had not entered the electronic game business and was losing $2.5 million on $75 million in sales. Hasbro had been introducing fifty new products per year and sold over one hundred eighty toys in its product line. Nobody knew product costs and the company kept any product that might add to overhead. The philosophy was as follows,

> If it covers a little overhead, leave it in. More new products seemed to mean more chances to hit it big, despite the fact that it also meant stretching the resources of the company so thin that none of the products had enough marketing muscle behind them to ensure success. No one at Hasbro had attempted to stay current with the true cost of launching a new product. "We all sort of grew up when the costs of product development, tooling and advertising weren't as great as they are today, a time when perhaps the cost of failing wasn't as great as it is today." [1]

By 1980, Hasbro made $4.6 million on sales of $104 million. Hassenfeld limited Hasbro's product line to preschool toys, 3D skill and action games like Hungry Hippos, and design toys like Lite Brite. Marginal toys and those outside these markets were eliminated. New product introductions were limited to 25 with a 120-toy product line. Licenses were limited to established names such as

[1] Steven Flax, "You Could See It in Their Eyes . . . 'Has Been,' " *Forbes,* May 25, 1981, pp. 84–91.

Sesame Street and *Peanuts* characters. Hassenfeld stayed out of electronic games, and because of his product strategy, Hasbro missed the price cutting that occurred in obsolete electronic games. The 30 preschool line toys grew sixty-three percent since 1978. Over 60 per cent of the products were carried into 1981 with less than 10 per cent of sales being tied to any one product. Operations are more efficient, inventory turnover is up, stocks are down, borrowings are down, and cash is up. Hassenfeld's philosophy now prevails:

> Firms of our size, in this industry, can't bring many products to market and give every element of every product the kind of tender loving care it must have. The commercial and media plans have to be right if it's a promoted product, also the price, the packaging, quality, delivery . . . that's a full boat. Attention to detail is critical. If you fall down in two areas, you're almost sure to be in trouble.

In addition to changing strategy, top management determines how the organization operates. Consider the impact that a change in management has had on Gillette as described by *Forbes* in 1981:[2]

In 1976, Coleman Mockler was promoted to president of Gillette. He was the exact opposite of Gillette's CEO, Vincent Ziegler. Mockler's background was finance rather than sales. After graduating from Harvard and the Harvard Business School in 1957, Mockler came up through the finance and accounting area to vice-chairman. Then, as president, he faced the rebuilding of Gillette's slumping position following the 1974 recession.

Mockler began by cutting all marginal products and businesses that had accumulated under Ziegler. Cost savings of nearly $70 million were put into advertising and into product development of products that fit Gillette's marketing competence. Overhead was slashed and has been maintained at the 1974 level. In addition, Mockler insisted that direct operating costs be cut 4 per cent per year to reach his goal of 40 per cent cost reductions using technical improvements.

At the same time, Mockler worked on restructuring and finding the right people for the jobs. Of the top 50 jobs, 38 went to new executives. The net result was a major turnaround in key product areas. The safety razor division held its position against new competition while capturing 70 per cent of the disposable razor market. The Paper Mate division's Eraser Mate nearly doubled that division's profitability. Reducing 225 products to 27 has channeled promotional money for the introduction of Dry Idea and Silkience. While working to improve margins, returns, and earnings per share, Mockler also worked to develop sustained growth and strong financial discipline.

Top management actions, as seen in Hasbro Industries and Gillette, have the impact of changing the "rules of the game" for the corporation. It is important, then, that top management concern itself about the climate of the organization. For example, consider the concern and strategy that Pat Haggerty had for Texas Instruments' organization in 1974:

> It is a fundamental tenet of TI's management philosophy to direct our efforts to achieve company goals in such a fashion as to yield genuine satisfaction of important employee needs. This philosophy obviously has a great effect on *how* we manage, *how* we pursue our objectives, *how* we use our human resources. It has significance both in the selection of goals and the development of the means to achieve

[2] Robert V. Flaherty, "The Patient Honing of Gillette," *Forbes*, February 16, 1981, pp. 83–87.

> them. It says that an essential requirement of the manager's job is to strive for the integration of individual TIer's goals with department or company goals.
>
> An underlying premise of this philosophy is that the vitality of TI depends upon the personal commitment of TIers. Compatible goals result not in mere passive compliance with management's wishes, but spontaneous and creative contribution to their fulfillment. An aim of TI management is the generation of conditions in which personal and company goals are not only consonant but mutually catalytic.

To create a proper climate in support of cooperation was seen as management's responsibility. Haggerty explained:

> Our philosophy requires that as managers we maintain a high degree of sensitivity to on-the-job attitudes and the needs TIers have. This requirement is reflected in our many programs of self-scrutiny: attitude surveys, post-performance review analysis, TI motivation research, etc. These are valuable management tools to provide us with insights upon which to base corrective action and to monitor our effectiveness in managing our human resources.

From these examples, it should be apparent that top management's decisions and philosophy impact heavily on organizational goals, strategy, structure, systems, staff, and skills. There is very little in an organization that will not be affected by management's beliefs about business and how organizations should operate. As organizations grow in size and complexity, strategic business decisions often come from lower levels in the organization. Management's style and philosophy then become the critical elements in developing an organizational culture that will influence the way such decisions are made. Ideally, top management would like all managers to come to the same decisions as themselves. However, that requires extensive indoctrination and training of such managers. The success of strategy implementation depends on consistency of decisions throughout the organization.

THE NEED TO SOLVE STRATEGIC PROBLEMS

Although it is understood that top management decision making ultimately determines organizational strategy, the area of decision making in which top level strategic management is most critical is the area in which uncertainty as to strategic solutions is the greatest. Exhibit 11-1 shows how the responsibility for decision-making activities is likely to be located depending upon the nature of the organization's problems and the certainty with which solutions can be found. The vertical axis specifies that organizational problems can range from those which have already been "identified" to those which are not yet known or are "unidentified." The horizontal axis shows the range of solutions that can be applied to an organization's problems. These solutions can be "known" and very specific or may still be "unknown" or untried. This problem-solution matrix then incorporates all varieties of problem-solutions from those totally unknown to those totally known.

To understand the impact that these problem-solution combinations have on top management, let us consider the simplest of known problems and solutions found in the lower left-hand corner of the matrix. For example, if the costs

EXHIBIT 11-1: Typology of Organizational Decision Making

Nature of Problem	Nature of Solutions: Specified Solutions ⟷		⟷ Unknown or Untried Solutions
Unspecified or Generalized Problems	Structural, operations-focused decisions (top management)	Tactical, intermediate-range decisions for sub-units (top management)	Strategic long-range decisions for organization (top management)
↕	Allocate funds to subunits to identify and resolve problem (staff and subunit managers)	Establish subunit planning and decision-making procedures (subunit managers, top management and staff)	Fund general area research, i.e., government grants and organization's basic research (top management and research staff)
Specified or Known Problems	Purchase and installation of Turnkey systems (sub-unit managers)	Analysis and design of specific solution or system (staff and subunit managers)	Fund problem-oriented research to find potential solutions or systems (research and development staff)

of labor make a product unprofitable to produce, management can search for high-speed equipment that can automate the job and reduce production costs. In the same sense, if management finds it difficult to keep accurate or timely operating reports, it is likely that a "turn-key" computer-based accounting system can be installed to overcome the information problem. At the opposite, upper right-hand corner of the matrix, problems and solutions are totally unspecified or unknown. For example, determining in what product or country the company should invest to overcome its slacking sales requires assessment of political risks, social risks, economic risks, and technological risks such as the likelihood of new electronic or communication technology obsoleting the company's product-line or marketing approach. Deciding what the company should do to overcome such threats and take advantage of new opportunities in these areas can cause the future success or failure of the organization.

Mixed combinations of problem-solution uncertainty are shown in either the upper left- or lower right-hand corners of the matrix. Problem-solution combinations at the upper left-hand corner can be seen as rather unknown or general problems that can be dealt with through rather specific solutions. For example, an organization in which managers have difficulty coping with the complexity and volume of information or with the lack of appropriate information for making decisions or recognizing problems may require a shift in organization structure or additional systems to collect information. At the lower right-hand corner of the matrix, problems may be known whereas solutions have yet to be found. Finding cures to cancer or meeting EPA automobile emission standards for 1985 are representative of such unfound solutions.

The focus of decisions in an organization are seldom stable and will migrate across the matrix. For example, products or services that serve markets at one point in time are likely to be obsolete a decade later. If the products or services are not obsolete, then the process or procedures by which they were made or delivered will be. As a result, strategic managers must be constantly searching for new products or services or processes that represent potential threats or opportunities in the long run.

Technological change introduces the greatest variety of uncertainties into the strategic manager's world:

1. It may obsolete his products and/or processes.
2. Its impact is difficult to forecast in details that will aid decision makers.
3. It requires major investments, especially in production and marketing, to take advantage of new technologies.
4. Commitments to engineering, construction, and operations must be made before new technologies become stable.

As shown in Exhibit 11-2, investment recovery may lag far behind the decisions that commit the organization to new technologies or products.

Investment in basic and applied research has the greatest potential for impacting future replacements for current business strategies. However, this is only a small part of the total commitment necessary to take advantage of such opportunities. Investment in factories, employee training, distribution channel development, and promotions become the more significant investments, and is required before any guarantee of success can be made. As a result, those decisions

EXHIBIT 11-2: Financial Impact of the Product Life Cycle

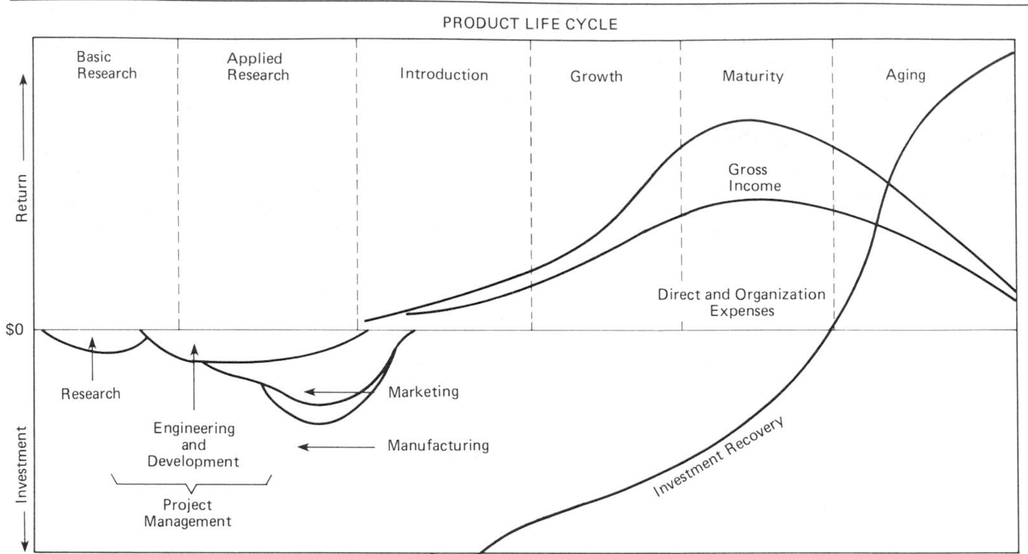

Source: Adapted from M. J. Mills, "The Boardroom Challenge of New Products," *Directors Handbook* (London: McGraw-Hill Publishing Co., 1979) p. 475.

that have the greatest potential for impacting the organization's future must be made under the most uncertain of situations.

As an organization's problems move into the "unknown" area of the problem-solution matrix, the more critical it becomes for the organization to establish a problem-solving "approach" for identifying problem-solution scenarios that can be evaluated in terms of the specific strengths and weaknesses of the organization. It is in this decision-making process that strategic management can instill discipline into the organization's culture. But once commitments are made, strategic management requires administrative skills in deciding how to allocate financial and human resources in a manner that will most effectively achieve desired ends. Exhibit 11-3 integrates the seven Ss described in Chapter 2 into the problem-solution matrix. Although we have artificially separated these management elements, such a separation can be helpful in determining which elements should be emphasized in the decision-making process. For example, the *uncertain* strategic decision area will likely require a heavy emphasis on shared goals and management style as organizational complexity increases. It is also the area in which top management involvement is essential because of the potential impact that such decisions may have on the future direction and growth of the organization.

The central area of the matrix, extending from upper left- to lower right-hand corners represents an area of intermediate risk where problem-solving responsibilities can be delegated through structure and/or the systems that allocate key staff and skills. A majority of staff and subunit managers will be involved in such intermediate risk-level decisions. The lower left-hand area of the matrix represents the area of lesser organizational uncertainty and can generally be handled through resource allocations in support of strategies that are implemented

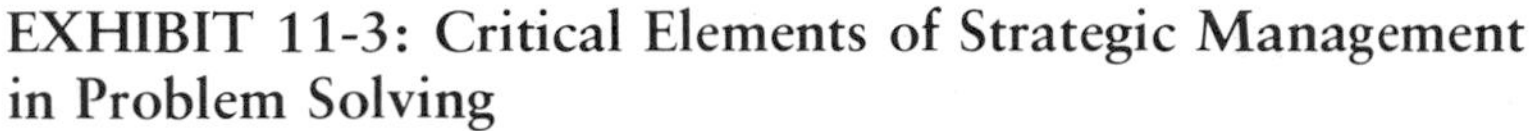

EXHIBIT 11-3: Critical Elements of Strategic Management in Problem Solving

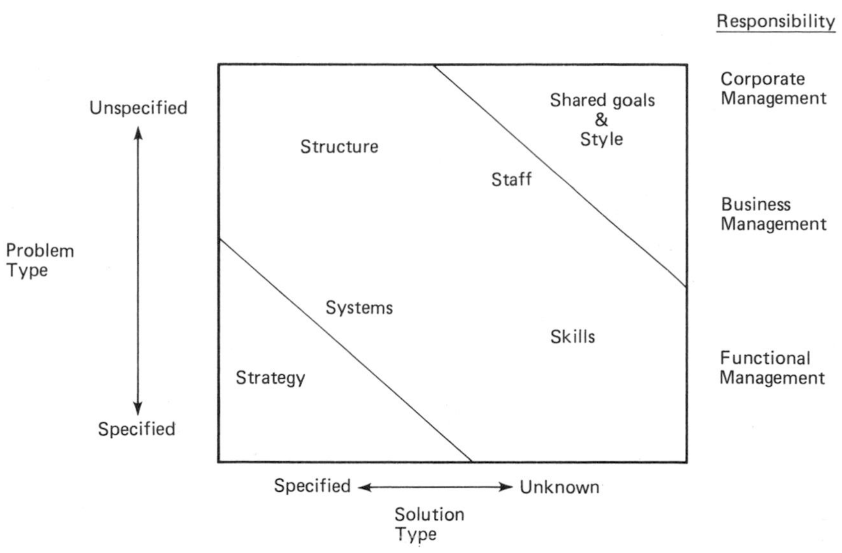

by functional specialists. The most critical concern in this area is the systems necessary to track performance of strategies against objectives agreed upon by management. Managing the organization's decision-making capabilities is then a key function of general management and the essence of delegating strategic management decisions and resources.

EVOLUTION OF STRATEGIC MANAGEMENT RESPONSIBILITIES

Since organizational strategy results from the consistency of decisions and behaviors of strategic managers and the organization's capabilities, we need to keep in mind that as organizations evolve they will increase the number of people involved in strategic management activities. Exhibit 11-4 depicts the change in responsibilities for strategic management functions as organizational evolution occurs. In small organizations, the chief executive will be the key decision maker and will carry the major burden of all strategic management responsibilities. As pointed out, heavy operating or administrative responsibilities can leave little time for more analytic, future-oriented, strategic planning. As the organization grows, the administrative and operating burdens are transferred to lower levels of the organization. Such change will require that the chief executive spend a greater amount of time making sure that strategic decisions "fit" with the shared goals and the organization's capabilities.

Whereas top management may be most concerned with strategic decisions confronting the organization, strategic management requires that problem-solving disciplines be explicitly incorporated into the organization's decision-making processes. Whereas responsibility for the future viability of the organization rests with top management, the organizational structure, staff, skills, and systems can

EXHIBIT 11-4: The Changing Role of the CEO as the Organization Becomes More Complex

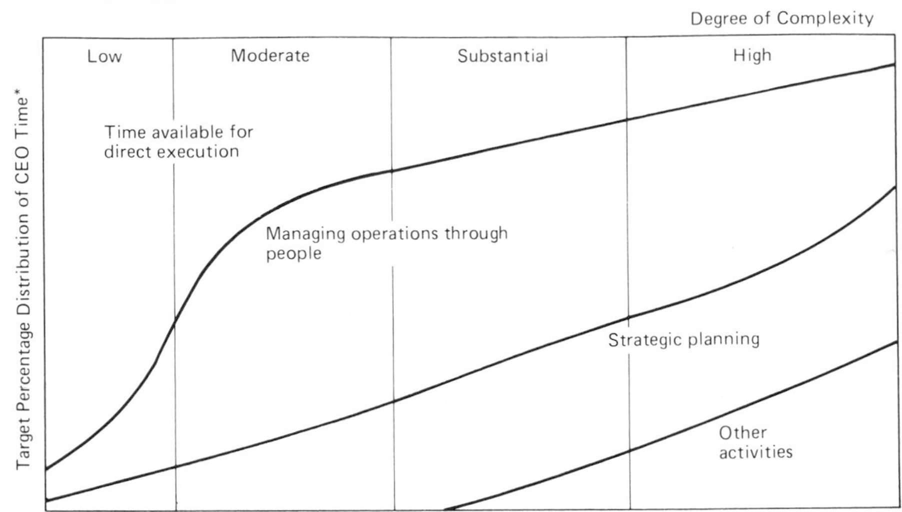

Source: Donald K. Clifford, Jr., *Managing the Threshold Company* (New York: McKinsey & Company, 1973), p. 21. Reproduced by permission.

be used to decentralize many administrative and operating decisions to lower levels. Tracking the performance of lower-level decision makers then becomes increasingly important to top management since even routine problems can become critical if they are poorly managed over longer periods of time.

The more complex the organization, then, the greater is the communication problem and the greater is the need for more formal decision-making procedures. In Exhibit 11-5, we have identified some of the elements that can signifi-

EXHIBIT 11-5: The Evolution of Strategic Management Responsibilities

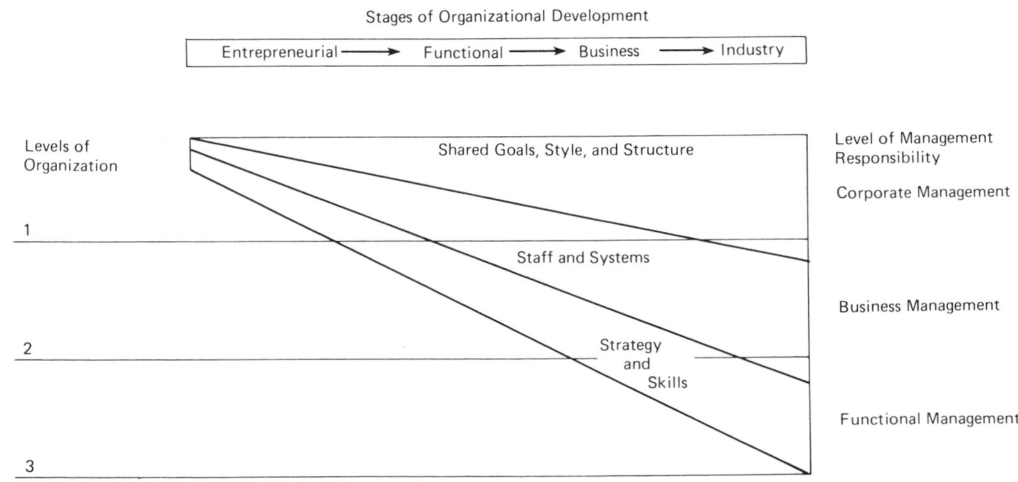

cantly affect strategic decision making. The importance and focus of decisions of strategic management can be identified by level as the size and complexity of the organization increases.

MAKING STRATEGIC DECISIONS

It should be obvious that decisions are seldom made unless there is a need for them. In essence, no decisions would have to be made if there were no problems to resolve. For this reason, problem solving and decision making tend to be the same process in strategic management. To understand the basic elements of this process, consider the following phases of decision making:[3]

1. monitoring the organization's environment as to whether problems exist.
2. defining the nature of the problem.
3. specifying the level of uncertainty in potential solutions.
4. determining what organizational capabilities will be required in the decision-making process.
5. appraising alternative courses of action in terms of organizational goals and problem-solving effectiveness.
6. selecting the best course of action to fit the situation and the organizational capabilities.
7. implementing the course of action and monitoring its effectiveness.

Since the organization's problem-solving capabilities will be key to its long-term success, top management must ensure their development. Recognition of problems before they become crises requires that performance standards be established against which results can be tracked. Setting organizational goals and tracking performance is one way to establish "crises identification" criteria for the organization.

MANAGING ORGANIZATIONAL PERFORMANCE

Most organizations have performance measures for individuals as well as for organizational units. The majority of these measures can be numerically specified, although it is not always easy to do so. At the functional level, Exhibit 11-6 lists the most frequently used measures as output, quality, and costs. At the business level, market share, growth in sales, profits, and return on investment are common measures. At the corporate level, sales, revenues, returns on investment, and productivity measures are popular. Individual measures can also be tied to financial performance such as sales and expenses, but are increasingly being focused toward market share, productivity, or program accomplishments. However, the vast majority of these measures are short-term measures.

The selection of performance measures should be tied to organizational objectives and strategies. The monitoring of these measures should then indicate the degree of strategy accomplishment. An indication of actual unit and/or in-

[3] Adapted from E. R. Archer, "How to Make Business Decisions," *Management Review* (February 1980): 54–61.

EXHIBIT 11-6: Organizational Performance Measures

	Long-Term Measures	Intermediate-Term Measures	Short-Term Measures
Corporate Management	• Purpose • Business Mix • Image (Values)	• Structure • Cash Flow • Risks	• Sales • Revenues • Returns • Productivity
Business Management	• Objectives • Stability • Market Position	• Staff • Investments • Strategies	• Market Share • Growth • Profits • Returns
Functional Management	• Milestones • Skills	• Capacity • Equipment • Materials	• Output • Quality • Costs

dividual performance requires that a goal be developed for current performance against which actual results can be compared. This often requires that special reporting documents be prepared to ensure that these measures are the ones which are tracked.

Tracking Financial Performance

The matrix shown in Exhibit 11-7 shows some general performance measures that might be used to measure strategic and operating performance. Measures of market development, for example, would project increased sales and marketing expenses. Costs affecting profitability levels would be monitored to ensure their stability. Withdrawal from businesses would expect reductions in sales and would require cutbacks in marketing expenses and investments in order to increase profitability. Measures of management performance would tie to productivity measures, reducing costs and expenses per unit sold, which affect overall profitability.

Other internal measures might include product development expenses, levels of value added, capacity utilization, process development expenses, bad debt levels, and cash flow. External measures might include supply prices, number of distributors and customers, market share of the firm and its competition, new market entry, and penetration. The variety of measures is endless, but should be tied to the objectives to be achieved.

Performance and Life Cycle

One would expect that the objectives and, therefore, performance measures would change over the life of an industry or product. Exhibit 11-8 indicates the kind of profit and cash flow that can be expected over the life of a new product from its conception through its termination. As one might expect, the major

EXHIBIT 11-7: Organizational Performance Measures

Strategy Focus \ Performance Measures	Sales	Cost of Goods Sold	Margin	Sales/Administrative Expenses	Profit	Fixed Asset Investment	Return on Assets
1. Marketing position	▲	√	√	▲	√		√
2. Go overseas	▲		√	▲	√	√	√
3. Production costs		▼	▲	▼	▲	▲	√
4. Efficient Management		▼	▲	▼	▲		▲
5. Harvest the business	▼			▼	▲	▼	▲

Source: Garrett E. Lion, "Measuring Strategic Performance," *A Management System for the 1980s* (Cambridge, Mass.: Arthur D. Little, Inc., 1979), p. 28.

investment and cash requirement comes in the earliest phases of development. Whereas sales may follow the normal life-cycle pattern after introduction, profits do not generally occur until sales reach a level that is adequate to support operations.

The expected level of investment recovery from profits and cash flow can be expected to increase over the life of the product. This is conditioned, however, on the strength of the organization's competitive position. As indicated, the stronger the competitive position the shorter is the period before investment recovery and profitability. Therefore, performance measures relating to competitive market position can be critical to financial performance. Exhibit 11-9 provides descriptions of other key financial measures.

Tracking Actual Performance

Tracking the actual performance of an organizational unit or individual requires that the specified performance measures and their target levels become formal reporting documents. Without a formal record of the contract (e.g., to agreed upon measures and their target levels), it is difficult to hold members

EXHIBIT 11-8: Financial Performance and Position Over the Product Life Cycle

	Life Cycle Stage			
Competitive Position	Introduction	Growth	Maturity	Aging
Dominant	Possible profit Cash user	Profit Cash user/ generator	High Profit Cash generator	Profit Cash generator
Strong	Loss Cash user	Profit Cash user	Profit Cash generator	Profit Cash generator
Favorable	Loss Cash user	Some profit Cash user	Profit Cash generator	Profit Balanced cash flow
Tenable	Loss Cash user	Loss Probable cash user	Some profit Balanced cash flow	Some profit Balanced cash flow
Weak	Loss Cash user	Loss Probable cash user	Loss Probable cash user	Loss Write off

accountable or to track all aspects of their performance. Exhibit 11-12 shows an example of the kind of format that can be used. Performance indicators are broken down between current highlights, intermediate targets (e.g., sales force levels and marketing expenses), and longer-term product-market measures. Variances between actual and planned performance can also be included in these forms. Other graphic forms of presentation can also be used. The actual report should be designed to meet the needs of the system.

WATCHING FOR RISKS

Thus far we have focused most heavily on techniques that can be used to monitor the organization's business environment and lead to the recognition of strategic alternatives. The actual selection of one course of action depends heavily on the situation involved, the players, the expected events, and the available resources. One might even consider the decision-making process as a form of gambling.

In making decisions that impact the organization's future, it is important to build on unique capabilities which are likely to be important in the future.

Past technology, production processes, and products may be obsolete in the future even though they were once competitive successes.

Recognizing the limitations of both your firm and your competition's capabilities can specify areas of risk and opportunity. By attacking the weak areas of competitors, your competitors can be diverted from building on their strengths, or vice versa. For example, a competitor's low price and heavy marketing approach may force a product innovator to divert funds from R&D areas to production and marketing areas. Such actions can change the assumed likelihood of success that originally caused a decision to be made. Competitive responses, therefore, must be appraised as part of the problem-solving process.

Effective decision making can reduce the basic risk level of an organization. For example, organizations that effectively monitor environmental changes and life cycles can take early advantage of such changes. For example, OSHA regulations created a new safety equipment industry. Market leadership changes as products move through the product life cycle and require new strategic thrusts. Being responsive to such changes protects current business positions and opens competitive opportunities.

It is also possible for top management to manage risk levels and encourage creativity through the use of small investments in mock-ups and production prototypes. Many firms today are instituting a form of "wild hair" program that allows employees to do initial development work on ideas of their own. Development of demonstration prototypes keeps organizations from making major investments in projects that still have "bugs" in them or may never be acceptable to the market. Developing a wide variety of prototypes opens the business alternatives that are available to the organization and increases the likelihood that one prototype may ultimately prove to be successful. As one executive explained, "It's like betting on the horse after it crosses the finishing line." It therefore reduces the uncertainty of the decision.

MANAGING RISK LEVELS

Whereas financial criteria are commonly used for decision making, they are very limited in actually assessing the level of risk inherent in a given alternative or course of action. As one evaluates decisions based upon inherent risk levels, it then becomes easier to adjust the probability levels of achieving a projected level of financial performance.

As part of the strategy decision-making process, that of selecting among business or functional alternatives, consider the analysis of general product/market alternatives shown in Exhibit 11-11. Alternatives can have risk levels assessed in response to their fulfillment of the criteria established for the decision. For example, market-oriented alternatives would have lower risk levels if there was high synergy with current operations and low investment requirements. The less in-house competence and the greater the required investment, the higher is the risk. Production alternatives that can use existing facilities will have lower risks than those requiring significant new capacity. Technology alternatives based on available know-how have less inherent risk than those requiring breakthroughs. At the same time, future success requires that manageable

EXHIBIT 11-9: Financial Performance Ratios

FINANCIAL PERFORMANCE:	MEASURE (RATIO)		OBJECTIVE INDICATION
Profitability	1. Gross profit margin	$= \frac{\text{Sales—Cost of Goods Sold}}{\text{Sales}}$	measures coverage of operating costs
	2. Operating profit margin	$= \frac{\text{After Tax Profits Before Interest}}{\text{Sales}}$	measures operating performance excluding cost of capital
	3. Return on Sales	$= \frac{\text{After Tax Profits}}{\text{Sales}}$	measures overall cost-price structure
	4. Return on Total Assets	$= \frac{\text{After Tax Profits + Interest}}{\text{Total Assets}}$	measures return on total investment excluding cost of capital
	5. Return on Net Worth	$= \frac{\text{After Tax Profits}}{\text{Total Equity}}$	measures return on stockholder's cash investment
	6. Return on Common Equity	$= \frac{\text{After Tax Profits—Preferred Dividends}}{\text{Total Equity—Preferred Stock}}$	measures return on stockholder's cash investment
	7. Earnings per share	$= \frac{\text{After Tax Profits—Preferred Dividends}}{\text{Number of Common Shares Outstanding}}$	measures earnings available to common share owners
Cash Liquidity	1. Current ratio	$= \frac{\text{Current Assets}}{\text{Current Liabilities}}$	measures coverage of short-term creditor liabilities
	2. Quick ratio	$= \frac{\text{Current Assets—Inventory}}{\text{Current Liabilities}}$	measures ability to pay off short-term creditor liabilities
	3. Inventory to working capital	$= \frac{\text{Inventory}}{\text{Current Assets—Current Liabilities}}$	up working capital
Operating Effectiveness	1. Inventory Turnover	$= \frac{\text{Sales}}{\text{Finished Goods Inventory}}$	provides measure of inventory adaquacy when compared to industry
	2. Fixed Asset Turnover	$= \frac{\text{Sales}}{\text{Fixed Assets}}$	provides measure of capital intensity and sales productivity when compared to industry

	Ratio	Formula	Description
	3. Total Asset Turnover	$= \frac{\text{Sales}}{\text{Total Assets}}$	provides measure of asset utilization and volume adequacy when compared to industry
	4. Accounts Receivable Turnover	$= \frac{\text{Annual Credit Sales}}{\text{Accounts Receivable}}$	measures average length of time required to collect from credit sales
	5. Average Collection Period	$= \frac{\text{Accounts Receivable}}{\text{Total Sales} \div 365 \text{ days}}$	measures average length of time (days) required to receive payment from sales
	6. Employee Productivity	$= \frac{\text{Sales}}{\text{Number of employees}}$	measures labor productivity when compared to industry
Capital Utilization	1. Debt to Assets	$= \frac{\text{Total Debt}}{\text{Total Assets}}$	measures the use of borrowed funds to finance operations
	2. Debt to Equity	$= \frac{\text{Total Debt}}{\text{Total Stockholders Equity}}$	measures the use of borrowed funds versus owners funds
	3. Long-Term Debt to Equity	$= \frac{\text{Long-Term Debt}}{\text{Total Stockholders Equity}}$	measures the balance between debt and equity in the long-term capital structure
	4. Interest Coverage	$= \frac{\text{Profit Before Int. \& Taxes}}{\text{Total Interest Changes}}$	measures riskiness of firm in its ability to pay interest
	5. Fixed Charge Coverage	$= \frac{\text{Profit Before Taxes, Int. \& Lease Charges}}{\text{Total Interest \& Lease Charges}}$	measures riskiness of firm in its ability to pay fixed charges
Stockholder Returns	1. Dividend Yield on Common Stock	$= \frac{\text{Annual Dividend Per Share}}{\text{Market Price Per Share}}$	measures annual return to shareholders
	2. Price Earnings	$= \frac{\text{Market Price Per Share}}{\text{After Tax Earnings Per Share}}$	measures market perception of firm's riskiness and growth potential
	3. Dividends Payout	$= \frac{\text{Annual Dividends Per Share}}{\text{After Tax Earnings Per Share}}$	measures percentage of profits paid to shareholders
	4. Cash Flow Per Share	$= \frac{\text{After Tax Profits + Depreciation}}{\text{Number Common Shares Outstanding}}$	

EXHIBIT 11-10: Tracking Actual Performance

PERFORMANCE INDICATORS

YEAR TO DATE				THIS MONTH		
Actual	Plan	Last Year		Actual	Plan	Last Year
			Current Highlights			
			Intermediate Goals			
			Product-Market Position			

Source: Adapted from Garrett E. Lion, "Measuring Strategic Performance," *A Management System for the 1980s* (Cambridge, Mass.: Arthur D. Little, Inc., 1979), p 32.

EXHIBIT 11-11: Analysis of Product/Market Alternatives

	Risk Assessment	
Strategic Questions	*Lower Risk*	*Higher Risk*
MARKETING ASPECTS		
What strategic need is filled?	Protect company position Meet future customer needs	Applications not developed Market not developed
What is product line effect?	Increase tie-in sales Little effect on existing line	Cut existing line sales Replace existing line
What is market trend?	Market is growing	Market is new Market is declining Market is static
What competition is there?	No competition Slight competition Some competition	Heavy competition
What is your product quality?	Superior to competitors No quality advantage	Product is inferior
What is your pricing position?	Distinct price advantage Price competitive	Can't meet competitor's price

Strategic Questions	*Risk Assessment* *Lower Risk*	*Higher Risk*
Will advantages last?	0–1 Years 2–4 Years	5–10 years 10–15 years
What service support is needed?	Negligible Moderate	Moderate Extensive
What is service position?	At customer's site Through current system	Requires new system Competition has unique system
What do customers demand?	They carry inventory	Need field inventories Need frequent deliveries
Will distribution change?	Use current modes	Require new modes
PRODUCTION ASPECTS		
Does the company have skills?	Use existing processes Use similar processes	Requires new technology
Does capacity exist?	Idle facilities available Some bexisting equipment can be used	Requires new facilities
Are raw materials and utilities available?	Available in-house long term Available on open market	Requires expanded facilities Not available on open market
How strong is competitor's technology	Little competition with in-house know-how Limited Competition	Few large competitors Readily available technology
What alternative uses exist?	Input to other products	Unique applications only
Are quality materials available?	Wide tolerances allowed Company has good controls	Standards will be tough to meet
Is the product hazardous?	Does not create hazards or pollution	Creates safety and pollution problems
RESEARCH AND DEVELOPMENT ASPECTS		
Is new technology required?	Available technology	Requires technological breakthrough
How much R&D is required?	Up to one year	Continuous support for over three years
Are patent rights available?	Rights can be leased	None exist Alternative must be developed

risks be taken. Few organizations can afford to gamble it all on one role of the dice, no matter how great the stakes.

Making the Best Decision

Until now, we have used a variety of matrices to help us understand organizational strengths and weaknesses and portfolio positions. Those same basic forms of analysis can be used to select between a variety of alternatives. Exhibit 11-12 shows how alternative decisions or courses of action might be selected according to potential outcomes and the ability to achieve those outcomes.

Consider three areas requiring trade-offs between strategic decisions: (1) resource decisions to ensure raw materials and hedge against inflation, (2) market niche decisions to enter high-growth areas, and (3) technology decisions to make product breakthroughs. We might find that heavy regulation, competition, and taxation, such as in oil distribution, makes our involvement very unattractive in the long run. Entering new markets, especially worldwide, may be virtually impossible for us. However, we might decide that a new product using our advanced technology might make obsolete current products and allow long-term leadership. In such cases heavy investments may be appropriate. Over the long term, decisions can be made to spread overall risks across all three of these areas.

With today's rapidly changing technologies, it will be increasingly difficult to determine the winning technologies of the future. Special attention will have to be given to identifying technologies with the highest probability of success and their highest volume applications. As was true in semiconductors, understanding the economics of the technology will allow the selection of applications to be consistent with the cost and value of the technology. With such deliberate

EXHIBIT 11-12: A Typical Decision Portfolio

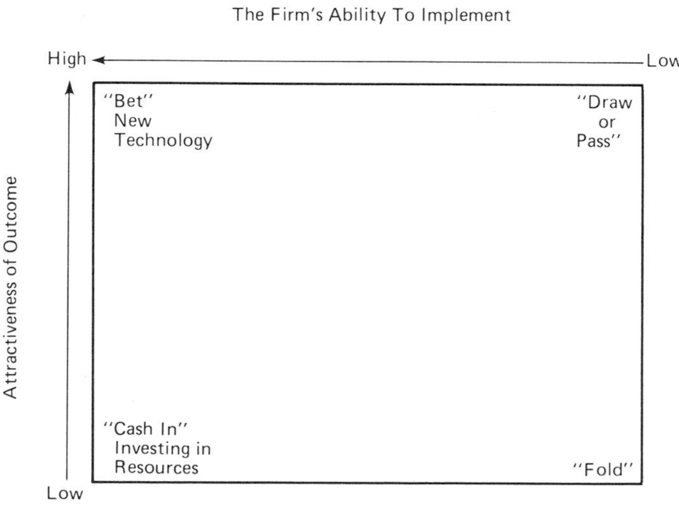

EXHIBIT 11-13: Comparing Decision Alternatives to Investments by Competition

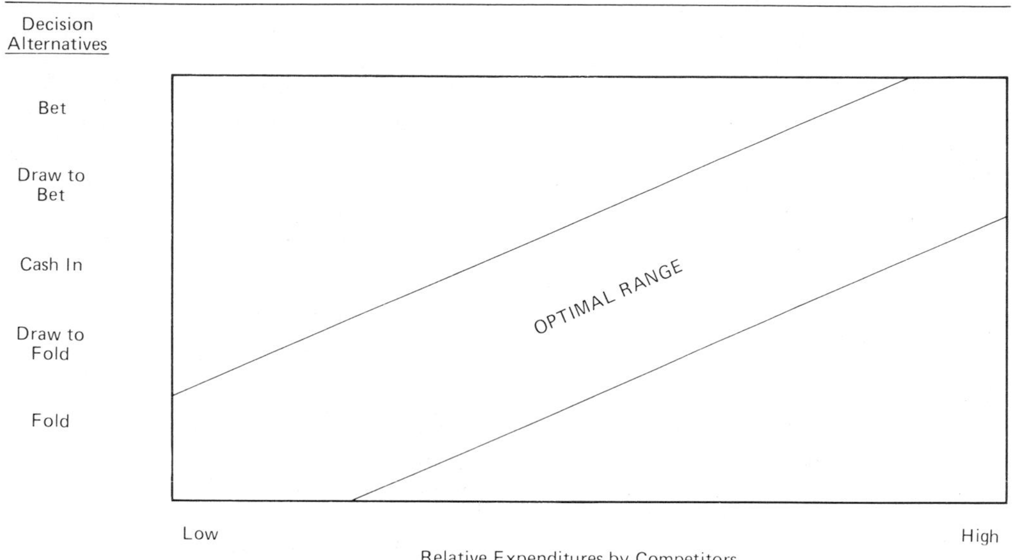

decision-making approaches, strategies can be developed to manage the risks and returns of one or more technologies.

In the same way that "alternative" matrices can be developed, we can also assess technology attractiveness and the technology position of the firm. However, an effective investment strategy must also be based on the level of spending planned by key competitors. Exhibit 11-13 provides a framework for assessing how quickly a decision is likely to have an impact based upon the support given by competition. For example, videotape players have had slow acceptance because of the lack of competitive support for a single technology. Once the technology is standardized, production economies are likely to reduce or hold prices while heavy competitive advertising expenditures generate growth in overall consumer demand. By deciding on those alternatives that have the greatest likelihood of success, risks can be reduced and returns maximized for the organization.

SUMMARY

We have concentrated on understanding key aspects of organizational decision making. It is the insistence and style of top management that causes problem-solving capabilities to develop within an organization. Education and practice are essential to the development of these problem-solving capabilities. Without an explicit determination on the part of management, it is unlikely that these capabilities will become a part of the organizational competence. Lack of such capabilities increases the organization's risk of failure.

FOCUS QUESTIONS

1. According to the four organizational styles described in Exhibit 10-3, how would you describe the organizational climate or atmosphere that is likely to result from each style? Which organization would you like to join? Why?
2. How does the role of top management change with organizational size? What management styles would be most appropriate for small organizations? For large organizations? Why?
3. How would you instill discipline into your organization if you were president of a large manufacturing company? How would you ensure the future growth of the firm? How would you control your risks?

ADDITIONAL READINGS

ALLISON, GRAHAM T. *Essence of Decision.* Boston: Little Brown and Co., 1971.

BARNARD, CHESTER, I. *The Functions of the Executive.* Cambridge, Mass.: Harvard University Press, 1968.

CHURCHMAN, C. WEST, et al., *Thinking for Decisions: Deductive Quantitative Methods.* Chicago: Science Research Associates, 1975.

CLIFFORD, DONALD K. JR., *Managing the Threshold Company.* New York: McKinsey and Company, 1973.

DRUCKER, PETER F. *Management: Tasks, Responsibilities, Practices.* New York: Harper & Row Publishers, 1974.

GANNON, MARTIN J. *Management: An organizational perspective.* Boston: Little, Brown and Co., 1977.

JONES, T. MORGAN. *Introduction to Decision Theory.* Homewood, Ill.: Richard D. Irwin, 1977.

LION, GARRETT E. *Measuring Strategic Performance: A Management System for the 1980s.* Cambridge, Mass.: Arthur D. Little, Inc., 1979.

STEINBRUNER, JOHN D. *The Cybernetic Theory of Decisions.* Princeton, N.J.: Princeton University Press, 1974.

12 Strategic Management: The Management of Change

As we approach the twenty-first century, it becomes increasingly evident that environmental and technological changes will affect us all. As with the industrial revolution, some two hundred years ago, new technology coupled with new societal goals and values have resulted in a steady increase in wealth and living standards through new levels of productivity and consumption. It was the corporation that provided the mechanism to harness this technology and achieve these new levels of productivity. Today, we again see significant changes in societal goals, needs, and values, as well as technology; and once again the corporation and its stockholders are in the center of this change.

Let us consider the likelihood that today's institutions will respond in a timely manner to this new set of changes. Because of its increasing influence over the corporation's future, perhaps the first stakeholder to consider is the government.

Government. In considering the motivation of government to change, we need to recognize that government is made up of elected officials, staffers, and bureaucrats—each having a different set of motivations. The elected politicians' objective is visible achievement and reelections. He or she needs to accomplish things, to be recognized, and, along the way, to achieve greater power. Although elected officials are charged with passing laws that reflect the needs and desires of society, such action is often not most expedient in assuring their reelection. Problems of energy, unemployment, inflation, stagflation, trade balances, rising interest rates, or dropping stock prices require solutions that may negatively affect the life-style of their constituents. Since the 1974 OPEC embargo, government has yet to pass a meaningful energy plan. The same lack of legislative activity exists with the Social Security system. Such action would necessitate life-style changes and, therefore, would reduce the probability of reelection.

Congressional staffers are probably one of the most powerful and influential groups in government. To have developed such a position, they first had to make the most powerful officials dependent on them. This required their knowing the needs and inclinations of their bosses and developing expertise in those areas of greatest interest. Bureaucrats who are most concerned with their own survival and advancement, achieve their goals by supporting those with power and influence. The increasing unionization of government employees also suggests a strong desire for maintaining the status quo. Taking on new activities is only supported when it creates new jobs and advancement for those in current positions.

Stockholders. Whereas the stockholder puts up equity and takes risk, only a small portion of today's equity is raised from the sale of stock. Also, most investing is done through mutual funds, pension funds, and trust funds with individuals being temporary investors with little continuing interest in the fate of the enterprise. In addition, over 60 per cent of the capital investment in the nation's one thousand largest manufacturing concerns has recently been financed internally under management control. Thus, corporate ownership is largely a legal fiction for claims on a fixed share of profits and nothing more. Societal desires in general will have more influence than stockholders.

Management. Many of today's successful organizations were established by an entrepreneur with a vision, such as Henry Ford and his Model T. or Dr. Land and his instant camera. But as the "founding father" leaves the corporation, other achievers will tend to rise to the top of the organization. As long as the corporation is considered to be growing faster than real GNP, these achievers will dominate management in search of prosperity, accomplishment, recognition, power, and status. Once the institution reaches maturity, it is no longer considered a growth company. Those who want to "hang on and survive" will take hold of the management reins while struggling to maintain the privileges and images of the past. These "preservers" will have difficulty breaking with the past and will struggle to maintain the status quo.

Society. Society's goals, needs, and values will ultimately determine the future of organizations. Obviously, self-seeking groups may cause short-term detours, but society will prevail in the long run. For example, when John Kennedy said "We shall place a man on the moon within this decade," he captured public support and was able to commit the resources necessary to do the job. However, when the U.S. defense industry attempted to get its commercial supersonic transport (SST), the impact on the societal values of environmentalists killed the project. Nuclear energy is in similar difficulty and, as a result of societal resistance, may never make a significant contribution to U.S. energy needs. In contrast, French and British politicians got support for their SST (the Concorde), and Japan and France are world leaders in nuclear power generation.

The largest portion of any society's population is going to be motivated by its cultural and religious values. In many Western countries, most individuals may be in search of their "own" security, pleasure, and friendships. Some Far Eastern countries are strongly religious and have societal values that stress "inner" serenity, wisdom, and accomplishment. Attempts to identify the future values of the majority in each society is of primary interest to many groups. In the United States, consensus suggests that "quality of life" will increase in importance as will the demand for income redistribution to close the rich-poor gap.

Although change is expected to increase in the future, it is also apparent that not all groups of individuals will be ready or motivated to change with the times. Thus change is an important management issue that will become even more pervasive in the future. It requires managers to be able to introduce changes in strategy, technology, and/or organizational characteristics that will enable their organizations to adapt to changes in their external environment. Exhibit 12-1 suggests that we have moved beyond strategic management to the need for "real-time" management of strategic issues and surprise. Such real-time management

EXHIBIT 12-1: Evolving Management Systems

		← Periodic Review		→	← Real Time Intervention	→
	Control	Long Range Planning	Strategic Planning	Strategic Management	Strategic Issue Management	Surprise Management
Objective	Control Deviations	Anticipate Growth	Change Strategic Thrusts	Change Strategic Thrusts and Capabilities	Prevent Strategic Surprises and Respond to Threats/ Opportunities	Minimize Surprise Damage
Basic Assumption	Past Repeats Itself	Past Trends Continue	New Trends and Discontinuities	New Thrusts Demand New Capabilities Organizations Resist Change	Discontinuities Are Happening Faster than Normal Response Time Can Handle	Strategic Surprises Occur
Limiting Assumption	Change is Slower Than Response	Future Will Be Like the Past	Change is Welcome. Past Strengths Future Thrusts	Future Is Predictable	Future Trends Are OK	Future Trends Are OK

Source: Adapted from H. Igon Ansoff, "Strategic Issue Management," *Strategic Management Journal* 1, (1980): 131–148.

will be directed toward efforts to keep current operations going during the periods of rapid change or crisis.

THE ADAPTIVE ORGANIZATION

It is unlikely that organizations that have operated in a stable environment over a long period of time will be prepared to make rapid changes. Such organizations may still be very successful and have highly effective strategies and very efficient organizations. However, as was evident in the U.S. automobile industry, that does not mean that the organization has the capacity to engage in an ongoing self-reexamination which is aimed at identifying incongruities between organizational elements (McKinsey's 7-Ss) and planning for needed changes in those components. The uncertainties of environmental and organizational changes can, in fact, create chaos, unless the organization has developed change responsiveness behaviors. An organization must design flexibility into its system if there is to be minimal disruption during change.

Organizations that are responsive to change must design organizational elements to be consistent with the needs for change. Exhibit 12-2 describes some organizational characteristics that "fit" the demands for change in different environments. Our concern today is that unstable and turbulent environments are causing greater uncertainty, complexity, and conflict within organizations. To meet the demands of more turbulent environments, more specialized, temporary, and modular forms of organization will be required. Such organizational configurations, however, will render obsolete, traditional assumptions about authority, control, incentives, and hierarchy. In fact, it suggests organizations with characteristics similar to the successful companies described in Chapter 11.

An adaptive organization must be able to sense problems resulting from incongruities between organizational components, respond to such information

EXHIBIT 12-2: Matching Organizations and Environments

Environmental States	Stable: – slow changes – small changes	Transitional: – slow changes – large changes	Unstable: – rapid changes – small changes	Turbulent: – rapid changes – large changes
Organizational States	Directive	Delegative	Matrix (Distributive)	Modular (Distributive)
Organizational Characteristics	Functional Standardization	Decentralized Task Focus	Project or Product Task Focus	Temporary Teams That Self-destruct
	Authority Based Leadership	Delegated Decision Authority	Dual Technical Administrative Supervision	Problem-Solving Orientation
	Formalized Downward Communication	Management by Exception	Emphasis on Task Coordination	Mission Directed Coordination
	Control by Budgets and Standards	Control by Profit Incentives	Control by Rewards and Mobility	Control by Inter-team Competition

Source: Adapted from D. Basil and C. Cook, *The Management of Change* (London: McGraw-Hill Book Co., Ltd, 1974), p. 181.

with changes, and still continue to test new incongruities that may require future change. This capability to engage in ongoing self-examination to identify incongruities in organizational components determines the health of the organization. A healthy, adaptive organization is more likely to maintain organizational effectiveness through its strategic thrusts and efficiency in its implementation over the long term.

It is important also to understand that planned change is unlikely to occur until the organization is ready for change. That is, change will only occur when the costs to the individual members are outweighed by other positive factors. The relationship between the cost of change and support for change can be expressed as follows:[1]

$$\text{Change} = (D \times M \times P)/C$$

where D = Dissatisfaction with the status quo
M = A new model for managing the organization
P = A planned process for managing change
C = Cost of change to individuals and groups.

If one of these support elements is weak or lacking, then attempts to change the organization are likely to receive resistance or fail.

Change requires that the individuals responsible for the change process are sufficiently dissatisfied with the status quo (D); that there is a new approach for managing the organization (M); and that the planned methods for implementing the change are expected to be effective (P). Effective change efforts require that all three of these elements exist and that they provide sufficient impetus for change to overcome the perceived costs of change (C).

Dissatisfaction. Recognizing that current performance is inadequate to meet the needs of the organization is a fundamental requirement for change to take place. Managers will seldom attempt to change an organization without believing that an impending crisis exists. The more sensitive the organization is to organizational incongruities, the greater is its likelihood of proactively foregoing crisis through early adaptations.

The following are some of the conditions necessary for organizations to maintain their sensitivity:

1. Competent environmental-sensing functions, such as market research and technology assessments, to monitor changes in the external environment.
2. Ongoing processes for collecting data to assess the internal functioning of the organization, the efficiency of its operations, and the attitudes of its people.

Information gained from these sensing systems must be compared against established standards or assumptions. When variations occur, warning signals need to be sounded.

Plans for Change. Changes in the way organizational members behave requires a planned process of introduction. Several components of this process include:

[1] Michael Beer, *Organization Change and Development* (Glennview, Ill.: Scott Foresman and Co., 1980), pp. 31–32.

1. Creating an awareness of the need for change.
2. Diagnosing the situation and determining the direction and specifications of change.
3. Communicating the proposed change to those involved.
4. Monitoring the change and making the required adjustments.[2]

Underlying the change process is the assumption that explicit efforts are required to introduce and educate people about the need for and nature of change. This is imperative when change requires that members adopt new values and norms.

To encourage and support changed behaviors, explicit plans need to be developed. Several planning components include the need for:

1. Reinforcements of new behaviors through incentive systems, performance appraisal systems, and control systems.
2. Leadership role models to set an example.
3. Social interactions in which communication about changes can occur, individuals can be coached, and new group norms can be developed.
4. Selection of key people and replacements, and development of education programs to retrain displaced individuals.

It is essential to establish socialization mechanisms that will support changes. To this end, it is necessary to have managers who understand how to manage change, have the personal skills to do so, and have the mechanisms available to manage the change process.

Management Model. Preparing for changes in organizations requires the involvement of those who are in positions of power and authority. To ensure their involvement, it is necessary to (1) identify those affected: their backgrounds, experience, personality, and values; (2) make sure they understand how their current behavior and dispositions affect the organization and its behavior; and (3) have them understand the changes that will be required by them. To ensure that this type of self-evaluation and change is accepted, it is useful to have ongoing career development and performance evaluations that give managers data about themselves, and to develop their managerial skills and values. Without management's support, successful change is unlikely to occur.

BARRIERS TO ORGANIZATIONAL CHANGE

When an organization is not yet ready to change, as described previously, efforts to implement change are unlikely to be successful. However, delays can also occur for a variety of other reasons. For example, one organizational component may act as a roadblock to changes in another component. Exhibit 12-3 describes some of those components that may impinge on the responsiveness with which change occurs. Changes in style, skills, staff, or superordinate goals may, by their very nature, require the greatest amount of time to change. The lack of skills and staff can obviously impact on the ability of the organization to change its strategy or superordinate goals. The same problem might occur if interactions or information are not made available by proper structure and systems.

[2] Jay W. Lorsch, "Managing Change" ICCH Case #9-474-187.

EXHIBIT 12-3: Elements Impacting Organizational Change

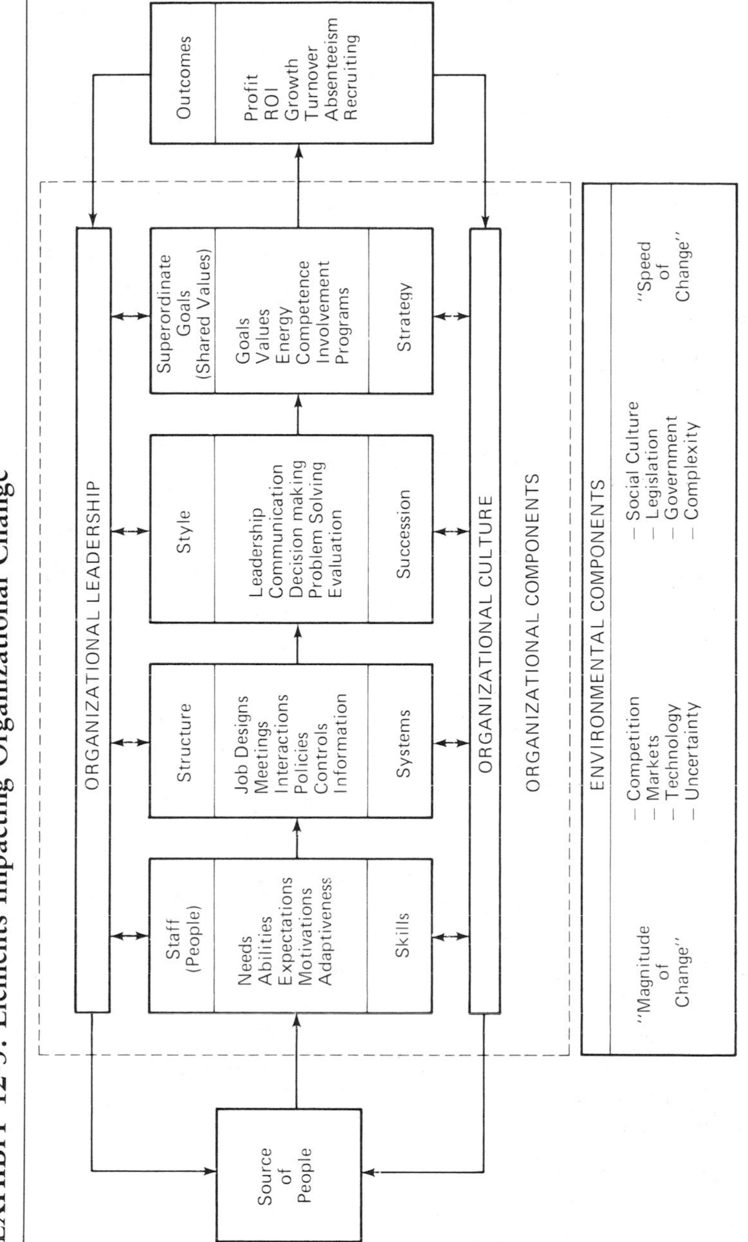

Source: Adapted from Michael Beer, *Organization Change and Development* (Glennview, Ill.: Scott Foresman & Co., 1980), p. 38.

Management style and organizational succession, however, are probably the areas of greatest concern in organizational change. When these behavioral components are not consistent with proposed change in other areas, change will be especially difficult to bring about. Some of the most likely problems include:

1. When top management is too involved in day-to-day decisions, changes impacting long-range performance will be neglected.
2. When change decisions are made by people who lack the knowledge, information, or competence to implement them, it is unlikely that these changes will have support (e.g. costs will be perceived as being too high).
3. When groups of individuals within the organization are predisposed or motivated not to change, as suggested in the introduction to this chapter, obtaining accurate information required to design changes may not be possible.
4. When the leadership or culture of the organization does not support open communication, diversity of opinions, or problem solving of conflicts; appropriate assessments and plans for change are unlikely to be adequate to support change.
5. When managers feel that their career opportunities are limited, and their position, power, or security is threatened, they will not be ready or motivated to support organizational change.

The combination of interactions between these organizational components will determine the organizational culture. The sheer momentum of culture, much like the ocean's currents, will then affect the ability of the organization to change. Such a culture will be adapted to the stability of its environment and, though it may be a success (both efficient and effective), it may place heavy constraints on the organization's ability to change. Until the new skills, systems, strategy, and goals are consistent, the changed organization will be inefficient.

CONSIDERATIONS IN PLANNING CHANGE

Thus far, we have discussed many of the concerns and problems which are likely to affect changes in organizations. With this background, let us now consider some of the factors which are most likely to impact the change process itself. These factors include:

1. the use of power.
2. the speed of change.
3. the likely resistance to change.
4. the behavioral norms about involvement.
5. the leadership style of management.
6. the size of the organization.
7. the locus of data.

The Use of Power

Power exists in all organizations and is used to influence behavior. Wherever consistency in the influence of behavior can be observed, a source of power can be identified. Let us consider the kinds of power that are likely to influence behavior within an organization.

"Law" and "societal norms" are two of the strongest sources of external power. They can affect every component in the organization. For example, equal employment laws affect the kinds of people that can be hired, health and safety laws affect the procedures and environment of operations, consumer protection laws can have a significant impact on the strategy, and securities laws have an impact on the style of management's relationship with its board of directors. Most of these laws originated from societal pressures.

The "actions," "charisma," and "resources/knowledge" displayed by, or at the disposal of, members of the organization are sources of power. In many cases, these may be linked to hierarchy. Job titles do not always help in the identification of these powers. For example, people who are known for their ability to "get the job done" can build a base for power, and those who are charismatic in attracting followers often move to higher positions by using such power. People who have control over budgets and cash flow decisions, or over human resource decisions become more powerful in times of economic decline.

Job security and control over one's own efforts are sources of power that are most important in changing times. When turbulent environments require greater organizational involvement by lower-level personnel, their decision to participate and stay in the organization is critical.

Power sources, however, are dependent upon the organization's leadership. The locus of power can be related back to the structure of organizations shown in Exhibit 12-2. In "directive" organizations, power will be kept at the top management levels. In "delegative" organizations, lower management levels are given control over specified tasks, resulting in their development of power over "actions" and "resources/knowledge." Delegative structures allow technical staff to develop power through their use of knowledge and contribution of efforts. In "distributive" organizations, power is allowed to build throughout the organization, leaving top management to rely heavily on its "charismatic" skills to coordinate the overall efforts of the organization.

Using power to influence behavior comes about in a variety of ways. Exhibit 12-4 lists a number of influence techniques that are commonly used in organizations. The use of threats may obtain compliance, but this would require also tight supervision and would create a bad working climate. Promises may achieve compliance, but would require rewards for support. Warnings and recommendations have little cost, but also have low levels of compliance. Totally indirect influence has little usefulness in organizations. Outside of direct control of rewards and punishments, influence can come through a variety of interview techniques such as disclosure, reflection, and probing of individual situations.

Within organizations, all of these techniques are used. Most individuals use some combination of these techniques. The success of an influencer's use of these techniques is dependent upon (1) his or her level in the hierarchy, (2) the use of positive or negative techniques, (3) the level of resources at his or her disposal, and (4) the level of skills or knowledge of the influencer. The greater the level of power, the more likely is the success one has in influencing others to change their behavior. Deciding the locus and structure of power is critical in determining what techniques will be used to implement change.

EXHIBIT 12-4: Usage and Benefits of Influence Modes

Mode	*Use Frequency*	*Advantage*	*Disadvantages*
Threat	3%	Highest levels of compliance	Produces dislike and requires surveillance
Promise	5%	Produces liking; moderate compliance levels	Requires high reward expenditures
Warning	5–10%	Little resource expense by user	Low compliance
Recommendation	7–12%	Little resource expense by user	Low compliance
Ecological control	Not measured	No influence appears exerted	Limited usefulness
Roundabout control	Not measured	Divorces actual influencer from attempt	Limited usefulness
Cue control	8–13%	Directed delivery of reward/punishment	Low effectiveness
Self-disclosure	3–25%	Provokes reciprocity	Requires disclosure of lying
Reflection	4–6%	Elicits information without delivering much in return	Nondirective
Probe	1–2%	Requires specific answers	Provokes counter-questions
All noninfluence	26–65%		

Source: From Thomas V. Bonoma and Gerald Zaltman, *Psychology for Management* (Boston: Kent Publishing Co., 1981), p. 173 © 1981 by Wadsworth, Inc. Reprinted by permission of Kent Publishing, a division of Wadsworth, Inc.

The Speed of Change

Change strategies should obviously be contingent upon the rapidity with which top management wants change to come about. The use of top management's power can speed up the introduction of change. Power-sharing approaches lead to more gradual change. The ideal form of change would be one that is consistent with the organization's culture and power structure. This would be most consistent with the organization's expectations. Where the speed of change is inconsistent with the culture, more explicit plans and mechanisms are required to overcome inherent resistance caused by the culture.

Change is bound to generate some anxiety on the part of affected individuals. The more slowly the change occurs, the greater the anxiety is likely to be. However, rapid change does not allow adequate time to deal with individual needs. Each manager needs to understand the approach that best suits the characteristics of his or her organization.

The Likely Resistance to Change

As described previously, for change to occur the motivation or perceived benefits of change must be considered to be greater than the cost. Whereas those in a position of power may make such a decision, individuals throughout the organization will not necessarily feel the same way. In fact, individual's jobs may be eliminated, or dramatically changed. Patterns of social relationships may be terminated and psychological contracts may be broken. At best, change is going to increase uncertainty for the individual by interrupting traditional patterns of behavior.

The variety of problems caused for an individual by change makes it only normal that some resistance will develop within the organization. The key to managing change, then, is to plan for resistance to occur and to develop mechanisms for dealing with it. Exhibit 12-5 describes six methods for overcoming resistance to change. Each method has its strengths and weaknesses and is dependent upon the time frame available for change to be carried out.

Educational and communication methods are most useful when information is inaccurate or inadequate. Participation and involvement methods are important where information and power is disbursed throughout the organization and are required for the design and implementation of change. Methods of facilitation and support are useful where people are having major adjustment problems. Methods of negotiation and agreement are needed when major power groups are going to lose out and can impede change. Where other techniques have failed, other methods of manipulation or co-option may work (e.g. transferring or promoting someone out of the way). When speed is most important, direct coercion through the use of power may be necessary.

The Behavioral Norms About Involvement

When organizational members take the thoughts, feelings, and attitudes of others into account before acting, there develops a convergence of viewpoints that we characterize as norms. Once these norms develop, members of the organization or group feel the need or pressure to conform to them. Such pressure is exerted independent of the manager, because individuals who deviate from the norms run the risk of isolation and rejection. Such norms, whether they are positive or negative, will tend to control individuals even though they may be outmoded or detrimental to the individual, group, or organization. For example, even though unions today support increased productivity, worker norms place "rate busters" under tremendous pressure. It takes crises as great as Chrysler's to cause restructuring of such norms to take place. In fact, managers often rely on the "clean sweep" of group members to restructure inappropriate norms.

In large and complex organizations, changes are likely to involve a great number of people. People who participate in the change process are likely to be much more committed to it and have a personal stake in its success. When the norms alienate members from being involved, it becomes very difficult to define

EXHIBIT 12-5: Methods Dealing With Resistance to Change

Approach	*Commonly used in situations*	*Advantages*	*Drawbacks*
Education + communication	Where there is a lack of information or inaccurate information and analysis	Once persuaded, people will often help with the implementation of the change	Can be very time-consuming if lots of people are involved
Participion + involvement	Where the initiators do not have all the information they need to design the change, and where others have considerable power to resist	People who participate will be committed to implementing change, and any relevant information they have will be integrated into the change plan	Can be very time-consuming if participators design an inappropriate change
Facilitation + support	Where people are resisting because of adjustment problems	No other approach works as well with adjustment problems	Can be time-consuming, expensive, and still fail
Negotiation + agreement	Where someone or some group will clearly lose out in a change, and where that group has considerable power to resist	Sometimes it is a relatively easy way to avoid major resistance	Can be too expensive in many cases if it alerts others to negotiate for compliance
Manipulation + co-optation	Where other tactics will not work, or are too expensive	It can be a relatively quick and inexpensive solution to resistance problems	Can lead to future problems if people feel manipulated
Explicit + implicit coercion	Where speed is essential, and the change initiators possess considerable power	It is speedy, and can overcome any kind of resistance	Can be risky if it leaves people mad at the initiators

Source: Reprinted by permission of the *Harvard Business Review*. Exhibit from "Choosing Strategies for Change" by John P. Kotter and Leonard A. Schlesinger (March–April 1979), p. 111.

or plan the need for change at the bottom of the organization. In such situations, it becomes especially important to manage the change process well and to include strategies for changing norms.

Some techniques that may aid attitude and behavior changes through changes in norms include the following:

Involve the Reference Group. All individuals who are expected to have the greatest impact need to be involved in determining the character of the new norms. Their support for the new behavior patterns or norms is fundamental to the success of change efforts. If those who strongly encompass the old norms are not a part of the change effort, it is unlikely that they will support the new norms.

Involve the Decision Makers. Those members of the organization who have the greatest amount of power and influence over organizational decisions need to understand the limitations of prevailing norms and be prepared to provide the leadership in establishing new norms. Whether the new norms support productivity improvements, quality improvement, or involvement, without the involvement and powerful impact of the "boss," it is unlikely that subordinates will be able to change their own behavior.

Take a Problem-Solving Approach. Since norms are not likely to be explicit, it becomes necessary to get participants to recognize the norms that regulate their behavior. A variety of techniques can be used to aid a group in developing problem-solving skills and applying those skills to their own problems (e.g., excessive absenteeism, high product returns). Through such approaches, they can identify the underlying causes for such problems.

Problem solving requires that objective facts and data be made available to the members. Through their discussions about the reasons for such problems, members become involved in the process. As emotions and feelings come to the surface, norms can be recognized and agreements reached about the need for new norms. Explicit statements then need to be developed about agreed-upon norms and follow-up procedures must be established to keep the organization from backsliding.

The Leadership Style of Management

Change strategies need to be consistent with the leadership styles of management. Leadership pertains to the way in which leaders get others to do what they want. Without followers, there are no leaders. If approaches are tried that are not consistent with the organization's norms about the use of power, then followers are likely to see the change process as synthetic, poorly designed, and unworthy of their support.

Managers' personalities and preferences affect their leadership styles. Although "participative" management concepts continue to be stressed, such training does not cause all leaders to practice participative management techniques. Managers' personalities and cognitive processes are not always logical or rational. For example, managers' approaches to leadership and problem solving depend on their perception and judgment of organizational activities.[3] Managers

[3]See Carl Gustav Jung, *Psychological Types* (New York: Harcourt Brace, 1923).

can "perceive" situations through either sensation or intuition. Sensation relies on the five body senses in determining reality whereas intuition uses unconscious inputs to determine realities. Managers can then make "judgments" about the situation through logical, analytical processes of thinking, or through their totally personal and subjective feelings. Exhibit 12-6 shows the kinds of distinctions that are made.

From these managerial preferences comes leadership and problem-solving styles that characterize most organizations. Based on preferences for judging and feeling, four management styles include:

1. autocratic managers (Intuition-Thinking).
2. autocratic-consultative managers (Sensation-Thinking).
3. Consensus managers (Sensing-Felling).
4. Stockholder managers (Intuition-Feeling).

These classifications can be used to describe basic approaches to leadership and problem solving, as shown in Exhibit 12-7.

Autocratic managers with intuitive-thinking preferences tend to enjoy ill-defined situations that require abstract skills for dealing with theoretical problems which can be dealt with in an impersonal manner. Autocratic-consultive managers with sensing-thinking preferences generally emphasize facts and details, use logic in reaching decisions, develop rules and regulations for judging performance, emphasize control and certainty, and concentrate on short-term goals. Consensus managers with sensing-feeling preferences emphasize the human side of problems, structure organizations to benefit people, and stress facts about people instead of tasks. Stockholder managers with intuitive-feeling preferences rely on gestalt perceptions of broad, human themes and avoid rules, regulations, and specifics.

The autocratic manager, then, is likely to generate new ideas and push for progress with enormous drive. Unfortunately, feelings of others can get badly hurt in the process through the manager's impatience and increasing challenges.

EXHIBIT 12-6: Managerial Preferences

I. APPROACH TO PROBLEM IDENTIFICATION

Sensing Types	*(Check)*	*Intuitives*	*(Check)*
Dislike new problems unless there are standard ways to solve them.	_____	Like solving new problems.	_____
Like an established routine.	_____	Dislike doing the same thing over and over again.	_____
Enjoy using skills already learned more than learning new ones.	_____	Enjoy learning a new skill more than using it.	_____
Work more steadily, with realistic idea of how long it will take.	_____	Work in bursts of energy powered by enthusiasm, with slack periods in between.	_____

I. APPROACH TO PROBLEM IDENTIFICATION

Sensing Types	*(Check)*	*Intuitives*	*(Check)*
Must usually work all the way through to reach a conclusion.	______	Frequently jumped to conclusions.	______
Are impatient when the details get complicated.	______	Are patient with complicated situations.	______
Are patient with routine details.	______	Are impatient with routine details.	______
Rarely trust inspirations, and don't usually get inspired.	______	Follow their inspirations, good or bad	______
Seldom make errors of fact	______	Often tend to make errors of fact.	______
Tend to be good at precise work.	______	Dislike taking time for precision.	______
Total	(______)	Total	(______)

II. APPROACH TO PROBLEM SOLVING

Thinking Types	*(Check)*	*Feeling Types*	*(Check)*
Are relatively unemotional and uninterested in people's feelings.	______	Tend to be very aware of other people and their feelings.	______
May hurt people's feelings without knowing it.	______	Enjoy pleasing people, even in unimportant things.	______
Like analysis and putting things into logical order. Can get along without harmony.	______	Like harmony. Efficiency may be badly disturbed by office feuds.	______
Tend to decide impersonally, sometimes ignoring other people's wishes.	______	Often let decisions be influenced by their own or other people's personal likes and wishes.	______
Need to be treated fairly.	______	Need occasional praise.	______
Are able to reprimand people or fire them when necessary	______	Dislike telling people unpleasant things.	______
Tend to relate well only to other thinking types.	______	Relate well to most people.	______
May seem hardhearted.	______	Tend to be sympathetic.	______
Total	(______)	Total	(______)

Source: Adapted from the Manual of the Myers-Briggs Type Indicator, 1962.

EXHIBIT 12-7: Managerial Style and Leadership Model

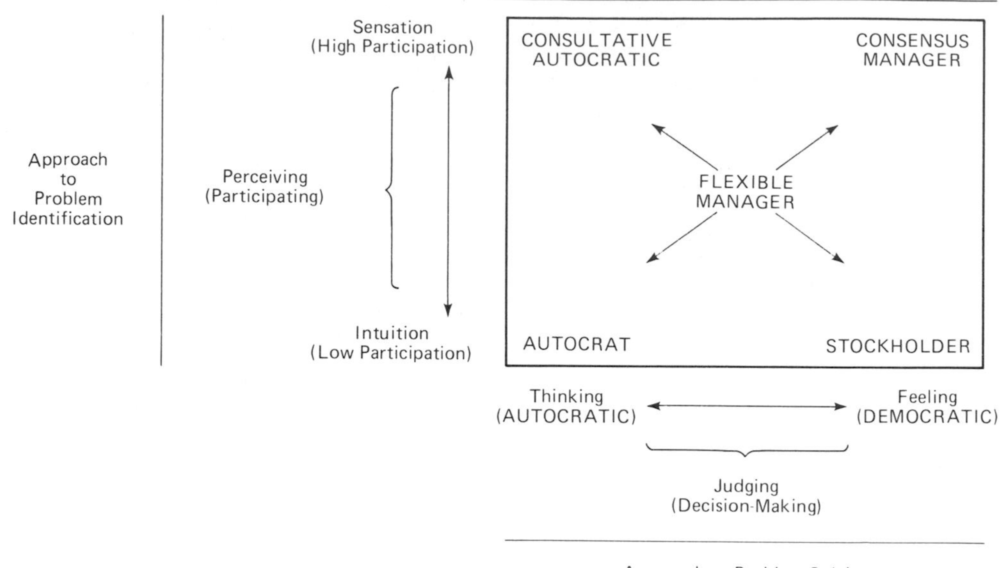

This manager enjoys problem solving and admires individuals showing logic, reason, and intelligence. Results are very important to this manager.

The autocratic-consultive manager is more likely to establish a stable system with effective managerial routines. Details will be kept under control and few decisions will be made on error of fact. Procedures and projects will be clear, well defined, and settled. Meetings will be efficient, well planned, and ordered. A formal, impersonal style will develop for managing the organization. Unfortunately, obsolete rules and procedures may have difficulty getting changed and may result in interpersonal problems. Efforts to develop the perfect organization may result in slow adjustments to external changes and create tensions for all those involved.

The consensus manager keeps in close touch with the organization's environment and is able to use the organization's people and system effectively to solve problems. High levels of abstraction are unlikely to be used, and, therefore, concepts of strategy and purpose will be thought academic. This creates a problem of inconsistent behavior and a short-term problem orientation.

The stockholder manager will encourage a democratically run organization and is likely to be quite charismatic as a leader. The organization is likely to be less structured with group-centered administration and decision making. Unfortunately, decisions are likely to be made based on personal likes and wishes rather than facts. Use of authority will be in conflict with personal values for "esprit de corps."

Each of these management styles will impact the kind of organization that is developed. Exhibit 12-8 incorporates some of the organizational characteristics that are likely to develop as a result of such leadership. Autocratic organizations will be characterized by top-down management that uses rigid performance standards and motivates through fear and punishments. Autocratic-

EXHIBIT 12-8: Impact of Management Style on Organizational Characteristics

	Organizational Characteristics					
Management Style	Objective Setting	Action Planning	Communication	Implementation	Control & Appraisal	Motivation
Autocratic	At top	Top determines plans and tasks	Top down	Follow orders	Rigid standards	Use fear, threats, & punishment
Autocratic-consultative	At top with some inputs	Top determines plans & tasks	Top controls policy	Follow directions	Use standards	Use rewards & some punishment
Consensus	Subordinates participate in goal making	Subordinates participate action planning	Consult subordinates in job related decisions	Moderate commitments	Use multiple performance measures	Use rewards, involvement, & some punishment
Stockholder	Networks of goals through participation	Subordinates determine tasks and activities	Groups set goals at all levels	Open communication based on trust & confidence	Track critical goals and standards	Use team involvement to achieve goals

consultative organizations will maintain top level control, but use some inputs and motivation. Consensus organizations will "involve" subordinates in all phases of management, but top management will still be involved. Stockholder organizations will be run by its members through the use of teams with minimal control of strategic issues by top management.

From these descriptions, it should be apparent that management style will significantly affect change strategies. The expectations of organization members will be that change decisions and their implementation will be carried out in the same manner as currently practiced. Changes directed at changing the organizational model to "fit" new environmental conditions (review Exhibit 12-2) will require special effort, a new management style, and heavy involvement of top management to convince members that "the new style is for real."

The Size of the Organization

As described in Chapter 8, the size and complexity of the organization is likely to have a significant impact on how quickly it can be changed. The larger the organization, the more complex are the interrelationships between organizational components and, therefore, the greater is the job of changing those interrelationships. Rather than describing those elements again, we direct the reader back to Chapters 8 and 10 for review.

The Locus of Data

The availability of relevant data is especially important in planning for organization change. If planners do not have such information, it is unlikely that they will be able to determine the exact need, direction, or likely consequences of change. The more disbursed the information is across the organization, the greater will be the need for widespread participation in the planning of change.

Today, pressure is increasing for top management to have more widespread access to information so that problems can be identified earlier. Increased turbulence is also requiring that more rapid changes take place, suggesting less participation in the change process. To meet these pressures, corporate computer-based information systems are being developed to provide for more widespread and timely access to information.

SUMMARY

Planning for organizational change requires explicit management. Without effective management, change is most likely to throw the organization out of balance. Effective organizational change requires a proper balance between the seven organizational elements of strategy, structure, systems, shared goals, staff, skills, and style. Finally, organizational change implies the deliberate management of succession since change is carried out through people.

Shared goals may have the greatest impact on organizational change. These goals may relate to specific organizational elements, especially skills. For example, the following goals have provided consistency for some very successful organizations. Service and staff innovation and productivity are fundamental to long-term success:

Organization	*Shared Goals*
AT & T	"universal service"
IBM	"customer service"
G.E.	"progress"
H.P.	"innovative people"
Dana	"productivity"
3M	"new products"

These goals become the focus for decision making and the driving logic for the organization's development.

"Strategy" translates these goals into customer value and competitive actions. "Structure" is used to manage organizational specialization and interaction and to ensure that properly trained "staff" are in the proper jobs. "Systems" provide for information transfer throughout the organization to ensure consistency and appropriateness of decisions. Top management's "style" will affect the organization's environment and determine what "goals" or "skills" will be maintained by the organization.

These seven organizational factors add to the complexity of strategic management functions, but allow for each to be understood and simplified. The key obviously is in finding the appropriate "fit" between all seven factors for a given organization. Exhibit 12-9 points out some of the issues in finding that fit. For example, small organizations may be the goal, but dewiring complex structures is not an easy task. To get simple, focused, externally oriented systems requires meticulous design and a consistent theme. Developing people and a culture that get the job done takes a long time. Developing a basic theme is easy, but getting people to believe and preach this theme is difficult. Limiting skill development may be impossible in complex environments. Focused strategies still require skills for the organization to achieve them. Developing a culture requires a separation of daily activities, a challenge to any manager.

EXHIBIT 12-9: McKinsey's 7-S Framework Summary

S Area	*Simple Message*	*Complex Message*
Structure	suboptimal units	"dewire"
Systems	simple, focused	all head same way
Staff	aimed at double tasks	"get on with it" environment
Superordinate goal	*A* theme	singling it out—not just a drill
Skills	sharpen the basics	manage complexity, bureaucracy
Strategy	execution	make execution a key skill
Style	attend to basics, a theme	manage busy agenda to free time
	"Keep it simple—keep it short"	

Source: "Findings from the Excellent Companies" (New York: McKinsey & Company, 1980), p. 117

FOCUS QUESTIONS

1. In planning for the future, what changes do you expect to have the greatest impact on business organizations? What actions are necessary to meet these changing conditions?
2. What strategic management philosophies do you expect to be most successful in the future?
3. In attempting to adapt an organization to changing environments, what would you be most concerned about? How would you go about changing an organization? How would the size of an organization affect your approach?

ADDITIONAL READINGS

ANSOFF, J. IGOR. "Strategic Issue Management." *Strategic Management Journal* (January 1980): 131–148.

BASIL, D. and C. COOK, *The Management of Change.* New York: McGraw-Hill Book Company, 1974.

KOTTER, JOHN P., and L. A. SCHLESINGER. "Choosing Strategies for Change." *Harvard Business Review* (March–April 1979).

MCCLELLAND, DAVID C., and D. H. BURNHAM. "Power Is the Great Motivator." *Harvard Business Review* (March–April, 1976): 100–110.

NEUSTADT, RICHARD E. *Presidential Power.* New York: John Wiley & Sons, Inc., 1960.

PART IV

Cases in Organizational Missions and Objectives

CASE ONE

Mr. Gatti's

ED D. ROACH and JACK D. EURE, JR.
Southwest Texas State University

Assignment Questions:

1. What is Jack Eure's business? How would you measure his success?
2. What has been Jack Eure's strategy? How would you evaluate it?
3. What should Jack Eure do now?

As he neared age 60, James R. Eure began to reflect over his career and business involvement of the past ten years. In those brief years he had built a substantial financial empire in the pizza business—one any entrepreneur would be proud of. Building the empire, though, had had its costs as Eure had devoted long, hard hours in establishing the business. He wondered if maybe he shouldn't try to "enjoy life" a little more. He looked at the construction delays on his new pizza restaurants and considered the impact the energy crisis would have on the eating habits of Americans. Eure thought again about his naturally pessimistic nature.

As he reflected upon the direction he ought to take, Eure thought about the earning capacity of the business and the volume it was doing. Perhaps, he thought, he should look for a quality buyer—someone whom he thought would continue the business as it was intended to be. Should he decide to sell, he wondered about the asking price he should attempt to establish for the business. Then his mind flashed back to how it all got started.

"I guess I was born an entrepreneur," said James R. Eure, describing how he came to go into the pizza business. A product of the depression, Eure recounted how, even at an early age, he displayed signs of being a potential entrepreneur.

> During the depression, I would grow peanuts off the farm and sell them for five cents per bag, which was pretty good money in those days. When I graduated from high school in 1936, it was in the midst of the depression and there was little hope of going to school that year.
>
> My brother and I borrowed $75 and rented what had been an old drug store in this little drying up town in West Texas where we were living. With just $75

Reprinted by permission of the authors and the Case Research Association.

> we put in what we called a confectionary—a little soda fountain, a little ice cream and school supplies, hamburgers, and some drugs and sundry items.
>
> But typically I suppose, I didn't know what I wanted to be so I drifted from that to selling magazines and taking my pay in chickens (which I had to catch myself).

After bouncing around awhile, Eure decided to go into the Air Force. He spent twenty-five years in the service and retired with the rank of Lt. Colonel in 1964. His career in the Air Force was spent as a communications electronics officer.

HISTORY AND DEVELOPMENT

When Eure retired from the Air Force, by his own account, he did not have anything specific in mind. He was, however, determined that he would not let occupation determine where he would live. He wound up in Stephenville, Texas (population 7,000 with a small college), about 60 miles southwest of Ft. Worth. He and his wife built a new home with their own hands. Then he decided to think about going into the restaurant business.

> I knew that it was the one sure way for me to make some money. I knew that you can make money in any service business if you give good service. There is always a shortage of good things.

James R. Eure managed to scrape up enough money to open a "hole in the wall" in Stephenville. Before that time, no one had ever tried to sell pizza there. Eure indicated that at the time it was generally believed that pizza could succeed only in larger cities. In addition to pizza, the restaurant served charburgers and submarine sandwiches. Eure called his new business venture the "Yucca Hut."

> The charburgers were a whole lot better than the pizza because I knew how to make a good hamburger. I didn't know the first thing about pizza. I figured that by the time I got opened I would learn how to make pizza. Sure enough I didn't learn. The cheese companies, the tomato companies, etc. would give you all sorts of recipes to make pizzas, None of them worked and none of them were good.

Despite his failure to invent "the perfect pizza" by opening day, Eure indicated that the people in this small town were so hungry for something besides chicken-fried steaks and Dairy Queen hamburgers that they "mobbed" him the first day. In fact, the response was so unexpectedly large that he had run completely out of food before 6:00 o'clock.

> As bad as the pizza was, they even liked that. We had no idea of the people that were going to mob us. We weren't stocked, manned, or equipped. We had good intentions and that's about all. So we actually shut down. We put up a sign on the reader board saying "Oops, we goofed!! We will reopen in a few days." This was my first experience and worst.

After this rather unexpected start in business. Eure set about to deal with the surprising level of demand. While on a trip to Dallas to look for a used walk-in cooler, he met a person who was to change the course of his business. This individual was in the pizza business, and Eure noted that he "had some sharp looking methods." Eure asked him to help him learn the pizza business.

For a modest contract, essentially based on 2 percent of sales in two years, this pizza entrepreneur agreed to share some of his secrets with Eure and to furnish the spices to mix the pizza sauce. He showed Eure how he did everything except the spices.

"Yucca Hut" apparently was a tongue-twister for the people of Stephenville and after a few months, everyone had more or less changed the name to "Pizza Place." In the meantime, Eure had purchased the property next door with the anticipation of building a restaurant large enough to accommodate the ever-increasing demand for his pizza, charburgers, and submarine sandwiches. He closed his restaurant on the last day of school and began preparation for building and moving to the property next door. With this restaurant, Eure started on a long journey of growth and innovation in the pizza business which was to change his life drastically.

THE PIZZA PLACE AND ATMOSPHERICS

By Eure's assessment, the Pizza Place was pretty innovative for the town and the time.

> That was my first venture into split-level dining and to my little privacy booths and to the showing of old movies. I found that people loved to go up and down steps. They seemed to go first to the available seating which was hardest to get to. I also found that people like lots of privacy. People are territorial. The more that a customer can stake out his territory and say "This is mine," the more comfortable he will be. So it's not so much privacy as the satisfying of the territorial urge.

Eure observed that the little privacy booths came to be one of his most important gimmicks. Eure believes that gimmicks are very, very important.

> You have to create a gimmick to create good advertising. You have something that generates your own advertising by making people talk about you. You have something different and they will go and say, "You should go to that place; they even have this." So you try to put something that is different in each one.

For the size of town, Eure believed the Pizza Place to be very successful. However, in 1968, because of school problems of his handicapped son, he leased the business and moved to Austin, Texas.

FROM PIZZA PLACE TO MR. GATTI'S

After a brief and unsuccessful attempt at selling real estate, Eure decided that he would "back his ears and get back into the kitchen making pizza." So he picked a spot in Austin.

> I don't know why I picked it except that the rent was cheap. It was a location which many of my subsequent locations have been—dismal failures—but these are the locations you can get on your own terms. It was originally to be a Utotem Store [a chain of small, convenience stores] and it was a different design. Utotem had a 15-year lease for $300 per month and a Seven-Eleven had already opened around the corner. There was an informal arrangement between Seven-Eleven and

> Utotem that they wouldn't get that close to each other. Anyway, Utotem never opened the store, and I got it cheap.

Eure indicated that he knew immediately that the new pizza operation would be a success, but it was not an immediate, raging success. Within six months, however, traffic was very heavy. Too many people were coming in, in Eure's opinion, for the size of the restaurant. Therefore he started looking for a second location, more in the thought of an overflow to take some pressure off the first rather than to put in a second resturant to "make lots of money." Number two was opened one year after the first Austin "Pizza Place." It was in a shopping center store front. The location had just failed as a pizza operation. About this time, Eure began to see, according to his accounts, the potential for growth and expansion. He was, however, determined to do it very cautiously and to do it only out of cash flow.

One year after the opening of Number 2, additional space was leased to double the seating capacity of this unit. Sales grew from first-month sales of $6,800 to better than $15,000 per month sales within a relatively short time span. Number 3 was soon opened opposite the main gate of the Air Force base located on the outskirts of Austin. It was housed in a building which had seen a succession of failures in its five-year life. Its immediate success prompted negotiations for a larger facility.

> Before Number 1 had been open a year we had three places opened. In opening Number 3 I discovered how easy it was to open a pizza restaurant. If you have a central commissary, you can put in an oven and some tables and chairs and some refrigerators. Then you send some people that you have taught how to put some pizzas together. You control the quality in the commissary.

Number 4 was opened 16 months after Number 1 opened. It also contained the first complete commissary, supplying other stores with preportioned and "idiot-proofed" supplies [see below for a discussion of the commissary concept]. Its sales increased steadily from a first-month of $7,000+ to a volume in excess of $24,000 per month.

Number 5 opened in August of 1971 in a large regional shopping center in Austin. Eure believes this to have been the first pizza operation in a shopping mall. Several of the better known chains now have mall locations. Eure noted that this store not only enjoyed a steady increase in sales but provided much publicity and recognition for other outlets. It quickly reached a volume of $20,000 per month in sales and was highly profitable.

Cautious expansion was continued in Austin. In addition, in September of 1972, San Marcos Number 1 [San Marcos is a small city of around 20,000 population located 28 miles south of Austin] was opened. Second month sales were $11,000 or approximately $10 per square foot.

Writing in 1973, James R. Eure observed that

> . . . this business has easily survived the transition from "Mom and Pop" operation. After taking accelerated depreciation and every permissible write-off for tax purposes, our net profit is thirteen percent. Our salaries and wages are equal to or above the industry average; salary and bonuses of the two top executives this year will total $84,000.

MR. GATTI'S

Eure indicated that the name "Pizza Place" was getting more and more confusing.

> I would call up somebody and say, "I'm 'so and so' with the Pizza Place." They would say, "Which one? The one over on Guadalupe." "No," I'd say, "We don't have one on Guadalupe. That's Shakey's." "The one on so and so?" "No. That's Pizza Inn." So many people thought "pizza is pizza," and maybe some still do. That's one reason why we decided to change our name. I wanted to leave pizza completely out of the name. I wanted the name to be "Mr. Gatti's," comma, and then in smaller print, "Pizza, etc." I was convinced the vagueness of the name "The Pizza Place" would hamper future expansion.

Eure explained that the name "Mr. Gatti's" was decided upon after reviewing names submitted by employees in a contest to rename "The Pizza Place." "Gatti" is the maiden name of Eure's wife.

MANAGEMENT AND ORGANIZATION

Upon reaching the decision to go into business in Austin, Eure decided to ask relatives to enter a partnership with him. His sister and his nephew agreed to a partnership arrangement. They remained a partnership until January 1971 when a Subchapter S corporation was formed by the original partners. At the same time, Jonathan D. Wilson*, who had been accountant and operations manager, was permitted to buy stock equivalent to one-seventh ownership. The original three partners retained the remaining stock (two-sevenths each).

Four locations were in operation before the first full-time employee was hired. Eure used nothing but students and other parttime workers.

> Nobody had any responsibility. I did all the scheduling and all the hiring. I didn't have a single person other than my wife who had any responsibility for the stores when they were not there. In other words, they came in and worked and then they went home.

As things began to get more and more complex with the addition of other locations, Eure decided that what he needed was someone whose main job it would be to figure what the stores needed each morning and figure up how much the commissary should make that day to get ready for the various locations. From the product delivered to them this person should be able to calculate how much money should be in each restaurant.

> We had Number 4 opened and this young man who had just graduated from the University of Texas with a degree in finance went to work for us. He had worked his way through college working at Shakey's. Prior to going to college he had been a naval pilot. He was a whiz at mathematics and accounting. He knew quite a bit about computers. He was very good for the business.
>
> We were a good combination. He never questioned philosophies and policies. If he didn't think that everything I wanted to do was the greatest he did not let on. He backed me 100 per cent in everything.

* Name disguised.

Eure began to give more and more decision making authority to Wilson, although at first it was very difficult to part with the authority.

> He had been given 95 percent of the decision making. But it took a long time for him to get to that level. Buying was the hardest thing for me to turn loose of. I wanted to buy everything. If we needed a pound of nails, I wanted to buy them. I soon found that I couldn't do all these things, and I gradually turned bigger and bigger things over to other people once I gained confidence in them.

The second full-time employee hired had the responsibility of going around and collecting the money and making the deposits. Then as the number of restaurants increased, stronger and stronger people were hired to work in the headquarters office. Eure desired that one headquarters person should be held responsible for about four stores.

Eure recognized himself to be a stern taskmaster, a perfectionist. He indicated that one of his faults was to initially not have enough confidence in people.

> I'm too much of a perfectionist. I don't give people enough credit for being able to do the job initially. Once they prove themselves to me then I'm inclined to give them too much leeway. I know I'm a very difficult person to work for. However, I'm very good to my people. I pay them well. On the other hand, I've given lots of thought as to why the way I pay people why I can't get the same kind of longevity and loyalty and dedication that [some people get].

Knowing that people find him difficult to work for, Eure indicated that he tried to isolate himself two or three steps from employees. He said, "I put one trusted person who can put up with me between me and the employees."

STRATEGIC DEVELOPMENT

Eure described his business as a well-above average pizza restaurant. Mr. Gatti's never did advertise cheap prices. Their prices, according to Eure, were known to be a little higher than the competition. As an above-average pizza restaurant, Mr. Gatti's sought to cater to a sophisticated, mature crowd.

> Steak and Ale and that type of restaurant is our competition. The better restaurants, the ones catering to a lively crowd, are our competition.

Eure indicated that he never was afraid of taking on the likes of Pizza Hut, Pizza Inn, and Shakey's. He gave the following account as to why.

> I once knew a fellow who had a little hamburger joint. I had a friend who owned the property and he asked me to go by and visit with this fellow and kind of evaluate his operation. So I did. The significant thing that came out of the conversation was that he was going to turn out a good product, but he was in no way going to attempt to be as good as McDonald's.
>
> I think that the big boys are sitting ducks for any single, quality operator. I mean you are not going to hurt them but you can operate all around them. You must take advantage of them because you are a single owner-operated enterprise, and you should be able to do so much better in quality, size, and product.
>
> So I don't think the little operator needs to fear the big boys if he knows this and applies it.

PRICE AND QUALITY

Gatti's, under Eure's direction, did not price according to competition. The best ingredients were figured into the product; the products were then priced to keep food costs around 20 to 25 percent. No resistance to the company's pricing policies has been encountered according to Eure.

> At times we've had to raise the prices to maintain food costs and we have not hesitated one minute to do so. I did have a price-raising strategy. I leap-frogged prices. That is, I would never raise prices across the board. There were always some products that were dragging heels, some that were underpriced anyway. So those would go and become over-priced. I would leave some things alone. For example, one time I'd raise the price of small and leave the large and medium alone. Next time I would raise the medium and leave the small and large alone.

PRODUCT MIX

Eure stressed the philosophy of "keeping it simple" and doing what you do well. His strategy was not to try to satisfy everyone. The theme was to do what you do well and leave the rest up to somebody else. In the first Austin location, he started out with pizza only. He then added the submarine sandwich. However, he indicated that the submarine sandwich was not added until the pizza was established.

> I haven't really developed a new product since Stephenville that succeeded. We have never sold a dessert because we have not come up with anything that would not take away from our efforts to sell pizza.
>
> When Shakey's a few years ago first came out with their big announcement that they were going to serve fried chicken and mojo potatoes I laughed and said that was wonderful. I said that if they can't make pizza they sure can't make pizza and chicken. And I was right in thinking that it would make their pizza worse, their service worse, and their business worse. People who think they have got to grab whatever somebody wants to eat think they are missing out if they're not there to satisfy them. We want our customers to go somewhere else to eat chicken.

ADVERTISING AND PROMOTION

In the early phases of operation, Gatti's was so small that the only promotion was through "Welcome Wagon." After four locations opened, one-inch, one-column ads simply stating "Mr. Gatti's—South Congress" were run in the paper. These ads got larger as the number of stores grew. Seldom, however, was anything run in the newspaper except the logo and the name. The radio spots were kept as short as possible, never more than 30 seconds. Many of the spots were for 20 seconds. Eure indicated that he wanted the customers to be so happy that he wasn't "bugged for a whole minute" that they were left with a good feeling toward Mr. Gatti's. In other words, Eure said, "Give our name and what we do and then we're gone."

Promotion coupons that we handed out never used a discount or "you buy one get one free" theme. The promotion coupons were always no strings attached. This was in keeping with the quality image which Mr. Gatti's tried to promote. "When we gave away beer, we would say 'come in for a free Michelob'." That may cost us only one cent more.

OPERATIONS

James R. Eure expressed "a terrible fear of deterioration of products." This led him to develop two concepts which became a trademark of his operations. These two concepts were the "commissary principle" and "idiot-proofing" as he labeled it. Essentially this meant doing the important part of the food preparation in the back of the restaurant. Then the people who were to put the pizza together in the rush at night would have everything laid out for them. Eure observed that the important steps are cooking the sauce, mixing the dough, and even chopping the onions.

Eure found that he could get stable, permanent-type help from people who were looking for daytime work. Then, he relied on students and parttime help to put the pizzas together and cook them at night.

As noted previously, Eure did all of the hiring, interviewing, and scheduling for all the stores in the early history of Mr. Gatti's. At the stage where he had four restaurants, he bought a little pick-up and put a cooler on the back of it to haul the groceries. It was while doing this that Eure says that he "perfected the method of restocking the stores."

> The concept was to sell out. Theoretically, it meant they were not supposed to have a scrap of food left. But in practice they would have some left. The more perishable the item was the more often it was required that they run out of it. That was one of the biggest battles—overcoming the fear of running out of something. One of the most important things is running out of something often. If something has only a two-day shelf life and you are afraid of running out of it, you are going to be selling about 90 percent of the time a product which is on the tail-end of its shelf-life and is deteriorating. If you have enough before you run out, you have too much and today when you like to be serving a nice, fresh product you are still serving yesterday's left-overs.

Another thing which Eure believed had made his operation profitable was the fact that he had no losses on products. He required that stock would be maintained at a level that they would run out of one size of pizza crust in a store every night. The attempt was made to schedule the "run-out" just after the rush hour. Eure scheduled his salads to run out at some point during the supper rush. He maintains that no one was offended if they ran out of salads.

The commissary principle and "idiot-proofing" allowed Eure to manage his operations in such a way that the people in the stores had nothing to do with how much merchandise was brought to a particular restaurant. The employees in a restaurant had nothing to do with scheduling, etc. Therefore, Eure alleges, "there was nothing to manage."

> Whoever got there first was the manager. Usually someone had already been there and put the stuff in the refrigerator for him before he got there.
>
> Eventually, we started the commissary at three or four in the morning and we had restocking procedures laid out. With brief calculations, we would know how much to start producing to build the stores back up to a Monday, Tuesday,

> etc. stock level. It really worked quite well. It made each store identical. You could go into any one of them and get exactly the same quality food.

Eure's operations manager "knew computers." For a long time prior to the hiring of Wilson, Eure had been interested in computers and in "teaching a computer how to stock and control his restaurants." The type of control he ultimately was able to achieve he attributes to the use of computers and to Wilson's knowledge of how to use them.

FINANCE

Consolidated balance sheets and income statements are shown for Mr. Gatti's (Tables 1 and 2) on the following pages.

GROWING PAINS AND OTHER PROBLEMS

Reflecting upon the strains that almost any business experiences that has been successful enough to grow, James R. Eure rather philosophically observed:

> I know many businesses have been a booming success as a single operation and they make good money and have decided to expand. They didn't take into consideration that they and their families were doing a large share of the work. They often use the family automobile and their personal tools to fix things and he's able to do all the repairs. They use their garage for their warehouse. You do your own bookkeeping, etc. When you start growing suddenly you have to hire someone to do your maintenance and you have to buy them a set of tools and a truck and rent a warehouse. You suddenly stop working and start spending. Labor and capital become strained.

In the specific case of Mr. Gatti's, Eure noted that he ultimately got up to eighteen stores. The pressures and the work resulting from such a large number of stores made Eure wonder about the desirability of continued expansion when he was already making more money than he "really wanted to spend." He remarked, however, how that it was difficult to stop once the venture is started and some talent is attracted by the expansion.

> You are committed from then on. You can't stop because the minute you stop everybody will abandon ship. So I had this pressure of "You got to keep rolling." We had passed the "one-at-a-time, we conceive one, build it, finish it, and open it" stage. At one time we had four big ones going, and this was at the time the recession [of 1973] hit. We had construction delays and we had other problems.

Among those "other problems" was the loss of Eure's key man, Jonathan Wilson. Along toward the latter part of his tenure with Mr. Gatti's, Wilson, according to Eure, began wanting to inject himself into advertising, design, etc. These were areas in which Eure felt himself particularly qualified in the case of Mr. Gatti's and even more that Wilson lacked proven expertise in.

> He came back from a restaurant show once with a whole bunch of propaganda. He wanted us to hand out buttons to everyone saying "Pizza Makes Me Passionate." Also, he wanted to hand out balloons for the kids. I said, "Jonathan, we are not Shakey's; we are not Pizza Hut. This is an important thing. A business has to

TABLE 1: Consolidated Balance Sheets

Financial Statement	*1969*	*1970*	*1971*	*1972*	*1973*	*1974*
ASSETS						
Current Assets						
Cash	$ 2,620	$ 7,395	$ 13,713	$ 28,253	$ 52,760	$ 39,879
Accounts Receivable		1,342	2,532	3,346	5,637	26,823
Inventories	951	8,471	12,385	14,251	37,734	106,003
Other Current Assets			23,392	4,639	25,507	24,288
Total Current Assets	3,571	17,208	52,022	50,489	96,131	196,993
Loans to Shareholders					5,000	9,609
Building and Other Fixed Deprec. Assets	12,199	68,196	129,349	331,791	586,828	732,370
Land			2,000	12,958	32,317	32,317
Other Assets	2,370	6,173	5,244	8,112		10,314
Total Assets	$18,140	$91,577	$188,615	$403,350	$745,783	$976,603
LIABILITIES AND CAPITAL						
Current Liabilities						
Accounts Payable		$25,551	$ 27,183	$ 65,658	$ 97,064	$354,362
Notes Payable in less than 1 Year		25,424	17,545	17,655	48,651	41,775
Other Current Liabilities			27,078	44,175	81,250	92,502
Total Current Liabilities		50,975	71,806	127,488	226,965	488,639
Notes Payable in more than 1 Year				73,986	125,275	179,471
Partner's Capital	$18,140	40,602				
Capital Stock			64,890	64,890	69,890	66,640
Paid-in or Capital Surplus			22,730	22,730	48,840	37,270
Retained Earnings Unapprop.			(1,094)	(3,294)	44,457	73,443
Shareholders Undistributed Taxable income Previously Taxed			30,283	117,550	230,356	131,140
Total Liabilities & Shareholders Equity	$18,140	$91,577	$188,615	$403,350	$745,783	$976,603

TABLE 2: Consolidated Profit and Loss Statements

Financial Statement	*1969*	*1970*	*1971*	*1972*	*1973*	*1974*
Net Sales	$70,871	$313,981	$479,426	$1,050,791	$1,772,123	$2,952,548
Cost of Sales	20,166	92,240	124,760	271,644	480,201	805,077
Gross Profit	50,615	221,741	354,666	779,147	1,291,922	2,147,471
Total Expenses	39,405	193,371	302,641	658,982	1,119,581	1,875,042
Taxable Income	$11,210	$ 28,370	$ 52,025	$ 129,165	$ 172,341	$ 272,429

> decide who it is, who are you, and constantly—everything you do—to work toward that image. We worked to be a quality place and we deliberately avoided gimmicks and give aways, promotions, and the like such as balloons and things to encourage kids to come in."

When Wilson left he took two or three of Eure's top people with him. By the time Wilson decided to leave, Eure had got almost completely out of operations. He was leaving the "nuts and bolts" up to Wilson and concentrating upon the strategy and policy side of the business.

At this stage, Eure began to search for a replacement for Wilson. He ran ads in paid publications such as the *Wall Street Journal.* He got numerous applications from all over the country. He read through the piles of resumes and sorted out those which appeared to have any promise at all.

> I'd get on the phone and talk to them. I'd go to Denver and then swing over to New York City and talk to them. . . . I'm a great pessimist. People who are looking for jobs—you don't want to hire them.

Eure indeed knew that it was hard to find good people. As he again thought of the construction delays, energy crisis, his advancing age and naturally pessimistic nature, maybe it was time to sell the business. But that would bring a whole new set of problems.

APPENDIX:

A Note on the American Pizza Industry

INDUSTRY HISTORY

Pizza has become as American as hot dogs and hamburgers, but it didn't start out that way. Pizza goes back in history many years. Naples and Sicily, Italy were responsible for developing the pizza in the forms we are now familiar with. From the 1700's until the 1940's, pizza traveled the length of Italy picking up local refinements and embellishments. Meat was added in Rome, mushrooms were added in Sicily, anchovies were added in Italian fishing areas, and so on. The crust varied from region to region, with the extremes being the very thin Neapolitan crust and the one-inch thick Sicilian crust.[8]

Somewhat later, some of the Italian chefs traveled to France because the King of France had heard about how delicious Italian food was, and he wanted to try it. These Italian chefs taught the French chefs how to cook Italian foods, and before long they became world famous for "French cooking." Eventually, some of these French chefs traveled to the United States, and that's how pizza made the journey to our country and became one of our favorite foods.[8]

Pizza may have arrived in the United States as early as the 1890's, but America's passion for pizza is only about 20 years old. It was originally sold by peddlers from wagons and pushcarts or from corner stands in immigrant Italian neighborhoods, mostly along the Atlantic coast from New York City to Providence. This early American pizza was just a slice of bread, already baked, over which the peddler ladled fresh tomato sauce.[14]

According to Henry Weil, the first chef to bake bread and topping together—or so he insisted—was the late Frank Pepe, an immigrant from near Salerno who opened a pizzeria in New Haven in 1925. Pepe claims his place was the first sit-down pizzeria in America and the first to make a king-sized shareable pizza. None of this can be documented, but Pepe's is at least known to be the first American pizzeria to be granted a beer license.[14]

Until the early 1950's, a non-Italian person had to go to an immigrant community to get a pizza. Then, suddenly, pizza's popularity in America erupted. In 1954, Sherwood (Shakey) Johnson founded Shakey's in Sacramento. Four years later, Frank and Don Carney started Pizza Hut. The first Pizza Hut restaurant opened on June 15, 1958. Their tiny Pizza Hut restaurant became an almost overnight success.

REGIONAL DIFFERENCES

America's taste for pizza varies regionally. Mid-America and the two coastal markets are complete extremes from one another. In the Southwest a different kind of dough is used. The sauce is put on top of the cheese in Pennsylvania. The people in Milwaukee cut pizza into little pieces. A Greek style is prepared in Boston. Deep dish is the "thing" in Chicago. Only Sicilian pan pizza sells well in New York, and San Francisco serves yet another version.[5]

Americans also vary in the type of toppings they prefer. Most Americans prefer a thin crust with cheese and pepperoni, though the Southwesterners like to liven things up a bit with jalapeno peppers. There are even regional variations in where and when people like to eat pizza. Table 1 and Table 2 give some recent analyses of eating locations by regions and the time of meal.[9]

According to a 1978 survey, cheese pizza is the biggest seller nationally, and per capita consumption of cheese pizza in Philadelphia is higher than any other city in the country. The place where cheese pizza is least popular is Minneapolis. Sausage pizza is the second-most popular type of pizza nationally and the leader in the Mid-West. The entire Northeast is at the bottom of the barrel for sausage pizza sales. Pepperoni pizza has found the greatest intensity of demand in the South, but can scarcely be found in large cities like New York and Chicago. The beef-raising states prefer hamburger pizza, but very little of it is on sale in the Northeast. Denver and Seattle residents buy more deluxe combination pizzas than any other cities, and a variety on the rise in the Northwest is Canadian bacon.[5]

MAJOR SEGMENTS OF THE INDUSTRY

The major segments of the pizza industry consist of franchise chains, (both national and regional), independents, and frozen and dry pizza processors.

Chains/Franchises. Americans ate a mere $700 million worth of pizza at restaurant chains in 1974, but spent $1.6 billion on the dish in 1978.[7] Projections called for more than 20% growth in 1979. Pizza Hut is the undisputed leader of franchised pizza operations, with 2820 units in 1977. It accounts for 22% of total sales for pizza-only chain restaurants.[15]

Table 3 and Table 4 give some detailed information about some selected

TABLE 1: Eating Locations for Pizza by Regions

	Total U.S.	*N.E.*	*N.C.*	*S.*	*W.*
Any Pizza	100	124	120	77	73
Away From Home	100	151	82	86	83
Carry In	100	180	112	33	89
Frozen/Refrig.	100	100	140	82	66
Homemade	100	95	134	89	66
(Indexed at 100 on total U.S.)					

Source: *Mainstream,* National Frozen Foods Association, p. 9.

TABLE 2: Regional Differences in Consumption Patterns by Meal Occasion

Any Pizza	*Total U.S.*	*N.E.*	*N.C.*	*S.*	*W.*
Midday	20	34	23	33	31
Evenings	54	45	59	55	65
Snacks	16	21	18	12	4
Total	100	100	100	100	100
(Figures are percentages)					

Source: *Mainstream,* National Frozen Foods Association, p. 9.

leading pizza chains and the top 20 pizza chains in the U.S. Pizza Hut dominates the pizza-chain market even more than McDonald's does the Hamburger market. "However, pizza is more fragmented and less chain-dominated than the hamburg segment," says Michael Esposito of Bache-Halsey-Stuart-Shields, Inc. "In 1975, there were 5,000 units of pizza chains but 23,000 hamburger-chain units. By 1977, pizza had grown about 15% to 7,250 units, while hamburger increased almost 9% to 25,070 units."[15]

Table 5 exhibits the growth rates in sales at franchise restaurants. Sales of

TABLE 3: The Top Twenty Pizza Chains' Sales

	1975 (in millions)	*1976 (in millions)*	*1977 (in millions)*
Pizza Hut, Inc.	$177.3	$250.0	$317.4
Pizza Inn, Inc.	75.7†	98.0†	129.1
Shakey's, Inc.	122.4	124.7	130.0
Pasquale Food Co.	42.0*	46.0	35.0
Village Inn Pizza	31.0*	32.0*	34.1*
Straw Hat (Saga)	31.1	33.9	33.2
Round Table Pizza	23.6	29.5	33.0
Ken's Pizza	20.0	21.8	31.2
Domino's	23.0	24.5	30.0
Happy Joe's Pizza	14.2	20.0	27.3
Cassano's	18.5	18.9	20.9
Dino's	16.0	19.0	18.5
Noble Roman's	7.0	11.5	18.5
Pizza King	7.5*	8.0*	10.0
Pizza Haven	5.0	6.1	8.4
P. K. Management	2.4	3.0	4.3
Pasta House Co.	2.0*	2.5*	3.6
Lou Malnati's	1.5	2.3	3.3
Numero Uno	1.5*	2.0	2.6*
Original Pizzaman		1.7	1.3

* estimated figures.
† eliminates promotional sales.
Source: *Institutions, Volume Feeding,* May 15, 1978, p. 34.

TABLE 4: Selected Leading Pizza Chains

Chain (Hq.)	*Year Founded*	*Past + Curr. Est. Fiscal Year Sales (Millions)*	*Past + Curr. Fiscal Year Est. Net Income (Millions)*	*Avg. Est. Per Year Sales*	*Avg. Est. Per Person Ticket*	*No. of Units*	*No. New Units Projected '79*	*Main, Extra and Test Menu Items*
Pizza Hut (Wichita) [a]	1958	$650–$850	$25–$20	$225,000	$2.25	3,700	450	Super style pizza, chili, soups, desserts, salad bar
Pizza Inn (Dallas)	1960	125–160	2.1–N.A.	240,000	2.05	730	155	Gourmet Pizza, taco pizza, salad bar
Shakey's (Dallas) [b]	1954	130–145	(1)–1	320,000	2.10	500	40	Spaghetti, sandwiches, salad bar
Straw Hat (Dublin, Calif.) [c]	1943	56–65	N.A.	310,000	2.50	220	25	Hot hat sandwiches, deli sandwiches, salad bar
Pasquale's (Birmingham, Ala.)	1962	50–65	0.6–N.A.	225,000		275	50	Salads
Mr. Gatti's (Louisville)	1974	25–38	1–1.5	350,000	2.00	105	90	Sandwiches, salad
Noble Roman's (Bloomington, Ind.)	1969	25–30	2–2.5	525,000		55	20	Deep dish pizza
Papa Gino's (Needham, Mass.)	1958	20–25	1–1.2	350,000		75	18	Hamburgers, desserts
Cassano's (Dayton, Ohio)	1953	18–21	1–N.A.	250,000	2.75	95	10	Sandwiches, seafood, soup
Gigi's (Atlanta)	1959	8–8	N.A.	375,000	N.A.	20	0	Sandwiches, sausage
Pietro's (Seattle) [d]	1964	N.A.	N.A.	500,000	2.75	15	10	Wines, salad bar

[a]owned by PepsiCo [b]owned by Hunt Int'l [c]owned by Saga Corp. [d]owned by Campbell Soup
Source: *Restaurant News*, January 8, 1979, p. 123.

TABLE 5: Per Cent Change in Sales of Franchise Restaurants by Major Activity, 1975–78*

	Sales 1976 (in millions)	*% Change 1975–76*	*% Change 1976–77*	*% Change 1977–78*
Seafood	$ 439,762	+48.7	+49.1	+39.2
Pizza	1,091,534	+18.1	+20.3	+22.7
Mexican (taco, etc.)	309,113	+13.4	+17.4	+21.8
Hamburger, Hot Dog, Roast Beef	8,030,623	+18.8	+17.7	+20.3
Pancake, Waffle	464,462	+23.8	+12.5	+17.0
Steak, Full Menu	2,585,786	+17.0	+13.0	+15.2
Chicken	1,609,270	+17.1	+ 9.0	+10.2
Sandwich & Other	75,763	+39.8	+22.5	+48.0
Total	$14,606,313	+19.1	+16.9	+19.4

* estimated by respondents for 1977–78.
Original data source: National Restaurant Association.

franchise pizza chains are increasing faster than those of any other type except seafood in the most recent year.[15] Five of the leading pizza chains are owned by other corporations. For example, PepsiCo owns Pizza Hut; Hunt Resources International owns Shakey's; Saga, Saga Corp. owns Straw Hat; and Campbell Soup owns Pietro's.[1] Even though the major chains have a lower cost advantage, the smaller regional chains have a more important advantage in that they can become more customized—more attuned to their market. This advantage is more important in the ethnocentric areas of the U.S. The national chains have another problem caused by large corporate structures. To state it simply, the problem is a lack of capable managers.

Regional and medium-sized pizza chains appear to be taking an increasing share of the market from the big three chains (Pizza Hut, Pizza Inn, and Shakey's). But, inflation has slowed their growth, at least in absolute numbers. Most of the small regional pizzerias plan to open only a few (0–10) stores in the near future, whereas the larger chains have been very aggressive in their growth attempts (almost 100 per year). This situation may be a blessing in disguise for the "little guy." Growing pains may have gotten the best of a couple of the larger chains. Costs are rising rapidly, and they are eating away at the marginal profitability of the newly opened pizza restaurants. The regional chains, by restricting their growth to familiar areas, will achieve a higher profitability per store.[9]

Because regional differences are so wide, it is hard for any single chain to customize one product on a nation-wide basis. This pattern of pizza acceptance is so diverse and decisive that it would be next to impossible for any company in the business—even the large ones—to achieve market saturation. For these reasons, the small independent pizzeria has an advantage over a national chain operation.

Independents. There are more independent operators of pizza parlors than national chains in the U.S. This is because of regional differences in taste. (It is not feasible for chain operators to differentiate their pizzas for all regions.) Independents have the advantage of superior quality in their pizzas because of the individual attention given to each pizza. It is harder to make pizza in multiples than hamburgers or chicken. Therefore, most chains make compromises with their dough. For this reason some people feel the national chains' pizza is somewhat plastic, and they prefer "homemade" pizza.

The independent's main disadvantage is that their pizza's quality is not consistent. They are not standardized like the big chains because the quality of the ingredients they buy is not constant. Many experts do believe that pizza is likely to taste better at an independent's restaurant than at a chain's unit. But the independents pay for that advantage with higher food cost. "The food cost at Pizza Hut may be 22% or at Shakey's may be 32%—there's a difference in weight and the toppings used," says one observer. "An independent operator may run a food cost of 40–45% using all fresh, made-to-order methods."[3]

Frozen and Dry Pizza Mixes. The frozen pizza business is well over half a billion dollars annually, and there still are signs of continuous growth. Pizza was once known as junk food, but that image is changing. *Quick Frozen Foods* has shown that pizza is highly nutritious and suitable as a main dish of a meal.[12]

"Frozen pizza is the pie of the future," says Richard A. Blott, Vice-president of Sales and Marketing for Ore-Ida Food, Inc., Boise, Idaho. The growth in space allocated to frozen pizza in grocery stores exemplifies this. In the last four years the amount of retail freezer cabinet space devoted to frozen pizza in chain stores has increased 60%, and sales now exceed $500 million a year.[11]

It is generally thought that the major competition to frozen pizza comes from pizzerias, and this is true; but, there is another form of competition, and that is from dry pizza mixes. There are many different types of pizza mixes, some with containers of cheese and tomato sauce. The advantage of dry pizza mix is the psychological feeling of accomplishment that accompanies its preparation. The maker feels like a real pizza chef. An average retail price for the product would be about 90¢, and it could make a 9–16 inch pizza.[6]

SPECIAL PROBLEM AREAS

The American pizza industry faces two special problems and challenges. One is the energy crises—an uncontrolled factor affecting all segments of American life. The other is controllable, at least to an extent, and that involves pizza's junk image and the nutrition issue.

Energy Crisis. In 1973 the Arabs placed an embargo on oil. This led to higher energy costs for many major fast-food restaurant chains, as well as decreasing sales of pick-up orders by the customers. During the months of May and June in 1979 the gasoline supply crunch further weakened the business pace of the fast-food restaurant chains. Eateries in areas where the wait for gasoline didn't extend beyond 30 minutes had matched or exceeded the 6% average increase in nominal sales of the industry. But in regions where gasoline waiting periods went beyond 30 minutes, nominal sales of the restaurant industry were up only 1.5%.[4]

Table 6 lists 17 major chains and the percentage changes from a year earlier in real sales, adjusted for price increase.[4]

TABLE 6: The Percentage Change in Real Sales, Adjusted for Price Increase (1979)

	April % *Change*	*May* % *Change*	*June* % *Change*
Burger King	− 3	− 4	− 4
Captain D's	+ 6	− 2	− 6
Church's	+ 3	+ 2	− 3
Denny's	− 6	−12	−12
Friendly's	− 6	− 5	− 5
Howard Johnson	− 2	−11	− 8
Jack in the Box	− 1	+ 2	− 2
Kentucky Fried Chicken	− 4	0	0
Long John Silver	+10	+10	+ 3
McDonald's	− 4	− 4	− 4
Pizza Hut	+ 1	− 3	0
Ponderosa	− 1	− 7	−11
Sambo's	−12	−10	−15
Shoney's	+ 2	− 2	− 7
Taco Bell	0	− 4	− 1
Wendy's	− 6	− 9	−16
Winchell's	− 7	− 7	− 9

Source: *Wall Street Journal,* July 17, 1979, p. C 37.

Nutrition. Present studies of pizza indicate that there are high levels of protein, vitamins and minerals, rendering the product suitable for meals and snacks, thus nullifying the "empty calories" stigma of junk foods that has been plaguing pizza for many years. Table 7 shows the nutritional value of pizza versus home-cooked meals and other fast food meals.[13]

The laboratory results in the table indicate that both fast foods (including pizza) and popular home-cooked meals are a rich source of most essential vitamins, while lacking in others. For example, vitamin A is lacking in most fast foods, but pizza is an exception. Dairy products like cheese and milk are good sources of calcium; a very high level of these are found in pizza. Red meats, enriched flour and pasta are prime sources of iron—these are found in pizza also.[13]

In addition, a recent test of fast foods by Consumer's Union showed that a Pizza Hut pizza was the most nutritious fast food tested. One serving (7¾ ounces) provided from one-third to one-half the recommended daily allowance (RDA) for most essential vitamins and minerals. But it also had over 500 calories—about equal to hamburger entrees, and it was very high in sodium.[2]

Industry Trends

Industry trends to be discussed include expanding menus in pizza restaurants, changing atmospheres, and the increasing popularity of pizza.

Expanding Menus. Major changes are reshaping the entire pizza chain idea. Many people feel that there is no way that you can make it on just pizza

TABLE 7: The Nutritional Value of Pizza and Fast Foods vs. Home-Cooked Lunch/Dinner Dishes

	Calorie	*Protein*	*Fat*	*Carbo.*	*Sodium*	*Vit. A*	*Calcium*	*Iron*
Fast Foods								
Hamburgers								
Regular	255	13	9	30	.5	2	5	15
Quarter LB.	420	26	21	33	.7	3	8	28
Specialty	575	27	32	45	.9	9	12	29
French Fries	210	3	10	27	.1	0	1	2
Chicken Dinner	830	52	46	56	2.3	15	15	25
Cheese Pizza (½ 10″ pie)	370	26	10	44	1.0	10	50	20
Fried Fish & Potatoes (2 pieces)	640	23	33	60	.5	4	3	5
Home Cooking								
Tuna Salad Sandwich	325	20	13	32	.7	6	7	16
Soup & Grilled Cheese Sandwich	550	24	25	56	1.7	23	57	12
Spaghetti & Meatballs	670	36	26	71	1.7	38	17	35
Pot Roast & Vegetables	570	30	45	14	.8	150	7	30

Source: *Good Housekeeping,* May, 1979, p. 268. (listed in grams—U.S. RDA)

today. Pastas, all types of sandwiches, hamburgers, chili, soups and dessert are creeping onto the menus in necessary bids for incremental sales. Salad bars are almost becoming a staple at most of the operations. Some chains are going as far as billing themselves as Italian restaurants. Ethnic foods are selling like "hot-cakes" these days, and pizza is no exception. Most of the growth in the fast food industry has been in ethnic foods.[1] Pizza is riding the crest of popularity shared by many ethnic specialties, including Mexican food. People are more adventuresome eaters than they used to be.

Atmospherics. The old time "beer hall" and carry out atmospheres are being discarded in favor of modern decor and adequate seating as the chains strive for a family image with a broader menu. A change in atmosphere can do a lot for sales. For example, President Huse of Noble Roman's explains, "In our units, we have a man hand-toss all the pizzas near a window in the restaurant. People like the show."[3] Pizza parlors in general are trying to create a new, relaxed atmosphere. Their strategy is to reduce the emphasis on gimmicks and entertainment and to become more a family restaurant.

Some chains are zeroing in on one particular market segment where there may be a gap—for example, the advent of deep-dish pizza. Others are trying to emphasize thin, thick and deep-dish to capture every market segment. Meanwhile, most are still looking for "the perfect pizza."

Pizza Popularity. Pizza's mass appeal makes it an American concept. No

TABLE 8: Pizza Popularity Crosses Market Segments

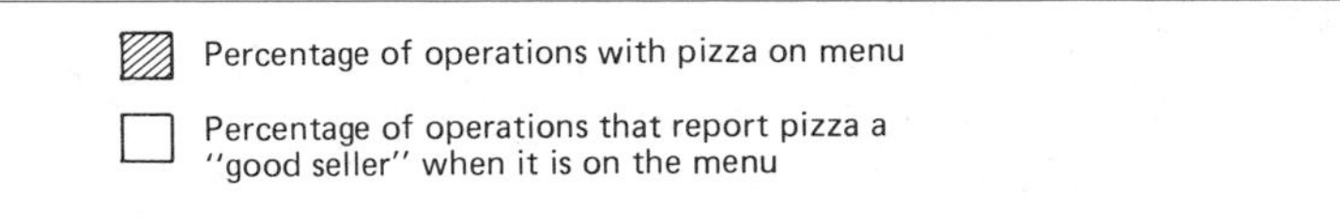

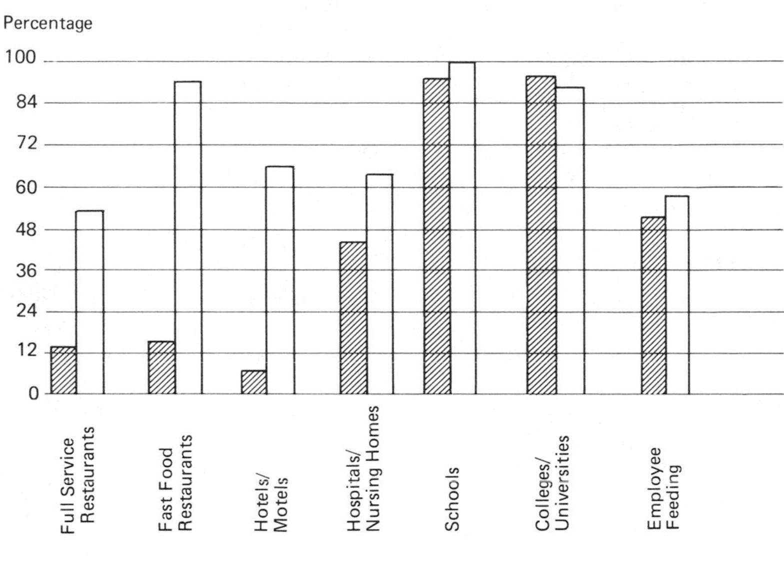

Source: 1978 Menu Census, *Institutions,* January 1, 1978, p. 81.

longer just a teenage favorite, pizza appeals to all age groups. Sales growth over the years has been steady, and the percentage of the population raised on pizza keeps increasing. This gives an added dimension to pizza's popularity growth. Table 8 gives an indication of its popularity.[10]

High demand for pizza may be seen on this chart developed from data in *Institutions'* 1978 Menu Census. Even in operations where it's unlikely that pizza would be on the menu (full-service or hotel/motel), operators observe pizza is a "good seller" when offered. The advent and continued use of pizza on school and college-university menus underscores its newfound nutritional advantage.[3]

In final analysis it can be said that pizza varies significantly by geography and meal. People like variety in flavors, crusts, sizes and prices because pizza is fun as well as nutritional. Pizza is not about to knock off hamburgers as the nation's number one fast food. (In 1978, Americans spent about $11 billion at hamburger restaurant chains.) But pizza, according to trend watchers, has more room to expand.[7]

BIBLIOGRAPHY AND FOOTNOTES

1. Bernstein, Charles, "Regionals Push Giants for Bigger Slice of Pizza Pie," *Restaurant News,* January 8, 1979, pages 122–24.

2. "Fast-Food Chains—Which Fast Foods are Best?," *Consumer Reports,* September 1979, pages 508–513.
3. "Food Service/Lodging Update," *Institutions,* April 15, 1978, page 4.
4. "Gasoline Pinch Blamed for Further Weakness in Fast-Food Outlets' Already Faltering Sales," *The Wall Street Journal,* July 17, 1979, page C-37.
5. MARTIN, SAM, "Frozen Pizza Preferences by City Drawn from Household Purchases," *Quick Frozen Foods,* April 1979, pages 14–25.
6. MARTIN, SAM, "Seasonal Sales Curves for Frozen Pizza by Region Compared to Dry Pizza Mixes," *Quick Frozen Foods,* January 1978, pages 16–20.
7. MOFFETT, BARBARA S., "Hamburgerized Society Takes Time Out for Pizza," *Pottsville, PA Republican,* March 21, 1979, p. 28.
8. NORTH AMERICAN PIZZA ASSOCIATION, "A Brief History of the Pizza."
9. NATIONAL FROZEN FOOD ASSOCIATION, INC., "State of the Industry," *Mainstream,* April 19, 1978, pages 8–10.
10. "Pizza Kitchens' Italian Menu Shifts from Pasta to Full Dinner Concepts," *Institutions,* January 1, 1978, page 81.
11. "Pizza's Linear Footage in Retail Cabinets Climbed 60 Per Cent in Last Four Years," *Quick Frozen Foods,* April 1979, pages 28–32.
12. "Processor Seeks to Elevate Consumer Image of Frozen Pizza to Restaurant Level," *Quick Frozen Foods,* November 1977, pages 208–212.
13. SMITHIES, RONALD R., "The Good News About Fast Foods," *Good Housekeeping,* May 1979, pages 266–269.
14. WEIL, HENRY, "Mom, the Flag, Apple Pie and Pizza," *Good Housekeeping,* May 1979, pages 20–21.
15. WILEY, JUDY, "Pizza," *Institutions/Volume Feeding,* May 5, 1978, pages 31–34, 39.

CASE TWO

Majestic Hardware Co., Inc.

JEANNE M. LYNCH
Rensselaer Polytechnic Institute

Assignment Questions:

1. What business is Arthur Elman in? How did this evolve?
2. How would you describe the atmosphere and culture of Elman's stores?
3. What problems do you see in the future?

By the end of 1976, Arthur Elman, president of Majestic Hardware Co. of West Warwick, Rhode Island, was the tenth largest Honda motorcycle dealer in the United States. In addition to owning two Honda stores with automobile and motorcycle franchises, Elman also carried Yamaha motorcycles at his downtown hardware store. By February, 1977, with sales of over $5 million and profits of some $150,000, Elman had decided how to cover rapidly increasing costs. He explained:

> Our fixed costs for heat, light, taxes, insurance, everything, are going up and up with no end in sight. We have a $350,000 mortgage at 9% on the West Warwick Honda store, and an $800,000 line of credit on 30-day notes at a quarter over prime rate, 6.5%, on which we currently owe $600,000.
>
> The problem is that we can't pass these added costs on to our customers. The only thing we can do is increase our volume. That's why I decided to go into used cars.
>
> I say that I won't go into anything else. I said that a month ago, and two weeks ago I went into the used car business. We've already spent about $50–$60,000 on used cars, and we'll be spending another $100,000. This is like going into another business entirely.
>
> As much as I say I'm not going to do anything else, I get caught up in things. It seems that something will come along, and it just happens and I do it. But I won't go into something if I can't see a good legitimate profit in it. I don't think profit is a dirty word, like a lot of people do. I'm not adverse to making a profit. I want to see my people make money. I'd like them to make a lot of money.

History of the Business

The original business was started as a partnership between Arthur Elman's father and uncle in 1919 in Providence, Rhode Island. In the 1920s they opened a second store in West Warwick, and in 1932 decided to form separate companies, with the uncle taking the Providence store and the father the West Warwick store, Majestic Hardware Co., Inc.

By 1962 Arthur Elman and his sister, Mrs. Burt Charren, had inherited the business as equal partners. In that year he decided to carry Vespa scooters in the store. The reason was simple. They were selling chainsaws by then and the repair work required a part-time mechanic. He added the scooters so that there would be enough repair work to give the mechanic a full-time job. The results were unexpected, as Elman explained:

> I figured we'd sell about ten a year, or something like that. The first year we sold 150. It was phenomenal! Then I started seeing ads for Honda motorcycles; 'You meet the nicest people on a Honda'; and I noticed they were advertising in *Life* and *Ladies Home Journal* rather than the 'cycle magazines, so I decided to try selling them in the small store next to the hardware store.

Looking back, Elman can see that he caught the beginning of a new trend; the shift of the motorcycle from a subculture machine to a recreation vehicle. Honda, with a full profit line from minibikes to touring machines, became the leading maker, with 50 per cent of the United States motorcycle market. Majestic sold every motorcycle they could get from Honda, with a one-third markup on the wholesale price, plus a $40 freight and setup charge.

In 1967 and 1968 motorcycle sales slumped. The effect on Majestic was softened somewhat when a major competitor, with two Honda franchises within 30 miles of West Warwick, decided to drop the line, giving Majestic a larger share of the smaller market. Arthur Elman saw no point in getting out of the motorcycle business.

> Even with the lower volume, there was nothing else that would give us a better return on the space we were using. Motorcycles are seasonal. You order them a few months in advance, pay for them when you take delivery, then sell almost all of them out in the four months from April to July.

From 1969 into the early 1970s motorcycle sales came back stronger than ever, helped first by the economic boom, then by rising gasoline prices. "It was nothing," one employee explains, "to sell three or four motorcycles in a half an hour during the motorcycle season. Customers came in ready to buy. We were writing up orders as fast as we could."

In 1971 the Honda sales representative talked with Elman about having an "open point" in northern Rhode Island; room for another dealership with a good drawing area. Elman took a ride with him up Route 146 through Lincoln, Rhode Island, to look at the area.

> I'd lived in this state all my life, but I don't think I had been up that road six times. I was impressed with the area and the amount of traffic, so I decided to take the franchise.
>
> At that time we had gone through a lot of good years in motorcycles, so I bought a piece of land, had it filled, put up a 10,000 sq. ft. building, stocked it

> with motorcycles, equipment, parts, and accessories, and didn't owe anybody a dime.
>
> At the same time, I asked Honda for an automobile franchise, but they turned me down. Motorcycles and automobiles are two separate businesses with Honda, with two separate organizations. The automobiles were new, but doing well. But Honda wasn't even offering the franchises to their motorcycle dealers; most were going to General Motors dealers. I had the space for cars, so I took on a Subaru franchise.
>
> But I kept pushing, pushing, pushing with Honda, and about a year after we opened they gave me the automobiles. The first shipment came in with part Honda 600s and part Civics. After a few months we dropped the Subaru.

The Civic introduced an engine that burned gasoline so completely it required no emissions control equipment and had an EPA rating of 34 miles to the gallon on the highway. As the energy crisis worsened, and gasoline prices rose, Honda introduced the CVCC with a highway rating of 41 mpg, and at the beginning of 1977, the five-speed CVCC rated at 54 mpg highway and 41 mpg city was introduced.

In the latter part of 1976 Honda brought out the Accord, a somewhat larger car that was so popular that, by February of 1977, there was a three-month waiting period for it. Some dealers were charging a premium for early delivery. Elman refused to consider such a practice, even though he had 70 customers waiting for delivery of Accords.

By 1974, with the automobiles selling well in Lincoln, R.I., Elman asked for an automobile franchise for West Warwick. Honda pointed out that there was no room for automobiles at the hardware store location, but agreed to the franchise on the condition that Majestic would build another showroom. Elman found a site on Route 2 in West Warwick and bought it. A week later, Metropolitan Life Insurance Co. announced their purchase of the site directly across the highway for a new regional center that would employ about two thousand clerical personnel.

Majestic was offered twice what it had paid for the site, but turned the offers down and started construction on a building with 15,000 sq. ft. on the first floor, and 4,000 sq. ft. on the second floor to be used for offices and storage. The building costs ran far over estimate.

> When we first took on motorcycles in West Warwick, we bought the motorcycles, the tools, parts, accessories; the whole ball of wax; for $5,000. When we turned the key on this new building, we had $1,000,000 invested here. That's the difference between then and now.

As automobile sales rose, the 1975 and 1976 motorcycle seasons became what Elman termed, "a disaster":

> The whole ecomomy was off, plus the fact that our main market in motorcycles is still the 18-to-24-year-olds. They're the last ones in on a job, the first ones to get laid off, and the hardest people to finance. The gasoline scare was over, so people weren't that concerned about fuel. From '74 to '76, our volume dropped by 50 percent and our profits by 75 percent. Luckily we had the automobiles. We're doing about 70 cars a month now.

Not every decision worked out as well as that of taking on the Hondas. In the four years it had been in automobiles, Majestic had carried Subarus, Alfa

Romeos, and Bricklins, but it discontinued each when either sales or service failed to meet Elman's expectations:

> I've made plenty of bad investments. If they don't turn out, I don't ride them to death; I take my shellacking then and there. They don't improve by sitting and crying over them, so if you get back fifty cents on the dollar and get out, at least you've got fifty cents to invest in something else. The other way, you just sit and watch it go down the drain, trying to prove that you were right.

THE HARDWARE STORE

When it opened in the 1920s, the hardware store was in a countrified section of West Warwick known locally by its old name, Artic, R.I. The store had two types of business: retail, based on a full line of hardware for urban and rural homes, and commercial, based on industrial hardware and supplies, chiefly for textile mills. Over the years, the balance of the business had shifted from 50–50 to 75 percent retail. In 1976 the store carried an inventory with a retail value of $250,000 and had sales of approximately $400,000. Burt Charren, Arthur Elman's brother-in-law who managed the hardware store, explained:

> We're an old-fashioned country hardware store with a big inventory. We carry slow-turning items. We could cut the inventory and get more stock-turns, but if we did that, we wouldn't have what the other fellows don't have.
>
> We can't compete with the discount stores on price, so we compete by having a big variety and plenty of stock. And we have the "goodies", things that you can hardly find anymore. For example, we have kerosene lanterns, stove mica for the door of a pot-bellied stove, galvanized buckets, "perfection" wicks for kerosene stoves, scrub boards; you name it. We carry stone crocks in three sizes, V-belts up to 100″ long, including heavy-duty belts for 7–8 horsepower motors. If someone wants a wall plug receptacle, we carry six different kinds.
>
> This used to be a shopping town. Years back, we'd have so many people in here on a Friday night, we'd have to have a policeman directing store traffic. But that's changed. We don't even keep a traffic count anymore. But, while the volume of traffic is down, we make more money than we did.
>
> Part of this is because of inflation. When you have a big inventory, and prices keep going up, you make more on it. Then we carry a big supply of items you don't have to discount, and on competitive merchandise, we buy right.
>
> We're one of about 5,800 partners in the Carter & Co. buying cooperative out in Chicago that owns the True Value brand. They have eight or nine distribution warehouses around the country, one up in Manchester, New Hampshire. We order from them at 10 per cent over their cost, and they deliver weekly. You can set your clock by the time the truck arrives. And we usually get a year-end rebate of 25 per cent of the premium we pay.
>
> We can also buy some merchandise on "relay." The cooperative pools the orders from a number of stores and gets the carload price. We pay 6 per cent over carload, and usually get a rebate of 2 per cent. Another thing we can do is order direct from manufacturers in Carter's name and have the merchandise "drop shipped" to our store. We get Carter's price and pay them 2 per cent, of which we get back about half.
>
> Being in business as long as we have, we can buy direct from some manufacturers. That way, we save the 1 per cent and get a cash discount from manufac-

turers that ship 10, 10, net 30.* When we buy through Carter, we lose any cash discounts.

With so many different purchase plans, breakage, inflation, and the fact that Majestic sold to many of its commercial hardware accounts at a discount, it was difficult to know the margin on every item sold. Because of this, Majestic estimated the average cost of goods. In the early part of 1976 it had been using 60 per cent, and Burt Charren felt that, if anything, this was a little high. Elman disagreed. He felt that the hardware store financial statements were showing more profit than they were making. To be on the safe side, they shifted to a 65 per cent estimated cost.

Talk with Burt Charren for even a short while, and you realize that the people in the hardware store put a heavy emphasis on customer service. As he explained:

> Every day people come in with problems and we can tell them what to do. I'm not a plumber, but if a pipe comes up an inch and a half from where it's supposed to be, I can tell them what to do, and how to do it. We talk to our customers and help them, and it doesn't matter if they're just buying a small item. We want to be sure they get the right thing.
>
> We can do that because we have 10 people in the store, and most of them have been with us a long while. Our pay averages $3.75 to $4.00 an hour, and we give them a lot of fringes. Compared to a discount store, having 10 people eats up the money. In a discount operation, they'll have two men stocking, two girls on the registers, and a manager. We have hardware people.
>
> But it pays off. A few years ago the Johnson Wax people did a survey on us and found that people knew about Majestic Hardware as much as 100 miles away. We draw customers from Connecticut, Massachusetts, and New Hampshire as well as here.

One of the decisions that Majestic's management had to make in 1976 when they moved the Honda motorcycle franchise to the new showroom was what to carry in their place at the hardware store.

> We were looking for a big-ticket item that carried a good markup. We weighed sporting goods, but there's too much discounting in that. In the end we decided to take on a Yamaha motorcycle franchise. Honda's share of the market is now 40 per cent, Yahama's 20 per cent, and Kawasaki's 17 per cent.
>
> Even if the motorcycle business isn't great, it's one we know and a few sales are like found money. We sell 2 or 3 a week right now, with an average margin of $250. You'd have to sell more than two tons of fertilizer to make as much. We took the Yamahas on in October and we've sold about 40 to date.

Before the annual inventory was taken, and using a 65 per cent estimated cost of goods, the hardware store was showing a 1976 before-tax profit of $43,000, up from $34,000 in 1975. Their accountant, Martin Dittleman, was reserving judgment on the accuracy of that figure saying, "They moved the office staff over to the Honda showroom. I want to check on whether they transferred the office expenses from this statement to that one." But he felt that the figures

* 10,10, net 30 means 10 percent discount is given if the bill is paid in 10 days; but the net bill is due in 30 days.

might not be too far off, in light of the conservative cost estimates, and commented, "Their stock-turn is worse than average, but their profits are better. They're doing something right."

How long they could continue to do "something right" in the hardware business was a matter in question. As Burt Charren explained:

> The business has changed in the last 25 years. We have half as many customers, but we've held the dollar volume. The way costs are going up, we figure the volume has to grow at 10 per cent a year just to keep the same profit. This is why we decided to use this as a base and branch out into automobiles; to take the plunge while we were still young enough.
>
> We saw the handwriting on the wall; the day of the corner grocery store is gone. If we had a fair offer, I guess we'd sell this store. Otherwise, we'll just milk it without adding any new capital. When it starts losing money, we'll just have to close it.

THE HONDA STORES

The business of the two Honda dealerships, or "stores" as they were called throughout the Majestic organization, was divided into Sales, Automobile Service, Motorcycle Service, and Parts and Accessories. In January 1977, a Used Car department was added at each dealership, but since the Lincoln store was out of space and out of land, this department was not expected to grow to any significant size at that store until they found a way to expand its facilities.

Only one of the Majestic managers (Bill Mahlerwein, general manager of the Lincoln store) had had any experience in the automobile business before joining Majestic. Most managers felt that the industry had a bad reputation, earned through questionable business practices. They did not want to be associated with the industry, and prided themselves that Majestic was different; that they were not automobile "dealers," but operated automobile "stores." Elman commented:

> We started off in hardware. We don't base our business on other automobile dealerships. We don't even know how they operate, and I could care less. I don't want any sharpie automobile salesmen around here, and we don't have them. I don't like the lingo that automobile sales use. I don't allow it in here. I don't like any of those sharp dressers. In other words, when someone comes in here to buy a car or a bike, I want them to feel the same way they'd feel if they went into the hardware store to buy a pound of nails. And we treat them the same way.
>
> Naturally, we try to sell them, but we don't use any of the tactics used in a lot of places. Our compensation to salesmen is entirely different. In a regular automobile agency salesmen work on a draw of \$50–\$75 a week against commissions. Their commissions are based on the gross profit of a deal.
>
> We never went into that, because I have always felt there is nothing sadder looking than a commission salesman who hasn't made a sale. Plus the fact we're open long hours—65 hours a week—and I feel that if people are going to put in these long hours they should be paid for them.
>
> Our salesmen punch in on a timeclock, just like everyone else. I don't think there's another place where salesmen punch a timeclock. They get paid \$2.75 an hour, and time and a half after 40 hours. So their base pay is usually around \$200—that's whether they sell anything or not—which is not enough to live on

comfortably, but at least it puts food on the table so they don't have to worry that they're not going to eat this week if they don't sell anything. And they don't have to worry about paying it back.

The commission structure, which Arthur Elman changed whenever he felt he should, was used as a reminder and as an incentive system to encourage sales, but it was deliberately kept low enough that salesmen would not "high pressure" customers. For example, when Martin Dittleman pointed out that Majestic was selling few retail financing contracts, and thus losing the 2–3 per cent commission, or "reserve" as it was called, from the bank, Elman instituted a system to pay a salesman $5 for each year of any retail financing contract he sold, or $15 for a typical three-year contract. Almost immediately, the sale of financing started to increase.

Occasionally, mistakes were made, such as when it was discovered that the commission offered for selling air conditioning in a car was more than Majestic made on the air conditioning. When this happened, the commission was changed. Arthur Elman continued:

Salesmen get 1 per cent commission on anything they sell. If there's a trade-in, it's 1 percent of the price difference. If not, it's 1 per cent of the total retail price, including accessories. They also get an extra commission on accessories, and a commission on any parts or accessories they sell separately. They get the commission on the retail financing contracts, and a percentage—I think it's 10 per cent—on the insurance, if they sell that.

You have to remember that the Honda is not a high-priced car with a big margin. The Civic lists for just under $3,000, on which Majestic gets just about 10 percent. But even at that our full-time salesmen average between $17,000 and $21,000 a year. If they can't make at least $15,000, they're no good to us or to themselves. We don't set quotas or harass them. We don't have sales meetings every morning.

The only thing I ask them is to be neat and wear a tie. I don't allow any beards. I allow stylishly long hair, but I don't like the kooky look. These people are on display the same as the merchandise.

The mechanics go under the same rules; no beards, no overly long hair, clean clothes; because they're on display as well. We want people to get the feeling that they're dealing with ordinary people like themselves; that they're not running into a bunch of slobs or kooks out in the shop. Most people don't take any offense at beards nowadays, but for the few that do, I don't want it. We had problems at the beginning when we enforced this, but they worked out. Now we make it a condition of employment.

Elman felt that the chief incentive Majestic offered its mechanics was the opportunity for overtime. As he reported it:

Most of them work on cars and motorcycles because they love it. Some of them would work for nothing if they had to. We start mechanics at the bottom of the heap, and if they work out well we send them to Honda school. They can work as much as they want, up to 80 hours a week with time and a half for everything over 40 hours.

Our hourly rate is pretty much standard. The difference is the overtime and fringes. A good mechanic who wants to work can make $16,000 to $17,000 a year. I'd like to get them over $20,000. Then they get all paid holidays, a week's vacation after the first year and another week for each five years with us, Blue Cross and Major Medical for themselves, and for their families, if they want to pay the difference, and after they've been here a year—if they're over 25—they get in on our new profit-sharing plan.

We pay mechanics up to . . . let's see . . . the highest one is $6.00 an hour, and we figure it averages about $5.00 an hour. With all the fringes and overtime it comes to about $9.00 an hour. Since we estimate all our costs at 65 per cent, we bill mechanics' time out at $14.00 an hour. We know this is low, so I think we're going to have to start billing it at $16.00 an hour, which is about average for around here.

Ordering Merchandise

The four major types of merchandise carried by Majestic in the Honda stores were automobiles, motorcycles, parts, and accessories. Each was ordered differently. In fact, automobiles were not ordered at all. As Arthur Elman explains:

> We've never ordered a Honda car since we've been in business; we've never ordered a color, a model or a quantity. They call us up to tell us what we're going to get, and whatever we can get, we take.
>
> We're not as subject to a "season" as American cars. When the model changeover comes at the first of the year, we'll get in a load of cars with half '76s and half '77s. The next load might be all '76s, and the next all '77s. People don't seem to care. The Civic went up about $150 at retail, so given the choice, they take the '76s for the difference.
>
> Of course, we discount the leftovers $50–$100, but we don't have any big year-end clearance sale. Honda gets the same amount for the last car of the year as the first. No rebates.

Motorcycles were different; these were not only ordered by year, type, model, and color, they were picked up in New Jersey by Majestic's own trailer truck. Elman continues:

> Motorcycles we play by ear. A sales analysis won't work, because motorcycles are a fad business. This year one model may be the in thing; next year this may not go at all. So we have to play it by ear.
>
> I sit down with (Lloyd Paterson and Bill Mahlerwein) my managers once a week—if we don't sit down, we use the tie-line to Lincoln—and we discuss it. We make up our motorcycle orders. We try to order at least 40 crates at a time, because we do our own pick-up with our own trailer truck. 'Cycles are packed one or two to the crate, depending on size. Whatever is moving, we replenish. We know about what we want in inventory, and what we don't.
>
> Storage is no problem. The bikes that are not on display are stored over at the mill, along with a lot of the parts inventory, at no charge. This helps, because we've got a big inventory right now.
>
> Honda had so many bikes left over when business slumped that they're still selling '75s and '76s as well as '77s. Last year we bought some '72s. Prices have gone up, and some people would rather save the money than have this year's model. We're still buying '75s, but I've stopped ordering any '76s because I figure they're going to start discounting them pretty soon, like they do the '75s.
>
> On '77s, we're using Honda's suggested retail price, which gives us a 20 per cent margin, the lowest we've ever gotten, and this year, for the first time, Honda is rebating the set-up charge in the form of a credit on parts.

Elman explained the decision to buy a trailer truck and handle their own motorcycle deliveries in the following way:

> Freight rates are now a disaster; that's the reason we got into the trucking business. A full trailerload of motorcycles—40 crates—out of Newark costs us 800 and some odd dollars by common carrier. It costs us $141 to pick them up with our own truck, with tolls, fuel, driver, and coffee and doughnut money at the warehouse. Of course, this doesn't include the depreciation and insurance.
>
> We decided to put the truck in a separate leasing company to limit our liability. We carry a million-dollar policy on it, but I'm not sure if that's even enough if . . . God forbid . . . the truck should hit a school bus. Occasionally we lease the truck to a manufacturer or the textile company to help to cover some of the costs.
>
> Insurance rates have gone crazy. A few years ago, I took a million-dollar umbrella policy on the business, and it cost me about $700. Last year it went to $1,800, and this year they tell me the premium will be $3,600. And I'm beginning to worry that $1,000,000 isn't enough; that we should have a $2,000,000 policy.
>
> It's gotten so bad that I've thought of making each of the stores a separate business, so that if we get sued in one, and the insurance isn't enough, at least we won't lose the whole business.

The Honda stores also did what was termed, "a big business" in parts and accessories. Most parts and accessories were ordered by mail and delivered by freight within two weeks. Rush orders could be placed by phone and delivered by express in about four days. On orders that filled 50 lines or more of the order form, Majestic received a discount of 7 per cent from the dealers' list price, a discount which Bill Mahlerwein pointed out, "just about covers the freight costs." The company truck was rarely used to pick up parts or accessories even though most of these came from Newark. The orders were seldom large enough to warrant sending the truck, and when it was picking up motorcycles it was usually full.

Parts were ordered for each store separately on the basis of what the service and parts managers of that store felt were needed or what they would like to have in inventory. They based their decisions on inventory levels, current needs, and seasonal projections. Accessories were ordered for each store by the parts manager and the general manager on the basis of inventory levels and what the general manager felt could be sold in his store.

Parts were sold through the service departments in conjunction with repairs, and over the counter through the parts department to people who did their own repairs. Some of the latter were sold to other automobile and motorcycle dealers in Massachusetts, Connecticut, and Rhode Island, at prices ranging from 10 per cent to 20 per cent over dealers' cost.

Honda offered only a limited number of automobile accessories, such as air conditioning, custom trim and wheels, and roof racks. Since the cars were not custom ordered, these were not factory installed. Most were sold with new cars and installed by the automobile service department at the time of delivery.

Motorcycles generated a far larger accessories business in the form of equipment for the rider and equipment for the machine. Each store had some 1,500 square feet of display space in its showroom for rider equipment, such as helmets, jackets, gloves, and boots; and for bike equipment, such as windscreens, luggage carriers, mirrors, radios, gauges, backrests, and the like. It was not uncommon for a large road bike to carry $500 to $1,000 worth of accessories, or for a rider to spend a few hundred dollars on personal equipment.

Whereas each store ordered its parts and accessories separately, if one needed an item that was available at the other, it could have the item merely by asking for it. This was so common that inventory flowed back and forth between the two stores almost daily. No records or invoices were kept on these inventory transfers.

In February, 1977, it was estimated that the combined parts and accessories inventory—on display, in the parts departments, and in storage at the West Warwick store and at the mill—had a value in excess of $250,000 at cost. Commenting on this Arthur Elman said:

> In a foreign car franchise like ours, we can't run down to the corner parts store for parts, so we stock many, many times more parts than an American car dealer. A regular dealer, if he has $70–80,000 in parts, he feels loaded. We have over $250,000 in parts at our cost, but we do a big parts business. We keep the counter open 8:00 to 5:00 on Saturdays, and until 9:00 at night on weekdays.

One of the costs of carrying inventory in stock was the local inventory property tax. In February, the tax rate in West Warwick was $52 per $1,000 with a 65 per cent valuation, approximately the same as that in Lincoln. The tax rate was expected to go up in March.

Estimating Costs

Honda offered its dealers a real-time computerized inventory control system that would allow a dealer to know exactly what he had on hand and on order, his purchase price, the retail price, and the actual margin earned on inventory sold during a period. The terminal could also be used for ordering parts and accessories. Elman had considered it, but rejected it:

> It costs a fortune; somewhere around $20,000 a year. And it would mean that every item sold, every nut and bolt, would have to be punched into the computer. The trouble with a lot of these systems is that they cost more than they save.
>
> The system we have now is kind of archaic, but it works. If a parts man takes something out of a box, and he sees the supply is getting low, he puts a clothespin on the box. The parts manager checks these every day or so. The date and the amount of the last order are written on the box, so he can tell how fast the part is moving. If it's getting obsolete, he just Xs-out the box. If it's moving fast, he checks with the service manager to see if they should increase the order.
>
> We use Honda's suggested retail price, and the markup varies all over the place—from 10 per cent to a few hundred per cent—so we use an estimated cost of 65 per cent. I don't care what we make on an individual part of an individual deal. What difference does that make? I just want to know the average. When we take inventory, if we find the estimate is off, we change it.

The system of estimating costs was applied to service work, as well. Most jobs, whether degreasing and setting up a new car or bike or repairing a customer's vehicle, had a standard for the time it should take and the amount to be charged. The charges were applied against the dealer allowance on new vehicles, to Honda on warranty work, or to the customer on repair work. On all of these, labor was estimated at 65 per cent and the margin at 35 per cent.

On nonstandard jobs that involved diagnosing what was wrong with a vehicle and repairing it, the mechanics were suppose to record the actual time spent on the job, and this was billed at $14.00 an hour to allow a 35 per cent margin. If the service manager felt that the diagnosis or repair work had taken longer than it should, he could, and often did, charge the customer for less than the actual hours worked.

The bookkeeper kept a monthly "labor inventory" for the service departments, based on the number of paid hours of labor. The inventory was reduced by the "billed hours"—those billed to customers, to warranty work, and to internal charges, such as vehicle preparations and repair work done on company cars. The time that mechanics spent going to the other store or the mill complex for vehicles or parts, and any time spent waiting at the parts counter during rush periods, was charged to the parts department. In spite of all efforts to keep accurate records, there was usually a "surplus" of $300 to $400 in paid time that had to be written off at the end of the month.

Elman credited this to poor record keeping, a problem that kept coming up again and again. He commented:

> Sure, I know we're loose on a lot of things. Nobody is really forced to comply on the record work. We're probably estimating our costs too low on labor and too high on parts. I don't know. Our system isn't 100 per cent, but then neither is a computer.
>
> We have this computer service for bookkeeping, and that thing is always out of whack. Take sublet repairs—the work, like bodywork, that we have to send out to be done by somebody else. We were keeping that on the computer and it looked terrible. We had all these bills we had paid for sublet repairs, and none of it was shown as billed out to customers.
>
> So one day I told the office girls to track it down. It took three of them most of a day, and they found almost every single thing had been billed, but it had been billed as parts or as labor, and that put the parts and labor inventories out of whack. Ridiculous! I told them to just take the sublet repairs off the computer and forget it. We weren't losing anything except what we were paying to print the stuff on the computer sheets . . . at 75¢ a line.
>
> This computer . . . I don't know what it costs us, but between the girl punching it in, and the rent of the machine and the supplies, it's very, very expensive. It's at least $10,000 a year. And for what?
>
> We have to have it because we have to furnish a four-page financial statement to Honda every month, and there's no way we can do it manually. It's impossible. The statement is standard in the industry. You can't just give the manufacturer a little profit and loss statement. They want everything analyzed to the nth degree.
>
> We get tons and tons of stuff out of the computer every month that I don't even look at; don't even need. For instance, we get a big sheet that ages every one of our motorcycles. Now who cares! I don't care if one motorcycle is six months old and another is one month. It's the same model, same price, same everything. If we wanted to take them in order, it would mean a forklift operator over at the mill for an extra hour just digging around in the cases to find the right serial number. It's not worth it!
>
> Look at the gasoline inventory. Every few months it gets up so high that it's twice our storage capacity, so we have to adjust it. It's been used. What does that mean, that people are stealing it? No! They're just not writing it down!

Look . . . my people are not perfect, but they're better than 90 per cent of the people in this industry, and I know that for a fact. There's practically never a complaint. You should hear how customers rave about the sales people and the service.

I'm not going to act like Big Brother, watching them all the time, telling them what to do. If you do that, you never find out what they can do for themselves; they never learn anything. They make mistakes. Who doesn't? When they make mistakes, they hear about it. I don't threaten them or cajole them. And very rarely does a mistake come up the second time.

I treat my people the same as if they were my partners here. After all, their livelihood depends on this business. Right now, we have a profit-sharing plan. When the time comes, I want to give them part of the business. I'm not going to live forever.

I still consider us a country hardware store. That's what we are. The volume is a lot higher, but it's still the same thing, and we run the same way as we always did. Sure, we're more sophisticated on a lot of things, but this sophistication isn't all for the good.

FINANCING

Until the West Warwick automobile dealership was opened, Majestic used little financing, and what there was was seasonal:

> In the hardware business, every once in a while we'd have "spring dating" on a lot of merchandise, so I'd borrow $10,000. When I did, I wouldn't sleep for a month saying, "How am I ever going to pay back $10,000?" Then spring would come and I'd sell the merchandise and we'd pay back the $10,000, and that would be the end of it for a year.
>
> Now I've been as high as $800,000 on 30-day notes, and it doesn't seem to bother me. Well, it bothers me, but not a lot more than the $10,000. No . . . it bothers me a lot, and sometimes, if I owe a lot and go through a month of slow business, I start panicking . . . start worrying about it.

Honda motorcycles and automobiles are shipped "cash on delivery." Until 1975, Majestic needed little financing. Then three factors combined to force it to use heavier and more continuous borrowing. The first was the decision to invest in the new West Warwick building. The second was the cost overrun. The third was that Honda, which had been rationing cars to the extent that most were sold before or shortly after delivery, increased production and shipped some 250 cars to Majestic in the summer of 1976. Arthur Elman commented:

> Until then, I didn't know what it meant to have an overhead. Now I have a $350,000 mortgage at 9 per cent on the West Warwick building, plus the 30-day notes.
>
> But we have a very, very good relationship with the bank. We borrow on the 30-day notes, and we renew, pay back, or take more, whatever the case may be. We don't use floor planning. Right now, we borrow money at about 3 per cent less than any dealer that floor plans, which is about 99 per cent of the dealers. We're paying, right now, 6.5 per cent, a quarter over prime rate, which is pretty unheard of in this industry. We get the preferred rate because I cosign all the notes personally.

Elman's relationship with the bank started in 1966 when he decided to invest some of his personal funds in a textile business with a friend who was an expert in weaving narrow elastic fabrics. The original plan was to buy some obsolete equipment that was for sale, modify it, and start in a small way. During the negotiations, Elman decided that instead of buying the obsolete equipment, Majestic should borrow some funds and buy out the selling company completely. Later, when he found he couldn't get satisfactory repair and maintenance on the mill complex in which the business was housed, he bought that as well.

> We had no trouble getting the mortgage here, or getting a line of credit, first \$500,000, then \$800,000. The bank takes both businesses into consideration when they set our rates.
>
> At first, the bank wanted a 10–10 compensating balance on the notes; 10 per cent of the line of credit, and 10 per cent of the amount in use. I said, "No way! I don't make anything on that money unless it's invested in merchandise." 10–10 on a \$500,000 line, with all of it in use, would mean I'd have to keep a compensating balance of \$100,000. We talked, and finally they agreed.

In the fall of 1976, the bank asked that Majestic start sending it copies of the monthly financial statements so that the bank could have a better "risk profile" on the loans. After an extended discussion, Elman agreed to send the bank Majestic's quarterly statements, but he knew that if his borrowing got too far out of line with his equity the bank might suggest he go into floor planning or pay a higher interest rate.

The preliminary figure for 1976 showed that Majestic had done just over \$5,000,000 in business between the hardware store and the two Honda automobile and motorcycle dealerships, and that it had made money, somewhere around \$150,000 before taxes. Elman didn't know exactly how much, and wouldn't know until the annual inventories were completed, and all year-end adjustments were made on the financial statements.

In Elman's mind this was not a problem; it was just the price you paid for simplifying the business by using estimated costs instead of actual costs. They would have the actual earnings within a week or two.

There were more important things to worry about. One was fixed expenses, which seemed to be going up and up with no end in sight; heat, light, insurance, taxes, everything, and he had just had to add dump service at the West Warwick dealership—one more thing he was going to have to pay for that he hadn't paid for in the past.

And there was the interest expense. In the last year, between the mortgage on the West Warwick dealership and the 30-day line of credit used to finance the cars and bikes, Elmer had paid more than \$75,000 in interest charges. A few weeks earlier, he had reached the \$800,000 maximum on his short-term borrowing, and even though he had now paid it down to \$600,000, he didn't like owing that much.

Elman could have paid more, but delayed doing so because he was expecting a shipment of cars. A series of snow storms had hit the East Coast, and the shipment would not be in for a week or two. As a result, he had found himself holding almost \$200,000 of borrowed money in his checking account. He was now using that money to get into the used car business.

ENTERING THE USED CAR BUSINESS

The used car opportunity had been with Majestic for some time. In the four years since Majestic had opened its first Honda store in Lincoln, it had sold automobiles and taken used cars in trade. Most trade-ins were sold at wholesale prices to other dealers, and a few were sold at retail to individual customers.

In the spring of 1976, Martin Dittleman, Majestic's accountant from Laventhol and Horwath, questioned Elman about going into the used car business. Dittleman recalls:

> He was wholesaling the used cars because he didn't want to be in that business. Used cars take a different strategy and different techniques. He didn't want to be bothered with it. This way, he knew what his profit was. He'd get rid of the cars, and he knew where he stood at all times.
>
> But he was throwing away a tremendous market. People were coming to him, but he had nothing to show them except the few used cars that might be there for a few days. I thought this was the last thing he should be doing, especially in the springtime when students were looking for cars to use on summer jobs and there was just no supply around.
>
> Then he was talking with another dealer who said to him, "You're not wholesaling? My God! I make more money on my used cars than on my new car sales. You tend to offer a little less for a trade-in on a Honda Civic, so you're buying your used cars a little bit better than I am!" He found it was true; other dealers were making more on used cars than new.
>
> One day I told him, "Arthur, it's another aspect of the business that you can't be out of. It's part and parcel of it. If you're going to make money and be successful in the automobile business, you have to be successful in all phases. You can't throw away the used car part of it."

Elman hesitated to get into the used car business because it differed from his current businesses in two ways: the first was that it was more responsive to short-term supply and demand and to the prices that competitors were asking for the same car; and the second, that used cars depreciated if they were kept on the lot for any length of time, a fact that had to be kept in mind when pricing or trading.

There was one thing more: accounting presented a number of problems when dealing in used cars. If the price of a trade-in was inflated because the car might bring a good price on the used car lot, this cut the commission of the salesman selling the new car. If the new and used car departments were separate, there were questions about how to determine the profitability of each—questions that could turn into major issues if the department managers earned bonuses on the basis of profitability.

If a car taken in trade needed repairs, service, cleaning, or bodywork, which was almost always the case, this went to the service department and had to be costed into the resale price of the car. And, finally, a used car was seldom a single sale; it was part of a chain of sales that continued until the last trade-in was wholesaled or junked.

ELMAN SUMS UP THE PROBLEM

Arthur Elman admitted that Majestic "backed into" the automobile business, that he ran it differently than most people in the business, that, in fact, he ran it like "a country hardware store." He talked about the business, and what he saw as his problem.

> Sure, we run it like a country hardware store. What's wrong with that? That's what we are. When we were just selling motorcycles, we made a lot more at it than most automobile dealers were making selling automobiles.
>
> When we started in automobiles, we sold about six to eight cars a month. Now, with two stores, we can sell 70 when we can get them. The motorcycles dropped "way down." We could double our motorcycle business without increasing our overhead at all. These places were set up with the idea that we were going to sell 1,600 motorcycles a year, plus the cars. We're not selling them, but we're capable of it. The economy is off. We're not big enough to reserve a nationwide trend.
>
> We look at the statements, and we say, "We're weak on financing cars. We can do something about that." We talk to our salesmen and tell them we'll given them a commission on financing, and try to build that up.
>
> We do a big parts business because we have the counter open when people can get here. So now we're going to try opening it at 7:30 in the morning to see if we get more. We're going to put in a drop-off service for people working at the new Metropolitan Insurance building, with a shuttle bus going back and forth, so we'll get more service and repair work.
>
> So . . . where do I cut? I can sit here and pick out every mechanic and tell you what he's doing. I can't eliminate this one; I can't eliminate that one, so I can't change that.
>
> I can't change the money that we have to pay in interest to the bank. We have to have the money—that's all there is to it—and we have to pay for it. The mortgage on the building has to be paid. There're no two ways about it; it's a fixed expense.
>
> Our telephone bills? We can't cut that because the bulk of it is Yellow Pages advertising. We have quite a few long distance calls, but calls are cheaper than writing a letter. When parts people call up instead of mailing an order, they see if there are any specials, as well as finding out if they're going to get the part they want and when. We have a tie-line between the two stores that costs us $116 a month, but before we had it, it used to cost us $250–$300 a month for calls.
>
> You look at all these things and you say, "Where am I going to chop?" You cut out the overtime, and the work won't get out. You hire kids in here at $3.50 an hour to work the second shift, and the work will go out sloppy. You put your mechanics on straight time, and what do they do in their spare time? They moonlight. At what? Repair work. So the next thing you know customers are saying to mechanics, "Gee, this job is going to cost a lot. Why don't you do it on your own time? I'll save money and you'll make more on the job." I'd rather have them working for me on overtime.
>
> Our only problem . . . our main problem . . . is that fixed expenses keep going up, and we can't pass them on to the customers. So we try to sell more volume to make up for it.
>
> I have to admit that I don't spend as much time on statistics as I should. Paperwork overwhelms me. I look at the financial sheets, but there are just too many variables in there. That's why I tell you they don't mean a thing to me. The bottom line is the thing that's important.

I look at the computer sheets and they'll show a good month and a bad month, but I don't think the computer sheets are showing as much profit as we're making because we're averaging a lot of things, and naturally I'm going to take them on the low side.

The only thing I worry about is paying our bills, which we do—religiously—on the 10th of the month. If I have to borrow the money to do it, I do. Many accounts we don't have to pay the 10th. They wouldn't say a word because we're such good customers, but I don't want to do that.

My objective is to get everything going and reduce our debt. We are reducing it, but I'm impatient because we were on a cash basis for so many years.

Our main problem, as I've said, is that we can't pass on our added costs. So we have to go for more volume. That's why I've decided we should go into used cars. What else can we do?

So in January 1977, Elman talked with Vincent Flynn, a used car dealer from Providence, Rhode Island, who had acted as his agent in wholesaling Majestic's used cars. If it was to go into the used car business, Majestic would have to become a buyer rather than a seller in the wholesale market. Flynn agreed to change roles, and act as Majestic's buyer at the wholesale automobile auctions throughout the Northeastern states, for 10 per cent of the net volume Majestic did in used cars, plus $200 a week toward expenses. Elman agreed.

A week later Elman took another step and hired two professional used car salesmen for the West Warwick store; one as a salesman, the other as the manager of the Used Car Department. The new salesman was to receive $2.75 an hour plus commissions, the same as the other salesmen; the manager was to receive a weekly salary, sales commissions, plus a 10 per cent on the net volume of the Used Car Department.

It was agreed that all sales personnel could sell both new and used cars, and motorcycles as well. On the new cars, motorcycles, accessories, financing, and insurance, the commissions would be the same as in the past. On Accords, the commission was cut to ¾ of 1 per cent retroactive to the beginning of 1977.

On used cars, the commission structure would be based on the gross profit of a sale: the selling price, less the purchase price of the vehicle, the charges for putting the car in condition for sale, and a $100 lot charge to cover Majestic's expenses. The commission rates were to be as follows:

5% on the first $200 of gross profit
10% on the next $300 of gross profit
15% on all of a $500 gross profit
20% on all gross profit over $500

In the Automobile Service Department at West Warwick, manager Billy Albro bought what he called, "a big tune-up cabinet" for servicing and reconditioning used cars, plus a stock of tires, oil filters, wiper blades, and other small parts, and commented:

For anything big we need, we can call the NAPA* place a mile down the road and have it delivered free in 15 minutes. We get a 25 per cent discount on those, and just charge the customer the suggested retail price.

I'd like to have a "scope" (oscilloscope) and some electro-testing equipment,

* National Automobile Parts Association

> and more parts. A "scope" is expensive—about eight grand—but you need it and it saves time.

At the Lincoln store, the decision to go into used cars meant little or no change, as Bill Mahlerwein, the Lincoln general manager explained:

> We don't have room for used cars. You need room for reconditioning, and someone who can be working on the used cars. I only have four repair bays—West Warwick has eight—and with the volume of Honda service we're doing right now, there just isn't room.
>
> Our problem is that we have no room to expand. We're built as close as we can be to the brook in front of our property, and what little space we have beside the building has to be used for the driveway and parking.
>
> We've tried to buy about an acre of land next to ours, but it belongs to the city water department. It's of no use to them, but we haven't been able to get them to sell. We've even offered to trade them another acre we own down the street, but just when it looked like we were making progress, the town officials changed and we had to start over. If we don't get the property, we have a problem.

By the second week in February, Lloyd Paterson, the general manager of the West Warwick store, started noticing a problem of his own; a problem of personnel rather than property. How serious it might become, he wasn't sure:

> It's starting to get a little "gamey" here. I'll put it that way. The two new salesmen we hired have been in the business so many years they're very aggressive; very hungry.
>
> We should take turns on the next customer, but we don't. It goes to whoever's on the floor. But the new men are watching the parking lot. Sometimes they'll ask me, or one of the other salesmen, to run an errand because they saw someone drive in, and they'll take the customer.
>
> As soon as our salesmen get a taste of selling used cars—that can pay a bonus that's three times as much as the bonus on a new car—you might see a little more scrambling for the customer that comes in and heads for the used cars.
>
> When I realize I can pick up more money on a used car, I'll be more aggressive for that used car sale than I was on the new cars. I'm more aggressive now. I used to be shy. Sometimes it's a little frightening to me.
>
> It's changing the nature of the business, but there's a lot more money in the used car business for the sales person and for the house. We've always been a little country store operation, but now we're getting bigger and bigger.

CASE THREE

Bankers Trust of South Carolina (A)

WILLIAM R. BOULTON
University of Georgia

Assignment Questions:

1. Do you consider Bankers Trust to be successful? Why?
2. How would you describe Bankers Trust's organizational strategy?
3. What problems do you see in the future? What would you do? Why?

By 1981, Bankers Trust of South Carolina had joined the ranks of banks with over a billion dollars in assets and over ten million in net operating earnings (Exhibit 1). In September 1981, after a fifteen-year compounded growth rate of 17.5 per cent for assets and 19.5 per cent for earnings, chairman W. W. Johnson expressed concern about the banking industry's future:

> Our strategy over the past two decades had been to establish ourselves as a statewide bank, being in principal markets, having a strong management team, and a profitable bank, and contributing to the growth of South Carolina. We probably achieved this in about 1978. We've made a few bank acquisitions since that time. However, its a totally new ballgame today.

Johnson's concern for Bankers Trust's future was a result of rapid changes in the banking industry as he explained:

> Two things have changed today's ballgame. First is, of course, the Deregulation Act of 1980. The second is that we now have one hell of a lot of brick and mortar and people for a bank our size. As long as we were operating in a protected environment with cheap money, we could aggressively market our services and make a good spread. I don't think we'll be able to do that three years from now.

Background and History

Bankers Trust of South Carolina (BTSC) is the largest state-chartered bank in South Carolina and ranks among the top three banks in assets and deposits and second in number of branches. As of June 30, 1981, assets reached $1.1 billion with deposits of $891 million (see Exhibits 2, 3 and 4 for current financial data).

EXHIBIT 1: Past Performance

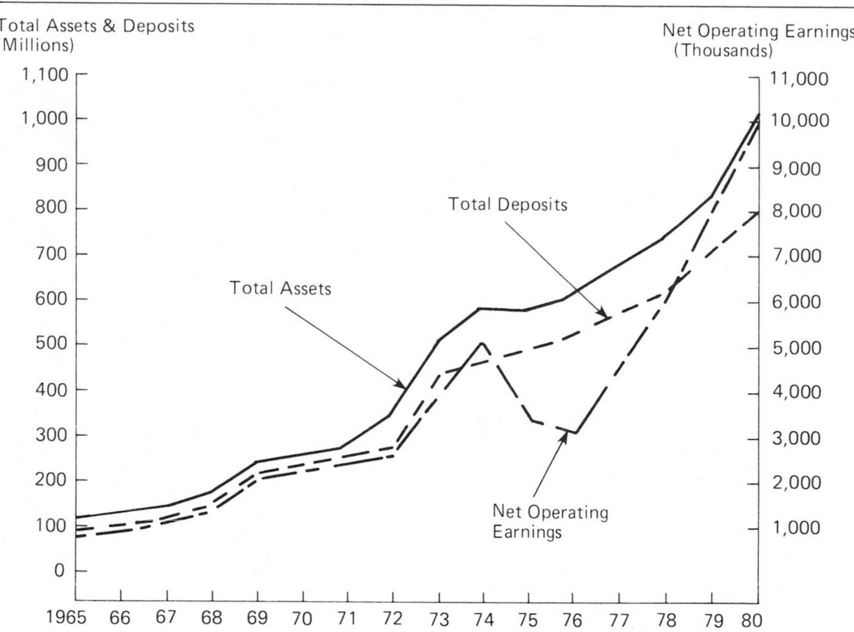

Bankers Trust of South Carolina began as the Bank of Greenwood, a small, moderately successful $5 million country bank, in which Dewey H. Johnson and his friends acquired controlling interest in 1943. The Bank of Greenwood had been chartered by the state in 1886 and had begun operation in 1888. Under Johnson's leadership, the bank soon became the fastest growing bank in South Carolina. As described in the bank's history:

> He moved against the grain of conventional money lending; he took credit to the little man. He urged farmers to set their sights beyond the one-crop cotton economy. He counseled merchants to build their own communities. He lent small sums to people who had never borrowed from a bank before.

In 1955, Johnson changed the bank's name to State Bank and Trust Company to reflect its expanding growth and range of services in serving the textile and farming communities of the area. That year also marked the beginning of the bank's merger activity and expansion outside of the Savannah River Valley. Prior to Johnson's death in 1961, he had merged with banks in Wagener, Columbia, Whitmire, Cayce, and Abbeville, South Carolina.

At Dewey Johnson's death in 1961, the bank had grown to more than $60 million in assets with eighteen offices. His eldest son, Wellsman Johnson, served as president until 1965, when he became chairman of the board, and Dewey's second son, W. W. "Hootie" Johnson, was elected president. As a result of this continued family leadership, the bank's history states:

> Management has supported the simple precept that the bank must help the community grow if the institution itself is to grow. Repeatedly, the leadership has vindicated this belief. It has committed capital for growth or re-growth of areas where others have waited for the "trend" to happen. And, the commitment has

EXHIBIT 2: Consolidated Balance Sheet (June 30, 1980–1981)

Bankers Trust of South Carolina and Wholly-Owned Subsidiaries

	June 30,	
Assets	*1981*	*1980*
Cash and due from banks	$ 94,130,766	$ 93,939,290
Temporary investments:		
Federal funds sold and securities purchased under agreements to resell	104,958,684	10,150,000
Trading account securities	23,034,913	32,700,593
Other temporary investments	5,915,908	21,604,220
Total temporary investments	133,909,505	64,454,813
Investment securities:		
U.S. Treasury securities	127,305,832	112,608,927
Securities of other U.S. government agencies and corporations	40,985,073	19,330,089
Obligations of states and political subdivisions	127,280,151	121,194,498
Other securities	966,020	682,461
Total investment securities	296,537,076	253,815,975
Loans		
Commercial and Industrial	182,356,222	143,540,835
Residential real estate	82,158,959	66,798,317
Mortgages held for resale	11,270,356	16,694,955
Construction and land development	21,947,733	15,356,513
Installment	180,427,815	167,019,477
Credit card	73,606,985	57,731,952
Gross loans	551,768,070	467,142,049
Less: Unearned income	(28,997,221)	(23,424,874)
Reserve for possible loan losses	(8,993,013)	(7,791,519)
Net loans	513,777,836	435,925,656
Premises and equipment	31,815,317	20,583,511
Other assets	33,288,242	24,133,859
Total assets	$1,103,458,742	$892,853,104
Liabilities and Subordinated Notes		
Deposits		
Demand deposits	$ 356,123,151	$347,533,135
NOW accounts	62,544,893	—
Time deposit open accounts	45,292,899	63,481,440
Savings deposits	118,712,654	117,568,618
Savings certificates	212,736,518	131,700,489
Certificates of deposit	92,041,277	73,662,364
Other time and savings deposits	3,913,980	3,469,128
Total deposits	891,365,372	737,415,174
Federal funds purchased and securities sold under agreements to repurchase	117,786,000	72,303,000
Other liabilities	14,276,578	13,469,408
Total liabilities	1,023,427,950	823,187,582
Subordinated notes	15,000,000	15,000,000

Bankers Trust of South Carolina and Wholly-Owned Subsidiaries

			June 30,	
Assets			*1981*	*1980*
Shareholders' equity				
Preferred stock, $18 par value,	1981	1980		
Series A $1.80 convertible	327,945	335,208		
authorized, issued and outstanding			5,903,010	6,033,744
Common stock, $10 par value				
authorized	4,000,000	4,000,000		
issued and outstanding	3,065,080	2,642,636	30,650,800	26,426,360
Surplus			17,157,571	10,268,142
Undivided profits			11,319,411	11,937,276
Total shareholder's equity			65,030,792	54,665,522
Total liabilities, notes and shareholder's equity			$1,103,458,742	$892,853,104

helped regenerate the inner cities. The bank has generously supported efforts for schools and colleges, for art and music, for minority interests, and for business ventures that promised to add to the stature or the quality of life in a community.

Soon after Hootie Johnson became president, banks were allowed to pay 4 per cent on thrift savings. Believing that the day of free money was limited, BTSC continued to aggressively seek paid-for funds, being the leader in introducing new high-interest offerings. By 1980, BTSC had a 29 per cent share of the state's top five banks in time deposits and open accounts.

Under Hootie Johnson, BTSC also accelerated its thrust into statewide banking coverage. Mergers were completed in Newbery in 1966 and Batesbury and Pickens in 1968. In 1969, management moved to enter other large markets besides Columbia and merged with banks in Charleston, Orangeburg, Johnston, and North Augusta. That year management also changed the name of the bank from State Bank and Trust Company to Bankers Trust of South Carolina in an attempt to shed its "country bank" image. Management also laid plans for a major office building in Columbia to give prominence to the $200 million bank.

In 1969, BTSC management reaffirmed its commitment to the consumer market by issuing Master Charge cards. As Bob Isbell, executive vice president, explained, "We decided to jump into credit cards with both feet. We came in charging, and we were the first bank in the state to later offer dual cards." In 1972, BTSC was also the first bank in South Carolina to put automatic teller machines into service.

During the early 1970s, Hootie Johnson continued the bank's merger activity into the rich Piedmont area of South Carolina:

> In late 1971, Peoples National Bank of Greenville agreed to a proposal to merge. It would become the largest ever in South Carolina. But circumstances were not

EXHIBIT 3: Bankers Trust of South Carolina Quarterly Operating Results 1980–1981

	1981 Quarters		*1980 Quarters*		
(dollars in thousands, except per share)	*Second*	*First*	*Fourth*	*Third*	*Second*
Interest income—taxable equivalent	$ 35,169	$ 30,169	$ 27,211	$ 24,982	$ 24,525
Interest expense	17,785	16,786	12,820	10,491	10,650
Net interest income—taxable equivalent	17,384	13,383	14,391	14,491	13,875
Provision for loan losses	(600)	(600)	(900)	(900)	(900)
Opening income other than interest	4,595	5,001	3,533	3,092	3,744
Operating expenses other than interest and provision for loan losses	(15,140)	(13,278)	(12,681)	(11,922)	(11,816)
Earnings					
Income before income taxes and securities gains (losses)—taxable equivalent	6,239	4,506	4,343	4,761	4,903
Less taxable equivalent adjustment	(2,379)	(2,354)	(2,171)	(2,147)	(1,908)
Applicable income tax benefit (expense)	(643)	370	347	(70)	(447)
Income before securities gains (losses)	3,217	2,522	2,519	2,544	2,548
Securities gains (losses), less related tax effect	(1)	(896)	4	(37)	(117)
Net income	$ 3,216	$ 1,626	$ 2,523	$ 2,507	$ 2,431
Earnings Per Common Share					
Primary:					
Income before securities gains (losses)	$ 1.04	$ .90	$ .90	$ .91	$ .91
Net Income	$ 1.04	$ .56	$ .90	$ .89	$ .86
Fully diluted:					
Income before securities gains (losses)	$ .99	$ .86	$ .85	$ .86	$ .86
Net income	$ .99	$ .55	$ .86	$ .85	$ .83
Cash dividends declared:					
Preferred	$ .45	$ .45	$ .45	$ .45	$ .45
Common	$ .30	$ .30	$ .30	$ .30	$ .30
Weight average common shares outstanding:					
Primary	2,960,249	2,644,316	2,643,095	2,642,935	2,642,636
Fully diluted	3,259,930	2,946,837	2,946,837	2,946,837	2,946,837

Totals may not agree due to rounding.

EXHIBIT 4: Cash Flow Statement 1980–1981

Bankers Trust of South Carolina and Wholly-Owned Subsidiaries

	Six Months Ended June 30	
Source of Financial Resources	*1981*	*1980*
Funds provided from operations:		
Net income for the period	$ 4,842,248	$ 4,859,844
Charges or credits to income not affecting funds:		
Provision for loan losses	1,200,000	1,800,000
Amortization of premium and discount on investment securities	(6,089)	(95,567)
Depreciation and amortization	1,864,954	1,270,814
Total	7,901,113	7,835,091
Issuance of common stock	10,728,027	—
Sale of Bankers Trust Plaza, Greenville	—	4,901,062
Increase in: deposits	81,125,895	38,848,865
federal funds purchased and securities sold under agreements to repurchase	1,374,000	—
other liabilities and other	—	5,050,711
Decrease in: cash and due from banks	6.367,044	—
federal funds sold and securities purchased under agreements to resell	—	47,100,000
trading account securities	5,599,919	—
other temporary investments	7,686,092	—
Investment securities	17,812,713	—
net loans	—	17,886,686
Total	$138,594,803	$121,622,415
Application of Financial Resources		
Cash dividends declared	$ 2,010,318	$ 1,815,197
Additions to premises and equipment	9,461,279	2,187,838
Acquisition and retirement of common stock	3,244,892	—
Increase in: cash and due from banks	—	3,343,918
federal funds sold and securities purchased under agreements to resell	70,507,567	—
trading account securities	—	18,424,565
other temporary investments	—	20,304,220
investment securities	—	66,603,196
net loans	44,596,670	—
other assets and other	4,573,076	6,320,481
Decrease in: federal funds purchased and securities sold under agreements to repurchase	—	2,623,000
other liabilities and other	4,021,001	—
Total	$138,594,803	$121,622,415

encouraging. Indeed, for two years the growth of each bank was penalized while litigation was framed by the Justice Department under its "potential competition" theory. Finally, terms were reached [in 1973] and at last Bankers Trust entered South Carolina's most potent market.

With this $110 million in assets merger, BTSC gained the geographic reach it needed to become a major bank as well as gaining a position in commercial banking which it had not yet held. With the acquisition of the last two mortgage loan companies in South Carolina in 1972, Aiken Loan and Security in Florence and N. G. Speir in Charlotte, BTSC also entered into the mortgage banking business.

In 1973, with $511.7 million in assets, BTSC moved from a state to national charter—a move which was reversed a year later. In explaining the move back to a state charter, Ed Sebastian, vice-chairman of BTSC, explained:

> We were one of the first banks to go from a national bank back to a state bank charter. We did that because we liked the laws of the state better. We also felt that we would maintain deposits with our correspondents to assist with our clearing activities and loan participation activities. After analyzing the situation we realized that we could get back about $26 million in reserves that weren't earning. Secondly, we could clear our cash letter items just as fast, if not faster, through our correspondents rather than the Federal Reserve System. So there was really no benefit. The only thing we lost was safekeeping, which we never used, and currency shipments which we can buy from anyone. So we converted back. That just shows that we try to be avant garde.

In 1974, BTSC merged with Peoples Bank of Beaufort and also moved its central offices into the new 330,000 square foot, $12.7 million Bankers Trust Tower. With the Bankers Trust name overshadowing downtown Columbia, BTSC displayed its existence and demanded recognition. However, this also marked the beginning of consolidation as chairman Johnson explained:

> We got too large in 1974. We also got into construction lending which was financed by the bank. We had just increased the size of the bank about 50 percent, bought two mortgage loan companies, and brought in some credit experts in the field of construction lending. We should have been making those decisions ourselves, and we took some pretty good lumps in 1975 and 1976 getting out of those bad credits. In 1977 and 1978, the mortgage company just lay dormant.

In recounting BTSC's history and experiences through the 1970s, John Boatwright, vice-chairman of BTSC, explained:

> Let me give some background. The bank started under Hootie's father. He achieved the bank's statewide presence and financed other banks or cash depositories all over the state. He financed businesses all over the state and traveled an awful lot on dirt roads. He started the merger growth and Hootie kept that up through the sixties. We had a lot of merger activity. In 1972, we merged with Aiken Loan and Security. In 1973, we accomplished the large merger of the bank in Greenville. In the mid-seventies, many got into the doldrums and we did too. It wasn't just real estate loans, but we had pinned some money on trees trying to fill up that pipeline and expand the mortgage company.
>
> Because of mergers, we had stretched our people and needed to reconsolidate. So the mid-seventies was a time of consolidation, of improving our internal reporting and of shuffling around to get that behind us. If you look at our perfor-

mance, our charge-offs, they were pretty high during that period. We got them behind us. The other banks that didn't do that still have to face it. Our state laws say you have to charge off real estate acquired through foreclosure over five years at increasing rates of 10, 15, 20, 25, and 30 per cent. We took those right along; wrote them down to market on foreclosure and then wrote them off. We write those off through the loan loss reserves. Many banks set up a separate reserve so they don't have to show these writedowns in loan losses. So as you compare us to other banks you'll see that.

As president of Bankers Trust for fifteen years, Hootie Johnson has had time to develop his own management team. He explained:

I was elected president when I was thirty-three and I had to plan the management transition. I had a chairman and vice-chairman who just retired in the last several years and I had to bring younger guys in. In the last twelve to fourteen years, we have attracted top people because we were aggressive, dynamic, growing, profitable, and a fun place to work. A man knew that if he worked and did a good job that he'd have an opportunity because the bank was growing.

These two older men were invaluable to me, but I saw it was going to get crowded at the top at a point in time. So I worked out an arrangement with them about ten years before they retired for them to retire at age 62. They retired two years apart. As they moved out, I had these four younger men coming along. I never had a number two man, so to speak, because I managed with those two and these younger men under them.

As the two older men moved out it got more complicated. I decided that I would have a four-man team. John Boatwright is our credit specialist and policymaker for the bank. Jim Finch is in charge of systems and operations. Marketing, branch operations, nor anyone else can do anything without checking with systems and operations so he is a very key part of what we do. Julian Turner is president of the bank, is our branch administrator and is in charge of all branch operations. He is responsible for motivating and training our branch people in procedures and services. Ed Sebastian is in charge of the mortgage company.

Ed Sebastian went to Penn State and, before coming with us, worked for Price Waterhouse. Finch was a bank consultant for Arthur Anderson after graduating from Georgia Tech. Boatwright finished Princeton, was in the Navy, and worked for United Virginia Bankshares for about ten years before coming with us eleven years ago. Turner went to the University of Virginia and worked for a Virginia bank before coming here. That's my management team.

John Boatwright, Jim Finch, and Ed Sebastian were also vice-chairmen of BTSC. In commenting on the titles of the management team, Mr. Johnson said, "I guess you would call this the office of the chairman."

BTSC's Objectives and Strategies

In BTSC's annual report for 1980, Chairman Johnson reported to shareholders:

Well-managed banks strive for a 1 per cent return on assets and a 15 per cent return on equity. We are pleased to report that for the third straight year we have exceeded these benchmarks, achieving a 1.13 per cent return on assets and a 19.06 per cent return on equity. Earnings were the highest in the bank's history.

In explaining BTSC's goals, Jim Finch described what he felt was important:

> We're not striving to be number one in the market. We would like to be larger, but South Carolina National has a pretty big lead. I think our interest is to do what we do best which is making money and having growth in shareholder's earnings. The goal is to have consistent and increased growth rather than being the largest bank.

Johnson commented further:

> I'm not thinking about being number one right now, I'm thinking about survival. There will be a lot of banks that go the road of S&Ls. I don't see our bank going that way, but I can see us earning 10 per cent on equity instead of 20 per cent.

At Bankers Trust, strategic planning was not a formal process that resulted in a written plan. In describing the bank's approach at setting strategy, Jim Finch explained:

> We don't have a written strategic plan in the classical sense. We work together so closely that we all have a pretty good perception of where we're going. Broadly we're looking for several key things to do. We have strategic directions to improve our customer service and the business, to provide good information systems, to face the future, and to generate fee income[1] because we know what that is going to mean to us to offset increased interest expense. Fee income reflects our strategic move with the mortgage company. Another of our strategic endeavors is to plan how we are going to run our bank more productively. Like most banks, personnel expense is over 50 per cent of our total noninterest expense. Being a widespread branch bank operation, spreading those deposits on a per branch basis becomes an expensive operation when compared to a unit bank. Because of this we've always pushed for high yields and expense control.
>
> I'd say we follow the strategic planning process. We go through the process of objective and priority setting, and go through all of our options on a long-range basis. We're not like a General Electric where you have a definitive business unit and you can specify what product you're going to make four years from now. Some of our products are dictated by the vagaries of the marketplace and deregulation.

Bankers Trust's competition in South Carolina included a variety of banks. James Finch, vice-chairman, explained:

> Statewise our competitors are C&S, South Carolina National, First National, and some from Southern. Then we get into local communities where we have a different kind of competition such as Farmers and Merchants in Aiken, County Bank in Greenwood, and Bank of Beaufort down in the Hilton Head-Beaufort area (See Exhibit 5).
>
> We keep track of competition with periodic reports. We get that from a variety of services and do our own special reports. Also, we joined Cole survey for salary and for other noninterest expenses. Not everyone is on the noninterest expense comparison.

Financial Strategies

Edward J. Sebastian, vice-chairman and chief financial officer, had been with Bankers Trust for eight years. Prior to joining BTSC, he had experience as a CPA:

[1]Fee income is revenue generated from services provided to customers. In the mortgage company, fees are charged for collecting mortgage payments for the investor.

EXHIBIT 5: Total Deposit Share of Market for Ten Largest Banks, June 30, 1975–June 30, 1980 ($000)

	1975		*1976*		*1977*		*1978*		*1979*		*1980*		*Annual Growth Rate*	
	Total Deposits	*% of SC*	*Total Deposits*	*% of SC*	*Total Deposits*	*% of SC*	*Total Deposits*	*% of SC*	*Total Deposits*	*% of SC*	*Total Deposits*	*% of SC*	*75/80*	*79/60*
SCN	802.510	20.4	796,500	19.4	844,580	18.5	972,956	19.2	1,053,575	19.5	1,134,924	19.2	7.2	7.7
C&S *	505,393	12.8	534,350	13.0	584,906	12.8	649,612	12.8	713,779	13.2	765,934	13.0	8.8	7.3
Bankers Trust *	498,697	12.7	516,633	12.6	577,292	12.7	609,976	12.0	659,512	12.2	737,415	12.5	8.1	11.8
First National	438,101	11.1	476,764	11.4	525,783	11.5	595,509	11.7	619,571	11.4	651,271	11.0	8.3	5.1
Southern B&T *	267,419	6.8	296,905	7.2	321,678	7.1	330,439	6.5	337,556	6.2	378,168	6.4	7.2	12.0
First Citizens *	240,514	6.1	256,393	6.2	245,285	5.4	248,005	4.9	257,488	4.8	274,461	4.7	2.7	6.6
NCNB *	104,197	2.6	111,296	2.7	122,962	2.7	137,873	2.7	142,367	2.6	151,769	2.6	7.8	6.6
F&M, Aiken	46,079	1.2	50,547	1.2	60,981	1.3	70,198	1.4	84,207	1.6				
First Nat'l,											94,726	1.6	15.5	12.5
O'burg.	57,350	1.5	59,873	1.5	67,306	1.5	75,251	1.5	76,336	1.4	85,474	1.5	8.3	12.0
Lexington State	38,392	1.0	46,971	1.1	55,739	1.2	62,748	1.2	72,829	1.3	84,522	1.4	17.1	16.1
TOTAL TOP TEN	2,998,652	76.1	3,146,232	76.5	3,406,512	74.8	3,752,567	73.9	4,017,220	74.2	4,358,664	73.9	7.8	8.5
TOTAL SOUTH CAROLINA	3,941,278	100.0	4,111,099	100.0	4,557,490	100.0	5,081,294	100.0	5,416,714	100.0	5,901,514	100.0	8.4	9.0

* Deposits adjusted to reflect mergers consummated between 1975 to 1980 reporting period.

> Most of my background is with Price Waterhouse. I'm a certified public accountant and was with them in New York, Washington, Charlotte, and Columbia. That's the base of my business experience. My undergraduate degree was in aeronautical engineering and business administration. It gives you the capability of understanding the business world. Although, through my Price Waterhouse experience, I understand how organizations work, how they make profits, how they report their profits, and how they utilize their reporting as a tool to accomplish the main goal of the corporation of making profits for their shareholders. As I see it, that makes profits for our community and then, hopefully, for ourselves.

In describing his current responsibilities, Sebastian explained:

> My current duties and responsibilities include being vice chairman of the board of directors and cashier to the bank, plus having charge of the overall financial structure. I'm also president and chief executive officer of Bankers Mortgage Corporation—our mortgage banking subsidiary. I'm also president and chief executive of BT Building Corporation which is our premises subsidiary. I'm on the executive management committee of the bank and report to the chairman. I'm a member of the construction loan committee of both the bank and of the mortgage company, so I get involved in major lending decisions.[2]

BTSC was not a holding company as was generally the case with banks its size. Sebastian explained the reason:

> In the state of South Carolina, we have a law that allows a nonmember state bank to engage in any activity that a holding company can engage in through its wholly owned subsidiaries. They don't have to be wholly owned, but you have to own 80 percent of the stock. So through our corporate structure, we can do anything that a holding company can do. So we have never had a reason to form a holding company.

BTSC's management was also concerned about the capital adequacy of the bank. In explaining the bank's perspective, Sebastian stated:

> We look at capital adequacy differently than other financial institutions. We think capital adequacy should be determined by the market, not just some general rule for the nation made by regulator agencies. It's our feeling that you have to also look at liquidity and profitability. Penn Central proved that. They had unbelievable assets and not that many liabilities. The problem was that they didn't have enough cash to make payroll. They just didn't have any liquidity.
>
> In inflationary times, the only way to build capital is through the retention of profits, assuming debt or equity is so costly that its not feasible. So you want to be as profitable as you can, give the shareholders the return they deserve for starting the company, and still retain as much as you possibly can by being profitable.
>
> We also look at the use of capital. Its great to say that we have the strongest capital base in relationship to deposits[3] on total assets. The truth of the matter may be that you're denying your shareholders a fair return. Excess capital is as bad as not enough. If the shareholders had that money, they could either buy more stock or invest in an alternative opportunity.

Feeling that overcapitalization penalized the shareholders had resulted in a relatively high dividend payout. Sebastian felt that this had also had a positive effect on their stock price as he explained:

[2]Loans are the primary assets of a bank as shown in Exhibit 2.
[3]Deposits are the primary liabilities of a bank as shown in Exhibit 2.

Our dividend payout ratio is 35 to 36 per cent. We have gone up to 38 per cent. Our dividiend yield is about 6.5 per cent. Compared to our competitors, that's about 700 basis points higher on a market yield basis. We try to keep that yield high.

If you go back into the mid-seventies, you'll see that Bankers Trust's market value has always approximated book. Some of our competitors are lucky if their market yield is 70 per cent of book. We feel that always having a good dividend yield, along with our appreciation in stock and the aggressiveness of the company, has kept our value up. We don't think our shareholders feel we are just retaining capital for the sake of retention, and have therefore stayed with us. That has also helped keep our market value up. Not many places can say that.

Credit and Loan Administration

Before joining Bankers Trust in 1970, John Boatwright had served in various jobs at Virginia Bankshares since 1961. During that time, he had spent several years in credit, had been a lending officer, had worked in the correspondent and national areas, and had moved to branch manager of its main office before leaving. Since coming to BTSC, he had become the bank's senior credit officer and loan administrator.[4] He explained:

I moved down here as city executive for Columbia. In 1973, we lost a senior officer who had effected the mergers with N. G. Spier and Aiken Loan and Security over in Florence. At that time, I took over the responsibility for managing those mortgage subsidiaries as well as the branches. In 1974, we began surfacing bad loans that we had made during that period, and in 1976 I was asked to head up the credit area because of my credit background.

So my primary responsibility today is the credit area. I am senior loan officer of the bank responsible for credit administration and also have responsibility for the international division, the correspondent division, the national division, the credit card and consumer loan areas, and the construction loan department.

Bankers Trust provided a wide range of traditional commercial banking and related financial services to customers engaged in manufacturing, wholesaling, retailing, service industries, real estate, agriculture, institutions, and governmental agencies. Commercial loans were made for working capital, real estate financing, and floor plan loans.[5] As of June, 1981, commercial loans accounted for 33.0 per cent of BTSC's total loans, or $182 million of its $551.8 million loan portfolio. This was an increase of over 27 per cent from June 1980.

In 1981 BTSC was also increasing its residential real estate loans. Representing nearly 15 per cent of the loan portfolio in June 1981, $82 million, it had grown nearly 23 per cent since the previous year. Construction and land development loans had increased nearly 43 per cent, reaching nearly $22 million by July 1981. Mortgages held for resale, however, had declined 48 per cent, down from $16.7 to $11.3 million. In commenting on construction-related loans, Boatwright explained:

After the mid-seventies, we thought we would never get into construction lending again, but we found a darn good man. Construction lending takes a good man on

[4]Determining the amount of credit and the size of loans a customer should have is key to managing a banks assets.

[5]Floor plan loans are used to finance automobile dealers' inventories.

the scene. You need a good, hard-nosed underwriter or you had better stay out of the field.

Bankers Trust maintained correspondent accounts with some thirty banks located in the United States and fourteen in foreign countries. Thirty-eight banks in South Carolina maintain correspondent accounts with Bankers Trust, as did eighteen banks in other states and four foreign banks. Correspondent bank services included loans financing, investments, collections, bank card services, credit information, compliance, and financial planning.

International banking activities were primarily directed at aiding customers in foreign travel and international transactions. Boatwright explained:

> We have not done a great deal of international lending. Our philosophy is that the international department is primarily a service department for our customers. We give good service on foreign exchange trades, on letters of credit, on documentary collection, and other basics.[6] We upgraded this department last fall. We began to see more demand for a good, sharp operation and we brought in a man with experience. The department has grown steadily and very profitably since then. It's getting out of the loss area and we will probably make about $300,000 a year on that operation within a year or two. We still don't intend to become an international bank per se, because our market is too small to support that kind of organization.

Bankers Trust provided consumer installment loans for cars, boats, trailers, campers, taxes, medical expenses, education, home improvements, furniture, appliances, recreational goods, and the like. By June 30, 1981, these loans amounted to over $180 million, nearly 33 percent of BTSCs total loans, and had increased 8 per cent over the previous June.

Bankers Trust also provided a variety of credit card services, offering both Master Charge and Visa charge accounts. Its "Sunmaker" automated teller devices offered seven-day-a-week, twenty-four-hour-a-day banking services. The American Express Gold card was also offered to credit card customers with a $2,000 credit line that provided additional American Express services. Credit card loans amounted to over $73.6 million by June 30, 1981, up 27.5 per cent over the previous year.

The heavy commitment that BTSC made to consumer loans had its impact on its financial statements as Boatwright explained:

> We will always have higher losses when you compare us to our peer group, because our credit card plan is a lot larger and our installment commitment is a lot higher than other banks of our size. We expanded our credit card business very rapidly in the late 1970s, but our return is at the top of all banks in the country. In spite of higher losses, we get higher returns even after losses by running an efficient shop.

To show how BTSC compared to other banks in its bankcard operations, Boatwright explained the report comparing his bank's results with other banks for 1980 (Exhibit 6):

> This report compares our credit card operations against the Federal Reserve's data for all banks. It shows that "net operating income (NOI) before funds cost" has an average yield of 6.1 per cent for all banks. Ours is 11.0 per cent compared to

[6]This service allows international traders to transfer the title of goods at the same time financial payments are made.

EXHIBIT 6: Bankcard Division, Comparison of 1980 Card Operating Performance to Other Banks Reporting to FRB, September 14, 1981

		Federal Reserve Data		*Bankers Trust: More or (Less)*	
	Bankers Trust	*Av. all Banks*	*High Earners*	*Av. all Banks*	*High Earners*
A. REVENUES					
1. Finance Charges	16.9%	13.7%	15.3%	3.2%	1.6%
2. Merchant Discount	2.5%	4.6%	7.3%	(2.1%)	(4.8%)
3. Net Interchange	.4%	.8%	.8%	(.4%)	(.4%)
4. All Other	.4%	1.6%	.9%	(1.2%)	(.5%)
TOTAL REVENUES	20.2%	20.7%	24.3%	(.5%)	(4.1%)
B. OPERATING EXPENSES					
1. Salaries & Wages	2.0%	5.0%	3.2%	(3.0%)	(1.2%)
2. Data Services	1.5%	1.3%	1.4%	.2%	.1%
3. Advertising	.2%	.3%	.3%	(.1%)	(.1%)
4. All Other	2.1%	5.3%	7.4%	(3.2%)	(5.3%)
TOTAL OPER. EXPENSES	5.8%	11.9%	13.2%	(6.1%)	(6.5%)
C. NOI BEFORE LOSSES AND FUNDS COST	14.4%	8.8%	12.0%	5.6%	2.4%
D. LOSSES					
1. Credit	3.2%	2.4%	1.4%	.8%	1.8%
2. Fraud	.2%	.3%	.2%	(.1%)	0
TOTAL LOSSES	3.4%	2.7%	1.6%	.7%	1.8%
E. NOI BEFORE FUNDS COST	11.0%	6.1%	10.4%	4.9%	.6%
F. FUNDS COST	10.6%	8.0%	7.9%	2.6%	2.7%
G. NOI	.4%	(1.9%)	2.5%	2.3%	(1.9%)

> 10.4 per cent for high earners. Our operations are centralized so there is no guessing at the numbers. But you see our credit losses are a high 3.4 per cent compared to the 2.7 per cent for the average bank and 1.6 per cent for the high earners. The reason we do so well is that our operating expenses are lower. Salaries and wages are only 2 per cent for us compared to the 5.0 per cent for the average and 3.2 per cent for high earners. Our finance charges are a little higher because of our mix of business, and our merchant discounts are lower because we've been more consumer oriented over the years. Of the total, our losses are a big proportion because its such a large operation for our size, relative to other banks, and it's a high loss area.

For 1980, Bankers Trust had charged off over $3.8 million in loan losses, of which $2.2 million had come from its credit card operations and $1.0 million from installment loans.

Given the importance of the credit area to the bank, Boatwright had taken actions to strengthen his organization. He explained:

> As to the credit area, we reorganized it, set up regional loan administrators which we hadn't had before, and upgraded the quality of the job so people could look at it as a career job rather than just a temporary job. We also maintain a staff of field monitors—a staff that looks at the loan portfolio on site in the field.

Management had also just instituted a new policy for charging credit card customers. Johnson explained:

> We now charge interest on float. We don't charge a fee. The state passed legislation which allows us to charge 24 per cent. We already had a fee option so when they went to 24 per cent, we went up to 21 per cent and put in a $12 fee. They raised Cain because they hadn't expected us to raise our fee charge. So I said, "Ok, you win!" because they have to renew the 24 per cent figure again after two years and I did not want to make them mad. So we went to 22 per cent, dropped the fee, and eliminated the free period.
>
> We were using $4 million of our money with that float. At 15 per cent, that is $600,000 per year. We're the only ones eliminating the float. If we lose some accounts, we will just lose them; but we will at least have our money back. We communicated this to our customers about two months ago and, as I hear, have had very little flack.

Branch Administration

Julian B. Turner was president of Bankers Trust and, like John Boatwright, came from Virginia with credit and commercial loan experience in 1970. He explained his experiences since joining BTSC:

> I came to Bankers Trust in 1970, a couple of months ahead of John, to head up the credit department. We were a $200 million bank then so we were all pretty close together. In about six months, I went up on the commercial platform as commercial loan officer. In 1971 someone left the bank and I became the senior lending officer of the main office. When John went upstairs, I became the city executive in Columbia.
>
> When we merged with Peoples Bank in Greenville, I was sent up to head up the Piedmont region of the bank in 1973. That region included the Bankers Trust offices in the region plus all of the Peoples Bank's offices. In 1978, I was also given the Western region which was in the Greenwood-Abbeville-Newberry area. In early 1980, I was asked to come down to Columbia and take over all the regions. By the end of 1980, I instituted a statewide business development department here in Columbia and put in business development offices in each of the nine regions across the state. We have now merged the business development area with the marketing department which is also under me. That was just accomplished in the third quarter of 1981.

In September 1981, BTSC had 108 branch offices in forty-five cities and towns in South Carolina. These offices covered twenty-two counties, still less than half the counties in the state. In addition, BTSC had thirty automatic teller machines. See Exhibit 7 for branch locations.

The consumer banking services offered by Bankers Trust included checking accounts, travelers checks, and safe deposit boxes. During the past year, BTSC had introduced two new checking services. Their "Young Budgeter Account"

EXHIBIT 7: Branch Locations in South Carolina

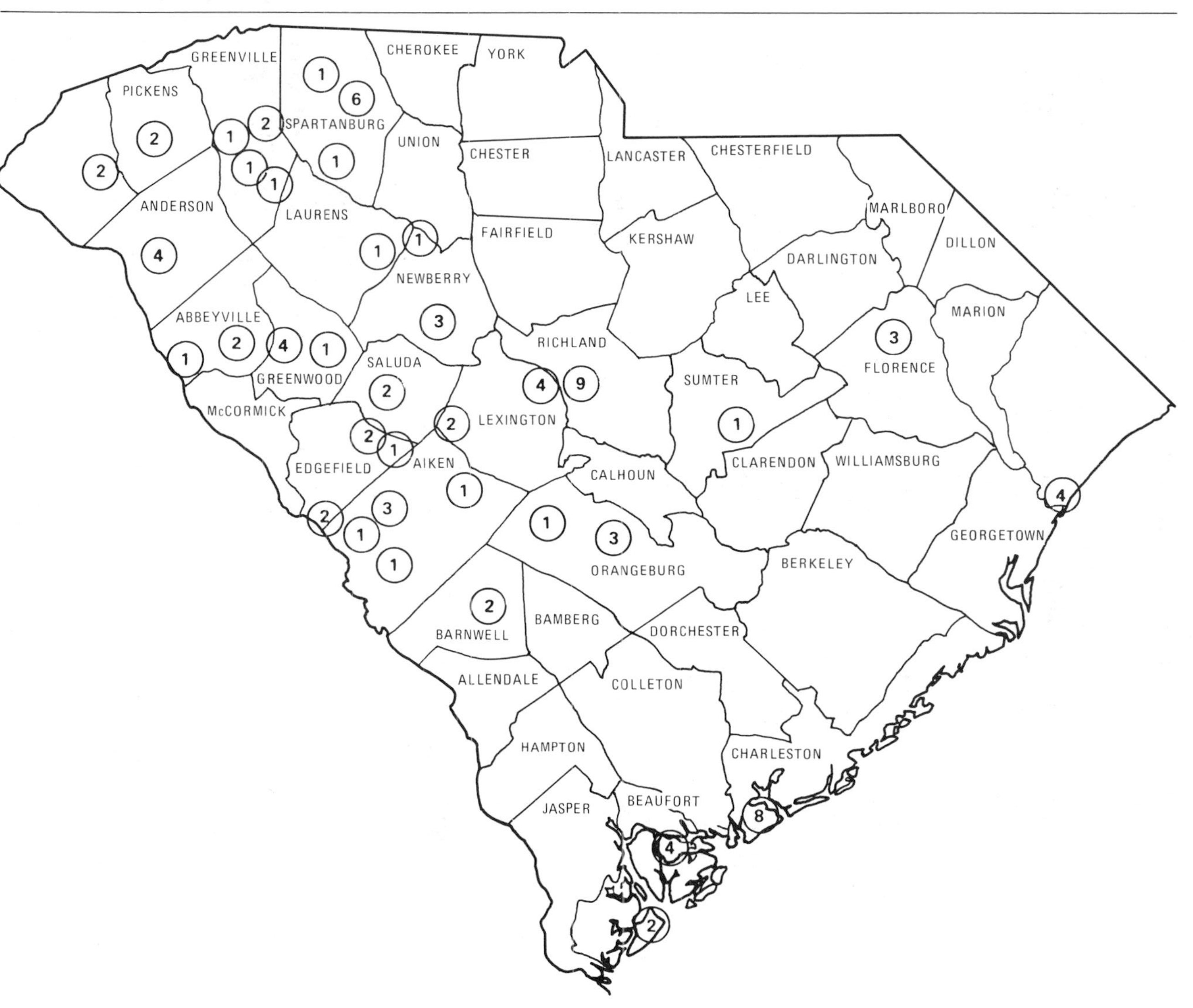

was a special checking account for people under 30 which provided fifteen free withdrawals, or unlimited free withdrawals when balances were over $100. New NOW interest checking accounts required a daily balance of $1,000. Regular checking waived charges with $150 balances. In addition, BTSC offered a new "Anywhere Check"—a Visa debit card—which provided check cashing and cash advance services anywhere in the world, in addition to being used in BTSC's "Sunmaker." Bankers Trust was the first in South Carolina to offer the debit card. From June 1980 to June 1981 Bankers Trust's demand deposit base had grown to $356 million, up only 2.4 per cent from the previous year. However, it had also added $62 million in NOW accounts.

Bankers Trust had also offered money market certificates (MMCs) since 1979. By the end of 1980, it had over $120 million in six-month, high-interest certificates. In 1980, the "Big 30" was introduced, offering thirty-month MMCs at high interest rates. Over $23 million in Big 30 certificates were obtained during the year. By mid-1981, savings certificate deposits had reached over $212 million, a 61.5 per cent increase over the previous June. Finch commented on the bank's success in attracting time deposits:

> We have more time deposits than those competitors our size, so we end up paying a little more for our money. We've gone after time deposit dollars over the years such as the thrift account. We went big after money market certificates, and we got some new accounts with that.

Management was now in the process of changing the branch's emphasis to sales, as Turner explained:

> One emphasis that we are really involved in is creating a new direction for our 108 offices across the state. That emphasis is to bring them from service-oriented offices—we still must give good service—to making them dynamic sales operations by retraining the tellers, retraining the customer service reps, the branch managers, and the assistant branch managers in product knowledge and the art of selling, and completely rejuvenating the sales effort. With 108 offices we have to gain more deposits and really develop the offices that we have. We have too many offices for a bank our size. With the shrinking margins that we're seeing in the banking side, we have to get more business per office. We'll have a smaller margin, but we'll make more money by having more business.

In addition to improving the selling efforts of its branches, BTSC's management was also planning to continue branch expansion. However, future branching efforts would be much more focused as Turner explained:

> We're still opening new branches, but we'll be closing branches that are in areas that are not growing, or areas that we can service with an automatic teller machine. We'll probably close some of the unprofitable offices and continue opening offices in areas of growth where we can see a profit two or three years down the road.

Break-even analyses had also become important in determining the size of new branches. Turner continued:

> In the past we used to build 2400 square foot branches. We had a branch manager with a staff of five or six. Now we're looking at building three sizes: a minibranch with two to three people; a midibranch of 1800 square feet with four to five people; a maxibranch would be 2500 square feet with a full staff; but that wouldn't

come along until we prove the market. The break-even for a mini-branch takes a deposit base of about $1.1 million. The largest office takes a deposit base of about $2.6 million.

We analyze the market very closely and decide what we can do over a certain period of time. We then go in and develop the market and add physical plant and equipment as the market develops. We're also looking for the minibranch to be a very dynamic sales platform. We're retraining the customer service rep to handle that job and opening an avenue of advancement for tellers and service reps to become branch managers. It is having a tremendous effect in the field and we've seen dynamic results in the first five months of the program in new business booked, growth, and increased employee morale.

ATMs also had special importance in South Carolina as vice chairman James H. Finch explained:

Banks have a lot of ATMs in this particular market and several years ago South Carolina probably had more ATMs per deposit dollar than any place in the country. Other competitors now have large numbers. We probably have half the number that C&S has in South Carolina. They have around sixty-five. South Carolina National and First National are in the thirty to forty range. We have thirty and have ten more on order for installation over the next six months. We will keep adding. It's kind of like having drive-ins, we will keep having them in strategic locations. We won't hesitate to move them around either. If we find one that's not really producing, we will move it. We were the first in the state to have them and we moved some of them around.

Bankers Trust used ATMs in both branch and stand-alone applications. In describing the bank's location strategy, Finch continued:

We find that strategically most ATMs probably belong in walls of a branch. People know where the branch is. It is easy to find. We have already centrally located the branch in a particular geographic area. We will also locate ATMs as stand-alone units, for example, at certain large shopping centers. We have three or four stand-alone units now, two in Columbia. We'll include ATMs with our minibranch concept. They will act as a depository, take loan applications, and have ATMs.

ATMs cost from about $47,000 for branch units to $60,000 for stand-alone units. There aren't too many companies in the state of South Carolina that would warrant putting an ATM in a company. We've looked at putting ATMs in convenience stores and supermarkets, but the volume just isn't there. It would be a nice splashy thing to do, but you're talking about a $60,000 or more investment if it's remote, including the building, facade, and electricity. ATMs make sense in companies if they have eight or ten thousand employees at one location. Hospital complexes are interesting because you have a lot of doctors' offices along with the hospital itself.

Systems and Operations

James H. Finch was vice-chairman of BTSC responsible for the more traditional "back room" operations of the bank. Prior to joining the bank in 1971, he had worked nine years for Arthur Anderson & Co. after graduating from Georgia Tech in industrial management. He explained his responsibilities at BTSC:

I'm responsible for all the account services and data processing. We have an internal consulting group called "administrative systems" that reports to me. The per-

> sonnel division reports to me. Internal auditing reports to me administratively, but has a direct line to the chief executive officer and reports to the board of directors. I also get involved in new things. For example, when the deregulation committee introduced the four-year certificate and the all savers certificate, I generally got these projects started even though someone else may do most of the work. My role has changed over the years, because I'm kind of the projects guy.

One of Bankers Trust's most important systems was its settlement of branch transactions. With continued mergers and branch expansion activities, this had been an important area to the bank as Finch explained:

> That's been one of the best things we've done. We have a system that is very centralized with a structure that allows us to accept anything from anywhere. For example, a lot of branch banking operations have to make transactions from branch A to branch B by sending, in effect, a cash letter. You then have a day delay in that process before accounts get posted. Here, we truck all transactions into Columbia. We've had remote processing centers before but they weren't economical. Columbia is the geographic center of the state and the farthest point is about three hours away.
>
> All transactions get entered into our systems and get posted each night. We have what is called an automated interoffice reconcilement system. So everything gets reconciled between all branches and departments and comes out in a report that we have on our desk at 8:30 the next morning. So we're very current. We have a policy of no holdovers of deposits or transactions. We pay a certain price for that, but we just work our schedule so we get it done. But that's been very beneficial to us from an operating standpoint. If there is a customer, for example, that moves from Beaufort to Columbia, they don't have to change their checkbook.

Supporting BTSC's automatic teller machines (ATMs) was also a key part of Finch's responsibility. In describing the importance of ATMs, Finch explained:

> We see ATMs as a way to service our customer base by extending branch banking hours, as most people need. We have our young budgeter program to focus on people under thirty. That obviously ties into ATMs. We have also structured our ATM network so you can use any one of five cards in it. A lot of people just go with the proprietary debit card—that's our Sunmaker card. We also have a Visa debit and a Visa credit card. We're one of the few people in the country to have a Visa debit. We have Master Card and Medallion, a prestige-type private label card. We're structured to provide a lot of flexibility for what people want to use. There is a lot of complexity in the thing, but we work around it. We're supporting that network as an operating system.

In 1979, BTSC replaced its computer with an IBM model 3031 to handle its continued systems expansion, new Anywhere Check and Young Budgeter accounts, growth in certificates of deposits, and development of customer information files (CIF), and to support on-line automatic teller machines (ATMs). However, BTSC's management was still assessing the need for on-line branch information as Finch explained:

> One of the things we'll have that is different from other banks is overnight turnaround for some key reports. We are assessing the need for fast response, immediate response, overnight response, or one-week response. For example, an overnight item will be a credit report. For a commercial credit analysis, we usually don't need that information on an instant response basis. So what we do is print the

whole report and give it to the proper person for their file. We will do that for the credit reports we mail to other banks.

We're trying to focus on the information needs, as opposed to just building a fast response inquiry system, which is what most people do in CIF. We're focusing on the information side first and the fast inquiry side last. We already have inquiries, we're just improving the existing operation there. What we want to do is get something we've never had before. We're in the early part of that—we're building our files and have been cleaning up our records over the last couple of years. The CIF project will go on for several years and, obviously, will become the cornerstone of any branch automation. So that's an exciting area.

In describing BTSC's current branch information systems, Finch continued:

We do have on-line information to the branches through audio-response, so they can check balance information, place holds on accounts, stop payments, and those sort of things. So we do have information on-line for key information that they need. And we're not in an area where customers take advantages of our check cashing limits. We run some risk there, but its an effective way to work it. But we can't tie everything together as we might through branch automation. That's one of the benefits we can't put a direct dollar figure on.

One of the things we are using in our branch network is our CIF. We're not going to put it on-line right away because we want to work out how we want to use the information. It'll be broken down into eight or nine modules of information: one for consumer business development, one for commercial business development, one for solicitations, statistical analyses, on-line inquiries, etc. We have some inquiries handled centrally at Rivermont.

In considering how far BTSC would take branch automation, Finch explained:

Branch automation is very modern but also very expensive. So we're looking at the cost-benefit side of that. We've already solved some of the problems people use branch automation to solve because of our interoffice reconcilement system, because we don't have passbook savings, and other problems some banks are trying to solve. So the benefits that we're going to get will relate to having better information, a consistent way to train tellers, and things like that. They don't translate into direct dollar savings, but may cost $4 million up front plus operating costs. We have about 400 tellers in our network, and if you get a machine for each one of them at $4,000 each plus equipment for customer service representatives, telephones lines, and so on, it adds up in a hurry. But we may still need to sell services better.

BTSC had embarked on programs that could streamline or simplify current operations. Finch explained:

We're putting together a comprehensive program and have placed a lot of responsibility on the division managers to figure out what kinds of things they can do without. In other words, what are we doing that we don't have to do? That gets us results. For example, how many loans should we be collecting at certain size levels? Charge offs may not be as high as labor expenses.

We have some programs under way to automate collection of credit card accounts. We're doing that with an outside service bureau right now. We're putting the collection side of that business on-line with prompting so collection workloads can be specified for a workday. That'll save some staff in collection and bookkeeping. That's a major change in how we operate. We will perform bulk filing in our account services area.

> Then we're going to bring some training into our management seminars on how managers can apply work simplification techniques to their operation such as combining certain operations and eliminating others. We want to put this training into our management associate program so that, from day one, these techniques get built into the way we think about managing. We've had people like that in the past, but, hopefully, this will add consistency to our training and development.

BTSC's management had also decided to use its capabilities to process checks for savings and loan associations' new NOW accounts. Finch explained the strategy:

> Our strategy with S&Ls is to service the check collection part of their transactions, but we're not in the business of doing the deposit accounting for them. We have four or five long-standing correspondents that we do that for, but we include their transactions right along with our work and process the transactions as we do. But we believe that's an unprofitable business to be in so we're restricting our activities with the S&Ls to check clearing, cash management, lending services, and credit card services. We don't think processing individual accounts is profitable. I think that is evident by the fact that banks that were big in that business, such as NCNB and Wachovia, have gotten out of the processing business.

Management Reports

James Finch, vice-chairman of Bankers Trust of South Carolina, had been instrumental in providing BTSC's management team with key information. This was especially true with regard to asset and liability reporting, as he explained:

> From the management standpoint, I provide the asset and liability information and the management reports. I dream up the ways to present the information and participate in the decision-making process from various points of view. My major role, however, is related to financial reporting and management reporting, as well as new things that come along outside of marketing or lending.

In fact, Finch had developed the asset and liability report that had become a key tool in aiding management's attempt to manage the bank's interest gap.

The management team felt that its reports were quite good. For example, vice-chairman John Boatwright described an experience the team had previously had with a New York bank:

> I think our systems are as good as any I've seen. When we borrowed money several years ago from Manny Hanny, we sent them our management books—we have a book put out by each department. The account officer said he wished he had something like that in his shop. We have a capsule way of seeing what's happening in each function, each month. He didn't have comparable information in his organization which informed managment about what was going on. They probably have briefings by department, but not as handy data in as simple a form.

In explaining their current management focus, Boatwright continued:

> Today we're trying to manage the interest sensitivity gap and its taken us a while to get that complex system in place. But, from what I've seen, its a better system with far superior reports than what I've seen anyone else come up with. Most are still using some "back of the envelope" type systems. Interest sensitivity is something you have to get a feel for—what changes are taking place. For example, all of our thrift accounts are spread into the five-year and over maturity category on these reports while these accounts are actually shrinking. That means

> that these accounts are more sensitive than initially indicated. But only over time can you track your experience in a category of accounts because it will change with different interest rate environments. We've seen that happen. Passbook accounts are a parking place when interest rates fluctuate, so they can go up and down in surprising patterns. You can get a handle on instruments with scheduled maturities. So we're talking about those patterns, looking at them, looking at them constantly, and looking at them a lot more than a lot of people.

Finch commented further on the asset and liability report:

> The asset and liability report is monthly because we're still in the early stages of developing our system. It's a presentation of what has transpired during that period. Our information is coming from different systems and we wanted to have this information as a first order of business. The next step will be to get this kind of data base and then have a faster turnaround. We found these needs are not that dynamic.
>
> There are more dynamic needs in the components of that report, such as the net short-term position, trading activities, and so on. We do get supplemental reports for some of the key components, such as weekly loan reports, so we know how many loans are being put on the books, at what rates and maturities, for the installment and commercial sides. For example, we get daily reports on what's happening with our balance sheet. So this supplemental information allows us to get to the gutsy operating aspects. That's all automated, but its not on-line.

Finch was still working to improve BTSC's management information. He continued:

> We're pretty much automated on all major operating applications and are now turning our direction to improve management information and more advanced systems, maybe replacing the old ones. There are some things we're starting to outgrow, can afford to change, and even have the time to change.

Vice-chairman Ed Sebastian explained further the bank's belief about the need for incremental reporting:

> What corporation could operate without cost accounting? How many financial institutions have cost accounting? In the 1960s you didn't have to worry about it. You had a normal yield curve and you had the spreads. You made profits no matter what. You made profits by the regulations. You were protected by the market environment with natural yields curves. That changed in the seventies because of economic conditions and is really going to change in the eighties because of the lack of regulatory protection. So you are hit twice.
>
> What manufacturer doesn't look at incremental change. They look at production costs, logistics costs, transportation costs, advertising and promotional costs on a current basis. They have to price off that, so they're always current. Financial institutions haven't done that. They've been unrealistic.

In commenting on BTSC's system, Ed Sebastian explained further:

> We don't feel we need cost accounting. We feel we're above it. We have "liquidation-addition" reports where we look at the incremental change. We have been developing our software, and tying it into our trial balances for incremental change reporting on earning asset additions and liquidations, and liability additions and liquidations. We've been working on this for a year and a half. I think we're pretty far advanced in the concept.
>
> Some financial institutions may never be able to go to this concept because

they already have all their software programs. To develop the weighted average system on their data bases may triple the size of their data base. It may be too costly for them to do. They may also be too short to have the need.

BTSC's financial forecasting model was another key management tool. In describing Bankers Trust's use of forecasting, James Finch explained:

Since 1974, we've had a financial model with which we could do forecasts and ask "what if" questions. We're getting more and more sophisticated about how we use it. We're not using it in a simple manner any more. We actually go through and forecast the rate that loans come off the books. We forecast the rates that loans go on. That allows us to purify the forecasting process. We still have things we would like to do in all of this. We feel we're kind of on the leading edge of using information, though I know there are still a lot of things we can do as we go on down the path.

Results of Asset-Liability Reporting

BTSC's asset-liability reporting system had revealed a number of critical trends that chairman W. W. Johnson was contemplating. He explained:

This report [Exhibit 8] shows our portfolio of total earnings assets and liabilities broken down by maturity—what we have maturing over the next three months, three to six months, six to twelve months, the total due within a year, one to two years, two to five years, and over five years. Our return on over $390 million in assets due within one year is over 17 per cent. That's pretty good for a bank with a billion dollars in assets. Now the longer term assets, about $380 million, get 12.7 per cent return for one to five years, and 14.7 per cent over five years. This high level is because our credit card business is stuck in there. If it wasn't, it would be about 12 per cent. On the liquidity side, we have about $270 million for which we're paying almost 15 per cent. Most of that is money market certificates.

This second report [Exhibit 9] shows the changes in assets and liabilities for last month. These are the incremental changes. We added $34 million in loans due within a year at an average rate of 20.14 per cent. We added $59 million in liabilities, mostly money market certificates and CDs, at an average cost of 16.5 per cent. We then show the monthly summary of these changes over the last six months by each category of asset and liability, and by maturity.

We also show what is happening to our interest-bearing liabilities. The per cent of major time deposits to total earning assets, for example, has increased from 22 per cent in March of 1980 to 33 per cent in August of 1981. That's expensive money. [See Exhibit 10.]

We track our interest-bearing liabilities to total earning assets. This is where it worries me. In March 1980, it was 63 per cent. Its now up to 72 per cent in August 1981. Now those are just trends, but you don't have to be too smart to see what's happening.

We also track our cost of funds. That includes time deposits, which might cost 11.5 per cent, and other demand deposits that used to be free. That cost of funds has increased from 5.76 per cent in March 1980 to 8.2 per cent in August 1981. If that goes to 10 per cent on a billion dollars in assets, your costs go up $18 million, or $9 million after tax. We have about $105 million in savings deposits which the DDIC is talking about raising interest on to 10 per cent. If they do, that's a 5 per cent increase in cost or $5 million, which is $2.5 million after tax. We'll only make about $12.5 million this year.

Johnson was especially concerned about these trends as he explained:

> I see my cost of funds going up every month. I see money shifting. I see that the proportion of my liabilities which supports my earning assets increase from 60 per cent time deposits to 72 per cent in one year. I see the cost of those funds increasing. Then I see my overhead, currently $55 million per year, growing at 15 per cent per year. That means I need $8 million more in net interest income or service charges just to stay even.
>
> Increases in net interest income is hard to come by. We have good usury rates in South Carolina, but we're bumping up against that ceiling. We've been able to increase our rates on loans, but that pipeline is about full and our cost of funds continues to rise. The question now is what to do given these circumstances. If you anticipate this will continue, what alternatives do you have?

Looking at the Future

Chairman Johnson saw the changing nature of competition in the banking industry. He described the major contenders in the future:

> Besides the other large banks, Sears just announced it is going to establish a money market fund. I happen to believe that it will be more competitive than Merrill Lynch. If the average American can get 16 per cent on his checking account, he would rather do business at Sears. He is more comfortable at Sears & Roebuck than walking into a Merrill Lynch office. That is going to be a big factor. Then there is American Express.
>
> In regional cities like Atlanta there are at least twenty-five loan production offices of major banks. We've seen them issuing credits as low as a million dollars. Three years ago we never dreamed we'd see Continental-Illinois or Bank of America in South Carolina giving million dollar credits. There will be a lot of them in the future. These people will provide a new dimension to the market that will be substantial.

Ed. Sebastian, vice-chairman, saw these changes as a growth in merchant banking. He stated:

> I think banks will become merchant bankers. I think insurance companies will become merchant bankers. I think credit card companies, Carte Blanch and American Express, will become merchant bankers. And I think you'll see some retail chains, J.C. Penney, Sears, and Montgomery Ward, also become merchant bankers.
>
> I think the retail side of the business will go to those financial institutions with under a billion dollars in business. They're the ones who will be able to give the service. That will include a savings account, a checking account, and participation in some kind of consumer lending. But the average checking account will be below $1,000. Excess cash will be in higher yielding items.

Sebastian also expected the continuing changes in the tax laws and regulations to have an effect on the nature of competition. He explained:

> Take individual retirement accounts which come into effect on January 1, 1982. That ballgame is wide open to insurance companies, brokerage houses, mutual funds, S&Ls, and commercial banks. I mean everyone is going to be bidding for that business. One article claimed that would be a $38 billion business. Products

EXHIBIT 8: Portfolio Asset/Liability Spread Management

(Amounts in Thousands, Except Yields)
AUGUST 1981

	Portfolio Total		Less Than 3 Months		3–6 Months		6–12 Months		Due Within 1 Year		1–2 Years		2–5 Years		More Than 5 Years	
	Dollars	Yield	Dollars	Yield	Dollars	Yield	Dollars	Yield	Dollars	Yield	Dollars	Yield	Dollars	Yield	Dollars	Yield
ASSETS																
Prime Sensitive Coml. Lns.	115,401	21.72	115,401	21.72	—	—	—	—	115,401	21.72	—	—	—	—	—	—
Fixed Rate Coml. Lns.																
Coml. R/E	38,072	11.77	3,409	13.70	1,933	12.76	3,713	12.01	9,055	12.81	5,222	11.24	11,813	11.72	11,983	11.27
R/E Resid. & Gov't	31,632	12.99	3,734	15.23	2,695	14.77	2,803	12.97	9,232	14.41	4,091	11.77	10,558	12.45	7,751	12.68
Other Coml.	31,580	16.58	11,550	18.94	4,752	17.27	4,735	15.50	21,037	17.79	3,817	14.13	5,431	13.99	1,295	15.00
Personal	18,922	17.93	12,248	18.62	3,543	17.85	768	16.13	16,559	18.34	785	14.78	1,069	14.79	508	16.10
State & Mun.	15,403	15.13	1,748	17.38	2,508	18.10	1,733	16.56	5,989	17.44	3,381	13.23	3,446	13.67	2,585	14.19
Other	4,379	15.57	1,000	15.49	532	16.46	553	16.44	2,085	15.99	497	14.87	1,077	15.10	719	15.50
Spartanburg	13,904	15.23	6,322	18.94	1,050	15.74	1,001	14.10	8,373	17.96	1,007	11.07	2,048	11.45	2,476	10.83
Total Fixed Rate Coml. Ln.	153,891	14.52	40,011	17.89	17,016	16.49	15,307	14.28	72,334	16.80	18,800	12.53	35,441	12.66	27,316	12.29
Total Commercial Loans	269,292	17.61	155,412	20.73	17,016	16.49	15,307	14.28	187,735	19.82	18,800	12.53	35,441	12.66	27,316	12.29
Mortgages Held for Resale	17,754	17.29	—	—	17,754	17.29	—	—	17,754	17.29	—	—	—	—	—	—
Installment Loans	146,475	15.20	18,054	15.80	16,803	15.83	29,658	15.54	64,515	15.69	41,951	14.79	35,620	14.80	4,389	15.34
Credit Card	75,080	18.22	—	—	—	—	—	—	—	—	—	—	—	—	75,080	18.22
Total Loans	508,601	16.99	173,466	20.22	51,573	16.55	44,965	15.11	270,004	18.67	60,751	14.09	71,061	13.73	106,785	16.58
Net Short-Term Position	—	—	—	—	—	—	—	—	—	—	—	—	—	—	—	—
Securities	274,117	12.30	37,948	13.39	68,831	14.35	17,239	11.58	124,018	13.67	49,220	11.05	42,851	11.09	58,028	11.30
Total Earning Assets	782,718	15.35	211,414	18.99	120,404	15.29	62,204	14.13	394,022	17.10	109,971	12.73	113,912	12.74	164,813	14.72

LIABILITIES																
Time and Savings																
Money Market Cert.	173,288	14.34	98,497	13.98	74,792	14.81	—	—	173,288	14.34	—	—	—	—	—	—
100M+ CD	93,465	16.22	74,543	16.54	10,393	15.27	8,529	14.58	93,465	16.22	—	—	—	—	—	—
Big 30	35,598	12.21	—	—	—	—	2,436	10.73	2,436	10.73	22,605	11.28	10,557	14.55	—	—
Thrift Savings	105,732	5.39	—	—	—	—	—	—	—	—	—	—	—	—	105,732	5.39
Other Time	66,934	6.38	—	—	—	—	—	—	—	—	—	—	—	—	66,934	6.38
Total Time and Savings	475,017	11.44	173,040	15.08	85,185	14.87	10,965	13.72	269,189	14.96	22,605	11.28	10,557	14.55	172,666	5.77
Net Short Term Position	3,491	16.49	3,491	16.49	—	—	—	—	3,491	16.49	—	—	—	—	—	—
Total Scheduled Liabilities	478,508	11.48	176,531	15.11	85,185	14.87	10,965	13.72	272,680	14.98	22,605	11.28	10,557	14.55	172,666	5.77
Demand Deposits Supporting Earning Assets	304,210				Gross Yield on Earning Assets					15.45						
Total Time and Demand Deposits Supporting Earning Assets	782,718				Net Yield on Earning Assets					7.25						
					Cost of Funds Supporting Earning Assets					8.20						
Gap	–0–															

EXHIBIT 9: Additions Asset/Liability Spread Management

(Amounts in Thousands, Except Yields)
AUGUST 1981

	Portfolio Total		Less Than 3 Months		3–6 Months		6–12 Months		Due Within 1 Year		1–2 Years		2–5 Years		More Than 5 Years	
	Dollars	*Yield*	*Dollars*	*Yield*	*Dollars*	*Yield*	*Dollars*	*Yield*	*Dollars*	*Yield*	*Dollars*	*Yield*	*Dollars*	*Yield*	*Dollars*	*Yield*
ASSETS																
Prime Sensitive Coml. Lns.	15,761	21.46	15,761	21.46	—	—	—	—	15,761	21.46	—	—	—	—	—	—
Fixed Rate Coml. Lns.																
Coml. R/E	1,749	15.52	788	14.14	264	17.62	206	15.00	1,258	15.01	86	16.47	261	16.85	145	16.98
R/E Resid. & Gov't	2,399	17.61	588	18.08	420	18.48	112	16.45	1,120	18.07	92	16.66	324	16.66	863	17.46
Other Coml.	6,056	19.35	3,420	20.00	1,122	18.94	1,001	18.34	5,543	19.49	168	17.79	326	17.95	20	19.11
Personal	5,292	18.86	3,782	19.05	1,343	18.41	90	18.19	5,215	18.87	26	18.11	27	17.87	24	18.01
State & Mun.	2,789	19.08	—	—	1,600	19.46	1,000	18.63	2,600	19.14	189	18.30	—	—	—	—
Other	392	19.35	227	18.59	71	20.79	48	19.94	346	19.23	8	20.91	14	20.62	23	21.33
Spartanburg	2,293	20.58	2,028	20.72	197	19.38	20	18.59	2,245	20.58	12	20.35	36	20.09	—	—
Total Fixed Rate Coml. Ln.	20,971	18.81	10,832	19.24	5,018	18.90	2,479	18.12	18,329	19.00	580	17.69	988	17.35	1,074	17.50
Total Commercial Loans	36,732	19.95	26,593	20.56	5,018	18.90	2,479	18.12	34,090	20.14	580	17.69	988	17.35	1,074	17.50
Mortgages held for Resale	—	—	—	—	—	—	—	—	—	—	—	—	—	—	—	—
Installment Loans	7,895	18.78	494	21.96	754	21.45	1,580	21.26	2,828	21.43	2,203	18.27	2,633	16.53	231	17.23
Credit Card	1,470	20.00	—	—	—	—	—	—	—	—	—	—	—	—	1,470	20.00
Total Loans	46,097	19.75	27,087	20.59	5,772	19.23	4,059	19.34	36,918	20.24	2,783	18.15	3,621	16.75	2,775	18.80
Net Short-Term Position	—	—	—	—	—	—	—	—	—	—	—	—	—	—	—	—
Securities	9,443	17.30	—	—	9,443	17.30	—	—	9,443	17.30	—	—	—	—	—	—
Total Earning Assets	55,540	19.33	27,087	20.59	15,215	18.03	4,059	19.34	46,361	19.64	2,783	18.15	3,621	16.75	2,775	18.80

LIABILITIES																
Time and Savings																
Money Market Cert.	22,736	15.68	—	—	22,736	15.68	—	—	22,736	15.68	—	—	—	—	—	—
100M+ CD	36,737	17.01	35,085	17.05	1,652	16.13	—	—	36,737	17.01	—	—	—	—	—	—
Big 30	5,065	16.78	—	—	—	—	—	—	—	—	—	—	5,065	16.78	—	—
Thrift Savings	—	—	—	—	—	—	—	—	—	—	—	—	—	—	—	—
Other Time	—	—	—	—	—	—	—	—	—	—	—	—	—	—	—	—
Total Time and Savings	64,538	16.52	35,085	17.05	24,388	15.71	—	—	59,473	16.50	—	—	5,065	16.78	—	—
Net Short Term Position	3,491	16.49	3,491	16.49	—	—	—	—	3,491	16.49	—	—	—	—	—	—
Total Scheduled Liabilities	68,029	16.52	38,576	17.00	24,388	15.71	—	—	62,964	16.50	—	—	5,065	16.79	—	—
Demand Deposits Required to Support Earning Asset Additions	(12,489)	—														
Total Additions Interest Spread	—	2.81														
Net Yield on Additions Earning Assets	—	(6.81)														

EXHIBIT 10: Trend of Interest Bearing Deposit Ratios

(Monthly Averages, Amounts in Thousands, Except Ratios)

	1980				1981							
	March	*June*	*Sept.*	*Dec.*	*Jan.*	*Feb.*	*March*	*April*	*May*	*June*	*July*	*August*
Bank Total Earning Assets	745,615	750,737	812,318	829,473	849,445	872,130	888,196	887,469	938,268	930,745	957,724	954,322
Major Time Deposits	165,666	177,464	187,053	222,963	253,874	287,089	295,119	271,365	281,689	280,848	306,583	315,706
Major Time Deposits/ Bank Total Earning Assets	22%	24%	23%	27%	30%	33%	33%	31%	30%	30%	32%	33%
Total Interest Bearing Liabilities	466,724	469,495	500,965	532,168	586,786	630,842	642,487	627,772	667,216	655,790	685,971	685,814
Total Interest Bearing Liabilities/Bank Total Earning Assets	63%	63%	62%	64%	69%	72%	72%	71%	71%	70%	72%	72%
Gross Yield on Earning Assets	12.86%	12.39%	12.08%	13.20%	14.00%	14.47%	14.17%	14.49%	15.07%	15.40%	15.68%	15.45%
Cost of Funds Supporting Earning Assets	5.76%	5.46%	5.18%	6.83%	7.56%	8.09%	7.81%	7.51%	7.80%	7.93%	8.17%	8.20%
Net Yield on Earning Assets	7.10%	6.93%	6.90%	6.37%	6.44%	6.38%	6.36%	6.98%	7.27%	7.47%	7.51%	7.25%

Major Time Deposits include 100M+ C.D's, MMC's, and Big 30's.

are going to change. People aren't going to accept 8 per cent. Prudential just came out with an annuity program based on what you contribute. They'll pay you or your spouse an annuity at retirement age even if you pass away. That is going to be big business.

Johnson was also concerned about the future of such financial institutions as S&Ls and Credit Unions. He explained:

I'm concerned they will go broke. I'm not concerned about them as competitors. Reg Q is going to be lifted and you're going to see real competition.

As today's consumers become more demanding of a fair return on their savings, Sebastian believed it could have a significant impact on how investments were made, and on interest rates. He explained:

People are asking why Reagan economics aren't working. One reason could be that everyone is wondering what will happen in the future and, therefore, they want to stay in short-term investments. Back in the early sixties you would take inflation and add 1 per cent. That was all people wanted. In the late sixties they wanted 3 per cent. In the early seventies they wanted 8 per cent. Now they want 10.

I think the average person on the street is recognizing that the government has restricted financial institutions so they could only pay them a minimum rate. We are the only nation that hasn't paid at least the inflation rate on deposits for the last forty years. It's about time for the saver, rather than the borrower, to benefit. I think we're there.

I think the average investor is insisting on a minimum amount of interest or he's not going to buy. If that's true, you won't see the cost of money go below the inflation rate. If that happens, you won't see a shift from short to long term. If cash won't go into long-term investments, you have a problem. The government debt is over a trillion dollars and averages three years. The average saver is looking short term because that's the only place he can get a return, or thinks he can get a return. You can't change inertia quickly. It took us forty years to get here. It'll take at least ten years for the pendulum to swing back again.

CASE FOUR

Bankers Trust of South Carolina (B)

WILLIAM R. BOULTON
University of Georgia

Assignment Questions:

1. How does Bankers Trusts' management philosophy and style fit into its organizational strategy? The way it manages people?
2. How does Bankers Trusts' management philosophy relate to its acquisition strategy?
3. What kinds of organizational problems do you see for Bankers Trust in the future?

Bankers Trust of South Carolina had experienced fifteen years of growth in assets and earnings. By September 1981, the bank had reached $1.1 billion in assets with earnings of over $10 million. Much of the bank's growth had come from its aggressive management team's expansion into South Carolina markets through a variety of acquisitions. However, now that it has become a statewide bank, there was concern about the future of its acquisition strategy. Ed Sebastian, vice-chairman of Bankers Trust, explained:

> Until we have relief under the Clayton Act defining our competition, we really don't have more markets in the state of South Carolina to expand into. The whole universe is considered to be commercial banks. We'll probably see a breakdown of this with the Federal Home Loan Bank Board wanting S&Ls to be able to give all services that a commerical bank gives. If that happens, then the courts are going to have to say that the universe, from the Clayton Act competition standpoint, includes S&Ls and commercial banks. Then more market areas may open up to us through consolidations and mergers in South Carolina. Unless these regulations erode, we probably won't do many more mergers.

Bankers Trusts' Management Structure

W. W. (Hootie) Johnson, chairman of Banker's Trust, had handpicked his management team and they worked closely together. This was his deliberate management style, as Johnson explained:

> When the last of the senior managers retired, I made Boatwright, Finch, and Sebastian vice-chairmen and Turner president. I brought them in and I said, "Guys, I am not looking for a number two. We're all working together and that is the way it is going to be for a long while. Anybody who doesn't like that, I'll be glad to help look for another job. I don't want any fighting for number two."

In describing the way the management team worked together, Johnson continued:

> It's not too structured. Several times a month the five of us have what we call a strategy meeting. But we're all right here on one floor. Boatwright may be working on a credit that is relating to the mortgage company, and I'll call in both him and Sebastian and we'll talk about that problem. I am working closely with Julian Turner on putting together our "all-savers" package, and Boatwright might have some input into that.
>
> We don't have a dozen meetings a week that are structured. That can be good or bad. Some banks' top guys are in meetings every time I call. If all you do is sit in meetings, you don't have time to work. I have never gone to the Harvard Business School. I learned from my father. I think you can get things too structured. But we have close communication. When any important memorandum is written in any one of these disciplines, everyone gets a copy of it. If Finch makes an equipment change in data processing, Boatwright and Turner are informed.

John Boatwright, vice-chairman, also emphasized the close communication that the management team had with themselves and with the organization:

> I am constantly amazed when I look at banks about our size at the lack of their management's knowledge. We know our people better. We know our systems better. We know what is going on. Some of those banks have more impressive documents to track it, and they may be making talks about it around the country, but they get so much information that they end up not being able to absorb it or even find it.
>
> Our senior management is all on this floor. We talk constantly back and forth and meet formally every two weeks to talk about the situation and what is going on.

James Finch, vice-chairman, commented further on the absence of an organization chart for the overall bank:

> We have organization charts for our own areas, but for the bank as a whole, we don't have one. I guess part of the reason for that is that we grew from a small operation to a large operation thinking that structure creates boundaries. Almost by definition one says that's mine and that's yours. Now we have to have that too, but we don't worry too much about crossing over organization lines when there is a need.
>
> You don't have to go up the organization and down to talk to someone when you need to talk about an operating matter. For example, I may go directly to one of Julian Turner's managers and let him know what I am doing if it's important. If it's a policy matter, I talk to Julian first.
>
> If we had a real structured organization chart, I think we could lose some of this flexibility. We have a structure from the overall standpoint. It is just not all put together on a chart and we've never really had any serious misunderstandings. We look at organization when we assess how we should operate and we may even draw some boxes. We're very mindful of the need for structure and the kind of people you put in a slot. We know what the organization is and we do delegate.

> We kind of all work as a team, so when these things come up, we just harness all of our resources and form a team to get things put together. Depending on availability and whose expertise is needed, one of us takes the operating leadership on a specific project.

Tom Connor, senior vice-president in charge of the personnel division, expressed his feelings about the bank's management philosophy:

> Bankers Trust is an organization that is concerned about its people. It's demanding of them but is humane. It has a corporate heart. It believes very strongly in a team commitment, team effort, and team spirit. It believes that backbiting and backstabbing cause you to become fragmented and will tear you down. We don't condone that. It demands a lot of its people, but also demands a lot of itself as an organization. That starts with Hootie, who demands a lot of himself, and that permeates the rest of the organization. But he is a compassionate individual as well.
>
> People are also given leeway to identify problems and make decisions, and influence the outcome of the organization. I think we have winners who are willing to perform in that environment and take the consequences when they make mistakes.
>
> We believe in the active involvement of our people. We couldn't have done a lot of things without super, extracommitted, bright people who were dedicated to hard work. We've been a winner and a lot of esprit de corps has come out of our growth. If you have winners, they like to be associated with winning and we've won. That has given us a lot of esprit de corps.

Ed Sebastian also believed in the bank management structure:

> It is pretty simple. Everyone at this level knows what his job is. They all have charts for their own areas. If there is any overlap, it takes place at this level, and I don't think anyone underneath knows that or needs to know that.
>
> The overlap up here is primarily an information overlap; kind of a community effort. Hootie is not a tyrant. He doesn't sit there and tell people what to do. He wants people to think for themselves and think about the future. Rather than each of us specializing, though we have specialties and everyone knows it, I believe most of us know what is happening in all forms of the industry and can communicate that. I might know more about rules and regulations in some areas than the person who has that specialty. But we'll communicate and understand. We'll get into a meeting and hammer it out. Someone will say, "Hey, I don't think that's the way you should be doing that."
>
> When you have a rigid organization and the guy is nearsighted, you don't keep in touch with what's happening. If one guy is responsible for reading the FTC sheets to see what products are passed, while the other is in research and development, there can be a lack of communication. When people become nearsighted in their specialty, you can never have a strategy or achieve your goals. It may be on paper, but it's never communicated because the specialists really don't care. That doesn't ever happen here.

Personnel and Training

Thomas G. Connor, senior vice-president in charge of the personnel division, had been with BTSC for over fourteen years. His primary job since graduating from the University of South Carolina had been to develop the personnel department as he explained:

> I graduated from the university here and came with the bank in 1967 as personnel director. It was a much smaller organization than it is today. My initial assignment was to bring together some personnel functions that were fragmented and create a foundation to build on. It didn't have a formal division before that.

In describing the role that BTSC's personnel division played in the organization of 2,200 persons, Connor continued:

> We try to maintain the heartbeat or pulse of the organization and of the people within the organization; ensure that we remain demanding of our people, but sensitive as well; that we have programs that address the philosophies of executive management; that we have people to meet the challenges in the coming years; that we have programs and systems that will track those people, motivate, and help us retain those people. We're not a keeper of records, but need to be as creative as the other areas of the bank.

Connor had primary responsibility for recruiting new members into the organization. He articulated the kind of people that BTSC was looking to recruit:

> We're looking for the same thing that IBM, Wachovia, or G.M. is looking for. We're looking for bright, alert, good students who performed well academically. But, beyond that, we're looking for people who know where they are, where they want to go, and what it's going to take to get there. They are goal oriented, have done a self-analysis and know what it will take to make them happy. That they will and can be self-motivated when they get here, have self-determination and can be team players. We look for a lot of integrity, a lot of character. I think those are the things every organization wants. We want competitive people who want to make things happen.

New employees at BTSC participate in a basic training program about a month after they are hired. This program provides employees with an early orientation to the bank and describes the bank's history, benefits, and belief in free enterprise. As Connor explained, "We are trying to get an early identity and commitment from those folks, regardless of position, to the organization." In describing BTSC's specialized training programs, Connor continued:

> We have a management associate program where we try to teach new people to be bankers. We'll compare this program with any in the Southeast. It has learning modules which include activities, productivity requirements, and learning requirements with assignments and follow-ups. It is to develop general commercial bankers, lenders, credit persons, or business development contact people.
>
> We also have an operations associate program which is for people who will be involved in the administrative areas of the bank, the operations area, the controller's area, the planning area, and the back office areas. That is also modular with learning objectives in each assignment.
>
> Regarding general programs, we have devoted most of our time in the recent past to customer service, customer relations, and business development skills. We're now moving into the area of management skills training. We consciously chose to do the others first because we felt we could get a return on our training dollar more quickly by training employees to listen to customers, to refer customers to the proper people, and to sell customers. We felt this training would put tools in the hands of the people more quickly. We have done a good job in training people to be bankers. We haven't done quite so well in training them to be managers.

> Now the game is changing and we need to be more productive and better utilizers of resources.

In September 1981, BTSC's management was also moving to improve the bank's performance appraisal system. Connor explained:

> We're not pleased with what we have now and we're working on it. We have a more traditional system that is used for salary increases and is more trait oriented than quantitative. We review nonmanagement people formally twice per year, in April and October. We refer to those as progress report months. It is a progress report form. We hope that the supervisors sit down with their people in a coaching fashion, tell them what they have done, their strong points, weak points, what they need to work on, set a plan of action, tell them what is expected, and what they will do to help them get there.
>
> With management people we do it a little differently because we want benchmarks to compare against earnings and expenses. We're looking to set a foundation to be more precise, more accurate, and more quantitative. I say more accurate because we're engaged in a job analysis to give us a more scientific description of the job content. From that we can better establish standards against which performance can be measured in a more quantitative way. We're looking at three jobs right now which will cover about 25 per cent of the jobs in the bank: the branch managers, the commercial loan officers, and tellers. If we like the results, we'll continue.

In spite of the limitations in BTSC's current appraisal system, Connor felt that management had a good feel for the employees' abilities. This was the result of the relative small size of the organization and the style of management, as Connor explained:

> We have not been so large that tracking people is a problem. Size has been on our side. Hootie knows most of the officers in the bank by their first names. Our structure helps us, because those people in charge of others are constantly aware of people under them. We're aware that this will become more difficult as we grow and that communication will become more difficult, but we work to meet that challenge.
>
> We use a number of information-type meetings to gather and impart information within the organization. Julian Turner meets with his regional managers and Jim Finch meets with his division people monthly about the bank's performance. It's not just a passing of information downstream, but is also taking it upstream. We also have an annual meeting of regional people and division heads at a location away from the office to discuss business and have some fellowship. Top-management members present their objectives, discuss last year's performance, and discuss their roles in this. It is not that we have the solution to communication, but we may do more than some other organizations. To help that, you need to be a team player.

In addition to having provided promotional opportunities for his branch personnel, Turner felt that BTSC's management were knowledgeable about the people in the organization. He cited his own example:

> I had a car, which I just traded in after 19 months, with 62,000 miles on it. My phone stays busy all the time. We're a bank that does communicate. We keep in touch with our people. I think our people feel that senior management is aware of them and their needs and the door's open. We're not a formalized organization. We're still small enough to be close to our people. I think that's very important.

Ed Sebastian summarized the bank's philosophy:

> Everyone wants to be a part of a growing company. If you give the people the right to feel that they're making part of those decisions on growth and production and systems design and operations, and if they're busy, we find that they are a lot happier. They don't have time to be disgruntled and the productivity increases.

BTSC's Acquisition Strategy

Acquisitions had played an important role in BTSC's growth and profitability. This successful strategy had given BTSC a statewide presence. Gary Page, vice-president for corporate compliance and planning, was heavily involved in recent acquisitions. He explained the bank's approach to acquisition:

> We're naturally interested in the numbers and what effect they'll have on Bankers Trust. Some of that is quantifiable and much of it is not. Anytime you are dealing with the future you are guessing, even though you might substantiate your guess with lots of assumptions and lots of forecasts. We've also had cases where the performance of an institution wasn't that exciting, but a merged institution with greater financial resources could perform more favorably than the smaller independent institution. For example, Peoples National Bank had showed flat earnings prior to the 1973 merger. But its location in the Piedmont section of South Carolina and the fact that it was 50 per cent of our size allowed us to be a more formidable competitor with other South Carolina banks. That proved to be true even though it took time. It just doesn't happen on the merger date.
>
> That has led to the merger of Bankers Trust and Spartanburg Bank and Trust Company. It is a natural affiliation with Spartanburg county being adjacent to Greenville county. While it would be nice to have answers about the future, all the forecasting in the world will not predict what will actually happen. It all boils down to a matter of judgment. Risk is inherent in our decision to acquire a firm or offer a new service. Its judgmental even though you might try to quantify it.

Regarding the process of actually putting mergers together, Page described his involvement:

> I'm not involved in actual negotiations and that sort of thing. But I'm involved in putting them together from an analytical standpoint, putting performance numbers together for both organizations, looking at exchange ratios of stock for stock, and financial ramifications of the merger.

BTSC had used a variety of accounting techniques to accomplish mergers while minimizing dilution of its stock. Ed Sebastian, vice-chairman, explained:

> We've accomplished mergers in a lot of different ways. We've used regular common stock pooling of interests. When we merged with Peoples National Bank of Florence, we used convertible preferred stock. That allowed us to utilize purchase accounting, so we sold off the securities portfolio and took the losses before merger date, used a 10-year NOL (net operating loss) carryback, recovered that tax money, and increased the yield on the portfolio 500 to 600 points.
>
> We feel we were very avant garde in our merger with Spartanburg Bank and Trust Company, because we issued common stock and retired stock simultaneously. That prevented dilution of our earnings per share. The retirement of stock was an integral part of the merger. As far as I know, we are the only nonmember bank or financial institution to ever utilize the issuing and retirement of stock to

accomplish a merger. We issued a $21.08 tender offer and retired $3,250,000 worth of shares within 25 days.

BTSC's mergers required an extensive amount of planning and involved the whole management team. Exhibit 1 shows the areas of planning and the degree of executive involvement. Page described the merger plan:

> We have a work plan for each area that is involved in an acquisition. There is a corporate area, a legal-regulatory area, a personnel area, a marketing area, and an operations area, which are all very important. Each of these areas is meshed in an acquisition to make an entire corporation.

EXHIBIT 1: Bankers Trust and Spartanburg Bank & Trust Company Merger

DATED: *August, 1980*
ISSUED BY: *L. J. Sebastian*

INDEX TO SUMMARY PROJECT PLANS

Area of Responsibility	*Assigned*
I. Corporate and Legal (see Vol. 1(a) for "Correspondence"	Weeks(retired) Sebastian Page
II. Reorganization of SB & T	Johnson Turner Boatwright Weeks(retired) Finch
III. Financial	Weeks(retired) Finch Sebastian Page
IV. Portfolio and Safekeeping	Bell
V. Marketing	Isbell
VI. Personnel	Connor
VII. Credit	Boatwright Sperry Moore
VIII. Credit Cards	Boatwright Dougherty
IX. Profit Planning	Page Bush
X. Operational Procedures—Manuals	Reynolds
XI. Computer Services, Operations, and Purchasing	Thirkell Oliver
XII. Insurance	Gorham Sebastian
XIII. Internal Audit	Ireland
XIV. Corresponent/National	Capell
XV. Trust	Duffie
XVI. Administration of Project	Finch Sebastian

The Spartanburg Bank and Trust Company acquisition plan included seven three-inch binders. The paperwork is tremendous. Two of these were the corporate-legal-regulatory area. We document our acquisitions and the work plan for every step required to integrate the organizations. The last two have been quite formalized. It's a highly technical thing because you have to make that procedure mesh with this procedure, and those individuals have to be integrated. It's a real experience.

Bankers Trust's management also found it useful to integrate personnel across organizations. John Boatwright, vice-chairman, explained the strategy:

> We use the scrambled egg theory. As someone said of mergers, "If you leave the same people there entirely, they may dance to the same tune, but they won't dance cheek to cheek." To really get them on board, you have to begin moving their people into your organization and your people into their organization. Hopefully, for most of their people, that represents a move up. They have more opportunity than they would with a small bank, which is one of the advantages of merger to a small bank. Of course, it also opens up opportunity for our people who show management promise. They may become a senior loan officer or city executive in one of those regions.
>
> I don't know of any situation where we haven't scrambled people over time to give it the Bankers Trust flavor.

Julian Turnover, president, commented further:

> We've had some situations where the scrambling has almost been a cleaning of the house. We haven't done anything with the merger we just completed. They have a good, aggressive, solid organization. This one probably has less requirement for scrambling than any of the others. Our 1979 merger in Florence resulted in early retirement by the manager who was put on a consulting contract, so we moved someone in immediately to take over his position, and moved another man in to head up the loan platform and cover business development. We moved people into several branches in the Myrtle Beach area. That merger resulted in a fairly wholesale scrambling because we wanted to beef up their staff to capitalize on the market. In several mergers, we did a complete scrambling to overcome some problems in management.

Local advisory boards were also used to help keep contact with the communities in which BTSC did business. Turner explained the boards' position in the organization:

> We have local boards in most of our communities—many formed from the boards of merged banks. They are used as a sounding board of the community and help you market the bank's services. We have one in each area and they meet eight times per year.

The division plans were developed under the guidance of the top management team to integrate all operations. Gary W. Page, vice-president for corporate compliance and planning, explained:

> Annually, there is a meeting down at the beach, away from the bank, of key division heads and officers in charge of the regions, held over a two-day period. One function of that meeting is to allow the chairman of the board, the president, and other executives to stand up in front of seventy some officers and tell them our objectives and how we'll plan to get there.
>
> In the profit planning process, the senior officers present their profit plans to

the executive management of the bank. Of course, those plans are in writing, but there is also a verbal presentation and discussion among all the individuals. The objective of that is to ensure that the executive management of the bank is aware of what the manager is planning, to ensure that his plan is in accordance with the overall corporate objectives of the bank. That's not just for 1982, but for the next five years.

Looking to the Future

Mergers would continue to play an important role in BTSC's overall strategy because of the potential they brought to improving the efficiency of the bank's operations. Johnson explained:

> If I look where you get economies, it is where you can dramatically cut fixed costs. When I talk about mergers, all I have to do is look at the balance sheet and I can see how much we can save. We have a computer and they have a computer. We spend on advertising and they spend on advertising. We have a trust department and they have a trust department. We have an audit function and they have an audit function. We have 107 branches and they have branches which overlap in locations. So mergers provide opportunity, even though they may not save us over the long haul. But they can buy us some time to develop new products and position ourselves as an efficient operation. We'd be a more attractive acquisition.
>
> Since we're already making good money, we can only do better if we can improve those economies of scale. And the environment for mergers is so much better than it has been. The Justice Department may require selling off some branches, but it looks good.

With the recent push toward interstate banking, Johnson had also considered the impact this might have on BTSC:

> I've been giving serious thought to interstate banking for almost a year. South Carolina is in the Sunbelt and would be a good market, but it is not a Texas, Florida, Georgia, North Carolina, Louisiana, or Oklahoma—the energy states. We'd be one of the less attractive states for banks to enter even if we passed legislation to allow money center banks to acquire banks in South Carolina. But it would make us the only game in town.
>
> On the other hand, we could acquire a bank like Columbus Bank and Trust in Georgia. However, that wouldn't make sense because we wouldn't achieve any economies of scale. We'd be a two billion dollar bank with the same operating ratios. And we'd compound our management problem tenfold. That's not a viable option to improving economies of scale. We don't see ourselves doing that.

Ed Sebastion summed up BTSC's approach to accomplishing its objectives:

> We're always trying to think about what is going to happen. We think that these changing times open opportunity, because people who are ready to accept change, think about it, utilize their skills and talents, and use their capital base can find opportunities. Those who take advantage of those opportunities are going to be successful. That's the way we look at these times. We're not going to stand still and let the grass grow under our feet. We're going to be out there looking for opportunities, structuring and restructuring the organization, merging, and every other thing we can do to continue to make ourselves profitable.
>
> We're always trying to think and stimulate thoughts, find new areas, new

products, new mergers, new acquisitions, new regulations that allow us to get into new products and services, and find income opportunities.

As far as the bank goes now, the name of the game is productivity. Finding fees and increasing profits through better productivity methodologies. A lot of things can be done there. A lot of opportunities exist.

CASE FIVE

Hewlett-Packard (A)

ROGER M. ATHERTON and DENNIS M. CRITES
University of Oklahoma

Assignment Questions:

1. Do you consider Hewlett-Packard to be successful? Why?
2. How would you describe Hewlett-Packard's organizational strategy?
3. What problems do you see in Hewlett-Packard's future? What would you do? Why?

In May 1978 John Young was appointed chief executive of Hewlett-Packard. He was simultaneously handed the difficult task of charting a path through a rapidly growing and increasingly complex competitive jungle. Forbes reported that Young would be paid $280,000 to lead the classy electronics company into the rapidly changing, new computer market in which the biggest competitor (IBM) had vastly greater resources.[1] Although handpicked by the company's two founders, Bill Hewlett and Dave Packard, who between them owned 39 percent of the stock, he would be watched carefully. Whether he could continue the growth, the success, and the same egalitarian leadership style of his predecessors was a real question. Whether he should even try to adopt the same general strategy and tactics of recent years was also a real question.

This case depicts some of the major facets of the 1975–1978 transitionary period for Hewlett-Packard. In summary, the period appears to have been marked by a continuation of impressive growth; by repeated affirmation of, and only slight changes in, the company's basic objectives and policies; by a smooth transfer of top executive responsibilities; and by a changing product mix and marketing strategy which had brought Hewlett-Packard into increasingly more competitive markets and direct confrontation with IBM and other major computer companies.

Hewlett-Packard: A Brief Sketch

Innovative products have been the cornerstone of Hewlett-Packard's growth since 1939, when Hewlett engineered a new type of audio oscillator and, with

[1] "Welcome to the Hot Seat, John Young," *Forbes*, July 24, 1978, pp. 62–63.

Reprinted with permission of the author and the Case Research Association.

Packard, created the company in Packard's garage. The product was cheaper and easier to use than competitive products, and it was quickly followed by a family of test instruments based on the same design principles. Hewlett-Packard has since become one of the giants of the high-technology electronics industry. Their products include electronic test and measuring systems; medical electronic products; electronic instrumentation for chemical analysis; and solid-state components. According to company sources, Hewlett-Packard has remained a people-oriented company with management policies that encourage individual creativity, initiative, and contribution throughout the organization. It has also tried to retain the openness, informality, and unstructured operating procedures that marked the company in its early years. Each individual has been given the freedom and the flexibility to implement work methods and ideas to achieve both personal and company objectives and goals.

Both Hewlett and Packard have indicated that their corporate objectives, first put into writing in 1957 and modified occasionally since then, have served the company well in shaping the company, guiding its growth, and providing the foundation for its contribution to technological progress and the betterment of society. Last updated in 1977, the corporate objectives were, according to company sources, remarkably similar to the original versions developed from management concepts formulated by Hewlett and Packard in the company's early years.[2]

The following is a brief listing of the Hewlett-Packard (HP) objectives in 1978.

1. Profit objective: To achieve sufficient profit to finance our company growth and to provide the resources we need to achieve our other corporate objectives.
2. Customer objective: To provide products and services of the greatest possible value to our customers, thereby gaining and holding their respect and loyalty.
3. Fields of interest objective: To enter new fields only when the ideas we have, together with our technical, manufacturing, and marketing skills, assure that we can make a needed and profitable contribution to the field.
4. Growth objective: To let our growth be limited only by our profits and our ability to develop and produce technical products that satisfy real customer needs.
5. People objective: To help HP people share in the company's success, which they make possible; to provide job security based on their performance; to recognize their individual achievements; and to help them gain a sense of satisfaction and accomplishment from their work.
6. Management objective: To foster initiative and creativity by allowing the individual great freedom of action in attaining well-defined objectives.
7. Citizenship objective: To honor our obligations to society by being an economic, intellectual, and social asset to each nation and each community in which we operate.

[2] "Revised Corporate Objectives," *Measure,* May 1977, pp. 7–10.

Except for slight changes in wording, the objectives were the same as in 1975.

The 1973–1974 Redirection

Adversely affected by computer and aerospace downturns in 1970, Hewlett-Packard had at first welcomed the 30 percent increase in sales in 1972 and the 40 percent increase in 1973. Problems arose, however, as inventories and accounts receivable increased substantially. A 32 percent increase in employees to handle the increased sales, administrative, and manufacturing activities required extensive training efforts and organizational readjustments. Some products were put into production before they were fully developed. Prices were sometimes set too low for an adequate return on investment. Short-term borrowing increased substantially to $118 million and management seriously considered converting some of its short-term debt to long-term debt, a practice the company had traditionally avoided, preferring to operate on a pay-as-you-go basis.

In 1973–74, top management decided to avoid adding long-term debt and to reduce short-term debt by controlling costs, managing assets, and improving profit margins. As Packard made clear to the management at all levels, they had somehow been diverted into seeking market share as an objective. So both he and Hewlett began a year-long campaign to reemphasize the principles they developed when they began their unique partnership. Packard toured the divisions to impose this new asset-management discipline. In addition, while other companies dropped prices to boost sales and cut research spending to improve earnings, Hewlett-Packard used quite different tactics. It raised prices by an average of 10 percent over the previous year, and it increased spending on research and development by 20 percent, to an $80 million annual rate. These two strategies were intended to improve company profitability, to slow the rate of growth that had more than doubled sales in the previous three years, and to enable it to compete primarily on the basis of quality and technological superiority.

The improvements in 1974 performance compared with 1973 were quite dramatic. During fiscal 1974, inventories and receivables increased about 3 percent while sales grew 34 percent to $884 million. The effect of this better asset control combined with improved earnings, resulted in a drop in short-term debt of approximately $77 million. Earnings were up 66 percent to $84 million and were equal to $3.08 per share compared to $1.89 per share. Only 1,000 employees were added compared to 7,000 in the previous year.

Both Hewlett and Packard were reportedly dismayed that they had been forced to initiate and personally lead the efforts to get the company back on the track. It was particularly disconcerting to them because they believed the issues were fundamental to the basic strategy of the company. They had also had to intervene directly in day-to-day operational management, which was counter to their basic philosophy of a decentralized, product-oriented, and divisionalized organization structure.

Growth, 1975–1978

The dramatic growth that followed the 1973–74 redirection was in essence maintained through the 1978 fiscal year. The sales increase from $981 million in 1975 to $1.73 billion in 1978 averaged almost 21 percent per year. Net earnings, growing from $84 million in 1975 to $153 million in 1978, averaged 22 percent per year with an 8 percent increase in 1975–76, a 33 percent jump in 1976–77, and a 1977–78 growth of 26 percent. A four-year consolidated earnings summary, strategic ratios, financial ratios, contributions to sales and earnings by business segments, and a percent of sales analysis are presented in Exhibits 1, 2, 3, and 4. Total employees, about 29,000 at the beginning of the 1975 fiscal year, grew about 11 percent a year to a level of about 42,400 at the end of the 1978 fiscal year. The total number of products increased from roughly 3,400 in late 1975 to over 5,000 in mid-1978. The number of new product introductions increased significantly from about 90 major new products in 1975 to 130 in 1978. In keeping with its traditional attention to research and development, these expenditures grew from $90 million in fiscal 1975 to $154 million in fiscal 1978. Data on growth are given in Exhibit 5.

Structure

In a 1978 statement of philosophy, HP emphasized as a basis for high-level achievement their provision of a realistic and simple set of long-term objectives on which all could agree and on which people could work with a minimum of

EXHIBIT 1: Consolidated Earnings Summary For the Years Ended October 31, 1975–1978 ($ millions)

	1975	*1976*	*1977*	*1978*
Net sales	$981.2	$1,111.6	$1,360.0	$1,728.0
Other income, net	8.3	12.0	13.9	23.0
Total revenues	989.5	1,123.6	1,373.9	1,751.0
Costs and expense:				
Cost of goods sold	462.7	535.6	622.2	805.0
Research and development	89.6	107.6	125.4	154.0
Marketing	162.0	176.6	207.5	264.0
Administrative and general	124.5	139.1	185.4	226.0
Interest	2.2	4.1	4.2	6.0
Total costs and expenses	841.0	963.0	1,144.7	1,455.0
Earning before taxes on income	148.6	160.6	229.2	296.0
Taxes on income	65.0	69.8	107.7	143.0
*Net earnings	$ 83.6	$ 90.8	$ 121.5	$ 153.0
Earnings per share:				
Net earnings	$ 3.02	$ 3.24	$ 4.27	$ 5.27
Cash dividends	.25	.30	.40	.50
Common shares outstanding at year-end	27.6	28.0	28.5	29.0

Note: Figures may not add exactly due to rounding.
Source: Hewlett-Packard annual reports, 1975–1978.

EXHIBIT 2: Strategic and Financial Ratio

A. Strategic ratios

	Net earnings / Total revenues	×	Total revenues / average assets	=	Net earnings / average assets	×	Average assets / average net worth	=	Net earnings / average net worth
1975	8.5%	×	1.39	=	11.8%	×	1.39	=	16.4
1976	8.1	×	1.32	=	10.6	×	1.38	=	14.7
1977	8.8	×	1.31	=	11.6	×	1.40	=	16.2
1978	8.7	×	1.34	=	11.7	×	1.44	=	16.8

B. Financial ratios

	1975	*1976*	*1977*	*1978*
Current ratio	2.51	2.62	2.58 (*a*)	2.29
Acid test	1.36	1.59	1.62	1.44
Collection period (days)	75	76	72 (*b*)	77
Accounts payable T/0 (days)	25	21	27	32
Inventory T/0	2.31	2.42	2.41	2.54
Debt to net worth	.33	.35	.37 (*c*)	.42
Interest coverage	66.9	38.2	53.6	48.3
Gross profit margin	.53	.52	.54	.53
Net profit to net sales	.086	.082	.089 (*d*)	.089

Note: *Dun's Review*'s (December 1977) figures are the averages of the electronic component and scientific instrument business lines. Comparable figures for 1978 were not published.
(*a*) *Dun's Review* indicated the industry median was 2.64.
(*b*) *Dun's Review* indicated the industry median was 65.
(*c*) *Dun's Review* indicated the industry median was .85.
(*d*) *Dun's Review* indicated the industry median was .047.
Source: Developed by casewriters from Hewlett-Packard annual reports, 1975–1978.

EXHIBIT 3: Contributions to Sales and Earnings For the Years Ended October 31, 1975–1978 ($ Millions)

	1975	*1976*	*1977*	*1978*
Sales:				
Test, measuring, and related items	$ 453	$ 501	$ 593	$740
Electronic data products	395	453	580	761
Medical electronic equipment	99	119	135	163
Analytical instrumentation	53	58	76	98
Total sales	1,000	1,131	1,384	1,762
Less sales between business segments	(19)	(19)	(24)	(34)
Net sales to customers	$ 981	$1,112	$1,360	$1,728
Earnings:				
Test, measuring, and related items	$ 94	$ 103	$ 134	$ 180
Electronic data products	68	69	106	124
Medical electronic equipment	13	21	22	26
Analytical instrumentation	8	7	12	16
Operating Profit	183	200	274	346
Less eliminations and corporate items	(34)	(39)	(45)	(50)
Earnings before taxes on income	$ 149	$ 161	$ 229	$ 296

Source: Hewlett-Packard annual reports, 1975–1978.

EXHIBIT 4: Percent of Sales Analysis

	1975	*1976*	*1977*	*1978*
Earnings:				
Cost of goods sold	46.8%	47.7%	45.3%	46.0%
Research and development	9.1	9.6	9.1	8.8
Marketing	16.4	15.7	15.1	15.1
Administrative and general	12.6	12.4	13.5	12.9
Interest	.2	.4	.3	.3
Total costs and expenses	85.0	85.7	83.3	83.1
Earnings before income taxes	15.0	14.3	16.7	16.9
Taxes	6.6	6.2	7.8	8.2
Net earnings	8.5%	8.1%	8.8%	8.7%
Sales by business segment (percent of total):				
Test, measuring, and related	45.3%	44.3%	42.8%	42.0%
Electronic data products	39.5	40.1	41.9	43.2
Medical electronic equipment	9.9	10.5	9.8	9.3
Analytical instrumentation	5.3	5.1	5.5	5.6
Earnings by business segment (percent of total):				
Test, measuring, and related	51.4	51.5	48.9	52.0
Electronic data products	37.2	34.5	38.7	35.8
Medical electronic equipment	7.1	10.5	8.0	7.5
Analytical instrumentation	4.4	3.5	4.4	4.6

Note: Figures may not add exactly due to rounding.
Source: Developed by casewriters from Exhibits 1 and 3 in the case.

EXHIBIT 5: Selected Growth Indicators for Years Ended October 31, 1975–1978

	1975	*1976*	*1977*	*1978*
Employees				
Domestic	22,000	22,800	25,400	31,000
International	8,200	9,400	9,700	11,400
Total	30,200	32,200	35,100	42,400
Total customers	35,000	n.a.	Over 50,000	n.a.
Domestic orders (millions)	$500.4	$592.4	$768.8	$977.0
International orders (millions)	$501.3	$557.6	$664.1	$898.0
Backlog of orders (millions)	$145.0	$175.0	$252.0	n.a.
R&D expenditures (millions)	$ 89.6	$107.6	$125.4	$154.0
Patents held and pending	770/151	837/158	850/165	n.a.
Number of products	~3,400	~3,600	~4,000	~5,000
Major new products introduced	~90	~100	~115	~130
Capital expenditures (millions)	$ 66.0	$103.4	$115.5	$159.0
Increases in plant capacity (sq. ft.)	760,000	768,000	696,000	741,000
Increases in sales and service (sq. ft.)	n.a.	175,000	183,000	253,000

n.a. = Not available.
Source: Hewlett-Packard annual reports, 1975–1978, form 10-Ks, and correspondence with HP.

supervision and a maximum of responsibility.[3] They stated that to attain such a participative working environment requires special attention to the basic organizational structure of the company. At Hewlett-Packard, a product division was an integrated self-sustaining organization with a great deal of independence that performed in much the same way as the company had 22 years ago. The fundamental responsibilities of a division, extending worldwide, were to develop, manufacture, and market appropriate products. Acting much as an independent business, each division was responsible for its own accounting, personnel activities, quality assurance, and support of its products in the field. Coordination of the divisions was achieved primarily through the product groups. Group management had overall responsibility for the operations and financial performance of its divisions. Each group had a common sales force serving all of its product divisions. To keep an atmosphere that encouraged the making of problem-solving decisions as close as possible to the level where the problem occurred, HP has striven over the years to keep its basic business units—the product divisions—relatively small and well-defined.

Selected Strategies and Related Policies

Hewlett-Packard's product-market strategy has concentrated on developing quality products, which make unique technological contributions and are so far advanced that customers are willing to pay premium prices. Products originally limited to electronic measuring instrument markets have expanded over the years to include computers and other technologically related fields. Customer service, both before and after the sale, has been given primary emphasis. Their financial strategy has been to use profits, employee stock purchases, and other internally generated funds to finance growth. They have avoided long-term debt and have resorted to short-term debt only when sales growth exceeded the return on net worth. Their growth strategy has been to attain a position of technological strength and leadership by continually developing innovative products and by attracting high caliber and creative people. Their motivational strategy has consisted of providing employees with the opportunity to share in the success of the company through high wages, profit-sharing, and stock-purchase plans. They have also provided job security by keeping fluctuations in production schedules to a minimum by avoiding consumer-type products and by not making any products exclusively for the government. Their managerial strategy has been to practice "management by objective" rather than management by directive;[4] they have used the corporate objectives to provide unity of purpose and have given employees the freedom to work toward these goals in ways they determine best for their own area of responsibility. The company has exercised its social responsibility by building plants and offices that are attractive and in harmony with the community, by helping to solve community problems, and by contributing both money and time to community projects.

Division Review. A principal vehicle for effecting communication between corporate management and the basic operating units has been the division re-

[3] "Working Together: The Hewlett-Packard Organization," *Measure,* June 1978, pp. 10–11.

[4] "Management by objective" is Hewlett-Packard's phrase for using corporate objectives primarily as a framework for coordination, decision making, and planning rather than for performance appraisal as in typical MBO programs.

view conducted annually at almost every division and sales region. Described as the natural outgrowth of the personal interest and hands-on style so characteristic of HP, reviews by 1978 were covering a full range of business matters: financial performance for the past year; outlook for orders, shipments, and facilities for the next three years; detailed presentations on product development strategy and key programs; and a look at people management including training, recruiting, and affirmative action goals and results. A very broad cross section of division personnel as well as a visiting group of reviewers were involved in organizing, presenting, and participating in the reviews. The visiting reviewers generally included several members of the corporate executive committee, corporate staff heads such as personnel and controller, appropriate group and related division managers, and on occasion even outside directors.

MBWA. Another concept has received considerable attention at HP as "an extra step that HP managers needed to take in order to make the HP open-door policy truly effective." Developed by John Doyle, vice president, personnel, earlier in his career at HP, it has been termed "management by wandering around" or MBWA.[5] It has been described as friendly, unfocused, unscheduled, and—to any employee at their work with whom a wandering manager stops to chat—an invitation to repay the visit and walk through that open door whenever they choose. To encourage MBWA it has been the subject of management briefings and seminars. A two-part video program on MBWA has been taped and made available to all HP organizations. The three corporate personnel administrators have also begun to encourage it wherever they go on their liaison missions. One division general manager said of MBWA, "it's really a body chemistry kind of thing. You've got to really want to wander around and communicate at all levels." A manufacturing manager, talking about MBWA, indicated that "management by involvement" was more descriptive of the HP way than would be "management by overview." A sales region personnel manager, however, citing their communication problem as "a certain sense of isolation," noted that a "manager can't do much spontaneous wandering around" a sales territory.

Corporate Organization and Leadership Transition, 1975—1978

The April 1975 restructuring which led to speculation on who would later be taking the corporate reins had three main parts: (1) it expanded the product groups from four (test and measurement, data products, medical equipment, and analytical instrumentation) to six (instruments, computer systems, components, medical, calculators, and analytical); (2) it added a new management level of top vice presidents; and (3) established an executive committee to oversee day-to-day operations of the company. The June 1978 corporate structure—except for some changes in the personnel holding various positions, a growing number of divisions within the product groups, and an increasing emphasis on computers and calculators—was basically the same structure as in 1975. (See Exhibits 6 and 7.) The company magazine *Measure,* introducing the 1978 organization, wrote that, "Except for an official transfer of titles and responsibilities plus a birthday celebration, you would hardly have known that HP made a rather sig-

[5] "What Is This Management by Wandering Around?" *Measure,* April 1978, pp. 8–11.

EXHIBIT 6: Corporate Organization, April 1975

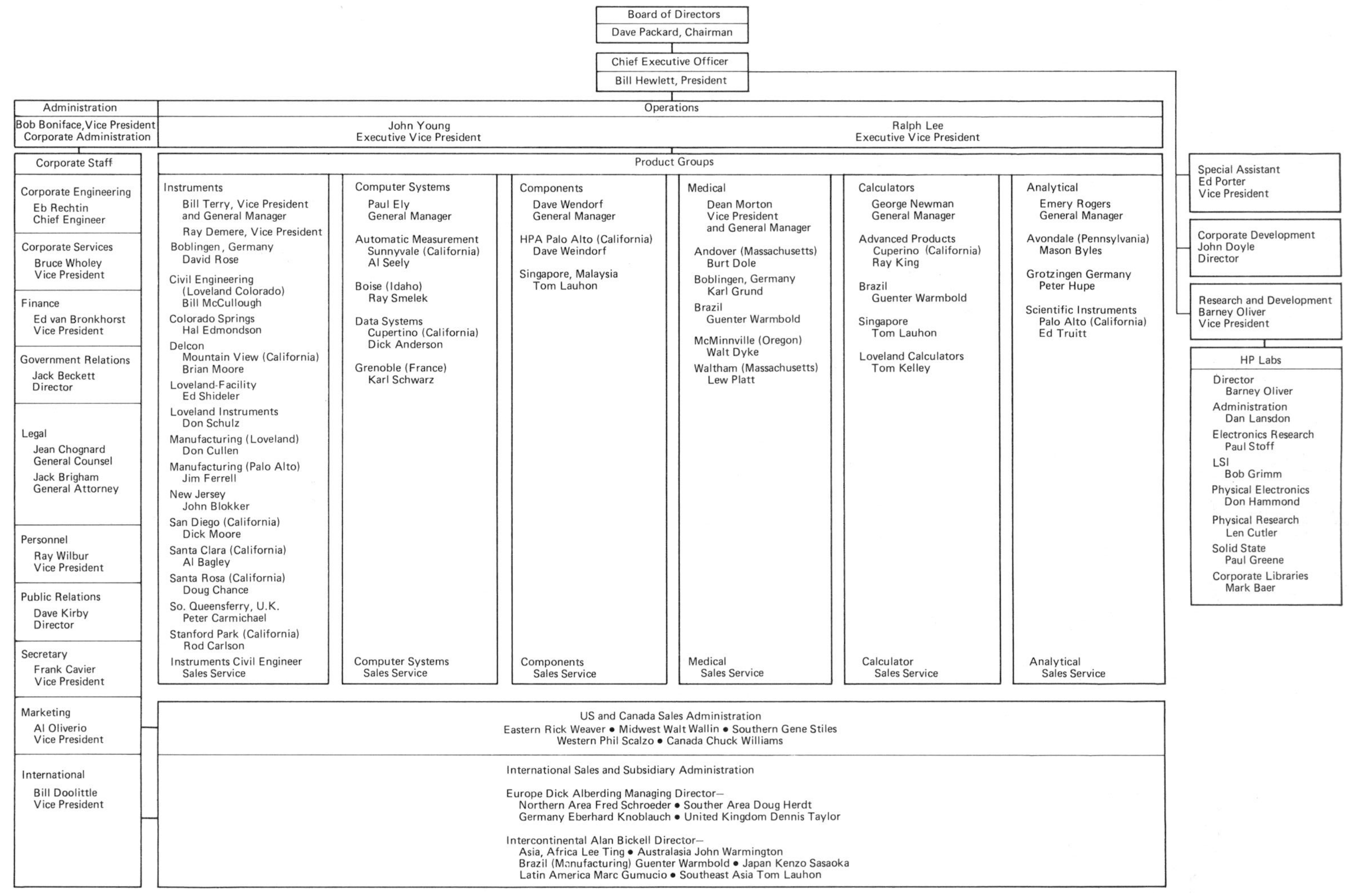
Board of Directors
Dave Packard, Chairman
Chief Executive Officer
Bill Hewlett, President
Administration
Bob Boniface, Vice President
Corporate Administration
Operations
John Young
Executive Vice President
Ralph Lee
Executive Vice President
Corporate Staff
Corporate Engineering
Eb Rechtin
Chief Engineer
Corporate Services
Bruce Wholey
Vice President
Finance
Ed van Bronkhorst
Vice President
Government Relations
Jack Beckett
Director
Legal
Jean Chognard
General Counsel
Jack Brigham
General Attorney
Personnel
Ray Wilbur
Vice President
Public Relations
Dave Kirby
Director
Secretary
Frank Cavier
Vice President
Marketing
Al Oliverio
Vice President
International
Bill Doolittle
Vice President
Product Groups
Instruments
Bill Terry, Vice President
and General Manager
Ray Demere, Vice President
Boblingen, Germany
David Rose
Civil Engineering
(Loveland Colorado)
Bill McCullough
Colorado Springs
Hal Edmondson
Delcon
Mountain View (California)
Brian Moore
Loveland-Facility
Ed Shideler
Loveland Instruments
Don Schulz
Manufacturing (Loveland)
Don Cullen
Manufacturing (Palo Alto)
Jim Ferrell
New Jersey
John Blokker
San Diego (California)
Dick Moore
Santa Clara (California)
Al Bagley
Santa Rosa (California)
Doug Chance
So. Queensferry, U.K.
Peter Carmichael
Stanford Park (California)
Rod Carlson
Instruments Civil Engineer
Sales Service
Computer Systems
Paul Ely
General Manager
Automatic Measurement
Sunnyvale (California)
Al Seely
Boise (Idaho)
Ray Smelek
Data Systems
Cupertino (California)
Dick Anderson
Grenoble (France)
Karl Schwarz
Computer Systems
Sales Service
Components
Dave Wendorf
General Manager
HPA Palo Alto (California)
Dave Weindorf
Singapore, Malaysia
Tom Lauhon
Components
Sales Service
Medical
Dean Morton
Vice President
and General Manager
Andover (Massachusetts)
Burt Dole
Boblingen, Germany
Karl Grund
Brazil
Guenter Warmbold
McMinnville (Oregon)
Walt Dyke
Waltham (Massachusetts)
Lew Platt
Medical
Sales Service
Calculators
George Newman
General Manager
Advanced Products
Cupertino (California)
Ray King
Brazil
Guenter Warmbold
Singapore
Tom Lauhon
Loveland Calculators
Tom Kelley
Calculator
Sales Service
Analytical
Emery Rogers
General Manager
Avondale (Pennsylvania)
Mason Byles
Grotzingen Germany
Peter Hupe
Scientific Instruments
Palo Alto (California)
Ed Truitt
Analytical
Sales Service
US and Canada Sales Administration
Eastern Rick Weaver • Midwest Walt Wallin • Southern Gene Stiles
Western Phil Scalzo • Canada Chuck Williams
International Sales and Subsidiary Administration
Europe Dick Alberding Managing Director–
Northern Area Fred Schroeder • Souther Area Doug Herdt
Germany Eberhard Knoblauch • United Kingdom Dennis Taylor
Intercontinental Alan Bickell Director–
Asia, Africa Lee Ting • Australasia John Warmington
Brazil (Manufacturing) Guenter Warmbold • Japan Kenzo Sasaoka
Latin America Marc Gumucio • Southeast Asia Tom Lauhon
Special Assistant
Ed Porter
Vice President
Corporate Development
John Doyle
Director
Research and Development
Barney Oliver
Vice President
HP Labs
Director
Barney Oliver
Administration
Dan Lansdon
Electronics Research
Paul Stoff
LSI
Bob Grimm
Physical Electronics
Don Hammond
Physical Research
Len Cutler
Solid State
Paul Greene
Corporate Libraries
Mark Baer

Source: "Working Together: The HP Organization," *Measure,* April–May 1975, pp. 16–17.

EXHIBIT 7: Corporate Organization, June 1978

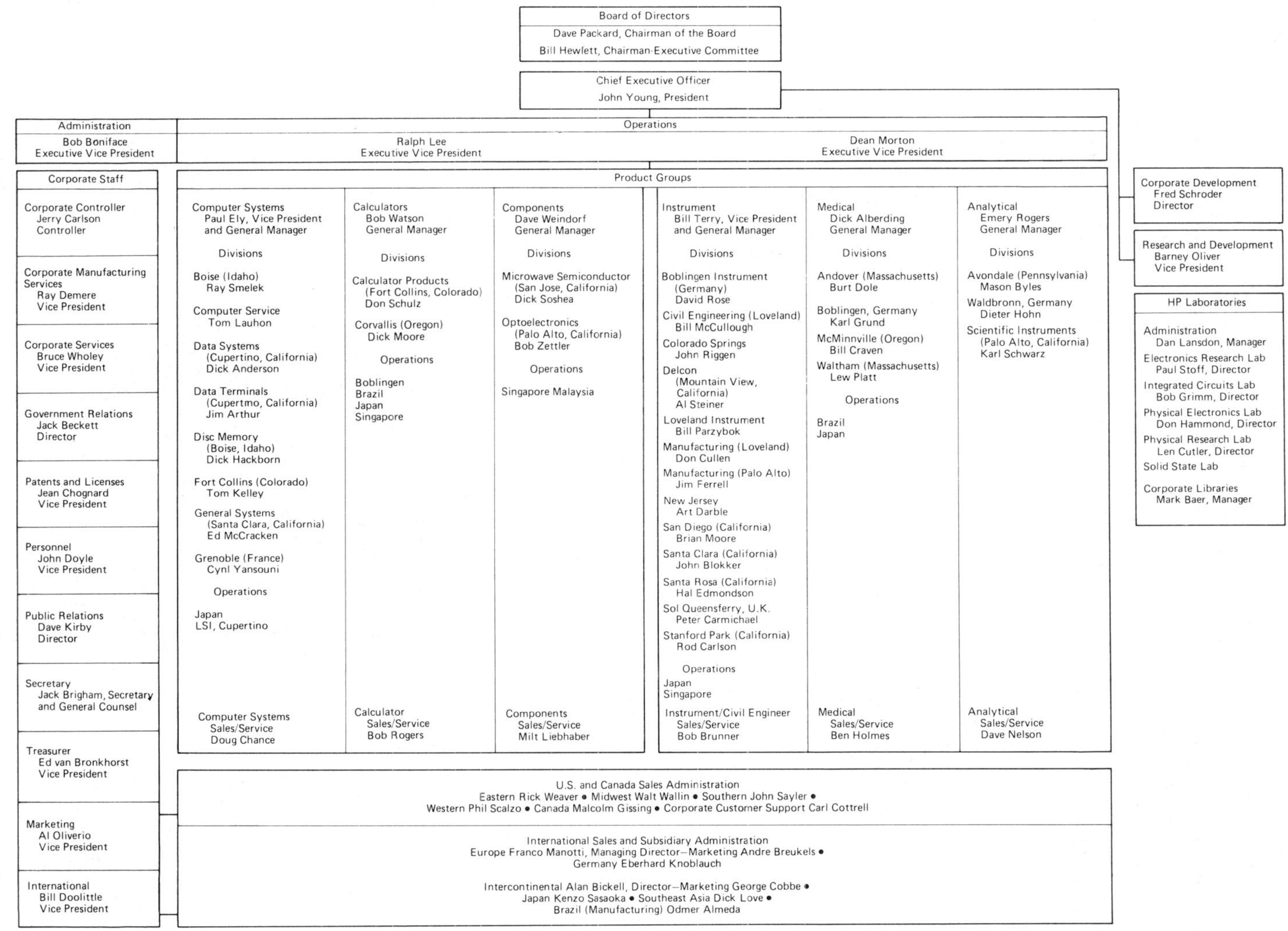

nificant change in its organizational character last month."[6] One day before his 65th birthday, Bill Hewlett's resignation as chief executive officer was made official in a brief announcement; thereupon, John Young, who in 1974 had been designated as "the leading contender," became CEO as well as president. Elevated to one of the then-new executive vice presidencies and to the board of directors in 1974, Young had fulfilled the numerous predictions made during the 1974–1977 period by succeeding Bill Hewlett as president and chief operating officer in November 1977. Thus, by June 1978 John Young had completed a four-year preparation for the top spot wherein HP for the first time in its 39-year history would be managed by a team of managers developed within the organization rather than by its original founders.

Although Bill Hewlett, as chairman of the executive committee, and David Packard, as chairman of the board of directors, were still spending about half their time at HP, it was John Young who had been handed the tough task of taking Hewlett-Packard deeper and deeper into the unfriendly territory of computational technology.

Computational Technology

Hewlett-Packard has always been heavily engaged in electronic technology. Even as recently as 1977, a special section of their annual report indicated that nowhere else did technological innovation show more momentum than in electronics and its offspring, electronic computation. The environment, as pointed out by *Forbes,* is friendly indeed for HP in the field of measuring instruments, where the company has made a big name for itself and the competition was comparable in size or more often specialized and smaller (e.g., Beckman, Tektronix, and Varian.)[7] But the instrument business had slowed in rate of growth; *Forbes* claimed the company, in order to keep its growth record intact, has had to move into a more competitive environment where the opposition is bigger and tougher (e.g., Digital Equipment, Texas Instruments, and IBM). See Exhibit 8 for asset size, debt position, and financial strength for typical instrument, electronic, and computer companies. See Exhibit 9 for key performance data for selected companies.

HP first became involved in the use of computational technology in the early 1960s when its engineers began to design instruments that could work together automatically in computer-controlled systems. The company carried the concept one step further in the mid 1960s with the introduction of a computer designed specifically to work with its instruments. The principal contribution offered by HP in that first computer was ruggedness—the ability to function outside a controlled environment, exposed to wide variations in temperature, humidity, and pressure. In subsequent years, HP products have been prominent in engineering and scientific applications, where there was a high premium on advanced instrumentation to solve complex problems of instrumentation and measurement, in widely varying environmental conditions.

More recently, the need for precise measurement and computation had become widespread in many different industries, businesses, and professions. Among

[6]"The HP Organization: Reaching a Landmark Quietly," *Measure,* June 1978, p. 7.
[7]"Welcome to the Hot Seat."

EXHIBIT 8: Selected Financial Position Data on Selected Firms

Company	*Total assets 1978 ($ millions)*	*Total debt 1978 ($ millions)*	*Short-term debt as a percent of total investment capital 1978*	*Long-term debt as a percent of total investment capital 1978*	*Common equity as percent of total investment capital*	*Stock price as percent of book value P/S 9/22/78*
Beckman Instruments	277.0	79.3	17.7	17.8	64.4	244.4
Data General	322.1	59.6	0.0	25.4	74.6	349.2
Digital Equipment	1,436.5	119.2	3.4	10.6	86.1	237.0
Fairchild Camera	387.9	91.0	8.4	23.4	68.2	99.1
General Instrument	363.5	72.7	0.1	26.1	69.1	141.9
Hewlett-Packard	1,295.8	105.2	9.4	1.0	89.6	278.9
IBM	19,114.1	428.2	1.3	2.0	96.7	313.6
National Semiconductor	278.9	24.9	15.0	1.0	84.1	276.8
Raytheon	1,966.1	97.1	2.3	11.2	86.5	219.5
Texas Instruments	1,350.7	78.8	6.0	3.6	90.4	246.2
Tektronix	491.1	47.4	2.8	9.9	87.3	255.6
Varian Associates	312.6	62.7	13.7	14.5	71.8	86.2

Source: "A Significant Swing to Short-Term Debt," *Business Week*, October 16, 1978, pp.122–36.

EXHIBIT 9: Selected Performance Data on Selected Firms, 1974–1978

A. Sales growth (percent of change)		*1974–1975*	*1975–1976*	*1976–1977*	*1977–1978**
Beckman Instruments		17%	6%	18%	18%
Data General		30	49	58	47
Digital Equipment		27	38	44	36
Fairchild Camera		−24	52	44	15
General Instrument		−11	24	8	8
Hewlett-Packard		11	13	22	24
IBM		14	13	11	13
National Semiconductor		10	38	19	28
Raytheon		16	10	14	16
Tektronix		24	9	24	32
Texas Instruments		−13	21	23	21
Varian Associates		6	10	3	14
Average		8.9%	23.6%	20.7%	22.7%
B. Net Profit margin (percent)	*1974*	*1975*	*1976*	*1977*	*1978*
Beckman Instruments	4%	4%	5%	6%	7%
Data General	12	12	12	11	11
Digital Equipment	11	9	10	10	10
Fairchild Camera	7	4	3	2	5
General Instrument	3	3	4	5	6
Hewlett-Packard	10	9	8	9	9
IBM	15	14	15	15	15
National Semiconductor	8	7	6	3	5
Raytheon	3	3	4	4	4
Tektronix	8	8	8	10	10
Texas Instruments	6	5	6	6	6
Varian Associates	3	3	3	4	3
Average	7.5%	6.8%	7.0%	7.1%	7.6%
C. Earnings on net worth (percent)	*1974*	*1975*	*1976*	*1977*	*1978*
Beckman Instruments	8%	9%	10%	13%	15%
Data General	21	14	17	20	21
Digital Equipment	13	12	12	15	16
Fairchild Camera	17	6	7	6	13
General Instrument	7	7	9	12	14
Hewlett-Packard	18	15	13	15	15
IBM	18	17	19	21	21
National Semiconductor	35	25	20	10	17
Raytheon	14	15	16	18	20
Tektronix	12	13	13	16	17
Texas Instruments	17	11	15	16	16
Varian Associates	6	6	6	8	8
Average	15.5%	12.5%	13.1%	14.2%	16.1%

* Estimated by *Value Line Investment Survey* (Arnold Bernhard & Co., July 7, 1978), p. 187.

the company's newest customers were those involved in business data processing. The first HP product aimed exclusively at this market was a hand-held calculator for financial analysis. At the other end of the size scale was the development in the early 1960s of HP's first minicomputer-based time-share system which found wide use in science and engineering, and was particularly well received in the educational market. The next generation of computers, introduced in the early 1970s, also found a ready market in the educational field because it could accommodate many different programs and computer languages. HP has steadily upgraded this computer as a result of applying the computer to HP's own business problems. This development has proved particularly useful to HP customers with similar worldwide manufacturing operations.

The relative success, however, of HP's excursions into hand-held calculators and minicomputers have been quite different. Erratic market conditions and heavy competition characterized both industry segments. There were marked differences, however, in the ability and willingness of the company to adapt and respond to these product/market changes.

Hand-held Calculators. More widely known to college students and the general public than its broad line of basic products was the company's line of hand-held calculators. David Packard described HP's entry into this field in *The AMBA Executive* newsletter in September 1977: "Actually we got into the electronic calculator business by accident. We hadn't planned it at all."[8] In 1966 calculators were largely mechanical; a young man working for one of the calculator companies brought to HP a model for an electronic calculator. His own company was not interested in it because they didn't have the electronic capability. An HP team was put together and the first electronic calculator, with a great deal of power, was designed for the engineers at HP. It was, however, a large device about one foot square. Coincidentally, HP was also doing research on large-scale integrated circuits and on light-emitting diodes. Bill Hewlett realized that these technologies could be combined into a calculator, that these light-emitting diodes would make it possible to have a small readout, and that the result would be something that could be put into a pocket. A year later, the HP-35, the first hand-held calculator was introduced.

Forbes has reported that for a brief period, HP made itself the leader in the business and scientific hand-held calculator field, which in 1974 was estimated to have yielded roughly 30 percent of company profits.[9] Shortly after, HP's high-priced, high-quality calculators fell before the competition led by Texas Instruments. Rather than compete across the board, HP decided to remain in the specialized upper end of the market. In 1978 the division was reputed to be barely profitable, but with relatively stable sales.

Minicomputers. HP had become, by 1978, a well-integrated minicomputer manufacturer, competing with International Business Machines, Digital Equipment Corporation, and Data General. This business had long been characterized by high technological risk and erratic earnings. During the late 1960s, HP successfully directed sales efforts toward the educational, scientific, and engineering markets, where it was an established supplier of instruments. Subse-

[8] "Hewlett-Packard Chairman Built Company by Design, Calculator by Chance," *AMBA Executive*, September 1977, pp. 1 ff.

[9] "Welcome to the Hot Seat."

quently, in entering the minicomputer market, the company chose to service the time-sharing sector, which fell apart in the 1970s, causing profit reversals.

Recently, however, the picture has improved and HP's electronic data processing product category has contributed over 40 percent of sales and almost the same proportion of profits, despite the drag from hand-held calculators. (See Exhibit 4.) HP has expanded its computer line into the area where others hold strong positions. HP's minicomputer line consisted basically of two products, one for business and one for scientific/technical use. Big customers often bought several systems at a time complete with peripherals-terminals, disc-drives, printers, and even instruments that could be attached. A single sale could easily exceed $1 million. The company was well aware of the dangers of its thrust into computers. Many big and smart companies had tried to take on IBM and lost. Hewlett-Packard has mounted its effort carefully. The division's domestic sales force has been almost doubled in the previous year to 500 people. The sales force has been split between business and engineering systems. Young has reportedly spent 10 percent of his time making sales presentations to customers' top management, since commitments in the $1 million range typically require board-of-directors' approval. The company has also limited its marketing efforts by foregoing well-covered markets like banks and insurance companies in favor of large manufacturing companies which could use systems that HP had developed initially for its own operations. Such firms could take a whole computer line from the technically slanted machines on the factory floor and near engineers' desks to business systems for payrolls and customer billing.

To effectively compete in minicomputers, the company has had to continue to be extremely innovative and creative, as well as efficient. The minicomputer environment was difficult, rapidly changing, and extremely competitive. In this market, Hewlett-Packard has started to kick at the shins of IBM, which was 15 times larger (see Exhibit 8). A June 1976 article in *Business Week* quoted a former HP marketing executive, then president of Tandem Computers, Inc., as saying, "The first rule of this business is not to compete with IBM."[10] And in October 1978, *Business Week* described an incredibly fast adjustment in HP's marketing strategy.[11] It also noted some rough spots in the road that HP had already traveled in the field of computational technology: (1) its early reliance on techniques that worked well with sales to engineers, but not with the applications-oriented commercial EDP customers; (2) the difficulty of selling the idea of distributed processing, a concept involving pushing data processing out of the central computer room, HP's primary strategic difference from IBM; (3) a period in 1973 when the HP 3000 had to be taken off the market and redesigned because its software was too powerful for the hardware; (4) the different requirements, buyer attributes, and decision processes that characterized the larger and more fragmented market of commercial systems; (5) the tough task of meeting systems repair and maintenance response standards set by the main-frame companies it was now up against; and (6) the hard push by its customers for more applications software that would allow customers to perform specific tasks.

[10] "Hewlett-Packard Takes on the Computer Giants," *Business Week,* June 7, 1976, pp. 91–92.

[11] "Hewlett-Packard Learns to Sell to Business Managers," *Business Week,* October 26, 1978, pp. 62B and 62G.

Included in the same *Business Week* article were two items that must have intrigued long-time observers of HP and the computer industry. The product manager for HP's new HP 3000, Series 33, noting how, since 1974, they had concentrated on expanded capability for the 3000 at about the original price, was quoted, "Now let's use the technology to drive down the price." *Business Week* also indicated that HP is likely "to see more competition in distributed processing, especially from IBM, which is expected to announce a powerful new series of low-cost main-frame computers this fall."

CASE SIX

Hewlett-Packard (B)

ROGER M. ATHERTON
University of Oklahoma

Assignment Questions:

1. How well has Hewlett-Packard performed under John Young?
2. What changes have you seen in Hewlett-Packard's organizational strategy?
3. What problems do you see for the future? What would you do? Why?

In May 1978, one day before his sixty-fifth birthday, Bill Hewlett resigned from his position as chief executive officer of Hewlett-Packard, the company he had helped found in 1939. He was appointed chairman of the executive committee and joined David Packard, chairman of the board of directors, in semi retirement. John Young, who had succeeded Bill Hewlett as president and chief operating officer in November 1977, was promoted to the vacated CEO position. For the first time in its thirty-nine-year history, H-P was to be directed by an executive who had been developed from within the organization rather than being led by its original, almost legendary founders. It had become John Young's responsibility to manage the rapidly growing company as it headed deeper and deeper into the unfriendly territory of computational technology, where the competition was both bigger and tougher than in H-P's traditional businesses—electronic test and measurement, medical electronic equipment, and analytical instrumentation. The question raised by the trade press, Wall Street analysts, and some employees was whether John Young could provide the needed strategies and leadership in this more hostile environment for continued successful growth.

STRATEGIC CHANGES[1]

Electronic Office Systems

By 1981 H-P had become the world's third largest minicomputer manufacturer, exceeded only by IBM and Digital Equipment Corporation. In October

[1]See Acknowledgments for sources.

1981, the *Wall Street Journal*[2] reported that H-P had decided to expand from their traditional base of data-processing equipment for business, factory, and scientific purposes into the word-processing and office terminal field dominated by IBM and Wang Laboratories. John Young indicated that H-P's strategy would be to place computer power in the form of interactive, information-processing networks directly into the hands of all office professionals, specialists, and managers, as well as secretaries and the data-processing staff. To implement this strategy, H-P introduced twenty-seven new office products, including two new minicomputers, new word-processing terminals, improved computer terminals for creating graphic representations of numbers, new low-cost disc memories, and four new data communications products to tie all these elements together. Electronic mail and electronic filing packages were due to be introduced within a year. Combined with its previously announced products, such as laser printers and a low-cost personal computer, these new products gave H-P a fully integrated office system. For the first time, H-P had the potential to penetrate the full spectrum of business computer uses.

Although in 1979 and 1980 Hewlett-Packard had enjoyed an average annual growth rate of 45 per cent in electronic data products revenues, that growth rate dropped in 1981 to 17 per cent. According to *Business Week*,[3] a growing number of its data-processing customers had begun to purchase equipment from such companies as Wang Laboratories, Datapoint, and Lanier Business Products, which offered systems aimed directly at the automated office. Growth in the market for conventional minicomputers had slowed to 25 per cent, so that H-P needed to tap into the market for the larger so-called superminis and the market for office systems, since both were expanding at about 40 per cent a year, if it wanted to continue its healthy growth rate.

A major target for H-P's thrust into office systems would be manufacturing companies. H-P had focused its efforts in minicomputers on this market segment, which accounted for 40 per cent of the company's business computer sales. H-P wanted to offer these same customers systems that integrated everything from measurement instruments and data-collection terminals on the factory floor to word processors in the front office in a single data-processing network.

The office market presented H-P with new marketing challenges. Minicomputer makers traditionally sold to data-processing departments, but to sell office equipment they would have to identify a whole new set of buyers among their large corporate customers. H-P had developed plans to expand its business computer marketing force by 25 per cent and service force by one-third. It also intended to go after new customers in financial services, retailing, and other nonmanufacturing sectors. John Young has indicated that H-P would not aggressively go after new customers in these other areas except as there were spare resources to do so. These markets were seen as highly opportunistic sectors of the market, where perhaps some additional business could be picked up, but they were not seen a part of the basic strategic program.

Whether H-P could win sales outside its own manufacturing customer base remained to be seen. But few industry watchers doubted the company's new

[2] "Digital Equipment and Hewlett-Packard Enter Electronic Office Systems Market," *Wall Street Journal,* October 30, 1981, p. 48.

[3] "Two Giants Bid for Office Sales," *Business Week,* November 9, 1981, pp. 86–96.

products would appeal to a large proportion of their regular customers. One competitor believed that if they could execute their strategies and followed them up with service and support, there was no question that H-P would gain market share at the expense of word-processor vendors with narrower offerings. Conversely, a Wang Laboratories vice-president indicated that H-P didn't concern them that much because H-P's strength was selling to data-processing managers. Wang and IBM had much more experience selling directly into the office.

The office automation market was expected to triple to $36 billion by 1990, according to a market research report released in October, 1981 by International Resource Development, Inc. No doubt the major contenders would compete fiercely to dominate the market while the multitude of small firms, which had just entered the new market, would have to scramble to survive. But in 1981, no single company had managed to secure for itself a corner on the market. *Electronics,*[4] a major trade journal, predicted that the main contenders would be IBM, AT&T, Xerox, and very possibly Wang and Datapoint. It also indicated that DEC and H-P had the background for especially good chances of success. The unanswered question was whether Hewlett-Packard could manage this new growth and whether the company could manage to remain technologically competitive in this new business and its traditional businesses at the same time.

Electronic Calculators

In sharp contrast to the rapid-growth market in electronic office equipment, the market for electronic hand-held calculators was largely saturated. Texas Instruments had been the pioneer in inexpensive hand-held calculators and dominated the market for years, until low-priced Japanese models had taken over the lower end of the market. In 1981–82 the different calculator makers were attempting to develop specific market niches that they believed would provide opportunities for further growth. The big Japanese producers had added gimmicks like solar calculators and games such as boxing matches and electronic cube puzzles. Casio was trying to get more business by driving prices still lower. It was also offering low-cost printer calculators that could fit in a shirt pocket. At the high-priced end of the market, companies were developing—or were already producing—products that could compete in the newly formed hand-held computer market. This market had only developed recently when Tandy (Radio Shack), Casio, and others introduced their pocket computers. In fact, *Business Week*[5] even questioned whether there was still a market for calculators with $300 price tags since the Japanese and Radio Shack had begun to sell hand-held computers that cost less. One consultant asserted that hand-held computers would replace programmable calculators in the following three to five years. Other experts felt that the market might flatten out, but that the market for programmable calculators would die slowly and hard.

The essential difference between hand-held calculators and computers is the way the units are programmed. On advanced calculators, programs are written by pressing a series of fixed-function keys in the order needed to step through

[4] "H-P: A Drive into Office Automation," *Electronics,* November 3, 1981, pp. 106–110.
[5] "When 'Calculator' Is a Dirty Word," *Business Week,* June 14, 1982, p. 62.

calculations. Hand-held computers, however, use a conventional programming language which consists of short statements that tell the machine what to do. Both TI and H-P were working to reposition their products in this developing market segment.

Hewlett-Packard had dominated the top end of the market from the beginning with its highly successful scientific calculator, the HP-35, introduced in 1972. With its late 1981 introduction of several new products, H-P put its calculator somewhere in the increasingly gray border between programmable calculators and hand-held computers. For example, the Hewlett-Packard Interface Loop (HP-IL) provided a link that let the HP-41 calculator control and communicate with other machines and computers, including the company's HP-80 personal computer. Complementary products included a battery-operated printer, a digital cassette drive, cassettes that significantly expanded the calculator's memory, and a device that other companies could build into their computers to make them compatible with the system. The company aimed the new system at its favorite customers: engineers and scientists. The products would allow H-P to sell accessory products to people who already owned the popular HP-41 series calculators, and to attract new customers who would prefer to pay $325 and add components later, instead of paying $2,000 or more for a personal computer.

Analysts expected both Texas Instruments and Tandy Corporation (Radio Shack) would be strong competitors, especially at the high-priced end of the market. However, as *Business Week*[6] and the *Wall Street Journal*[7] were quick to point out, the Japanese producers were not limiting their horizons to the high end of the calculator market. They were clearly working on strategies and products that would expand pocket computers to the mass market. One of Casio's vice-presidents eventually expected to have a pocket computer low enough in price to do away with all the scientific calculators in the market. It seemed clear that H-P would have to be both technologically innovative and cost-effective if it intended to be competitive in this market.

Business Segment Performance (1978–1981)

Hewlett-Packard reported data by business segment, with both electronic office systems and hand-held calculators and computers included in electronic data products. The other business segments were electronic test and measurement, medical electronic equipment, and analytical instrumentation. Exhibit 1 provides data on net sales, earnings before taxes, identifiable assets, and capital expenditures for these four business segments. Exhibit 2 compares electronic data products with the other business segments combined together to provide a summary comparison of their comparatively newer, more competitive, and higher risk line of business with their basic and more traditional business activities. The electronic data products appeared to have provided greater growth in profit margins (ebt/sales), asset turnover (sales/assets), and return on assets (ebt/assets), although the level of returns was higher in the more traditional businesses.

[6] Op. cit.

[7] "Calculator Makers Add Features and Cut Prices to Find a Niche in a Crowded Market," *Wall Street Journal*, December 21, 1981, p. 23.

EXHIBIT 1: Selected Data on Business Segments (Millions)

	1978	*1979*	*1980*	*1981*	*Percent Average Annual Growth 1978–81*
Net Sales					
Electronic data products	$715	$1,060	$1,510	$1,771	36
Electronic test and measurement	731	986	1,200	1,349	23
Medical electronic equipment	163	193	230	273	19
Analytical instrumentation	98	122	159	185	24
Earnings Before Taxes					
Electronic data products	$124	$ 183	$ 285	$ 319	38
Electronic test and measurment	180	242	271	284	17
Medical electronic equipment	26	27	37	50	25
Analytical instrumentation	16	16	24	32	28
Identifiable Assets					
Electronic data products	$587	$ 767	$1,000	$1,169	26
Electronic test and measurement	452	594	709	817	22
Medical electronic equipment	120	131	146	175	14
Analytical instrumentation	71	83	94	99	16
Capital Expenditures					
Electronic data products	$ 90	$ 115	$ 148	$ 174	25
Electronic test and measurement	49	46	85	89	28
Medical electronic equipment	7	5	11	18	52
Analytical instrumentation	7	6	11	9	17

Source: Hewlett-Packard *Annual Reports*.

STRATEGIC IMPLEMENTATION

Structural Changes

The January, 1982 Hewlett-Packard Corporate Organization Chart (Exhibits 3 and 4) showed that a number of changes have been made since Mr. Young became chief executive officer. Ralph Lee, executive vice-president-operations retired in 1980 after thirty-five years with H-P. Paul Ely, vice-president and general manager-computer systems, and Bill Terry, vice-president and general manager-instruments, were subsequently made executive vice-presidents-operations.

Bill Doolittle had been promoted from vice-president-international to senior vice-president-international. Al Oliverio had been promoted from vice-president-marketing to senior vice president-marketing. Ed van Bronkhorst had been promoted from vice-president to senior vice-president, corporate treasurer,

EXHIBIT 2: Comparison of Electronic Data Products and Other Business Segments Combined[1]

Summary Data	*1978*	*1979*	*1980*	*1981*	*Percent Average Annual Growth 1978–81*
Net Sales (millions)					
Electronic Data Products	$715	$1,060	$1,510	$1,771	36
Other Segments Combined	992	1,301	1,589	1,807	22
Earnings Before Taxes (millions)					
Electronic Data Products	$124	$ 183	$ 285	$ 319	38
Other Segments Combined	222	285	332	366	18
Identifiable Assets (millions)					
Electronic Data Products	$587	$ 767	$1,000	$1,169	26
Other Segments Combined	643	808	949	1,091	19
Capital Expenditures (millions)					
Electronic Data Products	$ 90	$ 115	$ 148	$ 174	25
Other Segments Combined	63	57	107	106	26
Strategic Ratio Analysis					
EBT/Sales (percent)					
Electronic Data Products	17.3	17.3	18.9	18.0	2
Other Segments Combined	22.4	21.9	20.9	20.3	−3
Sales/Identifiable Assets (times)					
Electronic Data Products	1.22	1.38	1.51	1.51	8
Other Segments Combined	1.54	1.61	1.67	1.66	3
EBT/Identifiable Assets (percent)					
Electronic Data Products	21.1	23.9	28.5	27.3	9
Other Segments Combined	34.5	35.3	35.0	33.5	−1

[1] Electronic Test and Measurement, Medical Electronic Equipment, and Analytical Instrumentation.

and chief financial officer. Franco Mariotti had been promoted from managing director-Europe to vice-president-Europe. Dick Alberding had been promoted from general manager-medical group to vice-president-medical group. Dr. Bernard Oliver retired as an officer and director of the company in May 1981. He had been with H-P for twenty-nine years as head of corporate research and development activities. John Doyle, vice-president of personnel, replaced Oliver as vice-president-research and development. Appointed director of personnel,

EXHIBIT 3: Hewlett-Packard Corporate Organization January, 1982

Viewed broadly, Hewlett-Packard Company is a rather complex organization made up of many business units that offer a wide range of advanced electronic products to a variety of markets around the world. Giving it common direction and cohesion are shared philosophies, practices and goals as well as technologies.

Within this broad context, the individual business units—called product divisions—are relatively small and self-sufficient so that decisions can be made at the level of the organization most responsible for putting them into action. Consistent with this approach, it has always been a practice at Hewlett-Packard to give each individual employee considerable freedom to implement methods and ideas that meet specific local organizational goals and broad corporate objectives.

Since its start in 1939, the HP organization has grown to more than 40 product divisions. To provide for effective overall management and coordination, the company has aligned these divisions into product groups characterized by product and/or market focus. Today there are ten such groups or segments. Six sales-and-service forces, organized around broad product categories, represent the product groups in the field.

HP's corporate structure is designed to foster a small-business flexibility within its many individual operating units while supporting them with the strengths of a larger organization. The accompanying chart provides a graphic view of the relationship of the various groups and other organizational elements. The organization has been structured to allow the groups and their divisions to concentrate on their product-development, manufacturing and marketing activities without having to perform all the administrative tasks required of a company doing business worldwide. Normal and functional lines of responsibility and communication are indicated on the chart; however, direct and informal communication across lines and between levels is encouraged.

Here is a closer look at the company's basic organizational units:

Product Divisions

An HP product division is a vertically integrated organization that conducts itself very much like an independent business. Its fundamental responsibilities are to develop, manufacture and market products that are profitable and which make contributions in the marketplace by virtue of technological or economic advantage.

Each division has its own distinct family of products, for which it has worldwide marketing responsibility. A division also is responsible for its own accounting, personnel activities, quality assurance, and support of its products in the field. In addition, it has important social and economic responsibilities in its local community.

Product Groups

Product groups, which are composed of divisions having closely related product lines, are responsible for coordinating the activities of their respective divisions. The management of each group has overall responsibility for the operations and financial performance of its members. Further, each group has worldwide responsibility for its manufacturing operations and sales/service forces. Management staffs of the four U.S. sales regions and two international headquarters (European and intercontinental operations) assist the groups in coordinating the sales/service functions.

The group management structure provides a primary channel of communication between the divisions and corporate departments.

Corporate Operations

Corporate operations management has responsibility for the day-to-day operation of the company. The executive vice presidents in charge of corporate operations are directly responsible to HP's president for the performance of their assigned product groups; they also provide a primary channel of communication between the groups and the president.

Corporate Administration

The principal responsibility of corporate administration is to insure that the corporate staff offices provide the specialized policies, expertise and resources to adequately support the divisions and groups on a worldwide basis. The executive vice president in charge of corporate administration also reports to the president, providing an important upward channel of communication for the corporate staff activities.

The marketing and international offices, through the U.S. sales regions and two international headquarters, insure that—on a worldwide basis—all corporate policies and practices are followed and that local legal and fiscal requirements are met.

Corporate Research and Development

HP Laboratories is the corporate research and development organization that provides a central source of technical support for the product-development efforts of HP product divisions. In these efforts, the divisions make important use of the advanced technologies, materials, components, and theoretical analyses researched or developed by HP Labs. Through their endeavors in areas of science and technology, the corporate laboratories also help the company evaluate promising new areas of business.

Board of Directors

The board of directors and its chairman have ultimate responsibility for the legal and ethical conduct of the company and its officers. It is the board's duty to protect and advance the interests of the stockholders, to foster a continuing concern for fairness in the company's relations with employees, and to fulfill all requirements of the law with regard to the board's stewardship. The board counsels management on general business matters and also reviews and evaluates the performance of management. To assist in discharging these responsibilities, the board has formed various committees to oversee the company's activities and programs in such areas as employee benefits, compensation, financial auditing, and investment.

President

The president has operating responsibility for the overall performance and direction of the company, subject to the authority of the board of directors. Also, the president is directly responsible for corporate development and planning functions, and for HP Labs.

Executive Committee

This committee meets weekly for the purpose of setting and reviewing corporate policies, and making coordinated decisions on a wide range of current operations and activities. Members include the executive committee chairman, the chairman of the board, the president and the executive vice presidents for operations and administration. All are members of the board of directors.

Operations Council

Primary responsibilities of this body are to review operating policies on a broad basis and to turn policy decisions into corporate action. Members include the executive vice presidents, product group general managers, the senior vice presidents of marketing and international, the vice president—Europe, and the managing director of intercontinental.

EXHIBIT 4: Hewlett-Packard Corporate Organization, January 1982

Hewlett-Packard
Corporate Organization
January, 1982

BOARD OF DIRECTORS — Dave Packard, Chairman of the Board; Bill Hewlett, Chairman—Executive Committee

CHIEF EXECUTIVE OFFICER — John Young, President

ADMINISTRATION

Bob Boniface, Executive Vice President

CORPORATE STAFF

- Corporate Controller — Jerry Carlson, Controller
- Corporate Services — Bruce Wholey, Vice President
- Government Relations — Jack Beckett, Director
- International — Bill Doolittle, Senior Vice President
- Patents and Licenses — Jean Chognard, Vice President
- Personnel — Bill Craven, Director
- Public Relations — Dave Kirby, Director
- Secretary — Jack Bingham, Secretary and General Counsel
- Marketing — Al Oliverio, Senior Vice President
- Treasurer — Ed van Bronkhorst, Senior Vice President

EUROPE

Franco Mariotti, Vice President

Field Sales Regions: Germany; France; United Kingdom; South/Eastern Europe; Northern Europe

Manufacturing: United Kingdom; Germany; France

INTERCONTINENTAL

Alan Bickell, Managing Director

Field Sales Regions: Japan; Far East; Australasia; South Africa; Latin America

Manufacturing: Singapore; Malaysia; Puerto Rico; Brazil; Japan

U.S./CANADA SALES

Field Sales Regions: Eastern; Mid-West; Southern; Neely (Western); Canada

Corporate Parts Center

OPERATIONS

COMPUTERS

Paul Ely, Executive Vice President

TECHNICAL COMPUTER GROUP — Doug Chance, General Manager
- □ Data Systems
- □ Roseville
- □ Desktop Computer
  - ○ Engineering Sys.
- □ Boblingen Desktop
- □ Computer I.C.
  - ○ Cupertino I.C.
  - ○ Systems
  - ○ Technology

COMPUTER PERIPHERALS GROUP — Dick Hackborn, General Manager
- □ Boise
- □ Disc Memory
- □ Greeley
- □ Vancouver

BUSINESS COMPUTER GROUP — Ed McCracken, General Manager
- □ Computer Systems
- □ Information Networks
  - ○ Pinewood
- □ Boblingen General Systems
- ○ Application Systems

COMPUTER TERMINALS GROUP — Cyril Yansouni, General Manager
- □ Data Terminals
- □ General Systems
- □ Grenoble
- ○ Puerto Rico

Computer Marketing Group — Jim Arthur, General Manager
- □ YHP Computer
- ○ Systems Remarketing
- □ Computer Support
- Worldwide Sales
- ○ Computer Supplies

INSTRUMENTS

Bill Terry, Executive Vice President

MICROWAVE AND COMMUNICATION INSTRUMENT GROUP — Hal Edmondson, General Manager
- □ Colorado Telecom
- □ Queensferry Telecom
- □ Stanford Park
- □ Spokane
- □ Manufacturing
- □ Signal Analysis
- □ Network Measurement
- ○ Santa Rosa Technology Center

ELECTRONIC MEASUREMENTS GROUP — Bill Parzybok, General Manager
- □ Boblingen Instrument
- □ San Diego
- □ Colorado Springs
  - ○ Logic Systems
  - ○ Oscilloscope
  - ○ Graphics Displays
- □ YHP Instrument
- □ Loveland Instrument
- □ Lake Stevens Instrument
- □ New Jersey
- □ Santa Clara
  - ○ Lasers

Instrument Marketing — Bob Brunner, Group Marketing Manager
- □ Instrument Support
- Worldwide Sales

Dean Morton, Executive Vice President*

COMPONENTS GROUP — John Blokker, General Manager
- □ Microwave Semiconductor
- □ Optoelectronics
- ○ Malaysia
- Components Sales/Service Worldwide

ANALYTICAL GROUP — Lew Platt, General Manager
- □ Avondale
- □ Scientific Instruments
- □ Waldbronn
- Analytical Sales/Service Worldwide

MEDICAL GROUP — Dick Alberding, Vice President
- □ Andover
- □ Boblingen Medical
- □ McMinnville
- □ Waltham
- Medical Sales/Service Worldwide

PERSONAL COMPUTATION GROUP — Dick Moore, General Manager
- □ Corvallis
- □ Personal Computer
- ○ Brazil
- ○ Singapore
- Personal Computation Marketing Worldwide

HP LABORATORIES

John Doyle, Vice President, Research and Development

Research Centers: Computer Research; Physical Research; Technology

Corporate Development — Fred Schroder, Director

Internal Audit — George Abbott, Manager

Corporate Manufacturing Services — Ray Demere, Vice President

□ DIVISION
○ OPERATION (Product line, international locations)

succeeding Doyle, was Bill Craven, general manager of the McMinnville division (medical group) since 1976. Exhibit 5 provides background information on these executive officers.

Corporate manufacturing services had been shifted from being part of corporate staff reporting to administration to having a direct reporting relationship to operations. An internal audit department had been set up and reported

EXHIBIT 5: Executive Officers of Hewlett-Packard

David Packard; age 69; chairman, H-P. Mr. Packard is a co-founder of the company and has been a director since 1947.[1] He has served as chairman of the board of directors since 1972 and was the company's president from 1947 to 1964. Mr. Packard also served as chairman of the board and chief executive officer from 1964 to 1968 when he was appointed U.S. Deputy Secretary of Defense. Mr. Packard is a director of Caterpillar Tractor Company; Standard Oil Company of California; The Boeing Company; and Genentech, Inc.

William R. Hewlett; age 68; chairman of the executive committee, H-P. Mr. Hewlett is a co-founder of the company and has served on its board of directors since 1947. Mr. Hewlett served as executive vice-president of the company from 1947 to 1964 when he was appointed president. He served as president and chief executive officer from 1969 to 1977 and was chief executive officer and chairman of the executive committee from November 1977 to May 1978 when he retired as chief executive officer. Mr. Hewlett remains the chairman of the company's executive committee. He also is a director of Chrysler Corporation and Utah International, Inc., a mining company.

John A. Young; age 49; president and chief executive officer, H-P. Mr. Young has served as president and chief executive officer of the company since May, 1978. He was appointed president and chief operating officer of the company as of November 1, 1977, and has been a member of the company's board of directors since 1974. Prior to his appointment as president and chief operating officer, Mr. Young served as executive vice-president from 1974. Mr. Young is a director of Wells Fargo & Company; Wells Fargo Bank, N.A.; Dillingham Corporation; and SRI International. He also serves on the board of trustees of Stanford University.

Robert L. Boniface; age 57; executive vice-president, H-P. Mr. Boniface has been a director of the company since 1974. He has served as an executive vice-president of the company since 1975 and was vice-president, administration from 1974 to 1975. Mr. Boniface served as vice-president, marketing from 1970 to 1974.

Paul C. Ely, Jr.; age 49; executive vice-president, H-P. Mr. Ely was named an executive vice-president of the company in July 1980 and was elected to the board of directors effective September 1980. Mr. Ely is responsible for the company's computer groups. Prior to his appointment as executive vice-president, Mr. Ely served as computer group general manager from 1974 and as vice-president from 1976.

Dean O. Morton; age 49; executive vice-president, H-P. Mr. Morton was elected a director of the company in September 1977. He was appointed a vice-president of the company in 1973 and was also appointed general manager of the company's medical products group in 1974. Mr. Morton served in those dual capacities until he assumed his present position in November, 1977. Mr. Morton is also a director of State Street Investment Corporation and Cobe Laboratories, Inc.

William E. Terry; age 48; executive vice-president, H-P. Mr. Terry was named an executive vice-president of the company in July 1980 and was elected to the board of directors effective September 1980. Mr. Terry is responsible for the company's In-

EXHIBIT 5: Executive Officers of Hewlett-Packard

strument groups. Prior to his appointment as executive vice-president, Mr. Terry served as vice-president and general manager of the company's instrument group from 1974. Mr. Terry served as general manager of the company's data products group from 1971 to 1974. Mr. Terry is a director of Applied Magnetics Corporation; Altus Corporation, a manufacturer of lithium batteries; and Kevex Corporation, a manufacturer of X-ray spectrometers.

William P. Doolittle; age 63; senior vice-president, international, H-P. Mr. Doolittle has been a director of the company since 1971 and served as vice-president, international from 1963 until he assumed his present position in July, 1981. Mr. Doolittle is also a director of Machine Intelligence Corp. and Creative Strategies International.

Alfred P. Oliverio; age 54; senior vice-president, marketing, H-P. Mr. Oliverio served as vice-president, marketing from 1974 until he assumed his present position in July 1981.

Edward E. van Bronkhorst; age 57; senior vice-president, treasurer, H-P. Mr. van Bronkhorst served as vice-president and treasurer of the company from 1963 until his appointment as senior vice-president and treasurer in July, 1981. He also serves as the company's chief financial officer. He was named a director of the company in 1962 and currently serves as a director of ROLM Corporation, a manufacturer of computerized communication systems; Northern California Savings and Loan Association; and TRIAD Systems Corporation, a manufacturer of microcomputer-based data-processing systems primarily for the auto parts distribution industry.

Richard C. Alberding; age 50; vice-president, medical products group, H-P. Mr. Alberding was appointed to his present position in July 1981 and has served as general manager of the company's medical products group since 1977. Mr. Alberding was director of the company's European operations from 1970 until 1977.

Jean C. Chognard; age 57; vice-president, patents and licenses, H-P. Mr. Chognard has been patent counsel for the company since 1958 and has been a vice-president of the company since May 1976.

Raymond M. Demere, Jr.; age 60; vice-president, manufacturing services, H-P. Mr. Demere has been a vice-president of the company since 1971 and served as operations manager of the instrument group of the company from 1974 until September 1977 when he was appointed vice-president, manufacturing services.

John L. Doyle; age 48; vice-president, research and development, H-P. Mr. Doyle was appointed corporate director of personnel in June 1976 and thereafter elected vice-president, personnel in July 1976. In June, 1981 Mr. Doyle assumed his present position as vice-president, research and development.

Franco Mariotti; age 46; vice-president, Europe, H-P. Mr. Mariotti was appointed to his present position in July 1981 and has served as managing director of the company's European operations since 1977. From 1976 to 1977 Mr. Mariotti served as marketing manager for Europe.

W. Bruce Wholey; age 60; vice-president, corporate services, H-P. Mr. Wholey has been vice-president, corporate services since January, 1973.

S. T. Jack Brigham III; age 42; secretary and general counsel, H-P. Mr. Brigham was elected assistant secretary of the company in May 1974. He served in that capacity as well as general attorney of the company until May 1976 when he was elected secretary and general counsel of the company.

[1]Mr. Packard did not serve as a director during his service as United States Deputy Secretary of Defense from January 1969 to December 1971.

Source: Hewlett-Packard 1981 Form 10-K.

directly to John Young. The computer systems group had been split into four separate entities—the technical computer group, the business computer group, the computer peripherals group, and the computer terminals group. The products of these four groups continued to be marketed through one organization, the computer marketing group. The instruments group had been divided into the microwave and communication instrument group and the electronic measurements group. The products of these two groups continued to be marketed through one organization, instrument marketing. The hand-held calculator and personal computer activities had been elevated to product group status, the personal computation group. As a result, there were ten product groups instead of the six in 1978. There remained, however, the same six marketing organizations.

Leadership

According to the *San Jose Mercury*[8] John Young's team of employees was learning to play the electronics game by Young's rules which demanded diligent planning, close attention to cost effectiveness, and no last-minute surprises. Although many had originally doubted that he could fill the shoes of the two founders, these critics have since admitted they like the way Young has changed and redirected the firm. He has placed added emphasis on manufacturing and marketing, dropped technological programs when they weren't cost effective, and monitored day-to-day details to correct problems before they have snowballed. At the same time he has balanced his approach by stimulating efforts on new products and technologies, such as electronic office systems and hand-held computers with the associated H-P integrated loop. Young has not emphasized formal planning done by corporate planners. Instead, he has pushed a pragmatic system with the operating people doing the planning. Young believed his contribution was having put emphasis on having a lot more time spent in thoughtful consideration of what the company was doing, but not in a formal planning regime.

John Young was reported to be a serious chief executive with a dry sense of humor, a logical thinker who often asked leading questions to get his managers to come around to his way of thinking, and an efficient worker who did not tolerate incompetence. Associates saw him as a "numbers man" with a top priority of profits. Despite his devotion to numbers and planning, Young also followed two basic and more subtle tenets of the H-P way of life managing by wandering around and showing respect and empathy for employees. Exhibit 6 provides a brief outline of "The H-P Way." For all his formal position power, Young has relied heavily on consensus-style management. He has met often with his executive committee, and few major decisions have been made without the agreement of everyone around the table. Members of the committee were expected to be independent thinkers, but Young has used a subtle approach based on logic to bring people around to his point of view. When Young has not agreed with a colleague's opinion, he has asked questions. These were not confrontational kinds of questions, but they were penetrating. Young would then go along with whatever course the executive eventually recommended. Young

[8] *San Jose Mercury*, "H-P—Now It's the House That Young Built," August 24, 1981, pp. 1D and 7D.

EXHIBIT 6: The H-P Way

Business Practices

Pay As We Go—No Long-Term Borrowing
- — Helps to maintain a stable financial environment during depressed business times.
- — Serves as an excellent self-regulating mechanism for H-P managers.

Market Expansion and Leadership Based on New Product Contributions
- — Engineering excellence determines market recognition of new H-P products.
- — Novel new-product ideas and implementations serve as the basis for expansion of existing markets or diversification into new markets.

Customer Satisfaction Second to None
- — Sell only what has been thoroughly designed, tested, and specified.
- — Products must have lasting value, having high reliability (quality) and customers discover additional benefits while using them.
- — Offer best after-sales service and support in the industry.

Honesty and Integrity in All Matters
- — Dishonest dealings with vendors or customers (such as bribes and kickbacks) not tolerated.
- — Open and honest communication with employees and stockholders alike. Conservative financial reporting.

People Practices

Belief in Our People
- — Confidence in, and respect for, H-P people as opposed to dependence on extensive rules, procedures, etc.
- — Trust people to do their job right (individual freedom) without constant directives.
- — Opportunity for meaningful participation (job dignity).
- — Emphasis on working together and sharing rewards (teamwork and partnership).
- — Share responsibilities; help each other; learn from each other; provide chance to make mistakes.
- — Recognition based on contribution to results—sense of achievement and self-esteem.
- — Profit sharing; stock purchase plan; retirement program, etc., aimed at employees and company sharing in each other's success.
- — Company financial management emphasis on protecting employees' job security.

A Superior Working Environment
- — Informality—open, honest communications; no artificial distinctions between employees (first-name basis); management by wandering around; and open-door communication policy.
- — Develop and promote from within—lifetime training, education, career counseling to give employees maximum opportunities to grow and develop with the company.
- — Decentralization—emphasis on keeping work groups as small as possible for maximum employee identification with our businesses and customers.
- — Management-By-Objectives (MBO)—provides a sound basis for measuring performance of employees as well as managers; is objective, not political.

Management Style

Management By Wandering Around

- To have a well-managed operation, managers and supervisors must be aware of what happens in their areas—at several levels above and below their immediate levels.
- Since people are our most important resource, managers have direct responsibility for employee training, performance, and general well-being. To do this, managers must move around to find out how people feel about their jobs—what they think will make their work more productive and meaningful.

Open-Door Policy

- Managers and supervisors are expected to foster a work environment in which employees feel free and comfortable to seek individual counsel or express general concerns.
- Therefore, if employees feel such steps are necessary, they have the right to discuss their concerns with higher-level managers. Any effort through intimidation or other means to prevent an employee from going 'up the line' is absolutely contrary to company policy—and will be dealt with accordingly.
- Also, use of the Open-Door policy must not in any way influence evaluations of employees or produce any other adverse consequences.
- Employees also have responsibilities—particularly in keeping their discussions with upper-level managers to the point and focused on concerns of significance.

Source: *Measure,* September–October, 1981, p. 14.

saw himself as being good at the nondirective approach and worked hard at being a good coach.

High on Young's list of priorities for the 1980s was for H-P to become a low-cost manufacturer. Young admitted this had not been one of H-P's strengths. His concern for cost effectiveness was almost legendary. When he initially assumed the presidency, he put a lot of effort into convincing his management team that the company could do a better job of managing assets, particularly inventory and accounts receivable. One of the first things he axed was research for research's sake. Yet about 70 per cent of total company product orders in 1981 resulted from products developed after 1977. Under Young, technology has received more of a profit-and-loss kind of consideration and evaluation. In 1981, research and development was increased to 9.7 per cent of sales, an increase of 1.1 per cent over the previous year. Further, John Young has restructured H-P Laboratories entirely. He has also created over the last three years a computer and semiconductor research facility staffed with one hundred professionals. He thought this would become one of the top such facilities in the United States.

In September 1979, an attitude survey was taken in which 7,966 employees were asked to evaluate more than 100 topics at H-P, including pay, benefits, supervision, management, job satisfaction, and many other items. Exhibit 7 provides results on major items and a comparison to national norms. With a 67 per cent favorable response, employees rated H-P management well above the national norm of 46 per cent. The rating covered such questions as the fairness of management decisions and the concern of managers for the well-being of the

EXHIBIT 7: H-P Attitude Survey

	Percent Favorable Responses	
	H-P Employees	*National Sample*
Work organization	70	65
Work efficiency	67	63
Management	67	46
Job training and information	61	56
Work associates	81	78
Supervision	70	61
Overall communications	58	41
Performance and advancement	75	58
Pay	52	39
Benefits	70	53
Job satisfaction	76	66
Organizational identification	84	59
Organization change	28	25
Working conditions	59	44
Job stability	56	60
Policies and practices	81	69
Reactions to the survey	77	55

[1] 200 Top U.S. Companies.
Source: *Measure,* "Open Line," March–April, 1981, p. 12b.

people they managed. As reported in the March–April issue of *Measure*[9] (H-P's magazine), four of the top twenty-two issues generated by the survey analysis showed concern about top management and the application of management philosophy. The quality of some managers was questioned; management-by-objective and management-by-wandering-around were criticized for not being used widely enough, and the use of the open door policy was sometimes frustrated by a feeling of threat of retribution. The fundamental responses to these concerns were seen by top management as chiefly matters of local responsibility and action, although corporate support in the form of training, communication, and management evaluation was believed to be important. The start-up of more than three hundred quality teams at many locations was believed to improve both productivity and the practice of MBO. The open door policy as well as MBWA were topics of messages by Young in various issues of *Measure.* Both of these policies were seen by John Young as important to the creation of a feeling of openness and providing informal opportunities for everyone to hear and be heard. He believed the desired result was to achieve mutual trust and respect for both the people and the process involved. He has tried to make it clear both in his communications and his actions that the H-P manager has no greater responsibility.

Performance (1978–1981)

Since 1978, when John Young became CEO, Hewlett-Packard has grown rapidly. The annual growth rate of net sales has averaged 27.4 per cent and that

[9] "Open-Line," *Measure,* March–April, 1981, pp. 12 a–h.

EXHIBIT 8: Four-Year Consolidated Summary*
—For the years ended October 31
(Millions except for employee and per share amounts)

	1978	*1979*	*1980*	*1981*
Net Sales	$1,737	$2,361	$3,099	$3,578
Cost and expenses				
Cost of goods sold	808	1,106	1,475	1,703
Research and development	154	207	272	347
Marketing	264	362	459	526
Administration and general	215	291	370	422
	1,441	1,963	2,576	2,998
Earnings before taxes	296	398	523	580
Provision for taxes	143	195	254	268
Net earnings	$ 153	$ 203	$ 269	$ 312
Per share:*				
Net earnings	$ 1.32	$ 1.72	$ 2.23	$ 2.55
Cash dividends	$ .12	$ .17	$ .20	$ .22
At year-end:				
Total assets	$1,462	$1,900	$2,337	$2,758
Long-term debt	$ 10	$ 15	$ 29	$ 26
Common shares outstanding*	116	118	120	123
Thousands of employees	42	52	57	64

* Reflects the 2-for-1 stock splits in 1979 and 1981.
Source: Hewlett-Packard *Annual Reports*.

of net earnings has averaged 26.9 per cent. The growth rates for 1980–1981, however, were substantially lower than previous years, 15.5 per cent and 16.0 per cent respectively. The 1981 *Annual Report*[10] indicated that the major cause of the reduced growth was the adverse economic conditions in the United States

EXHIBIT 9: Financial Analysis

	Per Cent Increase from Prior Year				*Per Cent of Net Sales*			
	1978	*1979*	*1980*	*1981*	*1978*	*1979*	*1980*	*1981*
Net sales	27.0	35.9	31.3	15.5	100.0	100.0	100.0	100.0
Cost of goods sold	29.3	36.9	33.4	15.5	45.7	46.8	47.6	47.6
Research and development	23.2	32.5	33.3	27.6	8.9	8.6	8.8	9.7
Marketing	26.9	37.1	26.8	14.6	15.2	15.3	14.8	14.7
Administrative and general	18.8	35.3	27.1	14.1	12.4	12.3	11.9	11.8
Earnings before taxes	29.3	34.5	31.4	10.9	17.0	16.9	16.9	16.2
Provision for taxes	32.4	36.4	30.3	5.5	8.2	8.3	8.2	7.5
Net earnings	26.4	32.7	32.5	16.0	8.8	8.6	8.7	8.7

[10] "1981 Annual Report," *Hewlett-Packard Company*, pp. 2–4.

EXHIBIT 10: Consolidated Balance Sheet*

	1978	*1979*	*1980*	*1981*
Current assets:				
Cash and temporary cash investment	$ 189	$ 248	$ 247	$ 290
Accounts and notes receivable	371	491	622	682
Inventories:				
Finished goods	99	120	148	186
Purchased parts and fabricated assemblies	257	358	397	456
Other current assets	36	52	77	91
Total current assets	952	1,269	1,491	1,705
Property, plant, and equipment:				
Land	44	53	69	78
Buildings and leasehold improvements	405	491	645	789
Machinery and equipment	272	348	447	581
	721	892	1,161	1,448
Accumulated depreciation	245	301	372	469
	476	591	789	979
Other assets	34	40	57	74
	$1,462	$1,900	$2,337	$2,758

Liabilities and Shareholder's Equity

	1978	*1979*	*1980*	*1981*
Current liabilities:				
Notes payable and commercial paper	$ 85	$ 147	$ 143	$ 144
Accounts payable	71	109	104	143
Employee compensation, benefits, and accruals	171	237	297	308
Accrued taxes on income	88	106	147	109
Total current liabilities	415	599	691	704
Long-term debt	10	15	29	26
Deferred taxes on earnings	35	51	70	108
Shareholders' equity:				
Common stock	29	59	60	123
Capital in excess of par	247	267	333	358
Retained earnings	727	909	1,154	1,439
Total shareholders' equity	1,002	1,235	1,547	1,920
	$1,462	$1,900	$2,337	$2,758

* In millions; for fiscal years ending October 31.

Source: Hewlett-Packard *Annual Reports*.

EXHIBIT 11: Consolidated Statement of Changes in Financial Position*

	1978	*1979*	*1980*	*1981*
Funds provided:				
Net earnings	$153	$203	$269	$312
Items not affecting funds:				
Depreciation and amortization	56	72	93	120
Other, net	11	21	27	53
Total from operations	220	302	389	485
Proceeds from sale of stock	29	37	50	67
Increase in accounts payable and accrued liabilities	59	104	55	50
Total funds provided	308	443	494	602
Funds used:				
Investment in property, plant, and equipment	159	191	297	318
Increase in accounts and notes receivable	99	120	131	60
Increase in inventories	77	122	67	97
Increase in other current assets	8	16	25	14
Decrease (increase) in accrued taxes	(26)	(18)	(41)	38
Dividends to shareholders	14	20	24	27
Other, net	(1)	(5)	(12)	6
Total funds used	330	446	491	560
Increase (decrease) in cash and temporary cash investment, net of notes payable and commercial paper	$ (22)	$ (3)	$ 3	$ 42
Net cash at beginning of year	126	104	101	104
Net cash at end of year	$104	$101	$104	$146

* In millions; for fiscal years ending October 31.
Source: Hewlett-Packard *Annual Reports*.

and abroad. Net sales were somewhat below projections, and incoming orders were considerably lower than expectations. These shortfalls, coupled with a high level of committed expenses for new product development and product introductions, put heavy pressure on operating profit. Two changes were made in 1981 that somewhat modified earnings. The first was a $14 million reduction in accrued pension expense for the year, which increased net earnings by $7 million. This change resulted from a scheduled five-year review of the initial funding assumptions used for the U.S. Supplemental Pension Plan begun in 1976. The second was an $8 million reduction in income taxes, resulting from the Economic Recovery Tax Act of 1981. Without these two adjustments, the company's net earnings would have been $297 million, up only 10.4 per cent from 1980. Exhibit 8 provides a four-year consolidated summary of various measures of performance. Exhibit 9 provides an analysis of operating results. Exhibit 10 is a consolidated balance sheet. Exhibit 11 is a consolidated statement of changes in financial position, showing how funds were provided and how they were used. Exhibit 12 provides a strategic ratio analysis of H-P's performance during

EXHIBIT 12: Strategic Ratio Analysis

Fiscal Year	*Profit Margin: Earnings / Sales (Per Cent)*	*Asset Turnover: Sales / Assets (Times)*	*Return on Assets: Earnings / Assets (Per Cent)*	*Financial Leverage: Assets / Net Worth (Times)*	*Return on Net Worth: Earnings / Net Worth (Per Cent)*
1978	8.81	1.19	10.5	1.46	15.3
1979	8.60	1.24	10.7	1.54	16.4
1980	8.68	1.33	11.5	1.51	17.4
1981	8.72	1.30	11.3	1.44	16.3

this period. Exhibit 13 includes information on sales, profits, and research and development expenses for selected companies and industries.

A TIME FOR EVALUATION

John Young had just reviewed the changes made in strategy and strategic implementation while he had served as chief executive officer. He wondered whether the strategic changes made had been the right ones and whether any additional changes might be needed. He believed the performance of the various business segments might offer a valuable point of departure for his analysis. He also felt that this seemed like an appropriate time to review the changes made in organization structure, his management and leadership of the company, and the organization's overall corporate performance during these recent years of growth and strategic change. He believed that enough time had passed that a reasonably objective assessment could be made as to whether he had provided the necessary strategies and leadership to the Hewlett-Packard Company during this difficult transition period.

REFERENCES

"When 'Calculator' Is a Dirty Word," *Business Week,* June 14, 1982, p. 62.
"Two Giants Bid for Office Sales," *Business Week,* November 9, 1981, pp. 86–96.
"H-P: A Drive into Office Automation," *Electronics,* November 3, 1981, pp. 106–110.
"Annual Reports" 1978, 1979, 1980, 1981, *Hewlett-Packard Company.*
"Form 10-K," *Hewlett-Packard Company,* 1978, 1979, 1980, 1981.
"Open Line," *Measure,* March–April, 1981, pp. 12a–h.
"Why Do HP People Do Things the Way They Do," *Measure,* September-October, 1981, pp. 11–14.
"H-P—Now It's the House That Young Built," *San Jose Mercury,* August 24, 1981, pp. 1D and 7D.
"Digital Equipment and Hewlett-Packard Enter Electronic Office Systems Market," *Wall Street Journal,* October 30, 1981, p. 48.
"Calculator Makers Add Features and Cut Prices to Find a Niche in a Crowded Market," *Wall Street Journal,* December 21, 1981, p. 23.

EXHIBIT 13: Sales, Profits, and R&D Data on Selected Companies and Industries

	Sales		*Profits*		*R&D Expense*			
	1981 millions of dollars	*Percent annual change (1977–81)*	*1981 millions of dollars*	*Percent annual change (1977–81)*	*1981 millions of dollars*	*Percent of Sales*	*Percent of Profit*	*Dollars per Employee*
SELECTED COMPANIES								
AT&T	58214	12.2	6888	10.6	507.2	0.9	7.4	594
Datapoint	396	40.1	49	53.8	34.7	8.8	71.2	5091
Digital Equipment	3198	31.1	343	33.2	251.2	7.9	73.2	3987
Hewlett-Packard	3578	28.4	312	27.9	347.0	9.7	111.2	5422
Lanier Business Products	303	35.9	26	39.4	4.7	1.5	18.4	1163
IBM	29070	12.3	3308	5.4	1612.0	5.5	48.7	4542
Texas Instruments	4206	21.0	109	2.7	219.4	5.2	202.2	2621
Wang Laboratories	856	60.2	78	73.3	66.9	7.8	85.7	4240
Xerox	8691	14.3	598	8.4	526.3	6.1	88.0	4350
INDUSTRY COMPOSITES								
Instruments	14106	18.6	740	17.4	647.5	4.6	87.5	2571
Information Processing								
Computers	60057	15.5	5311	9.4	3845.5	6.4	72.4	4231
Office Equipment	14716	17.9	771	13.2	729.2	5.0	94.6	3324
Peripherals and Services	5800	29.3	365	35.7	344.1	5.9	94.2	3284

Source: "R & D Scoreboard," *Business Week*, July 5, 1982, pp. 54–72.

PART V

Cases in Business and Corporate-Level Strategies

CASE SEVEN

Note on the Analytical Instruments Industry[1]

JAMES J. CHRISMAN and WILLIAM R. BOULTON
University of Georgia

Assignment Questions:

1. What makes the analytical instruments industry fragmented?
2. What are the positions and roles of buyers and suppliers in this industry? How have they changed?
3. What strategies will dominate this industry in the future?

Analytical instruments are high-technology products designed to detect, analyze, and measure the composition of chemicals. The most important and rapidly growing instruments, chromatographs and spectrophotometers, have grown from sales of over $326 million in 1978 to $544 million in 1982. With the advent of microprocessor technology, new products and applications have rapidly opened up new markets while changing the nature of competition. Rivals included well-diversified firms with diverse electronic technologies who often sold components to other competitors. It was not uncommon for these competitors to also sell substitute products. To understand the nature of this industry and the impact of recent electronic technology, this report will look at industry rivals, potential entrants, substitutes, buyers, and sellers.

ANALYTICAL INSTRUMENTS

Chromatographs and spectrophotometers accounted for over 60 per cent of industry sales by 1982 as shown in Exhibit 2. No other instruments, including mass spectrometers, nuclear spectrometers, electron microscopes, ph meters and ion-selective electrodes, thermal analyzers, and nuclear and X-ray analyzers, account for more than 7 per cent of industry sales. Because of their relative importance, the following discussion focuses on chromatographs and spectrophotometers.

[1]Analytic instruments account for a major portion of products included under SIC Code 3832 (Optical and Analytic Instruments). See Exhibit 1 for financial ratios for the total industry.

EXHIBIT 1: Financial Ratios

(SIC) code 3832)	*1980 Industry*	*1979 WA*	*1981 BI*	*1980 PE*	*1980 HP*	*1980 VA*	*1981 TR*
Current Ratio	2.3	2.2	2.6	2.7	2.2	2.1	2.9
Net Profits/Sales (%)	5.8	7.2	6.0	7.0	8.7	3.6	5.0
Net Profits/Total Assets (%)	13.1	8.5	9.5	15.0	17.2	8.9	10.5
Net Profits/Equity (%)	19.8	17.2	12.0	17.4	17.4	11.3	13.0
Sales/Net Working Capital	5.1	3.3	2.2	2.7	3.9	3.0	3.8
Sales/Inventory	8.6	3.9	2.8	4.1	5.7	2.9	7.7
Sales/Equity	4.3	2.4	2.0	2.5	1.6	3.1	2.6
Sales/Total Assets	2.9	1.2	1.0	1.4	1.2	1.2	1.5
Accounts Receivable Collection Period (days)	49	94	82	71	72	82	69
Total Debt/Equity (%)	51	101	99	77	40	154	73
Price/Earnings Ratio	14	na	15	12	18	28	10
Earnings Per Share ($)	—	na	1.76	1.81	2.24	2.77	2.00

na = information not available
WA = Waters Associates (acquired by Millipore Corporation, 1980)
BI = Beckman Instruments (acquired by Smith Kline, 1982)
PE = Perkin Elmer
HP = Hewlett-Packard
VA = Varian Associates
TR = Tracor, Inc.

Note: All financial ratios for the individual firms may not match up with industry averages. This is because of the fact that many of these companies are included in other industries for the purpose of determining industry averages. However, since this report deals with analytical instruments that are a part of SIC code 3832, averages for this industry have been used.

Sources: *The Value Line Investment Survey*, October 1981, pps. 154, 167, 174, 1012, 1052, 1075, 1100, *Dun & Bradstreet's Key Financial Ratios*, 1980.

Chromatographs

Chromatographs are analytical instruments designed to detect, separate, and identify the contents, in parts per billion, of a wide variety of chemical substances. Chromatographs are used in gas and liquid applications though gas chromatographs are most common. Column chromatographs, developed in 1938, were used to separate chemicals by passing them through a column of finely ground materials. The first gas chromatograph was invented in 1950 by H. J. P. Martin, an English chemist. It worked on gases using the same principles developed earlier. It wasn't until 1956 that the first commercially produced instruments were available. By 1959, a dozen firms had entered the market, but little has changed in the basic technology since then. The growth in products, technology, and competition in recent years had come mostly from developments in support equipment.

By the mid-1960s, liquid chromatography was rediscovered to solve one basic problem. The problem was that certain compounds decomposed when they were converted to gases and, as a result, could not be properly analyzed. However, it was only through the development of support technologies that liquid chromatographs were made effective. Today, even though gas chromatographs are faster, easier to use, and less expensive, liquid devices have a broader range of applications and are slowly gaining favor over gas devices.

Liquid chromatographs were growing in popularity despite their higher purchase price and operating costs. Liquid chromatographs could analyze larger

EXHIBIT 2: Analytical Instrument Sales By Product 1978–1980 (in millions of dollars)

	1978	*1980*	*1981E*	*1982E*
Chromatographs, Total	139.8	224.6	267.7	306.6
Gas	93.8	115.0	133.0	152.5
Liquid	46.0	90.0	110.0	124.5
Ion	—	19.6	24.7	29.6
Spectrophotometers, Total	186.6	191.0	212.8	237.5
Infrared	35.2	35.1	38.5	42.1
Ultraviolet-Visible	54.0	45.1	49.0	53.3
Atomic Absorption	37.4	42.8	51.0	63.0
Other	60.0	68.0	74.3	79.1
Mass Spectrometers	40.0	48.0	53.0	59.3
Nuclear Magnetic-Resonance Spectrometers	18.5	26.5	29.0	31.8
Electron Microscopes	—	13.0	13.0	13.2
ph Meters and Ion-Selective Electrodes	27.0	33.0	36.0	40.5
Thermal Analyzers	17.2	19.0	23.5	29.4
Nuclear and X-ray Analyzers	47.0	52.0	55.0	59.1
Other	84.0	73.8	76.8	87.9
Total	560.1	680.9	766.8	865.3

E = estimated

Source: Electronics-Electrical Current Analysis, *Standard & Poor's Industrial Surveys,* June 4, 1981, vol. 149, no. 23, sec. 1, pp. E18.

molecular structures and greater amounts of material. Since liquid chromatographs were relatively new products, product obsolescence caused by technological changes was rapid. The application of microprocessor technology to chromatography had greatly improved the science. Microprocessors allowed much of the analytic work previously performed by skilled technicians to now be done by machines that ranged in price from $5,000 to $100,000.

Spectrophotometers

Like chromatographs, spectrophotometers were first developed in the 1930s. Since that time the basic machine had changed very little. Equipment that existed in the 1950s was almost identical to today's equipment except for the support technologies which had been added. Thus, like chromatographs, the basic product was mature, but the growth phase had been extended as a result of the application of computer and other electronic technologies.

Spectrophotometers were used in chemical research, drug identification, new product development, and monitoring of carcinogenic chemicals. There were several types of spectrophotometers, the most common being the infrared, ultraviolet-visible, and atomic absorption devices. The spectrophotometer operated on the principle that the frequency of vibrations in a specific molecule was unique. The spectrophotometer passes a beam through the material to be analyzed. If all the molecules vibrated at the same frequency (e.g. no foreign substances were present) the beam's energy would be reduced. Likewise, if the molecules were not vibrating at the same frequency, the beam would pass through unaffected. The spectrophotometer charted these energy differences that, when compared to known molecular patterns, enabled the chemist to determine the molecular structure of the sample. Spectrophotometers, as well as other analytical instruments, were used in applications requiring digital spectrums rather than analog information. Spectrophotometers on the low end of the price spectrum were relatively mature and have changed little from year to year. Those on the high end of the price range had been adapted to included microprocessors and were characterized by rapid technological improvements and new applications. These products were not in direct competition because the higher-priced machines could perform many more tasks and were used for different purposes than low-end machines. Prices range from as low as $1,000 to as much as $150,000.

THE ANALYTICAL INSTRUMENTS INDUSTRY

To understand the analytical instruments industry, it is necessary to understand its fragmented nature, the importance of key competitors, and the products themselves.

Major Competitors

Although only about sixty competitors were listed as part of the optical and analytical instruments industry (SIC code 3832), no single competitor was dominant across the board. However, Perkin-Elmer was recognized as the industry leader in most segments. Another broad-line competitor was SmithKline-Beckman. More focused companies included Varian Associates, Tracor, and Hewlett-Packard. Specialist companies included Millipore, Spectra-Physics, Kevex, Nicolet, Finnigan, and Baird. Perkin-Elmer, SmithKline-Beckman, Hewlett-Packard, Varian Associates, Tracor, and Millipore were the recognized leaders in various industry segments or in their strategic groups.

To understand the relative position of the six industry leaders, Exhibits 3 and 4 provide comparative financial performance data for 1980 and 1981. The largest and most profitable competitors continue to be Hewlett-Packard and SmithKline-Beckman, followed by Perkin-Elmer. Hewlett-Packard and Smith Kline also had the lowest debt leverage ratios in 1981, with debt-to-equity ratios of .436 and .536, respectively. Varian was losing money and had the largest debt-to-equity ratio of 1.578 in 1981. The strengths of these competitors in research and development is shown in Exhibit 5. With $347 million in R&D expenses, Hewlett-Packard spent more than double SmithKline's $163 million and four times Perkin-Elmer's $83 million R&D expenses. It should be noted that these are total corporate data and do not relate to company performance in the analytical instrument industry.

Broad Line Producers. Perkin-Elmer's (P-E) total sales reached $1 billion in 1981 with its largest division, the analytical instruments group, accounting for about 30 per cent of sales and profits. Even with a heavy reliance on foreign customers (40–45 per cent of sales) and a poor economy, P-E's strong domestic

EXHIBIT 3: Comparative Financial Data 1980 (in millions of dollars*)

	Perkin-Elmer	*Hewlett-Packard*	*SmithKline-Beckman*	*Varian*	*Tracor*	*Millipore*
Sales*	996.0	3099.0	1772.0	621.0	313.7	265.0
Operating income*	149.0	700.0	492.0	58.4	33.2	41.1
Operating income/Sales	15%	19.6%	27.8%	9.4%	10.6%	15.5%
Capital expenditures*	55.0	297.0	147.0	33.2	19.5	26.9
Depreciation*	17.9	93.0	39.4	11.3	7.2	8.4
Interest expense*	12.5	NA	25.2	15.4	5.7	5.6
Net income*	68.2	269.0	308.0	21.2	14.1	18.5
Dividend payout	21%	9%	37%	17%	13%	19%
Total assets*	741.0	2337.0	1554.0	515.0	185.0	241.0
Equity*	381.0	1547.0	987.0	195.0	97.4	142.0
Long-term debt*	106.0	29.2	136.0	114.0	39.5	35.9
Long-term debt/Total Capital	21.0%	1.8%	12.1%	35.1%	28.8%	19.4%
Current ratio	2.7	2.2	2.5	2.1	3.0	2.7
Debt/Equity	94.5%	51.1%	57.4%	164.1%	89.9%	69.7%

Sources: *Moody's Industrial Manual,* 1982, *Standard NYSE Stock Report,* Standard and Poor's Corporation, 1982, and *Standard OTC Stock Report,* Standard and Poor's Corporation, 1982.

markets allowed profits to soften only slightly as sales and profit margins declined. Other sales areas included data systems, semiconductor equipment, optical equipment, flame spray equipment, Bodenseewerk, and Geraetetechnik.

As shown in Figure 1, P-E had evolved a wide product line that included chromatographs, spectrophotometers, thermal analyzers, and others. Perkin-Elmer had developed a strong reputation for its quality products, breadth and expertise in technology, and support services. As one industry analyst noted about P-E, "its position is unique in that P-E is the leader or nearly so in most major classes of instruments."

Horace G. McDonald, president of Perkin-Elmer Corporation, explained the nature of his company's involvement in analytical instruments:

EXHIBIT 4: Comparative Financial Data 1981 (in millions of dollars*)

	Perkin-Elmer	*Hewlett-Packard*	*SmithKline-Beckman*	*Varian*	*Tracor*	*Millipore*
Sales*	1115.8	3578.0	1985.3	638.4	371.1	253.5
Net Profit*	78.1	312.0	370.0	−3.6**	19.0	10.6
Return on sales	7.0%	8.7%	18.6%	negative	5.1%	4.2%
Return on assets	9.3%	11.3%	19.6%	negative	8.5%	4.2%
Return on equity	17.4%	16.3%	30.2%	negative	16.4%	7.0%
Dividend payout	23%	9%	38%	192%	14%	42%
Total assets*	840.0	2758.0	1883.0	495.0	223.5	251.1
Equity*	450.0	1920.0	1226.0	192.0	115.9	151.2
Long-term debt*	106.0	26.0	153.0	110.0	49.4	34.4
Long-term debt/Total Capital	18.5%	1.3%	11.1%	34.6%	29.9%	18.5%
Current ratio	2.7	2.4	2.4	2.0	2.7	2.7
Debt/Equity	86.7%	43.6%	53.6%	157.8%	92.8%	66.1%

** includes losses from discontinued operations.

Sources: *Moody's Industrial Manual,* 1982, *Standard NYSE Stock Report,* Standard and Poor's Corporation, 1982, and *Standard OTC Stock Report,* Standard and Poor's Corporation, 1982.

EXHIBIT 5: Total R&D Expenditures* 1980–1981 (in millions of dollars)

	1980	*1981*
Hewlett-Packard	272.0	347.0
Millipore	16.1	17.2
Perkin-Elmer	69.8	83.5
SmithKline-Beckman	135.8	163.9
Tracor, Inc.	7.4	7.0
Varian Associates	34.0	38.6

* does not include customer sponsored R&D.
Source: *Moody's Industrial Manual,* 1982.

While Perkin-Elmer covers more of the field of analytical chemistry than most other suppliers, we are a long way from covering it all. Yet, the number of technologies, or product lines, we are in today in order to cover just our segments of the industry's total requirements in sixteen and its still growing. Within these 16 technologies, P-E offers more than 150 distinct instruments, not counting the thousands of accessories and configuration options we market. As we say at Perkin-Elmer, there are no large targets.

To the instrument company, the fact that the targets are small means that if you don't hit them squarely, you won't survive. The market is a honeycomb of

FIGURE 1: History of Analytical Instrument Techniques at Perkin-Elmer

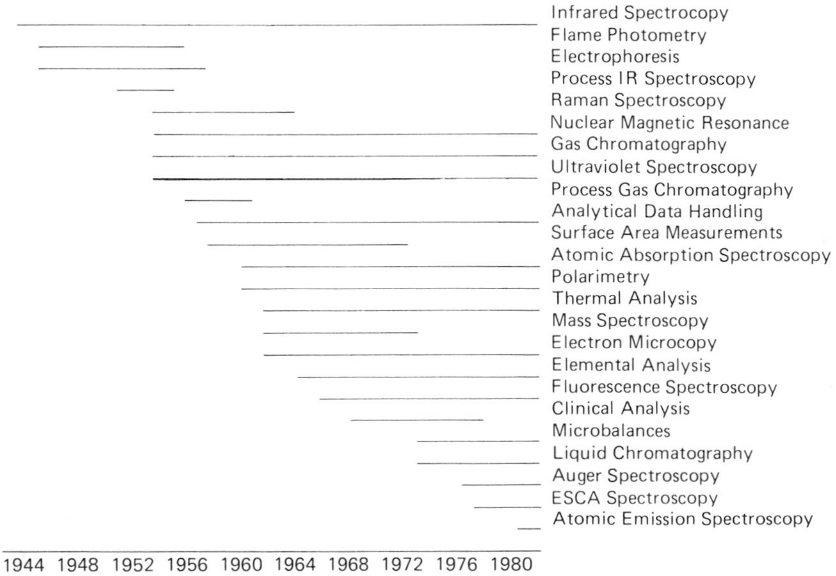

Infrared Spectrocopy
Flame Photometry
Electrophoresis
Process IR Spectroscopy
Raman Spectroscopy
Nuclear Magnetic Resonance
Gas Chromatography
Ultraviolet Spectroscopy
Process Gas Chromatography
Analytical Data Handling
Surface Area Measurements
Atomic Absorption Spectroscopy
Polarimetry
Thermal Analysis
Mass Spectroscopy
Electron Microcopy
Elemental Analysis
Fluorescence Spectroscopy
Clinical Analysis
Microbalances
Liquid Chromatography
Auger Spectroscopy
ESCA Spectroscopy
Atomic Emission Spectroscopy

1944 1948 1952 1956 1960 1964 1968 1972 1976 1980

Source: "Evolution on Analytical Instruments—The Perkin-Elmer Story," *31st Pittsburgh Conference on Analytical and Applied Spectroscopy,* Pittsburgh Conference Paper No. 379, March 1980, pp. 2.

> small pockets with special requirements. None or at least few of these pockets are large enough to reward enormous investments of capital or technology to be amortized in that target alone. Yet the technology demands of each segment are very high. The system, therefore, favors the adaptive organization.[2]

In March 1982, Smith-Kline, a successful pharmaceutical firm, acquired Beckman Instruments, the number two competitor in the industry. Smith-Kline (Beckman) now does about 40 per cent of its business overseas Smith-Kline was a health care firm with sales in ethical pharmaceutical products, animal health products, proprietary drugs, ophthalmic and optical products, clinical laboratories, industrial instruments, and medical instruments. The acquisition of Beckman broadened Smith-Kline's sales into electronic instruments while also providing backward integration into an important source of supply.

Beckman's full line of analytical instruments included nuclear counting devices, spectrophotometers, liquid chromatography systems, electrochemical analyzers, and others. Prior to the merger in 1981, Beckman's instruments division, of which analytical instruments was a major part, accounted for 65 per cent of its $650 million in sales and 75 per cent of its $37 million in profits. Like other competitors, with 30 per cent in foreign sales, performance had been affected by currency exchange losses and a slow economy.

Focused Producers. In 1981, Hewlett-Packard's (H-P) analytical instruments division contributed $185 million of the company's $3.6 billion in revenues. H-P was the largest of the industry's competitors though analytical instrument products were less extensive than Perkin-Elmer's. Products included gas and liquid chromatographs, mass spectrometers, and related analytical equipment. Analytical instruments accounted for only about 5 per cent of H-P's sales, its smallest business segment. However, H-P was the largest producer of test and measurement equipment (sales of over $1.35 billion in 1981); and second largest producer of electronic data products ($1.8 billion in 1981). Medical electronic equipment also contributed about 8 per cent to revenues and to profits.

Hewlett-Packard had a strategy of controlled, internally financed growth. Since 1972, H-P's growth rate had averaged 20 per cent with increasing return on sales investment. This strategy was likely to constrain its expansion into other segments of the analytical instruments industry since commitments were being made to major business areas. However, with over 64,000 employees, 200 U.S. sales and service offices, and 30 overseas locations, H-P still had a strong position in the analytical instruments industry. Major markets for H-P's instruments were the chemical, energy, pharmaceutical, medical, and food industries.

Varian Associates (VA) instruments group accounted for $138 million of 1981's sales of $638 million. VA's core business was microwave power tubes with other sales in medical and industrial products. Losses of $1 million pretax, and a $3.5 million net loss (including write-offs), were caused by the phaseout of VA's UV-visible spectrophotometer products whose $5 million in sales had brought $2 to $3 million in operating losses. According to VA's president, Thomas Sege:

> The instrument group's performance, poor in 1981, is expected to improve gradually as a result of strengthened products and market positions for gas and liquid

[2]Horace G. McDonald, "Evolution of Analtical Instruments—The Perkin-Elmer Story," presented at the symposium on "Analytical Instrumentation-Evolution in the last 40 years," *31st Pittsburgh Conference on Analytical and Applied Spectroscopy,* Pittsburgh Conference Paper No. 379, March 1980.

chromatography, new product introductions in atomic absorption and optics, and aggressive new management which is currently implementing a number of steps designed to improve efficiency and reduce costs.

The internal problems caused the change in our top management, including my appointment as CEO and president about a year ago. The management represents a very significant change in the corporate personality from technology for its own sake to a clear profit aim.[3]

In developing VA's future strategy, Sege continued:

We are intent on gaining market share, particularly in the instrument area. Our range of products is wide. They are considered among the most user-friendly. We have a strong number two position in gas chromatography. . . . [We] are the only major supplier of both liquid chromatographs and gas chromatographs. That combination gives us an edge—not just a market edge, but a technological edge—that we intend to take advantage of.

Our strong emphasis in '82 has been profits performance and asset management. We have focused on our important businesses and divested others.[4]

Varian's major instrument market sales were broken down as follows:

Chemical	25%
Petroleum	8%
Environmental	15%
Life Sciences	23%
Drugs	11%
Others	18%

With this market base, VA's market position and technical reputation, management felt that the company was in a strong position for the future.

Tracor Incorporated was a diversified electronics firm that provided a broad range of technological services, analytical instruments, sophisticated science systems, and electronic components to military, medical, industrial, and university customers. With 1981 sales of $371 million and $19 million in profit, instruments accounted for 18 per cent of Tracor's sales and 16 per cent of its profits. Other divisions included applied sciences with 34 per cent of sales and 23 per cent of profits, aerospace with 28 per cent of sales and 30 per cent of profits, and components with 20 per cent of sales and 31 per cent of profits. Whereas an aggressive acquisition strategy had developed Tracor's aerospace business in particular, recent acquisitions had expanded product lines and markets in every division.

Tracor's analytical instrument sales were about $45 million in 1981. Major products included gas chromatographs, X-ray analyzers, beta and gamma counters, and nuclear analyzers. Tracor was the leader in the manufacture of detectors for gas chromatographs with 60 per cent of that market. New product introductions included a new gas chromatograph, the TN-7200 nuclear analyzer, and the spectrochrome 512 color video monitor. The color monitor was used with other devices as a part of Tracor's move to instrument systems and won an award as one of the 100 most significant new products in 1981. With 21 per cent in

[3] Thomas D. Sege, "Presentation to Investment Meetings—Los Angeles, Boston, New York," Varian Associates, Inc., August 24–26, 1982.

[4] Ibid.

foreign sales, and a slow domestic economy, Tracor's instrument sales had slowed since 1980.

Specialized Producers. In 1980, Millipore Corporation acquired Waters Associates to become the leading U.S. manufacturer of liquid chromatographs. Prior to the acquisition, Millipore's activities included the manufacture and marketing of products and systems for environmental controls, health care, food and beverage, and water purification customers. Analytical products were designed to analyze and process fluids to remove, separate, and identify biological, chemical, or inert substances. Waters also made accessories and supplies for both liquid and gas chromatographs and had sales of over $70 million and profits of over $5 million for 1979. Major customers of Waters included chemical producers, paint manufacturers, hospitals, and police crime labs.

Because of the nature of the industry, it was unlikely that any firm, even the largest competitors such as Perkin-Elmer and Hewlett-Packard, would dominate the overall market. Even though Hewlett-Packard's sales of analytical instruments surpassed $185 million in 1981, Millipore Corporation, with only a fraction of HP's instrument sales, enjoyed a dominant position in liquid chromatography.

Industry participants were characterized by individual entrepreneurs who had brought their new ideas to market, such as Hewlett-Packard and Tracor. However, the industry was not capital intensive but depended heavily on skilled personnel. Although customer needs were quite diverse, quality, service, and image were important competitive factors. This made it difficult for any one firm to be all things to all people. Furthermore, rapid technological changes allowed smaller firms to often respond more quickly to new product developments than larger firms. This permitted smaller firms to find niches that were too small or too costly for large firms to fill.

In the electronics industry, fragmentation had been overcome in some cases through the development of economies of scale and experience-curve strategies. However, the complexity of analytical instruments and the rapid technological advances that characterized many of the products had restricted such developments in this industry. Instead, manufacturers were concentrating on vertical, horizontal, and concentric diversification to build a critical mass in their operations and overcome the problems of fragmentation. In addition, many manufacturers had begun to build mobility barriers by emphasizing service, spare parts availability, and customer assistance. Others had attacked the problem by specializing or focusing on a particular product or product segment, such as Millipore Corporation in liquid chromatography.

Customer Segments

The key to industry success was to find new applications for existing, as well as developing, analytical instruments. As one industry participant commented: "Petrochemicals and pharmaceuticals are typical major business segments. In total, they represent a mature market that has entered a new period of long-term growth."[5] Because basic products and markets were relatively mature, instrument producers could not afford to neglect research and develop-

[5] Varian Associates, Inc., 1981 Annual Report.

EXHIBIT 6: Analytical Instrument Customer Survey

Product	*Plan to Acquire Per Cent*	*Presently Use Per Cent*
Spectrometers, electron	2	6
Analyzers, polarographic	3	9
Spectrometers, mass	4	14
Spectrometers, X-ray	4	14
Spectrophotometers, fluorescence	3	14
Analyzers, thermal	5	17
Chromatographs, thin layer	3	23
Spectrophotometers, atomic absorption	5	28
Chromatographs liquid	12	31
Spectrophotometers, infrared	7	39
Spectrophotometers, ultraviolet	5	41
Spectrophotometers, visible	4	46
Chromatographs, gas	11	48
ph Meters	9	71
Recorders, strip chart	11	75
Analytical balances	11	88

Source: *Industrial Research & Development*, February, 1981, p. 160.

ment. Without new technologies and applications, the industry could soon face a saturated market limited mostly to repeat sales.

Markets for analytical instruments included university, industrial, medical, and government laboratories. Exhibit 6 shows the current ownership of analytical instruments and planned purchases of new equipment. High demand is found for both gas and liquid chromatographs as well as for accessory equipment such as strip-chart recorders. In addition, new applications in pollution abatement and process control for chemicals, petroleum, pulp, and paper production had expanded markets for analytical instruments. In 1980, sales were approximately $700 million in the United States, which was about half the world market. In 1981 sales were estimated at $750 million in the United States.

In looking for market growth, industry participants had identified a number of specific product-market segments. For example, Tracor had gone after the nuclear and X-ray analyzer markets and was successful with its quality X-ray analyzer. Varian Associates was focusing on the separation-science half of the analytical instruments market, which it expected to grow at about 20 per cent. Varian also was concentrating on the fastest growing segment, that of chemical industry applications, which was applying analytical instruments to the detection and measurement of environmental contaminants.

Because of the complex technologies involved, customers required a wide range of support services and products. As William Buffo, Tracor's vice-president for instruments, noted: "One way we can build the business is increasing name recognition. Our increases in the servicing of the systems has been an important element in our marketing and name-recognition strategy."[6] As new technologies and applications were found for analytical instruments, customers

[6] "A Report to the New York Society of Security Analysts," Tracor, Inc., May 27, 1982.

sought out those suppliers that had previously met their needs. Both Perkin-Elmer and Varian Associates had become industry leaders as far as quality products and service were concerned. Beckman Instruments lacked the quality image in some circles, whereas Tracor had not yet achieved a natiowide reputation, though its quality was comparable to P-E and VA.

Unlike many products, sales for analytical instruments were generated from the need of a laboratory researcher or technician. For example, a university chemist who needed to acquire such equipment to solve a problem or conduct an experiment would initiate the process. After budgetary problems were resolved, the buyer and seller would make contact to discuss the problem. It was then the seller's task to demonstrate that his equipment could best solve the problem. Price was not as important as solving the problem so, if a $100,000 piece of equipment were required, it would generally be purchased. A less expensive machine would not be purchased if it could not solve the problem.

Customer service and training was also important as Hewlett-Packard had noted in its 1981 annual report:

> Hewlett-Packard's commitment to its customer isn't limited to delivering products of quality and reliability. The commitment also includes a variety of support services. H-P currently offers customers five courses in gas chromatography and two related to liquid chromatography, for example. In total, more than 16,000 employees around the world are part of the H-P customer support team.

Product delivery, performance, service, parts, and problem-solving assistance were all considered more important than price alone in selling analytical instruments.

Because of the complex nature of selling analytical products, Perkin-Elmer had restructured its direct sales function. Gaynor Kelley, senior vice-president for instruments, explained:

> On August 1st [1981] we introduced the final phase of a change in our U.S. analytical instrument field sales organization. This change essentially converts a classical horizontal management team with regional sales and branch managers to a vertical product line field sales organization, each with a national sales manager who directs product line field sales managers. The field managers are strategically placed throughout the country, and they in turn manage segments of the specialized field sales force. We felt our product lines had all reached sufficient size to support vertical organization, that a vertical product line sales organization would provide better and quicker penetration with new products or product lines and that we would serve our customer's needs better with highly trained specialized sales engineers. This new organization provides lines of communication which are short and straight.
>
> When you are trying to sell as many different products in as many different places as we are, and where each product line requires unique technical understanding for a proficient sales presentation, we perceived that the classical horizontal sales organization was not serving our effort particularly well. This is especially true since our competitors are inherently specialized due to their *limited* product line offerings.[7]

Since most analytical instrument purchases were considered capital expenditures, they were generally transacted by lump-sum payments. Except for pos-

[7]Gaynor D. Kelley, senior vice-president, Instruments Group, Perkin-Elmer, P-E Security Analysts meeting, November 1981.

sibly mature gas chromatographs and low-end spectrophotometers, leasing or financing by manufacturers was not attractive because of technological changes and product obsolescence. The move toward the sale of more expensive systems might change this situation in the future.

To maintain or improve product differentiation, research and development will become increasingly important. It will be important to keep abreast of technological changes and new product developments. Service and customer support will also affect buying decisions in the future as systems become more complex. To the extent that competitors were able to build switching costs into their products, their customers base would be insured. Less effective instrument producers could lose market share.

To protect future market positions, firms would need to supply more of their own component needs. Integrated firms such as Hewlett-Packard, Perkin-Elmer, and Tracor were well positioned to fend off forward integration of suppliers as well as satisfying the growing demand for systems.

Across-the-board market share strategies were expected to be risky as a result of changing technology, changing products and markets, and changing industry structure. Although opportunities existed for using leases for large systems, it would require a broad range of products, an outstanding sales and service organization, and a large financial commitment. Only Hewlett-Packard, SmithKline-Beckman, and Perkin-Elmer had the necessary resources. Firms such as IBM might be better positioned to enter the industry through leasing and systems strategies.

Small specialist firms would have to continue to develop market segments in which they might overcome their inability to match systems-selling approaches. The experiences of small firms in the computer industry might provide insights as to limited line strategies. Providing lower-priced, technologically advanced products that are compatible with major systems supplier's products could be key.

Analytical Instrument Trends

A primary difficulty was that analytical instruments were durable products. As such, they enjoyed long life spans that were affected only when new products made existing machines outdated or obsolete. However, a major development in industry sales had been the move toward sales of analytical instruments as a part of a system. The advent of microprocessor technology had allowed users to perform more complex analyses, with greater control and accuracy, in a shorter period of time. As Thomas Sege, president of Varian Associates explained:

> Throughout the product line the instruments are closely coupled to microprocessors for instrument control and microcomputers for data acquisition and applications. We intended to continue emphasis in these areas, but in addition, supply all software necessary to network our instruments to laboratory minicomputers.[8]

Tracor, Inc. was using a similar integrated equipment approach. As president Frank McBee explained, "Generally, our analytical instruments incorporate a

[8] Thomas D. Sege, "Presentation to Investment Meetings." Los Angeles, Boston and New York; Varian Associates, Inc., August 24–26, 1982.

detector, a data-processing system, and a display." Hewlett-Packard's efforts were concerned with improving customer productivity as stated in its 1981 annual report:

> Hewlett-Packard's efforts to automate the analytical process have focused on two fronts. The first is to simplify operator interactions with the equipment while producing results more quickly and with greater accuracy. The second is to continue improving the computational capabilities of lab systems that acquire, correlate, and store the data gathered by the analytical instruments.
>
> [Today] hundreds of chemical analyses can be performed, completely unattended from initial sample injection to final written report, using the capabilities of H-P's family of analytical instruments and associated computers. . . . Today H-P's lab automation systems can control and analyze data from as many as 60 instruments.

The extent of Hewlett-Packard's "system strategy" can be seen in Exhibit 7. In gas chromatography, for example, H-P offers a low-end, stand-alone machine; a gas chromatography system; and automated laboratory system; and is attempting to integrate the entire lab system to a complete information system designed to link together all aspects of an organization.

In commenting on analytical product development, an industry analyst noted: "The emergence of computer control—automation—is spurring the usefulness of biochemical instruments by cutting labor costs, allowing more tests per hour of instrument time, and more analysis by operators with lower skills. Perkin-Elmer leads this trend."[9] Gaynor Kelley, senior vice-president of Perkin-Elmer's instrument group, explained its systems approach:

> We have been promoting our computer aided chemistry products at three levels of power and sophistication. We begin with our intelligent microprocessed instruments, then go to the second level, our spectroscopy and chromatography data stations running our unique application software; then to the third level, our laboratory information management system (LIMS for short) which interfaces a Data Systems 3200 Series Computer operating with our LIMS/2000 Laboratory Management software through our data stations, in and out of our intelligent instruments.[10]

There had also been a move away from general purpose equipment to more specialized equipment. Specialized equipment had fewer applications but provided increased accuracy and sophistication. Newer firms such as Jarrell-Ash, Orion Research, Spectrophysics, Neotec, and Dickey John have taken advantage of this situation with products such as the "attenuated total reflectance spectrophotometer," which could analyze in seconds the composition of moistures, oils, and protein for agricultural applications.

Hewlett-Packard, Tracor, Varian, and Perkin-Elmer had all begun to market new or improved versions of their instruments within the past year. Hewlett-Packard's laboratories described future directions for its product development:

> Fields currently under investigation included all the traditional techniques such as gas chromatography, liquid chromatography, infrared spectroscopy and electro-

[9] E. White, Jr., and J. Wolpert, "Electronic and Biochemical Instruments: The Mid-Year Outlook." L. F. Rothschild, Unterberg, Towbin, June 30, 1982.

[10] Gaynor D. Kelley, "Perkin-Elmer Security Analysts Meeting," November 1981.

EXHIBIT 7: Hewlett-Packard's Analytical Products and Systems

HP 5700 SERIES
GAS CHROMATOGRAPHS

The HP 5710 dual column, single detector and 5730 dual column, multidetector gas chromatographs are low-cost, reliable instruments which bridge the gap between expensive research GC's and most routine units. Features such as the dual input/output electrometer, with electronic baseline compensation, two-column oven, temperature programmer, and optional capillary inlet provide the analyst with precise, consistent chromatographic performance.

Accessories for the 5700 Series GC's allow the chromatographer to select the levels of accuracy and automation needed. Some of these are a Gas Control Module, Gas Sampling Valve, the Automatic Sampler, and the Glass Capillary Inlet System. Interfacing the 5700 Series GC to the HP 3388A Integrator or one of the HP 3350 Series Laboratory Automation Systems gives an analytical laboratory extensive problem-solving capabilities.

HP 5580A Gas Chromatograph

The 5880A is much more than a gas chromatograph; it's a complete GC system. By choosing the appropriate components, the instrument needed can be designed. When those needs change, the 5880A can be upgraded in the lab. Beginning with a single column, single detector instrument with an isothermal oven, the 5880A can be upgraded to a programmed oven, four detector GC with dual channel integration and computation, a cartridge tape unit, and BASIC programming, capabilities.

VERSATILITY

A combination of sample inlets from two specialized packed column injection ports, a split/splitless/on-column capillary inlet system and automated gas sampling valves, can be selected.

A complement of up to four individual detectors, exactly tailored to the labs analytical needs can be used. Select from a flame ionization detector, a Ni63 electron capture detector, a nitrogen-phosphorus detector and a unique dual thermal conductivity detector.

A wide range of chromatographic accessories can be added for special needs. Valves, glass and metal effluent splitters, heated collection vents, cold traps and even a catalytic methanator can be readily installed.

AUTOMATION

All 5880A's have Run Time Programming, Clock Time Programming and Keystroke Programming. BASIC Programming is optional.

> *Run Time Programming* is used to execute commands at a preprogrammed time during each sample run. The analyst can change attenuation, switch to a different detector signal, actuate valves, change integration parameters and even label peaks by name.
>
> *Clock Time Programming* permits the execution of preprogrammed commands at specific times of day.
>
> *Keystroke Programming* sequentially executes preprogrammed commands just as though they were manually entered through the keyboard. Use it in conjunction with an automatic sample injector to develop a method overnight. After each run, the keystroke program changes the run conditions, orders a recalibration or even requests a new analytical method from the optional cartridge tape unit.

BASIC Programming extends the power of Keystroke Programming to include calculations and decision-making. A BASIC program can decide what set of conditions should be used on the next analysis, and change the conditions accordingly, thereby optimizing the method development procedure.

Complete automation is achieved with the addition of automatic switching, stream selection and gas sampling valves, and an automatic sample injector that can be preprogrammed to move from one injection port to another.

DATA HANDLING

Preprogrammed *Chromatographic Calculations* including internal standard, external standard, area per cent and normalization are available. A multipoint calibration procedure can be used to correct for nonlinear responses.

Methods, programs, instrument set-points, reports and other data are stored on the *Cartridge Tape Unit* and recall them as needed. A keystroke or BASIC program is used to set up every detail of a specialized analysis by retrieving the information from the cartridge tape.

COMMUNICATIONS

Options are available that allow the 5880A to output an analog detector signal for plotting or processing by an integrator, or data system; to accept an analog signal from another GC and process it as if it came from a 5880A detector; and to output a digital signal for use by an HP 3350 Series Lab Automation System.

REPRODUCIBILITY

The ultimate test of the total system is reproducibility. Extraordinary retention time reproducibility is the result of a new oven design coupled with sophisticated electronic and software control. Impressive peak area reproducibility is due to a superior integrator and injection systems.

The 5880A Gas Chromatograph sets the standard for chemical performance, automation and data handling for the 1980's.

HEWLETT-PACKARD
LABORATORY AUTOMATION SYSTEMS

HP 3350 Series Laboratory Automation Systems repay your investment with many benefits.

Systems accommodate from 30 to 60 instruments. Interface modules are arranged around a loop, making additions to existing systems easy. You can acquire and process data from GCs, LCs, atomic absorption spectrophotometers, differential scanning calorimeters, TM AutoAnalyzers, and other laboratory instruments; control HP 7670 Series Automatic Samplers; switch valves and other devices.

The turnkey software provides a full arsenal of chromatographic capability, while LAB BASIC lets you tailor the system to your data handling or reporting requirements. In 3356 systems FORTRAN is available for more difficult jobs.

All this capability means higher productivity. Perform hundreds of analyses a day—completely unattended from sample preparation to final report. And you can store data and reports automatically, for improved record keeping.

Four System Levels

Level II systems offer an easy-to-use chromatographic software package with a small or intermediate processor. Options include automatic sampler control, simulated distillation, LAB BASIC, and numerous hardware accessories.

EXHIBIT 7: (continued)

HP Systems: Working Together

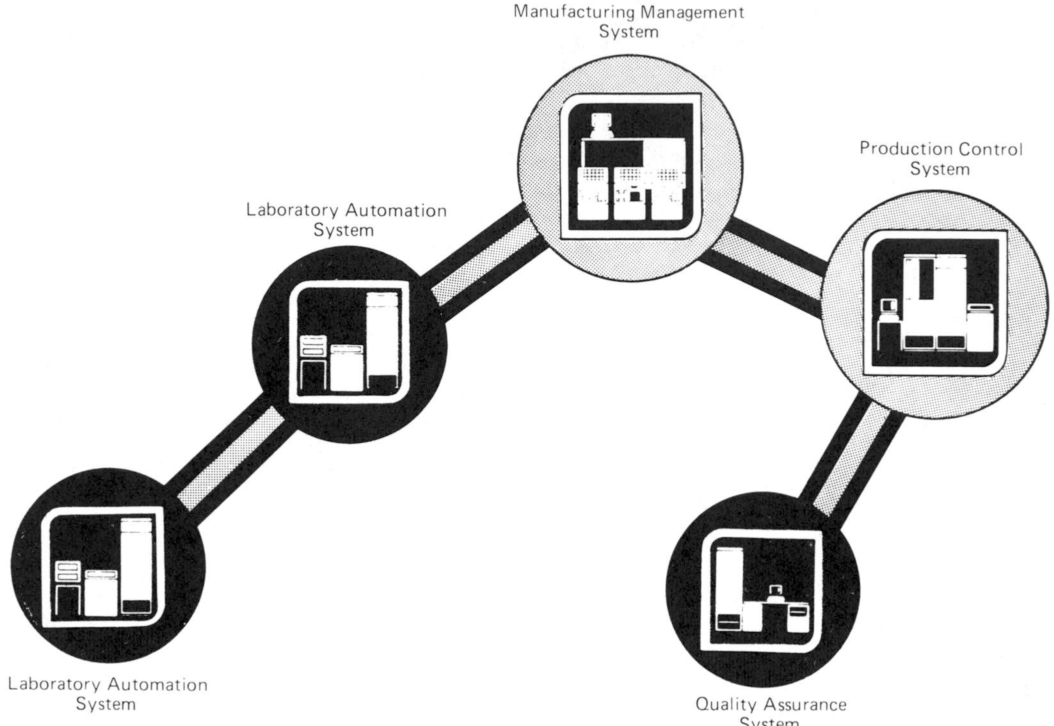

Level III systems are built around the powerful, 64K-word HP 2113E Computer. LAB BASIC and HP sampler control are standard, along with reintegration of raw data, preinjection events, and other features not available at Level II. You may include up to 30 interface modules in Level II or III systems.

The disc-based Level IV systems provide all the capability of memory-based systems plus added features like storage and reanalysis of area-slice or extended-processed-peak data and stream-mode BASIC. The 20-megabyte disc drive provides integral mass storage, which can be augmented by nine-track magnetic tape units. Up to 45 instrument interfaces are possible. Central system hardware can be mounted in a functional, space-saving 56-inch bay or an attractive, lowboy desk/cabinet.

The new HP 3356B/C (Level V) system supports up to 60 instument interface modules, one million words of main memory, and 370 megabytes of on-line disc storage. The RTE-IVB operating system provides great flexibility of configuration through on-line generation and dynamic control of operation with File Manager. Session Monitor manages user access to system resources and provides a system-use account structure. Programming in FORTRAN IV and Assembler augments LAB BASIC. FORTRAN programs can be scheduled from RTE or invoked by BASIC. The optional IMAGE/QUERY package facilitates development of data bases.

Upgrade kits allow conversion from one level to another, so that your system can grow along with your lab.

MPN: A Strategy for the '80s

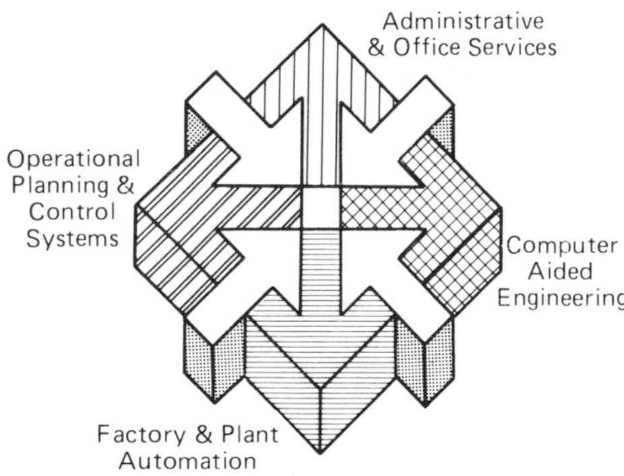

Large Selection of Peripherals

Choose from a wide array of HP peripherals for system expansion, including video display terminals with dual magnetic tape cartridges or built-in thermal printer; graphics terminals and printers; high-speed impact-printing terminals; quiet thermal printers, versatile, programmable plotters; and nine-track magnetic tape drives.

There was a time—not too many years ago, in fact—when it wasn't feasible for an individual department or division of an organization to have a computer system for its own use. Today it is. And today, Hewlett-Packard is one of the world's leading suppliers of small-to-medium-size computers for business and technical applications. By distributing systems to the various units of an organization, the ability of those units to employ computer power economically increases. That's because each system can operate autonomously on a relatively dedicated set of applications.

But the advantages of distributed processing are nullified unless there are means for separate systems to work together. HP offers this capability through the Distributed Systems Network, a family of hardware and software products that provide the necessary links. One set of these products, DS/1000-IV is available on some 3350 Laboratory Automation Systems.

With DS/1000-IV, 3350 Systems can communicate with each other, as well as with HP 1000 and HP 3000 Computer Systems. System-to-system communication adds an exciting new dimension to the concept of expandability, because your laboratory automation system can become part of a wide-ranging network of HP computers. We call this idea the "Manufacturer's Productivity Network"—MPN for short.

MPN is Hewlett-Packard's strategy for the '80s: a networking concept that will eventually integrate all information involved in a manufacturer's operations—from product design through sales and service. In addition, the network will distribute the information company-wide to any department requiring it for planning or decision-making. The increased speed and efficiency of departmental sharing of accurate, up-to-date information can bring significant benefits such as increased asset productivity, greater labor productivity, superior quality, and improved management information.

Source: "3350 Series, Laboratory Automation Systems—for Improved Productivity and Information Management" HEWLETT-PACKARD, 1982; "3357 Laboratory Automation System-Technical Information Bulletin" HEWLETT-PACKARD, 1981; "5790A Gas Chromatograph" HEWLETT-PACKARD, 1981; and "Hewlett-Packard Analytical Instruments 1981, HEWLETT-PACKARD.

chemistry. We are also interested in emerging technologies such as laser spectroscopy and super critical gas separation methods.[11]

CURRENT CONDITIONS AND TRENDS

The domestic recession of 1982 had unfavorably impacted the performance of nearly all instrument manufacturers. Foreign currency devaluations had made matters worse by raising the value of the dollar in foreign markets, thereby increasing the price of U.S. exports and reducing the price of U.S. imports. Along with reduced domestic demand, this had reduced sales of U.S. manufacturers as well as reducing the profitability of their foreign subsidiaries. Double-digit growth rates had been slowed by the recession to a near stop.

Despite current problems, long-term growth appeared likely. There was some uncertainty, however, as to the effect that cutbacks by the Reagan administration might have on government, university, and medical sales, or in other agencies that use analytical instruments for research. On the other hand, increased regulation, such as the Toxic Substance Control Act, was expected to increase demand for analytical instruments in areas of toxic materials control, environmental pollution, health and safety, and product liability.

With the increased development of integrated analytical instrument systems came an industry move toward vertical integration. With a growing dependence on component suppliers, and the growing value of component costs to total systems costs, the threat of supplier integration into analytical instruments sales was considerable. In fact, two of the six major instruments producers had been acquired by firms in related industries since 1980. More acquisitions might be likely. Thus, many instrument makers were attempting to acquire their own capabilities to produce components and other supporting technologies. Firms that already had these capabilities, such as Hewlett-Packard and Tracor, were best positioned to compete in this new environment.

In looking to the future of analytical instruments, Perkin-Elmer's president advised:

> Changes must be innovative, but gradual.
>
> Develop strong "breeding" strains and stick with them as long as possible; yet be at the forefront of the newest technologies. Microprocessors are an example of this.
>
> Be prepared to lose some bets—it is certain that you will.
>
> Learn from your experience and know your customer.
>
> Make the commitment. Be part of the analytical chemistry community. Live in it.[12]

[11] *Hewlett-Packard Laboratories*, 1981.
[12] Address by Horace G. McDonald to the Pittsburgh Conference on "Analytical Chemistry and Applied Spectroscopy" in March, 1981.

CASE EIGHT

Tracor Incorporated (A)

JAMES J. CHRISMAN and WILLIAM R. BOULTON
University of Georgia

Assignment Questions:

1. How would you evaluate Tracor's analytical instruments strategy?
2. What products and markets provide the greatest opportunities for Tracor? the greatest risks?
3. What should Tracor's future strategy be? What skills and resources will be required?

By 1982, Frank W. McBee, Jr., the chairman and president of Tracor Incorporated, was feeling the pressure of the general recession on his instruments group's performance. In 1981 the instruments group's sales increased only $700,000 to $65.7 million while profits actually declined from $7.5 million in 1980 to $7.1 million in 1981. In commenting on this decline, McBee stated that "The slight decline in revenues is due to general economic conditions and not from loss of market share."

The problem was that Tracor's instruments group was losing its relative position within the company. In 1981, the instruments group accounted for only 18 per cent of Tracor's total revenues, down from 21 per cent in 1980 as shown in Exhibit 1. The group's contribution to profits had also dropped from 23 per cent to 16 per cent between 1980 and 1981 while the relative performance of both the aerospace and applied sciences groups had improved. In reviewing the instruments' strategy and Tracor's commitments to the instruments group, McBee explained, "We have rather mixed emotions about our instruments' business." The problem was in deciding what direction to take.

TRACOR'S INSTRUMENTS GROUP

Tracor's instruments group produced over 250 different kinds of instruments. The major product lines included analytical instruments, process control equipment, shipboard navigators, and hearing testers.

EXHIBIT 1: Tracor Instrument Group Performance* (in millions of dollars)

	Sales		*Profits*		*Assets*	
	$	*Per Cent of Total Sales*	*$*	*Per Cent of Total Profits*	*$*	*Per Cent of Total Assets*
1977	28.0	17	3.1	19	20.5	23.4
1978	35.0	17	4.1	20	28.2	25.7
1979	52.4	20	6.3	23	39.9	26.9
1980	65.0	21	7.5	23	47.6	25.7
1981	65.7	18	7.1	16	48.5	21.7

	Capital Expenditures		*Depreciation*		*Operating Margin*	
	$	*Per Cent of Total Expenditures*	*$*	*Per Cent of Total Depreciation*	*Per Cent*	*Tracor Per Cent*
1977	0.5	6.0	0.3	8.8	11.1	9.7
1978	2.0	17.9	0.4	10.0	11.9	10.1
1979	4.5	25.4	0.6	11.3	12.0	10.5
1980	3.5	17.9	0.8	11.1	11.5	10.6
1981	2.4	14.1	1.1	12.8	10.8	11.6

* See Tracor Incorporated (B) for complete Tracor financial data.

Analytical Instruments

Analytical instruments accounted for about half of the instruments group's total revenues. In gas chromatographs (shown in Exhibit 2), sales had leveled off at about $7 million. Tracor was the leader in the manufacture of detectors for chromatographs and held a 60 per cent market share. However, in an attempt to stimulate sales growth, the group had introduced a number of new products, which included:

1. An automated gas chromatograph for customers ranging from oil refineries to government agencies.
2. The TN System 2000, which combined the TN X-ray analyzer system, X-ray detector, spectra-chrome color monitor, and TN 1310 modular automation controller to use with electron microscopes in industrial laboratories for nondestructive testing and materials research.
3. A compact, bench-top, manual gamma counter for use in clinical laboratories.

The system 2000 had been the most successful new product. Sales of the automated gas chromatograph also continued to grow. However, overall chromatograph sales remained flat.

Tracor had 10 per cent of the $80 million medical and clinical markets and had projected future annual growth rate of 10–15 per cent. Tracor had continued to focus on this market as William J. Buffo, the instruments group's vice-president, explained:

EXHIBIT 2: Tracor 570 Gas Chromatograph

570 System Features

OPERATOR ORIENTED DESIGN

The large CRT display provides continuous data for setting and monitoring instrument parameters. A programmed cursor leads you through the parameter setting process.

EASY TO USE KEYBOARD

No complicated alpha-numeric codes to learn. The 570 requires a minimum of pushbutton entries and uses "soft" keys for direct labeling of all entry/operational functions.

PERMANENT MEMORY

Electronically erasable PROMs completely eliminate loss of memory due to power interruption. On original start-up the system comes up to a present program, or comes back after power interruption to the exact program entered by the operator—no batteries, no programs lost.

PRINTER/PLOTTER OUTPUT

Results are automatically integrated and reported along with chromatogram and method on a single printout using a special printer/plotter integrator.

HIGH PERFORMANCE DETECTORS

Choose from seven Tracor designed detectors including the proprietary HALL®700 Electrolytic Conductivity Detector (HECD), a new Flame Ionization Detector, Thermal Conductivity Detector (TCD), new Photoionization Detector (PID), our patented Flame Photometric Detector (FPD), Nitrogen-Phosphorous Detector (NPD) and Electron Capture Detector (ECD). Any three may be installed in your 570 gas chromatograph.

CHROMATOGHAPHIC OPERATION

1. Injection System
    - Gas sampling
    - Auto sampling
2. Efficient Column Oven
    - Subambient operation
    - Stabilized pneumatics
3. Versatile Capillary Option
    - "All glass" system
    - Oval column analysis
    - "On column" injection
    - Capillary controls

The 570 combines the latest in microprocessor control and programming with Tracor's 20 years experience in gas chromatography technology. In addition to proven design features throughout the injection system, oven and pneumatic controls, we've incorporated a responsive CRT/keyboard interface for easy, reliable operation. From the simplest to the most sophisticated analyses, the 570 can be configured to meet your individual requirements.

INPUT/CONTROL

1. Method Entry
2. Method Storage
3. Method Linkage
4. Method/Run Editing
5. Soft Keys
6. Special
7. Instruction

A large format CRT provides an easy to read display. The size permits listing of most parameters on a single "page" which eliminates flipping from page to page to set or monitor the instrument. The CRT/keyboard combination lets you set controls instantly—no need to wait for the printer to interact with queries as in some "interactive" systems. The 570's logic is much easies to handle, yet as complete as any.

EXHIBIT 2 (continued)

SPECIAL CAPABILITIES

1. Multilevel Temperature Programming
2. Run Time Computation
3. Separate Control and Data Reduction Processor

The 570's advanced system features provide truly unlimited programming capability. Most important, however, is the *ease* of creating methods of any degree of complexity. On the CRT screen "page," all of the values are on the same display so the *complete* program is in front of you. Any value in the entire matrix can be changed by moving the cursor to that position and entering a new number. With this format, the time required to create a method is reduced to a minimum and programming errors are virtually eliminated.

DETECTORS

1. Flame Ionization (FID)
2. Flame Photometrix (FPD)
3. Hall 700A Electrolyic Conductivity (HECD)
4. Linear Ni63 Electron Capture (ECD)
5. Photoionization (PID)
6. Thermal Conductivity (TCD)

Tracor has an established reputation for state-of-the-art detector technology evidenced by our patents and licensing agreements with other GC manufacturers. The following Tracor designed detectors are available for Model 570 with up to *three* mounted simultaneously.

Only Tracor has all of these detectors available—each one optimally matched to the Model 570.

OUTPUT/RECORD

Detector outputs from the 570 are coupled to a special printer/plotter integrator. It is compact and easy to operate, yet has all the integration capabilities routinely required.

A full report—including the method, a chromatogram, and integrated results—is printed automatically after the run is completed. All the run information is clearly listed so that analysis, comparison with other runs, or duplication of previous runs is quickly and easily achieved.

For peak detection and integration this 570 output will:

1. Perform all desired chromatographic calculations—area per cent, external standard, normalization and internal standard based on area or height.
2. Store nine calibration methods—recalled by simple keystroke entry.

3. Update retention times by adjusting peak identification for small changes in peak retention times.
4. Recognize solvent peaks, track the solvent tail and calculate a tangent skimmed value.
5. Do baseline corrections for either upward or downward drifting baseline.
6. Automatically perform perpendicular drop calculation on all unresolved peak clusters.
7. Permit overriding of standard software decisions and tailor peak processing to your requirements.

Source: "Tracor 570 Gas Chromatograph," Tracor, Inc. 1982.

> Tracor Analytic made progress in expanding its products for the medical research and clinical markets with introduction of the GAMMATRAC 1290 automatic gamma counter; the BETATRAC 6895 liquid scintillation counter; and the GAMMA COMP, a data reduction system. New products for the neurological market are planned for introduction in 1982 as a result of joint development between Tracor Northern and Tracor Analytic.[1]

Unfortunately, 1982 had seen a 10 per cent decline in sales in both the medical and clinical markets. This had the worst impact on Tracor's gamma and beta scintillation line of products.

In addition to new product developments, Tracor had expanded facilities and acquired new product technologies. A new 140,000 square foot facility was located in Austin, Texas. Tracor also acquired detectors used in their TN X-ray analyzer systems. An acquisition, now Tracor X-ray, expanded Tracor's technical competence, allowing combined development of new products in X-ray fluorescence and optical spectrography for energy and other industrial research markets.

Tracor was best positioned to sell chromatograph and X-ray analyzer detectors, instruments, and related computer-based subsystems. However, more emphasis was being given to system-selling approaches. To this end, computer and semiconductor technologies were playing an important role in improving and introducing new products. William Buffo described Tracor's 570 system (see Exhibit 2):

> Recently announced, the new microprocessor-based gas chromatograph, model 570, features built in display, keyboard controller, and unique software with nonvolatile memory. Through creative use of computer technology in the model 570, it is now possible for complex analysis to be accomplished by individuals with only minimal training, saving laboratory technician time and costs.[2]

The TN system had also been designed as an automated and fully integrated system for electron beam microanalyses. However, Perkin-Elmer and Hewlett-

[1]Tracor, Inc. 1981 Annual Report.

[2]Ibid.

Packard had already made significant efforts in providing complete laboratory systems (see the "Note on the Analytical Instrument Industry" for a more complete description of P-E and H-P's commitments in this regard), a task that Tracor had not yet undertaken.

Process Control Equipment

The market for process control equipment had been growing and profitable for Tracor. It was an industry leader in both digital data acquisition systems and strip chart recorders produced by Tracor Westronics. After moving into new facilities, several new devices were introduced in mid-1982 for use by a broad range of industries to monitor and record variables in temperature, flow, and pressure. Tracor entered this segment of the process recorder market with a "nuclear qualified" 100 millimeter chart recorder and more extensive software for its 7800 digital data acquisition system. In broadening this product line, Tracor had acquired a temperature control product line from Paktronics in late 1980.

Tracor had both product and customer diversity in its process control business. Although primary markets were industrial process and laboratories, other customers were involved in the power generator, steel, food, beverage, pharmaceutical, and petrochemical industries. Major product sales for replacement parts and chart paper were basically immune to budgetary and cyclical business conditions and represented 30 per cent of the sales in this area.

Shipboard Navigators

Tracor had been involved in the shipboard navigator business for over twenty-five years, installing over 50 per cent of all OMEGA navigators. In 1982 Tracor held about 15 per cent of the OMEGA and satellite navigation system market. A recent acquisition of BE Industries strengthened that position by providing stabilized navigation platforms for shipboard satellite navigation systems. The satellite navigator receiver was the largest-selling instrument, sold mainly to foreign shipping customers. In spite of Tracor's strong position, sales had been sluggish with an overall decline in demand.

Sophisticated navigation systems incorporated microprocessor technologies and atomic frequency standards that would generate, monitor, and control time, accurate to the second, for 666 years. In developing new products, there was growing pressure to move from $10,000 to $5,000 navigators. To maintain leadership, Tracor had introduced several new products as described by Buffo:

> Two new Tracor satellite navigators have been introduced. The Transtar Sat Nav first marketed in 1981 was followed by a less expensive, fifth generation of Tracor satellite navigators, the Bridgestar. Both determine mid-ocean positions anywhere in the world with an accuracy to 1/10 nautical mile. Moreover, when combined in a system incorporating another upgraded navigator, the Tracor automatic OMEGA, continuous position accuracy is achieved.[3]

Unfortunately, demand was still sluggish along with world shipping demands.

[3] Ibid.

As in other groups, Tracor benefited from internal technologies and diversified product groups. The components group supplied a variety of navigator parts, and customers often overlapped with the applied science and aerospace groups. Tracor's research vessels also provided test sites for new products. Finally, customers were also known to sponsor specific research and development activities that crossed organizational boundaries.

Hearing Testers

Audiometric technology was an outgrowth of Tracor's original line of business—acoustics. Though overall sales were relatively small, Tracor held about 50 per cent of the screening audiometer market. In describing this businesses, Chairman McBee explained in 1981:

> The audiometric business, which is not of major significance, has been about $2 million per year. We commented [1976] that it was our expectation that with the advent of enforcement and implementation by OSHA of a hearing program for noisy industries, we would increase the sales of our audiometers by a multiple of 10 to 20. OSHA has, at this point, decided to implement its program in August, and our audiometer sales have already begun to increase.[4]

Along with audiometers, Tracor also sold a full line of sound booths and noise monitors for both government and industrial users.

INSTRUMENT MARKETING

As with most instrument producers, Tracor relied on industrial, medical, university, and government markets for the majority of its sales (Exhibit 3). Tracor used a network of corporate sales offices and, for less expensive items, independent dealers. Regarding sales to foreign markets, Buffo explained: "Our foreign markets are growing. We have our own marketing force headquarters in one area in Europe and sell most of the instruments through this operation in Amsterdam. We also sell throughout Europe and Asian countries."[5] Exhibit 4 shows the location of Tracor's worldwide sales and service outlets.

EXHIBIT 3: Major Instrument Markets

	1981 Sales	
	\$ Millions	(%)
Industry and Laboratory Electronics	39.2	60
Foreign Customers	22.9	35
U.S. Government	1.2	2
U.S. Defense	2.4	3
	\$65.7	100%

[4]"A Report to the New York Society of Security Analysts," TRACOR, INC., May 27, 1981.
[5]Ibid.

EXHIBIT 4: Tracor Sales and Services Outlets

Source: "Gas Chromatographs, Liquid Chromatographs," Tracor Instruments, 1981.

In attempting to develop customer relationships, Tracor stressed its customer support and warranty programs.

Customer Support. Tracor maintained a highly experienced applications laboratory to assist customers with chromatography before or after instrument sales. Training courses were offered at its new training center as part of the applications laboratory.

Warranty. Tracor offered one of the most comprehensive warranties in the industry. Defective parts were replaced for the first year. Any defects from materials or workmanship were repaired for the first ninety days. Optional service contracts were also available.

CURRENT OPERATIONS

Tracor's competitors were generally stronger in the instruments business. Most competitors had equivalent technical capabilities, but had greater resources and R&D capabilities. With environmental uncertainties and technological changes, it was felt that the competitive posture of the industry could change at any time.

Tracor's product quality, vertical integration, support technologies, and customer service operations had allowed the instruments group to compete head-to-head against much larger rivals. Its increase in market share and entrance into several new markets was not expected to elicit severe competitor reactions. In fact, Tracor had not yet developed a national reputation to the extent that Perkin-Elmer, Hewlett-Packard, and Varian Associates had done.

The instrument group's major problem related to the slow growth in sales relative to capital expenditures on a national level, as shown in Exhibit 5. To overcome the problem, management had made major commitments to product

EXHIBIT 5: Capital Spending on Plant and Equipment vs. Tracor Instrument Sales

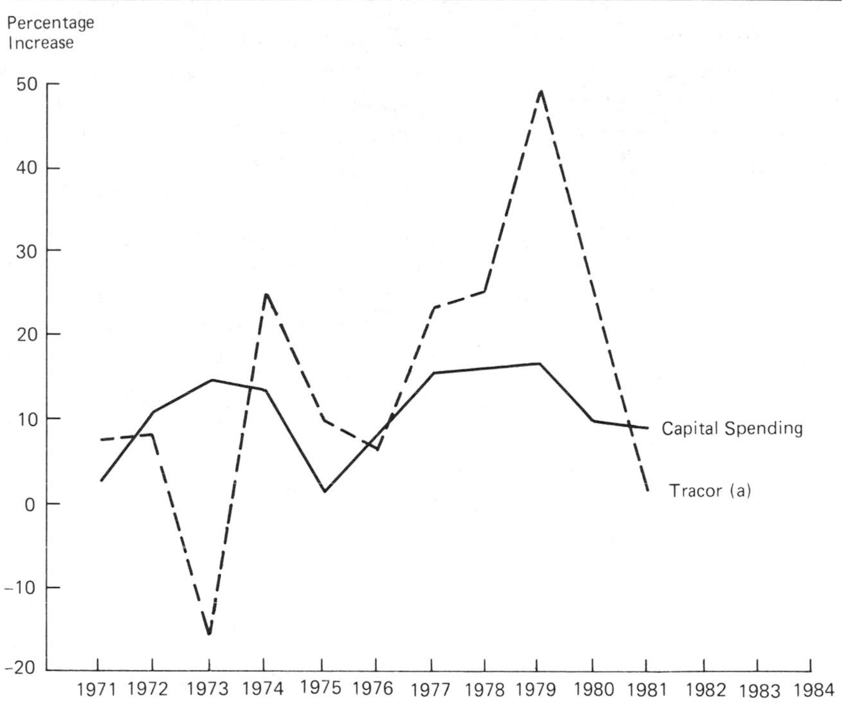

(a) 1973 results impacted by disposition of a subsidiary.

Source: Judith L. Comeau, "Tracor, Inc." Goldman Sachs Research, August 23, 1982.

and market developments and operating improvements. As Buffo explained: "We have designed new equipment, incorporated new technologies, brought in some people in sales, engineering and development, and we streamlined our firm's operations."[6] Chairman McBee also commented: "Product improvement programs, resulting both in manufacturing cost reductions and increased efficiencies in product performance, continue to be implemented by the instruments group during the second quarter. These efforts, along with increased bookings at the end of the quarter, should result in improved performance by this group for the balance of 1982."[7]

Despite management's efforts, it was still of concern that major competitors were spending more in R&D than Tracor had assets. Gaining market share and keeping up with competition would require that Tracor's board divert funds from other growth areas. If market growth in instruments did not materialize, it was felt that competition would become more intense and result, possibly, in intense price wars. On the other hand, if growth continued, as predicted, it was likely that new competitors, both components manufacturers and computer makers, would enter the market. In fact, two major competitors (Beckman In-

[6]Ibid.
[7]2nd Quarter Report 1982, Tracor, Inc.

struments and Waters Associates) had already been acquired by firms in related industries in the past two years.

Management knew that a major long-term commitment to the instruments business would require heavy capital expenditures. Tracor's instrument division was already operating near capacity and had been forced to farm out some of its needs for support equipment. In addition, skilled personnel were critical for research, equipment production, and support services of both in-house capabilities and customer needs. Finally, rapid technological changes and product development now characterized the instruments business.

With Tracor's past success in increasing market share in nearly all its business areas, management had mixed feelings about the instruments group. What should Tracor's future position be in instruments? What areas provided the greatest opportunity, profits, and growth? What should its strategy be relative to the nationally recognized competitors? These questions are still waiting for answers.

CASE NINE

Tracor Incorporated (B)

WILLIAM R. BOULTON and JAMES J. CHRISMAN
University of Georgia

Assignment Questions:

1. How would you evaluate Tracor's corporate strategy?
2. What role does each operating group play in the corporate strategy?
3. In light of this review, what strategy would you recommend for analytical instruments?

Over the past five years, Tracor Incorporated had more than doubled sales, from $164.6 million in 1977 to $371.1 million in 1981, while improving profits from $6.6 million to $19.0 million (Exhibit 1). Although this growth record had been achieved through both internal and external expansion, Tracor's chairman and president, Frank W. McBee, Jr., gave credit to his acquisition strategy (Exhibit 2). In commenting to security analysts, he stated: "Our basis for acquisition of companies is that they be involved in technologies and markets we know and understand. In the event an acquisition involves manufacturing, the same understanding must exist with regard to manufacturing technologies." In addition, the climate for growth in all of Tracor's major business areas had been exceptional, despite the recessionary pressures beginning in the 1980s. Tracor's research and development expertise had allowed the company to remain in the forefront of technological change. As McBee emphasized, "The backbone of our company is our scientists and engineers." In addition, Tracor's management team was considered strong, and was committed to growth and strategic planning.

Background

Tracor Incorporated began as Associated Consultants and Engineers, Inc. in 1955. The name was changed in 1956 to Texas Research Associates, Inc. and in 1962 to Tracor Incorporated. With headquarters in Austin, Texas, Tracor enjoyed the advantages of no state income taxes and an absence of unionized labor as was typical of the South. Until 1965, Tracor was primarily involved in acoustics research and development for government and private institutions.

Until the early 1970s, Tracor had successfully diversified into new areas.

EXHIBIT 1: Tracor, Inc. Financial Information

Income Statements	*1971**	*1977*	*1978*	*1979*	*1980*	*1981*	*First Half 1982*
(in $ millions)							
Sales	$71.1	$164.6	$191.2	$260.3	$313.7	$371.1	$193.5
Cost of Goods Sold	−52.5	−124.4E	−141.3	−189.8	−228.2	−273.4	NA
Operating Income	18.6	40.2E	49.9	70.5	85.5	97.7	NA
General Selling Expenses	−13.8	−25.3E	−32.2	−45.3	−54.5	−57.0	NA
Earnings Before Interest and Taxes	4.8	14.9	17.7	25.2	31.0	40.7	NA
Interest Expense	−1.8	−2.8	−3.4	−5.5	−5.7	−5.8	NA
Earning Before Taxes	3.0	12.1	14.3	19.7	25.3	34.9	17.6
Taxes	−1.7	−5.5	−6.5	−9.0	−11.1	−15.9	−7.8**
Net Income	1.3	6.6	7.8	10.7	14.2	19.0	9.8
Cash Dividend Paid	−0	−0.7	−1.1	−1.4	−2.0	−2.8	—
Retained Earnings	$ 1.3	$ 5.9	$ 6.7	$ 9.3	$ 12.2	$ 16.2***	—
Balance Sheet							
(in $ millions)							
Assets							
Current Assets	$28.8	$ 58.4	$ 73.8	$ 93.3	$111.6	$133.2	$138.3
Fixed Assets (Net)	13.0	24.9	32.1	44.1	62.1	84.5	90.6
Other Assets	6.3	4.2	3.9	2.9	3.0	6.1	6.3
Total Assets	$48.1	$ 87.5	$109.8	$140.3	$176.7	$223.8	$235.2
Liabilities and Equity							
Current Liabilities	$15.4	$ 20.6	$ 28.9	$ 32.6	$ 36.0	$ 48.9	$ 42.8
Long-term Liabilities + Capital Leases	29.1	34.3	41.0	58.9	47.4	59.7	68.7
Total Liabilities	$44.5	$ 54.9	$ 69.9	$ 91.5	$ 83.4	$108.6	$111.5
Net Stockholders' Equity	$ 3.6	$ 32.6	$ 39.9	$ 48.8	$ 93.3	$115.2	$123.7
Total Liabilities + Equity	$48.1	$ 87.5	$109.8	$140.3	$176.7	$223.8	$235.2

* before loss from discontinued operations of $27.9 million
** provision for income tax
*** includes $0.9 million in stock dividend
E = estimate, figures have changed several times because of restatements.
NA = information not available.
Source: Tracor, Inc. 1978–1981 Annual Reports 2nd Quarter Report 1982, Tracor, Inc.

However, in 1971 an unsuccessful venture into the computer business brought the firm to the edge of bankruptcy. It was then that one of the founders, Frank McBee, assumed control of Tracor and instituted a number of management and operating changes. In reflecting back, McBee commented, "We were probably broke and didn't know it." He also learned from that experience, "Don't attack IBM. Attack someone else."[1]

TRACOR'S RECENT FINANCIAL POSITION

By 1982, Tracor had diversified into the production and service of a variety of high technology electronic systems, components, and instruments. Despite the 1982 recession, Tracor expected to set new records in sales and earnings for the

[1] *The Christian Science Monitor,* March 31, 1982, pp. B1.

EXHIBIT 2: Acquisitions to Date

1964 Acquired:
Acurate Instrument Division of Atec, Inc.—Sulyer Laboratories

1965 Acquired:
General Technology Corp.

1966 Acquired:
Northern Scientific Inc.
Robert L. Store Co.
Micro Tek Instruments, Inc.
Allison Laboratories

1967 Acquired:
Astro Science Corp.
Petronics, Inc.
Westronics, Inc

1968 Acquired:
Coulson Instruments Co.
Aztec Research Co.
Littlefuse, Inc.
Frequency Control Corp.
Marine Acoustical Services, Inc.
Berkeley Scientific Laboratories, Inc.
Adams Electronics, Inc.
John I. Thompson and Co., Inc.
Dikewood Corporation

1969 Acquired:
Mel-Rain Corp.
Comel International Corp.
Richey Electronics
Kapco Electronics

1970 Acquired:
hardware products division of Tracor Computing Corp.
Datamark, Inc.
Bright Industries (minority interest)
Formed Tracor Data Systems, Inc. (subsidiary)

1971 Acquired:
Ownership increased in Remcom Manufacturing Co.
Sold assets of Computer Peripheral business

1973 Acquired:
Chromatic, Inc.
Sold Astro Science Corp.
Sold Remcom Manufacturing Co.

1974 Acquired:
Tracor Radcon
Sold Tracor Computing Corp.

1975 Acquired:
Certain assets of Marksman Corp.

1977 Acquired certain assets of:
Stabilized Optics Corp.
Norton Electronics, Inc.

1978 Acquired:
Scientific Systems division of Pinkerton Computer Consultants, Inc.
Tracor Analytic from G. D. Searle & Co.

1980 Acquired:
Tracor MB Associates

1981 Acquired:
United Scientific
Palolab Pharmaceuticals
Pak-Tronics (temperature controller product line)
Diagnostic Data (7.5% share)
Flight Systems
Aero Spacelines from Twin Fair
Olvis Utrecht
Olvis Mol
Olvis Grenchem

1982 Acquired:
BE Industries
Marcon
Letter of intent:
Scientific Communications, Inc.
Systems Engineering Associates Corporation

Source: *Moody's Indurtrial Manual 1981,* pp. 6051.

ninth consecutive year. Midyear sales of $193.5 million and profits of $9.8 million were 8 per cent and 11 per cent increases, respectively, over 1981. Record bookings for the second quarter raised management's expectations of reaching growth rates of 20 per cent by year's end, Tracor's average over the past five years. As shown in Table 1, backlogs had nearly reached 1980 levels by mid 1982.

TABLE 1: Tracor Backlogs ($ millions)

1977	75.2
1978	91.8
1979	108.1
1980	148.0
1981	130.0
mid 1982	142.5

Tracor's primary objectives for the future were stated as follows:

1. To grow from internal sources an average of 15 per cent per year in revenues and 20 per cent per year in profits.
2. To acquire, on a sound financial basis, companies of reasonable size, which are complementary to Tracor's technology, manufacturing, and marketing competencies.
3. To maintain Tracor's diversity which has served the company so well in the past."[2]

Major strategies evolved from Tracor's technological superiority, domination of market niches, diversification, and internal and external expansion.

In early 1982, Tracor's board of directors announced a five for four stock split that was distributed as a stock dividend in June 1982. This was the fourth such split in four years. Cash dividends were also increased for the fifth consecutive year.

To keep debt at a reasonable level, management had issued $25 million in stock in 1980. The new equity was used to retire intermediate term and floating rate debt, thereby reducing debt to the current level of 32 per cent of total capitalization. Future cash needs were expected to be covered through internal sources, and a $40 million revolving credit line was established with several banks in 1981. Jim A. Smith, Tracor's chief financial officer, explained: "Growth will require funding of additional receivables, inventory and property, plant and equipment. Tracor's internally generated cash flow should substantially cover these needs. Anticipated outside financing needs are adequately provided for by existing intermediate-term bank revolving credit agreements."[3]

TRACOR'S MANAGEMENT ORGANIZATION

Tracor's commitment to good management practices was reflected by its organizational chart (Exhibit 3). For example, only four of the eleven board members were Tracor employees. In addition, the operating committee, instituted in 1969, met monthly to review all activities of the organization from top to bottom. This committee also provided the forum for three-year plans and budgets. An operating report issued ten days following the close of each month was used to review performance and revise annual forecasts. An example of the operating report is shown in Exhibit 4.

[2] "Accomplishments, Outlook, Goals," *Tracor, Inc.*, October 1982.
[3] Tracor, Inc., 1981 Annual Report.

EXHIBIT 3: Tracor Organizational Chart

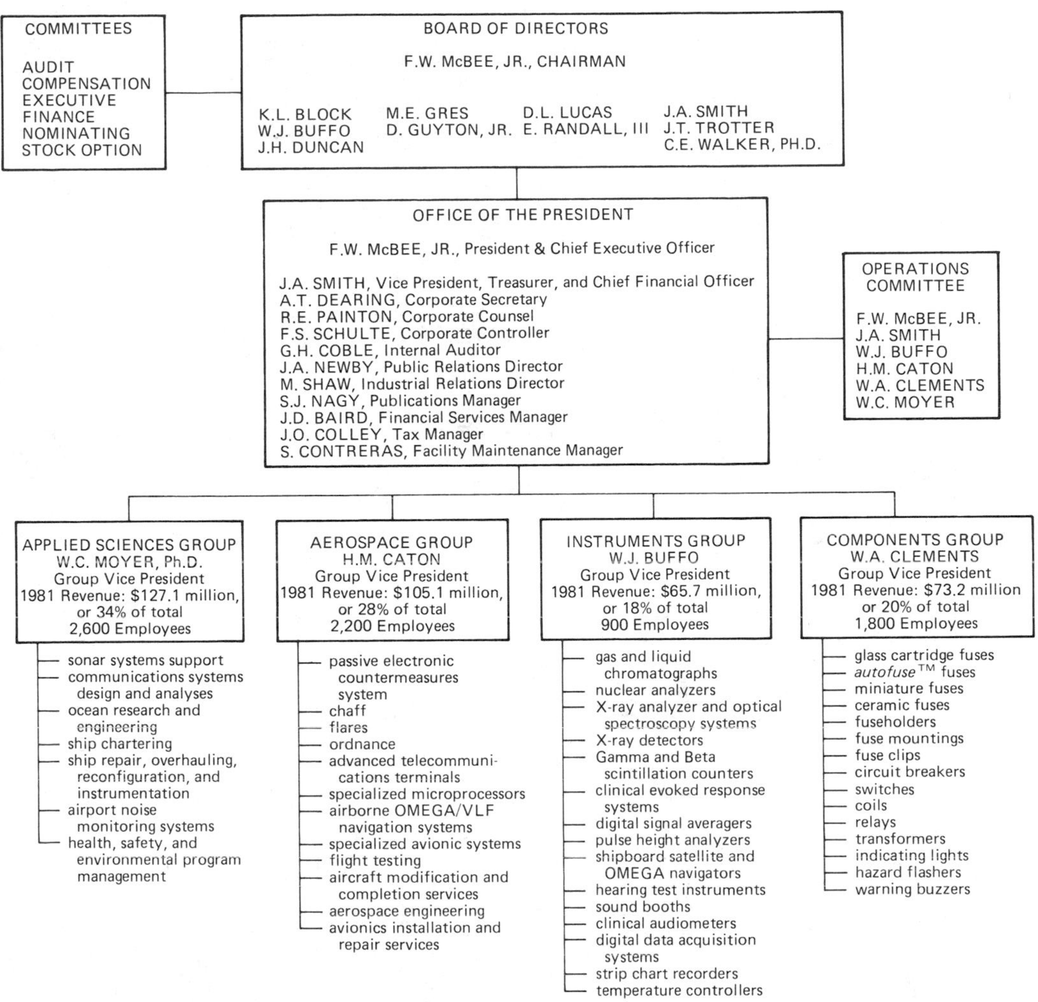

Sources: *Tracor, Incorporated 1981 Annual Report. Moody's Industrial Manual 1981*, pp. 4378.

TRACOR'S BUSINESS AREAS

Tracor was divided into four operating groups: applied sciences, aerospace, components, and instruments. The breakdown of sales and contributions from 1977 to 1981 are shown for each area in Exhibits 5–8. Although each area operated as an independent business unit, there were relationships between the groups. For example, applied sciences provided other divisions with research, development, and consulting services regarding customer needs. In some cases, these relationships created new markets or found new product applications. Likewise, the components division supplied a variety of electronic components to both the aerospace and instruments divisions.

EXHIBIT 4: Tracor Monthly Operating Report (Sample Page from Tracor Profit Center)

April	Year to Date			This Month		3 Months Projections			Qtr ended Mar		Qtr ending Jun		Total Year 1981		
Operations Report	*Actual*	*Plan*	*Prior*	*Actual*	*Proj*	*May*	*Jun*	*Jul*	*Actual*	*Plan*	*Proj*	*Plan*	*Proj*	*Plan*	*Prior*
Revenue	23655	19683	16796	6134	5400	6010	7100	5775	17521	14246	19244	18126	64740	64740	57927
Cost of Sales	19700	16285	13917	5098	4500	5000	5900	4800	14602	11785	15998	15000	53568	53568	48577
Gross Profit	3955	3398	2879	1036	900	1010	1200	975	2919	2461	3246	3126	11172	11172	9350
GP%	16.7	17.3	17.1	16.9	16.7	16.8	16.9	16.9	16.7	17.3	16.9	17.2	17.3	17.3	16.1
Operating Expenses:															
Marketing Exp	344	307	266	87	80	88	104	84	257	222	279	282	1006	1006	779
Mkt % of Revenue	1.5	1.6	1.6	1.4	1.5	1.5	1.5	1.5	1.5	1.6	1.4	1.6	1.6	1.6	1.3
IR&D	137	161	172	38	41	45	49	17	99	119	132	107	325	325	595
IR&D % of Revenue	.6	.8	1.0	.6	.8	.7	.7	.3	.6	.8	.7	.6	.5	.5	1.0
G&A Local	1383	1252	979	351	320	354	420	340	1032	908	1125	1147	4114	4114	3138
G&A % of Revenue	5.8	6.4	5.8	5.7	5.9	5.9	5.9	5.9	5.9	6.4	5.8	6.3	6.4	6.4	5.4
Total Oper Exp	1864	1720	1417	476	441	487	573	441	1388	1249	1536	1536	5445	5445	4512
% of Revenue	7.9	8.7	8.4	7.8	8.2	8.1	8.1	7.6	7.9	8.8	8.0	8.5	8.4	8.4	7.8
Op Inc Bef Int-Oth	2091	1678	1462	560	459	523	627	534	1531	1212	1710	1590	5727	5727	4838
Other Income (Exp)	4			1					3		1				1
Op Inc Bef Int	2095	1678	1462	561	459	523	627	534	1534	1212	1711	1590	5727	5727	4837
% of Revenue	8.9	8.5	8.7	9.1	8.5	8.7	8.8	9.2	8.8	8.5	8.9	8.8	8.8	8.8	8.4
Other Comparisons:					Plan	Plan	Plan	Plan	Prior		Prior				
Revenue					5437	5619	7070	6213	12759		13595				
Op Inc Bef Int					466	483	641	562	1110		1295				
Backlog Status:	Ytd	Feb	Mar	Apr					Previous Projections		Rev	Inc			
Beginning Backlog	22246	22065	19903	21482						Mar	18010	1545			
Bookings	28450	3515	9050	11693											
Revenue	23655	5677	7471	6134											
Ending Backlog	27041	19903	21482	27041											
Overhead-Rate Status:	Plan	Feb	Mar	Apr						Return on Assets	Plan	Feb	Mar	Apr	
Manufacturing	93.0	99.2	95.7	96.1							19.7	14.4	17.7	17.8	
Engineering	39.0	41.2	38.4	37.7											

Prev Projections—1981:	Jan	Feb	Mar	
Revenue	64740	64740	64740	
Net Oper Income	5727	5727	5727	
Accounts Receivable	Mar 80	Jan	Feb	Mar
Current	6120	4657	5983	6760
%	67.8	61.4	72.9	77.5
30–60	730	1164	1007	677
%	8.1	15.4	12.3	7.8
60–90	1087	543	348	586
%	12.0	7.2	4.2	6.7
Over 90	1087	1216	873	695
%	12.0	16.0	10.6	8.0
Total	9024	7580	8211	8717
Unreimb Costs and Fees	3633	6515	7623	8169
Total Accounts Rec	12657	14095	15834	16887
Days Sales in Accts Rec	89	80	87	87

	Dec 80	Jan	Feb	Mar
Employee Count	1325	1778	1818	1838
Inventory:	Mar 80	Jan	Feb	Mar
Raw Material	19	16	12	11
in Process				
Finished Goods	136	20	19	20
Total Inventory	155	36	31	31
Turnover—cost of Sales				
	Mar 81	Year 81		
	Actual	Proj	Plan	
Capital Expenditures	476	1746	1746	

Source: Tracor, Inc. 1981 Annual Report.

EXHIBIT 5: Tracor Applied Science Group Performance

$ in millions	Sales		Operating Profits		Operating Margins		Assets		Capital Expenditures		Depreciation	
	$	%*	$	%*	%	%***	$	%*	$	%*	$	%*
1977	51.1	31%	4.0	25%	7.8%	9.7%	**	—	**	—	**	—
1978	59.6	29%	4.6	22%	7.6%	10.1%	20.0	18.2%	2.2	19.6%	0.9	22.5%
1979	75.8	29%	6.1	22%	8.0%	10.5%	35.2	23.7%	2.9	16.4%	1.1	20.8%
1980	98.5	31%	7.6	23%	7.8%	10.6%	44.8	24.2%	4.3	22.1%	1.6	22.2%
1981	127.1	34%	10.1	23%	8.0%	11.6%	46.1	20.6%	3.2	18.8%	2.1	24.4%

*percentage of total company.
**Before 1980 the Applied Sciences and Aerospace Groups were combined into one group known as Science and Systems. Though some data were available for dividing the two groups for 1978–1979, no breakdowns were available for 1977. Science and Systems data for 1977 includes:
Assets = $36.5
Capital Expenditures = $5.2
Depreciation = $1.2
***Average operating margins for entire company.
Source: Tracor, Inc. 1978–1981 Annual Reports.

EXHIBIT 6: Tracor Aerospace Group Performance

$ in millions	Sales		Operating Profits		Operating Margins		Assets		Capital Expenditures		Depreciation	
	$	%*	$	%*	%	%***	$	%*	$	%*	$	%*
1977	30.1	18%	3.1	19%	9.6%	9.7%	**	—	**	—	**	—
1978	45.5	23%	5.3	25%	11.1%	10.1%	26.9	24.5%	3.9	34.8%	0.8	20%
1979	61.4	24%	7.3	27%	12.0%	10.5%	36.1	24.3%	7.3	41.2%	1.5	28.3%
1980	80.9	26%	9.3	28%	11.4%	10.6%	54.8	29.6%	8.3	42.6%	2.1	29.2%
1981	105.1	28%	12.8	30%	12.1%	11.6%	82.1	36.8%	7.2	42.4%	2.9	33.7%

*percentage of total company.
**Before 1980 the Applied Sciences and Aerospace Groups were combined into one group known as Science and Systems. Though some data were available for dividing the two groups for 1978–1979, no breakdowns were available for 1977. Science and Systems data for 1977 includes:
Assets = $36.5
Capital Expenditures = $5.2
Depreciation = $1.2
***Average operating margins for entire company.
Source: Tracor, Inc. 1978–1981 Annual Reports.

EXHIBIT 7: Tracor Instruments Group Performance

$ in millions	Sales		Operating Profits		Operating Margins		Assets		Capital Expenditures		Depreciation	
	$	%*	$	%*	%	%**	$	%*	$	%*	$	%*
1977	28.0	17%	3.1	19%	11.1%	9.7%	20.5	23.4%	0.5	6.0%	0.3	8.8%
1978	35.0	17%	4.1	20%	11.9%	10.1%	28.2	25.7%	2.0	17.9%	0.4	10.0%
1979	52.4	20%	6.3	23%	12.0%	10.5%	39.9	26.9%	4.5	25.4%	0.6	11.3%
1980	65.0	21%	7.5	23%	11.5%	10.6%	47.6	25.7%	3.5	17.9%	0.8	11.1%
1981	65.7	18%	7.1	16%	10.8%	11.6%	48.5	21.7%	2.4	14.1%	1.1	12.8%

*percentage of total company.
**Average operating margins for entire company.
Source: Tracor, Inc. 1978–1981 Annual Reports.

EXHIBIT 8: Tracor Components Group Performance

$ in millions	Sales		Operating Profits		Operating Margins		Assets		Capital Expenditures		Depreciation	
	$	%*	$	%*	%	%**	$	%*	$	%*	$	%*
1977	55.4	34%	6.0	37%	10.9%	9.7%	24.3	27.8%	2.2	55%	1.6	47.1%
1978	63.1	31%	6.9	33%	11.0%	10.1%	30.4	27.7	2.9	25.9%	1.6	40%
1979	70.6	27%	7.5	28%	10.6%	10.5%	31.8	21.4%	2.8	15.8%	1.8	34%
1980	69.3	22%	8.8	26%	12.7%	10.6%	33.6	18.2%	2.9	14.9%	2.5	34.7%
1981	73.2	20%	13.2	31%	18.0%	11.6%	39.5	17.7%	4.0	23.5%	2.3	26.7%

*percentage of total company.
**Average operating margins for entire company.
Source: Tracor, Inc. 1978–1981 Annual Reports.

Applied Sciences Group

The applied sciences group was the research branch of Tracor and as such represented the extension of its original line of business. With a service and technical orientation, the applied sciences group offered software and evaluation assistance to a large number of government departments and agencies, as well as to commercial and foreign clients. The group's major services and divisions are shown in Table 2.

Applied sciences became a separate operating group in 1980. Previously, applied sciences and aerospace had been included together in one group, which was then known as science and systems. Though growing rapidly, margins had not equaled those in other areas as a result of "cost-plus contracts" that restricted profits to about 4–8 per cent of operating expenses. On the other hand, these cost-plus contracts ensured a stable profit margin even given cost overruns and inflation. For this reason management could anticipate rather steady returns from this area.

Tracor kept at the forefront of technological advancements by actually playing a vital role in the research and development activities of customers. The applied sciences group also complemented other corporate activities and provided firsthand knowledge of market needs. By evaluating hardware systems and

TABLE 2

Services	*Divisions*
1. Sonar	1. Analysis and Applied Research
2. Fleet support	2. Electronic Systems
3. Marine life research	3. Systems Technology
4. Communications analysis and management	4. Special Programs
5. Marine services (Tracor Marine)	5. Tracor Marine
6. Health effects and biomedical program management (Tracor Jitco)	6. Tracor Jitco
7. Acoustical sciences	
8. Solar energy	

developing the accompanying software systems, the applied sciences group was in close touch with competitors, which allowed speedy reactions to new product developments. In commenting on the group's strong military ties, McBee explained: "Through this Group, we have had a long and very favorable relationship with the U. S. Navy, as close consultants. This relationship is so close that we are hardware excluded from the manufacture of large sonar systems."[4]

The government accounted for about 80 per cent of the group's revenues, with 70 per cent of that total related to the military. The outlook for this business unit appeared bright because of the Reagan administration's emphasis on defense spending. However, 1982 revenues were not quite up to plan because of delays in defense-related contract releases. In spite of these delays, over $21 million in new contracts were obtained in the first quarter of 1982 and in the second quarter the group received another from the U.S. Navy to provide technical services for fleet communications systems with a total potential value of $17 million. Additionally, services provided to foreign allies had expanded through technical support contracts with the Japanese and Saudi Arabian governments.

Applied sciences was also involved in a variety of nondefense-related support, although growth of this business was expected to be less dynamic than for the group as a whole. However, applied sciences was currently involved in one project to develop a communications system to link barge traffic on U. S. inland waterways and had worked for nine years with the National Cancer Institute on a project in bioassay testing to identify carcinogenic chemicals.

Many of these activities, such as Tracor Jitco's cancer contract, involved reserach fields and projects that related to other divisions. Testing for carcinogenic chemicals required equipment manufactured by the instrument group, for example. Thus, besides developing new markets and applications for other company products, the applied sciences group was also an in-house customer for many of the devices produced in other divisions.

The strong position of the applied sciences group should be further improved with the planned acquisition of Systems Engineering Associates Corporation (SEACOR). SEACOR specialized in technical and engineerng services for ship overhaul, repair, and alteration programs of the U.S. Navy. As in the past, this acquisition complemented existing activities within the group. SEACOR was profitable at present and was expected to add up to $20 million in sales.

Most of the efforts of the applied sciences group related to underwater research. For instance, Tracor also operated a fleet of privately owned research vessels, one of which the firm sold in 1982 for a pretax gain of $1 million. Its replacement in the future would be a ship more conducive to the types of research required by major markets, though no definitive plans had been made in this regard. Management considered this group as expert in all aspects of sonar and was committed to fleet support.

Aerospace Group

Like applied sciences, the aerospace group relies on the U.S. government for the majority of its revenues. However, since both groups served a large num-

[4]"A Report to the New York Society of Security Analysts," *Tracor, Inc.*, May 27, 1982.

TABLE 3

Product Lines	*Divisions*
1. Avionics	1. Tracor MBA
2. Countermeasures	2. Tracor Aviation
3. Telecommunications	3. Tracor Radcon
4. Digital Systems	4. Flight Systems
	5. Aerospace Austin
	6. Government Relations

ber of different agencies and departments, under a vast number of individual contracts, business activity was well diversified and not likely to be hurt significantly through the cancellation of any one project. Table 3 provides breakdowns of major aerospace product lines and group divisions.

Growth prospects appeared brightest for the aerospace group because of technological leadership in several areas and recent government commitments to defense spending. Most of Tracor's defense business in the aerospace group was contracted on a fixed fee basis, which kept margins relatively flat in recent years. However, considering inflation, the group's performance had indicated extremely efficient operations from a cost standpoint since contracts usually allowed for profit margins of only 4–14 per cent over estimated expenses.

Tracor's acquisition strategy was especially evident in aerospace, and recent additions accounted for almost 35 per cent of group sales. In August 1982 the company signed a letter of intent to purchase Scientific Communications, Inc., which further strengthened the group's already dominant position in the electronic countermeasures market.

Electronic countermeasures, like acoustic technology, was one of Tracor's base businesses and provides an example of the way the firm competed in most markets. The overall countermeasures market was estimated at $3.4 billion with competition from many large companies that concentrated on defense for the major portion of their business activity. On the other hand, Tracor's involvement was basically limited to passive countermeasures such as chaff and flare dispensers designed to confuse enemy radar. This market was estimated at only about $80 million in annual sales, yet the aerospace group held a 60 per cent share and had only one major U.S. competitor. From this solid foundation, the aerospace group also entered the active countermeasures market in 1981, which was expected to result in a new line of Tracor products.

Besides the rash of acquisitions that had significantly contributed to growth, the aerospace group had introduced a wide variety of new products. The recently developed computer emulator appeared especially promising because of its potential uses not only in defense-related applications but also in products produced by other company groups. However, the importance of the computer emulator was most notable in the aerospace group as McBee explained:

> We have two other programs to develop the emulator [complementary metal-oxide semiconductor, silicon-on-sapphire-emulator] as a computer substitute in military aircraft. We also have had a great deal of interest in its use from the major aircraft manufacturers. The emulator is radiation hardened and has other features that make it too expensive to be suitable in commercial applications. But it uses very

little power and very little space. Our entry in the market with the first one, we believe, is a real opportunity.[5]

Telecommunications terminals were another relatively new area with exceptional promise. These "intelligent" communications devices were expected to replace existing equipment in U.S. Military and NATO communications systems, and a recent contract with the U.S. Air Force for $35 million made Tracor's fixed station terminals the standard unit for military communication networks. McBee explained: "Another new device is a fixed station terminal with a CRT display, the Model 8000 selected by the Air Force as the standard terminal for all DOD fixed station communications worldwide. The contract was awarded after long protests from Data Products and Honeywell. We look to this area as a great opportunity."[6]

Tracor's aerospace group was not limited in its opportunities to these areas, however. The recently acquired Flight Systems and AeroSpacelines subsidiaries were very competitive in aircraft modification and flight testing of avionic and weapons systems. Several new nondefense contracts had been obtained, and sales of another new product, the "multiple radar emitter simulator," was expected to increase rapidly over the next several years.

Instruments Group

Tracor's instruments group had not performed as well as the applied sciences or aerospace groups over the past year. This group included a wide range of products and divisions shown in Table 4. Management had indicated that analytical instruments, 50 per cent of the group's sales, was the key to Tracor's competitive position in instruments. Tracor held a 60 per cent market share in gas chromatograph detectors. New product introductions in 1981 included Tracor Northern's Spectra-Chrome color video monitor, Austin Instruments' integrated gas chromatograph, Tracor Analytic's new gamma counting system, and Tracor Westronic's new shipboard automatic navigator.

TABLE 4: Instrument Group

Major Products	*Divisions*
Omega & Satellite Navigators	Austin Instruments
Time & Frequency Devices	Tracor Analytic
Audiometers	Tracor Northern
Chromatographs & Detectors	Tracor Westronics
Digital & Nuclear Multi-channel Analyzers	Tracor X-ray
X-ray Analyzers	Tracor Europa B.V.
Diode Array Rapid Scan Spectrometers	
Signal Averagers	
Chart Recorders	
Digital Indicator Systems	
Gamma & Beta Counters	

[5] Ibid.
[6] Ibid.

The recession had done little for the instrument group's sales and profits. Sales in 1981 were nearly flat at $65.7 million while profits declined slightly to $7.1 million. Foreign sales declined 17 per cent in 1981, medical and clinical markets declined 10 per cent, and OMEGA and satellite navigators sales also were down despite Tracor's 20 per cent market share. Despite these results, Tracor added a 140,000 square foot facility in 1981 and, in May 1982, acquired BE Industries to enhance its navigator product line.

In response to the recession's impact, the group introduced product-improvement and cost-reduction programs. The work force was cut from one thousand to nine hundred employees. With strong sales in new products, the group's position was expected to improve slightly in 1982.

Components Group

Tracor's components group produced nearly four thousand different electronic components, most of which sold for prices between $1.50 and $5.00. Sales in this division had remained relatively flat, $73 million in 1981, accounting for about 20 per cent of Tracor's sales. However, profits in 1981 reached $13.2 million, accounting for 31 per cent of Tracor's total profits. The group's product lines and divisions are shown in Table 5.

In describing the component group's business, McBee explained: "We make a wide variety of circuit protection devices for the general electronics area and the automotive industry. These include all kinds of fuses, fuse holders, and switches. One of these is the switch that turns on the light in your refrigerator when you open the door: We have about 95% of that market."[7]

One of Tracor's recent achievements had been the change in its component group's profitability. The group's sales mix had moved out of low-margin business. This shift, shown in Table 6, helps explain why sales were nearly flat between 1979 and 1981, whereas group profits increased from $7.5 million to $13.2 million. A key factor in sales mix had been the group's introduction of the "autofuse" in 1976, the first major innovation in autofuses in sixty years. Chairman McBee explained in 1981: "We introduced 'autofuse' in 1976. Today we are almost completely the sole source of this fuse. Our main competitor in the replacement parts market has never really been able to compete with us in

TABLE 5: Components Group

Products	*Divisions*
Components	Tracor Littlefuse Inc.
General Electronics	Tracor Littlefuse (G.B.) Ltd.
Industrial Electronics	Tracor Littlefuse S.H. de C.V.
Telecommunications	Olvis Smeltzekeringenfabriek B.V.
Automotive OEMs	
Autofuse	
Appliance OEMs	
TV OEMs	
Replacement Parts	

[7] Ibid.

TABLE 6: Component Group Customer Sales

	1979	*1981*
High Margin Business	51.4%	82.5%
• Autofuse		
• Consumer Replacement Parts		
• Industry/Laboratory Electronics		
• Foreign & U.S. Government		
Low Margin Business	48.6%	17.5%
• OEM Automotive Parts		
• OEM TV & Appliance parts		

the OEM market. All new U.S. automobiles are equipped with 'autofuse' fuses as are Japanese and about one-half of all European cars."[8]

With Tracor's control of autofuse sales, the group has been able to also achieve economies in fuse production. McBee described the fuse operations in Illinois: "We have a fully automated, fully integrated factory. About the only raw stocks we buy are plastic molding powders, and strip steel, copper or brass. We do our own slitting, cutting, bending, forming, plating, painting, stuffing and assembly. Autofuses are fabricated at a rate of 200 pieces per minute."[9]

The group also had a strong position with its customers. W. A. Clements, the group's vice-president, explained:

> We are well diversified. We also have 7,000 customers. One of the strengths our group enjoys is an anticipation of the needs of our customers. We know well in advance our customers' production plans from order rates. Our long familiarization with their products allows us to provide the right products at the right time. This knowledge allows us to redirect our production and marketing strategies and to implement internal cost controls."[10]

To strengthen its European position, Tracor recently acquired Olvis, a European fuse maker. New encapsulated color-coded subminiature fuses, Pica II, and a patented Omni-block fuse mounting had also been introduced.

Group Summary

To summarize the recent operations of Tracor's four operating groups, Table 7 shows some of the major contracts and events occurring for each group since August 1979 according to the *TRACOR NEWS*.

TRACOR'S MAJOR MARKETS

Though Tracor's businesses were quite diverse, its major markets were basically limited to defense electronics, analytical instruments, and electronic components. Because of the nature of these markets, Tracor's businesses were generally insu-

[8] Ibid.
[9] Ibid.
[10] Ibid.

TABLE 7: Major Tracor Contracts, Events (1979–1982)

Applied Sciences	
8/7/79	Tracor Receives 19.8 million from HBH Company for engineering support to Royal Saudi Naval Forces Program.
2/11/81	The Naval Sea Systems Command Department of the Navy awards $5.2 million contract to Tracor.
4/15/81	Navy awards Tracor $7.6 million contract.
6/10/81	Tracor Marine awarded $2.5 million Navy contract.
7/6/81	Tracor Marine wins $1.7 million contract.
7/8/81	Tracor acquired Palolab Pharmaceutical Corporation.
7/20/81	Tracor wins $8.3 million four year contract.
9/17/81	Tracor receives Navy communications and navigation contract.
12/7/81	Tracor receives $5.9 million for Navy program.
5/20/82	Tracor to support sonar technology systems under $3.9 million contract from Naval Sea Systems Command
6/7/82	Tracor receives $4.5 million contract from Naval Sea Systems Command
6/22/82	Tracor receives Navy contract to provide technological services for fleet communications systems.
9/14/82	Tracor announces acquisition of Marcon.
Aerospace	
12/31/79	Tracor enters embedded computer market.
1/22/81	Tracor wins $1.2 million contract for major DOD communications program.
2/19/81	Tracor wins USAF Computer Development Award.
5/4/81	Tracor to supply telecommunications terminals to NATO.
5/6/81	Air Force awards Tracor $6.4 million contract.
7/22/81	Tracor awarded $9 million contract for new generation of countermeasures.
7/27/81	Tracor MBA receives $6.7 million contract for electronic countermeasure products.
8/14/81	Tracor acquires Flight Systems.
9/11/81	Tracor completes acquisition of Aero Spacelines, Inc.
10/1/81	Air Virginia's BAC Intercity 748 outfitted by Tracor Aviation.
10/6/81	Tracor receives $1.1 million from India for OMEGA/VLF Systems.
10/20/81	Tracor to supply telecommunications system to SHAPE.
12/8/81	Tracor announces entry into active countermeasures decoy market.
4/26/82	Tracor to supply embedded processors for F-5G radar.
5/11/82	Tracor countermeasures contract with Navy reaches $3.7 million
6/19/82	Tracor's FSI subsidiary receives $6 million contract for B-1B program.
6/10/82	Tracor MBA receives $5.4 million contract for countermeasure expendables.
7/29/82	Tracor receives $5.8 million countermeasures award from Air Force.
8/5/82	Tracor builds data subsystem modules for Project Galileo Spacecraft.
8/5/82	Tracor radiation-hardened emulating computer receives MIL-STD-1750A validation.
8/12/82	Tracor awarded industrial technology modernization contract.
8/19/82	Tracor plans acquisition of SCICOMM.
9/13/82	Tracor receives $31.4 million for two MX missile systems programs.
9/29/82	Tracor MBA awarded 10.4 million plane production contract.
10/1/82	Tracor receives $11 million Air Force contract.
Instruments	
1/23/81	Tracor announces purchase of Data-Design Laboratories product line.
9/29/81	Tracor wins 3rd consecutive IR-100 award.
5/18/82	Tracor completes acquisition of B.E. Industries.
Components	
10/19/81	Tracor purchase of European Olvis Companies expands Tracor Components overseas fuse manufacturing.

lated from economic downturns. The applied sciences and aerospace groups did much of their business with the government and, therefore, were somewhat immune from recession. Over 50 per cent of Tracor's sales were dependent on defense-related business. A significant portion of foreign sales was defense business with NATO customers and U. S. allies. Exhibits 9 and 10 show the dependence of both the Applied Science and Aerospace groups on defense business and related contracts.

However, the components and instruments groups were less protected. The components group's sales moved with business cycles because of dependence of automobile, television, and appliance customers. The instrument group's sales were more closely related to capital spending because of the durable goods nature of their products. Therefore, instrument sales tended to lag economic downturns by about one year.

The Defense Electronics Industry

Though the overall defense market had been paying careful attention to the continual arguments on how to narrow the ever widening federal budget deficit, the fundamental outlook appeared very favorable. Amdec Security's analysts predicted a 15–20 per cent compounded growth rate through the next five years in the defense electronics industry. The real question according to Amdec was

EXHIBIT 9: Total Customer Market Breakdown 1979–1981 (in $ millions)

	1979		*1980*		*1981*	
	$	%	$	%	$	%
Automotive OEM	21.8	8	18.6	6	20.5	5
TV and Appliance OEM	9.2	4	7.7	2	5.9	2
Automotive and TV Replacement Parts	11.7	4	12.9	4	15.1	4
Industrial and Lab Electronics	49.3	19	56.4	18	68.0	18
Foreign Customers	42.5	16	64.7	21	77.8	21
Aviation Products and Services	7.7	3	7.0	2	14.0	4
Marine Services	7.8	3	7.8	2	7.3	2
U.S. Government N-D Systems Hardware	5.0	2	5.3	2	2.9	1
U.S. Government N-D Technical Support	18.1	7	22.9	8	29.9	8
U.S. Government Defense Systems Hardware	28.6	11	38.7	12	49.2	13
U.S. Government Defense Technical Support	58.6	23	71.7	23	80.5	22
TOTAL	260.3	100%	313.7	100%	371.1	100%

Sources: Tracor, Inc., 1979–1981 Annual Reports.

EXHIBIT 10: 1981 Customer Market Breakdown by Group (in $ millions)

	Applied Sciences		*Aerospace*		*Instrument*		*Components*	
	$	%	*$*	%	*$*	%	*$*	%
Automotive OEM							20.5	28
TV and Appliance OEM							5.9	8
Auto and TV Replacement							15.1	21
Ind. and Lab Electronics	2.9	2	3.1	3	39.2	60	22.8	31
Foreign Customers	17.0	13	29.0	27	22.9	35	8.9	12
Aviation P&S			14.0	13				
Marine Services	7.3	6						
U.S. Government N-D Systems Hardware			1.7	2	1.2	2		
U.S. Government N-D Technical Support	29.2	23	0.7	1				
U.S. Government Defense Systems Hardware			46.8	45	2.4	3		
U.S. Government Defense Technical Support	70.7	56	9.8	9				
TOTALS	$127.1	100%	$105.1	100%	$65.7	100%	$73.2	100%

Sources: Tracor, Inc., 1979–1981 Annual Reports.

whether the defense budget would grow as fast as the Reagan administration wanted, or at the more moderate rates proposed by opponents.

At any rate, the defense electronics segment was expected to grow, with its rate depending on the outcome of budget debates. The electronics segment was expected to capture a larger portion of the defense "pie." The United States had realized that the only way to nullify the Soviet Union's numerical superiority was through technological superiority. The fact that Soviet technology was rapidly improving served to magnify the importance of increased emphasis in this area on the part of the United States.

In the future the electronic content of weapons should continue to rise. Furthermore, as new or improved weapons were developed, new countermeasures would also be needed to defend against such devices. For example the Russians had developed twenty-five new radars since 1970 and each one required a different countermeasure system. To a certain degree then, the defense system was becoming more important than the weapons themselves.

The major electronic weapons and systems divided into several areas; smart offensive weapons, active and passive early warning systems, active and passive countermeasures, C^3I systems (command, control, communications, and intelligence), and underwater acoustics. Exhibit 11 provides a forecast for the total DOD budget and defense electronics segment for the years 1982–1991 prepared by the Electronic Industries Association.

The magnitude of growth in the defense electronics industry suggests significant opportunities for new entrants into the market as was common in nonmilitary high technology industries. In defense electronics, however, new competitors rarely appeared. According to Amdec this was largely because of the classified nature of the work and a customer perception that those who have not

EXHIBIT 11: Electronic Industries Association Defense Electronics Market 10-Year Forecast (in billions of dollars)

	DOD Budget		*Total Defense Electronics*		
	1982 $	*Annual Change*	*1982 $*	*Annual Change*	*% Of Electrical Content in DOD Budget*
1982	214.0	10.5%	34.7	18%	23.4%
1983	221.6	3.6%	37.3	7.5%	24.2%
1984	232.4	4.9%	41.1	11%	25.2%
1985	243.4	4.7%	44.6	8.5%	25.9%
1986	253.2	4.0%	47.9	7.4%	26.6%
1987	261.4	3.2%	50.6	5.6%	27.1%
1988	269.0	2.9%	53.7	6.1%	27.8%
1989	274.6	2.1%	55.7	3.7%	28.2%
1990	280.2	2.0%	56.8	5.2%	29.1%
1991	286.0	2.0%	60.6	3.4%	29.5%

Source: "Defense Electronics Market: Ten Year Forecast 1982–1991," *Electronic Industries Association,* October 1981.

done the work before probably could not do it adequately in the future, at least in the short run. Furthermore, unfriendly takeovers in the industry were practically nonexistent. Thus, growth in the defense electronics business should be shared, for the most part, by current industry competitors.

Industry analysts classified defense electronics competitors into six general categories:

1. Major commercial companies with large electronics markets. This group includes companies like IBM, Ford, and Westinghouse.
2. Large aerospace companies, such as Lockheed, McDonnell Douglas, United Technologies, and General Dynamics, all of which have developed an acquired expertise in electronics.
3. Medium-sized companies with a large part of their business in defense electronics. This group includes E-Systems, Loral, Sanders Associates, and Tracor.
4. Smaller, independent public companies, including names such as EDO Corporation, Hazeltine, Sierra Research, and Simmons Precision.
5. A new subgroup is emerging in the form of small companies which have evolved in the past ten years. Some of these have proprietary technology and strong records. Most are privately held, but one which went public recently is Technology for Communications International (TCI).
6. Component and service suppliers including Alpha Industries, Avantek, BDM International, and Narda Microwave.[11]

The Electronic Component Industry

The discussion of the Electronics Component Industry focuses on passive components (capacitors, resistors, coils, and transformers) and components

[11] N. B. Greene, Jr., CFA, "Defense Electronics," Hambrecht and Quist Investment Bankers, June 23, 1982.

classified as neither active nor passive (relays, switches, fuses, connectors, and others) and does not deal with the semiconductor segment of the market.

Passive Components

Passive components had been losing ground to semiconductors in terms of market share since 1975 though factory shipments were $3 billion in 1980, a 17 per cent increase. More modest growth was predicted in the future, however, and competitors had integrated operations or moved into the remaining growth areas such as multilayer ceramic capacitors. Markets such as instruments, automotive, military, and communication seemed to offer the best growth prospects. Price competition was severe and had been affected to some degree by the sluggish economy and softening demand on the part of industrial customers. Major competitors included Sprague (Penn Central Corporation), Kenet (Union Carbide), General Electric, and Matsushita Electric.

Other Components

Relays, switches, and connectors all registered flat sales in 1981. The market had been expected to pick up, but by mid-1982 the economy had shown no signs of a turnaround. The most promising component markets overall appeared to be in data processing and communications markets. The increased pervasiveness of electronic technologies in consumer products could also increase demand for testing equipment by those manufacturers.

The replacement parts segment of the industry offered high margins and good growth potential. In the automotive parts area, for example, demand was increasing as the average age of U.S. cars reached ten years in 1982. The increase in small cars, which operated at higher performance levels and used less expensive, lightweight materials, would also increase frequency of repairs. In addition, more car owners were doing their own repairs.

TRACOR'S FUTURE COMMITMENTS

Within each of the four groups, management had identified six opportunity areas:

Applied Sciences Group:	Technical support for defense and nondefense customers
Aerospace Group:	Military countermeasures and telecommunications
Instruments Group:	Analytical instruments and navigation systems
Components:	Circuit protection.

However, given the size and strength of competitors and the growing intensity of competition, there were still trade-offs to be made between the various product and market commitments.

Applied sciences and aerospace appeared to offer the greatest opportunities, but were limited in profitability. On the other hand, instruments could provide

EXHIBIT 12: R&D Expenditures 1977–1981 (in millions of dollars)

	Company Sponsored	*Customer Sponsored*
1977	3.5	18.1
1978	4.6	18.9
1979	6.1	22.8
1980	7.4	27.0
1981	7.1	35.8

Patents Owned & Pending 1978–1981

	Owned	*Pending*
1978	144	15
1979	143	12
1980	219	14
1981	227	13

Sources: Tracor, Inc., 1978–1981 Annual Reports.

significant opportunities for growth and profits should economic recovery be great. Little new was seen in the components business. Finally, the question of intergroup strategies remained as well as decisions about R&D commitments. As shown in Exhibit 12, in-house R&D expenditures appeared to be leveling off in recent years.

CASE TEN

EG&G, Inc. (A), Condensed

JESSE B. DOUGHERTY and MICHAEL E. PORTER
Harvard University

Assignment Questions:

1. What are the strengths of EG&G's business element planning system? What are its weaknesses?
2. How large can EG&G grow under this system? Can it handle one thousand business elements?

In 1974 EG&G was enjoying success as the manufacturer and marketer of a wide variety of technically oriented products. EG&G's operations were international in scope, and the financial community had recently sized up EG&G's performance very favorably.

> EG&G has reported successively higher quarterly sales and earnings comparisons with year-earlier results throughout the current economic recession. We believe that its energy technology related activities, successful acquisition, and strong financial management capabilities are chiefly responsible for its excellent earnings performance. . . . EG&G is uniquely associated with energy research and development and has a reputation for providing the highest quality products and services in its specialized field. (Merrill Lynch, *Institutional Report.*)

Exhibits 1 and 2 give EG&G's financial history and recent balance sheets and income statements.

BACKGROUND

During the course of America's development of nuclear energy, one of the more formidable problem-solving groups around was a trio of MIT professors named Edgerton, Germeshausen, and Grier. The three worked so well together that in 1947 they decided to form a company, whose name bore their initials, which would serve as a prime contractor to the Atomic Energy Commission and other government agencies in furnishing a variety of scientific and technical services in

EXHIBIT 1: Financial Highlights (as reported)

	Sales as reported ($000)	*Net income (loss) ($000)*	*Income (loss) per share*	*Assets ($000)*	*Shareowners' equity ($000)*	*Common shares outstanding*
1965	$ 51,441	$ 1,542	0.51	$12,884	$ 8,176	3,008,552
1966	64,655	2,012	0.59	16,331	10,148	3,439,978
1967	88,728	2,948	0.71	35,173	16,448	4,190,136
1968	111,628	3,619	0.78	50,327	24,800	4,554,364
1969	119,989	(2,175)	(0.49)	57,542	22,536	4,612,569
1970	112,925	1,009	0.20	52,546	23,084	5,717,712
1971	111,745	2,437	0.51	52,914	25,113	5,746,773
1972	125,387	3,393	0.65	64,580	32,063	5,765,551
1973	137,841	4,519	0.81	69,943	37,516	5,776,044
1974	162,949	5,716	0.97	77,084	44,079	5,781,898

Source: Annual reports.

the electronic and nucleonic fields. From the beginning the company was technically oriented, putting the emphasis on invention and entrepreneurship. During the 1950s revenue came primarily from government contracts. However, under the impetus of Bernard O'Keefe, one of the original employees, it was at this time that EG&G took its first tentative steps toward diversification into the commercial market, attempting at the same time to become more "hardware" than purely service oriented.

The 1960s was a period of success for high-technology firms, and the government continued its heavy demand for EG&G's services. EG&G went public in the early 60s and enjoyed a great reception, with P/Es as high as 100. In 1965 Bernard O'Keefe was made president. At about the same time, the environment

EXHIBIT 2: EG&G Inc. Financial Statements

Condensed Balance Sheets (recast) *Assets*	*1974*	*1973*
Current assets:		
Cash	$ 1,656,000	$ 2,277,000
Short-term investments, at cost which approximates market	8,362,000	8,170,000
Accounts receivable	24,733,000	22,089,000
Contracts in process	1,863,000	1,619,000
Inventories	20,316,000	14,340,000
Prepaid federal income taxes	—	803,000
Other current assets	800,000	474,000
Total current assets	57,730,000	49,772,000
Property, plant, and equipment:		
Land	964,000	776,000
Buildings and leasehold improvements	12,318,000	11,332,000
Machinery and equipment	22,723,000	22,002,000
Total property, plant, and equipment	36,005,000	34,110,000
Less: Accumulated depreciation	20,817,000	19,873,000
Net property, plant, and equipment	15,188,000	14,237,000

EXHIBIT 2: (Continued)

Assests (continued)	*1974*	*1973*
Investments	3,134,000	4,637,000
Other assets	1,032,000	1,144,000
Total assets	$ 77,084,000	$ 69,790,000
Liabilities		
Current liabilities:		
Notes payable and current maturities of long-term debt	$ 1,108,000	$ 1,606,000
Accounts payable	8,311,000	7,591,000
Accrued expenses	8,118,000	7,906,000
Accrued taxes	5,138,000	4,003,000
Total current liabilities	22,675,000	21,106,000
Long-term debt:		
3½ percent convertible, subordinated debentures	6,241,000	6,241,000
Other, less current maturities	3,395,000	3,113,000
Total long-term debt	9,636,000	9,354,000
Deferred federal income taxes	694,000	323,000
Shareowners' investment:		
Preferred stock	22,000	22,000
Common stock	5,792,000	5,783,000
Capital in excess of par value	6,469,000	6,399,000
Retained earnings	31,836,000	26,827,000
Total shareowners' investment	44,119,000	39,031,000
Less: Cost of shares held in treasury	40,000	24,000
Total shareowners' investment	44,079,000	39,007,000
Total liabilities	$ 77,084,000	$ 69,790,000
Consolidated Income Statement		
Net sales and contract revenues	$162,949,000	$143,997,000
Cost and expenses:		
Cost of sales	126,336,000	113,125,000
Selling, general, and administrative expenses	25,675,000	23,136,000
	152,011,000	136,261,000
	10,938,000	7,736,000
Net fee from operating contract	1,233,000	1,176,000
Income from operations	12,171,000	8,912,000
Equity in income of investments	310,000	319,000
Interest expense	(796,000)	(778,000)
Other income (expense), net	(267,000)	(227,000)
Income before income taxes	11,418,000	8,680,000
Provision for federal and foreign income taxes	5,702,000	3,846,000
Net income	$ 5,716,000	$ 4,834,000
Earnings per share	$0.97	$0.82

in which the company operated also began to change. Technology for technology's sake was becoming less sacrosanct, and the federal government began to shift its support from space programs into Viet Nam. O'Keefe decided it was time to take major diversification steps with the equity money then available in order to broaden the still relatively narrow focus of the firm's business. About 20 technically oriented companies were acquired during this period, which more than doubled the business areas in which EG&G was involved. During this period, the management systems used throughout EG&G were financial accounting procedures, which sometimes lacked consistency between business areas, and a periodic companywide forecast of sales and profits. Some of the more commercially oriented divisions were using an early planning system. Until 1969 EG&G returned outstanding financial results, with consistent earnings per share growth of 15+ percent and return on stockholders' equity of 15+ percent.

The year 1969 brought a number of traumas to EG&G. For the first and only time during its existence the company lost money (Exhibit 1) due to large cost overruns on a fixed price government contract. In addition, the stock market was no longer enamoured of high-technology companies, and thus EG&G's stock price, not to mention the value of senior management's accumulated equity holdings, took a nose dive. Several managers referred to this experience as their first realization that EG&G could make mistakes.

Following this experience, which one senior manager referred to as "an identity crisis," control became a popular goal at EG&G. Bernard O'Keefe, in particular, put great stress on planning and the ability to predict problems. He believed that management needed access to information on which to base decisions about which business units to keep in the company and which ones to spin off. The company began to pay attention to limiting the amount of resources tied up in accounts receivable and inventory. EG&G, which had always valued the innovative engineer, began to demand increased management skill as well.

O'Keefe also saw the need for planning throughout the company. The early long-range planning system which had been developed internally over the preceding eight years and used primarily in commercially oriented divisions was modified in order to make it uniform and applicable to all divisions. O'Keefe hired an outsider, Dean Freed, experienced in the use of planning, to take over the operational management of the business. At the same time he hired outside consultants, Arthur D. Little and some academics from the Boston area, to evaluate the company's planning system. Having been reassured that the system was a valid and consistent one, he encouraged operating managers to cooperate with the head of planning, George Gage, implementing the system throughout the company.

During the next two to three years, Freed and Gage worked with the operating managers to implement the system. George Gage said:

> When the planning system was being developed, much of my time was spent working on the system itself. Subsequently, as the system began to mature and stabilize, my time was increasingly spent on selling and applying the system throughout the company. Our experience indicates that about two years are required from the time a system is first introduced in an organization to the time when that organization is producing good plans.

EG&G IN 1974

Although EG&G did sell off some of the acquisitions it had made in the 60s after the loss in 1969, it still produced a wide variety of products and services. By 1974 EG&G provided scientific and technically oriented products, custom equipment, systems and related or specialized services to government and industrial customers. Its products and services were classified into six business areas: components for industrial equipment, scientific instruments, environmental testing systems and services, biomedical services, high-technology systems and services for the federal government, and Energy Research and Development Administration support.

Corporate goals were explicitly stated by top management in the *Planning Manual* developed by George Gage:

> EG&G is a company dedicated to develop and prosper from the commercial, industrial, and government application of technological products and services. Since technological progress and its market acceptance are not always predictable, the company strategy is to diversify its resources into a number of market areas, a variety of products and services, and a judicious blend of mature and emerging industries. Organizationally this translates into a number of self-sufficient divisional profit centers, grouped by market compatibility, with corporate emphasis on performance measurement, planning, and resource allocation. The corporation is thus uniquely qualified to identify and exploit opportunities in products and services for a variety of markets from mature as well as emerging technologies. . . .
>
> The long-term growth goal we have chosen is an appreciation in earnings per share of 15 percent per year while maintaining a minimum annual return of 15 percent on our stockholders' equity. These goals will require performance considerably above average, but are reasonable and achievable with above-average effort.

EG&G tried to meet these goals by participating in a large number of high-technology industrial and government markets. Typically EG&G was, or was striving to be, a leader in its market segments.

The Company Millieu

EG&G's corporate headquarters was in an industrial development in Bedford, Massachusetts, near Route 128. The area contained a great number of other technical firms, and at any given lunch hour a visitor would see groups of employees jogging around the buildings or playing frisbee. EG&G's head office, built in the 1960s, had simple decorations which attempted to alleviate the cinder-block walls.

The company's senior management were located in Bedford (see Exhibit 3 for an organization chart). The president, Bernard J. "Barney" O'Keefe, was a jovial extroverted man involved in many projects outside the company, such as organizing private business in Massachusetts to fund a Chicago consulting firm's study of the management of the Commonwealth of Massachusetts. He was on the board of directors of 11 companies.

Dean Freed, executive vice president in charge of directing all of the corporation's operating divisions and subsidiaries, had an office next to O'Keefe. He had a direct, efficient manner which quickly revealed a very thorough grasp

EXHIBIT 3: Organization Chart

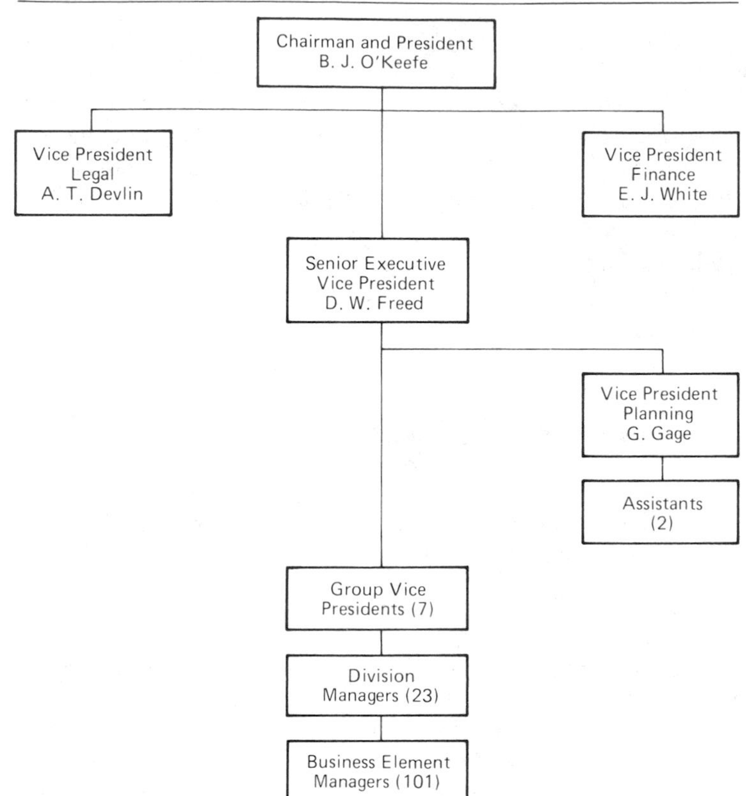

of all that went on in the company. He had joined EG&G in 1970, after having worked as a vice-president responsible for three divisions at Bunker Ramo and holding executive management positions at TRW, Inc., in manufacturing and marketing. He had received a B.S. in mechanical engineering from Swarthmore College and an M.S. from Purdue University. His office was decorated with aerial photographs, and two large battered briefcases were always kept nearby. In describing Freed a colleague said:

> Dean is really a superior manager. He's like a teacher. He knows how to improve an inventory system or marketing program. When he's dealing with other managers he is completely straightforward. He likes people to argue back at him and never bears a grudge against them the next day if they do.

George Gage was vice-president in charge of planning at EG&G and also had an office among the top executives at Bedford. He had joined EG&G in 1962 with the mission "to develop and implement a meaningful planning system to support long-term goals," and had recently been made a vice-president. When Dean Freed joined the firm, Gage switched from reporting to O'Keefe to reporting directly to Freed. Gage had two assistants. Otherwise, Freed and Gage had no staff support.

Many of EG&G's managers were rarely at Bedford since the company's businesses were so geographically dispersed. The company had operations in 20 states and 16 foreign countries. The majority of employees at EG&G had similar backgrounds. When asked about the type of person who worked at EG&G, George Gage said, "Oh, of course, we're all engineers."

Critical to the management process of EG&G was the monthly management meeting. It was held at corporate headquarters in Bedford. The meeting was chaired by O'Keefe and consisted of Freed, the seven group vice-presidents, and senior staff. There was a prescribed agenda which typically consisted of announcements, operations review, investments, acquisitions, and general discussion. O'Keefe used the announcement segment to inform the committee of new ideas he had gained in his travels around the country. A participant described the meeting as the "chief communication vehicle at EG&G."

A major committee within EG&G was the business development committee, which was composed of O'Keefe, Mr. Germeshausen (the retired chairman), Mr. White (vice-president and treasurer), Mr. Wallace (a group vice-president), Gage, and Freed. Mr. O'Keefe and Mr. Germeshausen did not attend all meetings. The major function of this committee was to review the five-year plans of the company's divisions. The reviews took place once a year at the divisional headquarters.

THE PLANNING PROCESS

The planning process at EG&G was divided into two major parts: the five-year plan and the profit plan. The major activities related to the two segments took place at different times of the year. The five-year plan focused on strategy setting. The profit plan was a financially oriented plan covering a 12-month period. Both were described in the EG&G *Planning Manual* which was provided to all managers in both a desk copy and a portable form.

In reflecting on his impression of the planning system, Dean Freed said:

> It is a great advantage for division managers to be given a framework of analysis, a way to test ideas. Basically, we want planning to test whether the things which a division manager wants to do with his assets are *consistent* with the strategy and competitive position of that particular division. In fact, I'd say going through our planning process and getting to fully understand all its implications is a magnificent business school.

Corporate Structure and the Planning Process

The lowest level at which EG&G required strategic planning was the "business element." This was defined as a "business system which involves a single product line or a particular service capability being supplied to satisfy the needs of a single market segment." George Gage brought the idea of business elements to EG&G when he joined the company in 1962. During the intervening years the idea grew from use only in the commercial products divisions to corporate-wide acceptance.

Top management believed that good definition of business elements was important because business elements were homogeneous products or services in a single market segment, and thereby particularly well suited for analysis and forecasting. As one manager put it:

> In many of our businesses EG&G has concentrated on specialized segments which business element managers are able to totally understand. The key is to describe the right battlefield; define the right business element.

EG&G had 101 separate business elements with total sales of $163 million, each the responsibility of a business element manager. These ranged in size from $5 million plus in sales for the largest business element to 23 business elements with less than $500,000 annual sales. In the last two years, EG&G had added 25 new business elements (16 through acquisition and 9 through internal development), divested 4, and discontinued 4 others.

Above the business element level were 27 divisions, each directed by a division manager. The division manager had responsibility for the delineation of business elements in the division and for their profit and loss and return on investment. Division managers were also responsible for developing strategies for their divisions as a whole, as well as being expected to be intimately involved in the development of the strategies of each individual business element within the division.

Divisions were grouped under seven group vice-presidents. These individuals were responsible for the performance of a number of divisions or one particularly large division. They also were part of the corporate administration. One group vice-president described his job as "an extension of Dean Freed." Therefore, the group vice-presidents were both closely involved in the development of strategy while at the same time were responsible for aiding top management in evaluating strategic plans.

In 1974 top management published the *Planning Manual* in a permanent form. Previously, a new planning manual and directions had been prepared every year incorporating the changes which had taken place. Management now felt that the system was sufficiently mature and did not expect any large changes in the future.

The Five-Year Planning Procedure

The first half of each year was dedicated to developing the company's five-year plan. Exhibit 4 presents a graphic representation of the system as well as a timetable for the different steps involved. Basically, the business development committee provided the group vice-presidents with planning guidelines which they in turn modified and cascaded down through division managers to the business elements. Then the business element and division and group managers created their own detailed five-year plans. There was a review by the business development committee of the plans. Finally, the consolidated corporate plan was reviewed by the board of directors.

1. Planning Guidelines. The first step of the five-year planning process took place in January of each year. After reviewing the previous five-year plans, George Gage wrote a preliminary draft of planning guidelines for the group vice-presidents. This draft was submitted to the members of the business development committee who modified it. In Gage's opinion it was Freed who had the major input into the final contents of the planning guidelines. These guidelines were on one-page forms and contained both quantitative and qualitative goals for the groups.

EXHIBIT 4: Five-Year Planning Process

January	Vice president planning and executive vice president review past performance and write new planning guidelines. Send to group vice presidents.
	↓
February	Group vice presidents assess and modify guidelines and set guidelines for divisions.
	↓
March	Division managers receive planning guidelines which they amend and send on to business element managers.
	↓
	Business element managers complete financial forms which result from Form K strategies.
	↓
April	Division managers work with the business element managers to perfect their plans.
	↓
	Group vice presidents work with their divisions on their plans.
	↓
May	Final review meetings are held at division headquarters.
	↓
June	Corporate consolidation of all results.
	↓
	Presentation to the board of directors.

Once the guidelines were received, the group vice-presidents began the cascading process which would eventually create guidelines for each business element based on the corporate guidelines modified by intervening levels of management. Top management expected to have its planning guidelines modified, and Gage described the procedure as "an opportunity to get all the ground rules and assumptions sorted out before the managers began the five-year plan."

Soon after the planning guidelines were received, the business development committee sent out a notice of the date on which each division would be reviewed. Accompanying this notice were any modifications in the planning procedure for that year and occasionally instructions to aid the uniformity of calculation such as foreign currency exchange rates.

The corporate planning staff did not provide the business element managers with any forecasts or environmental assumptions. Freed was skeptical about long-range economic forecasts. "After about one year's time I'd just as soon use astrology." Business element managers were expected to do their own environmental assessments appropriate for their units. "After all," said George Gage, "inflation is good for some of our businesses and bad for others. We don't want to provide our managers with pronouncements which will keep them from analyzing their own situations."

2. Five-Year Plan—The Business Elements. After receiving the division manager's planning guidelines, business element managers set to work developing the information for Form K, the "Long-Range Plan, Business Element Summary" (Exhibit 5). This was the only form which was devoted to strategy itself. The *Planning Manual* described Form K as follows:

EXHIBIT 5: Long-Range Plan: Business Element Summary (Form K)

Long-range plan: Business element summary

1. Product and/or service	2. Customers	3. End use

4. Direct competitors	Sales this market last year (CY)	Market share	5. Competitive advantages	6. Competitive disadvantages
Total direct market	$ K	100%		

7. Market alternatives (competing techniques)

8. Factors affecting future market growth

9. Summary of strategy

TYPE		Build
		Hold
		Harvest
		Withdraw
		Explore
DIRECTION		Base
		Market seg.
		Output diff.
		Market devel.
		Output devel.
POSTURE		Leader
		Me-too
		Performance
		Value
		Price
		Economy
		Prestige
		Quality

10. History/forecast										
Market										
Share of market, percent										
Sales										
Operating profit										

Date ______ ______ ______ ______

Form K (Rev. 1) (Subelement) (Business element) (Division)

The purpose of Form K is to provide a convenient one-page summary of its major strategic factors, a succinct statement of the business strategy, and a forecast of performance expected. The use of Form K greatly facilitates communication and discussion regarding the business element.

Once a business element manager was satisfied with the overall strategy of the element, there were several other forms to be completed in order to express the strategy in financial terms. The first was Form L which is "The Business Element Operating Statement" (Exhibit 6). This was an income statement which isolated certain expense items; the form also required actual results for previous years to be compared with those forecasted. Investment also had its own forms with which the business element manager had to contend. Form C, the "Investment Data" form (Exhibit 7), focused attention on the balance sheet and cash ratios.

3. Five-Year Plan—The Division. Division managers were also responsible for a strategic five-year plan. First, they worked with their business element managers in order to perfect the individual plans. After the division managers were satisfied with these individual plans, they were required to develop five-year plans for their divisions as a whole. Each consisted of (I) divisional goals, (II) divisional strategy, and (III) divisional summaries.

Divisional strategy was to discuss the direction and emphasis for the division as a whole, and provide a summary statement of the Form K for each existing business element and a summary statement of the strategy for any new business development and/or acquisition. The divisional summaries were provided on forms similar to the ones completed by the business elements.

4. Five-Year Plan—Groups. Once the business elements and divisions completed their plans, the group vice-presidents consolidated them. Their job, more than the other two levels, consisted mainly of summing the results of their subordinates. They needed to verify consistency and worked with any of their managers whose plans did not meet expectations. Also, if the overall financial results were inadequate when compared to the expectations of the planning guidelines previously negotiated, the group vice-president would work on improvements both in terms of existing operations and in developing new business ideas. At times group vice-presidents became aware of a weak plan among their elements. Although they would do their best to improve that plan they might well inform the business development committee about the problem in advance of the reviews.

5. Corporate Review. Prior to the corporate review, the business development committee received and reviewed copies of the five-year plan as submitted. The reviews themselves took place at the divisions' own headquarters. Each review considered all the business elements for which the division manager was responsible. Each division was represented by four or five people consisting of the division manager, his principal managers (including the controller), and possibly a divisional staff assistant. Depending on the preferences of the division manager involved and the need to explain a recent change which might be affecting a particular market, there was sometimes a brief presentation. One division manager said he used this presentation as an opportunity to give some visibility to an impressive manager in his division.

The question and answer period which followed was the heart of the review, however. Heated arguments could and often did take place during these. As one group vice-president said:

> The business development committee is sometimes wrong, and specifically, sometimes Dean Freed is wrong. His strength is his ability to comprehend the masses of

EXHIBIT 6: Business Element Operating Statement (Form L)

BUSINESS ELEMENT OPERATION STATEMENT										
Operating statement $000	CY*									
Market										
Share of market, percent										
Bookings										
Sales Cost of sales Gross margin										
Gross margin, percent to sales										
R&D Selling expense Local G&A expense Group G&A expense Corporate G&A expense										
Operating profit										
Operating profit, percent to sales										
SALES DETAIL										

Date ______ Form L	CY ___ sales mix	By type of contract		By geography		By source of funds		
		Cost plus fee	$ ______ 000	U.S.A.	$ ______ 000	Defense	$ ______ 000	______ (Business element)
		Fixed price standard	$ ______ 000	W. Europe	$ ______ 000	Other gov't	$ ______ 000	
		Standard price	$ ______ 000	Rest of world	$ ______ 000	Nongov't	$ ______ 000	______ (Division
		TOTAL	$ ______ 000	TOTAL	$ ______ 000	SUBTOTAL	$ ______ 000	

*CY = Calendar year.

EXHIBIT 7: Investment Data (Form C)

INVESTMENT DATA Investment detail $000	CY*									
1. Accounts receivable										
2. Contracts-in-process										
3. Inventories										
4.										
5. Accounts payable										
6. Accrued (prepaid) expenses										
7. Operating capital (1+2+4-5-6)										
8. Assigned fixed assets at cost										
9. Accum. depreciation, assigned assets										
10. Assigned net fixed assets (8-9)										
11. Allocated fixed assets at cost										
12. Accum. depreciation, allocated assets										
13. Allocated net fixed assets (11-12)										
14. Net other assets (liabilities)										
15. Net investment (7+10+13+14)										
16. Long-term lease commitments										
17. Total investment (15+16)										
CASH FLOW										
18. 0.5 X Operating profit (when negative, use as 1.0 X Operating profit)										
19. Depreciation and amortization										
20. Other sources (uses)										
21. Increase (decrease) in operating capital										
22. Capital additions										
23. Net cash flow (18+19+20-20-21-22)										
SUMMARY										
24. Sales										
25. RONI										
26. ROTI										
27. Operating profit, percent to sales										
28. Operating capital, percent to sales										
29. Net investment, percent to sales										
30. Accounts receivable, DSO										
31. Inventory turnover										

Date ____________ ____________ (Business element) ____________ (Division)

Form C

*CY = Calendar year.

details which make up the operations of this company. But he tends to get fixated on one little point which doesn't fit or bothers him in some way.

Another perspective on Freed at review meetings was:

He's a very involved manager. He likes to understand all the facts of the businesses. And sometimes the operating managers know better than he does. I guess if you had to fault him, it would be that he overmanages. Of course, that's easy to say about anyone until something goes wrong . . . and that doesn't happen very often around here.

The result of the question and answer period was either approval of the plan as presented or a consensus to do the plan again along the lines suggested by the business development committee. Every year there were three or four significant revisions of the 27 divisional plans presented.

The five-year plan was not directly linked with a manager's compensation. It did come into consideration when a manager was being considered for advancement. Although EG&G had a personnel department, it was Dean Freed and the group vice-presidents who made decisions about managers advancing to the division level.

A couple of division managers had been removed for not being able to come to grips with the planning expectations at EG&G. Dean Freed reflected on the seriousness with which the inability to plan strategically was viewed:

> It is a serious problem if a division manager has one business element whose five-year plan is not rigorous and consistent. If succeeding five-year plans exhibited the same problems, that division manager's career is in trouble. After all, if it's easy for me to see the fallacy of the strategy in the time I spend studying the plan, why didn't the manager?

When the committee was at a location evaluating a plan, they started by trying to understand the market involved, as described in Form K. From an understanding of the market, the committee then tried to evaluate whether the strategy was consistent with that market. Freed said, "If a business element has had 5 percent of a market and forecasted that it would have 30 percent of the market in five years, they need a more creative strategy than 'trying harder'." Once the business development committee approved a business element and division plan, the division and business element managers were finished with the formal preparation of the five-year plan for that year.

Although the planning process involved a great deal of time and effort on the part of EG&G managers, they seemed to appreciate the information it provided. One division manager said:

> It really takes a lot of work to complete the requirements, but once you learn the system with the aid of George Gage it becomes an extremely useful management aid. All the other managers have the same frame of reference so it makes communication easier. It's important to be forced to take a long look at what you're trying to do rather than constantly dealing with the day-to-day problems. Without the requirement I know I would postpone it in favor of the operating problems at hand. Beyond that, it is a great reference during the year with which to judge your progress.

6. Consolidation and Presentation to the Board. After careful review of the divisional five-year plans, Gage and Freed were chiefly responsible for producing the forecasts of sales and earnings on which corporate-wide planning was based. Bernard O'Keefe used these forecasts as part of his presentation to the board of directors of the consolidated five-year plans. Top management expected financial results to vary from forecast due to unforeseen and uncontrollable events, but EG&G had an excellent record in forecasting the performance of its ongoing businesses. The board had never rejected a corporate five-year plan but did offer suggestions, such as an adjustment in the procedure for treating inflation, which were used in planning the following year.

The Profit Plan (the One-Year Plan)

The annual profit plan was prepared in the fall of the year in the context of the five-year plan. Business element managers, division managers, and group vice-presidents were all required to prepare yearly profit plans. It was the ability of the managers to meet the yearly profit plan which was tied directly to a manager's compensation. If managers met their profit plans, they received a bonus. if they did better than their plan, they received a higher bonus, but one which was lower than if they had accurately forecasted the superior performance. At the division level approximately 10–20 percent of a manager's salary was variable depending on performance versus plan. Just how the allocation was made varied among divisions depending on the nature of the risk involved and the amount of flexibility available to the manager.

The profit plan was the basis for operations management and control of the business in the next 12-month period. Like the five-year plan, the one-year plan was reviewed by a group of senior corporate executives. In this case it consisted of Freed, Gage, Jack Dolan (the corporate controller),and the applicable group executive. The coordination of business strategy and financial control was achieved through these meetings and the one-year plan.

The Monthly Management Meeting

Each month at the management meeting, group vice-presidents had to present their division's monthly financial reports which consisted of bookings, sales, operating profit, and operating capital. Each group vice-president had the opportunity to fill in the narrative behind the cold financial results, and acquisitions and future acquisition candidates were also discussed as well as any new business ideas. Participants felt that the informality of this meeting led to a high degree of candor.

At approximately the same time as the management meetings were held, Dean Freed met individually with each group vice-president in order to review the financial results of the divisions. During the meeting the two discussed anything of interest which was happening in the divisions. Freed said:

> During these meetings I insist on discussing strategic issues. I am just not interested in the operating problems of the divisions. They can solve them better than I can. What I want to hear about is new ideas, staffing requirements, and potential problems.

Divisions and groups prepared monthly financial results which they were able to use in judging their performances. Although the division managers had complete discretion in the management of their divisions, many of them employed a monthly meeting format, analogous to the corporate one, in order to meet with their business element managers and discuss problems or new ideas in light of the data contained in the financial results.

Planning and Innovative Strategy for the Corporation

George Gage commented on the interaction of planning and innovation:

> Our planning system does an effective job of controlling and measuring our base operations. It even provides our managers with uniform methods of evaluating new business development. However, eliciting bright new ideas is beyond the scope of our system. Naturally in a firm like ours innovation and new business development are vital. At the very least, I hope the planning system doesn't stifle new ideas.

The compilation of element and division five-year plans identified needs of the corporation relative to its goals but did not generate innovative ideas. Many ideas for new business directions came from the business element level. There seemed to be a corporatewide belief in the ability of all managers to provide a creative input. For example, the divisional five-year plan asked for new business development ideas as the third section of its "strategy" requirement. One senior manager said, "There aren't many cases where the headquarters has been the source of creativity in terms of new products."

Top management, particularly Bernard O'Keefe and Dean Freed, did address the problem of corporatewide strategy. They held meetings from time to time specifically addressing the overall strategy of the company. In years past, EG&G had held retreat meetings in hopes that a new physical surrounding might elicit new perspectives. They were abandoned as not useful. Dean Freed felt that EG&G had less of a problem than some single-product, single-market companies in maintaining an unbiased perspective on the corporation's future. He said, "Heterogeneity is a great aid in avoiding irrational, emotional attachments to a particular strategy."

While recognizing the benefits of planning, not the least of which was a comparable basis for defending requests for capital, several managers expressed concern about continuing innovation. One group vice-president said, "Really good ideas are thought of in unorthodox ways, and planning imposes an orthodox system." He went on to speculate about the possible disincentives imposed on creativity by such an exhaustive planning system. "Innovative ideas can be successfully subjected to planning, but there's always a risk of their being stifled."

CASE ELEVEN

EG&G, Inc. (B)

JESSE B. DOUGHERTY and MICHAEL E. PORTER
Harvard University

Assignment Questions:

1. What should Dean Freed do about the Electro-Mechanical Division?
2. How should Dean Freed handle the strategy review meeting?

In May 1974 Dean Freed, executive vice-president of EG&G, wondered what he would do at the review meeting for the electro-mechanical division (EMD), scheduled for the following week. The division's previous year's results were disappointing, but division management expressed in their recently submitted 1974 five-year plan the belief that the situation could be turned around.

BACKGROUND

In the 1960s EG&G developed a new technology involving ceramic to metal seals. Management felt there was a good opportunity to exploit the new technology in connectors for electric cables. When two types of cables needed to be joined, connectors were clamped onto each end and these were fastened using mechanisms of varying complexity. The higher the frequency or voltage to be transferred, the more complex was the required connector. Depending on their complexity, connectors could cost from 5 cents to $5 or more. Higher technology, higher priced connectors were manufactured in the United States, while low-cost connectors were increasingly being manufactured abroad.

EG&G had a specific application for their new connector in the defense work they were then doing for the U.S. government's Sandia missile program. The high-technology connector was able to eliminate radio interference which affected the guidance of missiles in enemy territory. In order to be able to take advantage of the expected demand in the Sandia missile program, EG&G began to look for the best way to gain knowledge of the market and to develop the manufacturing capability necessary to produce this new connector.

The Strode Company, a small firm located in Franklin, Massachusetts, was brought to their attention. Strode was a manufacturer of standard technology connectors, had not been particularly successful, and was known to be available for sale. EG&G's management felt that the fixed costs of Strode's operation could be supported by EG&G's proprietary defense business. To this base EG&G's management hoped to enter other specialty markets in which their technological advantage could be exploited. In this way, EG&G planned to avoid Strode's competitive disadvantages in competing head to head with commodity producers who could manufacture connectors at lower costs because they produced and sold much greater standard volumes. However, the addition of specialty work to Strode's line would require the hiring of more engineers to do the designing and more highly skilled workers to produce the more varied products. EG&G acquired Strode in 1969, and it became the electro-mechanical division with all operations continuing in its existing facilities.

Strode's base businesses consisted of miniature, coaxial cable connectors for microwave applications and radio frequency (RF) applications. Coaxial cables were composed of a tube of electrically conducting material surrounding a central conductor held in place by insulators. They were used to transmit signals of high frequency. About one half of Strode's sales was in standardized connectors, the other half was in connectors for specialty applications.

The manufacturing process was straightforward and required only general-purpose machinery, though highly skilled machinists were necessary for some operations. Even experienced machinists, who were themselves in short supply, required about three months of training before they were competent to produce the new EG&G connector.

EMD was at a great cost disadvantage in the sale of standardized parts in comparison with its chief competitor, Amphenol Corporation, which controlled 25+ percent of the market. Strode's specialized work had greater profit potential, but this had not yet been realized because of problems with cost control and a small potential market. In an attempt to cover fixed costs, Strode produced standardized connectors in order to keep manufacturing at capacity despite the very low margins on these standardized items.

Freed remembered how Jim Sheets, the division manager, had been a driving force behind acquiring EMD. Sheets had been with EG&G for 15 years, and had had an outstanding record of achievement. As the manager of a highly successful business element, he had brought in a remarkable 10 percent of the corporation's profit in one year. Therefore, when Sheets began promoting the idea of a new division to exploit the ceramic to metal seal technology, Freed felt he had to be taken seriously. Sheets was familiar with the technology since it had been developed in his previous division. He had proven himself as a business element manager, and had earned, by part-time study, his MBA in 1968. There had been a general consensus among management that promoting Jim Sheets to division manager was a fitting reward for one of the company's outstanding young executives. EMD was placed in the technical products group under the direction of group VP Joe Giuffrida. The group consisted of six other divisions and 37 other business elements.

It was not long after its founding that EMD ran into its first problems. By early 1970 it became clear to the management of the EMD that the defense market for connectors which EG&G had planned on would not develop due to defense budget cuts. The business development committee, group management, and the management of the EMD jointly searched for other markets in which their new technology might be applicable and profitable. It was decided to explore the possibility of selling the high-quality connector as a component to the cable television industry.

CABLE TELEVISION

Cable television was a system for carrying television signals by wire rather than transmitting them through the air. It produced better reception and, in some cases, more channels. The wire used was a coaxial cable that could carry many different channels simultaneously. A typical cable system consisted of a television antenna placed in a location with good reception such as a high hill. The signal was then fed by cable to a "headend" which amplified the signal for the system's distribution cables which consisted of "trunk" cables which extended from the "headend," "feeder" cables which were along individual streets, and "drop" cables which went into subscribers' homes (Exhibit 1). EMD proposed to capitalize on the growth in this market by providing connectors between trunk and feed line cables. The connector market was primarily a new rather than replacement market. Each connector was designed to have a longer life than the system in which it was placed.

EXHIBIT 1: Diagram of Cable System

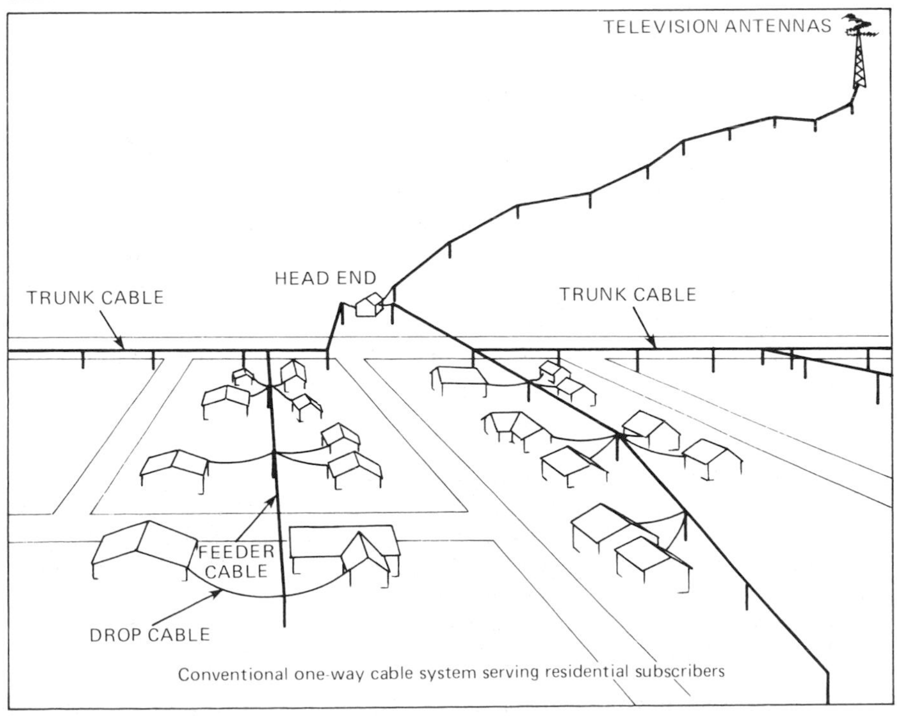

Source: The Rand Corporation.

Jim Sheets realized that there was no one in EG&G who was knowledgeable enough about the cable television industry to manage such a business element. Therefore, in a departure from usual EG&G procedure of advancement from within, an outside talent search was made in order to find a suitable business element manager. The search produced Mike Killion, who had a considerable track record as a marketer in the cable television industry having worked in sales for Jerrold, the leading cable television equipment producer. Killion was no longer with Jerrold and was working in sales at an electronics firm in Lawrence, Massachusetts. Killion expressed an interest in returning to the CATV business. He was impressed with EG&G's product and its prospects in the industry, and was able to communicate his enthusiasm and experience to Sheets and Giuffrida who decided to hire him after a joint interview.

Having hired Killion, EMD management looked forward with excitement to its participation in the CATV industry. In the past 15 years cable television had grown at a compound annual rate of over 20 percent. By 1970 cable television reached 7 percent of American households, and the industry had grown to a total of $500 million in annual revenue. Killion conducted extensive surveys and research in order to discover what qualities in connectors were valued by CATV builders so that EG&G's product would have distinctive features separating it from competitors.

The Rand Corporation, in a 1971 study of the cable television industry, predicted high growth for cable over the next two decades (Exhibit 2). *Barron's* said in 1971, "past success is dwarfed by future potential in the cable television industry," and predicted a total CATV market of $2.4 billion by 1980. One of the changes which led *Barron's* to predict such high growth was particularly interesting to EG&G. Before 1972, CATV was not allowed in major metropolitan areas by the Federal Communications Commission. By mid-1971 the FCC's new chairman, Dean Burch, let it be known that cable television would be allowed in cities. EG&G's connector had the distinguishing characteristic of being the best cable connector on the market for eliminating interference. This was a greater problem in urban than rural areas, and therefore EMD felt its product had a distinct advantage in the growth era ahead.

In the 1972 five-year plan, EMD expressed its strategy as one of improving margins in the base connector business by emphasizing specialty rather than standard products and by improving manufacturing techniques. EMD had reduced dependence on government contracts and wanted to maintain over 50 percent of their income in the commercial rather than government sector.

The 1972 plan went on to be more specific about the EMD's strategy for commercial business:

> The commercial business segment of the division business will include some share of the nonmilitary communications and instrument microwave markets. The major emphasis, however, will be directed at specific and concerted entry into the newly energized CATV connector market. The business in two facets, equipment manufacturers and cable distribution operators, has the proper size and growth potential to limit competition in number and size, but still be an attractive opportunity for the division.

Freed recalled that the move into CATV was seen as an entrance into a young, dynamic market with important future growth potential. See Exhibit 3

EXHIBIT 2: Growth of Cable Television

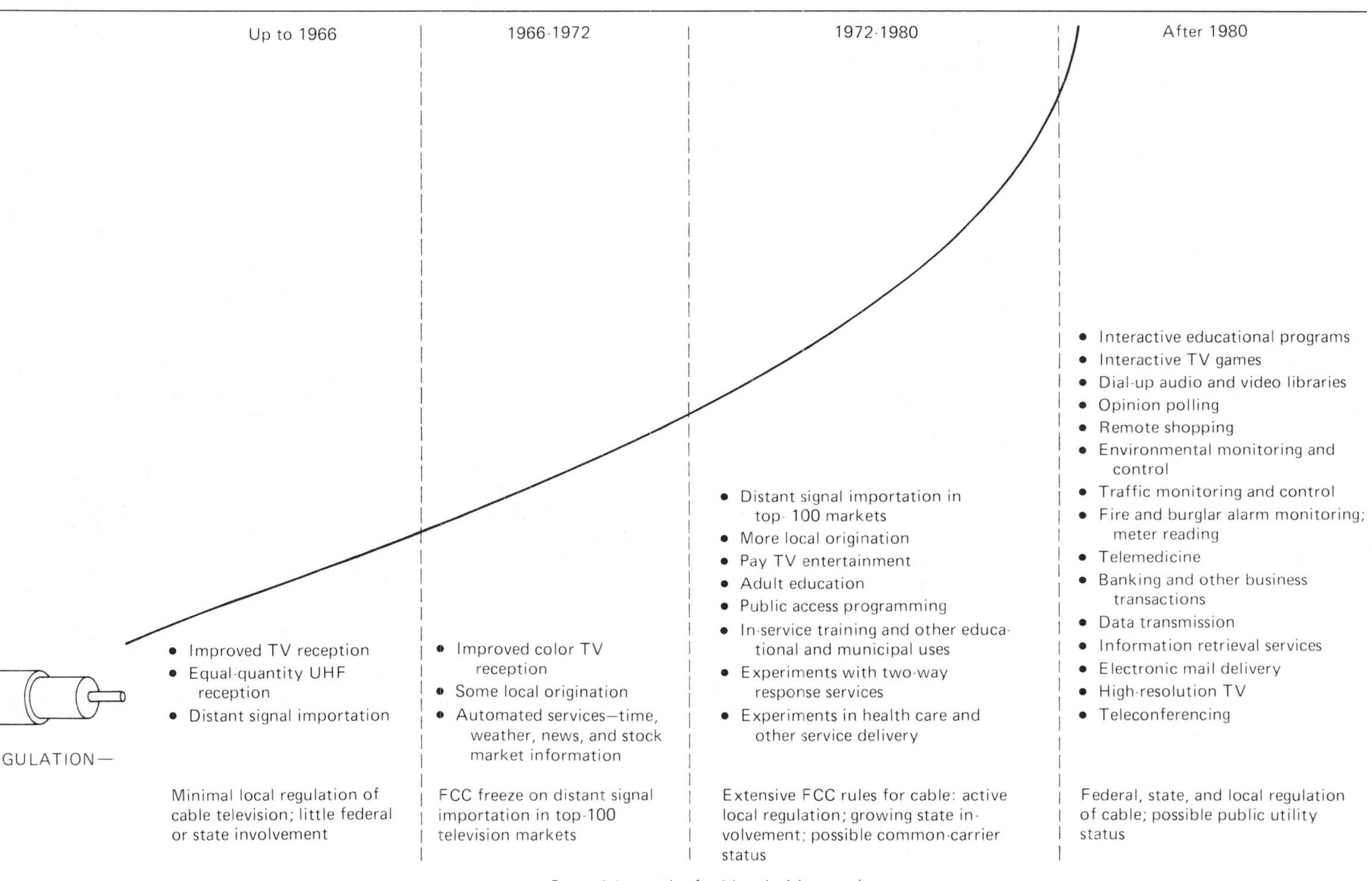
Up to 1966
1966-1972
1972-1980
After 1980
• Improved TV reception
• Equal-quantity UHF reception
• Distant signal importation
• Improved color TV reception
• Some local origination
• Automated services—time, weather, news, and stock market information
• Distant signal importation in top-100 markets
• More local origination
• Pay TV entertainment
• Adult education
• Public access programming
• In-service training and other educational and municipal uses
• Experiments with two-way response services
• Experiments in health care and other service delivery
• Interactive educational programs
• Interactive TV games
• Dial-up audio and video libraries
• Opinion polling
• Remote shopping
• Environmental monitoring and control
• Traffic monitoring and control
• Fire and burglar alarm monitoring; meter reading
• Telemedicine
• Banking and other business transactions
• Data transmission
• Information retrieval services
• Electronic mail delivery
• High-resolution TV
• Teleconferencing
REGULATION—
Minimal local regulation of cable television; little federal or state involvement
FCC freeze on distant signal importation in top-100 television markets
Extensive FCC rules for cable: active local regulation; growing state involvement; possible common-carrier status
Federal, state, and local regulation of cable; possible public utility status
—Potential growth of cable television services

EXHIBIT 3: EMD Strategy for Entry into the CATV Connector Industry—April 1972

CATV Connector

STRATEGIC ROLE

The strategic role of the CATV connector business element is to provide (1) divisional growth; (2) better balance between government and commercial funding sources in the electro-mechanical division and marketing mix, and (3) entrance into a young, dynamic market with important future growth potential.

STRATEGY

It is a major division goal to establish a significant (30 per cent) and ultimately leading market position in the specific area of outdoor connectors for aluminum sheath trunk and feed line distribution cable, capitalizing on the impending new growth predicted for the purely commercial CATV market. It will not be practical to establish the degree (percent) nor the timing for success until we are two or three years into the program. The necessary market penetration will be obtained by (1) exploiting an existing, unstable management situation of the present industry leader (Gilbert Electronics, a Transitron subsidiary); (2) exploiting existing EG&G-Startronics expertise in connector design and high-volume, reproducible manufacture; (3) concentration of prime sales efforts among the top 50 multiconstruction contractors; and (4) taking advantage of 17 years of personal contact and sales experience with many of the key principals among the largest MSO's and equipment manufacturers.

MARKET

Newly revised (March 31, 1972) FCC regulations governing the reuse, through cable distribution, of television signals in high-density population area (top 100 markets) have motivated a formerly dormant cable television equipment and construction industry to substantially increased activity. The resulting market for outdoor connectors estimated at $4 million level in 1971 is expected to reach the $8 million level by 1976. The new FCC regulations for the high-density markets require two-way capability. Because of these factors, in addition to the pure entertainment facet of cable distribution networks, the potential for use as a special purpose two-way communication link between subscribers and vendor/service organizations should realize a sustained high rate of new construction for the industry well beyond the time period of this business plan. Indeed, the industry which originally called itself Community Antenna Television, outgrew that small town image of itself and become Cable Television and now, with the local program organization and the exciting new two-way facilities, considers itself in the broadband communications business. At present only about 8 per cent of the 60 million TV homes in the United States are connected to a CATV system.

CUSTOMER GROUPS

The cable television customer groups can be viewed in the following segments: (1) multiple-systems operators (TelePrompTer), (2) equipment manufacturers (Jerrold), (3) construction contractors (Burnup & Sims), (4) single-system operators, and (5) distributors (Anixter-Pruzan). The current business plan is to concentrate on the 50 largest multiple system operator (MSO), 12 largest equipment manufacturer (OEM), and 20 construction contractor organizations for new/replacement business as appropriate. In the initial stages, all sales effort will be from the business element manager.

COMPETITION

The weatherproof, radiationproof aluminum connectors used in overhead and underground CATV distribution services are within the current technical and production capabilities of the electro-mechanical division. Current suppliers are Gilbert-Transitron (58 per cent of the market) and a number of smaller firms with comparably smaller market shares. These include Craftsman-Magnavox (11 per cent), LRC (11 per cent), Communication Dynamics (9 per cent), ITT Gremar Canada (6 per cent), and others (5 per cent).

The Gilbert-Transitron relationship is strained and unstable. The founder, Gilbert, who until recently directly controlled the operations of the company is no longer on the scene. Transitron is not noted for management prowess nor stability. Magnavox Craftsman and Communication Dynamics are not solely dedicated to the outdoor connector market as this is only a portion of their overall business. ITT Gremar (Canada) is hampered in the U.S. market by duties and customs-clearance problems resulting in slower response. LRC is a very small company in a remote location with limited expertise and resources.

The timing for immediate market entry seems particularly appropriate. A line of five types in each of four cable sizes is adequate.

Source: Company records.

for the unusually detailed strategy statement which EMD submitted in the 1972 five-year plan. Freed also reviewed the planning forms which EMD had completed in 1972. Two of these which were of particular interest to him are included in Exhibit 4: the business element strategy (Form K) for the CATV element and the division operating statement (Form B).

He also reviewed the Form Ks for the two other business elements in the division, "special seal and microwave devices" and "the RF connectors," both of which showed serious problems in 1972. The special seal and microwave devices were being sold mainly to Sandia as a method of eliminating radio interference. However, this limited the business element to one customer, the federal government, whose funds for and interest in such technology were being curtailed. The "summary of strategy" emphasized the need for "new product or new market activity." The RF connector also had serious problems. EG&G had a small market share, 7 percent, and ranked seventh in the market. Although EG&G had the advantage of a reputation for quality in the field, there was not enough demand for that quality to cover the fixed costs of the operation. EG&G was at a cost disadvantage to the larger producers when it came to standardized parts. EMD's "summary of strategy" discussed the need to develop better "linear programming techniques for production control, regulate operation, and business mix to optimize profit margin and growth." Sales to government contractors made up 94 percent of the RF connectors' sales.

At the first review session of a five-year plan for the new CATV business element, Freed recalled that Mike Killion had put on an impressive performance. He demonstrated a full grasp of the relationships among main actors within the cable television industry. He explained how the critical factor in selling connectors was the manufacturer's relationship with the distributors. CATV system installers were usually independent local contractors. They purchased their supplies from distributors who were organized in a number of layers. A key success

EXHIBIT 4: 1972 Form K—CATV Business Element

LONG-RANGE PLAN: BUSINESS ELEMENT SUMMARY

1. Product and/or service

CATV weather proof connectors for outdoor service in overhead and underground distribution installations

2. Customers

Multiple-system operators (50 largest)
Distribution equipment mfgs. (12-16 largest)
Construction contractors (20 major)

3. End use

CATV distribution cable interconnection devices for entertainment and broadband communications

4.

Direct competitors	*CY71 sales this market*	*Market share*
Gilbert (Transitron)	$2,500	58%
Craftsman (Magnavox)	500	11
LRC	500	11
ITT Gremar (Canada)	250	6
Communications Dynamics	400	9
Others	150	5
Note: Figures refer to noncaptive market. Jerrold & Vikoa (OEM's) make selected types for system use.		
Total direct market	$4,300,000	100%

5. Competitive advantages

Connector manufacturing expertise
Management stability
Dominant competitor in management difficulty
Other suppliers (small/distant)
Financial and technical resources for potential expansion

6. Competitive disadvantages

Lack of image and tangible experience in CATV market segments
Significant portion of components supplied in house by equipment OEMs

7. Factors affecting future market growth

Freedom from FCC restraints for entertainment rebroadcast
Deployment and utilization of two way, multichannel cable networks for nonentertainment uses
Average market growth rate, next 5 years: 15% per year

8. Competing techniques

Microwave relay links (Theta Comm) for municipal areas
Satellite communications

8. CY71 sales mix by

AEC & DOD	____%	CPFF	____%
Other gov't	____%	Fixed price	____%
Commercial	100 %	Std. prod.	100 %
Foreign	____%	Std. serv.	____%
Total	100 %	Total	100 %

10. Summary of strategy—Establish a significant market position in the CATV connector business: exploiting the following aspects:

1. New market growth for CATV as a result of FCC revision of rebroadcast regulations.
2. Unstable management position of industry leader, Gilbert, as part of Transitron and in the absence of the founder.
3. EG&G expertise in connector design and reproducible manufacture.

Date May 1972
Form K (72)

CATV Connector Business Element
Electro-Mechanical Division

Note: Form K varied slightly in its format from 1972 to 1974.

EXHIBIT 4: (continued) EMD Form B—Operating Statement, 1972

CY 1972-1976 PLAN: OPERATING STATEMENT	Actual					Forecast				
OPERATING STATEMENT $000	CY67	CY68	CY69	CY70	CY71	CY72	CY73	CY74	CY75	CY76
Sales	70	252	2,340	1,710	1,765	2,000	2,626	3,200	3,900	4,800
Cost of Sales	66	240	2,111	1,652	1,523	1,549	1,957	2,263	2,738	3,362
Gross margin	4	12	229	58	242	451	668	937	1,162	1,438
Gross margin, percent to sales	6	5	10	3	14	23	25	29	30	30
R&D	–	–	–	–	–	–	15	40	60	60
Selling expense	–	–	142	143	127	150	208	268	325	452
G&A (Noncorporate) expense	*	*	*	*	103	109	143	170	228	270
Other income (expense)					(6)	(17)	(23)	(28)	(35)	(45)
Corporate G&A expense	*	*	*	*	45	50	74	91	114	136
Operating profit, before taxes	4	12	87	(85)	(39)	125	205	340	400	475
Operating profit, percent to sales	6	5	4			6	8	11	10	10
SALES/OPERATING PROFIT BEFORE TAXES, BY BUSINESS ELEMENT						(*included in cost of sales)				
Sp. seal and microwave devices	70/4	252/12	328/21	392/17	416/42	350/32	375/42	400/53	435/58	475/66
RF connector			2,012/66	1,318/(102)	1,349/(81	1,650/93	1,900/113	2,000/130	2,000/162	2,000/167
CATV connector						–/–	350/50	800/157	1,465/180	2,325/242
Total sales/operating profit	70/4	252/12	2,340/87	1,710/(85)	1,765/(39)	2,000/125	2,625/205	3,200/340	3,900/400	4,800/475

Date May 1972
Form B (72)

Electro-Mechanical
(Division)

factor for a producer of CATV equipment was to establish a good relationship with a national distributor who in turn had contacts in all regions. Killion had conducted conversations with a number of major distributors and had reported that they all perceived the unique advantages of EG&G's connector and looked forward to selling it. Killion developed sales forecasts for the connector, designed a sales brochure, established sales representatives around the country, and helped work on engineering problems. In fact, Killion's performance was so impressive that the business development committee selected the CATV connector business element as one of its top five growth prospects for the 1972–77 period.

In the 1973 plan, the division once again submitted its optimistic projections about the opportunities for CATV:

> The electro-mechanical division strategy relates to a vigorous "build" role with special emphasis on the commercial business opportunity which is now posed by accelerated growth in the cable television industry. The market situation seems unique in terms of timing, demand, relative competitive weakness and close relation of expertise and facilities necessary to produce connectors for CATV and the microwave business.

The division also returned improved financial results in 1972 (Exhibit 5).

Due to its poor financial performance, the business development committee at EG&G studied the RF connector business of the electro-mechanical division in February 1973. The committee, with the assent of EMD management, decided that the RF connectors had to be phased out, since the product seemed to lack any real profit potential. It was felt that the CATV business would take up the slack. The business development committee stated in its 1973 planning guidelines, "The RF connector business element should go to 'Harvest' strategy, phasing down as CATV builds."

There were encouraging signs as 1973 proceeded. One of the objectives which the CATV element planned to achieve was to give the Gilbert Company, the number one supplier of connectors to the CATV market, some strong competition. Mike Killion was very optimistic about EG&G's ability to gain on Gilbert. Gilbert was having difficulty getting proper financing from its parent company, and Gilbert's main strength, its relationships with its distributors, also seemed to be deteriorating. When Killion was able to establish an exclusive distribution arrangement with Anixter/Pruzan, who had previously been the distributor for Gilbert, the division felt it was advancing according to plan. Anixter/Pruzan's initial order was for $300,000 worth of connectors at a time when EMD was carrying no inventory and EMD's previous orders had been about one tenth of that size. Also, improvements in manufacturing were enhancing the quality of the product.

Some of the interim financial results returned in 1973 were disappointing, however. Freed noticed that the CATV element was not making the sales or returning the profit that had been expected. Freed had also read that urban installation of cable systems was turning out to be more costly than expected but was not sure what impact this would have on the connector business. Financing was becoming increasingly hard to come by and expensive, and a recession had slowed economic growth. This squeeze caused those involved in CATV construction who had limited access to capital to buy their equipment from low-

EXHIBIT 5: EMD Form B—Operating Statement, 1973

	Actual				Forecast				
CY 1973-1977 PLAN: OPERATING STATEMENT									
OPERATING STATEMENT $000	CY69	CY70	CY71	CY72	CY73	CY74	CY75	CY76	CY77
Sales	2,340	1,710	1,765	1,887	2,480	3,150	4,000	5,100	6,050
Cost of sales	2,111	1,652	1,523	1,471	1,840	2,310	2,870	3,720	4,420
Gross margin	229	58	242	416	640	840	1,130	1,380	1,630
Gross margin, percent to sales	10	3	14	22	26	27	28	27	27
R&D	–	–	–	–	–	–	–	–	–
Selling expense	142	143	127	135	219	300	430	520	585
G&A (Noncorporate)	*	*	103	106	117	155	182	210	265
Other income (expense)	–	–	(6)	10	36	25	40	50	60
Corporate G&A	*	*	45	40	68	80	98	115	145
Operating profit, before taxes	87	(85)	(39)	125	205	280	380	485	575
Operating profit, percent to sales	4	(6)	(2)	7	8	9	10	10	10
SALES/OPERATING PROFIT BEFORE TAXES, BY BUSINESS ELEMENT									
CATV connector	–/–	–/–	–/–	–/–	600/100	1,200/150	2,000/300	2,800/300	3,600/375
RF connector	2,012/21	1,318/(102)	1,349/(81)	1,508/72	1,600/65	1,750/100	1,900/135	2,150/160	2,300/175
Sp. seal and microwave devices	328/21	392/17	416/42	379/53	280/40	200/20	100/20	150/25	150/25
Total sales/operating profit	2,340/87	1,710/(85)	1,765/(39)	1,887/125	2,480/205	3,150/280	4,000/380	5,100/485	6,050/575

Date April 1973
Form B(73)

Electro-Mechanical
Division

cost suppliers. Price cutting began to take place among suppliers of CATV components. Freed knew EMD could not compete for long on price, but he felt it was difficult to judge the danger of price cutting since EG&G's other high-quality products had tended to be immune to price cutting. When questioned about the financial results, Jim Sheets showed concern over them but insisted that headquarters was acting impatiently. Mike Killion continued to be extremely optimistic about the future of EG&G in the CATV connector market. He said at the profit plan review in 1973:

> All the clients I talk to say we have the best connector in the industry. After all, we just signed on with Anixter/Pruzan. Give us a chance to get that operation going. Gilbert is crumbling, and we are going to be the ones to take up the slack. We are now suffering from a cyclical problem of distribution, but it should be straightened out in nine months to a year. The quality which we build into our connector is very desirable in this business, but at times the higher price will temporarily cut into our sales volume.

Joe Giuffrida, the group vice-president, was sympathetic to the arguments of his two managers and felt they should be given more time to be allowed to prove themselves.

It was in this context that Freed received the results for 1973 and the next five-year plan from EMD. The financial results for 1973 were disappointing (Exhibit 6). Instead of making $100,000 in the CATV market, the division lost $98,000 in 1973.

When Freed reviewed the Form Ks for the two government-oriented connector business elements, he saw a deteriorating situation. The Form K for the "special hardware" connector forecasted a decrease in its already small sales and listed no market alternatives. It had the disadvantage of being more expensive than competitors' products, and thus saw little hope of expanding out of the specialty market, which while being profitable was just too small. The RF connector had slipped from 7 percent of the market to 3 percent and now was ranked 10th in terms of market share among the competitors. Freed also noted that lack of modern equipment was still a problem and that manufacturing costs in RF connectors were high relative to competitors. He was encouraged by the element's forecasted growth in sales and slight improvement in forecasted earnings, although he was not sure if the strategy summary for RF connectors could support such optimism:

> Continue responsive effort to build selective share of near standard connector business. Expand scope of coverage to increase marketing emphasis on individual OEM accounts served by the largest of the small competitors, nationwide. Concentrate on profitable near standard business opportunities and new client conversion list—exploiting long-term former customer relationships and organizational flexibility to provide responsive customer service and cost effective product. (Form K, 1974.)

However, CATV was the business element from which future growth was planned, and Freed wanted to review their Form K (Exhibit 7) at length. He also reviewed Form C (Exhibit 8) which highlighted the investment EG&G had in the entire EMD.

Freed tried to order his thoughts about the upcoming meeting with the EMD. EMD was not performing up to the level of EG&G's goals, and he knew

EXHIBIT 6: EMD Form B—Operating Statement, 1974

CY 1974-1978 PLAN: OPERATING STATEMENT

	Actual results				*Forecast*				
OPERATING STATEMENT $000	CY70*	CY71	CY72	CY73	CY74	CY75	CY76	CY77	CY78
Bookings			2,025	1,769	2,300	2,800	3,225	4,000	4,800
Backlogs		441	579	491	541	641	746	911	1,061
Sales	1,710	1,765	1,887	1,857	2,250	2,700	3,120	3,835	4,650
Cost of sales	1,652	1,523	1,471	1,646	1,750	2,050	2,340	2,850	3,455
Gross margin	58	242	416	211	500	650	780	935	1,195
Gross margin, percent of sales	3	14	22	11	22	24	25	26	26
R&D	–	–	–	–	–	–	–	–	–
Selling expense	143	127	135	192	210	255	285	340	400
G&A (Noncorporate)		103	106	105	115	130	140	165	190
Corporate G&A expense		45	40	52	55	70	80	100	120
Other (income expense		(6)	(10)	(18)	(20)	(20)	(25)	(35)	(40)
Under (over) applied overhead									
Operating profit, before taxes	(85)	(39)	125	(156)	100	175	250	345	445
Operating profit, percent of sales	–	–	7	–	4	7	8	9	10
SALES/OPERATING PROFIT BEFORE TAXES, BY BUSINESS ELEMENT									
RF	1,318/(102)	1,349/(81)	1,508/72	1,240/(85)	1,650/88	1,800/110	2,100/160	2,600/200	2,900/255
Special	392/17	416/42	379/53	259/27	250/22	150/15	120/10	135/15	150/15
CATV				358/(98)	350/(10)	750/50	900/80	1,200/130	1,600/175
Total sales/operating profit	1,710/(85)	1,765/(39)	1,887/125	1,857/(156)	2,250/100	2,700/175	3,120/250	3,835/345	4,650/445

Date April 1974
Form
*CY = Calendar year.

CY73 Sales Mix

AEC Cont.	$ 000
Other CPFF	200,000
Fixed price	59,000
Std. price	1,598,000
Total	$1,857,000

U.S.A.	$1,857,000
W. Europe	$ 000
Rest of world	$ 000
Total	$1,857,000

U.S.A. Sales Only

AEC	$ 000
DOD	$1,499,000
Other gov't.	$ 000
Nongov't.	$ 358,000
Subtotal	$1,857,000

CY73

Intercorporate Sales = $000

Electro-Mechanical (Division)

EXHIBIT 7: 1974 Form K—CATV Business Element

LONG-RANGE PLAN: BUSINESS ELEMENT SUMMARY

1. Product and/or service
CATV aluminum sheath cable connectors and adaptors

2. Customers
Cable television manufacutrers and service organizations

Distributors	24%
OEM	17
Multiple-system operators	42
Small-system operators	17

3. End use
Cable network distribution connectors
- —Cable-to-cable splice
- —Amplifier or tap to cable
- —Terminators
- —Adaptors

4.

Direct competitors	*Sales CY 73*	*Market share*
Gilbert	1,525	36%
LRC	1,000	24
EG&G	360	9
Coral	300	7
Cambridge	250	6
Tidal	250	6
ITT	200	5
Pyramid	50	1
Others	250	5
Total direct market	$4,185,000	100%

5. Competitive advantages
- —Superior product for areas and applications sensitive to radio frequency interference
- —Dominant competitor (Gilbert) unstable

6. Competitive disadvantages
- —Premium price
- —Emerging competitor (LRC) with cost effective product
- —Anixter-Pruzan distributor liaison temporarily ineffective

7. Market alternatives (competing techniques)
Conventional television reception

8. Factors affecting future market growth
- —MSO access to investment funds 2
- —Federal regulatory rulings
- —State and local franchise practices
- —Inflation-related subscriber rate hikes
- —Potential for two-way consumer services

9. Summary of strategy
- —Explore short-term viability of CATV business
- —Appraise Anixter-Pruzan distributor potential
- —Expand and improve distributor sales network selectively in key geographic areas of the United States
- —Continue to cultivate OEM liaisons through direct sales effort
- —Expand product line to provide adequate but lower price product for more general use in non-RFI and turnkey applications

10. History/forecast	CY72	CY73	CY74	CY75	CY76	CY77	CY78
Market compound growth 24% per year		4185	4500	5400	7000	9200	12100
Share of market		9	8	14	13	13	13
Sales		358	350	750	900	1200	1600
Operating profit, percent to sales		(3)	(3)	7	9	11	11

Date: April 1974 | CATV (Business element) | ELECTRO-MECHANICAL (Division)
Form K (74)

EXHIBIT 8: EMD Form C—1974 Investment Information

	Actual				Forecast				
INVESTMENT DETAIL $000	CY70	CY71	CY72	CY73	CY74 Estim.	CY75	CY76	CY77	CY78
1. Accounts receivable		396	424	518	525	580	640	780	950
2. Contracts-in-process			6	19	10	5	5	5	5
3. Inventories		542	493	709	5	700	755	830	900
4. Other		2	2	3	630	5	5	5	5
5. Accounts payable		73	117	247	120	140	160	190	230
6. Accrued (prepaid) expenses		75	165	137	140	170	195	210	260
7. Operating capital (1+2+3–5–6)		792	643	865	910	980	1,050	1,220	1,370
8. Assigned fixed assets at cost		678	715	712	742	782	832	832	942
9. Accum. depreciation		342	428	430	480	530	585	645	710
10. Assigned net fixed assets (8–9)		338	287	282	262	252	247	237	232
11. Allocated fixed assets at cost									
12. Accum. depreciation									
13. Allocated net fixed assets (11–12)									
14. Net other assets			7	2	–				
15. Net investment (7+13+18+14)		1,128	937	1,149	1,174	1,232	1,297	1,457	1,602
16. Long-term lease commitments									
17. Total Investment (15+19)		1,128	937	1,149	1,174	1,232	1,297	1,457	1,602

Giuffrida made it a policy to distribute the financial results of all his business elements at the monthly meetings held by his group. On the other hand, Sheets and Killion had warned from the beginning that the CATV connector would take a number of years to become established. In the past, EG&G had financed promising products, such as a component for the Xerox copier, for six years before they became profitable.

CASE TWELVE

Coca-Cola Wine Spectrum (A)

WILLIAM R. BOULTON
University of Georgia

PHYLLIS G. HOLLAND
Georgia State University

Assignment Questions:

1. Evaluate the acquisition of Taylor by Coca-Cola from Taylor's point of view; From Coca-Cola's point of view.
2. What is the potential effect of Coca-Cola's entry into the wine industry?
3. What factors should Albert Killeen consider in his decision about the taste test commercials? What do you recommend that he do?

Albert Killeen, general manager of Coca-Cola's newly formed Wine Spectrum division, was concerned about mounting delays in a "revolutionary" comparative advertising campaign for Taylor California Cellars wines. Not only was this the first major campaign of the Wine Spectrum division involving the California Cellars winery, the Taylor name, and bottling by Coca-Cola of New York's Franzia subsidiary, but issues had also arisen over the legality of comparative taste tests for wines. After three months of discussions with lawyers and federal officials, Killeen had still been unable to get a ruling; basically, it all boiled down to: "Do we wait for, probably, another year or go ahead and risk legal actions?"

Prior to the 1977 acquisition of Taylor Wine Company by Coca-Cola Inc., Taylor management had promoted the concept that wine was right for any time and any place in "Taylor territory." They had also worked to educate consumers to appreciate New York wines by using the "answer grape." Since California wines were blended into Taylor products, a later campaign used the term "Californewyork" to try to broaden the appeal of Taylor wines. However, Taylor's marketing organization had never seen wine commercials quite like the introductory campaign proposed by its new advertising agency (see Exhibit 1). The new ads were based on a comparative taste test that not only named Taylor California Cellars as the best, but named the competing wines.

The problem with the new ad campaign was that of determining whether

Prepared by William R. Boulton and Phyllis G. Holland.

EXHIBIT 1: Comparative Taste Test Advertisement Script

Program: "San Francisco Wine Test"		*Client: Taylor Wine Company*
VIDEO		*AUDIO*
OPEN ON:	Taster (male) inspecting glass and sniffing	*ANNOUNCER V/O:* a new California Rhine wine is judged against its competitors. Twenty-seven wine experts gather in San Francisco
CUT TO:	MASTER SHOT	
TITLE:	JULY 22, 1978	
CUT TO:	Taster (male) sniffing	to compare four
TITLES:	A-C.K. Mondavi Rhine B-Taylor California Cellars Rhine C-Almaden Mountain Rhine D-Inglenook Navalle Rhine	
CUT TO:	Taster (male) sniffing	California Rhine wines.
CUT TO:	Four glasses and hand writing	Which was judged best?
CUT TO:	Tasters in foreground, Judge and Nationwide Consumer Testing Institute Representatives in background	"Ladies and gentlemen, the wine you have judged best is
TITLES:	A, C, and D OUT REMAINING: B. Taylor California Cellars Rhine	Wine B."
CUT TO:	Four glasses. Hand places Taylor bottle in front	*ANN'R V/O:* Wine B. New Taylor California Cellars Rhine
TITLE:	OUT	Taylor California Cellars
TITLE:	Taylor Label	
CUT TO:	Glass A	
TITLE:	C. K. Mondavi Rhine	*ANN'R V/O:* Judged better than C. K. Mondavi
Pan to:	Glass C	
TITLE:	Almaden Mountain Rhine	Better than Almaden
Pan to:	Glass D	
TITLE:	Inglenook Navalle Rhine	Better than Inglenook
CUT TO:	Taylor Label	*TASTER (male) V/O:* "An interesting wine."
TITLE:		*ANN'R V/O:* But when you cost a little more, you better be better.

comparative advertising of wine was allowed under federal regulations. The Federal Bureau of Alcohol, Tobacco, and Firearms (BATF) had regulatory powers over the industry's advertising, but officials had refused to give any determination. The courts had also refused to hear the case prior to action being taken by Taylor. BATF was reviewing its regulations on the wine industry but contended that only after running the ads would competitors bring forward the evidence necessary for them to make their judgment. BATF would not protect Coca-Cola or Taylor from legal consequences should they be found in noncompliance with regulations. While it was generally known that misleading or disparaging ads were not permitted, specific guidelines on comparative taste tests in wines were not expected for another year.

THE WINE INDUSTRY IN THE UNITED STATES

In 1972, wine prices were rising dramatically and there was great interest in entering the industry. New wine grape acreage soared, with more acreage planted in 1971, 1972, and 1973 than the total of all previous plantings. In addition, speculators observed that foreign wines selling for $25 per case in the 1950s were selling for $500 to $1,000 per case and began to put bottles in storage. The 1972 vintage was bad and did not sell well, and the 1973 harvest was the largest in history. The increased supply led to a decline in prices that accelerated when the speculators put the hoarded wine on the market. By the time the first wine from the new plantings hit the market in 1974, inventories were at an all-time high and the oversupply was further increased by another large harvest in 1975. In 1972, the average return to a California grower per ton of grapes crushed was $217. In 1974 the return dropped to $131 and to $100 in 1975.[1]

By 1976 conditions were improving. Inventories were slowly being worked off and more grape vines were taken up than planted. Even though prices began to rise, producers were still cautious. In describing the future direction of the market, Taylor management indicated in 1976:

> In general, 1974 and 1975 were characterized by large grape harvests throughout the United States. It is believed that adverse weather conditions caused a smaller crop in 1976. However, increased grape harvests in the future may be anticipated as a result of substantial grape acreage which was planted in 1971 through 1974 and should mature approximately four years after planting. Grapes are a commodity which will continue to be affected by weather conditions, diseases and grower practices, which cause uncertainty for the crop until each annual harvest is near. Despite increases in many production costs, the abundance of grapes and large wine inventories have generally restricted wine price increases on an industry-wide basis. Furthermore, as discretionary income is believed to impact directly on wine consumption, recent economic conditions have contributed to relatively level industry sales.

Wine Consumption in the United States

Wine consumption in the United States was increasing both in absolute amounts and per capita. In 1977, 6 per cent more wine entered distribution channels than in 1976 and the same advance was predicted for 1978. Wine consumption was 400 million gallons in 1977 or 1.85 gallons per capita, as compared to 1.7 gallons in 1976:

> Wine sales in the foreseeable future should grow 8% a year, versus less than 3% for distilled spirits, according to Marvin Shanken, editor of *Impact,* a widely re-

[1]Gigi Mahon, "Everything's Coming Up Roses," *Barron's* 56, June 7, 1976, pp. 11–16.

> spected liquor industry newsletter (soft drink sales are growing 7% annually). By 1980, says Shanken, wines will overtake distilled spirits in gallons.[2]

Per capita consumption in the United States varied geographically, with the highest consuming states being on the east and west coasts. Highest per capita consumption was 5.41 gallons in Washington, D.C.—a far cry, though, from the Italian average of 26 gallons or the French average of 24. Twenty-two per cent of the wine sold in the U.S. was sold in California, 10.6 per cent in New York, 5.1 per cent in Illinois, followed by New Jersey with 4.5 per cent and Florida with 4.3 per cent.

Wine consumption was greatest in the 21–40 age group (which was growing as a percentage of the population) and was also greater among the more affluent income groups. Factors underlying increased wine consumption were said to be a growing preference for lighter, drier beverages, the availability of broadcast media to efficiently create a nationwide market, and growing purchases by women. A *Forbes* article stated that wine is

> increasingly purchased by women right along with groceries. According to *Progressive Grocer,* the trade publication, 35% of all wine is sold in supermarkets. In addition more wine (particularly dry white wine) is now being sipped before dinner—as a fashionable substitute for the Martini and Bloody Mary.[3]

Wine Production in the United States

In 1976 Taylor management noted several facts about U.S. wine production:

> California is the largest wine producing area in the United States, with New York State being the second largest producing area. Based upon the latest available industry estimates, California production increased 47 per cent from 239.6 million gallons in 1969 to 351.9 million gallons in 1975. During this same period, wine production in New York increased approximately 32 per cent from 26.3 million gallons to 34.7 million gallons. Based upon the most recent industry estimates, during 1975, 84 per cent of U.S. wine produced (but not necessarily sold) was produced in California and 8 per cent in New York. Taylor and many other non-California wine producers use California wines for blending purposes to achieve certain flavor characteristics.

In 1977 there were 615 wineries in 30 states, an increase of 41 per cent from 435 in 1970. California had the largest number with 353, followed by New York with 39. Ohio, Oregon, Michigan, and Pennsylvania each had 16. Average production was 20,000 gallons per year as compared to Gallo's production of 100 million gallons annually. Many of the smaller wineries were still waiting for their first vintage. Exhibit 2 shows the ownership of major brands in the wine industry.

Independent wineries are seldom publicly held and are rapidly being acquired by large firms who are increasingly aggressive marketers. Profiles of major competitors are included in Exhibit 3. At the same time, small "mom and pop" wineries have proliferated in the premium wine segment with sales going to local communities. There is little chance that they can expand beyond re-

[2]"Beverages: Basic Analysis," *Standards and Poors Industry Surveys,* October 19, 1978, p. B-71.
[3]"Coke Takes a Champagne Chaser," *Forbes,* 118: October 15, 1976, p. 66.

EXHIBIT 2: Major U.S. Wineries

Company	*Brands*	*Ownership (Date of Acquisition)*	*1977 Wine Sales***
E&J Gallo	Gallo	Private	$370,000,000
United Vintners	Colony Italian Swiss Colony Inglenook	Heublein (1969)	$201,751,000
Franzia-Mogen David	Franzia Mogen David	Coca-Cola Bottling (N.Y.) (1970, 1973)	$ 59,900,000
Almaden Vineyards	Almaden	National Distillers (1967)	$ 88,023,000
Canadaigua Wine Co.	Richard's Wild Irish Rose	Public	$ 35,605,000
The Taylor Wine Co.	Taylor Great Western	The Coca-Cola Co. (1976)	$ 59,600,000
Paul Masson Vineyards	Paul Masson	Seagram (1945)	$ 70,000,000*
Mont La Salle	Christian Brothers	Private	$ 50,000,000*

* Casewriter's estimate.
** Where companies are owned, sales figure is that of owner.

stricted market areas because of their small size, legal restrictions of interstate wine sales, and the wide variations in their product quality.

Most wine sold in the United States is produced in California. Exhibit 4 shows market share by origin of wine. Import prices have generally increased more than domestic prices because of inflation and the devaluation of the dollar. The packaging of some French wine in flexible plastic film pouches is one effort to maintain competitive costs.

Some wineries own grapevines while others buy from independent growers. For those depending on outside growers (Almaden uses 85–90 per cent outside grapes and Taylor 90 per cent) relationships with growers are very important. In hard times, the vintner buys grapes to subsidize the growers in order not to jeopardize future supplies. This practice can lead to large inventories and make storage capacity an important factor. Aging requirements for premium and sparkling wines also add to storage requirements. White wines require significantly less aging than red wines of comparable quality. Exhibit 5 shows storage capacities of twelve U.S. wineries, which account for 73 per cent of the storage capacities of the 100 largest wineries. All except Taylor are in California.

Advertising

The entry of large companies into the wine industry has been accompanied by an increase in advertising budgets and the advent of mass marketing techniques. Almaden has increased advertising by 100 per cent since 1974 while Taylor's advertising has increased 33 per cent. The largest advertiser, Gallo, on the other hand has increased its ad budget only about 9 per cent. In 1977, however, Gallo spent over $12 million on advertising while Taylor and Almaden spent about $2 million. Since all segments of the alcoholic beverage industry

EXHIBIT 3: Profiles of Major Competitors in the Wine Industry

E&J Gallo

With a sales volume nearly double its closest competitor, Gallo has more influence in the wine industry than any other U.S. company. Because Gallo purchases 40 per cent of the California grape harvest, the company is in the position of impacting grape prices throughout California. In addition to the winery, Gallo operations include vineyards, apple orchards, one of the West's biggest bottling plants, one of California's largest trucking companies, and several big wine distributors. The founders of the winery, Ernest and Julio Gallo, are active in the firm; Julio oversees the wine making and Ernest looks after everything else.

Gallo is the only large winery that doesn't offer tours and Ernest is noted for his secrecy about operations. At the same time, Gallo has served as a training ground for many vintners who have gone on to other companies.

In recent years, Gallo has upgraded its product line and its prices. Once known for pop wines like Thunderbird, Ripple, and Boone's Farm, the company stopped advertising these wines and began to emphasize the higher priced varietal and proprietary wines. Although sales and market share temporarily suffered, profits increased steadily.

Gallo is noted for producing a quality wine at a low price. Hearty Burgundy had been called the best wine ever made for the money and because of the cost advantage of the bottling plant, Gallo has sometimes been in the position of selling wine below cost while making a profit on the bottles.

United Vintners

United Vintners is 82 per cent owned by Heublein, Inc., the major U.S. producer of vodka (Smirnoff) and the owner of Kentucky Fried Chicken. The range of products of UV included pop wines (Annie Green Springs, T.J. Swann), Colony, Italian Swiss Colony, Inglenook table and dessert wines, and high-quality wines from Beaulieu Vineyards. The company also distributed Lancer's wine from Portugal.

United Vintners has been in the wine industry since the late '60s and is the second largest seller of wines; sales totaled $226.1 million in 1976, but fell to $201.8 million in 1977. Recent advertising campaigns have emphasized the personality of the drinker rather than attributes of its wines.

Franzia-Mogen David

Coca-Cola Bottling Company of New York purchased Mogen David in 1970 and Franzia Brothers in 1973. The former is known for sweet table, fruit, and specialty wines whereas the latter produces a range of California dry red and white wines, table wines; rosé, sparkling, and dessert wines; and brandy. In addition to bottling and distributing soft drinks (Dr. Pepper and Seven-Up besides the Coca-Cola line), the company's subsidiaries produce Igloo plastic coolers and other plastic products. The company owns two steamboats, the *Mississippi Queen* and the *Delta Queen*, and a TV station. It is one of the largest independent soft drink franchises in the world.

In 1977 wine sales of Mogen David and Franzia brands totaled almost $60 million, down slightly from $60.8 million in 1976; the operations of the Franzia unit were not profitable in 1977. Recent Mogen David commercials urged consumers to drink Mogen David because of its taste—even though it lacked "snob appeal."

EXHIBIT 3: (continued)

Almaden

National Distillers and Chemical Corporation acquired full ownership of Almaden in 1977. One of the four largest distillers in the United States, National Distillers was also active in chemicals, petrochemicals, brass mill products, and textiles.

Almaden had sales of $88 million and an operating profit of $14 million in 1977; in 1978 sales increased to $117.5 million and operating profits rose to $17.2 million.

Canandaigua Wine Co.

Canandaigua sold primarily dessert wines, and one product, Richard's Wild Irish Rose, accounted for over two thirds of its sales. The company owned wineries in New York, California, South Carolina, and Virginia and its 1977 sales were in the $35 million range.

Paul Masson Vineyards

Seagram Company Ltd., of which Paul Masson is a division, was in 1977 the world's largest producer and marketer of distilled spirits and wines. Case volume of Paul Masson wines was reported to be growing about 15 per cent annually. The Paul Masson brand enjoyed a good reputation in the industry and was one of the better known brands among consumers.

compete to some extent, the level of wine advertising is partly affected by promoting of beer and spirits.

Regulation

Wine is subject to regulation from all levels of government. State and local governments regulate the sales of alcoholic beverages and in some states legis-

EXHIBIT 4: Market Share by Origin of Wine (1977)

		Share	*Volume Increase (decrease) from '76*
Origin			
Domestic		82.8%	
California	86.1%		6.0%
Others	13.9%		(4.1%)
	100.0%		
Imports		17.2%	
Italy	43.0%		29.1%
France	19.4		12.2
Germany	15.3		18.5
Spain	9.4		(6.1)
Portugal	8.6		3.0
Other	5.0		
	100.0%		

EXHIBIT 5: Storage Capacities of Twelve U.S. Wineries

Winery	*Storage Capacity (millions of gallons)*
E. & J. Gallo	226
United Vintners (Heublein)	110
Guild Wineries	57
Vie Del Co.	37.1
Bear Mountain	36
Taylor (Coca-Cola)	31.3
Sierra Wine Corp.	30
Almaden (National Distillers and Chemicals)	29.4
Franzia Bros. (Coca-Cola, N.Y.)	28.3
Paul Masson (Seagram)	28
The Christian Brothers	27.5
A. Perelli-Minette & Sons	20

lation has been proposed to regulate packaging. At the federal level, the Treasury Department's Bureau of Alcohol, Firearms, and Tobacco (BATF) regulates advertising and labeling. New advertising guidelines were expected late in 1979, and new labeling requirements were to take effect in January 1983. These requirements state that if place of origin (e.g., California) is identified on the bottle, 75 per cent of the grapes must be from that place and if a viticultural area is identified (e.g., Napa Valley), 85 per cent of the grapes must be from there. These standards match those prevailing in the European Common Market.

In addition to regulation, wine is subject to taxation from all levels of government. Federal excise tax is $.17 per gallon on table wines, $.67 per gallon on dessert wines, and $3.40 per gallon on sparkling wines.

THE TAYLOR WINE COMPANY

The Taylor Wine Company, at the time of acquisition by Coca-Cola, was a leading domestic producer of premium still and sparkling wines, marketed under the "Taylor" and "Great Western" labels; it was also the largest producer of premium domestic champagnes. The record of Taylor Wine Company from 1972 to 1976 reflected the cyclical swings in the industry during that period. In 1973, record sales of $51 million registered an 18 per cent increase over 1972, with profits up 25 per cent to $6.8 million or $1.57 per share. In 1974, sales increased to $56 million while profits increased to $6.9 million or $1.58 per share. Results worsened as Taylor reported sales and profits of $57.6 million and $5.4 million, or $1.24 per share, in 1975 and $59.6 million and $5.6 million, or $1.30 per share, in 1976. In explaining these results, Taylor's management said:

> During the four years 1969–1972, the volume of wine entering U.S. marketing channels increased 10–14% per year. As a result of this growth and anticipated continued growth, substantial vine plantings and wine production occurred during

> the period 1971–1974. However, due to economic conditions in 1973 through 1975 the expected rate of growth in wine sales was not realized, and the industry faced a period of surplus wine inventories and grape crops. Taylor believes that its sales for the fiscal years 1975 and 1976 were adversely affected by competitive pricing conditions attributable to the foregoing factors. In its effort to maintain profit margins, Taylor has generally held or slightly increased its prices to distributors during this period, even though, based upon retail prices, it is believed that a number of wine producers have reduced prices. However, inflationary pressures, which increased costs, resulted in reduced profit margin percentages in fiscal 1974 and 1975. A decrease in some material costs and improved cost controls resulted in a modest improvement in profit margins for 1976, although gallons sold declined slightly.

Taylor's *1976 Annual Report* stated that the company had "successfully weathered the recession of the past two years and is in a strong position to take advantage of the recovery the wine industry appears to be experiencing." In addition to the recovery, 1976 also marked the end of the Taylor family's participation in the company's management and its merger with the Coca-Cola Company.

Merger with Coca-Cola

On August 6, 1976, Lincoln First Bank of Rochester, New York, put out a preliminary prospectus for sale of 603,000 of the 900,000 shares of Taylor stock it held for trust customers. The motive for the sale was to raise cash for the trusts involved and Taylor was informed of the proceedings because 10 per cent of the outstanding stock was involved. Several companies responded to the prospectus including Coca-Cola, PepsiCo, Beatrice Foods, Norton-Simon, and five private investors headed by Marne Obernauer (a former Taylor director and owner of Great Western before it was purchased by Taylor). Coca-Cola was interested in more than the 603,000 shares so when Coca-Cola and the Bank reached an agreement, the secondary offer was withdrawn and Coca-Cola entered into merger talks directly with Taylor.

After Taylor's board's approval of the proposed merger, Taylor's president, Joseph Swarthout, explained to the shareholders in the December 2, 1976, prospectus:

> The U.S. wine market has never been more competitive. As I stated at our Annual Shareholders' Meeting in September, our major competitors are stronger than ever. In several cases they have significantly stronger financial backing than we have. Under these conditions, it becomes increasingly difficult to improve, or even maintain, our share-of-market.
>
> I have had the pleasure of being an employee of this company for more than thirty years. I have been a corporate officer since 1955. They have been interesting years of growth and opportunity. It is now my firm belief that The Taylor Wine Company would enjoy substantially greater opportunities for success in the future through the financial strength and diversity of the Coca-Cola Company.

Industry observers speculated that Taylor management was frightened by several of the "unfamiliar" companies showing interest in the 603,000 shares of Taylor's stock and looked at the Coca-Cola merger as a way of preventing a greater evil. There did however appear to be possibilities for strategic fit with Coca-Cola, as indicated in Coca-Cola's description of its business:

> The Coca-Cola Company is the largest manufacturer and distributor of soft drink concentrates and syrups in the world. Its product, "Coca-Cola," has been sold in the United States since 1886, is now sold in over 135 countries as well and is the leading soft drink product in most of these countries.
>
> In 1978, soft drink products accounted for 76 per cent of total sales and 87 per cent of total operating income from industry segments. Soft drink products include Coca-Cola, Fanta, Sprite, TAB, Fresca, Mr. PiBB and Hi-C Brand. Coca-Cola accounts for over 70 percent of all Company soft drink unit sales, both in the United States and overseas.
>
> The worldwide soft drink operations of the Coca-Cola Company are organized into three operating groups: the Americas Group, the Pacific Group and the Europe and Africa Group. The Company's largest markets within its Americas Group are the United States, Mexico, and Brazil. The largest markets within the Pacific Group are Japan and Canada. The largest market in the Europe and Africa Group is Germany. In 1978, overseas markets accounted for some 62 per cent of total soft drink unit sales.
>
> In the United States, 67 per cent of soft drink syrup and concentrate is sold to more than 550 bottlers who prepare and sell the products for the food store, vending and other markets for home and on-premise consumption. The remaining 33 percent is sold to approximately 4,000 authorized wholesalers who in turn sell the syrup to restaurants and other retailers. Overseas, all soft drink concentrate is sold to more than 900 bottlers. Approximately 90 per cent of the syrup and concentrate is sold for further processing outside the Company before sale to the ultimate consumer, both in the United States and overseas. The remaining 10 per cent is converted into consumable soft drinks before being sold by the Company.
>
> Through the Foods Division, the Company manufactures and markets Minute Maid and Snow Crop frozen concentrated citrus juices, Minute Maid chilled juices and related citrus products, and Hi-C ready-to-serve fruit drinks and powdered drink mixes. The Foods Division also markets coffee and tea under the "Maryland Club," "Butter-nut" and other brands, as well as to private label and institutional accounts.

Exhibits 6, 7, and 8 show the combined pro forma summaries of operations, net profits, and balance sheet statements for the merged companies.

Under the terms of the merger agreement approved by stockholders of both companies in January 1977, all outstanding shares of Taylor stock were converted into shares of common stock of Coca-Cola at the rate of one share of Coca-Cola stock for each 3.75 shares of Taylor stock. No changes in Taylor management were planned and the company was to operate as a wholly owned subsidiary of Coca-Cola with Coca-Cola officials on its Board of Directors. Exhibit 9 shows the stock price movements for Coca-Cola and Taylor.

Taylor Wine Company Operations

At the time of the merger proposal, Taylor described its operations as follows:

> Taylor is a leading domestic producer of premium still wines. It is also the largest domestic producer of sparkling wines using the traditional French method of

EXHIBIT 6: The Coca-Cola Company and Subsidiaries and the Taylor Wine Company, Inc. Pro Forma Combined Summary of Operations (Unaudited)

						Six Months Ended June 30,	
	1971	*1972*	*1973*	*1974*	*1975*	*1975*	*1976*
	(In thousands except per share amounts)						
Net Sales	$1,772,029	$1,927,242	$2,201,410	$2,579,754	$2,932,457	$1,476,764	$1,508.416
Cost of Goods Sold	$ 949,124	$1,021,889	$1,179,168	$1,576,068	$1,745,238	$ 904,183	$ 835,472
Taxes on Income	$ 165,270	$ 179,661	$ 194,007	$ 173,899	$ 226,750	$ 106,372	$ 129,008
Net Profit (Note 1)	$ 173,238	$ 197,004	$ 221,862	$ 201,356	$ 224,951	$ 122,344	$ 144,483
Per Share:							
Net Profit (Note 1)	$2.85	$3.24	$3.64	$3.30	$4.01	$2.00	$2.37
Cash dividends declared	$1.58	$1.64	$1.80	$2.08	$2.30	$1.15	$1.32
Average Number of Shares Outstanding (Note 2)	60,730	60,860	60,937	60,996	61,050	61,049	61,078

Notes:

(1) In 1974 the Coca-Cola Company adopted the last-in, first-out accounting method for certain major classes of inventories as explained in the financial statements of the Coca-Cola Company and subsidiaries. For the year ended June 30, 1975, Taylor also adopted the last-in, first-out method of valuation for all its inventories as explained in the Taylor statement of income. These accounting changes had the effect of reducing pro forma net profit for 1974 by $32,329,548 ($.53 a share).

(2) The pro forma average number of shares outstanding represents the average number of shares of the Coca-Cola Company outstanding during each period after giving retroactive effect to the average number of Taylor shares outstanding during each period converted into shares of the Coca-Cola Company on a .267 for 1 basis.

(3) Estimated expenses of this proposed merger will be approximately $700,000. These expenses, which have not been included in the above pro forma presentation, will be deducted from operations of the resulting combined company for the period in which they are incurred.

EXHIBIT 7: The Coca-Cola Company and Subsidiaries and the Taylor Wine Company, Inc. Pro Forma Combined Net Profit and Per Share Data (Unaudited)

						Six Months Ended June 30,	
	1971	*1972*	*1973*	*1974*	*1975*	*1975*	*1976*
Net Profit (in thousands):							
The Coca-Cola Company historical	$167,815	$190,157	$214,981	$195,972	$239,305	$119,762	$141,763
The Taylor Wine Company, Inc., historical	5,471	6,847	6,881	5,939	5,646	2,582	2,720
Pro forma combined	$173,286	$197,004	$221,862	$201,365	$244,951	$122,344	$144,483
Net Profit Per Common Share:							
The Coca-Cola Company:							
Historical	$2.82	$3.19	$3.60	$3.28	$4.00	$2.00	$ 2.37
Pro forma combined (Note A)	2.85	3.24	3.64	3.30	4.01	2.00	2.37
The Taylor Wine Company, Inc.:							
Historical	1.29	1.57	1.58	1.24	1.30	.59	.63
Pro forma combined (Note B)	.76	.86	.97	.88	1.07	.53	.63
Cash Dividends Declared Per Common Share:							
The Coca-Cola Company historical	1.58	1.64	1.80	2.08	2.30	1.15	1.32
The Taylor Wine Company, Inc.:							
Historical	.48	.50	.56	.60	.62	.30	.31
Pro forma combined (Note B)	.42	.44	.48	.56	.61	.31	.35
Book Value Per Common Share:							
The Coca-Cola Company:							
Historical							21.57
Pro forma combined (Note A)							22.13
The Taylor Wine Company, Inc.:							
Historical							13.67
Pro forma combined (Note B)							5.90

Notes:
(A) Pro forma combined amounts per share for the Coca-Cola Company are based on average number of shares outstanding during each period and as of June 30, 1976, after giving retroactive effect to the conversion of Taylor shares into shares of the Coca-Cola Company on the basis of the exchange ratio for the merger, at .267 shares of the Coca-Cola Company for each share of Taylor.
(B) Pro forma combined amounts are based on .267 shares the Coca-Cola Company exchanged for each share of Taylor.

Source: prospectus.

EXHIBIT 8: The Coca-Cola Company and Subsidiaries and the Taylor Wine Company, Inc.
Pro Forma Combined Condensed Balance Sheet As of June 30, 1976 (Unaudited)

ASSETS	*The Coca-Cola Company*	*Taylor*	*Adjustment (Note)*	*Pro Forma Combined*
	(In thousands of dollars)			
Current Assets:				
Cash	$ 78,571	$ 1,173		$ 79,744
Marketable securities	229,793			229,793
Trade accounts receivable—net	250,947	4,356		255,303
Inventories	374,920	41,766		416,686
Prepaid expenses	28,467	180		28,647
Total current assets	962,698	47,475		1,010,173
Property, Plant and Equipment—net	647,684	26,462		674,146
Other Assets	209,641	902		210,543
Total	$1,820,023	$74,839		$1,894,862
LIABILITIES AND STOCKHOLDERS' EQUITY				
Current Liabilities:				
Notes payable including current maturities of Long-term debt	$ 24,891	$ 3,037		$ 27,928
Accounts payable and accrued accounts	337,129	3,656		340,785
Accrued taxes including taxes on income	121,763	1,729		123,492
Total current liabilities	483,783	8,422		492,205
Long-Term Liabilities and Deferred Taxes	44,092	6,904		50,996
Total liabilities	527,875	15,326		543,201
Stockholders' Equity:				
Common stock—No par value— The Coca-Cola Company	60,485		$ 1,173	
Common stock—$2 par value— The Taylor Wine Company, Inc.		8,707	(8,707)	
Capital surplus	87,938	9,930	7,534	105,402
Earned surplus	1,159,090	40,876		1,199,966
Treasury shares	(15,365)			(15,365)
Total stockholders' equity	1,292,148	59,513		1,351,661
Total	$1,820,023	$74,839		$1,894,862

Note:
The pro forma adjustment reflects the issuance of 1,161,000 common shares of the Coca-Cola Company upon conversion of each of the presently issued common shares of Taylor for .267 common shares of the Coca-Cola Company pursuant to the terms of the merger.

fermentation in the bottle, as contrasted with the bulk process in which the wine is fermented in large volume.

Taylor's 63 types of sparkling and still wines are produced and marketed exclusively under two trade names representing its two wine divisions. The Pleasant Valley division, the successor to the Pleasant Valley Wine Company, acquired by Taylor in 1961, produces and markets its wines under the Great Western name. Historically, these divisions have utilized separate production and marketing techniques, and the wines produced by each division traditionally have had different characteristics and consumer brand loyalties. As a result, they have continued as

EXHIBIT 9: Comparative Stock Prices

	TAYLOR COMMON STOCK		THE COCA-COLA COMPANY COMMON STOCK	
	High Bid Price	*Low Bid Price*	*High Sale Price*	*Low Sale Price*
1974				
First Quarter	$38.25	$23.75	$127.75	$109.50
Second Quarter	24.25	16.50	118.375	98.375
Third Quarter	17.75	12.25	109.00	48.00
Fourth Quarter	13.75	9.25	68.75	44.625
1975				
First Quarter	20.875	10.125	81.50	53.25
Second Quarter	19.50	16.00	93.50	72.75
Third Quarter	18.375	11.00	92.00	69.625
Fourth Quarter	15.375	10.75	89.75	69.875
1976				
First Quarter	17.50	13.50	94.25	82.00
Second Quarter	15.50	12.25	89.00	77.625
Third Quarter	19.375	12.875	89.625	82.875
Fourth Quarter				
November 20, 1976	20.25	16.875	86.25	76.25

The Coca-Cola Company announced that it had entered into merger negotiations with Taylor on September 8, 1976, and preliminary agreement on the exchange rate was announced on October 14, 1976.

separate divisions since 1961 and presently maintain their own advertising, marketing, production and storage capacity and operational staffs, although legal, financial, accounting, personnel and other functions are performed at the corporate level.

Wines are classified as either "still" or "sparkling." Still wines containing 14 per cent or less alcohol are generally referred to as "table" wines and those containing 14–21 per cent alcohol are generally referred to as "dessert" wines. Sparkling wines are those which are effervescent and contain not more than 14 per cent alcohol.

Employees

Taylor employed approximately 670 full-time employees. Because of the increased use of mechanized harvesting equipment, the number of seasonal workers hired by Taylor had declined in recent years. Approximately 15 seasonal workers were employed during the 1976 grape harvest as compared with approximately 200 such workers employed during the 1967 harvest. A few additional seasonal workers were sometimes employed at the winery for the grape pressing operations. Taylor maintained a pension plan to which it made annual contributions and which allowed employees to make voluntary contributions; it also provided group life and medical benefits for its regular full-time employees. The employees of Taylor were not represented by any unions, and Taylor believed that its employee relations were satisfactory.

Marketing

Taylor's wines were sold throughout the United States. Both Taylor and Pleasant Valley advertised through television, magazines, and newspapers. In addition, each division provided promotional materials to its customers for eventual use by retailers. In recent years, advertising, sales promotion and selling expenditures by Taylor approximated 17 per cent of net sales.

In 1976, the Taylor and Great Western product lines were marketed by 64 and 34 salesmen, respectively. Taylor's products were sold primarily to 490 wholesale distributors and through 27 brokers. With few exceptions, Taylor and Great Western wines were handled by different distributors in the respective geographic locations. Brokers were primarily used by Taylor to sell its products in states where no distribution agreements existed and in some of the 15 so-called "control" states where Taylor's customer was the local or state agency that controlled the purchase and distribution of alcoholic beverages. In some control states, such as Pennsylvania, sales were made directly by Taylor to the appropriate governmental agency. (A distributor purchases Taylor's products for resale to retailers, whereas brokers act on behalf of Taylor on a commission basis.) Taylor maintained one price list for all purchasers (F.O.B. the winery) and did not engage in selective discounting.

In 1976, no distributor accounted for more than 7 per cent of Taylor's net sales, and no state control agency accounted for more than 10 per cent of Taylor's net sales except Pennsylvania which accounted for 11 per cent. The largest markets, by state, for Taylor's products were New York, Pennsylvania, New Jersey, and Illinois. In addition to the wine sold through distribution channels outlined above, a small volume of wine was sold by Taylor directly to airlines and exported to United States armed forces, embassies and consulates abroad, and some foreign countries.

Taylor's sales volume was seasonal and was affected by price adjustments and the introduction of new products. Normally, sales volume was greatest in the last calendar quarter and smallest in the third calendar quarter. Sales volume for the first and second quarters was normally about the same. Preannounced price increases and new product introductions typically resulted in anticipatory buying by Taylor's customers.

In addition to normal and continuous product advertising, it was Taylor's practice to conduct individual promotional programs at various times during the year for certain of its wines and brands.

The vast majority of Taylor's products were bottled in one-fifth gallon (25.6 oz.) and 1.5 liter (50.7 oz.) sizes. Metric conversion was legally required as of January 1, 1979, and, at that time, the one-fifth gallon size was expected to be converted to a .75 liter (25.4 oz.) size. In early 1976, Taylor converted the half-gallon (64 oz.) size to 1.5 liter size. Taylor did not produce wine for bulk sale to other wineries. Exhibit 10 shows the market sizes and Taylor's position in the table, dessert, and sparkling wine segments.

EXHIBIT 10: Marketing of Wines in the United States (thousands of gallons)

	1971	*1972*	*1973*	*1974*	*1975*
Table Wines (1)					
U.S. produced	159,510	182,640	190,469	201,634	219,171
Foreign produced	26,356	37,741	45,658	42,153	40,524
Total	185,766	220,381	236,127	243,787	259,695
Taylor	2,840	3,504	4,574	5,123	5,264
Taylor market share (2)	1.5%	1.6%	1.9%	2.1%	2.0%
Dessert Wines (1)					
U.S. produced	87.551	86,976	82,637	78,447	80,659
Foreign produced	8,023	7,325	7,487	7,437	6,867
Total	95,574	94,301	90,124	85,884	87,526
Taylor	4,420	4,465	4,577	4,752	4,683
Taylor market share (2)	4.6%	4.7%	5.1%	5.5%	5.4%
Sparkling Wines					
U.S. produced	22,005	20,323	18,935	18,008	18,424
Foreign produced	1,877	1,976	2,081	1,804	1,928
Total	23,882	22,299	21,016	19,812	20,352
Taylor	1,697	1,738	1,763	1,688	1,605
Taylor market share (2)	7.1%	7.8%	8.4%	8.5%	7.9%
Total of all categories					
U.S. produced	269,066	289,939	292,041	298,089	318,254
Foreign produced	36,156	47,042	55,226	51,394	49,319
Total	305,222	336,981	347,267	349,483	367,573
Taylor	8,957	9,707	10,914	11,563	11,552
Taylor market share (2)	2.9%	2.9%	3.1%	3.3%	3.1%

(1) Still wines with less than 14 per cent alcohol have been included in table wines and those with greater than 15 per cent alcohol have been included in dessert wines.
(2) Taylor as a percentage of total.
Source: Wine Institute Statistical Reports for other than Taylor statistics.

Wine Production

During the last five years, vineyards owned and operated by Taylor supplied approximately 10 per cent of its annual grape requirements. Taylor had over 850 acres of vineyards in production, with an additional 450 acres of such plantings not yet in full bearing. Of the 450 acres, 420 acres overlooking Seneca Lake, the largest of the Finger Lakes, were recently purchased and planted and were expected to be in full bearing by 1980. The balance of Taylor's annual grape requirements was supplied by more than 450 independent growers from approximately 11,500 acres, located principally in the Finger Lakes region of New York State. A portion of Taylor's grape requirements was purchased from counties in the far western part of New York State.

Taylor had contracts with all independent growers from whom it purchased grapes, and a large number of these growers had been supplying Taylor for many years. These contracts required Taylor, on or before August 1 of each year, to announce the prices it would pay for grapes to be purchased in the Fall harvest as well as the quantities it would purchase. Taylor financed its grape purchases through short-term financing. Harvesting generally occurred for approximately eight weeks in September and October. Growers had the right to cancel their contracts during the first two weeks of August; and during November of each year, either the grower or Taylor could cancel the contract. In the past five years, four growers exercised their cancellation rights. On July 30, 1976, Taylor announced it would purchase approximately 70 per cent of the grape tonnage purchased in 1975; this was the first time that the announced quantities did not constitute substantially the entire crop of its growers under contract. The average per-ton price paid to growers for grapes for the 1976 harvest was approximately 86 per cent of that paid in the 1975 harvest. The company maintained an advisory service program for its independent grape growers, providing them with information with respect to fertilization, cultivation, soil analysis, disease control and planting. In addition, it conducted experimental work in its own vineyards and in conjunction with the New York State Agricultural Experiment Station located in nearby Geneva, New York.

Taylor purchased about 25 per cent of its wine needs from several California suppliers for blending purposes and also bought ingredients for certain wines the flavor characteristics of which were derived from grapes not grown in the eastern United States. In addition, wine spirits, sugar and other ingredients, and packaging materials were obtained from several sources. The company believed its sources of supply were adequate and anticipated no shortage in the foreseeable future of grapes supplied by independent growers or of land suitable for growing the varieties and quality of grapes required for its wines.

Taylor's current manufacturing facilities had a total bottling capacity of approximately 4,070 cases per hour. Aging of Taylor's sparkling and still wines normally took up to two years, although wines could be stored for substantially longer periods. As a result of this aging process, and to guard against crop shortages, Taylor, like many companies in the wine industry, maintained inventories that were large in relation to sales and total assets. The company's inventories usually peaked in late October shortly after the grape harvest. In October 1975, Taylor's wine inventories totaled 25.2 million gallons. This figure declined to 20.7 million gallons in July 1976 and then rose again to 25.5 million gallons in October 1976. Taylor had approximately 31.1 million gallons of wine storage capacity, of which 24.7 million gallons was tank storage and 6.4 million gallons was bottled storage. Because of operating limitations, the effective tank storage capacity was limited to approximately 85 per cent or 21 million gallons. On June 30, 1976, the cost (LIFO basis) of Taylor's inventory of still wines in bulk and sparkling wines in process was approximately $30.8 million.

Acquisition by Coca-Cola

Analysts on Wall Street identified several factors that seemed to make the Taylor acquisition a bargain for Coca-Cola. By maintaining premium prices while others were cutting prices, Taylor had maintained its profitability and its record of increasing dividends. Although not investing heavily in such capital projects as a bottle factory, the company had kept its facilities up to date and in good shape. The slipping market share and lack of national image for Taylor were the kind of problems that Coca-Cola's $387 million in cash could solve. Taylor was not deep in debt, was profitable, and in a position to capitalize on what Coca-Cola saw as another wine boom.

Coca-Cola's decision to enter the wine industry was discussed in its publication, *Refresher USA:*

> Our Company's figurative foray into the vineyards came only after a very careful study of the market, a study which revealed some extremely positive indication of growth potential for wine in this country.
>
> The study's major conclusion was that the wine boom that began in the United States in the 1960's will continue through the 1970's and beyond. In other words, the popularity of wine is here to stay.
>
> "More than 60 per cent of the adult U.S. population now consumes wine, which has become an everyday dinner beverage in many households," says Thomas Muller, manager of administration and development for the Wine Group (Changed to Wine Spectrum in 1978). "And as distribution expands from specialty stores to supermarkets, women are becoming an increasingly important group of purchasers as well as consumers of wine."
>
> Another major factor favorably affecting sales, says [Albert] Killeen [President of the Wine Spectrum] "is an accelerating general cultural interest in wine. There's almost an art form to it that could be called 'winesmanship' as people gain more knowledge about wine.
>
> There's a great interest in such activities as wine tasting, vineyard tours, and wine with food. Many people are studying how to develop a wine cellar, the ritual of chilling, de-corking, decanting, and serving wine."
>
> "Among college students there is a decided preference for wine over other alcoholic beverages," observes Grant Curtis, vice-president and marketing services manager for Taylor Wine. "To give you an idea of what an important growth factor that is, there are 28 million college graduates in the United States today; by 1985, there will be nearly double that number—45 million. And these young adults are carrying their preference for wine into their post-college lives."

BUILDING THE WINE SPECTRUM DIVISION

After the Taylor acquisition, Coca-Cola purchased two California vineyards. Sterling Vineyards was the one hundredth largest winery in the United States with a capacity of 60,000 cases per year. Sterling president Michael P. W. Stone described his product:

> We are one of the half dozen or so of the smaller California wineries which seek to position their products at the extreme upper spectrum of the premium line of wines. Wines generally are classed as standard, medium-range and premium: we are aiming to be what you might call "super-premium."

The winery's four red and four white wines were grown and bottled on premises and were classified as estate-bottled, vintage wines. Killeen commented on plans for Sterling:

> Sterling Vineyards' development as a wine growing and producing enterprise will remain unchanged. It will continue to have as its objective the production of the finest Napa Valley premium estate bottled wines in the U.S. Production will con-

> tinue to be restricted and the uncompromising practices that have made Sterling Wines highly respected will be continued by the existing staff at Calistoga.[4]

The purchase of the Monterey Vineyard near Gonzales, California, was announced by Coca-Cola in November 1977. Monterey County was one of the last regions in California to be planted in wine grapes and its wines have been characterized as having "an intense varietal flavor, thinner body, and more fruitiness and crispness." Monterey was completed in 1975 and much of the production equipment was designed by its president, Richard Peterson, a Ph.D. in agricultural chemistry and former employee of Gallo and Beaulieu. The construction of the winery was somewhat unorthodox—the foundation was laid, then the production equipment was installed, and finally the walls and roof were put up. Monterey owned no vineyards and produced eight varietals and one blend. Production capacity was 7 million cases and storage capacity was 2.2 million gallons.

Taylor, Great Western [Pleasant Valley], Sterling, and Monterey became the components of the Wine Spectrum Division of the Coca-Cola Company; together, these wine operations made Coca-Cola the fifth largest factor in the U.S. wine industry. Albert E. Killeen served both as executive vice-president of Coca-Cola and president of the Wine Spectrum. He had responsibility for directing and coordinating the company's wine interests and served as chairman of the board of directors of each winery. He had previously served as corporate marketing director and executive vice-president for marketing at Coca-Cola.

Killeen assessed the strengths of the components of the Wine Spectrum as follows:

> Taylor is the keystone of the Company's wine business because of its reputation for quality, its strong distribution system, and its fine sales organization. The Sterling and Monterey wineries add geographic balance as well as new brands of varietal wines to our product mix. We now have really the best of both worlds—the distinguished tradition of wine-making from the Finger Lakes region of New York State known for its fine champagne and sherries, and the fresh and exuberant ambience of the California growing regions, known for their table wines. Even the two California wineries were carefully chosen to balance one another. One is in a region that produces a very fine Cabernet Sauvignon grape, for example; the other in a much cooler region, fosters some of the best Johannisberg, Riesling and Gruner Sylvaner grapes available anywhere. So our combination of vineyards puts us in a prime position for taking advantage of opportunities to produce a wide variety of high-quality American-grown wines for optimum acceptance among American consumers and consumers around the world.[5]

The importance of the Taylor name to Coca-Cola was illustrated in the following news item:

> Walter S. Taylor, a grandson of the founder of the giant Taylor Wine Company, must take his last name off the labels of bottles containing wine produced by his own company, Bully Hill.
>
> So said Federal Judge Harold Burke in the United States District Court in Hammondsport, N.Y., yesterday. The judge upheld a request by the Coca-Cola

[4] "The Coca-Cola Company Acquires Sterling Vineyards," Coca-Cola press release, August 8, 1977.
[5] *Refresher, USA*, 4 (1977), p. 15.

Company, of Atlanta, for an injunction forbidding Mr. Taylor to use the name because of confusion over the wine made by Taylor Wine Company, which Coca-Cola had purchased last year. Mr. Taylor had been a vice-president of Taylor Wine, but left some years before Coca-Cola acquired control.

Mr. Taylor said he planned to appeal the ruling. However, he added, the family name will be scratched out by hand on the Bully Hill bottles, pending resolution of the case. The "Walter S." will stay.[6]

National Status Sought for Taylor

The immediate result of Coca-Cola's acquisition was the introduction of a new line, Taylor California Cellars. The line was composed of four generic wines—chablis, rhine, rose, and burgundy—which were developed and blended by Dr. Peterson of Monterey Vineyards. The wines were bottled at Franzia Brothers, a subsidiary of Coca-Cola of New York. Taylor provided the label name and the distribution system. Prices for California Cellars were set slightly higher than other premium generic wines. The introductory ad campaign for California Cellars became the reason for the BATF dispute.

Taylor's advertising agency had commissioned a national consumer group to conduct a series of taste tests to compare the new wines with more established names in California premium wines. The results of the tests placed three California Cellars wines in first place in generic categories and one in second place. (See Appendix.) Their results were used as a basis for the introductory ad campaign for the fall of 1978 in the East and in Southern California.

Comparative advertising was a break with traditional wine advertising and there was some question also about whether it was allowed under federal regulations. Taylor sought clearance to use the ads from the Bureau of Alcohol, Tobacco, and Firearms, but was refused. The BATF also refused to prohibit the ads. Taylor then sought court action to gain approval for its commercials but the court ruled that there were no grounds for suit because the ad had not been ordered stopped. Part of the problem resulted from the fact that the Bureau was about to review advertising regulations and new guidelines were not expected for a year after the California Cellars campaign was scheduled to begin. The Bureau was unwilling to pre-clear taste test advertising until it had held hearings and developed standards for review. Prohibitions against taste test ads were based on a 1954 ruling dealing with beer. One BATF official stated:

> It is not the bureau's position that all comparative taste test advertising is misleading and therefore prohibited. It is the Bureau's position that misleading advertising of wine be prohibited.[7]

The decision as to whether or not Taylor's ads were misleading was to be left until the ads were aired and complaints were filed. In view of the uncertainty surrounding the campaign an alternate series of introductory ads was prepared which did not use taste test information.

Penalties for improper advertising ranged from a "letter of admonition" to suspension of vintners' license to criminal prosecution. The possibility of suits from competitors was also present.

[6] "People and Business," *New York Times*, August 16, 1977, p. 58.

[7] Richard C. Gordon, "Try Taste Test Ads, Taylor Told, But U.S. Won't Give Prior OK," *Advertising Age*, 49 (August 21, 1978), pp. 1, 70.

Strategies and Future Outlook

Regarding the prospects for the Wine Spectrum division, Coca-Cola stated the following in its *1978* Annual Report:

> The United States wine market is expected to grow at a healthy rate in the years ahead; annual growth in table wines alone may surpass 10%. United States wine consumption today is at only 5% to 10% of the per capita levels of many European markets. Production, packaging, marketing, merchandising, advertising and promotional programs are now being developed to take advantage of this unique growth opportunity.
>
> The Wine Spectrum units are attempting to exceed industry growth by following these strategies: (1) establish strong production and distribution bases; (2) develop a balanced industry position with quality products from both coasts of the United States; and (3) employ strong and innovative marketing, merchandising, and advertising programs targeted at both the trade and the consumer.

APPENDIX I

Coca-Cola Wine Spectrum (A): Background Information on the Advertising Campaign for "Taylor California Cellars"

I. Wine Tasting Test

The advertising for the introduction of Taylor California Cellars is based on a scientifically structured and carefully monitored wine tasting test, a study that relied on the objective ratings of a panel of twenty-seven recognized wine experts and which clearly establishes this new brand of premium generic wine as one of the finest of its genre.

To ensure the validity and accuracy of the competition, Kenyon & Eckhardt, agency of record for Taylor California Cellars, commissioned the Nationwide Consumer Testing Institute, Inc. (NCTI) to design and implement the tasting test.

The NCTI project sought to determine the rank preference of four brands of California wine in four different categories.

Specifically, the wine tasting competition included the following four tasting tests:

A) *Chablis Tasting*

- Almaden Mountain White Chablis
- Inglenook Navalle Chablis
- Sebastiani Mountain Chablis
- Taylor California Cellars Chablis

B) *Rosé Tasting*

- Almaden Mountain Nectar Vin Rosé
- Inglenook Navalle Vin Rosé
- Sebastiani Mountain Vin Rosé
- Taylor California Cellars Rosé

C) *Rhine Tasting*

- Almaden Mountain Rhine
- Inglenook Navalle Rhine
- C. K. Mondavi Rhine
- Taylor California Cellars Rhine

D) *Burgundy Tasting*

- Almaden Mountain Red Burgundy
- Inglenook Navalle Burgundy
- Sebastiani Mountain Burgundy
- Taylor California Cellars Burgundy

II. Panel of Experts

To reach the highest standards of integrity, the tasting tests required a panel of qualified and unbiased wine tasters, in a blind study, to rank each wine according to preference.

Careful and detailed screening procedures governed the search for the wine tasters to participate in the test. NCTI specified, for instance, that no taster could have any financial interest in or affiliation with: a wine producer, wholesaler or retailer; any publication dealing with wine or reviewing the quality of wine; or a restaurant. Nor could any participant be associated with an advertising agency or market research firm.

As a further requirement, each participant had to have a minimum of five years tasting experience and was required to average at least twelve tastings per year.

NCTI chose the San Francisco Vintners Club, a nonprofit private wine tasting group, as a starting point for recruitment because of its reputation within California wine tasting circles. The club also is not affiliated with any wine producer and its members routinely participate in weekly wine tastings, generally organized according to the identical principles and twenty-point Davis rating system the NCTI intended to use in its own study.

Sixty-four per cent of the twenty-seven-member panel was chosen from this group. The remainder was composed of other serious wine tasters who were members of such other respected wine tasting societies as Les Amis du Vin, Knights of the Vine, and Berkeley Food and Wine Society. Like the tasters from the Vintners Club, each participant was chosen for his or her experience and familiarity with tasting protocol.

The resulting line-up of participating tasters far exceeded those initial qualifications. Most of the respondents had well over five years of tasting experience and several had 20 years of more. In fact the 27 panel members averaged 12.3 years of wine tasting experience.

Likewise, the frequency with which each panel member participated in wine tasting tests averaged fifty per year, far exceeding the minimum standards established by NCTI.

III. Test Procedure

The details of the testing procedure itself were no less demanding than those governing the selection of the panelists. The wine tasting format of the Vintners Club was chosen as the model to be followed by NCTI, specifically because of the club's meticulous and established protocol, including the use of the twenty-point Davis rating system.

The tastings were conducted on July 22, 1978, in San Francisco at the Stanford Court Hotel.

Identical settings and procedures were replicated for each of the four wine tastings. All wine was served in odorless glasses marked only by A, B, C, or D.

In accordance with standard tasting procedures, the panelists moved from tasting the drier wines first to the sweeter wines. Within this order—chablis, rosé, rhine, burgundy—the individual wines were also rotated so that, for example, Glass A contained a different brand of wine in each test.

Great care was also taken in the purchase of the competitive wines to ensure that the competitive wines in the tasting were also recently bottled. Naturally, each of the wines was served at the appropriate temperature.

IV. The Results

Using the twenty-point Davis rating system, the tasters evaluated ten different properties of each wine and ranked the four wines in each test in order of preference.

When the results were tabulated, Taylor California Cellars was judged superior in the rosé, burgundy, and rhine tastings and a very close second in the chablis testing.

CASE THIRTEEN

Republic Steel (A)

DONALD W. SCOTTON and ELEANOR B. SCHWARTZ
Cleveland State University

Assignment Questions:

1. How would you evaluate Republic Steel's commitment to environmental concerns?
2. How are environmental concerns included and controlled through public and governmental actions?
3. What are the problems facing Republic Steel in 1978? What would you recommend that it do now? Why?

Republic Steel was founded in 1899 with corporate headquarters in Cleveland, Ohio. It was the fourth largest steel maker in the United States with net sales of approximately $3.5 billion in 1978.

The Cleveland district was the company's largest steel producing facility, accounting for 35 percent of the corporation's total shipments. It is the largest steel plant in Ohio and one of the top 10 in the United States. Operations conducted within the Cleveland district included blast furnaces, basic oxygen furnaces, primary rolling mills, bar mills, hot and cold strip mills, and a zinc plating line. Also, there were coke ovens for producing a high carbon substance used in iron making; and powerhouses existed for the production of steam and power generation to facilitate the manufacturing operations. Cleveland district capital expenditures exceeded $800 million between 1950 and 1978, of which $161 million was allocated to environmental control equipment and devices.

Concern for environmental control continued over the years and required significant planning, investment, and administration.

Environmental Control

Various kinds of air emissions and waste water are by-products of steel manufacturing. For example, a basic oxygen furnace makes steel by blowing pure oxygen into molten iron and steel scrap. The oxygen combines with the carbon in the molten metal and forms carbon monoxide. This off-gas contains particulate matter that is primarily iron oxide (red dust). Other impurities are

Reprinted with permission of the authors and the Case Research Association.

removed in the form of liquid slag. If the red dust enters the air, the environment can be affected. Another form of air and water pollution can result from the manufacture of coke in steel making.

Steel manufacturers, government groups, and the public at large have been concerned that excessive quantities of these emissions could damage the environment.

Action by Republic. The February 1966 issue of *Republic Reports,* "The Fight against Pollution," revealed that various steel companies supported anti-pollution research programs at Mellon Institute in Pittsburgh since 1938. It was also reported in the article that in the post-World War II years Republic had been active in minimizing pollution emerging from coke ovens and the open hearth furnaces. Specific actions taken at the Cleveland district were reported to include:

1. A process to be completed in 1969 to eliminate the drainage of waste acids into the Cuyahoga River.
2. Installation of connections to newly constructed city of Cleveland interceptor sewers to redirect the plant's sanitary sewerage from the Cuyahoga River to the city's treatment plants.
3. A recycling system for soluble oil and development of an automatic scale pit cleaning system to make the oil available for reuse in the plant rather than disposal in the river.
4. An electrostatic precipitator system to clean air of emissions from the no. 2 open hearth shop and two new oxygen furnaces.

There was increased activity during the 1960s and 1970s by government groups in specifying environmental controls and by Republic Steel in meeting these requirements. The increasing impact of the environmental control program was revealed in the *Republic Steel 1978 Annual Report.* It was reported that almost 20 percent of the corporation's capital outlay in 1978 was for environmental facilities; and pretax profits were reduced by more than $86 million required to maintain and operate environmental control equipment.

Organization for Environmental Concerns. Directly concerned on a day-to-day basis were the division of Government Affairs and Environmental Control. Governmental Affairs was headquartered in Washington, D.C. and concerned itself with federal matters as well as directing the activities of the State Government Affairs Department in Cleveland. Charles A. Hesse, assistant director, State Government Affairs, indicated that the mission of his department was to ensure that Republic's interests and opinions were properly considered when the actions of state and local governments affect the corporation or its products. Personnel were required to conduct continued surveillance of state and local legislative and regulatory actions and to maintain ongoing liaison with government and trade association personnel. The department was also a source of information on government contacts, operations, and specific legislation and activity; and it disseminated pertinent information to the corporation and coordinated corporate responses to legislative and regulatory agencies. Also, it administered programs that encouraged employee participation in government and political activities that fostered good citizenship.

It was the responsibility of the Republic Steel Division of Environmental Control to coordinate corporate effort in meeting partinent regulations. William

L. West, the current Director, indicated that his group was responsible for interpreting regulations and working within the firm to provide adequate control devices. This activity included gaining knowledge of the state of technology available to meet the requirements and suppliers of materials and contractors who could install and build the controls. This Division was also concerned with the monitoring of emissions. David M. Gubanc, Staff Environmental Engineer, analyzed emissions in relation to the standards for control. He was also involved in the economic analysis of emission reduction achieved through additional capital investment. Finally, the Division of Environmental Control cooperated with the Division of Government Affairs in hearings and other public contacts about the role of Republic Steel in environmental controls.

The Division of Public Relations, under the directorship of Randall L. Woods, cooperated with the Divisions of Governmental Affairs and Environmental Control in communicating environmental concerns to the concerned publics and government groups.

The Coke Ovens Controversy

Indicative of the complexity of meeting environmental regulations for environmental control was the coke ovens controversy. This incident extended from 1974 through 1979 and was not completely resolved at the latter date. The matter was presented in detail in an institutional publication, November 26, 1976. Glen A. Johnson, then director of environmental control, wrote the article as follows.

> *The Cleveland Coke Ovens Controversy—A Review and Commentary*
>
> For years Republic's Cleveland district has operated six coke oven batteries to produce coke for ironmaking operations at the district's blast furnaces. These batteries, containing a total of 354 separate ovens, have had an annual cokemaking capacity of approximately 2 million tons per year. Coke, of course, is crucially important to the production of steel and accordingly an adequate supply must always be on hand.
>
> A few years ago, it became apparent to Republic's management that the no. 5 Cleveland coke battery built in 1943 would have to be replaced as rapidly as possible with a new battery. Engineering began promptly and builders of the necessary components of the battery—companies whose capabilities were then very much in demand—were lined up and committed for deliveries in time to have the new battery on stream before the old one was no longer operable. *From the very outset, Republic's plans included the installation of the best available pollution controls on all aspects of cokemaking.*
>
> Pressed to proceed with the construction of the new ovens as soon as possible, Republic commenced field operations in October 1974 in preparation for the erection of the new battery. On October 23, 1974, Republic filed an application with the Ohio Environmental Protection Agency for a permit to install the battery of ovens, specifying the proposed environmental controls. In keeping with prescribed procedures, this application was submitted to the state through the Cleveland Division of Air Pollution Control. On December 7, 1974, the city of Cleveland asked Republic to submit to it a similar permit application, including additional details and drawings concerning the ovens, their operational and technical features, and environmental controls. At this point, it must be mentioned that even the best coke-oven pollution controls are not capable of fully complying with certain Ohio

environmental regulations when interpreted literally. The regulations simply were not drawn up to accommodate the extraordinary technical problems involved in controlling all emissions from such a complex source as a coke battery. However, it was Republic's feelings that recognition of this fact by governmental agencies and realistic negotiations between the company and the agencies would lead to agreement as to the precise controls to be installed and the level of performance to be attained. Nevertheless, the problem led to complications, controversies, and delays in receiving approvals of our permit applications from the state and from the city of Cleveland.

Meanwhile, construction of the vitally needed new coke battery continued and on March 18, 1975, Republic committed itself to the installation of coke-side shed technology to control emissions during the pushing operations, which present the most vexing pollution control problem involved in cokemaking. The shed was to be completed and in operation when the battery was ready for production. At that time, the shed technology—a very costly method—was regarded by the federal EPA as the most satisfactory control approach.

Then we ran into a mid-project technology crisis. As construction of the battery proceeded, we began to receive strong indications that the coke-side shed method of control might not be acceptable to the federal Occupational Safety and Health Administration (OSHA). *In other words, the problem lay not with any unwillingness on Republic's part to install satisfactory pollution controls but rather with an inability on the part of the various governmental agencies involved to decide what kind of pushing controls would be acceptable.* After the passage of many months without satisfactory resolution of this problem, Republic on September 3, 1975 withdrew its commitment to install a coke-side shed in order to avoid the possibility of spending millions of dollars on a control system that might end up being unacceptable. However, Republic recognized that pushing controls, in some form, were needed and that the company would be expected to install whatever control technology was approved by all of the governmental agencies involved.

Late in 1975 and in early 1976—more than a year after Republic submitted its permit applications—the applications were denied by both the state and the city, principally on the grounds that the pushing control controversy had not been resolved. The attention given these denials brought Cleveland's City Council and the media into the dispute and resulted in Republic's receiving a great deal of adverse publicity for purportedly seeking to construct and operate a battery without adequate pollution controls.

After months of extensive negotiations with the various governmental agencies involved, consent agreements were signed in July 1976 with the city and state environmental protection agencies. Under these agreements, Republic was authorized to operate the battery provided the company selected an acceptable pushing control technology by September 1 of this year and agreed to have the controls in operation by September 1978. By this time, there were strong indications that the acceptable technology would be either the one-spot quench car—a system costing about $5 million—or an alternative method being developed by the Donner-Hanna Coke Corporation in Buffalo. Federal authorities participated in these negotiations and subsequently also signed a consent order with Republic containing terms similar to those with the city and state. These actions by the involved parties seemed sensible and equitable, since Cleveland's air quality would benefit by the shutdown of the old battery and since even without pushing controls the new battery would be far cleaner than the battery it was replacing. So, at long last it appeared the problem of satisfying all of the governmental environmental control agencies had been resolved and that the way was cleared for a smooth transfer of cokemaking from the old battery to the new one.

Subsequent events proved this to be optimistic. To begin with, the old battery deteriorated even faster than had been anticipated and in July it had to be withdrawn from service to protect the safety of employees working at the facility. This put Republic into a severe race against time in the effort to get the new ovens on stream and producing coke before our Cleveland coke supply diminished to the point where we could not adequately sustain the required production of steel and keep our normal work force employed.

But this proved to be the lesser of the unforeseen problems that were to plague Republic's efforts. After the company was well along with the 60- to 90-day oven heating and seasoning process required prior to actual cokemaking, citizen groups known as The Neighborhood Environmental Coalition, challenged Republic's agreements with the city and state and requested public hearings before the Ohio Environmental Board of Review—hearings which they hoped would lead to a denial of cokemaking by the new battery until all pollution controls were installed.

This action led to weeks of involved hearings during which the board, on October 8, issued an order prohibiting the startup of cokemaking by the battery until even further hearings could be held and a final decision on the plea of the citizen groups could be rendered. At that time, the board also established the requirement that the citizen groups post a bond of $5,000, ostensibly to compensate Republic for losses incurred by the delay should the company's position ultimately prevail. (As a practical matter, the compensatory worth of the bond was insignificant, since the delay was costing Republic *each day* several times the value of the bond.)

When the board attempted to delay the hearings, Republic appealed to the Ohio Supreme Court asking that the board be ordered to proceed with the additional hearings without interruption or delay. On October 27, the Supreme Court ruled in Republic's favor and ordered the board to proceed with further hearings without interruption. Two days later, based on an earlier legal action by Republic, the Ohio Court of Appeals in Cuyahoga County found that the board's order prohibiting coke production by the battery was invalid, thereby seemingly paving the way for the startup of the battery.

But, again, this proved not to be the case, because on November 1, the citizen groups filed a new motion with the Environmental Board of Review seeking a second order prohibiting startup of the battery. The board complied with this request by issuing a second order prohibiting the startup of cokemaking, again requiring the posting of a $5,000 bond. Republic again appealed to the Ohio Court of Appeals contesting this second action by the board, and a ruling of the court is awaited.

To grasp the breadth of participation in this wasteful procedural controversy that has consumed more time in the effort to obtain permits than was required to construct the facilities themselves, the following is the list of organizations and institutions involved in the dispute:

Republic Steel Corporation
Cleveland Division of Air Pollution Control
Cleveland Board of Building Standards and Appeals
Ohio Environmental Pollution Authority
U.S. Environmental Pollution Authority
Ohio Environmental Board of Review

Cleveland City Council
Cuyahoga County Court of Common Pleas
Cuyahoga County Court of Appeals
Ohio Supreme Court
Ohio Attorney General
The Neighborhood Environmental Coalition
Northern Ohio Lung Association
Southwest Civic Association
Broadway United Methodist Church
Broadway Christian Church
Broadway Retirees Fellowship
Forest City Civic Association

Despite the regulatory ordeal just described, Republic intends to persevere in its efforts to achieve an equitable resolution of this issue. But the episode serves as a striking example of the difficulties a company can face in seeking to make an improvement that will benefit everyone concerned.

Tentative Resolution. A consent decree was issued by the Federal Court of Appeals in December 1976. Republic Steel opened the new coke ovens battery in January 1977. In excess of $8 million was spent for emission controls in this new $30 million facility. The original design included all emission control facilities except pushing emission control. Republic was in the process then of installing pushing emission control. Pertinent air emission controls and Republic's performance are summarized as follows:

1. Federal Environmental Protection Agency.
   a. Control of emissions when charging batteries with coal and containment of leaks through doors, lids, etc.
   Standard: No visible dust for more than 84 seconds over seven consecutive charges.
   Republic Steel performance: Meets standard.
   b. Pushing emissions, occurring when unloading finished coke from coke ovens into quenching cars.
   Standard: Not greater than 0.03 lbs. of particulate matter per ton over 90 percent of total activity of pushing coke into quenching cars.
   Republic Steel performance: Cannot meet standard; results from 0.05 to 0.06 lbs. per ton under existing technology.
2. City of Cleveland Division of Air Pollution Control (with cooperation of Ohio EPA) pushing emission limitations.
   Standard: 0.1 lb. of particulate matter per dry ton of coal charged, or 0.8 lb. of particulate matter of coke produced.
   Republic Steel performance: See (*b*) above. The standard is met and is four times less demanding than the federal standard.

The consent decree included the provision that the standards for pushing emission controls must be met by September 1978. However, when it became known that the state of technology would not make this possible, an extension until September 1979 was granted. As this latter date was approached, there was little confidence that a technological breakthrough would occur to enable the corporation to conform.

The Future—Ambient Air Quality Standards and Source Performance Standards

The passage of the Federal Clean Air Act of 1970 established clean air as a national goal and set up a regulatory organization with the responsibility of achieving the goal within a specified period of time. The agency first defined *clean air* by establishing air quality standards. These are concentrations of specific air pollutants that will not affect human health under conditions of long-term exposure. This standard is called the "primary air quality standard" or "health standard." The primary air quality standard for total suspended particulate (TSP) is an annual average concentration of 75 micrograms per cubic meter, and a 24-hour maximum of 260 micrograms per cubic meter. Subsequent regulations concerning emission performance such as the coke oven emission limitation described in the previous section were written to reflect the technological state of the art of air pollution control. The agency proceeded on the premise that if point sources of pollution conformed to the mandated performance standards which were technology based, then the primary air quality standards would be achieved.

The Cleveland air monitoring network has one station located in a public parking lot that reports its daily average readings of ambient air quality to the media which then disseminates the information to the general public. The 1978

EXHIBIT 1: Total Suspended Particulate at St. Vincent Monitoring Station, Cleveland, Ohio

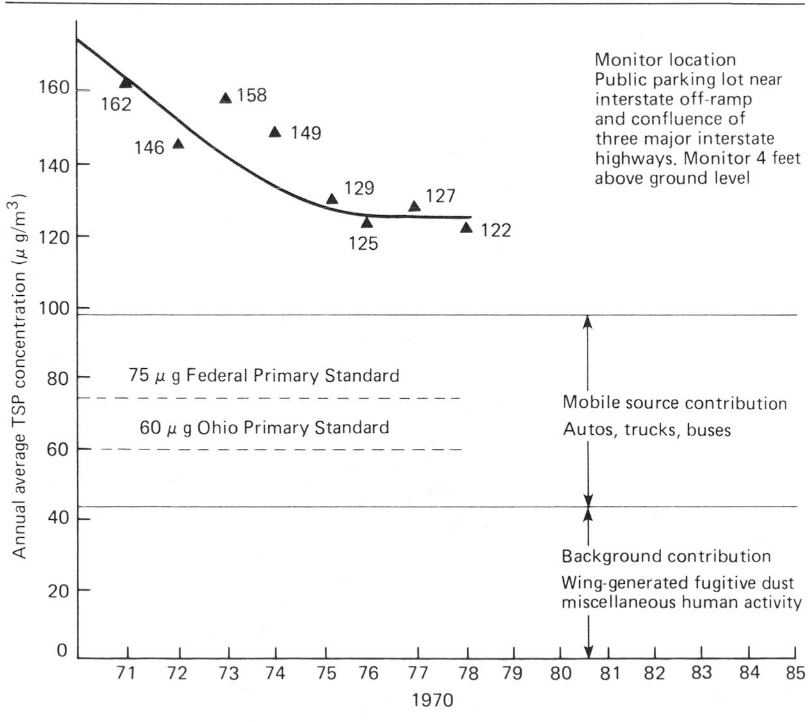

Source: Republic Steel Environmental Control Department, April 1979.

annual average TSP concentration recorded at this station was 122 micrograms/cubic meter which exceeded the primary air standard by 47 micrograms. Exhibit 1 shows the eight-year trend of the annual average TSP level. Analysis of the 1978 TSP level by source reveals the following.

Contributing source	*Total suspended particulates (TSP) in micrograms per cubic meter*
Wind-generated fugitive dust, miscellaneous human activity	42
Autos, trucks, buses	55
Other, including Republic Steel	25
Total	122

Exhibit 1 and the TSP data reveal that the 75 microgram per cubic meter TSP health standard is exceeded by background levels and mobile source contribution before any industrial or point source pollution is added to the ambient air.

David M. Gubanc noted that the regulatory agencies recognized the invalidity of the premise that controlling point source pollution would result in air

EXHIBIT 2: Annual Average Air Quality Measurements (Total Suspended Particulates) and Republic Steel Cleveland District's Capital Investment in Air Pollution Control Equipment

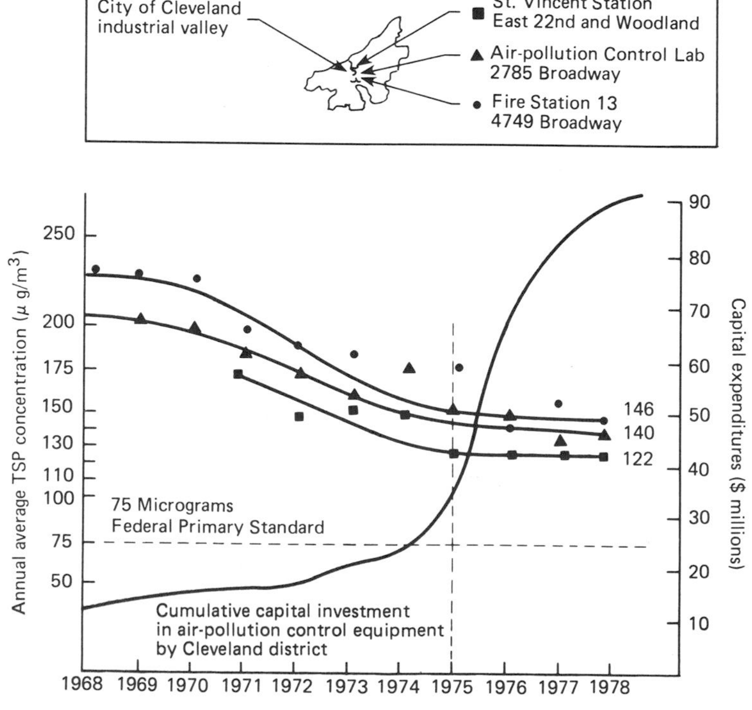

Source: Republic Steel, Environmental Control Department, April 1979.

quality that met the primary air quality standards. The U.S. EPA stated as much when it submitted an urban particulate assessment study for Cleveland in 1976 that concluded that despite full compliance by point sources with mandated emission limitations, a few air monitoring stations would continue to exceed the TSP standards due to the topography, land use patterns, and meterology of the area. Rather than deal with this false premise, the public strategy of the agency and legislative bodies was to extend the legislated dates for primary air quality standard attainment from 1975 to the end of 1982. The agency then continued to insist upon additional industrial source control based on the same premise it had proven false through its own assessment study.

West and Gubanc expressed their firm's concern for the increased capital outlays for environmental control capital equipment and the decreasing rate for achieving reductions in air pollution. The Environmental Control Division of Republic compared the cumulative capital investment in air pollution control equipment to TSP concentration trends at the air sampling stations closest to Republic's Cleveland district as shown in Exhibit 2. Measurements taken at the three air quality monitoring stations in Cleveland revealed approximately equivalent geographical effectiveness in reducing pollution; but the rate of return in air quality to investment was decreasing markedly.

There were heavy capital outlays for point source emission controls by other industries within the urban area. The possibility remained that other solutions should be considered.

CASE FOURTEEN

Republic Steel (B)

DONALD W. SCOTTON and ELEANOR B. SCHWARTZ
Cleveland State University

Assignment Questions:

1. What impact have public attitudes had on Republic Steel?
2. How would you evaluate Republic Steel's public awareness program?
3. What programs would you recommend for the future?

The Cleveland district of the Republic Steel Corporation assumed a low profile to the public for many years. Although the corporation wanted to be known as a good citizen in the community which supported civic endeavors and provided jobs, income, and nationally needed products, there was no active strategy to communicate and build this image. Little was done to inform business, government, civic groups, and the public at large of the firm's contributions and importance in the community.

Possibly, the highest visibility resulted from the incident referred to as the coke oven controversy. For three years Republic was involved with government and civic groups in obtaining a permit to build a new coke oven battery. The matter of environmental controls was the source of the controversy, and publicity was not always favorable for Republic.

In 1976, it became apparent that Republic Steel should review its low profile strategy and consider an active program of informing the public as to its role and contributions to the community.

Strategy to Increase Public Awareness and Favorable Attitudes

The Concept. Republic Steel believed that action should be taken to increase the public awareness of its activities, contributions to the community, and efforts to establish effective pollution controls. L. T. Young, director of marketing and advertising communications, indicated that the public had scarce information about and understanding of his firm. For example, substantial support was given to civic groups, charities, and the Cleveland Orchestra; however, these activities had not been publicized.

Randall L. Woods, director of public relations, related the firm's concern

Reprinted with permission of the authors and the Case Research Association.

about the public's lack of knowledge and adverse reactions among the news media and local groups to Republic's pollution control measures. Meldrum and Fewsmith, Inc., Republic's advertising agency, indicated in an action proposal that:

> lack of awareness . . . makes members of the community groups more receptive to vocal critics of Republic whose attacks frequently contain distorted information, whose charges are emotionally appealing, and whose demands indicate a lack of understanding of the problems facing those who must devise, construct, and finance equipment to reduce or eliminate industrial emissions. . . .

Meldrum and Fewsmith had run an environmental control communications program in 1971 for Republic in Cleveland, Chicago, and Buffalo over a three-month period. The results showed that there were dramatic changes in awareness and attitudes held by the public. Important findings were (1) attitudes toward Republic changed because of their specific environmental control programs, and (2) public awareness of Republic's efforts varied quite closely with the intensity of the communications program.

Thus, it was determined that a new reportable communications program should be run to increase public awareness and provide a basis for the public forming attitudes toward Republic Steel.

The Program. Meldrum and Fewsmith was retained to conduct the program, and presented tentative objectives which are summarized as follows:

Corporate objectives

1. Reduce public criticism of Republic as it relates to environmental control and a lack of accurate information about what Republic has done to control industrial emissions.
2. Increase public acceptance and support of Republic Steel as a community good neighbor in the specified audiences.

Communications objectives

1. Increase awareness and understanding in Cleveland mill-fence-line communities, general public, and target "thought leader" audiences of what Republic Steel has done, is doing, and plans to do to control industrial emissions and the relative costs of these actions as they relate to viability of the Cleveland district.
2. Increase awareness of Republic Steel as a good neighbor that is doing its best to protect the environment and maintain employment as a result of maintaining itself as a reliable supplier of steel to the marketplace.
3. Increase awareness of Republic's contributions to the community: employment, taxes, etc.

Tactical objectives

1. The program is to be comprehensive, straightforward, reportable, and use a multimedia campaign format based on a common theme.
2. The tone and degree of impact created should be midrange. Sufficient impact and frequency of message should be developed to assure that audiences will receive messages. But overstatement should be avoided.

All problems are not solved; steel making will always be a dirty process. Communicate in a rational approach that Republic has done a lot to solve its problems, quite a lot, and there are dramatic improvements and public benefits, but no implications should be made that the job is finished.

3. The primary audience is located within a two-mile radius of the Cleveland district and is described in this campaign as "fence-line community." But the publics of the entire city of Cleveland and its suburbs are equally important to Republic in its quest for an informed public.
4. Substantive technical communications content would be based on information contained in Cleveland district environmental data sheets, April 1978, and counsel of G. A. Johnson, director of environmental control, and David M. Gubanc, staff environmental engineer.

The current program was patterned after the 1971 environmental control communications program. Plans were made for (1) a benchmark survey of the community to determine existing awareness patterns and attitudes, (2) a corporate advertising program, and (3) a postcampaign survey of the community to determine possible changes in awareness and attitudes.

The Benchmark Survey

The benchmark survey was designed by Meldrum and Fewsmith in consultation with Republic Steel. Its specific purpose was to establish base levels against which future changes, as measured in follow-up studies, could be compared. Changes between the benchmark and follow-up studies findings would be evaluated in terms of total communication program contribution. The sample selection, field work, and preliminary findings were completed by Business Research Services, Inc. of Cleveland. Interviewing began May 3, 1978 and was completed by May 6, 1978, so that the corporate advertising program could be started during May.

Research Design. (1) *Sample.* Householders were chosen as the group to be interviewed. The city of Cleveland, which surrounds the Republic Steel facilities, was chosen as the area of study. Next, it was recognized that those persons living within two miles of the installation were affected particularly by any unfavorable industrial environment. This group was defined as the fence-line community; and they could be identified and selected by using a crisscross directory for the census tracts within the two-mile range of Republic. The decision was made to choose a sample consisting of 600 respondents. Because one third of the households were located within two miles of Republic facilities, 200 were to be selected randomly from the fenceline communities and 400 from the remainder of the city of Cleveland. (2) *Method of collecting information.* The survey was conducted by means of telephone calls to householders as described above. (3) *Questionnaire.* It was designed to obtain the respondents' knowledge and perceptions about (*a*) causes of pollution, (*b*) which industries and firms caused it, (*c*) effect, concern, and control of pollution by the three leading steel manufacturers in Cleveland, and (*d*) impressions about Republic as to its contribution to the city as a citizen and economically. Not only was this information to provide a base line for measuring changes after the institutional advertising campaign, but it was to provide information as to items to be communicated for better awareness and perceptions.

Findings. A summary of findings was included with the detailed report submitted by Business Research Services. (See the Appendix for comparative tables containing condensed information about this and the postcampaign survey.) This study was interpreted in a memorandum by Bruce Childers, director of research, for Meldrum and Fewsmith as follows:

> . . . Republic Steel is considered as a good company . . . beneficial to the community . . . however, there is a lack of specific knowledge of the environmental control steps taken and the magnitude of these steps, as well as the contribution to the community in terms of employment, salaries, and taxes.
>
> . . . the steel industry and Republic Steel are seen as major contributors to pollution—particularly air pollution . . . Republic is seen as . . . trying to control pollution. But, a sizable portion of the respondents were unable to make an assessment of efforts in general or specific terms.
>
> . . . the three steel companies in the area . . . were rated about equally on "efforts to control air and water pollution," "concern for Cleveland's environment," and "support of the community."
>
> . . . due to Republic's higher visibility, I would expect to see a much more critical view of the environmental issues and a more positive view on the community support issue. We could assume that this "similar" rating of the three companies is due to a lack of awareness of specific company environmental control efforts or contributions to the community.
>
> . . . there appears to be a feeling that while Republic is thought of as a major cause of pollution, they are also thought of as being important in the area.
>
> To summarize. . . . First, the attitudes toward Republic are a good foundation upon which to build . . . the communication program need not concentrate on the difficult task of reshaping, rebuilding, or even reversing basic attitudes. A positive base is imperative if desired messages are to be accepted rather than rejected. Second. . . . an awareness void exists in terms of specific environmental control accomplishments, efforts, and contributions to the community. These two points indicate that the communication of basic hard facts about accomplishments and contributions will be accepted and are necessary to overcome the awareness void.

The research study and Bruce Childers' analysis were forwarded to Republic by Norton I. Satz, senior vice-president and account executive for Republic Steel. He recommended that the findings and interpretations be used as the base line of awareness and attitudes; and they should be used also in composing the content of the advertising program.

CORPORATE ADVERTISING PROGRAM

A multimedia advertising program, based upon the benchmark survey findings, was established to present facts about Republic Steel. This program was run from mid-May through mid-November 1978.

Messages. The advertising messages covered both air and water pollution controls used by and the economic impact of Republic Steel in the community. The messages were allocated by subject and media as follows:

Media	*Percent of messages by topic*	
	Economic	*Pollution*
Television	21%	79%
Radio	2	98
Print media	15	85

They were classified under the categories of (1) pollution control, which included scrubbers, water treatment, red dust, coke oven gases, and smoke; and (2) economic impact, which included payroll number of employees, investment and taxes paid. (See Appendix Exhibits 1, 2, and 3.)

Typical of message content was the story told in the 60-second TV commercial entitled, "Coke." Appropriate film showed a coke oven in operation. The following key phrases are representative of the meesage:

Spokesman: [*on camera*] In these big events at Republic Steel, coal is converted into coke.

We have to do this, because coke is something we absolutely need as an ingredient when we're making steel.

[*open oven*] What you're looking at now is the usual way that the red hot coke is emptied from an oven, cooled and transported.

Up to now, it has always been pushed into an open quench car.

That makes for a lot of smoke and gas . . . and a tough, environmental problem.

[*on camera*] But technology is catching up—and now Republic Steel is beginning to use a new kind of *closed* quench car, designed just to solve this problem.

The hot coke is never in the open, but it is pushed directly into the car, where the dirty gases are captured and cleaned by water sprays.

What comes out the exhaust vent is only steam and cleaned gas.

It's another way we're working at Republic Steel to make Cleveland a *better* place for all of us.

Media and Schedules. Detailed information about the media and schedules are presented in Appendix Exhibits 1, 2, and 3. The media mix tactical decisions included:

1. A variety of media was needed to reach a broad socioeconomic audience range.
2. Radio and television (considering station and time selections) were chosen to reach industrial plant employees and municipal government, Cleveland voters, and other important audiences. Considered also was the necessity to reach black and ethnic audiences.
3. Newspapers, citywide, plant neighborhood, foreign language, ethnic, and black, were used to contact the target publics.
4. The upscale audiences, thought leaders, community influentials, and those who sway opinions within the city were reached through two Cleveland media networks—business and opinion. The affluent, young, active, pacesetters were reached through *Cleveland Magazine.* This package covered that segment of the market having upper educational, income, and managerial/professional demographics.
5. Outdoor billboards were used to contact the mobile and pedestrian traffic, particularly within the fence-line community area.

To the extent possible, an alternating strategy of heavy and maintenance message exposure was carried out. This followed the principle that concentrated exposure is required to penetrate and command attention; and once this is achieved, fewer exposures are required to maintain the level of awareness for a short period of time. Then, the cycle must be repeated. Finally, media usage was to be held below the "irritation-factor level" that can occur with heavy sustained exposures.

Postcampaign Survey and Findings

This portion of the program was conducted in mid-November 1978 and after six months of the corporate advertising program. It was designed to measure pertinent changes between May 1978 and November 1978 in awareness and attitudes of the Cleveland public. This second survey was designed and conducted identically to the benchmark survey to obtain comparable data. Meldrum and Fewsmith and Business Research Services assumed the same responsibilities as they had for the May survey.

Summary Findings. Because of their roles in designing the program and serving as the agency for the corporate advertising phase, Meldrum and Fewsmith requested that Business Research Services summarize the findings and report them directly to Republic Steel. Summary tables prepared by the research firm are included in the Appendix. The interpretations presented below were extracted from the Business Research Services report.

1. *Overview.* The corporate advertising campaign was highly successful in informing the public of Republic Steel's pollution control efforts and its position in the community. There were positive changes in public attitudes and perceptions since the start of the campaign.

2. *Changes in awareness of pollution control.* Awareness of Republic's pollution control efforts changed significantly. Increases from May to November of 300 percent and 171 percent occurred in the fence-line area and the remainder of Cleveland, respectively. (See Appendix, Table 1A.) Not only was the fence-line community more aware, but 37 percent were able to cite corrective action taken to include water filtration and 23 percent named new systems to filter smoke stacks and other devices for air purification. (See Appendix, Table 1B.)

3. *Perceptions about the control of pollution.* Republic was viewed as doing the best job of controlling air and water pollution at the end of the corporate advertising program. (See Appendix, Table 2.) In fact, it was the only one of the three steel firms whose measurements increased significantly. This is particularly significant when it is noted that no one company was really distinguished as doing the best job of pollution control in the benchmark survey.

4. *Favorable impressions of pollution control efforts.* The respondents were asked to rate the three steel companies in four characteristics: efforts to control air pollution; efforts to control water pollution; concern for Cleveland's environment; and overall support of the community. The results contained in Appendix, Table 3 revealed that Republic increased its favorable ratings in every measurement in both samples. The ratings given by the fence-line respondents who live nearest the industrial areas are of particular interest. Their attitudes toward the other two steel companies did not change significantly in any of the four measurements since the benchmark survey. However, attitudes toward Republic Steel were more positive in every measurement.

5. *Republic as a corporate citizen.* Although specific economic facts were not known by the respondents, they indicated that Republic was valuable to Cleveland, because it provided jobs. (See Appendix, Tables 4A and 4B.) There was a dramatic change in opinion between May and November concerning Republic's attempt to clean up pollution. There were 525 percent more respondents in the fence-line area and 125 percent more in the remainder of Cleveland who believed that Republic Steel was trying to stop pollution. In summary, Republic Steel was rated as good to have in the community.

6. *Increased awareness of steel industry as a polluter.* Business Research Services noted that the advertising program not only increased knowledge of efforts to control pollution, but also called attention to pollution. (See Table 5.) The increased recognition of pollution caused by steel makers was limited to the fence-line sample and water pollution. Business Research Services said: "The problems of pollution are very real . . . to fence-line residents . . . it is logical to expect a more intense, more personal reaction to a pollution advertising campaign among fence-line respondents than among respondents from the city as a whole."

APPENDIX

EXHIBIT 1: 1978 Corporate Advertising Program (Television)

Commercials run during test period:
Benchmark interviewing completed May 6, 1978
Follow-up interviewing completed November 1, 1978

Total commercials:
177—60s, 10—30s during test period.

Commercial title		*Times run*	*Basic subject*
Pockets	60 sec.	36	Economic
	30 sec.	4	Economic
Coke	60 sec.	56	Environmental control
	30 sec.	6	Environmental control
Red Dust	60 sec.	32	Environmental control
Water Treatment	60 sec.	53	Environmental control

By basic subject:
Economic, 36—60 sec; 4—30 sec. (21%)
Pollution, 141—60 sec; 6—30 sec. (79%)

Stations used:
WKYC = 52; WJW = 54; WEWS = 36; WUAB = 45

Time period:
Early and late news, prime rotator (3, 5, and 8); prime move (43)

Number of spots by week:
First spots—mid-August 1978
8/14/78 = 22—60s; 8/21/78 = 17—60s; 8/28/78 = 23—60s; 9/3/78 = 17—60s
9/11/78 = 21—60s, 2—30s; 9/18/78 = 19—60s, 4—30s; 10/9/78 = 19—60s, 4—30s
10/16/78 = 23—60s; 10/23/78 = 16—60s posttest conducted
10/30/78 = 15—60s, 2—30s; 11/6/78 = 18—60s; 11/27/78 = 17—60s
12/4/78 = 17—60s; 12/11/78 = 17—60s

EXHIBIT 2: 1978 Corporate Advertising Program (Radio)

Commercial run during test period:
Benchmark interviewing completed May 6, 1978
Follow-up interviewing completed November 1, 1978

Total commercials:
1,064—60 sec. spots during test period.

Commercial title		*Times run*	*Basic subjects*
Scrubber	(R3)	76	Environmental control
	(R1)	55	Environmental control
Water treatment	(R2)	115	Environmental control
	(R5)	276	Environmental control
Red dust	(R4)	203	Environmental control
Coke	(R6)	317	Environmental control
Investment	(R8)	11	Economic
	(R7)	11	Economic

By basic subject:
Pollution control—1,042 (98%); economic—22 (2%)
First spots end of May 1978

Stations used:
WZAK-FM, WERE-AM, WJMO-AM, WHK-AM, WQAL-FM, WWWE-AM

EXHIBIT 3: 1978 Corporate Advertising Program (Print Media)

Ads run during test period:
Benchmark interviewing completed May 6, 1978
Follow-up study interviewing completed November 1, 1978

Publication	*Number and size ads*	*Time period/month run*
IMC Reporter	2—2P4CB	September and October
Bring Back Broadway Program	1—1PB&W	October
Cleveland Athletic Club Roster	1—1P4CB	September
Torchlight Roster	1—1P4CB	September
Ad Club News	2—1/3PB&W	September and October
Plain Dealer	11—7cx215 lines	May 6–October 19
Program-Tennis Tournament	1—1PB&W	July
Cleveland Press	11—7cx215 lines	May 6–October 19
Call & Post	8—7cx215 lines	May 20–October 21
Neighborhood News—Garfield Hts Tribune	6—7cx215 lines	May 17–October 4
American Home (Slovenian)	8—6cx210 lines	May 26–October 19
Driva (Lithuanian)	8—5cx224 lines	May 26–October 19
Hungarian News	9—6cx210 lines	May 25–October 19

EXHIBIT 3: (continued)

Publication	*Number and size ads*	*Time period/month run*
Kuryer (Polish)	6—6cx210 lines	May 25–October 12
Wolfsblatt (Saxon-German)	9—6cx210 lines	May 22–October 16
Szabadsag (Hungarian)	8—6cx210 lines	May 26–October 20
Wachter & Anzeiger (German)	8—6cx210 lines	May 26–October 20
Com Corp—		
Sun Herald	7—7cx215 lines	June 22–October 19
Lakewood Sun Post		
News Sun		
Perma Sun Post		
West Side Sun News		
Sun Currier		
Sun Press		
Sun Messenger		
Southeast Sun		
Herald Sun		
Strongville-Royalton Sun Star		
Cleveland Business Network	2—1P4CB	August and October
Cleveland Opinion Network	1—1P4CB	September
Cleveland Magazine	3—1P4CB	July, September, and October
Billboards:		
Airport		August, September, and October
Huron Road		August, September, and October
Westside Superior Bridge		October
Rotating Boards (34 boards)		July, August, and September

Total ads: 114 run during test period

Ad title	*Times run*	*Basic subject*
Pockets (A-2484)	17	Economic
Smoking habit (A-4568)	28	Environmental control
Coke (A-4509)	13	Environmental control
Water treatment (A-4598)	38	Environmental control
Water treatment (A-4497)	6	Environmental control
Super scrubber (A-4498)	12	Environmental control
Billboards/smoking habit (A-4570)		

By basic subject; Pollution control—97 ads (85%): economic—17 ads (15%)

TABLE 1A: Awareness of Pollution Control Efforts

Question: *Are you aware of anything that has been done or is being done by any of these companies to control air and water pollution? (If yes) Which company?*

Awareness or Republic's efforts to control air and water pollution increased significantly since May 1978: In Cleveland, Republic's measurement went from 17 to 46 percent, a 171 percent increase. In the fence-line, Republic's measurement went from 15 to 60 percent, a 300 percent increase.

	City of Cleveland					*Fence-line*				
	May	*November*	*Percent change*	*Point change*	*Signi-ficant*	*May*	*November*	*Percent change*	*Point change*	*Signi-ficant*
Yes, Republic	17%	46%	+171	+29	Yes	15%	60%	+300	+45	Yes
Yes, Jones & Laughlin	7	8	+ 14	+ 1	No	4	8	+100	+ 4	No
Yes, U.S. Steel	7	7	0	0	No	4	5	+ 25	+ 1	No
Base	(400)	(400)				(200)	(200			

TABLE 1B: Recall of Republic's Activity to Control Pollution

Question: *What do you recall has been done or is being done by Republic Steel to control air and water pollution?*

Thirty-seven percent (37 percent) in the fence-line, and 24 percent in Cleveland recalled Republic's water filtration facility; and 23 percent in the fence-line and 10 percent in Cleveland recalled Republic's air filtration systems.

	City of Cleveland					*Fence-line*				
	May	*November*	*Percent change*	*Point change*	*Significant*	*May*	*November*	*Percent change*	*Point change*	*Significant*
New system for smoke stacks/ screens and filters installed to purify air	7%	10%	+ 43	+ 3	No	6%	23%	+ 283	+17	Yes
Water filtration facility/ improved water pollution control methods	3	24	+700	+21	Yes	1	37	+3600	+36	Yes
Making a general effort to fight pollution/spending money on improvements	1	8	+700	+ 7	Yes	7	12	+ 71	+ 5	No
Base	(400)	(400)				(200)	(200)			

TABLE 2: Best Job of Controlling Pollution

Question: *Which one of these companies do you feel is doing the best job of controlling air pollution? . . . The best job of controlling water pollution?*

Perceptions of Republic doing the best job of controlling air pollution increased 126 percent in Cleveland (from 23 to 52 percent) and 108 percent in the fence-line (from 25 to 52 percent). Perceptions of Republic doing the best job of controlling water pollution increased 194 percent in Cleveland (from 17 to 50 percent) and 194 percent in the fence-line (from 17 to 50 percent).

	City of Cleveland					*Fence-line*				
	May	*November*	*Percent change*	*Point change*	*Significant*	*May*	*November*	*Percent change*	*Point change*	*Significant*
Best job of controlling air pollution:										
Republic	23%	52%	+126	+29	Yes	25%	52%	+108	+27	Yes
U.S. Steel	18	15	− 17	− 3	No	21	11	− 48	−10	No
J&L	13	17	+ 31	+ 4	No	18	13	− 28	− 5	No
Best job of controlling water pollution:										
Republic	17	50	+194	+33	Yes	17	50	+194	+33	Yes
U.S. Steel	12	13	+ 8	+ 1	No	12	10	− 17	− 2	No
J&L	8	14	+ 75	+ 6	Yes	11	9	− 18	− 2	No
Base	(400)	(400)				(200)	(200)			

TABLE 3: Positive Ratings of Characteristics*

Question: *I'd like you to rate three steel companies in the Cleveland area on several characteristics. Let's use a scale of from 1 (lowest, most unfavorable rating) to 5 (highest, most favorable rating).*

Republic Steel significantly increased its favorable ratings (5 and 4) in every measurement in both samples. Republic's largest increase in Cleveland was in efforts to control water pollution, which increased 135 percent; Republic's largest increase in the fence-line was in concern for Cleveland's environment, which increased 93 percent.

	City of Cleveland					*Fence-line*				
	May	*November*	*Percent change*	*Point change*	*Significant*	*May*	*November*	*Percent change*	*Point change*	*Significant*
Efforts to control air pollution:										
Republic Steel	22%	42%	+ 91	+20	Yes	22%	34%	+55	+12	Yes
J&L	16	21	+ 31	+ 5	No	19	14	−26	− 5	No
U.S. Steel	18	23	+ 28	+ 5	No	13	15	+15	+ 2	No
Efforts to control water pollution:										
Republic Steel	17	40	+135	+23	Yes	19	36	+89	+17	Yes
J&L	13	20	+ 54	+ 7	Yes	15	12	−20	− 3	No
U.S. Steel	13	22	+ 69	+ 9	Yes	15	15	0	0	No
Concern for Cleveland's environment:										
Republic Steel	21	46	+119	+25	Yes	15	29	+93	+14	Yes
J&L	19	28	+ 47	+ 9	Yes	16	16	0	0	No
U.S. Steel	17	26	+ 53	+ 9	Yes	14	15	+ 7	+ 1	No
Overall support of the community:										
Republic Steel	25	54	+116	+29	Yes	18	33	+88	+15	Yes
J&L	23	27	+ 17	+ 4	No	15	17	+13	+ 2	No
U.S. Steel	22	29	+ 32	+ 7	Yes	13	18	+38	+ 5	No
(Base)	(400)	(400)				(200)	(200)			

* Combination of 5 and 4 ratings in a 1 to 5 rating scale.

TABLE 4A: Impression of Republic Steel

Question: *Overall, what is your impression of Republic Steel?*

Without aid, respondents perceive Republic Steel as providing jobs (22 percent in Cleveland, 26 percent in fence-line), having a good reputation (18 percent in Cleveland, 25 percent in fence-line), and trying to stop pollution (18 percent in Cleveland, 25 percent in fence-line).

	City of Cleveland					Fence-line				
	May	*November*	*Percent change*	*Point change*	*Significant*	*May*	*November*	*Percent change*	*Point change*	*Significant*
Positive response:										
They provide jobs/hire people	20%	22%	+ 10	+ 2	No	27%	26%	− 4	− 1	No
They have a good reputation/ a good company	17	18	+ 6	+ 1	No	23	25	+ 9	+ 2	No
They are environmentally concerned/ are trying to stop pollution	8	18	+125	+10	Yes	4	25	+525	+21	Yes
They are a large company	8	8	0	0	No	13	10	− 23	− 3	No
They are good for Cleveland	8	14	+ 75	+ 6	Yes	8	14	+ 75	+ 6	No
Negative response:										
They pollute the air/do not control pollution	12	9	− 25	− 3	No	17	15	− 12	− 2	No
Base	(400)	(400)				(200)	(200)			

Note: Only comments with 10 percent or more mentions listed.

TABLE 4B: Reactions to Republic Steel Being Located in Cleveland

Question: *Do you feel it is good for Cleveland to have Republic Steel in the community? Why do you say that?*

Ninety-five percent (95 percent) of the respondents said, yes it is good for Cleveland to have Republic Steel in the community. The major reason cited was that Republic provides jobs for Cleveland.

	City of Cleveland					*Fence-line*				
	May	*November*	*Percent change*	*Point change*	*Significant*	*May*	*November*	*Percent change*	*Point change*	*Significant*
Do you feel it is good for Cleveland to have Republic Steel in the community?										
Yes	93%	95%	+ 2	+ 2	No	91%	96%	+ 5	+ 5	No
No	5	2	− 60	− 3	No	8	4	− 50	− 4	No
Yes reasons:										
They provide jobs for Cleveland	81	80	− 1	− 1	No	77	88	+ 14	+11	Yes
Cleveland needs companies like Republic	11	17	+ 55	+ 6	Yes	9	14	+ 56	+ 5	No
They help Cleveland by paying taxes	10	7	− 30	− 3	No	2	5	+150	+ 3	No
They are good for the image of Cleveland/Cleveland needs them	10	6	− 40	− 4	No	14	13	− 7	− 7	No
They are good for Cleveland's economy	6	16	+167	+10	Yes	22	18	− 18	− 4	No

TABLE 5: Causes of Air/Water Pollution

Question: *What particular industry do you think of as the major cause of air/water pollution? What specific companies do you consider as major causes of air/water pollution?*

Perceptions of the steel industry in general, and Republic Steel in particular, as causes of water pollution increased in the fence-line. Unaided mentions of Republic as a cause of water pollution went from 9 to 24 percent, a 167 percent increase.

	City of Cleveland					Fence-line				
	May	*November*	*Percent change*	*Point change*	*Significant*	*May*	*November*	*Percent change*	*Point change*	*Significant*
Industry causing:										
Air pollution:										
Steel mills	61%	58%	− 5	−3	No	70%	74%	+ 6	+ 4	No
Automobile industry	8	8	0	0	No	1	7	+600	+ 6	No
Factories	4	12	+200	+8	Yes	3	3	0	0	No
Water pollution:										
Steel mills	21	26	+ 24	+5	No	15	39	+160	+24	Yes
Chemical plants	10	12	+ 20	+2	No	19	9	− 53	−10	Yes
Factories	2	11	+450	+9	Yes	8	11	+ 38	+ 3	No
Company causing:										
Air pollution:										
Republic Steel	33	27	− 18	−6	Yes	42	49	+ 17	+ 7	No
J&L	18	15	− 17	−3	No	28	33	+ 18	+ 5	No
Ford	7	5	− 29	−2	No	1	5	+400	+ 4	No
All steel companies	3	6	+100	+3	No	6	4	− 33	− 2	No
Water pollution:										
Republic Steel	9	10	+ 11	+1	No	9	24	+167	+15	Yes
J&L	5	9	+ 80	+4	No	7	16	+129	+ 9	Yes
Harshaw Chemical	2	2	0	0	No	4	4	0	0	No
Base	(400)	(400)				(200)	(200)			

CASE FIFTEEN

DuPont de Nemours & Company (A)

WILLIAM R. BOULTON
University of Georgia

Assignment Questions:

1. How had the titanium dioxide (TiO_2) industry changed between 1970 and 1975?
2. How did DuPont's TiO_2 strategy take advantage of industry changes?
3. What are the risks in adding the $200 million De Lisle plant? Should these risks continue?

On October 10, 1975 A. H. Geil, vice-president of DuPont's Pigments Department had just completed his presentation to the executive committee to justify continuation and completion of its titanium dioxide plant in De Lisle, Mississippi. He was now wondering what decision they would make. In his presentation, Geil had presented four alternatives: (1) the continuation of the De Lisle project; (2) an alternative program that would provide for a maximum reasonable time "delay" of the De Lisle project and its consequences; (3) an alternative program, at less cost, that would allow them to maintain market share; and (4) the consequences of abandoning their expansion altogether.

As a result of the precipitous downturn in business in late 1974 following the oil embargo, DuPont's management was faced with a tight cash-flow position which required the curtailment of some of its investment projects. The Pigments Department Task Force was then asked in 1975 to reexamine its titanium dioxide (TiO_2) growth strategy. Its current strategy called for rapid growth from 1976 to 1980 with increasing share of the TiO_2 pigments market to 52–55 percent. Geil felt that as long as DuPont was aggressive, the only U.S. expansion would be Kerr-McGee's 50,000-ton per year plant. High waste-disposal costs, low cash positions, and inability of competition to build large plants would keep competition from building new capacity. He also felt that a 3¢ per pound per year price increase would yield the necessary return for De Lisle, allow competition an adequate return to stay in business, but limit its ability to expand.

Background

Titanium dioxide (TiO_2) is a white chemical pigment employed in the manufacture of products such as paints, paper, synthetic fibers, plastics, ink, and synthetic rubber to make them whiter or opaque. It has no commercially satisfactory substitutes. TiO_2 can be produced from manufacturing processes using either (1) a sulfuric acid reaction on a relatively low-grade ilmenite ore or titanium slag feedstock (the "sulfate" process), or (2) a chlorine reaction upon either a high-grade titanium ore feedstock (rutile ore or synthetic rutile) or on lower grade ilmenite ore feedstocks (the "chloride" process). The sulfate process was a "batch" process as contrasted with the "continuous flow" operation of the chloride process.

Following World War II, DuPont decided to develop alternatives to its sulfate TiO_2 plants. In 1953, DuPont built its first fully operational chloride production unit using the abundant low-grade ilmenite ore in Edge Moor, Delaware. By 1958, it had built another plant at New Johnsonville, Tennessee, using its ilmenite chloride technology. Other manufacturers built sulfate process plants during this period.

With the discovery of abundant rutile ore deposits in eastern Australia in the late 1950s, all TiO_2 plants constructed through 1970, including DuPont's Antioch, California, plant, were designed to use high-grade rutile ore in a rutile chloride process. Overall production costs were substantially identical in the various processes until the late 1960s. DuPont enjoyed some economies of scale at its large New Johnsonville and enlarged Edge Moor chloride plants.

By early 1970, rutile ore became scarce and its price increased dramatically. At about the same time, environmental regulations required TiO_2 manufacturers using the sulfate process to embark on costly pollution abatement programs. Several rutile chloride plants were closed in 1970 and DuPont, with its ilmenite chloride process, was left with a substantial competitive cost advantage. It was estimated that DuPont's cost per pound for producing TiO_2 was 16¢ compared to 21¢ for competition. Ilmenite ore was also abundant in Florida, New Jersey, and New York.

In 1972, DuPont's management decided to capitalize on this cost advantage by engaging in a growth strategy. It continued the policy of refusing to license its ilmenite chloride technology, accelerated and increased the expansion of its Edge Moor and New Johnsonville plants and initiated plans to construct a large new plant using their advanced chloride technology in De Lisle, Mississippi. DuPont planned to supply the market with all its additional TiO_2 needs (including both growth in market and competitor withdrawals) through the 1980s. Management estimated that it would obtain about 65 percent of the TiO_2 market by 1985.

TiO_2 Competition

In 1975, DuPont had five manufacturing competitors in the domestic TiO_2 market, all of which manufactured a diversified product line. They were

EXHIBIT 1: Total Domestic TiO_2 Pigments Capacity 1970–1975 (In Tons). (Source: Chemical Economic Handbook, Stanford Research Institute, June 1978)[1]

	1970		1971		1972		1973		1974		1975	
	Tons	*Share*	*Tons*	*Share*	*Tons*	*Share*	*Tons*	*Share*	*Tons*	*Share*	*Tons*	*Share*
DuPont[2]	252,000	30.0%	277,000	33.0%	327,000	37.5%	368,000	39.7%	313,000	35.2%	368,000	38.9%
NL Industries	268,000	32.0%	268,000	31.9%	232,000	26.6%	221,000	23.9%	232,000	26.1%	232,000	24.4%
American Cyanamid	90,000	10.7%	82,000	9.8%	92,000	10.6%	112,000	12.1%	112,000	12.6%	112,000	11.8%
SCM	78,000	9.3%	78,000	9.3%	78,000	9.0%	78,000	8.4%	82,000	9.2%	112,000	11,8%
Gulf & Western	70,000	8.3%	70,000	8.3%	70,000	8.0%	70,000	7.6%	73,000	8.2%	73,000	7.7%
Kerr-McGee	37,000	4.4%	39,000	4.6%	45,000	5.2%	50,000	5.4%	50,000	5.6%	50,000	5.3%
Sherwin-Williams[3]	27,000	3.2%	27,000	3.2%	27,000	3.1%	27,000	2.9%	27,000	3.0%	—	—
PPG[4]	18,000	2.1%	—	—	—	—	—	—	—	—	—	—
TOTALS	840,000	100 %	841,000	100 %	871,000	100 %	926,000	100 %	889,000	100 %	947,000	100 %

[1] Because the capacity figures are year-end rather than an integrated average for the year, the calculated operating rate is not precise and is sometimes understated. It has generally been accepted that the effective operating capacity of most plants, taking into account normal downtime, is about 90% of nameplate. This table lists an estimated annual nameplate capacity history for the years 1970 through 1975.

[2] 55,000 tons of sulfate productive capacity located at Edge Moor, Delaware closed in 1974 and replaced by 55,000 tons of chloride located at Edge Moor. This chloride conversion is recorded in capacity figure of 1975.

[3] *Chemical Economics Handbook*, February 1975, p. 577.4204 P-Q. Sherwin-Williams' 27,000 TPY TiO_2 pigments plant located in Ashtabula, Ohio is allocated to Sherwin-Williams' capacity for 1974 even though the plant was acquired by SCM on October 12, 1974.

[4] PPG closed its sulfate plant in early 1970.

G&W, Cyanamid, Kerr-McGee, NL, and SCM. Exhibit 1 shows the capacity distributions of competitors in 1975. NL (National Lead Co.) was the oldest domestic producer of TiO_2 with its sulfate process plants built in Sayreville, New Jersey in 1918, and its St. Louis, Missouri plant in 1923. SCM entered the market in 1967 by purchasing Glidden Paint Company's sulfate process plant at Baltimore, Maryland, which had been built in 1956, and opened a rutile chloride plant there in 1968. In 1974, SCM also purchased Sherwin Williams' rutile chloride plant in Ashtabula, Ohio, built in 1970.

Cyanamid purchased Virginia Chemical Company in 1947, thereby acquiring its sulfate process plant, built in 1937. In 1955, Cyanamid built a second sulfate process plant in Savannah, Georgia, and opened a rutile chloride plant there in 1966. Gulf and Western, having acquired New Jersey Zinc Company in 1966, owned a Gloucester, New Jersey, sulfate process plant which had been built in 1956. In 1972, G&W leased Cabot Corporation's rutile chloride plant in Ashtabula, Ohio, built in 1964 and purchased that facility in 1975. Two rutile chloride plants, one owned by NL at Sayreville, New Jersey, and one by PPG at Natrium, West Virginia, were closed in 1970. Exhibits 2 and 3 show industry capacity in 1975 for sulfate and chloride TiO_2 production.

DuPont entered the TiO_2 business in 1931 when it acquired the Commercial Pigment Company which operated a sulfate process plant in Baltimore, Maryland. In 1935, DuPont built a second sulfate process plant at Edge Moor, Delaware. By 1952, Edge Moor also had the first ilmenite chloride process plant. DuPont started its 45,000 ton per year ilmenite chloride plant at New Johnsonville, Tennessee, in 1958 and rutile chloride plant at Antioch, California, in 1964. In 1956, a second chloride plant was built at Edge Moor that was expanded to 45,000 tons per year in 1965. The capacity at New Johnsonville was expanded to 70,000 tons per year in 1963, to 100,000 tons per year in 1964, and to 120,000 tons per year in 1968. By 1972, DuPont's New Johnsonville enjoyed substantial scale economies as well as a higher quality pigment, as noted in a management report:

> The success of the Johnsonville process resulted in a rapid increase in share of market as the quality and adequate supply of the improved pigment became the standard of comparison in the industry.

In addition, DuPont's net after tax return on investment in TiO_2 averaged 12.5 percent between 1965 and 1970, ranging between 10.5 and 15.5 percent.

In 1970, environmental legislation forced sulfate producers to incur substantial pollution-related capital investment costs. They were considered the worst of the chemical industry polluters, producing three and a half tons of iron sulfate and sulfuric acid waste for every ton of TiO_2. In contrast, the rutile and ilmenite chloride procesesses produced only about one-half ton of a dry anhydrous ferric chloride waste that was easier to dispose of. However, rutile ore developed an unexpected supply shortage in 1970, and by 1972 the cost of rutile ore reached an all-time high. This left DuPont with a significant 5 cent cost advantage over all its competitors. In addition, the shutdown of two rutile chloride facilities and reduced imports left a TiO_2 shortage in the domestic market. In 1974, DuPont

EXHIBIT 2: Total Domestic TiO_2 Pigments Production Via the Sulfate Process/1970–1975 (In Tons).

	1970		*1971*		*1972*		*1973*		*1974*		*1975*	
	Tons	*Share*	*Tons*	*Share*	*Tons*	*Share*	*Tons*	*Share*	*Tons*	*Share*	*Tons*	*Share*
DuPont	42,800	11.7%	41,700	12.0%	53,700	15.1%	53,000	13.9%	45,100	12.7%	—	—
NL Industries	192,888	53.0%	183,807	53.1%	162,702	45.7%	184,299	48.0%	166,257	47.0%	135,283	58.0%
American Cyanamid	47,349	13.0%	48,348	13.9%	53,561	15.1%	51,657	13.5%	50,480	14.3%	31,172	13.4%
SCM	48,370	13.3%	44,771	13.0%	45,613	12.8%	50,961	13.3%	48,814	13.8%	38,182	16.4%
Gulf & Western	33,067	9.1%	27,395	8.0%	40,499	11.4%	43,492	11.3%	43,020	12.2%	28,626	12.3%
Kerr-McGee	—	—	—	—	—	—	—	—	—	—	—	—
Sherwin-Williams	—	—	—	—	—	—	—	—	—	—	—	—
TOTAL	364,474	100 %	346,021	100 %	356,075	100 %	383,609	100 %	353,671	100 %	233,263	100 %

EXHIBIT 3: Total Domestic Production TiO_2 Pigments Via the Chloride Process/1970–1977 (In Tons).

	1970		*1971*		*1972*		*1973*		*1974*		*1975*	
	Tons	*Share*	*Tons*	*Share*	*Tons*	*Share*	*Tons*	*Share*	*Tons*	*Share*	*Tons*	*Share*
Dupont	161,000	57.4%	170,100	53.0%	200,900	58.4%	237,500	60.4%	272,400	63.1%	238,900	64.2%
NL Industries[1]	28,835	10.3%	20,805	6.5%	—	—	—	—	—	—	—	—
American Cyanamid	6,407	2.3%	23,961	7.5%	33,215	9.5%	31,634	8.0%	34,739	8.0%	28,710	7.7%
SCM	701	0.2%	12,784	4.0%	17,884	5.1%	21,113	5.4%	23,889	5.5%	40,346	10.8%
Gulf & Western	—	—	—	—	25,492	7.3%	28,789	7.3%	28,083	6.5%	14,491	3.9%
Kerr-McGee	33,472	12.0%	36,106	11.2%	41,952	12.1%	46,405	11.8%	48,120	11.1%	50,000	13.4%
Sherwin-Williams	18,407	6.6%	26,363	8.2%	26,398	7.6%	28,134	7.1%	24,773	5.7%	—	—
Cabot	21,416	7.6%	22,973	7.2%	—	—	—	—	—	—	—	—
PPG	10,366	3.7%	8,048	2.5%	—	—	—	—	—	—	—	—
TOTAL	280,604	100 %	321,140	100 %	347,841	100 %	393,575	100 %	432,004	100 %	372,447	100 %

[1]NL closed its chloride process TiO_2 pigments plant located at Sayreville at the end of 1972.

converted its Edge Moor sulfate process plant to a chloride process plant which came back on line in 1975.

DUPONT'S TiO_2 STRATEGY IN 1972

In 1971, DuPont's Pigments Department created a TiO_2 "Task Force" and "Core Group." The Core Group included the heads of the divisions in the Pigments Department who held various responsibilities for the TiO_2 business. The Task Force included individuals from the department at a level below the division heads. The Task Force also created subgroups called "Task Groups" to study various issues. The Task Force then reported to the Core Group, which in turn reported to Geil, vice-president and general manager of the Pigments Department, through Mr. Baird, the assistant general manager. In 1972, the Task Force engaged in a broad evaluation of DuPont's TiO_2 business and made recommendations for a long-range strategy, the final details of which were reported to DuPont's Executive Committee in May, 1972.

In his 1972 report to the Executive Committee on TiO_2 business opportunities, Geil reported:

> . . . A number of significant developments have occurred which make it desirable at this time to reassess the outlook for this business and to request your Committee's concurrence with the broad outlines of a program designed to take advantage of significantly enlarged opportunities.
>
> . . . The price competition of the 1965 to 1971 period narrowed profit margins for all producers in the industry, and brought home as never before the realities of the business. The most significant of these include:
>
> At substantial scale, the chloride process requires lower capital investment than the sulfate process.
>
> Disposal of wastes from the chloride process can be accomplished at a lower economic penalty than is the case with the sulfate process.
>
> With the exception of DuPont, all other producers by the chloride process require the use of either rutile ore or a beneficiated product having a low iron content. The world-wide shortage of rutile has resulted in an increase in price from $A65 in 1965 to $A110 in 1972.
>
> With completion of the conversion of the Edge Moor sulfate unit to a chloride process operation, DuPont will be entirely committed to chloride process operations at large scale. DuPont's unique ability to operate the chloride process with relatively low cost ilmenite ore provides a favorable operating cost capability. Technology for complete recycle of process wastes with an acceptable economic penalty is progressing. *This combination of factors puts DuPont in a unique position to increase its share of market by a substantial amount.*
>
> Competitive developments during the past six months provide support for this contention. PPG Industries recently announced the abandonment of its chloride process plant because of unfavorable prospective economics. This move coincided with the failure of the Sherbro project in Sierra Leone which was designed to provide the rutile feed for this unit. NL Industries has announced abandonment of its chloride process unit as a result of unfavorable economics. This producer has

also terminated its production of an extended titanium pigment under conditions which have alienated some of the customers formerly purchasing that product. Concurrent with these events has been the effect of the government's monetary actions on importation of titanium dioxide. The import surcharge and, subsequently, the devaluation of the dollar have made imported products less competitive in this market.

Assessment of the status of competitive producers leads to the conclusion that sulfate process operators, with the exception of NL Industries, will be unable to cope with waste disposal problems and will shut down eventually. Chloride process producers probably will continue operations, but it is difficult to see how they can cope with waste disposal and generate sufficient funds for major expansion.

The combination of these factors has narrowed the margin between total production capacity in this country and the level of consumer demand. The pigments Department has been oversold since early in the year, and information from the trade indicates that American Cyanamid and other producers in varying degree are in this position.

For the short term, the Pigments Department is taking steps to increase production capacity as expeditiously as possible. The plant shutdown of the Antioch unit has been deferred. The expansion at Johnsonville is being expedited in order to achieve partial expansion at the earliest date. Modest capacity increases at Edge Moor are being undertaken. In view of the prospects, however, these are stop-gap measures.

Continued growth of the TiO_2 market is forecast. While the rate of population increase has declined, TiO_2 has demonstrated a consistent increase in per capita consumption. In terms of total impact, TiO_2 can be described as a "standard of living" product. Its per capita consumption has paralleled the per capita consumption of electrical energy, for instance. Technologically, the only threats to TiO_2 as the major pigment of commerce are silicon carbide and "void hiding" products. It is concluded that silicon carbide would be too expensive to compete. Void hiding can be achieved by encapsulating tiny air bubbles and TiO_2 particles for certain emulsion paint and paper applications. Realistic potential for these products is included in sales projections.

It is expected that the domestic industry requirements will grow at a rate of about 3.5% per year for the balance of this decade. In terms of industry tonnage, this means that requirements will be between 1,000M[1] and 1,100M tons in 1980, as compared to 713M tons in 1971. The increase is equivalent to about four fully developed Johnsonville-type process lines. Even if growth should fall short of these expectations, any reasonable projection will require major expansion in the industry. *It is believed that the Pigments Department has the technology, the operating and construction capability, the cash generation capacity, and the waste disposal expertise to capture the major portion of this market growth. If this be true, there is the potential to increase market share from the current level of 31–32% to 56% by 1980, and with the trends persisting to approach 65% by 1985.* (See Exhibit 4 for impact of growth strategy).

A program designed to seize this opportunity would have specific implications, all of which would have to be resolved quantitatively at as early a stage as possible.

Adoption of a pricing policy which would provide adequate profit and cash generation for expansion.

[1] 100,000 Tons ("M").

EXHIBIT 4: Comparison of DuPont Market Share Projections: February/July 1972

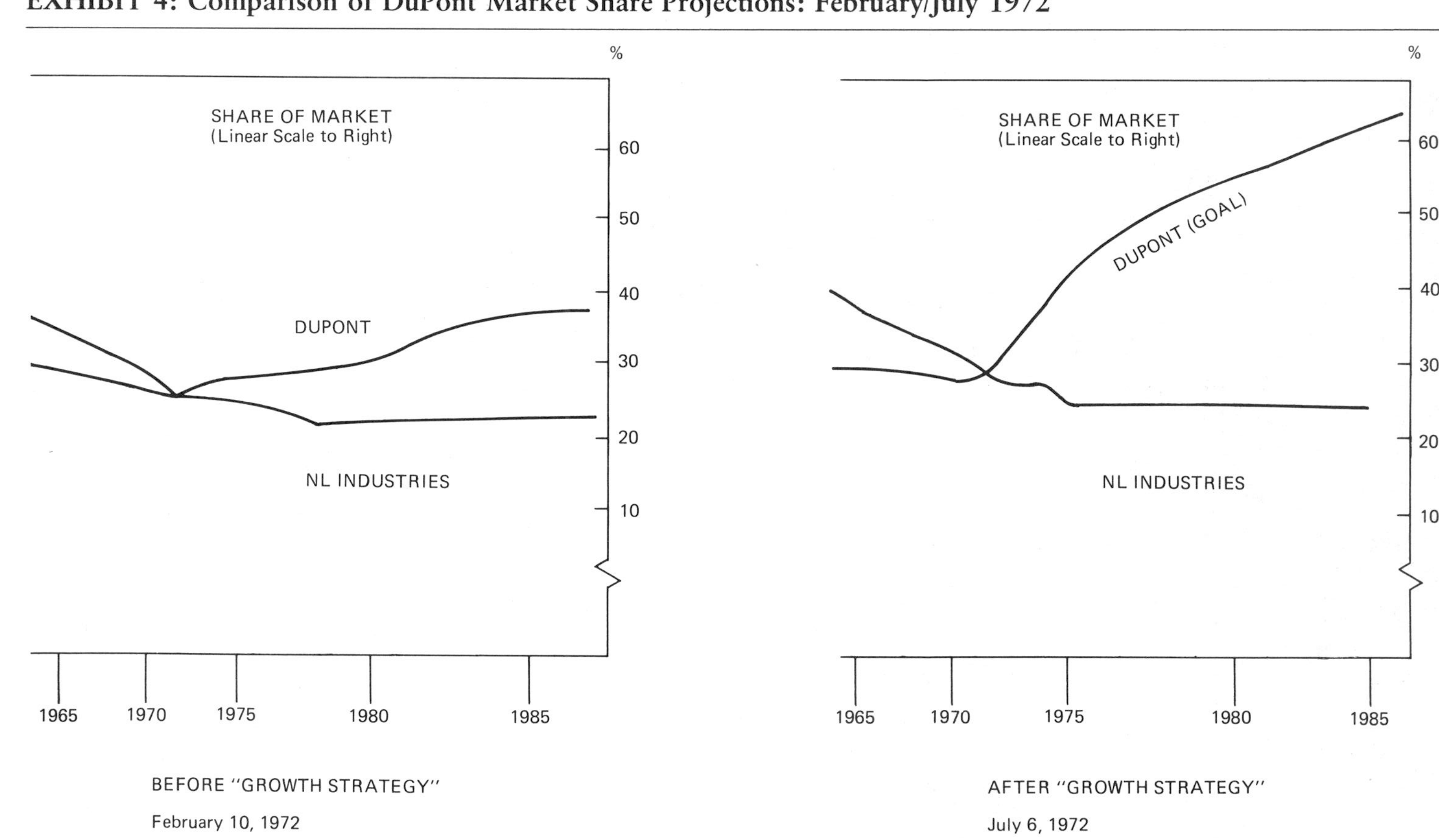

Decision on configuration of production facilities. It seems obvious that within this time period a fully developed third site would be necessary.

A substantial increase in our commitments for titanium mineral. There appear to be adequate possibilities for large-scale ilmenite supply.

Final decision between waste disposal alternatives including beneficiation of ore, electrolysis, or ferric chloride oxidation.

A program to acquire and train about 200 exempt salary personnel by 1977.

In summary, the Pigments Department finds itself in a unique situation. In technology, it is in a position of undisputed leadership not only in this country but in the world. Although the ability to use low grade ores in the chloride process has been known since 1950, no other producer has been able to achieve this capability. Most producers have directed their technical programs toward developing a beneficiated ilmenite which, at best, would show economics similar to rutile. In scale, Pigments Department is the only producer with large units which permit holding unit capital investment at low levels. We are not aware of any other producer with waste technology which can be accomplished without severe economic penalty. These same considerations apply to operations in foreign markets and separate studies to define the Department's participation in these markets are underway.

It is recommended that agreement in principle be granted to the Department to proceed with full development of this program. It is anticipated that substantial additional information will be provided in the Annual Report to be submitted in November 1972. In succession, appropriate requests requesting authorization of the expenditures necessary to provide the required facilities will provide your Committee with the detailed considerations necessary for your evaluation of each step prior to the authorization of the capital funds required.

On May 31, 1972, the Executive Committee approved Geil's proposal and granted "authority to the Pigments Department to proceed with full development of this program."

Pricing Decisions. By June 20, 1972, the Pigments Department was faced with its first pricing decision in response to Kerr-McGee's announcement of a 2¢ per pound price increase on rutile TiO_2, effective July 1, 1972. J. Kramer, director of the sales division, forwarded a recommendation that DuPont not increase its TiO_2 pigment prices because most large customers were "price protected" through 1972 and that any price increase would affect smaller customers. In addition, the price increase could be in conflict with the Economic Stabilization Act of 1970 and might be considered "grouping" by the trade after a substantial 1971 price increase. In addition, Kerr-McGee and G&W were actually selling TiO_2 pigments at prices below DuPont's list price. Current prices were also adequate to permit a respectable return on investment and adequate cash generation for expansion.

Between 1973 and 1974, the market for titanium pigments continued to grow while capacity remained stagnant, forcing TiO_2 allocations. On March 27, 1974, with removal of price controls, a report to the Executive Committee stated that rising raw materials costs and labor and pollution abatement costs would accelerate industry selling prices beyond forecast. It continued:

> Now that the Phase IV price controls have been modified on titanium pigments an additional increase of at least 3.5¢ per pound is expected almost immediately and thereafter an increase of about 1.75¢ per year.

This was expected to more than offset DuPont's cost increases. Prices in early 1974 were 28¢ per pound and projected at 36.77¢ per pound by 1977.

In January 1975, DuPont declined to follow several competitors' announced price increases of 5¢ per pound and the price increases were cancelled. The recession had caused sales of TiO_2 to drop substantially and competition began discounting from list price. However, by July 1975, DuPont led a 3.5¢ per pound increase in list prices that was followed by competition. A Pigments Department report explained:

> A 3½¢ per pound increase is expected to restore earnings to a satisfactory level for the balance of 1975 and through the first half of 1976 in the absence of any unforecasted energy cost increase. Major customers have been advised informally that an 8–10% increase would be necessary soon, and appear willing to accept this level. Such an increase is in keeping with projected prices in the 1974 Annual Report and Supplement, and Project 2613, and is believed to be the best compromise level for restoring earnings without shrinking the market (customers will probably not undertake gross reformulation to use less TiO_2 if the increase is held below 10%). We believe all domestic competitors will rapidly follow this increase, as three of the six attempted to initiate comparable increases in January 1975. Because demand at that time was so weak, we elected not to increase at that time.

Capacity Decisions. Competition appeared to be unable to expand by 1972 because of problems with small-scale chloride plants needing high-grade titanium ore and waste disposal equipment, and lacking advantages of scale. Sulfate plants required extra processing steps to meet the chloride quality standards, and had problems disposing of large volumes of pollutants. In July, 1972, the Executive Committee approved Geil's request to increase New Johnsonville's capacity from 141M to 196M tons per year. By December, 1973, requests were made to increase New Johnsonville's capacity to 228M tons per year.

In July, 1973, Geil proposed that DuPont take advantage of a developing shortage of TiO_2 pigment by constructing 110M tons and 220M tons per year production lines at Brunswick, Georgia, to start up in 1977 and 1979, respectively; and a 110M ton per year plant in Europe. By November 1973, programs were developed to build large scale plants in the United States for 1977, and Europe for 1978. Announcements were made that the U.S. plant would be in De Lisle, Mississippi. In July 1974, $8 million was released to begin designs and make equipment orders for the DeLisle plant. At the same time, a second press announcement was made giving a 1977 start up date for the plant, and reviewing plans to expand Edge Moor capacity to 167M tons per year and New Johnsonville to 228M tons per year.

Technology Decisions. Along with the Pigments Department's 1972 expansion strategy, DuPont decided not to release its unique technology or proprietary TiO_2 expertise to competition. In February, 1974, DuPont turned down a request by NL for a license for its ilmenite chloride technology.

THE TiO_2 STRATEGY IN 1975

By 1975, DuPont's TiO_2 strategy had changed little. In a report to the Executive Committee, the Pigments Department had stated the pertinent elements of their strategy as follows:

> *Business Description*
>
> . . . In spite of shortages in 1973–1974, only DuPont and Kerr-McGee have indicated plans for major expansions. DuPont's business is strongly focused on domestic markets where it is the undisputed leader because of superior manufacturing technology; lowest costs; good protection in titanium ore, a major raw material; experience and resources to respond rapidly to market opportunities; and a 41% market share.
>
> *Business Objective and Financial Goals (1975–1980)*
>
> The business objective is to complete implementation of the growth program outlined to the Executive Committee in the Department's report of May 25, 1972. This is, in essence, to exploit a unique opportunity to capture most of the domestic industry growth into the early eighties, thus increasing market share above 52% and operative earnings to about $200MM per year.
>
> *General Business Strategy*
>
> The strategic plan to implement the growth program capitalizes on the internal strengths and competitive factors that have yielded DuPont a position of leadership. Key elements are:
>
> Start-up new facilities at De Lisle, Mississippi, in 1978. This expansion, as the recently completed ones at Johnsonville and Edge Moor, exploits the ability to operate large scale plants utilizing low grade, lower cost titanium ore.
>
> Continuation of process innovation and improvement programs to maintain position as lowest cost producer. This work will affect both the product line and the development of new, more unique products. For example, the De Lisle design incorporates new lower cost (both manufacturing and investment) finishing technology.
>
> A pricing policy to bring operative margins to 25–35%. Prices are forecast to increase about 6% annually; assessments of competitor's costs indicate this is consistent with price increases they will require to recover increasing costs of ore and waste disposal.
>
> Continued focus on domestic opportunities. . . In addition there are world wide opportunities to license DuPont's chloride technology, capitalizing on it while it is still valuable to generate additional cash flow.

REVIEWING THE TiO_2 STRATEGY IN 1975

In the summer of 1975, the Pigments Department's task force engaged in an in-depth analysis of the TiO_2 business, its market strategies, and detailed projections of alternative business plans. This study was accelerated when the Executive Committee called for a reappraisal of the De Lisle project (one of 10 projects being reconsidered by the committee). On October 10, 1975, Mr. Geil made a presentation to the Executive Committee to justify continuation and completion of the De Lisle project. The presentation compared four alternatives: (1) continuation, (2) delay, (3) cutback to maintain share, and (4) abandoning the project.

In presenting continuation of the De Lisle project, Geil explained:

> We are the lowest cost producer in the world. A major part of this is based on low-grade ore and on scale of operation. We estimate that in ten years competitors will have solved these problems, particularly if they are encouraged to expand.
>
> We have publicized through the various press releases and speeches of Company officials that we plan to expand. This has made us into the most-favored supplier in the eyes of customers who depended upon us in the last shortage and are planning on our covering them in the next shortage. If we drop out of this leadership position by cancelling De Lisle we foresee we will lose some of our position as most-favored supplier.
>
> Because the big accounts must depend upon us as their major supplier, they also depend upon us to develop products which meet their needs. The way this has been carried out is that each new grade is generally developed with one or more big accounts. This cuts the lag time on grade introduction to almost zero. If we lose our credibility with these accounts by cancelling De Lisle, we will lose at least a part of this special product development relationship.
>
> One of our major strengths lies in the ability to operate large-scale plants. This gives us significant cost advantages. This advantage, however, incurs large capital outlays when a major expansion is undertaken. This means the plant must be operating at a high rate within 3–4 years to be economically viable.
>
> TiO_2 sales quantities have long followed GNP and Pigments and the Economist's office feels this relationship will continue during the period for which we are strategizing. Over this time, we expect TiO_2 use in the U.S. to grow at better than 5% (while the recovery is returning us to the long-term trend line), but then drop to about 2.7% in the 1980's. This means that in the immediate future we can fill a De Lisle in a little over three years; whereas by the end of this period, filling such a large plant will take about five years.
>
> A new site has value to Pigments. Pigments now has a very large portion of its production for the paint industry concentrated at Johnsonville. De Lisle would help minimize for our customers the risk of any kind of disturbance that was local in nature. Delays at De Lisle continuously increases our vulnerability to opposition in obtaining permits. If we delay by about three years from our original 1975 funding, we will have lost our current political support and, with it, our ability to keep permits active.
>
> Market share has value to us. In capitalizing on our strengths, we will increase our share. (See Exhibit 5 for impact of De Lisle project on market share).

With respect to the "Delay" alternative, Geil reported that "a one-year additional delay in funding to 1977 represents the maximum time delay," the principal disadvantage being lost sales and earnings.

With respect to the "Maintain Share" alternative, Geil outlined its considerations to alter some plans for completing Edge Moor to keep DuPont's grade structure in balance with the market and a "reamout" at Johnsonville, increasing capacity to 252M tons per year. It concluded:

> In the market place, as soon as it would become clear that DuPont had abandoned De Lisle, we would expect to see an additional price increase of about $2/cwt above our preferred case ["De Lisle"]. In addition, we would expect Kerr-McGee

EXHIBIT 5: Titanium Dioxide Sales and Capacity (Thousands of Tons)

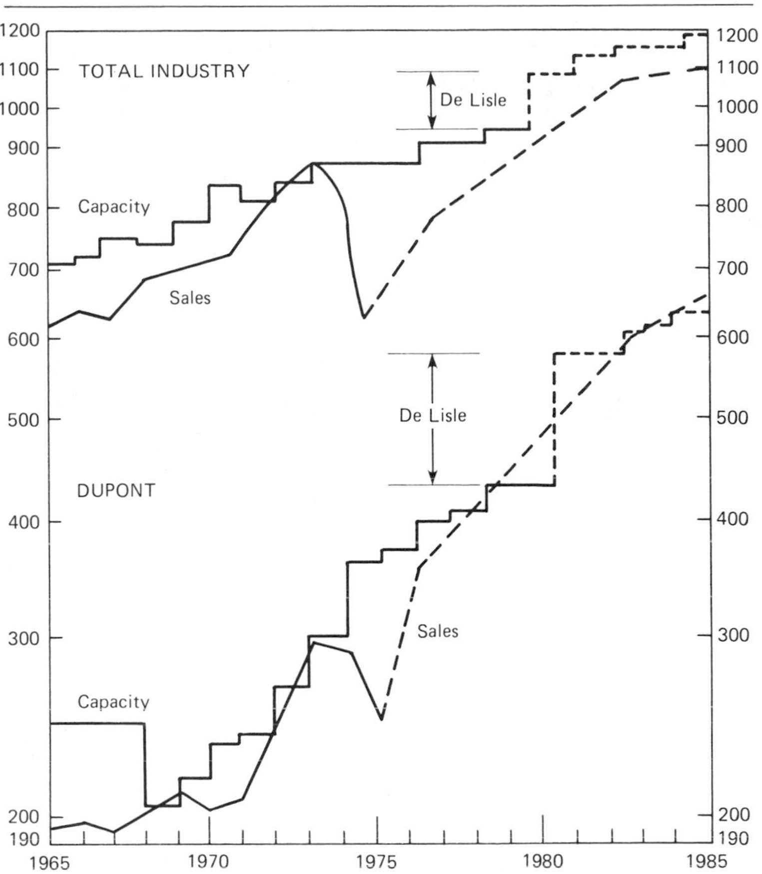

to build the plant they announced at Mobile but haven't started. We would also expect several others to expand. This might well be American Cyanamid and Glidden who have both told customers they would like to expand but haven't moved yet, apparently because of the pricing situation. When these expansions start up about 1980, we would expect a temporary oversupply which would cause some erosion of prices, so that by about 1982 we would expect to see the price drop about $2/cwt below the base case price structure.

Finally, with respect to the "No Expansion" alternative, Geil stated:

Abandoning the TiO_2 expansion program would mean simply maintaining the three existing plants. During our strategy re-analysis, we did not give this case the finely structured study that we gave the other cases. For purposes of this presentation, we've assumed that our plants would fill rapidly and stay full. We've also assumed pricing equal to the previous alternative. In fact, this is probably overly optimistic because badly timed expansions would probably periodically cause erosion of prices.

The presentation was summed up as follows:

> In summary, TiO_2 offers DuPont a low risk, high return business opportunity . . . [i]t is noteworthy that Reports on Accomplishment for TiO_2 projects over the last ten years have averaged 112% of forecast.

In assessing the continuation of their TiO_2 growth strategy, Geil noted an: "Increase [of] 3¢ per pound per year to 1980 will yield necessary return for De Lisle based on current cost projections, also giving competition generally adequate returns to stay in business."

CASE SIXTEEN

DuPont de Nemours & Company (B)

WILLIAM R. BOULTON
University of Georgia

Assignment Questions:

1. What has caused overcapacity to exist in the TiO_2 industry?
2. What should DuPont do now?
3. What should be done with the De Lisle project?

In December 1977, DuPont's domestic titanium dioxide pigments (TiO_2) business was experiencing problems of oversupply and price-discounting. The Executive Committee once again asked A. H. Geil, vice-president and general manager of DuPont's Pigments Department, to re-evaluate the investment plans for the De Lisle plant. The following comments were taken from his report:

> **The TiO_2 Business**
>
> The principal contribution [to the decline] is the sluggish recovery of the European and third world economies. This is encouraging a number of foreign producers to export to the United States at below market prices and in volumes estimated to be 62% ahead of last year. Softening domestic demand is aggravating the situation.
>
> In spite of these problems, the TiO_2 business is expected to achieve record sales volumes and pretax earnings in 1977. *Based on government data and reports from customers, it appears several of the larger domestic producers have been more adversely affected by the imports with sales significantly below 1973 levels. Our cost estimates indicate they may be operating at break-even or worse.*
>
> The situation has caused the forecast achievement of prices and volumes presented in the De Lisle project to be one year behind schedule. A price increase of two cents to 48.5 cents per pound for bagged rutile pigment announced around midyear will not become fully effective until the end of the year. Prices in Europe are equally sluggish running five to eight cents less than U.S. prices.

The TiO_2 Strategy

DuPont was the only TiO_2 producer in 1977 pursuing an active expansion program. In commenting on its expansion, Geil reiterated:

EXHIBIT 1: Total Domestic Shipments of TiO_2 Pigments (Including Imports, Excluding Exports) 1970–1977 (in 1,000 Tons)

(Shipments Rounded to Nearest 1,000, Market Share Rounded to Nearest Whole Number)

	1970		*1971*		*1972*		*1973*		*1974*		*1975*		*1976*		*1977*	
	Tons	*Share*	*Tons*	*Share*	*Tons*	*Share*	*Tons*	*Share*	*Tons*	*Share*	*Tons*	*Share*	*Tons*	*Share*	*Tons*	*Share*
DuPont	199	29%	214	30%	239	30%	286	34%	287	38%	239	40%	296	40%	320	41%
NL Industries	203	30%	202	29%	201	25%	208	25%	149	20%	115	19%	126	17%	128	16%
American/ Cyanimid	51	8%	70	10%	90	11%	87	10%	80	11%	63	10%	78	11%	80	10%
SCM	56	8%	62	9%	72	9%	71	8%	67	9%	76	13%	98	13%	99	13%
Kerr-McGee	31	5%	36	5%	45	6%	48	6%	44	6%	44	7%	51	7%	48	6%
Gulf & Western	30	4%	25	4%	61	8%	71	8%	63	8%	41	7%	51	7%	59	8%
Cabot	24	4%	23	3%	-0-	—	-0-	—	-0-	—	-0-	—	-0-	—	-0-	—
Sherwin/ Williams	15	2%	25	4%	29	4%	30	4%	26	3%	-0-	—	-0-	—	-0-	—
PGG	9	1%	9	1%	-0-	—	-0-	—	-0-	—	-0-	—	-0-	—	-0-	—
SUBTOTAL	618		666		737		801		716		578		700		734	
All Other Imports	58	9%	41	6%	58	7%	45	5%	35	5%	25	4%	37	5%	49	6%
TOTAL	676	100%	707	100%	795	100%	846	100%	751	100%	603	100%	737	100%	783	100%

> *The business objective is to complete implementation of the growth strategy and program outlined to the Executive Committee in the Department's report of May 25, 1972.* This is, in essence, to capitalize on a unique opportunity to capture most of the domestic growth into the early eighties, thus increasing market share above 51% and operating earnings to almost \$150MM per year by 1982.

Exhibit 1 shows the market share of major competitors through 1977.

In making his recommendations to the Executive Committee, Geil concluded:

> The current sluggishness of the TiO_2 business should not delay the De Lisle construction activities. A delay would have minimal effect on cash flow as \$140MM (of \$182MM authorized) has been expended or committed. Even under the pessimistic assumption that sales volume and prices slide two years versus project projections, the TiO_2 business would still break even in 1979 (the start-up year).
>
> A better choice is continuation of construction in the most economical way (e.g., no overtime or additional hiring to make up construction delays), leaving the option of temporary mothballing at time of completion. This approach could delay start-up now scheduled for the first quarter of 1979, by at least one to two quarters. Further study by Engineering will provide more definitive schedule information by mid-December. This construction route offers the advantage of having the plant available to meet a sudden surge of demand brought about by a turn around in the world economic situation or by removal of TiO_2 capacity from the market due to competitive environmental or profitability pressures.

In order for competitors to eliminate or reduce DuPont's cost advantage in the manufacture of TiO_2, it would have to develop a low-grade ore technology and build large-scale chloride process plants which required substantial learning time. DuPont's management estimated it would take competitors 5 to 10 years to come close to their cost of production. In addition, they felt that three plants like New Johnsonville could supply the market through 1985. Exhibit 2 shows estimated costs of TiO_2 producers.

The Problem of Overcapacity

The TiO_2 industry had been operating at about 70 percent of capacity during 1975 and 1976. Even with this level of slack in production, DuPont's customers had accepted price increases in 1975 and 1976 of 3.5¢/lb. (9%) and 3¢/lb. (7%), respectively, to ensure future capacity. In estimating the impact of price increases on demand, management stated in 1976:

> Prices are forecast to increase 5–7% annually from current levels through the early 1980's. Several elements are at work to sustain these rates of increases. We estimate the inflation in the general economy coupled with more stringent pollution control requirements will force competitive costs up about 8% per year over the next several years. The old sulfate plants cannot be expected to achieve productivity increases to offset these increased costs. Selling prices for project return purposes are considered to be conservative estimates because they do not allow for full recapture of estimated competitive cost increases of the sulfate producers by as much as two cents per pound. *The high investment cost required to provide additional capacity should prevent overcapacity developing to depress prices.*

EXHIBIT 2: Mill Costs of Titanium Dioxide Producers

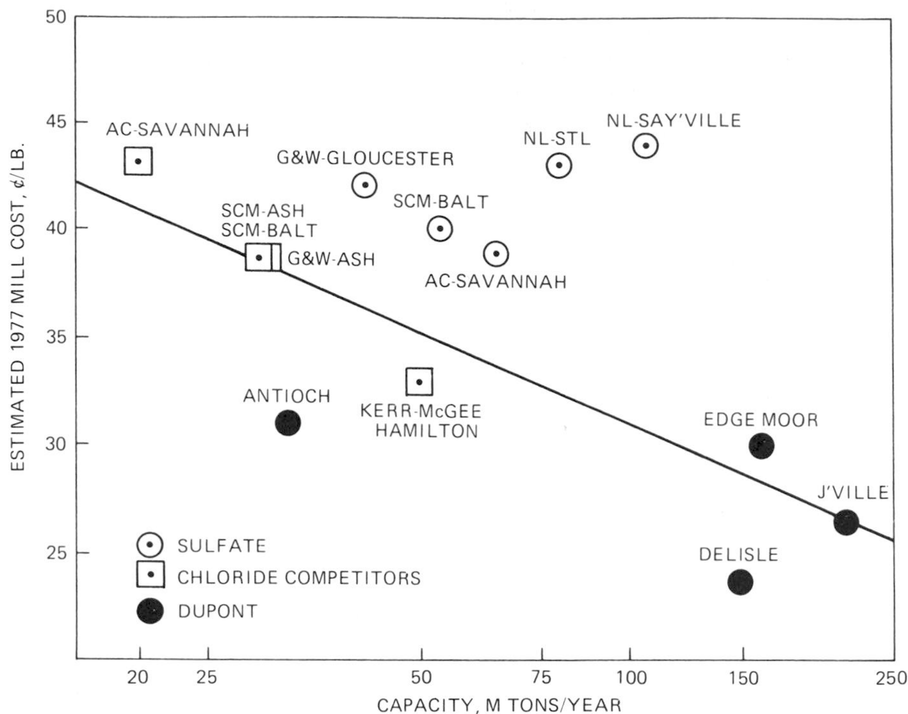

However, when competition (SCM and NC) announced 5¢/lb. price increases in 1977, DuPont raised prices only 2¢/lb. The rationale for such action identified the potential of attracting offshore competition. It stated:

> *The market is still not firm as there are many deals in all the industries we serve either by discounting price 3 to 4¢/pound, sale of "substandard" material at distressed price, or the use of extended terms. Through the first quarter, we sold 18% of our product at reduced prices as a result of meeting competitive action.*
>
> A worldwide supply and demand imbalance of ± 300,000 tons exists. Imports of titanium dioxide have increased during 1977 and substantially higher prices would invite offshore producers to have a larger U.S. market share.
>
> A deterrent for customers to formulate their products to lower TiO_2 levels, and an incentive for restoration toward historical levels [is necessary]. This is highly important to us, as our growth depends on an expanding market.
>
> Smaller price increases are more palatable to our customers as they can pass the increases along easier.
>
> *Reverse downward trend of market share; we do not need De Lisle if we can not capture the market growth. When we aggressively priced from 1972 through 1975, we substantially gained market share even during the 1975 recession. From March, 1976 on we have not been aggressive in the marketplace from a pricing standpoint and as a result, our market share eroded 2.5%.*
>
> Two cents per pound increase, effective June 1, 1977, and in place 100% by 11/1/77 is expected to yield additional earning of $4.5MM during 1977.
>
> Current average selling price is 44.9¢/pound and this increase should put us

> ahead of the price forecasted in both the Annual Report and Project 2613-14 (De Lisle) of 45.4¢/pound.

However, by December, 1977, it was apparent that the 2¢/lb. price increase was not holding, and sales personnel recommended a price rollback:

> The announced June 1977 titanium dioxide price increase is not holding. I propose that we promptly announce that pre-June prices are in effect through the first quarter, and try to initiate an increase in the second quarter if conditions appear more favorable.
>
> Thirty-eight per cent of "TiPure" sales were at the current list price in December, but of this 38 per cent, over 8 per cent was as R-O (slip) codes or RPS with performance guarantees. In effect, 30 per cent is conventional grades at current list, and the number of pricing actions we are asked to meet indicates this could drop below 25 per cent by February.

CASE SEVENTEEN

DuPont de Nemours & Company (C)

WILLIAM R. BOULTON
University of Georgia

Assignment Questions:

1. What are the charges against DuPont?
2. What implications do the FTC's actions have for corporate strategies?

On April 5, 1978, the Federal Trade Commission issued a complaint charging E. I. DuPont de Nemours and Company (DuPont) with unfair methods of competition and unfair acts and practices in or affecting commerce in violation of Section 5 of the Federal Trade Commission Act, as amended (15 U.S.C. 45).

The Commission charged that DuPont had, since as early as 1972, engaged in certain practices in an attempt to monopolize the production of titanium dioxide pigments ("TiO_2") in the United States. The Commission alleged that the practices challenged included, but were not limited to, the following:

a. adoption and implementation of a plan to expand the company's domestic TiO_2 production capacity by an amount sufficient to enable the company to capture substantially all growth in domestic demand for TiO_2 through at least the 1980's; and
b. adoption and implementation of a pricing policy designed to frustrate the growth of smaller domestic TiO_2 producers and to forestall entry by foreign producers.

The complaint alleged that DuPont's practices had the tendency and capacity to restrain, lessen, or eliminate competition or to create a monopoly in the relevant TiO_2 market and were to the prejudice and injury of the public and constituted unfair methods of competition in violation of Section 5.

In the notice of contemplated relief that accompanied the complaint, the Commission suggested, among other things, (1) the divestiture of DuPont's De Lisle, Mississippi, TiO_2 production facility as a viable, independent entity; (2) divestiture of either DuPont's New Johnsonville, Tennessee, TiO_2 facility or of DuPont's Edge Moor, Delaware, TiO_2 facility as a viable, independent entity; and (3) royalty-free licensing of all "technology and know-how" used by DuPont in connection with the production of TiO_2.

RESULTS OF FTC ACTIONS

The following is the judgment handed down by Miles J. Brown, administrative law judge in the matter of E. I. DuPont de Nemours and Company vs. the Federal Trade Commission.

> Section 5 of the Federal Trade Commission Act empowers the Federal Trade Commission to prohibit certain "unfair methods of competition" and certain "unfair or deceptive acts or practices."[1] Section 5 was intended to be a broad and flexible statute under which the Commission could designate as "unfair methods of competition" conduct that, although not previously deemed violative of statutes governing trade practices, had the anticompetitive effects that such legislation was designed to prevent. See H.R. Rep. No. 1142, 63d Cong., 2d Sess. 18–19 (1914). It is well settled that Section 5 covers conduct that either violates the prohibitions of the Clayton Act and the Sherman Act or conduct that could lead to unreasonable restraints on competition if not prohibited. See *Federal Trade Commission v. Brown Shoe,* 384, U.S. 316, 321 (1966); *Federal Trade Commission v. Cement Institute,* 333 U.S. 683 (1948).
>
> An illegal attempt to monopolize constituting a violation of Section 2 of the Sherman Act involves a "specific intent" to control prices or destroy competition in a relevant market, predatory or anticompetitive conduct directed to accomplish those ends, and a dangerous probability of success. *Purex Corp. v. Proctor & Gamble Co.,* 596 F.2d 881, 890 (9th Cir. 1979). *Janich Bros. Inc. v. American Distilling Co.,* 570 F.2d 848, 853 (9th Cir. 1977); *Golden Grain Macaroni Co.,* 78 FTC 63, 164 (1971), *enforced in part,* 472 F.2d 882 (oth Cir. 1972), *cert. denied,* 412 U.S. 918 (1973). It is generally accepted that monopoly power exists when an industry member has the power to raise prices or exclude competition when it so desires, and that such monopoly power is unlawful if it is willfully maintained or acquired as distinguished from arising from growth or development as a consequence of a superior product, business accumen or historical accident. *Purex Corp.* v. *Proctor & Gamble Co.,* 890 *supra; Golden Grain Macaroni Co., supra,* 78 FTC at 157.
>
> Complaint counsel contend that DuPont had (and continues to have) the intent to prevent competition, to control prices and to gain a dominant share of the TiO_2 market. In this respect, complaint counsel allege that DuPont has engaged in certain strategic business conduct designed to perpetuate a so-called "investment asymmetry" between DuPont and its TiO_2 competitors, namely, the existence of business conditions under which competitors would not choose to construct large scale TiO_2 production facilities.
>
> Complaint counsel assert that as part of its strategy DuPont priced its TiO_2 products low enough to discourage competitors' expansion, yet high enough to fund DuPont's own expansion, engaged in premature expansion of its own TiO_2 facilities and capacity, made exaggerated announcements relating to its expansion plans, and refused to license its TiO_2 technology to its competitors. They contend that this exclusionary scheme was anticompetitive, and that through such strategy DuPont has insulated its substantial cost advantage from erosion over time. Complaint counsel contend that without large-scale construction no competitor would be in a position to substantially reduce or eliminate DuPont's cost advantage through

[1]"Sec. 5(a)(1). Unfair methods of competition in or affecting commerce and unfair or deceptive acts or practices in or affecting commerce, are hereby declared unlawful."

"(2). The Commission is hereby empowered and directed to prevent persons, partnerships, or corporations . . . from using unfair methods of competition in or affecting commerce and unfair or deceptive acts or practices in or affecting commerce."

the necessary "learning by doing," inherent in the development of an ilmenite technology, or by scale economies, available from large chloride process plants. Complaint counsel contend that the intended effect of DuPont's strategy was to limit the funds available for competitive expansion, decrease the return that competitors could expect from expansion and increase the risks of such expansion. Complaint counsel conclude that if the results of this challenged course of conduct are not reversed DuPont will eventually obtain the power to raise prices or prevent competition at will.

Characterizing DuPont's challenged course of conduct as an "exclusionary growth strategy," complaint counsel take the position that such conduct violates Section 5 of the Federal Trade Commission Act because it constitutes an illegal attempt to monopolize the TiO_2 market violative of the Sherman Act, threatens an incipient violation of the Sherman Act, violates the spirit of the Act, and violates public policy insofar as it causes undue harm to competition, competitors or consumers.

DuPont argues that there is nothing anticompetitive about an industry member attempting to gain market share and that such an "attempt" is the very substance of effective competition. It also contends that no one element of its challenged conduct ("growth strategy") is unlawful: that it did nothing illegal in obtaining its cost advantage over its competitors; that its plant expansion and new construction were reasonable and necessary responses to anticipated increase in market demand for TiO_2; and that it was under neither a legal nor a moral obligation to give its competitors (particularly NL) its ilmenite technology through licensing. DuPont contends that its competitors had and continue to have the means and technical ability by which to develop their own ilmenite technology or other low grade ore technology and their competitors' choice not to undertake the required investment in the past or present should not be held against DuPont.

DuPont claims that complaint counsel have made unwarranted assumptions about its growth strategy by attributing to DuPont's management certain policies that appeared in certain planning or analysis documents. For example, DuPont claims that it never engaged in the strategic pricing alleged by complaint counsel, that it did not forecast higher prices for TiO_2, should its growth plans prove successful and that it never considered itself to have or to be able to obtain through its growth plans a monopoly share of the TiO_2 market. DuPont also claims that it never made announcements about its expansion plans that were not accurate and for a legitimate reason.

Although the record does not support complaint counsel's overall view of DuPont's growth strategy, it does support their view of the exclusionary effect of DuPont's expansion program on competitor's expansion, and the probability that DuPont will obtain substantial market (monopoly) power. There is no doubt that the Federal Trade Commission Act was designed to prevent unfair trade practices that have the tendency or capacity to create a monopoly or lessen competition. But in any proceeding brought under the Federal Trade Commission Act, the Commission, before it may issue orders deemed remedial or preventative, must find that a respondent's conduct constitutes an *unfair* method of competition or an *unfair* or *deceptive* act or practice.

No matter how DuPont's officials may have analyzed their future business opportunities that arose upon the advent of DuPont's substantial cost advantage in the early 1970's, and no matter how they have appraised the nature or effect of their growth strategy, I can find no *conduct* that can be considered "unfair" within the meaning of the Federal Trade Commission Act. Even complaint counsel do not assert that any individual action taken by DuPont, whether in acquiring its cost advantage, in its TiO_2 pricing, in its expansion of capacity or in its choice not to license its TiO_2 ilmenite technology was illegal or even unreasonable. Complaint counsel challenge the exclusionary *effect* of all of these actions taken together, along with their claim that DuPont *intended* such an exclusionary effect.

In my opinion, the ultimate question in this matter is whether DuPont had *alternatives* to its aggressive growth strategy that it was required to take, in lieu of the actions it did take, in order not to run afoul of the antitrust laws.

Dr. Shepherd testified that "DuPont should have done whatever it wanted to do, subject to the proviso that it not choose a strategy whose effect was to transform the TiO_2 industry into a virtual monopoly." In this respect Dr. Shepherd noted that DuPont had made analyses of various directions it could have taken. His testimony on the various elements of the strategy indicates that in his opinion DuPont should not have priced as low as it did or should not have embarked on such a large expansion program (especially the construction of the De Lisle facility). He was of the opinion that one alternative DuPont had was to license its ilmenite technology to its competitors (including NL) at some point in time after 1972.[2]

I am not convinced that DuPont was required to take actions different than those it did take. DuPont's cost advantage was the result of business foresight, intelligent planning, dedicated technological application to a most difficult production problem, the taking of economic risk, and its competitors' choice during the 1960's to build production facilities designed to use high-grade rutile ore. The development of the shortage of rutile ore and the advent of high costs of pollution abatement for TiO_2 producers were not accidental. Although DuPont's gain was not unexpected, the magnitude and the timing of this new cost advantage was unexpected. But this cost advantage was not "fortuitous" in the sense that it was either accidental or unearned.

I do not believe that DuPont was required to price its TiO_2 products high enough to insure its less efficient competitors sufficient revenue to finance expansion. The resulting higher cost of TiO_2 to user-customers (and ultimately to the consumer) and the resulting exorbitant profits to DuPont would be more antisocial in the long run than the natural exclusionary effect of the so-called "investment asymmetry" that developed in the TiO_2 industry before 1972. As detailed above, I do not believe that DuPont's actual pricing in the period from May 1972 to 1978 could have been much different than it actually was, given price controls, the mid-70's recession and the slow recovery of the TiO_2 industry during 1976 and 1977 (see tr 1602-03 [Adelman]). In those situations where DuPont failed to match its competitors' price raises, the market conditions did not justify such price increases. During the period 1975 to 1977 there was an over supply of TiO_2, producers were operating at approximately 70 percent of capacity, and there were substantial TiO_2 sales at prices discounted from list. If DuPont had raised its TiO_2 list prices substantially, and then sold at those prices, it would have placed itself at a competitive disadvantage and would have been considered a "price gouger" by customers.

The lowest cost producer's choice to expand capacity in a situation of short supply, is a sound business judgment that is economically justified. In 1973, where there was a severe shortage of TiO_2, DuPont was entirely justified in planning to build a new plant. The record shows that a plant the size of De Lisle was necessary to take advantage of scale economies. The record also shows that DuPont thought

[2] Dr. Shepherd testified: I would like especially to consider another alternative that DuPont could have adopted—that of licensing its technology. DuPont had many opportunities to license its chloride technology. A policy which permitted licensing would have lowered production costs throughout the industry, while letting DuPont harvest extra profits in line with the cost savings made possible by its chloride technology. With licensing, the cost-saving benefits of DuPont's technology would not have been limited to its own production. . . .

the future of the sulfate process plants was in doubt. Any theory that higher cost producers must be protected against the effects of expansion by their lower cost competitor is not sound economic theory. And certainly the construction of a plant at less than scale is not socially desirable. In the circumstances, the De Lisle expansion was a reasonable business choice in 1972, and was still a reasonable choice in 1975. DuPont's announcements of its plans for De Lisle were for legitimate reasons and were not necessarily for the purpose of restraining competitive expansion.

DuPont was not required to license its ilmenite technology to its competitors (or potential entrants, if any). The choice to look to long run profitability instead of immediate revenue from royalties is not unfair. There is no showing on this record that competitors could not develop that technology, if they had chosen to take that course of action. The fact that these competitors found themselves five to ten years behind DuPont in 1972 did not obligate DuPont to give up its technological advantage.

The final question is whether DuPont's course of conduct, neither unreasonable nor unfair, becomes unfair because DuPont, in forecasting the effects of its actions, i.e., limited or no competitive expansion and its own increase in market share, knew or should have known that it would acquire substantial market power. With knowledge that the success of its growth program depended on either minimal or no expansion by its competitors, DuPont nevertheless put a growth strategy into operation in 1972 and has continued that growth strategy to date. DuPont was aware that TiO_2 prices were low enough to discourage competitive expansion and acknowledged that increase in market share was important to its profitability. As the dominant TiO_2 producer in the 1980's, DuPont predicted that it could be in a position to increase the profitability of that portion of its business in the foreseeable future.

In other words, the question is whether DuPont was prohibited from engaging in any conduct, the *effect* of which might be to transform the TiO_2 industry into a virtual monopoly. I do not think that business awareness of the nature of and the probable results of otherwise completely legitimate business conduct changes that conduct into an illegal anticompetitive practice or supplies an illegal intent to lessen competition or create a monopoly. I have found no prior "attempt to monopolize" case in the courts or before the Commission and not one has been cited by complaint counsel, that transforms lawful conduct into unlawful conduct without the presence of some overt or anticompetitive act considered unreasonable in the regular conduct of a competitive business.

I am not persuaded on the record considered as a whole that DuPont created, or unfairly maintained, the "investment asymmetry" which has existed in the TiO_2 industry since 1970 and which now is an effective barrier to the competitive expansion required by DuPont's competitors to place them in a position to challenge DuPont's impending dominance in the TiO_2 industry. Regardless of its market share, DuPont, in 1972, acquired the means to develop market power when it obtained a substantial cost advantage over its competitors. In my opinion whether DuPont adopted a less aggressive growth strategy program that complaint counsel and Dr. Shepherd appear to think it should have engaged in or the aggressive growth strategy challenged in this case, the so-called "investment asymmetry" would have nevertheless prevailed and the future prospects for effective competition would be just as tenuous as they appear today.[3]

[3]Dr. Shepherd was of the opinion that DuPont's behavior was that of a dominant firm and that its share of 40 percent of the TiO_2 market (where its nearest competitor's share was only 16 percent) indicates it already has substantial degree of monopoly power. I do not agree that DuPont already has monopolized the TiO_2 market within the meaning of Section 2 of the Sherman Act. The record shows that DuPont does not

Section 5 of the Federal Trade Commission Act can be invoked to effect structural changes in an industry only where it is clearly demonstrated that the competitive disequilibrium is the result of some conduct that could be designated as "unfair." If the challenged conduct is not unreasonable and not the cause of the trend toward monopoly power, no violation of Section 5 exists, merely because the effects upon competition may be undesirable from an economic point of view.

Conclusion

I conclude that DuPont did not engage in the "strategy" attributed to it in the complaint and by complaint counsel in their proposed findings in that DuPont did not *engage* in "strategic pricing," but rather established its TiO_2 prices relative to market forces over which it had no control.

I also conclude that DuPont's conduct of its business, insofar as it is challenged in this proceeding, was neither unreasonable nor unfair and that its conduct did not constitute an illegal attempt to monopolize the domestic TiO_2 market in violation of Section 2 of the Sherman Act and did not constitute unfair methods of competition or unfair and deceptive acts or practices in violation of Section 5 of the Federal Trade Commission Act, as amended.

Order

IT IS ORDERED that the complaint in Docket 9108, E. I. DuPont de Nemours & Company, is dismissed.

Miles J. Brown
Administrative Law Judge

August 31, 1979

have control over TiO_2 prices. It does not have the power to establish prices without regard to its competitors' pricing. However, when the De Lisle facility is in full production and the demand for TiO_2 increases as DuPont expects it will, a different case may appear. In this respect, Dr. Shepherd testified:

> . . . DuPont's market share seems to be likely to grow further, rather than suffer erosion. The record suggests that the sulfate TiO_2 plants now operating in the U.S. have a limited future. Meanwhile, DuPont has over 66 percent of all chloride-process TiO_2 production in the U.S. market, and this share will rise in the next year or two as the De Lisle plant opens. That plant, with up to 16 percent of U.S. TiO_2 capacity, will raise DuPont's total market share to at least 55 percent, and approximately 75 percent of the chloride-process TiO_2 production. Other producers have no major expansion under way, nor any present access to comparable chloride technology. Their sulfate-process plants are at an increasing cost disadvantage.

PART VI

Cases in the Global Competitive Business Environment

CASE EIGHTEEN

The Japanese Steel Industry

WILLIAM R. BOULTON and J. MICHAEL ALFORD
University of Georgia

Assignment Questions:

1. What has been the strategy for developing Japan's steel industry?
2. How would you describe the structure and strategic groupings of the Japanese steel companies?
3. What do you expect the structure to look like in the future? Who will have the power?

"[O]*ur objective is . . . to strongly promote rationalization of the steel industry which is the most important both as an export and basic industry and at the same time to lower the price level of coal through various measures to rationatize the coal mining industry, so that with efforts of the two industries, a foundation for self-sustenance of the Japanese will be established in the target year [1953]*"[1]

Industrial Rationalization Council
August 1950

By 1975, the Japanese steel industry had probably become the most productive and efficient in the world. Over 80 per cent of the total steel produced in Japan used the most efficient basic oxygen furnace, the LD converter, capable of producing over 3.5 million metric tons per year. Only 56 per cent of U.S. steel production used this system and only U.S. Steel Corporation and, perhaps, Bethlehem Steel Corporation had adequate cash flow to build such large furnaces.

In terms of size, five fully integrated steel companies had over $26.7 billion in assets and, with production of 117 million metric tons of crude steel and pig iron, produced over 80 per cent of Japan's total production. By 1975, Japan ranked as the third largest steel producer behind only the United States and the USSR. Japan's steel production had grown from 8 to 19 per cent of world production in only ten years. Of the ten largest free-world steel companies, four were Japanese, including the world's largest, Nippon Steel Corporation.

[1] Kawahito, Kiyoshi. *The Japanese Steel Industry, with an Analysis of the U.S. Steel Import Problem* (New York: Praeger Publishers, 1972), p. 24.

In Japan the steel industry accounted for about 20 per cent of total exports in 1974, approximately $12 billion. In fact, it was steel exports that helped absorb the massive payments deficits which would have otherwise occurred following worldwide oil price increases. The steel industry also became the major supplier of other key Japanese industries such as automobiles, heavy equipment manufacturing, construction, and shipbuilding.

BACKGROUND AND HISTORY

Japan's rise from the ashes of World War II to the third largest producer of steel in 1974 was part of the Japanese government's official policy. The government backed its policy with financial support from three government-owned banks, foreign-exchange loans, corporate bond and stock issues, duty-free imports of equipment, and depreciation rates 150 per cent above normal for three years.

In addition to government policy, the Japanese steel industry benefited from demands of the Korean conflict. This reduced the industry's financing needs by commercial banks to only 11.2 per cent of total funds.[2] By 1956, equipment modernization and production efficiencies made the Japanese steel industry competitive in the international marketplace. This year also began the second modernization program aimed at increasing capacity for iron- and steel making to supply rapidly growing domestic needs. In fact, capacity problems had caused export restriction in 1955.

Japan's second modernization program also included construction of giant ore and coal carriers. Japan depended upon imports for 85 per cent of ore and 40 per cent of its coking coal. This construction was a cooperative effort between the steel and shipping industries and the government. As shown in Exhibit 1, commercial banks funding 41 per cent of the funding requirements of the second modernization continued their favorable treatment and, in spite of low profits, public confidence enabled the steel firms to easily sell stocks and issue bonds.[3]

Japan's second modernization efforts resulted in the following improvements by 1960:

1. Iron-making capacity increased 197.6 per cent.
2. Steel-making capacity increased 278.9 per cent.
3. Hot-rolling capacity increased 224.0 per cent.
4. Labor productivity increased an average 29 per cent.
5. Crude steel production of 84 tons per worker in 1961 surpassed that of Great Britain and West Germany. U.S. steel production was 170 tons per employee.
6. Steel exports increased 2.3 times in ten years.

As a result, steel was established as the primary business of Japan by 1961.

Along with the government's support and growing demand came a simultaneous reforming of the industrial and financial groupings. These groupings

[2] Ibid., pp. 25–27.
[3] Ibid., pp. 28–41.

EXHIBIT 1: Sources of Funds for the Second Modernization, 1956–60 (in per cent)

Development Bank	5.5
Industrial Bank	5.5
Long-Term Credit Bank	4.0
Commercial Banks	1.1
Trust Companies	6.7
Insurance Companies	5.9
World Bank	8.6
Export-Import Bank	2.4
Other Foreign Sources	1.3
Stocks	20.2
Corporate Bonds	11.8
Internal Sources	31.9
Others	0.1
Totals	100.0

Note: Figures are on net-increase basis.
Source: Compiled from Ministry of International Trade and Industry, *Tekkogyo no Gorika to Sono Seika* (Tokyo: Kogyo Tosho Shuppan, 1963), pp. 156–57.

allowed the steel industry to concentrate only on the production of steel. Acquisition of up-to-date steel-making technology and the raw materials necessary for mass production of steel was handled by each group's trading houses. The trading firms also applied their domestic marketing and distribution capabilities to the developing steel industry. Although the majority of steel was sold domestically in the early years, it eventually provided the foundation for later international marketing activities of these trading firms. Through their sales function, the trading companies also allowed the steel industry to quickly turn its inventories into needed cash. As part of the industry groups, the Japanese banks also provided long-term capital needs, which was deceptively labeled "short-term" debt.

All of these factors created an environment that stimulated the steel industry's rebuilding process. By 1975, the steel industry had become the most modern, most productive, and most efficient in the world.

Japan's Steel Production

In 1974, the Japanese steel industry produced nearly 19 per cent of the world's steel production. As shown below, whereas only West Germany matched Japan's recent percentage growth in steel output, West Germany's output in tonnage was only 45 per cent that of Japan's.

		Japan	*EEC Total*	*F.R. Germany*	*U.S.A.*	*U.S.S.R.*
	1971	88,557	128,136	40,313	109,266	120,637
	1974	117,131	155,757	53,233	132,018	136,300
Increase	$\left(\frac{1974}{1971}\right)$	32.2%	21.6%	32.0%	20.8%	13.0%

Unit: 1,000 metric tons.
Source: Japan Iron and Steel Federation.

As shown in Exhibit 2, Japan's average annual growth since 1963 had more than doubled that of the total world's.

Japan's growth in steel output had also been accomplished by only a limited number of steel-making firms. For example, five steel firms produced 79 per cent of Japan's 117.1 million metric tons of crude steel, ranking four of these firms in the top ten shown in Exhibit 3. By 1975, the depreciated assets of these top four steel makers represented $11.3 billion. In addition, nine of the twelve largest blast furnaces in the world, including the largest, belonged to Japanese steel companies as shown in Exhibit 4.

By 1975, some of the largest industrial firms in the world had become Japanese firms according to *Fortune's* list of the 300 largest outside the United States. According to *Fortune,* 13 of the top 50 were Japanese, of which 10 were primary steel producers or users such as shipbuilding, automakers, and appliance manufacturers. By 1972, Japanese steel exports had represented 22 per cent of the total world steel trade. As shown in Exhibit 5, outside of the common market, these exports represented nearly 30 per cent of the steel trade and had grown rapidly since then. There was little doubt that steel would continue its importance in Japan and in the world.

Japan's Steel Productivity

Unlike other major steel-producing nations, Japanese steel was produced in high-capacity, efficient blast furnaces called LD Converters. The LD, or Linz-Donawitz, converter was a basic oxygen process developed in 1951 in Austria.

EXHIBIT 2: Steel Output Market Shares

	Japan	*United States*	*USSR*	*West Germany*	*United Kingdom*	*France*	*World Total*
Market Share (%)*							
1973	17.1	19.6	18.8	7.1	3.8	3.6	100.0
1974	16.4	18.6	20.7	8.1	5.6	4.5	100.0
Annual Growth (%)							
1963–1973	14.2	3.3	5.0	4.6	1.5	3.7	6.1
1968–1973	12.3	2.8	4.2	3.8	0.3	4.4	5.7

*Per cent of total world production of crude steel.

EXHIBIT 3: Top-Ranking Steel Manufacturers in Free World (1973) (Raw Steel Basis: 000 MT)

1. Nippon Steel (Japan)	41,080
2. U.S. Steel (U.S.)	31,750
3. British Steel (U.K.)	23,980
4. Bethlehem Steel (U.S.)	21.500
5. Nippon Kokan (Japan)	16,050
6. Sumitomo Metal (Japan)	14,490
7. Kawasaki Steel (Japan)	14,370
8. A.T.H. (West Germany)	13,900
9. ESTEL Netherlands)	11,570
10. Italsider (Italy)	11,460

Source: Japan Iron and Steel Federation

EXHIBIT 4: World Giant Blast Furnaces (1974)

Rank	*Works and Furnace No. (Steel Company)*	*Country*	*Inner Volume*
1	Fukuyama No. 5 (Nippon Kokan)	Japan	4,617 m^3
2	Dunkerque No. 4 (USINOR)	France	4,526
3	Mizushima No. 4 (Kawasaki Steel)	Japan	4,323
4	Fukuyama No. 4 (Nippon Kokan)	Japan	4,197
5	Oita No. 1 (Nippon Steel)	Japan	4,158
6	Schbergern No. 1 (August Thyssen Hutte)	West Germany	4,084
7	Kashima No. 2 (Sumitomo Metal)	Japan	4,080
8	Kimitsu No. 3 (Nippon Steel)	Japan	4,063
9	Kakogawa No. 2 (Kobe Steel)	Japan	3,850
10	Tobata No. 4 (Nippon Steel)	Japan	3,799
11	Ijmuiden No. 7 (Hoogovens)	Netherlands	3,667
12	Mizushima No. 3 (Kawasaki Steel)	Japan	3,363

Source: The Industrial Bank of Japan, Ltd.

EXHIBIT 5: Japan's Steel Exports (million MT)

	World Exports (A)	*Within EC (B)*	*(A)–(B)*	*Japanese Exports (D)*
1972	94.9	23.2	71.7	20.9

Japanese Share	
D/A	*D/A–B*
22.0%	29.2%

Source: United Nations statistics compiled by Baker, Weeks Co., Inc.

EXHIBIT 6: Crude Steel Production and Productivity in Principal Steel Mills in the World

Steel Mill	*Name of Steel Maker*	*Country*	*Crude Steel* Production (1,000 tons)*	*Number of Workers*	*Production/ Worker (Tons)*
Sakai	Nippon Steel Corporation	Japan	3,730	3,468	1,076
Nagoya	Nippon Steel Corporation	Japan	5,170	8,845	585
Kimitsu	Nippon Steel Corporation	Japan	7,660	6,815	1,124
Fukuyama	Nippon Kokan Kabushiki Kaisha	Japan	10,360	10,492	987
Chiba	Kawasaki Steel Corporation	Japan	5,510	12,916	427
Mizushima	Kawasaki Steel Corporation	Japan	6,430	11,560	556
Wakayama	Sumitomo Metal Industries, Ltd.	Japan	7,160	12,005	596
Kashima	Sumitomo Metal Industries, Ltd.	Japan	2,890	4,325	668
Gary	United States Steel Corporation (U.S. Steel)	U.S.A.	8,300	25,000	332
Sparrows Point	Bethlehem Steel Corporation (Bethlehem)	U.S.A.	7,300	23,000	371
Weirton	National Steel Corporation	U.S.A.	5,900	12,500	472
Indiana Harbor	Inland Steel Corporation	U.S.A.	8,100	21,000	386
Duisburg-Hamborn	August Thussen Huttle Group (A.T.H. Group)	West Germany	8,400	24,000	350
Huckingen	Mannesmann A.G.	West Germany	3,500	10,000	318
Dunkerque	Usinor	France	3,320	4,200	790
Ijmuiden	Hoogovens	Holland	5,120	18,000	284
Spencer	British Steel Corporation	U.K.	2,200	9,000	244
Pt. Talbot	British Steel Corporation	U.K.	3,250	16,000	203

* 1972 Actual Production for Japanese Mills and Dunkerque and Limuiden.

Source: The Industrial Bank of Japan, Ltd.

By 1973, almost 80 per cent of Japan's total crude steel output used this process. Use of the low-efficiency, open-hearth process declined from 68 per cent of 1960 production to only 2 per cent by 1972. In contrast, efficient production accounted for only 65 per cent for West Germany, 56 per cent for the United States, 46 per cent for France, 42 per cent of the United Kingdom, and 19 per cent for the USSR.

Using LD technology had also raised Japan's crude steel production per worker per year to increase from 85 metric tons in 1960 to 357 metric tons in 1972. This compared to an increase in the United States from 170 to 261 metric tons, and in France from 135 to 211 metric tons during the same period. With such high productivity, the Japanese continued to compete aggressively in world markets. As shown in Exhibit 6, only France came close to productivity of Nippon Steel or Nippon Kokan.

In addition to productivity, Japan's raw material and steel transport operations were highly efficient. As a consequence of not having adequate land space on which to build steel plants, major production facilities had to be located on reclaimed land areas that were surrounded by water. This resulted in low-cost importation of raw materials and export or intracompany transfer of finished products. As suggested by Exhibit 7, this gives Japan a major cost advantage over major steel-making countries.

In cooperation with shipbuilders, the steel industry developed large ore carriers capable of hauling over 100,000 tons of ore, giving coastal plants a decided advantage over inland plants. The delivered cost of materials accounted for as much as 40 per cent of total product costs. Costs of loading, unloading, and transport were a major portion of that cost. In fact, one Japanese producer had built a mammoth ocean carrier designed to self-load, transport, and unload large tonnage of slabs.

EXHIBIT 7: Steel Mills Located on Seashores

	Seashore Steel Mills (Unit: 1,000 tons)			*Production Share of Seashore Steel Mills in Total Production of Respective Countries*
Country	*No.*	*Crude Steel Production*	*Name of Company*	
Japan	17	81,250	Seashore steel mills of six steel-making companies	79%
United States	2	9,450	Fairless, Sparrows Point	6
West Germany	1	4,000	Bremen	9
France	1	3,320	Dunkerque	14
United Kingdom	2	5,250	Spencer, Pt. Talbot	21
Italy	4	10,500	Taranto, Bagnoli Cornigeliano, Piombino	53
Belgium	1	2,470	Gent	17
Holland	1	5,120	Ijmuiden	92

Source: The Industrial Bank of Japan, Ltd. (1974).

Government Influence in Japan

The steel industry in most industrialized nations impacts on governments' economic goals. In the United States, for example, the government had been involved in price setting, helping with wage negotiations, and providing tariff protection in the steel industry. However, U.S. steel firms still had much autonomy. In Japan, government administrations maintained strict control of the industry since it was a major exporting industry and supplier of low-cost, high-quality raw materials to other key industrial sectors.

In 1966, Japan's Industrial Structure Council established its steel industry section. The council, under the control of and adviser to the Ministry of International Trade and Industry (MITI), had extremely broad and undefined powers. Through this council, for example, MITI must approve all major construction or expansion projects, any proposed price changes, and planned export levels. In cooperation with the Ministry of Finance, the council also had regulatory power over much of the steel industry's financial policies.

In addition to direct control of the steel industry, MITI also supervised the resolution of intraindustry policy questions. For example, in coordination with industry members, MITI established an "offsetting shut-down rule" in 1971. This rule required companies that bring new plants on line with capacity of over 4 million tons per year to simultaneously shut down 2.5 million tons of existing furnace capacity. This ruling has allowed the industry to operate at near full capacity and has avoided frequent price competition by controlling relative market shares. It should also be noted that Nippon Steel Corporation, as industry leader, negotiated contracts and acquired raw materials for all industry members. A long-term coal supply contract with Jim Walter Corporation of Australia was in excess of $2 billion.

Raw Materials Supplies

Japan, in 1973, imported over 99 per cent of its iron ore and 71 per cent of its hard coal requirements for marketing steel. Over 48 per cent of its ore and 43 per cent of its coal requirements were imported from Australia. India was the source of another 14 per cent of Japan's ore imports, whereas the United States provided 31 per cent of its coal imports.[4] U.S. ore exports to Japan had fallen from over 3.6 million tons in 1967 to 439,105 tons in 1974.[5]

As shown in Exhibit 8, Japan surpassed all major steel-producing countries in its import of ore and coal. Only Italy required a greater percentage of its total import requirements. West Germany and the United Kingdom required ore imports amounting to over 94 and 88 per cent of their requirements, respectively, compared to 34 per cent for the United States. France, importing 28 per cent of its coal requirements, was the second largest importer of coal. Other countries had their own coal supplies.

[4] Julian Szekely, ed., *The Future of the World's Steel Industry* proceedings of the Fifth CL Furnace Memorial Conference (New York: Marcel Dekker, Inc., 1976).

[5] *Iron Ore 1976,* American Iron Ore Association, Cleveland, Ohio, p. 31.

EXHIBIT 8: Dependence on Overseas Supplies of Steel-Making Materials (1973)

	Japan	*United States*	*United Kingdom*	*West Germany*	*France*	*Italy*
Iron Ore						
(%)	99.2%	34.7%	88.2%	94.6%	38.4%	97.6%
1,000 tons	128,761	44,027	23,920	50,325	11,530	14,193
Hard Coal						
(%)	71.8%	N.A.	1.4%	7.9%	28.4%	100.0%
1,000 tons	56,904	87	1,871	7,107	9,907	10,760

Source: The Industrial Bank of Japan, Ltd.

CONDITION IN 1975

Both the rising costs of raw materials and the domestic recession of 1974 put considerable strain on the Japanese steel industry. Whereas exports offset this in 1974, prices and volume had both declined through March, 1975 (Exhibit 9). As a result, steel inventories were extremely high at all levels, including dealers and users. Higher costs and lower demands caused the steel industry's earnings to be squeezed during the latter half of 1974. Over 80 per cent of domestic steel

EXHIBIT 9: Steel Capacity Utilization (1974–1975) (million tons)

	Crude Steel		*Pig Iron*	
	1974(9/30)	*1975(3/31)*	*1974(9/30)*	*1975(3/31)*
Nippon Steel Corp.				
Capacity	47.9	46.8	44.0	42.1
Utilization Rate (%)	81.6	74.1	84.8	81.6
Nippon Kokan K.K.				
Capacity	19.4	19.4	16.3	16.3
Utilization Rate (%)	84.6	79.3	91.3	82.3
Sumitomo Metals Ind., Ltd.				
Capacity	20.1	20.6	14.8	15.5
Utilization Rate (%)	72.4	70.6	89.0	87.7
Kawasaki Steel Corp.				
Capacity	36.6	39.1	14.5	14.5
Utilization Rate (%)	77.9	71.5	98.6	95.1
Kobe Steel, Ltd.				
Capacity	19.3	19.3	9.4	8.8
Utilization Rate (%)	44.7	41.2	82.2	87.6
TOTAL (Big 5)				
Capacity	143.4	145.3	99.0	97.2
Utilization	74.8	69.2	88.3	85.2

EXHIBIT 10: Crude Steel Production per Worker per Annum (Unit: tons)

	1960	*1965*	*1970*	*1971*	*1972*	*Average Annual Growth Rate*
Japan	95	160	326	314	357	11.7%
United States	170	222	238	236	261	3.6
West Germany	122	146	197	190	211	4.7
France	135	156	220	215	N.A.	N.A.
Italy	95	110	209	196	N.A.	N.A.

Source: The Industrial Bank of Japan, Ltd.

sales were on long-term contracts, and user industries were reluctant to renegotiate prices. MITI's policy was to let corporate profits be squeezed by inflation.

Total domestic demand declined 19.5 per cent in 1974 to 51.6 million metric tons. Declines in construction and public works projects amounted to 27.4 and 27.3 per cent, respectively, from 1973 levels. The construction industry had accounted for 50 per cent of total domestic sales in 1973.

International steel sales for 1974 had increased 24.2 per cent over 1973, to 34.3 million metric tons. As a result of average prices increasing from $107 per ton in 1973, to $348 per ton in 1974, total steel export revenues increased 90.9 per cent to $12 billion. Capacity shortages for coke ovens in the United States and ore shortages in Europe had benefited Japan just as domestic demands had declined.

Raw material costs increased rapidly in 1974. Labor problems in the United States and Australia had reduced coke supplies 11.0 per cent while prices increased from $23.80 per ton in 1973 to $55.00 per ton in 1974. Costs for total energy consumption also increased even with cutbacks in overall crude steel production.

Even with current adversity, Exhibit 10 shows the productivity and efficiency of the Japanese steel industry and its comparative ability to absorb price increases. Given the importance of steel to Japan, it was also expected that government policies would ensure the industry's long-term viability. However, slower growth and rising prices would put continued pressure on the industry as the supplier of low-cost, high-quality steel to Japanese industries. With expected losses from four of Japan's top five steel producers in 1975, it was expected that MITI would allow domestic price increases to offset some of those losses by year-end.

International Outlook

It was projected that world steel supplies would be 10 to 61 million metric tons short of demand by 1980. If Communist countries failed to add capacity, the short fall was expected to reach 61 million metric tons. The actual shortage would depend on expected actions of both raw material and steel-making countries. In any case, Japan was expected to benefit.

EXHIBIT 11: World Iron Ore Production (million metric tons)

	1973	*Per Cent Share*	*Estimate 1980*	*Per Cent Share*
"Big Four"	175	24.3	380	33.9
All Others	545	75.7	740	66.1
Total	720	100.0	1,120	100.0

Source: Julian Szekely, ed., *The Future of the World's Steel Industry,* Proceeding of the Fifth C. L. Furnace Memorial Conference (New York: Marcel Dekker, Inc., 1976), p. 9.

The big four iron ore producers were Brazil, Australia, Canada, and Sweden, which together accounted for 24.3 per cent of 1973's ore production as shown in Exhibit 11. By 1980, they were expected to account for over one-third of total ore production.

Steel-making capacity was probably even more important. Total share of the big three producers (Japan, the United States, and West Germany) was expected to decline from 61.9 per cent in 1973 to 54.2 per cent by 1980. Lack of water ports, rising labor costs, limited capital, raw material shortages, and demands for pollution controls and quality of life were all considered to affect future growth of the big three.

"Ore rich" countries were expected to become an important force. Exhibit 12 shows that Brazil, Sweden, South Africa, Canada, and Australia were expected to add 16 million metric tons in their steel-making capacity by 1980. This would increase their share from 7.9 per cent in 1973 to 11.1 per cent in 1980, as shown in Exhibit 13.

"Oil rich" countries were also expected to add steel-making capacity. Saudi Arabia, Venezuela, Algeria, and Iran had natural gas supplies and large oil revenues. Electric arc furnaces and continuous-casting plants were being planned. Brazil was rumored to be considering a 40 per cent interest in Saudi Arabian

EXHIBIT 12: Semifinished Steel Plants Planned for 1980

County	*Location*	*Initial Capacity (million metric tons raw steel)*
1. Brazil*	Tubārao	3.0
2. Sweden*	Luleå	4.0
3. South Africa*	Saldanha Bay	3.0
4. Canada	Nova Scotia	3.0
5. Australia	West Australia	3.0
Total		16.0

* Definite.

Source: Julian Szekely, ed., *The Future of the World's Steel Industry* (New York: Marcel Dekker, Inc., 1976), p. 18.

EXHIBIT 13: Projected Free World Raw Steel-Making Capacity by Groups (million metric tons)

	1973	*Per Cent Share*	*Estimate 1980*	*Per Cent Share*
"Big Three"	332	61.9	371	54.2
"Ore-rich"	42	7.9	75	11.1
"Oil-rich"	2	0.4	22	3.2
"Other"	160	29.8	216	31.5
Total Free World	536	100.0	684	100.0

Source: Julian Szekely, *The Future of the World's Steel Industry* (New York: Marcel Dekker, Inc., 1976), p. 17.

steel on an "ore for oil" basis. Egypt, Tunisia, Nigeria, and Tobago had announced plans for plants that would produce reduced iron and lead toward production of semifinished steel. This would increase the market share of these countries from 0.4 to 3.2 per cent by 1980.

Overall steel capacity expansion, then, was expected to come most from ore-rich and oil-rich countries. As shown in Exhibit 14, the "big three" were only expected to round out current production needs. "Ore-rich" countries were expected to increase their share of semifinished steel as "oil-rich" countries entered into direct reduction plants. This latter strategy would have the greatest impact on steel scrap since that would be the primary raw material.

JAPANESE STEEL PRODUCERS

In recent years, the Japanese steel producers continued to expand and modernize their plants using the latest technologies. The vast majority of investment was financed through the use of debt as shown in Exhibit 15. Since steel industry

EXHIBIT 14: Free World Expansion Strategies

	"Big Three"	*"Ore-Rich"*	*"Oil Rich"*
Main Expansion	Rounding Out	New Semis Plants	New Direct Reduction Plants
Production Process	Blast Furnace BOF Rolling Mills	Blast Furnace BOF	Direct Reduction Electric Furnace
Major Advantage	Market for Steel	Iron Ore	Oil and Natural Gas
Main Drawback	Lack of Funds to Expand		Plant Operating Difficulties

Source: Julian Szekely, ed., *The Future of the World's Steel Industry* (New York: Marcel Dekker, Inc., 1976), p. 19.

investments were considered low risk, Japanese banks made funds readily available to the steel producers. By 1975, total debt of the top six Japanese steel companies averaged 8.9 times its total net worth. This compared to debt/equity ratios of .73 and .81 for U.S. Steel and Bethlehem Steel, respectively.[6] The major portion of this debt was short-term, with long-term debt accounting for only 35.8 per cent of the total.

With such high levels of debt, interest payments represented a significant percentage of total sales. Of the top six Japanese producers, interest to sales ranged from 7.99 per cent for Kobe Steel to 5.70 per cent for Nippon Steel Corp. Both bankers and government officials viewed long-term debt as short-term, and viewed short-term debt as long-term.

These differences in financial structure made "cash flow" analysis an important measure of financial health. By adding depreciation and other pretax reserves to net income, one could better assess a company's financial strength. Referring back to Exhibit 15, net cash flow analysis shows the strength of Nippon Steel with 90 billion yen ($322 million) in cash flow, compared to the need of Kobe Steel and Nisshin Steel for over 16 billion yen ($57 million) in additional cash. Yet Nippon Steel had the weakest earnings ratio, only average depreciation, and the highest dividend payout ratio.

To further assess the financial stability of these top steel companies, consider the current portion of long-term debt that is due for payment. In cases such as Kobe Steel and Nisshin Steel, where the debt payment cannot be made, with the heavy investments also came heavy depreciation write-offs as shown in Exhibit 16. Depreciation ranged from 4.20 per cent of sales for Kobe Steel to 7.37 per cent for Nippon Kokan. Depreciation averaged 5.72 per cent of sales for the Japanese steel industry as compared to 4.1 and 3.9 per cent for U.S. Steel and Bethlehem Steel, respectively.

With high interest and depreciation expenses, profits in the Japanese steel industry were relatively low. For the year ending March 31, 1975, profit as a per cent of sales averaged 1.52 per cent for the top six firms. Nisshin Steels' profits were a high of 1.72 per cent of sales compared to 6.8 and 6.3 percentage for U.S. Steel and Bethlehem Steel. Even though dividend payments were a high 50 to 77 per cent of net income, since interest on debt was a pretax expense, the overall cost of capital was less expensive for Japanese firms than for U.S. steel firms.

Finally, the current ratios for the top six Japanese steel producers averaged a low of .92 in 1975. Kawasaki Steel showed a current ratio of .85 with Nippon Steel only slightly better at 1.0, as shown in Exhibit 17. The top six steel firms averaged negative working capital of 48.4 billion yen (over $170 million). Whereas Nippon Steel showed 53 billion yen in positive working capital, the remaining five were negative with Nippon Kokan's deficit mounting to over 114 billion yen.

The weaknesses of the Japanese current financial position stems from their heavy reliance on short-term debt. Despite the fact that legally these are short-term instruments, there is a firm understanding between financial institutions and borrowers that such debt will never be repaid but rolled over in perpetuity.

[6] Equity was generally issued at par in Japan and required dividend payments equal to 10–12 percent of par. This raised aftertax cost to 20–24 per cent.

EXHIBIT 15: Major Integrated Steel Manufacturers Capitalization Analysis (3/31/75) (¥ 000,000's omitted)

	Equity Capital (TWN)	*Long-Term Debt (LTD) 1.*	*Short-Term Debt 2.*	*Current Position LTD*	*Total Capital*	*Short-Term Debt/ Total Capital*	*Current Portion LTD/ LTD*	*LTD/ Total Debt*
Nippon Steel Corporation	318,245	925,493	1,126,246	70,869	2,691,207	41.8%	7.7%	42.7%
Nippon Kokan K.K.	145,440	484,345	853,917	77,980	1,648,333	51.8%	16.1%	34.2%
Sumitomo Industry, Ltd.	109,349	429,692	742,529	66,815	1,475,967	50.6%	15.6%	34.2%
Kawasaki Steel Corporation	117,293	393,788	683,017	46,746	1,339,244	51.0%	11.9%	34.5%
Kobe Steel Corporation	93,985	328,130	617,417	48,928	1,117,183	55.3%	14.9%	33.9%
Nisshin Steel Co., Ltd.	43,269	88,245	154,783	21,340	306,554	50.5%	24.1%	35.0%
Average						50.1%	15.1%	35.8%

1. Excludes current portion LTD.
2. Includes current portion LTD.
3. Includes reserve accounts.
4. LTD + 50% of NIBT + Depreciation + Net changes to reserves − Dividends.
5. NIBT + Interest Expense ÷ Interest Expense.

Source: Ministry of Finance.

As a consequence, this debt can be viewed as equity capital. The companies would renegotiate these maturities by refunding them into long-term or short-term debt, depending on interest rates. Even with these considerations, at present level of cash generation, long-term debt repayment for the Japanese steel industry could be made in an average 6.3 years. But to better understand individual company strengths, one has to further assess the strength of its group relationships.

NIPPON STEEL CORPORATION

Nippon Steel Corporation was the largest steel company in Japan and the world. Although it began in 1857, it was organized in 1874 into the Kamaishi Iron Works. Later, in 1896, the government-owned Yawata Steel Works began operations. In 1934, the government merged the Yawata Steel Works with Kamaishi Iron Works and with Rinsai Steel Works, Fuji Iron and Steel, Mitsubishi Steel, Kyushu Iron and Steel, and Toyo Steel. The resulting company, called Japan Iron and Steel, was broken up into the former Yawata Iron and Steel Corporation and the Fuji Iron and Steel Corporation after World War II by American occupational authorities. Even though these independent companies grew rapidly during the 1950s and 1960s, they merged under government direction in March 1970 into Nippon Steel.

In March 1975, Nippon Steel had sales in excess of $7.6 billion (Exhibit

LTD/ Capital	*Years to Repay LTD 3.*	*Years to Repay Total Debt*	*Times Interest Earned 5.*	*Dividends/ Net Income*	*Total Debt*	*Cash Flow Factor per Footnote 4.*	*Total Liabilities/ Total Net Worth*
34.4%	5.8 years	13.6 years	1.4x	77.0%	2,167,588	158,735	6.8
29.4%	4.9 years	14.3 years	1.5x	50.3%	1,418,165	98,852	9.7
29.1%	5.7 years	16.5 years	1.7x	52.5%	1,256,780	75,722	11.5
29.4%	5.9 years	16.9 years	1.3x	69.8%	1,140,334	67,205	9.7
29.4%	8.7 years	25.5 years	1.3x	73.3%	964,711	37,900	10.3
28.8%	6.5 years	18.5 years	1.4x	73.9%	251,958	13,580	5.8
30.1%	6.3 years	17.5 years	1.4x	66.1%			8.9

18). With 11 blast furnace sites that produced nearly 79 million tons of pig iron and crude steel plus 34.9 million tons of manufactured steel products in 1974, Nippon Steel produced 2.8 times the output of the third largest steel maker, Sumitomo Metals Industries. Nippon Steel's overall sales for 1974 were as follows:

Steel bars and shapes	18%
Steel plates and sheets	60%
Special steel	7
Steel tubes, pipes	9
Other	6
Total	100%

Nippon Steel was the primary purchaser of iron ore and coking coal for the industry exporters of finished products and the primary participant in technical cooperation and exchanges. As industry leader, it had been the prime influence in developing Japan's international steel position.

Group Connections

Because of its unique history, Nippon Steel has a unique status, as an industrial company, in its relationship with the Japanese government. Two of its directors are from the Ministry of International Trade and Industry and one is

EXHIBIT 16: Integrated Still Manufacturers Comparative Income Statement Analysis (3/31/75) (¥ 000,000's omitted)

	Nippon Steel Corp.		*Nippon Kokan K.K.*		*Sumitomo Metal Ind.*		*Kawasaki Steel*		*Kobe Steel*		*Nisshin Steel*	
	Amount	*% of Sales*	*Amount*	*% of Sales*	*Amount*	*% of Sales*	*Amount*	*% of Sales*	*Amount*	*% of Sales*	*Amount*	*% of Sales*
Net Sales	2,287,025	100.00%	1,192,124	100.00%	1,030,045	100.00%	879,529	100.00%	768,832	100.00%	253,871	100.00%
Depreciation	135,845	5.94%	87,842	7.37%	49,141	4.77%	62,776	7.14%	32,424	4.20%	12,518	4.9%
Income from Operations	177,759	7.77%	118,489	9.94%	131,030	12.72%	104,469	11.88%	77,756	10.1%	20,089	7.91%
Interest Expense	131,385	5.70%	81,732	6.86%	63,234	6.14%	51,090	5.81%	61,428	7.99%	15,950	6.28%
N.I. before Taxes	54,856	2.40%	37,942	3.18%	46,441	4.5%	23,686	2.69%	18,064	2.35%	6,779	2.67%
Taxes and Taxes/N.I.B.T	25,000	45.57%	17,650	46.52%	30,300	53.30%	13,900	58.68%	7,670	42.46%	2,400	35.40%
Net Income	29,856	1.31%	20,292	1.70%	16,141	1.57%	12,786	1.45%	10,294	1.35%	4,379	1.72%
Dividends and Div./N.I.	23,000	77.04%	10,206	50.3%	8,476	52.5%	8,926	69.81%	7,616	73.27%	3,240	73.99%
Net Changes to and (from) Reserves	18,462		5,545		11,837		12		4,060		913	
Gross Cash Flow[1]	184,163		113,679		77,119		75,574		46,878		17,810	
Current Portion L.T.D.	(70,867)		(77,980)		(66,815)		(46,746)		(48,928)		(21,340)	
Cash Flow before Dividends	113,296		35,699		10,304		28,828		(2,050)		(3,530)	
Dividends	(23,000)		(10,206)		(8,476)		(8,926)		(7,616)		(3,240)	
Net Cash Flow	90,296		25,493		1,828		19,902		(9,666)		(6,770)	

[1]Net income plus depreciation plus net changes to reserves.

Source: Ministry of Finance.

EXHIBIT 17: Integrated Steel Manufacturers Comparative Balance Sheet Analysis (3/31/75)
(¥ 000,000's omitted) **Prepared from the MOF Report**

	Tangible Net Worth	*Accounts Receivable Net*[1]	*Inventory*	*Current Assets*	*Fixed Assets (Net)*	*Current Liabilities*	*Long-term Debt*	*Total Liabilities*	*T.L./ T.N.W.*	*Current Ratio*	*Working Capital*	*Receivables Net Sales*	*Inventory Net Sale*
Nippon Steel Corporation	318,245	340,791	448,769	1,179,291	1,256,246	1,126,246	925,493	2,167,588	6.8x	1.0x	53,045	14.9%	19.6%
Nippon Kokan K.K.	145,440	387,602	329,509	739,448	771,033	853,917	484,345	1,418,165	9.8x	.87x	(114,469)	32.5%	27.6%
Sumitomo Metal Industries, Ltd.	109,349	194,404	208,490	652,402	702,610	742,529	429,692	1,256,780	11.5x	.88x	(90,127)	18.9%	20.2%
Kawasaki Steel Corporation	117,293	189,007	241,751	582,205	666,305	683,017	393,788	1,140,334	9.7x	.85x	(99.812)	21.5%	27.5%
Kobe Steel Corporation	93,985	286,237	207,414	590,064	447,503	617,417	328,130	964,711	10.3x	.96x	(27,353)	37.2%	27.0%
Nisshin Steel Co., Ltd.	43,269	57,892	44,656	143,338	139,809	154,783	88,245	251,958	5.8x	.93x	(11,445)	22.8%	17.6%
Total	827,581				3,983,607			7,199,536					
Average									8.9x	.92x –	(48.360)	24.6%	23.3%

[1]Includes accounts and notes receivable plus notes discounted.

Source: Ministry of Finance.

EXHIBIT 18: Top Six Japanese Steel Producers Financial Highlights (3/31/75) (¥ 000,000 omitted)

	Nippon Steel Corporation	*Nippon Kokan*	*Sumitomo Metal Industries, Ltd.*	*Kawaski Steel Corporation*	*Kobe Steel Ltd.*	*Nisshin Steel Co., Ltd.*
Net Sales	7,623,417	3,973,746	3,433,483	2,931,763	2,562,773	864,236
Depreciation	452,817	292,806	163,803	209,253	108,080	41,726
Income from Operations	592,530	394,963	436,767	348,230	259,197	66,963
Net Income	99,520	67,633	53,803	42,620	34,647	14,596
N.I/Shares*	1.31%	1.7%	1.57%	1.45%	1.35%	1.68%
Depr./Sales*	5.94%	7.4%	4.77%	7.14%	4.22%	1.83%
Interest Exp./Sales*	5.70%	6.9%	6.61%	8.89%	7.99%	6.28%
Tangible Net Worth	1,060,816	484,800	364,497	390,977	313,283	144,230
Fixed Assets	4,187,823	2,570,110	2,342,033	2,221,017	1,491,677	466,030
Total Liabilities	7,225,293	4,727,216	4,189,267	3,759,523	3,215,703	839,860
Working Capital	176,816	(381,561)	(300,417)	(332,707)	(91,177)	
T.L./T.N.W.*	6.81x	9.75x	11.49x	9.62x	10.26x	5.82x
Current Ratio*	1.05x	0.87x	0.88x	0.85x	0.96x	0.93x
Number of Employees	78,422	41,209	30,359	34,078	34,410	10,181

* Industry Comparisons:	*Average of Top Six Steel Companies*
N.I/Sales	1.52%
Depr./Sales	5.72
Interest Exp./Sales	6.46
T.L./T.N.W.	8.97x
Current Ratio	0.92x

Source: Ministry of Finance.

from the Tax Administration Agency. Although other corporations in the ferrometals industry are associated with Nippon Steel, none are as significant or influential as their leader.

Nippon Steel is not affiliated with the traditional industrial groupings. However, because of its size and strength, a large number of the group's financial institutions were creditors, as shown:

Nippon Steel's Debt Structure (1975)
(billions of yen)

	Long-Term	*Short-Term*	*Total*
Mitsubishi Group	87.4 (11%)	17.1 (10.8%)	104.5 (11.0%)
Mitsui Group	68.4 (8.6)	8.7 (5.5)	77.2 (8.1)
Sumitomo Group	77.2 (9.7)	13.0 (8.2)	90.2 (9.5)
Fuyo Group	86.8 (10.9)	13.8 (8.7)	100.6 (10.6)
Dai-Ichi Kangyo Bank Groups	20.4 (2.6)	9.1 (5.8)	29.6 (3.1)
Sanwa Group	74.6 (9.4)	13.8 (8.7)	88.4 (9.2)
Foreign Banks	44.8 (5.6)	9.5 (6.0)	54.3 (5.7)

Japan's largest bank, Dia-Ichi Kangyo Bank, provided only 3.1 per cent of Nippon Steel's total debt financing. Dia-Ichi Kangyo Bank group had its own steel company, Kawasaki Steel Corp., to which it applied 20 per cent of its financing needs. Sumitomo and Fuyo groups also had major steel companies within their groups.

NIPPON KOKAN K.K.

Nippon Kokan K. K., founded in 1912 as Japan's first manufacturer of steel pipe, had become Japan's second largest steel company. Developing without government support, Nippon Kokan fired its first blast furnace in 1937 and managed to avoid mergers and nationalization during World War II. Following the war, the company acquired an adjacent shipyard and began vertically integrating into other industries.

In 1974, Nippon Kokan produced 31 million tons of crude steel and pig iron and 27.8 million tons of plates, sheets, shapes, pipe, and section. By 1975 this represented sales of over $3.9 billion (Exhibit 18). Unlike other steel companies, Nippon Kokan is also in shipbuilding and repair and in construction of buildings, large span bridges, and heavy machinery. Shipbuilding and repair activities represent 11 per cent of total revenues and construction represents 9 per cent. There is some question as to the impact that the current downturn in shipbuilding will have on the company. Nippon Kokan's Fukuyama works were the largest and most modern in the world with capacity of over 16 million tons of crude per year.

Group Connections

Nippon Kokan K. K. is one of the largest and most important members of the "Fuyo-kai" business council along with the Fuji Bank (the group's focal point), the Yasuda Trust and Banking Co., Marubeni Corporation (Japan's fourth largest trading company), and Kubota, Ltd. (a major producer of industrial machinery). Fuji Bank was the largest shareholder of Nippon Kokan, owning 4.4 per cent of the stock, whereas Nippon Kokan owned 3.7 per cent of Fuji Bank stock and was its largest shareholder. Although this relationship was very strong, other group ties were less strong.

In 1975, the Fuyo group's financial institutions provided 16.9 per cent of Nippon Kokan's short-term debt and 29.4 per cent of its long-term debt. As shown, no other groups were nearly this important:

Nippon Kokan's Debt Structure (1975)
(billions of yen)

	Long-Term	*Short-Term*	*Total*
Mitsubishi Group	18.5 (3.8%)	10.8 (6.6%)	29.3 (4.5%)
Mitsui Group	7.5 (1.6)	1.3 (0.8)	8.8 (1.4)
Sumitomo Group	22.7 (4.7)	3.8 (2.3)	26.5 (4.1)
Fuyo Group	81.8 (16.9)	47.8 (29.4)	129.6 (20.0)
Dia-Ichi Kangyo Bank Group	21.6 (4.5)	19.0 (11.7)	40.6 (6.3)
Sanwa Group	13.8 (2.9)	1.6 (1.0)	15.4 (2.4)
Foreign Banks	27.3 (5.6)	4.1 (2.5)	31.4 (4.6)

Of the Fuyo group's 47 billion yen ($167.8 million) in short-term debt, Fuji Bank provided 80 per cent (40.1 billion year) plus 29 billion of long-term debt. This represented about 34 per cent of Fuiji Bank's total capital and reserves.

SUMITOMO METAL INDUSTRIES, LTD.

Sumitomo Metals Industries, Ltd., Japan's third largest fully integrated steel producer, was originally established in 1897 as Sumitomo Copper Rolling Mill in Osaka. Its sister company, Sumitomo Steel Works introduced the first open hearth furnace to Japan in 1901. In 1935, the two companies were merged into Sumitomo Metal Industries. After being almost totally destroyed during World War II, the remaining company merged with Kokura Steel Co. in 1953 to become an integrated manufacturer of steel and steel products. With the beginning of its modernization program in 1957, the nonferrous metals division was spun off into Sumitomo Light Metals Industries, and its precision aircraft parts division into Sumitomo Precision Products Co. In 1963, its electromagnetic products division was spun off into Sumitomo Special Metals Co.

By 1975, Sumitomo Metals' five major plants were producing annually 27.9 million tons of crude steel and pig iron and 11.6 million tons of steel pipe, shapes, sheets, forgings, and rolling stock. Sumitomo Metal's sales were over $3.4 billion for 1974, which broke down as follows (Exhibit 18):

Sheet and plates	39.4%
Tubes and pipes	34.7
Wire rod	10.4
Castings	7.7
Rolling stock	7.8
Total	100.0%

Over 47 per cent was produced for export. In addition, Sumitomo Metals exported production facilities, having established in Brazil plants for forging automobile parts and producing welded pipe. Sumitomo Metals also imported raw materials and exchanged technology.

Group Connections

Sumitomo Metals was one of 16 companies represented on the closely knit Sumitomo group's "Hakusui-Kai" council. Group members owned 16.4 per cent of the company's stock with Sumitomo Bank owning 5.0 per cent, Sumitomo Trust and Banking Company owning 4.9 per cent, and Sumitomo Mutual Life Insurance company owning 4.6 per cent. Sumitomo Metals also owned 3.1 per cent of Sumitomo Bank stock and 4.0 per cent of Sumitomo Trust and Banking Company. As seen, the Sumitomo group's financial institutions provided 38.6 per cent of short-term debt and 23.6 per cent of long-term debt requirement:

Sumitomo Metal's Debt Structure (1975)
(billions of yen)

	Long-Term	*Short-Term*	*Total*
Mitsubishi Group	23.5 (5.0%)	8.1 (4.4%)	31.5 (5.1%)
Mitsui Group	9.5 (2.2)	1.2 (0.6)	10.7 (1.7)
Sumitomo Group	101.3 (23.6)	71.0 (38.6)	172.3 (28.1)
Fuyo Group	9.1 (2.1)	2.8 (1.5)	12.0 (1.9)
Dia-Ichi Kangyo Bank Group	7.7 (1.8)	1.4 (0.8)	9.1 (1.5)
Sanwa Group	20.4 (4.8)	3.0 (1.6)	23.4 (3.8)
Foreign Banks	24.9 (5.8)	10.1 (5.5)	35.0 (5.7)

The close relationships within the Sumitomo group helps account for the 11.5 debt/equity ratio of Sumitomo Metals, compared to 8.97 for the industry.

KAWASAKI STEEL CORPORATION

Kawasaki Steel Corporation, the fourth largest in 1975, had started steel making in 1906 as Kawasaki Heavy Industries, a producer of heavy machinery. In 1916, it began producing steel plate for shipbuilding. After World War II, the steel manufacturing division was separated by the occupational authorities to become Kawasaki Steel Corporation. In 1951 and 1967, Kawasaki Steel established full integrated complexes.

By 1975, Kawasaki Steel produced 28.9 million tons of crude steel and pig iron and 12.9 million tons of plates and sheets, steel wire and rods and pipes annually. Sales for 1975 were over $2.9 billion (Exhibit 18). With about 32.7 per cent exported, 31.5 per cent went to Asian countries. Plants were also being built in the Philippines and in Brazil.

Group Connections

Kawasaki Steel was most closely associated with the Kawasaki companies that were grouped around Japan's largest bank, Dia-Ichi Kangyo Bank, and the

Long-Term Credit Bank, Ltd. (not a group member). Although the members of the group were not closely coordinated, there was a strong relationship between Dai-Ichi Kangyo Bank and Kawasaki Steel. The two banks were Kawasaki Steel's largest shareholders and Kawasaki was a major shareholder in Dai-Ichi Kangyo Bank. As shown, this group's financial institution held the largest portion of Kawasaki's short-term debt:

Kawasaki Steel's Debt Structure (1975)
(billions of yen)

	Long-Term	*Short-Term*	*Total*
Mitsubishi Group	30.0 (7.6%)	4.4 (2.9%)	34.5 (6.3%)
Mitsui Group	26.3 (6.7)	3.9 (2.5)	30.2 (5.5)
Sumitomo Group	28.8 (7.3)	4.1 (2.7)	32.9 (6.0)
Fuyo Group	10.1 (2.6)	1.7 (1.1)	11.8 (2.2)
Dai-Ichi Kangyo Bank Group	23.8 (6.1)	31.6 (20.7)	55.4 (10.2)
Sanwa Group	35.7 (9.1)	5.1 (3.4)	40.8 (7.5)
Foreign Banks	28.3 (7.2)	4.9 (3.2)	33.2 (6.1)

While the Long-Term Credit Bank was not associated with any group, it provided 61.3 billion or 11.2 per cent of Kawasaki Steel's total debt and over 15.2 per cent of their long-term debt.

KOBE STEEL, LTD

Kobe Steel, Ltd., Japan's fifth largest steel company, began in 1905 as part of Suzuki and Co., a leading trading company in Kobe, Japan. It was incorporated under its present name in 1911 and expanded into copper and aluminum metals. After surviving near destruction during World War II, it rebuilt its construction operations and set up Shinko Electric Co. and Shinko Metal Industries to handle the metals business. In 1957 it reversed direction by setting up Shinko Construction Co. and absorbing Shinko Metals Industries. In becoming an integrated steel producer, it completed its Kobe works in 1959 and merged with Amagasaki Iron and Steel Manufacturing Company in 1965.

By 1975, Kobe Steel produced 15.7 million tons of crude steel and pig iron and 6.7 million tons of bars, wire rods, and plates, about 20 per cent of Nippon Steel. Being rather diversified, Kobe's steel division's sales were about 62 per cent (nearly $1.7 billion) of total revenues of over $2.5 billion (Exhibit 18). The second largest machinery division, a producer of heavy construction equipment, chemical industry machinery, and cutting and shaving tools accounted for 20 per cent (over $550 million) of sales. Nonferrous metals were 11.8 per cent of sales with the welding electrodes division being the smallest with 6.2 per cent. Kobe Steel's exports were 22.5 per cent of sales. The company also exported a plant and technology to Qatar.

Group Connection

Kobe Steel was considered to be a member of the Sanwa Bank group of companies and was one of seventeen companies represented on their "Sansui-

Kai" and "Clover-Kai" directing councils. By not being on the group's "Midori-kai" council, it appeared that Kobe Steel was considered an affiliate number of the group. Whereas Sanwa Bank held 4.4 per cent of Kobe Steel stock, Dai-Ichi Kangyo Bank owned an equal share. However, Kobe Steel did not own a major share of Sanwa Bank as did Nippon Steel. Nevertheless, as shown, Sanwa financial institution provided 13.8 per cent of Kobe Steel's total debt and was the largest supplier of both long- and short-term funds:

Kobe Steel's Debt Structure (billions of yen)

	Long-Term	*Short-Term*	*Total*
Mitsubishi Group	18.2 (7.0%)	6.5 (5.9%)	24.7 (6.7%)
Mitsui Group	10.0 (3.9)	1.7 (1.6)	11.7 (3.2)
Sumitomo Group	8.0 (3.1)	1.4 (1.3)	9.4 (2.6)
Fuyo Group	25.2 (9.7)	6.1 (5.5)	31.3 (8.5)
Dai-Ichi Kangyo Bank Group	21.6 (8.4)	14.6 (13.2)	36.3 (9.8)
Sanwa Group	34.0 (13.1)	17.0 (15.3)	51.0 (13.8)
Foreign Banks	22.3 (8.6)	8.8 (7.9)	31.1 (8.4)

Sanwa group support was not as great as was group support for Sumitomo Metals or Nippon Kokan. This was further indicated by the fact that the debt of foreign banks was 8.4 per cent, 3.4 per cent higher than the 5 per cent average foreign debt of the other steel companies.

NISSHIN STEEL CO., LTD.

Nisshin Steel Co. was the result of a 1959 merger of Nihon Teppan, a galvanized steel producer founded in 1911, and Nichia Steel Works, a producer of cut steel plates founded in 1908. The combination of their facilities and technologies allowed Nisshin Steel to produce both steel products and stainless, galvanized, and treated steel. In 1962 the company fired its first large-scale blast furnace and established the first integrated stainless steel production system in Japan.

By 1975, Nisshin Steel produced 1.6 million tons of steel plate, strip and polished steel strip, and 1.2 million tons of coated and semifinished steel products. Although it is a significant producer of stainless, galvanized, and coated steel products, Nisshin Steel is the smallest of the major producers and is not included in most discussions about the Japanese steel industry. Its $864 million in sales were as follows (Exhibit 18):

Steel plate	35.0%
Steel strip	20.1%
Coated steel product	26.3%

Of this, only about 30 per cent was exported.

Group Connections

Although Nisshin Steel was considered part of the Nippon Steel group, its financial affiliation was with the Sanwa group. However, Nippon Steel owned 13.1 per cent of Nisshin Steel's stock as compared to Sanwa Bank's 3.9 per cent ownership. Since the Nippon Steel group had no bank, this relationship allowed Nippon Steel access to Nisshin's coated steel technology and products and still provided Nisshin's financing needs. As shown, Sanwa Bank provided 30 per cent of the short-term and 25.9 per cent of the long-term debt of Nisshin steel:

Nisshin Steel's Debt Structure (billions of yen)

	Long-Term	*Short-Term*	*Total*
Mitsubishi Group	2.9 (3.9%)	2.1 (5.6%)	5.0 (4.5%)
Mitsui Group	1.6 (2.2)	.5(1.3)	2.1 (1.9)
Sumitomo Group	1.3 (1.7)	.3 (0.9)	1.6 (1.5)
Fuyo Group	.7 (0.9)	.9 (2.4)	1.6 (1.4)
Dia-Ichi Kangyo Bank Group	1.5 (1.9)	1.0 (2.7)	2.5 (2.2)
Sanwa Group	19.3 (25.9)	11.0 (30.0)	30.3 (27.2)
Foreign Banks	1.4 (1.9)	.2 (0.5)	1.6 (1.5)

Sanwa Bank provided 4.8 billion yen of the group's 11 billion yen in short-term debt and 3.8 billion in long-term debt. Toyo Trust and Banking Co., part of the Sanwa group, provided 11.6 billion yen in long-term debt. The firm's debt-to-equity ratio was 5.8 as compared to the 8.97 average of the top six steel companies. It had not invested to the same degree in new facilities as the other firms.

CASE NINETEEN

Toyo Kogyo Co., Ltd.

WILLIAM R. BOULTON and J. MICHAEL ALFORD
University of Georgia

Assignment Questions:

1. Why did the Japanese auto industry grow so rapidly in the early 1970s?
2. Why had Mazda been so successful?
3. Why was Mazda saved? How was it saved? What are its future prospects?

In the early 1970s, Toyo Kogyo Company began its invasion into the U.S. automobile market with its unique rotary engine Mazda branded cars. As described in the April 8, 1972, issue of *Business Week:*

> Four low-volume Japanese makes are coming on fast. Mazda Motors, importers of the Toyo Kogyo rotary (Wankel) engine cars, is now eighth among the foreigners with distributors in 21 states, mostly in the West, and 1972 sales of 10,009 units. By fall, Mazda will expand into the East and Midwest and hopes to finish the year in fifth place with 60,000 cars sold.

By the end of 1973, Mazda had become the fifth largest auto importer with U.S. sales of 104,328 units.

Mazda's invasion came to an abrupt halt in 1974 as its U.S. sales plummeted by 46.9 per cent to 55,392 units. Mazda dropped to seventh largest importer, and on March 24, 1975, made the *Wall Street Journal*'s front page. As Japan's number three automaker, Toyo Kogyo's management was up against the wall and faced a serious cash shortage as inventories surpassed the current level of annual sales. Toyo Kogyo's survival was in deep question (see Exhibit 1).

THE JAPANESE AUTO INDUSTRY

The automobile industry in Japan became a high priority for development in the late 1950s. By 1958, industry-wide research and development efforts were well under way:

EXHIBIT 1: Financial Information (1974)

Toyo Kogyo

7261
東洋工業

Est.: January, 1920 **Fiscal Year Ended:** October, (Mid) April
Head Office & Factory: 6047, Fuchumachi, Akigun, Hiroshima Pref. 730
Tel.: 0822-82-1111 **Telex:** 0652333
Branch(es): Tokyo (Tel. 03-449-4111), Osaka (Tel. 06-252-1261)
President: Kohei Matsuda
Reference(s): Sumitomo, Sumitomo Trust, Mitsubishi Trust, Industrial Bank, Hiroshima

Capital Change:

Month & Year	Allotment Ratio	New Capital (¥ mil.)
(May '49	R	150)
Aug. '60	1:1	8,000
May '61	1:1, PO	16,800
Sept. '63	1:2	25,200
June '70	1:50SD	25,704
*	N	

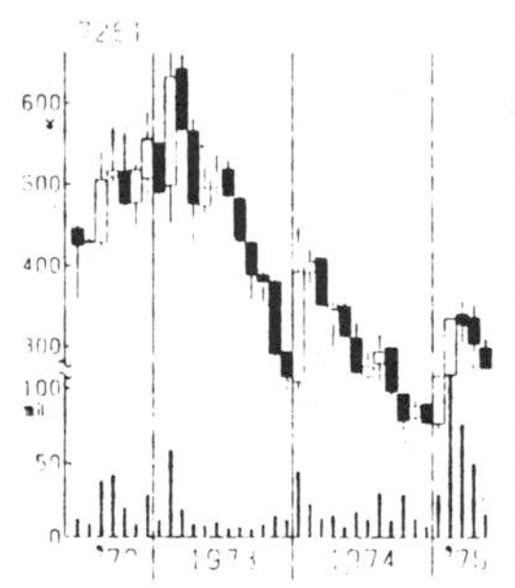

Capital: (¥50 par value)	25,704
Total Assets: (Oct. '74)	633,328
Stockholders' Equity: (Oct. '74)	93,054
Employees: (Oct. '74)	35,325
Average Age:	33
Monthly Starting Pay: (1975)	91,820
No. Stockholders: (Oct. '74)	59,804
Major Stockholders:	(1,000) %
Nippon Life Ins.	26,710 (5.2)
Sumitomo Bank	20,400 (4.0)
Tokio M. & F. Ins.	15,000 (2.9)
Yasuda F. & M. Ins.	15,000 (2.9)
Asahi M. Life. Ins.	14,000 (2.7)
Sumitomo Trust.	12,330 (2.4)
Foreign Ownership	14,477 (2.8)
No. Shares Out.: (Oct. '74)	514,080

Listed: All markets
Underwriter(s): Nomura

Sales Breakdown in %: (Oct. 1974)
Passenger cars (39), trucks (45), auto parts (8), rock drills (1), others (7)
Export Ratio: 45%

Business Results: (¥ mil.)

	Sales	Current Profit	Profit	Earnings Per Share	Dividend Per Share	Equity Per Share
Apr. 1972	158,383	6,541	4,051	¥7.9	¥4	¥167.1
Oct. 1972	185,881	6,643	4,113	8.0	4	171.1
Apr. 1973	217,711	6,863	4,313	8.4	4	175.4
Oct. 1973	238,474	5,894	4,051	7.9	4	179.2
Apr. 1974	268,226	6,182	4,014	7.8	4	182.4
Oct. 1974	250,016	2,033	1,363	2.7	2.5	181.0
Oct. 1975*	480,000	(–)12,000	2,200	4.3	3~5	

Characteristics: Third largest automobile manufacturer. Management of Matsuda family. Closely related to Sumitomo group. Succeeded in mass production of rotary engines for the first time in the world.
Remarks: Registered ¥10 billion deficit in current phase in first half. However, giving ¥3 dividend at minimum for term by selling assets. Deficit and inventory adjustment will continue. Concluded technical tie-up with General Motors in rotary engine field in April. **Plans** to market RE fuel saving cars in autumn. Plans to halt increase of borrowings in summer.

* Estimated

Source: Japan Company Handbook, 2nd Half, 1975, *The Oriental Economist*, Tokyo, 1976, p. 654.

- MITI, through the establishment of the Motor Vehicle Technology Institute in 1955, established a three-year project to standardize motor vehicles with academics and technicians of the automakers participating.
- Major research was under way on producing higher speed vehicles for

export, standardizing parts, transmissions and engines, and simplifying manufacturing methods.

- Major studies were being conducted on time skidding and small car diesel engines.
- The Technical Research Laboratory of the Ministry of Transportation studied brake systems and safety driving.
- The railway's Technical Research Laboratory studied air springs for motor vehicles.
- The Small Motor Vehicle Industry Association studied parts standardization.
- The Motor Vehicle Parts Association examined radiators.

In 1958, the Motor Vehicle Technology Institute sponsored two conferences in which fifty-one research papers were presented.

To speed up the development of their automobile production capabilities, the Japanese automakers imported additional technological know-how from other countries. Between 1965 and 1971, ninety-five contracts were signed for know-how from nine countries. The United States accounted for about 55 per cent of the contracts. Toyo Kogyo (Mazda) and Nissan (Datsun) were the major users of foreign know-how, with Toyota developing most of its own technology.

Toyo Kogyo's rotary engine research was one key example of the Japanese ability to further develop outside technology. In 1963, Toyo Kogyo licensed Europe's NSU's Wankel engine technology. By December 1964, the company had tested an engine for 672 hours that used new seals developed by Nippon Carbon Company. The new seals eliminated a primary problem of chatter marks caused by wear. By 1967 the Cosmo Sports (Mazda 110S) was introduced with the new rotary engine. The company claimed that its seals had a life of over 30,000 miles or twice that of NSU.

The number of vehicles produced per employee, or labor productivity, also increased through the 1970s. Japanese automakers, with Toyota and Nissan as leaders, recognized that capital expenditures for automated equipment could not only provide for increased productivity but for higher quality products as well.

Government support had encouraged the growth and protection of the Japanese auto industry, a major user of steel. Growing domestic demand for vehicles helped the effort and, by the early 1970s, MITI had provided guidance in merging weaker firms with less proficient marketing, manufacturing, or management. The mergers were felt to improve overall economies of scale as well as to prepare the automakers for the expected inflow of foreign investment and competition.

By 1971, Japan's auto industry could be grouped into four groups: Toyota, Nissan, those with foreign capital tie-ins, and independents. These included:

- *Toyota Group:* Hino Motors, Ltd.; Daihatsu Kogyo Co., Ltd.; and Toyota Motor Co., Ltd.
- *Nissan Group:* Aichi Machine Industrial Co., Ltd.; Fuji Heavy Industries; Nissan Diesel Motor Co., Ltd.; and Nissan Motor Co., Ltd.
- *Foreign Tie-ins:* Isuzu Motors, Ltd. with General Motors; and Mitsubishi Motors Corporation with Chrysler.
- *Independents:* Honda Motor Co., Ltd.; Suzuki Motor Co., Ltd.; and Toyo Kogyo Co., Ltd.

EXHIBIT 2: Imported Cars into the United States

IMPORTED CARS IN OPERATION BY MODEL YEAR, AS OF JAN. 1, 1975

	1974	*1978*	*1972*	*1971*	*1970*	*1969 and Earlier*	*Total*
Alfa Romeo	2,988	2,485	2,003	1,802	1,274	9,633	20,185
Audi	48,442	46,240	26,211	20,050	5,622	—	146,565
Austin	4,752	4,632	913	5,621	12,164	28,389	56,471
Aus.-Healey	—	—	—	—	974	42,315	43,289
BMW	14,700	13,797	13,261	11,189	9,785	20,684	83,416
Capri	76,663	113,431	79,764	52,548	14,148	—	336,554
Citroen	338	991	1,753	1,290	1,051	6,830	12,253
Colt	41,242	34,472	29,763	26,410	—	—	131,887
Cricket	—	3,919	12,366	25,264	—	—	41,549
Datsun	183,578	225,370	166,960	175,888	90,012	128,236	970,044
Eng. Ford	—	—	—	674	8,540	69,843	79,057
Fiat	69,653	57,327	50,869	42,098	33,601	112,773	366,321
Honda	41,388	35,789	17,274	9,280	2,888	—	106,619
Jaguar	4,914	6,840	4,664	5,600	6,641	32,219	60,878
Jensen	3,036	1,366	—	—	—	—	4,402
Lotus	902	951	854	605	643	1,284	5,239
Mazda	54,949	102,355	45,664	18,099	2,007	—	223,074
Mer.-Benz	37,105	41,808	37,718	33,580	30,003	124,178	304,392
MG	25,017	31,441	27,873	29,617	27,896	113,331	255,175
Opel	55,588	68,793	59,399	83,118	75,244	233,271	575,413
Pantera	886	1,505	1,156	119	—	—	3,666
Peugeot	7,177	3,987	4,184	5,870	4,836	29,502	55,556
Porsche	21,193	23,688	18,534	16,199	12,389	35,065	127,068
Renault	6,412	6,643	9,942	17,259	17,444	115,858	173,558
Rls.-Royce	630	590	587	460	351	3,967	6,585
Rootes	—	—	—	313	1,489	40,098	41,900
Rover	—	—	—	626	1,366	8,496	10,488

Saab	13,090	16,615	11,709	12,691	10,469	44,749	109,323
Simca	—	—	282	4,363	4,919	35,547	45,111
Subaru	20,993	30,363	13,651	11,952	3,647	1,403	82,009
Toyota	230,666	271,343	248,441	272,121	166,950	181,696	1,371,217
Triumph	18,291	21,937	19,235	18,558	14,497	91,642	184,160
Volks.	329,125	466,321	478,760	500,357	528,401	2,287,823	4,590,787
Volvo	52,959	60,567	46,857	49,327	44,074	158,049	411,833
Misc.	719	412	274	383	366	34,855	37,009
TOTAL	1,367,396	1,695,978	1,430,921	1,453,331	1,133,691	3,991,736	11,973,053

Source: *Automotive News*, April 7, 1975, p. 15.

EXHIBIT 3: Market Share of Imported and Japanese Vehicles in the United States (by per cent)

	1973	*1974*
Imported cars/total market	15.1	15.7
Japanese/imported cars	42.4	47.7
Japanese cars/total market	7.9	8.0

Source: The calculations are based on sales figures compiled and published by *Automotive News* (Detroit: Marketing Services, 1973–75).

Export Growth. As demands grew in the early 1970s for high-quality, fuel-efficient vehicles, Japanese automakers were well positioned. By 1974, Japan surpassed West Germany in the export of vehicles. Exhibit 2 shows the rapid growth of Japanese imports into the United States. Mazda, for example, even with its 1974 sales decline, had increased sales 27 times over 1970 levels. Subaru imported six times as many cars in 1974 as 1970, Datsun twice as many, and Toyota nearly 50 per cent more. Between 1973 and 1974, Japanese automobile imports grew from 42.4 per cent to 47.7 per cent of all imports as shown in Exhibit 3. The growing importance of exports to the automakers is further shown in Exhibit 4.

Growth in U.S. demand for Japanese automobiles had come in spite of the dollar's devaluation in 1972. As the U.S. trade deficit grew from $2 billion in 1971 to $6.4 billion in 1972, the U.S. dollar was devalued 7.89 per cent while Japan revalued the yen by 16.88 per cent and West Germany revalued the mark by 13.57 per cent. The impact of this move is shown on prices listed in Exhibit

EXHIBIT 4: Ratio of Export to Production (in Percentages)

Makers	*1971*	*1974*
Daihatsu	3.99	7.38
Fuji (Subaru)	15.48	30.65
Hino	12.57	22.31
Honda	13.95	35.90
Isuzu	15.59	42.69
Mitsubishi	17.83	35.89
Nissan (Datsun)	39.66	47.76
Nissan Diesel	10.20	26.24
Suzuki	.96	6.39
Toyo Kyogo (Mazda)	33.46	52.53
Toyota	40.22	40.49
Total	30.62	39.96

Source: Japan Automobile Manufacturers Association.

EXHIBIT 5: Manufacturers' Suggested Retail Prices of Selected Models of Imported and American Subcompact Passenger Cars

	1971	*1972*	*Price Change (per cent)*
Toyota Corolla 1200	$1,798	$1,956	8.79
Pinto	$1,919	$1,960	2.14
Datsun 1200	$1,736	$1,976	13.82
Volkswagen Beetle	$1,899	$1,999	5.27
Gremlin	$1,999	$2,021	1.10
Vega	$2,090	$2,060	−1.44
Colt	$1,924	$2,095	8.89
Toyota Corolla 1600	$1,918	$2,109	9.96
VW Super Beetle	$2,049	$2,159	5.37
Cricket (4 door)	$1,915	$2,017	5.33
Opel	$1,878	$2,049	9.11

Note: Vega, Opel, and 1972 Gremlin prices include dealer preparation charges, and the others do not. 1971 prices are as of August 14, before the freeze and before removal of the federal excise tax.

Source: *Automotive News*, February 7, 1972, p. 1. Reprinted with permission from *Automotive News*. Copyright 1972.

5. Whereas Toyota and Nissan remained cautious in pushing 1972 U.S. sales, Mazda's sales of its unique rotary engine car grew by 50 per cent. As shown in Exhibit 6, the Japanese continued to build their dealer networks.

By 1973, the U.S. Chamber of Commerce held a conference in Tokyo to encourage Japanese manufacturers to make capital investments in the United States. Labor leaders also supported investments that would create new jobs. It was becoming apparent that lessons might be learned from the Japanese in developing technology and managing people.

EXHIBIT 6: Japanese Franchises in the United States

	Jan., 1973	*Jan., 1974*	*Jan., 1975*
Arrow-Sapporo	—	—	—
Colt/Challenger	1,492	1,661	1,820
Datsun	937	948	940
Honda	212	352	435
Mazda	308	350	375
Subaru	509	560	562
Toyota	932	951	946
Opel	—	—	—
Total figures	4,390	4,822	5,078

Source: *Automotive News* (Detroit: Marketing Services, 1973–75). *Automotive News*. Copyright 1973–75.

THE RISE AND FALL OF TOYO KOGYO

Toyo Kogyo grew from a small truck maker in the early 1960s to a fully integrated automaker in the 1970s. With the grandson of the company's founder as its head, Toyo Kogyo reached sales of over $1.6 billion in 1974. Exhibit 7 depicts major milestones in Toyo Kogyo's history. The rotary (Wankel) engine it introduced into the U.S. market in 1970 was quiet, lightweight, and nonpolluting, and it also performed well. Unfortunately, the rotary engine achieved only

EXHIBIT 7: Toyo Kogyo Company Milestones

1920	Founded in Hiroshima City named—Toyo Cork
1927	Renamed Toyo Kogyo Co., Ltd.
1928	Began Machinery Production
1930	Began Machine Tool Production
1931	Began Mazda Three-wheel Truck Production
1935	Began Rock Drills and Gauge Block Production and Introduced Machine Tools on the Market
1945	Reorganized for Production of Machine Tools, Rock Drills, and Three-wheel Trucks
1957	Assembled 200,000 Trucks
1958	Began 4-wheel Truck Production
1959	Began Ductile Cast Iron Production
1960	Completed New Painting and Final Assy Shop Introduced Passenger Car "R360 Coupe"
1961	Concluded Technical Collaboration Agreement With NSU and Wankel for Joint Development of NSU/Wankel Rotary Piston Engine
1962	Announced Two New Passenger Cars—Reached Highest Annual Output in Japan Auto Industry—235,455 Vehicles
1963	Assembled One-Millionth Vehicle—introduced IBM 7074 and Electronic 1620 Computers—Added 68th Ship to Auto Transport Fleet—Introduced "Mazda Familia Van."
1964	Introduced Cab-over, 4-wheel Truck—Began Bridge/Road Construction to Connect Plants
1965	45th Anniversary—Constructed New 300 Acre Province Ground—Completed Bridge/Road Connecting Plants—Tie Up with Perkins Diesel(UK).
1966	Introduced New Diesel Cab-over Truck and Two Career Sedan Model Cars—Produced the Two Millionth Vehicle—Completed New Car Assy Plant (10,000/mo.)
1967	Mazda 110S (2 rotor-rotary piston engine) Introduced
1968	Completed New Stamping Plant—Entered Canadian Market (Total 24 Countries) with Total Exports of 30,435 units.
1970	Introduced Rotary Engine Auto to U.S. Market This (1970) began an exciting time in the history of Toyo Kogyo. From the sale of only 2,007 cars in the U.S. market in 1970, there were 18,099 of the 1971 models sold, 45,664 of the 1972 models, 102,355 in 1973.
Late 1973–1974	The Iranian oil embargo and increasing gas prices caused a drop in sales to 54,949. Toyo Kogyo was having cash flow problems.

12 to 13 miles per gallon. As the oil embargo brought on by OPEC raised fuel prices, buyers backed off from the Mazda for more fuel-efficient cars. By 1974, Mazda sales fell by nearly half their 1973 levels with rotary engine car sales falling from 240,000 to 120,000 units to only 32.5 per cent of the plant's capacity.

Officials of Sumitomo Bank, Toyo Kogyo's second largest shareholder and major lender, advised the company's president, Mr. Matsuda, to control production of its 1975 export models in order to seal off 1974 model inventories. Matsuda, however, argued that the slump was only temporary and that sales would quickly recover. By October 31, 1974, sales continued off with net income dropping 66 per cent. At the same time, long-term and short-term debt increased to over $1.2 billion. The Sumitomo group lent over $285 million for cash needs whereas the large inventory of 1974 and 1975 model cars drained off some $2 million a month in dock storage fees and interest charges.

As Matsuda belatedly recognized the severity of his company's position, he turned to the Sumitomo group for help. Two Sumitomo executives joined Toyo Kogyo's board of directors. Shozo Hotta, the seventy-six-year-old chairman of the Sumitomo Bank, began calling on both business and government colleagues to aid in saving Toyo Kogyo.

TOYO KOGYO'S MARKETING FOCUS

In May 1973, Toyo Kogyo had reorganized its four U.S. distribution companies into Mazda Motors of America, located in Compton, California. Each of its six regional branches was headed by a distribution director. The new organization also consolidated advertising responsibilities to the national level. Mazda America's advertising expenditures were then more than doubled to over $15 million. Mazda's primary advertising focus was to promote the novelty of its rotary Wankel engine. In addition, Mazda offered a 24-month or 24,000 mile warranty, which was twice the industry's standard to offset fears of the rotary engine's failure.

By mid-1973, Mazda had about 350 dealers covering the West Coast, East Coast, and Midwest, and planned to increase dealers to 650. Nearly 90 per cent of the dealers had multiple dealerships. However, with nearly 4,000 applications for the remaining dealerships, Dick Brown, president of Mazda Motors of America, had intended to increase sole-Mazda dealerships. Dealers were required to have $150,000 in cash plus land and building for the dealership, ensuring that the dealers were well respected and well financed. Brown also intended to limit the number of dealerships for ease of operations.

Mazda America's sales goal for 1975 had been 350,000 cars, averaging 45 cars per dealer per month. The 1973 goal of 120,000 units was actually 104,328 units sold. Exhibit 8 compares Mazda's U.S. sales with other imports. While total imports declined 20.4 per cent between 1973 and 1974, Mazda sales declined 46.9 per cent. This disastrous collapse in sales slowed Mazda America's advance, delaying new dealerships as well as reducing the total exclusive dealerships to 221 out of 350 in 1975.

EXHIBIT 8: Import Auto Sales in the U.S. (Twelve Months)

1974 Position		*Make*	*1973 Position*	
1	327,488	Volkswagen	469,082	1
2	231,360	Toyota	276,720	2
3	184,500	Datsun	229,115	3
4	76,894	Capri	115,153	4
5	69,723	Fiat	58,669	8
6	55,532	Opel	69,798	6
7	55,392	Mazda	104,328	5
8	53,065	Volvo	61,042	7
9	48,539	Audi	46,800	9
10	41,638	Honda		*
		Mercedes Benz	42,102	10

* Not in top ten.
Source: *Automotive News,* March 10, 1975, p. 3.

JAPAN INCORPORATED TO THE RESCUE

Although the Sumitomo Bank alone could not cover Toyo Kogyo's capital requirements, Hotta was not without influence in Japan's banking and business circles. In addressing his first concern for Toyo Kogyo's poor cash position, he had Sumitomo buy hundreds of Mazdas for its own vehicle fleet. Officials at Sumitomo's 191 branch banks were also ordered to direct bank customers to Mazda dealers. Hotta spoke for Toyo Kogyo at meetings with bankers and businessmen, stressing Hiroshima's need for a healthy Toyo Kogyo and Japan's need for the nonpolluting rotary engine.

To spur overseas sales, Hotta formally requested C. Itoh and Company, Sumitomo's leading trading company, to start distributing Mazdas in the eastern United States. As the fourth largest Japanese trading company, with $17.4 billion in sales, C. Itoh had not expressed an interest in handling the distribution of Mazdas. In fact, C. Itoh already had close ties with General Motors and its Japanese affiliate, Isuzu Motor Company. However, since Sumitomo held about $375 million in C. Itoh debt and 9 per cent of its outstanding stock, C. Itoh did not refuse.

Hotta also convinced Shigano Nagano, head of the Japan Chamber of Commerce and former chairman of Nippon Steel, to act as supreme adviser and counselor to Toyo Kogyo. The 74-year-old Nagano was considered even more eminent than Hotta and was an old friend of the Matsuda family. Sumitomo Bank was Nippon Steel's sixth largest shareholder and a major lender to the company. Nippon Steel was, in turn, Sumitomo's fifth largest shareholder and Toyo Kogyo's largest supplier (see Exhibit 9). Before agreeing to help Toyo Kogyo, Nippon Steel sought, and obtained, assurances from Toyota and Nissan Motor Companies that they would not object to Nippon Steel's intervention.

EXHIBIT 9: Toyo Kogyo Co., Ltd. Interfirm Relationships

I. STOCKHOLDERS OF TOYO KOGYO AND C. ITOH AND COMPANY

	Per Cent of Ownership	
Shareholders	*Toyo Kogyo*	*C. Itoh & Co.*
Nippon Life Insurance Co.	5.0	3.7
Sumitomo Bank	4.0	8.7
Tokio M. & F. Life Insurance Co.	2.9	3.4
Asahi Mutual Life Insurance Co.	2.7	3.0
Sumitomo Trust & Banking Co.	2.4	0.0

II. OTHER RELATIONSHIPS

A. Sumitomo Bank and Simitomo Trust had arranged loans of over $400 million to Toyo Kogyo.
B. Sumitomo Bank had loaned $375 million to C. Itoh & Co.
C. Sumitomo Bank owned 1.7 per cent of Nippon Steel.
D. Nippon Steel owned 2.5 per cent of Sumitomo Bank.
E. Nippon Life Insurance Co. was a major shareholder in Sumitomo Bank, Sumitomo Metals, Nippon Steel, Toyo Kogyo, and C. Itoh & Co.

Source: *Japan Company Handbook*, 2nd half 1975. The Oriental Economist: Tokyo, 1976.

According to Robert Ballon of Tokyo's Sophia University, "Nagano's coming in means that all of Japan is standing behind Toyo Kogyo." The support of Hotta and Nagano enabled Sumitomo Bank to interest more than 50 other banks in putting together a $119 million loan to see Toyo Kogyo through April 1975. At the February 1975 meeting of the Sumitomo group's Hakusui Kai (White Water Club), the policymaking and planning council consisting of the heads of Sumitomo's 16 largest companies, the group agreed to help Toyo Kogyo in any way it could (see Exhibit 10).

To further support Hotta and Nagano's efforts, Hiroshima officials enacted an antipollution measure that reduced the local tax on Mazdas by 50 per cent and increased taxes on some competitors' cars by 10 per cent. Hiroshima's representatives introduced national legislation to provide Toyo Kogyo with similar tax relief at the national level. MITI, the ministry for international trade and industry, also provided low-cost loans and subsidies to Toyo Kogyo's subcontractors. In some cases, suppliers extended Toyo Kogyo's credit from the normal 30 days to as long as 210 days. Further, it was rumored that supporters would insist on a merger if Toyo Kogyo's condition did not turn around. Toyota and Nissan would be prime candidates if that were to happen.

A group of Japanese businessmen formed the Kyoshin Kai (Home Heart group) to promote Mazda's sales. It had five full-time employees who arranged purchases of Mazdas by fleet operators and individual government and business officials. This group was directly credited with increasing Mazda's market share in the Hiroshima area from 20 to 34 per cent.

EXHIBIT 10: The Sumitomo Group

Key Companies[1]	*Estimated Fiscal 1975 Sales (millions of dollars) (April 1974–March 1975)*
Chemicals:	
Sumitomo Chemical	$1,607*
Sumitomo Bakelite	229*
Construction:	
Sumitomo Construction	333
Electric & Electronics:	
Nippon Electric Industry	1,317
Sumitomo Special Metals	47
Finance and Insurance:	
Sumitomo Bank	2,020**
Sumitomo Trust & Banking	385**
Sumitomo Marine & Fire Insurance	290
Sumitomo Mutual Life Insurance	NA
Forestry:	
Sumitomo Forestry	425**
Glass/Cement/Ceramics/Carbon:	
Nippon Sheet Glass	240
Sumitomo Cement	293

Key Companies[1]	*Estimated Fiscal 1975 Sales (millions of dollars) (April 1974–March 1975)*
Iron and Steel:	
Sumitomo Metal Industries	$ 3,381
Machinery-General:	
Sumitomo Shipbuilding & Machinery	767
Sumitomo Precision Products	42
Mining:	
Sumitomo Coal Mining	48
Nonferrous Metals:	
Sumitomo Metal Mining	541
Sumitomo Light Metal Industries:	280
Sumitomo Electric Industries	814
Real Estate:	
Sumitomo Realty & Development	153
Trading and Commerce:	
Sumitomo Shoji Kaisha	17,344
Warehousing and Transportation:	
Sumitomo Warehouse	84

[1]Underlined companies are represented on the (Hakusuikai) or White Water Club.
*Actual sales for calendar 1974.
**Actual sales for year ended Sept. 1974.

Source: *Business Week*, March 31, 1975, p. 45.

TOYO KOGYO'S EFFORTS TO SURVIVE

As the leader of Toyo Kogyo, Matsuda also took immediate actions to improve the company's cash position and show his cooperation with outside supporters. To begin with, all capital expenditures would be closely reviewed with only those considered essential being approved. In addition, the actions included:

- Reducing planned 1975 output from 740,000 to 640,000 units.
- Laying off production workers for two to three days each month, with 70 per cent pay for the days off.
- Paying the normal year-end lump-sum bonus in three monthly increments.
- Canceling all raises for managers.
- Selling its Tokyo office building.
- Selling an Osaka building to Sumitomo's real estate company.
- Selling off undeveloped land.
- Selling Toyo Kogyo's interests in some Sumitomo group companies.
- Intensifying marketing efforts to reduce inventories.

To deal with the sales decline in Japan, Toyo Kogyo transferred 1,150 workers from its manufacturing and assembling operations to its dealerships to aid in sales efforts. Employees received their regular salaries and no commissions. It was planned that 7 per cent of the work force would move from production to sales. The tactic was so successful that Mitsubishi and Fuji (Suzuki) automakers followed suit.

Mazda America introduced a $500 rebate program in April 1975 for its U.S. dealers. This spurred April sales to 9,064 units, about triple March sales and double the prior April sales.

Mazda Motors of America was reorganized in February 1975 to further increase its financial resources, improve administrative controls, and increase its responsiveness to its 385 dealers. Mazda America's headquarters remained in California with responsibility for twelve western and south central states. A new Toyo Kogyo subsidiary located in Chicago, Mazda Motors of America (Central), and in New Jersey, Mazda Motors of America (East), were established to serve the rest of the country. Sumitomo Shoji Kaisha (Sumitomo's trading company) was induced to buy Mazda Motors of America (Central). C. Itoh and Company owned MMA (East).

The reorganization of Mazda America changed the normal factory-to-dealer distribution concept used by importers. Mazda, yielding to Hotta's influence, moved to use the trading company's expertise in distribution and marketing. For Mazda America's vice-president of sales, Sidney H. Fogel, the sales job was still not easy. The 1974 models had to be moved out with 1975 models being introduced in January 1975 and 1976 models planned for November 1975.

FUTURE OF THE ROTARY ENGINE

In late 1974, Rand Corporation, the California "think tank," issued a report to Congress stating that a super-charged, stratified charged rotary engine could offer the best gasoline-saving potential of any auto engine by 1980. It stated:

"Compared with the conventional spark ignition engine, it (super-charged stratified rotary engine) yields about twice the fuel economy, requires about 40 per cent less lifetime energy, and reduces initial and lifetime per vehicle costs by over 25 per cent."

Mazda planned to introduce a fuel-efficient rotary engine car in 1976. Volkswagen was also planning to introduce a luxury model car powered by a rotary engine in 1976. General Motors had not finalized its plans to use the rotary engine because of pollution emission problems.

Mazda continued to advertise the high performance and high power-to-weight ratio of its rotary engine. Mazda's RX-4 was about the size of the Chevrolet Monza (a small, U.S. car), but equaled the performance of G.M.'s V-8 engines and Ford's V-6 and provided comparable gas mileage. Unfortunately, consumers compared the gas mileage of Mazda's rotary engine with other small Japanese imports and the Volkswagen. Getting away from small car competition and their fuel-efficient image was a real problem.

CASE TWENTY

The World Motorcycle Industry

WILLIAM R. BOULTON and JAMES J. CHRISMAN
University of Georgia

Assignment Questions:

1. Why have the Japanese been able to dominate the U.S. and European motorcycle industries?
2. How has the industry structure changed between the 1950s and 1975? What has caused this change?
3. What are the strategic issues facing each strategic group in 1975? What strategies should they adopt?

The Japanese in the early 1960s began changing the motorcycle rider's image at a time when Americans were ready for a new leisure-time sport. By the late 1960s, motorcycle market in the United States began to take off, allowing the Japanese to invest in new, highly modernized plants and equipment. Between 1969 and 1973, Japanese sales of large (450cc) motorcycles in the United States increased from 27,000 to 218,000 units, whereas the well-established British companies stayed at about 30,000 units. Then, in 1975, just as the U.S. market began to mature (with a slight sales decline), the newly affluent European market began to grow. The size and importance of these marekts is shown in Exhibit 1. This case describes the nature of the world motorcycle industry and its competitive structure.

DEVELOPMENT OF THE MOTORCYCLE INDUSTRY

Prior to World War II, the motorcycle industry was mostly national, with local producers satisfying the needs of their own markets. By 1959, the image of this 1885 German invention had been tarnished in America by hoodlums wearing leather jackets. At best, motorcycles were seen as "basic" transportation. This restricted market growth as Americans fell in love with, and became able to afford, automobiles, which were more desirable for this type of usage. Less developed countries in Europe had a strong demand for basic transportation such

[1]This material comes from "Strategy Alternatives for the British Motorcycle Industry" (London: Her Majesty's Stationery Office, 1975).

EXHIBIT 1: The World Motorcycle Industry Major Markets

	Market Size 1968 ('000 units)	*1974 ('000 units)*	*Market Growth Per Cent P.A. (1968–1974)*
North America	458	1,066	15%
United Kingdom	38	91	16
Europe	100	290	19

as mopeds, motor scooters, and motorcycles. In Japan, Honda (started in 1948) found a strong demand for small-sized motorcycles and, by 1959, became the world's largest manufacturer with sales of over $55 million. As Honda began to move abroad with its low-cost, high-volume, capital intensive production strategy; supported with effective R&D and distribution; such well-known names as Indian, Matchless, and Harley-Davidson began to fade.

In 1959, Honda entered the U.S. market with a superior machine and an innovative marketing strategy. Honda stressed the fun of riding motorcycles and, thereby, created a new recreational motorcycle market. By 1965, Honda's sales of motorcycles in the United States had reached $77 million. Honda's commitment to low price, style, high performance, and reliability could not be matched by the industry leaders. Early industry leaders, such as Harley-Davidson, Norton Villiers, and B.S.A., began to have financial difficulties. In 1973, Norton Villiers and B.S.A. merged, becoming NVT (Norton Villiers Triumph) to save the insolvent B.S.A.

JAPAN'S SUCCESS

With Honda's 1959 introduction of lightweight motorcycles that were fun and easy to ride, consumers also found a machine that was inexpensive and problem-free compared to traditional products. In 1969, Honda began to enter the traditional "superbike" market with its technically superior CB 750. Its unique product features and design were a result of Honda's heavy commitment to R&D. Products were designed for specific market segments and also stayed in the forefront of technical developments.

In addition to product design, Honda placed heavy emphasis on sales volume and market share. To achieve results in these areas, key functional strategies included:

1. Updating or redesigning products whenever a market threat or opportunity was perceived.
2. Pricing to achieve market share objectives, cutting price if necessary.
3. Developing effective marketing systems in all markets where serious competition was intended, regardless of short-term costs.

EXHIBIT 2. Growth in Japanese Motorcycle Production (1959–1974)

	Production in 1959 ('000 units)	*Production in 1974 ('000 units)*	*Average Annual Growth Rate (per cent p.a.)*
Honda	285	2,133	14
Yamaha	64	1,165	21
Kawasaki	10	355	27
Suzuki	96	840	16
	455	4,493	

Source: Japan Automobile Industry Association

As other Japanese competitors, such as Yamaha, Kawasaki, and Suzuki, went abroad, they followed similar policies. As a result, their growth between 1959 and 1974 averaged nearly 19 per cent as shown in Exhibit 2.

Product development and introduction were considered especially important in maintaining growth. New entries, if successful, would normally have a two- to three-year life cycle—moving from rapid sales, to level and then declining sales, and finally model phaseout. The Honda CB 750, for example, was introduced in 1970, and by 1974 its sales had ceased growing in North America and were declining in Europe. New models appealed first to the fashion segment of the market because they incorporated the most up-to-date technology and design concepts. In later years, major modifications or face-lifts as with the restyled Honda 750 could keep sales levels up. However, as new up-to-date models were introduced by competitors the effectiveness of restyling eventually faded.

New model introductions were determined by the growth rate in a specific market class, designated by the cubic centimeters (cc) displacement of the engine. For example, the 47 per cent annual growth rate in superbikes between 1968 and 1974 had been attractive to new entrants. Exhibit 3 shows the number of new, large motorcycles introduced by the Japanese by 1975. These new models continued to gain market share in this growing market.

EXHIBIT 3. Japanese Superbike Introductions: 1968–1975 Number of Superbike Models

	750cc		*>750cc*		*450–749cc*	
	1968	*1975*	*1968*	*1975*	*1968*	*1975*
Honda	—	1	—	1	1	2
Yamaha	—	—	—	—	—	2
Kawasaki	—	1	—	1	1	1
Suzuki	—	—	—	1	1	3
Total	—	2	—	3	3	8

Source: R. L. Polk.

MOTORCYCLE CLASSIFICATIONS

Motorcycles could be classified as on-road, off-road, or combination bikes. On-road motorcycles, intended only for street and highway use, were the most prevalent and appealed to the general public. They were larger than off-road machines and had features such as lights, disc brakes, and electric starters. Off-road bikes, or trail bikes, were generally lighter, had lower gear ratios, and more front-end torque for hill climbing and mud use. These specialty machines had been growing since 1968 with 38 models being offered in 1975. There were thirty-nine combination models also offered, which included features of off-road machines but were legal for on-road driving.

The primary distinction between motorcycles in each class is by engine size (its cc rating). On-road machines range from 50cc to 1200cc. Increased size corresponds to increased speed, acceleration, and the amount of skill required to safely operate the machine. Two-stroke (rather than four-stroke) cycle engines, which were lighter and more powerful for their size, were used most often in off-road models. Four-stroke engines were used in larger machines because they used less gas, were more dependable, and had a longer life.

There had been little attempt to classify motorcycles by features. However, market share was heavily influenced by product features, price, and distribution. For example, a 1972 survey showed the relative importance of such features as handling, quality, economy, power, styling, and price. As shown in Exhibit 4, quality and handling were primary considerations in all purchases, with power and styling becoming more important in larger machines and price more important in smaller machines.

Price tended to be broadly related to engine size, although models could differ up to 10 per cent in price without affecting sales at each displacement level. A premium or discount of over 10 per cent was expected to affect sales volume between models with comparable features. Models with outstanding features, such as the BMW, did command a premium whereas those with poor features, such as the Yamaha 750, did not sell even with a substantially lower price. The Japanese had typically introduced models at low prices and then held those prices. This resulted in rapid growth for such large models as the Honda

EXHIBIT 4. Importance of Features for Street Motorcycles

*Per Cent**	*125cc*	*125–250cc*	*251–449cc*	*450–650cc*	*651cc*
Handling	57	33	44	60	57
Quality of Workmanship	67	65	73	67	80
Economy of Operation	27	24	12	(8)	(7)
Power	22	18	34	49	62
Styling	17	26	37	45	56
Price	55	46	38	27	7

* Per cent of purchasers rating attribute a very important influence on purchasing decision less those rating it of little or no importance (street motorcycles only).

Source: Ziff-Davis Market Research Department, AHF Market Research, Survey Data, 1972.

750, Yamaha 650 and 500, and Kawaski 900. The price advantage combined with new, attractive features generated high sales volumes.

Mopeds and motorscooters dominated the lowest price segments of the market. Mopeds had engines of not more than 50ccs and could also be propelled by the use of pedals. Although mopeds were seldom seen in the United States, they were common in Europe with the French company Motobecane producing over 700,000 units per year. Cycles Peugeot and Honda both produced about 400,000 units per year. Motorscooters had smaller wheels, were built close to the ground, and were easy to maneuver in traffic. Motorscooters ranged in size from 75ccs to 250ccs.

MAJOR MOTORCYCLE MARKETS

The North American Market

Although the primary use of motorcycles has been for basic transportation, the development of a leisure market for motorcycles began in North America. As incomes rose, consumers replaced basic motorcycle transportation with the increased comfort and convenience of the automobile. During the 1950s, motorcycle ownership fell to only about 0.3 per cent of the population in the United States. By 1974, ownership had increased to 2.4 per cent of the U.S. population with America's rediscovery of the motorcycle. Sales increased at an annual rate of over 20 per cent between 1960 and 1974, growing from 80,000 to a million units in sales during that period. Exhibit 5 shows how this growth developed by class and size of motorcycle.

Whereas the U.S. market began its growth in lightweight, low displacement, street machines, by 1970, market growth had shifted to larger street machines, competition bikes, and on/off road combination motorcycles. Exhibit 6 shows the shift in growth to larger bikes. The major reasons for this event were considered to be as follows:

1. Motorcycle riders typically "traded up" over time from smaller to larger machines. The growth of each cc class can be related to earlier growth of lower cc classes. Growth in larger bikes was, therefore, dependent on the earlier growth in small bikes. Whereas the rapid 1960s growth of motorcycles under 450cc began fading in 1971, growth in larger machines was now apparent. This growth, however, was limited by the tendency of older riders to drop out of the market.
2. Before 1970, there were few large motorcycles on the market. Large bikes, however, were now available and were being actively promoted by the competition.

With the growth rate leveling off since 1967, it appeared that the market was becoming saturated. Growth was expected only in new-user segments of the market, such as in competition, off-road, and superbike markets. Additional segments had yet to be found, and expected growth caused by the energy crisis had failed to mature.

Future growth in the U.S. market was expected to reach 2¾ to 3 per cent of the population if trends in usage and income levels continued through 1980.

EXHIBIT 5. The U.S. Motorcycle Market by Class and Size (1968–1974)

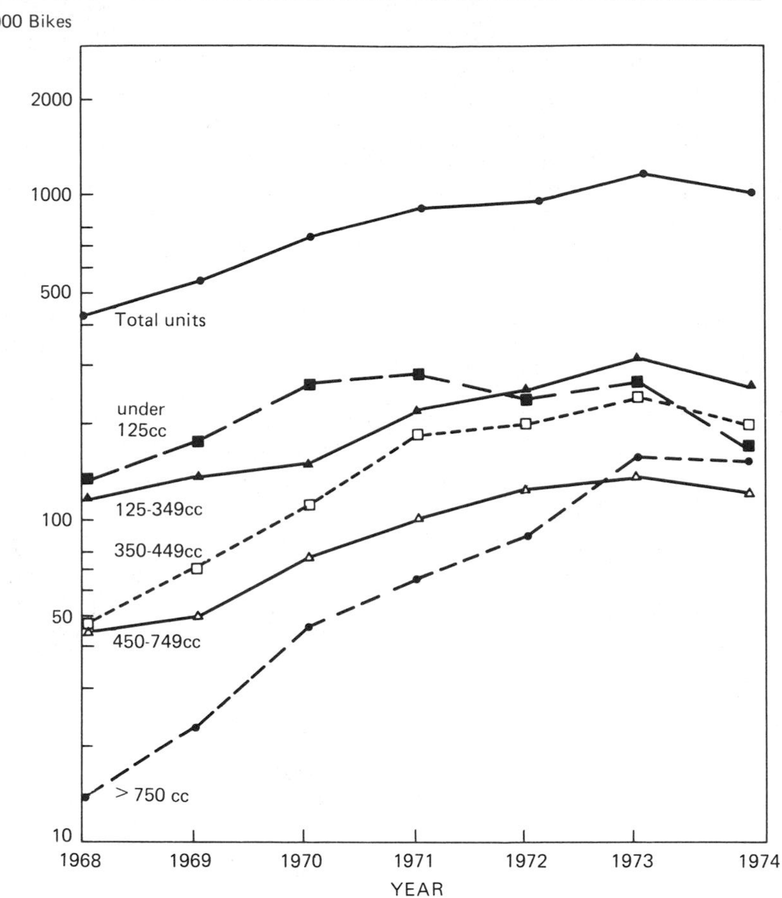

Source: R. L. Polk.

EXHIBIT 6: Sales of Big Bikes in the United States

	1968 Sales ('000 units)	*1974 Sales ('000 units)*	*1968–1974 Growth (Per Cent p.a.)*	*1968–1974 Volume Increment ('000 units)*
450–799cc	57	139	16	82
>799cc	17	168	47	151

Source: R. L. Polk, BCG Forecasts.

EXHIBIT 7: Forecasted Sales of Motorcycles in the United States

	1974 Sales ('000 units)	*1980 Sales ('000 units)*	*1974–1980 Growth (Per Cent p.a.)*	*1974–1980 Volume Increment ('000 units)*
Total Market	1,011	1,205	3	194
450–749cc	139	169	3	30
750cc	91	133	7	42
>750cc	77	108	6	31

Sales of Motorcycles in Canada

	1974 Sales ('000 units)	*1980 Sales ('000 units)*	*1974–1980 Growth (Per Cent p.a.)*	*1974–1980 Volume Increment ('000 units)*
Total Market	55	81	7	26
450–749cc	8(e)	11	6	3
750cc	5(e)	9	10	4
>750cc	4(e)	7	10	3

(e) = estimate.
Source: R. L. Polk, BCG Forecasts.

Trade-up sales were expected to be more limited in the future, and a rash of new models of 750cc and above were expected over the next three to four years. As shown in Exhibit 7, projected sales in the United States and Canada were expected to be far below the overall 15 per cent growth rate of the past 15 years. Canada's maturity was only two to three years behind that of the United States.

The European Market

The European market appeared to be a decade behind the United States. Declining demand for motorcycles as primary transportation occured in the 1960s as the automobile displaced it. The level to which usage of motorcycles had fallen by the late 1960s was very different in each country. The proportion of the population owning a motorcycle in each of the major European countries in 1969 is shown:

	Per Cent of Population
Italy	2.3
United Kingdom	1.2
France	0.6
West Germany	0.4

EXHIBIT 8: European Market Growth (1969–1973)

	Per Cent p.a. Growth in Total Sales	*Per Cent p.a. Growth in Total Ownership*
United Kingdom	25	(3)
France	32	3
West Germany	45	4
Italy	22	5

It can be seen that the UK and particularly Italy maintained a high level of usage, whereas France and Germany had fallen much farther. This indicates that the use of motorcycles for basic transport remained higher in Italy and the United Kingdom than in Germany and France.

The dynamics of market growth in Europe since the late 1960s have, therefore, involved a complex combination of riders entering the market for secondary uses (as in the United States), other riders moving from primary to secondary uses, and yet other primary use riders dropping out of the market entirely. The net result of these changes has been substantial growth rates in overall sales and the beginning of a growth in actual usage. Exhibit 8 shows growth rates in the major European countries.

Considering the U.S. motorcycle experience and the effect of per capita income, car usage, population density, insurance, legislation, and weather, projected growth in the secondary market is expected to more than offset declines in primary use of the motorcycle. West German and French sales are expected

EXHIBIT 9: Forecasted Sales of Motorcycles in the United Kingdom

	1974 Sales ('000 units)	*1980 Sales ('000 units)*	*1974–1980 Growth (Per Cent p.a.)*	*1974–1980 Volume Increment ('000 units)*
Total Market	91	110	3	19
450–749cc	3	8	18	5
755cc	2	7	23	5
Over 755cc	2	5	17	3

Sales of Motorcycles in Continental Europe

	1974 Sales ('000 units)	*1980 Sales ('000 units)*	*1974–1980 Growth (Per Cent p.a.)*	*1974–1980 Volume Increment ('000 units)*
Total Market	290	510	10	220
450–749cc	28	60	14	32
755cc	25	55	14	30
Over 755cc	14	40	19	26

Source: Society of Motor Manufacturers & Traders, BCG Forecsts.

to be greatest since primary transportation usage is low. The growing use of motorcycles for secondary use could stimulate growth in larger motorcycles. Forecasts for both the United Kingdom and continental Europe are shown in Exhibit 9.

The Japanese Market

Whereas Japan's motorcycle market grew rapidly in the 1950s and 1960s, sales remained steady in smaller cc bikes. With motorcycles still being purchased as primary transportation, sales had leveled off since 1967 and were 1.2 million units in 1974. Unlike Europe and the United States, the secondary markets had failed to develop. This was thought to be the result of the high traffic density on Japanese roads that discouraged many people from shifting to automobiles. A second factor was the rigorous requirements of acquiring a driver's license for either cars or large displacement motorcycles.

The primary nature of the Japanese market appeared to be price competition. Compared to U. S. prices, Japanese consumers were paying 20 to 40 per cent less for similar models, as shown in Exhibit 10. Even allowing for packing, freight, and duty, the Japanese appeared to be obtaining a premium for machines sold in the secondary market in the United States. This suggests that competition in the Japanese home market was much more fierce than in the United States.

Other Markets

Markets outside Europe, North America, and Japan were less developed economically and were not expected to develop secondary markets for motorcycles for some time. However, the Japanese were expecting growth in the primary market for small motorcycles. According to MITI., growth projections for less-developed markets were:

Southeast Asia	11%
Central and South America	18%
Middle East	20%
Africa	12%

IMPACT OF RELATIVE COST STRUCTURES

The ability of a company to keep its costs below those of its competitors was based on its access to technology, level of experience, and economies of scale. As seen in the research and development area, economies of scale had a major impact on overall costs of R&D per unit of sales. It was also normal for labor inputs into a product's production cost to decrease with accumulated volume. This relationship between costs and volume had been found to apply to total product costs involved in the manufacturing, distribution, and marketing of products.

Each time the accumulated experience of manufacturing a particular product doubled, the total cost in real terms, or constant dollars, could be made to

EXHIBIT 10: Honda Price Difference: USA vs. Japan

PREMIUM ON RETAIL LIST PRICES, 1974

Model	*Japan Price* ¥ 000	*Japan Price* $ Equivalent	*U.S. Price ($)*	*Premium*
CB 750	395	1,411	2,024	43%
CB 550	355	1,268	1,732	37%
CB 450	303	1,082	1,471	36%
CB 360	253	904	1,150	26%
CB 350	275	982	1,363	39%
MT 250	218	779	965	24%
MT 125	158	564	743	32%
CB 125	166	593	640	8%

Premium allowing for freight, duty, and packing
CB 750, U.S. retail list price 1975 = $2,112

Price to dealer	$1,584 (75% of 2,112)
Price to distributor	$1,373 (65%)
Japan list price	¥400,000 or $1,517 (equivalent)
Price to distributor	$ 986 (65%)
Ocean freight to Los Angeles	60
Duty	63 (3% U.S. Retail Price)
Packing costs	40
	$ 163

Thus, indicated price to U.S. distributor for equal manufacturer's margin to that sold in Japan = $ 986 + 163
= $1,149

Thus, premium in United States even after allowing for freight, duty, and packing = (1,373/1,149 − 1) × 100
= 20%

Note: The versions of the smaller bike models shipped to the United States may be slightly more expensive than their Japanese equivalents (extra lighting, etc.). The versions of the larger bikes are, however, reported to be identical in both markets.

decline by 20 to 30 per cent. The experience inherent in volume could influence the product design itself, either in terms of technical or performance characteristics, or in terms of cost effectiveness in manufacturing the product as described at Honda. This experience could also affect the technology of production equipment, factor organization, control methods, and administration. It could also affect purchases, raw materials, and components. Experience also affected marketing effectiveness and distribution expenses. The failure to grow or to bring costs down as fast as competitors could be a critical disadvantage.

Exhibit 11 shows the overall price trends for Japanese motorcycles. These curves show a consistent reduction in price for three sizes of motorcycles. The larger 126–250cc machines had shown the sharpest decline, following a 76 per cent experience curve slope. Smaller machines had shown 81 and 88 per cent

EXHIBIT 11. Japanese Motorcycle Price Experience Curves (1959–1974)

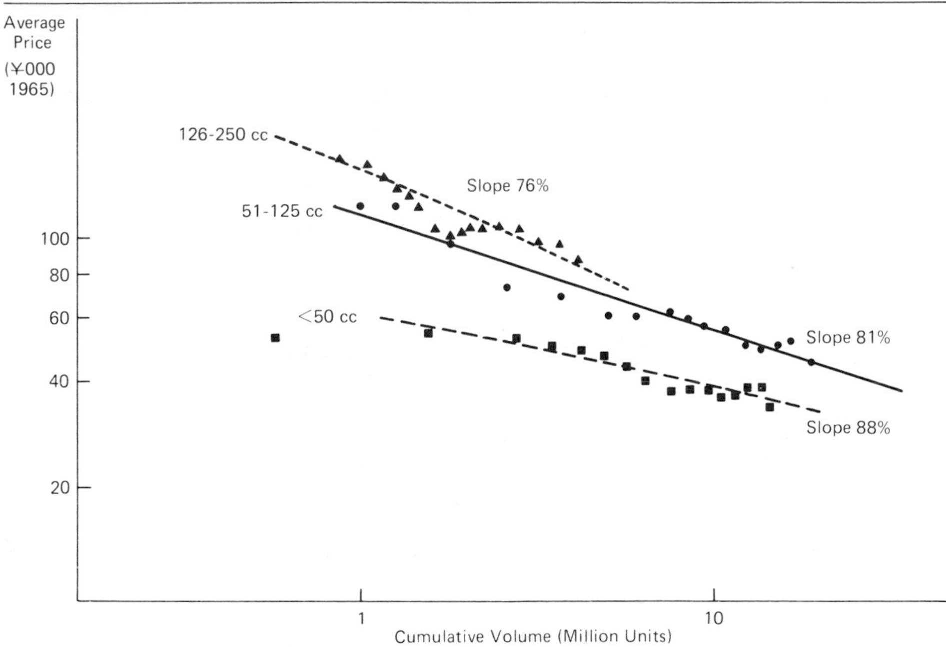

Source: MITI.

curves. Exhibit 12 shows similar price experiences with Honda's larger 350–750cc machines that were considered comparable to other Japanese manufacturers. However, because of changes in the yen-dollar exchange rate, the actual price to U.S. retailers had remained constant. The following discussion looks at how R&D, production, materials and components, and selling and distribution experience contributed to declining prices in the industry.

Product Research and Development

Product research design and development had proven to be critical to the motorcycle industry. Its level of importance stemmed from key facts:

1. Motorcycle models had relatively short life cycles.
2. Appearance, ease of maintenance, and performance were key factors in buyers' decisions.
3. Production costs were closely related to design.
4. R&D capabilities were necessary in responding quickly and effectively to new product introductions.

R&D "effectiveness" appeared to be the highest for the Japanese competitors. Honda claimed to take an idea from conception to production in eighteen months; Suzuki claimed two years. It would take three years minimum for the British competitors. Honda had the largest R&D facilities, but, because of its high sales volume, it had the lowest number of R&D employees per million units of sales and the lowest R&D cost per unit produced as shown:

	R&D Employees Per 1 million of Sales	*Total R&D Employees **
Honda	1.8	1,300
Yamaha	3.2	800
Suzuki	2.7	1,000
NVT	4.0	100

* Includes all R&D employees, not just professional engineers.

EXHIBIT 12: Honda Large Bikes: Price Experience Curves

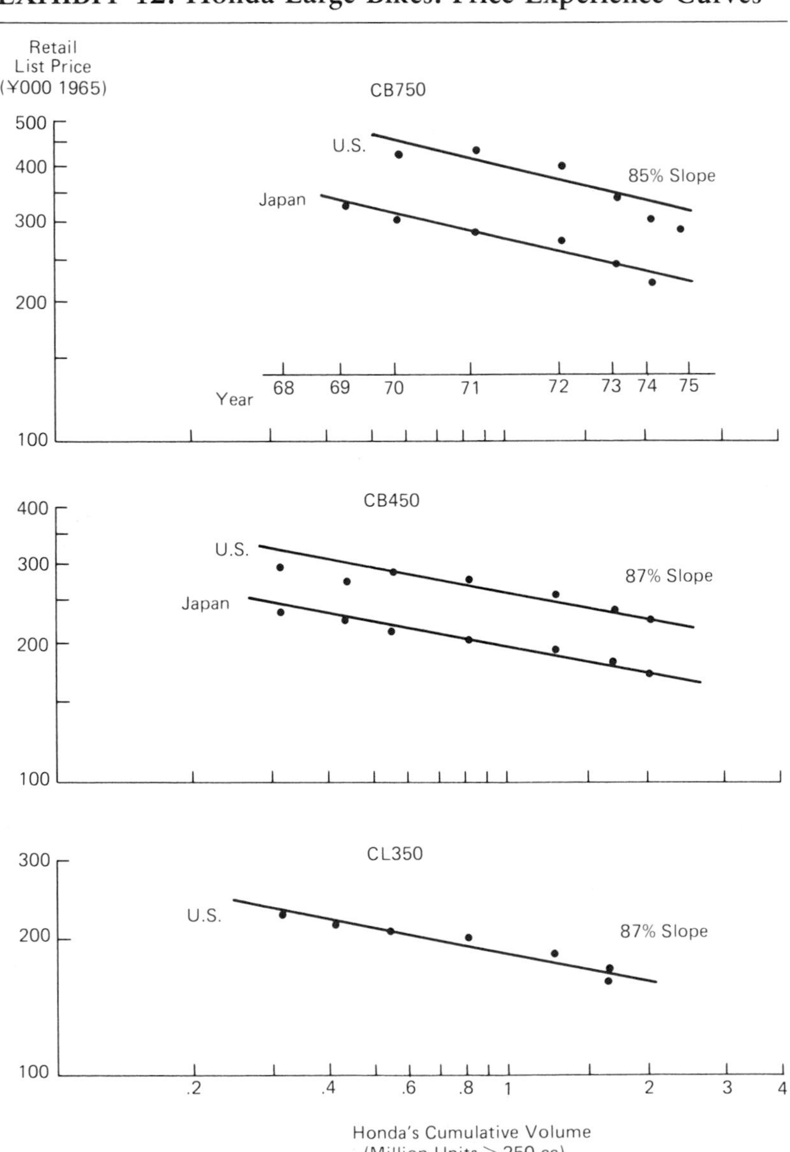

The Japanese also worked to develop an effective balance between "pure" engineering, production engineering, and the marketing requirements of a new product. Before design work began, preliminary cost assessments and commercial evaluations were made. Programs for research, development, and production were made explicit. Production engineers were involved early in the project teams to ensure that production needs were not being overlooked. Cost projections and commercial prospectors were reevaluated at regular checkpoints, with rigorous review prior to production. All design features were carefully evaluated for cost and acceptability. This design process was seen as a critical service for production and marketing.

NVT had a smaller R&D facility than the major Japanese companies although its ratios of costs and staff to sales were higher. This put NVT at a cost disadvantage as well as a limited ability to respond to competitive introductions. Honda kept a backlog of design projects that had already reached advanced stages of development which could be quickly brought to the market. Honda's rapid introduction of a superb two-stroke, off-road bike when the U.S. dirt bike market took off was such an example.

Production

Production incorporated those tasks that were carried out in the factory to add value to the end product. For motorcycles, this included engine part machining, parts manufacture, and assembly of both engines and finished bikes. Cost reduction could be achieved in each of these areas through (1) technological and organizational influences and (2) taking advantage of volume and size to apply up-to-date technology and specialized production facilities.

The growing competitor was in the best position to apply up-to-date technology since investment in new equipment was necessary for expansion. This allowed the manufacturer to maximize learning by using current technology and the most updated production equipment and methods. To the extent that this increased productivity by reducing labor content through capital expenditures, average costs would continue to decline.

The majority of production technology used in the motorcycle industry was available from independent machine tool manufacturers. In Japan, manufacturers had been designing and making their own specialized equipment. This had allowed them to apply their own cumulative production experience to motorcycles. The potential for production cost reduction in the motorcycle industry varied at each stage of manufacturing. Overall, the company's accumulated experience in the business would affect its engineering experience, technology, machine tool availability, and manufacturing methods. As Japan's producers continued to use modern, complex technologies and became more capital intensive, they had increased their fixed costs and reduced their variable costs. This move allowed them to achieve very low unit costs if they could keep output volumes high.

The greatest opportunity for cost reduction had come in the area of engine and transmission parts production. At low volumes, these were highly labor-intensive parts. Only with high volumes had it been economical to invest in special-purpose equipment that was highly automated. However, advanced product designs for high-volume production had allowed greater automation.

EXHIBIT 13: The Effect of Volume on the Choice of Production Methods and Costs (Schematic)

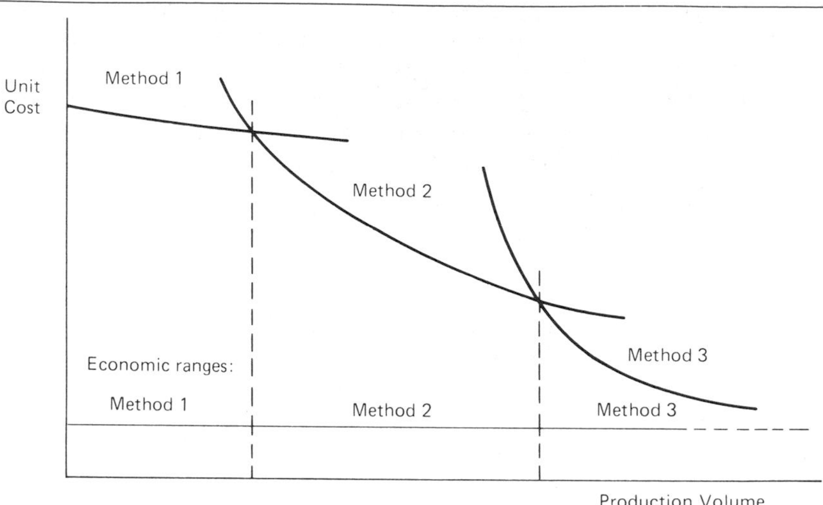

Notes

Method 1 has low fixed costs but high variable costs. It is labour intensive and economic only at low volumes. At higher volumes, Method 2 is economic. This has a higher capital content, higher fixed costs, and lower variable costs. At even higher volumes, Method 3 offers the lowest costs. This is even more capital intensive and has the lowest labour content, but requires very high volumes to amortise the fixed costs.

Initial moves to rotary index machines required 5,000 units per month. More expensive in-line transfer machines required over 10,000 units per month. Parts standardization for volume production was, therefore, critical to cost reduction as shown in Exhibit 13.

Cycle parts contained a lower portion of value added. Electrical parts were essentially purchased complete and assembled into the bike. Production of frames, fork legs, exhaust systems, and wheels could be automated only slightly if high model volumes were sustained. Use of pressed, rather than milled, frames had large cost-savings potential.

Assembly of low volumes was mostly done in groups, using jigs and trolleys for transfer. At high volumes, motorized assembly lines, using specialized and simplified assembly jobs, could raise output per employee to much higher levels. However, high-volume assembly required special administrative skills to manage the logistics of model changeovers to make sure that all the parts were available at the right time and in the right place.

Materials and Components Purchasing

Materials and components accounted for roughly half the costs of production. Cost reduction was related to buying power in volume purchases and to improvement of supplier operations. Once manufacturers became large customers, they could get better service and response from their suppliers in terms of delivery and quality.

Selling and Distribution Systems

Overall selling and distribution activities included a wide range of activities, especially for international sales. These activities included:

1. obtaining dealers.
2. obtaining floor space.
3. obtaining sales support.
4. parts and cycle distribution.
5. warranty and service support.
6. dealer support.
7. advertising and promotion.
8. market planning and control.

Exhibit 14 compares the selling and distribution systems of the four full-line Japanese manufacturers selling in the United States.

Good dealers and dealer support led to improved market shares. Active competition between dealers led to product price discounting that would stimulate total sales. Manufacturers could affect both of these areas through their dealer network strategies. Outstanding products also led to higher market share and vice versa for poor products. For the Japanese, typical market shares were

Honda	40–50%
Yamaha	15–25%
Kawasaki	10–15%
Suzuki	9–12%

Maintaining strong selling and distributions systems could protect against the erosion of these positions. In the United States, exclusive dealerships gave incentive for dealers to sell the full range of a manufacturer's models. In Europe, shared dealerships would place emphasis on those models that had the greatest sales potential.

The major opportunity for cost reduction in selling and distribution was in administrative expenses. Large systems would allow those expenses to be spread across the sales force, dealer training, advertising, and promotional support. Such costs as duty, freight, and landing were generally fixed. Overall marketing expenditures, however, tended to rise with market share and size rather than de-

EXHIBIT 14: The Selling and Distribution Systems of Japanese Companies in the USA

	Estimated Total S & D Expenditure by Sales Company 1974 ($m)	*Advertising Expenditure 1972 ($m)*	*Dealers 1974*		*1974 Per Cent Share of Total Market (units)*	*Lowest Per Cent Share of any cc Class*	*Highest Per Cent Share of any cc Class*
			Numbers	*Units Sold per Dealer*			
Honda	90–100	8.1	1,974	220	43	34	61
Yamaha	40–45	4.2	1,515	135	20	4	34
Kawasaki	30–35	2.2	1,018	127	13	9	19
Suzuki	25–30	3.0	1,103	98	11	5	16

Sources: R. L. Polk, *Motorcycle Dealer News,* Ziff-Davis Market Research Dept., BCG Estimates.

cline. This appeared to be a deliberate decision by manufacturers to protect and build a market position, thereby allowing the greatest savings to come in production and improved quality.

To support high-volume strategies, the Japanese dealers often gave discounts of 5 to 10 per cent on high-volume models. The increased turnover still allowed dealers to achieve good returns on their investment.

COMPETITORS' POSITIONS

The position of competitors in the world motorcycle industry depended on their relative competitive strengths. This section describes the capabilities and strategies of the major world competitors.

Honda Motor Company

Honda was the world's largest producer of motorcycles with an output of 2.1 million units in 1974. By producing a wide range of products that met the requirements of the vast majority of riders at affordable prices, Honda had developed the leading position in nearly every market it entered, as shown in Exhibit 15.

Honda's largest markets were Japan and North America. Local producers and local trade barriers had made Honda's recent efforts to penetrate European markets more difficult than it had found in the United States. Honda was now setting up subsidiaries in many lesser-developed countries where primary demand for lightweight machines was emerging.

Honda generally introduced its new products into markets at prices below those of comparable competitive products in order to develop sales volume. In instances where it found itself selling at a price disadvantage, Honda would give special price cuts to keep the competition from gaining market share. In entering new markets, Honda was prepared to sustain losses for as long as necessary to establish its marketing channels.

Despite these strengths, Honda had lost share in world markets in recent years, as a result of increased competition, especially in larger bikes, by Yamaha, Suzuki, and Kawasaki. Before Honda developed its range of two-stroke motocross bikes in 1973, these competitors were able also to take advantage of the

EXHIBIT 15: Per Cent Market Shares of Total Units Sold: 1974

	USA	*Canada*	*UK*	*France*	*Germany*	*Italy* *
Honda	43	41	54	37	39	17
Yamaha	20	18	19	19	20	1
Kawasaki	13	17	5	5	5	8
Suzuki	11	12	13	13	6	4
Total	87	88	74	74	70	30

* Japanese competitors are not allowed to import machines of less than 380cc.

off-road market that preferred two-stroke engines over Honda's heavier four-stroke machines. In addition, Honda had turned much of its attention toward the expansion of its overseas automobile activities between 1969 and 1974.

Honda's introduction of new motorcycles and new capacity in 1975 appeared to be a reversal of this policy. Its 1,000 cc Goldwing was the first of a new generation of superbikes and its modified CB 750 Supersport also had improved performance and handling characteristics. This suggested a major push by Honda to capture or maintain its share of the larger engine market as shown:

Honda Market Shares (%) 1974

	Total Market	*Superbikes*
United States	43	36
United Kingdom	54	4
France	37	27
Germany	39	22
Italy	17	17
Netherlands	41	32

Honda's R&D activities are said to be back to their previous high levels indicating its commitment to holding onto its leadership in all product classes.

Yamaha Motor Company

Yamaha had grown more rapidly than Honda since 1962 to become the world's second largest producer of motorcycles. Much of Yamaha's success had come from off-road and competitive cycle markets where it had developed a "sporting" image with numerous racing successes. Yamaha was the last of the Japanese to enter the larger 500cc and 650cc markets, but its entries were doing well. Yamaha now planned to bore out its 650cc model to 750cc after the 1972 750cc entry failed and was withdrawn. The new entry was expected to be a very price-competitive model in its class. A heavy, 1,000 cc four-stroke, three-cylinder touring bike was also being planned. Yamaha had used a volume strategy and had tripled its capacity in low cc machines despite estimated losses of $20 per unit on sales in Japan.

Kawasaki Heavy Industries

Kawasaki was the last of the big four Japanese firms to enter the motorcycle industry, but was now competing with Suzuki for third place. In the early 1960s, Kawasaki diversified out of shipbuilding and heavy industrial products to get closer to the consumer. Motorcycles provided a logical extension from its industrial engine business. Poor results in the Japanese market during the 1960s led Kawasaki to a re-evaluation and decision to set up a U.S. subsidiary. Kawasaki was reported to have broken even for the first time in 1974.

Kawasaki's products, stressing speed and performance, had not had all-around success. Its 500cc and 750cc two-stroke machines were fast, but lacked the handling, styling, and features of its new 900cc four-stroke Z-1 model. The Z-1 was well regarded in the industry and represented Kawasaki's R&D departments' success in building a motorcycle with real "class." Although small compared to Honda, Kawasaki's financial backing and product successes made it a formidable competitor.

Kawaski planned to upgrade its Z-1 to 1000cc and to introduce a new low-priced 750cc model in the $1,800 price range. It introduced an inexpensive 400cc model in 1975, which was being assembled in Kawasaki's new Lincoln, Nebraska, plant. Management was also considering production of the Z-1 in the United States.

Kawasaki was beginning its push into the European market with a small number of exclusive dealerships. It hoped to build a more loyal dealer network with heavier Kawasaki support than was possible in the typically European shared-dealership situation.

Suzuki Motor Company

Suzuki had been gaining world market share since 1972. Like Yamaha, Suzuki had concentrated on two-stroke off-road and competition machines. It had stressed comfort and solid design more than speed, since its performance had not been particularly good. Its introduction of on-road machines at 380cc and 550cc had some success but has not taken share from the market leaders. In the depressed U.S. market, Suzuki had offered rebates on several models that ranged from $50 to $100. The latest entry, the Rotary RE-5, had not been well received. Suzuki's next development was said to be a 1000cc four-stroke, three-cylinder, water-cooled machine. Exhibit 16 shows the relative resource base of the Japanese competitors.

Harley-Davidson

Harley-Davidson was the only remaining U.S. producer of motorcycles. In the United States, Harley produced only large 1,000cc and 1,200cc motorcycles, relying on Aermacchi, its Italian subsidiary, for smaller machines to fill out its line. With Harley's primary market being in the United States, it had customer loyalty that foreign motorcycles could not match as well as a distinct advantage in obtaining contracts with the police and the army. Thus, customers were willing to pay a premium for Harley-Davidson machines. Harley's dealers were also believed to be among the best in the country.

In spite of strong competition, Harley's market share had held steady since 1971. Production capacity had constrained sales until its capacity was recently doubled. It is expected that Harley will replace its 1000cc Sportster over the next several years with a 880cc model. It is also working on a new 1200cc model. Although Harley is expected to keep its V-engine configuration, it is also expected to introduce a four-cylinder model.

BMW

BMW, part of the German automobile group, produced only 25,000 machines per year. Its motorcycles, in the 600cc to 900cc range, had a high-quality image that commanded premium prices. In the United States, the 900cc BMW R90-6 sold for 28 per cent more than Kawasaki's 900. Despite higher prices, BMW had been able to gain market share in the United States and Europe. A

EXHIBIT 16: The Japanese Motorcycle Industry

	Honda (1974/5 Sales £730m, 19,000 Employees)	
Factories	*Employees*	*Products*
Suzuka	8,500	High vol. 125 cc bikes 550 cc, 750 cc bikes Civic and 145 cars TN 360 Truck
Hamamatsu	3,100	50 cc plus 125–500 cc bikes Generators, outboards, tillers, etc.
Sayama	2,800	Cars 1000 cc bikes
Wako	2,000	Engines
Other		
Honda R & D Co.	1,300	R & D
Honda Engineering	1,400	Machine tools
	Yamaha (1974/5 Sales £250m, 5,500 employees)	
Factories	*Employees*	*Products*
Iwata	2,200	Bike and Engine Assembly Snowmobiles
Hamakita	1,600	Parts machining Machine tools
Niii	700	N/A
Other		
R & D (at Iwata)	800	R & D
	Suzuki (1974/5 Sales £270m, 10,000 employees)	
Factories	*Employees*	*Products*
Hamamatsu	4,500	Parts machining, some assembly Machine tools
Toyama	800	Bike assembly
Toyokawa	700	Bike assembly
Kosai	1,100	Car and Truck assembly
Iwata	1,400	Car and Truck assembly
Osuka	350	Castings
Other		
Technical Centre	1,000	R & D
	Kawasaki (Motorcycle Activities 1974/5 Sales ca. £60m, 1,700 Employees)	
Factory	*Employees*	*Products*
Akashi	1,700	Motorcycles

Source: Interviews, Annual Reports, Company Histories. All figures approximate.

sporty version of the R90-6 was selling well at a $500 premium over the regular model. Although its smaller models had done well, BMW withdrew its 350cc and 500cc models.

BMW had clearly gone for the market segment looking for a superior machine. All of its products were variations of the same basic engine and frame design. Although the design was not new, it incorporated features that led *Motorcyclist Magazine* to rate the BMW 750 as the best superbike on the market in July 1973. BMW was planning to increase production to 45,000 units in 1980.

British Competitors (NVT)

British motorcycles had retained an image of high performance, superior handling, elegant style, and a premium finish. Increased Japanese competition, however, had narrowed their lead. A primary weakness was felt to be in the reliability of British machines, a weakness made worse by poor spare parts availability and by a reluctance of the British to accept warranty claims. Although NVT claimed to have improved reliability, oil leaks suggested continued problems in the basic design.

Since the British had not introduced a new model since the 1968 Trident, it was easy to understand why the competitive gap between them and the Japanese had closed. Features such as electric starters, four-cylinder engines, disc breaks, and five-speed transmissions were lacking on British machines. Japanese introductions were generally lower priced than the low-feature British models. British attempts to update features and increase displacement were generally perceived only as modifications and not new models and were priced above competitive Japanese models. Since 1968, Triumph had lost market share every year except 1973, when it sold its Bonneville 750 at a price 12 per cent below the Honda 750.

The British manufacturers had generally withdrawn from lower 175 to 650cc markets. They uprated the Bonneville and Commando models to 750cc and over. These superbikes sold lower volumes and had higher margins even for the Japanese. With rather constant sales, the British had continued to lose market share. Recent research showed that only 28 per cent of Triumph owners were repurchasing that same brand. The financial strength of British manufacturers continued to suffer as shown in Exhibit 17.

Moto-Guzzi, Benelli, and Ducati

Since 1972, Italy's Moto-Guzzi and Benelli had been part of the deTomaso group. They produced a full line of motorcycles (40,000 units per year) and mopeds (80,000 units per year) of which half were exported. Models under 380cc could not be imported into Italy and high duties and deposits were imposed on other larger models. Honda had, in fact, been forced to open a factory in Italy. Guzzi-Benelli's new models for 1974 were based on Japanese designs. With a strong dealer network and protection from Japanese competition, their market share in Italy had been maintained.

Ducati had an image of high performance, good handling, and elegant styling similar to that of the British. Ducati's sales had declined to 10,000 units in 1974 and its losses had led the Italian government to assume ownership. Even with loss of market share in its home market, new production facilities were planned along with a new model range.

EXHIBIT 17: Motorcycle Manufacturers: Financial Summary

	Norton		*BSA/Triumph*		*Honda Motor*		*Yamaha Motor*		*Suzuki*	
	Earnings	*ROI*	*Earnings*	*ROI*	*Earnings*	*ROI*	*Earnings*	*ROI*	*Earnings*	*ROI*
1969/70 } 1970/1 }	£0.37m	4.5%	£0.4m	N/A	¥35.0b	24.6%	¥2.4b	16.2%	¥8.4b	18.8%
			£(7.2)m	loss	¥35.0b	20.4%	¥3.4b	17.0%	¥10.0b	16.2%
1971/2	£0.38m	7.3%	£(3.1)m	loss	¥35.4b	19.6%	¥5.6b	30.2%	¥11.4b	15.8%
1972/3	£(0.02)m	loss	£(2.9)m	loss	¥34.2b	18.6%	¥8.8b	35.0%	¥10.6b	13.2%
1973/4					¥34.4b	14.8%	¥8.4b	22.8%	¥10.0b	11.4%
1974/5 (Est)	£(5.1)m (Norton and BSA/Triumph combined)				¥32.0b	12.4%	¥9.5b	21.6%	¥9.0b	10.4%

Notes: 1. Earnings are expressed before tax and interest, and include provisions for reorganization, etc., in the case of BSA/Triumph, for which company the results of the motorcycle activities only are quoted.
2. ROI equals earnings divided by net assets at the end of the year.
3. In 1975 Y1 billion = £1.5 million.
4. Year-ends: July for NVT, February for Honda, March for Suzuki, April for Yamaha. Data for Japanese companies is for Parent Company, not Group.

Source: Annual Reports, NVT Group Accountant, BCG Tokyo.

EXHIBIT 18: Financially Sustainable Growth Rates 1970–74

Company	*Average Return on Net Assets, R (AT, BI)*	*Average Gross Debt/Equity Ratio, D/E*	*Average After Tax Interest Rate on Debt, i*	*Average Dividend Payout, p*	*Sustainable Growth Rate, g**	*Actual Net Asset Growth*
Honda (*Group*)	7%	3.0	2.5%	0.30	14%	14%
Yamaha	12%	1.0	3.0%	0.15	18%	21%
Suzuki	6%	2.7	3.0%	0.50	7%	10%

**Sustainable Growth Rate*

The rate at which a company can internally finance growth is a function of its earning power, the proportion of earnings it retains, and the extent to which it gears up these retentions with debt. The relationship can be expressed in a simple formula, as follows:

$$g = \{D/E(R - i) + R\}(1 - p)$$

For a fuller description of this "sustainable growth formula," see *Growth and Financial Strategies*, The Boston Consulting Group, Boston, 1971.

Other Competitors

Communist countries had recently begun producing cheap models of motorcycles with styling, finishes, and performance below Western standards. Motorcycles had been accepted in these countries as basic transportation and were not expected to achieve much share in developed markets. Few other producers of motorcycles were of any significance outside their national markets.

THE SITUATION IN 1975

The Japanese had developed a distinct advantage in R&D, production, and marketing of motorcycles. Continued profitability combined with a relatively high use of debt and low dividend payout should allow the Japanese to sustain their current high rate of growth as shown in Exhibit 18. The British typically used little debt and had high dividend payouts.

The short-term problem, however, was related to the depressed state of the North American market. The impact on sales of all cc classes was not yet known. BMW and Harley-Davidson's superbikes had not been affected to the same extent as other segments of the market. Honda's exports of bikes over 500cc reportedly had not declined, and its production of 1000cc bikes had been increased from 4,000 to 5,000 units per month. Superbike sales in the United States had declined only slightly, but Norton and Triumph were reported to have lost market share because of price competition. The high prices of British bikes were expected to continue to hurt their position.

CASE TWENTY-ONE

The British Motorcycle Industry (A)[1]

WILLIAM R. BOULTON and JAMES J. CHRISMAN
University of Georgia

Assignment Questions:

1. How does the British motorcycle industry's strategy differ from that of the Japanese? BMW? Why has it been unsuccessful?
2. How would you compare the current positions of the British, Japanese, and BMW in the world motorcycle market? How does this relate to their strategies?

Although sales of British motorcycles began to decline in the 1950s, it was not until the late 1960s and early 1970s that severe losses raised questions as to the continued survival of the British motorcycle industry. In fact, by 1973, heavy losses forced a merger between the last of the British manufacturers, BSA/Triumph and Norton Villiers, so as to avoid bankruptcy. The surviving company, NVT, continued to lose money after the merger and was struggling to determine a strategy for survival.

BACKGROUND

Although the world motorcycle industry had grown rapidly since the early 1960s, spurred by rapid expansion of the North American market, the British did little to stop the Japanese invasion of the market. In fact, the British had lost nearly 90 per cent of their market share since 1968 as shown in Exhibit 1. Whereas the Japanese began developing economies of scale in small motorcycles, the British response was to withdraw from those markets in which Japanese competition and lower prices were a problem. The British believed that the Japanese would not become a threat to their "more difficult to make" large bike markets. However, by the mid-1960s, most small British producers had been driven out of the market and only the largest, BSA/Triumph, was still profitable as shown in Exhibit 2.

[1]This material comes from "Strategy Alternatives for the British Motorcycle Industry (London: Her Majesty's Stationery Office, 1975).

EXHIBIT 1: The British Motorcycle Industry (A)

BRITISH MARKET PERFORMANCE: 1968–74

	Market Size		*Market Growth*	*British Market Shares*	
	1968 ('000 units)	*1974 ('000 units)*	*1968–1974 per cent p.a.*	*1968 per cent*	*1974 per cent*
North America	458	1,066	15	11	1
United Kingdom	38	91	16	34	3
Europe	100	290	19	2	1

British orientation toward short-term profitability fostered complacency among British managers. As profits declined, funds became inadequate to permit investments that were comparable to the Japanese. Continued profitability then depended on the growth in large bike sales that was required to offset sales lost in their retreat. During the 1960s, their narrowing large bike segment was growing rapidly and annual production was maintained at about 80,000 units. The British retreat was felt to be successful so long as the Japanese were still weak in their market segments and they remained profitable.

The British Retreat

Segment retreat strategies are common in industry. They often result from needs for short-term profitability and can succeed for quite long periods of time, as with the British motorcycle industry. The long-term risk comes from allowing the competition to penetrate higher-volume segments where it can experience cost-curve reductions and high profits. As the competition takes over vacated

EXHIBIT 2: The British Motorcycle Industry (A)

BSA FINANCIAL PERFORMANCE DURING THE 1960S

Year	*Sales*	*Earnings Attributable to Ordinary Shareholders*	*Net Assets*	*ROA Per Cent*
1960	N/A	1.54m	21.1m	7.3
1961	N/A	1.25	27.1	4.6
1962	N/A	0.67	21.5	3.1
1963	N/A	0.48	23.5	2.0
1964	33.1m	0.71	24.0	3.0
1965	40.3	1.97	25.9	7.6
1966	46.6	2.16	30.2	7.2
1967	35.5	1.88	31.8	5.9
1968	36.5	2.01	26.8	7.5
1969	33.9	0.41	29.4	1.4

Note: Data no longer exist for separating the results of the motorcycle activities from those of the Group for this period. It would seem, however, that motorcycles were major contributors to Group profits throughout the period.

Source: Moodys.

market segments, its power continues to grow until it begins to penetrate the last segments into which the smaller retreating competitors have withdrawn.

Retreat strategies can be successful when market growth in those segments continues to create an avenue of retreat. However, it appears that the motorcycle industry has reached a "natural" limit with respect to manageable size and power. In such cases, retreat strategies may call for a halt to retreat and an attempt to maintain a volume position within the segment, keeping segment production and sales costs below competitors.

For the British there was some question as to whether there was a real retreat or simply a lack of product availability. With limited production and distribution, dealers had difficulty in getting products into the showrooms in sufficient quantity and timely enough to capitalize on the underlying demand. For example, it had been BSA/Triumph policy to "sell out" of its products rather than to increase capacity to meet market demands. Such constraints on supply ensured maintenance of prices and margins, product exclusivity, and easy production scheduling to meet market sales. Although this policy appears to have worked in the 1960s, there was little evidence that any lack of availability existed in the 1970s. In fact, all manufacturers tended to run short of their most popular models. At Honda, the Goldwing was in short supply.

In 1971, BSA/Triumph introduced a "new look" that failed to find favor within the market. By late 1972, BSA/Triumph had returned to its traditionally "British look." However, its continuing loss of market share was considered to be the result of several factors:

1. New competitors had entered the British segment with a variety of new and up-to-date models.
2. The British had not introduced a new model since the Triumph in 1968.
3. The British had withdrawn from the 500 cc and 650 cc segments into the more limited 750 cc and above segment.

MAJOR BRITISH MOTORCYCLE MARKETS

North America. NVT was represented in the United States by its subsidiary, Norton Triumph Corporation, Inc. Although the company attempted to offer a full range of dealer support, it was limited by relatively low levels of current sales. Norton Triumph's advertising and promotion budget, for example, was only $800,000 compared to Honda's $10 million. Furthermore, low sales volumes had led to a cut in Norton Triumph's staff and sales support, which resulted in further decay of its dealer network and market share, as shown in Exhibit 3.

In 1972, BSA/Triumph had 850 U.S. dealers and Norton had 750. By 1975, a *Motorcycle Dealer News* survey showed only 408 dealers claiming to have Triumph franchises. After consolidation of the Norton and Triumph dealer networks, only 400 dealers were expected to be active.

The long history of British motorcycles in the U.S. market gave Norton Triumph some firm and loyal contacts in all parts of the trade. Along with Honda, Yamaha, Suzuki, Kawasaki, and Harley-Davidson, Triumph was regarded as one of the "big six." Consequently, British products got good press coverage and had high public awareness and surprising dealer loyalty for such a

EXHIBIT 3: The British Motorcycle Industry (A) Market Shares of Motorcycles ≥440 cc USA 1968–1974

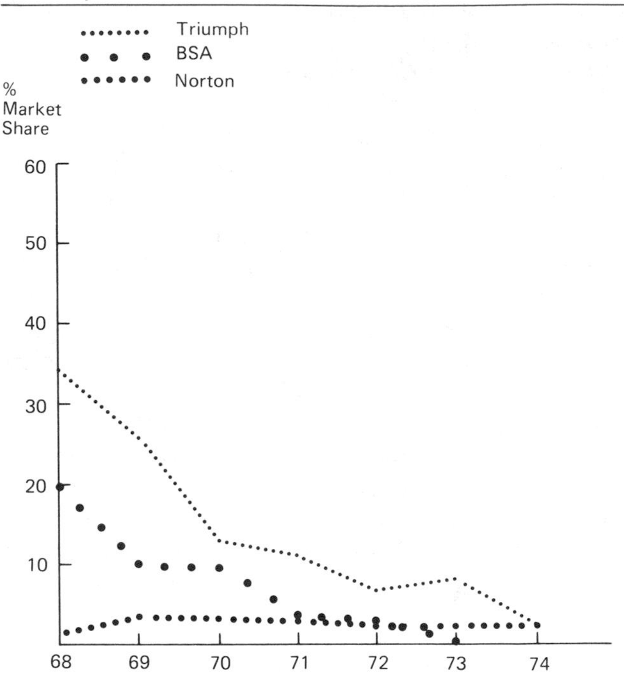

Source: R. L. Polk.

small market share. The Bonneville even continued to play starring roles in Hollywood films. British distribution in Canada was handled by Norton Triumph Canada, Ltd.

The United Kingdom. Nationalism had been a strong force with motorcycle purchasers in the past. As a result, Norton and Trimph had enjoyed market shares of superbikes in the United Kingdom of 33 per cent and 38 per cent, respectively. These market shares also reflected the strength of NVT's dealer network and selling and distribution system in the United Kingdom. Even with NVT's lack of product range, it had still been able to exercise considerable hold on the British market.

Other Markets. Norton Triumph Europe was responsible for sales in European countries outside the United Kingdom. Its low market share was considered to be the result of the unsuitable nature of British products for European riding conditions. Its lack of consistent reliability was regarded as particularly damaging by European riders who liked to travel long distances without trouble and who valued handling, styling, and performance less highly than the British and Americans.

The British had never given the European market the same commitment in selling and distribution as in North America and the United Kingdom. Furthermore, prices were held high to importers, which restricted margins and the development of sales and distribution systems. In fact, European sales were considered to be incremental to the total sales effort, providing high contribution margins for a minimal investment in market development. In Germany, for example, NTV had been unwilling to invest $7,200 to pass legal requirements for selling its 1974 models. As a result, it became the dealer's responsibility to clear each machine he sold with authorities.

In most markets outside North America, Europe, and the British Commonwealth, NVT had little representation. An Australian subsidiary handled sales there and in New Zealand. Some sales were made to South Africa and the Middle East.

THE BRITISH COST POSITION

By 1975, the Japanese had created a massive disparity in cost effectiveness compared to the British. Exhibit 4 compares the productivity levels of major competitors. High productivity appears to be directly related to high-output vol-

EXHIBIT 4: The World Motorcycle Industry

MOTORCYCLE INDUSTRY PRODUCTIVITY COMPARISON

	Motorcycle Output	*Motorcycles per Man-Year*
BRITAIN		
Small Heath Factory 1975	10,500	10
Wolverhampton Factory 1975	18,000	18*
Meriden Factory 1972/3	28,000	14*
JAPAN		
Honda		
Total Company	2 million	106 bikes *plus* 21 cars
Suzuka Factory	1.5 million	350 (Estimate)
Hamamatsu Factory	500,000	174
Yamaha		
Total Company	1 million	200
Suzuki		
Motorcycle Activities†	800,000	114
Kawasaki		
Akashi Factory	300,000	159
OTHER		
Moto-Guzzi/Benelli	40,000	13 *plus* 20 mopeds
BMW	25,000	20‡
Harley-Davidson	38,000 (1974—includes 3-month strike)	11
	50,000 (Projected full year)	15

* Higher proportions of bought-in components than Small Heath.
† Head Office and Main Plant (machining) plus Toyama and Toyokawa motorcycle assembly factories.
‡ Very low proportion of bought-in components.

Sources: Annual reports, company histories, published articles. Plant data in Britain direct from NVT manufacturing records. Information on other non-Japanese companies partly derived from interviews with the companies concerned.

EXHIBIT 5: The British Motorcycle Industry

JAPANESE MOTORCYCLE MANUFACTURERS: VALUE ADDED PER EMPLOYEE

	Honda		*Yamaha*		*Suzuki*	
Year *	*'000 Yen* **	£	*'000 Yen*	£	*'000 Yen*	£
1967/8	6,300	7,400	3,300	3,900	N/A	—
1968/9	7,400	8,600	3,700	4,300	6,300	7,300
1969/70	8,200	9,600	4,100	4,800	6,200	7,300
1970/1	8,600	10,700	5,200	6,500	6,800	8,500
1971/2	8,500	12,000	6,500	9,200	6,900	9,700
1972/3	9,000	13,900	6,500	10,000	6,900	10,600
1973/4	9,700	13,700	6,600	9,300	6,300	8,900
1974/5 (1st 6 months)	11,900	17,800	N/A	—	N/A	—

* Based on year ends of August 31 for Honda, October 31 for Yamaha, and September 30 for Suzuki.
** $1 = 270 yen.
N/A = not available.
Source: Annual Reports and Security Analysts' Reports.

umes. At the total company level, Honda produced over 100 bikes and 20 cars per employee—equivalent to over 200 bikes per employee per year. At the factory level, Japanese productivity ranged from 100 to 200 bikes per employee. Honda's Suzuki plant, the world's largest, produced over 300 bikes per employee.

In contrast, the British produced 10 to 18 bikes per employee. The British planned to double output at the Meriden plant over 1972–73 levels, but such an achievement using existing equipment and methods was questionable. The productivity of other non-Japanese competitors was similar to the British. Moto-Guzzi and Benelli produced 13 bikes and 20 mopeds per employee with new, general-purpose machine tools. BMW achieved about 20 and Harley-Davidson 15 bikes per employee. Only BMW was able to charge a price premium that allowed profitability. All other manufacturers were under profit pressure.

In 1975, British factories added about $12,000 per employee in value that, if subtracting current losses, would amount to about $10,000 per employee. This compared to over $44,000 (11.9 million yen) per employee for Honda in 1975, as shown in Exhibit 5. This Japanese cost advantage was based on volume output, rather than government support or labor rate differentials. In fact, the Japanese labor costs had surpassed British labor costs in 1975 by nearly 30 per cent. The dramatic difference in output can be seen in Exhibit 6. This certainly hurt British production effectiveness and left only raw materials as a way to cut costs. With the contraction of selling and distribution activity, these expenses remained a rather constant percentage of sales.

Product Design

NVT's engineering staff numbered about 100. Most were detailers and draftsmen with little concern for low-cost production. In fact, designs tended to

EXHIBIT 6: The British Motorcycle Industry British versus Japanese Production (Motorcycles and Mopeds)

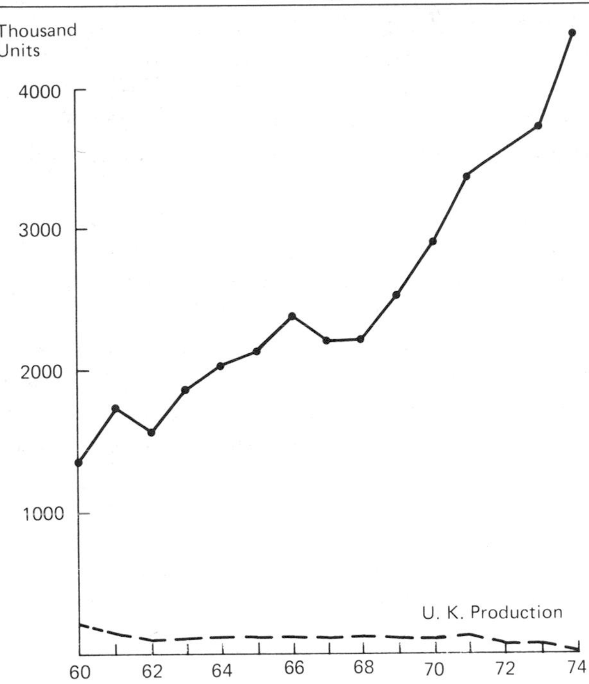

Source: Japan Automobile Industry Association.

include nonstandard fixtures that required special machining and added cost. The Trident had been designed to use existing equipment, making it a high-cost machine. The engine design, causing the crankcase and cylinder block to meet at a "T," virtually guaranteed an oil leak. None of the existing motorcycle designs had been considered for high-volume production techniques.

With regards to design, British motorcycles did have better handling than competition. Their appearance and styling had also been very effective. However, the design function had not been linked to the cost requirements of marketing or production.

New model developments included the Cosworth (P86), Wankel, and "Safety Bike." The Cosworth (P86) was under joint development of Cosworth Engineering and NVT using a 750 cc Formula 1 racing engine. There was hope that its racing success would continue at NVT if it could prove reliable service. Whereas NVT had several air-cooled, rotary Wankel engines in operation, there were questions as to whether this new, lightweight engine would be accepted in the traditional market. Although the Wankel could be put into production cheaply, it still had some technical and pollution problems. British producers were also involved in developing a safe bike for the U.S. government. However, safety in bikes was not considered an important selling feature.

British Production

NVT was the result of mergers and acquisitions during the 1960s and 1970s. The closing of Norton Villier's Woolwich and Andover plants and BSA/Triumph's Redditch plant had been unsettling. The threatened closure of the Meriden plant resulted in the workers' occupation of the factory in 1973. Continued reorganization had dissipated any potential for experience-based cost reductions. Complete motorcycle assembly had been carried out at the Wolverhampton plant only since 1972, and operations had yet to become functionally specialized as in Japanese plants.

Current employment in the British motorcycle industry was about 4,000 employees. As shown in Exhibit 7, about 800 of these were in subcontracted engineering (Small Heath) and industrial engines (Wolverhampton) rather than motorcycles. Factory buildings were pre-World War I and lacked efficient working conditions. Small Heath was a multilevel building, and Wolverhampton was a confused, multibuilding site. Morale at both these plants was low, since few expected them to survive. Morale at Meriden seemed high, but was probably the result, at least in part, of the success of the employee's occupation two years earlier.

The factories were labor intensive with over 80 per cent of Wolverhampton's equipment being more than 15 years old. The general-purpose equipment was not capable of producing close tolerances or high volumes. Since workpieces were moved between a large number of machine tools, each performing a sepa-

EXHIBIT 7: The British Motorcycle Industry

Factories		*Employees*	*'000 Square Feet*
Wolverhampton:	Motorcycles	1,115	—
	Industrial Engines	447	—
	Total	1,562	480
Small Heath:	Motorcycles	1,245	—
	Subcontract	330	—
	Total	1,575	1,000
Meriden (Plan):	Motorcycles only	590	350
Other Departments			
Engineering Staff Wolverhampton and Kitts Green)		110	
Norton Triumph International (Marketing, etc.)		87	
Norton Triumph Europe (Andover)		55	
Villiers engines Limited (Industrial Engines)		35	
Group HQ (Allocation)		5	
		292	
Total U.K. E	Total U.K. Employees	4,000 (approx.)	

rate operation, it was difficult to restrict the number of inaccuracies that crept into the products. Investments of $3,120 per employee compared to $12,000 for Honda. Plans to automate Small Heath operations had been scrapped years ago when volume declined. The three rotary index tables at Small Heath and Meriden were seldom used.

The Japanese commitment to high-volume models and advanced production engineering was absent in Britain. The British did not use automated high-pressure die casting at the metal-forming stage, which saved 20 to 40 per cent over gravity methods. This process was believed to produce castings of dubious strength and porosity, even though Honda used it exclusively to fabricate crankcases and cylinder blocks. However, the process also required that about 50,000 units be manufactured per year in order to be economical. The British lacked the experience and technical know-how to take advantage of the process.

Pressure die castings also created precision parts. This resulted in savings in the machine process, taking less time and equipment, as well as saving material. The British also trailed in other techniques, such as sintering, which reduced waste and machining of gears, sprockets, and other forged parts. Honda used rotary index and in-line transfer machines to manufacture its less popular models of only 70,000 units. In addition, nearly 10 per cent of Honda's employees (1,400) were engineers working on machine tool design or production engineering. Automated machinery methods also improved Honda's product quality. Tolerances could be controlled for all holes, bores, faces, and their relative positions. General-purpose machines lacked such reliability.

Parts Supply

Purchased materials and components accounted for about half of the factory cost of a bike. Unfortunately, NVT's low production volumes did not allow suppliers to use the best or lowest cost technology. In addition, NVT was a relatively small customer for auto industry suppliers such as Dunlop, Girling, Lucas, or Smiths. As a result, NVT stood behind British Leyland or Ford for service. Less service meant that new product lead times would be longer, and investments in production equipment would be slow.

NVT was also a supplier of industrial engines and subcontract engineering. Industrial engines and parts reached $6 million in 1975 with engineering contracts reaching $3.6 million. These activities approached one-third of the volume for Wolverhampton and Small Heath facilities and generated some profits.

As in motorcycles, NVT had withdrawn into the high-quality, long-life engine segment away from Briggs and Stratton's "throw-away" variety. Compared to the U.S. giants, Briggs and Stratton's production of 8 million units per year, NVT produced 40,000 to 50,000 units per year and employed about 500 people in this area. At a growth rate of 5 to 10 per cent per year, it was felt that NVT could maintain its present market share and obtain some experience curve cost reductions.

Small Heath's engineering subcontract work was highly competitive with low margins. This business also required specialized equipment to be used for relatively rare projects. In addition, the business often got confused with the requirements of motorcycle operations.

BRITISH MARKETING PHILOSOPHY

The British appeared to be most concerned with the profitability of each of their models. It was expected that each model would yield a profit over its cost throughout its life cycle. With this as their primary goal, the British carried out the following policies:

1. Products were uprated or withdrawn whenever the accounting system showed them to be unprofitable.
2. Prices were set at levels that guaranteed a profit.
3. The costs of marketing were only acceptable in established markets that were profitable. New markets were developed only if front-end costs were low.
4. Objectives and plans were directed toward the profitability of current operations rather than long-term industry strength.

The question now was, "How far would these policies carry them in today's market?"

CASE TWENTY-TWO

Group Lotus Car Companies Ltd.

R. JEFFERY ELLIS
Boston College

Assignment Questions:

1. How has Lotus Car Company's strategy changed since 1960? Why has it changed?
2. What was critical for success in this industry by 1980?
3. What future strategic alternatives exist for Lotus? What should Mr. Chapman do next?

Group Lotus Car Companies were famous throughout the world for its road cars and for seven world Formula One Championships (1963, 1965, 1968, 1970, 1972, 1973 and 1978). The road car manufacturing company was one of only a few independent specialist car manufacturers in Europe. Success for such companies was rare:

> In Britain alone it has been calculated that over 40 specialist manufacturers have appeared since the war and then driven into obscurity. The successes are few—Lotus, and Rolls Royce. (1)

In the 1970's the auto industry had suffered many setbacks and the specialist high performance manufacturers had been particularly affected. All over Europe these manufacturers had had difficulties. For example, Maserati had been acquired by Citroen, Alpine by Renault and Ferrari by Fiat. In 1975 Maserati was sold to the Italian State Industrial Recovery Agency for a token fee of about $200.

From early beginnings in hill climbing events in the 1950s, Group Lotus had grown in 1979 to a producer of high performance, luxury cars with sales of nearly £15 million and profit (before an extraordinary item) of £635,000. The Lotus Turbo Esprit, for example, offered its drivers sumptuous comfort, a top speed of more than 150 mph, impeccable roadholding, 0–60 mph in 5.5 seconds, a standing quarter mile in 14.4 seconds (98 mph) and fuel economy of almost 30 mpg at 55 mph. In 1980, however, the company's position did not look so bright. The beginnings of the world recession brought on by the

1979/1980 oil price increases, the consequences of tight money supply policies in the United Kingdom, the exceptionally high value of the pound sterling which raised prices to export markets and major government subsidy of other car companies in Britain and elsewhere caused a plunge in the number of cars manufactured.

In 1980 the volume of cars produced by Lotus fell by 63 percent and the value of cars produced by Lotus fell by 49 percent. Many did not expect the economic conditions to recover to the comparitively bullish atmosphere of the 1970s for some time to come. Prolonged low demand as most of the world's major economies sought expansion with deflation could be severe for the company. This case study presents the development of the Lotus Car Company from its early days to the present.

THE LOTUS MARQUE

Lotus has been prominent on the world's Formula I racing circuit for more than two decades and was well known for the distinctive black and gold "John Player Special" livery. Lotus had been known for its sports road cars, first in Britain and then through most of the world, since the late 1950s. The earliest product was very simple but today the Lotus marque included some of the most luxurious, highest performance and exotic road cars.

Lotus Seven

The Seven was introduced in 1957 and was the first Lotus road car available to the ordinary motorist. The Marque was already famous for performance and roadholding since Lotus racing cars had been almost invincible in the small, enthusiast 1172 c.c. Formula hill climbing events for two years.

The overall design concept of the Seven was spartan in the extreme. There was no provision in this car for doors, luggage space, or elbows, and the seat was made of wood slats. This car was just about the closest thing to a racing car that could be driven legally on public roads. The Lotus Seven was an immediate commercial success and, with modifications, was still being manufactured in the 1980s by Caterham Cars limited as the "Caterham Seven." The primitive but powerful design made possible a top speed of more than 100 mph and 0–50 mph in 6.4 seconds (1961 model).

One major reason for the success of the Lotus Seven was its exploitation of a tax loophole. At that time a "kit car" could be sold in Britain without the imposition of a substantial car purchase tax that had to be paid by buyers of already constructed automobiles:

> The Seven presented excellent value for money to the enthusiast who could build this high performance car for himself at just over £500 [$1,400]* in 1957. If however, he was lazy and could afford it, the little open two seater could be purchased complete for £690 [$1,932] to which, unfortunately, Purchase Tax had to be added making the total rather formidable at £1036 [$2,900]. (2)

*The British pound sterling (£) is converted to U.S. dollars at the rate holding at the time of the example which is discussed (for example £1.00 approximately equalled $2.80 in 1957).

Thus a high performance very exciting sports car could be bought for much the same price as a small family car so long as the buyer assembled the car himself.

The Elite and Elan

The Elite joined the Seven in 1959 and was the company's front runner until it was replaced by its derivative, the Elan, in 1962. Both cars were strictly 2-seaters until the Elan +2* was introduced in 1967. In addition to the legendary Lotus performance these two cars offered elegance and luxury. The Elan, for example, had electric windows, cigar lighters, and other amenities as standard equipment as well as a long list of mechanical "goodies" from twin carburetors and disc brakes on all wheels to twin tone horns. All these cars could only be bought from Lotus in kit form.

A conspicuous feature of these cars was the highly streamlined and distinctive body shape which was made possible by the use of fiberglass (the Seven used aluminum panels to provide mudguards and a cover for the engine). The Elite was the first car in the world to be constructed of this material. The use of fiberglass presented many technical problems which A.C.B. Chapman, the acclaimed automotive engineer and founder of the Lotus Company, grappled with for some time before the material could be used for the Elite body.

The disadvantages of fiberglass relative to pressed steel were considerable:

- high material cost.
- high volume production was uneconomical and impractical.
- metal parts could not be fixed to fiberglass.
- an extensive steel chassis had to be incorporated to support the entire car (such a chassis was unnecessary in most automobiles where a much lower cost unitary pressed steel body could be used).

Among the many advantages that fiberglass presented relative to pressed steel were:

- low weight which was essential for a small-engined, relatively low priced, high performance car.
- low tooling costs.
- low breakeven volume.
- the ability to make changes to the body shape quickly and inexpensively.
- no reliance on monopsonistic supply**

Overall the use of fiberglass provided the Lotus sports car with a distinctive performance and a distinctive appearance despite the technical and commercial difficulties associated with its use.

The engineering of the Elite and the Elan relied heavily on the Lotus racing traditions using the most advanced understanding of aerodynamics, breaking, suspension, engine performance and other considerations conceived, tested and "perfected" on the race track. For example, the Lotus Formula 2 racing car (the Lotus company had now graduated to Formula 2 racing) provided the design of the brakes and the suspension system. The suspension system used the now fa-

* The +2 designation refers to "plus two" seats.

** There was effectively a monopoly in the supply of pressed steel automobiles in Britain and the supplier [Pressed Steel Fisher] was said by many to be interested only in high volume production of standard autobodies such as bought only by the world's largest automobile manufacturing companies.

mous "Chapman Strut" which was later adopted by most automobile manufacturers.

Because of the links with motor racing and for other reasons many of the large suppliers of specialized automobile parts were happy to cooperate with Lotus in supplying critical, purpose designed components for Lotus road cars. For example the Firestone Tire Company was happy to design and supply a tire specifically suited for the unusually low weight of 60kg (0.55 ton) for the Elan in 1964, together with the high speeds of up to 120 mph, exceptional acceleration of 0–50 mph in 6.5 seconds, and the rapid braking and dramatic cornering through which Lotus owners enjoyed pacing their cars.

Indeed, the Elan was largely constructed of parts supplied by other motor manufacturers and automobile component manufacturers. For example, the engine in the Elan was a bored-out Ford 1500c.c. Triumph (now part of Britain's Leyland Motors) was also a major supplier of some parts and other manufacturers provided specialized components such as radiators and ball bearing races. Many of these items and components were modified for use in Lotus cars to reduce weight or boost performance and were Lotus branded.

New Products and Upgraded Models

The Europa. The Europa was a mid-engined two seat sports car with a fiberglass body introduced in 1967 but upgraded in 1971 to the Europa Twin Cam.

With perfectly equal weight distribution on all four wheels and the traditional high performance, low weight configuration of other Lotus cars, the Europa provided even higher standards of performance and comfort than the previous Lotus cars with a top speed of 125 mph and 0–50 mph in 4.8 seconds for the 1973–74 Europa Special.

The Sprint and +2S130. Upgraded versions of the Elan and Elan +2 were introduced around 1970. The Elan Sprint was an improvement of the Elan introduced in the early 1960s and the Lotus +2S130 was an improvement of the Elan +2 introduced in the middle 1960s. An important distinction between these new models and the previous models was that they were only available in fully built form and not as kit cars. The introduction of the Europa and the upgraded Elan and Elan +2 helped to counter the impact of the termination of the tax advantages for kit cars. After January, 1973 the same value added tax and special car tax applied equally to kit cars and to fully built cars. Lotus stopped supplying kits in 1972.

Two Liter Engine. Lotus introduced a two-liter engine in 1972. This was the first engine manufactured entirely by the company which did not rely on parts supplied by other firms. It was not only outstanding for its performance but also met stringent pollution standards, being the first engine without cumbersome and impractical cleaning appendages from any manufacturer in the world to be awarded the United States Emission Certificate for a "clean air package" (1973).

This two-liter engine was used in all Lotus automobiles from the early 1970s and was supplied to other motor manufacturers. It was supplied first to Jensen-Healey (an independent motor manufacturer) for use in a high performance sports car. After Jensen folded in 1975, sales agreements with other manufacturers, including Chrysler of Europe (now part of Peugeot), were arranged for small quantities.

Overseas Sales. With the growing international reputation of Lotus cars, overseas sales had increased. In 1971 60 per cent of total car sales were made in the United Kingdom, 30 per cent in North America and 10 per cent in the rest of the world. The commitment to reducing dependence on the home market in Britain was exemplified by the introduction of the Europa, Elan Sprint, and Lotus +2S130 in the United States before Britain, by the naming of "The Europa," and by the introduction of that wholly new car in the national markets on the continent of Europe before its introduction to Britain.

Some Problems for the 1970s

The 1970s were to bring about a series of shocks to the auto industry and to specialized automobile manufacturers in particular. As well as the closing of the home market tax loophole for kit cars discussed above, Lotus was affected by: the legislated move to pollution free engines in the United States; the passing of stringent safety legislation for automobiles in the United States; complicated difficulties in the supply of components in the United Kingdom; suddenly high energy costs and some shortages of auto fuel in the industrial world; and a general increase in road congestion together with the imposition of low speed limits in almost all countries.

United States Safety Legislation. The United States safety regulations following publication of Ralph Nader's book "Unsafe at Any Speed" threatened the ability of Lotus to sell to the crucial American market which constituted about 30 percent of sales. Continued sales to the United States were essential to the survival of the company and adapting the proportion of manufactured cars destined for the United States in order to meet specifically the American legislation was deemed impractical and uneconomic because of the very small volumes of cars that would be involved. Cars would have to be manufactured to a universal standard applicable to all the markets essential to the survival of Lotus.

In some ways the consequences of the legislation were worse for small high performance cars because of their capability for high speeds, the complexity and density of their layouts and the need to keep weight to a minimum. This last factor was of fundamental importance to Lotus in particular in order to maintain their characteristic performance and handling. Problems were perhaps aggravated further for Lotus because it was felt that many Americans considered a light car such as a Lotus car to be inherently unsafe. But most critical to the future of Lotus was that it was technically impossible at that time to manufacture fiberglass bodies so that they could withstand the impact collision regulations of the United States.

Supply Difficulties. Increasing labor unrest in the British Automobile Industry except for Lotus and some other specialist car manufacturers resulted in many damaging strikes in the 1970s. These stoppages and strikes had the unfortunate effect of frustrating supplies of key components. The company had to hold contingent stocks and duplicate sources of supply, thereby increasing the unit cost of components. On some occasions the production of Lotus cars was brought to a standstill by a continuing strike at a component supplier. Lotus built cars extensively from parts bought from other companies and the company was therefore unusually vulnerable to problems of this sort.

The company's position was further worsened in the early 1970s because many of the parts that were used in the Elans and the Europa were no longer used by the large manufacturers from which they were purchased. For example, the engine block which was bought from Ford was still available but since it was no longer used by Ford its continued availability was in doubt. Supplies of all essential items were still available in the early 1970s but were becoming more difficult and more expensive. From 1970 onwards general cost inflation on supplies and direct labor, too, had become a major problem for Lotus and for the auto industry more generally.

Energy Problems. At the beginning of 1974 the Western World was subjected to massive increases in the price of fuel oil resulting in a near doubling of the retail price of automobile fuel in most of Europe. This development led to a collapse in the sales of larger and less economical cars by some 50 percent in the immediately subsequent years and overall sales of automobiles showed declines of 40 percent from 1972 levels in most European markets. Lotus' Europa, Elan, and Elan +2 range of cars on the market at that time faced a relatively disadvantageous position by offering expensive motoring of a largely non-practical character, but not to the very high price luxury market where running costs may be inconsequential.

In addition, the United Kingdom faced a particular industrial energy crisis in the early part of 1974 as a result of a coal miners' strike. Under government legislation manufacturers were only permitted to continue operations for three days out of every week. Lotus was the first company in the country to receive government permission for exemption from the three day week but the dramatic loss in the production of the companies that supplied Lotus with components resulted in a protracted shortage of many key components.

The increase in the cost of fuel oil in 1974 also precipitated a sudden and severe surge in the cost of all forms of energy, components, raw materials, and ultimately, labor. Lotus was particularly affected by the increase in oil prices because the fiberglass resin from which the bodies of Lotus cars were manufactured was a derivative of fuel oil. Similarly, Lotus was particularly affected by the uncertainties of supply because of its exceptional dependence on outside manufacturers.

To remain profitable at lower levels of production nearly half of the labor force were let go in 1974. The total number of employees in the company was reduced from about 800 to 429 by the end of that year. Management reported, however, that because of the company's policies on labor relations and their open management style the dismissals were executed without great bitterness or opposition from the work force. It was also necessary to bring inventories into line with new production levels and to achieve this the company went so far as turning around their suppliers' trucks and refusing to take delivery of goods.

Congestion and Lower Speed Limits. Increasing congestion on the roads throughout most of the industrialized world was compromising the sheer fun of driving a sports car. Speed restrictions were becoming widespread on all roads in almost all the markets in which Lotus cars were sold, making high speed and high performance road driving practically impossible. These circumstances were expected to dampen demand for cars which offered the kinds of features for which Lotus cars were famous.

Finance

Comparative results for 1968 to 1980 are given in Exhibits 1 and 2. Until 1968 Lotus operated as a private company legally exempted from declaring its financial performance but it is popularly acknowledged that the company's founder had no significant capital at its inception. In 1968 the company went public with its shares quoted on the London Stock Exchange. With 7,500,000 shares of 10p each authorized, about 5,750,000 shares were issued and have not changed significantly. Chapman (with family interests) had until about 1974 or 1975 owned over 50 percent of the quoted shares. This had prevented the firm from being bought out. In 1980 Chapman owned approximately 460,000 shares and other directors owned a total of nearly 250,000 shares. A policy of high dividend payouts was maintained until 1975:

	1970	*1971*	*1972*	*1973*	*1974*	*1975*	*1976*	*1977*	*1978*	*1979*	*1980*
Dividends/ After Tax Profit	60%	54%	30%	37%	87%	—	—	—	12%	—	5%

In 1968 an agreement was struck between Group Lotus Car Companies Limited and Team Lotus Limited where amounts could be advanced from Group Lotus to Team Lotus. Eighty two and a half percent of the issued share capital was held by directors of Group Lotus. For example, a charge of £75,000 was made to Group Lotus for Team Lotus in 1976 for which no interest was charged. Similar arrangements were also made for other companies. "Amounts due from companies controlled by directors" constituted £142,000 in 1979 and £87,000 in 1980 (see Exhibit 3). The consolidated accounts refered to the whole corporate group.

The Company entered a profit throughout its public history except for a loss of more than $1 million for the year 1975. Commenting on this loss Mr. Chapman stated:

> During 1975 the company concentrated its efforts on completing development and preparing for production of the Lotus Eclat and Esprit. Following the presentation of these new models in October the Eclat was in production in December and the Esprit in June, 1976. . . . Financially the Company's sales suffered a £3,000,000 reduction from a one model range [the Elite] and the loss of engine sales following the financial failure of its engine customer [Jensen]. . . .

In 1976, £110,000 of the £127,000 after tax profit was due to the extraordinary item of a sale and leaseback agreement of plant and machinery at the Hethel site.

The company was substantially refinanced in 1976. The American Express International Banking Corporation (AEIBC) agreed to a six-year loan to Lotus of £2,000,000 (almost $5,000,000) and an overdraft privilege of £600,000 (almost $1,500,000) freeing the company of dependence on previous overdraft facilities. The loan was secured by the company's fixed assets. Chapman, the di-

EXHIBIT 1: Group Lotus Car Companies Limited Comparative Operating Results (1968–1975)

		1968 *£'000's*		*1969* *£'000's*		*1970* *£'000's*
OPERATING:						
Lotus Cars Produced	3,048		4,506		3,373	
Total Employees—Average for year	618		865		684	
Group Turnover		4,443		5,285		4,932
EMPLOYMENT OF FUNDS:						
Fixed Assets		802		943		1,106
Net Current Assets plus Development		298		221		146
Total Net Assets		1,100		1,164		1,252
SOURCE OF FUNDS:						
Ordinary Shareholders Interest (Net Worth)		701		772		870
Deferred Taxation		99		92		82
Secured Loans		300		300		300
Capital Employed		1,100		1,164		1,252
PROFITS AND RATIOS:						
Group Pre-Tax Profits		731		607		322
Profit on Net Worth	104.0%		79.0%		37.0%	
Profit on Turnover	16.5%		11.5%		6.5%	
Development Written off		121		160		149
Depreciation		55		90		89
Retained Earnings		209		84		77
TOTAL REVENUE CASH FLOW		385		334		315

rectors and members of their families held 50.17 percent of the voting stock at that time, and irrevocably agreed to the terms of the AEIBC loan. As part of the deal the AEIBC have an option to purchase ordinary shares of the Lotus Company.

It was always the policy of the company to treat development expenditure as a capital asset on the balance sheet with the expenditure selectively written off against the profit and loss account as shown in Exhibit 4 and 5. No capital reserve was made by the company. In 1980, for example, £735,000 was recorded in the balance sheet for development expenditure. In that year development expenditure was £700,000 and £160,000 was written off as a charge on the profit and loss account according to normal company policy. An additional amount of £1,200,000 for prior development expenditures was also written off as an exceptional item in that period.

1971		*1972*		*1973*		*1974*		*1975*	
£'000's		*£'000's*		*£'000's*		*£'000's*		*£'000's*	
2,682		2,996		2,822		1,447		535	
654	4,456	726	5,953	787	7,344	696	7,504	385	4,003
	1,189		1,559		2,602		2,689		2,658
	359		685		1,120		1,482		311
	1,548		2,244		3,722		4,171		2,969
	1,099		1,608		2,597		2,630		2,026
	149		312		799		1,164		564
	300		326		326		377		379
	1,548		2,244		3,722		4,171		2,969
	736		1,127		1,156		294		(1,238)
67.0%		70.0%		44.5%		11.2%		—	
16.5%		19.0%		15.7%		3.9%		—	
	72		184		180		222		914
	67		89		85		103		127
	204		483		314		17		(604)
	343		756		579		342		437

Management

The managerial relationships at Lotus were closely defined (see Exhibit 6) but the overall management style was open and casual. The impression on entering the air conditioned offices on the factory floor was one of quiet and informal diligence. Offices were open plan in concept with senior management positioned at various points on the floor area as determined by efficient work practices. There was a small office lounge which office staff could use at will situated at the edge of the floor near to the door connecting the offices to the factory.

As the size and complexity of the firm grew, management controls became necessary and a management-by-objectives system, integrated with a corporate planning system, was introduced in 1971. Following requests from managers, at

EXHIBIT 2: Group Lotus Car Companies Limited Comparative Operating Results (1976–1980)

		1976 £'000's		*1977 £'000's*		*1978 £'000's*		*1979 £'000's*		*1980 £'000's*
OPERATING:										
Lotus Cars Produced	940		1,070		1,200		1,031		383	
Total Employees—Average for year	479		479		518		682		613	
Group Turnover including Engineering Activity		5,635		8,171		9,357		14,943		14,280
EMPLOYMENT OF FUNDS:										
Fixed Assets		2,972		2,878		3,391		3,639		4,490
Net Current Assets plus Development		233		2,276		2,232		2,357		1,261
Total Net Assets		3,205		5,154		5,623		5,996		5,751
SOURCE OF FUNDS:										
Ordinary Shareholders Interest (Net Worth)		2,153		2,319		2,621		2,977		5,007
Deferred Taxation		683		965		1,344		1,830		—
Secured Loans		369		1,870		1,659		1,189		744
Capital Employed		3,205		5,154		5,624		5,996		5,751
PROFITS AND RATIOS:										
Group Pre-Tax Trading Profits		17		557		716		1,283		461
Profit on Net Worth	0.8%		24.0%		27.3%		43.1%		9.2%	
Profit on Turnover	0.3%		6.8%		7.7%		8.6%		3.2%	

EXHIBIT 3: Group Lotus Car Companies Limited

Notes to the Accounts

1. ACCOUNTING POLICIES

Basis of Preparation.
The accounts have been prepared under the historical cost convention as supplemented by the revaluation of freehold properties. Comparative figures for the period ended 28th December 1979 are shown in blue.

Depreciation
Depreciation of the cost or value of fixed assets is provided on a straight line basis so as to write them off over their estimated useful lives as follows:

Freehold Building:	50 years
Leasehold land and buildings:	period of lease
Plant and machinery:	10 years
Aircraft and motor vehicles:	5 years
Furniture and equipment:	4 to 10 years
Tooling (including tooling held by suppliers):	3 to 5 years

Development expenditure
Development expenditure carried forward relates to expenditure (comprising materials, labour and related overheads) on new models and engines and major variations thereto. This is written off at a specified amount for each unit produced, calculated by reference to anticipated production in the 5 years following the introduction of the new model or major variation. Development expenditure on continuous engineering and minor variations to models is written off as incurred.

Stock
Stock is valued at lower of cost (including related manufacturing overheads) and net realisable value.

Deferred taxation
Taxation deferred as a result of material timing differences is provided at the rate of taxation applicable at the current year end ("the liability method") except to the extent that there is reasonable probability that the liability will not arise in the foreseeable future.

Foreign currency translation
Assets and liabilities in foreign currencies are translated into sterling at the rates ruling at the balance sheet date.

Warranty provision
Provision is made for the estimated liability on all products under warranty in addition to claims already received.

2. TURNOVER

Turnover comprises invoiced sales to customers for goods and services and is net of commission paid to dealers and VAT.

EXHIBIT 3 (continued)

3. FIXED ASSETS CONSOLIDATED

Cost and Valuation	*Freehold Land and Buildings £'000's*	*Short Leasehold Land and Buildings £'000's*	*Plant Equipment etc. £'000's*	*Motor Vehicles and Aircraft £'000's*	*Tooling £'000's*	*Total £'000's*
At 28th December 1979						
valuation	2,050	—	—	—	—	2,050
at cost	32	159	1,146	837	882	3,056
Additions	48	91	128	510	75	852
Less Disposals	—	(4)	(17)	(560)	—	(581)
Revaluation surplus	895	—	—	—	—	895
At 2nd January 1981	3,025	246	1,257	787	957	6,272
Depreciation						
At 28th December 1979	68	63	581	188	567	1,467
Less Disposals	—	(4)	(4)	(113)	—	(121)
Charged for period	35	20	92	168	224	539
Revaluation Surplus	(103)	—	—	—	—	(103)
At 2nd January 1981	—	79	669	243	791	1,782
Net book value						
At 2nd January 1981	3,025	167	588	544	166	4,490
At 28th December 1979	2,014	96	565	649	315	3,639

FIXED ASSETS PARENT COMPANY

Cost and Valuation	*Freehold Land and Buildings £'000's*	*Short Leasehold Land and Buildings £'000's*	*Motor Vehicles and Aircraft £'000's*	*Plant Equipment etc. £'000's*	*Total £'000's*
At 28th December 1979					
valuation	2,050	—	—	—	2,050
at cost	32	155	427	70	684
Additions	48	91	19	1	159
Less Disposals	—	—	(156)	—	(156)
Revaluation surplus	895	—	—	—	895
At 2nd January, 1981	3,025	246	290	71	3,632
Depreciation					
At 28th December 1979	68	59	109	29	265
Less Disposals	—	—	(60)	—	(60)
Charge for period	35	20	79	11	145
Revaluation Surplus	(103)	—	—	—	(103)
At 2nd January 1981	—	79	128	40	247
Net book value					
At 2nd January 1981	3,025	167	162	31	3,385
At 28th December 1979	2,014	96	318	41	2,469

The freehold land and buildings of the Company were revalued as at 2nd January, 1981 on the basis of open market value in existing use by Percy Howes & Co., Chartered Surveyors as follows:

Freehold land	£460,000
Freehold buildings	2,565,000
	£3,025,000

EXHIBIT 3 (continued)

	Consolidated £'000's	*Parent Company* £'000's
Capital commitments		
Contracted	5	—
Authorised, not yet contracted	52	32

4. SUBSIDIARY COMPANIES

	£'000's	£'000's
Shares at cost, less amounts written off	—	—
Amounts due from Subsidiary companies	948	1,171
	948	1,171

All trading operations were carried on by Lotus Cars Limited. The other subsidiaries are Lotus North America (Holdings) Limited, Lotus North America Inc. and Lotus Engineering Company Limited. All subsidiaries are wholly owned by the Company and registered in the UK except for Lotus North America, Inc. which is registered in the U.S.A.

5. DEVELOPMENT EXPENDITURE, JANUARY 1981 (DECEMBER 1979)

Development expenditure in the period was £700,000 (£767,000) and the amount written off on the basis of the Group accounting policy during the period was £160,000 (£335,000); As explained in the Chairman's Statement an additional amount of £1,200,000 has been written off development expenditure and charged in the profit and loss accounts as an exceptional item. Continuous development expenditure incurred in the period of £180,000 (£210,000) was written off.

	Consolidated		*Parent Company*	
	£'000's	£'000's	£'000's	£'000's
6. CURRENT ASSETS				
Stock—note (a)	3,426	4,811	—	—
Amounts due from companies controlled by directors	87	142	—	—
Debtors	2,034	1,479	59	7
Cash at bank and in hand and on deposit	327	1,288	239	102
	5,874	7,720	298	109

6a. Stock may be analysed as follows:		
Finished stock including cars at dealers	1,421	2,280
Cars in course of production and raw materials	1,244	1,718
Service stocks etc.	761	813
	3,426	4,811

EXHIBIT 3 (continued)

	Consolidated		Parent Company	
	£'000's	£'000's	£'000's	£'000's
7. CURRENT LIABILITIES				
Creditors and provisions—note (a)	2,634	4,574	90	36
Deposits against stocks with dealers	684	1,722	—	—
Current taxation	18	18	18	18
Bank overdraft (£1,263,000 secured)	1,527	—	272	—
Secured loans (note 8)	444	444	444	444
Proposed Dividend	41	—	41	—
	5,348	6,758	865	498

7a. Warranty provision is £231,000 (£306,000).

8. SECURED LOANS £1,188,000

£888,000 repayable by 4 remaining consecutive installments, the next due on 19th March 1981 and balance half-yearly thereafter; interest at sterling deposit rate +3 per cent. During the term of the loan dividend payments except with the prior consent of the lending bank, must only be met out of current earnings and must be limited to an aggregate amount, including related tax credit, of not more than 12½% of the Company's issued ordinary share capital and consolidated reserves in any financial year.

Installments payable within twelve months are included in current liabilities.

£300,000 payable 1992, interest at 8½ per cent per annum.

9. DEFERRED TAXATION

The total amount of liabilities for deferred taxation which would arise if the Group's assets were sold at their book value as shown below:

	Consolidated		Parent Company	
	£'000's	£'000's	£'000's	£'000's
Provided in the accounts:				
Excess of net book value of assets over corresponding tax written down value	771	1,220	—	33
Stock appreciation relief	—	1,306	—	—
Short term timing differences	(120)	(70)	—	—
Capital Gains on re-valued properties and arising by way of roll over relief	—	270	—	253
Less: Relief for trading losses carried forward	(651)	(739)	—	—
Less: Advance Corporation tax recoverable	—	(157)	—	(17)
	—	1,830	—	269
Not provided for in the accounts:				
Stock appreciation relief	1,533	—	—	—
Capital Gains on re-valued properties and arising by way of roll over relief	539	—	521	—
Excess of tax written down value of				

EXHIBIT 3 (continued)

	Consolidated		Parent Company	
	£'000's	£'000's	£'000's	£'000's
assets over corresponding net book value	(52)	—	(52)	—
Industrial Buildings Allowances	355	314	355	314
Trading losses carried forward	(166)	—	—	—
Advance Corporation Tax recoverable	(175)	—	(35)	—
	2,034	314	789	314
	2,034	2,144	789	583

The tax credit of £236,000 based on the loss for the period has been restricted to the extent that the unutilised losses and ACT recoverable exceed the timing differences provided for in the accounts.

Stock relief has been calculated in accordance with the provisions of the Finance Act 1981. Because of the resulting change in the basis of taxation for stock relief it is no longer felt necessary to provide for deferred taxation in respect of stock relief and accordingly the provision of £1,306,000 at 28th December 1979 has been released in the period.

10. SHARE CAPITAL

Authorised—7,500,000 shares of 10p each	750	750	750	750
Issued—5,830,030 shares of 10p each, fully paid	583	583	583	583

11. RESERVES

	Consolidated		Parent Company	
	£'000's	£'000's	£'000's	£'000's
Distributable				
Undistributed profits at start of period	1,773	1,417	589	540
Undistributed profits/(losses) for period	762	356	(22)	49
Distributable profits at end of period	2,535	1,773	567	589
Undistributable				
Unrealised profits at start of period	585	585	585	585
Surplus on revaluation of freehold property in the period	998	—	998	—
Provision for capital gains tax transferred from deferred taxation account	270	—	253	—
Share premium	36	36	36	36
	1,889	621	1,872	621
Total reserves	4,424	2,394	2,439	1,210

12. DIRECTORS' REMUNERATION

(exclusive of pension contributions)

	£'000's	£'000's
Chairman	34	27

EXHIBIT 3 (continued)

	Number	*Number*
Other Directors		
Under £5,000	1	1
£20,001 to £25,000	—	1
£25,001 to £30,000	1	—

13. EARNINGS PER SHARE

The calculation of earnings per share is based on earnings after tax of £803,000 (£635,000) and issued share capital of 5,830,000 ordinary shares.

14. CONTINGENT LIABILITIES

Lotus Cars Limited is a defendant of various actions in respect of accidents in the U.S.A. involving Lotus cars. These claims in which Lotus Cars Limited will dispute liability are not fully covered by insurance. The Directors have little doubt but that, regardless of liability, these claims are excessive but insufficient evidence is available for them to form a precise view of the amount involved.

15. DIRECTORS INTERESTS IN TRANSACTIONS

The Group has engaged in transactions during the period with the following companies which A. C. Chapman and F. R. Bushell control or in which they hold more than 1/5 of the share capital:

Team Lotus International Limited
Hethel Properties Limited
Delamare Estates (Cheshunt) Limited
Technocraft Limited
Crystic System Limited
Ludham Plastics Engineering Limited

A summary of the transactions with the Group and the total amounts outstanding at the beginning and end of the year is as follows:

Net amount due from the companies at 29th December 1979	£136,253	
Sales of Cars	17,267	
Sundry expenses recharged by the group	113,645	
Sundry expenses recharged to the group		£43,290
Rental charged by the group	4,700	
Rental charged to the group		52,000
Net cash payments by the group	331,939	
Team Lotus support charge to the group		75,000
Purchases of specialist services by the group		327,960
Building repairs and maintenance charged to the group		46,020
Administration and other charges	27,052	
Net amount due from the companies at 2nd January 1981		86,570
	£630,856	£630,850

The maximum amount in aggregate outstanding during the year was £238,350.

In accordance with the arrangements envisaged in the Agreement dated 26th September 1968 between Group Lotus Car Companies Limited and Team Lotus Inter-

EXHIBIT 3 (continued)

national Limited amounts have been advanced to Team Lotus International Limited and indebtedness incurred by that company from Group Lotus Car Companies Limited in connection with the racing activities of Team Lotus International Limited from which the Group derives benefit and for which a charge of £75,000 was made for the period. Having regard to the benefits so derived no interest has been charged on the amounts due Team Lotus International Limited.

EXHIBIT 4: Group Lotus Car Companies Limited Consolidated Profit and Loss Account

		Fifty-Three Weeks Ended 2nd January 1981		*Fifty-Two Weeks Ended 28th December 1979*	
	Notes	*£'000's*	*£'000's*	*£'000's*	*£'000's*
Turnover:	2		14,280		14,943
Group Trading Profit before exceptional item, taxation and extraordinary item is arrived at after charging/(crediting)			461		1,283
Depreciation		539		406	
Development expenditure written off	1 & 5	160		335	
Leasing Rentals		23		204	
Directors' remuneration—including fees £2,000	11	65		55	
Auditors' remuneration		29		26	
Interest payable:					
Bank overdraft and other short term loans		196		148	
Long term loans (including £25,500 on loans repayable after 5 years)		251		284	
Net proceeds of accident insurances		(209)		—	
Surplus on disposal of other fixed assets		(11)		(31)	
Exceptional item—additional amount written off development expenditure	1 & 5		(1,200)		—
Group (Loss)/Profit after exceptional item, before taxation and extraordinary items			(739)		1,283
less Taxation:					
Transfer (from)/to deferred taxation account	9	(236)		648	
Exceptional Transfer from deferred taxation account	9	(1,306)	1,542	—	(648)
Group Profit after taxation before extraordinary item			803		635
Extraordinary item			—		(279)
Group Profit after extraordinary item includes Profit of £19,000 (1979 Profit £50,000) dealt with in the accounts of the Parent Company			803		356
less Proposed Dividend			41		—
Undistributed Profit for the period			762		356
Earnings per share	13		13.8p		10.9p

EXHIBIT 5: Group Lotus Car Companies Limited Consolidated Balance Sheet

	Notes	2nd January 1981 £'000's	2nd January 1981 £'000's	28th December 1979 £'000's	28th December 1979 £'000's
Fixed assets	3		4,490		3,639
Development expenditure	5		735		1,395
Current assets	6		5,874		7,720
			11,099		12,754
less					
Current liabilities	7	5,348		6,758	
Secured loans	8	744		1,189	
Deferred taxation	9	—	6,092	1,830	9,777
			5,007		2,977
Representing:					
Issued share capital	10		583		583
Reserves	11		4,424		2,394
			5,007		2,977

A C B Chapman
F R Bushell
Directors

Parent Company's Balance Sheet

	Notes	2nd January 1981 £'000's	2nd January 1981 £'000's	28th December 1979 £'000's	28th December 1979 £'000's
Fixed assets	3		3,385		2,469
Subsidiary companies	4		948		1,171
Current assets	6		298		109
			4,631		3,749
less					
Current liabilities	7	865		498	
Secured loans	8	744		1,189	
Deferred taxation	9	—	1,609	269	1,956
			3,022		1,793
Representing:					
Issued share capital	10		583		583
Reserves	11		2,439		1,210
			3,022		1,793

A C B Chapman
F R Bushell
Directors
2nd October 1981

EXHIBIT 6: Group Lotus Car Companies Limited Organization Chart

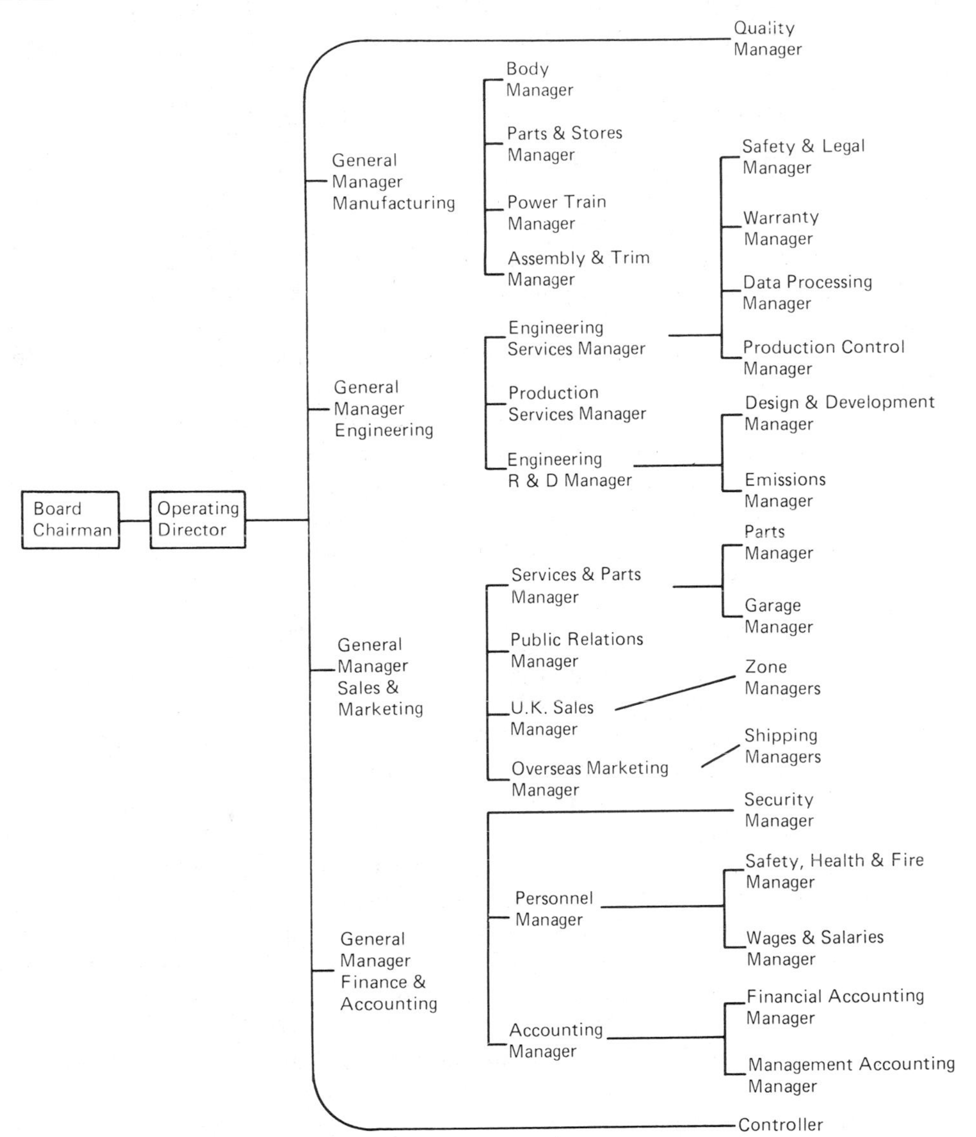

the end of 1972, a profit sharing scheme was introduced where a bonus was paid to managers. This bonus varied according to company profits and upon an individual manager's performance against a personal set of objectives as measured directly in terms of contribution on sales.

Product Development and Research and Development

Product development and research and development were major and continuous activities in the Group Lotus Car Companies. Winning world Formula I championships recognized persistent research and development with ideas being incorporated and tested month by month. The engineering of the Elite, Eclat, Esprit range demonstrated the capacity of the Lotus Company for product development and research and development in road cars. In particular, the new range necessitated the discovery of a wholly new manufacturing process, a challenge readily met by Colin Chapman and his team.

In the automobile industry it was usual for the decision to build a new car to be taken some five or more years before the car was brought to market. It took about three years for the new Elite, the first car in the range, to be introduced to the market place from the first decision to go ahead. The concept started with Chapman briefing the selected Italian design consultant and within two weeks sketches were available for consideration. It had already been decided to use the new 2-liter engine and to incorporate the customary fiberglass body. After the car reached the prototype stage it was shown to the dealers and the press for comment. Artists' impression of "The Coming Generation" were provided in the 1972 Annual Report to Stockholders.

Development proceeded apace with many engineers and draftsmen working "eight day weeks." Chairman Chapman played an important part in the decision making because of his experience and judgment of the market and products. Senior management played a continuously active part in supervising and controlling both the technical and the commercial aspects of the project.

Particularly critical to the development of a new range of cars that would meet the safety legislation of the United States was the need to incorporate structural strength into the fiberglass body. In the existing model range the fiberglass all but totally collapsed on impact because fiberglass does not have structural properties similar to steel. This was a very difficult problem for the engineers at Lotus because the two liter Lotus engine could not have provided much more than family car performance with a heavier steel body. Much of the fine automobile engineering developed by Lotus from experience on the race track as well as experience with their road cars assumed light bodies and high maneuverability and would have been of limited value for the building of a heavier car. But another important consideration was that the legendary Lotus performance admired by all owners was distinguished from other high performance cars by the exceptionally high power to weight ratio together with the intrinsic lightness of the car.

The need to embody structural strength in the automobile body was the death knell for the Marcos car company, which had used wood for their cars but Chapman and the management of Lotus Car Company were determined to find a way of using fiberglass that would give the automobile body structural strength. Technically the need was to find a way of introducing differential thickness in the fiberglass so that the body would have a planned pattern of stresses to direct impacts to reinforced body sections. Mr. T. Enright, one of the directors of the company, described how Chapman had discovered what was termed the "resinject process" that enabled the company to manufacture bodies that satisfied the collision safety legislation:

> One night Mr. Chapman could not sleep for thinking through the problems of producing a fiberglass body with the necessary structural properties. Eventually, he left his bed and drove to the factory where he set about a series of experiments and trials to test and develop his ideas. There, on his own in the middle of the night, the resinject process was born. The process involved the production of whole fiberglass bodies in a mold.

Previously, fiberglass bodies largely were manufactured by layering the material on a male mold until the necessary thickness was achieved. The surface of the fiberglass was then finished off and paint applied. The resinject process reduced the number of tools required for manufacture from twenty to just two. It also required a shorter manufacturing time, produced at constant quality and had the capability to make self colored bodies. The cost savings relative to the old method were said by management to be enormous. Theoretically there was no limit to the size or shape of structures that could be made by the process. Management believed that with this revolutionary process the company was the world leader in fiberglass technology and bettered the quality and cost of the back street manufacturers which constituted most of the industry.

Thus it was that the Lotus management were prepared to meet the collision safety legislation of the United States. However, the new Elite failed on its first testing for technical reasons. To measure collision damage to the roof, cars were catapulted to about thirty miles per hour into a large water bath. The rapid deceleration on the nose caused the cars being tested to spin over onto a concrete surface and roll over several times. The damage to the roof was then assessed. The Lotus Elite did not, however, roll over because of the car's exceptional stability. Instead, the car slid into the bath of water and then "teased" the testing method further by refusing to sink in the water as other cars would have done. The fiberglass body was completely watertight. Eventually a way was found to roll the car and the Lotus Elite, therefore, passed this test as well as the others required by United States safety legislation.

A Product Line for the '70s

Between the spring of 1974 and the summer of 1975 the whole Lotus product line was discontinued and replaced by an entirely new line of cars, the new Elite, Esprit, and Eclat. The development costs of this range approximated £1.5 million.

A *Fortune* article summed up the product range change on which work had begun in 1971 in this way:

> With survival in mind, Lotus's chairman and founder, Colin Chapman, dramatically decided to bet the shop when he scrapped his entire product line in the middle of the 1975 economic slump. Though at the time the Lotus position was not an unstable one, Chapman realized that his small, light cars were not designed to carry the cumbersome safety equipment that the government wanted hung on them.

> His only hope was to produce a new car that would meet the laws rather than artfully dodge them with cobbled-up versions of present designs. (3)

The monthly production of Lotus cars from 1973 through 1975 illustrates the scale and suddenness of the transition that the company accomplished over this period.

	J	*F*	*M*	*A*	*M*	*J*	*J*	*A*	*S*	*O*	*N*	*D*
1973												
All Cars	321	264	273	187	292	234	154	209	245	220	220	211
1974												
All Cars	127	104	162	160	156	151	149	102	106	99	92	58
1975												
All Cars	61	64	72	*	60	45	48	28	48	36	63	72

* Unavailable.

Source: Society of Motor Manufacturers and Traders, London.

The new Elite, a four seat luxury car headed the range and was introduced first. Later the Eclat was added which was also a four seat car but with a "fast back" body design, less luxurious appointments, and a lower price than the Elite. The range was completed by the Esprit which was a very fast, very luxurious, two seat sports car. All cars used the same two-liter engine and had many common parts and components; for example, the lower body mold was the same for all cars.

The Elite was obviously of "Lotus Pedigree" being high powered with low weight,exceptional handling and luxurious appointments.It was a full four seater and represented a dramatic up-market move by Lotus to a retail price of well over £6,000 ($13,000) compared with their previous "flagship" the Elan +2S130 at a price of just over £3,000. The boldness of this move by Lotus, particularly in the spring of 1974 with its gasoline lines and general uncertainties, was noted by many. Patrick Sargeant, a financial journalist, commented: "The gamble Lotus is taking on producing a new car would have been large enough even without the added burden of acute component shortages and a gasoline problem." (4)

But Chapman and the Lotus senior management had taken the trouble to design a car that was apparently right for the times as amplified by its sales literature:

> The Lotus Elite is the only luxury four seater that gives ultimate performance with true economy. Energy will never be cheap again. Tomorrow's car must run on lower octane fuel. Tomorrow's car must not pollute the world's shrinking atmosphere. Tomorrow's car will be small on engine, big on performance, light on materials, strong on safety. Will carry four people and luggage in luxury and absolute safety. Tomorrow's car must have optimum performance and perfect road-handling. Energy conserving low drag lines. Light weight, safety proved, fiberglass construction. A totally new motoring concept. Designed for tomorrow.

The motoring press almost unanimously endorsed the excellence of the Elite as illustrated by the following:

> So highly do we regard this superb car in its latest form that all members of the test team were duty bound to sample it in order to renew the standards by which

they must now judge rivals, some of them very much more expensive than the Lotus. (5)

The enthusiasm of the non-motoring press was, however, more tempered. As the Motoring Correspondent of the *Times* (London) pointed out, Lotus was then competing with the Jaguars, Ferraris and Maseratis and selling to the 40-year-old company director. He claimed that it was difficult for a 6′0″ (1.8m) person to sit in the rear seat without his head butting against the roof. He also noted the difference between a Jaguar's smooth pull away from 30 m.p.h. (50 k.p.h.) in top gear and the relative hesitation of a Lotus engine performing the same task. Further, the nonspecialist motoring press drew attention to the small luggage space. Comparisons of the Elite with some of its competitors is provided in Exhibit 7.

The new car reduced the company's dependence on outside suppliers. Richard Morley the Managing Director stated that Lotus now made 95 percent of the parts of the cars themselves and that only tires, glass, and electrical instruments were bought outside. (6) Although many felt this to be something of an overstatement, in-house manufacture of components was extensive, even automobile air conditioners being self-manufactured. Becoming independent of suppliers was a critical need in the middle 1970's. While at one time major manufacturers had been only too pleased to supply components and help out with engineering advice, most suppliers were now far too occupied with their own cash problems to become involved in low volume and low priority activities. Also making parts internally permitted higher quality designs than were commonly available on the open market as well as tighter control over manufacturing quality.

LOTUS OPERATIONS

Marketing

The typical owners of Lotus cars in the 1950s and 60s were the "cloth cap brigade," wearing dungarees and carrying a tool kit in the back, who enjoyed constructing the car from a kit and then maintaining and repairing the car themselves. These owners were fiercely proud of their Lotus' astounding performance, all the more so because they felt a command of the road comparable to or better than that of the drivers of the most expensive cars that money could buy. An extra nut or bolt was often in each kit just to confound a new owner. After the ruse was discovered, the new owner often framed the extra part. Owners often, in fact, "patched" the kit together just enough to drive it to the nearest dealer who would reassemble the car properly.

Promotion during this era was largely accomplished by word-of-mouth, a few advertisements in motoring enthusiasts' magazines and press reports of Lotus racing accomplishments. Owning a Lotus car was probably the most prestigious trapping for the young professional. The enormous costs of insuring and maintaining such a car made it accessible only to the *nouveaux riches* in their early twenties who typically also needed some flair for the highly masculine domain (as then perceived in Britain) of automobile engineering.

In the early days the cars and their natural image more or less provided the

EXHIBIT 7: Group Lotus Car Companies Limited

The Elite and Some Competitors 1975	*Capacity cc*	*Price £*	*Max mph*	*0.60 sec*	*Overall mpg*	*Weight cwt*	*Trunk cu ft*	*Body Type*
Lotus Elite 503	1,973	6,973	120.1	7.8	21.7	23.0	6.6	4 seat
Alfa Romeo Montreal	2,593	6,299	135.2	8.1	13.8	25.1	—	4 seat
Citroen SM EFI	2,970	7,226	142†	8.3	14.9	29.5	9.0	4 seat
Ferrari Dino 308 GT.	2,926	9,217	150†	6.4	14.8	25.3	5.0	2+seat
Jensen Interceptor III (auto)	7,212	8,717	129†	7.7	10.0	35.1	8.5	4 seat
Maserati Marak	2,965	7,821	140.0†	7.5	13.2	27.3	6.6	2+2 seat
Porsche 911S Targa	2,687	8,898	140.0†	6.5	19.8	21.3	4.3†	2+2 seat
Reliant Scimitar GTE o/d	2,994	3,722	123†	8.7	21.7	22.8	—	4 seat

†Estimated. Trunk space not recorded for Alfa Montreal or Reliant Scimitar.

Source: *Motor,* May 24, 1975.

only need advertising and public relations. Later, as the company began to move upmarket, away from kit cars, marketing strategy changed to reach more established buyers from higher age ranges and with, perhaps, less active leanings in favor of engineering, self-repair and so on. These older buyers were more removed from the close networks of racing enthusiasts and the like.

All sales of Lotus cars were made through appointed main dealers which were typically independent sports car retailers. Consequently, Lotus cars were usually sold in the same outlets and side-by-side with direct competitors. Ford or other major motor manufacturers often had sole dealerships with which the large automobile manufacturer could negotiate and enforce a rigorous dealership contract. The "leverage" of Lotus over the dealerships was therefore more limited. Matters were made difficult for the retail dealers of specialized cars by the often major demands and idiosyncrasies of the owners of expensive, specialized automobiles.

While many Lotus dealers were top quality automobile retailers and repairers, the efficiency of Lotus dealers had been criticized in many circles and managers of Lotus agreed that their dealers were of mixed standard up to the early 1970s. Damage had been done to the Lotus image by owners dissatisfied with the actions of their dealers, and hence with Lotus themselves. An extreme case occurred when an owner, speaking on a BBC national broadcast, stated that he was going to drive to the Lotus offices in his new Europa and set it on fire outside. The threat was not actually carried out although the car and owner did arrive outside of the head office. The number of Lotus dealers approximately halved through the 1970s.

The market for Lotus cars was always small and specialized in each of the national markets in which the cars were sold. The selling emphasis was on prestige with the Team Lotus (the international motor car formula racing subsidiary of Group Lotus) adding to the prestige rather than creating a racing image for the cars. The customers, as would be expected, were often enthusiastic about the company and followed the racing activities of Lotus.

From the early 1970s onwards use of the media included:

- Advertisements in the glossy magazines and the color supplements of quality newspapers.
- The racing team's accomplishments as publicized
- Editorial matter in newspapers and journals

Expenditures on advertising and public relations constituted only a few percent of sales.

Manufacturing

Until 1966 the company had manufactured in a series of locations in and around London. The growth in sales of the Elan and the Seven and the introduction of the Europa demanded a move to new premises. The company purchased a 37 acre freehold site on the outskirts of Hethel, a tiny village outside of the small city of Norwich. This site is set in a rural area and approached by many miles of poor main roads (until about 1980) and then through narrow country roads. It is relatively isolated from the industrial centers of England, being some 130 miles from the West Midlands center of the auto industry and 150 miles from the financial center of London.

In spite of these disadvantages, the plant's size allowed spacious single floor offices and factory and also accommodated an airfield and hanger for the two company airplanes together with land surplus to immediate requirements. Also on the site was a racing test track with viewing stand to which company executives sometimes retreated late on Friday afternoons if the weather was favorable to enjoy car testing and racing.

The production of cars was labor intensive requiring about 300 man hours per car. Lotus cars were not built on a production line and production workers were assigned stages of work rather than a single operation. For example two workers did all the exterior trim rather than repetitively fixing just, say, a door.

There was a substantial degree of flexibility between jobs and the preference of an operator for a particular type of work was accommodated where possible. In the assembly shop there was little in the way of mechanization, automation, production belts and overhead conveyors seen at the major car plants. The cars, their parts and sub-assemblies were manufactured in batches of eleven. They were assembled individually rather than by a flow line sequence. No employees were paid hourly but received a weekly salary with some remuneration linked to performance. The skill levels required for the Lotus production system were much lower than usual for an automobile plant.

About 70 percent of the workers were employed in the production department and were mainly male. The few women in the manufacturing area were mainly employed in stitching trim. The workforce was drawn from within a radius of about 30 miles of Hethel and substantially from agriculture. Production workers saw themselves as quiescent craftsmen rather than militant car workers, and displayed an enthusiasm for the product that was shared throughout the company. The employees were relatively well paid compared with other employment in the area, even though their pay was substantially less than unionized auto workers in the manufacturing centers of Britain. When the company had moved from the London area in 1967 about 80 percent of the employees transferred to Hethel.

In contrast to the car itself, manufacture of the Lotus engine was highly automated through the use of numerically controlled machine tools. Three raw castings were delivered to the factory with the main chambers and other wide bore holes already in place but finished roughly. Each type of casting was then clamped into the respective one of three custom made machines and when the switches were pressed, a series of drills and other tools automatically finished off all the details of each of the three pieces of the final engine. The three pieces were then bolted together, exhaust manifolds and supply lines were connected and the engine was started, run for a few hours and then final adjustments were made before installing it in a car or shipping it to a buyer. The numerically controlled machining principle meant that any small modifications or design changes could be coped with very quickly by reprogramming the machines. Production times were about one third of those needed if conventional equipment and methods were used.

Although most of the Elite, Eclat, and Esprit range was made in-house there were certain parts such as tires, windscreens and instruments that were made, sometimes exclusively, for Lotus by suppliers such as Smiths Industries (for instruments). Because Lotus was a minor customer of these suppliers compared with Ford, Leyland Motors and other automobile manufacturers, it was important to hold sufficient stocks to be sure of availability when needed. The stocks were also a protection against strikes and stoppages at the suppliers. A prime reason for so much in-house manufacture was to be free of loss of production due to labor and other troubles in the auto industry which had bedevilled the manufacture of previous models extensively using outside components.

Lotus had no formal labor relations policy until 1972 when one was formulated following militant intervention by trade union *agents provocateurs*. Management stated that democratic participation was the principle on which the policy was founded. Employees were allowed to join a union or not until the maintenance of a closed shop became a legal necessity in the late 1970's and collectively elected at 6-month intervals representatives to a Staff Council and a Joint Negotiating Council.

Minor complaints were dealt with by a 48 hour rule where a worker was able to lodge a complaint at successively higher points in the hierarchy and obtain a reply within 48 hours from each level; the director being contractually obligated to settle the complaint. Any outstanding issue was put to a ballot of all employees and a two thirds majority allowed the workers to be represented by the national level of the Transport and General Workers Union which was one of the largest and most militant British unions.

Work force remuneration was partly geared to performance where each section, such as "the spray shop," received a bonus depending upon the extent to which the workers in that section exceeded or fell short of the average labor cost per unit. The notional cost per unit against which their performance was judged was arrived at as a percentage of the retail price of the product. The system was very sensitive to cost and volume changes and quickly detected an output/labor imbalance. It therefore allowed the company to adjust the deployment of its work force and redress the balance in a way less drastic than the sudden large-scale adjustments common in the automobile industry at that time. Management claimed that this system made the teams of work study specialists, standard times and the other cumbersome devices typical of large automobile manufacturers unnecessary at Lotus.

LOOKING TO THE FUTURE

New Products. Four new Lotus products were introduced in the Spring of 1980. These comprised series two versions of the Elite and Eclat, both of which were reengineered to accommodate an uprated Lotus 2.2 liter engine which not only produced considerably more power but also achieved better fuel economy standards. Additionally, the Turbo version of the Esprit was introduced. This version was fundamentally redesigned to cope with the 210 bhp output of the Turbo engine. Press comment concerning the Turbo Esprit was considerable and very flattering and it was commonly thought that this car deserved a place among the world's most exotic automobiles.

United States Distribution. Concerted efforts were made in 1979 to strengthen the company's distribution arrangements in the United States which had been found somewhat troublesome and something of a roadblock in developing sales in that country. Previous arrangements with independent distributors were terminated in 1979 and Lotus set up its own distribution operation with a view to establishing in due course a new network of dealers. Lotus North America Inc. was established, based at Costa Mesa, California, to supervise this process.

In view of past omissions by the previous distribution organization, it was necessary to support the market and to assume liability for customer satisfaction. The cost of this support was shown in the accounts as part of an extraordinary item. Launching the marketing operation was a long-term project in view of the problems left from the past and the state of the market in the wake of the fuel shortage in the USA during the early summer of 1979 with resultant reluctance by dealers to take up a new franchise.

During this reconstruction process, Lotus entered into discussions with the American distributing company of Rolls-Royce Motors for them to undertake the marketing and distribution of Lotus cars in the United States. After careful evaluation by both companies, an agreement was finalized in October, 1979 and the Lotus operation thereafter wound down, this cost being the balance of the extraordinary item in the 1979 accounts. The marketing of the Lotus product through an established dealer network of the standing of Rolls Royce was expected to be mutually advantageous and to generate a satisfactory volume of sales.

Consulting Activities. Lotus also developed a relatively new source of earnings through 1980. Engineering, consulting and other services accounted for 65 percent of the 1980 sales and several substantial consultancy assignments were awarded to Lotus on an ongoing basis in that year. The techniques and expertise demonstrated in research and development projects both in engine technology, such as turbo power, and lean burn concepts together with the Lotus application of plastic processes played a large part in obtaining these outside contracts. A large proportion of the 1980 consulting activities were associated with the design and development of the DeLorean sports car to be manufactured in Northern Ireland.

The British Economy. At the turn of the decade, Britain, a difficult place to do business at the best of times, was entering a period of major economic uncertainty. Interest rates, currency exchange rates, and inflation were at record levels.

Typically, a company like Lotus would be able to borrow money at two or three percentage points above the Bank of England minimum lending rate. As shown in Exhibit 8, the Bank of England minimum lending rate had increased from above 7 percent at the end of 1977 to a prevailing rate of 16 percent or 17 percent through most of 1980. In the early part of 1981 the rate had fallen to 14 percent. High interest rates increased the costs of doing business, dampened business activity, and helped to hold down consumer demand for major purchases.

Currency exchange rates for the pound Sterling suddenly reached unparallelled heights compared to recent years as shown in Exhibit 8. In 1980 the pound Sterling reached $2.44 to £1 Sterling which contrasted with much lower exchange rates of about $1.90 to $2.20 through the preceeding few years. The spring of 1981 saw a slight fall in the high value of Sterling (February 1981 $2.20 = £1.00) but this reflected mostly an increase in the strength of the United

EXHIBIT 8: Group Lotus Car Companies Limited
Some Economic Indicators for the United Kingdom

	1967–1967	*1967–1974*	*1974*	*1975*	*1976*	*1977*	*1978*	*1979*	*1980*	*1981 Jan.*	*1981 Feb.*
INTEREST RATES percent per annum, and of period Bank of England minimum lending rate						7.00	12.50	17.00	14.00	14.00	14.00
EXCHANGE RATES pounds sterling expressed as United States Dollars (end period market rate)	2.80 ± 0.02	2.40 ± 0.02	2.35	2.02	1.70	1.91	2.03	2.22	2.38	2.38	2.40
PRICES											
Raw Material						146.6	143.7	167.1	198.9	205.6	209.8
Fuel						138.1	151.1	169.8	215.7	240.2	239.4

Source: Interest Rates and Prices: OECD Main Economic Indicators
Exchange Rates: International Financial Statistics, International Monetary Fund.

EXHIBIT 9: Group Lotus Car Companies Ltd.
High Price Sports Cars, United States Sales or Registrations (number of cars)

Make	*Model*	*1972*	*1973*	*1974*	*1975*	*1976*	*1977*	*1978*	*1979*	*1980*	*First Quarter 1980*	*First Quarter 1981*
Domestic:												
Chevrolet	Corvette	25,149	29,303	29,114	39,493	40,579	41,818	40,426	40,076	36,507	9,611	8,580
Imported:												
Bricklin	Bricklin	—	—	400	2,190	300	—	—	—	—	—	—
Ferrari	All Models	255	410	338	188	265	458	617	675	779	184	219
Lincoln/ Mercury	Pantera	1,173	1,515	890	472	—	—	—	—	—	—	—
Lotus	All Models	200	200	200	200	200	200	287	120	100	16	41
Maserati	All Models	100	100	100	100	100	100	125	125	150	38	45
Mercedes	450 SL	6,656	6,234	5,940	6,015	5,893	7,180	6,920	6,610	7,287	1,730	1,848
Porsche	911/911 SC	5,120	5,838	4,868	5,013	4,300	5,709	4,484	3,267	3,463	856	872
Porsche	924	—	—	—	—	4,534	13,676	10,433	7,710	3,443	1,137	952
Porsche	924 T	—	—	—	—	—	—	—	635	1,921	651	439
Porsche	928	—	—	—	—	—	13	1,535	1,555	1,468	445	427
Porsche	930 T	—	—	—	—	—	—	566	652	198	149	11
Subtotal		13,504	14,297	12,736	14,178	15,592	27,336	24,967	21,349	18,809	5,206	4,854
Total		38,653	43,600	41,850	53,671	56,171	69,154	65,393	61,425	55,316	14,817	13,434

(1) Registrations for 1972–1979; sales for 1980 and 1981.
(2) Sales except for Ferrari; registrations for Ferrari for 1972 through 1980 and sales for 1981.
(3) Total registrations are based upon published data; registrations by year are estimated by Williamson, Merrill, Taylor & Darling. The Bricklin was manufactured in Canada; it was, however, marketed in the United States as a domestic sports car.
(4) Motor management estimates for Lotus and Maserati.

Source: DeLorean prospectus.

States dollar and consequently the pound sterling remained at similar high levels relative to most other of the currencies of the industrial world. These high exchange rates made the exports of the Lotus Car Company more expensive in the foreign markets and also made imports of competitive cars more attractive in the British home market.

General inflation had been touching 20 percent in Britain in the late 1970s (see Exhibit 8). In late 1980 and early 1981 there was some cause to believe that these rates were falling for raw materials but for fuel inflation rates there was less cause for optimism and this was of consequence to Lotus because fiberglass contains a high proportion of petroleum derived product. But the cost of fuel to consumers was of special importance to Lotus because the price of auto fuel could reasonably be expected to influence the demand for their products. Auto fuel prices "at the pump" had increased more than 50 percent through 1980 in Britain.

It was difficult in late 1980 and early 1981 for even the most strident economists or managers to come to any confident conclusions on the near term or long-term future of the British economy. The implications of the situation for the Lotus Car Company were no clearer than for other companies.

However, Lotus did face some other more specific problems around this period:

> The world market for high price, sports automobiles was showing every sign of being squeezed. The number of Lotus cars sold in the United States together with the sales of direct competitors are given in Exhibit 9 where it can be seen that Lotus unit sales for 1980 were about 35 per cent of the sales for two years previous and sales for the first quarter of 1981 totalled 41 cars.
>
> The management of Lotus felt they were being subjected to "unfair competition" as a result of large government subsidies to the British automobile industry. In the case of the DeLorean Motor Company alone, a potentially major competitor of Lotus, government equity capital grants, loans and bank guarantees totalled more than £80 million.[7]

As a result of these and other problems, Colin Chapman stated: "It is, I believe, remarkable that we were able to record virtually an unchanged level of sales of £14 million for 1980."

The Lotus Car Company was almost alone in the world as an independent specialist automobile manufacturer. Many believed that the coming decade would be even more challenging than the past for Colin Chapman and his managers to continue to disprove the doomsayers.

REFERENCES

1. Foster, Peter, *The Financial Times,* London, October 15, 1974.
2. Smith, Ian H., "Lotus the First Ten Years," Motor Racing Publications Limited, 1958.
3. Bohr, Peter, "Exotic Cars: In Perilous Pursuit of Excellence," *Fortune,* New York, June 4, 1979, p. 114.
4. Sargeant, Patrick, *The Daily Mail,* London, January 9, 1975.
5. *Motor,* London, May 24, 1975.
6. Foster, Peter, *The Financial Times,* London, March 6, 1976.
7. *Wall Street Journal,* New York, October 19, 1982, p. 39.

PART VII

Cases in Managing the Organization

CASE TWENTY-THREE

Lou Holtz's Razorback Football Image

ROBERT D. HAY
University of Arkansas

Assignment Questions:

1. How would you describe the Razorbacks' image? How did they develop it?
2. How important is their image to the Razorbacks? The University?
3. How could you destroy the Razorbacks' image? How free is Lou Holtz to become involved in the beer distributorship? What should he do?

"Image? You bet we're concerned with our image!" Lou Holtz, Head Football Coach of the University of Arkansas Razorbacks, stated these words emphatically.

"There are several images which our football program has. One is the image we try to project to our fans. Another is the one we have with other collegiate football programs. Another is the one we have of our players versus other players of teams we play. And there are others—the image we have with our peers in the profession, with the general public, and other people with whom we do business.

"What's more important—image or winning? Well, I think that the two go together. Image is probably an offshoot of a traditional winning program. If we were to start losing, our image certainly would suffer. But image, a good one, is one of our program objectives. I'd be kidding you if I said it was not.

"But I will not subscribe to win at all costs. We play by the rules. We try to be highly ethical in everything we do. We do not cheat or lie; we keep our promises; we try to be fair. And our football program has been run as a clean one. And Frank Broyles has stated many times that if he even suspects we've done anything wrong, he will personally turn us in.

"What strategies do we use to project a good image? A successful image? Well, everything I do is to try to project a 'class' program. We want to be a 'class' team. By 'class' I mean one in which our people—players, coaches, administrative assistants—everyone connected with our football program will exhibit behavior that he/she knows is 'right' in dealing with other people. I believe

Reprinted by permission of the author and the Case Research Association.

in the 'do right' principle. Do things which you know deep down are the right things to do.

"For example, by a 'class' team I mean one on which all the players don't do anything to embarrass or tear down the opposing team. Our players do not taunt other players. We do not spike the ball, argue with officials, swear at other players, showboat, do jigs and dances, and so forth. Such behavior exhibits a lack of class, in my opinion. We keep our mouths closed and try to do a high class professional job on the field as well as off the field. The same is true of the Texas Longhorns. They are a 'class' team.

"Our assistant coaches are 'class' coaches. They have a high regard for their professional bearing. They wear ties on the job in their office. Their offices are expected to be kept clean, neat, orderly and project a class image to all the players, fans, coaches, faculty, students, and other people who visit our coaching staff. The same is expected of our secretaries and clerical staff.

"Our physical facilities are always kept clean and neat. We even, occasionally, have our whole team of Razorbacks police the field and the area. We try to design any facility to show some evidence of beauty in its surroundings.

"When we go on road trips, our athletes wear a white sport shirt with a red helmet on it which they have to purchase, and coaches wear suits and ties. We want to be well groomed. We don't want to project a sloppy image.

"But our biggest concern is our image with our fans and the general public. We want them to support us in our athletic endeavors. Frank Broyles, my athletic director and boss, has stated many times that a successful, positive image has many advantages: financial support from our booster clubs, additional season ticker holders, recruiting assitance from people all over the country, additional students attracted to the University, support from the State legislators, help from potential employers for our athletes, and many others. And I agree with him!

"Our image is remarkable. When I travel all over the United States and people find out who I am (and I'll bet I travel more than anyone in the country), they say, 'Oh, you're the Coach of the Razorbacks (not the University of Arkansas), the Razorbacks!' They associate the Razorbacks with hog hats, whoo pig sooie, University of Arkansas, and the whole State of Arkansas. And I don't want the whole State of Arkansas and its fans to be split up and divided. I want them to give us 100% support in attendance, recruits, money, and other resources. (See Exhibit 1).

"Our fans and people in the State are unique. They follow us to bowl games. They like to be associated with a winner (and Frank Broyles' teams had established a winning tradition before I came here). They wear hog hats and dress in red. They are hard working people, church-going people who have Christian values of bible-belt tradition (many of them don't appreciate swearing, drinking, carousing, gambling, and so forth). I don't know if their support would diminish if we started to have losing seasons, but I suspect that we do have a hard core of supporters—win or lose.

"One of our main strategies is to have excellent press relations. Our sports information director is always sending out news releases about our team, our players, our coaches. In fact, we have a very unique situation regarding newspapers, radio, and television reporters. As far as I know, we are the only college in the country which has two full time newspaper reporters (living near the

EXHIBIT 1: Six-Year Statistical Summary U of A Athletic Program

Revenues	*Six Years Ago*	*Five Years Ago*	*Four Years Ago*	*Three Years Ago*	*Two Years Ago*	*Last Year*	
Football Revenue	$1,080,000	$1,208,000	$1,400,000	$1,410,000	$1,900,000	$2,059,000	
TV & Radio (primarily football)	290,000	300,000	393,000	355,000	484,000	545,000	
Other Revenues	600,000	872,000	908,000	635,000	1,566,000	2,346,000	
Total	$1,970,000	$2,380,000	$2,700,000	$2,400,000	$3,950,000	$4,950,000	
Win/Loss Record	6–4–1 Broyles	10–2–0 Broyles	5–5–1 Broyles	11–1–0 Holtz	9–2—1 Holtz	10–2 Holtz	
Little Rock Stadium Attendance (games) 53,555 cap.	200,309(4)	201,575(4)	194,462(4)	214,991(4)	164,266(3)	221,686(4)	
Fayetteville Stadium Attendance (games) 41,221 cap.	120,500(3)	118,460(3)	121,657(3)	131,611(3)	135,284(3)	132,345(3)	
Total	320,809(7)	320,035(7)	316,119(7)	346,601(7)	229,550(6)	354,031(7)	
Wire Service Rankings	—	7 AP 6 UPI	—	3 AP 3 UPI	11 AP 10 UPI	8 AP 9 UPI	
Season Tickets Sold Ahead of Schedule	—	—	—	—	Sold Out	Sold Out	Sold Out Next Year

campus) representing the two papers in Little Rock who are assigned by their superiors to cover Razorback sports. Every single day in the year, there is some coverage of our athletic program.

"When we have a spring practice session and the practice is over, before I walk off the field, I am surrounded by at least five newspaper reporters and five TV reporters everyday to find out how we practiced, who did well, who got injured, and so forth. That kind of press coverage builds a good image for us.

"Why do the two full time newspaper reporters from Little Rock cover us so thoroughly? One of the papers surveyed its readers and found that 90% of them liked to read about the Razorbacks. And readership sells newspapers as well as creates an image of our football program! I do my best to have good relations with all reporters.

"When people anytime mention the top football programs, I want them to say that out of the top five or ten, Arkansas is automatically included. So you need to win, and you need to have national exposure. That's why national and regional television exposure is so important to us.

"Years ago Alabama's Bear Bryant said that he'd play games at midnight if TV asked him to so do. TV is so important to a national image. During my short tenure here, our teams have a 30-5-1 record. We've only lost to Texas, Houston, and Alabama. And we've played on TV nine times. When ABC moved the Arkansas-Texas game to September 1 (to which we agreed), it was to be the lead off game of the decade of the 1980's, on prime time on a holiday, the start of Monday night football. We had a chance to play before 50–60 million people. You could not buy that type of exposure. And yet they're paying us! Even if we lose to Texas on that first game, we can gather momentum for the remaining games (if we are a good team) and possibly end up in a bowl game.

"Our TV exposure has brought in countless dollars to our revenues, to the Southwest Conference coffers, and to the other teams in our Conference who believe in sharing the wealth.

"I always shoot to become a national winner, to be our conference winner, and to go to a bowl game. If we can accomplish any of those three goals, we get on TV and hopefully our image will be improved. Remember our win over Oklahoma 31–6 in the Orange Bowl? That's when we won with three of our star players staying at home because they did not follow the 'do right' principle. I'm sorry the three of them had to be disciplined, but they didn't 'do right.' But even without them, we were able to win and improve our image as having a disciplined program that appealed to the personal value system of millions of people. That Orange Bowl game and its surrounding factors have been instrumental in building our image.

"I'll tell you about another unique aspect which we are practicing. Every one of our coaches takes a group of players into the local community and performs some type of community service. I personally approve each project. And there is no fanfare about it. We don't publicize these community projects at all. But you should read the letters I get praising and thanking our players for mowing lawns of old retired ladies, for painting houses, for cleaning up parks, and so forth. As far as I know, we are the only school in the country doing this type of community service.

"Every coach and several of our players make speeches for a variety of reasons. But a collateral offshoot of these speeches is an improved image of our program.

"We try to stress a positive attitude in all of our contacts with people—as coaches and players. We try not to run down any person. We try to run a class program."

With those words, Lou Holtz expressed some of the strategies that he uses to build a good image of the University of Arkansas Razorback football program.

Recently Lou Holtz was confronted with a financial opportunity to become involved as a partial owner of a Coors beer distributorship in Northwest Arkansas. Lou has four children whose college education needs have to be taken care of. Lou stated that this Coors beer deal was a very lucrative one which could insure a high degree of financial security for him, his wife, and family. So he agreed to become a part owner. (Coors beer had never been sold in Arkansas before. But the chance arose to take advantage of a fairly sure financial return, according to Lou.)

When it was announced in all the newspapers that Lou Holtz had a financial interest in a newly proposed Coors beer distributorship in Northwest Arkansas, Lou received a deluge of letters from people in the State of Arkansas. About half of them stated that Lou should not get involved in the Coors distributorship. The other half stated that there was nothing wrong with his ownership in the beer business—that the free enterprise system should be available to anyone, a coach included.

Coach Holtz went to ask Frank Broyles, the athletic director, about whether Lou should go ahead with the investment or whether he should get out of it. Frank told Lou, "You do what you think is right."

CASE TWENTY-FOUR

BCI Ltd.

CHARLES E. SUMMER
University of Washington

Assignment Questions:

1. How would you describe the strategies of BCI and Harrogate?
2. How well have Denham and Lampton performed their jobs?
3. Is Denham really sick? What should Lampton do now?

"In today's world, we do not think that our subsidiary companies can expand to their full potential without some help from central advisory services provided by our headquarters staffs," stated Mr. Henry Lampton, one of BCI's executives and a leading contender to succeed the BCI managing director, who would retire within one year. British Commercial Investments Ltd. (BCI), a London-based industrial holding company, comprised 16 subsidiary companies, with operations ranging from the manufacture of oil drilling equipment to electrical components and from special steel fabrication to the construction of agricultural buildings. Originally, the company had been involved solely with Malayan rubber plantations, but in the fifties it was decided to diversify entirely out of these politically risky activities through acquisition of small- to medium-size private companies, mainly in the United Kingdom. During the preceding seven years, partly through acquisition and partly through internal growth, gross tangible assets had risen from £9 million to £31 million and pretax profits from £900,000 to £3.4 million. A recent shift in emphasis had occurred, however. According to one executive:

> Our present investment effort is directed mainly towards internal expansion by existing subsidiaries and the acquisition of no new subsidiaries unless they complement technologically those we already have. These two efforts, growth from within and acquisition of *related* companies, is what will produce the kind of profit we are interested in. Also, we have instituted what we call the BCI Three-Year Forecast, which involves much forward thinking-in-detail. This kind of planning is accepted as essential in modern company planning, but, even if it wasn't, something very similar would be needed to ensure the continued strength of BCI.

PARENT-SUBSIDIARY RELATIONSHIPS

The shift in emphasis in corporate objectives as well as the increased attention to formal planning had also led to changes in the relationships between BCI and its subsidiaries. According to Mr. Lampton, who had been instrumental in bringing about these changes:

> We have been trying recently to provide additional help to our subsidiary companies. Until very recently, however, we were rather diffident about providing these services to give specialized advice in particular fields; it would be fatal to try and force them on unwilling subsidiary managements. But recently the success of our operations research group, the welcome accorded to the monthly economic bulletins of our chief economist, and the demand for the services of our BCI marketing adviser all attest to the need felt by subsidiary managers. Only in the last three weeks a computer adviser has joined our staff and has begun to familiarize himself with existing EDP installations and projects. We have been too slow in recognizing the part which EDP techniques will play in the future. We hope to provide companies individually too small to justify their own EDP units with access to facilities, and to reduce costs for all by organizing a coordinated network available on a BCI-wide basis.
>
> It is, however, a part of our philosophy that our underlying principal subsidiaries (or, if you like, divisions) should be of a size that they can support their own local functional staff of a high caliber. We are not suffering under the delusion that we can operate a large central services team capable of resolving the local problems of such a diverse organization. Our advisory staff are used as catalysts.
>
> Finally, I would like to say something about the services rendered to subsidiary operating companies by our BCI nominee director. We like to think that the personalities, experience, and sometimes wider contacts which our directors have are an important source of help to managements of BCI subsidiary companies.

Another executive elaborated:

> BCI maintains a (nonexecutive) director on the board of each of its subsidiaries, usually as chairman. Although nonexecutive, the BCI nominee normally visits each of his two or three companies about once a week, or twice every three weeks. The BCI nominee typically has had considerable industrial experience before joining our organization, either with a firm of accountants or management consultants, or with some other industrial corporation in an executive capacity. Many of them have university education and have also attended advanced management programs such as the Administrative Staff College at Henley, Harvard Business School, Stanford Business School, or IMEDE in Lausanne.

Mr. Lampton continued:

> The position of a BCI nominee director involves a rather heavy responsibility. We are not bankers, interested only in the financial aspects of the business. We are not there to take a normal dividend and let it go at that. In some financial holding companies, the local managements have the idea that they are entirely self-sufficient, except for dividends. At the same time, the directors nominated by the parent company to the boards of those subsidiaries create the impression that they are banker types—somewhat superior to getting into real operating problems. I personally believe that in some such holding companies the subsidiary managers are being supine; they sit there with talent which could add to operations, but which they abdicate. Specifically, I am certain that in this day of complex technology and society, the director has a moral responsibility to help his managers—to encourage

them to do planning for the future, to aid them in selecting and staffing their operations, and to give advice where the director has talent or knowledge.

I can give you one example. Most recently, BCI acquired the L. M. Trowbridge Company from the Trowbridge family. This company specializes in construction projects using asphalt products—parking lots, tennis courts, large industrial asphalt areas. It is to the benefit of everyone—BCI, Harrogate [another subsidiary which produces asphalt materials] and Trowbridge managers, and employees of both companies—to merge the operations of the two companies. In this way, both will be more profitable, enjoy more growth, and stand a much better chance of survival in the British economy. Next year we plan to form a company to hold both Harrogate and Trowbridge in the interest of better all-round operations. The move was, inevitably, initiated by the BCI nominee chairman; the managers of Harrogate and Trowbridge don't have the same chance of standing back and taking an overall view of their operations. Without our BCI man, the merger would never have been initiated.

This shows how far we have moved from our position when BCI was still mainly involved in Malayan plantations and when our United Kingdom subsidiaries were regarded merely as diversified investments to be bought and sold, managerial responsibilities resting wholly with the underlying unit. Gradually we have come to acknowledge that this is an untenable position and have taken on full responsibility for the underlying units while allowing them a very wide degree of local autonomy in the main areas of their businesses.

THE ACQUISITION OF HARROGATE

Seven years ago, Mr. Jack Stanley, a man of 82 and the owner of a number of family companies including Harrogate Asphalt, wanted to put his estate in order so that it could be passed on to his heirs. His brother approached a member of BCI management in London with the idea that BCI might be interested in acquiring Harrogate Asphalt. Mr. Lampton, then 31 years old and living in Birmingham as the BCI Midlands representative, was assigned the job of doing a management evaluation of the Harrogate company, which was located in Frampton, a small town in Yorkshire near Harrogate.

Lampton's general conclusion was that Harrogate represented an excellent investment. He based this on a thorough analysis of finances, management, marketing, production, and raw material procurement. He also found that the Harrogate management had sold a less profitable coal business some years earlier, had concentrated on the more profitable asphalt operations, had introduced a revolutionary technological process in the late fifties, and had expanded production and sales. He found that the company was in sound financial condition and that profits had increased at a fast pace.

Mr. Lampton's management evaluation report described Mr. Paul Denham, Harrogate's managing director and secretary, as follows:

> Mr. Denham is 48 years old. He has spent the last 25 years with Mr. Stanley and has grown up with the business. He has been the prime mover in the expansion of Harrogate over the past several years. Despite Harrogate's rapid growth, the company is still relatively easy to administer and Denham has a tight personal control over it. He has a very pleasant personality. He is a strict disciplinarian and is respected for it. As the company is in a rural area and there is a very low labor

> turnover, Denham regards the employees with Edwardian paternalism. He has three sons at public school; the eldest (at 16) works in the company during vacations. Denham hopes one of the three will join him in the business later.

The works, transport, and sales managers were seen by Lampton as capable but "only one is likely to grow to sufficient stature."

Lampton pointed out that the workers in the plant earned very good wages compared to general conditions in British industry. The wages were exceptionally high in relation to the surrounding agricultural area. Wages of between £30 and £40 per week were due to the fact that when the new revolutionary production machinery was purchased, neither the manufacturer of the machinery nor the Harrogate management knew that it would be so productive. Piece rates were established based on what the machines were estimated to produce, but these were "grossly wrong."

Lampton continued:

> The company (in the event, wisely) did not change these rates but reserved the undisputed right to trim all production units to a bare minimum of labor. As the company has constantly expanded, no surplus labor has been laid off but merely transferred to new units.
>
> Needless to say, at these rates competition for jobs at Harrogate is very high. There was an intensely "brisk" air about the whole place. It is nonunion labor. There is no pension scheme. Hours worked are long (normally 07:30 to 18:30) and annual holidays are split, a week in the summer and another in the winter. The work is arduous and in the winter conditions are not good by the very nature of the business. As the rates are all fixed by team output, there is no room for individual slacking. Relations with management appear to be good. Total labor force has risen rapidly in the past year to around 100.

Lampton concluded his report:

> The reason for the company's success is probably due to its geographical position (both for raw materials and markets), the fact that it invested early in a revolutionary production machinery (outside engineers reckon that Harrogate has more of these than anyone else, but Denham has no proof of this), very efficient management (mainly by Denham), and because it is supplying a material in increasing demand over the past decade.

As a result of this report, BCI made an offer to Mr. Jack Stanley for his company. This was accepted, and Harrogate became a subsidiary of the London holding company. At the time of acquisition, Jack Stanley, with his wife, daughters, and grandchildren, owned 90% of Harrogate, and Paul Denham and his wife owned 10%. This latter represented an interest which Stanley had permitted Denham to buy. During the first three years of BCI ownership, Denham retained his minority ownership, but this was subsequently sold to BCI on recommendation of his own financial adviser.

Because the future of the company's sales and profits looked so good, Stanley had proposed that Denham receive £4,000 net salary per year, and 2½% of net profits over £100,000. Previously, he had received a lower salary (£2,000) plus 5% of total net profits. Lampton stated that Denham agreed with this, and that at the time it meant a total take-home of £5,000. His total earnings had risen consistently over the years, culminating in £17,000. This was considered by the casewriter to be a relatively high remuneration in British industry.

The First Five Years of Operation

During the first year, the board of directors of Harrogate consisted of Jack Stanley, Paul Denham, and Gerald Kemp, a full-time executive of BCI who was assigned as the parent-company representative.

During those years, Mr. Henry Lampton was serving as BCI representative in the Midlands and as nominee director of two BCI subsidiaries located near Birmingham. Nevertheless, Mr. Lampton recalled certain things which he knew went on during the first five years.

> In this period, the new equipment installed from Mason & Grant gave Harrogate an overwhelming competitive advantage in a business mainly served by fairly small companies, with the result that profits, sales, and return on new capital increased dramatically. Here is a company whose return on net worth was among the highest of any BCI company. Nevertheless, in my judgment, there were definite signs of trouble. Stanley died at the end of the second year. This left the BCI director and Paul Denham. About a year later, these two directors recommended as the third director Roger Sample, a young man who was hired by Denham in the second year of our ownership. I'll have more to say about him later, but I acknowledged Roger from the first time I met him to be a capable chap, though his experience in Harrogate was limited.
>
> The board meetings of those days consisted of a rather formal, cut-and-dried reporting of figures, once a month.

At this point, the casewriter asked: "Was Paul Denham making the policy decisions?" Mr. Lampton responded: "If there were any policy decisions being made—though I doubt there were."

Lampton continued:

> Also, in about the second year, Harrogate suddenly found itself with a strike on its hands. Denham was at loggerheads with the union and he was at a loss as to what to do. The BCI director had to go up there and deal with the union, and a settlement was reached. As I recall, Denham simply gave up and said that he could not deal with them.
>
> Also, Denham operated by turning up at 8 A.M., opening the mail, then sitting in the sales (internal) office for two hours, returning to his own office where he would incarcerate himself and merely look at figures of past performance. He rarely went to see customers off site or saw customers when they came in.

Recent Events

About two years ago, while some other changes were being made in the BCI organization, Mr. Lampton, at age 36, returned from Birmingham to the BCI London head office as a director of BCI; at the same time he was also assigned to the board of the Harrogate subsidiary. Mr. Lampton commented on his new Harrogate assignment as follows:

> I arrived on the scene of this highly successful company (60% on net worth is remarkable by any criteria) full of youthful bounce and asking why they don't look at the situation in the building products industries for growth. I knew that the company was doing no real forward planning, and that with the addition of a lot of hard work along this line the company could do much better. I also had a

certain amount of good will and ambition—and the knowledge that I would have a delicate time with Paul Denham.

But I soon found that it was an unusual company. I saw a managing director making £15,000 a year but no other men of responsibility. His four top men, including Roger Sample, were making £3,000 or under. This came as a surprise. Here was an outstandingly successful company, profit-wise, with no staff in depth. In fact, in addition to Roger Sample, the only talent I could see was a good production assistant who had just given notice of his termination.

First let me say that I am not adverse to local autonomy—I believe it is best—but not for one local autocrat. Let me also say that my relationship with Denham was a good relationship, personally speaking, but when I tried to bring some things up for improvement around the board table (I had instituted more frequent board meetings and insisted that we discuss company policy problems rather than just review figures of past performance) he did not want to discuss them. Instead, he would say, "This is not a matter for formal board—why don't you come around to my office and let's talk about them informally." Nevertheless, I thought that all three board members (including Sample) should be in on important matters, and that there should be formal board meetings, with the board having the responsibility for making decisions.

Let me give you an example. Our operators in the plant were getting very high piece rates, but it was physically very hard work, 58 hours a week, and two one-and-a-half-week holidays that had to be split, one-and-a-half weeks in summer and one-and-a-half in winter: anyone absent without a doctor's note got instant dismissal. When Denham asked me not to bring this up in the board but to come to his office, I said, "No, this is board matter." I could see that these conditions would mean trouble, and Roger Sample was telling me—not as a moral issue at all, but as a practical issue—we couldn't keep things this way. For my own part, I regarded it as a practical issue *and* a moral issue. In a way, we were blackmailing the workers with high pay and not providing opportunity for recreation. They were spending money in considerable amounts in gambling and drinking (this seemed to be a problem in the town). So I proposed that we allow them to take their two one-and-a-half weeks together, thus affording more of a real holiday and rest away from the job.

As I persisted in placing this matter before the board, Denham finally said: "I don't want any part of this discussion. If you want to make board policy, do it." Notice that he wasn't saying, "I am the managing director, I will think and be responsible about this." Instead, he was abdicating the managing directorship to us.

I mentioned Roger Sample. Denham had hired him some years ago from a local construction firm, and he subsequently became production manager. While he had rather narrow experience working locally up there in Yorkshire, he is a man of talent. He knew I thought highly of him, but he was reticent with me at first because he didn't know what kind of game I was playing. He did not have much confidence in pushing his ideas, because when Denham resisted he did not know if I would back him. Gradually, however, we established a relationship of trust. It came about through situations like the following. On my side, I could see great need for looking beyond the narrow confines of present products and processes. The company needed market research and research on new technology. On Roger's side, he had been reading magazines of the industry and had become aware of some new processes which were being developed in Sweden. He wanted to go there to investigate but had been forbidden by the managing director. Later, I raised this at the board table, but Denham's reaction was, "Don't let's meddle outside the company now. We have a system which is producing high profit." Why he took this attitude I don't know. I suspect that the real trouble lay in the fact that Denham had been outgrown by the company he managed, and he was afraid that anything new might put him still further out of his depth. Harrogate's very success was against him.

Some time later, the accountant for the plant quit. I think it was because he was mistreated by Denham. At this point, I tried to get Denham to go out and find a really top-flight managerial accountant, one who could think and plan rather than simply be an audit clerk. As things proceeded, I could see that Denham just wasn't capable of doing this, so I persuaded him that we should go out and hire an outside firm of consultants to do the recruiting. The consultants presented four candidates for our approval. I was party to interviewing them. We rejected two immediately, and there were two left, in my opinion, who were suitable. About this time I left to attend the 13-week Advanced Management Program of Harvard University in the United States. When I returned, I found to my amazement that he had rejected both of them and instead had hired a local accountant at £1,800 a year rather than the £4,000 man I had envisaged.

About this time I recognized that Paul Denham was a man who was going to reject any sort of idea, and any sort of talent, that he was not familiar with. I was utterly disenchanted with what he was doing. When I got back from Harvard, Paul Denham also recognized that I was a chap who was going to stick to his guns. I could see trouble ahead and was determined to do something about it, even though the company's profit record continued to be outstanding.

Mr. Lampton continued:

At the second board meeting after I returned, Roger Sample brought up a subject which I had encouraged him to study. (I had encouraged him to look at all facets of the business.) Our office staff had very high turnover. The staff was working on Saturday mornings, but there was no need, no work, for this. When Roger proposed it, Paul again said he wanted no part of it. He wasn't even fighting it. I suspect it was because he knew it was going to be put into effect anyway.

At any rate, I was intent on pursuing this to some sort of conclusion. The meeting became heated and intense. Denham said: "Hell, why do we waste our time on these matters; go out and find out what the order position is and let's get down to work." At this point, and in front of Roger, I blew my top. "This is real business," I said, "and if we don't pursue it, we have a real crisis."

One BCI executive commented that during this time,

Lampton was very conscious that the company's success was in some measure due to the tremendous pace which Denham had set for the company in earlier years. Indeed, the competitive edge which Harrogate had gained came largely from the fact that the company utilized its machines so intensively—the credit for which, at any rate initially, was Denham's.

(See Exhibit 1 for Harrogate's sales and profit performance.)

After the above incident, Mr. Lampton upon returning to London wrote Denham a letter stating:

I have given myself some cooling time since our last meeting to consider its implications. I believe that it is most important that you and I meet away from Harrogate to discuss both the future of the business and the way in which you and I can operate together constructively for its good.

The letter then requested Denham to come to London for a meeting. According to Lampton:

EXHIBIT 1: Harrogate Asphalt Products Ltd.
Selected Financial and Operating Results

Year	*Sales*	*Profits Before Taxes*
−14	£ 31,000	n.a.
−13	55,000	£ 22,000
−12	83,000	28,000
−11	110,000	39,000
−10	178,000	62,000
− 9	224,000	87,000
− 8	361,000	136,000
− 7	520,000	150,000
− 6	867,000	260,000
− 5	1,053,000	310,000
− 4	1,096,000	300,000
− 3	1,638,000	450,000
− 2	1,922,000	595,000
− 1	2,050,000	600,000
Current year	2,500,000	750,000 (estimated)

Figures are rounded to nearest £1,000.
n.a. = not available.
Source: Company records.

I felt that it was stupid to keep this up and that we must resolve it somehow. Anyway, Denham had not once been to London in all the years we owned the company. I always invited him to the annual dinner we hold for subsidiary managing directors, but he always accepted and then sent a last-minute excuse.

The night before the meeting was to take place here at the head office, Paul Denham telephoned to say that he was not feeling well. He had shut himself off and did not realize that someone else owns the company and that he was not, as he thought, master of his own domain. I drove all the way to Yorkshire the next day. He was surprised to see me. I said that it is intolerable to go on this way and that we must cooperate if the company is going to progress. I told him also that we must educate Roger Sample in a wider sphere, that we must move him out of the production manager position and give him experience on the commercial side. He agreed to this, and to promote Roger's assistant to production manager.

On his return from Yorkshire, Mr. Lampton also sent to Denham the letter which appears as Exhibit 2. He continued:

During this entire period I had been getting close to Roger Sample, but at this point I got very close. He said, "I don't want to be disloyal to the managing director. You are moving me from an area where I know the work and feel secure to an area where I do not. But I am going to be of no use to anybody if I go on not being allowed to be in contact with customers. I wonder if Paul, who is 54, knows that, at 38, I am cornered?"

Mr. Lampton said that he then offered Sample a service agreement (contract) to insure that he would not be summarily fired. Sample responded, according to Lampton, "No, that is not what I want. I will give you a pledge to

EXHIBIT 2: BCI Ltd.

Mr. Paul Denham, Managing Director
Harrogate Asphalt Products Company
Frampton, Yorkshire

Dear Paul:

Although I was disappointed that you did not feel fit enough to come down here yesterday, I am glad that we had our discussion about the future, and I hope that you now understand and sympathize with our determination to strengthen the management at Harrogate so that it can be in a position to maintain its leadership in its own field and to exploit other opportunities in allied fields. I am sure that our decision to put Roger in full charge of sales is sound.

At the same time I hope that you understood that the BCI management is insisting that the individual subsidiaries institute, this year, a formal approach towards three-year planning and forecasting (the majority of the companies did this last year, of course). This is not an academic exercise but, in our opinion, an essential step both for the operating companies and for BCI. The preparation of such a report must essentially be a team effort that has your full backing, and as it is sometimes difficult to start viewing the future in this way I have, as I told you, arranged for James Kemp, our management accountant and planning specialist, to be free for a week (or more, if necessary) at the end of this month or in September to give you any help you may need. I sincerely hope that I have managed to persuade you that one is not just looking for a "figure pledge" that you would consider you had broken were it not achieved. When you look at the framework around which such a report is constructed, you will see that it requires the participation of the whole management team.

Naturally, I am anxious about your health and I do hope that you can soon discover what is wrong with your arm. What you said about overworking and the need for a really worthwhile break of two months or more seems to me not only desirable but necessary if you are going to be able to maintain your energies in the future. You have our complete backing for this, and I hope you can manage this as soon as possible.

Yours,

H. Lampton

Source: Company records.

stay three years, but I will leave if there aren't some changes in the way the company is running."

Mr. Lampton continued:

> Naturally, I did not put it to Denham that way. I told him it would be a good thing to send Roger to a three-week marketing course I knew about at the University of Glasgow. He said that this is not productive for the company, but that if Roger wants it and I approve, he would go along.
>
> On the very day that Roger left, Paul Denham took sick. Roger phoned from Glasgow (Paul had phoned him) and wanted to know if he should go back to Frampton.

CASE TWENTY-FIVE

Nichols Equipment Incorporated

J. OWEN WEBER
West Virginia University

WARREN A. DEBORD
University of South Florida

Assignment Questions:

1. What is the Nichols Equipment strategy?
2. Why was a consultant called in? What did the consultant do?
3. What needs to be done now?

Nichols Equipment Incorporated is a multi-million dollar construction equipment distributorship with headquarters in a major midwestern city. Having started the company nearly twenty-seven years ago, Mr. Robert E. Nichols, founder and President, has seen Nichols Equipment grow from a small distributorship employing seven persons, to the present organization with over 150 employees who collectively own 51% of the company. Of these employees, nearly two-thirds are located in the headquarter facilities with the remainder being dispersed over five branch locations.

Having had a meteoric beginning, the last four years have been very difficult for Mr. Nichols. The economic and political decisions during this period have reaped havoc on the construction equipment market in general and Nichols Equipment in particular. Table 1 graphically illustrates Nichols' machine sales performance over the past four years while Table 2 displays the profit picture for Nichols during the same period.

This regressive financial picture not only applies to Nichols Equipment but to other concerns as well. Campbell Equipment, a John Deere distributor, had a net loss of $861,000 for fiscal year 1978. Although 1979 improved for Campbell, they had a $565,000 loss for the first three months of 1980. The president of the company attributed his company's performance to the economic downturn and a high degree of business uncertainty. "When that hits you, it hits you hard. The whole industry has been caught in a downturn since late 1979." Similar conditions prevailed with the local Case dealership who likewise attributed their 1980 deficit to a "soft-market."

Outside reports suggest that Caterpillar experienced a similar economic

Reprinted by permission of the authors and the Case Research Association.

TABLE 1: Nichols Equipment's Annual Machine Sales

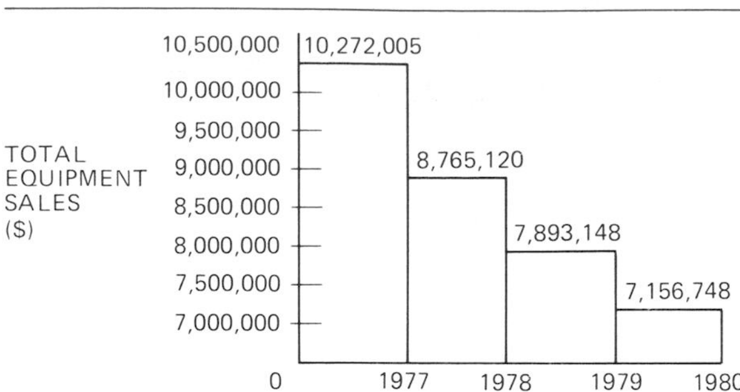

downturn in 1980. Furthermore, a recent magazine interview with a vice-president for Goodyear Tire and Rubber Co. revealed that sales of heavy-duty tires were just beginning to move upward after plummetting over the past four years. Overall, the scenario seems to have been bleak for most major construction and construction-related businesses during this period.

However, the question at hand pertains not to what has happened, but, to what can be done to turn this situation around; in essence, to identify ways in which Nichols Equipment can compete more effectively in the marketplace. To answer these questions, Mr. Nichols has just received a report from a management consulting firm he retained to examine the internal and external mechanisms of Nichols Equipment and to provide recommendations necessary to put Nichols back on the road to financial recovery. As Mr. Nichols settled into his favorite chair to read his voluminous report, he wondered aloud: "was it purely marketplace economics or was it something that he could have prevented?"

CONSULTING REPORT

In an effort to assess Nichols Equipment's overall operations, Management Efficiency, Inc., an internationally renowned management consulting firm was retained. After preliminary discussions with Mr. Nichols, consultants at Management Efficiency, Inc. (MEI), felt that the best approach would be to consolidate

TABLE 2: Nichols Equipment's Annual After Tax Profit

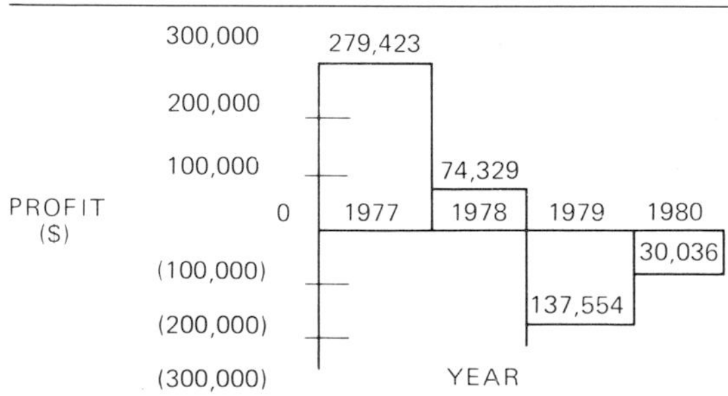

their study into three major subsections. Each subsection, organizational management, marketing and sales activities, and financial management, address the specifically related problems. A second report soon to be forthcoming, would enumerate the various recommendations that MEI proffered for each given area.

ORGANIZATIONAL MANAGEMENT

From an organizational management standpoint, the research design consisted primarily of two phases. First a written survey was distributed to all Nichols Equipment personnel to elicit information pertaining to the organizational climate as well as to several key components. The second phase of the research consisted of personal interviews with key employees using a series of specially designed questionnaires for each management level and department. The major purposes of this phase were to supplement the climate data, enable the respondent to elaborate on those areas felt most critical, and provide supportive data for branch location analysis.

Organizational climate refers specifically to the motivational properties of the organizational environment; that is, to those aspects of company management and surroundings that lead to the arousal of different levels of motivation and performance. Climate is usually determined through the use of a questionnaire and consists of several groups of questions known as dimensions. For Nichols Equipment, the dimensions selected for analysis were:

1. Clarity—How clear are the company goals, job duties, policies, etc.?
2. Standards—Does the department and/or company set realistic and challenging standards for performance?
3. Rewards—Is corporate emphasis on rewards or criticism?
4. Spirit—Does a feeling of team effort and helpfulness prevail within the organization?

In addition to assessing the climate of Nichols Equipment, the questionnaire was designed to ascertain the level of satisfaction that prevailed within the organization. Since satisfaction is such a broad, all-encompassing term, it was decided to break it down into subsections that indicated the satisfaction with:

1. Accomplishment—Self-satisfaction from responsibilities and accomplishments
2. Supervision—Style of leadership of immediate superior
3. Management—View of top management's fairness and competency
4. Overall Company—Desirability of the company as a place to work

Of the 160 Nichols Equipment employees surveyed, 84 or 52.5% returned completed questionnaires. The geographical breakdown by branch location of completed questionnaires is given in Table 3.

A summary of the findings pertaining to Nichols' level of climate and degree of satisfaction follows:

Climate and Satisfaction Analysis

Clarity: Nichols Equipment as a whole does a favorable job of explaining their rules and procedures. The strong point was Lover where they consistently

TABLE 3

	Total Employees	*Completed Questionnaires*	*Per Cent of Employees Completing Questionnaires*
Middleton	11	5	45.5%
Overland	10	4	40.0%
Hayfield	12	11	91.7%
Red Lion	11	3	27.3%
Lover	16	9	56.2%
Upton (Headquarters)	100	52	52.0%
Total	160	84	52.5%

scored higher than the mean while Overland and Red Lion repeatedly scored below the average.

Standards: A majority of the employees felt that goals were not difficult or challenging enough. Lover again scored the highest while Overland scored the lowest.

Rewards: This dimension was the low point for the Nichols Equipment climate study. Employees tended to feel that:

A. Rewards and recognition were generally lacking.
B. The promotion system is inadequate.
C. Rewards were not proportionate with job performance.

When compared to individual branches, it appears that no single branch is dominant.

Spirit: The spirit dimension is used to ascertain the feeling of general "good teamwork." Although overall the company scored favorably, no single branch location emerged as a leader over the remaining branches or overall mean. In fact, Middleton consistently scored below the mean while Lover had low scores pertaining to the degree of warm relationships and the aloofness of management.

Accomplishment: The overall results were favorable with the exception of reward recognition. This result seems to confirm the previous finding.

Supervisor: This subsection of satisfaction dealt with employee satisfaction of their immediate supervisor. Although Nichols Equipment scored favorably in this section, one particular question indicated that nearly half the respondents felt that they did not get an adequate amount of guidance and encouragement from their supervisor. This was especially apparent at Red Lion where the score overall and for that given question was quite low.

Management: Of all the satisfaction subsections, this section had the lowest favorable score. The strong branches in this category were Middleton and Red Lion which consistently scored lower in other areas throughout the study. On the other hand, Lover's low score on the question that dealt with top management being fair seems to support the finding previously noted concerning the aloof (but efficient) manner of Lover's management.

Overall Company: Overall satisfaction pertained to the overall feelings the respondent had toward his job and toward Nichols Equipment. The overall results were quite favorable except for that question dealing with employees leaving for work elsewhere. The results to this question were low at every branch except Lover. Similarly, Lover was by far the strongest branch in this area as opposed to Hayfield which was the lowest.

Additional analyses of Nichols Equipment's employee questionnaire responses indicate the existence of a significant degree of teamwork with very little conflict among departmental employees. Similarly, interdepartmental relationships were evaluated highly since only 12% felt such relationships were poor. Furthermore, teamwork among similar departments in different branches outpolled conflict among the same departments by a 4 to 1 ratio.

However, when given the opportunity to suggest changes that would bring together more cooperation and effectiveness throughout the company, nearly half of the respondents indicated better communications between departments was needed. Also, over one-fourth of the answers pertained to improving management/employee relations as a means of securing more cooperation. This latter statistic is consistent with the results of the satisfaction with management where many of the same feelings were expressed.

Thirty-one percent of the individuals completing the survey indicated good management as a strength of Nichols Equipment. Good people (40.8%) was another strength that was most often given. However, 36% of the same group indicated that poor management was the major weakness of their company. An additional 34% felt that the facilities were poor and that the work force was not sufficient to handle the volume of business. Furthermore, improving branch management (44%) was singled out as the area of weakness that needed the most attention from top management; while 20% of the employees felt that top management should review the low pay of personnel.

Branch Location Analysis

Middleton. During fiscal year 1980 Middleton lost $50,482 on sales of $712,545. This latter figure represented a decrease of nearly 75% from the previous year. Equally disturbing was that there was only one (1) new equipment sale for the year while used equipment accounted for an additional seven units sold. This was the worst performance of all the Nichols Equipment branches. The question thus becomes: Was this performance based on the economy, management, personnel, or a combination of the three?

Middleton has been particularly hard hit by the economic downturn as a result of their dependency on the quarrying and water and sewer construction markets. Similarly, although the smallest of Nichols Equipment's branch locations, Middleton is beset with a high level of competitive activity in a relatively small market. Caterpillar, Case, John Deere and Komatsu all play an important role in the Middleton market.

A good record of parts sales have helped offset a serious decline in new equipment sales; while it is further hoped that the recent acquisition of an industrial equipment line will strengthen branch performance. However, the addition of the I. E. line is questionable from a profit standpoint as a result of lack of decisive policy from the manufacturer.

Middleton personnel evaluated their branch above average in satisfaction with management. This was the highest score of any branch in this particular area. However, the same employees evaluated the branch below average in clarity of objectives, accomplishment and spirit.

During the personal interviews, it was apparent that the spirit or morale was low throughout the branch. The parts manager was bitter toward Upton concerning a recent mandate that required a severe reduction in inventory levels. Similarly, the senior salesman and the branch manager were despondent over their inability to penetrate the market. These types of attitudes manifested a branchwide morale problem which permeated every department. This was specifically highlighted by a service mechanic who would not even answer the questions concerning department or branch problems that presently exist.

Even more importantly was the way the branch manager and senior salesman responded to the interviews. Both were unprepared, nervous, not sure of themselves and unaware of the conditions that existed within the distributorship. John Syes, the branch manager, indicated he spent the majority of his time handling customer problems as opposed to actually selling. On the other hand, Bill Kayo, the senior salesman had no clear system of calling on customers. He presented himself as totally disorganized and unprofessional in his manner. Conversely, Tim Jackson, a young salesman recently hired, came across completely organized and professional. His system of calling on customers was the best in the organization. Furthermore, he understood the problems at Middleton—internally and externally—and was prepared to cope with them in the short run. He seemed to demonstrate the potential necessary to move ahead within the total organization.

Exhibit 1 illustrates the organizational flow chart for the Middleton branch. Also included are the salaries for management and sales personnel.

Overland. Machine sales increased by approximately 10% at the Overland branch. This was accomplished even though they had one less salesman than the previous year; the only salesman being Pat Hill, the branch manager. This sales increase may be attributable to the Overland market base. At present 60–70% of the market is oriented toward forest products which have enjoyed a mild respite from the economic turmoils that have affected other markets. Additionally, 25–40% of the market is aggregate and quarrying with the remainder split between mineral, mining and construction. However, like Middleton, Over-

EXHIBIT 1: Middleton Organization Chart

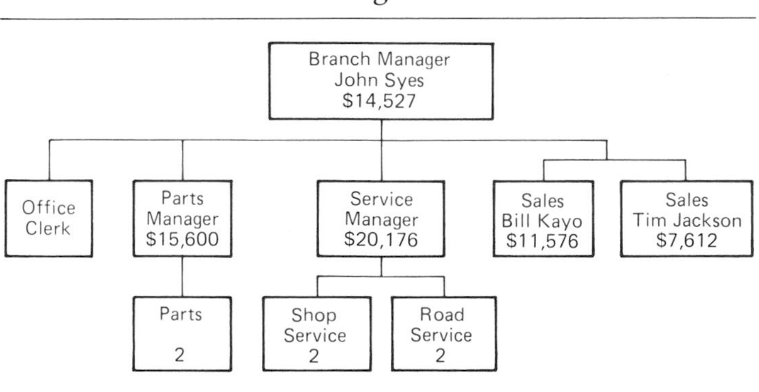

Total Salary of Management and Sales = $69,491

land is operating in a highly competitive environment with Caterpillar, Case, John Deere, Eaton Yale, Wabco, and Komatsu all having an impact.

The correlative results of the employee survey indicate that the employees feel their branch is neither the most desirable nor, on the other hand, the least desirable. However, some isolated problems were discovered which should be looked into. These were:

1. Management does not set challenging goals
2. Present promotion system is unfair
3. Rewards are not proportionate with performance

Conversely, the employees evaluated Overland the highest of all the other branches in reference to:

1. Equity and fairness of supervisor
2. Demonstration of appreciation by supervisor

The results of the survey were basically borne out by the personal interviews. Morale was very high and was particularly apparent in the service department. The service manager has done an excellent job in creating a very friendly work atmosphere where teamwork is the rule and not the exception. Servicemen responded favorably during the interviews and on several occasions openly admitted to their leaving work early when business was slow or else working on their cars when everything else was completed.

From an organizational standpoint, Overland is very similar to Middleton. Exhibit 2 illustrates Overland's organizational flow chart.

Hayfield. Machine sales dropped 30% from 1979 to 1980. Similarly, parts and service revenues decreased during the same period making Hayfield the only branch experiencing declines in all three departments. Nevertheless, Hayfield has been a consistent profit contributor for Nichols Equipment having the second highest five year average net profit/sales (5.7%). However, this same net profit/sales dropped significantly in 1979 and again in 1980. This may be a result of the market base being primarily aggregates and quarrying, plus construction; all having suffered serious setbacks over the last four years.

Additionally, survey results were the lowest among all branches. Hayfield's best score was with standards, but scored the lowest overall in areas of rewards, accomplishments, and management, supervisor, and overall satisfaction.

Specific questions which resulted in low scores:

EXHIBIT 2: Overland Organizational Chart

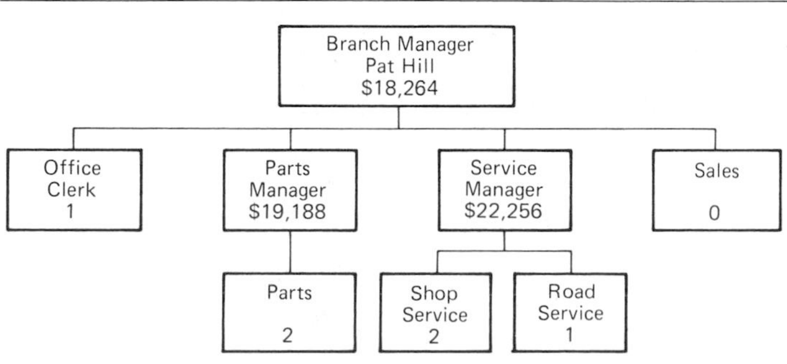

Total Salary of Management and Sales = $59,708

1. Management sets difficult and challenging goals in this company.
2. There isn't very much personal loyalty to the company.
3. We have a promotion system that helps the best rise to the top.
4. People are rewarded in proportion to performance.
5. Rewards and encouragements outweigh threats and criticism.
6. Good work is recognized.
7. We have a competent top management staff.
8. Employee needs are considered before changes are made.

Even though Mark Wilson, the Branch Manager has been at Hayfield a relatively short period of time, the results of the survey are discomforting. During the interviews he indicated that he was "sales oriented versus management oriented." His primary contact at headquarters is with Terry Creamer, Director of Sales, but little or no communication with B. L. Cappo, his immediate supervisor. Joe Cali, Hayfield's parts and service manager, presented himself as a competent individual capable of making contributions to the organization. He was assisted by two able supervisors. Exhibit 3 illustrates the overall organizational chart for the Hayfield branch.

Red Lion. Machine sales in Red Lion experienced a decline of approximately 60% during 1980, while the parts and service departments increased marginally. As was true with Overland, these sales figures were generated by only one sales person—the branch manager.

Fifty-five percent of Red Lion's sales volume is dependent on the forest products industry. Like other Nichols Equipment branches, Red Lion is confronted with a myriad of competitors in a relatively limited market area. The one strong point for Red Lion is that they are an established business enterprise in the market area.

The employee survey results indicate that sales are not the only problem at Red Lion. Of all the branches, Red Lion scored the lowest in the areas of clarity of objectives and supervisor satisfaction. Specific question areas where the majority of respondents answered unfavorably were:

EXHIBIT 3: Hayfield Organizational Chart

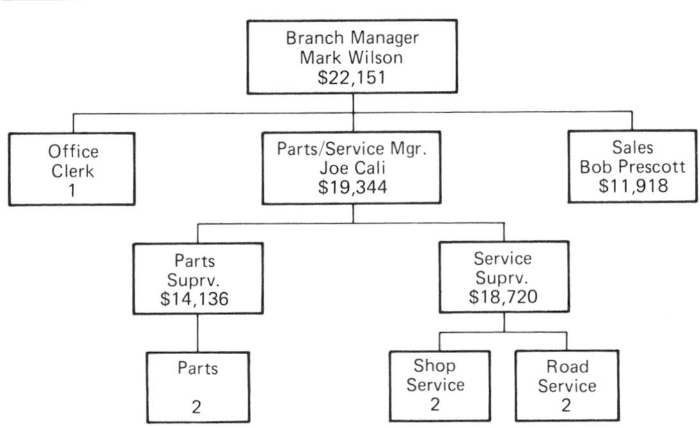

Total Salary of Management and Sales = $67,029

EXHIBIT 4: Red Lion Organizational Chart

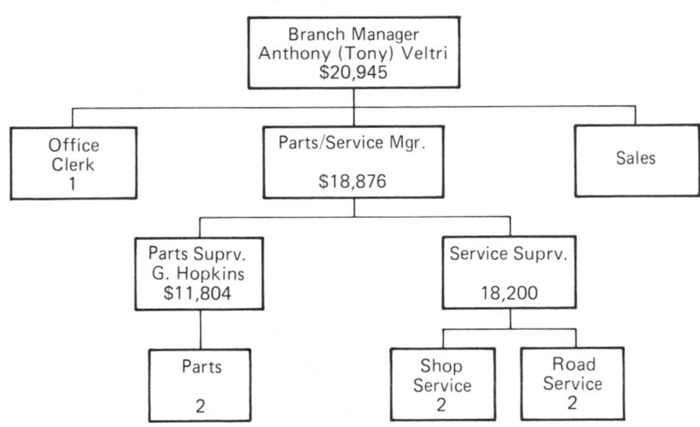

Total Salary of Management and Sales = $69,825

1. Productivity suffers from lack of planning and control.
2. The work group relies on the supervisor for guidance and encouragement.
3. I find it difficult to talk to my supervisor.
4. My supervisor doesn't show enough appreciation.

During the personal interviews several individuals referred to some of the same areas mentioned above and simultaneously expressed concern over "the change in Tony." Upon probing it was discovered that some employees are under the impression that their branch manager is "having personal problems." Although Mr. Veltri gave no indication of having personal problems during his interview, the fact, nevertheless, remains that employee perceptions may be interfering with the work situation.

Recognizing the need for an additional salesman, Mr. Veltri indicated during the interview process that he felt his parts supervisor would be an "ideal candidate" for the position. However, George Hopkins, the parts supervisor, has no knowledge of this; in fact, he indicated that in the ten years he has been with Nichols Equipment he "has never known where he stood." His feelings are that "because of the present management structure he will not be able to go any further." This is unfortunate. George impressed the interviewers with his gregarious personality and keen perceptions. As was true with the young salesman at Middleton, George has all the capabilities to be successful with Nichols Equipment.

The organizational flow chart and corresponding salaries for management and sales personnel are illustrated in Exhibit 4.

Lover. Machine sales and parts revenues each increased by approximately 40% in 1980 over 1979 while service revenues increased by 15%. More importantly, however, was that Lover contributed $316,708 to before tax profits in 1980 and has had a strong net profit/sales ratio over the past six years averaging approximately 10%.

In comparison to other branches, Lover is confronted with limited competition. Only Caterpillar and John Deere play a role in a market that is 75%

dependent on the forest products industry. Furthermore, Nichols Equipment has been the leading supplier of heavy construction equipment in Lover for several years thereby gaining the edge in momentum.

Of all the branches, Lover had the highest climate analysis scores in the area of clarity, standards and spirit. Similarly they had the highest score in the overall satisfaction score. Although from an overall standpoint Lover's answers to questions were very favorable, there were several questions which were lower than the other branches. These questions were:

1. Top management is fair and equitable
2. Difficult to talk to supervisor
3. Not enough reward and recognition
4. People in department tend to be cool and aloof
5. There is a lot of warmth between management and other personnel

Although the people are basically satisfied overall, they see Randy Thomas, the Branch Manager, as "removed" from the ongoing interpersonal relationships. This was also expressed verbally by several employees interviewed at the branch. While they have a great deal of respect for Randy and his ability as branch manager, they nevertheless find him "cool" and "distant." One individual interviewed stated that on one occasion Randy came walking through the branch facilities showing off his commission check. While the personnel are proud of his performance and that of the branch, they nevertheless cannot relate to the kind of money a branch manager makes. This is the kind of action that could suddenly turn a branch around.

Exhibit 5 illustrates the organizational flow chart and salaries for managerial sales personnel at Lover.

Upton. Total new and used machine sales, plus rental equipment declined by nearly three-quarters of a million dollars for fiscal year 1980. Similarly, before tax losses amounted to $299,910. As the corporate headquarters and largest branch location of Nichols Equipment, Upton is confronted with: (1) a weak construction market, (2) increasing competition, (3) high inventory levels and (4) high overhead—especially interest charges. On the other hand,

EXHIBIT 5: Lover Organizational Chart

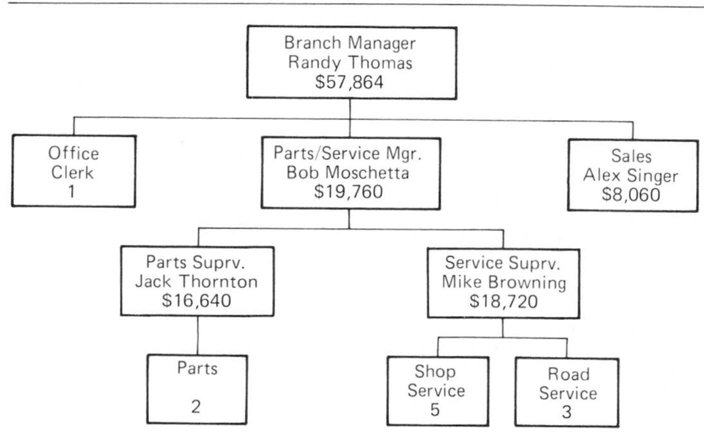

Total Salary of Management and Sales = $121,044

EXHIBIT 6: Upton Branch and Corporate Organizational Chart

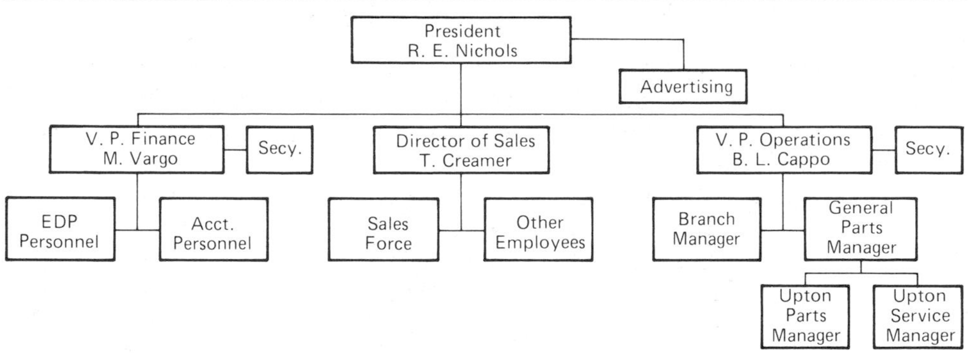

Nichols Equipment has a good corporate identity in Upton, excellent physical facilities, experienced management and local employees.

Upton is by far the largest single branch yet no one person is responsible for its performance. In fact, present financial reports combine Upton branch data with a variety of unallocated corporate accounts making it impossible to compare Upton performance with other branches. Similarly Upton branch functions are spread across the organization chart with certain administrative functions reporting to the V. P. Finance, sales reporting to the corporate Director of Sales and parts and service reporting through to the V. P. Operations. No one individual seems to have bottom line responsibility for the Upton branch.

Of the 100 employees at Upton, 52 returned the employee surveys. These responses accounted for nearly 61% of the total completed questionnaires. On the whole, attitude and moral should be considered good at the Upton branch. Compared to other branches the results would be average. Analysis of the interviews, however, have revealed some subtle nuances that may be portentous. Brief biographical sketches of key Upton personnel are provided below while their respective organizational positions are illustrated in Exhibit 6.

- R. E. Nichols—57 year old founder and President. Perceived avuncular and patriarchal with excellent communication skills. Well liked by employees. Delegates all work to subordinates. Little involvement in day-to-day activities.
- M. Vargo—V. P. of Finance. Organized and detail oriented. Good grasp of financial data. Excellent rapport with banking community. Pragmatic.
- T. Creamer—Director of Sales. Sales oriented rather than marketing oriented. Gregarious, back-slapping individual who is respected by sales force. Believes strongly in letting others make decisions. Was once top salesperson four years in a row for Nichols Equipment.
- B. L. Cappo—V. P. Operations. Has been the mainstay of Nichols Equipment for past three years. Firm but fair. 28 years experience in construction related business. Problem-solver based on analytical reasoning. Upward mobile.
- Paul Linton—General Parts Manager. 30 years parts experience; 22 with Nichols Equipment. Actually makes decisions for Upton parts depart-

ment. Respected for parts knowledge but weak in service department. Tendency to be dogmatic.

- Tom Lyons—Upton Parts Manager. Young manager (28 years old) with high aspirations and presently doing a credible job. However, also perceived as "second-fiddle" to Mr. Linton in terms of making parts decisions for Upton branch. People oriented with tendency to overpay employees for work received.
- Ralph Hixon—Upton Service Manager. 18 years service experience with Nichols Equipment. Very respected for knowledge, organization, planning and creativity. Developed organizational booklets 5 years ago for service departments which also had interdepartmental applicability; but as of yet, has not received approval for dissemination. Feels management not receptive to new ideas or suggestions. Handles all personnel problems in service department because his assistant is task oriented and has the uncanny ability of alienating other employees.

Marketing and Sales Activities

The purpose of the marketing situation analysis was to assess and profile the performance of the marketing and sales efforts within the Nichols Equipment organization. In order to accomplish this objective, personal interviews were conducted with all sales management personnel, individual salesmen in each branch, and a cross-sectional sample of Nichols Equipment customers and non-customers located throughout the six branch locations. As a result of these interviews, combined with additional sales call information, two broad categories of findings have been delineated:

1. Sales management findings
2. Competitive market findings

Each of these will be discussed separately in this section.

Sales Management Findings

Sales management has very little control over the individual salesman's daily sales calls, and seems to have very little influence over the planning of these calls. Although salesmen submit weekly call reports to Upton, this information is not fed back to branch sales management for use in decision making. One of the reasons for this is a lack of appreciation of how this type of information can be used. Other than posting sales calls each week (which takes place in Upton) no further analysis of the data took place. It was difficult to determine if any subsequent review of the posted sales call data takes place, however, it was clear that branch management did not recognize the form showing sales call postings to the customer list.

According to the customer lists for each salesman in the Upton office, anywhere from 4% to 42% of the customer accounts were not called on during 1980, depending on the territory. An average of 63% of the Upton customer accounts were called on less than four times during 1980. This represents a problem of retaining "customer" on the list who may not be viable prospects or customers, which in turn represents a cost to Nichols Equipment. This raises the obvious question—how many customer accounts, actual and potential, are not on the customer list who should be on the list? Each and every missing customer and/or prospect is another cost to Nichols Equipment.

When asked how they went about prospecting or soliciting new business, 80% of the Nichols Equipment sales force responded with something similar to: "I beat the bushes" or "if I'm driving down the road and see a new construction job starting I stop in." A few salesmen indicated that they made use of telephone directories, Road Builders Association material, trade magazines, and referrals from other customers.

Sales support should be distinguished from product support, at least for communication purposes in this report. Sales support here refers to the advertising, direct mail, sales promotion, market information and any other marketing related activities that directly or indirectly help a salesman make an equipment sale. Direct mail efforts at Nichols Equipment are at a minimum as is market information pertaining to customers, growth trends by market segments, and competitive activity information. Advertising and sales promotion are the responsibility of the President of Nichols Equipment who apparently consults with an independent advertising specialist for media, theme, and scheduling decisions. Little if any input comes from elsewhere in the organization.

Perhaps the only true sales incentive for a salesman is provided to those salesmen who open a new account. Presently salesmen and sales management are pushing for an increase in the base salary from the present annual level of $8,300 to a base of $12,000. As they state it, "this assures the salesman that he will not starve during the slow periods," and "$12,000 is the market rate for construction equipment salesmen."

Based on the information obtained from sales management interviews, sales quotas are assigned based on the previous three-year performance record plus an allowance factor for economic forecasts of the level of business activity for the market area. No systematic method is used nor are estimates of market potential by territory available for sales management in assigning quotas to salesmen. There was no indication of possibly linking sales performance relative to quotas to the salesmen's compensation program.

For the most part, salesmen and sales managers are satisfied with the level and types of training programs. Typically, a new sales trainee will spend an indefinite amount of time (from a couple of months to a year or more) working in the Upton office until a territory becomes open. This system provides a good opportunity for the trainee to learn product, parts and service departments and to become familiar with the internal operation of the distributorship. Unfortunately, the trainee's maximum point on the learning curve probably takes place within 5–6 months on the job, which in some cases might be only half-way through the trainee's program.

Although expressing satisfaction, branch managers may also be the recipient of insufficient training. The path to branch management is typically through sales, and the very successful salesman usually has a reasonably good chance of being promoted to a branch manager's position. A branch manager not only is responsible for managing the entire branch operation including the branch's salesmen, but he also has major responsibility for producing equipment sales himself. He has an assigned territory, perhaps geographically smaller than the other salesmen, and works that territory just as any salesman would be expected to do. The problem that could arise, of course, is that the branch manager begins to devote more time to what he knows (and possibly what he prefers) best; to the exclusion of managing the branch's other resources, such as physical, financial, information, and human resources.

Finally, there would appear to be a significant lack of "professionalism" among salesmen. Professionalism has to do with the proper balance of such things as the individual's appearance, self-confidence, attitude, communicative skills, customer treatment, actual behavior with customers and prospects, and more. Several of the Nichols Equipment's sales personnel would probably rate above average on the so-called "professionalism scale." Others are clearly unprofessional for one or more reasons. An unprofessional salesman reflects poorly on the organization each day that he is in the field making sales calls. Given the choice, and all other factors being equal, the customer prefers to do business with the professional salesman. Therefore, the distributorship with the most professional sales force and sales management team actually gains a competitive edge in a highly competitive marketplace.

Competitive Market Findings

As noted earlier, personal interviews were also conducted with Nichols Equipment's customers and non-customers in each of the six branch locations. The major thrust of these interviews was to obtain information pertaining to the strengths and weaknesses of the construction equipment distributors serving that customer's geographic area. Additional information was collected on the customer's equipment inventory and the customer's perception of the most important services a distributor can provide to a customer. A summary of these competitive profile findings as measured by customer perceptions for each branch location follows:

Upton

- *Nichols Equipment's* major strength is customer treatment. Several customers complained about the machine inventory and service received offsetting ratings.
- *Caterpillar* offers good product support but falls short on machine productivity and the overall attitude of the people in the organization.
- *John Deere* has a competitive product at a better than competitive price.

Hayfield

- *Nichols Equipment* is known for good service and good management, however, the Hayfield branch is weak on parts availability and parts pricing.
- *Caterpillar* has a good product but is perceived as having an independent (almost arrogant) attitude in dealing with customers.
- *John Deere* sells equipment at a favorable price, offers good service and

has a good man in the field. They are having trouble on parts availability and their location is not the most desirable.

- *Case* is similar to John Deere in the Hayfield area.
- *Michigan* markets a good product, but its management seems questionable.

Middleton

- *Nichols Equipment* handles a good product line and provides good product support. Several customers rate Nichols Equipment poorly on trade-in deals, engine problems on equipment, and the manufacturer(s) Nichols Equipment represent(s).
- *Caterpillar* is very strong on product and service, but this comes at a high price as far as customers are concerned.
- *John Deere* markets a good product at a good price with an organization that is perceived as poor by one of the customers interviewed.
- *Case* and *Michigan* could be significant competitors.

Red Lion

- *Nichols Equipment* is strong on product support and personnel, but perceived as a weak organization that has trouble filling parts orders.
- *Caterpillar* again is strong on product and service. Their equipment's fuel consumption came out as a negative factor as perceived by several customers.
- *John Deere* is vulnerable on parts and service, but has good branch management.
- *Case* and *Michigan* did not come out as really strong or weak competitors by the customers interviewed.

Overland

- *Nichols Equipment* is strong on product support, especially service. Also strong on customer treatment. Nichols prices perceived to be too high on parts.
- *Caterpillar* has the product and the service customers want, but customers pay the price, both in terms of dollars and an independent attitude they are forced to deal with.
- *John Deere's* location is a problem as are Case's and Komatsu's locations.
- *Michigan* is price competitive.

Lover

- *Nichols Equipment* has respected management offering a questionable product with strong parts and service backup.
- *Caterpillar* is perceived strong on product and parts, however, both are high on price. Attitude comes out negatively once again.
- *Case* turned out negatively among customers interviewed.

FINANCIAL MANAGEMENT

The purpose of the financial management analysis was to assess the branch locations as to operating profitability and to ascertain the reasons behind the increasing debt levels and the extent to which these could be reduced. As true with the previous sections, the results of this section were based largely on interviews with key personnel at Nichols Equipment as well as analysis of available financial data.

FIGURE 1: Nichols Equipments' Sales and Inventory Trends

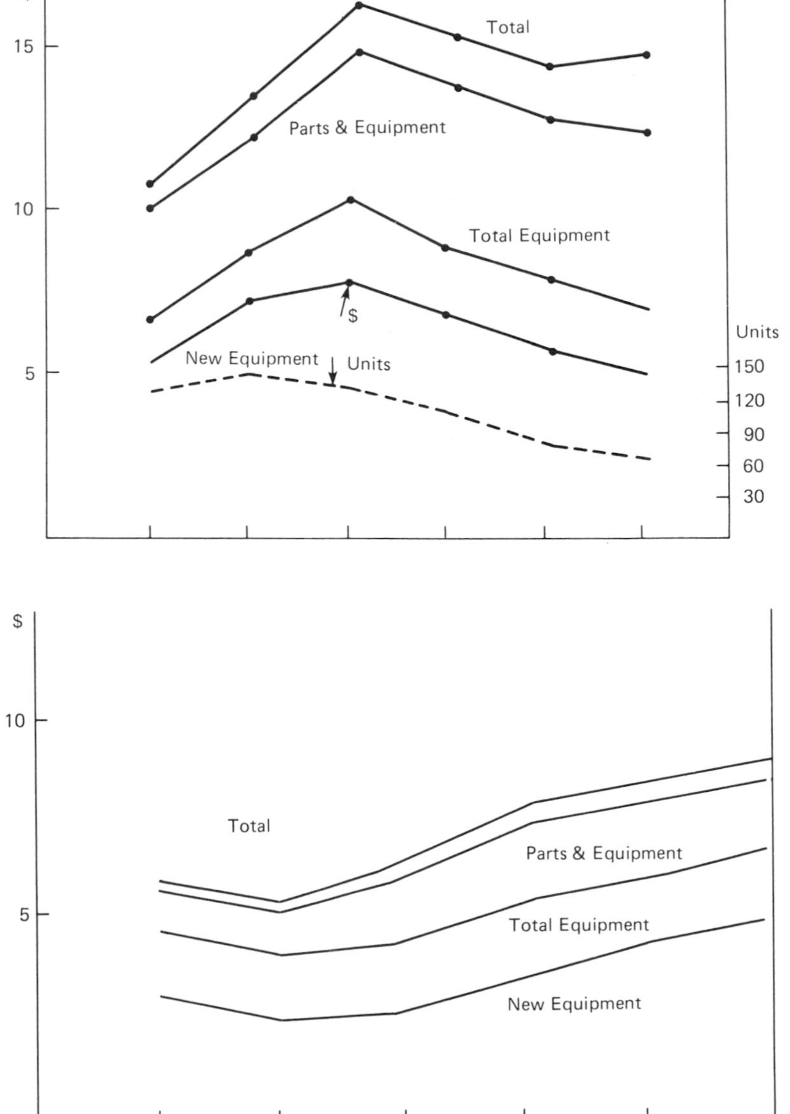

Nichols Equipment's Profitability

Nichols Equipment has been experiencing declining sales since 1977, especially in sales of new equipment, with Middleton and Red Lion showing significant declines in new equipment sales during this period. Figure 1 graphically illustrates Nichols Equipment's sales and inventory trends since 1975.

In 1980, equipment sales, parts, and service accounted for 56.0%, 37.2% and 6.8% of total sales respectively. In fact, sales of both parts and service have been relatively stable in the 1975–80 period showing some dollar growth each year except for mild declines of parts in 1979 and service in 1980.

Primarily as a result of declining machine sales, profits have also been de-

TABLE 4: Nichols Equipment Company
Balance Sheet, December 31, 1980

Assets	
Current	
Accounts receivable	$ 1,905,852
Income taxes recoverable	—
Inventories	8,753,454
Prepaid expenses	9,491
Total Current Assets	10,668,797
Property, plant and equipment	3,398,478
Less accumulated depreciation	834,299
Total Property, Plant and Equipment	$13,232,976
Liabilities	
Current	
Bank indebtedness, secured	$ 2,352,715
Accounts and notes payable and accrued charges	5,708,520
Current portion of long-term debt	415,028
Total Current Liabilities	8,476,263
Long-term debt	3,474,443
Deferred income taxes	—
Total Liabilities	$11,950,706
Stockholders' Equity	
Capital stock	
Authorized 6,000 7% cumulative preferred stock par value $100: 4,000 shares issued and outstanding	$ 400,000
Authorized 6,000 shares common stock with no par value: 2,365 shares issued	236,500
Total Capital Stock	636,500
Retained earnings	703,325
	1,339,825
Treasury Stock at cost	57,555
	1,282,270
Total Liability and Stock Equity	$13,232,976

clining since 1977 culminating in after tax losses of $137,554 in 1979 and $30,036 in 1980. In fact, the five year ('76–'80) after-tax profits have ranged from a high of 1.7% of sales in 1976 and 1977 down to the 1979 and 1980 losses of 0.96% and 0.21% of sales respectively.

Nichols' financial statements for 1980 are included in Tables 4 and 5. Similarly, Table 6 provides income statement for each branch location while Table 7 provides a departmental overview expense analysis by branch for 1980.

Debt Levels

Nichols Equipment is presently confronted with an untenable cost structure. The major contributing factors to the present high cost structure were determined to be:

- Increased debt levels and related interest charges. Between 1975 and 1980 interest charges (interest and exchange account only) went from approximately $394,000 to $925,000 in 1979 and $863,000 in 1980. In the same period, after tax profit decreased by nearly $300,000.

TABLE 5: Nichols Equipment Company
Income Statement, Period Ending December 31, 1980

	Sales	*Parts*	*Service*	*Total*
Sales	$7,885,260	$5,237,468	$959,946	$14,082,674
Cost of Goods	6,794,217	3,199,461	322,937	10,316,615
Gross Profit	$1,091,043	$2,038,007	$637,009	$ 3,766,059
Adjusted Gross Profit*	1,121,886	2,363,555	657,807	4,143,248
Expenses				
Operating Expenses	492,949	576,993	424,348	1,494,290
Administrative and General Expenses				2,057,062
Interest and loss on Foreign Exchange				863,000
Total Expenses				$ 4,414,352
Other Income and Income Adjustments				
Building—Rent				52,260
Interest Earned				145,920
Cash Discounts				21,598
Bad Debts Recovered				16,025
Total				235,803
Grand Total Expenses				4,178,549
Net Loss Before Taxes				(35,301)
Recovery of Income Taxes				5,265
Net Loss for the Year				$ (30,036)

* Adjustments include
A. Miscellaneous Sales
B. Parts Inventory Appraisal
C. Warranty

TABLE 6: Nichols Equipment Company
Income Statement By Branch Location For Period Ending December 31, 1980

	Middleton	*Overland*	*Hayfield*	*Red Lion*	*Lover*	*Upton*
Sales	$712,545	$1,214,687	$1,289,970	$1,035,472	$3,115,023	$6,714,987
Cost of Goods Sold	449,613	867,920	972,211	746,721	2,413,259	4,489,712
Gross Profit	262,932	346,767	317,759	288,751	701,764	2,225,275
Operating Expenses	131,874	146,708	131,244	132,251	162,019	790,194
Administrative and General Expenses	181,540	197,960	180,672	166,059	223,037	1,107,794
Other Expenses and Income (net)	—	—	—	—	—	627,197
Total Expenses	313,414	344,668	311,916	298,310	385,056	2,525,185
Net Loss Before Taxes	$(50,482)	$ 2,099	$ 5,843	$ (9,559)	$ 316,708	$(299,910)

TABLE 7: Nichols Equipment Company
Overview Departmental Expense Analysis & Volume Per Employee By Branch Location

	Middleton 1980	*Overland 1980*	*Hayfield 1980*	*Red Lion 1980*	*Lover 1980*	*Upton 1980*	*Total*
Sales Department	$180,100	$ 566,945	$ 709,731	$ 472,778	$1,914,268	$4,041,798	$ 7,885,260
Department Expenses	$ 47,844	$ 42,103	$ 49,013	$ 45,072	$ 53,835	$ 255,082	$ 492,949
% Total Expenses of Branch	15.3	12.2	15.7	15.1	14.0	10.1	11.8
% Department Sales	26.6	7.4	6.9	9.5	2.8	6.3	6.3
Number of Employees	2½	½	1½	½	1½	12	18½
Volume per Employee	$ 72,040	$1,133,890	$ 472,914	$ 945,556	$1,276,179	$ 336,817	$ 426,230
Parts Department	$477,219	$ 542,867	$ 496,449	$ 459,560	$1,076,529	$2,214,847	$ 5,237,468
Department Expenses	$ 49,227	$ 57,145	$ 57,370	$ 51,636	$ 73,782	$ 287,833	$ 576,993
% Total Expenses of Branch	15.7	16.6	18.4	17.3	19.2	11.4	13.8
% Department Sales	10.3	10.5	11.5	11.2	6.9	13.0	11.0
Number of Employees	3	3	3½	3½	3½	16	32½
Volume per Employee	$149,073	$ 180,956	$ 141,843	$ 131,030	$ 307,580	$ 138,428	$ 161,153
Service Department	$ 85,226	$ 104,875	$ 84,150	$ 103,134	$ 124,226	$ 458,335	$ 959,946
Department Expenses	$ 34,803	$ 47,460	$ 24,861	$ 35,543	$ 34,402	$ 247,279	$ 424,348
% Total Expenses of Branch	11.1	13.8	8.0	11.9	8.9	9.8	10.2
% Department Sales	40.8	45.2	29.5	34.4	27.7	54.0	44.2
Number of Employees	4	4	5½	5½	7½	33	59½
Volume per Employee	$ 21,306	$ 26,219	$ 15,300	$ 18,752	$ 16,563	$ 13,889	$ 16,134
Administration							
Department Expenses	$181,540	$ 197,960	$ 180,672	$ 166,059	$ 223,037	$1,107,794	$ 2,057,062
% Total Expenses of Branch	57.9	57.4	57.9	55.7	57.9	43.9	49.2
	—	—	—	—	—	—	—
Number of Employees	1½	1½	1½	1½	1½	32	39½
Volume per Employee	$475,030	$ 809,791	$ 859,980	$ 690,315	$2,076,682	$ 209,843	$ 356,523
Other Expenses & Income Adjustments	—	—	—	—	—	$ 627,197	$ 627,197
Grand Total	$712,545	$1,214,687	$1,289,970	$1,035,472	$3,115,023	$6,714,977	$14,082,674
Total Expenses	$313,414	$ 344,668	$ 311,916	$ 298,310	$ 385,056	$2,525,185	$ 4,178,549
% Sales	44.0	28.4	24.2	28.8	12.4	37.6	29.7
Number of Employees	11	9	12	11	14	106	163
Volume per Employee	$ 64,777	$ 134,965	$ 107,498	$ 94,134	$ 222,502	$ 63,349	$ 86,397

TABLE 8: Nichols Equipment Company Inventory Turnover Rates By Branch

Location	*Inventory Turnover*	*Machine Inventory Turnover*	*Parts Inventory Turnover*
Middleton		.09:1	1.77:1
Overland		1.74:1	3.30:1
Hayfield		1.26:1	3.07:1
Red Lion		.77:1	4.07:1
Lover		2.04:1	3.71:1
Upton		.84:1	1.36:1

- Inventory levels increased ($) during a period of declining sales (Figure 1). Total company inventory turnover has gone from 2.49 in 1974 to 1.65 in 1979 and 1.29 in 1980.
- High cost of branch operations (controllable) in relation to available sales and margins (not controllable).
- High initial five year cost of the new Upton premises.

The significant inventory increase has been in New Equipment (Figure 1). On the other hand, new equipment inventory turnover has gone from 2.7 in 1976 and 1977 to 1.2 in 1979. This is significantly below the suggested guideline that inventory levels should be equal to 90 days sales, or, in this case, an inventory turnover figure of 4.0. Furthermore, unit sales of new equipment have decreased from 149 in '76 to 85 in '79 to less than 70 in 1980.

The new equipment inventory problem is aggravated by the combination of decreasing unit sales and increasing unit value. The prices of 4 typical units increased by an average of 150% between 1976 and 1980. Similarly, figures for 1976 thru 1980, for total inventory as a percentage of total sales and new equipment inventory as a percentage of new equipment sales are shown below:

	1976	*1977*	*1978*	*1979*	*1980*
Total Inv. / Total Sales	42.3%	40.3%	53.2%	60.7%	62.4%
New Equip. Inv. / New Equip. Sales	36.7%	37.9%	55.5%	87.6%	85.1%

Though the largest inventory increases have been in the new equipment category, the parts inventory has increased from 16.5% of total inventory in 1975 to 28.1% in 1980. Parts inventory turnover in the same period declined from approximately 3.5 to 2.1. Table 8 illustrates turnover rates by branch locations for 1980.

CASE TWENTY-SIX

Independent Publishing Company

WILLIAM R. BOULTON
University of Georgia

DAN R. E. THOMAS
Stanford University

Assignment Questions:

1. What are John Ginn's problems?
2. What should John Ginn do?
3. How should Bob Marbut evaluate John Ginn in this situation?

John Ginn was quite proud of his accomplishments since joining the Harte-Hanks Newspaper (HHN) chain as President and Publisher of the Independent Publishing Co. (IPC). Since February 1, 1974, he had succeeded in improving both the internal operations and the community relations of IPC. His greatest coup had been in getting President Ford to come to Anderson, South Carolina, to be the keynote speaker of IPC's October 19 Anniversary Celebration and to dedicate their new newspaper building. A commemorative plaque of the occasion read:

> The Anderson
>
> INDEPENDENT/DAILY MAIL
>
> Dedicated October 19, 1974
>
> Address by President Gerald R. Ford

The ceremony, which received national television news coverage, had also been attended by Senators Thurmond and Hollings, South Carolina's Governor West, and HHN's top executives—Chairman Houston Harte, Director Andrew Shelton, President Bob Marbut, and Allan Johnson III (President of the Southern

Metro Group). As a result of this event, John's relations and image with HHN, IPC, and the Anderson community had become quite strong.

However, in spite of his successes, by early December John Ginn was faced with the possibility of losing his bonus for the year because of a rapid deterioration in the local economy. An increase in unemployment, from 2.1 percent in October to 8.4 percent in early December, had caused IPC's revenues and circulation to decline so rapidly that John had missed his budgeted managerial margin in November by nearly $60,000.[1] With this decline expected to continue through December, John Ginn was faced with the problem of taking some immediate actions to meet budget, or lose his profit sharing bonus for the year.

BACKGROUND

John Ginn, at age 37, had spent a major part of his career in the newspaper business. John was the son of a newspaper pressman in Longview, Texas. After graduating from the University of Missouri School of Journalism in 1959, he worked as a reporter, night wire editor, and chief copy editor for the Charlotte, (N.C.) *Observer*. In 1962 he spent a year as editor for the Kingsport (Tennessee) *Times-News* where he was given an award for "Best Editorial of the Year" in 1963. He then became city editor of the *Charlotte News* until 1966 when he became Public Relations Coordinator for Celanese Corporation. In 1967, John was appointed Manager of Advertising and Public Relations for Celanese Coatings Company. In 1970 he decided to attend the Harvard Business School where he received his MBA with high honors in 1972. He then became director of corporate development for the *Des Moines Register*, part of an Iowa-based newspaper group.

In December 1972, the group made him editor and publisher of the Jackson (Tennessee) *Sun*—a newly acquired paper. Though the Jackson position fulfilled John's long-term goal, the Anderson position offered even more opportunity. As John explained:

> I had had a great year in Jackson. There are great ego trips working in a local community as a publisher. I didn't think things could be as exciting the second year. But with Harte-Hanks I could do it again. This was an acquisition having problems and it had a high profile. Bob Marbut (President of HHN) also knew that I was turned on by being a "hero" and his "pitch" worked.

John Ginn had joined Harte-Hanks on February 1, 1974, as president and publisher of IPC's two Anderson newspapers—the *Independent* and the *Daily Mail*. John knew when he was hired that the Anderson newspapers had several problems which would require much of his time. When Bob Marbut and Allan Johnson talked with John, they had expressed three major concerns. First, the corporate internal auditors had found IPC's business controls totally inadequate. Second, neither the *Independent* nor *Daily Mail's* news reporting staffs were displaying the degree of professionalism considered appropriate by management. A third, and particularly delicate problem, was related to the morale of IPC employees and the company's relations with the community. John explained the challenges and problems that he had dealt with during the past ten months.

[1]Some numbers have been disguised.

> One of the most important challenges was building a business control system and getting a handle on the business office. In 1973 there were almost $250,000 of bad-debt write-offs on $4,000,000 in revenues. In late 1973 internal auditors had found practices where people had put checks in drawers for several months before depositing them. There were inadequate accounts receivable records, no linage planning, no credit control or budgeting. There was no atmosphere of questioning "why?" The same situation was found in marketing—there had been no analysis of why or how we did well or badly.
>
> When I arrived, we sent off information to headquarters and the computer sent back a profit statement which showed how well we had done. It surprised us all! My goal now is to know what our profit is before we sent it to headquarters. It has really been a challenge to get a handle on it—it was running wild.
>
> The second challenge was in the news area. Some of the people we had weren't very accomplished and, had they been, there weren't enough of them. One measure of this, for example, was the fact that we had never won a state press association award in 75 years of news reporting.

The most delicate problem John had dealt with was the deteriorating morale within the newspaper and the community, due to the uncertainty created by continued changes in IPC management. As John explained:

> Harte-Hanks had bought the newspapers in February, 1972 and had brought new people into the firm. Between March and June of 1973, the papers were moved out of town into a new facility. It was a whole new "ball-game." As a newcomer, I didn't really have much idea of how weak or strong the leadership of the former management had been.
>
> Bob Marbut had explained that the previous publisher had been fired and that this left inherent morale problems caused by the uncertainty it created. I was told that my predecessor had been well liked by the community and that there had been some discussion by the Anderson business community about getting on a plane and flying out to Texas to ask Bob to reconsider. This kind of action is not unusual. Since it's the community's newspaper, people often feel you can't just change it without their input.

CORPORATE EMPHASIS

Bob Marbut, President of HHN, considered the publisher as the focal point of HHN's professional management. His position as leader of his community's basic institutions led to a high profile and active role in the community. Bob commented in a company memorandum:

> A Harte-Hanks publisher has a most enviable job. He has the satisfaction that comes from running all facets of an exciting business—market research, product development, manufacturing, sales, distribution, personnel administration and policy. He has complete profit center responsibility and accountability.
>
> He is in the middle of all that goes on in his community. His advice is sought; his influence carries great weight. He is among the handful of key people who have the wherewithal to move a community or to hold it back.
>
> Yet, there is another dimension of his job—the most important and exciting part. A publisher has the great privilege and public trust to communicate infor-

mation—particularly the news—with integrity and dispatch. This is so important that his is the only profession specifically protected by the Constitution.[2]

One of Bob Marbut's main goals for Harte-Hanks was to improve its franchise in each local market. With respect to meeting its (HHN's) growth and profit goals, Bob commented:

> There's plenty of growth in the old girl yet. We should be able to meet our goals for the next three to five years with the companies we have now. Our goal is to improve our operating margin by one percent each year. In the meantime, we're constantly looking for new properties.

Each publisher was required to write a monthly report for Marbut including information on (1) his objectives achieved, (2) the objectives missed, (3) problems, (4) market information and (5) the outlook for next month. These reports were sent to the group head who summarized them and sent the individual reports and summary to Bob Marbut. Each month the financial figures for the first ten days were compiled into "flash reports" to provide red flag warnings of potential problems. Allan Johnson commented:

> We don't want to react to a bad quarter. With the flash reports, we can react to problems on a monthly basis, long before the end of the quarter.

Once John had accepted the job, he had worked with Allan Johnson, President of the Southern Metro Group, to develop IPC's objectives. However, since he knew little about IPC, Allan had made the major contribution, as John explained:

> Once I got here, objectives were developed with Allan Johnson. They were primarily to stabilize the situation, but didn't really get into strategy. It wouldn't make sense to talk strategy without knowing much about the newspaper. The only exposure I had was coming in once, as a visiting publisher, and looking around. Coming up with a strategy was one on my first tasks.
>
> I had set my objectives for the year the first month I came, but it was a great leap of faith on my part because I didn't have enough information to know. Allan said, "These are what the objectives should be," and I said, "O.K."

Publishers in HHN were held responsible not for net income, but for their "managerial margin" which included only the costs they could control. If a publisher met his profit goal, he would receive a substantial bonus, but Marbut would always negotiate another, higher goal. Marbut commented on his usual procedure:

> I sit down with each publisher and we eventually agree on a reasonable set of objectives for him. Then I tell him that if he does some other things I think are important we'll give him the "big bucks." The individual performance bonus can range from 20%–35% of base salary. Combined with profit sharing bonus, a publisher can earn an additional 50% of his base salary in bonuses. While a higher managerial margin is usually one of the objectives, other things that I think are important may also be included. For example, we may agree on some needed personnel changes.[3]

[2] Robert G. Marbut, "Responsibilities of a Harte-Hanks Publisher," Company memorandum.

[3] Quotes taken from Harte-Hanks Newspapers case ICCH No. 4-376-081. Published with permission.

For John Ginn, the objectives included the following:

	Must	*Good*	*Outstanding*
(1) Managerial margin	$1,050,000	$1,125,000	$1,200,000
(2) Operating revenues	$3,926,735	$4,144,887	$4,363,039
(3) Paid space	52%	53%	54%
(4) Bad debt write-offs	$ 77,000	$ 73,000	$ 70,000
(5) Circulation	50,000	54,000	55,000
(6) Nonunion status	no union	no elections	no threats

The bonus system offered two pay-off levels depending on the level of managerial margin achieved. No bonus would be paid until John achieved a level of $1,125,000. If John reached the "Good" level of managerial margin, he was able to go for a bonus pot of $4,000. The "Outstanding" level of managerial margin yielded a bonus pot of $12,000. The actual bonus received, once the pot was determined, depended on the number of goals achieved as a percentage of the total possible goals. This was then the percentage he would receive of the pot.

John was shooting for the "big" pot which he had planned to use to pay off the $7,000 balance he owed on the loan he had taken out while going to graduate school.

STRATEGY

Each of HHN's newspapers was a separate operation, with its own publisher and news staff. Each newspaper was expected to tailor its product to meet the specific needs of the individual community. Each newspaper was editorially autonomous from corporate headquarters to ensure freedom of the press and editorial independence in local markets.

IPC, located in Anderson, South Carolina, published a local and regional newspaper. The regional *Independent,* a morning newspaper, was distributed 7 days per week in two morning editions—a Georgia edition which averaged 29 pages and a South Carolina edition which averaged 27 pages with an average 36-page Sunday edition. The local *Daily Mail,* which averaged 24 pages per issue, duplicated the *Independent's* coverage in the Anderson area but provided an evening newspaper 5 days per week which was helpful in maintaining IPC's local franchise by making it difficult for new competition to enter the area.

The duplicate coverage of the two newspapers required that John develop a strategy which would distinguish them so that people could subscribe to both without feeling they were getting two versions of the same newspaper. John described the basis for such a strategy:

> The strategy is to get two papers in households where distribution overlaps. This has real validity for our advertisers since it provides them with a *reach* (circulation) of 40,000 copies with the morning *Independent,* plus *frequency,* with the two papers, of almost 10,000 copies of the afternoon *Daily Mail* which is distributed to those households closest to the Anderson trade area.

In June 1974, a memo from John Ginn and his editors, J. B. Hall and L. S. Hembree, was sent to all news staff defining the roles of the morning *Inde-*

pendent and the evening *Daily Mail* and establishing policies for implementing an ambitious growth plan.

The memo presented targeted growth of IPC's combined circulation reaching 85,000 within the next 48 months, up from 54,000 in June 1974. The following information and goals were included in the memo:

	Present Circulation	*Circulation Goal*	*Per Cent Increase*
Daily Mail	9,000	20,000	122%
Independent			
Georgia	14,000	26,000[4]	86%
S.C. (not Anderson)	12,000	20,000	67%
Anderson County	19,000	19,000	0%
Total *Independent*	45,000	65,000	44%
Total Both Papers	54,000	85,000	57%

The memo then proceeded to explain the underlying assumptions and the basic strategy for achieving these growth targets:

> You can see from the percentages shown here that these constitute very ambitious goals. However, we are convinced that you and your colleagues in news and elsewhere in this company are capable of achieving this kind of growth.
>
> To achieve this kind of growth, we will have to convince many households—especially in Anderson County—that it makes sense for them to subscribe both to the *Daily Mail* and to the *Independent.* In our opinion, superficial distinctions between the two papers will not be enough to accomplish this. The distinctions must be significant and deep rooted—factors that impact the way staff members are assigned, writing styles, how the wires are edited, typography, and decisions on the play of stories and pictures.
>
> This will mean a thorough understanding of each paper's role by all concerned and continued awareness of what we are trying to achieve as we publish each edition each day.
>
> Before getting into the several ways we plan for the newspapers to differ, we want to touch on some important *similarities* we want to achieve and/or sustain. We want both papers to strive to maintain high standards of journalism as they relate to fairness, accuracy, clear thinking, and clear statement. We believe the function of our news columns should be to serve readers, not to reward news sources. We want the papers to be independent of outside influence while avoiding the temptations to seek power for power's sake or to do harm to those who happen to disagree with us as individuals. We hope both papers will covet praise from readers that centers on integrity and compassion.

THE INDEPENDENT PUBLISHING CO.

Of IPC's 190 employees, about 25 were part-time and there were no union employees. The newspaper's new building, which President Ford had recently dedicated, had been completed and occupied between March and June 1973.

[4]See Exhibit 1. While the Georgia PAT counties of Franklin and Stephens had only 11,000 households, IPC had meaningful circulation in five other Georgia counties. The seven Georgia counties had a total of 41,000 households in 1974 and were growing at about 2 percent a year.

EXHIBIT 1: The Independent Publishing Company Definition of Market Sales Areas

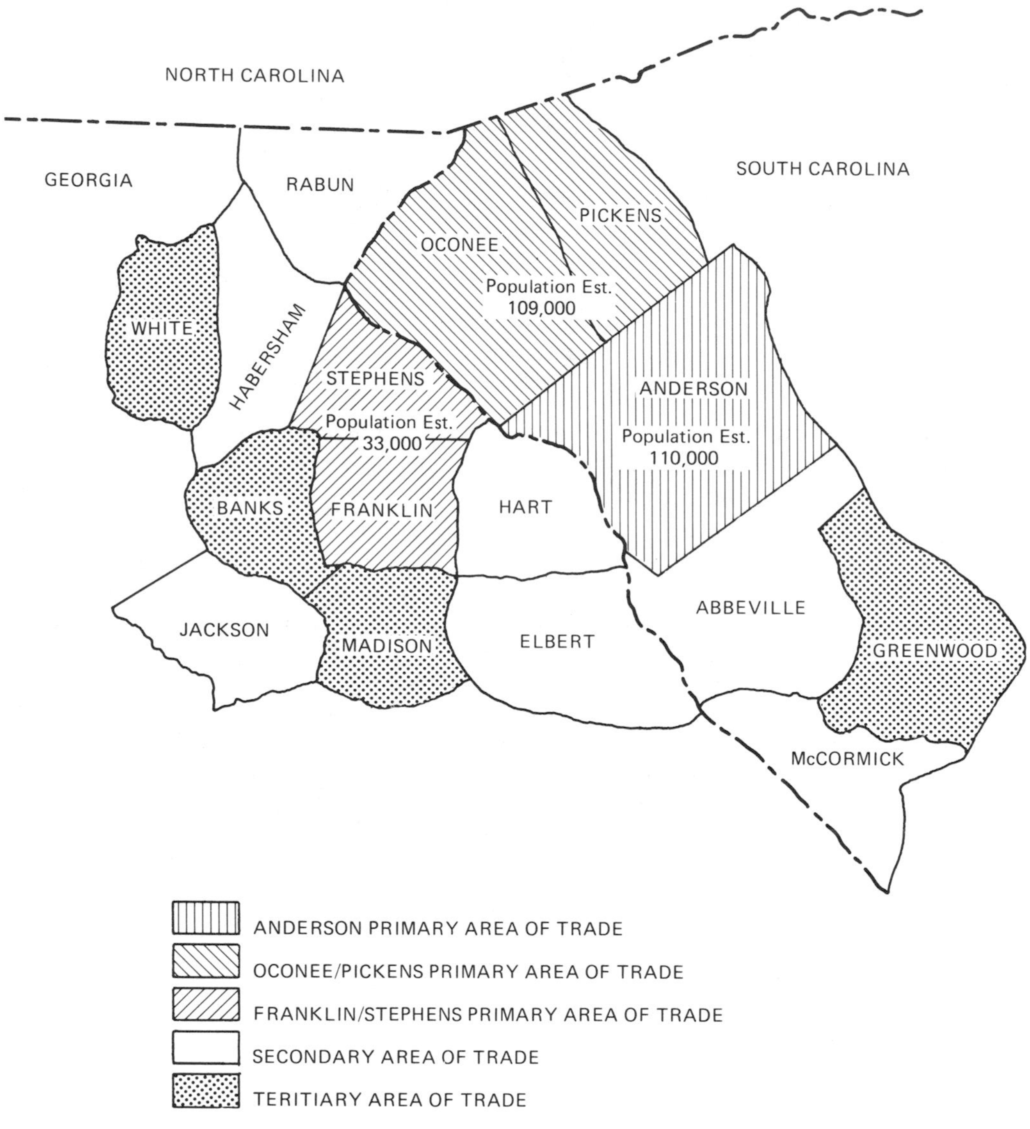

The newspapers had, at that time, been moved out of their old downtown facilities into this new building with all new equipment. The newspapers were printed using photo-composition methods together with an eight-unit Goss Urbanite press with one color unit.

IPC's primary area of trade (PAT) included three major zones. (See Exhibit 1). The dominant PAT zone was Anderson county with a population of almost 110,000 including over 36,000 households. The second PAT zone included Oconee and Pickens counties, located northeast of Anderson county, with a population of about 109,000 representing over 35,000 households. IPC's third PAT zone included Georgia's Stephens and Franklin counties, located west of Anderson county, with a population of about 33,000 which included over 11,000 households. This Georgia zone was the primary source of revenues for IPC's Georgia bureau located in Lavonia, Georgia.

Of the major trade centers in the three PATs (Anderson, Toccoa, and Senaca), Anderson with a population of 30,000 continued as the dominant city of the three due to its major educational, medical, and shopping facilities.

Competitive media within IPC's three PAT zones includes the following:

County	*Radio*	*TV*	*Weekly Newspapers*
Anderson	5	1	3
Oconee/Pickens	5	0	6
Franklin/Stephens	2	0	4

Radio and TV stations accounted for about 9 percent of the total advertising dollars spent in Anderson county with 1 percent going to the weekly newspapers. In the Oconee/Pickens zone, the six competitive weekly newspapers and five radio stations accounted for 85 percent of the advertising dollars spent in those counties. In the Franklin/Stephens zone, the four weekly newspapers and two radio stations accounted for approximately 80 percent of the advertising dollars spent in those counties.

THE DAILY MAIL

John Ginn saw the *Daily Mail* as a local newspaper emphasizing Anderson County news and features. He wanted to distinguish it from the *Independent* as an "especially lively, friendly, people-oriented, fun-to-read newspaper that features a good deal of reader involvement." To encourage subscriptions, the *Daily Mail* was priced at $2.05, about 60 percent of the *Independent's* price of $3.50 per subscription. A combined rate of $5.25 was offered. The carriers were billed directly for these papers at about 50 per cent of the subscription rate.

To encourage home subscriptions, single copy prices of both newspapers were kept ahead of home delivery rates. As John explained:

> This allows us to emphasize the service we provide to the subscriber. We tell subscribers that it's not only delivered but has a lower price than the single copy.

However, pricing was also a complex issue for single copies. Because of the coin-operated vending machines, pricing was a step function, i.e., prices must be changed by five cent intervals from 10 to 15 cents, etc.

THE INDEPENDENT

John saw the *Independent* as a serious, regional newspaper emphasizing investigative reporting, crime news, politics, government, etc. He felt, however, that the key to developing the *Independent's* circulation was through publishing multiple daily editions tailored to the area it served. His memo explained three editions he foresaw:

> The three editions we will move toward are (1) Georgia, (2) South Carolina (actually serving Abbeville, Greenwood, McCormick, Oconee and Pickens counties),

and (3) Anderson County. This three-edition arrangement will require significantly more replating than we now do, because the emphasis of each edition will vary.

The Georgia edition would feature better Georgia wire news, sports, women's news, and editorial commentary. In addition, a separate masthead would say, "Enjoy Northeast Georgia's Best-Read Newspaper," while the South Carolina editions would read, "South Carolina's Best Newspaper."

The South Carolina editions would emphasize more state wire news and investigative reporting in the region, state, and Anderson. The third edition would include more news, features and pictures from Anderson, but would still differ from the *Daily Mail* as described in the memo:

> . . . The *Independent's* Anderson coverage will focus more on the big spot local news, investigative reporting, government issues, politics, etc. For instance, had we experienced the recent Village B story under this strategy, both papers would have sought the hard news story. But when it came time to do follow-ups on the announcement, the *Daily Mail* would have focused on the people involved, the human interaction that leads to success, and possibly a profile of David Vandiver and/or other key leaders. The *Independent's* follow-up efforts would have focused more on the economic implications, how the project is scheduled to progress from announcement to completion, where employees are likely to come from, etc.
>
> The wire report in all editions of the *Independent* will be more complete and involve more depth and analysis than will the *Daily Mail's.*

In discussing the importance of the newspapers' franchise, it was continually pointed out that maintaining an established franchise was critical. As John explained:

> There are two important aspects of the franchise. First it allows you to keep out any competition because readers' habits become established and are hard to change. Secondly, if you give up, or lose your franchise, it is very expensive and extremely difficult, if not impossible, to rebuild it in the same area.
>
> My predecessor had cut off Georgia's unprofitable district, but I felt the Georgia circulation was important to the franchise. I felt we should make it profitable rather than cut it, so I have worked hard to establish the new bureau there.

EDITORIAL POLICY

Corporate policy required that when an HHN paper was the only newspaper in town, it covered both sides of a story regardless of its editorial stand. However, determining editorial policy was left up to the publisher. To carry out the function of determining IPC's editorial policies, John Ginn established an Editorial Board when he became the Publisher of IPC. Through the majority decision of the editors and managers who sat on the board, editorial issues would be resolved and supported by the newspapers.

By July 28, 1974, John had found himself in disagreement with the Board's decision that the newspaper's gubernatorial endorsement be for Bryan Dorn. John Ginn had deep personal convictions that Charles "Pug" Ravenel should get the endorsement, but he did not try to overrule the board. On July 29, 1974, John sent a letter to Ravenel to explain the papers' endorsement. Some excerpts follow:

> When I came here six months ago, my priority objectives involved building our integrity with readers, news sources and advertisers, and increasing the involvement of some talented editors and managers in our decision-making process. I feel we have made some progress to date in these directions.
>
> One element in this effort has been the establishment of our Editorial Board to determine editorial policy. I realize in establishing this board that there would be times when my own ideas would not prevail in determining the positions taken on our editorial pages. Indeed, if this were not the case, the existence of the board would be a farce.

After explaining that the split decision of the board members had gone to Dorn, John continued to explain his support of the process:

> I was personally very disappointed, because I have a deep conviction that your election to the governor's chair would be a hallmark for this state. But my priority is to build a newspaper organization with the characteristics I believe are essential to good journalism. Thus, while disappointed in the outcome of this decision, I remain devoted to the process that produced it.
>
> My intention with this letter is not to apologize for our endorsement. Rather I have detailed what for me was a personal dilemma because I am convinced your intellect and compassion are sufficient to appreciate my position.

In addition to the editorial board's involvement in political issues, it was also involved in decisions relating to the presentation of economic issues. John saw this as critical in maintaining credibility with the readers:

> We pay a lot of attention to how we handle economic news. Since the consumer confidence index is influenced by news, we have obligations that relate to our credibility. We have discussed internally what to put in and how much to say. We must say enough to reflect conditions accurately. But we must avoid sensationalizing—especially in bad times—because we have a role that could make matters worse.

COMMUNITY RELATIONS

As publisher of IPC, it was not surprising that John Ginn should become an important member of Anderson's community. Though he had declined membership on local corporate boards, John was actively involved in the Chamber of Commerce, YMCA, and United Fund. He also enjoyed his membership in the "Management Lunch Bunch" which consisted of a small group of local executives. In discussing his role in the local community's leadership, John explained:

> The previous owner of the Anderson newspapers had been one of the key leaders in Anderson. He, and the others, have now retired and have left a vacuum. The community now has a lot of old members who have not been used to having control, and a lot of new younger people who have recently come to Anderson. There is no clear leader or power broker and it is fun to be in the middle of it and watch it developing. Though I don't have any particular urge to be in the running, I wouldn't be unhappy if it happened.
>
> My commitment to the community is based on my commitment to Harte-Hanks and its franchise here. I am still new here and feel more identification with the company. How the company is perceived by the community is critical.

In an effort to improve the newspaper's interaction with its community, a new "action line" column had been established in May, called I-Line. John explained its purpose:

> We initiated the I-Line to improve reader involvement and not as a market research tool. It is the epitome of news reporting. In the past we had to guess at what our readers were interested in, but I-Line removes the guess-work because we know what the reader is interested in. This is key to our efforts to tailor all news to our local needs and interests.

ORGANIZATION

In an effort to tackle IPC's problems, John initiated some changes in personnel in March 1974. The first area of concern had been in IPC's editorial policies, and John had found it necessary to dismiss IPC's editor-in-chief. This action, however, created a vacancy which could not be filled without approval of IPC's prior owner. Nominations of L. S. Hembree in April and J. B. Hall in June 1974 had both been rejected and this vacancy continued. In April, J. B. Hall had taken ill and had an operation which kept him out of work until June.

However, in spite of editorial vacancies, John took immediate action to improve the editorial and news staffs through recruiting new university graduates. John explained:

> We decided to use the University of Missouri's Journalism School to recruit new graduates. I had gone to school there and felt it was a good school. I also had four good faculty contacts there who could tell me who was good. So I sat down with the editors and we figured out how many jobs we might fill with a low salary of around $150 per week. We felt we could use ten people so I called my faculty friends. They each sent a list of candidates on which 15 people were mentioned two or more times. I then called the school and arranged an interview room. Then I called the 15, one of whom had already accepted another job, and had 14 to dinner at the Ramada Inn on Saturday. After showing them slides and talking with them, I sent around a sign-up sheet and they all signed up for interviews on Monday. We eventually flew ten out here in a chartered airplane for the weekend. They all accepted and began work in June and July 1974.
>
> We were able to recruit them even against some strong competition. We know we can't keep them forever, but we can give them experience, provide a nice living environment, and help them find a job when they want to go.
>
> These hirees have increased the size of our news staff, which had been understaffed, by six people.

In the business office, John hired an experienced bookkeeper in an effort to begin improving accounting records. In March, however, the credit manager took ill and required the business manager, Ron Lentz, to take up with slack until a new credit manager, Laurie McWheene, joined IPC in May. With training and changes of business personnel, IPC began to gain some control over receivables and by the end of May receivables had been reduced from 70 days in 1973 to 40 days of sales. However, after finding a $10,000 accounting error in July, the business office was reorganized. In October John was still not satisfied as an internal audit by the corporate staff had revealed inadequate controls.

The advertising and circulation departments had also been affected. New people were hired and internal training was initiated in May and June to improve performance of both departments. In September a Circulation Sales Seminar was held for the 14 district sales managers and John was pleased with its success.

John Ginn had become personally involved in the development of IPC's management. He explained the importance of this role in a small organization like IPC.

> In an organization of this size, the education role of the general manager is very important. It requires that he be directly involved. It's not like being in a large firm where the personnel or training department are responsible for providing appropriate programs.
>
> In this industry, management development has been traditionally ignored. You would just be promoted and be expected to be a general manager.

John had previously used the Xerox Management Discussion Skills program in Jackson and found it a useful training program which also allowed him to learn about his managers. John explained about this two-day program which he held away from the office:

> This program is designed to improve problem-solving between the supervisor and subordinate. The key concepts developed are information gathering—decision-making versus information-giving. It uses a self-programmed text, a random numbers chart for answering questions, video tape for role playing, and questions for the leader to use.
>
> This has been a major training approach to develop management skills in both the business and editorial departments. It was traumatic for some of the older employees and I learned a lot from that, too.

John initiated the first MDS program in April and included eight of his key staff and managers. (See Exhibit 2). Another eight managers went through the program in June.

In order to maintain employee morale so that unionization would not become a threat, Harte-Hanks' managers had to keep in touch with employee attitudes so that situations did not develop which would attract unionization. As John Ginn explained:

> Keeping unions out means that I have to keep on top of employees' needs. We have initiated the employee attitude survey to get the kind of feedback we need. In order to minimize any threat to the employee, all employees return their survey to an appointed secretary, without names. They are then compiled by the secretary so that management can not know who has commented on what. Headquarter's industrial relations man is our major resource for this. He provides any support or information we might need.

The employee survey was completed in August with what management considered "surprisingly positive results."

On September 15 an employee picnic was held at Sadler's Creek Park. About 225 employees *and* family members attended. On September 18 the first edition of the Employee Reporter, a newly established employee newsletter, was issued. Other corrective programs were being formulated to deal with problems identified through the employee survey. The employee health insurance benefits had already been substantially improved at a lower cost through the Corporate Plan initiated in March. Employee evaluation and training programs were also being improved.

EXHIBIT 2: Independent Publishing Company

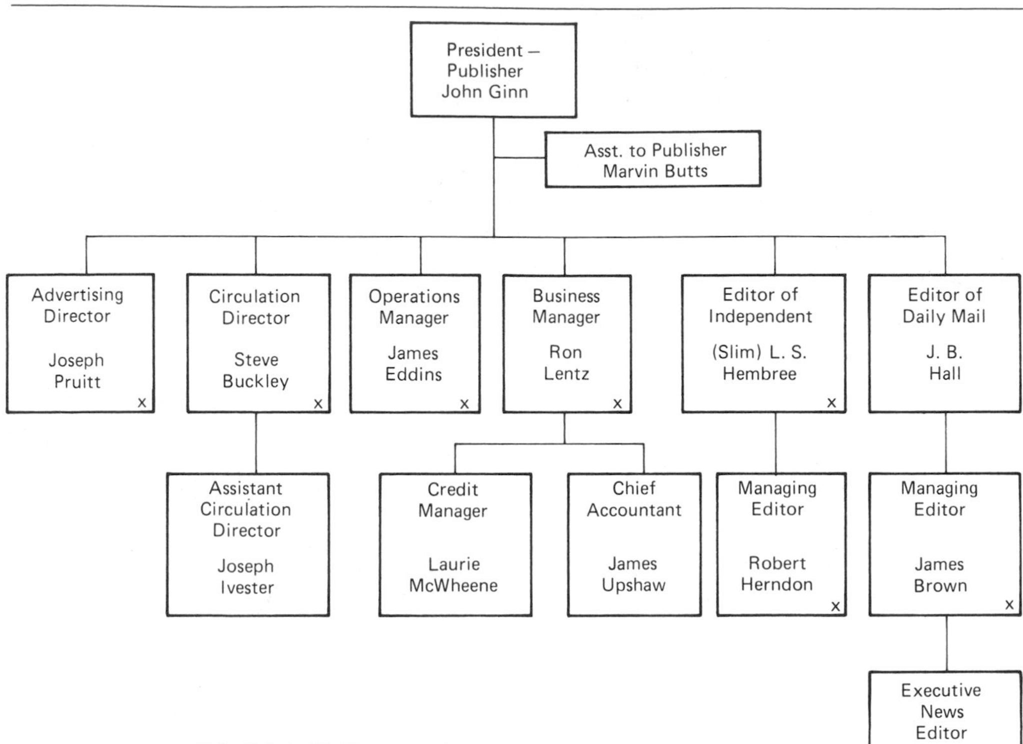

PRESIDENT'S VISIT

Nineteen-seventy-four represented two very significant anniversaries for the Anderson newspapers. October 1974 would be the 75th year of operation for Anderson's *Daily Mail* and the 50th year of the Anderson *Independent.* After a discussion of the anniversaries during the June management meeting, IPC management decided to have a public event and to do something special to reward IPC's advertisers and readers. John explained how President Ford became the keynote speaker.

> We hadn't decided on a speaker, yet, when Ford became President. At our staff meeting, while we were still debating as to whom to get, I said, "Let's go for Ford." It was a real lark, but we couldn't lose. If he said "no" we were simply back where we started. I assigned three men to specific tasks: one contacted the White House Staff, one went through Senator Thurmond and one through a Republican Congressional Candidate who had served in the Small Business Administration in Washington.
>
> I was so skeptical that I knew it wouldn't happen right up till the morning of October 19. When it came off, the high visibility of the President coming to Anderson to dedicate our new facility and participate in our anniversary celebration really helped our community image.

The preparations were substantial and consumed management's time for nearly a month prior to the celebration as John explained:

> In October we were working full-time getting ready for the President's visit. If he came, I was willing to do whatever was necessary, but I insisted that there be no politicizing on our grounds.

With the scheduled anniversary celebration, John and his staff knew that it would be difficult to make Harte-Hanks' November 1, 1974, deadline for submitting 1975 budgets. However, it proved to be another opportunity to be a "hero" and IPC's 1975 budget was completed on October 11, 1974. John commented on his projected budget after the celebration:

> We submitted our 1975 budget in October before the President's visit. Even though we had the perfect reason to miss the November 1 deadline, we wanted to be heroes. By November 1, corporate will have already put our next year's budget figures into the computer.
>
> We have budgeted an increase of 15 percent in revenues and 18 percent in managerial margin for next year. We don't think this will be too difficult to achieve. To date this year, all of our revenue accounts have been ahead of budget, and expenses are about one percent under budget. This gives us a margin of about 7 percent over budget and a 36 percent improvement in margin over 1973.
>
> As a matter of fact, we have decided to sacrifice about $60,000 in December revenues by moving our annual Progress[5] edition from December to January. The problem was that my predecessor had moved it into December to gain sales, but it didn't do well because salesmen were still busy selling Christmas advertising. Though we had budgeted it for December, we decided to bite the bullet and move it back into January.

UNEMPLOYMENT

While unemployment in Anderson and Oconee counties had been at about 2.1 per cent in early October, by November the economy was beginning to decline. On November 3, 1974, the *Independent/Daily Mail* carried an article indicating the seriousness of the situation:

> The nation's unemployment rate jumped to six percent in October for the first time in three years, emphasizing the economy's deepening slump. . . .
>
> Administration economic advisors, who now acknowledge the current economic condition is likely to be judged a recession, predict unemployment will rise to seven percent. . . .
>
> We don't expect any improvements in the employment situation. More cutbacks are expected. . . .
>
> In my opinion, if there are any improvements coming anytime soon, it will probably be in the second quarter of next year . . .

By November 26, total unemployment in Anderson County had reached six percent. The softening economy caused more than 2,000 layoffs in Anderson during November and early December. About 2,000 more employees experienced shorter work weeks. Though the community's industrial base had been

[5]The Progress edition was published annually by IPC as a service to the community and as a vehicle for selling space to firms which did not normally advertise. This edition would highlight events of the area over the past year and developments within the community.

diversifying, the textile industry remained dominant and was the major industry being affected. By early December unemployment in Anderson county had reached 8.4 per cent with no near-term prospect for improvement in sight.

As a result of the downturn, IPC's retail, classified, and circulation revenues dropped rapidly. Due to decreased levels of advertising, revenues were down \$28,800 in retail, \$24,100 in classifieds, \$2,600 in general, \$8,900 in inserts, and \$3,100 in other advertising for a total of \$67,500 below budget. This was partially offset by over-budget performance of \$8,200 in circulation and \$19,200 from the first large (2 million unit) commercial press run for a net decline in revenues of \$40,200 in November. In addition, there were also 1,822 subscription cancellations in November with "no job" as the main reason given for cancellation. Expenses were \$18,300 over budget due to \$9,100 in unbudgeted circulation promotion expense and \$9,200 in commercial newsprint expense. (See Exhibit 3 for financial details.)

Results for November were

	Actual	*Budget*	*Per Cent Variance*
Revenues	384.3	424.5	− 9.5
Expenses	315.6	297.3	+ 6.2
Managerial Margin	68.7	127.3	−46.0

In early December, the major commercial printing customer, which had contributed \$19,200 to November revenues, decided against printing their December newsprint insert. John Ginn felt the "Flash" report for December was optimistic:

	Budget	*Flash*
Revenues	474.6	415.0
Expenses	308.5	299.8
Managerial Margin	166.1	115.2

This meant that with November's results being \$58,600 below budgeted margin, plus an estimated \$51,000 decline in December, John's bonus was in jeopardy. Given current projections, he would miss the \$1,125,000 level of managerial margin by \$20,000.

ALTERNATIVES

Since no single action appeared to be available for resolving the problem John reviewed the various options which he felt were available. In a memo to his management group, John outlined those alternatives which he felt provided the greatest potential for improving performance and asked his managers to make appropriate recommendations for actions. Since he had sent off his December Flash Report that same day, he wanted to be prepared for inquiries from Allan Johnson and have begun implementation of appropriate action before he heard from top management.

Opportunities for cutting expenses included:

Circulation: On October 1, 1974, IPC had raised its subscription and single copy rates for both the *Independent* and *Daily Mail.* Street sales prices increased from 10 cents to 15 cents daily and from 25 cents to 35 cents on Sunday. Home delivery rates increased from $1.70 to $2.05 for the *Daily Mail* and from $3.15 to $3.50 for the *Independent.* In addition, a combined rate of $5.25 was offered.

IPC's management had expected this price increase to cause subscription cancellations so John had hired an outside circulation solicitation firm. Though their efforts had yielded IPC a net circulation gain of 1,051 in October, there was a net decline of 712 in November, as reported:

	November 1974	*October 1974*	*November 1973*
Morning	45,536	45,787	44,172
Evening	9,424	9,511	7,861
Total	54,960	55,298	52,033
Sunday	49,352	49,726	47,004

The solicitation firm had managed to offset the 1,973 cancellations in October with 3,024 new subscriptions. In November, however, the firm had failed to completely offset the 1,822 cancellations experienced by IPC.

Though cancellation would save IPC about $10,000 per month in circulation promotion expense, John wondered whether furloughing the firm would require even greater retrenchment and cost cutting action to overcome the loss of new subscription revenue.

Georgia Bureau. In an effort to increase the *Independent's* readership, John's first major action had been to expand the Georgia Bureau into a full-service bureau. Though the bureau had provided a positive contribution, it continued to remain below budget, as shown:

Georgia Bureau Results

	November		*October*		*September*		*August*	
	Budget	*Actual*	*Budget*	*Actual*	*Budget*	*Actual*	*Budget*	*Actual*
Revenues	$21,175	$14,370	$20,052	$14,404	$14,625	$7,810	$11,550	$11,219
Expenses	7,555	9,164	7,759	10,765	7,456	7,732	7,483	5,110
Contribution	$13,620	$ 5,206	$12,293	$ 3,639	$ 7,168	$ 78	$ 4,067	$ 6,109

Though the bureau cost $9,164 (charged to advertising) to operate in November, it had generated $3,120 in advertising revenues and $11,250 in circulation revenues. John knew that closing the bureau would result in total loss of advertising revenues, but he did not know what effect the closure would have on circulation revenues.

Zoning Strategy. John wondered what effect cutting out the Georgia Bureau would have on his zoning strategy. Though he knew IPC would still sell newspapers in Georgia without a bureau, it would reduce IPC's ability to tailor the *Independent's* Georgia edition to that community.

This also raised the option of discontinuing the zoning strategy and selling the same paper to both Georgia and South Carolina residents. Currently, IPC averaged five replates per day which John estimated to cost about $50 per plate. Thus a change in strategy would represent a savings in direct materials of about

EXHIBIT 3: Independent Publishing Company Divisional Contribution Summary November 1974

(1) Operating Revenues	*Current Month*			*Year to Date*		
Description	*Actual*	*Budget*	*Last Year*	*Actual*	*Budget*	*Last Year*
Advertising Revenue						
Retail advertising revenue	190,777	219,587	197,909	1,952,373	1,940,816	1,761,630
General advertising revenue	17,227	19,865	17,177	186,981	171,906	144,581
Classified advertising revenue	38,053	62,188	57,049	636,040	688,974	684,624
Paid inserts	15,402	24,350	20,727	182,481	183,375	188,522
Other advertising revenue	4,366	7,493	1,164	56,171	67,905	7,694
Total advertising revenue	265,825	333,483	294,025	3,014,046	3,052,976	2,787,251
Circulation revenue						
City zone—circulation	31,276	28,475	26,151	315,854	310,360	270,869
Retail zone—circulation	57,412	51,961	40,151	548,990	536,844	451,651
Other zone—circulation	6,504	6,508	5,261	63,970	70,265	69,401
Total circulation revenue	95,192	86,944	71,562	928,814	917,469	791,921
Other operating revenue						
Other operating revenues	23,274	4,120	5,689	67,656	39,080	33,383
Total other operating revenue	23,274	4,120	5,689	67,656	39,080	33,383
Total operating revenue	384,291	424,547	371,276	4,010,516	4,009,525	3,612,556
(2) Total Expenses by Category						
Payroll expense	135,578	135,436	110,683	1,347,027	1,384,878	1,253,227
Fringe benefits	5,178	3,300	4,679	46,447	35,700	44,221
Payroll taxes	10,164	7,500	5,399	102,471	87,200	82,567
Employee expense	7,600	7,938	5,456	102,511	73,110	58,356
Outside services	37,097	41,333	36,016	428,693	416,991	383,904
Newsprint expense	84,575	72,677	51,663	577,885	638,419	610,096
Other direct materials	20,077	10,657	7,662	170,612	148,581	82,139
Indirect materials	8,307	9,043	5,681	65,428	82,547	712,720
Supplies	5,923	4,517	8,478	66,079	45,752	51,266
Promotion expense	15,543	2,740	1,915	75,232	37,145	23,268
Repairs and paint	1,574	1,516	2,046	19,818	18,371	14,123
Other managed expense	4,551	1,460	57,939	36,438	51,424	202,073
Managed depreciation						309

Depreciation expense	8,012	7,900	5,617	86,584	78,254	74,873
Leased facilities						2,655
Taxes	4,775	4,200	8,883	48,862	34,700	25,955
Management services	4,136	4,400	4,907	41,850	46,000	50,028
Interest expense						534
Capital gains and losses				1,049		
Misc. operating income						830
Total	333,489	314,617	317,026	3,221,286	3,185,132	3,030,554
Profit before tax	50,801	109,930	54,251	789,230	824,393	582,001
(3) *Managed Expenses by Department*						
Advertising department	26,347	25,279	51,163	248,824	251,012	341,741
Business office	10,614	8,048	5,178	80,359	66,647	34,956
Circulation department	33,863	39,849	55,429	387,924	423,836	387,798
Editorial department	43,693	47,748	34,566	457,012	459,843	490,487
Production department	51,283	52,423	47,266	54,056	573,306	540,822
Production commercial work	17,175	1,260	3,138	18,900	11,340	15,350
Direct materials department	71,947	83,013	58,646	735,475	780,111	684,422
Service departments	19,810	8,746	6,446	125,499	103,611	61,152
Management	22,454	19,368	21,534	257,235	220,807	196,084
Other managed expense	18,247	11,550	10,599	172,645	131,450	136,227
Total managed expense	315,633	297,284	294,035	3,019,928	3,022,013	2,459,037
Managerial margin	68,657	127,263	77,242	990,587	987,512	753,519
(% margin/revenue)	22	30	21	25	25	21
Other div. income and expense	17,856	17,333	22,991	200,309	163,119	171,813
Divisional contribution	50,801	109,930	54,251	790,278	824,393	581,706
(% contribution/revenue)	18	26	15	20	21	16
Interest expense						534
Net profit from operations	50,801	109,930	54,251	790,278	824,393	581,171
(% net profit from oper./rev)	18	26	15	20	21	13
Nonoperating income and expense				1,049		830
Profit before tax	50,801	109,930	54,251	789,230	824,393	582,001
(% profit before tax/rev)	18	26	15	20	21	16

$7,500 per month. Obviously, this would eliminate IPC's ability to run zoned advertising and would encourage fall-off in Georgia circulation.

The strategy of maintaining a strong distinction between the *Independent* and *Daily Mail* also led to increased production costs in both staff and production facilities. The difference in emphasis on news coverage and features allowed for few economies of production between the two newspapers. By reducing the variation between the two papers, John felt he could significantly reduce the production hours per page. However, he questioned what the long-range effect would be on the franchise and the ability of IPC to maintain dual subscriptions in the Anderson area. A reduction in density of coverage due to a loss in dual subscriptions would require a reduction in full-line advertising rates and possibly a greater loss in revenues than the increased production economies. At best, the *Daily Mail* could break even under present operations, but it allowed IPC to maintain the franchise through its evening paper thereby keeping out potential competition.

John also saw the option of concentrating circulation on the higher density primary markets. Cutting out the less profitable outlying subscriptions would reduce circulation by about 7,100.

Telephones. John had become concerned with the telephone expense which was $8,374 in November. Though he was not aware of what savings could be made, he felt a telephone log system would allow individual accountability for long-distance calls. The problem with such a system would be in taking away from time otherwise used in gathering news, selling ads, etc.

Newsprint. In IPC's newspaper production, newsprint accounted for about 20 per cent of total operating costs, or about $130,000 per month.

John saw an alternative of reducing the width of the newspaper. He estimated the cost of altering equipment to reduce the width from 60 inches to 58 inches at about $1,000. Reducing the width to 56 inches or less would cost about $20,000, because of more drastic equipment alterations. He estimated monthly savings of $2,000 for the 58 inch width and $4,000 for the 56 inch width. He had no idea what impact such a change might have on readers or advertisers.

Personnel. The largest monthly expense incurred by IPC was payroll and associated personnel expenses. This accounted for 50 per cent of IPC's operating costs. Some of the alternatives discussed for reducing personnel expenses included laying off copy boys and having editors absorb their tasks, laying off some secretarial help and having managers absorb their tasks, laying off part-time night-watchmen and phone operators and consolidating some of these jobs into full-time positions for other production and clerical people, and laying off two reporters, two copy editors and one district circulation manager. Though this would result in an estimated savings of $5,000 per month John was concerned as to what impact such layoffs might have on IPC's existing nonunion labor environment and the quality of their products.

In addition to these expense cutting measures, John also saw some revenue-generating alternatives which included:

Advertising Revenues. Increasing the percentage of paid advertising to over 53 per cent of total space would require a basic change in editorial policy. At present, it was IPC's policy that there would be no advertising on key pages, including the front page, the front page of each section, the stock page, the editorial page, and the comic section. John explained the resulting problem:

> By the time we insert all of our ads the way they fit, we use all the remaining space. On the average, we have only 53 per cent space left and any change in that would require a change in policy.

However, given the economic decline, operating revenues were falling and the problem was in maintaining 53 per cent of paid space.

There was also the option of raising advertising rates. The last rate increase had been a 12 per cent increase May 1, 1974. Though John felt an 8 per cent to 10 per cent increase in rates beginning next month might yield $20,000 or so in additional revenues, he also knew that advertisers were undergoing a similar economic pinch and might stop advertising if rates were to increase.

Another alternative was to increase advertising rates of contracted advertisers. Though large advertising accounts committed to one year volumes, about 40 per cent had not yet been moved to the May 1 rates. Though a contract provision allows for such rate increases with a 30–day notice, IPC had not previously enforced the provision and was concerned as to what effect it might have on these advertisers. He estimated $7,000 to $8,000 an increased monthly revenues if there was no loss in volume.

Circulation Rates. With a 12 per cent rate increase just two months ago, John was concerned that an additional increase might seriously jeopardize IPC's circulation base. However, he felt another 10 per cent increase might yield $8,000 to $9,000 in revenues depending on how much circulation volume was lost.

After determining that no specific alternative actions could possibly reduce IPC's operating costs to a level required for maintaining profitable operations, John had to decide what his strategy should be in this regard. He explained his dilemma:

> As an organization, we have to work together. I have a commitment to the bright young people who we have hired and who have worked hard. We have worked together as management and are a team.
>
> As employees, I feel we're in it together. Whatever we create, we have to live with. I don't want to make decisions that will hurt our product, the organization's morale, or our long-term franchise in the community.

CASE TWENTY-SEVEN

The Lincoln Electric Company

ARTHUR D. SHARPLIN
Northeast Louisiana University

Assignment Questions:

1. Why has Lincoln Electric been so successful?
2. What role does their merit rating system serve?
3. What changes are needed in the future?

INTRODUCTION

The Lincoln Electric Company is the world's largest manufacturer of welding machines and electrodes. Lincoln employs 2400 workers in two U.S. factories near Cleveland and approximately 600 in three factories located in other countries. This does not include the field sales force of more than 200 persons. It has been estimated that Lincoln's market share (for arc welding equipment and supplies) is more than 40%.

The Lincoln incentive management plan has been well known for many years. Many college management texts make reference to the Lincoln plan as a model for achieving high worker productivity. Certainly, Lincoln has been a successful company according to the usual measures of success.

James F. Lincoln died in 1965 and there was some concern, even among employees, that the Lincoln system would fall into disarray, that profits would decline, and that year-end bonuses might be discontinued. Quite the contrary, fifteen years after Lincoln's death, the company appears stronger than ever. Each year since 1965 has seen higher profits and bonuses. Employee morale and productivity remain high. Employee turnover is almost nonexistent except for retirements. Lincoln's market share is stable.

A HISTORICAL SKETCH

In 1895, after being "frozen out" of the depression-ravaged Elliott-Lincoln Company, a maker of Lincoln-designed electric motors, John C. Lincoln took out his second patent and began to manufacture his improved motor. He opened his new business, unincorporated, with $200 he had earned redesigning a motor

Reprinted by permission of the author and the Case Research Association.

for young Herbert Henry Dow, who later founded The Dow Chemical Company.

Started during an economic depression and cursed by a major fire after only one year in business, Lincoln's company grew, but hardly prospered, through its first quarter century. In 1906, John C. Lincoln incorporated his company and moved from his one-room, fourth-floor factory to a new three-story building he erected in east Cleveland. In his new factory, he expanded his work force to 30 and sales grew to over $50,000 a year. John Lincoln preferred being an engineer and inventor rather than a manager, though, and it was to be left to another Lincoln to manage the company through its years of success.

In 1907, after a bout with typhoid forced him from Ohio State in his senior year, James F. Lincoln, John's younger brother, joined the fledgling company. In 1914, with the company still small and determined to improve its financial condition, he became the active head of the firm, with the titles of General Manager and Vice-President. John Lincoln, while he remained President of the company for some years, became more involved in other business ventures and in his work as an inventor.

One of James Lincoln's early actions as head of the firm was to ask the employees to elect representatives to a committee which would advise him on company operations. The Advisory Board has met with the chief executive officer twice monthly since that time. This was only the first of a series of innovative personnel policies which have, over the years, distinguished Lincoln Electric from its contemporaries.

The first year the Advisory Board was in existence, working hours were reduced from 55 per week, then standard, to 50 hours a week. In 1915, the company gave each employee a paid-up life insurance policy. A welding school, which continues today, was begun in 1917. In 1918, an employee bonus plan was attempted. It was not continued, but the idea was to resurface and become the backbone of the Lincoln Management System.

The Lincoln Electric Employees' Association was formed in 1919 to provide health benefits and social activities. This organization continues today and has assumed several additional functions over the years. By 1923, a piecework pay system was in effect, employees got two-week paid vacations each year, and wages were adjusted for changes in the Consumer Price Index. Approximately thirty percent of Lincoln's stock was set aside for key employees in 1914 when James F. Lincoln became General Manager and a stock purchase plan for all employees was begun in 1925.

The Board of Directors voted to start a suggestion system in 1929. The program is still in effect but cash awards, a part of the early program, were discontinued several years ago. Now, suggestions are rewarded by additional "points," which affect year-end bonuses.

The legendary Lincoln bonus plan was proposed by the Advisory Board and accepted on a trial basis by James Lincoln in 1934. The first annual bonus amounted to about 25 percent of wages. There has been a bonus every year since then. The bonus plan has been a cornerstone of the Lincoln Management System and recent bonuses have approximated annual wages.

By 1944, Lincoln employees enjoyed a pension plan, a policy of promotion from within, and continuous employment. Base pay rates were determined by formal job evaluation and a merit rating system was in effect.

In the prologue to James F. Lincoln's last book, Charles G. Herbruck writes regarding the foregoing personnel innovations,

> They were not to buy good behavior. They were not efforts to increase profits. They were not antidotes to labor difficulties. They did not constitute a "do gooder" program. They were expressions of mutual respect for each person's importance to the job to be done. All of them reflect the leadership of James Lincoln, under whom they were nurtured and propagated (Lincoln, 1961, p. 11).

By the start of World War II, Lincoln Electric was the world's largest manufacturer of arc-welding products. Sales of about $4,000,000 in 1934 had grown to $24,000,000 by 1941. Productivity per employee more than doubled during the same period.

During the War, Lincoln Electric prospered as never before. Despite challenges to Lincoln's profitability by the Navy's Price Review Board and the tax deductiblity of employee bonuses by the Internal Revenue Service, the company increased its profits and paid huge bonuses.

Certainly since 1935 and probably for several years before that, Lincoln productivity has been well above the average for similar companies. Lincoln claims levels of productivity more than twice those for other manufacturers from 1945 onward. Information available from sources other than the company tends to support these claims.

COMPANY PHILOSOPHY

James F. Lincoln was the son of a Congregational minister and Christian principles were at the center of his business philosophy. The confidence that he had in the efficacy of Christ's teachings is illustrated by the following remark taken from one of his books:

> The Christian ethic should control our acts. If it did control our acts, the savings in cost of distribution would be tremendous. Advertising would be a contact of the expert consultant with the customer, in order to give the customer the best product available when all of the customer's needs are considered. Competition then would be in improving the quality of products and increasing efficiency in producing and distributing them; not in deception, as is now too customary. Pricing would reflect efficiency of production; it would not be selling a dodge that the customer may well be sorry he accepted. It would be proper for all concerned and rewarding for the ability used in producing the product.[1]

There is no indication that Lincoln attempted to evangelize his employees or customers—or the general public for that matter. The current Board chairman, Mr. Irrgang, and the President, Mr. Willis, do not even mention the Christian gospel in their recent speeches and interviews. The company motto, "The actual is limited, the possible is immense," is prominently displayed but there is no display of religious slogans and there is no company chapel.

Attitude Toward the Customer. James Lincoln saw the customer's needs as the *raison d'être* for every company. "When any company has achieved success so that it is attractive as an investment," he wrote, "all money usually

[1] James F. Lincoln, *A New Approach To Industrial Economics* (New York: The Devin Adair Co., 1961), p. 64.

needed for expansion is supplied by the customer in retained earnings. It is obvious that the customer's interests, not the stockholder's, should come first."[2] In 1947 he said, "Care should be taken . . . not to rivet attention on profit. Between 'How much do I get?' and 'How do I make this better, cheaper, more useful?" the difference is fundamental and decisive."[3] Mr. Willis still ranks the customer as Lincoln's most important constituency. This is reflected in Lincoln's policy to "at all times price on the basis of cost and at all times keep pressure on our cost . . ."[4] Lincoln's goal, often stated, is "to build a better and better product at a lower and lower price."[5] It is obvious, James Lincoln said, "that the customer's interests should be the first goal of industry."[6]

Attitude Toward Stockholders. Stockholders are given last priority at Lincoln. This is a continuation of James Lincoln's philosophy: "The last group to be considered is the stockholders who own stock because they think it will be more profitable than investing money in any other way."[7] Concerning division of the largess produced by incentive management, Lincoln writes, "The absentee stockholders also will get their share, even if undeserved, out of the greatly increased profit that the efficiency produces."[8]

Attitude Toward Unionism. There has never been a serious effort to organize Lincoln employees. While James Lincoln criticized the labor movement for "selfishly attempting to better its position at the expense of the people it must serve,"[9] he still had kind words for union members. He excused abuses of union power as "the natural reactions of human beings to the abuses to which management has subjected them."[10] Lincoln's idea of the correct relationship between workers and managers is shown by this comment: "Labor and management are properly not warring camps; they are parts of one organization in which they must and should cooperate fully and happily."[11]

Beliefs and Assumptions About Employees. If fulfilling customer needs is the desired goal of business, then employee performance and productivity are the means by which this goal can best be achieved. It is the Lincoln attitude toward employees, reflected in the following quotations, which is credited by many with creating the record of success the company has experienced:

> The greatest fear of the worker, which is the same as the greatest fear of the industrialist in operating a company, is the lack of income . . . The industrial manager is very conscious of his company's need of uninterrupted income. He is completely oblivious, evidently, of the fact that the worker has the same need.[12]

> He is just as eager as any manager is to be part of a team that is properly organized and working for the advancement of our economy. . . . He has no

[2]Ibid., p. 119.

[3]"You Can't Tell What a Man Can Do—Until He Has the Chance," *Reader's Digest,* January 1947, p. 94.

[4]George E. Willis' letter to author of 7 September 1978.

[5]Lincoln, 1961, p. 47.

[6]Ibid., p. 117.

[7]Ibid., p. 38.

[8]Ibid., p. 122.

[9]Ibid., p. 18.

[10]Ibid., p. 76.

[11]Ibid., p. 72.

[12]Ibid., p. 36.

desire to make profits for those who do not hold up their end in production, as is true of absentee stockholders and inactive people in the company.[13]

If money is to be used as an incentive, the program must provide that what is paid to the worker is what he has earned. The earnings of each must be in accordance with accomplishment.[14]

Status is of great importance in all human relationships. The greatest incentive that money has, usually, is that it is a symbol of success. . . . The resulting status is the real incentive. . . . Money alone can be an incentive to the miser only.[15]

There must be complete honesty and understanding between the hourly worker and management if high efficiency is to be obtained.[16]

Lincoln's Business

Arc-welding has been the standard joining method in the shipbuilding industry for decades. It is the predominant way of joining steel in the construction industry. Most industrial plants have their own welding shops for maintenance and construction. Manufacturers of tractors and all kinds of heavy equipment use arc-welding extensively in the manufacturing process. Many hobbyists have their own welding machines and use them for making metal items such as patio furniture and barbeque pits. The popularity of welded sculpture as an art form is growing.

While advances in welding technology have been frequent, arc-welding products, in the main, have hardly changed except for Lincoln's Innershield process. This process utilizing a self-shielded, flux cored electrode, has established new cost saving opportunities for construction and equipment fabrication. The most popular Lincoln electrode, the Fleetweld 5P, has been virtually the same since the 1930's. The most popular engine-driven welder in the world, the Lincoln SA-200, has been a gray-colored assembly including a four-cylinder Continental "Red Seal" engine and a 200 ampere direct-current generator with two current-control knobs for at least three decades. A 1980 model SA-200 even weighs almost the same as the 1950 model and it certainly is little changed in appearance.

Lincoln and its competitors now market a wide range of general purpose and specialty electrodes for welding mild steel, aluminum, cast iron, and stainless and special steels. Most of these electrodes are designed to meet the standards of the American Welding Society, a trade association. They are thus essentially the same as to size and composition from one manufacturer to any other. Every electrode manufacturer has a limited number of unique products, but these typically constitute only a small percentage of total sales.

Lincoln's research and development expenditures have recently been less than one and one half percent of sales. There is evidence that others spend several times as much as a percentage of sales.

Lincoln's share of the market has been between thirty and forty percent for many years and the welding products market has grown somewhat faster than the level of industry in general. The market is highly price-competitive, with

[13] Ibid., p. 75.
[14] Ibid., p. 98.
[15] Ibid., p. 92.
[16] Ibid., p. 39.

variations in prices of standard products normally amounting to only a percent or two. Lincoln's products are sold directly by its engineering-oriented sales force and indirectly through its distributor organization. Advertising expenditures amount to less than one-fourth of one percent of sales, one-third as much as a major Lincoln competitor with whom the casewriter checked.

The other major welding process, flame-welding, has not been competitive with arc-welding since the 1930's. However, plasma-arc-welding, a relatively new process which uses a conducting stream of super heated gas (plasma) to confine the welding current to a small area, has made some inroads, especially in metal tubing manufacturing, in recent years. Major advances in technology which will produce an alternative superior to arc-welding within the next decade or so appear unlikely. Also it seems likely that changes in the machines and techniques used in arc-welding will be evolutionary rather than revolutionary.

Products. The company is primarily engaged in the manufacture and sale of arc-welding products—electric welding machines and metal electrodes. Lincoln also produces electric motors ranging from half horsepower to 200 horsepower. Motors constitute about eight to ten percent of total sales.

The electric welding machines, some consisting of a transformer or motor and generator arrangement powered by commercial electricity and others consisting of an internal combustion engine and generator, are designed to produce from 30 to 1000 amperes of electrical power. This electrical current is used to melt a consumable metal electrode with the molten metal being transferred in a super hot spray to the metal joint being welded. Very high temperatures and hot sparks are produced and operators usually must wear special eye and face protection and leather gloves, often along with leather aprons and sleeves.

Welding electrodes are of two basic types: (1) Coated "stick" electrodes, usually fourteen inches long and smaller than a pencil in diameter, which are held in a special insulated holder by the operator, who must manipulate the electrode in order to maintain a proper arc-width and pattern of deposition of the metal being transferred. Stick electrodes are packaged in six to fifty-pound boxes. (2) Coiled wire, ranging in diameter from 0.035″ to 0.219″, which is designed to be fed continuously to the welding arc through a "gun" held by the operator or positioned by automatic positioning equipment. The wire is packaged in coils, reels and drums weighing from fourteen to 1,000 pounds.

Manufacturing Operations

Plant Locations. The main plant is in Euclid, Ohio, a suburb on Cleveland's east side. The layout of this plant is shown in Figure 1. There are no warehouses. Materials flow from the half-mile long dock on the north side of the plant throughout the production lines to a very limited storage and loading area on the south. Materials used at each work station are stored as close as possible to the work station. The administrative offices, near the center of the factory, are entirely functional. Not even the President's office is carpeted. A corridor below the main level provides access to the factory floor from the main entrance near the center of the plant.

A new plant, just opened in Mentor, Ohio, houses some of the electrode production operations, which were moved from the main plant. The main plant is currently being enlarged by 100,000 square feet and several innovative changes are being made in the manufacturing layout.

Manufacturing Processes. The electrode manufacturing process is highly capital intensive. Metal rod purchased from steel producers is drawn or extruded down to smaller diameters and cut to length and coated with pressed-powder "flux" for stick electrodes or plated with copper (for conductivity) and spun into coils or spools for wire. Some of Lincoln's wire, called "Innershield," is hollow and filled with a material similar to that used to coat stick electrodes. Lincoln is highly secretive about its electrode production processes and the case-writer was not given access to the details of those processes.

Welding machines and electric motors are made on a series of assembly lines. Gasoline and diesel engines are purchased partially assembled but practically all other components are made from basic industrial products, e.g., steel bars and sheets and bare copper conductor wire, in the Lincoln factory. Individual components, such as gasoline tanks for engine-driven welders and steel shafts for motors and generators are made by numerous small "factories within a factory." The shaft for a certain generator, for example, is made from raw steel bar by one operator who uses five large machines, all running continuously. A saw cuts the bar to length, a digital lathe machines different sections to varying diameters, a special milling machine cuts a slot for a keyway, and so forth, until a finished shaft is produced. The operator moves the shafts from machine to machine and makes necessary adjustments. Another operator punches, shapes and paints sheetmetal cowling parts. One assembles steel laminations on a rotor shaft, then winds, insulates and tests the rotors. Finished components are moved by crane operators to the nearby assembly lines.

Worker Performance and Attitudes. Exceptional worker performance at Lincoln is a matter of record. The typical Lincoln employee earns about twice as much as other factory workers in the Cleveland area. Yet the labor cost per sales dollar at Lincoln, currently 23.5 cents, is well below industry averages.

Sales per Lincoln factory employee currently exceeds $157,000. An observer at the factory quickly sees why this figure is so high. Each worker is

FIGURE 1: Factory Layout

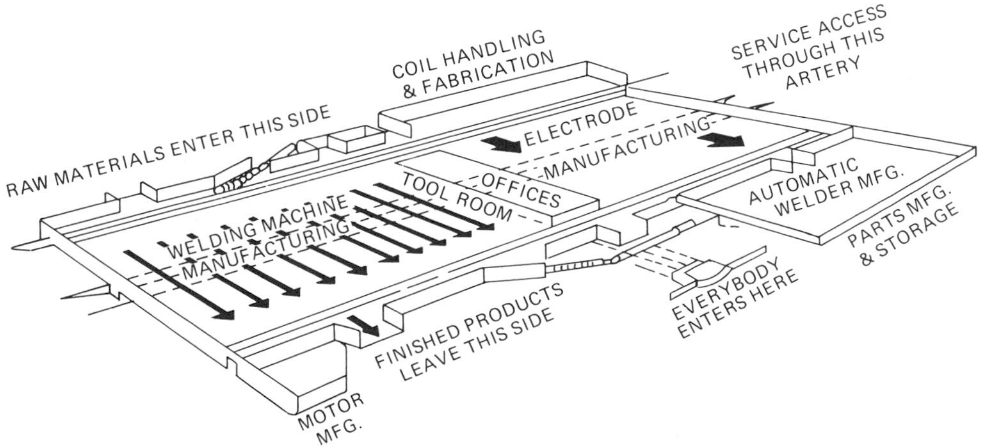

proceeding busily and thoughtfully about his task. There is no idle chatter. Most workers take no coffee breaks. Many operate several machines and made a substantial component unaided. The supervisors, some with as many as 100 subordinates, are busy with planning and recordkeeping duties and hardly glance at the people they supervise. The manufacturing procedures appear efficient—no unnecessary steps, no wasted motions, no wasted materials. Finished components move smoothly to subsequent work stations.

Worker turnover at Lincoln is practically nonexistent except for retirements and departures by new employees. Appendix A includes summaries of interviews with Lincoln employees.

Organization Structure

Lincoln has never had a formal organization chart.[17] The objective of this policy is to insure maximum flexibility. An open door policy is practiced throughout the company and personnel are encouraged to take problems to the persons most capable of resolving them. Perhaps because of the quality and enthusiasm of the Lincoln workforce routine supervision is almost nonexistent. A typical production foreman, for example, supervises as many as 100 workers, a span-of-control which does not allow more than infrequent worker-supervisor interaction. Position titles and traditional flows of authority do imply something of a organizational structure, however. For example, the Vice-President, Sales, and the Vice-President, Electrode Division, report to the President, as do various staff assistants such as the Personnel Director and the Director of Purchasing. Using such implied relationships it has been determined that production workers have two or, at most, three levels of supervision between themselves and the President.

Personnel Policies

Recruitment and Selection. Every job opening at Lincoln is advertised internally on company bulletin boards and any employee can apply for any job so advertised. External hiring is done only for entry level positions. Selection for these jobs is done on the basis of personal interviews—there is no aptitude or psychological testing. Not even a high school diploma is required except for engineering and sales positions, which are filled by graduate engineers. A committee consisting of vice-presidents and superintendents interviews candidates initially cleared by the Personnel Department. Final selection is made by the supervisor who has a job opening. In 1979, out of 3500 applicants interviewed by the Personnel Department fewer than 300 were hired.

Job Security. After one year, each employee is guaranteed that he will not be discharged except for misconduct and he is guaranteed at least thirty hours of work each week. There has been no layoff at Lincoln since 1949.

Performance Evaluations. Each supervisor formally evaluates his subordinates twice a year using the cards shown in Figure 2. The employee perfor-

[17] Once, Harvard Business School researchers prepared an organization chart reflecting the below-mentioned implied relationships. The chart became available within the Lincoln organization and present Lincoln management feels that it had a disruptive effect. Therefore, the casewriter was asked not to include any kind of organizational chart in this report.

FIGURE 2: Merit Rating Cards

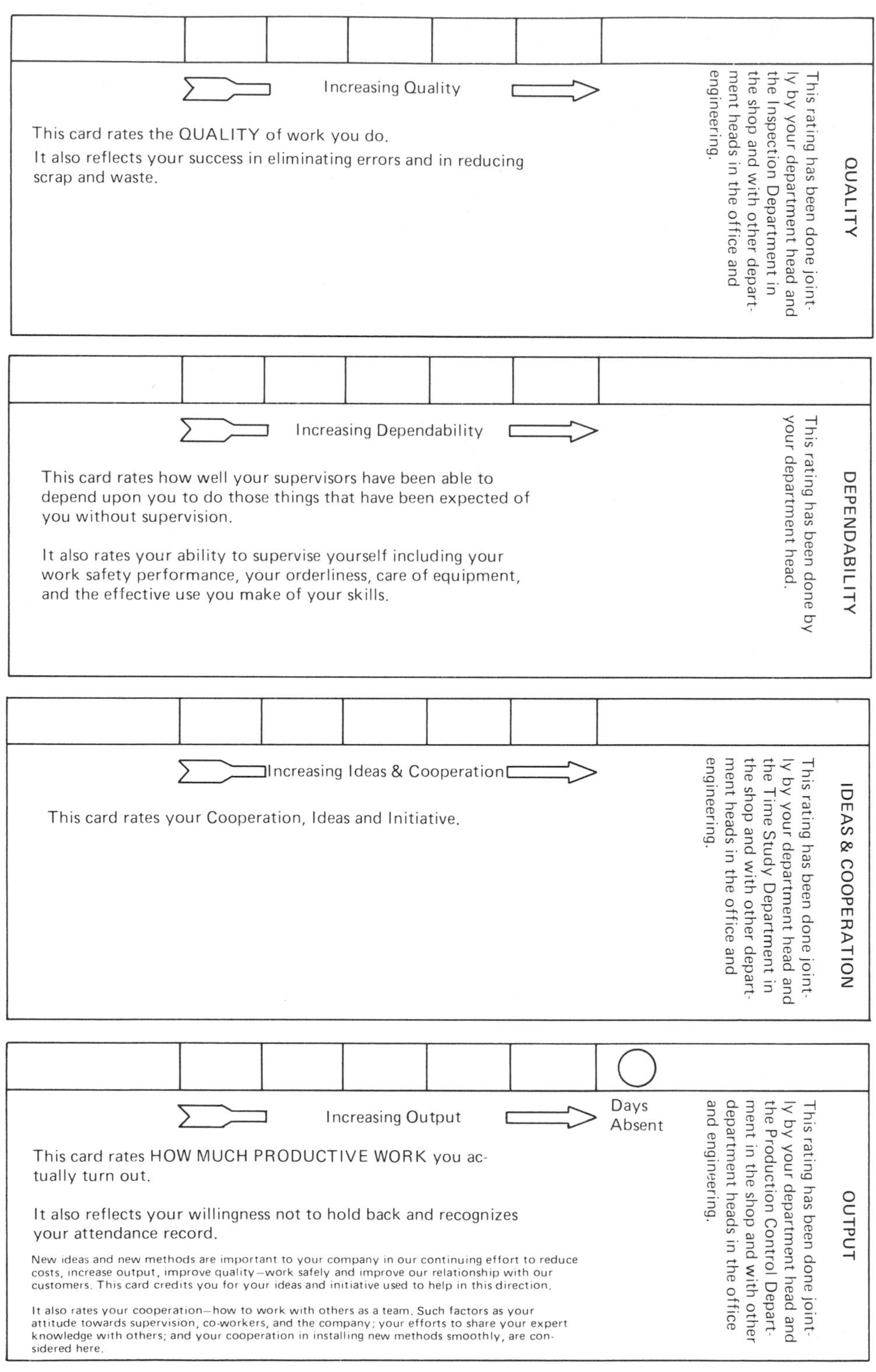

mance criteria, "quality," "dependability," "ideas and co-operation," and "output," are considered to be independent of each other. Marks on the cards are converted to numerical scores which are forced to average 100 for each evaluating supervisor. Individual merit rating scores normally range from 80 to 110. Any score over 110 requires a special letter to top management. These scores (over 110) are not considered in computing the required 100 point average for each evaluating supervisor. Suggestions for improvements often result in recommendations for exceptionally high performance scores. Supervisors discuss individual performance marks with the employees concerned.

Compensation. Basic wage levels for jobs at Lincoln are determined by a wage survey of similar jobs in the Cleveland area. These rates are adjusted quarterly in accordance with changes in the Cleveland Area Consumer Price Index. Insofar as possible, base wages rates are translated into piece rates. Practically all production workers and many others—for example, some fork-truck drivers—are paid by piece rate. Once established, piece rates are never changed unless a substantive change in the way a job is done results from a source other than the worker doing the job. In December of each year, a portion of annual profits is distributed to employees as bonuses. Incentive bonuses since 1934 have averaged about the same as annual wages and somewhat more than after-tax profits. The average bonus for 1980 was about $17,500. Individual bonuses are exactly proportional to merit-rating scores. For example, a person with a score of 110 would receive 110 percent of the standard bonus as applied to his regular earnings.

Work Assignment. Management has authority to transfer workers and to switch between overtime and short time as required. Supervisors have undisputed authority to assign specific parts to individual workmen, who may have their own preferences due to variations in piece rates.

Employee Participation in Decision Making. When a manager speaks of participative management, he usually thinks of a relaxed, nonauthoritarian atmosphere. This is not the case at Lincoln. Formal authority is quite strong. "We're very authoritarian around here," says Mr. Willis. James F. Lincoln placed a good deal of stress on protecting management's authority. "Management in all successful departments of industry must have complete power," he said ". . . Management is the coach who must be obeyed. The men, however, are the players who alone can win the games."[18] Despite this attitude, there are several ways in which employees participate in management at Lincoln.

Richard Sabo, Manager of Public Relations, relates job-enlargement to participation. "The most important participative technique that we use is giving more responsibility to employees." Mr. Sabo says, "We give a high school graduate more responsibility than other companies give their foremen." Lincoln puts limits on the degree of participation which is allowed, however. In Mr. Sabo's words,

> When you use "participation," put quotes around it. Because we believe that each person should participate only in those decisions he is most knowledgeable about. I don't think production employees should control the decisions of Bill Irrgang. They don't know as much as he does about the decisions he is involved in.

[18] Lincoln, *Incentive Management* (Cleveland, Ohio: The Lincoln Electric Company, 1951), p. 228.

The Advisory Board, elected by the workers, meets with the Chairman and the President every two weeks to discuss ways of improving operations. This board has been in existence since 1914 and has contributed to many innovations. The incentive bonuses, for example, were first recommended by this committee. Every Lincoln employee has access to Advisory Board members and answers to all Advisory Board suggestions are promised by the following meeting. Both Mr. Irrgang and Mr. Willis are quick to point out, though, that the Advisory Board only recommends actions. "They do not have direct authority," Mr. Irrgang says, "and when they bring up something that management thinks is not to the benefit of the company, it will be rejected."[19]

A suggestion program was instituted in 1929. At first, employees were awarded one-half of the first year's savings attributable to their suggestions. Now, however, the value of suggestions is reflected in performance evaluation scores, which determine individual incentive bonus amounts.

Training and Education. Production workers are given a short period of on-the-job training and then placed on a piecework pay system. Lincoln does not pay for off-site education. The idea behind this latter policy is that everyone cannot take advantage of such a program and it is unfair to expend company funds for an advantage to which there is unequal access. Sales personnel are given on-the-job training in the plant followed by a period of work and training at one of the regional sales offices.

Fringe Benefits and Executive Perquisites. A medical plan and a company-paid retirement program have been in effect for many years. A plant cafeteria, operated on a break-even basis, serves meals at about sixty percent of usual costs. An employee association, to which the company does not contribute, provides disability insurance and social and athletic activities. An employee stock ownership program, instituted in about 1925, and regular stock purchases have resulted in employee ownership of about fifty percent of Lincoln's stock.

As to executive perquisites, there are none—crowded, austere offices, no executive washrooms or lunchrooms and no reserved parking spaces. Even the company President pays for his own meals and eats in the cafeteria.

FINANCIAL POLICIES

James F. Lincoln felt strongly that financing for company growth should come from within the company—through initial cash investment by the founders, through retention of earnings, and through stock purchases by those who work in the business. He saw the following advantages of this approach:[20]

1. Ownership of stock by employees strengthens team spirit. "If they are mutually anxious to make it succeed, the future of the company is bright."
2. Ownership of stock provides individual incentive because employees feel that they will benefit from company profitability.
3. "Ownership is educational." Owner-employees "will know how profits

[19] Incentive Management In Action, *Assembly Engineering,* March 1967, p. 18.
[20] Lincoln, 1961, pp. 220–228.

are made and lost; how success is won and lost. . . . There are few socialists in the list of stockholders of the nation's industries."

4. "Capital available from within controls expansion." Unwarranted expansion will not occur, Lincoln believed, under his financing plan.
5. "The greatest advantage would be the development of the individual worker. Under the incentive of ownership, he would become a greater man."
6. "Stock ownership is one of the steps that can be taken that will make the worker feel that there is less of a gulf between him and the boss. . . . Stock ownership will help the worker to recognize his responsibility in the game and the importance of victory."

Lincoln Electric Company uses a minimum of debt in its capital structure. There is no borrowing at all, with the debt being limited to current payables. Even the new $20 million plant in Mentor, Ohio, was financed totally from earnings.

The unusual pricing policy at Lincoln is succinctly stated by President Willis: "at all times price on the basis of cost and at all times keep pressure on our cost." This policy resulted in Lincoln's price for the most popular welding electrode then in use going from 16 cents a pound in 1929 to 4.7 cents in 1938. More recently, the SA-200 Welder, Lincoln's largest selling portable machine, decreased in price from 1958 through 1965. According to Dr. C. Jackson Grayson of the American Productivity Center in Houston, Texas, Lincoln's prices in general have increased only one-fifth as fast as the Consumer Price Index since 1934. This has resulted in a welding products market in which Lincoln is the undisputed price leader for the products it manufactures. Not even the major Japanese manufacturers, such as Nippon Steel for welding electrodes and Asaka Transformer for welding machines, have been able to penetrate this market.

Huge cash balances are accumulated each year preparatory to paying the year-end bonuses. The bonuses totaled $46,500,000 for 1979. This money is invested in short-term U.S. government securities until needed. Financial statements are shown in Tables 1 and 2.

HOW WELL DOES LINCOLN SERVE ITS PUBLIC?

Lincoln Electric differs from most other companies in the importance it assigns to each of the groups it serves. Mr. Willis identifies these groups, in the order of priority Lincoln ascribes to them, as (1) customers, (2) employees, and (3) stockholders.

Certainly Lincoln customers have fared well over the years. Lincoln prices for welding machines and welding electrodes are acknowledged to be the lowest in the marketplace. Lincoln quality has consistently been so high that Lincoln "Fleetweld" electrodes and Lincoln SA-200 welders have been the standard in the pipeline and refinery construction industry, where price is hardly a criterion, for decades. The cost of field failures for Lincoln products was an amazing four one-hundreths of one percent in 1979. A Lincoln distributor in Monroe, Louisiana says that he has sold several hundred of the popular AC-225 welders and, though the machine is warranted for one year, he has never handled a warranty claim.

TABLE 1: Summary of Balance Sheet Information ($000)

	1975	*1976*	*1977*	*1978*	*1979*	*1980*
Assets:						
Cash	$ 3,392	$ 1,744	$ 2,203	$ 1,588	$ 2,261	$ 1,307
Govt. Securities & C.D.'s	26,822	23,548	24,375	28,807	38,408	46,503
Notes & Accounts Rec.	27,101	25,343	34,093	38,786	41,598	42,424
Inventories (Lifo Basis)	24,635	23,148	28,449	35,916	37,640	35,533
Deferred Taxes & Prepmts.	2,758	2,464	2,275	1,729	1,437	933
	$ 84,708	$ 76,247	$ 91,395	$106,826	$121,344	$126,700
Other Intangible Assets	6,330	9,703	14,172	19,420	19,164	19,723
Investments in Foreign Subs.	4,696	4,696	4,696	4,976	4,986	4,695
	$ 11,026	$ 14,399	$ 18,868	$ 24,396	$ 24,150	$ 24,418
Property, plant, equipment						
Land & Bldgs. (Net)	12,791	23,412	23,137	22,622	22,496	23,895
Machinery & Tools	12,742	13,426	17,035	18,458	21,250	25,339
	$ 25,713	$ 36,838	$ 40,172	$ 41,080	$ 43,746	$ 49,234
Total Assets	$121,447	$127,484	$150,435	$172,302	$189,240	$200,352
Liabilities:						
Accounts Payable	$ 10,510	$ 8,735	$ 9,891	$ 14,330	$ 16,590	$ 17,599
Accrued Wages	686	666	839	882	917	1,504
Taxes Payable	14,306	5,351	8,057	9,116	9,620	5,622
Dividends Payable	3,398	3,978	4,327	5,730	5,889	5,800
	$ 28,900	$ 18,730	$ 23,114	$ 30,058	$ 33,016	$ 30,525
Shareholders' Equity						
Common Stock	3,878	3,631	4,479	4,502	4,423	2,917
Retained Earnings	88,669	105,123	122,842	137,742	151,801	166,910
	$ 92,547	$108,754	$127,321	$142,244	$156,224	$169,827
Total Liabilities & Shareholders' Equity	$121,447	$127,484	$150,435	$172,302	$189,240	$200,352

Perhaps best-served of all Lincoln constituencies have been the employees. Not the least of their benefits, of course, is the year-end bonuses, which effectively double an already average compensation level. The foregoing description of the personnel program and the comments in Appendix A further illustrate the desirability of a Lincoln job.

While stockholders were relegated to an inferior status by James F. Lincoln, they have done very well indeed. Recent dividends have exceeded $7 a share and earnings per share have exceeded $20. In January 1980, the price of restricted stock committed by Lincoln to employees was $117 a share. By July 16, 1980, the stated value, at which Lincoln will repurchase the stock if tendered, was $132. A check with the New York office of Merrill, Lynch, Pierce, Fenner and Smith on July 16, 1980 revealed a bid price on Lincoln stock of $219 a share, with none being offered for sale. Technically, this price applies only to the unrestricted stock owned by the Lincoln family, a few other major holders, and employees who have purchased it on the open market, but it gives some idea of the value of Lincoln stock in general. The risk associated with Lincoln stock, a

TABLE 2: Summary of Income Statement Information

	1975	*1976*	*1977*	*1978*	*1979*	*1980*
Income:						
Net Sales	$260,870	$249,232	$276,947	$329,652	$373,789	$387,374
Other Income	5,245	6,720	5,768	7,931	11,397	13,817
	$266,115	$255,952	$282,715	$337,583	$385,186	$401,191
Costs and Expense:						
Cost of Products sold	$158,707	$157,285	$175,733	$210,208	$244,376	$260,671
General & Admin. Exp.	21,468	21,547	23,821	28,126	35,048	39,004
Incentive Bonuses	26,130	26,255	29,263	39,547	44,068	43,249
Pension Expense	3,728	3,579	4,062	5,881	6,131	6,810
	$210,033	$208,666	$232,879	$283,762	$329,623	$349,734
Income Before Taxes	$ 56,082	$ 47,285	$ 49,836	$ 53,821	$ 55,563	$ 51,457
Provision for Taxes	27,764	23,874	25,936	27,548	29,998	28,085
Net Income	$ 28,318	$ 23,874	$ 25,936	$ 27,548	$ 29,998	$ 28,085
Eligible Employees	2,369	2,412	2,431	2,533	2,611	2,637

major determinant of stock value, is minimal because of the absence of debt in Lincoln's capital structure, because of an extremely stable earnings record and because of Lincoln's practice of purchasing the restricted stock whenever employees offer it for sale.

A CONCLUDING COMMENT

It is easy to believe that the reason for Lincoln's success is the excellent attitude of Lincoln employees and their willingness to work harder, faster, and more intelligently than other industrial workers. However, Mr. Richard Sabo, Manager of Publicity and Educational Services at Lincoln, suggests that appropriate credit be given to Lincoln executives, whom he credits with carrying out the following policies:

1. Management has limited research, development and manufacturing to a standard product line designed to meet the major needs of the welding industry.
2. New products must be reviewed by manufacturing and all production costs verified before being approved by management.
3. Purchasing is challenged to not only procure materials at the lowest cost, but also to work closely with engineering and manufacturing to assure that the latest innovations are implemented.
4. Manufacturing supervision and all personnel are held accountable for reduction of scrap, energy conservation and maintenance of product quality.
5. Production control, material handling and methods engineering are closely supervised by top management.
6. Material and finished goods inventory control, accurate cost accounting

and attention to sales costs, credit and other financial areas have constantly reduced overhead and led to excellent profitability.

7. Management has made cost reduction a way of life at Lincoln and definite programs are established in many areas, including traffic and shipping, where tremendous savings can result.
8. Management has established a sales department that is technically trained to reduce customer welding costs. This sales technique and other real customer services have eliminated nonessential frills and resulted in long-term benefits to all concerned.
9. Management has encouraged education, technical publishing and long range programs that have resulted in industry growth, thereby assuring market potential for the Lincoln Electric Company.

Appendix A: Employee Interviews

During the late summer of 1980, the author conducted numerous interviews with Lincoln employees. Typical questions and answers from those interviews are presented below. In order to maintain each employee's personal privacy, the names used for the interviewees are fictitious.

I

Interview with Betty Stewart, a 52-year-old high school graduate who had been with Lincoln thirteen years and who was working as a cost accounting clerk at the time of the interview.

Q: What jobs have you held here besides the one you have now?
A: I worked in payroll for a while and then this job came open and I took it.
Q: How much money did you make last year, including your bonus?
A: I would say roughly around $20,000, but I was off for back surgery for a while.
Q: You weren't paid while you were off for back surgery?
A: No.
Q: Did the Employees-Association help out?
A: Yes. The company doesn't furnish that, though. We pay $6 a month into the Employee Association. I think my check from them was $105.00 a week.
Q: How was your performance rating last year?
A: It was around 100 points, but I lost some points for attendance, with my back problem.
Q: You lose points for attendance even when you're sick?
A: Yes. But after a certain period they don't deduct any more points for that.
Q: How did you get your job at Lincoln?
A: I was bored silly where I was working and I had heard that Lincoln kept their people busy. So I applied and got the job the next day.
Q: Do you think you make more money than similar workers in Cleveland?
A: I know I do.
Q: What have you done with your money?
A: We have purchased a better home. Also, my son is going to the University

of Chicago, which costs $10,000 a year. I buy the Lincoln stock which is offered each year, and I have a little bit of gold.

Q: Have you ever visited with any of the senior executives like Mr. Willis or Mr. Irrgang?

A: I have known Mr. Willis for a long time.

Q: Does he call you by name?

A: Yes. In fact he was very instrumental in my going to the doctor that I am going to with my back. He knows the director of the clinic.

Q: Do you know Mr. Irrgang?

A: I know him to speak to him and he always speaks, always. But I have known Mr. Willis for a good many years. When I did Plant Two cost accounting I did not understand how the plant operated. Of course you are not allowed in Plant Two because that's the Electrode Division. I told my boss about the problem one day and the next thing I knew Mr. Willis came by and said, "Come on, Betty, we're going to Plant Two." He spent an hour and a half showing me the plant.

Q: Do you think Lincoln employees produce more than those in other companies?

A: I think with the incentive program the way that it is, if you want to work and achieve, then you will do it. If you don't want to work and achieve, you will not do it no matter where you are. Just because you are merit rated and have a bonus, if you really don't want to work hard then you're not going to. You will accept your ninety points or ninety-two or eighty-five because, even with that, you make more money than people on the outside.

Q: Do you think Lincoln employees will ever join a union?

A: I don't know why they would.

Q: What is the most important advantage of working for Lincoln Electric?

A: You have an incentive and you can push and you get something for pushing. That's not true in a lot of other companies.

Q: So you say that money is a very major advantage?

A: Money is a major advantage but it's not just the money. It's the fact that having the incentive you do wish to work a little harder. I'm sure that there are a lot of men here, who, if they worked for Pontiac or some other place, would not work as hard as they do here. Not that they are over-worked—I don't mean that—but I'm sure they wouldn't push.

Q: Is there anything that you would like to add?

A: I do like working here. I am better off being pushed mentally. In another company if you pushed too hard you would feel a little bit of pressure and someone might say "Hey, slow down; don't try so hard." But here you are encouraged, not discouraged.

II

Interview with Ed Sanderson, 23-year-old high school graduate who had been with Lincoln four years and who was a machine operator in the electrode division at the time of the interview.

Q: How did you happen to get this job?
A: My wife was pregnant and I was making three bucks an hour and one day I came here and applied. That was it. I kept calling to let them know I was still interested.
Q: Roughly what were your earnings last year including your bonus?
A: $37,000.00
Q: What have you done with your money since you have been here?
A: Well, we've lived pretty well and we bought a condominium.
Q: Have you paid for the condominium?
A: No, but I could.
Q: Have you bought your Lincoln stock this year?
A: No, I haven't bought any Lincoln stock yet.
Q: Do you get the feeling that the executives here are pretty well thought of?
A: I think they are. To get where they are today they had to really work.
Q: Wouldn't that be true anywhere?
A: I think more so here because seniority really doesn't mean anything. If you work with a guy who has twenty years here and you have two months and you're doing a better job, you will get advanced before he will.
Q: Are you paid on a piece rate basis?
A: My gang does. There are nine of us who make the bare electrode and the whole group gets paid based on how much electrode we make.
Q: Do you think you work harder than workers in other factories in the Cleveland area?
A: Yes, I would say I probably work harder.
Q: Do you think it hurts anybody?
A: No, a little hard work never hurts anybody.
Q: If you could choose, do you think you would be as happy earning a little less money and being able to slow down a little.
A: No, it doesn't bother me. If it bothered me I wouldn't do it.
Q: What would you say is the biggest disadvantage of working at Lincoln, as opposed to working somewhere else?
A: Probably having to work shift work.
Q: Why do you think Lincoln employees produce more than workers in other plants?
A: That's the way the company is set up. The more you put out, the more you're going to make.
Q: Do you think it's the piece rate and bonus together?
A: I don't think people would work here if they didn't know that they would be rewarded at the end of the year.
Q: Do you think Lincoln employees will ever join a union?
A: No.
Q: What are the major advantages of working for Lincoln?
A: Money.
Q: Are there any other advantages?
A: Yes, we don't have a union shop. I don't think I could work in a union shop.
Q: Do you think you are a career man with Lincoln at this time?
A: Yes.

III

Interview with Roger Lewis, 23-year-old Purdue graduate in mechanical engineering who had been in the Lincoln sales program for fifteen months and who was working in the Cleveland sales office at the time of the interview.

Q: How did you get your job at Lincoln?
A: I saw that Lincoln was interviewing on campus at Purdue and I went by. I later came to Cleveland for a plant tour and was offered a job.
Q: Do you know any of the senior executives? Would they know you by name?
A: Yes, I know all of them—Mr. Irrgang, Mr. Willis, Mr. Manross.
Q: Do you think Lincoln salesmen work harder than those in other companies?
A: Yes. I don't think there are many salesmen for other companies who are putting in fifty to sixty-hour weeks. Everybody here works harder. You can go out in the plant or you can go upstairs and there's nobody sitting around.
Q: Do you see any real disadvantage of working at Lincoln?
A: I don't know if it's a disadvantage but Lincoln is a Spartan company, a very thrifty company. I like that. The sales offices are functional, not fancy.
Q: Why do you think Lincoln employees have such high productivity?
A: Piecework has a lot to do with it. Lincoln is smaller than many plants, too; you can stand in one place and see the materials come in one side and the product go out the other. You feel a part of the company. The chance to get ahead is important, too. They have a strict policy of promoting from within, so you know you have a chance. I think in a lot of other places you may not get as fair a shake as you do here. The sales offices are on a smaller scale, too. I like that. I tell someone that we have two people in the Baltimore office and they say "you've got to be kidding." It's smaller and more personal. Pay is the most important thing. I have heard that this is the highest paying factory in the world.

IV

Interview with Jimmy Roberts, a 47-year-old high school graduate who had been with Lincoln 17 years and who was working as a multiple drill press operator at the time of the interview.

Q: What jobs have you had at Lincoln?
A: I started out cleaning the men's locker room in 1963. After about a year I got a job in the flux department, where we make the coating for welding rods. I worked there for seven or eight years and then got my present job.
Q: Do you make one particular part?
A: No, there are a variety of parts I make—at least twenty-five.
Q: Each one has a different piece rate attached to it?
A: Yes.
Q: Are some piece rates better than others?
A: Yes.
Q: How do you determine which ones you are going to do?

A: You don't. Your supervisor assigns them.
Q: How much money did you make last year?
A: $47,000.
Q: Have you ever received any kind of award or citation?
A: No.
Q: What was your merit rating last year?
A: I don't know.
Q: Did your supervisor have to send a letter—was your rating over 110?
A: Yes. For the past five years, probably, I made over 110 points.
Q: Is there any attempt to let others know . . . ?
A: The kind of points I get? No.
Q: Do you know what they are making?
A: No. There are some who might not be too happy with their points and they might make it known. The majority, though, do not make it a point of telling other employees.
Q: Would you be just as happy earning a little less money and working a little slower?
A: I don't think I would—not at this point. I have done piecework all these years and the fast pace doesn't really bother me.
Q: Why do you think Lincoln productivity is so high?
A: The incentive thing—the bonus distribution. I think that would be the main reason. The pay check you get every two weeks is important too.
Q: Do you think Lincoln employees would ever join a union?
A: I don't think so. I have never heard anyone mention it.
Q: What is the most important advantage of working here?
A: Amount of money you make. I don't think I could make this type of money anywhere else, especially with only a high school education.
Q: As a black person, do you feel that Lincoln discriminates, in any way, against blacks?
A: No. I don't think any more so than any other job. Naturally, there is a certain amount of discrimination, regardless of where you are.

V

Interview with Joe Trahan, 58-year-old high school graduate who had been with Lincoln 39 years and who was employed as a working supervisor in the tool room at the time of the interview.

Q: Roughly what was your pay last year?
A: Around $55,000: salary, bonus, stock dividends.
Q: How much was your bonus?
A: About $23,000
Q: Have you ever gotten a special award of any kind?
A: Not really.
Q: What have you done with your money?
A: My house is paid for—and my two cars. I also have some bonds and the Lincoln stock.
Q: What do you think of the executives at Lincoln?

A: They're really top notch.
Q: What is the major disadvantage of working at Lincoln Electric?
A: I don't know of any disadvantage at all.
Q: Do you think you produce more than most people in similar jobs with other companies?
A: I do believe that.
Q: Why is that? Why do you believe that?
A: We are on the incentive system. Everything we do we try to improve to make a better product with a minimum of outlay. We try to improve the bonus.
Q: Would you be just as happy making a little less money and not working quite so hard.
A: I don't think so.
Q: You know that Lincoln productivity is higher than that at most other plants. Why is that?
A: Money.
Q: Do you think Lincoln employees would ever join a union?
A: I don't think they would ever consider it.
Q: What is the most important advantage of working at Lincoln?
A: Compensation.
Q: Tell me something about Mr. James Lincoln, who died in 1965.
A: You are talking about Jimmy Sr. He always strolled through the shop in his shirt sleeves. Big fellow. Always looked distinguished. Gray hair. Friendly sort of a guy. I was a member of the advisory board one year. He was there each time.
Q: Did he strike you as really caring?
A: I think he always cared for people.
Q: Did you get any sensation of a religious nature from him?
A: No, not really.
Q: And religion is not part of the program now?
A: No.
Q: Do you think Mr. Lincoln was a very intelligent man, or was he just a nice guy?
A: I would say he was pretty well educated. A great talker—always right off the top of his head. He knew what he was talking about all of the time.
Q: When were bonuses for beneficial suggestions done away with?
A: About fifteen years ago.
Q: Did that hurt very much?
A: I don't think so.
Q: Is there anything you would like to add?
A: It's a good place to work. The union kind of ties other places down. Electricians only do electrical work, carpenters only do carpenter work. At Lincoln Electric we all pitch in and do whatever needs to be done.
Q: So a major advantage is not having a union?
A: That's right.

PART VIII

Cases in Managing the Organization's Future

CASE TWENTY-EIGHT

Texas Air Corporation (A)

TIMOTHY SINGLETON and ROBERT McGLASHAN
University of Houston at Clear Lake City

Assignment Questions:

1. How would you describe Frank Lorenzo? His goals? His achievements?
2. How do you evaluate Lorenzo's business strategies?
3. What is the future of the industry? Of Continental? Of Texas Air?

Frank Lorenzo, Chairman and Chief Executive Officer of Texas Air Corp. ("TAC"), once said that "by 1990 there will be only six (6) major airlines in the United States. I intend to own one of them."[1] Since coming to the Houston based carrier at the age of thirty in late 1971, most of his efforts have been directed toward that goal. By December, 1980, Texas Air could boast of an operation which generated almost $300 million in revenue on an asset base of almost $400 million, employed 3,500 people, and produced profits in seven of the nine years under Lorenzo's control. In 1981, Texas International acquired controlling interest in the much larger Continental Airlines. These were significant accomplishments for a carrier which eleven years earlier was on the brink of bankruptcy. Some observers believe that the TI-Continental merger is a significant step by Lorenzo to achieve his goal of owning one of the major airlines in the U.S. by 1990.

THE PRE-LORENZO YEARS: 1947–1971

Trans Texas Airways (TTA), the forerunner of Texas International (TI) and Texas Air Corp. (TAC), began official operations on Saturday, October 11, 1947. It was a rather inauspicious start. R. Earl McKaughan mortgaged everything he owned to purchase two World War II surplus DC-3 aircraft. Each had seating capacity for 21 passengers. Trans Texas employed 96 people and its route struc-

[1]Author unlisted, "The Great Texas Air War," *Texas Monthly*, November, 1975), p. 97.

ture included eight Texas cities: San Angelo, Brownswood, Fort Worth, Dallas (Love Field), Palestine, Houston (Hobby), Victoria and San Antonio. Due to its size, the nature of the airline industry, governmental regulation, and its regional nature, Trans Texas was besieged by problems from its infancy. Even its airline code letter, TTA, bore the brunt of many remarks such as Tinker Toy Airlines, Tree Top Airways, and Try Try Again.

To really appreciate TTA's position during the pre-Lorenzo years, one must first recognize the regulated condition of the industry. In most business activities, profits are realized by out-performing the competitors. Tactics such as producing a superior product, obtaining patents and better management potential, or reducing costs could be effectively employed. Prior to deregulation in 1978, the Civil Aeonautics Board (CAB) strictly controlled activities within the airline business. Basically, the industry had two types of companies, the trunk or cross-country carriers and the local or intrastate feeder lines.

The trunk carriers were essentially government franchised by the CAB, thus almost guaranteed to make money. Losses occurred due to mismanagement and overzealous acquisition plans for aircraft rather than market forces. The real competition among the trunk carriers took place in the offices of the Civil Aeronautics Board rather than the marketplace. The CAB's major purpose was to control the airline industry through approval of new routes, a process which could take as long as thirty months. The degree of control was remarkable: [2]

1. Sixteen trunk carriers were chartered by the CAB in 1938.
2. By 1975, eleven of these were still operating; the remaining five disappeared through merger.
3. None of the original sixteen had ever been bankrupt.

Life for the local or so called "feeder lines", such as Trans Texas, which were not as regulated by the CAB was radically different. They were "created to lose money, to fly the routes where passengers ain't."[3] With the aid of government subsidies which decreased each year, the feeder lines were relegated to service small cities such as Jonesboro, Arkansas; Big Springs, Texas and the like. Of the original nineteen local airlines authorized in 1945, all but ten were lost through bankruptcy by 1975.

In spite of these conditions, a fleet of aging aircraft, and a route structure composed primarily of small Texas towns, Trans Texas Airways registered revenue growth and modest profits until 1966 when a group of "Minnesota investors" purchased the airline. They immediately embarked upon an ill conceived expansion program from an already highly leveraged financial base which included additional routes into more unprofitable cities and purchase of the Tropicana Hotel in Las Vegas. Net income fell dramatically and a revolving door of presidents followed. The small Texas airline would not have a profitable month from 1966 to 1972. By 1971, Texas International, as it became known in 1969, was $20 million in debt and facing bankruptcy. Its stock, which was traded in the over-the-counter market, fell from $20.25 per share in 1969 to $3.50 per share by 1971. It was then that Frank Lorenzo entered the TI picture.

[2] Author unlisted, "The Great Texas Air War," *Texas Monthly*, (November, 1975), p. 92.
[3] Author unlisted, "The Great Texas Air War," *Texas Monthly*, (November, 1975), p. 90.

FRANCISCO A. LORENZO: ENTREPRENEUR

"My aim is to build the most successful, low fare, airline in the United States."[4] Francisco A. Lorenzo is an enigma, publically quiet and unassuming, yet an energetic and highly ambitious individual. Lorenzo has been described in many terms; a pure entrepreneur, a listener rather than a talker, the maverick of the airways. He seems to be highly regarded in financial circles both in the United States and abroad, but viewed with apprehension by his peers within the industry. When reminded that Wall Street investors had highly acclaimed his financial dealings, his reply was typically modest. "People think we're financial geniuses when all we do is add."[5]

Frank Lorenzo is not unfamiliar with the airline industry. Born in Queens, New York in 1940, to a beauty shop owner, he is a licensed pilot. By the age of twenty-three, his academic credits included a degree in Finance from Columbia University and an MBA from Harvard. Prior to forming Jet Capital Inc. with fellow Harvard classmate, Robert Carney, Frank Lorenzo worked for three years in the financial departments of both Eastern and Trans World Airlines. The latter has been a successful conduit for many of Texas Air Corp.'s top executives.

Lorenzo seems to feel most comfortable when surrounded by highly talented professionals and willing to gamble on creative ideas. Carl R. Pohlad, an investment banker and director at Texas Air describes him as "the initiator who sets the tone (of the board) and provides the broad perspectives."[6] However, Pohlad quickly adds that the company is by no means "a one man show."

Jet Capital Inc. (formerly Lorenzo-Carney Enterprises) was and still is Lorenzo's investment base. He and Carney launched the highly speculative, financial venture in 1966 with the expressed intention of leasing airplanes. However, the underlying implications were clear; Lorenzo wanted an airline. The more official intent was expressed in Jet Capital's charter "to provide a meaningful platform for successful participation in the exciting but beleaguered field of air transportation."[7] They were thwarted by Allegheny in the first acquisition attempt, Mohawk Airlines. Unsuccessful in this effort, Jet Capital shifted gears and acted as a consulting firm to airlines for large New York banks. It was a time when many investment contacts were made on both Wall Street, within the industry, and abroad.

THE EARLY YEARS: 1971–1974

By the Spring of 1971, Texas International was a financial shambles. Losses were running over one million dollars per month. Employee morale was low and creditors were about to foreclose and liquidate the carrier. These events were viewed as an opportunity by Lorenzo. The Chase Manhattan Bank of New York retained Jet Capital for a $15,000 per month fee to help Texas Interna-

[4] Author unlisted, "Texas International's Quiet Pilot," *Business Week*, (July 30, 1979), p. 78.
[5] Author unlisted, "Texas International's Quiet Pilot," *Business Week*, (July 20, 1979), p. 80.
[6] Author unlisted, "Who Are The TI Whiz Kids?," *The TI Flyer*, (May, 1979), p. 21.
[7] Author unlisted, "The Great Texas Air War," *Texas Monthly*, (November, 1975), p. 94.

tional out of their dilemma. The Lorenzo-Carney management team went to work. One year later, Frank Lorenzo, at the age of 31, was President and Chief Executive Officer and Robert Carney was Chief Financial Officer of TI. Together, either directly or through ownership of Jet Capital, they controlled 59% of TI's voting stock. The results of their work were dramatic. The carrier's net loss for 1972 was $1.707 million versus a loss of $7.416 million the year before and total debt (current and long term) was reduced by $24.123 million.

The airline industry had caught the first glimpse of Lorenzo's wizardry of debt leverage at work. He worked out a 35 million dollar debt restructuring plan with the Chase Manhattan Bank. This was no small feat considering TI's financial condition. In addition, through reinvesting that $180,000 in consultants' fees and $60,000 in "finder's fees" from Chase for arranging the new loans, he was able to leverage the Jet Capital venture to provide an additional capital infusion of $1.150 million into Texas International.

Lorenzo's expertise went to work in other areas as well. A management housecleaning ensued which formed the nucleus of his new team. Expense reduction areas were identified and plans implemented. The tropicana operation, a severe drain on profits, was sold. More lucrative routes to large cities such as Denver, Albuquerque, and Mexico City were obtained. The groundwork to replace the aging Convair aircraft with more fuel efficient McDonnell Douglass DC-9's was laid. Productivity improvements were implemented. Route structures were put to the pencil. These were thoroughly analyzed in an attempt to reduce Texas International's dependence on federal subsidies. Through "creative scheduling," service to many of the small, marginal cities which plagued profits was discontinued.

Once again, the tactics produced positive results. In 1973, Lorenzo's first full year, the carrier produced a $121,000 profit, its first in eight years. By 1974, passenger load factor and yield per revenue passenger mile, key profit criteria in the industry, had risen to 50.4% and .0981 from 47.2% and .0796 in 1971. In the process, profits of $257,000 in 1974 more than doubled 1973 levels.

THE STRIKE: DECEMBER 1, 1974–APRIL 3, 1975

Frank Lorenzo was in his element. Eight years had passed since the formation of Jet Capital and he was finally building his airline. In spite of fierce competition from the major trunks and smaller, regional carriers such as Southwest, his hand picked management team had turned a company from bankruptcy to a profit-generating enterprise in just two short years. However, the storm clouds of change were brewing.

If Lorenzo has a weakness, it is his relationship with Texas International Unions. The Texas carrier has some of the toughest in the industry with which to deal:

A. ALEA—Airline Employees Association (1968–1980) (Clerical/Secretarial)
B. Teamsters—1980 to present (clerical)
C. ALPA—Airline Pilots Association (pilots, stewards and stewardesses)
D. IAM—International Association of Machinists (mechanics)

The friction has always centered around the unions' versus Lorenzo's perception of how the company should be operated in order to allow it to compete within the industry. Pay and benefits have always been competitive and are seldom the root issues involved. On December 1, 1974, the carrier's union personnel walked out in a bitterly contested four month strike which curtailed the momentum gained in the previous two years.

A lawyer representing the union employees expressed resentment concerning the changes made by Lorenzo with the following interview in *Texas Monthly Magazine* in 1975:

> "Management had to weather the strike to keep the company afloat. It's the easiest thing in the world to avoid a strike, all you have to do is give in. It's harder to make the necessary judgement of what the company can sustain in the long run."

Numerous small issues were involved. However, each side used these merely as negotiating chips. The major areas of concern could be boiled down to two key points of differences.

1. Management's contention that they had the right to hire part-time help in lieu of later furloughing full-time employees in order to handle peak traffic periods.
2. Management's contention that they had the right to have employees work split shifts at premium pay in order to operate the unique flight scheduling requirements at the smaller stations.

On the surface, it may seem that the strike issues were not critical. However, underlying currents of mistrust had grown in the early Lorenzo years. The unions, especially ALEA, viewed these actions as attempts to usurp their authority and weaken them. They had become very apprehensive about the constant changes taking place within the company. Lorenzo, on the other hand, felt that Texas International's survival was at stake. He firmly believed that unless such actions were adopted, the feeder airlines would not be able to compete against the major trunk lines and Southwest Airlines, a non-union, very aggressive regional carrier.

Both sides dug in for the mini-war which followed. It is fair to point out that there was sharp disagreement among union members about the major issues. Management's hand was further strengthened when 19% of the membership refused to honor the picket lines and worked system-wide during the strike. This enraged the pro-union faction and deep bitterness and resentment persisted for a long period after the strike had ended. By April 3, 1975, the unions had exhausted their resources and settled for essentially the same package offered in December 1974. The end was welcomed by both sides. The airline had been kept afloat primarily because of a package called Mutual Aid, which was unique to the airline industry. Mutual Aid was a fund, contributed to by all airlines based upon revenues. Its purpose was to provide capital to maintain skeleton operations during labor difficulties.

Financially, the strike was devastating to Texas International. The net loss for 1975 was $4,249,000 versus income in 1974 of $257,000. More importantly, it had allowed Southwest Airlines to entrench itself as the number one carrier into "The Valley," a group of very lucrative vacation/business routes into the McAllen-Harlingen-Brownsville areas of Texas. Heretofore, these stations represented some of the most profitable in the TI system. The corporate intrigue and court room dealings which followed between Texas International and Braniff against Southwest could fill volumes and was referred to as "The Great Texas Air War." The litigation portion came to an end when Braniff and TI were found guilty of conspiracy and antitrust violations against Southwest.

On the union front, ALEA, the clerical union, became the real loser. It was the one which initiated the strike and from whom most of the "scab-labor" came. For all practical purposes, it was broken and wielded considerably less influence. In 1980, its membership voted to have it replaced by the Teamsters to handle contract negotiations.

PEANUTS AND PRE-ACQUISITION: 1976–1978

The concurrent forces of the strike, hints of deregulation, the antitrust suit and recession produced a dismal atmosphere at Texas International. Both morale and profits had reached their lowest ebb under Lorenzo. He needed a gimmick to infuse increased revenue and purpose. It was found in the "Fly for Peanuts" marketing program.

The advantages of the strike concessions were the key ingredients. Lorenzo's management team began a route-by-route analysis of revenues versus costs, an almost unheard of practice in the industry prior to its adoption at TI. The major thrust of the "peanuts campaign" was to attract a new class of traveler, one who would normally drive or take trains and buses. The economics were clear. It requires nearly as much in operating costs to fly a jet 20% full as it does at 60%. TI opted for higher load factors by reducing prices. The results of this innovative marketing ploy were phenomenal. Load factors increased to 53.6% in 1976, 57.7% in 1977, and 60% in 1978. Net income for the same period was $3.479 million, $8.238 million, and $13.151 million. By 1978, Texas International ranked fourth in terms of traffic among the regional lines, experienced thirty-nine consecutive months of record earnings and was heralded as the fastest growing regional airline in the United States. The infusion of profits allowed it to continue its upgrading to a strictly jet fleet and petition the Civil Aeronautics Board for permission to carry its "peanut fares" into twenty-three new markets. Some of the more lucrative included Las Vegas, Baltimore, Kansas City, Salt Lake City, and the Mexican resort communities of Cancun, Cozumel and Merida.

Such expansionist moves were viewed with suspicion by the large trunks such as Delta, Eastern, Continental, Allegheny (U.S. Air), North Central (Republic) and National. Industry-wide fare discounting ensued but they found it difficult to compete against Texas International's cost structure, said to be near the lowest in the industry. TI responded to these competitive threats by reducing prices further. In the highly contested Houston-Baltimore route, its fares were 50% below those charged by Delta on certain late evening flights. By late 1978, "peanuts fares" accounted for 34% of all seats sold.

The mood in Washington toward the airline industry was beginning to change. A more consumerist Congress applauded the fare discounting methods employed by the regionals. By the end of 1978, the regulatory environment which stabilized the industry and strangled competition for so many years was being phased out. The major trunks found themselves in a crucial position. Their cost structures could not compete and the regionals were aggressively pursuing their lucrative routes.

"MR. PEANUT" MEETS NATIONAL AND TWA: 1978–1979

Either by design or happenstance, Lorenzo had prepared his airline for the deregulatory environment more than any other large regional or major trunk airline. As airlines were still reeling under the effects of the new government regulations and discount fares, Lorenzo took both Wall Street and the industry by surprise. After obtaining major European and South American financial agreements, he announced that Texas International owned 9.2% of National's stock and was intent on merger.

Possessing attractive Sun-Belt routes, a relatively debt-free balance sheet, and a grossly underpriced stock, National was a plum ready to be picked. Other large trunk carriers immediately joined in the bidding. Pan Am desired the domestic routes to complement its international network. Air Florida submitted a plan to liquidate National so that it could buy its planes. Eastern wanted merger so that National's western routes would provide it access to the West Coast. Eastern's proposal came under severe antitrust scrutiny due to the natural competitive nature of Eastern and National on the eastern seaboard and Florida. While recommendations as to what to do about National were bantered about, Lorenzo methodically increased Texas International's holdings of National to 24.5% before it was frozen. By April of 1979, the contestants had been whittled down to Texas International and Pan Am. Bidding had reached $40 per share.

Publicly, Lorenzo was confident and wore his gambler's mask. Internally, things were much different. National's board rejected TI and highly favored Pan Am as their "white knight." In addition, the burden of $400,000 per month in interest charges was beginning to take its toll on profitability. Lorenzo realized his airline probably could not afford the hostile merger attempt and set the stage for one of his patented financial gambles. In mid-May he insinuated in a speech before a group of Wall Street analysts that the book value of National's assets was at least $76 per share rather than the $46.50 indicated by National's board. It was a risk that paid off. Pan Am promptly offered $50 per share which Lorenzo accepted. The after tax profit realized by Texas International was said to be around $46–50 million. TI's stock was selling at eleven times earnings.

The industry was still guessing where Lorenzo would strike next. It didn't take long. On September 13, 1978 Texas International announced that it had acquired 4% of TWA's 16 million shares of stock. Trans World Corporation, the holding company for such diverse ventures as the airline, the Hilton Hotel chain and Century 21 Real Estate, was almost four times Texas International's size and announced on September 19 that it would fight the takeover attempt.

Through complex lending agreements and commitments by Lorenzo to liquidate or sell off the non-airline related ventures, he seemed to have adequate financing leverage. Robert J. Joedick, an analysis from Lehman Bros. remarked:

> "Financing such an acquisition would be attractive to lenders primarily because of the reputation of Lorenzo and Texas International. When you have a track record such as his, a lot of people will back you a second time around."

Though hostile toward merger, Trans World Corp. opted to meet with Lorenzo personally rather than fight him in the press. Both factions were very familiar with one another. Some of Texas International's top management had been recruited from the larger airline, Lorenzo had once worked at TWA, and all parties were familiar with his financial dealings. After a series of meetings, Lorenzo, for whatever reason, decided not to press merger talks further. It is said that Texas International realized approximately $6 million in profits from the sale of TWA stock. It is interesting to note that Continental stock, once mentioned as a possible TI acquisition, fell to $12 per share during the merger talks.

MORE PEANUTS, "TAC" AND NEW YORK AIR: 1979–1980

Primarily due to the sale of National stock, profits in 1979 rose to over $41 million dollars. Only $6.5 million came from operations, down almost $9 million from the year before. The primary factors for decreased earnings from operations were a 68% increase in fuel costs and 30% increase in other expenses. Revenues were up only 30% to offset these increases. Passenger load factor of 62.1% had reached an all time high and yield per passenger mile had decreased slightly.

The company began to utilize its windfall from Pan Am. Contracts were negotiated to purchase twenty used DC—9—30 aircraft, now the standard for the TI fleet. The highly acclaimed peanuts program was expanded. New "stations" such as St. Louis, Tulsa, and Guadalajara were added to the system. Six marginal cities were dropped and the airline operated without a dollar in federal subsidies for the first time since inception. During the period, a common stock dividend ($.04 per share) was paid for the first time in history.

By late 1979, Lorenzo's seven year tenure had produced an airline whose book value assets totaled over $319 million of which approximately $141 million consisted of cash and short term investments which could be utilized for another merger attempt, expansion, or both. To manage such an asset portfolio, the carrier decided to reorganize. In March of 1980, it formed a holding company in the name of Texas Air Corp. In Lorenzo's own words,

> "The holding company structure will permit greater business and financial flexibility. For example, the company would be able to raise funds on either the credit or the holding company, the airline, or any subsidiary. We may find it easier to pursue diversification should we find it advisable to enter into either regulated or non-regulated business activities without necessarily being under the jurisdiction of the Federal Aviation Act."[8]

With the formation of the holding company concept in 1980, Texas International was transformed into a subsidiary. In the face of a recessionary environment during 1980, the airline decided to change some fundamental strategic directions.

1. Greater emphasis would be placed on the business traveler who is affected less by a changing economic environment. Efforts were made to

[8] Author unlisted, "Trans World to Fight Takeover," *Aviation Week & Space Technology* (September 24, 1979), p. 25.

raise the ratio to a 60–40 mix in favor of business travel. Prior to that time, the carrier had near the reverse.
2. Consolidate the two major hubs, Dallas/Ft. Worth and Houston. Route expansions would spring from those points only.
3. Re-establish ties with travel agents to expand their marketing network rather than relying solely on incoming calls to their reservation center.

In short, 1980 was a year of consolidation. However, the company remained committed to expansion. Houston's Intercontinental Airport is the eighth busiest in the United States and twentieth in the world according to the Airport Operator's Council International. In June of 1980, Texas Air Corp. announced that fifteen of the twenty-six new gates added upon completion of terminal C would belong to the airline. The other eleven were reserved by Continental. At the time of the announcement, Texas Air was operating fifty-nine flights from five gates in Terminal A at Houston Inter-Continental.

Financial and operating data for Texas Air Corporation for the year 1971–1980 are shown in Exhibit 1.

In January of 1980, a "falling out" occurred between Lorenzo and part of his management team concerning among many things the new "Peanuts Payola" marketing plan. The result was the resignation of some key personnel: Don Burr, President of Texas International and a member of TAC's Board; Jerry Gitner, Senior Vice-President of Marketing & Planning; and Bob McAdoo, Controller and Vice-President of Information Systems. The group left with other Texas Air management personnel to form People's Express, a low cost "commuter line" between New York and Washington.

Not to be outdone, Lorenzo announced his version of People's Express, New York Air, on September 12, 1980. The newly formed subsidiary was formed when $24 million and six DC–9–20's from Texas International's fleet were provided by Texas Air. A public offering of stock was made to raise additional capital. However, Texas Air maintains about an 80% interest in New York Air.

New York Air's system is planned to ultimately span fifteen cities in seven states and the District of Columbia. The hub is planned to be the New York/Newark area with no destination requiring more than two hours in flight time. Cities listed in its initial filing included Detroit, Boston, Newark, Albany, Buffalo, Rochester, Syracuse, New York City, Cincinnati, Cleveland, Columbus, Dayton and Pittsburgh. The airline competes directly with Eastern, the entrenched shuttle system master in the area. Through creative advertising programs such as requiring passengers to take the New York Oath "to never, ever again fly the Eastern shuttle" before receiving the discount fares, the airline has become the darling of the press. Dubbed "Son of Shuttle" by the New York City media, its passenger load factor has been in the 65–70% range.

The venture has not been without its detractors. Being a nonunion subsidiary of Texas Air has caused an uproar from ALPA, Texas International's pilots union. They claim that their contract forbids the use of non-union pilots and that New York Air is in violation. Lorenzo contends that their contract is with Texas International and that New York Air is a subsidiary of Texas Air, not TI. Therefore, he sees no justification in their complaints. The issue is crucial in that if TAC wins, a new non-union precedent will be established in a highly unionized industry.

EXHIBIT 1: Texas Air Corporation Financial and Operating Data 1971–1980 ($ thousands except for share date)

	1980	*1979*	*1978*
Summary of Operations			
Passenger Revenues	$ 266,837	$ 213,218	$ 158,185
Other Revenues	24,659	20,943	22,007
Total Operating Revenues	$ 291,496	$ 234,161	$ 180,192
Total Operating Expenses	284,949	218,825	164,118
Operating Income (Loss)	$ 6,547	$ 15,336	$ 16,074
Interest and Debt Expense—Net	$ 19,650	$ 15,092	$ 6,656
Other (Income) Expense—Net	(20,402)	(48,051)	(3,733)
Provision for Income Taxes	2,630	6,900	5,174
	$ 1,878	$ (26,059)	$ 8,097
Income (Loss) from Continuing Operations	$ 4,669	$ 41,395	$ 7,977
Income (Loss) from Tropicana Hotel	—	—	—
Extraordinary Items	—	—	5,174
	$ 4,669	$ 41,395	$ 13,151
Earnings (Loss) per Common and Common Equivalent Share	$ .64	$ 5.88	$ 2.17
Earnings (Loss) per Common Share Assuming Full Dilution	.64	4.84	2.05
Financial Information (At Year End)			
Current Assets	$ 196,169	$ 156,927	$ 39,785
Current Liabilities	82,871	68,452	44,578
Working Capital (Deficit)	113,298	88,475	(4,793)
Net Investment in Flight Equipment	158,062	143,824	83,592
Total Assets	386,428	319,201	194,955
Total Long-Term Debt	217,790	175,295	113,213
Net Worth (Deficit)	89,903	81,218	40,784
Common Stock Price Range	14¾–6⅜	13⅝–7½	16⅜–7⅜
General Statistics*			
Employees at Year-End	3,500	3,400	3,000
In Scheduled Service for the year:			
Passengers Boarded	3,970,197	4,073,019	3,699,079
Revenue Passenger Miles (000's)	2,241,586	2,186,297	1,560,553
Available Seat Miles (000's)	3,898,422	3,523,128	2,601,677
Passenger Load Factor	57.5%	62.1%	60.0%
Breakeven Load Factor	55.8%	57.6%	55.0%
Average Fare	$ 67.10	$ 52.35	$ 42.76
Yield per Revenue Passenger Mile	$ .1189	$ .0975	$ .1014

* Texas International only.

1977	*1976*	*1975*	*1974*	*1973*	*1972*	*1971*
$ 122,038	$ 102,051	$ 60,594	$ 74,431	$ 62,758	$ 58,181	$ 56,203
22,749	18,342	18,529	17,345	14,547	14,907	13,788
$ 144,787	$ 120,383	$ 79,123	$ 91,776	$ 77,305	$ 73,088	$ 69,991
132,623	114,375	79,833	87,711	73,618	70,348	71,591
$ 12,164	$ 6,018	$ (710)	$ 4,065	$ 3,687	$ 2,740	$ (1,600)
$ 4,305	$ 3,496	$ 3,510	$ 4,267	$ 4,128	$ 4,324	$ 4,821
(379)	(957)	29	(459)	(562)	(63)	156
1,034	822	—	43	13	—	—
$ 4,960	$ 3,361	$ 3,539	$ 3,851	$ 3,579	$ 4,261	$ 4,977
$ 7,204	$ 2,657	$ (4,249)	$ 214	$ 108	$ (1,521)	$ (6,577)
—	—	—	—	—	$ 199	$ (839)
1,034	822	—	43	13	(305)	—
$ 8,238	$ 3,479	$ (4,249)	$ 257	$ 121	$ (1,707)	$ (7,416)
$ 1.52	$ .70	$ (3.48)	$ .02	$ (.03)	$ (1.42)	$ (6.19)
1.52	.70	(3.48)	.02	(.03)	(1.42)	(6.19)
$ 37,266	$ 27,287	$ 21,457	$ 18,846	$ 19,127	$ 18,793	$ 16,216
44,433	33,401	30,301	26,160	23,698	21,748	36,726
(7,167)	(6,114)	(8,844)	(7,314)	(4,571)	(2,955)	(20,510)
55,661	43,723	46,856	47,790	46,262	52,152	56,604
108,796	78,868	73,575	73,998	80,076	75,307	78,946
61,610	49,966	50,302	51,739	56,548	55,476	64,621
11,749	4,267	760	4,932	4,573	5,214	(7,527)
8–2⅛	3⅝–1⅝	2¾–1¼	3⅞–1	4¾–1⅞	7–4	8–3½
2,600	2,300	2,150	2,000	2,153	2,019	2,089
3,002,913	2,397,256	1,515,196	2,116,605	2,045,933	2,160,928	2,220,515
1,167,059	946,756	580,269	758,949	681,904	686,353	705,853
2,022,907	1,767,488	1,167,349	1,506,193	1,484,787	1,374,167	1,494,642
57.7%	53.6%	49.7%	50.4%	45.9%	49.9%	47.2%
53.9%	51.9%	53.3%	50.1%	45.5%	51.5%	52.7%
$ 40.64	$ 42.57	$ 39.99	$ 35.17	$ 30.67	$ 26.92	$ 25.31
$ .1046	$ .1078	$ .1044	$ .0981	$ .0920	$ .0848	$ .0796

THE ATTEMPT TO ACQUIRE CONTINENTAL 1980–1981

Western and Continental were very near a corporate marriage when Frank Lorenzo announced in early 1981 that Texas International (i.e., *not* Texas Air) had acquired 9.4% of Continental's stock and intended a takeover. Western negotiations terminated and the Los Angeles based carrier was in the fight of its life. On February 9, 1981, Lorenzo announced a tender offer for 4.3 million shares of Continental stock (48% of the outstanding stock) for $13 per share, a quote which bore a 25% premium over the price at which Continental closed on February 5. In a carefully worded statement to Continental shareholders, Texas International reminded them of some facts about the proposed Western merger:

1. There was no guarantee that the merger would either equal or exceed TI's cash offer.
2. The combined loss for Continental and Western in 1980 was $52.7 million.
3. The combination would have produced a net loss of $1.94 per share on Continental Stock versus the .64 per share actually recorded.
4. The combination would have $321.2 million in debt coming due within the next five years.
5. The proposed company would have a total long term debt structure of over $763.8 million, a 132% increase over current levels.

Almost 4.3 million Continental shares were tendered to TI within four days.

By the first week of April, Continental was desperate. It proposed a $185 million ESOP offering in which employees would be able to buy the airline and effectively dilute the ownership of existing shareholders, including Texas International, by 50%. The battle has raged for months. In late June, 1981, the New York Stock Exchange ruled that it would de-list Continental if the ESOP plan was implemented. The California Commissioner of Corporations, the first governmental authority to issue an opinion, ruled that Continental could not issue the additional 15 million ESOP shares without a vote from shareholders and employees. In addition, it acted to neutralize Texas International's voting power by allowing it to vote only in the same proportion as the remaining small investors.

CASE TWENTY-NINE

Texas Air Corporation (B)

ELIZABETH GATEWOOD and WILLIAM R. BOULTON
University of Georgia

Assignment Questions:

1. What has happened to the airline industry since 1980?
2. How has Lorenzo done since 1980?
3. What should Lorenzo do now?

"Frank's got a lot of guts, but he may have bitten off more than he can chew this time," said Lamar Muse, the chairman of Muse Air Corporation, which operated a small Texas airline. "The timing for bringing three airlines together couldn't be worse. It could all go down the drain."

Frank Lorenzo, president of Texas Air Corporation, a holding company for Texas International, Continental Airlines, and New York Air, planned to make Texas Air one of the major airlines in the United States by 1990. Given recent developments in the airline industry, this challenge could be even more than Frank Lorenzo can handle. (See Exhibit 1.)

INDUSTRY HIGHLIGHTS

The twelve major U.S. airlines were expected to post a cumulative operating loss of nearly $500 million for 1981. This loss followed on the heels of a $297.2 million operating loss in 1980, the worst financial performance in the history of the industry until 1981. Net 1981 losses for parent companies with major airline operations were expected to run $600 million or higher compared to $366.4 million in 1980 (Exhibit 2). Parent companies losses were expected despite gains from asset sales and nonairline activities. Recession, deregulation, and soaring labor and fuel costs had combined to decrease profits and cut into already weak balance sheets.

The economic recession and the Professional Air Traffic Controllers Organization (PATCO) strike in August 1981 resulted in a decline in passenger traffic. After the strike, mandatory cutbacks ordered by the Federal Aviation Agency (FAA) reduced major carrier flights by 25 per cent, and as much as 50 per cent

EXHIBIT 1: Texas Air Corporation (B)
Texas Air Corporation (5 Year) Financial Statement

FIVE YEAR FINANCIAL SUMMARY (DOLLARS IN THOUSANDS EXCEPT PER SHARE DATA)

	1981	*1980*[1]	*1979*	*1978*	*1977*
Total Operating Revenues	$ 719,400	$291,496	$234,161	$180,192	$144,787
Total Operating Expense	760,246	284,949	218,825	164,118	132,623
Operating Income (Loss)	(40,846)	6,547	15,336	16,074	12,164
Non Operating Income (Expense)	(11,132)	73	32,959	(2,923)	(3,926)
Pre-Tax Income (Loss)	(51,978)	6,620	48,295	13,151	8,238
Provisions for Income Taxes (Credit)	(4,793)	2,630	6,900	5,174	1,034
Extraordinary Items	—	—	—	5,174	1,034
Net Income (Loss)	(47,185)	3,990	41,395	13,151	8,238
Earnings (Loss) per Common and Common Equivalent Share (Primary)	$ (8.11)	$ .55	$ 5.88	$ 2.17	$ 1.52
Total Assets	$1,301,316	$385,749	$319,201	$194,855	$108,796
Current Assets	352,549	195,490	156,927	39,785	37,266
Current Liabilities	670,356[2]	82,871	68,452	44,578	44,433
Cash and Cash Equivalents	129,848	141,949	116,128	14,356	12,467
Net Investment in Flight Equipment	852,035	158,062	143,824	83,592	55,661
Total Long-Term Debt	833,409[2]	217,790	175,295	113,213	61,610
Net Worth[3]	44,853	89,224	81,218	40,784	11,749

[1] Restated.
[2] Includes long-term debt classified as current.
[3] Includes redeemable preferred stock.

EXHIBIT 2: Texas Air Corporation (B)
Industry Profits

THE NOSE DIVE IN AIRLINE OPERATING PROFITS

Carrier	*Quarter Ended Dec. 31, 1980*	*Quarter Ended Dec. 31, 1981*	*1980*	*1981*
		(millions of dollars)		
American Airlines+	−$7.5	−$39.7	−$112.9	$43.9
Delta Air Lines	53.7	2.1	164.2*	86.5*
Eastern Air Lines	6.9	− 29.4	1.9	−49.9
Frontier Airlines	11.2	9.0	36.4	50.9
Pan American+	−60.4	−127.7	−129.6	−359.7
Trans World Airlines+	−29.1	− 31.3	−18.4	13.6
United Airlines+	40.6	−123.3	−65.6	−148.8
USAir	32.5	16.7	91.4	58.5
Western Air Lines	−10.2	−43.7	−45.8	−66.0

+ Airline operations only.
* Calendar year; fiscal year ends June 30.
Data: Salomon Bros.

in some markets. By the fall of 1982 the system had gradually increased to 86 per cent of its prestrike capacity.

After a decade of growth at an annual compound rate of 7 per cent, the airlines experienced two consecutive years of decline. In 1980, the twelve major carriers enplaned 223.2 million passengers on domestic flights, 7.3 per cent below the 1979 level, as shown in Exhibit 3. Continuing poor economic conditions and inflation resulted in another year of traffic decline in 1981. The airlines estimated a decline of 6 per cent in 1981 traffic compared to 1980.

Equally damaging to industry profitability had been the intense competition resulting from deregulation of the airline industry in 1978. Deregulation had allowed the airlines to change routes, flight schedules, and fares. The immediate impact of deregulation was to allow carriers to choose which routes to enter, and which routes to pull out of. Though many routes had been discontinued since 1978, scheduled flights had increased in over 100 cities, and 35 carriers started flying 231 flights that had been kept dormant by the airlines that had permission to fly them.

In an effort to establish market share in new routes, many airlines chose to utilize reduced and discounted air fares. According to International Air Transportation Authority, for the first seven months of 1980, reduced fare traffic accounted for 54.2 per cent of total domestic revenue passenger miles. In 1981 deep discount fare tickets represented 70 per cent of total tickets sold.

Airline carriers had also turned to marketing variables to gain a competitive advantage. Marketing programs had been developed that aimed at the repeat passenger or "frequent flier," the airlines' best customer. More than 90 per cent of these customers traveled on business trips. Some 20 per cent of these passengers provided as much as 70 per cent of several major carriers' traffic.

EXHIBIT 3: Texas Air Corporation (B)
Decrease in Traffic

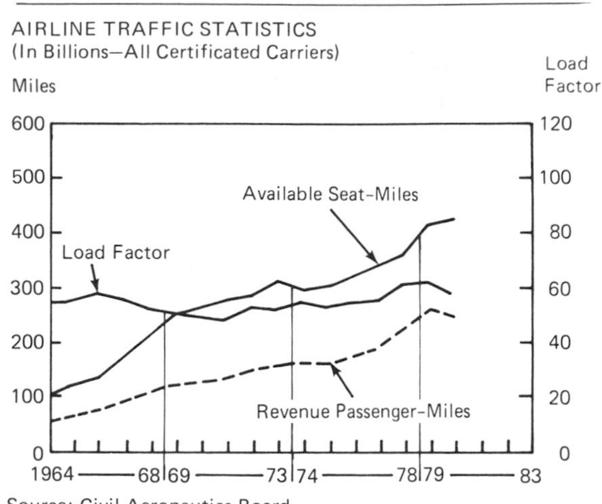

Source: Civil Aeronautics Board

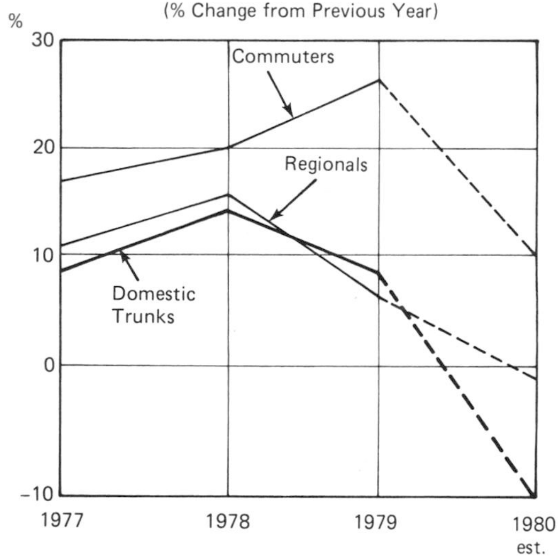

Source: Air Transport Association

In the past, airlines courted these valued customers with VIP airport lounges and similar promotions. But the latest customer inducements allowed frequent fliers to earn free travel when they consistently booked with one line. American introduced its promotion in May 1981 when it offered AAdvantage, which allowed a flier of 12,000 miles to upgrade for free from coach to first class on one round trip or to earn a 25 per cent discount on a round-trip ticket for flying 20,000 miles. Competing carriers quickly answered with promotions of their own, adding discounted or free hotel room and rental cars.

The promotions had become powerful marketing tools. Said one New York-based traveler, "I really like flying New York Air to Boston and Washington, but I take the shuttle to earn free travel on Eastern." American, noticing unusual booking patterns, checked with customers only to discover that these peculiar routings were selected to earn AAdvantage miles. What had surprised the airlines was the number of awards taken as upgrades to first class.

Those airlines that had the most sophisticated computer systems had the easiest time administering their promotional programs, and carriers with computer capability had been the most successful in targeting their market and efficiently promoting to it. Domestic airline advertising had been increasing over the last decade. The major domestic airline carriers spent approximately $475 million in 1981, up from $393 million in 1980. United Airlines, the largest advertiser, spent $75 million in 1981, as shown in Exhibit 4.

Another major problem the airlines had been facing was rising fuel and labor costs. In 1973, the average jet fuel price was 11¢ per gallon accounting

EXHIBIT 4: Texas Air Corporation (B)
U.S. Airline Advertising
Advertising Expenditures ('000)

Majors	*1970*	*1975*	*1979*	*1980*	*1981*	*Per Cent Change (1981–1980)*
American	24,145	30,259	42,093	55,772	62,238	15.2
Braniff	5,385	8,529	12,423	21,485	21,086	−1.9
Continental	11,203	10,907	22,310	19,390	18,881	−2.6
Delta	9,531	18,746	34,557	39,195	42,741	9.0
Eastern	20,696	22,521	40,232	52,810	57,551	9.0
National	6,193	7,667	15,864	N.A.	N.A.	N.A.
Northwest	7,101	9,788	12,815	17,489	22,375	27.9
Pan Am	36,912	38,530	50,739	50,313	52,346	4.0
Republic	N.A.	N.A.	14,833	14,048	14,742	4.9
TWA	30,546	40,444	45,205	59,056	68,941	16.7
United	28,753	27,964	52,494	62,776	75,379	20.0
U.S. Air	N.A.	N.A.	9,367	9,930	12,177	22.6
Western	8,089	9,209	13,354	15,085	20,170	33.7
Subtotal	188,555	224,566	366,286	417,349	468,627	12.3
National						
Capitol Air	N.A.	N.A.	N.A.	2,299	5,339	132.2
Frontier	N.A.	N.A.	2,897	2,467	3,822	54.9
Hawaiian	N.A.	N.A.	N.A.	1,513	2,695	78.2
Piedmont	N.A.	N.A.	3,609	5,198	7,653	47.2
PSA	N.A.	N.A.	N.A.	3,089	4,242	37.4
Ozark	N.A.	N.A.	2,800	3,165	3,710	17.2
Texas International	N.A.	N.A.	2,399	2,554	2,408	−5.7
Transamerican	N.A.	N.A.	N.A.	1,825	2,045	12.0
Subtotal	N.A.	N.A.	11,705	22,110	31,914	44.3
Grand Total	188,555	224,566	377,991	439,459	500,541	13.9

N.A. = Not Available.

EXHIBIT 5: Texas Air Corporation (B) Fuel Costs

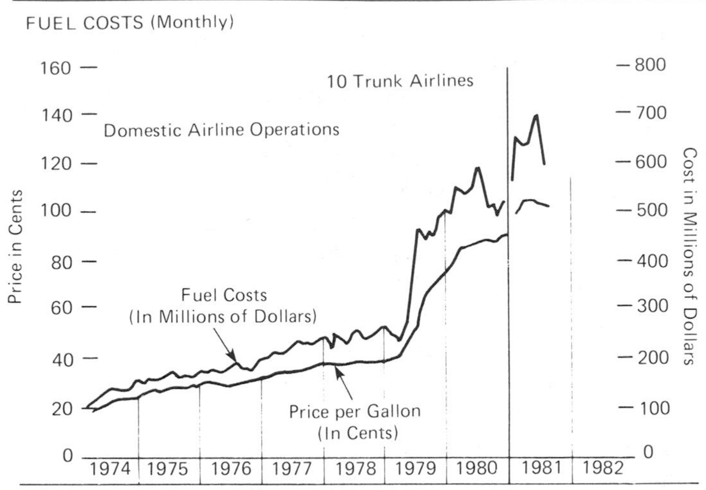

Source: Civil Aeronautics Board.

Fuel Cost and Consumption
Year 1981

Type of Operation	*Gallons Consumed ('000)*	*Cost per Gallon (cents)*	*Gallons Consumed Per Cent Change 1981/1980*	*Cost per Gallon Percent Change 1981/1980*
DOMESTIC SERVICE				
Majors				
Scheduled Service	7,220,290	101.838	(10.00)	17.90
Non-Scheduled Service	43,125	103.174	(33.65)	18.61
TOTAL	7,263,415	101.846	(10.18)	17.90
Nationals				
Scheduled Service	1,049,777	103.260	9.212	16.84
Non-Scheduled Service	69,212	111.396	(13.15)	26.64
TOTAL	1,118,989	103.763	7.69	17.45
Large Regionals				
Scheduled Service	95,807	109.683	90.93	11.35
Non-Scheduled Service	53,098	117.828	70.48	38.65
TOTAL	148,905	112.588	83.10	20.64
Medium Regionals				
Scheduled Service	17,732	117.512	106.81	6.57
Non-Scheduled Service	622	123.822	(78.35)	14.77
TOTAL	18,354	117.726	60.34	7.34
Total Domestic	8,549,663	102.318	(7.26)	18.02
Total International	2,032,427	114.641	(2.90)	10.63
Total All Carriers	10,582,090	104.685	(6.45)	16.54

Source: CAB Form 41, Schedule P121(A).

for 19 per cent of total operation costs. As of December 1979, fuel was 75.8¢ per gallon, accounting for 28 per cent of operation costs. In 1979 a 1 per cent per gallon increase in fuel costs resulted in a $106 million increase in the airline industry's operating expenses. In 1981, the average fuel cost of $1.04 a gallon represented approximately 30 per cent of total expenses for the industry. (See Exhibit 5.)

The problem of increasing prices of jet fuel was likely to continue throughout the 1980s. Fuel prices stabilized during the latter months of 1980, but this was considered a temporary condition. The stabilized price had been attributed to a surplus of crude oil resulting from the stagnated economies of the industrialized nations. Although price rises were expected to be modest in the next few years, by 1985 fuel was expected to account for 65 per cent of airline operating expenses.

One of the ways in which the industry attempted to control fuel supply and cost was through vertical integration. The airlines were investing in independent refineries and forming their own energy exploration projects. It was estimated that carriers could cut 30 per cent of their fuel costs just by controlling their own fuel distribution.

Rising labor costs had also contributed to the increase in operating expenses. Although most airlines had decreased their work forces, labor costs had continued to increase. In 1980 Pan American Airlines laid off 11 per cent of its work force, yet its labor costs increased 6 per cent.

TEXAS AIR CORPORATION

In October 1981, President Reagan approved the acquisition of Continental Airlines by Texas International. This was one of Frank Lorenzo's first strategic moves to parlay Texas Air, a near bankrupt regional carrier in 1970, into a major airline by 1990. The financial performance of Texas Air Corporation was heavily affected by recent events and reported a $47 million loss for 1981. (See Exhibits 6 and 7 for details.)

Lorenzo, chairman and chief executive officer of Texas Air Corporation, planned to combine Texas International's short-haul planes and routes with Continental's long-haul capacity and create a hub-and-spoke system similar to other major airlines as shown in Exhibit 8. Texas Air Corporation was the holding company for Texas International, Continental Airlines, and New York Air. New York Air was a discount airline founded to compete directly with People's Express, a low-cost commuter line flying between New York and Washington. People's Express had been started by a group of former key Texas International personnel after Lorenzo balked at starting their proposed airline.

Texas International

Despite a reputation as a financial whiz, Lorenzo had his hands full. In the summer of 1981, Texas International moved the hub of its route structure from Dallas to Houston, where Continental also had significant operations. Unfortu-

EXHIBIT 6: Texas Air Corporation (B)
Texas Air Corporation and Subsidiaries
Consolidated Statement of Operations
(Dollars in thousands, except per share data)

	For the Years Ended December 31,		
	1981	*1980*	*1979*
Operating Revenues:			
Passenger	$649,491	$266,837	$213,218
Cargo, mail and other	69,909	24,659	20,943
	719,400	291,496	234,161
Operating Expenses:			
Fuel	228,919	87,796	54,960
Flying operations	80,072	27,564	24,040
Maintenance	59,182	28,561	21,538
Aircraft and traffic servicing	137,925	56,287	49,315
Passenger service	64,737	15,139	14,313
Promotion and sales	96,476	32,400	25,948
General and administrative	48,772	21,674	16,958
Depreciation and amortization	44,163	15,528	11,753
	760,246	284,949	218,825
Operating Income (Loss)	(40,846)	6,547	15,336
Other Income (Expense):			
Interest and debt expense	(63,662)	(20,858)	(16,205)
Interest capitalized	3,083	1,208	1,113
Interest income	19,615	15,412	4,025
Disposition of property and equipment	1,490	3,019	2,589
Sale of income tax benefits	23,386	—	—
Gain on sale of investments	7,740	437	41,545
Equity in loss of Continental Air Lines, Inc.	(11,139)	(679)	—
Minority interest in loss of subsidiaries	12,077	27	—
Other, net	(3,722)	1,507	(108)
	(11,132)	73	32,959
Income (Loss) before Income Taxes	(51,978)	6,620	48,295
Provision (Credit) for Income Taxes	(4,793)	2,630	6,900
Net Income (Loss)	$(47,185)	$ 3,990	$ 41,395
Earnings (Loss) per Common and Common Equivalent Share	$ (8.11)	$ .55	$ 5.88
Earnings (loss) per Common Share Assuming Full Dilution	$ (8.11)	$ .55	$ 4.84

nately, the transfer was interrupted by the PATCO strike that resulted in Texas International's loss of passengers and nearly $20 million in annual revenues.

Texas International was also undergoing a marketing change. Started as a low-cost carrier in the Texas market, deregulation had brought in new competition offering similar fares. As a result, Texas International had been searching for a new, yet undefined, niche.

New York Air

New York Air, originally conceived as a cut-rate alternative to Eastern Air Lines Inc.'s New York-Washington Shuttle service, had early successes in the marketplace. Within a few months of its conception it had achieved a 25 per cent market share. As New York Air began adding other routes, established competitors matched fares and increased their schedules.

New York Air's major airports—Boston, New York LaGuardia, and Washington National—were among those hardest hit by flight restrictions imposed by the FAA in the face of the PATCO strike. New York Air was forced to reduce its number of flights from 60 to 40 in its daily schedule, and it also abandoned its Boston-LaGuardia route because it could not get the frequency of flights it thought it needed to be profitable. Operational losses mounted when New York Air ran into a contractual problem with United Airlines Inc., a provider of ground air services to New York Air at LaGuardia. New York Air posted a loss of nearly $12 million in 1981.

Continental Airline

At the first board meeting after the Continental acquisition, Lorenzo discovered that Continental's financial condition was much worse than he had previously suspected. Continental's president, George Warde, told the board that the airline expected 1981 losses to exceed $60 million even after $30 million from tax credits and gains from selling equipment. (See Exhibits 9 and 10.)

"A very grim meeting," Lorenzo recalled. "I never expected them to lose $60 million—$30 million, maybe." Continental's actual operating losses for 1981 turned out to be more than $100 million. A few days after the announcement of the operating results for 1981, Continental's lenders withdrew from its revolving-credit agreement. The airlines was forced to negotiate a $25 million short-term credit.

In March 1982, Peat, Marwick, Mitchell & Co. qualified Continental Airline's 1981 financial results. Citing its continuing losses and the month-to-month amendments governing its long-term debt, the auditors questioned its continued existence. Previous to Peat, Marwick, Mitchell & Co.'s actions, Continental announced that it had failed to meet a deadline for labor cost cuts the airline was seeking in an attempt to control costs and improve the profit picture. The airline termed the concessions necessary for the continued existence of Continental in its existing form.

Continental was attempting to negotiate labor productivity concessions totaling $60 million with its unions, and had laid off 1,500 of its 11,000 employees in a cost-cutting move. This paralleled a cost-cutting program at Texas In-

EXHIBIT 7: Texas Air Corporation (B)
Texas Air Corporation and Subsidiaries Consolidated Balance Sheet
(Dollars in Thousands)

	December 31,	
Assets	*1981*	*1980*
Current Assets:		
Cash and temporary cash investments	$ 129,848	$141,949
Other investments	2,469	12,482
Accounts receivable	160,911	29,481
Inventories of spare parts and supplies	43,484	7,121
Prepayments and other	15,837	4,457
Total current assets	352,549	195,490
Property and Equipment, at cost:		
Flight equipment	709,495	181,353
Aircraft purchase deposits	1,400	8,050
Other	142,451	24,157
	853,336	213,560
Less: Accumulated depreciation	(77,478)	(48,030)
	775,858	165,530
Property and Equipment Under Capital Leases:		
Flight equipment	172,084	27,448
Other	6,607	6,607
	178,691	34,055
Less: Accumulated amortization	(26,191)	(21,597)
	152,500	12,458
Total property and equipment	928,358	177,988
Other Assets	20,409	12,271
Total Assets	$1,301,316	$385,749

Liabilities and Stockholders' Equity	*December 31,* *1981*	*1980*
Current Liabilities:		
Current maturities of long-term debt	$ 51,961	$ 7,583
Current obligations under capital leases	5,212	2,624
Long-term debt classified as current	280,376	—
Notes payable to banks	—	4,500
Accounts payable	119,125	24,380
Advance ticket sales	124,608	15,797
Accrued payroll and pension costs	35,030	14,704
Accrued interest	20,210	5,668
Accrued taxes	9,864	3,168
Other accrued liabilities	23,970	4,445
Total current liabilities	670,356	82,871
Long-term Debt, net	339,647	196,236
Obligations Under Capital leases, net	156,213	11,347
Deferred Federal Income Taxes	—	5,933
Other Deferred Credits	23,467	—
Minority Interest in Subsidiaries	66,780	138
Commitments and Contingencies		
Redeemable Preferred Stock—Series A—26,402 and 28,536 shares outstanding at liquidation value	4,400	4,899
Non-Redeemable Preferred Stock and Common Stockholders' Equity:		
Preferred stock, at liquidation value—		
Series B—66,075 shares outstanding	—	165
Series C—2,040,000 shares outstanding	1,275	1,275
Common stock, 5,999,094 and 5,759,848 shares issued	60	58
Additional paid-in capital (less note receivable from affiliate of $3,335,000 in 1981)	49,543	42,682
Retained earnings (deficit)	(8,419)	40,145
Treasury stock, 174,354 shares at cost	(2,006)	—
Total non-redeemable preferred stock and common stockholders' equity	40,453	84,325
Total Liabilities and Equity	$1,301,316	$385,749

EXHIBIT 8: Texas Air Corporation (B) Airline Network

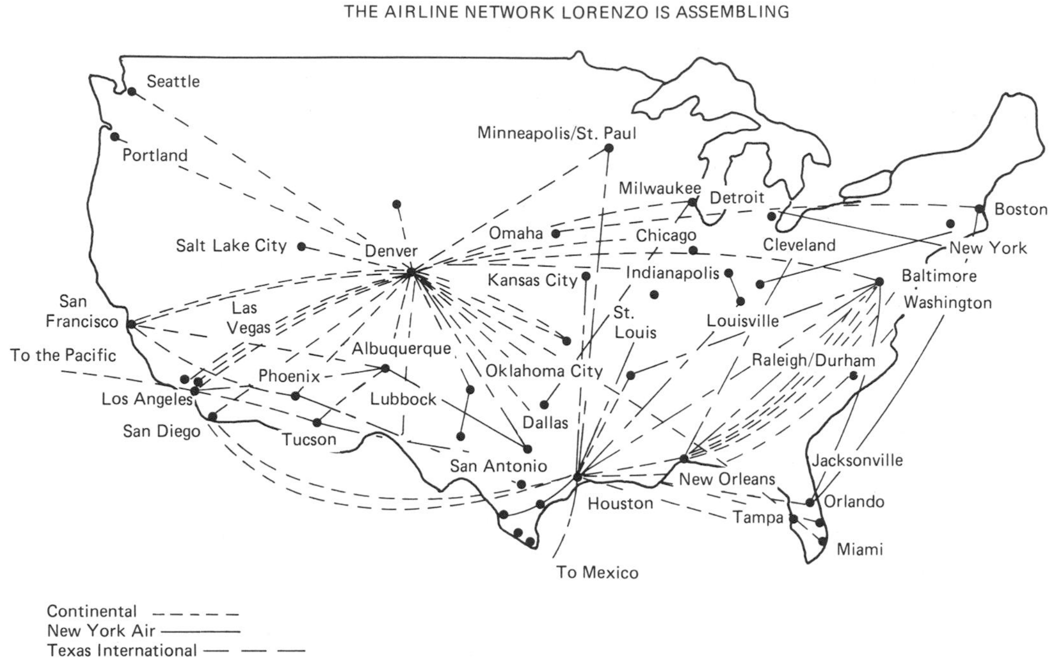

Source: *Business Week*, June 7, 1982.

ternational that included laying off 15 per cent of its 3,265 employees and asking its unions for productivity increases and compensation cuts. Complicating the problem were bitter feelings that had remained at Texas International after a contract fight between Lorenzo and Texas International's pilots dragged on for a year and a half before it was settled. New York Air's nonunion status had also added to Lorenzo's antiunion image at both Continental and Texas International at a time when both airlines were pushing their union employees for productivity and wage concessions.

Continental's senior vice-president Roy Rawls warned that if the concessions weren't adopted, Continental's work force could be "dramatically cut back by as many as 5,000 more employees." These concessions were seen as critical because of the poor financial condition of Continental's balance sheet. The airline's net worth had fallen to $131 million at the end of 1981 from $190.9 million a year earlier. The airline had approximately $205 million in long-term debt. A spokesman for Continental said it would report most bank and institutional debt as "current maturities" on its 1981 balance sheet because of the uncertainty cited by Peat, Marwick, Mitchell & Co.

Concern for the Future

By the end of 1981, Lorenzo's three airlines had a combined debt of $700 million. Texas Air Corporation's losses totaled $47.2 million for 1981 compared to a profit of $4 million in 1980, prior to the acquisition. In May 1982 Lorenzo

EXHIBIT 9: Texas Air Corporation (B)
Continental Income Statement
Continental Air Lines, Inc. and Subsidiaries
Consolidated Statements of Operations
(In thousands of dollars except per share amounts)

	Years ended December 31,		
	1981	*1980*	*1979*
Operating revenues:			
Passenger	$ 968,135	$ 879,593	$ 807,694
Cargo	83,554	77,903	89,262
Contract services and other	27,947	16,824	12,245
Other operations	11,141	17,699	18,781
Total operating revenues	1,090,777	992,019	927,982
Operating expenses:			
Wages, salaries and related costs	427,846	401,481	380,089
Aircraft fuel	336,104	295,255	227,614
Depreciation and amortization	68,768	59,262	56,353
Other	301,528	282,229	271,847
Total operating expenses	1,134,246	1,038,227	935,903
Operating loss	(43,469)	(46,208)	(7,921)
Nonoperating expense and (income):			
Interest expense	63,001	42,099	30,182
Interest capitalized	(2,169)	(4,974)	(1,673)
Sale of income tax benefits	(23,386)	—	—
Disposition of property and equipment, net	(12,649)	(41,961)	257
Other, net	(1,210)	(5,539)	(4,902)
Total nonoperating expense (income), net	23,587	(10,375)	23,864
Loss before income tax credits	(67,056)	(35,833)	(31,785)
Income tax credits	(6,700)	(15,129)	(18,600)
Net loss	$ (60,356)	(20,704)	(13,185)
Net loss per common share:			
Primary and fully diluted	$ (3.92)	(1.35)	(.87)
Weighted average shares outstanding:			
Primary and fully diluted	$15,402,491	15,345,304	15,118,031

was dealt another blow when Arthur Andersen & Co. qualified his holding company's financial statements. The auditors believed their action was necessary because of the possibility of Continental's bankruptcy bringing down Texas Air Corporation. There was little optimism that Lorenzo could pull this one out.

EXHIBIT 10: Texas Air Corporation (B)
Continental Airlines, Inc. and Subsidiaries Balance Sheet
(in thousands of dollars)

	December 31,	
Assets	*1981*	*1980*
Current assets:		
Cash	$ 24,372	16,717
Short-term investments, at cost, which approximates market	21,292	15,000
Receivables, principally traffic, less allowance for doubtful receivables ($2,424 in 1981 and $1,023 in 1980)	123,160	106,381
Spare parts and supplies, less allowance for obsolescence ($8,695 in 1981 and $9,060 in 1980)	35,602	36,938
Prepaid expense	12,869	5,816
Total current assets	217,295	180,852
Investments and other assets	4,422	5,038
Property and equipment, at cost:		
Flight equipment owned	720,588	638,062
Flight equipment held under capital leases	144,735	115,544
Other property and equipment	202,976	198,886
	1,068,299	952,492
Less accumulated depreciation and amortization	425,993	382,928
	642,306	569,564
Advance payments on equipment purchase contracts	—	28,695
Net property and equipment	642,306	598,259
	$ 864,023	784,149

Liabilities and Stockholders' Equity	*December 31,* 1981	1980
Current liabilities:		
Current installments of long-term obligations	$ 29,186	39,936
Long-term debt classified as current	280,376	–
Accounts payable	85,938	64,549
Air traffic liability	105,157	98,732
Accrued expenses	54,859	43,218
Total current liabilities	555,516	246,435
Long-term obligations:		
Debt	12,485	213,306
Capital leases	140,988	115,491
Deferred credits:		
Income taxes	1,300	8,000
Other	22,791	10,043
Stockholders' equity:		
Preferred stock without par value. Authorized 15,000,000 shares; none issued	—	—
Common stock of $.50 par value. Authorized 50,000,000 shares; issued 15,414,865 in 1981 and 15,355,267 in 1980	7,707	7,678
Capital in excess of par value	81,671	81,275
Retained earnings	41,565	101,921
Total stockholders' equity	130,943	190,874
	$ 864,023	784,149

CASE THIRTY

The Chrysler Corporation (A)

CHRISTINE A. BLOUKE and DAN R. E. THOMAS
Stanford University

Assignment Questions:

1. How did Chrysler get itself into such difficulty?
2. Who are the stakeholders that will be involved in finding a viable solution? What will they demand from Chrysler?
3. What alternative strategies are available to Chrysler's management? What are their consequences? Which would you select?

In October 1979, the Chrysler Corporation faced its third survival crisis in a decade. Allegedly shortsighted management policies and the costs of compliance with government regulations had contributed to an anticipated loss of $1.07 billion in 1979. The collapse of the nation's tenth largest company seemed highly possible unless rapid remedies could be found.

Chrysler's future rested on Lee A. Iacocca, the company's new chairman and chief executive officer. Chrysler had approached the Treasury Department on September 15, 1979, with a request for a $1.2 billion federal loan guarantee. The request was immediately rejected as excessive by Treasury Secretary G. William Miller, so Chrysler officials had gone back to Detroit to prepare a scaled down request which met Miller's criteria. Time was short. If approved by the Treasury, the second proposal would have to be submitted to Congress, where prolonged debate was anticipated; and the outcome of that debate, held in an election year, was not at all predictable.

Assuming that financial aid could be acquired, Iacocca's plans to regain Chrysler's profitability hinged on a line of compact cars scheduled for introduction in 1981. The new line had been designed to compete directly with General Motors' (G.M.) fast selling front wheel drive compacts which had been introduced in the spring of 1979. Even with financial aid, Chrysler expected to have a $482 million deficit in 1980. Sales of the new line of compacts were anticipated to generate a $393 million profit in 1981, and projected sales gains were expected to raise profits to $996 million in 1985.

Reprinted from *Stanford Business Cases 1979* with permission of the publishers, Stanford University Graduate School of Business, © 1979 by the Board of Trustees of the Leland Stanford Junior University.

Iacocca's options were limited. The Treasury Department had made it clear that government support through loan guarantees would be forthcoming only if Iacocca could secure written commitments of help from the United Auto Workers (UAW) union, Chrysler's principal banks, and certain state and local governments. Without loan guarantees, it appeared that the company would have to choose between bankruptcy and acquisition—probably by a foreign manufacturer.

THE AUTOMOBILE INDUSTRY

The automotive industry in the United States was highly competitive with respect to price, appearance, size, special features, distribution organization, warranty, product reliability, and, by 1978, fuel economy. Four domestic passenger car manufacturers dominated the industry in 1978: (1) General Motors (GM), the industry leader, was the largest industrial manufacturer in the United States, with sales of $63.2 billion for that year; (2) Ford Motor Company had sales of $42.8 billion; (3) Chrysler Corporation had sales of $16.3 billion; (4) American Motors Corporation (AMC) had sales of $2.6 billion. Unlike the Big Three, AMC was a producer of specialized vehicles and did not manufacture a full line of passenger cars.

Annual sales of the industry and of individual manufacturers had fluctuated over the years. Table 1 shows the market share of manufacturers in the domestic market.

Exhibit 1 shows detailed data on share of market by segment and manufacturer for 1972 through 1979.

Sales fluctuations were due to a number of factors. The purchase of an automobile was a deferrable item and the tendency of owners, when business conditions were adverse, was to keep their cars longer and postpone replacing them. When economic conditions appeared more favorable, this tendency was reversed. The degree of consumer acceptance of new models could also significantly affect sales and earnings. Other factors included competition from other products and services for the consumer dollar, as well as competition from vehicles imported from abroad or assembled in the United States by foreign manufacturers.

TABLE 1: Manufacturers' Share of the Domestic Automobile Market (Model Years)

	1972	*1973*	*1974*	*1975*	*1976*	*1977*	*1978*
GM	44.6	44.3	42.4	42.6	46.7	46.6	46.9
Ford	24.4	23.4	24.6	22.8	23.4	22.0	23.3
Chrysler	13.9	13.6	13.6	11.7	12.8	11.3	10.3
AMC	2.8	3.2	4.1	3.6	2.7	1.9	1.6
Foreign	14.3	15.5	15.3	19.3	14.4	18.2	17.9
	100.0	100.0	100.0	100.0	100.0	100.0	100.0

Source: Casewriter's Estimates from Multiple Sources.

EXHIBIT 1: The Chrysler Corporation (A)

CORPORATE SEGMENT TRENDS BY MANUFACTURER'S SHARE OF SEGMENT 1972–1979

	(Model Years)							
	1972	*1973*	*1974*	*1975*	*1976*	*1977*	*1978*	*1979†*
*Subcompact**								
Chrysler—Domestic	0%	0%	0%	0%	0%	0%	7.7%	7.7%
—Imported	3.8	2.3	2.2	4.2	4.5	7.0	3.3	4.4
GM —Domestic	21.1	22.7	23.6	19.3	23.0	16.0	23.8	15.5
—Imported	4.5	3.8	3.3	3.6	0.9	1.6	1.1	1.0
Ford —Domestic	26.4	25.0	24.4	21.2	20.4	14.5	10.5	10.5
—Imported	0	0	0	0	0	0.7	3.9	3.5
AMC	6.0	6.2	7.8	4.6	3.8	2.5	1.1	2.1
Non-Captive Foreign	38.2	40.0	38.7	47.1	47.4	57.7	48.6	55.3
Memo: Segment Share of Industry	14.6	16.9	16.8	17.6	14.5	16.0	18.1	20.7
Compact								
Chrysler	35.4	33.0	34.8	30.1	39.7	38.5	23.2	21.2
GM	26.0	27.4	26.8	29.4	32.5	36.7	27.8	32.4
Ford	21.2	19.6	18.3	14.3	10.5	8.4	31.8	29.3
AMC	5.8	7.0	7.8	6.8	5.8	4.7	7.3	6.5
Non-Captive Foreign	11.6	13.0	12.3	19.4	11.5	11.7	9.9	10.6
Memo: Segment Share of Industry	13.8	15.5	18.5	16.6	15.8	14.0	15.1	13.8
Small Specialty								
Chrysler—Domestic	6.3	5.7	2.9	0.1	0	0	0	5.9
—Imported	0	0	0	0	0	0	1.9	1.8
GM	19.3	19.6	26.4	39.5	47.6	46.3	43.7	42.9
Ford —Domestic	24.1	21.9	32.5	21.3	16.6	13.6	15.5	22.9
—Imported	11.5	14.3	9.5	6.6	3.0	2.1	1.0	0
AMC	0	0	0	6.9	7.8	5.1	1.9	0
Non-Captive Foreign	35.1	34.9	26.0	25.5	25.0	32.9	35.9	26.7
Memo: Segment Share of Industry	6.7	6.5	9.0	11.8	11.0	10.8	10.3	15.9
Basic Middle								
Chrysler	13.5	17.8	17.3	12.1	8.5	12.0	18.2	15.4
GM	50.2	42.4	44.2	38.0	40.2	37.3	39.9	53.4
Ford	25.6	29.2	25.7	36.2	42.6	41.8	31.1	23.2
AMC	2.3	2.6	4.7	4.3	2.4	1.4	0.7	0
Non-Captive Foreign	8.4	8.0	8.1	9.4	6.3	7.5	10.1	8.0
Memo: Segment Share of Industry	21.4%	17.2%	16.8%	17.9%	18.1%	16.3%	14.8%	11.2%
Middle Specialty								
Chrysler	0%	0%	0%	15.9%	15.3%	10.2%	9.3%	6.1%
GM	100	100	81.5	67.1	69.9	66.9	64.6	72.6
Ford	0	0	18.5	17.0	14.8	22.9	26.1	21.3
Memo: Segment Share of Industry	2.6	6.6	8.9	11.0	15.2	16.5	16.1	15.2
Basic Large								
Chrysler	14.5	15.1	13.1	12.0	9.7	9.0	3.7	6.6
GM	58.0	56.9	59.0	61.8	61.8	67.6	74.2	71.8
Ford	26.5	26.8	26.9	26.2	28.5	23.4	22.1	21.6
Memo: Segment Share of Industry	36.0	32.2	24.7	18.9	19.2	20.0	19.0	16.6

EXHIBIT 1: (continued)

	(Model Years)							
	1972	*1973*	*1974*	*1975*	*1976*	*1977*	*1978*	*1979*†
Luxury								
Chrysler	2.6	2.4	2.4	2.0	0	0	0	0
GM	65.8	61.0	61.0	63.3	63.8	59.7	60.8	59.6
Ford	21.1	26.8	24.4	22.4	25.4	30.5	31.4	21.0
Non-Captive Foreign	10.5	9.8	12.2	12.2	10.6	9.8	7.8	19.4
Memo: Segment Share of Industry	3.8	4.1	4.1	4.9	4.8	5.0	5.1	6.6
Bus (Vans/RV's)								
Chrysler	26.4	34.8	42.9	40.4	40.4	37.8	33.3	N.A.
GM	14.7	15.3	15.8	19.3	18.9	25.4	26.7	N.A.
Ford	19.6	15.7	15.9	20.3	27.0	21.0	26.7	N.A.
VW	39.3	34.2	25.4	20.0	13.7	15.8	13.3	N.A.
Memo: Segment Share of Industry	1.1	1.2	1.2	1.4	1.4	1.4	1.5	N.A.

†Data for 1979 is estimated.
* See Exhibit 2 for examples of cars in each segment.
Source: Industry Analyst.

Model Classification

There was no accepted rule for the classification of passenger cars. During the late 1970s the industry had been decreasing the size and weight of its new models in efforts to meet federal regulations for fuel economy.

Cars were generally classified as subcompact, compact, middle-sized or intermediate, and large or full-sized. Because large cars were becoming smaller annually to allow greater fuel economy, the distinctions between middle-sized and large models were becoming blurred. (Exhibit 2 contains a listing of models by manufacturer.)

Subcompacts were the smallest cars on the market. They had seats for four persons, usually had four-cylinder engines, performed best with manual transmissions, and offered the highest fuel-economy of any size group.

Compacts were slightly roomier than subcompacts, accommodated four or five passengers in moderate comfort, and were available with four-cylinder or small six-cylinder engines that had enough power to handle automatic transmissions and air-conditioning. (Exhibits 1 and 2 include an additional category, "small specialty." These cars were generally "sporty" versions of the compacts or slightly larger cars. Aimed specifically at the "sporty" car market, they included more optional equipment and larger engines.)

Middle-sized models offered increased comfort for five or six passengers, and larger six-cylinder engines or small eight-cylinder engines with ability for moderate hauling. (Exhibits 1 and 2 divide this category into "Basic Middle" and "Middle Specialty." The specialty cars tended to have more optional equipment and often were aimed at the "sporty" car market.)

Large/Luxury models could accommodate six persons in comfort. They were available with six- or eight-cylinder engines and were the lowest in fuel economy. Some full-sized models were marketed as luxury cars. As manufacturers' top-of-the-line models, they were the most expensive and were available with extensive optional equipment and gadgetry.

EXHIBIT 2: The Chrysler Corporation (A)

EXAMPLES OF CARS BY SEGMENT FROM EXHIBIT 1

Subcompact

Chrysler—Domestic:	Omni, Horizon (1978–79)
—Imported:	Colt, Cricket (1972–73), Arrow (1976–79)
GM —Domestic:	Vega/Monza, Chevette (1976–79), Sunbird/Astro (1975–79)
—Imported:	Opel
Ford —Domestic:	Pinto, Bobcat (1975–79)
—Imported:	Fiesta (1977–79)
AMC —Domestic:	Gremlin/Spirit

Compact

Chrysler:	Valiant/Volare, Dart/Aspen
GM:	Nova/Citation, Ventura/Phoenix, Omega (1973–78) Apollo/Skylark (1973–79)
Ford:	Maverick/Fairmont, Comet/Zephyr
AMC:	Hornet/Concord

Small Specialty

Chrysler—Domestic:	Barracuda (1972–74), Challenger (1972–74), TC3 (1979), 024 (1979)
Imported:	Sapporo (1978–79), Challenger (1978–79)
GM —Domestic:	Camaro, Firebird, Starfire (1975–79), Skyhawk (1975–79), Corvette, Monza (1976–79), Sunbird (1976–79)
Ford —Domestic:	Mustang, Cougar (1972–73), Capri (1979)
—Imported:	Capri (1972–78)
AMC —Domestic:	Pacer (1975–78)

Basic Middle

Chrysler:	Fury/Satellite (1972–78), Coronet (1972–78), LeBaron (1977–79), Diplomat (1977–79)
GM:	Chevelle/Malibu, LeMans, Cutlass (base), Century (base)
Ford:	Torino/LTD II, Granada (1975–79), Montego/Cougar (base), Monarch (1975–79)
AMC:	Matador

Middle Specialty

Chrysler:	Cordoba (1975–79), Charger/Magnum (1975–79)
GM:	Monte Carlo, Grand Prix, Cutlass Supreme, Regal
Ford:	Elite/T'Bird (1974–79), Cougar XR-7 (1974–79)

Basic Large

Chrysler:	Grand Fury (1972–77), Royal Monaco/St. Regis, Newport/New Yorker
GM:	Impala/Caprice, Catalina/Bonneville, 88&89, La Sabre/Electra, Toronado (1972–78), Riviera (1972–78)
Ford:	LTD, Marquis, T'Bird (1972–76)

EXHIBIT 2 : (continued)

Luxury	
Chrysler:	Imperial (1972–75)
GM:	DeVille, Eldorado, Seville (1975–79), Toro-Riviera (1979)
Ford:	Lincoln, Mark IV/V, Versailles (1977–1979)
Bus	
Chrysler:	Sportsman, Voyager (1974–79)
GM:	Sportvan
Ford:	Club Wagon

Source: Industry Analyst.

Styling

An automobile's body style was one of its principal sales attractions. Most models were available in two-door (coupe) and four-door (sedan) forms. Design options available included "fastback" styling wherein the back of the car sloped, presenting a sleeker, less boxy silhouette. Some models were available as "three-door" coupes or "hatchbacks." The third door or hatch was a large, hinged rear window that could be raised for access to the luggage area. The rear seat of a hatchback could be folded down flat to provide a longer cargo floor. The rear end of a "station wagon" was squared off like a box, providing increased cargo capacity which was accessible through a rear door. As in the hatchback, the rear seats folded flat.

"Sporty" cars were often basic two-door models that had been "dressed up" with optional equipment. Larger engines, manual transmissions, wire wheels, bucket seats, and racing stripes were just a few examples of the myriad options available.

Trucks and vans provided the largest and most versatile cargo areas and were frequently sold as commercial, as well as personal, vehicles. A truck provided a two-door enclosed seating area for two or three passengers and an open back for cargo. Vans were squared off in front and back and could be designed with a wide variety of window and door configurations. Both trucks and vans had wide appeal as recreational vehicles.

Industry Economics

Due to strong competitive pressures, particularly from foreign manufacturers, and the impact of government regulations, the performance of individual manufacturers had been erratic. Table 2 shows the return on assets of the "Big Three" U.S. manufacturers from 1960 to 1977.

The poor performance of the U.S. auto companies was reflected in the trends in the market value of their stocks. Although part of the downward turn might be attributed to general market trends, the relative changes in price are interesting (see Exhibit 3).

Obviously, the various manufacturers faced different cost structures, and these related to their profit performance. Although no exact numbers were avail-

TABLE 2: Return on Total Assets

	GM	*Ford*	*Chrysler*
1960	12.2%	11.4%	2.3%
1965	18.5	9.3	8.1
1970	4.3	5.2	(0.2)
1971	10.6	6.3	1.7
1973	11.8	7.0	4.2
1975	5.8	2.3	(4.1)
1977	12.5	8.7	2.1

Source: Chase Information Services. *A Cost-Benefit Analysis of the 1979 to 1985 Fuel Economy Standards.* December 1978, p. 241. Reprinted with permission.

able, Chrysler generally had the highest cost/unit of the Big Three auto manufacturers.

These profit problems unfortunately came at a time when the Big Three had an almost insatiable thirst for capital to meet new product and government regulation needs. Table 3 shows one projection of capital expenditure needs versus net income during 1978–85.

Sales Forecasts

In October 1979, the future of the U.S. automobile industry was uncertain. Forecasting sales was a tenuous business.

Exhibit 4 shows several different forecasts made by professional analysts during 1978. These forecasts indicated some variability among forecasters, but similar general trends.

Federal Regulations and the Cost of Compliance

All automobile manufacturers were required to meet a number of fuel economy, safety, and emissions regulations, and standards that had been issued under the following statutes: National Traffic and Motor Vehicle Safety Act of 1966, Clean Air Act, Titles I and V of the Motor Vehicles Informations and Cost Savings Act and Noise Control Act of 1972.

TABLE 3: Capital Expenditures vs. Net Income, 1962–1985, Big Three (billions of dollars)

	1962–69	*1970–77*	*1978–85*
Average Capital Expenditure	2.9	4.1	9.5
Average Net Income	2.4	2.8	3.9
Capital Expenditures as a Per Cent of Net Income	121%	146%	244%

Source: Chase Information Services. *A Cost-Benefit Analysis of the 1979 to 1985 Fuel Economy Standards.* December 1978, p. 236. Reprinted with permission.

EXHIBIT 3: The Chrysler Corporation (A)

FIVE YEAR AVERAGE RANKING OF AUTO FIRMS AMONG 1,000 LARGEST FIRMS, 1972–1977

	General Motors		*Ford*		*Chrysler*		*American Motors*	
	5 Year Average	*Ranking*	*5 Year Average*	*Ranking*	*5 Year Average*	*Ranking*	*5 Year Average*	*Ranking*
Profitability								
Return on Equity	16.9%	274	12.2%	597	4.2%	929	1.1%	954
Return on Capital	15.4	133	10.2	447	4.0	925	2.2	958
Growth								
Earnings per Share	5.6	675	6.4	643	−8.1	898	N.A.	N.A.
Sales	10.3	718	10.8	684	11.1	655	15.1	370
Stock Market Performance								
5 Year Price Change	−18.6	583	−30.3	688	−66.5	946	−48.5	848

Source: *Forbes,* January 9, 1978, 30th Annual Report on American Industry.

EXHIBIT 4: The Chrysler Corporation (A)

FORECASTS OF SALES AND GROWTH
LONG TERM INDUSTRY FORECAST COMPARISONS, CALENDAR YEARS
(MILLIONS OF UNITS)

	1979	*1980*	*1981*	*1982*	*1983*	*1984*	*1985*
U.S. Car							
Chase Auto	10.4	10.5	11.1	11.2	11.4	11.7	11.9
D.R.I.	10.6	10.3	11.0	10.8	11.1	12.9	12.2
Wharton	10.6	10.6	11.5	12.5	13.0	13.2	12.9
Merrill-Lynch	10.3	9.7	11.2	12.3	12.5	12.5	12.5
Average	10.5	10.3	11.2	11.7	12.0	12.6	12.4
Chrysler	10.4	10.5	11.1	11.2	11.4	11.7	11.9
U.S. Trucks							
D.R.I.	3.5	3.4	3.9	3.7	4.0	4.4	4.7
Merrill-Lynch	3.5	3.5	4.2	4.3	4.4	4.6	4.6
Average	3.5	3.5	4.1	4.0	4.2	4.5	4.7
Chrysler	3.5	3.4	3.9	3.7	4.0	4.4	4.7

ANNUAL RATES OF INDUSTRY GROWTH, CALENDER YEARS

	U.S. Car	*U.S. Truck*	*Total*
1960–1978	3.0%	8.9%	4.1%
1968–1978	1.6	8.4	3.0
1978–1985 Forecast	1.8	1.3	1.7

Source: Chrysler Corporation: "Analysis of Chrysler Corporation's Situation and Proposal for Government Assistance." September 15, 1979.

The Clean Air Act required Chrysler to meet stringent emission standards for 1979 and substantially more stringent standards commencing with the 1980 and 1981 model years. These standards were designed to reduce certain exhaust emissions from passenger cars by 90 per cent from levels for the 1970 and 1971 model years. Similar standards affected light-duty trucks.

Chrysler adamantly blamed mandatory government regulations for its financial problems. The 1978 annual report states the Company's position:

> Chrysler faces the serious anti-competitive effect of government regulation. Regulation, by its very nature, places a disproportionately heavy burden on the smaller companies in an industry. Its invariable result is a reduction of competition in direct contradiction to other government policies which attempt to promote competition.
>
> By law, every standard and every regulation must be met at the same time by every manufacturer regardless of size. Not only do these regulations place the smaller company at an economic disadvantage because it has fewer units over which to spread the cost, the burden of these requirements on the smaller companies also forces them to commit the majority of their resources to meeting government stan-

TABLE 4: Model Year Average Fuel Economy Standards (miles per gallon)

1978	*1979*	*1980*	*1981*	*1982*	*1983*	*1984*	*1985 and Thereafter*
18.0	19.0	20.0	22.0	24.0	26.0	27.0	27.5

> dards leaving little for use in developing the unique competitive edge so vital to success and growth. . . . If strong competition is to be maintained, the government must recognize the anti-competitive effects of its regulatory actions. . . . We urge the federal government to conduct a serious cost benefit analysis of all regulations and to establish a fair and equitable set of standards which will achieve the national goals we all support, while insuring continued strong competition.

Iacocca contended that the regulations were "regressive" and "always hurt the small the most."

> Over the next few years we are being forced to rebuild and retool all our products, develop all-new engines and drive trains, develop three-way catalysts and airbag systems, not to gain a competitive advantage, or to sell more cars, or to put more people to work, but to meet the law.[1]

Chrysler certainly was not alone in this view. "There is no choice in the United States but for the major auto companies to spend massive amounts of money to develop new products on a time schedule that has nothing to do with business at all," complained Donald E. Peterson, Ford's Executive Vice-President for Internal Automotive Operations.[2]

Assistant Secretary of Commerce, Jerry J. Jasinowski, was quoted by *Newsweek* magazine:

> Chrysler absolutely must have some relief from the present regulatory burden that it faces. It simply can't meet the current light-duty-truck mileage standards, the passenger-car mileage standards, the heavy-duty truck air emission standards, and the safety standards now mandated by the various regulatory groups. It just doesn't have the money.[3]

The Motor Vehicle Information and Cost Savings Act, as amended by the Energy Policy and Conservation Act required that for passenger cars the corporate average fuel economy (CAFE)* must be 19.0 miles per U.S. gallon (mpg) for the 1979 model year and 20.0 mpg for 1980. These standards, set by the Secretary of Transportation, increased 2 mpg per year from 1981 to 1983. As shown in Table 4, by 1985 CAFE had to reach 27.5 mpg. The Secretary had also set fuel economy standards for certain vans and light trucks in 1979 and more stringent standards for a wider range of such vehicles for 1980 and 1981.[4]

Failure to meet the average fuel economy standards would result in the

[1] *Fortune,* October 22, 1979, p. 47. "Chrysler's Pie-in-the-Sky Plan for Survival" by Peter Bohr.
[2] *Business Week,* August 20, 1979, p. 103.
[3] *Newsweek,* August 13, 1979, p. 53. "Can Chrysler Be Saved?"
[4] *Business Week,* August 20, 1979, p. 104.

* CAFE was the *average* fuel economy of all the cars produced by a manufacturer in a model year. The "average" was calculated by multiplying the average mpg/model × the number of that model sold and dividing the total by the number of units sold.

imposition of a substantial penalty amounting to $5 for each one-tenth of a mile by which the standard was not met multiplied by a manufacturer's total production.[5]

The industry had unsuccessfully gone to battle with the Transportation Department in early 1979 attempting to even out or "straight line" the annual increments between 1980 and 1985. "Detroit had argued that a modified schedule (increasing only one mpg per year) would save it and the car-buying public, which ultimately pays the tab, some $7 billion, while increasing fuel consumption during that period by only 0.3 per cent."[6]

Ironically, it was not a lack of technology for getting a CAFE of 27.5 mpg by 1985 that was creating the problems Chrysler and Ford faced. The auto makers *had* the technology. The problem was raising enough additional capital to allow production of a full mix of models that would permit them to be competitive. It cost Chrysler $620 per car to comply with the rules, nearly twice GM's figure of $340 because of GM's greater sales volume.[7] A Chrysler-sponsored study of the impact of regulations conducted by H. G. Wainwright and Company of Boston concluded that because of existing federal standards, Chrysler's operating profit margin would have to grow at an annual rate of 15 per cent between 1979 and 1985 for the company to break even.[8]

Four independent studies conducted in 1978 and 1979 concluded that the mileage standards and, to a lesser extent, the safety and emission standards worked to decrease competition in the U.S. auto industry. General Motors could meet the standards and even gain market penetration while smaller companies had to engage in a life-or-death struggle to meet them.[9]

The four major studies—by Harbridge House, The Futures Group, the National Highway Traffic Safety Administration, and the Automotive Division of the Chase Manhattan Bank—all concluded that Chrysler had been pushed to its limits by the cost of federal regulations.

The study done by Boston's Harbridge House for the Transportation Department in November 1978, estimated that the Big Three auto makers (GM, Ford, and Chrysler) would have to spend nearly $44 billion between 1979 and 1983, specifically to make government-mandated improvements in their cars.

Both Chrysler and Ford were under tremendous financial pressure to meet federal standards that would take effect for autos in 1981. The convergence of regulatory requirements had collapsed the normal 15- to 20-year cycle for complete turnover of all product lines and manufacturing facilities to just five years.

In an editorial published in the *Wall Street Journal,* September 4, 1979, David A. Stockman, a Congressman from Michigan, observed that Congress' decision to reach European levels of fuel economy [27½ mpg] by 1985:

> . . . fails to recognize that the European auto fleet averages about 25 miles per gallon in a large measure because stiff gasoline and horsepower taxes have produced a radically different mix of vehicles. Typically, 80% are four-passenger or less compared to 20% here. . . . In 1977, GM's American fleet was 64%—1,400 pounds—heavier than its European fleet.

[5]*Newsweek,* August 13, 1979, p. 53.
[6]*Business Week,* August 20, 1979, p. 104.
[7]*Automotive Industries,* March, 1979, p. 25. "Regulations Threaten Chrysler's Future."
[8]*Business Week,* August 20, 1979, p. 104.

> Studies have demonstrated that the U.S. autos are actually more efficient than foreign vehicles on a pound-for-pound basis. It is thus evident that the high fleet average fuel economy in Europe is due to drastically less car, not better technology.

Auto emission standards were also scheduled to drop to their most stringent level ever in 1981. To effect the drop in emissions, GM had developed a computer-controlled fuel management system which was expected to cost $240 per car in GM models. Iacocca had secured federal permission to purchase this three-way catalyst from GM for use in Chrysler cars.

In addition, by the end of 1981 passive seat belt or air-bag systems would be required in full-size cars. All automobiles were to be fitted with such automatic safety equipment by 1983.

> The National Highway Traffic Safety Administration figures that air bags, which burst from the steering wheel or dashboard to cushion occupants in frontal crashes, will cost consumers $119 per car. Skeptical carmakers put the tab closer to $325 per car and estimate that replacing an air bag once it has been triggered could cost $600 or more.

Stockman's *Wall Street Journal* editorial also commented on the air bag:

> [The air bag's] estimated cost has escalated nearly 500% in recent years. Its reliability and cost effectiveness have been called into question repeatedly, most recently by the General Accounting Office. Equipping the entire automotive fleet at a cost in excess of $50 billion will gain fatality and injury reductions that could be achieved with only a modest increase in the seat belt usage rate—from the present 20% to perhaps double that rate.

THE COMPANY

Chrysler's Internal Organization and Financial Standing

The Chrysler Corporation operated in two segments: automotive operations which accounted for more than 95 per cent of total dollar sales between 1973–78, and nonautomative operations.

Chrysler, Dodge, and Plymouth passenger cars, Dodge trucks, and related automotive parts and accessories were manufactured, assembled, and sold in the United States and Canada. The passenger cars were offered in subcompact, compact, middle-sized, and large models. Some of Chrysler's subcompact models were manufactured in Japan by Mitsubishi Motors Corporation, in which Chrysler had a 15 per cent interest. Chrysler produced light-duty trucks and vans that were marketed by the Dodge and Plymouth divisions. Overseas subsidiaries and associated companies of the corporation manufactured passenger cars, trucks and related parts and accessories which were sold outside the United States.

In 1977 and 1978 the Big Three manufacturers had the number of dealers shown in Table 5.

Defense operations were the major portion of nonautomotive operations. The company also manufactured and sold outboard motors, boats, inboard marine engines, and industrial engines. Defense operations produced combat vehicles, fire control components, and other military equipment under government contracts.

TABLE 5: Number of Domestic Dealers

	1976	*1977*	*1978*
GM	11,670	11,610	11,565
Ford	6,712	6,722	6,723
Chrysler	4,811	4,822	4,786
AMC	1,690	1,612	1,661

Source: Industry Analyst.

During 1974, 1975, and 1978 Chrysler operated at a net loss and its nonautomotive operations produced a modest profit. In 1976, nonautomotive operations produced 9.9 per cent of total operating profits and in 1977 produced 13.2 per cent of total operating profits.

In 1978 Chrysler incurred a loss of $204.6 million compared to a 1977 profit of $163.2 million. Worldwide sales in 1978 reached $13.6 billion, compared to $13.1 billion in 1977. Worldwide sales of motor vehicles were 2,211,535 units in 1978, compared to 2,328,302 in 1977.

Table 6 shows Chrysler's mix of car and truck sales in the United States, Canada, and overseas from 1974 through 1978.

The company had piled up 58 cents of debt for every dollar of equity, and return on sales during those years the company was not losing money had dropped to less than 1 per cent after taxes.[9] Chrysler had become a $12 billion marginal business enterprise.

> [Chrysler] did manage to generate [cash totalling] $1.4 billion during 1975–76 when the industry was recovering. But since then Chrysler has had worsening cash problems. Indeed when interest and dividend charges of nearly $200 million a year are considered, the company apparently used borrowed funds to service its debt and equity costs in 1978, when it produced cash from operations of only $5.2 million.[10]

TABLE 6: Chrysler's Mix of Car and Truck Sales: U.S., Canada, and Overseas[1]

	United States			*Canada*			*Outside U.S. and Canada*[2]			
	Cars	*Trucks*	*Total*	*Cars*	*Trucks* *(In thousands of units)*	*Total*	*Cars*	*Trucks*	*Total*	*Total*[2]
1974	1,221.2	296.3	1,517.5	198.4	53.6	252.0	185.1	60.4	245.5	2,015.0
1975	1,039.1	275.0	1,314.1	206.5	43.1	249.6	141.2	68.4	209.6	1,773.3
1976	1,428.7	442.0	1,870.7	224.2	50.1	274.3	164.3	61.2	225.5	2,370.5
1977	1,354.7	499.6	1,854.3	206.1	47.1	253.2	159.6	61.2	220.8	2,328.3
1978	1,229.5	502.6	1,732.1	180.6	43.8	224.4	166.5	88.5	255.0	2,211.5

[1] Unit sales as reported by Chrysler are recorded when the vehicle is sold to a dealer or purchaser which is not a consolidated subsidiary or when the vehicle is licensed for highway use. This method of reporting unit sales conforms with the method of reporting dollar sales.

[2] Restated to exclude deconsolidated operations.

Source: Company 10K, 1978.

[9] *Fortune*, June 1, 1978, p. 54. "Chrysler Goes for Broke" by Peter J. Schuyten.

[10] *Business Week*, August 20, 1979, p. 106. "Is Chrysler the Prototype?"

EXHIBIT 5: The Chrysler Corporation (A)

TEN YEAR FINANCIAL STATISTICS

Operating Data	*1978*	*1977*	*1976*	*1975*	*1974*	*1973*	*1972*	*1971*	*1970*	*1969*
Motor vehicles sold (in thousands of units)	2,212	2,328	2,371	1,773	2,015	2,423	2,192	1,898	1,794	1,851
Net sales	$13,618	13,059	12,240	8,572	8,389	8,983	7,749	6,431	5,606	5,793
Interest expense	$ 166	106	101	121	101	72	63	66	74	45
Maintenance and repairs	$ 426	439	351	230	277	328	251	204	175	220
Taxes other than on income	$ 308	278	249	190	187	189	156	423	362	433
Research and development	$ 344	286	237	161	202	211	161	123	113	140
Depreciation	$ 154	130	108	93	131	123	129	133	136	158
Amortization of special tools	$ 198	190	229	149	124	168	173	165	161	164
Taxes on income (credit)	$ (81)	72	152	(9)	(61)	163	167	47	(20)	87
Earnings (loss) from continuing operations	$ (205)	125	328	(207)	(41)	266	226	92	—	107
per common share (in dollars)	$ (3.54)	2.07	5.45	(3.46)	(0.73)	4.99	4.38	1.82	—	2.26
Net earnings (loss)	$ (205)	163	423	(260)	(52)	255	220	84	(8)	99
per common share (in dollars)	$ (3.54)	2.71	7.02	(4.33)	(0.92)	4.80	4.27	1.67	(0.16)	2.09
Average shares outstanding (in thousands)	61,679	60,278	60,205	59,942	56,421	53,182	51,643	50,214	48,693	47,391
Common stock dividends paid	$ 52	54	18	—	79	69	47	30	29	95
per share (in dollars)	0.85	0.90	0.30	—	1.40	130	0.90	0.60	0.60	2.00
Net earnings as a per cent of sales	$ (1.5%)	1.2%	3.5%	(3.0%)	(0.6%)	2.8%	2.8%	1.3%	1.3%	1.7%
Expenditures for facilities other than special tools	$ 338	386	227	164	226	331	169	114	174	375
Expenditures for special tools	$ 333	337	197	220	242	298	166	136	242	272

Source: Company annual report 1978.

Exhibits 5 through 10 present the company's balance sheets and income statements.

To understand how Chrysler could reach such a crisis point for the third time in a decade, it is necessary to review the company's managerial history.

Company History

In 1921, Walter P. Chrysler purchased the failing Maxwell Motor Company. Seven years later he bought up the flourishing factory of Horace and John Dodge, establishing Chrysler as a major force. By 1946, the Chrysler Corporation had achieved a reputation for sound engineering and a record 25.7 per cent market share, second only to General Motors (GM). However, in 1950, Ford surpassed Chrysler and Chrysler's downward slide began.

EXHIBIT 6: The Chrysler Corporation (A)

TEN YEAR FINANCIAL POSITION*
(IN MILLIONS OF DOLLARS)

Financial Position—Year End	*1978*	*1977*	*1976*	*1975*	*1974*
Current assets	$ 3,562	4,153	3,878	3,116	3,697
Current liabilities	$ 2,486	3,090	2,826	2,462	2,709
Net current assets	$ 1,076	1,063	1,052	654	988
Net property, plant, equipment & tools	$ 2,023	2,425	2,087	2,115	2,062
Total assets	$ 6,981	7,668	7,074	6,267	6,733
Long-term debt	$ 1,189	1,240	1,048	1,054	981
Shareholders' investment	$ 2,927	2,925	2,815	2,409	2,660
Shares outstanding (in thousands)	63,634	60,290	60,247	60,102	59,266
Shareholders' investment per common share (in dollars)	$ 42.06	48.51	46.73	40.09	44.89
Number of shareholders	209,153	210,701	217,359	233,915	232,435

Financial Position—Year End	*1973*	*1972*	*1971*	*1970*	*1969*
Current assets	$ 3,238	2,896	2,411	2,167	2,230
Current liabilities	$ 2,094	1,941	1,648	1,548	1,644
Net current assets	$ 1,144	955	763	619	586
Net property, plant, equipment & tools	$ 1,926	1,680	1,729	1,803	1,753
Total assets	$ 6,105	5,497	5,000	4,816	4,742
Long-term debt	$ 946	784	816	791	587
Shareholders' investment	$ 2,728	2,489	2,269	2,156	2,154
Shares outstanding (in thousands)	54,442	52,359	50,950	49,499	47,942
Shareholders' investment per common share (in dollars)	$ 50.10	47.54	44.53	43.55	44.94
Number of shareholders	208,771	188,914	201,945	204,329	174,066

* Restated to exclude deconsolidated operations.

Source: Company annual report 1978.

EXHIBIT 7: The Chrysler Corporation (A)

CONSOLIDATED STATEMENT OF NET EARNINGS 1977–1978

	1978	*1977*
	(In millions of dollars)	
	Year ended December 31	
Net sales	$13,618.3	$13,058.6
Equity in net earnings of unconsolidated subsidiaries	22.1	20.4
Net earnings from European and certain South American operations	29.4	(27.9)
	13,669.8	13,051.1
Costs, other than items below	12,640.1	11,725.9
Depreciation of plant and equipment	154.0	129.8
Amortization of special tools	198.2	190.1
Selling and administrative expenses	572.1	453.3
Provision for incentive compensation	—	5.6
Pension plans	262.3	274.4
Interest expense—net	128.9	74.9
	13,955.6	12,854.0
EARNINGS (LOSS) BEFORE TAXES ON INCOME	(285.8)	197.1
Taxes on income (credit)	(81.2)	72.3
EARNINGS (LOSS) BEFORE EXTRAORDINARY ITEM	(204.6)	124.8
Extraordinary item—Effect of utilization of foreign tax credit carryforward benefits	—	38.4
NET EARNINGS (LOSS)	(204.6)	163.2
Dividends on preferred shares (includes amortization of discount)	13.6	—
NET EARNINGS (LOSS) ATTRIBUTABLE TO COMMON STOCK	$ (218.2)	$ 163.2
Earnings per share of Common Stock:		
Earnings (loss) before extraordinary item	$ (3.54)	$ 2.07
Extraordinary item	—	0.64
Total	$ (3.54)	$ 2.71
Average number of shares of Common Stock outstanding during the year (in thousands)	61,679	60,278

Source: Company annual report 1978.

During the 1960s Chrysler came under the direction of former accountant, Lynn A. Townsend, who initiated a worldwide expansion program. Townsend built plants in Europe, South America, South Africa, and Australia. Domestically, he attempted to match every Ford and GM product line while neglecting to update his core facilities. As a result, concluded a study by Harbridge House

EXHIBIT 8: The Chrysler Corporation (A)

CONSOLIDATED BALANCE SHEET 1977–1978

	1978	*1977*
	(In millions of dollars)	
Assets	December 31	
Current Assets:		
Cash	$ 123.2	$ 207.6
Time deposits	248.8	41.7
Marketable securities—at lower of cost or market	150.8	159.5
Accounts receivable (less allowance for doubtful accounts: 1978—$16.7 million; 1977—21.9 million)	848.0	896.7
Inventories—at the lower of cost (substantially first-in, first-out) or market	1,980.8	6,622.6
Prepaid insurance, taxes and other expenses	109.7	141.2
Income taxes allocable to the following year	60.5	83.5
Refundable taxes on income	40.0	—
TOTAL CURRENT ASSETS	3,561.8	4,152.8
Investments and other assets:		
Investments in and advances to associated companies outside the United States	449.1	56.5
Investments in and advances to unconsolidated subsidiaries	896.9	918.2
Other noncurrent assets	41.8	77.6
TOTAL INVESTMENTS AND OTHER ASSETS	1,387.8	1,052.3
Property, Plant and Equipment:		
Land, buildings, machinery and equipment	3,391.3	4,218.3
Less accumulated depreciation	1,963.9	2,463.8
	1,427.4	1,754.5
Unamortized special tools	595.5	670.7
NET PROPERTY, PLANT AND EQUIPMENT	2,022.9	2,425.2
Cost of Investments in Consolidated Subsidiaries in Excess of Equity	8.7	37.9
TOTAL ASSETS	$6,981.2	$7,668.2
Liabilities and Shareholders' Investment		
Current Liabilities:		
Accounts payable	$1,725.0	$1,911.9
Accrued expenses	698.0	733.4
Short-term debt	49.2	249.9
Payments due within one year on long-term debt	12.4	90.8
Taxes on income	1.2	63.9
	2,485.8	3,089.9
Other Liabilities and Deferred Credits:		
Deferred incentive compensation	1.6	4.3
Other employee benefit plans	89.4	86.8
Deferred taxes on income	107.1	122.4

EXHIBIT 8: (continued)

CONSOLIDATED BALANCE SHEET 1977–1978

	1978	*1977*
	(In millions of dollars)	
Unrealized profits on sales to unconsolidated subsidiaries	66.4	79.6
Other noncurrent liabilities	96.1	88.4
TOTAL OTHER LIABILITIES AND DEFERRED CREDITS	360.6	381.5
Long-Term Debt:		
Notes and debentures payable	1,082.6	1,120.3
Convertible sinking fund debentures	105.9	120.0
TOTAL LONG-TERM DEBT	1,188.5	1,240.3
Obligations Under Capital Leases	15.0	12.6
Minority Interest in Net Assets of Consolidated Subsidiaries	4.8	19.3
Shareholders' Investment:		
Represented by		
Preferred stock—no par value	217.0	—
Common Stock—par value $6.25 a share	397.7	376.8
Additional paid-in capital	683.1	648.7
Net earnings retained for use in the business	1,628.7	1,899.1
TOTAL SHAREHOLDERS' INVESTMENT	2,926.5	2,924.6
TOTAL LIABILITIES AND SHAREHOLDERS' INVESTMENT	$6,981.2	$7,668.2

Source: Company annual report 1978.

of Boston, "Chrysler's direct manufacturing costs per vehicle have been 10 per cent higher than those of GM."

> Lynn Townsend seemed more like an old-style Hollywood film czar than a midwestern auto company chief. He was a handsome and dictatorial leader who enjoyed a high reputation as a numbers man, but he never seemed to understand the fundamental business of his company . . . at one point the company was running marginal or losing operations on every continent except Antarctica.[11]

In 1961 Townsend engineered a badly needed financial turnaround, but there were unhealthy side effects on long-term earnings from his maneuvers. His European acquisitions, Simca in France, and Rootes Motors, Ltd. in Britain, were failing companies when acquired. They became enormous cash drains that siphoned off funds just as the Company should have been capitalizing at home to meet fuel economy, emission, and safety regulations.

Townsend made a major strategic error when he chose to redesign Chrysler's big cars rather than developing a subcompact car to compete with GM's Vega and Ford's Pinto, both introduced in 1971. Chrysler's new big cars were

[11] *Fortune,* June 1, 1978, p. 55.

EXHIBIT 9: The Chrysler Corporation (A)

CONSOLIDATED STATEMENT OF CHANGES IN FINANCIAL POSITION 1977–1978

	1978	*1977*
	(In millions of dollars)	
Additions to working capital	Year ended December 31	
From operations:		
Earnings (loss) before extraordinary item	$ (204.6)	$ 124.8
Depreciation and amortization	352.2	319.9
Depreciation and amortization—European and South American operations	46.5	68.1
Changes in deferred income taxes—noncurrent	26.0	(9.9)
Equity in net earnings of unconsolidated subsidiaries	(22.1)	(20.4)
Loss on translation of long-term debt	2.5	18.5
	200.5	501.0
Extraordinary item—Effect of utilization of foreign tax credit carryforward benefits	—	38.4
Proceeds from long-term borrowing	347.4	279.0
Proceeds from sale of common stock	37.2	.4
Proceeds from sale of preferred stock and warrants	234.4	—
Proceeds from PSA Peugeot-Citroen transaction	230.0	—
Retirement of property, plant and equipment	9.8	5.0
Other	12.1	20.7
TOTAL ADDITIONS	1,071.4	844.5
Dispositions of working capital		
Cash dividends paid	65.0	54.3
Increase (decrease) in investments and advances	32.2	(47.9)
Expenditures for property, plant and equipment	337.9	386.3
Expenditures for special tools	332.8	336.8
Reduction in long-term borrowing	49.2	104.9
Decrease (increase) in minority interest	1.2	(.4)
Deconsolidation of European and South American operations	240.0	—
TOTAL DISPOSITIONS	1,058.3	834.0
Increase in working capital during the year	$ 13.1	$ 10.5
Changes in components of working capital	Increase (Decrease) in Working Capital	
Cash and marketable securities	$ 114.0	$(163.2)
Accounts and notes receivable	(48.7)	99.1
Current and deferred taxes on income	79.7	60.5
Inventories	(641.8)	268.6
Accounts payable and accrued expenses	262.3	(193.7)
Short-term debt	200.7	(77.5)
Other	46.9	16.7
	$ 13.1	$ 10.5

Source: Company annual report 1978.

EXHIBIT 10: The Chrysler Corporation (A)

EARNINGS AND BALANCE SHEET, SEPTEMBER 30, 1979

Earnings, 9 mos. to Sept. 30 (Consol.—$000 omitted):

	1979	*1978* [3]
Net sales	8,936,500	9,637,500
Equity earnings	16,500	8,100
European, etc. earn.[1]	—	30,700
Total revenues	8,953,000	9,676,300
Costs	8,615,700	9,005,300
Sales expense	430,900	418,600
Depreciation	125,100	118,200
Spec. tool amortization	151,900	155,600
Pension plans	201,700	216,300
Interest, net	160,600	89,900
Income taxes	*cr*11,400	*cr*79,800
Net loss	721,500	247,800
Mar. quarter	*d*53,800	*d*119,800
June quarter	*d*207,100	30,500
Sept. quarter	*d*460,600	*d*158,500
Earnings per com. sh.[2]	*d*$11.41	$4.15
Mar. quarter	*d*0.95	*d*1.98
June quarter	*d*3.31	0.51
Sept. quarter	*d*7.15	*d*2.68
Aver. no. com. shs.	65,168,000	61,210,000

[1] Net earnings from European and certain South American operations.
[2] As reported on average shares.
[3] Restated to reflect deconsolidation of European and South American operations.

Balance Sheet, as of Sept. 30 (Consol.—$000 omitted):

	1979	*1978*
Assets:		
Cash & mkt. secur.	553,100	334,000
Receivables, net	667,900	1,027,400[1]
Tax claim	64,400	68,400
Ref. inc. taxes	488,000	33,000
Inventories	2,228,000	2,085,100
Prepaymts., etc.	110,000	118,500
Total current	3,672,200	3,666,400
Net prop., etc.[1]	2,273,700	1,974,500
Invest., etc.	1,207,800	1,357,600
Total	7,153,700	6,998,500
Liabilities:		
Notes, etc. payable	788,000	193,600
Accts., etc. pay	1,670,700	1,745,100
Income taxes	—	36,900
Accruals	857,900	731,500
Total current	3,316,600	2,707,100

EXHIBIT 10: (continued)

Balance Sheet, as of Sept. 30 (Consol.—$000 omitted):

	1979	*1978*
Long-term debt	1,043,400	1,080,000
Cap. lease obligations	13,400	16,300
Def. income taxes	110,900	69,700
Minority interests	36,900	12,500
Other liabilities	432,700	226,100
Preferred stock	218,200	216,700
Common stock ($6.25)	416,900	391,500
Addition to pd-in. cap.	692,200	679,500
Retained earnings	872,500	1,599,100
Total	7,153,700	6,998,500
Net current assets	355,600	959,300
Depr. & amort.	2,060,200	2,041,800

[1] Incl. $230,000,000 cash proceeds to be received from PSA Peugeot-Citroen.
Source: *Moody's Industrial Survey,* 1979.

introduced in the fall of 1973, just months before the Arab oil embargo destroyed the luxury car market.

> In the fall of 1974, when the auto market all but disappeared, Townsend hatched a plan to lower the company's breakeven point to a level where it could make money even if the market for domestic automobiles dropped to the unheard-of level of six million cars. (In a normal year it was above nine million.) The cost cutting required to even approach that goal was awesome; the effect on future car development at Chrysler nearly fatal. Thousands of designers and engineers were either laid off or fired . . . and product programs were so seriously delayed that every model the company has introduced since then has been from four to eight months late.[12]

Townsend retired in mid-1975, passing a crippled company and the biggest loss in history, $260 million, to John Riccardo. Riccardo had been appointed to Chrysler's presidency after the Company's severe retrenchment in 1969 and 1970 and, "displaying the tough-minded management style that had previously earned him the nickname of 'Flamethrower,' launched a major cost cutting program to turn the company around."[13] After the company sank into the red in 1975, Riccardo was elected chairman and chief executive officer.

His first task was to solve organizational problems. For instance, product plans had always been on one calendar, profit plans on another.

Riccardo realized that to compete with GM and Ford and meet federal standards for fuel economy, safety, and emissions, Chrysler was going to have to "downsize,"—build smaller, lighter cars. To do so, Chrysler's antiquated plants would also have to be rebuilt.

> By the end of 1976, the rescue plan was ready. Each year for four years, starting with its 1979-model cars, Chrysler was to bring out all new models—first the

[12] Ibid.
[13] *Wall Street Journal,* September 18, 1979, p. 3. "Chrysler's Riccardo to Quit This Week."

standards, then the intermediates, then compacts, and finally, trucks and vans. While each new line was being made ready for production, the plant that was to produce it would be gutted and refitted. . . .

The company couldn't move ahead, however, until the government had set those emission, safety, and fuel-economy standards. When those numbers finally came down (in late 1977) and Chrysler put a price tag on its program, management was shocked to discover that the tab, estimated earlier at $5.5 billion, had risen to $7.5 billion. That quashed Chrysler's hope of financing its plan internally.[14]

Sale of Preferred Stock

In the summer of 1978, in order to help finance the $7.5 billion capital spending program necessary to restore Chrysler's competitive strength, the Company issued a block of preferred stock plus warrants to buy common stock. The issue was rated as speculative by Moody's and Standard and Poors investment services and was poorly received by the underwriting syndicate. The issue was managed by First Boston Corp. and Merrill Lynch. In spite of a lack of institutional interest, Merrill Lynch was so successful in promoting the offering to retail customers that the issue was increased from $150 million to $250 million. Its strongest selling point was an 11 per cent dividend yield on the preferred stock. "It was a dangerous issue," comments one Wall Street broker. "Merrill Lynch deserves a lot of credit for how they marketed it. I hope it doesn't come back to haunt them."[15]

Marketing History

In the past Chrysler had offered a wide range of products to fill wide consumer preferences. By 1978 Chrysler had only one luxury model (a 4-door sedan) available. The Company's share of full-sized models had dropped below 5 per cent from close to 30 per cent in 1972.

Until the 1973–74 energy crisis Chrysler had been the small car leader. It sold roughly 40 per cent of the compact car volume in 1972 and offered over 43 per cent of available models. In 1978 Chrysler's share stood at barely over 10 per cent.

Chrysler had offered 77 models in 1972—over 25 per cent of the domestic total. In 1978 they had only 29 distinct products, or roughly 12 per cent of total domestic offerings (See Table 7).

In 1972 Chrysler's full-sized and intermediate models were among the least expensive in their respective segments. Their compact models were competitively priced. By 1978 the company's full-sized and luxury intermediate products were at the high end of the price spectrum. Exhibit 10 shows model price comparisons between 1972 and 1979.

Plans to Recover Market Share

Chrysler bounded back into the compact car market in the 1976 model year with the new Volaré and Aspen models. With gasoline again available,

[14]*Fortune,* June 1, 1978, p. 56.
[15]*Financial World,* November 15, 1978, p. 21. "Will Chrysler Drown in Red Ink?" by Ronald Nevans.

TABLE 7: Chrysler Number of Models Offered

	1972*		1978		1979	
	Number	Per Cent of Total	Number	Per Cent of Total	Number	Per Cent of Total
Standard High	8	30.8	2	9.5	1	5.3
Full Size	38	29.2	2	4.4	2	4.4
Intermediates	21	25.3	30	34.5	16	23.5
Compacts	10	43.5	6	10.7	6	10.3
Subcompacts	—	—	2	13.3	4	18.2
Total Chrysler	77	25.8	42	16.2	29	11.7

* Barracuda/Challenger not listed.

Source: Chase Information Services. *A Cost-Benefit Analysis of the 1979 to 1985 Fuel Economy Standards.* December, 1978, p. 236. Reprinted with permission.

small-car sales promptly began to soften. Forced to neglect its larger models in order to concentrate its limited resources on the compacts, Chrysler was two years behind GM in down-sizing the top of its line. In the fall of 1978, to beef up sales of its big cars, the company announced full-sized Chrysler New Yorker and St. Regis models.

> . . . When it introduced its standard-sized St. Regis, the company blew it. Not only was the market unreceptive to large cars, but Chrysler couldn't get the models to its dealers in time to coincide with the promotion. By February, the Company had an appalling 381-day supply of St. Regises—and there are only 307 days in the sales year![16]

In January, 1978, Chrysler introduced the virtually identical Dodge Omni/Plymouth Horizon. This boxy subcompact had a sideways-mounted engine and front-wheel drive. The model earned rave reviews for Chrysler and was two years ahead of GM's front-wheel-drive car. *Motor Trend* magazine named it car of the year.

> Then disaster struck. The July '78 issue of *Consumer Reports* featured on its cover the same Omni and Horizon photo used by *Motor Trend* but with one difference: The words "Not acceptable" were stamped across the photo. According to the Consumers Union, the car had a dangerous directional instability—a tendency to sway from side to side when, at the speed of 50 miles per hour, "we twitch the steering wheel smartly and then let go with both hands. . . ." It was the first time in 10 years that Consumers Union had found an American-made car to be "not acceptable."[17]

Although auto experts rallied to Chrysler's defense and federal safety experts agreed that the car was not dangerous and that the faults appeared only under highly unusual circumstances, the damage was done. The impact on 1978 sales of the Omni/Horizon was catastrophic, and other Chrysler models were affected as well. Expense items associated with plant conversions and rearrangements plus introductory costs of the Omni/Horizon were major contributors to Chrysler's $204.6 million loss in 1978.

[16] *Fortune,* October 22, 1979, p. 48.
[17] *Financial World,* November 15, 1978, p. 19.

Enter Lee Iacocca

In December 1978, Riccardo appointed Lee A. Iacocca, former president of Ford Motor Company to Chrysler's presidency. Riccardo announced plans to retain the chairmanship, turning over the duties of chief executive officer to Iacocca after one year.

Iacocca was a graduate engineer with a formidable reputation as a marketing wizard. He had been fired the year before by Henry Ford, Jr., presumably over a difference of opinion in timing the introduction of smaller, more fuel-efficient models.

Industry observers and Chrysler dealers greeted Iacocca's appointment with hearty enthusiasm. He also had the support of Chrysler's bankers who were said to have recommended him. Certainly, Iacocca's marketing skill was badly needed. He pledged to "stop the bleeding," restore Chrysler's profitability, and to fill some of the "gaping holes" in the ailing corporation's product line.

Iacocca would be assisted in his product planning and design efforts by Harold Sperlich, a former Ford vice-president hired by Riccardo two years earlier after a similar disagreement with Henry Ford, Jr. Sperlich and Iacocca had been widely credited in the industry with the development of Ford's very successful Mustang in the mid-1960s. Many Chrysler supporters hoped they could repeat that success.

THE TURNAROUND PLAN

Iacocca accepted the presidency of Chrysler determined to maintain the company's position as a full-line rival to GM and Ford, competing in every category from subcompacts to pickup trucks. He set out to correct some of Chrysler's long standing problems in styling, advertising, and marketing.

First, separate Chrysler-Plymouth and Dodge divisions were established to increase competition among dealer groups. Iacocca switched Chrysler's advertising to the Kenyon and Eckhardt Agency which had been Ford's agency for many years. Advertising policy was changed to separate the Dodge and Plymouth lines. The Dodge was presented as a sporty, fun-to-drive car, while virtually identical Plymouth models were sold for their stability and road-handling characteristics. As executive vice-president R. K. Brown explained in *Fortune,* "some things are what you say they are."

Iacocca's next move was to reorganize the company's system of car building. "I'll be damned if I'm going to build one car without a dealer order," he said in a September 10, 1979, interview with the *Wall Street Journal.*

Unlike the system used by GM and Ford wherein no car was built without a dealer order, Chrysler had dealer orders for only half the cars it built. The other half of the cars built went into what the Company called a "sales bank" or company inventory. Units were then sold to dealers from that inventory. As Iacocca explained to *Automotive Industries,* July 1979:

> There's only one thing wrong with that. You miss the market, usually because you don't know what the hell to put in the bank. Also you carry hundreds of millions of dollars in carrying costs. The cars are in there 30, 60, or maybe 90 days. When

> you add all the concomitant damage that goes with it—it's not the way to do business.
>
> [I'm] putting in place in the company a dealer-ordering system whereby he signs for an order of cars and trucks one and then two months in advance. Then our schedules would be built up on the aggregate of those orders. [This] system has been in use in the industry for 30 or 40 years.

In addition, Iacocca had instituted incentive programs and rebates to dealers to help boost sales and had added 5-year or 50,000 mile warranties on some slow-moving models. He made numerous top-level management changes, hired away from Ford a few key officials and engineers, and eliminated about 1500 positions in a cost-cutting move.

Sale of Foreign Subsidiaries

When Townsend resigned he said that his proudest achievement had been taking Chrysler overseas for a third of its sales. Once Riccardo became chairman, he immediately began to unload Chrysler's overseas businesses. He worked out a deal with the British government to help bail out Chrysler U.K. Aid from the British government stabilized the ailing subsidiary long enough for Riccardo to arrange its sale, along with all other Chrysler European manufacturing and financing companies, to Peugeot-Citroén in 1978. Chrysler got $300 million in cash, 15 per cent equity in the French company, and wiped almost $400 million in debt from the company's balance sheet.

With Iacocca on board, Chrysler moved to complete overseas retrenchment with a "fold or fix" strategy.

> VW agreed in January [1979] to triple the capitalization of Chrysler do Brazil, acquiring two-thirds equity in that company by providing all the additional funds involved. In February, Chrysler sold GM its car and truck assembly facilities in Venezuela and its equity in a Colombian assembly operation. And in May it struck a deal with Mitsubishi Motors Corp. and Mitsubishi Corp. under which the two would pump $30.2 million into Chrysler Australia Ltd. in exchange for a combined one-third equity in the company. [In August 1979], Chrysler [was] discussing yet another deal with VW, this time to shed facilities in Argentina.[18]

In addition Chrysler sold its Turkish plants and all but 25 per cent of its South African company.

Sales Slump Jeopardizes Long-Range Plans

In the spring of 1979 the United States experienced a gasoline shortage which caused an abrupt swing of the U.S. market to 30 mpg cars. Meeting consumer demand was more difficult than satisfying federal standards. Sales of Chrysler's big cars, pickup trucks, and vans "dropped like a rock." Chrysler reported first quarter 1979 losses of $53.8 million.

Demand for the Omni/Horizon surged in the spring of 1979. Ironically, Chrysler's production of the fast-selling Omni/Horizon was limited by a worldwide shortage of four-cylinder engines. Iacocca found that neither Volkswagen, Chrysler's original supplier of 300,000 engines for the Omni, nor Mitsubishi of

[18] *Business Week*, August 20, 1979, p. 106.

Japan, which built the Colt and Sapporo models for Chrysler, would have additional four-cylinder engines available before August 1980. Chrysler's own Trenton, Michigan, plant was being retooled to produce four-cylinder engines with production there expected to begin in the spring of 1980. By 1981 Chrysler would have the ability to provide its own four-cylinder engines.

An all new fuel-efficient compact line had been developed for introduction in the 1981 model year. Iacocca's plans to return Chrysler's profitability hinged on the projected sale of close to one million of these new front-wheel drive compacts. Scheduled to replace the Aspen/Volaré, this new line of "K-cars" would compete with GM's spectacularly successful "X-cars" (e.g., Chevrolet Citation) that were introduced in 1978.

Iacocca had scheduled the introduction of slightly larger front-wheel drive cars in 1984 and 1985. Downsized vans and trucks were planned for 1983 and 1986 that would be added to Chrysler's full-sized lines.

However, Chrysler's second quarter 1979 losses made it grimly apparent to Iacocca and Riccardo that the company had to find a way to ride out its losses in 1979 and 1980 until sales of the 1981 models could boost Chrysler's income and market share. The company could not proceed with its recovery plans without assistance.

Decision to Seek Federal Assistance

In early June 1979, Riccardo began a Washington lobbying blitz to spotlight Chrysler's financial problems. He mobilized a lobby of dealers, suppliers, the United Auto Workers union, and most of the Michigan Congressional delegation to emphasize that a Chrysler collapse would start an economic tidal wave. Riccardo maintained that the slump in car sales could not have been anticipated and the immovable product spending schedule dictated by Washington regulators had therefore made profitability temporarily impossible. To test public opinion Riccardo suggested a program of special tax credits to cover part of the expenditures necessary to meet regulations. Chrysler would repay its obligation to the U.S. Treasury with higher than normal tax payments on future earnings. In addition, Riccardo proposed a two-year postponement in complying with federal exhaust-emission standards, a concession which would save the Company $600 million.

Democratic Senator Donald W. Riegle, Jr. of Michigan was quoted in the August 13, 1979, issue of *Newsweek:* "We are headed into a recession already, and 500,000 people directly or indirectly obtain their livelihoods from Chrysler's activities. These people must be helped."

Trouble at Chrysler Financial

In July 1979, Chrysler reported a second quarter loss of $207 million and indicated there was more red ink to come. As a result, the entire commercial paper market slowed to a crawl. The reason—Chrysler Financial, the company's financing arm, had $1.3 billion worth of such paper outstanding. Investment rating services, including Standard and Poors and Moody's Investors Service, downgraded Chrysler Financial. Its credit standing lost, Chrysler Financial was shunned by investors. Corporations that usually sold paper, fearing the collapse of the market, began to activate bank credit lines* instead.

Chrysler itself, now blocked from obtaining funds in the short-term money market, was forced to turn to its backup lines of credit at about 300 banks. The company negotiated a $400 million credit line in Japan, $70 million in Canada, and $94 million from Prudential Insurance Company and Aetna Life Insurance Co., Chrysler's two largest long-term lenders.

Some confidence in Chrysler Financial was regained when, in August 1979, it arranged to sell retail receivables (car loans to retail customers) to Household Finance Corp. for $500 million and wholesale receivables to General Motors Acceptance Corp. for $230 million. The subsidiary then moved to convert its backup credit lines to revolving credit.**

CHRYSLER REQUESTS FEDERAL AID

The first week in August 1979, John Riccardo called a press conference. "We have taken all the prudent steps that could be taken to make our way," Riccardo declared. Chrysler was asking the U.S. Government for a $1 billion cash advance against future income. Riccardo maintained: "We are not talking about bailout, we are not talking about handout, we are not talking welfare. We are talking equity. We are talking about money we intend to repay."[19]

Three days later Iacocca met with United Auto Workers' (UAW) president Douglas A. Fraser and asked that Chrysler be exempted from August contract negotiations and that a two-year freeze on both wages and benefits be granted. Fraser promptly rejected the proposal but it was clear that he was impressed with the gravity of Chrysler's plight. "They've hollered wolf so many times, I'm concerned about people taking them seriously," Fraser said. "I think they *must* be taken seriously."[20]

Commentary and discussion about "to rescue or not to rescue" filled the press. The initial response was predictable. Fiscal conservatives seemed sympathetic to the idea of relaxing regulatory restraints, but opposed financial handouts. Environmentalists took exception to any easing at all. For the most part, congressmen were waiting to see how the situation developed politically. The key issue was seen to be whether Chrysler had done enough to help itself.

> Two weeks before Chrysler Corporation surprised the world with its public plea for a government rescue, Michigan's two senators personally took the word to President Carter. . . . The Senators' involvement, at that level and at that early stage, was characteristic of Chrysler's handling of its financial crisis. The mid-July meeting with the President was part of a long, carefully choreographed campaign to build advance political backing before asking the government for radical relief.[21]

*A line of credit was the amount a bank had stated it would be willing to lend a corporation if the borrower's financial or operating conditions met certain criteria stipulated in the agreement.

**A revolving line of credit was a contractual agreement to provide loans. When a loan was paid off under such an agreement, the amount was again available to the borrower.

[19] Ibid., p. 102.

[20] *Newsweek,* August 13, 1979, p. 52.

[21] *Wall Street Journal,* September 6, 1979, p. 1. "How Chrysler Orchestrates Support of Bid for Federal Aid."

The administration rejected Chrysler's opening pitch for a direct $1 billion cash bailout and requested a detailed company survival plan be submitted to the Treasury. Riccardo was spending four to five days a week in Washington to drum up support from federal officials and legislators. "This despite having been hospitalized in May for a 'cardiac insufficiency'."[22] Iacocca got down to business in Detroit.

Iacocca moved in several directions. Common stock dividends were suspended, as was an employee "thrift stock" plan under which the Company matched half the funds invested by salaried employees in Chrysler stock. In 1978 Chrysler contributed $15.8 million to the plan; its resumption was scheduled to coincide with Chrysler's return to profitability, hopefully in 1981.

All price increases from suppliers were rejected and Iacocca requested extended payment terms. Most suppliers agreed, but promptly purchased insurance to cover their accounts receivable.

Meetings, continued between Iacocca and the United Auto Workers Union. In August, industry observers were speculating that the UAW, whose contract would expire in September, would agree to a one-year extension of their current contract.

Iacocca put the Company's public relations and advertising operations to work. Chrysler bought full-page ads in 50 major metropolitan newspapers, and many leading magazines outlining its situations under the headline, "Would America Be Better Off Without Chrysler?" The ad emphasized "we're going to get well . . . because it will be good for the automotive business. And for America."

In addition, Iacocca: (1) Negotiated the sale of Chrysler Realty Corp.; (2) instituted a rebate offer to help move the backlog of 1979 models and generate badly needed cash; (2) began layoffs of blue- and white-collar employees; (4) announced salary cuts for top management; and (5) initiated price cuts on slow-moving models.

(1) Domestic Subsidiaries—Sale of Chrysler Realty

Continuing its retrenchment drive, in late August 1979, Chrysler sold its Chrysler Realty Corp. unit to Abko Realty Inc., a privately held real estate investment concern in Wichita, Kansas, that was formed specifically to purchase the realty unit. The sale netted Chrysler about $200 million in cash, and cleared its books of some $70 million in debt. As a unit of Abko Realty, Chrysler Realty became a new company with a new name, but continued to lease its 780 dealership facilities to Chrysler dealers.

The only unconsolidated subsidiary remaining was Chrysler Financial Corp. Capital generated by this subsidiary was used to finance wholesale purchases of cars and trucks by Chrysler dealers and retail purchases by consumers.

Chrysler held on to its diversified products group which consisted largely of its defense business and small auto-parts manufacturing operations. Chrysler was the nation's 13th largest defense contractor in 1978 with $742.5 million in military business.

Industry observers indicated that Chrysler had been trying unsuccessfully

[22] Ibid.

to find a buyer for its marine division which made boats and marine engines. The marine division consisted of three manufacturing plants. One of Chrysler's smaller operations, it was estimated that sale of the division would net about $20 million.

(2) Rebate Offer

In Mid-August 1979, Chrysler instituted a rebate offer in a bid to boost its faltering sales and provide an influx of much needed cash, to counter the downturn in consumer demand.

Chrysler's decision to revive cash rebates, a form of price-cutting it first introduced during the 1975 auto sales slump, created debate among sales and marketing strategiests. Some sales strategists maintained that rebates really did not expand the market but merely prompted people who were going to make purchases anyway to do so sooner than they otherwise would. It was felt that sales would fall off by as much as they had increased once rebates were stopped.

However, rebates were popular with Chrysler's dealers whose inventories stood at more than 350,000 vehicles on August 1, 1979.

> Chrysler sold 28,500 recreational vehicles in the second quarter of 1978, but in this year's second quarter [1979] it sold only 2,345—and just twelve during the three-week period in June. "Is that a drop in a market?" asks Iacocca. "No, that's a complete *disappearance* of a market."[23]

All Chrysler's 1979 light trucks, vans, and cars, except the Dodge Omni/Plymouth Horizon subcompacts, were subject to $400 cash rebates made directly from the factory to customers. Once the dealer's inventories started to turn over they were willing to take additional models from Chrysler's "sales bank," a corporate inventory of 80,000 cars and trucks, representing $700 million, that had been produced without dealer's purchase orders.

In an inverview with the *Wall Street Journal,* September 10, 1979, Iacocca explained that although the rebate offer had been costly it had trimmed the company's 80,000 car inventory by 53,000 cars in five weeks. Iacocca said that this left the company in a "pretty good position" except for fat inventories of trucks which hung "like an albatross" around Chrysler's neck. "Some of the gas hysteria has gone away," Iacocca observed. But he added that because of intense competition from other companies' small cars, "we aren't going to burn up the track."

In referring to Chrysler's plans to have fuel-efficient cars available in 1981, Iacocca quipped that the ousting of the Shah of Iran in 1979 came just two years too soon.[24] According to late 1978 government forecasts, the price of gasoline would rise to 76.6 cents per gallon in 1981. Prices of $1-a-gallon were not anticipated before 1985, as indicated in Table 8.

As part of Chrysler's advertising programs, Iacocca joined Frank Borman of Eastern Airlines as one of the few company presidents to promote his products on nationwide TV. Beginning in mid-August, Iacocca appeared in television ads announcing the Company's rebate offer, stating sternly, "I'm not asking anyone to buy a car on faith—I am asking you to compare."

[23] *Automotive Industries,* July, 1979, p. 77. "Can Iacocca Turn Chrysler Around?"
[24] *Newsweek,* August 13, 1979, p. 53.

TABLE 8: Gasoline and Diesel Price Forecasts (cents per gallon)

	Gasoline *	*Diesel Fuel*
1976	58.7	52.1
1977	62.5	56.5
1978	63.9	57.7
1979	67.8	58.1
1980	70.7	62.8
1981	76.6	68.0
1982	83.6	74.2
1983	91.2	81.5
1984	95.0	84.8
1985	101.0	90.2
1986	108.1	96.5
1987	115.0	102.6
1988	122.3	109.1
1989	130.2	116.2
1990	138.6	123.6

* Gasoline price is full service-regular grade.
Source: Chase Information Services. *A Cost-Benefit Analysis of the 1979 to 1985 Fuel Economy Standards.* December, 1978, p. 26. Reprinted with permission.

(3) Layoffs

With the elimination of the sales bank policy which had maintained production levels in spite of the absence of dealers' orders, Chrysler found layoffs were necessary. By August 1979 Chrysler had laid off 25,800 from a total of 100,000 hourly workers.

Following Riccardo's request for aid, the company announced it would reduce output of its slowest selling large cars. At plants which manufactured Dodge St. Regis and Chrysler New Yorker and Newport models, 1,800 hourly workers were indefinitely laid off. Over 2,500 employees of Chrysler in Canada were similarly laid off.

Chrysler's layoffs left the company with a bare minimum of new models to send to its dealers as the 1980 model year began in October.

All nonessential white-collar employees were also laid off department by department, as, under Iacocca's scrutiny, further belt-tightening continued.

(4) Salary Cuts

At the end of August, as part of their effort to convince the government that the company was making every sacrifice to cut costs, Riccardo and Iacocca announced they had given up all but $1 per year of their salaries until the company returned to profitability.

By disclosing its salary-reduction program Chrysler "defused a potentially explosive issue; several public officials have been sharply critical of the $360,000 annual base salaries Chairman John J. Riccardo and President Lee A. Iacocca have been drawing."[25]

Over 17,000 other top executives also took salary cuts averaging 10 per cent for the vice-presidents and 2–5 per cent for executives with lower base salaries. The cuts were expected to save the company less than $3 million per year, but the move was a highly visible expression of the top managers' commitment to turning Chrysler around. The salary reduction plan allowed recovery of the deferred salaries if Chrysler returned to profitability on schedule in 1981.

(5) Pricing Tactics

In mid-September, concerned that sales could fall off when the rebates ended, necessitating further shutdowns and layoffs, Chrysler announced pricing tactics to stimulate dealer orders for slow-selling models.

Prices on the slow-moving Aspen and Volaré models were set below 1979 prices, achieving price cuts of more than $100. These models were priced several hundred dollars below the popular Omnis and Horizons.

Chrysler announced new three-year, unlimited mileage corrosion warranties on all its cars and trucks. The new warranties were similar to those introduced in 1979 by the rest of the U.S. industry, and did not cover exhaust-system parts.

In spite of its incentive efforts, the company anticipated a loss of at least 200 of its dealers by 1980.

THE ADMINISTRATION'S POSITION

On August 9, 1979, in his first full-scale interview since he moved from the Federal Reserve Board to the Treasury Department, G. William Miller was asked about the Chrysler situation by *Wall Street Journal* reporters:

> The self-confident Treasury Chief appears to be playing a subtle game in the Chrysler situation. Determined to keep the government's role and financial exposure as small as possible, he is putting pressure on the company to do all it can to solve its problems. The more successful Chrysler is in helping itself, the less government assistance it will require.
>
> . . . Should he decide to press for loan guarantees for Chrysler, the Treasury Secretary said, he doesn't anticipate problems obtaining congressional approval. "A sound plan is one that would sell itself," he said.[26]

The administration's plan to bail out Chrysler by relying on federal loan guarantees was similar to previous government emergency efforts to assist Lockheed Corporation and New York City. Both of those actions averted possible failures that would have had ripple effects on the nation's economy.

In the Lockheed case the government earned about $31 million in fees for guaranteeing up to $250 million in loans.

In mid-August, President Carter was asked at a town meeting in Burlington, Iowa, about the Chrysler situation. The President said he thought there

[25] *Wall Street Journal*, August 31, 1979, p. 2. "Top Chrysler Officials Give Up Salaries."
[26] *Wall Street Journal*, August 22, 1979, p. 3. "Miller Sees Chance of . . . Rescue Plan."

should be shared responsibility between Chrysler employees and officials, a heavy dependence on the private sector for assistance, a minimum involvement of the federal government, and maximum security for any loan the government did guarantee. It "would be a good investment, I believe, if we do it that way" he said. This package would keep Chrysler operating, enhance auto industry competition, hold prices down, and keep several hundred thousand Chrysler workers employed.

On September 8, 1979, Iacocca and Riccardo met informally with Treasury Secretary G. William Miller to make a preliminary report on Chrysler's situation and to suggest tax credits as an acceptable remedy. Following the meeting, the Treasury released a statement indicating that it would *not* accept a plan that involved granting the company tax credits, "or the equivalent of the government's taking an equity interest in Chrysler." One of Miller's main objections to the use of tax credits was that the credits as outlined by Chrysler would have been interest-free.

Miller also emphatically indicated that $750 million would be the "outside range" of possible federal help for the company. He expected that the auto maker would have to show a "reasonable prospect of repayment."

If Chrysler's request were approved by the Treasury, it would go before the Senate banking committee chaired by Senator William Proxmire (D. Wisconsin). Proxmire was known to view Lockheed as a "terrible precedent." He had termed such guarantees a "gross interference with the private sector."

Chairman Henry Reuss (D. Wisconsin) of the House banking panel was equally unenthusiastic about a federal loan guarantee plan. Rep. Reuss said in a statement that the key question he would ask was: "Should we continue making the creaky structure of our economy . . . even more ramshackled by trying to save a company that is about to expire because it has insisted on making gas guzzlers . . ." at a time when buyers were looking for fuel-efficiency?

Survival Plan Submitted

On September 15, 1979, Chrysler formally presented its long awaited recovery plan to the Treasury, requesting $1.2 billion in federal loan guarantees. Chrysler had projected that it would be $2.1 billion short of what it needed by 1982 to finance its new product plans. It believed it could raise about $900 million without federal help. To raise the balance Chrysler proposed an immediate $400 million in federal loan guarantees, and $700 million in standby loan guarantees. The *Wall Street Journal* noted:

> Chrysler's request to the government, however, was surprisingly sketchy about how the auto maker hoped to muster either the initial $900 million or the $700 million that would otherwise have to be raised by the contingent loan guarantees. The auto maker said it would raise the $900 million from the sale of unspecified assets and "other actions." It didn't describe a strategy for generating the other $700 million or say what circumstances would allow it to do so.[27]
>
> . . . The plan Chrysler submitted to the government said that by 1982 it expects to realize $593 more a car than it does currently. Of this amount, the company expects to gain $257 a car because it's products will be more "competi-

[27] *Wall Street Journal,* September 17, 1979, p. 2. "Miller Rejects Chrysler's Aid Plan."

tive" and thus sell better, and because of design changes that will allow use of less-costly materials and manufacturing techniques.

Chrysler also expects to earn $89 more per unit by pushing more optional equipment such as tilt steering wheels, sophisticated sound systems, and other electronic gadgets.

The balance of this improvement in "variable profit margins" is supposed to come from other manufacturing efficiencies, less costly parts, and reduced warranty expenses stemming from design and manufacturing improvements.[28]

The recovery plan disclosed an anticipated loss of $1.07 billion for all of 1979. Even with federal help, a $482 million loss was forecast for 1980.

Exhibits 11 through 14 show Chrysler's estimates of the U.S. auto and truck markets through 1985, and Chrysler's planned penetration of those markets. Exhibits 15 and 16 show Chrysler's estimates of cash shortfall and how that shortfall will be funded. Exhibits 17 and 18 show Chrysler's planned capital expenditures for 1979–85 for cars, trucks, and the relevant powertrains.

In the plan, Chrysler announced negotiations with VW over the sale of an interest in its Argentine unit. The company also hoped to sell another part of its Australian unit to Japan's Mitsubishi group.

The plan did not contain firm loan commitments from local governments or statements from the UAW. While the plan indicated that the leadership of the UAW was sympathetic to Chrysler's request for special consideration, UAW officials had insisted on completion of their new contract neogiations with GM and Ford before they would consider a labor contract extension with Chrysler.

As part of its argument justifying federal assistance, Chrysler outlined a worst-case scenario. Utilizing studies conducted by the Department of Transportation and Data Resources Inc., Chrysler predicted tremendous hardships would fall on Detroit and other towns and cities where the company's plants were located.* The DOT study predicted that for every Chrysler production worker laid off, two people employed by Chrysler's suppliers and other related enterprises would also be forced out of work. Unemployment in Detroit could reach 16 per cent. Chrysler's plants were located primarily in older inner-city areas and employed a large proportion of blacks and minorities, a particularly sensitive segment of the population to be out of work in an election year.

David Stockman, a Republican Congressman from Michigan, took issue with Chrysler's projections:

> The longer-term prospects for Chrysler's 120,000 direct employees are not entirely bleak. Nearly two-fifths are white-collar, supervisory, or skilled production workers with strong prospects for re-employment. Another 22,000 are employed at modern efficient plants . . . with good prospects for a new owner. Even the 50,000 hourly employees in the Detroit area represent less than 20 per cent of total auto employment in the metro area.
>
> To be sure, during the transition period there would be substantial temporary unemployment within the Chrysler network . . . But nearly every Chrysler facility has already been certified for the full Trade Adjustment Assistance Package. This will guarantee every production worker 95 per cent of after-tax take home pay for

* For the years ended December 31, 1978, and December 31, 1977, the average monthly number of employees of Chrysler in the U.S. was 131,758 and 133, 572; wages and salaries paid to them totaled $2.9 billion and $2.7 billion respectively.

[28] *Wall Street Journal,* September 26, 1979, p. 5. "Chrysler is Pinning Profits, Hopes on Line of Compacts Similar to GM Cars."

a year, free retraining benefits, and 80 per cent of any job search or relocation expenses.[29]

Also at issue was the fate of Chrysler's pension plan. The Company's unfunded vested pension liability was $1.1 billion in 1979. Approximately $250 million of that amount was uninsured. The balance was insured by the Pension Benefit Guaranty Corp. (PBGC), a government agency. The PBGC had accumulated a net deficiency of $130 million in 1979 from the termination of 664 plans that had lacked enough assets to cover their pension liabilities and was not prepared to confront a major corporate liquidation. That raised the possibility that Chrysler's workers would lose more than $250 million.

However, upon examination that prospect did not appear likely. Henry Rose, general council to the PBGC was quoted in *Fortune:*

> If Chrysler did terminate its pension plan, the funded portion of the total liability ($1.4 billion) would be sufficient to meet the needs of the beneficiaries for the next seven years.[30]

That would be enough time for the agency to raise revenues by increasing premiums on other corporate plans. Besides, if Chrysler were to undergo a reorganization that continued operations, the pension plan would probably not be terminated and no one would lose anything.

ALTERNATIVES TO FEDERAL AID

Should federal assistance not be forthcoming it appeared that Chrysler could choose between liquidation or a takeover.

In the first week of July, 1979, the rumor of a Chrysler-VW merger swept Wall Street. The rumor was vehemently denied by Volkswagen and Chrysler officials. *Time* magazine noted:

> A Chrysler deal would make little sense for Volkswagen, which has just regained its old momentum after a long period of drift, during which Japanese automakers zipped past it in many major markets. Detroit executives point out that Volkswagen, which is the most firmly established foreign automaker in the U.S., does not need Chrysler's huge unsold inventory of big autos that could become the albatross of the gasless summer of '79.

In an analysis of the company, the investment house of Paine Webber Mitchell Hutchings declared:

> . . . We regard it as wishful thinking to expect a white knight to appear out of Europe, or elsewhere, to buy the company in its entirety. Realistically foreign car companies will wait for the "garage sale" which would accompany financial reorganization.

Some observers had begun to suggest that filing a Chapter XI bankruptcy might be Iacocca's wisest move. Under the recently revised federal bankruptcy code, the court could retain the present management rather than automatically appointing a trustee.

[29] Congressional Record-Senate, December 10, 1979, p. S18103 "The Chrysler Corp."
[30] *Fortune,* October 22, 1979, p. 52.

EXHIBIT 11: The Chrysler Corporation (A)

CHRYSLER'S FORECASTS OF U.S. CAR INDUSTRY BY SEGMENTS
CALENDAR YEARS
(RETAIL UNITS IN THOUSANDS)

	Actual		*Projection*						
	1977	*1978*	*1979*	*1980*	*1981*	*1982*	*1983*	*1984*	*1985*
Industry (Units)									
Sub-Compact	1,989	2,104	2,556	2,195	2,231	2,251	2,311	2,406	2,464
Compact	1,559	1,630	1,620	2,007	1,996	2,059	2,168	2,282	2,357
Small Specialty	1,063	1,205	1,465	1,443	1,576	1,654	1,704	1,773	1,844
Total Small	4,611	4,939	5,641	5,645	5,803	5,964	6,183	6,461	6,665
Basic Middle	1,915	1,615	1,114	1,038	1,256	1,217	1,217	1,215	1,189
Middle Specialty	1,650	1,852	1,439	1,512	1,649	1,667	1,717	1,755	1,785
Total Middle	3,565	3,467	2,553	2,550	2,905	2,884	2,934	2,970	2,974
Basic Large	2,270	2,138	1,715	1,727	1,785	1,753	1,697	1,686	1,678
Luxury	564	586	498	578	607	599	586	583	583
Total Large	2,834	2,724	2,213	2,305	2,392	2,352	2,283	2,269	2,261
Total Industry	11,010	11,130	10,407	10,500	11,100	11,200	11,400	11,700	11,900

Mix (per cent)									
Sub-Compact	18.1%	18.9%	24.6%	20.9%	20.1%	20.1%	20.3%	20.5%	20.7%
Compact	14.2	14.7	15.5	19.1	18.0	18.4	19.0	19.5	19.8
Small Specialty	9.6	10.8	14.1	13.7	14.2	14.8	14.9	15.2	15.5
Total Small	41.9%	44.4	54.2	53.7	52.3	53.3	54.2	55.2	56.0
Basic Middle	17.4	14.5	10.7	9.9	11.3	10.8	10.7	10.4	10.0
Middle Specialty	15.0	16.6	13.8	14.4	14.9	14.9	15.1	15.0	15.0
Total Middle	32.4	31.1	24.5	24.3	26.2	25.7	25.8	25.4	25.0
Basic Large	20.6	19.2	16.5	16.5	16.1	15.7	14.9	14.4	14.1
Luxury	5.1	5.3	4.8	5.5	5.4	5.3	5.1	5.0	4.9
Total Large	25.7	24.5	21.3	22.0	21.5	21.0	20.0	19.4	19.0
Total Industry	100.0%	100.0%	100.0%	100.0%	100.0%	100.0%	100.0%	100.0%	100.0%

Source: Chrysler Corporation: "Analysis of Chrysler Corporation's Situation and Proposal for Government Assistance," September 15, 1979, p. 55.

EXHIBIT 12: The Chrysler Corporation (A)

CHRYSLER'S FORECASTS OF CHRYSLER U.S. CAR AND PENETRATION BY SEGMENTS
CALENDAR YEARS
(RETAIL UNITS IN THOUSANDS)

	Actual		*Projection*						
	1977	*1978*	*1979*	*1980*	*1981*	*1982*	*1983*	*1984*	*1985*
Chrysler (Units)									
Sub-Compact (Omni 4 Dr.)	77	251	249	178	187	198	224	234	223
Compact (Aspen)	551	367	275	278	400	494	519	510	515
Sm. Specialty (Omni 2 dr.)	51	61	185	181	177	204	246	255	250
Total Small	679	679	709	637	764	896	989	999	988
Basic Middle (LeBaron)	262	284	144	158	167	125	122	201	172
Mid. Specialty (Cordoba)	180	154	93	170	169	168	163	136	199
Total Middle	442	438	237	328	336	293	285	337	371
Basic Large (Newport)	168	74	117	98	109	84	55	51	79
Luxury (Imperial)	—	—	—	8	24	27	28	28	32
Total Large	168	74	117	106	133	111	83	79	111
Total Chrysler	1,289	1,191	1,063	1,071	1,231	1,300	1,357	1,415	1,470

Chrysler Share of Segment (per cent)									
Sub-Compact	3.9%	11.9%	9.7%	8.2%	8.4%	9.1%	9.7%	9.7%	9.0%
Compact	35.3	22.5	17.0	13.9	20.0	24.0	23.9	22.3	21.8
Small Specialty	4.8	5.1	12.6	12.6	11.2	12.3	14.4	14.4	13.6
Total Small	14.7	13.7	12.6	11.3	13.2	15.0	16.0	15.5	14.8
Basic Middle	13.7	17.6	12.9	15.2	13.3	10.3	10.3	16.5	14.5
Middle Specialty	10.9	8.3	6.5	11.2	10.2	10.1	9.5	7.7	11.1
Total Middle	12.4	12.6	9.3	12.9	11.6	10.2	9.7	11.3	12.5
Basic Large	7.4	3.5	6.8	5.7	6.1	4.8	3.2	3.0	4.7
Luxury	—	—	—	1.4	4.0	4.5	4.8	4.8	5.5
Total Large	5.9	2.7	5.3	4.6	5.6	4.7	3.6	3.5	4.9
Total Industry	11.7%	10.7%	10.2%	10.2%	11.1%	11.6%	11.9%	12.1%	12.4%

Source: Chrysler Corporation, "Analysis of Chrysler Corporation's Situation and Proposal for Government Assistance," September 15, 1979, p. 56.

EXHIBIT 13: The Chrysler Corporation (A)

CHRYSLER'S FORECASTS OF U.S. TRUCK INDUSTRY BY SEGMENTS
CALENDAR YEARS
(RETAIL UNITS IN THOUSANDS)

	Actual		*Projection*						
	1977	*1978*	*1979*	*1980*	*1981*	*1982*	*1983*	*1984*	*1985*
Industry (Units)									
Bus—Small	24	20	20	20	20	20	64	243	368
—Standard	134	148	115	115	137	133	143	122	102
Total Bus	158	168	135	135	157	153	207	365	470
Van—Small	—	—	—	—	—	—	35	166	272
—Standard	508	608	458	473	571	549	566	493	445
Total Van	508	608	458	473	571	549	601	669	717
Pick-Up—Small	323	337	450	433	524	680	921	1,116	1,217
—Standard	2,047	2,206	1,707	1,620	1,776	1,474	1,371	1,301	1,293
Total Pick-Up	2,370	2,543	2,157	2,053	2,300	2,154	2,292	2,417	2,510
Motor Home—Van	90	114	51	51	88	91	102	110	118
—Light	42	52	25	26	'37	38	39	41	41
Utility	252	355	261	258	349	338	363	390	408
Car/Truck	78	80	80	75	65	65	65	65	65
Medium/Heavy	341	361	353	329	333	312	331	353	371
Total Industry	3,839	4,281	3,520	3,400	3,900	3,700	4,000	4,400	4,700

Mix (per cent)									
Bus—Small	.6%	.5%	.5%	.5%	.5%	.5%	1.6%	5.5%	7.8%
—Standard	3.5	3.4	3.3	3.4	3.5	3.6	3.6	2.8	2.2
Total Bus	4.1	3.9	3.8	3.9	4.0	4.1	5.2	8.3	10.0
Van—Small	—	—	—	—	—	—	.9	3.8	5.8
—Standard	13.2	14.2	13.0	13.9	14.7	14.8	14.1	11.2	9.4
Total Van	13.2	14.2	13.0	13.9	14.7	14.8	15.0	15.0	15.2
Pick-Up—Small	8.4	7.9	12.8	12.7	13.4	18.4	23.0	25.4	25.9
—Standard	53.3	51.5	48.5	47.7	45.5	40.0	34.4	29.5	27.5
Total Pick-Up	61.7	59.4	61.3	60.4	58.9	58.4	57.4	54.9	53.4
Motor Home—Van	2.4	2.7	1.5	1.5	2.3	2.5	2.5	2.5	2.5
—Light	1.1	1.2	.7	.8	.9	1.0	1.0	.9	.9
Utility	6.6	8.3	7.4	7.6	9.0	9.1	9.1	8.9	8.7
Car/Truck	2.0	1.9	2.3	2.2	1.7	1.6	1.5	1.5	1.4
Medium/Heavy	8.9	8.4	10.0	9.7	8.5	8.5	8.3	8.0	7.9
Total Industry	100.0%	100.0%	100.0%	100.0%	100.0%	100.0%	100.0%	100.0%	100.0%

Source: Chrysler Corporation, "Analysis of Chrysler Corporation's Situation and Proposal for Government Assistance," September 15, 1979, p. 59.

EXHIBIT 14: The Chrysler Corporation

CHRYSLER'S FORECASTS OF CHRYSLER U.S. TRUCK AND PENETRATION BY SEGMENTS
CALENDAR YEARS
(RETAIL UNITS IN THOUSANDS)

	Actual		*Projection*						
	1977	*1978*	*1979*	*1980*	*1981*	*1982*	*1983*	*1984*	*1985*
Chrysler (Units)									
Bus—Small	—	—	—	—	—	—	—	—	27
—Standard (Sportsman)	59	58	39	35	48	48	49	47	40
Total Bus	59	58	39	35	48	48	49	47	67
Van—Small	—	—	—	—	—	—	—	—	18
—Standard (Tradesman)	181	182	102	103	125	128	131	126	110
Total Van	181	182	102	103	125	128	131	126	128
Pick-up—Small	—	3	53	58	61	73	145	189	205
—Standard	192	184	132	124	138	112	75	75	75
Total Pick-up	192	187	185	182	199	185	220	264	280
Motor Home—Van	46	57	16	15	29	30	33	34	34
—Light	29	37	10	17	18	21	21	22	22
Utility (Ramcharger)	21	26	19	17	25	28	34	36	39
Car/Truck	—	—	—	—	—	—	—	—	—
Medium/Heavy	—	—	—	—	—	—	—	—	—
Total Chrysler	528	547	371	369	444	440	488	529	570

Chrysler Share of Segment (per cent)									
Bus—Small	—%	—%	—%	—%	—%	—%	—%	—%	7.3%
—Standard	44.0	39.2	33.9	30.4	35.0	36.1	34.3	38.5	39.2
Total Bus	37.3	34.5	28.9	25.9	30.6	31.4	23.7	12.9	14.3
Van—Small	—	—	—	—	—	—	—	—	6.6
—Standard	35.6	29.9	22.3	21.8	21.9	23.3	23.1	25.6	24.7
Total Van	35.6	29.9	22.3	21.8	21.9	23.3	21.8	19.1	17.9
Pick-up—Small	—	.9	11.8	13.4	11.6	10.7	15.7	16.9	16.8
—Standard	9.4	8.3	7.7	7.7	7.8	7.6	5.5	5.8	5.8
Total Pick-up	8.1	7.3	8.6	8.9	8.7	8.6	9.6	10.9	11.2
Motor Home—Van	51.1	50.0	31.4	29.4	33.0	33.0	32.4	30.9	28.8
—Light	69.0	71.1	40.0	65.4	48.6	55.3	53.8	53.7	53.7
Utility	8.3	7.3	7.3	6.6	7.2	8.3	9.4	9.2	9.6
Car/Truck	—	—	—	—	—	—	—	—	—
Medium/Heavy	—	—	—	—	8	—	—	—	—
Total	13.8%	12.8%	10.5%	10.9%	11.4%	11.9%	12.2%	12.0%	12.1%

Source: Chrysler Corporation, "Analysis of Chrysler Corporation's Situation and Proposal for Government Assistance," September 15, 1979, p. 60.

EXHIBIT 15: The Chrysler Corporation (A)

CHRYSLER'S ESTIMATES OF FUND REQUIREMENTS AND SOURCING: CHANGES IN FINANCIAL POSITION 1979–1985 ($ MILLIONS)

	1979	*1980*	*1981*	*1982*	*1983*	*1984*	*1985*
Funds Applied							
Net Tools, Facilities and Investments	$ 296	$ 454	$ 602	$ 621	$ 465	$ 483	$ 241
Reduction in Long-Term Borrowing	21	33	55	78	94	104	96
Selected Working Capital Items	(215)	174	79	(14)	68	29	7
Dividends—Common	12	—	—	—	—	—	—
—Preferred	29	29	29	29	29	29	29
Total Funds Applied	$ 143	$ 690	$ 765	$ 714	$ 656	$ 645	$ 373
Funds Generated							
Profits After Tax	$(1,073)	$ (482)	$ 393	$ 516	$ 610	$ 867	$ 996

Proceeds from Borrowing:							
Long Term	—	2	2	2	2	2	2
Short Term	(33)	(6)	—	—	—	—	—
Sale of Shares to Thrift-Stock Ownership Program	29	—	40	42	45	47	50
Financing Arranged	510	24	—	—	—	—	—
Change in Deferred Taxes and Other	3	(68)	(31)	(47)	2	(55)	55
Total Funds Generated	$ (564)	$ (530)	$ 404	$ 513	$ 659	$ 861	$1,103
Net funds (Applied)/ Generated	$ (707)	$(1,220)	$ (361)	$ (201)	$ 3	$ 216	$ 730
Decreases in Year-End Cash Balance	$ 373	$ —	$ —	$ —	$ —	$ —	$ —
Cumulative Funds to be Obtained	$ 334	$1,554	$1,915	$2,116	$2,113	$1,897	$1,167

Source: Chrysler Corporation, "Analysis of Chrysler Corporation's Situation and Proposal for Government Assistance," September 15, 1979, p. 24.

EXHIBIT 16: The Chrysler Corporation (A)

CHRYSLER'S PLAN FOR FINANCING OF CASH SHORTFALL, 1979–1985
($ MILLIONS)

	Current Availability 8/31/79	*1979*	*1980*	*1981*	*1982*	*1983*	*1984*	*1985*
Total Funds Required		$1,827	$3,090	$3,455	$3,706	$3,740	$3,587	$2,907
Funds Assumed Available[a]								
Supplier Payables	$ 700 Est.	$ 857	$ 800	$ 850	$ 900	$ 950	$1,000	$1,050
Eurodollar Bank Facilities	290	290	290	290	290	290	290	290
Japanese Bank Letter of Credit Agreement	244	346	396	400	400	387	400	400
Lease Financing in Progress	—	—	50	—	—	—	—	—
Total Funds Assumed Available	$1,234	$1,493	$1,536	$1,540	$1,590	$1,627	$1,690	$1,740
Shortfall—Cumulative		$ 334	$1,554	$1,915	$2,116	$2,113	$1,897	$1,167
—Annual		$ 334	$1,220	$ 361	$ 201	$ (3)	$ (216)	$ (730)

Assets Dispositions and Other							
Total Asset Disposition and Other—Annual	$ 101	$ 395	$ 232	$ 200	$ 130	$ 33	$ 64
—Cumulative	$ —	$ 496	$ 728	$ 928	$1,058	$1,091	$1,155
Balance to be Financed from Other Sources							
—Annual	$ 233	$ 825	$ 129	$ 1	$ (133)	$ (249)	$ (794)
—Cumulative	$ —	$1,058	$1,187	$1,188	$1,055	$ 806	$ 12

[a] These funds exclude unused borrowing capacity required for seasonal needs and short-term contingencies.

Source: Chrysler Corporation, "Analysis of Chrysler Corporation's Situation and Proposal for Government Assistance," September 15, 1979.

EXHIBIT 17: The Chrysler Corporation (A)

CHRYSLER CORPORATION PLANNED EXPENDITURES FOR CALENDAR YEARS 1979–1985—CAR PROGRAMS

Model Year	*Program*	*Memo: Total Lifetime Expenditures*	*1979–1985 Calendar Year Expenditures—$ Millions*							
			1979	*1980*	*1981*	*1982*	*1983*	*1984*	*1985*	*Total*
1979	Subcompact Specialty	$ 125	$ 4	$	$	$	$	$	$	$ 4
	Large	224	9							9
	Other Programs	123	1							1
1980	Middle Basic	113	80	9						89
	Middle Specialty	188	132	8						140
	Other Programs	184	107	4						111
1981	Compact	575	128	412	13					553
	Luxury	75	18	50	2					70
	Other Programs	102	20	52	11					83
1982	Programs	204	18	53	107	21				199
1983	Compact Specialty	294	1	20	135	132	6			294
	Middle Specialty	139		3	36	95	5			139
	Large	108	1	16	73	18				108
	Other Programs	277	2	20	104	141	10			277
1984	Subcompact Base & Spec.	90			4	25	57	4		90
	Middle Basic	576		5	18	145	388	20		576
	Other Programs	265		3	21	74	157	10		265
1985	Compact	127				4	34	84	5	127
	Compact Specialty	148				9	47	87	5	148
	Middle Specialty	314			3	15	89	196	11	314
	Large	106			1	3	29	70	3	106
	Luxury	164			1	6	46	104	7	164
	Other Programs	208			3	19	65	114	7	208

1986	Compact Specialty	139				1	4	36	98	139
	Other Programs	246				4	12	63	167	246
1987	Programs	1,057					5	32	302	339
1988	Programs	1,446						7	58	65
1989	Programs	805							3	3
	TOTAL CAR PROGRAMS	$ 8,422	$521	$ 655	$532	$ 712	$ 954	$ 827	$666	$4,867
			$2,420				$2,447			
	MEMO: Powertrain Programs	$ 2,491	$329	$ 390	$401	$ 382	$ 426	$ 244	$167	$2,339
	TOTAL (incl. Powertrain)	$10,913	$850	$1,045	$933	$1,094	$1,380	$1,071	$833	$7,206

Source: Chrysler Corporation, "Analysis of Chrysler Corporation's Situation and Proposal for Government Assistance," September 15, 1979, p. 42.

EXHIBIT 18: The Chrysler Corporation (A)

CHRYSLER CORPORATION
PLANNED EXPENDITURES FOR CALENDAR YEARS 1979–1985—TRUCK PROGRAMS

Model Year	*Program*	*Memo: Total Lifetime Expenditure*	*1979–1985 Calendar Year Expenditures—$ Millions* 1979	1980	1981	1982	1983	1984	1985	*Total*
1979	Standard Van/Wagon	$ 88	$ 5	$	$	$	$	$	$	$ 5
	Other Programs	35	2							2
1980	Programs	53	44	1						45
1981	Standard Pickup/Sport Utility	61	14	44	2					60
	Other Programs	44	12	29	1					42
1982	Programs	48	1	11	32	2				46
1983	Small Pickup/Sport Utility	593	5	33	230	314	11			593
	Other Programs	77		2	29	40	6			77
1984	Programs	47			2	11	32	2		47
1985	Programs	81				1	28	49	3	81
1986	Small Van/Wagon	774				13	26	302	433	774
	Other Programs	43				2	4	11	26	43
1987	Programs	410					2	9	106	117
1988	Programs	337						5	13	18
1989	Programs	591							3	3
	TOTAL TRUCK PROGRAMS	$3,282	$83	$120	$296	$383	$109	$378	$584	$1,953
			$882 (1979–1982)				$1,071 (1983–1985)			
	MEMO: Powertrain Programs	$ 430	$16	$ 71	$156	$ 70	$ 55	$ 54	$ —	$ 422
	TOTAL (incl. Powertrain)	$3,712	$99	$191	$452	$453	$164	$432	$584	$2,375

Source: Chrysler Corporation, "Analysis of Chrysler Corporation's Situation and Proposal for Government Assistance," September 15, 1979, p. 43.

> [Chrysler] would be protected against its creditors, and temporarily relieved of its burden of debt. The Company could fire unproductive managers, shed its unprofitable lines, continue to make cars and provide employment, and with any luck emerge a few years later a leaner, healthier company. "Chrysler will probably still be in business if it doesn't get any government help—just a smaller company than it is today," one analyst argued.[31]

Some of Chrysler's bankers were openly promoting bankruptcy as the preferable solution. One New York banker observed, "A reorganization could bring 70¢ to 80¢ on the dollar. With the government in, we don't know what our chances of recovery would be." Exhibit 19 outlines the provisions of Chapter XI of the Federal Bankruptcy Act.

Leaders of the UAW and key members of the Senate including Majority Leader Robert C. Byrd (D. W. Va.) and Russell Long (D. La.), chairman of the Senate Finance Committee, had suggested that government aid ought to be contingent on Chrysler workers' being able to own a chunk of the corporation, or at least to influence decision-making "at all levels of the corporation," as the UAW put it.

The White House had expressed interest in using employee stock ownership plans (ESOP) and White House aides had discussed the concept with ESOP experts. Two options were under discussion in the Senate:

> Under Long's tentative plans, Chrysler would have to set up an ESOP and give it 10 per cent to 20 per cent of company equity in new stock in return for federal loan guarantees. . . . [Byrd] proposes that Chrysler form an employee trust which would borrow money and transfer it to the company through some kind of debt instrument that could be converted into Chrysler stock. One Senate staff estimate figures that $1 billion in equity would give the trust about a one-third interest in the corporation.[32]

In the August 25, 1979, issue of *Nation* magazine Robert Lekachman endorsed Treasury acquisition of an equity interest in Chrysler:

> The virtues of Federal ownership of new, voting common stock are easily identified. As an owner, the U.S. Government will enjoy the privileges of other owners. Like any major stockholder, it will nominate one or several members of the board of directors. Through their agency, it will acquire detailed access to operational information and a strong influence over corporate investment and product policies. This is probably the most promising avenue of gradual socialization of the American economy. In the grim economic environment of the next decade, Chrysler will be only the first of numerous chances for the Government to become an active partner of corporate enterprise.[33]

THE OPPOSITION TO AIDING CHRYSLER

From July to September, 1979, Chrysler's request for federal assistance was continually in the news. Opposition to the plan was widespread, based on several philosophies. Some businessmen opposed the general principle of a federal at-

[31] *Newsweek,* August 13, 1979, p. 56.
[32] *Business Week,* October 1, 1979, p. 46. "Labor's Quid Pro Quo in the Chrysler Rescue."
[33] *Nation,* August 25, 1979, p. 133. "Saving Chrysler" by Robert Lekachman.

EXHIBIT 19: The Federal Bankruptcy Law

Under Chapter XI of the Federal Bankruptcy Act unsecured creditors agree to reduce the total amount of their claims, to extend the original time of payment, or both. The business continues to operate because the purpose of Chapter XI is to rehabilitate the business.

Proceedings under Chapter XI can only be initiated by the debtor. He/she files a petition in federal district court, stating that he/she is insolvent *or* unable to pay his/her debts as they mature. The debtor is usually allowed to continue in control of the business.

While a creditor may request that the court appoint a trustee, the court does not automatically do so. The creditor must prove the debtor should be disqualified on the basis of fraud or other similar serious charges, or convince the court that appointment of a trustee is in the best interest of the creditors.

The debtor in possession is generally granted 120 days to file a Plan of Arrangement, outlining steps for company reorganization that the court considers acceptable.

The court may appoint accountants to examine the books and records and appraisers to evaluate the firm both as a going concern and at liquidation value. This valuation gives the creditors more evidence by which to judge the proposed arrangement. The SEC acts in an advisory capacity in determining whether adequate disclosure is being made.

After the petition has been filed, the case goes to a referee who notifies the creditors of the date of the first meeting and sends them the proposed arrangement and schedules of the debtor's assets and liabilities. At the first meeting, proofs of claims are received and allowed or disallowed. The debtor must be present and make his books and records available for examination. A creditor's committee usually is elected if the debtor remains in possession of the business. Creditors and stockholders with distinct or separate interests can form individual committees that may examine the debtor before the referee, investigate the debtor's affairs, act as watchdogs over the operation of the business during the proceedings, and recommend to creditors that the arrangement be accepted or rejected.

After the first meeting of creditors has been adjourned, the creditors will meet to evaluate the debtor's plan in light of his testimony and other information made available at the first meeting. The creditors or the debtor may submit revised plans and negotiate with one another in subsequent court-supervised meetings. Once a suitable arrangement has been drafted, the plan is submitted to the creditors for their formal acceptance. A majority of *voting* creditors must approve the plan, and they must be creditors representing two-thirds of the debt or other interests of voting creditors. All creditors are aware that abstention may mean approval.

If the creditors accept the plan, it will be confirmed by the court if the provisions of Chapter XI have been complied with; the plan is in the best interests of the creditors and is "feasible"; the debtor has not been guilty of any acts which would be a bar to the discharge of a bankruptcy; and the proposal and its acceptance are in good faith. An arrangement is considered feasible if it is anticipated that the debtor will probably be able to follow through and emerge as a solvent enterprise.

The debtor is permitted to use collateral (excluding cash collateral) in the ordinary course of business. Cash collateral cannot be used without court authority or consent of each interested party.

Several provisions of Chapter XI can help the debtor during the Chapter XI phase of operations. For example, leases can be cancelled with only a three year payment

EXHIBIT 19: (continued)

penalty. The company can also obtain new lines of credit that allow a continuation of the business. Several companies have used these provisions to continue the business, and emerge as solvent, operating companies.

An arrangement in bankruptcy, when confirmed by the court, is binding on *all* unsecured creditors on the theory that the arrangement is "in the best interests of the creditors." Although Chapter XI proceedings do not affect agreements between a debtor and his secured creditors, debtors often enter into a voluntary arrangement with the secured creditors while implementing a Chapter XI arrangement with unsecured creditors.

---

tempt to rescue a failing private company. The possibility of setting an unfortunate precedent worried other executives. Some observers were concerned that Chrysler's situation was beyond repair from any quarter, and that federal loans would only forestall the inevitable.

The minority that favored assistance did so out of concern for possible job losses, some accepting Chrysler's premise that the government had created the company's problems.

> The ensuing debate [about federal assistance] quickly linked some unlikely allies and prompted some undiplomatic rhetoric. Consumerist Ralph Nader found himself agreeing with conservative economist Milton Friedman that Chrysler should fend for itself. But when General Motors Chairman Thomas A. Murphy weighed in on the same side, United Auto Workers president Douglas A. Fraser snapped: "Murphy is a horse's ass. He hasn't got any goddam business injecting himself into this!"[34]

Alfred H. Kingon, editor of *Financial World,* was typical of those who opposed any federal assistance to private business. In his July 15, 1979, editorial, "Chrysler and the Kremlin" he wrote:

> It would be one thing if Chrysler was an isolated instance, but it is simply one more example of a long and growing list of companies who, literally, cry "Uncle" when their failures catch up with them. And unless we stop the wave very soon, our concept of this nation as a capitalist or free-market economy will simply be a monumental self-deception.

Phil R. North, President of Tandy Corp., went further.

> The government should be trying to . . . help its winners instead of . . . help the losers. If government would pay as much attention to helping GM compete worldwide as they do to help Chrysler, which is only the victim of mismanagement, then GM might be selling a lot more cars abroad.[35]

Concern about possible job losses caused Howard S. Clark, a member of the executive committee of American Express Co., who was once a director of Chrysler, to change his mind. A self-described "political conservative," Mr. Clark initially opposed aid to Chrysler as an unsound practice but came to favor it:

> Government has become involved in lots of ways in business. Government spends as much as $15,000 per person training people for jobs, and here it has a chance

[34] *Newsweek,* August 13, p. 52.

[35] *Wall Street Journal,* September 17, 1979, p. 1. "Many Executives Oppose . . . Plea."

by guaranteeing loans for Chrysler to save 400,000 jobs. That's a pretty efficient way to go about maintaining employment levels.[36]

Walter D. Scott, executive vice-president for administration and finance at Pillsbury Co., believed that the government "should undertake a quick review of what its regulations are costing . . . and change the regulations if the benefits don't justify the costs."

Executives at GM and Ford heartily agreed. GM was not "opposed to federal government assistance . . . so long as the aid is in the form of relief from the excess burden of regulation and is applicable to all automotive companies," said Thomas A. Murphy, chairman. "The thought of my company's taxes being used as an incentive to sell against me doesn't give me a warm and comfortable feeling," commented Ford executive vice-president William O. Bourke.[37]

Former Treasury Secretary William E. Simon and other businessmen opposed to a bailout had formed the Council for a Competitive Economy in September 1979, to lobby against government aid, taking out newspaper advertisements to promote their opposition.

One disaffected former Chrysler financial analyst was cited by the *New York Times* on August 17, 1979, to the effect that the amount Chrysler would actually require to achieve a turnaround would be in the $7 billion to $8 billion range.

SURVIVAL PLAN REJECTED

On September 15, 1979, in a post-meeting news conference, Secretary Miller immediately rejected the proposal. Miller indicated that the government was unwilling to become the company's dominant financier. He repeated his intention to hold federal loan guarantees to no more than $750 million. Apparently one reason Chrysler's request was so high and Miller's rejection so swift was because the plan did not contain firm commitments of help from the UAW, local governments from areas where Chrysler had plants, the company's banks, or major suppliers. The Administration repeated its demand for Chrysler to secure financial aid from all quarters as part of its survival plan. On September 17, the *Wall Street Journal* noted:

> There are some signs that the Treasury's opposition . . . didn't completely surprise the company's management. . . . Aiming much higher and being turned down mightn't be bad for the auto maker in the long run, however. It has been clear for some time that any rescue plan is going to face tough opposition in Congress. And the final plan that goes to Congress will need active support of the administration if it is to have any chance for success, most observers agree. By shooting down two successive Chrysler proposals as excessive, the Treasury may be able to argue when it finally does go to Capital Hill that it has squeezed the Chrysler aid plan down to the bare minimum.[38]

[36] Ibid., p. 24.
[37] Ibid.
[38] *Wall Street Journal,* September 17, 1979, p. 2. "Miller Rejects Chrysler's Aid Plan."

MANAGEMENT CHANGES

On September 17, 1979, two days after Chrysler's meeting with Treasury officials, in a move which surprised industry observers, Riccardo announced his resignation as chairman and chief executive officer. His strenuous efforts in Washington on Chrysler's behalf had aggravated a heart condition that had surfaced earlier in the year.

In a statement quoted in the *Wall Street Journal* Riccardo said,

> In the minds of many, I am closely associated with the past management of a troubled company. It would be most unfair to the new management . . . if my continued presence as Chairman should in any way hinder the final passage of our request.[39]

It was understood that Riccardo made his assessment of the situation and his decision to step down on his own. Chrysler officials declared that neither Chrysler's directors, bankers, or the government had pressured Riccardo to leave.

On September 20, 1979, Lee A. Iacocca was elected chairman and chief executive officer by Chrysler's board of directors. Iacocca's control was strengthened when two of his long-time associates at Ford Motor Company who had recently joined him at Chrysler were named as president and executive vice-president, finance.

Replacing Iacocca as president and chief operating officer was J. Paul Bergmoser, a 63-year-old former Ford Motor purchasing vice-president. Bergmoser came out of retirement early in 1979 to join Iacocca.

The third member of the team was Gerald Greenwald who was elected to the new post of executive vice-president, finance. Greenwald, 44, had been lured from the presidency of Ford's Venezuelan subsidiary in May to join Iacocca at Chrysler.

In an interview following his appointment Iacocca indicated he would be spending "at least half" of his time running the company, and the rest negotiating with federal officials. "I came to run an auto show" he said flatly. "I don't want to do it in Washington. I'd rather do it in Detroit."

Iacocca was known not to be keen on the idea of turning to the government to help resolve Chrysler's financing crisis. At a press conference held in Detroit the week before Chrysler's proposal was submitted to Secretary Miller, Iacocca candidly said that going to the government for money "gets you in a bureaucratic and political tangle, and I don't like it. That should be stronger—I detest it."

Nevertheless, Iacocca had reluctantly conceded that Chrysler's deep trouble required some type of outside help. Chrysler's financial crisis was ". . . more than we're able to bear," he said. "Hell, I don't care what form [the aid] takes now. I'm very innovative."

It had fallen to Iacocca to prepare the plan which Secretary Miller would accept—a plan that had to include cash flow data on a month-to-month basis, information on concessions by the United Auto Workers union, and the names of the sources the company planned to tap in its borrowing.

[39]*Wall Street Journal,* September 18, 1979, p. 3. "Chrysler's Riccardo to Quit This Week."

BIBLIOGRAPHY

ARNOLD, JASPER H. and MICHAEL L. TENNICAN, "A Brief Note on Arrangements, Bankruptcy and Reorganizations in Bankruptcy," 1972. The President and Fellows of Harvard College.

EASTON, ELMER, "Surviving Bankruptcy," *INC.* December, 1979, pp. 12–17.

WECHSLER, JILL, "Bankruptcy: A New Ball Game?" *Dun's Review.* April, 1978, pp. 98–101.

CASE THIRTY-ONE

Georgia Federal Savings and Loan Association (A)

WILLIAM R. BOULTON and JAMES A. VERBRUGGE
University of Georgia

Assignment Questions:

1. How has Georgia Federal's strategy changed? How would you evaluate it?
2. How do the financial statements reflect competitors' strategies?
3. How would you evaluate Georgia Federal's alternatives for the future?

As was common throughout the savings and loan industry, by August, 1981, the management of Georgia Federal Savings and Loan Association was taking steps to counter the affects of deregulation and high interest rates. John B. Zellars, president and chief executive officer of the largest savings and loan in the state of Georgia explained (see Exhibits 1 and 2 for financial statements):

> We're in the highest risk business in the world—to borrow short and lend long. We did it for 40 years until double digit inflation and interest rates would not allow it to function. Now, we're changing our philosophy, or should I say we're changing our game plan. Three weeks from now, during our next planning session, we'll define what we want this institution to be in three years. What we want, as quickly as we can make it happen, is to reduce our interest sensitive risks. That means that rather than being 85 per cent loaned out, we're probably going to be 60 per cent.

Richard P. Trotter, senior vice-president, treasurer, and corporate planner of Georgia Federal, explained further:

> If we're going to survive in this business, we'll have to restructure our assets and liabilities, and that just suggests becoming more like a bank. I don't see a successful traditional S&L scenario!

EXHIBIT 1: Georgia Federal Savings and Loan Association (A)
Financial Statements for 1979–1980

STATEMENTS OF FINANCIAL CONDITION
DECEMBER 31, 1980 AND 1979

Assets	*1980*	*1979*
	(In thousands)	
First mortgage loans	$1,461,616	1,303,633
Other loans	28,547	33,884
Cash and investment securities	223,387	153,533
Federal Home Loan Bank stock	12,038	10,963
Office properties	18,324	15,019
Real estate owned	2,162	1,529
Investment in wholly owned subsidiaries	11,221	6,105
Other assets	25,847	11,909
	$1,783,142	1,536,575

Liabilities, Deferred Income and Retained Earnings		
Savings deposits	1,480,761	1,285,736
Federal Home Loan Bank advances	138,271	107,721
Loans in process	22,244	17,965
Other liabilities	21,642	11,653
	1,662,918	1,423,075
Deferred income	14,807	13,151
Retained earnings	105,417	100,349
	$1,783,142	1,536,575

STATEMENTS OF EARNINGS AND RETAINED EARNINGS
DECEMBER 31, 1980 AND 1979

	1980	*1979*
	(In thousands)	
Interest income:		
Loans	$127,005	111,255
Other	27,923	18,194
Total interest income	154,928	129,449
Interest expense:		
Savings	122,284	89,435
Other	12,556	10,447
Total interest expense	134,840	99,882
Gross margin on investments	20,088	29,567
Loan fees and other income	5,808	5,340
	25,896	34,907
Operating expenses	19,655	17,680

EXHIBIT 1: (continued)

	1980	1979
	(In thousands)	
Earnings before Federal income taxes	6,241	17,227
Federal income taxes	1,854	4,900
Net earnings	4,387	12,327
Retained earnings, beginning of year	100,349	88,022
Retained earnings of acquired association	681	
Retained earnings, end of year	$105,417	100,349

EXHIBIT 2: Georgia Federal Savings and Loan Association (A)
Sources and Uses of Funds Statement 1979–1980

STATEMENTS OF CHANGES IN FINANCIAL POSITION
YEARS ENDED DECEMBER 31, 1980 AND 1979

	1980	1979
	(In thousands)	
Sources of funds:	$ 4,387	12,327
Net earnings		
Noncash items:		
Interest accrued or credited to savings accounts	78,949	65,773
Depreciation and amortization expense	1,355	1,385
Funds provided from operations	84,691	79,485
Principal payments on first mortgage loans	99,976	122,517
Net savings deposits	89,029	14,084
Federal Home Loan Bank advances	48,200	45,181
	$321,896	261,267
Uses of funds:		
Investment in first mortgage loans	228,891	198,405
Repayment of Federal Home Loan Bank advances	19,850	19,590
Increase in cash and investment securities	69,854	32,675
Other, net	4,645	10,597
Acquired association's assets and liabilities:		
Loans	26,332	—
Other assets, excluding cash	917	—
Savings deposits	(25,712)	—
Federal Home Loan Bank advances	(2,200)	—
Net worth	(681)	—
	$321,896	261,267

HISTORY AND BACKGROUND

Georgia Federal Savings began as Atlanta Building and Loan Association on March 8, 1928. In 1933, a year when loans totalled little more than $20,000, Columbia Building and Loan Association merged into Atlanta Building and Loan. In 1935, Atlanta Building and Loan was coverted into a federal association and became Atlanta Federal Savings with assets of almost $600,000.

By 1936, assets topped one million dollars and Atlanta Federal moved into an old bank building in central Atlanta which had become available when Citizens and Southern Bank moved their offices to their acquired Atlanta Trust Company facilities. The vacated facilities, including teller counters and vault, were in an excellent location as Zellars explained:

> This was the first savings and loan in Atlanta to have a downtown office. There were no other savings and loan buildings of this magnitude. This was an old bank building and we look like a bank. The building gave a great deal of confidence to the people.

By 1940, Atlanta Federal reached three and a half million in assets, and its directors decided to appoint a fulltime manager. W. O. DuVall, a member of the law firm of McElreath, Scott, Duckworth, and DuVall and secretary of the association since 1931, became vice-president, manager, and attorney for Atlanta Federal. A graduate from Young Harris College, the University of Florida, and Atlanta Law School, Du Vall provided strong management and leadership in Atlanta Federal's growth as president from 1950 to 1966 and chairman from 1966 to 1976. In reflecting on his leadership, Zellars commented:

> The leadership in W. O. DuVall was dynamic. That helped us to move forward. There was always a willingness to make changes and to make things happen.

During the war years of the 1940s, Atlanta Federal continued to attract savers and pay interest though opportunity to make loans was limited except in government bonds. Liquidity, however, was readily available to make loans to returning veterans as Zellars recalled:

> This institution did not fail to accept savings during the war years when there were no outlets for it. They went ahead and accumulated capital so that after the war they had a head start on other institutions who did not have sufficient capital.
>
> We went into veteran loans and F.H.A. loans very heavily. I think that gave us a head start.

By 1950, the assets of Atlanta Federal reached 34 million, and management, convinced that the Marietta and Broad Streets location in downtown Atlanta should become its permanent headquarters, purchased the 17-story building. The decade of the fifties showed growth in assets to more than $173 million under the leadership of DuVall as president and McElreath as chairman.

Branch expansion began in 1951 with Atlanta Federal's West End office and continued throughout the Atlanta area. Brookhaven Federal Savings and Loan Association was merged into Atlanta Federal in 1961, and Southeast Savings and Loan Association in Lithonia in 1970 with the merged offices continuing as branches. By 1970, Atlanta Federal had 15 offices around Atlanta serving almost 150,000 savers.

In 1966, Bill Wainwright became the president of Atlanta Federal and was appointed chief executive officer in 1971. A family friend of Mr. DuVall, Mr. Wainwright attended the University of Florida and completed law school after being discharged from the military in 1945. DuVall continued as chairman.

Another important figure in the history of Atlanta Federal was Thomas Hal Clark, director and general counsel for Atlanta Federal until he was appointed by President Nixon in 1969 to a four-year term as a member of the Federal Home Loan Bank Board. Having worked with the United States League and American Bar Association, his experience played an important role during his appointment.

In 1975, John B. Zellars was promoted from executive vice-president to president of Atlanta Federal and developed a more formal approach to managing the $750 million in assets. As Zellars explained:

> We then began the usual management techniques—the planning sessions, the involvement of senior management in the plans, and the establishment of a corporate identity. We established a corporate management plan similar to a holding company which evolved as a result of our expansion into statewide banking with our acquisition of Home Federal of Augusta. I had the responsibility for mergers and became the expert in mergers.

The continued statewide expansion brought about the need for a new image and name for the association as explained by Zellers:

> It seemed to us as we moved into these statewide operations that the name Atlanta Federal was not as acceptable throughout the state as Georgia Federal. We were proud of our name, and it had nothing to do with a lack of identity in this market; but we felt that to have an appropriate statewide identity, it would be better to change the name to Georgia Federal. We did that in 1976.

By mid-1981, Georgia Federal had branches throughout the state including:

Atlanta	32 offices
Augusta	6 offices
Brunswick	2 offices
Columbus	2 offices
Dublin	3 offices
Macon	6 offices
Perry	5 offices
Savannah	5 offices
	61 offices

THE STRATEGY OF GEORGIA FEDERAL

As stated by W. O. DuVall in 1971, "Atlanta Federal is dedicated to the goals of thrift and home ownership and to community service." In 1981, the annual report read:

> To fulfill these purposes, the Association endeavors to provide its customers—the most valuable resource of the Association—with convenient, courteous, competitive and timely service.

With the addition of NOW accounts and consumer loans, Georgia Federal was attempting to reposition their consumer image using a promotion entitled "Can Do." Zellars explained:

> What we're attempting to do today is create an image that the savings and loan business "can do" anything. Everything that we did before was for savings and home ownership. Now we're trying to convince the public that the business is changing and that we can perform any service that you might need.

Georgia Federal's introduction of NOW accounts had proved successful as part of their "Can Do" campaign as Zellars explained:

> We have over $19 million in about 10,500 NOW accounts today. By the end of the year, we project 15,000 NOW accounts. We have a $250 minimum and a $5 fee under that.

With the introduction of NOW accounts, Trotter also saw a need for ATMs in providing consumer checking services:

> If you're going to be a "consumer bank," and we believe that to be a viable strategy, then you had darn well have the ATM capability. You'll find that most people are interested in convenience first. The only way we can make that service really convenient to the customer is not only to have a branch open where they can change accounts around, but also have ATMs.

Don DeLozier, Georgia Federal's group vice-president in charge of the Atlanta division, further explained the importance of ATM capabilities:

> We see the ATM, particularly in the Atlanta market, as essential because Atlanta has the highest usage rate for ATMs. ATMs also add convenience and we're committed to that. The question is what type of network we will have: how many, where, what kind of sharing, and those kinds of questions. There is no question in our minds that we have to have them to provide the services.

In fact, Trotter felt that Georgia Federal's lack of ATMs was restricting their growth in NOW accounts:

> We have the best priced checking account of the largest eight financial institutions in the greater Atlanta area. The only thing that really keeps us from moving ahead is the lack of ATMs. Once we have that, with the best price, a lot of people will switch to us.

Georgia Federal's initial move into ATMs was planned for the coming year. Trotter explained:

> ATMs are a must for an institution of our size. First Atlanta has 27. Trust Company has about 25. C&S has 50. I think you need about 20 to reasonably serve the metro area. I hope we'll be able to install 12 our first year and the balance the second year in existing branches. The next place might be some off-site remote units.
>
> You'll also find ATM interchange networks, not only locally, but nationally with Master Charge, Visa or American Express. If the banks will let them, you would go to any terminal and get money with your credit card. Wisconsin requires that ATMs interchange. We're talking with a commercial bank about interchange right now. I think we'll be able to work something out.

Zellars also explained the caution that Georgia Federal was taking in providing new services:

> We haven't jumped into the total spectrum of services that other institutions have because we're going a little bit slower. What we're trying to do is become as proficient in these new services as we can. We have a young man who formerly worked

for a bank that heads up our consumer lending operation. He came to work in January, so this is just beginning to get underway. If you're going to offer NOW accounts, you have to offer consumer loans, too.

Don DeLozier commented further on their introduction of new services:

> While we're a long way from providing all the new services, we're in an ideal position to provide them in an orderly fashion. I think we've positioned ourselves to implement the services we need and to do it well. It would be advantageous to have them all on stream right now, but its not essential. It takes time for people to become accustomed to the fact that we're a full service financial institution. I think the customer needs some time to recognize the changes and that gives us the time to make the adjustments.

In commenting on Georgia Federal's entrance into consumer loans, DeLozier continued:

> We were slow getting into consumer loans because they're not profitable and because people can obtain them from a number of places. As a result, there is not an overpowering need, and consumer loans won't do that much for our business. We see it as a vehicle to accommodate our deposit base and to accommodate our customers. We have held it to a minimum by only making it available to those who have a deposit relationship with us.
>
> From the asset side, consumer loans are short-term, and we like that; but everything is going to be short-term from now on. In fact, from our new perspective, consumer loans will turn out to be long-term investments.

While Georgia Federal moves to expand consumer services, Zellars planned to continue the "Can Do" campaign:

> We're going to stick with this "Can Do" campaign because we feel it is building a corporate image with the people we're trying to serve. Its done a lot for our name, too. People are now beginning to recognize the Georgia Federal name.

STATEWIDE OPERATIONS

The major element of Georgia Federal's continued expansion had been its success at acquiring and merging with S&Ls throughout the state. Zellars explained Georgia Federal's expansion strategy:

> We felt that mergers would give force in the way that branches did. Branches react by either producing capital or using capital. Mergers across the state offer either the utilization or creation of capital. We felt that by going statewide, we would have a greater diversity in accumulating capital or disbursing capital than if we stayed in the Atlanta market. Having an operation in Atlanta, in addition to statewide facilities, offered some added convenience to people coming into Atlanta or going out into other areas.
>
> The map (Exhibit 3) shows the areas where we are currently involved. Most of the counties around Atlanta have branches or multi-branches of Georgia Federal. In middle-Georgia we're fairly well covered—the merger with Home in Macon will give us a tremendous focus there. We cover the South Carolina line with Augusta and Savannah, and then down the coast to Brunswick. Savannah and Brunswick are our coastal branching operations. On the Alabama line, we have Columbus. So we're coving all but two SMSA's in the state. We may expand into other areas, too.

EXHIBIT 3: Georgia Federal Savings and Loan Association (A) Statewide Branch Operations

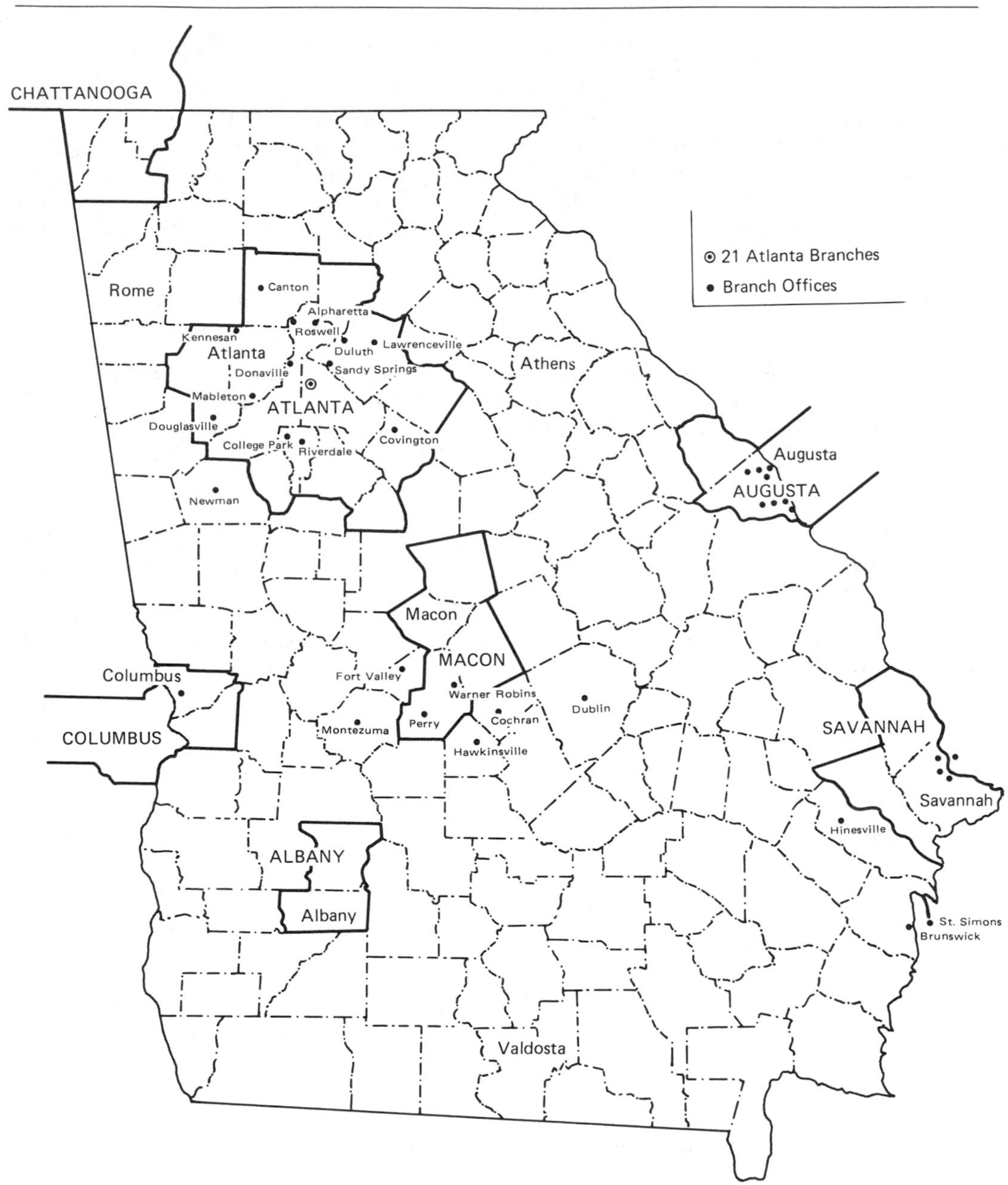

Trotter, as corporate planner, commented further on Georgia Federal's statewide expansion:

> We want to operate in the major market areas in the state of Georgia, and those markets, in some cases, jump across state lines like Columbus-Phoenix City, Augusta-North Augusta, Savannah-Hilton Head. The approach is to piggyback off those ongoing operations. If there is an S&L near one of our existing locations we

may consider it. If its 200 miles from any office that we have, we would probably wait on it. Its building on existing locations that we want.

GEORGIA FEDERAL'S PERFORMANCE

To keep track of Georgia Federal's overall operating performance, top management joined with 14 of the largest savings and loan associations in the United States to compare performance. As a result of this involvement, Georgia Federal's management felt they understood their major strengths and weaknesses. Trotter explained the differences between Georgia Federal's operations and the 14 peer groups associations:

> We exchange every conceivable ratio under the sun on a corporate basis with the peer group. Our first mortgage income has not been as high as the peer group because Georgia's usury restrictions have kept the yield on our portfolio low. However, we have a higher yield from investment and deposit income because of our liquidity. We also haven't emphasized consumer loan income as much as the peer group. We have a complete package in consumer loans, but have been late in getting it out (Exhibit 4).
>
> Our cost of funds has also been higher. Our interest on deposits, for example, has been 7.415 per cent compared to 7.068 per cent for the peer group. The reason for this difference, we found, is that the Atlanta market area has the highest cost of money of any major metropolitan market. There has been a lot of building and development here, and, consequently, there is a marked difference in the cost of money. When you match that against the lower investment yield resulting from the usury laws, it really creates a problem.
>
> Our "other income" is not as high because the peer group associations are more involved in subsidiary service corporation activities. That is an area that we're beginning to give more emphasis.
>
> When you look at expenses, you'll note that no one really comes close to us. That's because this association has, under W. O. and John, operated with very low overhead. We just do more with fewer people. Our fixed asset ratio is also .057 compared to .149 for the peer group. That's a non-earning asset, except for rental property. W. O. keeps that fixed asset schedule down in his right front drawer and he can tell you to the penny how much has ever been invested in fixed assets. We've written furniture and fixtures off until this year. Everything except the computer was written off to one dollar, but we're not doing that anymore.
>
> Another reason for our low occupancy expense is our horizontal branch site development strategy. We buy the land, build the branch, and then build a shopping center around it. The Federal Home Loan Bank Board has raised some questions about that sort of branch development; but, with Georgia Federal being the kind of institution it is, they have never done anything. It has been extremely profitable, along with some other real estate holdings.

In comparing Georgia Federal's portfolio with the peer group (Exhibit 5), Trotter continued:

> Our certificates are 84 per cent of total savings compared to 80 per cent for the peer group. The reason is that Atlanta's an aggressive savings market. If you compare us against the peer group members, you'd find that the only other institution even approaching Georgia Federal in cost of funds and certificates to total savings is in Dallas, Texas. No other market is like that, not Los Angeles, Seattle or Denver.

EXHIBIT 4: Georgia Federal Savings and Loan Association (A)
Operating Analysis
Georgia Federal vs. National Peer Group
1980

Each as Per Cent of Average Assets	*Georgia Federal*	*Peer Group Average*
Investment Income:		
First Mortgage Loans	7.423%	7.631%
Investment & Deposits	1.666%	1.112%
Profit (Loss) on Sale of Securities	0.002%	0.008%
Consumer Loans	0.235%	0.439%
Total Investment Income	9.326%	9.190%
Cost of Funds:		
Interest on Deposits	7.415%	7.068%
Interest on Notes Payable	0.761%	1.269%
Total Cost of Funds	8.176%	8.337%
Margin on Investment	1.150%	0.853%
Other Income:		
Fees: Loan Origination	0.219%	0.294%
Fees: Other	0.000%	0.111%
Other Operating Income	0.103%	0.234%
Total Income Less Cost of Funds	1.472%	1.492%
Expenses: Compensation & Benefits	0.531%	0.668%
Building Occupancy	0.057%	0.149%
Advertising	0.134%	0.121%
Furniture & Equipment	0.098%	0.131%
Other	0.244%	0.262%
Total Operating Expenses	1.064%	1.331%
Non-Operating Expenses	0.015%	−0.148%
Profit Before Tax	0.393%	0.308%
Taxes on Income	0.117%	0.089%
Net Income	0.276%	0.218%

In making mortgage loan comparisons with the peer group (Exhibit 6), Trotter explained:

> Georgia Federal's single family mortgages are 84 per cent of total loans compared to 69 per cent for the peer group. We've always been a single family lender. These other institutions have emphasized other investments. The Seattle association, for example, has a lot of commercial apartments which has helped its performance over the past several years. The problem with the single family market today is that those loans are long term and are hurting our performance because of their low yields.

EXHIBIT 5: Georgia Federal Savings and Loan Association (A)
Portfolio Analysis
Georgia Federal vs. National Peer Group
1980

	Georgia Federal	*Peer Group Average*
Weighted Average Mortgage Portfolio Yield	9.44%	9.60%
Average Portfolio Yield		
Mortgage Loans w/o fees	8.90%	9.25%
Mortgage Loans w/fees	9.16%	9.60%
Total Portfolio Yield w/fees	9.24%	9.70%
Certificates/Total Savings	84.28%	80.38%
Average Cost of Total Savings	8.84%	8.95%
Average Cost of FHLB Advances	9.76%	10.18%
Average Cost of Total Funds	8.95%	9.02%
Liquid Investments Portfolio Yield		
w/o gain (loss)	12.56%	11.52%
w/gain (loss)	12.57%	11.60%

GEORGIA FEDERAL'S COMPETITION

With the continued deregulation of financial institutions, Georgia Federal's competition was increasing. Trotter now saw their major competitors becoming commercial banks as he explained:

> We have always looked at Fulton Federal and Decatur Federal as major savings and loan competitors. Now we also look at the commercial banks—C&S, Trust Company and First Atlanta.

Trotter compared the financial results of Fulton Federal and Decatur Federal with that of Georgia Federal as shown in Exhibits 7, 8, and 9. He commented on the different strategies:

> Georgia Federal's lower loan growth is a result of our decision at the end of last year not to continue originating mortgage loans. That is a fundamental difference between us and Decatur Federal. Decatur has a ratio of about 110 percent between mortgages and deposits compared to our 90 percent. We have decided to restructure and shorten up our assets and have been aggressively working on that for nearly a year.
>
> Decatur Federal has continued to stay in the mortgage business and, as a result, it is showing up in their operating performance. For the first six months of this year, Georgia Federal's loss was about 40 percent of Decatur and Fulton Federal's losses (Exhibit 9). They each lost over five percent of their net worth in the first six months and we lost 2.2 percent. With Decatur's strategy, I think the loss will be accentuated in the next six months. We're predicting that they will each lose between 12 and 15 percent of their net worth this year. We'll lose between seven and eight percent. The difference comes from strategy. We have more liquid assets and our asset structure is far shorter than theirs.

EXHIBIT 6: Georgia Federal Savings and Loan Association (A)
Profitability, Balance Sheet, and Loan Analysis
Georgia Federal Vs. National Peer Group

	Georgia Federal	*Peer Group Average*
Net Income/Total Income	2.828%	2.172%
Return on Average Net Worth	4.169%	4.075%
Return on Beginning Net Worth	4.313%	4.249%
Return on Average Assets	0.276%	0.218%
Yield-Cost Spread	0.212%	0.537%
Yield-Cost Spread: Including Consumer Loans	0.283%	0.632%
Average Assets/Average Net Worth	15.100%	18.663%
Total Liquid/Total Deposits	14.985%	14.346%
Net Worth/Total Deposits	7.622%	6.652%
Borrowed Funds/Total Deposits	9.338%	17.370%
Mortgage Loans/Total Deposits	97.846%	102.856%
Total Loans/Total Deposits	98.138%	106.771%
As % of Total Loans:		
Single Family	84.158%	69.834%
2–4 Dwelling Units	1.177%	4.074%
Over 4	2.285%	9.461%
Other Real Estate	6.895%	6.633%
Consumer Loans	0.288%	3.524%
GNMA & FHLMC	2.722%	4.024%
Other	2.475%	2.450%
Mortgage Portfolio Turnover	7.484%	10.225%
—Including Refinancing	8.260%	10.782%
Purchase (Sales)/Loan Origination	16.185%	−10.856%
Loans Serviced By Others/Total Loans	13.080%	12.026%
Loans Serviced For Others/Total Loans	9.817%	18.810%
Slow Loans/Total Loans	0.068%	0.698%
Scheduled Items/Assets	0.331%	0.729%
Scheduled Items/Net Worth	5.189%	13.925%
#Employees per $1M in Savings	0.364%	0.460%

The difference between fee income for Georgia Federal and Decatur Federal also shows Decatur's emphasis on mortgage lending. We have made our income from our liquidity. It has increased $70 million so far this year and we expect it to increase another $40 to $50 million before year end. We have an average yield of nearly 15 per cent on over $300 million. That gave us nearly $3.7 million last month compared to $1.4 million net from our mortgage portfolios. If we could just add another 15 per cent in liquidity, we could ride this thing out. Our expenses are rock bottom and advertising is the only expense where we approach the others.

Deregulation, however, was now requiring that savings and loans be more competitive with commercial banks. This would require some basic restructuring of Georgia Federal's assets and liabilities as Trotter explained:

EXHIBIT 7: Georgia Federal Savings and Loan Association (A)
Comparative Summary Performance Statistics
Georgia Federal, Fulton Federal, Decatur Federal 1979, 1980

	Return on Average Assets		*Return on Average Equity*		*Assets*	
	1980	*1979*	*1980*	*1979*	*1980 (000,000)*	*1979*
Georgia Federal	0.27%	0.88%	4.15%	13.17%	$1,794	$1,545
Fulton Federal	0.09%	0.64%	1.71%	11.77%	1,140	1,104
Decatur Federal	0.22%	0.86%	3.38%	13.01%	1,187	1,057

	Borrowings/ Total Assets		*Net Worth/ Total Assets*	
	1980	*1979*	*1980*	*1979*
Georgia Federal	7.7%	7.0%	6.3%	6.8%
Fulton Federal	7.1%	9.3%	5.5%	5.5%
Decatur Federal	5.1%	6.2%	6.1%	6.7%

	Savings Growth		*Loan Growth*	
	1980	*1979*	*1980*	*1979*
Georgia Federal	12.8%	6.3%	8.7%	6.9%
Fulton Federal	7.3%	6.3%	5.3%	8.9%
Decatur Federal	14.7%	9.3%	13.5%	12.1%

If you compare the three or four major commercial banks in Atlanta with the savings and loans, they are 50 per cent loaned out and we're 85 per cent loaned out. When you look at retained earnings, ours are greater than any of the major Atlanta banks. The difference is in the capital account; they have the funds that they raised as a result of their capital issue and they have capital surplus. None of the four large banks in Atlanta have retained earnings over $100 million. So we're in a high equity position.

To reduce loans to the 60 per cent level of the banks, we have to create additional capital. Mortgage lending is going to be different. We're going to match book which means you have to reduce interest sensitive risks as much as possible. For the first time, we have the tools with variable rate mortgages and consumer lending. If we're buying money on 30 months, we ought to lend it on 30 months. If we buy money on 12 months, that ought to be on 12 month loans. The banks know this.

To point out the serious gap between their matching of short term assets and liabilities, Trotter continued:

Every bank tries to match its assets and liabilities which have maturities of under six months. They shoot for a ratio of 1.0. Georgia Federal has a ratio of .26. I think Decatur and Fulton Federal are around .15. Their risk is far greater than ours. Our goal is to ultimately achieve a ratio of .9 between maturing six month assets and six month liabilities. We have a long way to go, but that's the only successful scenario.

We're trying to formalize this objective into our structure with an asset-liability committee. It would look at our interest sensitivity and compare our performance to budget. The monthly balance sheets and operating statements, along with our daily investment report, should give that committee the guidance it needs to do the job.

EXHIBIT 8: Georgia Federal Savings and Loan Association (A)
Comparative Performance Statistics: Average Asset Analysis
Georgia Federal, Fulton Federal, Decatur Federal 1980

	Each as % of Average Assets					
	Interest Income	*Interest Expense*	*Net Interest Margin*	*Total Fees*	*Other Income*	*Non-Interest Income*
Georgia Federal	9.13%	8.01%	1.12%	0.21%	0.21%	0.43%
Fulton Federal	8.70%	7.75%	0.95%	0.37%	0.22%	0.67%
Decatur Federal	8.70%	7.75%	0.95%	0.79%	0.13%	0.92%

	Total Operating Expense	*Compensation & Benefits*	*Office Bldg. Expense*	*Advertising Expense*	*All Other Operating Expenses*
Georgia Federal	1.13%	0.49%	0.23%	0.13%	0.28%
Fulton Federal	1.43%	0.67%	0.32%	0.13%	0.31%
Decatur Federal	1.48%	0.59%	0.32%	0.11%	0.46%

		Liquidity		*Deposit Mix* — *Each as % of Total Deposits*	
	Average Mortgage Yield	*Cash & Invested Securities ÷ Total Assets*	*Total Borrowings ÷ Total Deposits*	*Savings Over $100 million*	*Passbooks*
Georgia Federal	8.7%	12.7%	9.3%	6.7%	15.6%
Fulton Federal	8.8%	5.8%	8.4%	7.4%	16.3%
Decatur Federal	8.7%	4.2%	4.9%	1.0%	14.4%

	Asset Mix — *Each as % of Total Assets*		*Income and Expense as % of Gross Operating Income*			
	Mortgage Loans	*Other Loans*	*Total Interest Income*	*Fees*	*Total Operating Expenses*	*Net Income*
Georgia Federal	81.7%	1.6%	95.8%	2.2%	11.9%	2.8%
Fulton Federal	87.0%	3.7%	94.6%	4.1%	15.5%	1.0%
Decatur Federal	89.9%	3.2%	90.6%	8.2%	15.5%	2.3%

**EXHIBIT 9: Georgia Federal Savings and Loan Association (A)
Balance Sheet Comparisons (Latest Six Months)**

	Georgia			*Decatur*			*Fulton*		
	6/30/81	*12/31/80*	*% Change*	*6/30/81*	*12/31/80*	*% Change*	*6/30/81*	*12/31/80*	*% Change*
Total Assets	1,846,844	1,783,142	3.6	1,238,943	1,187,182	4.4	1,168,816	1,139,799	2.5
Mortgage Loans	1,416,674	1,432,265	−1.1	1,109,478	1,073,703	3.3	1,008,151	979,996	2.9
Total Deposits	1,454,004	1,480,760	4.3	1,017,022	992,160	2.5	971,790	958,856	1.3
Net Worth	110,369	112,864	−2.2	69,045	72,793	−5.1	58,863	62,215	−5.4
Liquidity	299,020	227,312	31.5	60,042	50,440	19.0	66,003	66,640	−0.1
Borrowings	139,421	138,270	0.8	100,462	60,462	66.6	104,564	80,700	29.6

	Ratio		
	Georgia	*Decatur*	*Fulton*
Net Worth/Deposits	7.14	6.79	6.06
Net Worth/Assets	5.92	5.57	5.04
Mortgage Loans/Deposits	91.7	109.1	103.7
Liquidity/Deposits	19.4	5.9	6.8
Borrowing/Deposits	9.0	9.9	
ROA (Authorized)	−.27	−.62	−.58

In addition to restructuring Georgia Federal's balance sheet, the association was going to have increasing competition for future deposits. DeLozier commented on the challenge facing Georgia Federal:

> The most important thing for us is to maintain our share of the market. Its very competitive and we need to provide the services to maintain, build, and increase our market share. At the same time, we need to control our costs, though I don't think we have that much control. That's determined by the market. We need to keep our share of the deposit base in the face of broader based competition.

With regards to other competition from money market trusts, Trotter did not see any serious competition. He explained:

> I think the Merrill Lynch situation will cure itself. It's just a matter of time. Assuming that the government follows through with its plans to deregulate deposits, then we can compete easily and better. The reason for that is that Merrill Lynch may have an office in Atlanta, Athens, and Savannah, but they don't have a hundred offices in Georgia. I think convenience will make the difference. Even if you're automated and have ATMs all over, operating around the clock, the customer has to go talk to someone about their finances once in a while.
>
> We'll be able to compete with the money market funds out of sheer convenience once we have a deregulated structure and can compete with these guys. They aren't under any regulation. Their ability to draft those darn things is no different than having a checking account. Checking accounts are supposed to be under the control of the Fed. As you know, the Fed has been trying to gain control of the money supply since its inception and they made a big step last year. But just as they were reaching their objective, a big slug of about $150 billion slips right out from under their grasp. Now that makes no sense at all. Either we are going to regulate money supply or not. We're either going to have a Fed or not. But, if you give us the ability to compete, we'll do all right.

The deregulation of interest rates paid on 30-month money market certificates, however, was now posing a new problem for the savings and loan associations. Trotter explained:

> The problem is that we pay a differential of 25 basis points above the banks. On top of that, we compound the interest rate while government securities or agency markets pay only simple interest. For example, after they took the 12 percent interest cap off 30 month certificates, every 30 month rate has been over 17 percent compounded interest rate. Well we picked up $58 million in these certificates at an average yield of 17.5 percent, and there hasn't been a reinvestment alternative at higher rates. On top of that, we're losing nearly a million dollars per day in passbook savings and adding over $3 million per day in 30 month certificates.

The continued restructuring of the industry and recently announced interstate merger of three savings and loans concerned Trotter. He explained:

> Those who attempted years ago to eliminate the structural differences between financial institutions in this country are very successful. With the interstate S&L merger between Citizens in San Francisco, Washington in Miami, and Westside in New York, I'm very disturbed. I think the Federal Home Loan Bank Board had to do it because they wanted the S&L industry to solve its own problems. Besides, I don't think the Federal Reserve had the statutory authority to bring about an interstate merger like that. But I think the two problem cases in Florida and New York could have been broken up and spread between viable associations in their areas, or by letting the major commercial banks in those areas absorb them.

EXHIBIT 10: Georgia Federal Savings and Loan Association (A)
Comparative Performance Statistics[1]
Georgia Federal Vs. Major Atlanta Commercial Banks 1980

	George Federal	*Citizens & Southern National Bank*	*Trust Company Banks*	*First National Bank of Atlanta*	*Bank of the South*
Total Deposits (millions)	$ 1,481	$ 2,734	$ 1,276	$ 2,072	$ 708
Return on Average Assets	0.28	0.75	1.32	0.94	0.84
Return on Average Equity	4.17	12.48	21.33	15.70	16.46
Net Interest Spread	0.28[2]	6.10	7.29	7.94	5.37
Total Loans/Total Deposits	98.14	71.00	66.10	60.00	91.00
Savings Deposits/Total Deposits	100.00	48.10	35.30	41.40	50.50
Retained Earnings	$ N.A.	$ 97,721	$ 100,370	$ 69,472	$ 39,715
Total Capital	$ 112,864	$ 250,703	$ 186,726	$ 173,344	$ 65,085
Total Assets	$1,793,710	$4,340,720	$3,111,837	$3,147,111	$1,268,112
Retained Earnings/Total Assets	N.A.	.0225	.0323	.0221	.0313
Total Capital/Total Assets		.0578	.0600	.0551	.0513
Capital/Total Assets	6.29	4.95	5.25	6.81	6.31

[1]Numbers may not be directly comparable due to slight differences in definitions between commercial bank and S&L data.
[2]Defined as total portfolio yield less average cost of funds.
NA = not available.

> Setting up a national savings and loan now sets precedent for the big banks to go anywhere in the United States. This merger will also allow industrial corporations to get into the banking business, because Citizens is owned by National Steel. Sears and Roebuck owns Allstate Savings which is the 12th or 13th largest in the U.S. It's now possible for them to buy S&Ls all over the U. S. I think it could lead to 10 or 12 major banks in the U. S. It could end up like Europe or Canada where you have a few huge banks.

PLANNING FOR THE FUTURE

To plan for Georgia Federal's future in their rapidly changing environment, Zellars had involved his key managers in the strategic planning process. Planning sessions were important at Georgia Federal as he explained:

> Each year we conduct three or four corporate planning sessions. In addition to the senior vice-presidents that are involved in this, other people may be included depending on the focus of the session. Of course, in every corporate plan, you have to make certain assumptions; the environmental assumptions that you're going to operate under in that particular year, and assumptions about the most important things that will determine the priorities of the institution. Those have changed rather drastically year after year.
>
> We look at the environment that we have to deal with and then develop alternative strategies. For example, we have strategies for maximizing lending activities, using secondary markets, selling new loans, selling our loan portfolio, buying loans at discount, low interest loan tax swaps, development of aggressive construction loan programs, promoting second mortgages for home improvements, below market refinancing of customers with low interest rate mortgages, offering discounts for early payoffs on low interest mortgages, and renegotiable mortgage

rates when they become available. We try to go into each section of the business and establish programs which will be carried out in that year. At the same time, we realize that these things are going to change.

In analyzing the current environment facing Georgia Federal, a number of options had been discussed in their recent planning sessions. Trotter explained:

> We have looked at the options facing a savings and loan association today. There are really only four or five options: to continue as a traditional S&L; to become a mortgage banker; to become a full service family financial center; to become a commercial bank; or to merge with a large savings and loan. When you look carefully at these, the full service family financial center doesn't really look much different from the retail side of a commercial bank. We have looked at these options and have elected to become a full service family financial center. That may be just an interim step, however, assuming that S&Ls get the remaining commercial bank powers like lending and checking. I imagine those moving in this direction would take the next step and become a commercial bank.
>
> I think there is also a potential mortgage banking scenerio and there are two smaller Atlanta S&Ls following that strategy: Home Federal and United Federal. Home Federal is quite successful at it. We tried to merge with them years ago, but the Federal Home Loan Bank turned it down for antitrust reasons. I don't think they would do that today.

In commenting on continuing past merger activity, DeLozier explained:

> We would like to cover the whole state better than we do now. We want to be in every SMSA and do a more thorough job than we do now. We're not out to merge for merger's sake. We're very selective and we want economies of scale. We know it drains your resources, your people and your management. We look at the market areas and what they have to offer in market share. We look at their resources and what their managers can contribute. We're very selective.

In support of their move into family financial services, Georgia Federal's management was pushing to implement its ATM strategy. Trotter explained:

> We developed our ATM strategy. We are working to share our terminals. For example, I'm talking with American Express about a test in the Atlanta market using remote sites in all major shopping malls. These would dispense cash by using the Tilley Card, the Instant Banking Card, the Can Do Bank Card, and also dispense travelers checks with the American Express Card. We're also continuing to talk with a major commercial bank about sharing their ATMs and, if that doesn't work, we'll go to the larger S&Ls and middle sized commercial banks to develop a sharing effort.

To protect Georgia Federal's balance sheet through the restructuring period, Georgia Federal plans to do more hedging as Trotter explained:

> We have studied hedging and plan to hedge our deposits on the liability side when the time is right. We'll also hedge assets, particularly if we get involved in mortgage banking, and purchase commitments through Fanny Mae.

In addition to these efforts, Georgia Federal's management had taken actions to expand their service company operations. Don DeLozier, group vice-president responsible for the service corporation, explained their strategy:

> The service corporation is one vehicle where we might get some excessive profits to offset our low interest yield on the mortgage portfolio. Our strategy is to try as

many things as we can to make money, to learn, and to find out what we ought to be doing. We don't think there is one answer to the problem. We think it will take a multiplicity of activities. So we're entering into a number of different activities to generate income and experience, and get a better handle on what we ought to be doing.

DeLozier described several of the activities that he was pursuing:

> We have an office park condominium under construction in Cobb County. I bought a branch site and picked up additional land with it at a low cost. We got it rezoned and completed our branch. Now we're starting on the 60 unit condominium office park next to it. The second phase will be 64 units. We plan to sell it to make money. Before we make the permanent loans, we'll make a substantial profit.
>
> We're also breaking ground on a residential condominium. We're still committed to residential housing; but, if we're going to put up all of the money and take all of the risks, we think we're entitled to some of the return. Once we do some of these, we hope to repeat them. We have to get our feet wet.
>
> We have a civil engineering company which did surveys for Georgia Federal. We're doing our own engineering and real estate development on these projects. We will also be providing these services outside. In addition, we have a statewide appraisal for large institutional lenders, and we're entering the home inspection service market for people who want their house inspected prior to purchase. We don't believe the inspection market is being adequately serviced, and its not as mature as the appraisal business.

Regarding the contributions of the service corporation to Georgia Federal, DeLozier stated:

> No one of these activities will solve our problems, but a combination of them could have an impact. They will give us experience in a lot of fields and may give us capabilities we need for the future. I don't know what the future will look like; but, if we have a team with enough capabilities, we'll be able to capitalize on the opportunities when they come along. I see these activities as preparatory for the future, more than impacting the present.

The restructuring of Georgia Federal's balance sheet, however, remained of primary concern to management. Don DeLozier explained:

> The big challenge is to make adjustments in our portfolio, get more rate sensitive investments, and to divest ourselves as soon as possible of fixed rate investments. That's easier said than done, because we're saddled with those fixed rate mortgage contracts and you can't break them. So you have to use that area of your portfolio that is not on fixed rate contracts to generate returns to offset those low interest rate contracts. I see that as the biggest challenge.

Zellars continued:

> The orientation is going to change away from mortgage loans to family financing. Assuming very little new savings, we could bring our mortgage loan balance down $3 or $4 million per month. There is a difference and your total funds will not be in home mortgage, but in family financing.

Another alternative for making a significant change in the structure of their balance sheet was to issue stock. Zellars explained:

> I've always been for a mutual operation on a long-term basis because you can make decisions on a long-term basis that allows your institution to set a better

> foundation for growth. You don't have to make every decision based on the interest of stockholders. I'm changing a little bit now, purely because of the leverage that additional capital would give you. Down the road, as soon as we turn earnings around, you're going to see many conversions to stock. This will also give flexibility to acquire other businesses that you might not otherwise be able to buy.

In considering Georgia Federal's orientation in the future, Zellars concluded:

> Consumers feel that financial institutions should subsidize their needs. Financial institutions can't. We're in a business to make a profit. We have to make a profit.

CASE THIRTY-TWO

Georgia Federal Savings and Loan Association (B)

WILLIAM R. BOULTON and JAMES A. VERBRUGGE
University of Georgia

Assignment Questions:

1. How has statewide expansion affected Georgia Federal?
2. How would you evaluate Georgia Federal's organization? How large can it grow?
3. Will purchase method accounting solve the industry's problems?

John B. Zellars, president of Georgia Federal, believed that an aggressive acquisition strategy would allow his association to more rapidly develop its deposit base. However, the heavy losses being experienced by most savings and loan associations in late 1981 restricted their ability to continue their merger strategy. To overcome this problem, Zellars had submitted an acquisition to the Federal Home Loan Bank Board (FHLBB) using a purchase method of accounting rather than the traditional pooling of interest method. He explained:

> By using the purchase method, you can write the loans down to market, sell the loans, convert them to cash, and recover previously paid income taxes. The resulting goodwill will then be amortized over an extended period of time. The advantages are that you don't have to take the loss on those loans and it helps you match your assets and liabilities.
>
> We recently submitted a merger application requesting the permission to use the purchase method of accounting in the case of a merger of two mutual institutions. This question has never been presented to the FHLBB except in supervisory mergers. In order for the accounting firms to approve the use of the purchase method, it will be necessary to dispose of a significant portion of the assets of the disappearing institution. That suits us just fine.

GEORGIA FEDERAL'S MANAGEMENT AND ORGANIZATION

In 1975, Georgia Federal changed management and John Zellars became the president. His involvement in mergers and statewide expansion lead him to utilizing a divisional concept of management as he explained:

> Our statewide operations originated on the division concept. The division concept was not new, but it was new to the savings and loan business. It had been used by large corporations for a long time. The division concept allowed us to do this expansion because it solved the problem of having local identities within the communities and allowed them to keep their predecesser names—Home Federal as a division of Georgia Federal for example.

Through the divisional structures (see Exhibit 1), Zellars had delegated many responsibilities:

> I think the association really operates without me. We don't have an executive vice-president. It operates through the five senior people that are involved in the corporate organization. The corporate organization includes statewide operations, finance and corporate planning, the Atlanta division, administrative services, and marketing. Each of these people have an elaborate organization under them and they report directly to me. These people are the ones to make things happen. My job is to coordinate these people in an attempt to give some leadership to their operations.

In 1979 management decided that all division's would use the Georgia Federal name. This change allowed some basic changes to occur in the marketing area. Don DeLozier, group vice-president of the Atlanta Division, explained:

EXHIBIT 1: Georgia Federal Savings & Loan Association (B) Corporate Organization Chart (May 1, 1981)

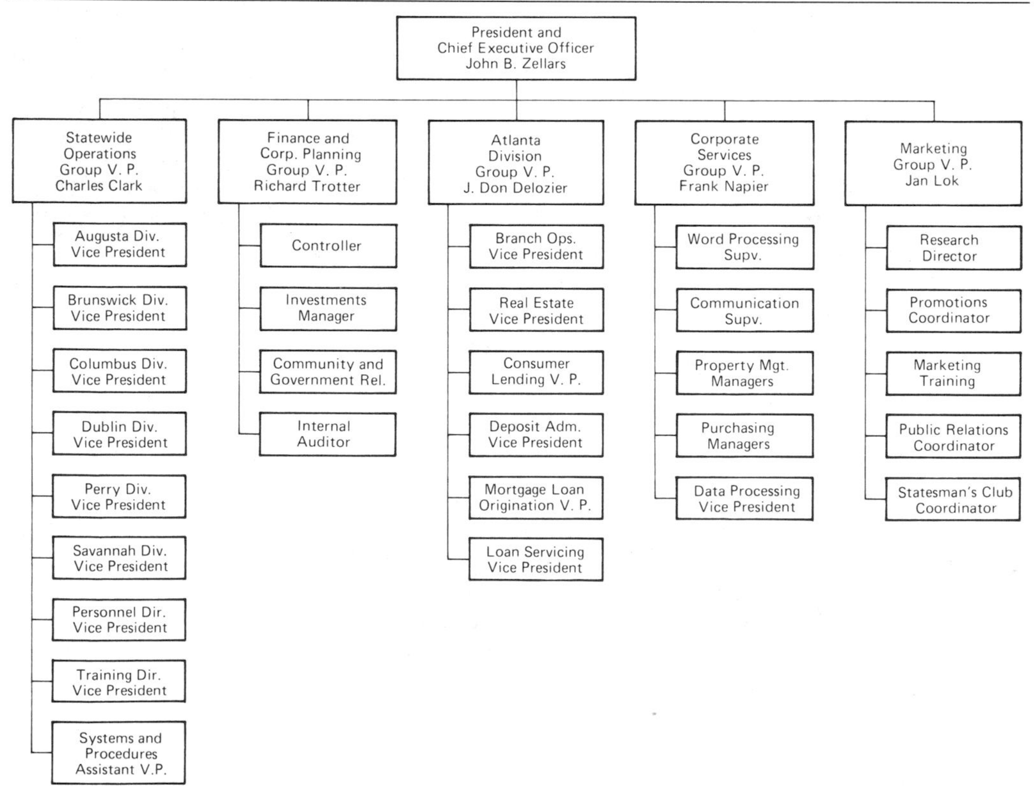

> When we started our mergers, they maintained their local identities and became a division of Atlanta Federal. When we changed our name to Georgia Federal to reflect our statewide expansion, they became divisions of Georgia Federal. At that time, Atlanta Federal also became a division of Georgia Federal. Georgia Federal was created with a structure similar to a holding company. The individual associations operate rather autonomously within that holding company concept.
>
> Georgia Federal takes care of many of the staff functions like accounting, data processing, and developing new products and services for the operating divisions. Although the divisions have autonomy, their operations are relegated to the traditional customer contacts.
>
> We do the lion's share of marketing out of the corporate level. That has been made simpler since we dropped the individual names and use Georgia Federal. It gives us the economies of scale that we had lost. One name and logo helps considerably.

Even with the coordinated marketing effort, divisional autonomy was quite high. Robert Joyce, vice-president for personal, explained:

> Generally speaking, we are dealing with separate entities. They have been operating for years and have their own management, their own management style, and their own way of conducting business. We don't interfere with that a great deal. They have to begin taking on our policies and procedures from an operating standpoint. We give them the current practices and procedures which they adopt immediately.

In describing Georgia Federal's management approach, DeLozier continued:

> Each division has a division manager who reports to Charlie Clark, who is in charge of statewide operations. He communicates on a day-to-day basis and through monthly meetings. The corporate functional areas also communicate any changes in policy or products to the divisions. Corporate creates it, prints the materials, and sends it to them for implementation. It sets the lending policies, for example, and sends it to them for application to their own markets. Each staff level visits and keeps in touch by phone. That works well.

As an example of the corporate role towards their divisions, Joyce explained the function of the personnel department:

> We leave personnel administration pretty much up to the division manager. The head of a new merger is given title of division manager and we allow them to determine local employment needs and handle personnel administration. We keep all the records here for each employee and bring them up to our level of benefits for sick leave, etc.
>
> Right after a merger, I will make a trip to the association and make a presentation to the employees about our benefit programs and answer any questions about our policies. I ask that the division managers consult with me when they have personnel problems. I'm responsible for all payroll changes or changes in title, so all changes are submitted to this office. But we're quite decentralized.

Zellars explained further:

> Statewide operations have helped us a lot in this area because we have people transferring in from other parts of the state. Young people have a greater opportunity through our mergers than ever before.

Performance reviews and salary recommendations were also held for Georgia Federal's employees. Joyce continued:

> Our appraisal system is more formal in the nonexempt areas than in the exempt areas. We use the Hay system of salary administration and evaluation. I also conduct a workshop which includes performance appraisal. We gear appraisals to the salary review and I use a form that includes performance review and salary recommendations. We have five performance ratings and require a formal narrative to support the performance rating. We do this every six months for our 375 nonexempt personnel.
>
> The exempt area uses the same forms. All 200 exempt personnel are reviewed once a year. They have consultation through the lines up to senior management. Its up to top management to decide the salary treatment.
>
> We put in profit sharing last year and 15 or 16 key managers were invited to participate. These are the managers who set corporate policies and procedures for the entire organization. Division managers did not participate in the first year. We also give a bonus the first week in December, but that is based solely on service and rate of pay.

In carrying out the ongoing operations of Georgia Federal, Zellars attempted to involve key managers and maintain communication as he explains:

> Every Tuesday afternoon at 3:30, I meet with my three senior officers of the Atlanta division, statewide operations, and finance and corporate planning. Every Wednesday morning at eight o'clock, I meet with fifteen people. These 15 represent, for the most part, the five corporate officers plus their key people. Those 15 are the ones who impact management decisions more than anyone else. During that meeting we ask each of them what they have to tell others. Every week they know that they are coming to that meeting. That is also the group that participates in any profit sharing—if we have any. They tell us what they think we need to know and the meeting is over in an hour—from 8:00 to 9:00 a.m. I don't want any lengthy discussion about what they have been doing other than the bottom line—give us the facts and let others know what has been happening. It has been a good vehicle.

Georgia Federal's top managers, the president, the vice-presidents of division operations and finance, are all involved in the merger process. Trotter described the nature of individual involvement.

> Several people are involved in mergers. John has the contacts with people in the industry. With his knowledge of the people, he is the principal person involved with all merger activities. Georgia Federal has more experience with mergers than any other institution in the state. It is in a better position to bring off a merger than any other institution in the state.
>
> The actors in the merger area change from time to time depending on the merger. For example, in 1975, when we merged with Home in Savannah, John brought it off entirely by himself. In 1976, when we merged with Security Federal Savings in middle-Georgia, I had very close personal ties with their managing officer from my days with the Federal Home Loan Bank Board. He had been vice-chairman of the Greensboro Federal Home Loan Bank Board. The last two, American in Columbus and Home in Macon, John and Charlie Clark, our group vice-president for statewide operations, were most involved. Of course, my department gets involved in the financial analysis.

In describing his own style of management, Zellars stated:

> I guess you would say that I am a participative manager, because I'm involved in lots of operations that would usually involve an operations manager. There are

some advantages in that I probably know more about what's going on in the organization than I would otherwise know. Secondly, in an organization of this size, there is no such thing as having two people who can run it. There is plenty of room for five, six, or seven people in senior positions.

INTEGRATING MERGER PARTNERS

With Georgia Federal's experience in mergers, Richard P. Trotter, Georgia Federal's chief financial officer and corporate planner, felt that the process of integrating new partners into their system was quite easy. He explained:

> We've done it so many times now it's just a matter of going through the motions. We have the data processing capacity and the knowhow. After converting five or six, one more is easy, especially Home in Macon, because it had data processing on an NCR system. We produce division balance sheets and operating statements every month. It's just a matter of cranking out the numbers.

Trotter commented on Georgia Federal's data-processing capabilities:

> We're near the top in data processing capabilities as far as hardware goes. Our system is relatively modern—we have a brand new Criterion computer which is the newest generation of NCR computers.
>
> We recently participated in a very costly study undertaken by the peer group. We contributed our share of approximately half a million dollars towards this project. The conclusion was that these companies could form a single data processing organization to perform all of the ultimate data processing needs of the peer group. Six of these institutions agreed to do that including some of the largest in the group. We felt it was premature for us, with our modern hardware and software, to be jumping into the project; by participating in the study, we preserve the option to join the system four or five years down the road.

Zellars also commented on the importance of Georgia Federal's processing capabilities:

> We were the first institution to go on-line in 1966. Of course, S&Ls for the most part are on-line with their NOW account operations. The big problem is in keeping our capacity up to date so we could get the job done. We're continuing to expand our own computer operations and have two mainframes now. This will continue to be a major problem area. I just lost my D.P. manager which also makes this a sensitive area.
>
> Our first priority has to be the computer and our information systems and their ability to deliver. We can't be held up because the computer can't perform.

Georgia Federal's divisional training programs were still limited as Joyce explained:

> We have teller training and financial counselor training. We will also have training for new products or procedures. We have a training department that confines most of its activities to the Atlanta area. Some of the division's key people come in for that, but not their tellers. We hope to change this in the future.
>
> We had a supervisors training program that was carried out statewide. That was completed when we lost our trainer so it hasn't been picked back up. Other management training is on the job.

ADVISORY BOARD OF DIRECTORS

As part of its merger and acquisition strategy, Georgia Federal had kept the local boards of directors in an advisory capacity. Trotter explained the advisory boards' present role:

> The division boards are a very important part of our strategy. They may function in an advisory capacity, but they are extremely important to the ultimate success of the merged institution. They are typically made up of community leaders and people who live and have worked in these communities all their lives. In order to have the relationship with the community, you really need to have these advisory boards. If you don't have one in an area, it suggests that you structure one.
>
> In middle-Georgia, we will need a board that represents at least every community in the area. We probably need someone from that area on the big board in Atlanta. In fact, all major cities should be represented on our board. Augusta, Savannah, and Columbus are now represented. We have an advisory director on the board from Perry. We need someone from middle-Georgia.

DeLozier commented further on the role of the advisory boards:

> The advisory boards meet on a regular basis with the division manager and provide contact with the community. They advise the division manager on the local scene and on local conditions. They have local information which is beneficial to the division manager. They're not involved in overall corporate decisions—that's not their purpose. They are the advisory board to that division.
>
> Some members of the advisory boards function on the division's loan committee. There are also some members from these division boards on our board of directors. Members are paid a modest fee. John Zellars makes decisions about new members with inputs from the division managers.

FUTURE MERGER OPPORTUNITIES

For Georgia Federal to implement an aggressive merger strategy, the Federal Home Loan Bank Board would have to give its approval of purchase method accounting. Such approval would allow an unprofitable savings and loan to show a profit for Georgia Federal, as Zellars explained:

> The difference between pooling and purchasing of an institution is $2.5 million on a $100 million institution. Let me explain: The average $100 million institution is losing $125,000 per month today. That means if I pool that institution, I'll have a $1.5 million loss. If I use the purchase method, bring their loans to market value, amortize the discounts on an accelerated basis, and amortize the goodwill over a longer period, I can generate $1 million in profit as compared to $1.5 million in losses. There is a point where you will still have goodwill to amortize, but hopefully, the operations of the merged institution would have improved prior to this occurrence.
>
> Another factor even makes this method better. You can take the liquidated loan portfolio and file for an income tax refund. On an effective 30 percent tax rate, you can bring in a substantial tax refund to reduce your goodwill. Well, we're pushing to do this.

Besides providing Georgia Federal with the basis for an aggressive acquisition strategy, Zellars felt that this provided a solution to one of the industry's most serious problems. He explained:

This could be a tremendous thing for the industry. Using this concept you can afford combinations of institutions without impacting the institution's earnings severely. Now, in order for an institution to use the purchase method, they must have several things. They need sufficient net worth to carry the capital they have acquired until that income stream is rebuilt. It may take three years to rebuild it. I don't think institutions that are losing money can afford to combine and create a greater loss. It doesn't make a lot of sense to merge with anyone today on any basis other than a purchase. If you do, you had better have on some rose colored glasses.

Trotter commented on the impact of their proposed strategy:

Once the current merger application is approved, then we have a great deal of flexibility and can be quite aggressive. At this point we have all the merger possibilities we could possibly want. John is called about every day from someone who is interested.

CASE THIRTY-THREE

Texas Instruments MODPLAN (A)

WILLIAM R. BOULTON
University of Georgia
CHARLES W. KIGHT
Republic National Bank

Assignment Questions:

1. What is the purpose of TI's corporate planning system?
2. What is MODPLAN? How does it relate to TI's planning system?
3. What are the problems with MODPLAN? How would you forecast its growth?

By April 1979, Texas Instrument's (TI) computer based financial planning and control system (MODPLAN) was being used throughout TI's world-wide operations. In fact, the continuing 100 per cent annual growth in the use of MODPLAN was beginning to cause longer response times for TI's MODPLAN users. In describing the problem, Fred Teter, manager of MODPLAN, explained in April 1979:

> You can look at what has been happening to MODPLAN by looking at its growth. For example, the number of data bases have grown from 31 at the end of 1976 to 62 in April 1979. The number of arrays being used grew from nearly 6,000 in 1976 to over 28,000 in April.[1] Our inquiry usage, which is on-line, has gone up from almost one million in 1976 to over 3 million in 1978, and nearly 1.4 million through April, 1979. We had 1,620 terminals authorized for MODPLAN usage in April, up from 349 in 1976. (See Exhibit 1).

Charles Kight, division manager within TI's information systems and services group, also commented on MODPLAN's growth:

> To understand the explosive growth of MODPLAN, you have to understand that technology is the driving force. The question is, "Why couldn't we have done MODPLAN even earlier?" Well, for one thing, we didn't have the worldwide computer network to be able to do it nor did we have the software expertise or organizational expertise in the user's camp to be able to do it. All three of these were missing.

[1]For each data base allocated to a MODPLAN user, there is the capability of storing three sets of data (usually revised estimates of budgeted numbers or forecasts) called arrays.

EXHIBIT 1: Texas Instruments' MODPLAN (A)
Information Systems and Services
Corporate Systems Strategy
Financial Planning Systems
MODPLAN GROWTH ANALYSIS

Growth Factors	*1976*	*1977*	*1978*	*1979 April YTD*
MODPLAN Terminals	349	593	1,448	1,620
Inq. Vol. (K)	949	1,440	3,087	1,367
% Growth Inquiries/Yr	41	52	114	
Arrays	5,965	10,117	22,835	28,460
% Growth Arrays/Yr	63	70	126	
Entries	4,192	7,068	17,101	21,247
Unique Data Bases	31	38	60	62
Cost Factors				
Total System Cost (K)	743	958	1,702	670
Total System Cost/Array	74	56	45	
Inquiries/Array	95	87	81	86
MODPLAN Staff				
Exempts	4	5	8	8
Non-Exempts	1	2	2	1

> Technology causes changes. We then hit a threshold of usage. There is now an opportunity to take advantage of TI's technology which has produced the TI 990 minicomputer.

In describing the problem of increased response time for MODPLAN users, Teter explained:

> The continued 100 percent growth in MODPLAN has also presented some problems. One problem is response time.
>
> Typically we see 8–10 second response time[2] except for peak demand periods during our monthly close, when everyone is using the system at once, and response time increases to as much as 1–2 minutes. Our international operations require another 15 seconds for communications. Anything over 8 seconds is probably too much from the user's point of view.

It was because of this growth and the problems in response time that management felt it was necessary to review MODPLAN's forecast and plans for the future. At the end of the MODPLAN Quarterly Review meeting in April, 1979, Charles Kight concluded:

> I think that we may be nearing a turning point in MODPLAN's life cycle and need to reexamine the alternative forecasts for MODPLAN's growth. We need three views of the future. First an aggressive plan. Second a conservative plan, and a model of the growth forecast. We need a description of the parameters which will determine which growth plan will occur. For example, we need to clearly state our

[2]Response time is the elapsed time between pushing the enter button (on-line), and receiving a response. TI's 8–10 second response time is at the 90th percentile which meant that only 10 percent of inquiries took longer than that as shown in Exhibit 7.

> assumptions about inflation and increases in salaries and wages; about the shift in people mix from clerical workers to more high priced professionals and specialists; about the annual decreases in computer costs; about the limits placed on hiring to meet our PEI[3] goals; about the availability of capital resources; and about our limits in the MODPLAN area to meet the expanding staffing needs caused by increased support requirements.

BACKGROUND: TI'S PLANNING CYCLE

Texas Instrument's planning cycle is a key part of its management philosophy and is at the core of the overall TI system of management. As such, it is a nearly continuous process which integrates near-term actions and constraints on profitability and resources with the long-range plans and corporate objectives. The planning cycle begins in August of each year when the operating committee sets the overall priorities which will guide TI for the upcoming year and the next three years. These priorities define the relative need for growth, profitability, productivity, new product or process development and similar issues.

TI's planning cycle is implemented through a "four loop" planning process as shown in Exhibit 2. The first loop is long-range planning which focuses on TI's direction for the next ten years and the strategies for getting there. The second loop is intermediate range planning which concentrates on planning for facilities, manufacturing equipment, and major product cost reductions for the next three years. In this second loop, the current year plus one is most critical because it ties the strategic plan, intermediate plan and rolling plan together.

The rolling plan, or third loop, is a quarterly update of the current year. It occurs in January, April, July, and October of each year. Rolling plans include a full set of P & L and resource objectives, or indices, along with the most current thinking as to volume levels and changing business conditions. The fourth loop is for monthly forecasting. In the first month of each quarter, PCCs[4] forecast for three months into the future. In the second month of a quarter, forecasts are five months; and in the third month, forecasts are four months. This final loop constitutes TI's short-cycle profit error signalling and control mechanism.

Throughout the planning process, TI's managers focus on key indices such as net sales billed (NSB), growth rate, gross profit margin (GPM) per cent, strategic investment (OST) per cent, organization profit per cent, and return on assets (ROA). Once these key indices are specified for an organization, then all other resources and P & L indices are developed. These indices are then referred to as "models" for an organization. In relating TI's models to the planning system, Mark Shephard, chairman and chief executive officer, explained to the case writer:

> In our models, we have what we call the "basic model." This is a model of key indices which together express the standard of achievable performance against which the performance of an organization will be measured. It is a stretch, but not an impossibility. We then also end up with "models of the year" in the intermediate plan. These models don't necessarily equal the basic model. The basic model itself

[3]PEI refers to TI's people effectiveness index which is equal to net sales billed divided by payroll plus benefits. See Exhibit 3.

[4]PCC stands for product-customer centers.

EXHIBIT 2: Texas Instruments MODPLAN (A)
Interrelated Financial Reporting Formats

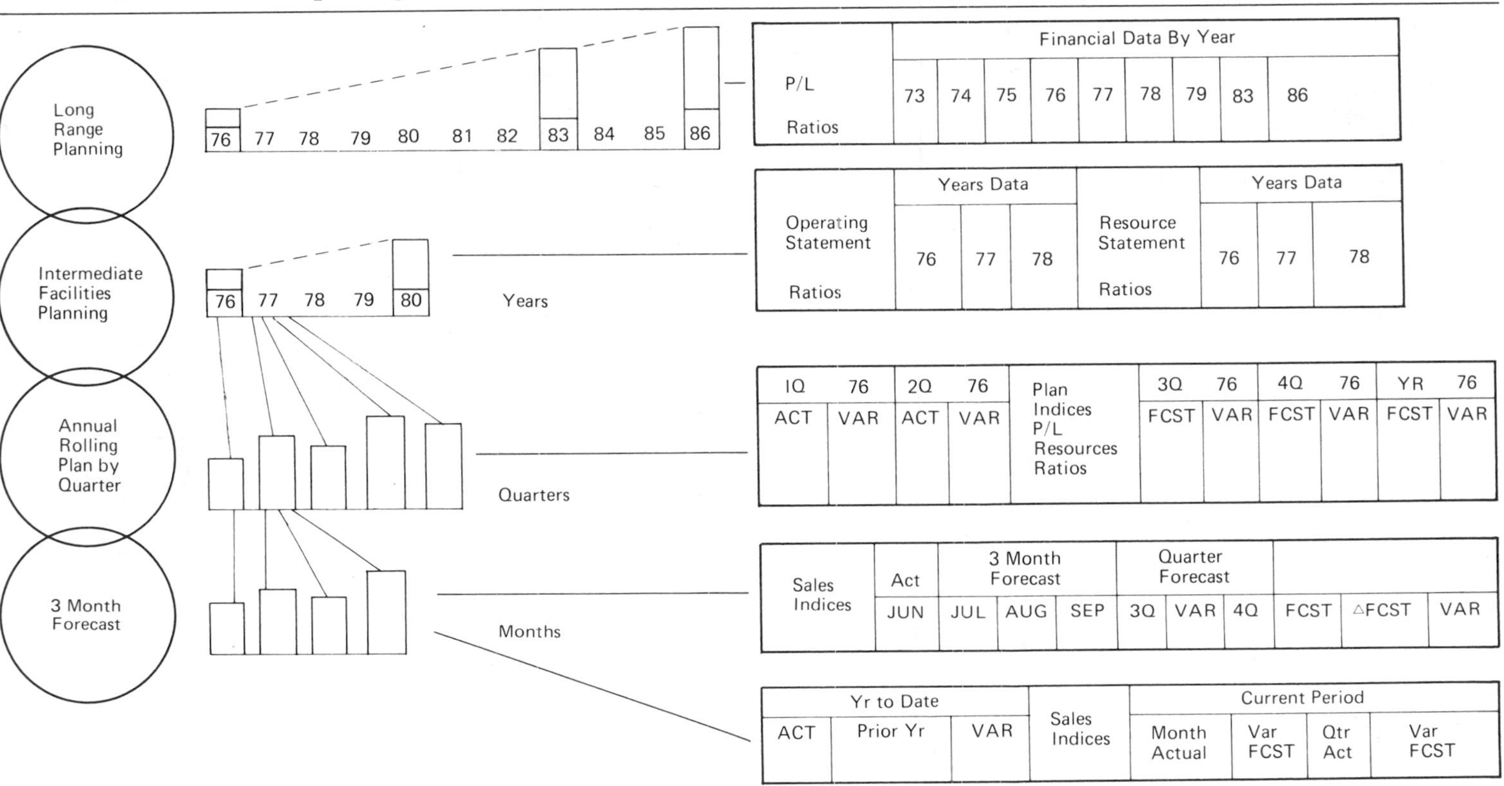

EXHIBIT 3: Texas Instruments MODPLAN (A)
Improving TI's Productivity

Texas Instruments had a formalized people and asset effectiveness (P&AE) system of programs which were aimed at improving the productivity of both the human and physical resources of the company. In 1979, president Bucy explained the impact of the P&AE system to stockholders:

> Through our productivity programs of capital investment and people effectiveness, we have brought the total cost of payroll and benefits plus depreciation down from 50.7% of TI's net sales billed in 1972 to 47.2% in 1978—an improvement of 3.5 points. This has been accomplished in a period when the costs of people, facilities and equipment has been rising at the highest rates in several decades.

ASSET EFFECTIVENESS GOALS

Ti's management set specific goals for asset turnover, return on assets, and profits which would allow TI to self-fund its own growth. Chairman of the board Shephard explained in 1974:

> Keeping our asset turns between 1.7 and 2.0 permits our achieving the 12% return on assets with profit after tax of 6% to 7% of net sales billed rather than to strive for some much higher level. This is a very important point. If we let our asset turns go down to one, our profit after tax would have to be almost 14% to self-fund 16% annual growth.

PEOPLE EFFECTIVENESS GOALS

In addition to asset goals, TI's management established the "people effectiveness index" (PEI) to use in measuring individual productivity improvement. This index was defined as net sales billed divided by total payroll costs. TI's goal for the 1980s was to improve productivity to achieve a people effectiveness index of 2.7, up from 2.4 in 1978. President Bucy commented to shareholders in 1979:

> PEI reached 2.4 in 1978, up from 2.3 in 1977 and 2.1 in 1971. This PEI improvement was made despite the increase in TI's total labor cost, including wages, salaries and benefits, of $195 million in 1978.
>
> At the level of 1978 net sales billed, the impact of an improvement in PEI of one-tenth of a point is approximately $10 million more in profit sharing for TIers and $25 million more profit before tax.

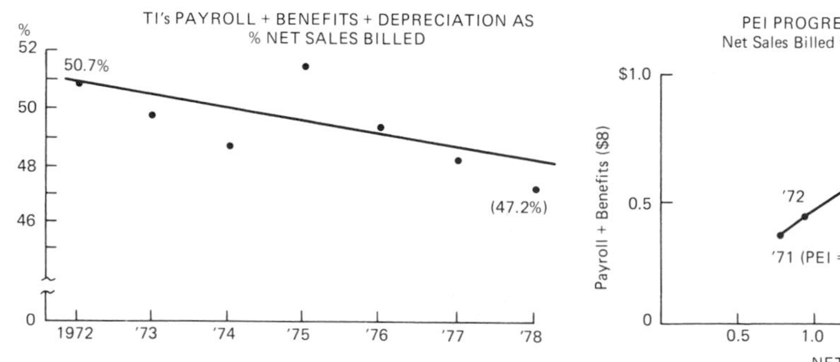

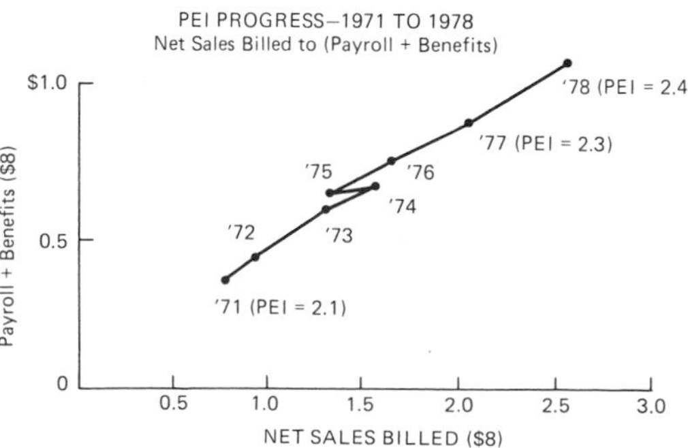

is not fixed in concrete, and can vary a great deal over time. One of the dangers in modeling is that people begin regarding them as more than bench marks. When you begin thinking of them as the gospel which can never be changed, you have problems. They have to be very living things.

The rolling-plan which is developed near year-end, and comes into print in January, is called the "bench-mark plan" from which our bench mark indices are established. Those indices are what we hold our managers' noses to the grindstone on for the rest of the year. We don't let them informally change each quarter as we produce these rolling plans. If they want to make a change, they have to come and negotiate it with me.

The ideal which we can strive for, though will never reach, is to understand our business well enough so that we can model it. We should be able to understand our business structure, the inter-relationships between the different businesses, and different parts of the same business, so that you can pick a billings number and have the computer tell you what you should have in every department. You have to be careful not to be a slave to that and must be able to recognize and investigate anomalies which may come out of such models.

The kind of measures which we use in these models include the output, what we call "net sales billed" or what some people call sales. We define a "sale" as an "order" which creates backlog. Our "net sales billed" are actual "shipments" of product to the customer. From net sales billed, we subtract manufacturing costs to get gross product margin. From this margin, we deduct operating expenses called D & A (distributed and allocated) expenses which leaves a sum that can either be invested in profits or in future OST[5] expenditures.

In the models, we have numbers which describe what percentage OST should be of net sales billed. This percentage includes some subjective inputs and some pseudo-mathematical derivations, but it varies a great deal from business to business. It becomes a function of the technical sophistication of your business, of your competition, and of the product life cycle. OST represents a much higher percentage of billings for products with short life cycles. If you have a life cycle of 40 years, it takes much less input each year to stay abreast or ahead than it does if you have a product life cycle of three years.

In discussing the early development of TI's models, Mark Shepherd, continued:

We're not as sophisticated as we would like to be with models, but we are making progress. What we try to do with this is to get our managers to look very hard at the structure of their business, rather than having them feel virtuous because they have pushed a pencil a lot. Pencil pushing is easy for the computer. We use a computer system called MODPLAN which does this for us.

I believe we're about half way, within a ten-year cycle, of getting models to do everything that they ought to be able to do for us, and in getting managers to accept them. The more "administrative" managers don't particularly like the idea of models, because models do automatically what he's been doing most of his life. Your innovators and entrepreneurs like models, because models give them more time to spend on things they're interested in.

[5]OST refers to TI's long range strategic planning system which specifies business objectives, strategies and tactics. Major resource commitments were a part of the OST process.

MODPLAN AT TEXAS INSTRUMENTS

MODPLAN is a management data base system for collecting, consolidating, and reporting of numerical information. MODPLAN was developed to help TI managers, planners, and analysts do their jobs easier and better. More specifically, it provides a tool which allows computer power to be applied to the tasks of collection, manipulation, analysis and reporting of any numerical data which can be arranged by time periods, such as is commonly done in forecasting, planning, budgeting, reporting, and controlling activities.

The original use of MODPLAN from the early 1970s was for the corporate "Blue Book" financial consolidations. As a result, the Blue Book consolidation system was commonly referred to as "the MODPLAN" or "the traditional MODPLAN" system. The "corporate" data base, called data base #61, is the source of the Blue Book management reporting data which is used to provide appropriate TI managers with a monthly analysis of operations and is used to consolidate and close TI's books each month.

By April, 1979, however, MODPLAN was being used for many applications besides corporate Blue Book consolidations. In fact, there were 104 different data bases which were being used for financial planning, manufacturing controls, cost centers and other modeling applications in TI's operations around the world. Exhibit 4 shows some of the users of MODPLAN data bases.

To understand MODPLAN's success at TI, it is necessary to understand the basic capabilities of the system. Most users of MODPLAN store historical data and forecast data within their own data base. This data may be specified as dollars, people, units, sites, or any other logical quantity which can be tracked by time periods. By working through the MODPLAN support organization, MODPLAN users are able to establish their own data bases and, thereby, reduce their need for manual calculations of their operating data.

Each MODPLAN data base is three dimensional with (1) data items called "line" items, (2) time periods, and (3) organizations called "entities", as shown in Diagram 1. Each data base has separate definitions for their "line" items, such as net sales billed, total people, direct material cost, manufacturing overhead, etc., which may or may not coincide with the names used in any other

DIAGRAM 1

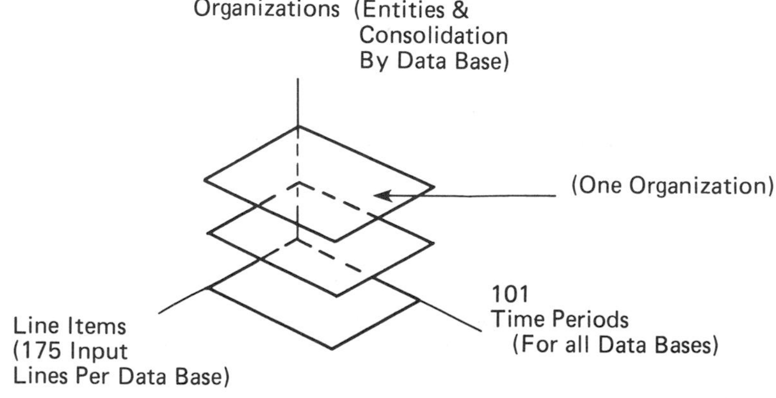

EXHIBIT 4: MODPLAN Data Bases

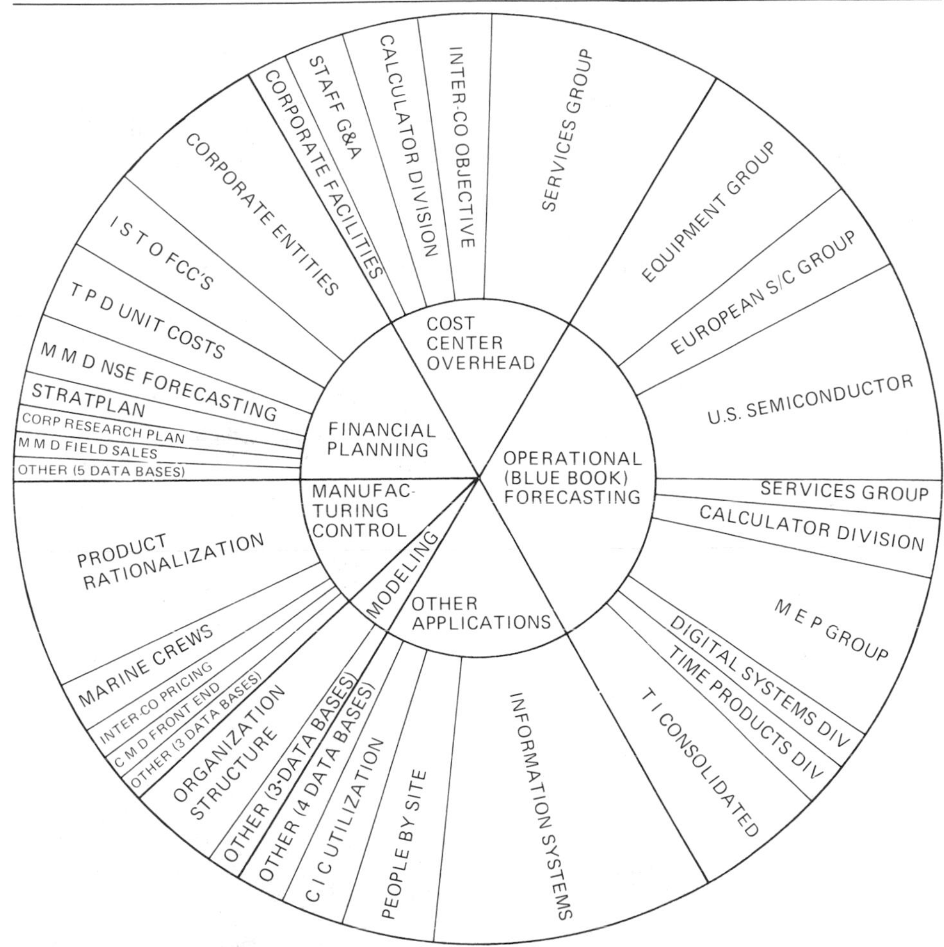

data base. Time periods include months, quarters, and years such as January, 1980, first quarter, 1980, or year 1980.

In order to save storage space, and thus reduce cost of operation, the MODPLAN system differentiates between calculated lines and non-calculated lines, and actually stores only those lines which are not calculated from other lines. Up to 175 of the 512 total lines available in MODPLAN may be stored lines. As long as data for a calculated line can be derived by some combination of stored data, there is no need to store the calculated result. Instead, MODPLAN retains a calculation formula along with data from actual stored lines to compute the desired data for the calculated lines.

Exhibit 5 shows a sample report of time period comparisons for 55 line items. MODPLAN calculated lines, such as per cent GPM (line 13) to sales, per cent OST expense (line 22) to sales, or net fixed asset as a per cent of sales (line 38), display ratios between sales, income statement items, balance sheet items, or other resources. The "number crunching" associated with ratio calculations, time period additions, organization consolidation, and clerical work, such as

EXHIBIT 5: Sample "Bluebook" Report Monthly Comparison

"Security Label" *Dummy Entity*	*December 1976*	*"Security Label"* *John Doe*
Operating Unit		*Responsibility*
12345678 *Year to Date*		*Current Period Comparison*

	Actual	*Last Year*	*Variance*	*Description*	*Month Actual*	*Variance FCST*	*QTR ACT/FCET*	*Variance PFST/FCST*	*Variance ORP*
1	62202	7051	55151	NSE-TOTAL	150	−56	12146	−56	−138
2	60306	3694	56612	BACKLOG-TOTAL	60306	102	60306	102	429
3	12772	6521	6251	BILLABLE ACT	1983	−310	3208	−376	−848
4	5550	6984	−1394	MSB-TOTAL	1406	−158	1591	−158	−567
5	3725	1610	−1665	DIRECT LABOR	394	46	1247	46	−40
6	4103	1644	−2455	DIRECT NATL	1099	−560	2418	−560	−759
7	3026	1417	−1609	MFG OVERHEAD	396	51	1079	51	135
8				OTH OVERHEAD					
9				COST ADJ-NET					
10	4	−7	−11	OTH MFG COST	4	−6	4	−4	−4
11	−5851	409	6260	INV REDUCTION	−675	484	−2940	484	903
12	1033	1911	−878	GPM%	188	−141	−217	−141	−332
13	18.5	27.4	−8.9	GPM% NSB	13.4	−7.6	−13.6	−9.3	−18.9
14	681	606	−75	OPER A	53	3	172	3	1
15	701	628	−73	OPER D+A	55	3	178	3	1
16	12.9	5.0	−3.5	OPER D+A% HSB	3.9	−.2	11.2	−.9	−2.9
17	67.9	32.9	−35.0	OPER D+A% GPM	29.3	−11.7	−82.0	−156.2	237.7
18				DIV OTH I/E					
19	332	1283	−951	OPER PROFIT	133	−138	−345	−138	−331
20	5.9	18.4	−12.5	OPER DFT% NSB	9.5	−7.8	−24.8	−10.1	−21.8
21	137	135	−2	DST D+A	15		37		10
22	2.5	1.9	−.8	DST D+A% NSB	1.1	−.1	2.3	−.2	−.1
23	838	763	−75	D+A O DOIE	70	3	215	3	11
24	81.1	39.9	−41.2	D+A EDOIE% GPM	37.2	−15.0	−99.1	−187.7	245.6
25	157	157		DEPT EXPENSE	17		43		10
26	195	1148	−953	ORGAN PROFIT	118	−138	−432	−138	−321
27	3.5	16.4	−12.4	ORG PFT% NSB	8.4	−8.0	−27.2	−10.4	−22.1
28	−14.4	−115.5	101.1	ORG PFT ROA	−237.0	−999.9	217.8	−22.2	430.9
29	179	156	17	CASH & OTHER	179	16	179	16	57
30	−2505	−3202	−700	RECEIVABLES	−2502	1527	−2502	1527	2322
31	−153	−700	−547	REC/MIL NSB	−153	83	−153	83	141
32	6857	1002	−5855	INV—NET	6857	−484	6857	−484	−903
33	1077	207	−870	INV/MIL NSB	1077	−166	1077	−166	−387
34	−5461	−554	4902	UNLIQ PRG PAY	−5461	786	−5461	786	996
35	−858	−115	743	UPP/MIL NSB	−858	190	−858	190	341
36	772	220	−552	NFA-FACIL DST	772	−24	772	−24	−5
37	772	519	−253	TOTAL NFA	772	−24	772	−24	−5
38	121	107	−14	TOT NFA/N NSB	121	−14	121	−14	−32
39	−155	−2044	−1889	ASSETS EQP	−155	1821	−155	1821	2467
40	−24	−422	−398	ASTS/NNSB EQP	−24	262	−24	262	292
41	−1352	0994	358	AVG ASSETS	−598	911	−794	304	1002
42	−1782	2272	−4054	ORG CASH FLOW	−820	1745	−1477	1745	2290
43				QP EXPEND TOT					
44				DEPR EXP TOT					
45				CAP AUTH TOT					
46	53	50	−3	DIR EX PED ID	53	1	53	1	7
47	24	20	−4	DIR NE PED ID	24	−2	24	–	−1
48				IND EX PED ID					
49				IND NE PED ID					
50	77	70	−7	TOTAL FEC EDP	77	−1	77	−1	6
51	74	66	−8	TOTAL AVG PED	76		73		3
52	172304	98554	73750	BILL ACT/APER	313105	−51345	174982	−20845	−37559
53	2631	17350	−14714	ORG PFT/A PER	18632	−22057	−23564	−7491	−17747
54				TOTAL PAYROLL					
55	.007		−.007	A IND/DIR PER	.007		.009		−.005

viewgraph presentation of financial and operating data, is greatly reduced by the system. "What if" considerations can be rapidly tested and consolidated in examining trade-offs between income and balance sheet factors, or employment levels, during the development of forecasts and plans. MODPLAN therefore performs the functions of collecting, calculating, consolidating, storing, and retrieving data in a very rapid and cost effective manner.

Time periods are universally defined in MODPLAN into 101* time periods for all data bases. For a particular data base, the organization or entity could be a cost center, product-customer center (PCC), product line, site, etc. As shown in Diagram 1, the arrangement of line items by time period for one entity is called an array. Each entity in the data base may have 1, 2, or 3 arrays (designated A-1, A-2, and A-3) depending on their need for multiple data sets. These entities can then be consolidated along organizational lines as desired.

These various MODPLAN capabilities were offered to TI managers through over 1600 on-line inquiry terminals plus batch (card deck) production terminals. This allowed user flexibility around the world.

In describing the motivation for the increased usage currently being experienced by MODPLAN, Teter explained:

> MODPLAN started as a financial forecasting system for corporate control. Eventually, as more people gained exposure, they began using it for their own operations. As the costs have been significantly reduced, from 5 to 13 percent per year, and it became easier to use; people began to increase their use of it in tracking their operations. That was coupled with managements' need for better information on how the businesses were doing.
>
> As businesses grew, it took more and more clerks to do the work and leverage of the system became quite high. People began moving to MODPLAN as a way to keep down the number of people that they had to hire and still know what their businesses were doing. Managers could track their own businesses by using the same system used by the corporation. Because of these obvious benefits, we have never had to actively go out to sell managers on using the MODPLAN system for their operations. We've had a constant backlog of requests throughout the system's life.

Corporate Consolidations

The original use of MODPLAN was for the corporate "Blue Book" financial consolidations. Each month, TI actual results for the current month and forecasts through year-end are updated worldwide. In addition, year plus one is forecasted each quarter and the long range plan for year plus ten is forecasted annually. John Alice, corporate P&L analyst, is responsible for consolidating the monthly forecasts for all TI operations. In describing his job, he also explained the role of MODPLAN:

> Each month we provide a detailed, consolidated profit and loss statement and balance sheet. MODPLAN is the sole means for doing this. Each group which consolidates to TI is asked via MODPLAN for input of NSB through profits on the P&L and assets on the balance sheet. Liabilities are forecasted at the corporate level. This includes nine or ten groups according to our operational structure such as Semiconductors, European Semiconductors, Equipment, Services, etc.
>
> By the ninth workday, every group will have completed their own bottoms-

* Time periods are actuals, forecasts, or prior forecasts of a month, quarter or year.

up forecast. Ten to fourteen days earlier, they will have had their PCCs make their inputs. The division levels will have consolidated their PCCs which then consolidate to the group level. Reviews of the forecast will have been made at each level and adjusted as necessary—to meet profit levels, etc. New profit goals may then be pushed back down to the PCCs. For TI consolidation purposes, only the group level inputs are needed.

We require all PCCs to have their forecasts in the base array on the tenth day, needing the information for management reporting. Forecasts are usually developed in the A-2 or "what if" array or sometimes, in the A-3 or "sum" array. The A-2 or A-3 arrays have no time period lockup protection of any sort and can be updated at any time during the month, if one knows the password. On the ninth workday, the groups turn it over to us. They roll the data into their A-1 or "base" array and call us to check it out. We then pull four or five reports to make sure it includes the correct time periods and line items to be forecasted. After we check it, we restrict the managers, even if they know the password, from updating the A-1 array by a security process to insure the integrity of our data.[6]

The line items vary based on the type of forecast being prepared. During the current year and year plus one, we have a fixed set of lines. As we go further out we require fewer and fewer lines. In the current year, for example, we require a detailed breakdown of manufacturing costs. For long-range plans, GPM is sufficient to show what percent of sales will go into manufacturing costs without a detailed backup. On the morning of the tenth workday, we begin actual consolidations for the P&L and balance sheet forecasts. It takes about eight hours to complete the forecast through earnings per share; having a full P&L, and a complete balance sheet of total assets, liabilities and stockholders equity for the whole corporation. This includes three to five months of forecasts, and one to three quarters forecast depending on the time of year. It takes an additional day to forecast the next year by quarter and another three or four hours per subsequent year for doing the long range plan. The long range plan, done in February, includes current year, year plus one, year plus 2, year plus 3, year plus 6, and year plus nine.

In describing the impact that MODPLAN has had on TI, Den Hiser, corporate operations controller, explained:

I can't say enough good things about MODPLAN. It has made control a lot more fun. In the last four years we've reduced the time it takes to consolidate by two days. Without MODPLAN, we couldn't hire enough people to do the job we do. A report that used to take us two hours to prepare now takes 10 minutes. As a result, we can recycle consolidations two or three times which means we have half a day to QC the numbers before we send them to top management.

I have only added one person in corporate financial analysis in the last six years. We reduced our staff by two when MODPLAN came in, so we have one less than in 1972. Our work load has gone up six times as sales and complexity have tripled since 1972. Even more important for a multi-national company is the use of standard definitions. Now people really understand the definitions.

MODPLAN USERS

TI's International Semiconductor Trade Organization (ISTO) is one of MODPLAN's major users. Karl Kehler, profitability manager for ISTO, explained his use of MODPLAN:

[6] No changes are made after the cutoff date for consolidations and reporting.

In ISTO, we make extensive use of MODPLAN with three data bases. Each data base has a unique set of lines we use to manage our business. Data base 11 is the corporate entity data base (for the ISTO group) which is used to put in statutory financial information. Data base 12 is the operational data base which is used for our operational management reporting and has our operational information in it. There is very little duplication between these two data bases because their purposes are very different. Of course, in the corporate entity data base the key is to have an income statement and balance sheet that conform to generally accepted accounting principals. The key lines are net sales billed (NSB), cost of goods sold, and expenses.

Both data base 11 and 12 do contain some common information. For example, NSB and profit before tax (PBT). We close both of these at the end of each month with our corporate legal entity close and our operational close.

We also have a third data base, which we call data base 63, which is a kind of performance maximization data base. We use it for collecting, forecasting and monitoring overhead expense. We also use it to monitor payroll which TI tracks closely. For example, this data base is designed to produce the payroll number once you've done an adequate job with the expense forecast. We have parameters on the number of people, the time they work, the pay per unit of time, etc., so it comes up with a payroll forecast consistent with the expense forecast. It also computes trends in wage rates, overtime per cents, etc. to help make sure you have a payroll plan that helps support your business plan.

Each cost center (FCC) is an entity in our cost center data base 63. In this data base the line numbers correspond to key account numbers from general ledger. We then have other lines for people counts, and hours worked, etc. The FCC's use this data base to prepare monthly their manufacturing overhead forecasts and their local department expense forecast. These two items are then summed across entities in data base 63 as general ledger items. You can then compare forecasts to previous time periods by each account number for all people, overhead and department expenses and see any discontinuities from time period to time period. We have an automatic feed from the general ledger of all the expense numbers.

In describing what he felt were some major strengths and weaknesses of MODPLAN, Kehler continued:

I've had mostly financial planning and staff budget coordination jobs while at TI and I am currently the corporate entity profitability manager for ISTO. I manage the intercompany transfer prices so that each corporate entity, or off-shore plant, is able to achieve the level of profit before tax (PBT) that we set as a goal. I couldn't do this without MODPLAN. In fact, I probably do as much work myself using MODPLAN as three or four professionals could do without MODPLAN. It gives you a lot of leverage.

The MODPLAN system has three or four really significant things that it can do. It stores both actuals and forecasts. It provides some line flexibility within the data base. It also has excellent reporting features that allow the users to define their own reports. You can do magic once you learn all the features of the system.

The system was never intended to be a simulator or a system that would take independent variables and give the answer. You have to build your own forecast based on your assumptions. Once you load that into the system you have a good tool for reporting it, analyzing it, or comparing changes and time periods. There is a whole structure below that which must be done with pencil and paper before its loaded into the data base. As a result, if the financial manager asks why a change caused your costs to go up, the manager has to take out his scratch paper. For example, the parts per hour on a specific machine can yield a certain output,

> plus your available labor force, gives a capacity constraint. We will be building other systems which will calculate these lines that are input lines to the MODPLAN data base.

Another major user of MODPLAN is TI's Consumer Electronic Products (CEP) group which includes calculators, watches, etc. Raj Seekri, manager of product planning, explained the development of CEP's MODPLAN data bases:

> When I started the product data base with MODPLAN, I used only one data base for calculators, watches and personal computers. As we grew, we put personal computers and calculators into a second data base. Now, with the addition of home computers, we have started a third product data base with personal and home computers.
>
> We use a fourth data base for people and expenses because we have to track all our customer marketing expenses. A fifth data base gives a capability to our market analysis people to look at the total availability of the market (TAM) for North America, Japan, Middle East, etc. and track our penetration in units and dollars.
>
> We also have to track sales by each salesman by each product because he is paid a bonus if he reaches his forecast. As MODPLAN capabilities increase, we can do all these calculations with MODPLAN.

In explaining how MODPLAN is used in CEP, Seekri continued:

> MODPLAN is used to calculate our month-to-date sales and to compare our projections to forecast. We have a forecast system to calculate net sales and units for each product model or series. We then look at sales month-to-date and compare our forecast to actual every week. We follow this closely because units don't always get shipped to the market as quickly as forecasted. At our weekly operating reviews, we look at our actual-to-date compared to forecast and then give our revised projection. At the end of the month, we then show our variance to forecast and explain the reasons for each variance.
>
> We use all three arrays in our forecast cycle. We get a rough forecast from the field which is reviewed by the area managers each month. They look at what NSB we can support with production and put that in array one. We then start making changes by analyzing each region's forecast and enter that in array two. We then review the forecast with our assistant vice-president and he may make additional changes in array two. We then go to the plants and review array two and make changes in array three. If I had additional arrays, I could use them to store historical data from obsolete models.
>
> Month-to-date numbers are automatically loaded into MODPLAN. We wrote a program that reads each model from the customer master file and automatically feeds it into MODPLAN. We used to do this manually, but as we began keeping sales by area we couldn't do this anymore. As we begin keeping records at the salesman level, it wouldn't be able to be done manually on a weekly basis.

In discussing some of the strengths and weaknesses in using MODPLAN, Seekri explained:

> MODPLAN is most helpful in forecasting. We used to do the forecasts manually, but nobody would want to do that now. Nobody likes forecasting the future but we need to do it well so we can depend on the numbers. We now change our forecasts about 20 times during the two or three days of our current forecasts cycle. With MODPLAN we can change the numbers and reconsolidate within five minutes while everyone is still in the conference room. Without MODPLAN we couldn't do that.

MODPLAN has also allowed us to add entities. First we were only tracking products at the area level. We have since moved to regional and are planning to go to salesmen levels with about 70 salesmen.

The only problem is that we are limited to 175 prime lines and 512 calculated lines. With only 175 prime lines and each product taking a line for net sales and net units, we can only have 87 models in a data base. When you count model changes and the need for historical data, we are too restricted. We have new models coming out every month which we put into obsolete model lines.

We also have so many models for calculators and watches that we have to sum up each model. For example, 625–1, 625–2, 625–3, etc. are also separated by employee sales and retail sales. Some models have 5 or 6 lines which have to be added together by model. We keep about 40 current models on the average in calculators and 35 models in watch series. When you add the new models coming out and try to keep history on old models, it uses all of the space very quickly. We are managing this, but it requires a lot of time to change the lines and make sure the history is correct.

INFORMATION SYSTEMS AND SERVICES

John White, assistant vice-president in charge of Information Systems and Services (IS&S), reports to Sam Smith, one of TI's six group vice-presidents. Reporting to White is the Corporate, MEP (metalurgical and electrical products), and EFO (electronic functions objective) systems division under Charles Kight. Reporting to Kight is the corporate systems department under Ron Green. (Exhibit 6).

EXHIBIT 6: Texas Instruments MODPLAN (A) IS&S Organization

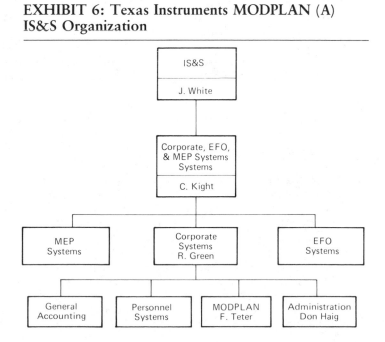

IS&S
J. White

Corporate, EFO, & MEP Systems Systems
C. Kight

MEP Systems

Corporate Systems R. Green

EFO Systems

General Accounting

Personnel Systems

MODPLAN F. Teter

Administration Don Haig

Corporate systems includes the general accounting systems, such as the general ledger, accounts payable, accounts receivable, and tax-treasury systems; the personnel systems, such as payroll, personnel file management, benefits, and personnel reporting; and the financial planning systems (MODPLAN). Each of these systems has been set up as a product line with its own cost center within IS&S.

MANAGING TI'S SYSTEMS

The basic concept used to manage TI's systems was considered rather unique, as Charles Kight explained:

> Industry wide, there are several aspects of systems management that are getting increased attention. Everyone is spending money for systems, but not feeling they have received appropriate value for their investment. Still the budget for systems keeps going up. It's probably one of the real growth sectors in business today—just look at IBM's growth. It's not uncommon for corporations to now spend between a half of a per cent and two per cent of their sales for data processing. Therefore it's probably one of the biggest functional growth areas in the U.S. Yet there are few approaches you can use to make sure you're getting the kind of performance you want. One of the things we have done at TI is to create pseudo-profit centers for systems. This is a common approach for products, but seldom used for systems.
>
> We treat systems as a business and have subdivided systems into major product lines. Financial systems, personnel systems, and general accounting systems are product lines. We treat each of these as businesses and have quantitative measures of their performance. For example, we look at the "fan out" of new capabilities—the per cent penetration of available market. We take a product line like our capital asset system and unit price it. We may charge five cents per asset to users around the world plus an adjustment where legal requirements demand different depreciation or currency fluctuation tracking. So the user pays five cents per asset and is sheltered from technical problems and development costs. Each year of operation lets us bring this system down a learning curve and allows us to charge users only for services rendered. That means that the system's budget has to have a certain amount of scrap in it just like in manufacturing. It then becomes possible to consolidate these systems, compare them, and provide tracking and motivational force for productivity improvements.
>
> We decided to treat planning systems as a profit center and force the learning curve into the systems area to get costs down. This idea began with our priority to have planning systems be one of the key systems over the past ten or twelve years. We did that because we felt "planning systems" would give us the highest leverage on payback to TI. This would then provide the resources to invest in other systems so you could grow the product line. The idea of having a "cash cow" in the systems area is kind of unique, but is one more step towards treating systems as a business. Now we can take funds from our cash cows and invest in shooting stars.
>
> Putting money into the financial planning area was like priming the pump. Now it is self sustaining with only a small per cent of its cash flow now being required to sustain it. We reviewed it and decided that we could use that money to prime the pump for new developments as well as for price reduction. This would let us operate like the product line areas where we designate a per cent of revenue for discretionary self-funding of growth.
>
> We chose "general accounting" as the second product line because we had over 40 corporate entities which were subdivided into operational entities. Since

> these corporate entities all needed their own payroll system, planning system, general ledger, etc., we couldn't do what we wanted in terms of management reporting if each system were unique. We then set a goal to get general accounting to be common throughout the company as soon as our planning system was up. We then started improving product cost accounting when the other two were working well.
>
> A good example of our self-funding was taking the financial planning product line (MODPLAN) and using its revenue to invest in the general ledger system—our "shooting star." For general ledger, we have reduced prices for on-line journal entries so that people can now do their operational statistical reporting as well as statutory reporting using the system. It becomes a self-fulfilling prophesy—reduced prices result in rapid growth in usage and revenues as fixed costs are spread over larger volumes and efficiency improves. Once this happens, you have another cash cow that you can invest in other areas.
>
> We use MODPLAN revenue and staff to invest in designated cost reduction for other areas. We usually can get a two-to-one return. If we take $40,000 for one person's expenses, we usually break even in that year. That is a fantastic return on your money. By taking this revenue and investing it in less mature product lines, such as our receivables and payables systems, we get a learning curve phenomena. As prices go down, people find new ways to use it.

More than using product line concepts and self-funding between product lines, Kight and Green were also concerned with the performance of TI's systems.

> In managing systems, we start off with three priorities. The first concern is that the system works, that it works right, is reliable and available. Secondly, we are concerned about the system's performance, how fast the function can be carried out and at what cost. Our third priority is developing new capabilities.
>
> To track the implementation of these priorities, we have measures of these concerns. Under availability, we have green and yellow charts for all our systems which show the band of acceptable performance levels for "on-time delivery" of reports, "response-time" on inquiries, unit cost reductions, etc. Green is good, yellow is acceptable but not good, and black is bad (Exhibit 7). We have numerous quantitative measures that we hold the product line manager responsible for.
>
> Once we begin measuring quantitative factors, such as the amount of paper per user, we begin to identify areas for making improvements. The only way we really make a breakthrough is by analyzing what is happening quantitatively. If we don't measure something, then we can't know for sure that we are making progress. It is therefore the development of performance measures that is key to achieving the productivity that we need and the culture that we want to foster in this operation.

Planning in IS&S

IS&S management participated in TI's planning system like all other operating groups. Don Haig, Ron Green's corporate systems administrator, explained:

> IS&S has a financial model like the rest of the corporation which the operating committee has approved. The model is supported by division and department forecasts and models, further subdivided into product lines.

In describing how the planning process applied to IS&S, Don Haig continued:

EXHIBIT 7: Texas Instruments' MODPLAN (A)
RPT 90% Response Time Green & Gold

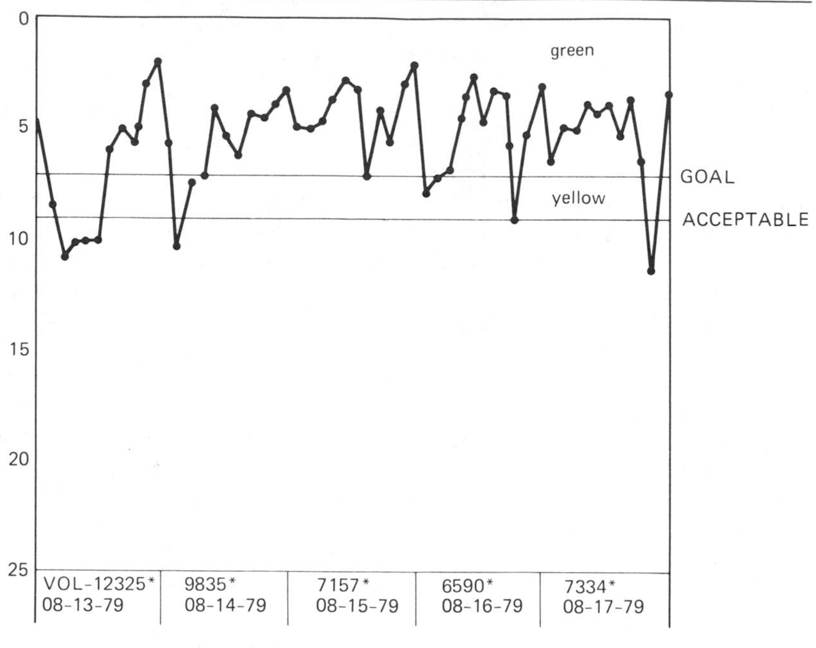

*Daily volume

Each product line manager makes a monthly forecast for various time periods. For example, in July we update the Rolling Plan forecast by month through September, plus the fourth quarter, 1979, and by quarter through 1980. My function is to organize and monitor these activities and to give managers guidelines for making forecast changes. I then arrange for Ron Green to examine changes made to prior forecasts, for approval and redirection if necessary, prior to consolidation of the numbers into IS&S total.

I issue a memo that has some general guidelines and a schedule with a set of forms that need to be filled out. It will show changes in sales taxes, social security rates, anticipated pay rate increases, etc. This is the mechanism for communicating corporate directives and guidelines to product line managers. I then set up the forms which are on MODPLAN to cover the time periods being forecasted. It is pretty much cookbook for the product line managers since they just look at the forms they have to fill out. They are basically sources and uses statements and income statements.

During our monthly reviews, first at the department level with Ron Green and then at the division level, each product line is reviewed and adjustments may be made. Then we have the IS&S review on the fifth working day with John White. These presentations change each month depending on the results and our priorities.

When we consolidate IS&S, we make adjustments at the top to judge out some of the things which were forecasted in some lower level organizations. To arrive at our goals in GPM, payroll and benefits, production computing costs, etc., we make "right way" judgments at the top. For example, we adjusted GPM to zero for the year for the consolidation. However, when all the product lines are

> consolidated we have $120,000 in GPM that can be applied against volume variances, performance variances, needed sustaining projects, or profit at the division level. That is about one percent of our total revenues. As we review all our goals, we also take judgments where something looks out of line so these can be reviewed to minimize anomalies in the future.
>
> Department managers take judgement on forecasts at their own levels. That requires that I look at their judgements before making my judgements. You can think of judgement as a slack variable in a linear programming problem where you have multiple constraints and a large number of variables. If the sum of the variables is greater than the constraint level that is defined, then the slack variable is negative. Otherwise it's positive. We have three slack variables within our entity structure. One is in general accounting systems and one is in personnel systems. They may or may not be used for any time period, but I have to be aware of them before using ours at the division level.

In discussing Charles Kight's operations, he explained the actual financial presentations which were compiled for the April rolling plan (Exhibit 8):

> We review operations monthly. Here is an example of our profit and loss report for MODPLAN. We show our unit price revenue, which comes from selling inquiries on-line. Operating revenue comes from user organizations who want us to do special work for them. Costs are then broken into sustaining costs related to production, and expenditures for new developments. Since MODPLAN is self sufficient, we aren't spending OST funds on it. Instead, MODPLAN shows expense for corporate systems projects which is funding cost reductions elsewhere. So we spent $95,000 out of revenues of $2.1 million to reduce costs in other product lines.
>
> If you subtract our people related expenses of $219,000, production costs of $1.2 million for keeping the system going and updated, and $139,000 for sustaining the system; it still leaves $363,000 in profit margin. At the division level, pluses and minuses balance out.
>
> We also have the new general ledger system which has now reached $780,000 in revenues. With costs of almost $900,000 we have a loss of $104,000. This loss is incurred as this is a new system which is in the process of being fanned out. In 1980, with full utilization and cost reduction, it is planned to break even. We fund it with $73,200 coming from MODPLAN and $31,000 coming from corporate OST. I break even as a division.

THE FUTURE GROWTH OF MODPLAN

With the continued growth and increasing complexity of doing business, Charles Kight and Ron Green felt that the growth in MODPLAN and other systems would continue. They discussed some of the reasons for this growth:

> If you look at the external business environment, you see the need for continued productivity improvements. For example, we're at about $3 billion in revenues today and plan to go to $10 billion (Exhibit 9). If we triple the number of plants, we would have nine times the number of interconnects. So complexity is increased with growth and vertical integration. What will be the impact of the increasing complexity that comes from this growth? What will be the impact of increased regulation on the internal operations? What will be the impact of continued very high inflation?

EXHIBIT 8: Texas Instruments MODPLAN (A)
MODPLAN Financial Review

MODPLAN	*1Q79*	*2Q79*	*3Q79*	*4Q79*	*YR79*	*1Q80*	*2Q80*	*3Q80*	*4Q80*	*YR80*
UN Price Rev	503	486	532	571	2,092	542	570	598	628	2,338
Operating	25	7	1		33	4				4
Corp Sys Proj	−20	−17	−27	−31	−95	−25	−25	−25	−25	−100
Total Funding	508	476	506	540	2,030	521	545	573	603	2,242
Sust:S&W Peo	52	46	60	61	219	77	77	78	78	310
CIC Prod	311	279	286	310	1,186	310	325	341	358	1,334
CIC Sust	40	37	31	31	139	45	45	45	45	180
Other	53	13	28	29	123	36	36	36	36	144
Sus Total	456	375	405	431	1,667	468	483	500	517	1,968
OST:S&W Peop										
CIC Cost										
Other										
Total										
Total Cost	456	375	405	431	1,667	468	483	500	517	1,968
Production Net	52	101	101	109	363	53	62	73	86	274
Int Price Sup	−61	−89	−64	−44						
GPM	−9	12	37	65	105	53	62	73	86	274

The work load is going up as a result of increased regulation by such agencies as the SEC, FASB, IRS, FTC, OSHA, and EPA. There is a demand for more information and there are more constraints being placed on actions. For example, FASB pronouncements increased from 5 in 1972 to 12 in 1978. Our footnotes in the annual report have increased from 3 pages in 1973 to 7 pages in 1978 while quarterly reports (10-Q's) have grown from 96 lines to 176 lines during that time.

To understand the impact of all this, we need to measure the expected work load of future managers. Assume, for example, that management information will grow at 10 percent, government information requirements grow at 10 percent per year, revenues increase at 10 percent per year, and complexity increases at some compounded rate of maybe more than 10 percent annually. If we want to increase profits by 10 percent per year and want the billings to payroll ratio to increase 20–30 percent over the next 5 to 10 years, we can't just work harder. We need improved tools to make step function improvements.

About the only tool you have to help manage the information needs of the indirect area is the computer. MODPLAN is one of the tools that has had a tremendous impact on how much work can get done by one person. We spend more time consolidating and planning now, because the utility of what we get has increased and the cost and time to do it has decreased. It's like growing crops by trailing sticks along the ground to plant seeds. When you give a farmer a hoe, he can do a lot more acres per person. You can now farm more land and be more profitable. It doesn't mean he has to work less either, because he still puts in a full day of hard work as he plows more ground. As the work unit becomes cheaper, the economic value of that work increases. We're like that with MODPLAN. If our decision is to have profitability with inflation in the external world, then we have to get better tools. This was shown to be the case in direct manufacturing where automation has payed off. Productivity in the future will depend more and more on indirect productivity which has two aspects. First is cost per unit of indirect work, i.e. efficiency, and second, the quality of decisions which will impact both direct and indirect areas, i.e. effectiveness.

In addition to productivity, TI's management was also concerned with the quality of the individual work environment. Charles Kight continued:

The second challenge we face relates to the kind of work that people are doing. We have a change in the expectations of employees. I can remember being told to work all night to close the books, but people aren't going to do that anymore. The goals of people in our society are changing and they aren't going to put in the long hours. We don't want people to spend their time in the monotonous drudgery of routine work so we have to automate and develop new productivity aids.

Demands for better decisions have also increased in areas such as asset and liability management, planning and control, and measurement of the impact of inflation. To do this we need better, and more readily available information. In addition to improving everyone's productivity, you have to change the mix of what people are doing. We need to change the mix of user effort from data preparation to data usage, and we need the ability to identify effects of change so that we can develop plans to respond more rapidly. This will only come about with use of the computer to do all the repetitive work and some decision assisting work. That's the only way we can achieve our productivity goals. For example, we now have technology in such areas as communication capabilities where we can transfer information around the world in just a few seconds at a very low cost.

The cost of labor has gone up 5 or 10 percent per year. If we compare

EXHIBIT: 9 Texas Instruments MODPLAN (A)
Financial Information for Texas Instruments Incorporated

Years Ended December 31	*1978*	*1977*	*1976*	*1975*	*1974*	*1973*	*1972*	*1971*	*1970*	*1969*
Summary of Operations *Thousands of Dollars*										
Net sales billed	$2,549,853	$2,046,456	$1,658,607	$1,367,621	$1,572,487	$1,287,276	$943,694	$764,258	$827,641	$831,822
Operating costs and expenses	2,296,338	1,835,619	1,495,981	1,252,833	1,403,105	1,141,824	860,625	705,094	773,113	769,983
Profit from operations	253,515	210,837	162,626	114,788	169,382	145,452	83,069	59,164	54,528	61,839
Other income (net)	12,249	9,261	23,782	11,971	4,159	6,746	7,178	6,840	4,529	3,936
Interest on loans	(8,370)	(9,179)	(8,310)	(10,822)	(10,741)	(6,654)	(5,676)	(6,526)	(7,014)	(5,474)
Income before provision for income taxes	257,394	210,919	178,098	115,937	162,800	145,544	84,571	59,478	52,043	60,301
Provision for income taxes	117,115	94,281	80,678	53,795	73,179	62,309	36,541	25,755	22,182	26,790
Net income	140,279	116,638	97,420	62,142	89,621	83,235	48,030	33,723	29,861	35,511
Earned per common share (average outstanding during year)*	$6.15	$5.11	$4.25	$2.71	$3.92	$3.67	$2.17	$1.53	$1.35	$1.53
Cash dividends paid per common share*	1.680	1.320	1.000	1.000	.920	.555	.415	.400	.400	.400
Common shares (average shares outstanding during year, in thousands)*	22,794	22,842	22,933	22,920	22,854	22,691	22,139	22,085	22,072	21,919

Financial Condition *Thousands of Dollars*										
Working capital	$278,336	$348,327	$364,754	$360,722	$314,302	$306,968	$282,049	$261,398	$210,957	$189,271
Property, plant and equipment (net)	572,652	394,093	302,873	253,709	280,449	219,941	154,992	154,954	171,436	182,377
Long-term debt, less current portion	19,069	29,671	38,169	47,530	72,755	67,690	71,373	94,778	86,801	94,595
Stockholders' equity	845,390	744,618	660,279	585,288	541,372	469,337	369,627	328,702	303,236	281,548
Employees at year-end	78,571	68,521	66,162	56,682	65,524	72,422	55,934	47,259	44,752	58,974
Stockholders of record at year-end	26,247	24,438	22,425	21,359	18,977	16,135	15,177	16,210	17,738	17,808

* Adjusted for stock split in 1972.

EXHIBIT 10: U.S. Labor and TI Computing Costs

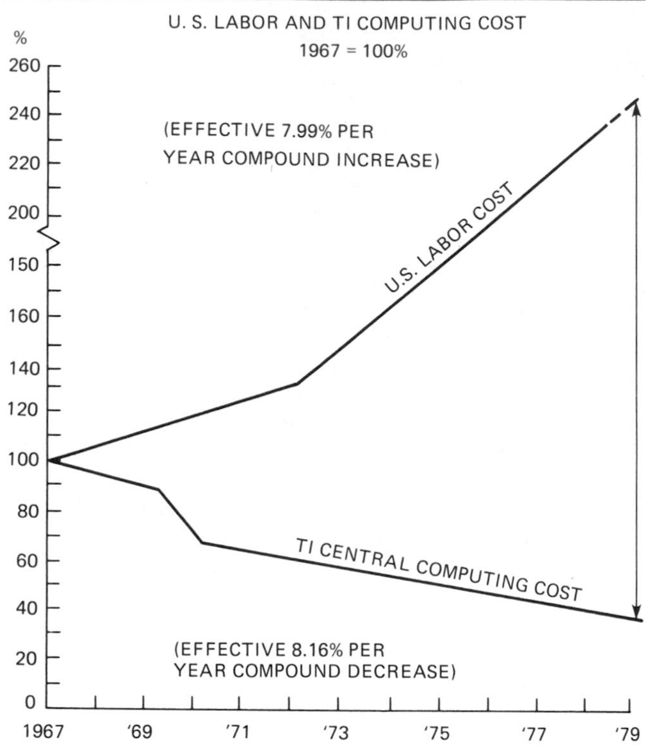

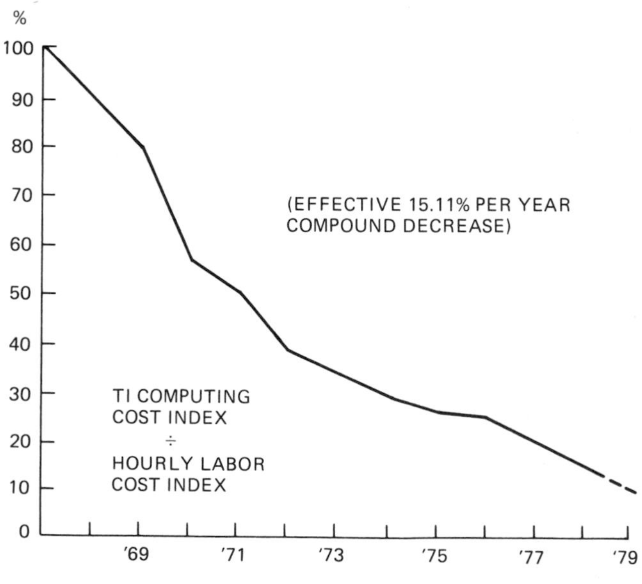

increases between 1967 and 1979 in labor costs to computing costs, we have almost 600 percent increase in cost using labor versus computer between 1967 and 1979. If we compare the decline in TI's computing cost index to the hourly labor cost index, we see over a 15 percent decrease each year by substituting computers for labor. The question then becomes one of deciding how fast you can automate. (See Exhibit 10).

CASE THIRTY-FOUR

CALMA Company (A)

CHRISTINE BLOUKE and L. J. BOURGEOIS III
Stanford University

Assignment Questions:

1. What is wrong with CALMA's current strategy?
2. Where are CALMA's greatest opportunities and risks?
3. What new strategies would you propose for CALMA given its strengths and weaknesses?

"You're quite right, Art," said Bob Benders, President of CALMA, to his Manager of R & D, Art Collmeyer. "Except for suggesting that our parent company avoid the 'no-growth' remote computing business, it's not clear to me what business strategy the ICI* people are recommending. Considering all the data and management time we have provided, it appears that they have hedged on making specific recommendations. You and I will have to sit down with Ron Hill (head of marketing) and Lem Bishop (finance), and hammer out our basic strategy for ourselves."

It was December 1979, and CALMA Corporation had just received ICI's final presentation after six months of intensive study and analysis. Having achieved a significant market position in the young and fast-growing CAD/CAM (computer-aided design and computer-aided manufacturing) industry, CALMA executives recognized the need to take stock of their current situation and formulate a coherent strategy to guide subsequent activity. Their sales growth from \$6.9 million to \$42.9 million in 4 years (see Exhibits 1 and 2) placed CALMA on the threshold of even more explosive growth. Benders wished to position his firm to handle this growth in a vigorous but orderly fashion.

*ICI (International Consultants, Inc.) was a management consulting firm whose identity has been disguised.

Funds for the development of this case were provided by the Program in Management of the Total Enterprise, major contributors to which are the Robert Denzil Alexander Fund, William H. Draper, III, Mr. Meyer Luskin, the Carlton A. Pederson Memorial Fund and Mr. Franklin Redlich.

EXHIBIT 1: CALMA Company (A)
Statement of Income 1971–1978

	Following U.T.I. Purchase Twelve Months Ending December 31		*Twelve Months Ending August 31*						
	1979	*1978*	*1977*	*1976*	*1975*	*1974*	*1973*	*1972*	*1971*
NET SALES AND SERVICE REVENUES	$42,797,602	$27,160,051	$14,278,552	$9,484,164	$6,919,332	$6,146,236	$3,461,912	$1,586,339	$ 670,215
Cost and Expenses:									
Cost and sales and service revenues	25,184,616	16,058,011	7,989,661	5,235,188	3,773,395	3,715,763	1,997,681	854,332	552,059
Research and development	3,698,410	2,419,039	1,430,367	1,057,548	866,365	524,436	320,662	151,542	124,119
Selling	7,874,392	5,393,815	2,102,508	1,391,221	991,925	791,915	448,903	238,957	173,499
General and administrative	1,175,514	1,017,897	520,946	404,411	446,401	335,820	186,566	88,593	51,689
Interest, net	1,740,588	709,608	125,078	129,309	108,335	110,841	64,501	60,804	61,894
Total Costs & Expenses	39,673,520	25,598,370	12,168,560	8,217,677	6,186,421	5,478,775	3,018,313	1,394,228	963,260
PROFIT FROM OPERATIONS* (1978, 1979)	4,864,670	2,271,289							
INCOME BEFORE PROVISION FOR INCOME TAXES	3,124,082	1,561,681	2,109,992	1,266,486	732,911	667,461	443,599	192,111	(293,045)
PROVISION FOR INCOME TAXES	1,279,000	356,903	880,000	519,300	335,000	255,000	223,000	105,000	
INCOME (LOSS) BEFORE EXTRAORDINARY ITEM (1971–1974)						412,461	220,599	87,111	(293,045)
EXTRAORDINARY ITEM Reduction of Federal income taxes arising from carry-forward of prior years' operating losses						150,000	191,000	92,000	
NET INCOME	$ 1,845,082	$ 1,204,778	$ 1,229,992	$ 747,187	$ 397,911	$ 562,461	$ 411,599	$ 179,111	$(293,045)
EARNINGS PER SHARE (1971–1977)									
Income before extraordinary item			$1.88	$1.22	$.66	$.70	$.38	$.18	$(.64)
Extraordinary item						.26	.32	.18	
Net income per share			$1.88	$1.22	$.66	$.96	$.70	$.36	$(.64)

* Net of interest expense.

Source: company records.

EXHIBIT 2: CALMA Company (A)
Balance Sheet 1971–1979

	Twelve Months Ending December 31		*Twelve Months Ending August 31*						
	1979	*1978*	*1977*	*1976*	*1975*	*1974*	*1973*	*1972*	*1971*
Assets									
CURRENT ASSETS:									
Cash	$ 976,649	$ 1,052,218	$ 19,144	$ 16,491	$ 6,854	$ 6,830	$ 1,511	$ 9,142	$ 2,160
Receivables, less allowances for doubtful accounts	11,908,769	10,412,117	6,000,238	4,612,847	2,668,684	1,982,341	1,283,143	498,224	322,631
Income taxes refundable	—	—	—	11,717	73,500	—	—	—	—
Inventories	15,541,102	10,647,684	3,347,010	1,996,896	1,225,457	1,185,500	751,340	275,323	254,659
Prepaid expenses	334,245	248,049	143,722	90,981	49,115	32,035	29,326	32,545	22,640
Total current assets	28,760,765	22,360,068	9,510,114	6,728,932	4,023,610	3,206,706	2,065,320	815,234	602,090
ADVANCES TO SUBSIDIARIES:	158,786	—	—	—	—	—	—	—	—
LONG-TERM RECEIVABLES:									
Equipment contracts, due after one year	—	—	183,070	77,894	178,249	29,841	53,676	47,575	—
Other			47,700	38,500	40,500				
			230,770	116,394	218,749				
EQUIPMENT, IMPROVEMENTS & LEASES:									
Communication, computer equipment & other property	6,649,946	4,580,463	—	—	—	—	—	—	—
Production equipment	—	—	341,116	276,113	78,017	77,072	70,225	62,748	48,128
Automotive equipment	—	—	11,788	11,788	11,788	14,448	12,423	15,084	10,032
Equipment leased to customers	—	—	150,037	160,702	122,834	53,647	24,058	24,058	25,446
Office furniture and equipment	688,060	251,781	79,012	58,187	39,517	36,840	28,257	20,174	19,663

Leasehold improvements	670,394	503,750	194,201	175,851	140,442	127,041	86,229	74,972	74,167
Demonstration system under capital lease	—	—	117,576	—	—	—	—	—	—
	8,008,418	5,335,994	893,730	682,641	392,598	309,048	221,192	197,036	177,436
Less-Accumulated depreciation and amortization	(1,810,732)	(841,985)	376,266	254,135	191,621	148,208	111,371	91,873	81,205
	6,197,686	4,494,009	517,464	428,506	200,977	160,840	109,821	105,163	96,231
TOTAL ASSETS	$35,117,237	$26,854,077	$10,258,348	$7,273,832	$4,443,336	$3,397,387	$2,228,817	$ 967,972	$ 698,321
Liabilities									
CURRENT LIABILITIES:									
Borrowings under bank line of credit/debt	$ 5,000,000	$ 8,500,000	$ —	$1,653,151	$ 937,360	$ 607,324	$ 624,011	$ 233,107	$ 140,000
Current portion of installment note payable to bank	527,624	455,150	466,300	290,625	—	50,000	—	—	—
Current portion of note payable to majority shareholder	—	—	—	62,264	62,264	71,175	72,345	35,000	651,100
Accounts payable	2,017,975	3,625,496	1,740,528	1,131,159	797,785	904,580	611,871	268,837	136,318
Accrued expenses									
Payroll and commissions	678,858	530,673	423,746	260,491	129,150	131,634	104,105	31,460	14,804
Other	2,260,691	737,959	265,898	197,134	256,758	176,761	38,647	—	91,043 (inc. int.)
Federal and state income taxes									
Currently payable	2,798,846	1,115,903	618,649	22,300	—	80,774	20,000	13,000	—
Deferred	—	—	1,103,906	861,232	408,091	—	—	—	—
Advance from UCS 1978, 1979:	4,665,587	1,040,858	—	—	—	—	—	—	—
Total current liabilities	17,949,581	16,006,039	4,619,027	4,478,356	2,591,408	2,022,248	1,470,979	610,674	1,033,265
LONG-TERM LIABILITIES:	1,144,425	1,669,889	2,140,157	481,168	237,460	256,592	201,912	213,131	—

EXHIBIT 2: (continued)

	Twelve Months Ending December 31		Twelve Months Ending August 31						
	1979	*1978*	*1977*	*1976*	*1975*	*1974*	*1973*	*1972*	*1971*
Shareholders' Equity									
After purchase by UTI:									
Shareholders' Equity	$10,216,213	$ 5,216,213							
Accumulated Earnings	3,961,936	3,961,936							
Current Year Earnings-1978	1,845,082								
1971–1977:									
Common stock, no par value-Authorized—800,000 shares Outstanding—at $.50 per share	—	—	312,633	304,134	298,173	280,667	280,587	280,507	230,507
Additional paid-in capital	—	—	814,544	775,528	769,080	688,576	688,496	688,416	438,416
Retained earnings	—	—	2,371,987	1,234,646	547,215	149,304	(413,157)	(824,756)	(1,003,864)
	16,023,231	9,188,149	3,499,164	2,314,308	1,614,468	1,118,547	555,926	144,167	(334,944)
TOTAL LIABILITIES	$35,117,237	$26,854,077	$10,258,348	$7,273,832	$4,443,336	$3,397,387	$2,228,817	$ 967,972	$ 698,321

Source: company records.

COMPANY BACKGROUND

"CALMA" is a combination of the names "Calvin" and "Irma," the couple who, in the early 1960s, founded the company in Santa Clara, California, to serve as sales representatives for a number of newly formed computer graphics components manufacturers.

In 1964, Ron Cone, a client from California Computer Products (Calcomp), sold his founders' stock in Calcomp and purchased CALMA. As a sideline, Cone began to manufacture digitizers (machines that convert a drawing into machine-readable form) in CALMA's back room. Cone gave Bob Benders, then an engineer with Lockheed, a night job designing digitizers. In 1968, Cone offered Benders the job of chief engineer and asked him to develop a new, more marketable product to take CALMA out of the hardware business and into complete graphics systems. As Benders, CALMA's current president, explains it:

> The offer appealed to me. It was a chance to get out of engineering and into management, and interactive graphics systems looked like they could offer us a good opportunity. The cost of computers was coming down, Tektronics had just introduced a memory tube display that drew pictures on a screen, and memory disk drives were coming down in price.
>
> We analyzed the semiconductor industry—integrated circuit "chips" were already getting too large for manual design methods—and after calculating our costs we figured we could build a single-terminal graphics system for about $50,000 and sell it for around $100,000. So we put together a system and began writing software to make it interactive. Well, we underestimated everything—costs and time to produce the software. Early in 1970, Cone got out. The recession was on and our banker called our loan. Cone said to me, "I've had enough of this. You can take this company if you want, but I can't give you any money; otherwise, we'll fold it." So I took it.
>
> I was lucky enough to find a banker who was an adventurer. He loaned me $100,000 and then we landed a government contract to develop a mapping system. The contract had progress payments which funded our integrated circuit CAD development, too.
>
> In late 1970 I approached Intel. They had one of our digitizers, were interested in automating, and there was nothing else on the market. We made a $150,000 deal with the specs and purchase order number written on a half a sheet of paper. CALMA shipped them our first system in 1971 and it worked. Then Motorola bought a system. It was famine to feast. We've been making money ever since.

Organizational Development

During the first few years, CALMA had a part-time financial manager, but by 1972 Benders decided CALMA's growth required full-time attention in that department. Lem Bishop was hired in May 1972. Bishop had been controller and financial officer for a subsidiary of GTE; he came to CALMA from the controller's job at a subsidiary of Pacific Lumber.

Bishop, a trim, unassuming man, describes himself as "constructively skeptical" in his dealings with other managers. He became the principal liaison between CALMA and its lenders, and a member of Bender's small top management team.

By 1974, CALMA's employment had doubled. Benders began to look for a professional manager to head the research and development department. He hired Art Collmeyer, who had been manager of CAD system development of Xerox. Collmeyer had a PhD in micro-electronics, and was a skilled line manager. He was well received as head of R&D, an area within CALMA (and the computer industry as a whole) which had a unique culture, often attracting "brilliant eccentrics"—a difficult group to manage, at best. Collmeyer was able to impose discipline on this group while still maintaining their creative productivity.

A lean, wiry man, Collmeyer radiated energy. "He's the first to arrive and the last to leave here," commented one of his employees, who credited Collmeyer with building a strong team spirit among his staff. "He makes us work like dogs and enjoy it." Of his own style, Collmeyer observed:

> I try to hire the best people, give them responsibility and accountability—the large picture of what they are part of—and I try to get their personal commitment to the job and to CALMA's and my own goals. Line management is a people-intensive job. I don't tell my people what to do or how to do it, I just tell them what results to get. And I give them plenty of chance to make mistakes. One mistake is OK. The second time, I'll get all over 'em. The third time the same mistake is made, I'll can them.
>
> I avoid creating staff functions; all my line managers are asked to do their own. Good line managers want to know what their jobs are. Staff guys want to know what *I* want them to do.

By 1976, Benders had begun to worry about marketing. "I saw that we were good hot-shot development types and could peddle what we designed, but we had no real marketing knowledge to help guide design. We usually worked on the guess that the 'product was right'." In 1977, Benders organized CALMA's first marketing department, and "went through two or three marketing bosses" with unsatisfactory results. Following this rapid succession of "technical people without a real understanding of the difference between marketing and sales," in May of 1978 Benders hired Ron Hill from Tektronix. With a PhD in engineering, an MBA, and marketing experience, Hill brought needed expertise to CALMA's marketing effort. Originally installed as vice president of corporate planning, and after a six-month experience as head of field engineering in Europe, Hill was named senior vice president for marketing in April 1979.

Within the marketing group, sales was organized by geographic region and sold the full array of products and applications to all markets and customers. The marketing department, on the other hand, specialized according to application (for example, microelectronic applications such as printed circuits and integrated circuits, or mechanical applications such as automotive design). In addition, the field engineering group, which provided after-sales service to customers, was brought under the marketing umbrella. (See Exhibit 3 for the December 1979 organization chart, Exhibit 4 for brief biographies of CALMA's top management team and Exhibit 5 for growth of facilities.)

Decision-Making Style

By the end of 1979, CALMA's executive team had developed an identifiable style. According to one executive, "CALMA has a strong top management;

EXHIBIT 3: Organization in December 1979

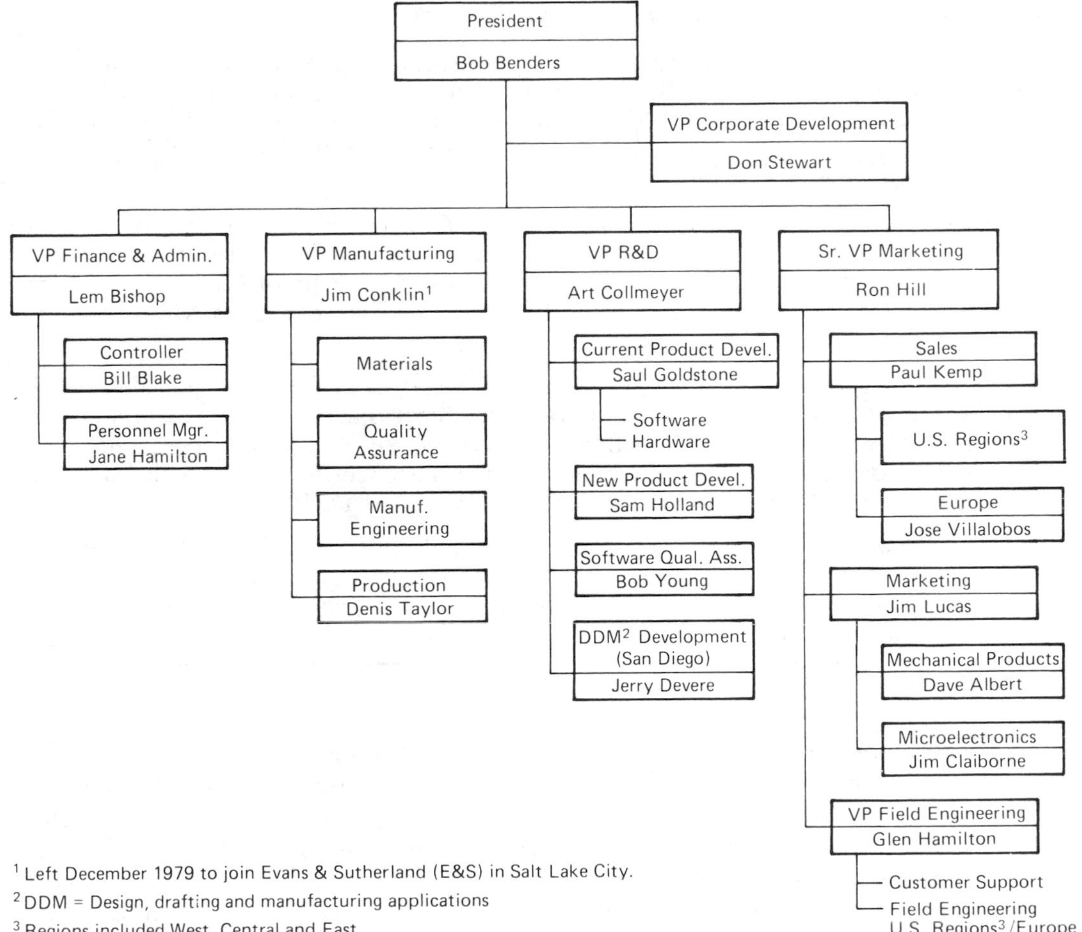

[1] Left December 1979 to join Evans & Sutherland (E&S) in Salt Lake City.
[2] DDM = Design, drafting and manufacturing applications
[3] Regions included West, Central and East.

it's not very participative, it's all top down. All the important decisions are made by three or four people."

While this perception was seen by several managers as a positive aspect of leadership, it was not uniformly shared. Another manager said that "like all CAD companies, CALMA's decision making is fairly flaky; we all run by the seat of the pants."

While CALMA had an annual operating plan and budgeting system, performance reviews and budget reviews were fairly informal. A company-wide MBO system was installed in 1980.

There were several guiding decision-making and management-style principles which were articulated by top management:

- If you have a good market position, you protect it. If you see a reasonable market, go after it. But we will not go into a market unless we can be among the top three competitors within three or four years.
—Bob Benders

EXHIBIT 4: CALMA Company

BIOGRAPHIES OF CALMA'S TOP MANAGEMENT, 1978

Robert Benders, President. Benders has been president of CALMA since 1971, directing the company's change from hardware manufacturing to systems supplier. Born in Latvia in 1936, Benders moved to Michigan from Germany at age fourteen. He received his BSEE from the University of Michigan in 1962, worked briefly for Boeing Digital Systems before moving to Lockheed in 1965.

Lemuel D. Bishop, Vice-President, Finance and Administration. Bishop joined CALMA in 1972. He was formerly controller for Victor Fluid Power, Inc. Born in Palo Alto in 1936, he received his BA in political science from the University of California at Santa Barbara, a BA in business administration from Menlo College, and an MBA from the University of Santa Clara.

Arthur J. Collmeyer, Vice-President, Research & Development. Collmeyer joined CALMA in 1974. He was formerly manager of CAD system development at Xerox Corporation. Born in southern Illinois in 1941, Collmeyer received a BS and MS degree in electrical engineering from the University of Illinois, Urbana. He spent four years with Motorola before earning a PhD from Southern Methodist University, Dallas.

Ronald V. Hill, Senior Vice-President, Marketing. Hill joined CALMA in 1978. He was formerly with Tektronix where he held various management positions in marketing and engineering. He holds an MS and a PhD degree in engineering from Washington State University and an MBA from the University of Portland.

- Bob has some very strong philosophies that guide him. For example, the superior competence of our technical people, the need for excellence—these are basic requirements for success. Also, he believes competitors will turn over every stone when competing with us. —Lem Bishop
- In the high-tech business, the superior product will win—assuming you do the other things reasonably well. —Bob Benders
- This business depends heavily on our R & D gurus for product innova-

EXHIBIT 5: CALMA Company (A)

HISTORY OF FACILITIES TO DECEMBER 31, 1979

	'68	'70	'72	'74	'76	'78	'79
1. 707 Kifer Rd. 12,000 sq. ft.	10/68 →						
2. 165 San Gabriel 19,208				12/73 →			
3. 185, San Gabriel 7,500 sq. ft.					2/77 →		
4. 527 Lakeside Dr. 67,174 sq. ft.					10/77 →		

Total sq. ft. 12/31/79: 105,882

Source: Company records.

tion and competitive dominance. The problem is that a lot of these people don't want to grow up. What they need is healthy doses of discipline without spoiling their enthusiasm. —Art Collmeyer

- Most people think marketing has to do with determining future directions and future products. But that just isn't something you do every month. The *real* marketing problem is getting the product to market—training the sales people, documenting the product for customer use, and providing after-sale support. —Ron Hill

Product Development

CALMA's first graphics system (GDS-1) was created to design integrated circuits (IC's). It made CALMA the market leader in IC CAD systems (a position it had maintained through 1979). Systems for printed circuit design were first introduced in 1974; in this market segment CALMA had strong competition from several other CAD vendors.

CALMA also sold mapping systems. However, by 1977 its initial product was experiencing data-base problems, as customers demanded more sophisticated software. CALMA chose to withdraw from the mapping market to concentrate on circuit design and to develop mechanical design software, which forecasts indicated would be the CAD application to experience fastest growth.

Bob Benders summarized the early years:

> We were just building and selling and hoping the product was right. In 1976, I realized that we really needed a separate marketing department. However, that's been a painful process. We still have not made a successful change from being a research and development-driven company to becoming a marketing-driven company. However, we have remained good at guessing what the market needs.

CALMA's geographic location was a key factor in its success. Located in the heart of Silicon Valley, a high-tech industry area, CALMA was surrounded by most of the nation's largest users and manufacturers of integrated circuits. "Close geography eliminated the necessity of a marketing department," according to one employee.

In the early years client needs were communicated directly to CALMA's R&D staff, who then developed the requested software. All integrated circuit designers could utilize the same software to produce ICs; but CALMA developed the most efficient graphics design system on the market and became "Goliath to the competitors' David." As a result, CALMA was the industry price leader.

As CALMA began to diversify its product line to include printed circuits and mechanical design applications, momentum slowed. The diversity of users presented a real dilemma as each new graphics customer requested different applications software and system capabilities. (See Exhibit 6 for product descriptions.)

Market diversification had its costs. CALMA's dominance in the IC market was challenged by Applicon's aggressive entry in 1978. "CALMA was squashed," according to one executive. "Applicon's entry caused a lot of instability in our sales force. We had to refocus and get back in control. To do so, we had to neglect the other markets."

EXHIBIT 6: CALMA Company

MAJOR PRODUCTS DESCRIPTION

CHIPS (Integrated Circuit Design System)

CHIPS is an advanced, minicomputer-based, interactive graphics system for very large-scale integrated circuit (VLSI) design work.

This turnkey system is based upon the industry standard GDS II base management system. It features 32-bit precision to support VLSI work, color graphics terminals for designers and software aids to enhance design implementation. Additional advantages include background processing for analysis programs and output formatting and application capabilities to tailor the system to the specific needs of the user. CHIPS is a total system applicable to all areas of graphic IC development.

CARDS (Printed Circuit Design)

CARDS is a comprehensive computer-based interactive graphic system for the design and production of printed circuits. The system encompasses all aspects of PC design and production from digitizing a schematic through final documentation and artwork, including features that handle net list generation; packaging, placement, and routing; automated design review; and NC drill and photoplot output.

DDM (Design, Drafting, and Manufacturing System)

Introduced in 1977 and now an industry leader, DDM is a powerful, minicomputer-based system for three-dimensional computer-aided design, drafting and manufacturing. This high-speed, flexible system enables a designer to explore several solutions to the design problem, perform engineering analysis, check clearances of moving parts and produce engineering drawings and documentation including the preparation of NC tapes. DDM systems provide design and manufacturing firms with greatly increased throughput, accuracy, and control of the product cycle from initial design concept through manufacture.

Source: Company documents.

By 1979, CALMA was back in control in ICs, but was "hanging by our fingernails" in the mapping, architecture, and mechanical design markets. "We were now David to Computervision's Goliath in the mechanical applications markets."

In the mid-1970s, CALMA, like its other graphics systems competitors, sold "on futures." Many sales were made upon the salesperson's promise that desired applications would be made available within six to eighteen months with a percentage of purchase price withheld until delivery. Since CALMA was operating on the leading edge of graphics technology, customers were willing to purchase less sophisticated systems because there were no better alternatives available. Customers occasionally were frustrated when promised developments could not be delivered on schedule; however, the problem was industry-wide.

Operations Flow

CALMA manufactured a very small percentage of the components of its graphics systems. Most of the hardware was purchased "off-the-shelf" from original equipment manufacturers (OEM's). Components were then assembled into various modules, placed in CALMA-designed cabinets, and CALMA's software was added to make the pieces of the graphics system work together. Once the system was assembled, diagnostic software was used to assure the equipment was properly connected and integrated (i.e., that the terminal could communicate with the disc memory, the plotter and the CPU, etc.).

During a quality control check, the equipment was externally examined for such things as paint chips, properly connected cable and wires, and the like. CALMA's graphics software was then added, and an "expert" trial user from customer support performed a software audit, using the system as its purchaser would use it. The equipment was then delivered to the customer. Representatives from field engineering set up the equipment, performed a quality check, and retested the equipment with diagnostic software. A customer support person then performed a final software check, demonstrated the system for the customer, and occasionally stayed for a short period to train the customer's staff to use the system.

Acquisition by UTI

In September 1978, CALMA was purchased by United Telecommunications, Inc., for $17 million. UTI had previously engaged the firm, International Consultants, Inc., (ICI) to assist several of their subsidiaries in strategic planning. It was suggested that ICI examine both CALMA and United Computing Systems (UTI's computer services subsidiary to which CALMA was now reporting) to assist both companies in evaluating their strategies and competitive strengths and weaknessess, and to assess their relative positions in the corporate portfolio.

MANAGEMENT CONSULTANT'S REPORT

In its report on Phase I of its study, begun in June 1979, the ICI team identified and examined major sources of information about the industry and the company. Orientation interviews with CALMA's upper and middle management had been performed. A four-part internal analysis had been made to examine CALMA's financial, marketing/sales/service, research and development, and manufacturing processes and procedures. CALMA's primary customers had been interviewed, a literature search had been performed, and a competitive analysis had been made.

In November, 1979, ICI made a presentation of their Phase I findings at a CALMA senior management meeting. The three-part presentation first described the evolution of the industry; second, outlined CALMA's competitive position and internal skills; and third, described the strategic issues facing CALMA.

Growth of the Graphics Industry

Automated computer graphics technology originated in the mid-1940s as a result of military research done at MIT and research for General Motors. During the 1960s, following the rapid development of computer hardware capabilities and sophistication, "view only" graphic data input and output became possible.

By 1970, graphic systems suppliers had entered the market. Hardware costs had dropped dramatically following technological advances which led to development of minicomputers and microprocessors. The graphics systems suppliers, operating on the leading edge of technology, developed increasingly sophisticated software which allowed graphic data manipulation in two and three dimensions.

Increasingly advanced software capabilities and breakthroughs in distributed systems were anticipated for the 1980s. This would lead to additional product innovations by turnkey systems suppliers, like CALMA, who had been historically most effective in matching software with improving hardware price performance trends.

ICI's presentation identified computer graphics—CAD/CAM—as a high-growth, rapidly evolving industry characterized by:

1. Product innovation, which first created and still drives the systems segment of the industry.
2. A favorable set of demand and buying characteristics which will generate increasing sales and service requirements, and
3. Moderate competitive pressures forecast to remain constant over the next few years."

As illustrated in Table 1, the CAD/CAM industry could be divided into four segments: Specialized Hardware, Stand-alone Software, Remote Services, and Turnkey Systems, which was CALMA's major emphasis.

The total world CAD/CAM market at the end of 1978 was $510 million, and the consensus of several industry observers polled by ICI indicated that the 1983 CAD/CAM market would reach $1,985 million.

TABLE 1: Structure of the Industry, 1979

Major Product Segments*	*Share of Total Market*	*Growth Rates (1978–1983)*
Specialized Hardware	58%	21%
Stand-alone Software	3%	26%
Remote Services	5%	22%
Turnkey Systems	34%	45%
	100%	31% av. growth rate

* Specialized Hardware—components for interactive graphics systems were manufactured by more than 70 companies, many of which had vertically integrated to sell complete graphics systems rather than single components.

Stand-alone Software, which worked for a variety of graphics equipment configurations, was available from several suppliers. Some were independent; others had formal cooperative agreements with turnkey systems suppliers or hardware manufacturers.

Remote Computing Services sold all types of data-processing services and applications; a few had begun to offer CAD services. The user bought time, not equipment.

Turnkey Systems Suppliers sold complete packages for graphics applications, including hardware, software, equipment servicing and training.

TABLE 2: Leading Competitors by Computer Graphics Segment

Specialized Hardware	*Software*	*Services*	*Systems*
Tektronix	ISSCO	Boeing	Applicon
Sanders	Manufacturing and Consulting Services	CDC	Auto-trol
Calcomp		McAuto	CALMA
	MDSI		
Versatec			Computervision
	SCRC		
			Gerber
			Intergraph

By 1978, all of the leading competitors in the four basic CAD/CAM segments had developed strength in a single segment only, as shown in Table 2. Whereas a few companies had begun movement across segment lines, the majority of 1978 sales, as well as new product introductions, were concentrated in the segment where each competitor was strongest.

Nature of Competition Within the Industry

ICI indicated that a dramatic increase in competition would be inevitable, in the long term, given the nature of the rapidly evolving systems segment. But between 1978–1980, competitive pressures were not expected to increase significantly:

> Existing competitors in each of the four computer graphics segments (Specialized Hardware, Stand-alone Software, Remote Services and Turnkey Systems) historically have tended to concentrate in their proprietary area, choosing not to enter other related segments.
>
> Even within the system's segment, competitors have tended to focus on special application niches.
>
> While a variety of new entrant competitors either have tentatively entered the systems business—or could, very easily—there appears to be little evidence of any significant competitive pressures from this area.

Forecast for the Future

In its presentation ICI indicated that the long-term future was unclear:

> Given the attractiveness of the computer graphics industry, it is likely to attract some new entrants, probably from the computer industry and with strong current/related involvement to one or more of the current computer graphics segments.

Possible new entrants included: Digital Equipment Corp., Exxon or Xerox in graphics hardware; General Electric, UCS, NIS or ISBD in services; and Tektronix, Calcomp or Evans & Sutherland in turnkey systems.

It was difficult to predict the nature and probability of technological breakthroughs which would impact the industry. ICI speculated:

Given the move to distributed data processing, the trends in hardware/software costs, and the revolution in microelectronics, new breakthroughs are likely to be applications-oriented, intelligent terminals. They will likely come from hardware or systems suppliers migrating to firmware capability.

So while it is difficult to determine specific responses to these potential developments in new competitors and technological breakthroughs, system suppliers can protect their current competitive lead by:

1. Monitoring vigilantly all competitive activity.
2. Staying abreast of all developments in microelectronics.
3. Ensuring a thorough understanding of core end-use applications.

Market Forecast for Turnkey Systems Segment

In 1978 three end-use industries accounted for 80% of the turnkey systems market: Aerospace, 30 per cent; Automotive, 25 per cent; and Electronics, 25 per cent. The remainder was divided among mechanical, construction, civil engineering and other industries. Turnkey systems sales were $165 million worldwide in 1978 and were forecast to reach $1.1 billion by 1983, an average growth rate of 45 per cent per year. Table 3 shows market segments by end-use industry and by systems application. (See Exhibit 7 for consensus forecasts of the systems market.)

Believing that the future would bring robust growth and limited cyclicality, ICI asserted that systems suppliers had a unique opportunity to develop "selling partnerships" with their customers, given the customer's reliance on their suppliers for expert advice. Sales and service were also considered of great importance to customers, whereby vendors could gain credibility and differentiate themselves.

Assessment of the Competition

Within the turnkey systems segment, six competitors accounted for 90 per cent of the total market (Table 4). ICI believed that CALMA's competitors were improving their competitive position through: "a combination of aggressive strategic actions and development of internal skills."

TABLE 3: Systems Market Segmentation (1978 Sales = $165 million)

End-Use Industry		*Systems Applications*	
Aerospace	30%	Mechanical	39%
Automotive	25%	Integrated Circuits	16%
Electronics	25%	Civil/Structural	15%
Mechanical	10%	Printed Circuits	13%
Construction	5%	Mapping	9%
Civil Eng.	2%	Other	8%
Other	3%		
	100% = $165 mill.		100% = $165 mill.

EXHIBIT 7: Turnkey Systems Market Forecast

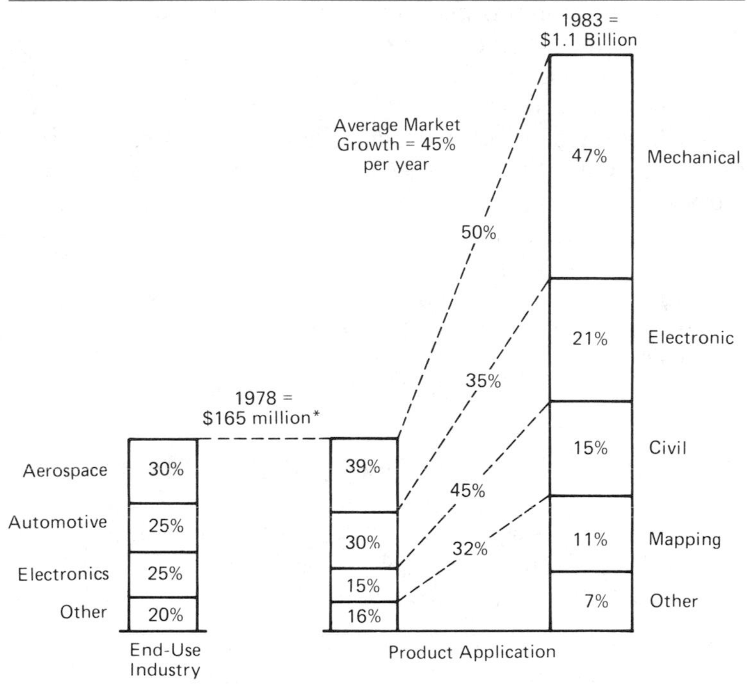

*U.S. sales = $124 million; Europe = $30 million; Japan = $11 million

Source: ICI report. Data compiled from research by Arthur D. Little, Inc., Merrill Lynch and others.

TABLE 4: Leading Turnkey System Competitors

Company	*1978 Sales ($ millions)*	*% Market Share (1978)*	*Projected Average Annual Sales Growth (1976–1979)*	*Major Application*
Computervision	$ 48.4	29%	76%	Mechanical
CALMA	$ 27.2	16%	58%	Integrated Circuit
Applicon	$ 22.0	13%	62%	Integrated Circuit
Auto-trol	$ 21.9	13%	68%	Structural
M & S	$ 20.1	12%	50%	Mapping
Gerber	$ 9.0			
	$148.6			

Since CALMA was growing slowly in the mechanical applications segment, ICI predicted that the company's total market share would drop to 14% by 1979. Exhibit 8 presents an overview of competitors' product-market strategies. Turnkey suppliers had historically focused on one application area and were just beginning to move into additional related areas in 1979.

CALMA was judged to have products with superior capabilities in its major lines: Integrated Circuits, Printed Circuits, and DDM (an interactive system for design drafting and manufacture). ICI cautioned that "while the systems generally provide good price/value, this may deteriorate unless capabilities continue to be enhanced and/or prices maintained at competitive levels." Exhibit 9 is ICI's assessment of CALMA's competitive position and projected market share. Exhibit 10 shows ICI's comparison of CALMA's relative performance on several financial indicators.

ASSESSING CALMA'S POSITION IN THE INDUSTRY

The ICI presentation suggested that CALMA's "current implicit business strategy needed rethinking." The consultants identified three factors that had positioned the company "on the threshold of becoming a broad-based market leader in computer graphics":

> Financial indicators of performance are quite favorable. However, success has been largely dependent on one product line and a few key customers.
>
> CALMA is in the process of introducing an array of new products. While

EXHIBIT 8: CALMA Company (A)
OVERVIEW OF PRODUCT-MARKET STRATEGIES

Company	*Apparent Strategy*
Applicon	—Establish product leadership in IC and build distribution —Shift emphasis in mechanical to low-end product
Auto-trol	—Dominate civil/structural applications by emphasizing price performance of 2D product and building distribution —Enter mechanical by introducing 3D product
CALMA	—Dominate IC through product leadership —Enter mechanical by introducing unique 3D product
Computervision	—Dominate mechanical by offering good product and emphasizing sales/service —Enter new segments (e.g., IC) with similar approach
Gerber	—Dominate 2D mechanical with sophisticated product and leverage established sales force —Enter PC segment with new product
M & S	—Dominate mapping through product leadership —Enter closely related segments (e.g., civil/structural) with similar approach

Source: International Consultants, Inc., analysis.

EXHIBIT 9: CALMA Company (A)
ICI's Assessment of CALMA's Competitive Position

MARKET SEGMENT	PRODUCT	PRICE	SELLING	SERVICE	OVERALL	Market Share 1978	Market Share 1979 est.
	SOURCES OF COMPETITIVE ADVANTAGE						
IC	Outstanding	Average/ Weak	Weak	Average	Outstanding/ Average	41%	43%
PC	Outstanding	Weak	Weak	Average	Average/ Weak	29%	12%
MECHANICAL	Outstanding/ Average	Average	Weak	Average	Average	10%	15%
CIVIL/ STRUCTURE	Average	Weak	Weak	Average	Average/ Weak	6%	7%
MAPPING	Average	Average	Weak	Weak	Average/ Weak	8%	3%
OVERALL	Outstanding/ Average	Average/ Weak	Weak	Average	Average	Total 16%	Total 14%

Source: International Consultants, Inc., research.

expectations are high, there have been some introduction problems and mixed results.

CALMA has aggressively expanded its staff to handle growth. However, the company still faces some critical operating problems.

CALMA had grown quickly and profitably. Average annual growth rates from 1975 to 1978 were 54 per cent in sales, 31 per cent in net income and 82 per cent in total assets. Sales were concentrated in one product line, CALMA's

EXHIBIT 10: CALMA Company (A)

CALMA'S RELATIVE FINANCIAL PERFORMANCE

Financial Performance (1978)	*Industry*	*CALMA*
Return on Capital (EBIT/Capital)	21.6%	10%
Operating Margin (EBIT/Sales)	11.7%	8.4%
Asset Turnover (Sales/Assets)	1.53x	1.01x
Expense Ratios (1978)		
SGA Expense/Sales	27.2%	23.6%
R & D Expense/Sales	9.3%	8.9%
Gross Margin	48.0%	40.9%

Source: Company records.

graphic display systems (GDS) I and II, and with a relatively small group of customers. CALMA was attempting to extend its success in electronics to other application areas; four new product introductions were planned for 1980.

Historically CALMA had made product commitments based on futures. Introductions timed for 1976–1978 had not gone as smoothly as anticipated, resulting in some internal pressures, as well as some customer discontent. For instance, in customer contacts between 1976 and 1978 CALMA had targeted high resolution VMD* on Graphic Display System I by 1979. In the fall of 1979, only low-resolution VMD was anticipated, for introduction in March 1980. CALMA had also been forced to abandon a proposed matrix plotter controller for Versatec, geared originally for several graphic display system customers, and had moved the completion date of a structural package sold in October 1978 from June 1979 to January 1980.

ICI's interviews with CALMA's customers indicated that mismanaged expectations appeared to be the major source of customer discontent. Typical of comments made to ICI interviewers was "CALMA has the most advanced Integrated Circuit product available. But they made unrealistic commitments to us, and the GDS II start-up has been fraught with problems."

To handle a projected average annual growth rate of 26.4 per cent, CALMA had been aggressively expanding its work force. As a result, in 1979, the average tenure was only 1.6 years, and 37 per cent of the employees had been hired within twelve months. The service department had the least number of new employees (30 per cent) whereas administration had 50 per cent. The influx of personnel had occurred at all levels—from senior management to the production floor—and it explained in part some of the operating problems identified by ICI:

Marketing: New department, performing sales support function, conducting little market research.

Service: Lacks total service concept; responsible for activities beyond department's control.

Production: Few cost-reduction efforts; poor procurement and MRP** with a new production planning program in the works.

Within CALMA's sales force, 36 per cent of 1979 sales revenue had been generated by its top four U.S. sales representatives; 25 per cent of sales revenue had come from the twelve other U.S. reps, 24 per cent from CALMA's Japanese agent, and 15 per cent from the European sales rep. Seventy-four per cent of CALMA's sales force had been hired since 1978.

In the fall of 1979 there were seven openings for sales representatives. According to ICI:

> This low staffing level and/or apparent lack of management interest accounts for the absence of badly needed controls. Staffing plans are done informally and nonroutinely. No formal prospect identification or account planning tools appear to be used. Methods for preparing proposals, negotiating corporate agreements, and requesting discounts are only beginning to be rationalized. Building CALMA's sales force appears to be an improvement opportunity with significant short-term benefit.

* VMD: Vector Memory Display.

** MRP: Material Requirements Planning.

TABLE 5

Company	Size of Sales Force	Sales Offices	1979 Production Level Forecast (Sales ÷ Sales Force Size)
CALMA	23	15	$1.7
Applicon	28	24	$1.5
Computervision	39	23	$2.4

Marketing:

ICI identified CALMA's marketing function as an area of slow development needing examination. The marketing department had recently been formed and its management turnover had been high. Its initial responsibility had been more toward sales support than marketing, and its product managers had limited end-use industry experience. Little market research had been conducted. CALMA's competitors appeared to be aggressively building their sales forces as shown in Table 5.

Service:

In the first eight months of 1979, CALMA customer service made an average of 16 calls for each system under service contract or "upon call." These calls required an average of 4.6 hours of direct efforts. ICI concluded that

> To deal with this growing volume and provide necessary service enhancements, management must continue building capabilities. Improvement opportunities appear to be: 1) Developing a CALMA service concept; 2) Adopting a more appropriate balance of account responsibility with the sales force, e.g., shift responsibility for sale of new software releases to sales force; 3) Establising a management information system to help monitor demand levels and provide management control.

Research and Development:

CALMA had a history of successful R&D. ICI indicated that CALMA's challenge would be to maintain creativity while installing controls. Major challenges were to establish a project planning and monitoring system, to ensure that deadlines were achievalble, and to coordinate with and take the lead from marketing.

Production:

ICI identified the production function as offering opportunity for major cost improvements. Efforts begun in January 1979 had resulted in savings per system of more than $18,000. Major additional opportunities were seen to exist in procurement and inventory management, as annual growth rates for inventory between 1975 and 1978 had averaged 106 per cent, while sales growth during the same period had averaged only 54 per cent.

ICI recommended that backlogs be increased to facilitate planning, procurement, and capacity management; that cost reduction initiatives be accelerated; and that production planning, MRP, and procurement programs be quickly upgraded.

ICI's Profile of Organizational Capability

ICI shifted its perspective to CALMA's internal organization to assess the company's strengths and weaknesses. CALMA's struggles were determined to be primarily product related. The company had been a highly innovative product developer. Within CALMA "winners" came from the research and development (R&D) department which was the largest single professional functional department.

New product development had been driven by R&D rather than by marketing, which ICI believed had led to a lack of customer and market orientation. CALMA was organized around functions rather than markets, and the marketing department had been organized around existing products. The top management team had no prior exposure to market-driven organizations.

As a result, ICI noted, sales and service capabilities were inconsistent. Sales and service plans were informal, management systems "embryonic, and internal communications poor." There was no structural specialization within the sales force around products and markets, and the focus had traditionally been on selling a system, not on developing an account.

ICI felt CALMA's cost control and asset management systems were weak; the CEO was the only person with true profit responsibility. Production planning and control systems had just been developed, and product line profitability figures had not been developed.

ICI suggested that CALMA needed a more effective compensation system to reward long-term performance and improve turnover rates. CALMA had not instituted a recruiting and management development function or a "CALMA culture" to build loyalty. As a result, team spirit was judged to be lacking.

ICI Identified Leadership Requirements

ICI identified three issues to be given top priority. First, of highest priority, was to upgrade the effectiveness of sales and service efforts. ICI recommended steps such as: "Launching a do-able account planning effort, upgrading sales force capability and management processes, and enhancing customer service efforts."

Next, ICI recommended that CALMA determine how to focus near-term product planning and development activities to other marketing efforts. Controlling R&D programs and supplementing R&D resources were recommended.

Cost and asset management were of low to moderate priority. ICI suggested improving procurement and materials management through interim manual systems, upgrading MRP systems activities, and establishing priority for product engineering cost-reduction efforts.

Determining alternatives and resource requirements for each market segment was also considered. Critical issues to be addressed were:

1. How much additional effort is needed to secure CALMA's leadership position in integrated circuits?
2. How to participate, if at all, in the printed circuit segment?
3. How to develop a meaningful position in mechanical?
4. How to participate, if at all, in other emerging segments?

ICI's recommendations for each issue included: 1) ensuring continued product leadership and providing a family of products for low-end niches; 2) understanding users' price performance requirements more clearly and determining the need for concurrency with other product lines; 3) meeting primary competitors head-on or identifying select niches to penetrate, and participating in all major end-use industries; and 4) determining market potential and current position for other markets like civil/structural and mapping.

Longer-term business strategy issues were also considered in ICI's presentation, particularly how product leadership could be maintained. Major issues presented for discussion included: 1) how to sustain a leadership position in the core business; 2) how to determine an appropriate sustainable level of vertical integration; and 3) how to develop a leadership role in the evolution of the office and factory of the future?

At the conclusion of the November 1979 presentation, ICI outlined the steps it would take during phase 2 of its investigation to develop strategic alternatives for CALMA. Those alternatives were to be prepared by the ICI task force for presentation at the December 1979 senior management meeting.

STUDY OF STRATEGIC ALTERNATIVES

On December 4, 1979, the ICI task force met with CALMA's senior management team. ICI had prepared a discussion draft of CALMA's strategic alternatives by product-market segment. For each of five markets (integrated circuits, printed circuits, mechanical, architecture/engineering, and mapping), ICI had analyzed CALMA's situation, its strategic position, and its strategic alternatives.

Also, for each product/market segment, CALMA's position was examined with respect to its sales volume and market share, customer base, product parity, and selling/service capability. Then, market attractiveness was discussed in terms of 1) size and growth, 2) demand pattern, 3) customers/concentrations, 4) product needs, and 5) buying patterns. This framework led to a discussion of CALMA's competitive situation, strategies, and strengths and weaknesses.

In further addressing CALMA's strategic position for each market, ICI highlighted the current strategies for 1; products, 2; costs, 3; selling, and 4; service. Incremental opportunities were then discussed.

Finally, strategic alternatives were explored and objectives, tactics, and requirements were identified which would allow either a modest or major redirection for each of CALMA's current strategies.

The discussion draft prepared by ICI follows as Appendix 1.

Conclusion

Following ICI's presentation, Bob Benders met with Lem Bishop, Art Collmeyer, and Ron Hill. The four men did not agree totally with ICI's perspective of the company or the issues presented, and had some misgivings about the value of the consultant's presentations. Benders had also begun to question ICI's objectivity, believing that ICI's conclusions were being dictated by what corporate headquarters might wish to hear. Nevertheless, it was clear that unless they moved quickly, some key opportunities might be lost.

APPENDIX 1 CALMA Company (A)

Outline of Calma's Strategic Alternatives By Product-Market Segment

This document contains summaries of Calma's strategic opportunities organized by segment. The segment covered and contents of each summary are as follows:

Segments	*Contents*
—Integrated Circuit (IC)	—Situation Analysis
—Printed Circuit (PC)	—Strategic Position
—Mechanical	—Strategic Alternatives
—Architectural/Engineering /Construction (AEC)	
—Mapping	

These documents were prepared on the basis of conversations with product managers, as well as the inputs from customers and other analysis performed by the task force.

It is important to recognize that these summaries are only a first cut. They are to be used for discussion purposes and it is expected that they will go through many iterations culminating in a more formalized product management process.

APPENDIX 1
Situation Analysis Segment: IC (Integrated Circuits)

CALMA Position:

VOLUME/SHARE:

—1978: $10.9M (41.2%)—Cumulative sales:
—1979: 15.0 (42.1%)—GDS I/IC:
—1980: 16.5 (34.3%)—GDS II/IC: 100
—1983: 22.0 (18.5%) · 65 operating/ 32 on-line design
· 21 in Japan

CUSTOMERS:

PAST	CURRENT	OPPORTUNITY
Natl. Semi (13)	IBM (2)	TI RCA
Intel (8)	Hitachi (4)	II-P AMD
Motorola (20)	Toshiba (5)	DEC Zilog
Plessey (12)		NEC Mostek

(·)—Systems sold

PRODUCT PARITY:

—Major strengths are edit features, analytic capabilities, manufacturing interfaces and overall reliability
—Product weaknesses are relatively slow display speed and lack of data management capability

SELLING AND SERVICE CAPABILITY:

—Core group of AEs and salesmen exist particularly on West Coast
—Hardware field service capability exists in major geographic locations only

Market Attractiveness

SIZE AND GROWTH:

—1978: $ 26.4M—Projected growth 35%/year
—1979: 35.6 —Volume figures represent only the available market
—1980: 48.1
—1983: 118.8 There is purportedly a market of equal size satisfied by in-house initiatives

DEMAND PATTERNS:

—Fundamental sources of demand very favorable
· Design constraints for VLSI
· Proliferating use of all ICs ($\Delta = 30\%$/year)
· Increasing number of designers/fabricators
—Lingering concern about cyclicality

CUSTOMERS/CONCENTRATION:

—Large captives (e.g., IBM)/
—Small captives (e.g., Atari)/
—Standard component (e.g., Intel)/
—Custom component (e.g., AMI)/
—Service bureau (e.g., Design Only)/
—User (i.e., Design Only)/

PRODUCT NEEDS:

GRAPHICS	ANALYSIS
Digitizing	Logic design
On-line design	Circuit simulation
Automatic design	Design rule checks
Auto/On-line	

BUYING PATTERNS:

—Customers tend to standardize on a CAD vendor—this has important implications for early penetration
—Trend toward CAD committees who are increasingly influential in purchase decisions
—Design systems usually assigned to major project teams
—First-time and less sophisticated customers generally more price sensitive

Competitive Situation

COMPETITION/SHARE: (1979 APPROXIMATE)

CALMA	42%
Applicon	33%
GCA/Mann	15%
Computervision	5%
Others	8%

STRATEGIES:

Applicon—Dominate segment by establishing product superiority (through Intel initiative) and building national account selling program

GCA/Mann—Establish meaningful position in CAD by introducing suitable product and leveraging contacts/expertise in IC fabrication

Computervision—Opportunistically sell low-end IC machine. And, if development efforts succeed, introduce new IC CAD systems

STRENGTHS AND WEAKNESSES:

Applicon—Good referenceable customer base; ongoing product development effort; new initiatives in sales and marketing
—Unproven product; poor service record

GCA/Mann—Unknown

Computervision—Excellent sales and marketing
—Obsolete product; small customer base

APPENDIX 1: (cont'd)
Strategic Position
Segment: 1C

Current Strategy	*Incremental Opportunities*
PRODUCT: —High-end graphic product on par or superior to competition —Current product development efforts directed at analytic capability (i.e., DRC*) and new terminal (i.e., VMD**), yet little attention being directed at data management	PRODUCT: —Current product line could be redefined to include three parts: (1) graphics systems; (2) analytic software; and (3) custom systems/software —While developing a "complete" product should be objective, there are a number of intermediate steps: (1) accelerate development of data management capability; (2) add more analytic software; (3) develop low-end graphics terminal; and (4) develop enhanced graphics systems (e.g., auto/on-line) —The hardware components provided should be rationalized to simplify selling, servicing and production requirements
COST: —Probably the high-cost producer. While customers are relatively price insensitive, it causes margin problems —Recent cost reduction efforts successful, but no logical action plan exists	COST: —Efforts at reducing product costs are the minimally acceptable alternative —Future pricing decisions should be based on: (1) economic value to customer; (2) payback; and (3) price performance (e.g., unbundle)
SELLING: —Selling activities are largely reactive and focus on only responding to established customers —Little initiative in this segment demonstrated in Midwestern or Eastern regions	SELLING: —Expanding sales force to enable increased coverage and frequency is the minimally acceptable alternative —A number of other steps are necessary: (1) leverage referenceable customer base and utilize some as Beta sites; (2) develop "account management" philosophy and prepare individual account plans; (3) establish prospecting and servicing priorities (e.g., current account; IBM/TI; competitors accounts; small accounts); (4) specialize sales effort (e.g., national accounts; dedicated sales force)
SERVICE: —Hardware service is adequate —Software service is dependent on R&D —Training activities are only in initial stages. And, little attention paid to account management	SERVICE: —Developing a "service concept" is essential for this as well as other segments —Additional opportunities include the following: (1) assigning AES to pre- or post-sale responsibilities; (2) developing multiple, application-specific training programs (e.g., operator, management, refresher); and (3) providing range of service contracts
SUMMARY: —Stated objectives are to dominate business, yet a realistic goal is only to hold share —Strategy hinges on maintaining product leadership and depending on customers to pull it through —Efforts to reduce cost, and particularly to improve sales and service capability, lack substantial management attention and resource commitment	

* DRC: Design Rule Check
** VMD: Vector Memory Display

APPENDIX 1: (cont'd)
Strategic Alternatives
Segment: IC

	Current Strategy (Including Planned Changes	*Modest Redirection*	*Major Redirection*
Objectives:	—Hold share (40%) by maintaining product leadership at high end	—Gradually increase share (e.g., 40 to 50 per cent over 5 years) by broadening graphics product capability and building a dedicated sales force capability	—Aggressively increase share (e.g., 40 to 70% over 5 years) by redefining product line and rapidly building dedicated sales force capability
Tactics:	—Continue current product development initiatives. In addition, a closer working relationship with NIS should be established and increased priority given to developing data management capability —Dedicate sales-force efforts to securing existing accounts —Develop contingency programs for Applicon product development efforts	—Current product development efforts must be expanded to include rapid development of low-end terminal —Expand regional sales force to include personnel with IC expertise and develop national account representatives responsible for key prospects (e.g., IBM) —Develop contingency program for computervision product development efforts	—Redefine product line to include three parts: (1) graphic systems; (2) analytic software; and (3) custom software. This implies providing a range of graphic system (i.e., low to end). And, it may require acquisition of IC analytic software house —Develop a dedicated sales force in U.S. and Europe, and establish account plans for *all* potential customers —Provide assistance to Japanese agent
Requirements:	—Capital requirements will be comparable to current projections —Product/market management effort must be increased by 2–3 times —Stabilizing current sales force and installing necessary controls will require additional management attention	—Capital requirements will be moderately higher —Product/market management efforts must be increased by 2–3 times —Sales force in Midwest, East and European regions must be expanded by 2–3 times; 3–4 people must be hired for NAM effort; and effort made to ensure solid efforts by Japanese agent	—Acquisition(s) may require $5–10 million —Establishing relationship with new processor supplier will involve start-up costs and building additional inventory —Specializing sales force will involve addition of 10–20 people, plus addition of new overheads

APPENDIX 1: (cont'd)
Situation Analysis Segment: PC (printed circuits)

CALMA Position

VOLUME/SHARE/PROFITABILITY:

—Market share declining sharply

	1978	*1979E*	*1980E*
Dollars	$6,000	$5,000	$5,000
SOM	20%	12%	9%

—Gross margin below average due to discounting
—Selling cost level unclear

CUSTOMERS:

—Significant installed base, directed towards large accounts with high-end product needs
—Reputation and image varies widely with current and potential customers
—Core customers are Burroughs (7), Hughes (7), Intel (7), ITT (8), and NCR (10)

PRODUCT PARITY:

—Above par high-end product now; but only par by 1981
—No product at low-end and mid-range
—Product development efforts behind and vulnerable to more slippage

SELLING AND SERVICE CAPABILITY:

—Little proactive selling; heavy repeat business
—Product and application selling skills in field minimal, e.g., few experienced AEs
—Very limited sales coverage; hardware service capability and training marginally adequate

Market Attractiveness

SIZE AND GROWTH:

—Overall segment $30M in 1978; overall growth at 35% although CALMA's core market may slip to 20% by 1983
—Geographic breakdown; U.S. 60%, Europe 30%, Japan 10%

DEMAND PATTERNS:

—Concurrency trends unclear
—Strong overall demand by all subsegments; little cyclicality
—Several emerging subsegments demanding low-end products
—Slow overall product mix shift

CUSTOMER/CONCENTRATIONS:

SUBSEQUENT	% OF MARKET	CONCENTRATION
—Computer peripherals	40%	High
—PC/mechanical (Auto, Aero, etc.)	25%	Very high
—Industrial controls	20%	Very low
—Consumer electronics	15%	Very high

PRODUCT NEEDS:

—Slowly emerging trends toward design automation continue, sequentially spreading to all segments
—Low-end digitize/edit niche concentrated in Consumer Electronic Customers

BUYING PATTERNS:

—First system penetration at 40–50% for U.S. buying centers but only 10–20% internationally
—Repeat buying patterns unclear but U.S.-based accounts probably committed to entrenched vendors

Competitive Situation

COMPETITION/SHARE/TREND:

—Computervision/35%/slowly declining
—CALMA/20%/rapidly declining
—Applicon/25%/slowly declining
—Gerber/5–7%/increasing rapidly at low-end
—S-C/5%/increasing rapidly at high-end
—Redac and 30 others/3–5%/fringe competitors

STRATEGIES:

—Computervision; maintain slow, steady product enhancements but use sales, service, low COGS, and installed base to slowly grow share; major focus on large, long-term customers
—Gerber and S-C; entering low and high-end respectively
—Applicon; unclear, appear vulnerable

STRENGTHS AND WEAKNESSES:

—Computervision; market coverage, mechanical reputation are major strength. Marginal product line is only weakness
—Applicon; installed base and image/weak sales and product others; software niche
—Others; software niche

APPENDIX 1: (cont'd)
Strategic Position
Segment: PC

Current Strategy	*Incremental Opportunities*
PRODUCT:	PRODUCT:
—Current efforts to improve high-end capability (e.g., design automation features) focused on rewriting Mark Revel package for MRD/Eclipse* —CARDS-N** project may need redirection	—Additional software enhancements to improve auto-check and design automation possible but CALMA lack application knowledge —Low-end dig/edit for consumer electronics may represent important new subsegment
COST:	COST:
—Clearly high-cost competitor with significant margin problems except for large, high-end buyers —Both product enhancements listed above will eliminate dual CPU requirement	—No apparent opportunities, except for fundamental redesign resulting from CARDS-N effort —Little pricing flexibility
SELLING:	SELLING:
—Sales effort largely focused on repeat, established customers —No apparent sales program in Japan —Little sales support for high-end product line	—Proactive fundamental account classification need to focus "new" selling effort —Product and application selling skills (e.g., how to sell the DA concept)
SERVICE:	SERVICE:
—Training aids inadequate and training process too complex, suggesting need for an improved application software package —Field service capabilities unknown	—Must develop base level of application engineering skills in U.S. and Europe —Application software support should be moved closer to major customers to counter product performance problems
SUMMARY:	
—Overall objective unclear; holding share may be difficult —Product development and sales effort lacks focus	

* MRD: Multicolor Raster Display
** CARDS: Computer-aided design and manufacturing system for printed circuits

APPENDIX 1: (cont'd)
Strategic Position
Segment: PC

	Current Strategy (Including Planned Changes	*Modest Redirection*	*Major Redirection*
Objectives:	—Stabilize declining share position during 1980–81 by Interim software development effort (by Mark Revel on MRD Eclipse. Maintain share longer term with high-end CARDS-N product to be sequentially introduced in 1981–82	—Stabilize current share position with new color Mark Revel product and introduce a low-end dig/edit product. Stretch out CARDS-N and develop sales capability of the general system sales force	—Double share by 1983 by accelerating product family enhancements through acquisitions/joint venture of a leading design automation software group, aiming for a series of product family introductions in late 1980–81
Tactics:	—Launch Mark Revel software development now for June 1980 shipment —Stress price/performance of new MRD and future compatability of CARDS-N in aggressive marketing promotion effort —Prioritize selling focus in U.S. better and prospect in Europe more	—Carry out planned efforts for new color Mark Revel product and slow CARDS-N effort —Piggyback onto NIS/CALMA Scorpio effort and introduce a low-end product by early 1981 —Sales and pricing tactics unclear	—Dedicate significant resources to introducing new product family during 1981 —Focus selling effort on benchmark customers during late 1980, then broadening customer focus during 1981–82 —Sharpen pricing based on competitive pressures, but maintain 10–20% premium
Requirements:	—Increase CALMA product management and development effort by 2–3 times —Develop contingency program for Mark Revel effort —Broaden general systems sales force effort to double-triple prospecting by year-end 1981	—Same as current strategy —Devote software modification effort to Scorpio project —Increase market management effort to obtain broader coverage	—Financial resources for acquisitions/joint venture? —Restructuring of product development effort —Start prototype development projects with key customers

APPENDIX 1: (cont'd)
Situation Analysis
Segment: Mechanical

CALMA Position

VOLUME/SHARE PROFITABILITY:

—Early market share increases have reached a plateau

	1977	*1979*	*1980*	*1983*
Dollars	$7,000	$16,000	$18,000	$28,000
SOM	10%	15%	12%	5%

—Gross marginn and operating margin below par to start up operating costs

CUSTOMERS:

—Established customer base fragmented but with some important niches in key segments
—Marketplace image limited
—Current and potential core customers unclear
—Strongest position in Japan

PRODUCT PARITY:

—Superior high-end product, but requiring significant customer application software development
—Expensive mid-range systems and no low-end systems
—Product family and next generation development program unfocused

SELLING AND SERVICE CAPABILITY:

—Selling largely reacting to many customer inquiries, lowering productivity
—Application and technical selling skills weak; no industry specialization
—Unable to provide demos to current prospects requesting them

Market Attractiveness

SIZE AND GROWTH

—Overall market largest and fastest growing ($105M/40%)
—Subsegments still unclear; probably tend towards buying pattern clusters
—Japan and Europe markets independent, but lag U.S.

DEMAND PATTERNS:

—Customer sophistication low
—Major amount of latent demand

CUSTOMERS/CONCENTRATIONS:

—Dominated by a few large customers with many, fragmented buying centers (i.e., automotive and aerospace make up 50% of today's market)
—Flagship customers are key influencers

PRODUCT NEEDS:

—Many latent demands in leading edge customers requiring in-depth, industry knowledge
—Distributed systems are a clear, major trend
—70 per cent of customers require full capability, i.e., layout, design, drafting, and manufacturing interface; 25% require PC/DDM product
—Slower rate-of-change in product requirements than in IC

BUYING PATTERNS:

—Large repeat-buy accounts standardizing on installed vendors
—First-time buyers follow complex, performance-oriented evaluation process
—Large accounts standardizing via CAD/CAM efforts

Competitive Situation

COMPETITION/SHARE:

—Computervision increasing rapidly holding key accounts and penetrating first-buy customers using broad sales coverage and substantial discounting when needed
—Second-tier competitor shares stable in key niches, e.g., Applicon in auto
—Minor inroads by new competitors

STRATEGIES:

Computervision—Future strategy a continuation of past; product strategy unclear

Applicon—Plans to devote major market resource to the mechanical market in the next 5 years. However, no outward signs, i.e., new product or sales effort indicate this

STRENGTHS AND WEAKNESSES:

Applicon—Entrenched based and joint customer development linkage is major strength/high-end product flexibility for new applications major weaknesses

Gerber and new competitors—unclear

APPENDIX 1: (cont'd)
Situation Analysis
Segment: Mechanical

Current Strategy

PRODUCT

—Superior product performance, but needs final packaging
—Next generation of enhancements include improved FEM, NC, and dimensioning capabilities plus surface package
—Introduce Scorpio low-end product (?)

COST:

—Cost reduction efforts unfocused
—Competitive costs, particularly Computervision's, lower than CALMA's

SELLING:

—Largely reactive due to people shortage
—Still developing basic skills, which lowers productivity
—Accounts focus unclear

SERVICE:

—Limited experience, but major customers would clearly buy a more aggressive hardware and software service package

SUMMARY:

—Ambitious goal to displace Applicon as number two largely unfocused
—Product leadership only source of clear competitive advantage

Incremental Opportunities

PRODUCT

—Data base management, multi-systems communication links, and enhanced application software packages (e.g., Auto-FEM) are clear next steps
—Refinement and extension of current line also critical

COST:

—Some opportunity to improve hardware procurement margins if volume grows, but limited to 2 to 3% improvement in GM by year end 1981. Other cost savings unclear
—Packaging software development may yield incremental revenues but gross margin impact unclear
—Repositioning of service agreements and repricing in late 1980 to early 1981 may have a 1% to 2% gross margin impact during 1981
—Traditional pricing structure can be reshaped and sharpened to improve share without decreasing margins

SELLING:

—General system sales force must be enlarged and skill level enhanced through more specialization
—More end-use industry and application knowledge critical, e.g., sales and application development

SERVICE:

—Major customers need and are demanding more software application support

APPENDIX 1: (cont'd)
Strategic Alternatives
Segment: Mechanical

	Current Strategy (Including Planned Changes)	*Modest Redirection*	*Major Redirection*
Objectives:	—Stable or declining market share while maintaining operating margins by leveraging product leadership across a broad range of subsegments. Market focus and competitive strategies still being formulated —Introduce low-end product (Scorpio) through combined NIS/CALMA efforts	—Build dominant niche positions through 1981 by committing major sales and service effort to a concentrated number of accounts/end-use industries with a broader market roll-out launched in 1982	—Leap frog established competitors through major product innovation and rapid expansion of sales/service. Substantial acquisitions and joint-venture will likely be needed for added service capability, software development, and sales-force expansion
Tactics:	—Extend current product development effort into multi-system, data-management area —Increase overall selling effort and broaden account focus in U.S.; international effort unclear —Competitive tactics and expected responses unclear —Maintain current operating margins	—Continue product development efforts internally but launch several joint-development projects with core customers —Sharpen selling focus through better intelligence efforts and avoid competitive confrontations outside target accounts —Introduce specialized marketing, sales, and service resources —Accept lower profitability to secure niche position and broaden product definition to include advanced software and application development	—Broaden sales and service through joint-venture with OEM supplier (e.g., DEC) or NIS or an acquisition of regional SBC distributors —Acquire major software development group (MDSI or SDRC) or build internal development —Broaden product line rapidly and introduce next generation product line in 1981
Requirements:	—Capital requirements largely working capital expansion and continued level of product development —Product/market management effort increased by 2–3 times —Significant (but unknown) increase in field sales and application development personnel needed	—Software development effort through 1981 double today's level —Supplement expanded general purpose sales effort with specialized sales effort	—Significant short-term operating cash drain through 1982 —Major acquisition funding needed —Significant changes in other administrative systems needed to manage change

Appendix: (continued)
Situation Analysis
Segment: AEC

CALMA Position

VOLUME/SHARE:

—1978: $ 1.5M (6.1%)—Cumulative sales:
—1979: 3.0 (8.4%) 10 systems
—1980: 4.5 (8.7%)—Projected growth:
—1983: 25.0 (15.2%) 75%/year

CUSTOMERS:

Past	*Current*	*Opportunity*
Procter & Gamble	Elin-Union	BC Hydro
Ontario Hydro	Stone & Webster	Boeing
Royal Graphics	Japan Gas	AECs ("50 good prospects")

PRODUCT PARITY:

—CALMA has the most advanced product spec, yet it is incomplete. Key features include: 3D database which facilitates analysis and dimensioning. Key weaknesses include speed and user interfaces, plus currently high price
—Competitors are successfully selling 2D schematic systems with complete AEC work packages at a low price. They have been promising a 3D capability
—Longer-term product needs include interference checking; auto hidden line removal; and a solids data base

SELLING AND SERVICE CAPABILITY:

—Very little sales-force effort has been dedicated to CADEC
—No track recoı

Market Attractiveness

SIZE AND GROWTH:

—1978: $ 24.7M—Projected growth = 45%/year
—1979: 35.8 —Potential market = 1,000 users
—1980: 51.9
—1985: 165

DEMAND PATTERNS:

—Major sources of demand are energy crisis; technological breakthroughs in low-cost terminals; and cumulative effects of product acceptance; and lack of enough engineers
—CAD systems are usually purchased for specific projects involving large structures

CUSTOMERS/CONCENTRATIONS:

—Independent AEC Firms (e.g., Sergeant & Lundy, Gibbs & Hill, Bechtel, Brown & Root)/Top 30 = 30% and Top 400 = 80%
—Commercial accounts (e.g., Procter & Gamble)/Top 500 = 80%
—Government

PRODUCT NEEDS:

Basic Needs	*Disciplines*
—Schematics	—Process (e.g., P&ID, Flow)
—Dimension drawings	—Electrical
—Analysis/reports	—Piping (e.g., Isometrice)
	—Structural steel (e.g., Flaming)
	—Structural concrete
	—Civil (e.g., Roads)
	—Architectural (e.g., layouts)

Competitive Situation

COMPETITION/SHARE: (1979 approximate)

Auto-Trol	33%
M&S	27%
Computervision	20%
Applicon	9%
CALMA	8%
Others	3%

STRATEGIES:

Auto-Trol—Dominate segment by leveraging established customer base and introducing new product

M&S—Dominate segment by rolling out superior product with aggressive pricing

Computervision—Establish meaningful position by pushing product through sales effort

STRENGTHS AND WEAKNESSES:

Auto-Trol—Adequate product; good position with AEC firms; excellent selling effort
—Inability to complete new product; potential risk of losing focus

M&S—Superior product (31) software, DEC hardware); good applications knowledge, improving position with AEC firms
—Modest selling skills

Computervision—Excellent sales and marketing; adequate product
—Product does not receive a lot of sales-force attention

—CAD systems have historically only been able to do schematics (2D). In mid 1970s, they were linked with report generators (e.g., bill of materials). More recently, the capability to do dimension drawings has been added, and 3D data bases created to allow stress analyses, etc.

BUYING:

—KBF are quite variable. However, minimum product requirements are schematics for process and electrical disciplines, and selling is increasingly important as competition intensifies

—An "easier" sale than mechanical

—Customers regarded as being very conservative and price sensitive

APPENDIX 1: (cont'd) Strategic Position Segment: AEC

Current Strategy

PRODUCT:

—High end product with specifications superior to competition
—Product development efforts dedicated to completing 10 work packages

COST:

—Probably the high cost producer. This reduces available market and flexibility considerably because it is perhaps the most price-sensitive segment
—Pricing is based on DDM—prices are 20% higher than two key competitors

SELLING:

—Product training and documentation has been provided to sales force by marketing
—Problems of small sales force complicated by fact that opportunities in DDM and IC are perceived as more significant resulting in essentially no attention being given to product

SERVICE:

—Efforts in service are similar to other product lines with exception that documentation is more complete

SUMMARY:

—Stated objective is to increase share, yet current approach is likely to result in no change or decrease
—While lack of a complete product is part of problem, the more serious shortcomings lie in poor understanding of customer needs/buying patterns and total lack of sales-force attention

Incremental Opportunities

PRODUCT:

—Immediate efforts must be dedicated to completing the product
—In addition, there are other necessary steps:
1. Providing display speed and user interface required for high-end product
2. Developing low to medium range product that provides basic 2D schematic and data management capability, plus flexibility to tradeup to high-end product

COST:

—Reducing product cost is minimally acceptable alternative
—Pricing changes have been proposed
• Lower base price to facilitate initial penetration
• Higher work package price to provide margin

SELLING:

—Adding one to two salesmen per region dedicated to this product is minimally acceptable alternative
—Providing these salesmen with more insight into specific customer needs and buying processes is also critical
—Specializing the sales effort (e.g., national accounts; dedicated salesforce) is more substantial opportunity

SERVICE:

—Developing a "service concept" is essential for this as well as other segments Additional opportunities include the following:
(1) assigning AES to pre- or post-sale responsibilities;
(2) developing multiple, application-specific training programs (e.g., operator, management, refresher); and
(3) providing range of service contracts

APPENDIX 1: (cont'd)
Strategic Alternatives
Segment: AEC

	Current Strategy (Including Planned Changes)	*Modest Redirection*	*Major Redirection*
Objectives:	—Stabilize current position (e.g., 10% share) by completing product development effort and adding one to two salesmen per region to focus on product	—Establish a meaningful position (e.g., 20–25% share) by maintaining product leadership and building specialized sales force	—Dominate segment (e.g., 40–50%) share by acquiring a significant competitor
Tactics:	—Product development effort will be completed according to current schedule —Product/market management efforts must be doubled —Pricing changes will be introduced (i.e., lower base price and increase package price to allow gradual customer tradeup) —Sales force additions will be made (i.e., salesmen in four or five cities with necessary support, each targeted at 10–15 customers)	—Current product development efforts must be expanded to include resolving current problems with high-end product as well as developing a low-to medium-range product —Product/market management effort must be increased 2–3 times —A national account sales force and perhaps a separate sales force must be built	—While corporate headquarters will contribute its marketing and product development efforts to acquisition, the acquired company will have overall responsibility for this segment —The candidate under consideration has a superior product in part due to outstanding hardware —Their sales force is dedicated to this and one other segment. It appears to have a good technical selling effort although it presumably faces typical problems of technology-oriented, threshold company
Requirements:	—Management must regard this as a discrete effort which will not distract its primary attention from more strategically important segments —If this cannot be ensured or if efforts to complete product/expand sales force fail, CALMA should exit the business	—Per current strategy, management must regard these internal initiatives as a discrete effort —Capital requirements will be moderately higher	—Acquisition may require $50–60 million Note: candidate under consideration would provide meaningful position in two segments —Substantial effort by corporate headquarters and CALMA will be required to acquire and integrate

APPENDIX 1: (cont'd)
Situation Analysis Segment: Mapping

CALMA/NIS Position

VOLUME/SHARE:

—30 CGI system sold through 1977
—1979: 3 systems
—1980: 6 systems
—1981: 13 systems
(Projections based on Corporate Business Plan)

CUSTOMERS:

Past	*Current*	*Opportunities*
Brooklyn Natural Gas	West Coast Engineering Firm	Con Ed
San Diego Gas & Electric		ARCO
Washington Gas & Light		PG&E
Columbus & Southern		UTI
Union Gas		

PRODUCT PARITY:

—Product is 6 years old. Product strengths include good input capability, yet it lacks a report writer
—Product development efforts significantly behind competitors
—Product requirements include intelligent terminal and color display
—CALMA's R&D is directed at other areas

SELLING AND SERVICE CAPABILITY:

—Corporate headquarters has only two sales representatives
—Service capability is inadequate to handle current accounts

Market Attractiveness

SIZE AND GROWTH:

—1979: $ 23M
—1980: 41
—1983: 125
—Market is generally regarded to be very latent (e.g., 1979 potential = $130M). Incremental growth is dependent on investment in marketing

DEMAND PATTERNS:

—Two distinct sources of demand: (1) automating the mapping of uncharted geology (e.g., energy companies); and (2) converting hard copy maps to automated data base (e.g., utilities)
—The underlying needs vary as well: (1) new maps = speed and flexibility; and (2) old maps = cost

CUSTOMERS/CONCENTRATIONS:

	Buying Center Concentration
Utilities	High
Petroleum company	Low
Natural resource company	Low
Federal and state government	Medium
Service bureaus	Low

PRODUCT NEEDS:

Service	*Product*
—Data collection and conversion (65%)	—Turnkey systems (5%) (i.e., digitize and edit)
—Software consulting (20%)	—Data storage (10%)

BUYING PATTERNS:

—Utilities are slow and conservative
—Government is slow and cumbersome
—Overall, buying centers and patterns are quite complex, and not well understood

Competitive Situation

COMPETITION/SHARE: (1979 approximate)

M&S	55%
Synercom	15%
Applicon	14%
Computervision	11%
Others	5%

STRATEGIES:

M&S—Sell consulting service with turnkey Systems: develop product for federal government then sell in commercial market
Synercom—Target municipalities and utilities
IBM—Introduced Geo-Facilities Graphic Support package (IGSS)

STRENGTHS AND WEAKNESSES:

M&S—Understand the product/market and have good related development skills
—No competitor offers full-service capability, i.e., data collection, conversion, and turnkey system

APPENDIX 1: (cont'd)
Strategic Position
Segment: Mapping

Current Strategy

PRODUCT:

—Enhance product slowly
- Build CGI/APEX product
- Develop macro library
- Add report generator
- Add data management capabilities

COST:

—Integrate into product new technology when feasible, e.g., new memory
—No cost reduction plan exists

SELLING:

—Sell with small sales force (three or four people) to large utilities
—No prospecting done; answer RFP that hit the street

SERVICE:

—Inadequate resources to manage existing accounts
—Hardware service marginal, but adequate

SUMMARY:

—Current strategy has NIS responsible for sales and CALMA responsible for R&D
—This strategy is doomed for failure because CALMA's R&D resources are being allocated elsewhere, and headquarters group has limited market knowledge and inadequate resources

Incremental Opportunities

PRODUCT:

—Add other DDM*-type application to product as well as drafting
—Add color graphics
—Develop breadth in product line

COST:

—Investigate a low-end product based on SI 30, i.e., piggyback on Scorpio project

SELLING:

—Work with prospects to develop their mapping requirements
—Create several Beta tests, for new CALMA/APEX product

SERVICE:

—Service current accounts better and leverage off this small base

* DDM: Design, Drafting and Manufacturing interactive graphics system.

APPENDIX 1: (cont'd)
Strategic Alternatives
Segment: Mapping

	Current Strategy (Including Planned Changes)	*Modest Redirection*	*Major Redirection*
Objectives:	—Maintain presence in market (i.e., 10% share) by selling CHI/APEX product through NIS. To succeed CGI must be rewritten with enhanced capabilities, i.e., improved data base capability, add Fortran, and other engineering capabilities (drafting)	—Establish meaningful position in market (e.g., 25% share) by developing a "complete" product. This will require adding data collection and conversion capability	—Dominate segment (e.g., 50% + share) by purchasing leading systems competitor and also developing a "complete" mapping product
Tactics:	—Target utilities segment only —Use small specialized sales force —Rewrite under DDM, which already had large data base, engineering and drafting capabilities —Move development effort from corporate headquarters	—Acquire a successful firm in this area such as Computer Graphics, Aero Services, or Vernon Graphics —Work with headquarters to develop complete product	—Developing a "complete" product involves same tactics contained under modest redirection —While headquarters will contribute its marketing and product development efforts to acquisition, the acquired company will have overall responsibility for this segment —The candidate under consideration has a superior product in part due to outstanding hardware —Their sales force is dedicated to this and one other segment. It appears to have a good technical selling effort although it presumably faces typical problems of technology-oriented, threshold company
Requirements:	—Obtain a commitment from CALMA to continue product development; will need to establish an R&D staff of about six people —Large file capacity on APEX	—Management commitment to a new expanded service —Funding of acquisition effort	—Acquisition may require \$50–60 million. Note: candidate under consideration would provide meaningful position in two segments —Substantial effort by headquarters and CALMA will be required to acquire and integrate

Index

E

F

G

H

I

J

L

M

N

O

P

T

U

W

DATE DUE

AUG 16 '85			
MAY 27 1988			
JUN 17 1988			
[illegible] 29 [illegible]			
DEC 22 [illegible]			